Interventional Radiology

Interventional Radiology

Edited by R. F. Dondelinger, P. Rossi, J. C. Kurdziel, and S. Wallace

with contributions by:

O. B. Adler
Y. Ben-Menachem
P. Bourquelot
J. H. Boverie
S. Bracard
C. H. Carrasco
W. R. Castaneda-Zuniga
C. Charnsangavej
P. Chastanet
V. P. Chuang
A. H. Cragg
M. Cremer
A. B. Crummy
K. S. Crystal
M. Darcy
A. N. Dardenne
C. Delcour
M. Delhaye
J. Devière
M. Dicato
R. F. Dondelinger
I. Enge
G. P. Feltrin
E. J. Ferris
J. Freilinger

J. C. Gaux
S. G. Gerzof
H. L. Giacobbe
C. Gianturco
J. H. Göthlin
V. V. Halbach
J. Hoevels
W. Hruby
V. Iaccarino
M. Jardin
F. Joffre
J. Karani
F. Karnel
B. T. Katzen
G. W. Kauffmann
J. C. Kurdziel
M. Labadie
J. L. Lamarque
P. Lasjaunias
C. L'Herminé
A. Liaras
F. Longtain
T. C. McCowan
J. C. McDermott
C. Manelfe

A. S. Mark
K. Mathias
G. B. Meloni
J. J. Merland
D. Miotto
J. Moret
B. E. W. Nordenström
D. Novak
H. B. Nunnerley
F. Olbert
R. C. Otto
R. Passariello
P. Pavone
S. Pedrazzoli
A. Per
L. Picard
T. G. Pickering
J. F. Reidy
D. Reizine
A. Remont
J. Rémy
W. R. Richli
G. M. Richter
A. Roche
M. J. Rodière

J. Roland
J. Rösch
A. Rosenberger
P. Rossi
H. Rousseau
A. Schilvold
G. Simonetti
T. P. Smith
R. Sörensen
T. A. Sos
E. Starck
E. Stoupel
J. L. Struyven
D. Swanson
J. Théron
U. Tylén
F. Urigo
A. L. van Breda
P. J. Van Cangh
S. Wallace
J. L. Westcott
K. C. Wright
E. Zeitler
C. Zollikofer

1088 Illustrations

1990
Georg Thieme Verlag
Stuttgart · New York

Thieme Medical Publishers, Inc.
New York

Library of Congress Cataloging-in-Publication Data

Interventional radiology / edited by
R. F. Dondelinger...[et al.] :
    with contributions by O. B. Adler...[et al.].
    p. cm.
    Includes bibliographical references.
    ISBN 0-86577-286-X (Thieme Medical)
    1. Radiology, Interventional. I. Dondelinger, R. F.
II. Adler, Olga B.
    [DNLM: 1. Radiography, Interventional.
    WN 200 I612]
    RD33.55.I58   1990
    617'.05--dc20
    DNLM/DLC
    for Library of Congress   89-20633
                                                    CIP

Important Note: Medicine is an ever-changing science. Research and clinical experience are continually broadening our knowledge, in particular our knowledge of proper treatment and drug therapy. Insofar as this book mentions any dosage or application, readers may rest assured that the authors, editors and publishers have made every effort to ensure that such references are strictly in accordance with the **state of knowledge at the time of production of the book. Nevertheless, every user is requested** to examine carefully the manufacturer's leaflets accompanying each drug to check on his own responsibility whether the dosage schedules recommended therein or the contraindications stated by the manufacturers differ from the statements made in the present book. Such examination is particularly important with drugs which are either rarely used or have been newly released on the market.

© 1990 Georg Thieme Verlag, Rüdigerstraße 14,
D-7000 Stuttgart 30, Germany
Thieme Medical Publishers, Inc., 381 Park Avenue South,
New York, N.Y. 10016

Typesetting by Götz KG, Ludwigsburg
(System Linotype 5 [202])

Printed in West Germany by K. Grammlich, Pliezhausen

ISBN 3-13-728901-7
(Georg Thieme Verlag, Stuttgart)

ISBN 0-86577-286-X
(Thieme Medical Publishers, Inc., New York)

2 3 4 5 6

To our patients

Foreword

During recent years, the patients and practitioners of diagnostic radiology have benefited from the enormous progress in technology, methodology and clinical applications which has taken place. *Interventional radiology* has played a very significant role in this progress, with the great variety of procedures and techniques which it offers. Many time-consuming operating procedures have been replaced by interventional radiological procedures, and in many instances, such procedures can also be used to prepare operative procedures or to follow them up. Saving time and money is of great importance here, but the benefits for patients from a more rapid and less traumatic therapeutic approach are most important of all.

Interventional radiology involves a great number of important fields of activity, and new fields for the refining of applied methods are continually being opened up. This is demonstrated most conspicuously in the contents lists of the leading radiological journals, in which the papers under the heading "Interventional Radiology" represent a great part of each issue.

It is interesting, too, to note that many papers and contributions to discussions in the journals are concerned with the problem of who should perform interventional procedures. Percutaneous transluminal coronary angiography (PTCA), in particular, has been a subject of heated discussion. The answer to the question is simple: since carrying out such procedures requires both talent and extensive experience, and since it makes cooperation between trained personnel and the use of highly specialized equipment necessary, the procedures should be performed by those who have the talent, experience and background, and who can offer short waiting times and low costs. These are usually radiologists and the radiology department; and, in any case, the radiologist's ambition must always be to be the best. The organization of departments of diagnostic radiology, with their autonomy, concentration of resources, and centralisation, facilitates this markedly.

For our colleagues working in this field, a deep and well-based knowledge of each of the procedures and its details is a must. Colleagues wishing to share their knowledge and experience in each of the many procedures available today have taken up an invitation to do so from the editors of this book, and specialists in each of the many fields have presented their rich experience here. The basic diagnostic and differential diagnostic situations, and the choice of the correct procedure for every specific situation, with its advantages and its risks, are presented here in a way that makes this book essential to everyone dealing with the new and rapidly expanding field of diagnostic radiology.

Olle Olsson
Lund, Sweden

Preface

Interventional radiology is a relatively young specialty within medical imaging which has been rapidly developing in many areas in the recent past. These developments have been made possible through the imaginativeness of interventional radiologists and their desire to introduce innovations; through the ultimate precision in anatomical representation achieved with modern imaging techniques; and through refinements in the percutaneous catheters, balloons, needles and other implant devices used. The creativity of interventional radiologists is supported by specialized international societies in Europe, the United States and Japan and by national societies in several countries, as well as through specialist journals and books.

We have now reached a stage at which interventional radiology has extended from isolated experiments to applications on a broad clinical basis. Unfortunately, in too many places the academic teaching of interventional radiology remains too limited, and the training of young interventional radiologists is still based on personal initiative through visits to departments, reading journals and attending meetings and courses.

Difficulties in teaching vascular interventional radiology arise from the fact that there has been a shift from many indications for visceral diagnostic angiography towards other techniques. The use of ultrasonography, computed tomography, and magnetic resonance imaging is already widespread and is adequately taught, but due to the decline in diagnostic visceral catheterangiography, training problems in interventional techniques limit the number of experts.

A lack of comprehensive English-language textbooks in Europe covering the major applications of interventional radiology was what gave us the stimulus to produce the present book. Recognized authorities from Europe and the United States in each particular field of interventional radiology agreed to contribute.

Overlapping and repetition among the different chapters of the book has been avoided, and it was possible to harmonize the style and presentation of all the contributions thanks to the discipline shown by the authors. Such an experiment could not be conducted in a short space of time. Since the techniques, indications and results of interventional radiology are changing rapidly, every effort has been made to include the latest developments.

This book should not give the impression that there is a division between diagnostic and interventional radiology. Interventional procedures are always based on precise imaging, the formulation of a diagnosis, and the choice of the appropriate interventional procedure.

It is impossible to predict today who will be responsible for carrying out interventional radiological techniques in the future. It is certain, however, that interventional radiology is promised a brilliant future, as the general trends in medicine move to meet the demand for more patient-friendly treatment with less aggression, less hospitalization and lower costs.

Radiologists should be conscious of their new potential and responsibility, and they should offer their patients all the interventional procedures required in their environment and technically feasible in their department.

Radiologic consultations, wards directly connected with the radiology department, and daytime hospitalization beds inside the department are imperatives which are already indispensable today. Constant cooperation with clinicians and surgeons is mandatory. However, interventional radiologists should not feel that they are restricted to providing a service: they must be willing to take a share of the responsibility for the choice of treatment. Diagnostic management has already taken the place of meeting requests for radiographs. Active participation in therapeutic management of the patient is the new challenge for interventional radiologists.

This challenge can only be met through perfect knowledge of each clinical problem and of the corresponding interventional radiological techniques. If the present book can contribute to achieving this, the aim of the editors and authors will have been fulfilled.

Autumn, 1989

The Editors
R. F. Dondelinger
P. Rossi
J. C. Kurdziel
S. Wallace

Contributors

O. B. Adler, M.D.
Clinical Associate Professor of Radiology
Technion – Israel Institute of Technology
Faculty of Medicine
Dept. of Diagnostic Radiology
Rambam Medical Center
Haifa 35254
Israel

Y. Ben-Menachem, M.D.
Professor of Radiology and
Adjunct Professor of Surgery
University of Washington;
Director
Dept. of Radiolgy
Harborview Medical Center
325 Ninth Avenue
Seattle, WA 98104
USA

P. Bourquelot, M.D.
Dept. of Cardiovascular Radiology
Hôpital Broussais
96, rue Didot
76674 Paris Cédex 14
France

J. H. Boverie, M.D.
Associate Professor of Radiology
University of Liège;
Chief
Dept. of Visceral Radiology
University Hospital Sart-Tilman
4900 Liège 1
Belgium

S. Bracard, M.D.
Staff Radiologist
Dept. of Diagnostic and Therapeutic
Neuroradiology
Centre Hospitalier Universitaire
Hôpital St.-Julien
1, rue Foller
54037 Nancy
France

C. H. Carrasco, M.D.
Associate Professor of Radiology
University of Texas;
Dept. of Diagnostic Radiology
M.D. Anderson Cancer Center
1515 Holcombe Boulevard, Box 57
Houston, TX 77030
USA

W. R. Castaneda-Zuniga, M.D., M.Sc.
Professor of Radiology
University of Minnesota School of Medicine
Dept. of Radiology
Box 292
University of Minnesota Hospital and Clinic
420 Delaware St. S.E.
Minneapolis, MN 55455
USA

C. Charnsangavej, M.D.
Professor of Radiology
University of Texas
M.D. Anderson Cancer Center;
Chief
Vascular and Interventional Radiology
Dept. of Diagnostic Radiology
M.D. Anderson Cancer Center
1515 Holcombe Boulevard, Box 57
Houston, TX 77030
USA

P. Chastanet, M.D.
Dept. of Radiology
Centre Hospitalier Universitaire
Place de Verdun
59037 Lille
France

V. P. Chuang, M.D.
Clinical Professor of Radiology
Emory University
Atlanta, GA;
Staff Radiologist
R.T. Jones Hospital
Canton, GA 30114;
Radiology Associates of North Georgia
110 Waleska Road
Canton, GA 30114
USA

A. H. Cragg, M.D.
Assistant Professor of Radiology
University of Iowa Medical School;
Director
Division of Interventional Radiology
Dept. of Radiology
University of Iowa Hospitals and Clinics
Iowa City, IA 52242
USA

M. Cremer, M.D.
Professor of Medicine
Free University of Brussels;
Chief
Dept. of Gastroenterology
Medicosurgical Dept. of Gastroenterology
Hôpital Erasme
808, route de Lennik
1070 Brussels
Belgium

A. B. Crummy, M.D.
Professor of Radiology
University of Wisconsin Medical School;
Dept. of Radiology
Clinical Science Center
600 Highland Avenue
Madison, WI 53792
USA

K. S. Crystal, M.D.
Cornell University Medical College
Dept. of Radiology
Division of Cardiovascular and Interventional
Radiology
The New York Hospital
Cornell Medical Center
525 East 68th St.
New York, NY 10021
USA

M. Darcy, M.D.
Assistant Professor of Radiology
Washington University School of Medicine;
Staff Radiologist
Section of Vascular and Interventional Radiology
Mallinckrodt Institute of Radiology
510 South Kings Highway
St Louis, MO 63110
USA

A. N. Dardenne, M.D.
Associate Professor of Radiology
Université Catholique de Louvain;
Chief
Genitourinary and Ultrasound Section
Dept. of Radiology and Diagnostic Imaging
University Hospital Saint-Luc
10, avenue Hippocrate
1200 Brussels
Belgium

C. Delcour, M.D.
Staff Radiologist
Free University of Brussels
Dept. of Radiology
Hôpital Erasme
808, route de Lennik
1070 Brussels
Belgium

M. Delhaye, M.D.
Free University of Brussels
Dept. of Gastroenterology
Medicosurgical Dept. of Gastroenterology
Hôpital Erasme
808, route de Lennik
1070 Brussels
Belgium

J. Devière, M.D.
Free University of Brussels
Dept. of Gastroenterology
Medicosurgical Dept. of Gastroenterology
Hôpital Erasme
808, route de Lennik
1070 Brussels
Belgium

M. Dicato, M.D.
Professor of Biology
Centre Universitaire Luxembourg;
Head
Department of Hematology and Oncology
Centre Hospitalier
4, rue Barblé
1210 Luxembourg

R. F. Dondelinger, M.D.
Associate Professor of Radiology
University of Liège;
Head
Dept. of Diagnostic and Interventional Radiology
Centre Hospitalier
4, rue Barblé
1210 Luxembourg

I. Enge, M.D.
Professor of Radiology
University of Oslo;
Chairman
Dept. of Radiology
Aker University Hospital
Trondsheimson 235
0514 Oslo 5
Norway

G. P. Feltrin, M.D.
Professor of Radiology
University of Padua;
Director
Dept. of Cardiovascular and Interventional
Radiology
Institute of Radiology
University Hospital
Via Giustiniani 2
35100 Padua
Italy

E. J. Ferris, M.D.
Professor of Radiology
University of Arkansas for Medical Sciences
Dept. of Radiology
University Hospital of Arkansas
4301 West Markham
Little Rock, AR 72205
USA

J. Freilinger
Société de Recherche Contre le Cancer et les
Maladies du Sang
Centre Hospitalier
4, rue Barblé
1210 Luxembourg

J. C. Gaux, M.D.
Professor of Radiology
University of Paris VI;
Faculty Chief of Medicine
Dept. of Cardiovascular Radiology
Hôpital Broussais
96, rue Didot
75014 Paris
France

S. G. Gerzof, M.D., F.A.C.R.
Professor of Radiology
Tufts University School of Medicine;
Chief
Section of Body Computed Tomography
Dept. of Radiology
Boston V.A. Medical Center
150 South Huntington Avenue
Boston, MA 02130
USA

H. L. Giacobbe, M.D.
Radiologist
Dept. of Diagnostic and Therapeutic
Neuroradiology
Centre Hospitalier Universitaire
Hôpital St.-Julien
1, rue Foller
54037 Nancy
France

C. Gianturco, M.D.
University of Texas;
Dept. of Diagnostic Radiology
M.D. Anderson Cancer Center
1515 Holcombe Boulevard, Box 57
Houston, TX 77030
USA

J. H. Göthlin, M.D., Ph.D.
Professor of Radiology
University of Bergen;
Chairman
Dept. and Institute of Diagnostic Radiology;
Director
Oncological Research Laboratory
Haukeland University Hospital
5016 Bergen
Norway

V. V. Halbach, M.D.
Assistant Professor of Neuroradiology
University of California – San Francisco
Dept. of Neuroradiology
UCSF Medical Center
505 Parnassus Avenue
San Francisco, CA 94143–0628
USA

J. Hoevels, M.D.
Professor of Radiology;
Chief
Dept. of Radiology
Städtische Krankenanstalten Bielefeld-Mitte
Posftfach 7908
4800 Bielefeld 1
West Germany

W. Hruby, M.D.
Associate Professor of Radiology
Dept. of Radiology
Krankenanstalt Rudolfstiftung
Juchgasse 25
1030 Vienna
Austria

V. Iaccarino, M.D.
Istituto di Scienze Radiologiche
I Cattedra
II Facoltà di Medicina e Chirurgia
II Policlinico
Via Pansini 5
80131 Naples
Italy

M. Jardin, M.D.
Service Central de Radiologie
Hôpital Albert Calmette
Boulevard du Professeur-J.-Leclerq
59037 Lille
France

F. G. Joffre, M.D.
Professor of Radiology
Paul Sabatier University
Toulouse;
Chief
Dept. of Radiology
Centre Hospitalier Universitaire Rangueil
1, avenue J. Poulhes
31054 Toulouse
France

J. Karani, M.D.
Consultant Radiologist
Dept. of Radiology
King's College Hospital
Denmark Hill
London SE5 9RS
England

F. Karnel, M.D.
Assistant Professor of Radiology
University of Vienna;
Angiography and Interventional Radiology Section
Zentrales Institut für Radiodiagnostik
Allgemeines Krankenhaus
Alserstrasse 4
1090 Vienna
Austria

B. T. Katzen, M.D.
Clinical Professor of Radiology
University of Miami School of Medicine;
Director
Miami Vascular Institute
Baptist Hospital of Miami
8900 North Kendall Drive
Miami, FL 33176
USA

G. W. Kauffmann, M.D.
Professor of Radiology
University of Heidelberg;
Director
Dept. of Radiology
Klinikum der Universität Heidelberg
Im Neuenheimer Feld 110
6900 Heidelberg
West Germany

J. C. Kurdziel, M.D.
Staff Radiologist
Dept. of Diagnostic and Interventional Radiology
Centre Hospitalier
4, rue Barblé
1210 Luxembourg

M. H. Labadie, M.D.
Chief Pathologist
INSERM U 45
Hôpital Edouard Herriot
Place d'Arsonval
69003 Lyon
France

J. L. Lamarque, M.D.
Professor of Radiology
University of Montpellier;
Chairman
Dept. of Medical Imaging
Hôpital Lapeyronie
555, route de Ganges
34059 Montpellier
France

P. Lasjaunias, M.D.
Associate Professor of Anatomy
University of Paris XI
School of Medicine;
Director
Dept. of Diagnostic and Therapeutic Angiography
Hôpital Kremlin-Bicêtre
78, rue du Général Leclerc
94275 Le Kremlin-Bicêtre
France

C. L'Herminé, M.D.
Professor of Radiology
University of Lille;
Chief
Dept. of Radiology
Centre Hospitalier Universitaire
Place de Verdun
59037 Lille
France

A. Liaras, M.D.
Pathologist
INSERM U 45
Hôpital Edouard Herriot
Place d'Arsonval
69003 Lyon
France

F. Longtain, M.D.
Dept. of Radiology
University Hospital Sart-Tilman
4900 Liège 1
Belgium

T. C. McCowan, M.D.
Research and Education Fellow
Radiological Society of North America;
Dept. of Radiology
University of Arkansas for Medical Sciences
4301 West Markham
Little Rock, AR 72205
USA

J. C. McDermott, M.D.
University of Wisconsin;
Dept. of Radiology
Clinical Science Center
600 Highland Avenue
Madison, WI 53792
USA

C. Manelfe, M.D.
Professor of Radiology
University of Toulouse;
Director and Chairman
Dept. of Neuroradiology and MRI
Centre Hospitalier Universitaire Purpan
Place du Docteur Baylac
31059 Toulouse
France

A. S. Mark, M.D.
Assistant Clinical Professor of Radiology
George Washington University Medical School;
Director of MRI
Dept. of Radiology
Washington Hospital Center
110 Irving Street N.W.
Washington, DC 20010
USA

K. D. Mathias, M.D.
Professor of Radiology;
Director
Institute of Radiology
Akademisches Lehrkrankenhaus
Beurhausstrasse 40
4600 Dortmund 1
West Germany

G. B. Meloni, M.D.
Università degli Studi di Sassari
Dept. of Radiology
Istituto di Scienze Radiologiche
Viale San Pietro 10
07100 Sassari
Sardinia
Italy

J. J. Merland, M.D.
Professor of Radiology
University of Paris VII
School of Medicine;
Chief
Dept. of Neuroradiology and Therapeutic
Angiography
Hôpital Lariboisière
2, rue Ambroise-Paré
75010 Paris
France

D. Miotto, M.D.
Research Fellow
University of Padua
Division of Cardiovascular and Interventional
Radiology;
Institute of Radiolgy
University Hospital
Via Giustiniani 2
University of Padua
35100 Padua
Italy

J. Moret, M.D.
Vice-Chief
Dept. of Radiology
Fondation Ophthalmologique Rothschild
29, rue Manin
75019 Paris
France

B. E. W. Nordenström, M.D.
Professor Emeritus of Radiology
University of Stockholm
Karolinska Institute;
Dept. of Radiology
Karolinska Hospital
Box 60500
10401 Stockholm
Sweden

D. Novak, M.D.
Professor of Radiology
University of Hamburg;
Director
Institute of Diagnostic Radiology
Adenauerallee 23
5300 Bonn 1
West Germany

H. B. Nunnerley, M.D., F.R.C.R.
Honorary Senior Lecturer
King's College School of Medicine and Dentistry;
Director of Radiology
King's College Hospital
Denmark Hill
London SE5 9RS
England

F. Olbert, M.D.
Professor of Radiology
University of Vienna;
Angiography and Interventional Radiology Section
Zentrales Institut für Radiodiagnostik
Allgemeines Krankenhaus
Alserstrasse 4
1090 Vienna
Austria

R. C. Otto, M.D.
Professor of Radiology;
Director
Institut für Röntgendiagnostik und Nuklearmedizin
Kantonsspital
5404 Baden
Switzerland

R. Passariello, M.D.
Professor of Radiology
University of L'Aquila;
Director and Chairman
Dept. of Radiology
Ospedale Colle Maggio
67100 L'Aquila
Italy

P. Pavone, M.D.
University of L'Aquila;
Staff Radiologist
Dept. of Radiology
Ospedale Colle Maggio
67100 L'Aquila
Italy

S. Pedrazzoli, M.D.
Professor of Surgery
University of Padua;
Chief
Dept. of Emergency Surgery
Dept. of Clinical Surgery
University of Padua
Via Giustiniani 2
35100 Padua
Italy

A. Per, M.D.
Anesthesiologist
Dept. of Anesthesia
Centre Hospitalier Universitaire
Hôpital Central
29, avenue Maréchal Delattre de Tassigny
54037 Nancy
France

L. Picard, M.D.
Professor of Radiology
University of Nancy I;
Chief
Dept. of Diagnostic and Therapeutic
Neuroradiology
Centre Hospitalier Universitaire
Hôpital St.-Julien
1, rue Foller
54037 Nancy
France

T. G. Pickering, M.D.
Cornell University Medical College
Division of Cardiovascular and Interventional
Radiology
The New York Hospital
Cornell Medical Center
525 East 68th Street
New York, NY 10021
USA

J. F. Reidy, M.D., F.R.C.R., F.R.C.P.
Guy's Hospital Medical School;
Consultant Radiologist
Guy's Hospital
St. Thomas' Street
London SE1 9RT
England

D. Reizine, M.D.
Dept. of Neuroradiology and Therapeutic
Angiography
Hôpital Lariboisière
2, rue Ambroise-Paré
75010 Paris
France

A. Remont, M.D.
Dept. of Visceral Radiology
University Hospital Sart-Tilman
4900 Liège 1
Belgium

J. Rémy, M.D.
Professor of Radiology
University of Lille;
Chief
Service Central de Radiologie
Hôpital Albert Calmette
Boulevard du Professeur-J.-Leclerq
59037 Lille
France

W. R. Richli, M.D.
University of Texas;
M.D. Anderson Cancer Center
Dept. of Diagnostic Radiology
1515 Holcombe Boulevard, Box 57
Houston, TX 77030
USA

G. M. Richter, M.D.
University of Heidelberg
Dept. of Radiology
Klinikum der Universität Heidelberg
Im Neuenheimer Feld 110
6900 Heidelberg
West Germany

A. Roche, M.D.
Professor of Radiology
University of Paris XI
School of Medicine;
Staff Radiologist
Dept. of Diagnostic Radiology
Institut Gustave Roussy
Rue Camille Desmoulins
94805 Villejuif
France

M. J. Rodière, M.D.
University of Montpellier;
Staff Radiologist
Dept. of Medical Imaging
Hôpital Lapeyronie
555, route de Ganges
34059 Montpellier
France

J. Roland, M.D.
Associate Professor of Anatomy
University of Nancy I
Faculty of Medicine;
Staff Radiologist
Dept. of Diagnostic and Therapeutic
Neuroradiology
Centre Hospitalier Universitaire
Hôpital St.-Julien
1, rue Foller
54037 Nancy
France

J. Rösch, M.D.
Professor of Radiology
Oregon Health Sciences University;
Director
Dept. of Vascular and Interventional Radiology
University Hospital
3181 S.W. Sam Jackson Park Road
Portland, OR 97201
USA

A. Rosenberger, M.D.
Associate Professor of Radiology
Technion – Israel Institute of Technology
Faculty of Medicine;
Chief
Dept. of Diagnostic Radiology
Rambam Medical Center
Haifa 35254
Israel

P. Rossi, M.D., F.A.C.R.
Professor of Radiology
University of Milan;
Chairman
Dept. of Radiology
Policlinico Building Zonda
Via F. Sforza 35
20122 Milan
Italy

H. Rousseau, M.D.
Dept. of Radiology
Centre Hospitalier Universitaire Rangueil
1, avenue J. Poulhes
31054 Toulouse
France

A. Schilvold, M.D.
Dept. of Radiology
Aker University Hospital
Trondsheimson 235
0514 Oslo 5
Norway

G. Simonetti, M.D.
Professor of Radiology
Università degli Studi di Sassari;
Director and Chairman
Dipartimento di Radiodiagnostica e Radioterapia
"Digitale"
Istituto di Scienze Radiologiche
Viale San Pietro 10
07100 Sassari
Sardinia
Italy

T. P. Smith, M.D.
University of Minnesota School of Medicine;
Dept. of Radiology
Box 292
University of Minnesota Hospital and Clinic
420 Delaware St. S.E.
Minneapolis, MN 55455
USA

R. Sörensen, M.D.
Professor of Radiology
Free University of Berlin;
Head
Cardiovascular and Interventional Radiology
Dept. of Diagnostic Radiology
Universitätsklinikum Steglitz
Hindenburgdamm 30
1000 Berlin 45
West Germany

T. A. Sos, M.D.
Professor of Radiology
Cornell University Medical College;
Director
Cardiovascular and Interventional Radiology
Dept. of Radiology
The New York Hospital
Cornell Medical Center
525 East 68th Street
New York, NY 10021
USA

E. Starck, M.D.
Professor of Radiology
Johann Wolfgang Goethe University;
Chief
Dept. of Diagnostic Radiology
Städtische Kliniken Kassel
Mönchenbergstrasse 41–43
3500 Kassel
West Germany

E. Stoupel, M.D.
Dept. of Radiology
Hôpital Erasme
808, route de Lennik
1070 Brussels
Belgium

J. A. L. Struyven, M.D.
Professor of Radiology
Free University of Brussels;
Chairman
Dept. of Radiology
Hôpital Erasme
808, route de Lennik
1070 Brussels
Belgium

D. Swanson, M.D.
University of Texas;
Dept. of Urology
M.D. Anderson Cancer Center
1515 Holcombe Boulevard
Houston, TX 77030
USA

J. Théron, M.D.
Professor of Radiology
University of Caen;
Chief
Dept. of Neuroradiology and Interventional
Radiology
Centre Hospitalier Régional et Universitaire
Avenue de la Côte de Nacre
14033 Caen
France

U. Tylén, M.D., Ph.D.
Professor of Radiology
University of Göteborg;
Chairman
Dept. of Radiology
Sahlgrenska Hospital
41345 Göteborg
Sweden

F. Urigo, M.D.
Dipartimento di Radiodiagnostica e Radioterapia
"Digitale"
Istituto di Scienze Radiologiche
Viale San Pietro 10
07100 Sassari
Sardinia
Italy

A. L. van Breda, M.D.
Associate Clinical Professor of Radiology
George Washington University Medical School;
Chief
Cardiovascular and Interventional Radiology
Dept. of Radiology
Alexandria Hospital
4230 Seminary Road
Alexandria, VA 22304
USA

P. J. Van Cangh, M.D.
Professor of Radiology
University of Louvain Medical School;
Chief
Division of Urology
Dept. of Surgery
Hôpital Universitaire Saint-Luc
10, avenue Hippocrate
1200 Brussels
Belgium

S. Wallace, M.D.
Professor of Radiology
University of Texas M.D. Anderson Cancer Center;
Deputy Department Chairman
Dept. of Diagnostic Radiology
M.D. Anderson Cancer Center
1515 Holcombe Boulevard, Box 57
Houston, TX 77030
USA

J. L. Westcott, M.D.
Clinical Professor of Diagnostic Imaging
Yale University College of Medicine;
Chairman
Dept. of Radiology
Hospital of St. Raphael
1450 Chapel St.
New Haven, CT 06511
USA

K. C. Wright, M.D.
University of Texas M.D. Anderson Cancer Center
Dept. of Diagnostic Radiology
1515 Holcombe Boulevard, Box 57
Houston, TX 77030
USA

E. P. Zeitler, M.D.
Professor of Radiology
University of Erlangen-Nuremberg;
Director
Dept. of Diagnostic Radiology
Radiological Center
Klinikum Nord
Postfach 910160
8500 Nuremberg 91
West Germany

C. Zollikofer, M.D.
Associate Professor of Radiology;
Chief
Dept. of Radiology
Kantonsspital Winterthur
15 Brauerstrasse
8401 Winterthur
Switzerland

Contents

Endoscopic and Percutaneous Management of Urinary Disease 233

Therapeutic Angiographic Techniques 283

Interventional Procedures in the Digestive Tract 729

Percutaneous Lysis of the Vertebral Disk 755
J. THÉRON

Percutaneous Lysis of Neural Structures 767

Index 781

Percutaneous Biopsy

Cytology

M. Labadie and A. Liaras

Description

Cytologic Technique

The radiologist who performs the biopsy puncture must bear in mind that the soundness of the final result depends to a large degree, namely, 60%, on the quality of the specimen and hence on his care in accomplishing the procedure.

Materials

Needles. Numerous needles specially designed for deep-seated lesions are currently available (9). They must be rigid to ensure accurate puncture, which rules out long needles. The best compromise between length and rigidity seems to be offered by a lumbar puncture type needle. The presence of "lateral windows" significantly improves the cellularity of the aspirate. Finally, some needles have a threaded tip that can be screwed into the lesion. The choice of diameter depends on the risk of spreading the malignant cells, which in turn depends on the particular lesion. Renal adenocarcinoma, often accompanied by extensive necrosis, is the type of malignancy for which this risk is high. Researchers who have evaluated the risk recommend using smaller than 20 G needles in order to reduce the risk to negligible levels (11, 35).

Syringes. Disposable 20 ml syringes should be used.

Aspirating Pistol. The aspirating pistol is an essential device. It exerts powerful suction and ensures better precision by leaving one hand free to immobilize the cutaneous plane. It is made of metal and so can be sterilized.

Puncture

Although the cytologist does not take part in performing the puncture, he should advise the operator on all aspects of specimen preparation. During the radiologist's training in this technique, the cytologist's presence can be helpful for on-the-spot checking of slide cellularity.

Slide Preparation

Smears. The aspirated material is placed on the slide, with the needle touching the slide (violent ejection is damaging). Two types of slides should be prepared:

A *small series* of smears fixed immediately, within 15 seconds (spray, 95° alcohol, methanol acetone). This requires the presence of a second person to do the fixation, since the operator is sterile and cannot handle the spray. Any delay in fixing the smears renders cytologic diagnosis impossible.

A *longer series* immediately and carefully smeared by the same technique as blood smears. Any delay in preparing the smears results in deterioration of the specimen.

Sections. The aspirate is processed in the same way as a conventional biopsy, namely, immersion in formol or Bouin's solution, followed by centrifuging, paraffin embedding, and finally cutting a series of sections. Although this procedure can be useful for immunologic marker studies, it is not, in fact, a cytologic technique and indeed betrays lack of faith in cytology.

Suspensions. Although cell morphologic characteristics are not much altered by osmotic phenomena resulting from suspending the cells in liquid, our findings indicate that detail is lost compared with smears. The tissue architecture largely disappears and accessory signs (necrosis, particular background, information on blood concentration) are no longer visible, although in practice the diagnosis is often established with the help of precisely these accessory signs. Suspension is nevertheless useful for handling liquid aspirates, such as those obtained from cysts, or cystic or necrosed tumors. The aspirate should be mixed with an equal volume of 50° alcohol. It is futile to attempt smearing the pure aspirate directly onto the slides. Rinsing the needle yields no useful material when the primary smears are acellular.

Filtering entails considerable manipulation and hence the likelihood of loosing information. Moreover, superimposition produces an inaccurate picture.

Centrifuging. The liquid aspirate is centrifuged for 5 min., at 3500 rpm, and the sediment processed in the same way as for direct smears.

Cytocentrifuging is useful for poorly cellular fluids. When cells are abundant, superimposition is very troublesome.

Finally, we recommend:

For *solid aspirates*, preparing several air-dried smears and a few slightly spread and fixed smears, for a total of 15 to 20 slides.

For *liquid aspirates*, placing the specimen in 50° alcohol.

The material can then safely wait several days for laboratory processing.

Staining

The choice of stain often depends on habit and training. For preliminary analysis, it is important to use two complementary stains systematically.

The *Papanicolaou* method stains both isolated cells and thick multilayered fragments. It can be applied only to perfectly fixed slides and is, unfortunately, not reversible.

Giemsa staining is used on air-dried smears and has the advantage of complete reversibility on immersion in methanol (15 to 20 min). This permits the subsequent use of all the special stains employed in histopathology (24). These special stains are used for revealing differentiation, which is not readily apparent with conventional staining. They can be used on slides to which Giemsa stain has been applied and then removed, thus limiting the total number of slides required. Should the pathologic diagnosis prove to be hematologic, the same slides can be stained anew with May-Grünwald-Giemsa.

Special stains. *Periodic acid-Schiff* (PAS) identifies either mucins in the form of vacuoles or glycogen in the form of granules. Certain parasites also stain well with this method.

Alcian blue selectively stains acid mucins.

Fontana-Masson demonstrates melanin.

The *Grimelius* stain can identify certain endocrine secretions: tumors of the amine precursor uptake and decarboxylation system (APUDoma).

With *Congo red,* amyloid can be identified because of dichroism in polarized light.

Immunomarking is a technique of the future and can be used with air-dried smears, embedded sections, and cell suspensions (1, 8). It is extremely precise and can establish a firm differential diagnosis between, say, lymphoma and anaplastic carcinoma.

Phenol toluidine blue gives excellent results within 20 seconds, enabling immediate on-the-spot reading. However, the stain is irreversible.

Cytologic Analysis

The cytology of an aspirate is meaningful only if the material comes from a malignant lesion. With rare exceptions, cytology is of no use for diagnosing benign conditions. Moreover, random passes through a solid organ have virtually no likelihood of obtaining significant material. Thus, it is essential to puncture only focal lesions, adequately defined by imaging techniques.

Cytologists trained in the Papanicolaou school of cervical cancer detection would tend to base their diagnosis on cell morphologic findings and more particularly on nuclear morphologic characteristics. For diagnosing deep-seated lesions, this approach is important but not sufficient. The nuclear abnormalities essential for diagnosing epidermoid cancers (cervical or bronchial) can sometimes be completely absent (hepatocarcinoma). This entails a complete rethinking of normal morphologic features and the pathologic state of the organs involved, leading to a recognition of characteristic architectural patterns. These can comprise omnipresent structures (vessels, connective tissue), elements by which the punctured organ can be identified (glomerular flocculus, pancreatic acinus, biliary canaliculus, etc.), and finally specific features of a lesion (neuroendocrine rosettes).

Cytologic analysis is dependent on clinical findings. It is essential to know the age, sex, preexisting pathologic conditions, previous treatment, and the possible diagnoses advanced by the clinician and the radiologist. An attempt should be made to select a number of plausible diagnoses in order to narrow down the possibilities. This aids the cytologist in his task of comparing the actual appearance of the slides with a hypothetical histologic picture by which the lesion could be diagnosed. Indeed, cytologic smears contain isolated cells that cannot always be identified, but also groups of cells that more or less reflect the hypothetical histologic section. This approach is especially necessary when the exact site of the lesion is not known and the puncture involves a region (abdominal or pelvic mass). The radiologist is better qualified than the cytologist to comprehend the anatomy of the sampled region. The soundness of the diagnosis will obviously depend on the radiologist's experience with respect to indications, puncture site and slide preparation, and also on the experience of the cytologist, whose presence during sampling is only necessary for difficult cases. The radiologist who wants to use the cytologic examination should do so systematically; otherwise, his puncture technique will lack precision. This also holds true for the cytologist, whose competence increases with experience.

Applications

Supraphrenic Region

Lung

The puncture is most often directed at peripheral pulmonary foci after failure of endoscopic techniques. Aspirates of normal lung tissue have poorly cellular elements, whereas tumors yield very cellular material. The aspirates are more specific than those obtained by scrape-aspiration and hence diagnosis is easier. The primary malignancy is easy to diagnose in small-cell undifferentiated carcinoma and in bronchioloalveolar adenocarcinoma, since the malignant cells exhibit very specific characteristics. Epidermoid carcinoma of the bronchi shows no distinctive features compared with other epidermoid carcinomas; except in cases of an already known epidermoid lesion, the malignancy is a primary tumor, since malpighian carcinoma metastasizes only late in the course. Paradoxically, primary bronchial adenocarcinoma is identified because of its poor differentiation. In contrast, there are other metastatic glandular tumors with specific cellular or architectural characteristics; adenocarcinoma of the colon and clear cell adenocarcinoma are prototype examples. A diagnosis of undifferentiated large cell carcinoma is not so much a positive diagnosis as an admission of failure in identifying the tumor. Correct identification of the tumor type can be obtained in 70 to 86% of cases (32, 34). The recognition of metastases depends on how experienced the cytologist is: some investigators have reported a very optimistic success rate of 92% (7); however, this is a very complex task and a rate of 70% is a more reasonable expectation (26) (Fig. 1).

The lesion can also be benign and pose no major diagnostic problems. Abscess, sarcoidosis, tuberculosis, encysted interlobar pleurisy, hydatid cyst, and hamartoma are some of the more common examples.

Mediastinum

Different lesions can occur in different sections of the mediastinum. In the anterior mediastinum, thymoma, dysembryoma, possibly of the seminomatous type, ectopic thyroid, goiter, parathyroid adenoma, or lymphoma (Hodgkin or non-Hodgkin) can be found. It is worth noting that the usual presentation of each of these disorders is rather different, which facilitates the diagnosis. In the middle mediastinum the possibilities are more limited, namely, bronchogenic cyst, lymphoma, or pericardial cyst. In the posterior mediastinum, schwannosis, neurofibroma, neuroblastoma, or lymphoma can occur. Finally, extension of a lung tumor can appear in any part of the mediastinum (13, 29, 31).

Subphrenic region

Liver

The puncture biopsy is taken in order to confirm that the focalized mass revealed by imaging techniques is indeed a tumor. However, the main purpose is to determine the exact type of the lesion. Puncture of nontumoral tissue is useful for assessing the hepatic background, which is essential for diagnosing certain hepatocellular carcinomas, and very helpful for evaluating the quality of the remaining parenchyma in the event of surgery. Biopsy of healthy liver reveals a main population of hepatocytes with uniform-sized nuclei, alongside a minority population of hepatocytes whose nuclei are twice as large. This doubling of nuclear size has been shown (22) to correspond to a twofold increase in chromatin material, that is, in the number of chromosomes. The cell size increases correspondingly and thus the nuclear to cytoplasmic ratio remains relatively constant. Such a clone of hepatocytes with 4N chromosomes (2N×2) appears during regeneration after hepatic necrosis of whatever origin. The clone persists even after regeneration has ceased. Thus, the healthy liver is particularly polymorphic because it is polyclonal.

Nontumoral Lesions. *Biliary cyst:* the smears do not show any diversity and only confirm the diagnosis established by imaging.

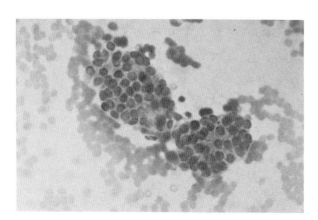

Fig. 1 **Fine-needle aspiration cytology of a pulmonary nodule.** The presence of genuine thyroid follicles even in the absence of atypical nuclei enables the diagnosis of metastasis from a well-differentiated follicular carcinoma of the thyroid

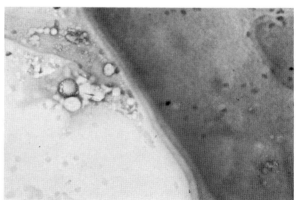

Fig. 2 **Fine-needle aspiration cytology of the liver.** This PAS-positive laminated cuticular membrane is typical of hydatid disease

Hydatidoma: there is no morphologic difference between the biopsy of a hydatid cyst and alveolar echinococcosis. Both contain fragments of PAS-positive cuticular membrane with a characteristic laminar appearance. Hooklets are only exceptionally seen (28). Differential diagnosis is based on the type of material, namely, liquid for hydatid cyst and solid for echinococcosis (Fig. 2).

Cirrhosis: hepatocyte polymorphism is more marked than in the normal liver owing to intensive regeneration.

Benign tumors. *Hepatocellular adenoma* is recognized by the particular background in which it occurs. The diagnosis can be established on the basis of the monoclonality of the hepatocyte population, associated with an increase in cell size and an increase of glycogen content (PAS) (12).

Focal nodular hyperplasia is cytologically indistinguishable from a focus of regeneration, since the hepatocyte population is polyclonal in both (30).

Hemangioma can be differentiated from metastasis by puncture biopsy, which ultrasonography cannot always achieve (14). It is rare for diagnosis to be established directly by the observation of hyperplastic endothelial cells. Rather, diagnosis is arrived at indirectly, by noting the absence of metastatic malignant cells and the presence of rare normal hepatocytes associated with large masses of blood platelets resulting from the turbulence produced by blood passing through the disorderly mesh of the angioma.

Primary malignant tumors. Diagnosis of *hepatocellular carcinoma* depends on the degree of differentiation of the neoplasm (19, 33). Well-differentiated tumors (54%) are composed of cells with perfectly regular nuclei. Certain investigators have considered cytologic diagnosis to be impossible, since the diagnosis is based mainly on architectural features seen on histologic section (6). The puncture of normal liver tissue is primordial here (Fig. 3a, b). Indeed, this disease is diagnosed by observing the contrast between monoclonal and hence monomorphic malignant tissue, and polyclonal polymorphic nonmalignant hepatic tissue (19). A whole range of signs can also confirm the diagnosis, notably microcellularity and decreased cytoplasmic glycogen (PAS) (19). Problems of differential diagnosis can arise with hepatocellular adenoma (different cell size and glycogen content) and with metastasis of clear cell adenocarcinoma (increased glycogen content).

With poorly differentiated tumors (9%), it can be practically impossible to recognize the hepatocyte origin of the malignant cells. A common error is to consider this to be a metastasis of a poorly differentiated carcinoma. The demonstration of minute amounts of glycogen by means of PAS staining may permit hepatocyte identification in some cases. Unlike focal lesions, the diffusely impaired liver is difficult both to sample and diagnose. There is no boundary between normal and pathologic tissue. Normal and malignant cells are closely intermingled, and the malignant cells can be extremely difficult to recognize in the well-differentiated types. PAS staining can again render diagnosis possible by demonstrating a difference in glycogen content between normal (PAS++) and malignant cells (PAS±).

In cirrhosis, a focus of regeneration can be diagnosed by ruling out hepatocarcinoma when biopsies of normal and pathologic tissues are the same.

Cholangiocarcinoma and *hepatocholangial carcinoma.* When the tumor is purely cholangial, which is uncommon, it simulates a metastasis; otherwise the transition between hepatocellular and cholangial components results in a picture of "metastasis within hepatocarcinoma", which is characteristic of this malignancy.

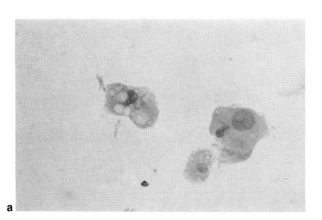

a

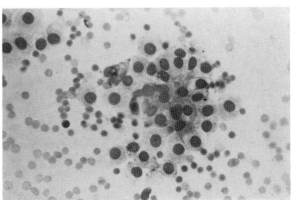

b

Fig. **3** **Fine-needle aspiration cytology of the liver.**
The contrast between the polyclonal cells **a** of the "healthy liver" and the monoclonal cells **b** of the pathologic liver enables the diagnosis of well-differentiated carcinoma of the liver

Metastasis is diagnosed when nonhepatocytic malignant cells are found to be mixed with normal hepatocytes. In 40% of the cases, puncture of a metastasis is done as part of assessing the extension of a known tumor, but in 60% of the cases it is done by first intention, before the primary neoplasm has been detected (4). The primary lesion is then sucessfully identified in just over half the cases (19) (Fig. **4**). The following malignancies, when they are differentiated, can be identified with a fair degree of certainty:

– Melanoma
– Epidermoid carcinoma
– Bronchial undifferentiated small cell carcinoma
– Non-Hodgkin malignant lymphoma
– Colon adenocarcinoma
– Colloid carcinoma
– Endocrine carcinoma
– Medullary carcinoma of the thyroid
– Any neoplasm with distinctive cell features

Identification of the following is more problematic:

– Exocrine adenocarcinoma of the pancreas
– Gastric adenocarcinoma
– Adenocarcinoma of the breast
– Adenocarcinoma of the prostate

In actual practice, the malignancies responsible for initial metastases are the following:

– Colon adenocarcinoma
– Undifferentiated small cell carcinoma of the bronchi
– Small intestine carcinoid
– Endocrine carcinoma of the pancreas

Cooperation between clinician, radiologist, and cytologist is valuable in the search for hypotheses that are consistent both with the clinical findings and the cytologic profile.

Pancreas

Percutaneous biopsy is performed on two types of lesions.

Solid tumors. The biopsy of a *focus of chronic pancreatitis* contains almost exclusively acinar clusters, which are actually foci isolated by postinflammatory sclerosis; inflammatory signs can be totally absent. In fact, little difference can be seen between biopsies of a normal pancreas and a focus of chronic pancreatitis (21).

The biopsy of an *exocrine pancreatic cancer*, of ductal origin by definition, contains ductal fragments that are more or less cancerous. A limited number of acini can be present. This radical difference between exocrine cancer and chronic pancreatitis warrants on-the-spot reading of cytologic smears during the puncture procedure. Noncancerous atypical ductal hyperplasia can be seen, and corresponds to pancreatic dysplasia (17). Although this precancerous lesion has been reported to be isolated, our own experience has shown it to be often perineoplastic. It is, therefore, wise to continue investigation and perform further biopsies.

Endocrine carcinoma develops in an acinar context. It is diagnosed on the evidence of endocrine cell morphologic characteristics, hypervascularization, and the presence of neuro-endocrine rosettes. Neuro-endocrine granulation stains positively with Grimelius in certain cases (Fig. **5**).

Cystic lesions. Puncture biopsy of *pseudocysts* contains purely inflammatory material that cannot be confused with that of adenocarcinoma even in its cystic form. The diagnosis of *cystadenocarcinoma* can only be based on a centrifuged liquid aspirate; the material is cellular and looks like an exocrine adenocarcinoma diluted in a mucous background.

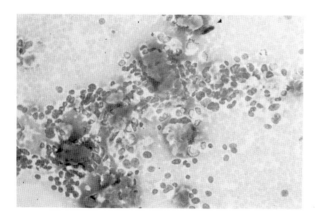

Fig. **4** **Fine-needle aspiration cytology of the liver.** The association of metastatic cells, and amyloid (dichroic Congo red stain) enables the diagnosis of metastasis from medullary carcinoma of the thyroid

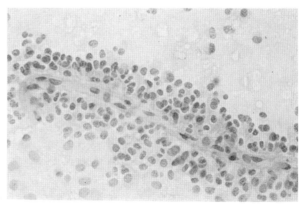

Fig. **5** **Fine-needle aspiration cytology of the pancreas.** The presence of small tumor cells, with a plasmocytoid appearance, arranged around hyperdeveloped vessels, is typical of an endocrine carcinoma

Differential diagnosis with *cystadenoma* is not difficult: in the latter the aspirates are poorly cellular and the cells lack atypia. It is important to discriminate between *serous* cystadenoma and *mucinous* cystadenoma, since malignant transformation is systematic in the latter. Finally, it must be remembered that the pancreas can be a site of *metastasis* (5, 13).

Bile Ducts

The cause of autonomic stenosis of the bile ducts, be it inflammatory, parasitic, or malignant, can be determined by studying the material obtained during percutaneous transhepatic cholangiography with drainage (10, 20, 25). Dysplasia often accompanies inflammatory stenosis. The principal difficulty in biliary cytology involves certain dysplasias that are difficult to distinguish from certain well-differentiated adenocarcinomas. Moreover, it is not always easy to decide between biliary neoplasm and pancreatic malignancy invading the bile ducts. Because of these difficulties, in order to achieve a good accuracy rate, it seems essential to perform both histologic and cytologic studies, especially since material for both techniques can be obtained during percutaneous transhepatic cholangiography and endoscopy. A diagnostic accuracy of 77 to 85% can then be reasonably expected (22, 27).

Kidney

Puncture biopsies can be taken from either the pyelocaliceal cavities, a cyst, or a solid focus. Biopsy of the pyelocaliceal cavities is of no interest and is, in fact, less informative than analysis of urinary sediment. Puncture of a cystic formation is useful only for confirming that it is really a simple cyst and not a necrosed tumor; the material is unvarying and identical to that in mammary or hepatic cysts. Although normal kidney aspirates show poor cellularity, renal adenocarcinoma aspirates generally contain an abundance of cells, but the ease of interpretation is variable and depends on the degree of necrosis, which often modifies the neoplasms. Most commonly, the cells are clear, reflecting a high cytoplasmic glycogen content (PAS). The presence of numerous vessels corroborates arteriographic evidence. Even when the smears exhibit only oncocytic cells, diagnosing oncocytoma should be avoided, since it requires examination of the whole operative specimen.

Extension to the kidney of transitional cell carcinoma is characterized by much more striking nuclear signs of malignancy and numerous mitotic figures. In angiomyolipoma the problem is more one of performing the puncture rather than of cytologic interpretation: only the small difficult-to-reach tumors need be sampled, since C. T. of the large tumors is specific (3).

The difficulties raised by metastases and lymphomas are the same as those described for the liver. The accuracy in detecting malignancy is 86 to 88% (15, 36), which is close to the rates obtained for the liver and the lung. However, all investigators report some false-positive results (18), arising from certain particular diagnostic difficulties. For instance, it is virtually impossible to discriminate between adenoma and welldifferentiated adenocarcinoma, since it is only by tumor size that the two can be distinguished.

Adrenal Gland

The main purpose of the puncture is to determine whether the malignancy is primary or metastatic, bearing in mind that adrenal cortical carcinoma is very rare and that pheochromocytoma can be diagnosed without recourse to puncture biopsy. Adrenal cytologic examination is most complex. Aspirates of normal adrenal parenchyma contain both medullary and cortical cells, forming a particularly polymorphous population, which is most difficult to analyze. Furthermore, hyperplasia of any one of the cell subsets can occur. Nuclear abnormalities are not particularly significant, since they are found both in benign lesions and in primary malignant tumors. Finally, the identification of metastases is beset by the same problems as in the other filtering organs (16).

Abdominal and Retroperitoneal Masses

This is the most complex situation that can be encountered. The cytologist must diagnose the malignancy and attempt to identify the type of tumor and hence the organ where it is seated. Cytology is fundamental here, since it can permit easy and rapid diagnosis. The lesion can be nontumoral, such as an abscess, hematoma, or malacoplakia. The mass most often proves to be a tumor: non-Hodgkin malignant lymphoma, metastatic adenopathy (2), adenocarcinoma of the colon, carcinoid, undifferentiated carcinoma, spindle cell sarcoma, mesenteric neoplasm. The diversity of the pathologic findings demands close cooperation between the cytologist and the radiologist in order to analyze each diagnostic hypothesis in terms of the site of the lesion. Despite the difficulty of diagnosing such masses, it is possible to achieve a sensitivity of 85% and a specificity of 94% (4, 30, 36).

Pelvic Mass

Many lesions can present as poorly defined masses. The mass can be a carcinoma of the bladder, rectum, or genital tract, or a recurrence thereof, which must not be confused with postradiotherapy fibrosis. Lymph node enlargement is frequent, most often as a result of lymph node metastasis of epidermoid carcinoma (cutaneous or gynecologic), melanoma, prostatic adenocarcinoma, or urothelial carcinoma, less often metastasis of abdominal or thoracic neoplasms. Lymphoma can originate in the pelvis. Finally, puncture biopsy of osteolytic lesions of the pelvis can be helpful for detecting a bone tumor: frequently chondrosarcoma, a chondroma, or most commonly a metastasis (colon, breast, kidney, thyroid, prostate) (23). Conversely, puncture biopsy in the first intention of an ovarian tumor is not advisable because of the high risk of peritoneal dissemination, owing to the mobility of the lesion and to the fact that it is often cystic.

References

1. Bejui-Thivolet F, Patricot LM, Vauzelle JL, Viac J. Keratins in malignant mesotheliomas and pleural adenocarcinomas: comparative immunohistochemical analysis with polyclonal and monoclonal antibodies. Pathol Res Pract 1984;179:67.
2. Bonfiglio TA, MacIntosh PK, Patten SF Jr, Cafer DJ, Woodworth FE, Kim DW. Fine needle aspiration cytopathology of retroperitoneal lymph nodes in the evaluation of metastatic disease. Acta Cytol (Baltimore) 1979;23:126.
3. Bret PM, Bretagnolle M. Small asymptomatic angiomyolipomas of the kidney. Radiology 1985;154:7.
4. Bret PM, Fond A, Bretagnolle M, Barral, F, Labadie M. Percutaneous fine needle biopsy (PFNB) of intra-abdominal lesions. Eur J Radiol 1982;2:322.
5. Bret PM, Nicolet V, Labadie M. Percutaneous fine needle aspiration biopsy of the pancreas. Diagn Cytopathol 1986; 2:221.
6. Carney CN. Clinical cytology of the liver. Acta Cytol (Baltimore) 1975;19:244.
7. Dahlgren SE. Aspiration biopsy of intrathoracic tumors. Acta Pathol Microbiol Scand [B] 1967;70:566.
8. Domagala W, Lubinski J, Weber K, Osborn M. Intermediate filament typing of tumor cells in fine needle aspirates by means of monoclonal antibodies. Acta Cytol (Baltimore) 1986;30:214.
9. Duvauferrier R. Aiguilles et trocards. In Duvauferrier R, Ramée A, Guibert JL, eds. Radiologie et échographie interventionnelles; vol. I. Montpellier: Axone,1986:65–71.
10. Elyaderani K, Gabriele OF. Brush and forceps biopsy of biliary ducts via percutaneous transhepatic catheterization. Radiology 1980;135:777.
11. Gibbons RP, Bush WH, Burnett LL. Needle tract seeding following aspiration of renal cell carcinoma. J Urol 1977; 118:865–867.
12. Gibson JB, Sobin LH. Types histologiques des tumeurs du foie, des voies biliaires et du pancréas. Classification histologique internationale des tumeurs. no 20. Genève: OMS, 1978.
13. Goodale RL, Gajl-Peczalska K. Cytologic studies for the diagnosis of pancreatic cancer. Cancer 1981;47:1652.
14. Haaga JF. New techniques for CT guided biopsies. AJR 1979;133:633.
15. Juul N, Torp-Pedersen S, Gronwall S. Ultrasonically-guided fine needle aspiration biopsy of renal masses. J Urol 1985;133:579.
16. Katz RL, Patel S, Mackoy B. Zornoza J. Fine needle aspiration cytology of the adrenal gland. Acta Cytol (Baltimore) 1984;28:269.
17. Kozuka, S, Sassa R, Taki T, Masamoto K. Relation of pancreatic duct hyperplasia to carcinoma. Cancer 1979;43:1418.
18. Kristensen JK, Holm HH, Rasmussen SN, Barlebo H. Ultrasonically guided percutaneous puncture or renal masses. Scand J Urol Nephrol. 1972;6(suppl 15):49.
19. Labadie M, Berger F, Liaras A, Bret PA, Bretagnolle M, Fond A, Minaire Y. Can cytological puncture-aspiration of hepatic lesions replace biopsy aspiration? Acta Endosc 1985;15:281.
20. Labadie M, Bouvet B, Berger F, Bret PA, Bretagnolle M, Minaire Y. Diagnosis contribution of cytological and histological study of endobiliary samples obtained by brushing and biopsy in the identification of stenosis of the biliary ducts: a preliminary study concerning 29 cases. Acta Endosc 1985;15:291.
21. Labadie M, Descos L, Berger F. La ponction cytologique du pancréas: étude préliminaire. Arch Anat Cytol Pathol 1980;28:175.
22. Laumonier R, Laquerrière R. Les variations de l'acide désoxyribonucléique (DNA) dans la régénération hépatique. Rev Int Hepatol 1962;12:633.
23. Linsk JA, Franzen S. Pelvis (non-gyn.). In: Linsk JA, Franzen S, eds. Clinical aspiration cytology. Philadelphia: Lippincott, 1983:207–219.
24. Lopes-Cardozo P. Atlas of clinical cytology. 's Hertogenbosch:Targa,1975.
25. Mendez G, Russel E, Levi JU, Koolpe EH, Cohen M. Percutaneous brush biopsy and internal drainage of biliary tree through endoprosthesis. AJR 1980;134:653.
26. Poe RH, Tobin RE. Sensitivity and specificity of needle biopsy in lung malignancy. Am Rev Respir Dis 1980;122:725.
27. Portner, WJ, Koople HA. New devices for biliary drainage and biopsy. AJR 1982;138:1191.
28. Retta JV, Manana G, Reissenweber NJ. The ctyologic diagnosis of hydatid disease. Acta Cytol (Baltimore) 1982;26:159.
29. Rosenberger A, Adler O. Fine needle aspiration biopsy in the diagnosis of mediastinal lesions. AJR 1978;131:239.
30. Staab EV, Jaques PF, Partain CL. Percutaneous biopsy in the management of solid intra-abdominal masses of unknown etiology. Radiol Clin North Am 1979;17:439.
31. Sterrett G, Whitabker D, Shilkin KB, Walter MN. The fine needle aspiration cytology of mediastinal lesions. Cancer 1983;51:127.
32. Taft PD, Szyfelbein WM, Greene, R. A study of variability in cytologic diagnosis based on pulmonary aspiration specimens. Am J Clin Pathol 1980;73:36.
33. Tao LC, Ho CS, McLoughlin MJ. The cytopathology of hepatocellular carcinoma. Montreal: The eighth International Congress of Cytology, 1983:78.
34. Thornbury JR, Burke DP, Naylor B. Transthoracic needle aspiration biopsy: accuracy of cytologic typing of malignant neoplasms. AJR 1981;136:719.
35. Von Shreeb T, Arner O, Skorsted G. Renal adenocarcinoma: is there a risk of spreading tumour cells in diagnostic puncture? Scand J Urol Nephrol 1967;1:270.
36. Zornoza J, Jonsson K, Wallace S, Lukeman JM. Fine needle aspiration biopsy of retroperitoneal lymph nodes and abdominal masses: an updated report. Radiology 1977;125:87.

Lung Biopsy

J. L. Westcott

In recent years, percutaneous transthoracic needle biopsy (PTNB) has become established as a safe and definitive method for diagnosis and management of pulmonary nodules and masses. The diagnostic accuracy has steadily improved, and several investigators have reported accuracies (sensitivity) of 93 to 98% for patients with lung cancer (2, 8, 13, 15, 18, 20, 26, 29, 30, 37).

The improved results from PTNB have resulted from progress in several areas. Improvements in imaging techniques have made it possible to visualize and carry out biopsy of lung nodules as small as 5 mm in diameter. Improvements in needle design have made it possible to use smaller needles (20 to 22 G) while maintaining the ability to obtain material for both cytologic and histologic study (1–3, 13–16, 19, 20, 24, 37, 38, 43). The use of smaller needles has made PTNB an extremely safe procedure. The risk of major hemorrhage has practically been eliminated, and biopsy of deep, central, and hilar masses is not only possible but safe. The relative ease and safety of the procedure has made it possible to perform several "passes" as needed to ensure that an adequate sample has been obtained. A cytologic diagnosis can usually be made within a few minutes, and, if necessary, the procedure can be repeated, at the same sitting, until a definitive diagnosis is obtained. Cytopathologists have developed remarkable accuracy in cytologic identification of cancer and in the ability to render accurate cell type determinations from cytology and small tissue fragments.

The increased accuracy of PTNB and fiber-optic bronchoscopy (FOB) warrants reevaluation of the approach to the diagnosis and treatment of suspected lung cancer. If it can be shown, with high statistical probability, that the lesion in question is benign, surgery is usually unnecessary (12, 18). Such patients can be managed conservatively, and, if the lesion is stable, followed with periodic X-rays. In the case of malignant disease, the patient should be staged accurately before surgery whenever possible.

In this chapter, the technique, results, complications, indications, and contra-indications of PTNB of the lung are reviewed. Suggested guidelines for the optimal use of FOB and PTNB will also be presented.

Technique

The techniques of PTNB have been described by numerous investigators (2, 8, 13, 15, 17–20, 26, 29, 35, 37, 42). For pulmonary lesions, it is usually easier and faster to use videofluoroscopy rather than computed tomography (CT) if the lesion is fluoroscopically visible. Occasionally, a lesion may be fluoroscopically visible, even when it cannot be seen on the standard chest radiograph (Fig. **1**). Before the procedure is undertaken, the exact position of the lesion should be ascertained from recent chest X-rays, tomograms, or CT scans. The depth of the lesion should be carefully measured roentgenographically before the biopsy procedure is done.

Several types of biopsy needles have been used by different investigators with good results (13, 15, 19, 24, 35, 37, 38, 43). For several years, we have used 20 and 22 gauge slotted needles almost exclusively (37, 38). The amount of material obtained has usually been sufficient for both cytologic and histologic analysis. The use of needles larger than 20 G has been restricted to bone or chest wall lesions and to the rare circumstance of a large tissue core being required. The 22 G and smaller needles probably are associated with a lower incidence of pneumothorax (15, 41, 43). Currently, we almost always routinely use the 22 G needle first. The 20 G needle is used only if the specimen is inadequate or if there is difficulty controlling the direction of the 22 G needle. The 20 G needle is more rigid, bends less, and is therefore easier to control. The added control and rigidity is sometimes an advantage in performing PTNB of small nodules and in penetrating hard lesions, such as hamartomas and granulomas.

Good videofluoroscopy and a movable table top are essential. Biplane fluoroscopy, rotating tables, and multidirectional intensifiers are all helpful (13, 18) but are not necessary. Premedication is rarely required. The patient is carefully instructed regarding details of the procedure and its overall safety, accuracy, and possible complications, such as pneumothorax and hemoptysis. It is important to inform the patient that the biopsy will be repeated one or more times if the initial results are negative, to ensure high diagnostic accuracy. There is much less resistance to repeat biopsy attempts if the patient and the referring physician understand the logic of repeat biopsy before the procedure is undertaken.

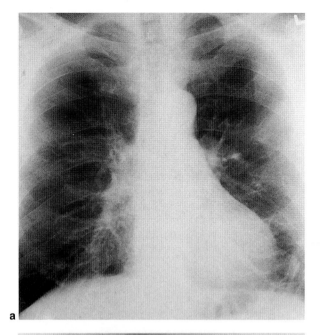

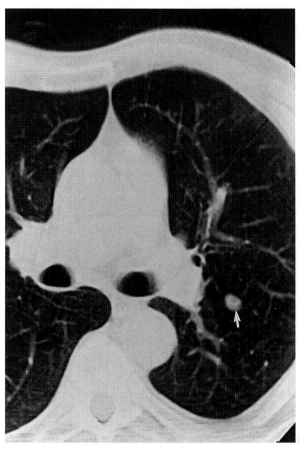

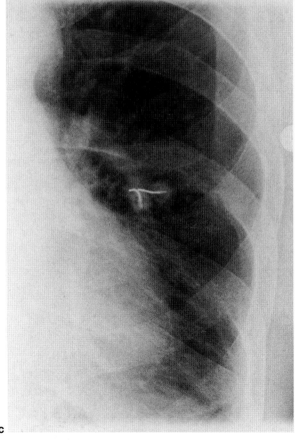

Fig. **1**   A 70-year-old man with recent onset of seizures. A CT scan of the head revealed multiple enhancing cerebral masses. Although the chest roentgenogram (**a**) was negative, a chest CT scan (**b**) revealed a 12 mm nodule in the superior segment of the left lower lobe. Needle biopsy was performed using a posterior approach; the lesion was faintly visible at fluoroscopy. Two 22 G needles were directed into the nodule (**c**). The aspirate revealed adenocarcinoma

The patient is placed on the fluoroscopy table in either the supine or prone position, depending on the location of the lesion. Occasionally, on oblique position is useful if the mass or nodule is difficult to visualize in the standard supine or prone position, or if it is situated directly beneath the scapula or a rib. The lesion is localized under fluoroscopy, and the skin directly over it is marked. Lidocaine 2% is generously infiltrated into the skin and soft tissues down to the estimated depth of the pleura. The instillation of anesthesia is important. If it is not instilled deeply enough, the patient will experience pain as the biopsy needle passes between the ribs. Any movement associated with the pain may misdirect the needle. If it is inserted too deeply, there is a small risk of pneumothorax. A small pneumothorax does not affect biopsy of large lesions. However, biopsy of a small nodule is extremely difficult in the presence of a pneumothorax because the lung tends to push away from the needle tip. For several years, we have used long, 1.5 to 3 inch 25 G needles for both superficial and deep local anesthesia. Since adopting this practice, we have not observed an anesthesia-induced pneumothorax.

After instillation of the anesthesia, the biopsy needle is inserted into the chest wall of the appropriate intercostal space. Before traversing the pleura, the needle position and direction are checked fluoroscopically to make certain that the tip is directed toward the lesion. Several minor readjustments of the needle direction may be required. The needle is directed into the lung on as straight a perpendicular axis as possible (Fig. **2**). The more "angling" of the needle that is used, the more difficult it is to triangulate the proper angle and depth of the needle with respect to the lesion. The immediate undersurfaces of the ribs and clavicle are avoided whenever possible to prevent damage to the intercos-

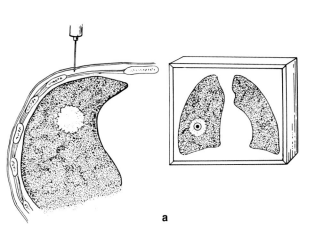

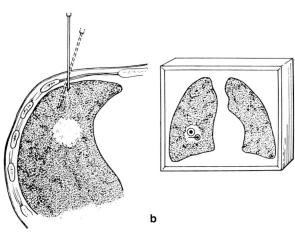

a

b

Fig. **2** **a** The position and direction of the lidocaine needle are carefully selected and adjusted fluoroscopically and visually to ensure that the needle is directed toward the lesion. This same position and direction is then used for the biopsy needle

b The biopsy needle is directed on a perpendicular toward the lesion, and the needle shaft and hub remain centered. Whenever possible, needle angulation is avoided, unless angled fluoroscopy or rotating table tops are available, because it is difficult to assess the proper angle required, particularly for small deep lesions. It is also difficult to redirect the needle after it has passed into the lung more than 2 or 3 cm. If it appears that the needle may bypass the lesion, it is advisable to retract the needle without complete withdrawal from the lung and redirect it. The needle is advanced intermittently 1 to 2 cm at a time with a fluoroscopic check after each advance. Respiration is suspended during advances, but the patient is otherwise allowed to breathe normally. When resistance is encountered, the needle is advanced into the lesion with a short thrust.

c–d The position is checked fluoroscopically, and a 50 ml glass syringe is attached. During maximum suction, the needle is jiggled up and down rapidly several times, and then slowly withdrawn during continued suction

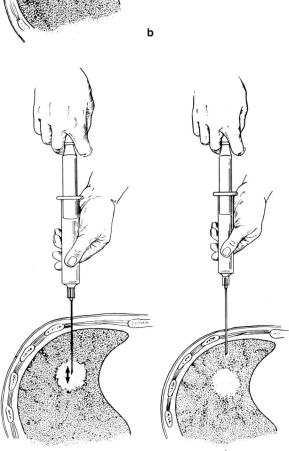

c

d

tal vessels; however, this principle may occasionally have to be violated. Fortunately, significant intercostal bleeding has not, to my knowledge, been reported with the use of needles 20 G or smaller. The needle is advanced into the lung during suspended respiration, and the position and direction are checked again. The patient is allowed to breathe normally at all times except when the needle is being advanced. The needle is never advanced during fluoroscopy because it is poor practice for the operator's hand to enter the fluoroscopic field. If the tip is not heading toward the lesion, it is usually best to retract, without complete withdrawal from the lung and to redirect the needle. Attempts to change the direction of the needle significantly by angulation are usually unsuccessful once the needle has penetrated the lung by more than 2 to 3 cm. The needle is advanced intermittently 1 to 2 cm at a time, with a fluoroscopic position check following each advance, until resistance is encountered at the edge of the lesion. Occasionally, little or no resistance can be appreciated. In such cases, biplane fluoroscopy, lateral fluoroscopy, or a lateral radiograph may be helpful for confirming the proper depth and placement of the needle. The needle stylet is withdrawn 2 to 3 cm, and the needle is advanced into the mass or nodule with a short thrust. Certain lesions, hamartomas, some granulomas, occasional neoplasms, are so hard that penetration requires a very rapid forceful thrust. The position of the needle tip is checked again fluoroscopically. If it is relatively certain that the needle is within the lesion, the stylet is removed, and a 30 or 50 ml syringe is attached to the needle hub. A 30 ml syringe is easier to use, but a 50 ml syringe creates greater suction. To prevent air embolism, respiration should be suspended, and the hub of the needle should be occluced with the operator's thumb or finger when the stylet is removed. The plunger is withdrawn as far as possible to achieve maximum suction. The operator's dominant hand is used to maintain suction while the other hand stabilizes the barrel of the syringe (Fig. 2c). The needle is jiggled up and down rapidly several times and then withdrawn slowly with continued suction (Fig. 2d). If the amount of material seems inadequate or if the operator is uncertain that the lesion was entered, a repeat biopsy is performed immediately. If it is obvious that the needle has missed the lesion, it is often advantageous to insert a second needle while the first needle is still in place. The initial needle tends to splint the nodule and adjacent lung and makes it easier to place the second needle correctly. With larger lesions, it is important to sample the periphery because many tumors have necrotic centers.

All of the aspirated material ist teased from the needle and from the barrel, hub, and sides of the syringe. The major portion of the aspirate is almost always in the syringe rather than the needle. A 5.5 inch flat nickel probe is helpful for extracting material from the syringe. The material is spread gently on frosted or albumincoated slides and immediately placed in 95% alcohol. Any larger pieces obtained are placed in 10% formalin for histologic sections. Usually, these pieces are small hemorrhagic or gelatinous fragments rather than solid cores of tissue, but they are usually adequate for histologic sections. The needle and syringe are washed with nonbacteriostatic saline or liquid culture medium for later bacteriologic study. To reduce cost, the bacteriologic material is processed immediately only when the patient has a known or presumed inflammatory process. When neoplasm is probable, the culture medium is held pending preliminary cytologic diagnosis; if neoplasm is confirmed, it is discarded.

If the initial biopsy report is negative and a specific diagnosis is rendered (granuloma, hamartoma, specific infectious agent), the biopsy is usually not repeated unless the suspicion of malignancy is extremely high. However, if the initial result is negative, no specific diagnosis, indeterminate, or unsatisfactory, the biopsy procedure should be repeated (12, 15, 29, 37). Within reason, aspiration attempts are repeated until both the radiologist and cytopathologist are reasonably certain that the material was obtained from a lesion and not just from normal lung. Rarely, it may be necessary to perform up to four or even five biopsies to satisfy these requirements. The usefulness of this approach was reported in a previous article (37). In this series, there were 105 patients with a negative, no specific diagnosis, or unsatisfactory result from the initial aspiration in whom the procedure was repeated one or more times. In 37 (35%), an initial reading of indeterminate or negative was changed, and the lesion was correctly identified as a malignant neoplasm. Of the total of 293 malignant neoplasms in this series, there were five false-negative results (1.7%). If the repeat biopsy approach had not been used, there would have been 42 false-negative results (14.3%).

Complications and Aftercare

The complications of PTNB are bleeding and pneumothorax. Significant bleeding which is life-threatening or requires treatment, almost never occurs. To my knowledge, there has been only one reported case of fatal hemorrhage after PTNB with a 20 G needle (21) and none with 22 G needles.

Hemoptysis, when it occurs, almost always takes place immediately and is usually preceded by a cough. The patient is turned into a lateral decubitus position with the biopsied side down on the principle that blood aspiration into the nonbiopsied lung should be less likely to occur in this position. The patient is assured that the bleeding will stop shortly. Nasal oxygen is administered if there is any respiratory distress. Although minor hemoptysis occurs in 5 to 10% of our lung biopsies, we have not personally encountered life-threatening hemoptysis using 20 and 22 G needles.

Radiographic evidence of bleeding around the lesion is frequently observed after the biopsy and is not of concern. However, it does make repeat biopsy of small nodules difficult. If a repeat is required, and if the nodule is obscured, we prefer to discharge the patient and postpone the repeat examination until the hematoma clears, usually in 1 to 2 weeks.

In our patients, the incidence of pneumothorax used to be approximately 25%, and approximately 40% of the pneumothoraces (10% of the total patients) were treated with small chest tubes. Currently, these figures are approximately 15%, 33%, and 5%, respectively. The reduced incidence of pneumothorax is presumably due to the more frequent use of 22 G needles.

Our routine for following and handling pneumothorax is as follows: after the procedure, an upright expiration radiograph is performed. If there is no pneumothorax, the patient ist returned to the floor with nursing instructions to check for shortness of breath every 2 hours for 24 hours. If there is a pneumothorax, and the patient is symptomatic, it is treated immediately. If there is a small pneumothorax that is asymptomatic, a repeat radiograph is taken within an hour. If the pneumothorax is progressing significantly, it is treated whether the patient is symptomatic or not. Treatment of a post-biopsy pneumothorax rarely requires a large chest tube. A 14 G, 15 cm two-piece Teflon sleeve needle containing 4 distal side holes is inserted percutaneously into the pleural space in the anterior second intercostal space and directed toward the apex of the thorax. A kit containing a 14 G Teflon needle with side holes, Heimlich valve, and connecting tube is available. The catheter is connected to a one-way Heimlich valve and left in place until the air leak seals. This is a modification of the technique described by Sargent and Turner (28). With large air leaks, the Heimlich valve can be inserted. The advantages of this system are firstly, that the chest catheter causes much less discomfort than does a standard chest tube and does not require special expertise for insertion and placement; and secondly, that the Heimlich valve allows the patient to remain ambulatory.

Outpatients are retained in the radiology department for 2 to 3 hours after PTNB. If the 2-hour expiration chest X-ray reveals no pneumothorax, the patient is discharged with instructions to call immediately if shortness of breath develops. If there is a significant pneumothorax, the chest catheter Heimlich valve system is inserted and the patient is hospitalized and monitored until the air leak seals, usually in 24 hours.

If there is a small asymptomatic pneumothorax that has stabilized, and if the patient is reasonably healthy, has transportation, and can return to the hospital, he or she may be discharged with instructions to return immediately if respiratory distress occurs.

Contraindications

There are no absolute contra-indications to performing PTNB. However, there are relative contra-indications when the risk of biopsy must be weighed against the alternatives.

Severely compromised pulmonary function is not a contra-indication by itself. However, if a pneumothorax occurs, it must be treated immediately. If the patient has severe emphysema, only one functioning lung, or severely compromised pulmonary function from any cause, a pneumothorax treatment catheter set should be ready for immediate insertion.

Coagulopathy. Initially, a blood coagulation profile was routinely obtained before all biopsies, but it is now performed only under special circumstances, such as immunosuppression, recent anticoagulation, bleeding disorders. Obviously, platelet and coagulation deficiencies should be corrected as much as possible before the biopsy.

Pulmonary hypertension. We have not considered severe pulmonary hypertension as a contra-indication to lung biopsy but have considered it a relative contra-indication to doing hilar biopsies.

If any of the above risk factors occur, use of a small-bore 22 G needle is recommended. Spread of tumor or infection along the biopsy site occurs so rarely with small-bore needles (10, 13, 39) that we do not believe it should be considered a contra-indication to needle biopsy.

Results

The reported results of PTNB vary, but accuracy rates of 90 to 98% have been reported by several investigators (2, 3, 8, 12, 13, 15, 18, 19, 20, 26, 29, 30, 31, 37). Significant bleeding has virtually been eliminated as a complication by using needles of 20 G or smaller, and this safety factor has made it possible to carry out biopsy on deep and centrally placed lesions routinely. Excellent results have been obtained with PTNB of both small nodules and larger masses; Sinner (29) reported 98% accuracy in a large series dealing exclusively with lesions measuring 2 cm or less in diameter. It is important to select those cases that are appropriate for PTNB properly. Patients with endobronchial lesions or atelectasis should undergo FOB rather than PTNB as the initial diagnostic procedure, because PTNB may result in a false-negative study if one samples an area of obstructive pneumonitis or collapse due to an endobronchial lesion.

PTNB has also been used for many years to obtain material for bacteriologic study in patients with pneumonias, abscesses, and chronic infections (4–6, 13, 22, 27, 37). Recently, Castellino and Blank (5) reported a 73% diagnostic yield in immunocompromised patients with focal infections. The comparative yield of PTNB and FOB for diagnosis of pulmonary infections is unknown. The major advantage of PTNB is that the problem of possible contamination from the mouth, nose, and pharynx is avoided. The major disadvantage of PTNB is a higher incidence of pneumothorax. However, in our experience, if the needle can be directed into an area of pleural-based consolidation, pneumothorax is uncommon.

PTNB is useful because it can eliminate the need for surgery. If it can be shown that the lesion in question is benign, surgery is usually unnecessary (11, 18, 37). Such patients can usually be followed with periodic X-rays. Our follow-up regimen for stable benign lesions is to repeat the chest X-ray at intervals of 1, 3, 6, and 12 months, and yearly thereafter for at least 3 years.

Proper interpretation and handling of the cytopathologic report is extremely important. If the diagnosis is benign and a specific diagnosis is rendered, such as abscess, specific infectious agent, hamartoma, or granuloma, it is usually accepted as such. If repeated biopsy is negative but no specific diagnosis is rendered, the patient may be followed if the suspicion of malignancy is low, if the biopsy sample is adequate, and if there are large numbers of inflammatory cells or multinucleated giant cells. If the suspicion of malignancy is high, FOB should probably be performed. If both procedures are negative but if suspicion of malignancy remains high, a management decision should be made based on input from the surgeon, chest physician, radiologist, and pathologist. In some patients, surgery may still be appropriate, particularly if there is any doubt regarding the adequacy of the biopsy specimen.

The handling of a positive result also warrants comment. False-positive results occurred early in our series but are now extremely uncommon. Therefore, a diagnosis of malignancy is usually accepted as such. Another important consideration is cell-type determination. Currently, the most important distinction is between small-cell and nonsmall-cell carcinoma. Fortunately, in our own and others' experience (19, 31, 34), accurate differentiation is usually possible from the needle aspirate. In questionable cases, electron microscopy of a portion of the aspirate is sometimes useful. If the pathologist is uncertain regarding the cell type, small-cell versus nonsmall-cell, repeat biopsy is performed. Usually, a repeat fine-needle

biopsy is sufficient, but occasionally larger needles or even open biopsy may be required.

Comparison of Diagnostic Methods

In addition to the need to optimize patient care, there are strong economic pressures to diagnose and stage patients with suspected neoplasms as accurately, inexpensively, and rapidly as possible. Results indicate that some diagnostic methods are better than others for different types of lesions. The following uses for FOB and PTNB are suggested for patients with suspected neoplasms of the lung. The choices expressed here assume reasonable and approximately equal competence in FOB and PTNB, as well as the availability of good cytopathologic examinations.

Solitary Pulmonary Nodule or Mass Measuring Less than 3 cm in Diameter

With solitary pulmonary nodules measuring less than 3 cm, assuming that there are no prior X-rays to determine the history of the nodule, chest tomograms or CT should be done to look for calcification (Fig. 3). If calcification is present and if it is either central, lamellated, or occupies a large portion of the nodule, no further evaluation is necessary. If calcifications are absent, small, eccentric, or scattered, a biopsy should be performed. We believe PTNB is the procedure of choice because it has the highest yield. As stated earlier, the accuracy of carefully performed PTNB including small nodules has usually exceeded 90% (2, 8, 13, 15, 20, 26, 29, 30, 37). Most series dealing with FOB have reported diagnostic yields of 60% or less in peripheral lesions measuring less than 3 cm in diameter and less than 50% when the lesion is 2 cm or smaller (7, 9, 25, 33).

If the biopsy reveals neoplasm, CT can be done for evaluation of the mediastinum. If CT reveals lymphadenopathy, we believe that mediastinal needle biopsy or mediastinoscopy is indicated for staging.

Endobronchial Lesion

If the clinical or radiographic presentation indicates an endobronchial lesion, atelectasis, hemoptysis, or radiographic evidence of bronchial narrowing, FOB is the procedure of choice because the diagnostic yield for lesions visible through the bronchoscope has been reported to be as high as 94% (40). If the results are negative or nondiagnostic, PTNB should be performed if there is a visible mass. If either test reveals neoplasm, CT should be performed if it has not already been done, followed by mediastinoscopy or needle biopsy of the mediastinum if CT reveals mediastinal disease.

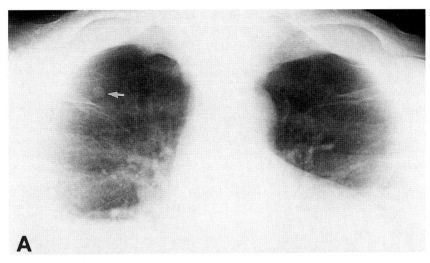

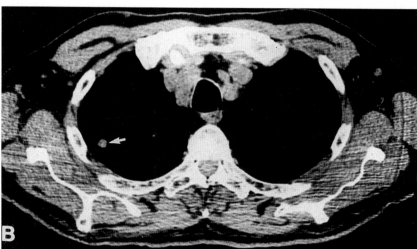

Fig. 3 This 56-year-old man had a slowly growing nodule (arrows) in the right upper lobe. Apical lordotic chest X-ray (**a**), CT scan (**b**), and chest tomograms failed to demonstrate calcification. Biopsy using a 20 gauge needle revealed class I, benign cytologic findings and cartilaginous fragments diagnostic of hamartoma. The patient is being followed with yearly chest X-rays

Suspected Metastatic Pulmonary Nodules

The yield from FOB for focal pulmonary metastases appears to be less than it is for primary lung carcinoma. Two studies have revealed a positive yield of only 37.5% in patients with metastatic pulmonary nodules (7, 40). With PTNB, the experience of several investigators (13, 15, 37) has revealed no significant difference in the percentage yields for primary versus metastatic lesions. Therefore, we believe PTNB is the initial procedure of choice for suspected metastatic nodules.

Diffuse Pulmonary Disease

PTNB is not recommended for diffuse interstitial pneumonitis and fibrosis because the yield is so poor. PTNB is sometimes useful in diffuse lymphangitic carcinomatosis. In our experience, the positive yield from PTNB in lymphangitic carcinomatosis has been approximately 50% when there is no focal lesion to

aim for. In patients with suspected lymphangitic carcinoma, we usually advocate FOB with biopsy as the initial procedure and reserve PTNB for cases in which the results from FOB are nondiagnostic.

Pulmonary Mass 3 cm or Greater in Diameter

The best diagnostic procedure in patients with a pulmonary mass greater than 3 cm in diameter depends on the presence or absence of bronchial involvement. If there is a visible lesion in the major bronchi, the best reported results of FOB and PTNB are similar: greater than 90% positive yield for primary neoplasms. However, the yield of FOB decreases sharply in peripheral lesions (7, 9, 25, 32, 33, 40). In this discussion, peripheral refers to non-endobronchial lesions and has nothing to do with the location of the mass within the thorax. Lesions in the central portions of the lungs may, therefore, be peripheral. When there is no endobronchial lesion, the reported yields from FOB have been less than with PTNB. According to Cortese and McDougall (7), the expected yield of FOB for all nonendobronchial lesions can be expected to be between 50 and 80%, although yields less than 50% have been reported (33). High yields of PTNB, exceeding 90%, have been achieved in patients with visible masses without regard to the presence or absence of bronchial involvement. We believe the bronchi should be evaluated initially with a chest radiograph and either bronchial tomograms or preferably CT (23, 36). If there is abnormality of the lobar or segmental bronchi, FOB is the logical initial procedure. PTNB is the procedure of choice if the major bronchi are not involved. If FOB or PTNB is positive, the patient should be staged for mediastinal or distant spread. If the biopsy is negative, patient management should depend on the adequacy of the biopsy specimen, whether there is a specific benign diagnosis and the index of suspicion for malignancy. If there is a strong suspicion of malignancy in a patient with nondiagnostic PTNB, FOB should be performed, and vice versa.

Distant Metastases

In many patients with distant metastases, determination of inoperability can frequently be accomplished without a needle biopsy of the lung. Needle biopsy of adrenal, soft tissue, and bony metastases is easily performed and can be used to stage as well as diagnose the problem without risk of pneumothorax.

Conclusions

Properly performed, PTNB is a relatively simple and safe procedure that can provide high diagnostic accuracy in patients with pulmonary lesions. The major complication is pneumothorax, but this is easily treated with small chest catheters. Its safety, ease, and accuracy render it the preferred initial diagnostic procedure in patients with pulmonary nodules and nonendobronchial masses.

References

1. Andriole JG, Haaga JR, Adams RB, Nunez C. Biopsy needle characteristic assessed in the laboratory. Radiology 1983;148:659–662.
2. Arnston TL, Boyd WR. Percutaneous biopsy using a safe effective needle. Radiology 1978;127:265–266.
3. Ballard GL, Boyd WR. A specially designed cutting aspiration needle for lung biopsy. AJR 1978;130:899–903.
4. Bandt PH, Blank N, Castellino RA. Needle diagnosis of pneumonitis: value in high-risk patients. JAMA 1972;220:1578–1580.
5. Castellino R, Blank N. Etiologic diagnosis of focal pulmonary infection in immunocompromised patients by fluoroscopically guided percutaneous needle aspiration. Radiology 1979;132:563–567.
6. Chaudhary S, Hughes WT, Feldman S, Sanyal SK, Coburn T, Ossi M, Cox F. Percutaneous transthoracic needle aspiration of the lung. Am J Dis Child 1974;131:902–907.
7. Cortese DA, McDougall JC. Biopsy and brushing of peripheral lung cancer with fluoroscopic guidance. Chest 1979;75:141–145.
8. Dahlgren S, Nordenstrom B, eds. Transthoracic needle biopsy. Stockholm: Almquist and Wiksell, 1966.
9. Ellis Jr. Transbronchial lung biopsy via the fiberoptic bronchoscope: experience with 107 consecutive cases and comparison with bronchial brushing. Chest 1975;68:524–532.
10. Engzelli U, Espost PL, Rubio C, Sigurdson A, Zajicek J. Investigation of tumour spread in connection with aspiration biopsy. Acta Radiol [Diagn] (Stockh) 1971;10:385–389.
11. Gobien RP, Bouchard EA, Gobien SB, Valicenti JF, Vujic I. Thin needle aspiration biopsy of thoracic lesions: impact of hospital charges and patterns of patient care. Radiology 1983;148:65–67.
12. Gobien RP, Valicenti JF, Paris BS, Danieleli C. Thin needle aspiration biopsy: methods of increasing the accuracy of a negative prediction. Radiology 1982;145:603–605.
13. Greene R. Transthoracic needle aspiration biopsy. In: Athanasoulis CA, Pfister RC, Greene R, Roberson GH, eds. Interventional Radiology. Philadelphia, Saunders, 1982:587–634.
14. Haaga JR, Lipuma JP, Bryan PJ, Balsara VJ, Cohen AM. Clinical comparison of small and large bore caliber cutting needles for biopsy. Radiology 1983;146:665–667.
15. House AJ, Thomson KR. Evaluation of a new transthoracic needle for biopsy of benign and malignant lung lesions. AJR 1977;129:215–221.
16. Isler RJ, Ferrucci JT, Wittenberg J, Muller PR, Simeone JF, van Sonnenberg E, Hall DA. Tissue core biopsy of abdominal tumors with a 22 gauge cutting needle. AJR 1981;136:725–728.
17. Jereb M, Sinner W. The use of some special radiologic procedures in chest disease. Radiol Clin North Am 1973;11:109–123.
18. Khouri NF, Stitik FP, Erozan YS, Gupta PK, Kim WS, Scott WW Jr, Hamper UM, Mann RE, Engleston JC, Baker RR. Transthoracic needle aspiration biopsy of benign and malignant lung lesions. AJR 1985; 144:281–288.
19. Lieberman RP, Hafez GR, Crummy AB. Histology from aspiration biopsy: Turner needle experience. AJR 1982;138:561–564.
20. Meyer JE, Gandbhir LH, Milner LB, McLaughlin MM. Percutaneous needle biopsy of nodular lung lesions. J Thorac Cardiovasc Surg. 1977;73:787–791.
21. Milner LB, Ryan K, Gullo J. Fatal intrathoracic hemorrhage after percutaneous lung biopsy. AJR 1979;132:280–281.
22. Mimica I, Donoso E, Howard JE, Ledermann GW. Lung puncture in the etiological diagnosis of pneumonia. Am J Dis Child 1971;122:278–282.
23. Nadich DP, Lee JJ, Garay SM, McCauley DI, Aranda CP, Boyd AD. Comparison of CT and fiberoptic bronchoscopy in the evaluation of bronchial disease. AJR 1987;148:1–8.
24. Nordenstrom B. New instruments for biopsy. Radiology 1975;117:474–475.
25. Radke JR, Conway WA, Eyeler WR, Kvale PA. Diagnostic accuracy in peripheral lung lesions: factors predicting success with flexible fiberoptic bronchoscopy. Chest 1979;76:176–179.
26. Sagel SS, Ferguson TB, Forrest JR. Percutaneous transthoracic aspiration needle biopsy. Ann Thorac Surg 1978;26:399–405.
27. Sappington SW, Favorite GO. Lung puncture in lobar pneumonia. Am J Med Sci 1936;191:225–234.
28. Sargent E, Turner AF. Emergency treatment of pneumothorax: a simple catheter technique for use in the radiology department. AJR 1970;109:531–535.
29. Sinner WN. Transthoracic needle biopsy of small peripheral malignant lung lesions. Invest Radiol 1973;8:305–314.
30. Sinner WN. Pulmonary lesions diagnosed by needle biopsy. Cancer 1979;43:1533–1540.
31. Sinner, WN, Sandstedt B. Small cell carcinoma of the lung. Radiology 1976;121:269–274.
32. Solomon DA, Solliday NH, Gracey DR. Cytology in fiberoptic bronchoscopy. Chest 1974;65:616–619.
33. Stringfiled JR III, Markowitz DJ, Bentz RR, Welch MH, Weg JG. The effect of tumor size and location on diagnosis by fiberoptic bronchoscopy. Chest 1977;72:474–479.

34. Thornbury JR, Burke DP, Naylor B. Transthoracic needle aspiration biopsy: accuracy of cytologic typing of malignant neoplasms. AJR 1981;136:719–724.

35. Vine HS, Kasdon EJ, Simon M. Percutaneous lung biopsy using the Lee needle and a tract obliterating technique. Radiology 1982;144:921–922.

36. Webb WR, Gamsu G, Speckman JM. Computed tomography of the pulmonary hilum in patients with bronchogenic carcinoma. J Comput Assist Tomogr. 1983;7:219–225.

37. Westcott JL. Direct percutaneous needle aspiration of localized pulmonary lesions: results in 422 patients. Radiology 1980;137:31–35.

38. Westcott JL. Percutaneous needle biopsy of hilar and mediastinal masses. Radiology 1981;141:323–328.

39. Wolinsky H, Lischner MW. Needle tract implantation of tumor after percutaneous lung biopsy. Ann Intern Med 1969;71:359–362.

40. Zavala DC. Diagnostic fiberoptic bronchoscopy: techniques and results of biopsy in 600 patients. Chest 1975;68:12–19.

41. Zavala DC, Schoell JE. Ultrathin needle aspiration of the lung in infectious and malignant disease. Am Rev Respir Dis 1981;123:125–131.

42. Zelch JV, Lalli AF, McCormack LJ, Belovich DM. Aspiration biopsy in diagnosis of pulmonary nodule. Chest 1973;63:149–152.

43. Zornoza J, Snow J, Lukeman JM, Libshitz HI. Aspiration biopsy of discrete pulmonary lesions using a new thin needle. Radiology 1977;123:519–520.

Mediastinal Biopsy

A. Rosenberger and O. B. Adler

The present state of the art in the diagnosis of mediastinal masses demands precise information about the nature of the lesion, before surgical or oncologic treatment is contemplated. The radiologist must be familiar with all the examinations and procedures to obtain this information, as well as with the capabilities and limitations of each modality. This knowledge will help him choose the most efficient method of investigation.

Clinical Findings

The clinical manifestations of mediastinal masses result from pressure or invasion of various mediastinal structures. The patient may complain about symptoms such as chest pain, dyspnea, cough, or fever. Superior vena cava and Horner's syndrome, and hoarseness due to recurrent laryngeal nerve paralysis point most often toward a malignant process.

Radiologic Findings

The presence of a mediastinal mass may be first suggested by the chest radiograph. The radiologic signs in favor of a mass are changes in the contour or width of the mediastinum. The mass may be of vascular or solid nature; the latter can be a primary process – benign or malignant – or a secondary one, i. e., hilar or mediastinal lymphadenopathy.

The location of the mass in the mediastinum may hint at the nature of the lesion; a posterior mediastinal mass is most likely of neurogenic origin.

Mediastinal Anatomy

The standard anatomic subdivisions of the mediastinum (54) include superior, anterior, middle, and posterior compartments.

The superior compartment lies above a line connecting the lower aspect of the manubrium of the sternum to the body of the fourth thoracic vertebra. The anterior mediastinum extends between the sternum and the pericardium; the posterior mediastinum lies behind a plane tangent to the posterior aspect of the pericardium, including the paraspinal extrapleural spaces. The middle mediastinum is the space between the anterior and posterior compartments.

This division of the mediastinum is the commonly accepted one and the one in use in textbooks.

Radiologic Anatomy of the Mediastinum

A somewhat different classification of the mediastinal anatomy has been proposed by Heitzman (27). This consists of:

the thoracic inlet, the lower border of which is a transverse plane through the first rib; the anterior mediastinum, which extends behind the sternum and in front of the great vessels from the thoracic inlet down to the diaphragm; and the mediastinal space lying behind the anterior mediastinum, which is separated into a right and left side due to the presence of two major vascular arches: that of the aorta and of the azygos vein. Accordingly, there are supra- and infra-azygos areas, and supra- and infra-aortic areas.

The reflection of the pleura about these two arches (28) can be identified on the chest radiographs and conventional tomographic images. This classification is more in accordance with the anatomic site of origin of a mass (27).

Mediastinal lung interfaces resulting in different lines visible on the radiologic images (28) form the basis of applied roentgenologic anatomy (8, 22).

The location of the hilar structures, whether pulmonary or mediastinal, is a controversial issue, since they are in continuity with the mediastinum and are often concomitantly involved by disease. They can be considered to belong to the mediastinum.

Radiologic Investigation

The number of radiologic examinations available for establishing the presence of a mediastinal mass or mediastinal and hilar lymphadenopathy is large (8). Some of them are of historic interest only, e. g. kymography to detect the pulsatile nature of a mass and thus its belonging to a vascular structure, and pneumomediastinography.

Today, the accepted radiologic examinations used to evaluate a mediastinal mass are the penetrated chest radiograph, with the possible addition of barium esophagogram, and computed tomography (15, 28). In a limited number of cases angiography, arterial or venous, may become necessary to obtain complete diagnostic information.

Presently, CT of the chest practically supplants conventional tomography; by its superior contrast resolution, it better distinguishes between tissue densities and delineates mediastinal anatomy in a transverse plane without superimposition (15, 37).

CT has the capability to detect pathologic conditions within the mediastinum, which on the chest radiograph would be too small to alter or widen the mediastinal silhouette. At the other end of the spectrum, a widened mediastinum on the chest radiograph or conventional tomographic image may turn out on CT to be a pseudomass due to abundant fat accumulation (5, 7). More laterally situated but normal vascular structures like a tortuous aorta can also contribute to enlargement of the upper mediastinum on the chest radiograph.

To improve delineation between vascular and soft tissue structures of the mediastinum, contrast material injection combined with rapid sequence dynamic CT has become routine in the evaluation of the mediastinum.

Despite these improvements, tissue diagnosis cannot be made by radiologic examinations alone, but with their aid planning and monitoring of percutaneous transthoracic needle biopsy becomes feasible.

The use of a fine needle through which aspirate for cytologic examination can be obtained makes this procedure, performed by the radiologist, a relatively minor invasive technique.

History

The technique of aspiration biopsy and fluoroscopy guidance dates back to the fourth decade of this century (10, 35). The development of cytology combined with the relatively atraumatic fine needle for aspiration biopsy contributed to the widespread use of this method for tissue diagnosis in different parts of the body (21, 26, 36, 46). Experience continues to accumulate up to the present day.

In the mediastinum, needle biopsy using a cannula, guide wire, and catheter system was proposed by Nordenstrom for the anterior mediastinum (38, 39) and for the posterior mediastinum (40). Through the catheter, contrast material could be injected and a biopsy needle and forceps inserted. Dahlgren and Ovenfors published their experience with aspiration biopsy of neurogenic tumors in the posterior mediastinum (16), but these methods did not gain widespread acceptance.

As experience with fine-needle biopsy of the lung became an established and reliable technique (46), the same modality was applied to mediastinal lesions (30, 41). The number of patients who have undergone fine-needle aspiration biopsy of the mediastinum is steadily increasing (1, 3, 6, 29, 44, 48, 49, 55, 56).

Surgical Procedures

The goal of surgical procedures (33) is to determine the histologic nature of a mediastinal mass, the presence of which has been established by radiologic methods.

Bronchoscopy has a limited value for this purpose, for the number of mediastinal masses protruding or eroding into the main airways is small. Bronchoscopy can be used to perform transtracheal or transcarinal needle biopsy (11, 45) for lesions situated along the trachea or at the bifurcation. Previous CT examination is very helpful in localizing precisely the mass to be punctured and in assessing the direction of the needle path.

Scalenus node biopsy (17) is used today in selected patients only and has been largely replaced by *mediastinoscopy* (12) and *anterior mediastinotomy* (34, 51). These two procedures permit direct visualization of both the pathologic lesion and its biopsy.

In mediastinoscopy, through an incision above the suprasternal notch, a rigid instrument is passed downward in front of the trachea to the level of the main bronchi. A mass of lymph nodes along the right side of the trachea down to the level of the azygos arch or along the left side of the trachea down to the level of the aortic arch can be explored.

For lesions situated in the anterior mediastinum, including internal mammary nodes as well as those of the aortopulmonary window, anterior mediastinotomy is recommended. Both procedures are surgical in nature, and require general anesthesia in the operating theatre. The location of the lesion will determine which procedure will be performed. Previous radiologic examinations, mainly CT, provide the surgeon with valuable information about the site and extent of mediastinal pathologic lesions. The drawback common to both techniques is their limitation to the anterior mediastinum only.

Exploratory thoracotomy, a major surgical procedure, is exceptionally performed as a diagnostic option.

The combination of radiologic examinations, fine-needle aspiration biopsy, mediastinoscopy, and anterior mediastinotomy usually permits assessment of an exact diagnosis.

Technique

The procedure of fine-needle aspiration biopsy of a mediastinal mass or lymphadenopathy will be discussed under several aspects:

– Indications and contra-indications
– Planning
– Guidance
– Technique

The goal of fine-needle aspiration biopsy of a mediastinal lesion is to obtain a specimen for cytologic examination while sparing the patient surgical procedures.

Indications. Practically all mediastinal masses are amenable to biopsy: masses of unknown etiology, or masses occurring in patients with known malignancy.

Superior vena cava syndrome. In patients with a mediastinal mass and the clinical signs of superior vena cava syndrome, it may be the fastest and, from the patient's point of view, the least traumatic procedure (43). No deleterious consequences were observed, despite the venous engorgement and collateral network present in the mediastinum in many patients with this syndrome (43).

Contra-indications. Contra-indications are vascular lesions and echinococcal cysts.

Vascular lesions. Dynamic CT or angiography can detect the vascular origin of a mass or assess the relationship between a mass to be biopsied and the great vessels of the mediastinum. Yet inadvertent entry into these vessels may occur, although without serious consequences when a fine-gauge needle is used (24, 56).

Echinococcal cysts are a rarity in the mediastinum. Personally (2, 44), we have not seen a single case among our patients, despite the fact that the parasite is endemic in our region and that our hospital is the center for chest surgery for a population of more than one million persons.

Planning. Age does not represent a limitation for the examination (Table 1); in infants and children, light anesthesia has to be given. In planning the biopsy procedure, four parameters need to be known: the size, site, and depth of the mass, and its relationship to adjacent structures.

Chest radiographs in two planes and sequential dynamic CT with bolus injection of contrast media serve this purpose.

Chest radiographs in posteroanterior and lateral positions usually provide sufficient information in planning the path of the biopsy needle. Problems may arise:

– Lesions close to the superior vena cava or in the aorto-pulmonary window have the same density on the plain radiograph and are not discernible from these major vessels.
– In lateral chest radiographs taken at a distance of less than 1.80 to 2.0 m, magnification and some distortion occur. In the presence of a large mass, small errors in depth calculation are not relevant, but for small lesions exact skin to target distance determination is most important.
– Small lesions lying entirely or partly behind the sternum and costal cartilages are difficult to appreciate when planning the needle path.

Computed tomography. Today, CT is routine for evaluating mediastinal masses. The transverse plane of the CT image inherently displays the size, site, and surroundings of the mass. Depth calculation by cursors and grids is most exact. Angulation, to avoid bony or vascular structures along the needle path, can also be estimated.

Needles. The technique of fine-needle aspiration biopsy implies by definition the use of small-gauge needles, i.e., 22 or 23 G. Originally, a spinal-type needle with a 25° bevel was used and this is still considered to be the least traumatic needle. In the course of time, different designs for needles have been proposed and introduced to increase the yield of the specimen, or to obtain tissue core for histologic examination (4, 32). In many of them, the angle of the bevel has been increased to 45° or 90°, sometimes with a serrated edge (4). Curved needles to circumvent skeletal or visceral structures have also been proposed (13). The discussion of which type of needle should be used is not yet settled.

Biopsy procedure. Before the biopsy, the procedure should be explained to the patient and informed consent obtained.

Biopsy guidance. According to the site of the lesion, the patient is positioned in supine or prone position on the examination table in order to determine on the skin the point for needle insertion. This can be

Table **1** Fine-needle aspiration biopsy of the mediastinum: age and sex distribution in 126 patients, at Rambam Medical Center (1978–1986)

	Total No.	Age (yr)			Sex	
		0–16	17–50	51–83	Male	Female
Anterior mediastinum	91	8	38	45	63	28
Middle mediastinum	9	0	0	9	5	4
Posterior mediastinum	13	3	3	7	9	4
Hilum	13	1	1	11	8	5
	126	12	42	72	85	41

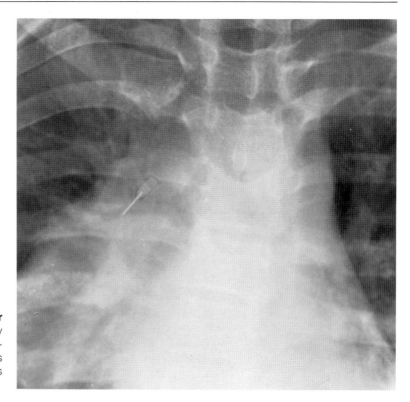

Fig. 1 **Fluoroscopy-guided fine-needle aspiration biopsy of anterior mediastinal mass** detected accidentally on routine chest radiograph in a 15-year-old boy. Needle tip inside the mass was verified by spot film. Cytologic diagnosis was lymphoma, confirmed by surgery

done by fluoroscopy or CT. The region is sterilely prepared; in apprehensive patients local anesthesia may be added. The depth of the lesion is marked on the biopsy needle, which is then advanced with a rapid thrust into the target. Very often, penetration of the needle into the mass is felt by change in tissue resistance.

Before aspiration, one must confirm that the needle tip lies within the mass. Biplane or C-arm television-monitored fluoroscopy permits 3-dimensional orientation for this purpose, but this equipment is less widely available, and single-plane fluoroscopy may also be sufficient (Fig. **1**). Guidance of the biopsy procedure by CT (2, 3, 18, 19, 23, 25) offers many advantages over fluoroscopy in addition to those already discussed (Fig. **2–5**). Repeat scans reliably and objectively verify the position of the needle tip, which can easily be redirected if necessary. Selective sampling from different portions of the mass can be achieved. The whole procedure is performed in daylight, without exposing the radiologist to radiation.

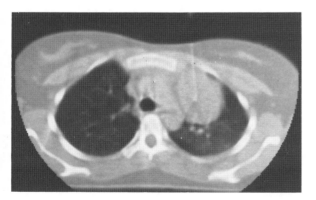

Fig. 2 **CT-guided fine-needle aspiration biopsy of left anterior mass** in 27-year-old woman with known malignant fibrous histiocytoma. Cytologic diagnosis was metastasis

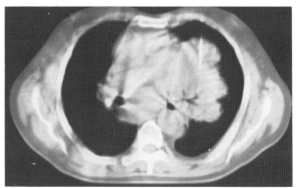

Fig. 3 **CT-guided fine-needle aspiration biopsy of left-sided lobulated anterior and middle mediastinal mass.** Cytologic diagnosis was probably thymoma, confirmed by surgery

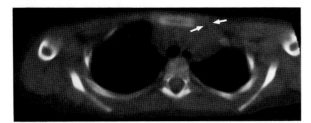

Fig. 4 **CT-guided fine-needle aspiration biopsy of mass in thoracic inlet** in 8-year-old boy. Clinically, cough and fever were present. Cytologic diagnosis was lymphoma

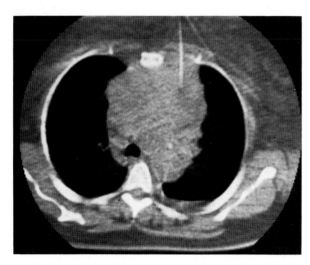

Fig. 5 **CT-guided fine-needle aspiration biopsy of lobulated anterior mediastinal mass.** Cytologic examination revealed blood. Mediastinoscopy indicated Hodgkin disease

Fluoroscopy and CT may be combined, with CT providing all the information for planning the biopsy, and fluoroscopy serving to monitor it (14, 44).

Aspiration technique consists of creating negative pressure in the syringe attached to the needle after the stylet is removed. Gentle rocking and rotating the needle increases the chances of better sampling. The needle is removed only after the negative pressure has been released. The content of the needle is blown onto glass slides, which are submitted to the cytotechnologist, who is present during the procedure in order to handle the sample properly.

The examination is completed with an expiratory chest film to check an eventual pneumothorax or by a repeat CT scan, which can detect even a minimal pneumothorax. Accuracy of needle placement can be increased by tandem or coaxial technique and CT for guidance (53).

Practical Considerations

The use of fine-needle aspiration biopsy of the mediastinum for cytologic examination is steadily growing (Table **2**). It accounts for the good results obtained by this relatively simple and fast procedure, with few complications, most often necessitating no further treatment (Tables **3, 4, 5**; Fig. **6–7**). Complications are similar to those of fine-needle aspiration biopsies of the lung, but rarer.

The effects on patient management are salient: shortening of diagnostic work-up, reduction in cost of health care (24), and a minimum of discomfort to the patient. According to experience accumulated, in about 60% of cases the mediastinal process is due to metastases in which only oncologic treatment would be considered.

In assessing the results, three large categories are considered:

– Conclusive biopsies, which furnish cytologic information about the nature of the mass – malignant or benign.
– Inconclusive biopsies, in which the cells of the specimen cannot be unequivocally classified or are not specific enough for definitive diagnosis.
– Unsatisfactory biopsies, when the aspirate contains only blood, or the number of cells is sparse or distorted that no diagnosis can be made.

Whenever histologic proof about the nature of the mass can be obtained, it is correlated with the results of fine-needle aspiration biopsy (Table **6**). An inconclusive or unsatisfactory result would delay further investigation by 24 hours only.

The success rate of fine-needle aspiration biopsy depends on:

– Sampling of a representative portion of the mass
– Obtaining a sufficient number of cells
– Cytologic interpretation

The first two conditions are in the realm of radiology. In **sampling,** the needle tip has to reach the mass; monitoring of this procedure can be done in a superior and indisputably more reliable manner by CT guidance. It permits sampling from the periphery of a necrotic mass that contains the viable cells, thus increasing the probability of a positive result. It is definitely preferable to guide the biopsy by CT in masses near or in the thoracic inlet, in hilar and middle mediastinal tumors, in paravertebral masses (57), in small mediastinal masses, and in patients with superior vena cava syndrome (3, 42).

The amount of cell material obtained can be improved by needle technology or an increase in the number of passes. Needles used can be of a large gauge (4), or core-cutting needles (1, 32), or modified thin-gauge needles with slots, serrated edges, or large-angle bevels for the purpose of obtaining larger pieces of tissue.

Table **2** Published results of fine-needle aspiration biopsies of the mediastinum

		No. cases	positive cytology	Complications
Jereb and Us-Krasovec (30)	1977	50	41	14
Westcott (56)	1981	91	88	28
van Sonnenberg et al. (53)	1983	7	7	1
Bartholdy et al. (6)	1984	132	88	
Gobien et al. (25)	1984	23	19	
Weisbrod et al. (55)	1984	116	83	22
Rosenberger	1986	126	91	11

Table **3** Fine-needle aspiration biopsies of the mediastinum in 126 patients at Rambam Medical Center (1978–1986)

	Guidance		No. puncture			Complications		
	Fluoros-copy	CT*	Fluoros-copy	CT	Pneumo-thorax	Drainage	Hemor-rhage
Anterior mediastinum	47	44	76	74	7	1	2
Middle mediastinum	0	9	0	16	0	0	1
Posterior mediastinum	3	10	4	15	0	0	0
Hilum	2	11	3	14	1	2	1
	52	74	83	119	8	3	4

* CT: computed tomography.

Table **4** Results of fine-needle aspiration biopsies of the mediastinum in 126 patients at Rambam Medical Center (1978–1986)

	Conclusive				Inconclusive		Unsatisfactory		Superior vena cava syndrome
	Malignant		Benign						
	Fl.*	CT*	Fl.	CT	Fl.	CT	Fl.	CT	
Anterior mediastinum	35	21	1	3	9	11	4	7	7
Middle mediastinum	0	9	0	0	0	0	0	0	6
Posterior mediastinum	3	7	0	0	0	2	0	1	0
Hilum	1	11	0	0	0	0	1	0	1
	39	48	1	3	9	13	5	8	14

Fl.: fluoroscopy; CT: computed tomography

Table **5** Summary of results of fine-needle aspiration biopsies of the mediastinum in 126 patients at Rambam Medical Center (1978–1986)

		Cytology			
Method	Total no.	Positive	Inconclusive	Unsatisfactory	Complications
Fluoroscopy	52	40	9	5	7
Computed tomography	74	51	13	8	4
	126	91	22	13	11

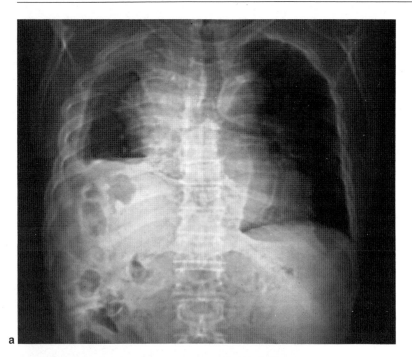

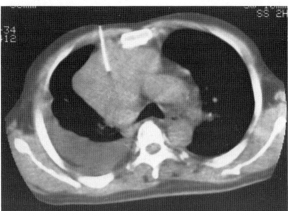

Fig. **6   Chest film. Elevated right diaphragm. a** Enlarge-ment of right upper mediastinum. **b** Computed tomogra-phy-guided fine-needle aspiration biopsy of the mass. Cytologic examination was inconclusive, lymphocytes. Diagnosis at surgery was thymoma

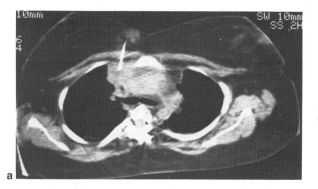

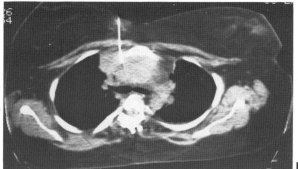

Fig. **7   CT-guided fine-needle aspiration biopsy of anterior mediastinal mass. a, b** Known lymphoma. State after therapy. Biopsy showed lymphocytes, morphologically identical to the histologic specimen. Residual lymphoma

Table **6** Fine-needle aspiration biopsy of mediastinal lesion in 126 patients at Rambam Medical Center (1978–1986): Correlation of cytologic results with other diagnostic procedures

Cytology	Mediastinum			Hilum	Superior vena cava syndrome
	Anterior	Middle	Posterior		
Total	91	9	13	13	14
Conclusive					
Metastases	48	6	5	11	9
Hodgkin disease	1	0	0	0	
Lymphoma	3	3	0	1	5
Myeloma	0	0	2	0	
Neurogenic tumor	0	0	3	0	
Thymoma	3	0	0	0	
Cyst	1	0	0	0	
Inflammation	3	0	0	0	
Teratoma	1	0	0	0	
Inconclusive					
Deferred	3	0	1	0	
Fibroma	0	0	1	0	
Hodgkin disease	2	0	0	0	
Inflammation	0	0	0	0	
Lymphoma	9	0	0	0	
Teratoma	1	0	0	0	
Thymoma	5	0	0	0	
Unsatisfactory					
Aneurysm	3				
Hodgkin disease	6				
Lymphoma	2	0	0	0	
Metastases	0	0	1	1	

The number of passes performed is at the discretion of the radiologist doing the biopsy. It can be assumed that the potential for complications grows by increasing the number of sampling attempts and even more with the use of large-gauge or core-cutting needles.

Although the number of cases reported of dissemination along the needle tract is scant (20, 41, 47, 50), it seems to be connected either to multiple passes or to use of needles different from the 25° beveled spinal needle.

In order to reduce the number of needle passes, the ideal solution would be an immediate cytologic assessment of the sample (31, 36), but this resource is not widely available.

An adequate sample is not synonymous with positive diagnosis; this is due to limitations in the ability of the cytologic examination to make a specific diagnosis or classification in some cases, most often in thymomas, lymphomas, and Hodgkin disease (52, 55) (table **6**).

In evaluation of metastases the results correlate well with the histologic examination. Electron microscopic analysis may be added to the standard cytologic examination when specific cell type diagnosis would significantly influence patient management (9).

Conclusions. It seems that after the diagnosis of a solid mediastinal mass has been made, the first step to elucidate the nature of the mass, benign or malignant, can be done by fine-needle aspiration biopsy, the results of which are often sufficient to institute proper therapy.

References

1. Adler O, Rosenberger A. Invasive radiology in the diagnosis of mediastinal masses. Radiology 1979;19:169.
2. Adler O, Rosenberger A. Computed tomography in guiding fine-needle aspiration biopsy of the lung and mediastinum. RöFo 1980;133:135.
3. Adler OB, Rosenberger A, Peleg H. Fine needle aspiration biopsy of mediastinal masses. AJR 1983;140:893.
4. Andriole JG, Haaga JR, Adams RB, Nunez C. Biopsy needle characteristics assessed in the laboratory. Radiology 1983;148:659.
5. Baron RL, Levitt RG, Sagel SS, Stanley RJ. Computed tomography in the evaluation of mediastinal widening. Radiology 1981;138:107.
6. Bartoldy, NY, Andersen MJF, Thommesen P. Clinical value of percutaneous fine needle aspiration biopsy of mediastinal masses. Scand J Thorac Cardiovasc Surg. 1984;18:81.

7. Bein NE, Mancuso AA, Mink JH, Hansen GC. Computed tomography in the evaluation of mediastinal lipomatosis. J Comput Assist Tomogr. 1978;2:379.

8. Berne AS, Gerle RD, Mitchell GE. The mediastinum: normal roentgen anatomy and radiologic technique. Semin Roentgenol 1969;4:3.

9. Berkman WA, Chowdhury L, Brown NL, Padleckas R. Value of electron microscopy in cytologic diagnosis of fine needle biopsy. AJR 1983;140:1253.

10. Blady J N. Aspiration biopsy of tumors in obscure or difficult location under roentgenoscopic guidance. AJR 1939; 42:515.

11. Brynitz S, Struve-Christensen F, Borgeskow S, Bertelsen S. Transcarinal mediastinal needle biopsy compared with mediastinoscopy. J Thorac Cardiovasc Surg 1985;90:21.

12. Carlens E. Mediastinoscopy: a method for inspection and tissue biopsy in the superior mediastinum. Dis Chest 1959;36:343.

13. Carrasco CH, Wallace S. Charnsangavej C. Aspiration biopsy: use of a curved needle. Radiology 1985;155:254.

14. Cohan RH, Newman GE, Braun SD, Dunnick NR. CT assistance for fluoroscopically guided transthoracic needle aspiration biopsy. J Comput Assist Tomogr 1984;8:1093.

15. Crowe JK, Brown LR, Muhm JR. Computed tomography of the mediastinum. Radiology 1978;128:75.

16. Dahlgren SE, Ovenfors CO. Aspiration biopsy diagnosis of neurogeneous mediastinal tumors. Acta Radiol. [Diagn] (Stockh) 1970;10:289.

17. Daniels AA. A method of biopsy in diagnosing certain intrathoracic diseases. Chest 1949;16:360.

18. Dondelinger R. Biopsies percutanées guidées par tomodensitométrie. J Belge Radiol 1982;65:227.

19. Dondelinger R. La tomodensitométrie d'intervention. Radiol. J CEPUR 1984;4:3.

20. Ferruci JT, Wittenberg J, Margolis MN, Carey RW. Malignant seeding of the tract after thin needle aspiration biopsy. Radiology 1979;130:345.

21. Ferruci JT, Wittenberg J, Mueller PR, Simeone JF, Harbin WP, Kirkpatrick RH, Taft PD. Diagnosis of abdominal malignancy by radiological fine needle aspiration biopsy. AJR 1980;134:323.

22. Figley MM. Mediastinal minutiae. Semin Roentgenol 1969;4:22.

23. Gatenby RA, Mulhern CB Jr., Broder GJ, Moldowsky PJ. Computed tomography guided biopsy of small apical and peripheral upper lobe lung masses. Radiology 1984;150:591.

24. Gobien RP, Bouchard EA, Gobien BS, Valicenti JF, Vujic J. Thin needle aspiration biopsy of thoracic lesions: impact on hospital charges and patterns of patient care. Radiology 1983;148:65.

25. Gobien RP, Stanley JH, Vujic J, Gobien BS. Thoracic biopsy: CT guidance of thin needle aspiration. AJR 1984;142:827.

26. Göthlin JH Post lymphography percutaneous fine needle biopsy of lymph nodes guided by fluoroscopy. Radiology 1976;120:205.

27. Heitzman ER. The mediastinum. Saint Louis: Mosby, 1977: 1–4.

28. Heitzman ER, Scrivani JV, Martino J, Moro J. The azygos vein and its pleural reflection: normal roentgen anatomy. Radiology 1971;101:249.

29. House AJ. Biopsy techniques in the investigation of diseases of the lung, mediastinum and chest wall. Radiol Clin North Am 1979;17:393.

30. Jereb M, Us-Krasovec M. Transthoracic needle biopsy of mediastinal and hilar regions. Cancer 1977;40:1354.

31. Johnsrude IS, Silverman JF, Weaver MD, McConnell RW. Rapid cytology to decrease pneumothorax incidence after percutaneous biopsy. AJR 1985;144:793.

32. Lieberman RP, Hafez GR, Crummy AB. Histology from aspiration biopsy: Turner needle experience. AJR 1982;138:561.

33. Mackenzie JW, Riley DJ. Diagnostic procedures: scalene node biopsy – mediastinotomy – thoracoscopy and lung biopsy. In: Glenn WWL, ed. Thoracic and cardiovascular surgery. 4th ed. New York: Appleton Century-Crofts, 1983:56

34. McNeill T, Chamberlain J. Diagnostic anterior mediastinotomy. Ann Thorac Surg 1966;2:532.

35. Martin HE, Ellis EB. Aspiration biopsy. Surg Gynecol Obstet 1934;59: 578.

36. Miller DA. Carrasco CH, Katz RL, Cramer FM, Wallace S. Charnsangavej C. Fine needle aspiration biopsy: the role of immediate cytologic assessment. AJR 1986;147:155.

37. Naidich DI. Zerhouni EA, Siegelman SS, eds. Computed tomography of the thorax. New York: Raven, 1984:43–82.

38. Nordenstrom B. Transjugular approach to the mediastinum for mediastinal needle biopsy. Invest Radiol 1967;2:134.

39. Nordenstrom B. Paraxiphoid approach to the mediastinum for mediastinography and mediastinal needle biopsy. Invest Radiol 1967;2:141.

40. Nordenstrom B. Paravertebral approach to the posterior mediastinum for mediastinography and needle biopsy. Acta Radiol [Diagn] (Stockh) 1972;12:298.

41. Rasleigh-Belcher HJC, Russel RCG, Lees WR. Cutaneous seeding of pancreatic carcinoma by fine needle aspiration biopsy. Br J Radiol. 1986;59:182.

42. Rosenberger A, Adler O. Fine needle aspiration biopsy in the diagnosis of mediastinal lesions. AJR 1978;131:239.

43. Rosenberger A, Adler O. Superior vena cava syndrome: a new radiological approach to diagnosis. Cardiovasc Intervent Radiol. 1980;3:127.

44. Rosenberger A, Adler O. Fine needle aspiration biopsy of mediastinal masses. Isr J Med Sci 1981;17:49

45. Schiessle W. La ponction transbronchique et transtracheale des adenopathies peribronchiques. J Fr Med Chir Thorac 1962;16:551.

46. Sinner WN. Wert und Bedeutung der perkutanen transthorakalen Nadelbiopsien für die Diagnose intrathorakaler Krankheitsprozesse. RöFo 1975;123:203.

47. Sinner WN. Complications of percutaneous transthoracic needle aspiration biopsy. Acta Radiol [Diagn] (Stockh) 1976;17:813.

48. Sinner WN. Directed fine needle aspiration biopsy of anterior and middle mediastinal masses. Oncology 1985;42:92.

49. Sinner WN. The direct approach to posterior mediastinal masses by fine needle biopsy. Oncology 1985;42:187.

50. Sinner WN. Zajicek J. Implantation metastasis after percutaneous transthoracic needle aspiration biopsy. Acta Radiol [Diagn] (Stockh) 1976;17:473.

51. Stemmer EA, Calvin JW, Chandor SB. Mediastinal biopsy for indeterminate pulmonary and mediastinal lesions. J Thorac Cardiovasc Surg 1965;49:405.

52. Thornbury JR, Burke DP, Naylor B. Transthoracic needle aspiration biopsy: accuracy of cytologic typing of malignant neoplasms. AJR 1981;136:719.

53. Van Sonnenberg E, Lin AS, Deutsch AL, Mattrey RF. Percutaneous biopsy of difficult mediastinal, hilar or pulmonary lesions by computed tomographic guidance and a modified coaxial technique. Radiology 1983;148:300.

54. Warwick RW, Williams PL, Splanchnology. In: Gray's anatomy. 55th ed. London: Longmans 1973:1195–1196.

55. Weisbrod GL, Lyons DJ, Tao LC, Chamberlain DW. Percutaneous fine needle aspiration biopsy of mediastinal lesions. AJR 1984;143:525.

56. Westcott JL. Percutaneous needle aspriation of hilar and mediastinal masses. Radiology 1981;141:323.

57. Williams RA, Haaga JR. Karagiannis E. CT guided paravertebral biopsy of the mediastinum. J Comput Assist Tomogr 1984;8:575.

Breast Biopsy

J. L. Lamarque and M. J. Rodière

Early diagnosis of breast cancer determines the prognosis. A 98% diagnostic reliability is achieved in the diagnosis of breast cancer by a combination of clinical findings, radiology and cytology. If these methods do not give definite results, a biopsy is performed for confirmation (6, 13, 14, 15). Whatever method for tissue sampling is used (aspiration cytology, percutaneous microbiopsy, surgical microbiopsy), imaging techniques offer precise localization of the lesion. Localization and sampling should be as atraumatic as possible.

Guidance Modalities

Mammography. The difficulties arising during percutaneous biopsy guided with mammography result from the fact that the biopsy itself is carried out in a different position from that used for the mammography. The lesion can be localized using markers on the skin and two perpendicular mammographic projections, or stereoradiographic techniques (1, 7). With growing experience, these methods, due to their precision, give excellent results. Proper technique and adequate equipment are mandatory (21, 22, 25, 26, 27). Needle placement can be checked with repeated biplanar mammography (28) (Fig. 1). A perforated plexiglass plate can be used to guide the needle to non-palpable lesions that can only be seen on mammography (19).

Computed tomography. CT can be used when a larger lesion has been identified within the breast. Lesions with a smaller diameter and microcalcifications cannot be localized by CT, however. Furthermore, many lesions are not visible within a dense fibrotic breast. Lesions located in a relatively hypodense breast can be localized with CT, and are easily biopsied without discomfort for the patient (Fig. 2).

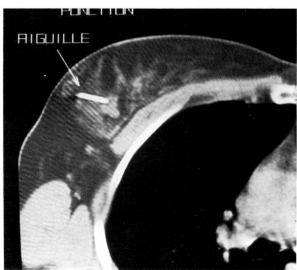

Fig. 2 **Puncture of a nodule in the breast with CT guidance**

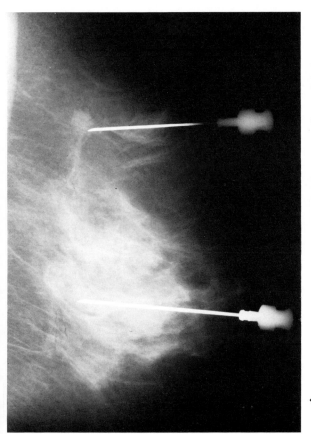

◀ Fig. 1 **Puncture of two nodules with mammographic guidance;** one lesion shows calcifications. Fibroadenoma and dystrophy with epithelial hyperplasia

Ultrasonography. Multiple ultrasonic (US) devices with special probes (perforated transducers) make percutaneous biopsy of the breast possible, but the positioning and identification of the needle tip is still difficult. Precise documentation of a solid lesion with a diameter of less than one centimeter is difficult with US guidance, especially when fibroneoplastic lesions are present in a dense or fatty breast.

Magnetic Resonance Imaging guidance. MRI is not yet routinely applied as a guidance method (6).

Sampling

Aspiration cytology, needle microbiopsy and surgical biopsy are standard techniques.

Aspiration cytology. A minimal percutaneous puncture is required. A few drops of fluid or cellular material are smeared onto a plate.

Aspiration biopsy. A larger needle is used, with or without lateral notches. When strong and continuous suction is applied, fragments of tissue are aspirated, the needle is rinsed, and the fragments are centrifuged (13). The diameter of the needles used varies from 0.6 to 0.9 mm; they produce samples that contain more cellular material than aspiration cytology provides. Smears can also be obtained with the aspiration biopsy technique.

Microbiopsy. This technique produces tissular fragments, using different types of needles. The Tru-cut (Fig. 3) and Rotex needles produce tissue fragments, the latter using a distal screw (20, 21, 22). These two needles are mainly used for lesions that have already been evidenced clinically or radiologically (2, 9, 12, 19, 24, 25, 26, 27). The application of percutaneous biopsy in the diagnosis of non-palpable lesions is doubtful, and the relative value of cytology and histology in the breast has not yet been established. We believe that cytology should be backed up by microbiopsy. Both procedures are performed during the same examination.

Surgical biopsy. Breast lesions can be localized prior to surgical biopsy by placing a wire in the lesion (Fig. 4) and injecting contrast medium (4, 10, 11, 21, 23) and carbon. The entry point is chosen on a previous mammogram and localized on the skin. The lesion is then punctured, and methylene blue is injected through the needle. A self-retaining wire is introduced, fixed to the skin, and its correct position is checked again by two perpendicular mammographic views (Fig. 5). The surgical specimen containing the suspect zones is also radiographed. Preoperative localization is carried out either the day before, or on the same day as surgery. The patient can easily move around with the fixed guide wire. This technique is readily accepted when the patient is informed that as a result of precise localization, surgery will be well-oriented and more limited. Reduction in the size of the surgical specimen also allows a more precise histologic examination. During surgery the wire in the breast is used as a traction hook, facilitating identification and dissection of the pathologic area.

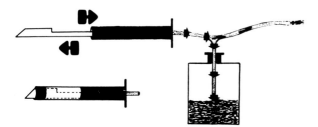

Fig. 3 **Microbiopsy technique** with continuous aspiration

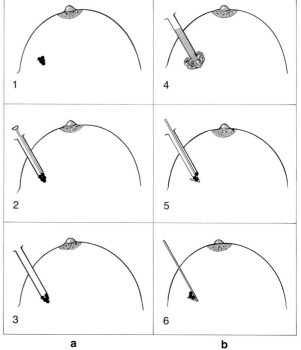

Fig. **4a, b Principle of placement of a localization** ▶ **wire.** 1 Mammographic detection of the lesion; 2 puncture of the lesion; 3 withdrawal of the mandril of the needle; 4 cytological aspiration (or microbiopsy); 5 introduction of the hooked wire or thread; 6 withdrawal of the needle

a   b

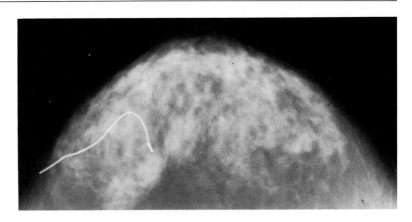

Fig. **5** **Mammographic control** after placement of the hooked wire

Results

Cytology has been proved sufficient to differentiate between benign and malignant cells in the breast, based on cytologic criteria of isolated or clustered cells. Many small-gauge needles also produce microhistological samples which are closer to histology than to cytology. Analysis of a histologic specimen is based on the cellular arrangement, and offers greater diagnostic capabilities than cytology alone. Cytology gives positive results in 75–80% of all cases (Table **1**).

The accuracy of clinical examination of the breast and of mammography is increased by cytology (Table **2**). A negative result does not prove that the lesion is necessarily benign, but sampling has to be repeated if there is any suspicion of malignancy. Cytology showing non-epithelial inflammatory cells should be considered acellular. On the other hand, a sample harboring a marked epithelial hyperplasia must be considered as suspicious of malignancy, even in the absence of malignant cells.

According to the literature, when cytology is doubtful, histologic sampling or a surgical biopsy must be performed.

The results obtained from histologic specimens with cutting needles are as reliable as cytologic smears (2). When lesions are sampled with radiologic guidance, results obtained with microbiopsy are similar to those achieved with cytology. There is no proof that histology is more reliable than cytology, although this seems probable.

Early Diagnosis of Breast Cancer

A combination of clinical examination, mammography and cytology establishes a correct diagnosis of malignancy in 95–98% of breast lesions. In this context, only suspicious lesions can be confirmed by cytology of histology. Radiographic detection of a lesion in the breast depends on the size and location of the lesion, the tissue density, individual immunological reactions and histochemical factors (8). Recognition of a lesion depends on all these factors, and the ease with which malignancy is confirmed varies from very easy (when a dense lesion is located in fatty breast) to impossible (when a lesion is located in a dense breast without microcalcifications).

Neoplastic tumors (Fig. **6**) grow over a long precancerous time-period (Fig. **7**) with high-risk mastopathy (3, 5). During this period, hyperplastic ductal and lobular lesions develop over a course of

Table **1**   Cytology in breast cancer: 2,800 procedures

Correct	79.7%
False negative	4.5%
False positive	2.0%
Suspicious	9.8%
Inadequate material	4.0%

Table **2**   Diagnostic accuracy in breast cancer (%)

Procedure	Correct Diagnosis	False positive	False negative	Suspicious	Inadequate
Cytology	77.5	4.5	4	9.8	4
Clinical examination	75.8	4.5	1.3	18.3	
Mammography	72.5	3.2	2	22.9	

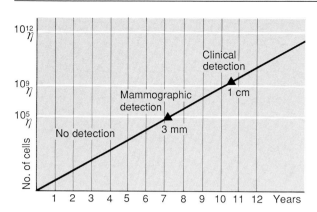

Fig. **6 Possible relation between mastopathy and neoplastic changes**

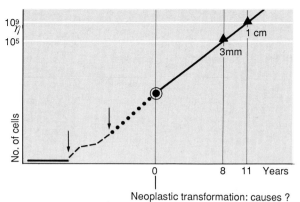

Fig. **7 Precancerous mastopathic development of neoplastic changes.** No epithelial hyperplasia (no risk): ———; hyperplasia but no cellular atypia (moderate risk): – – – –; hyperplasia with cellular atypia (high risk): •••••••

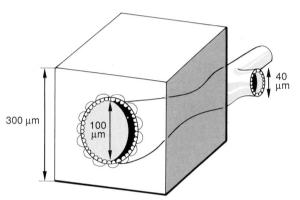

Fig. **8 Threedimensional diagram of an excretory duct in the breast.** Early lesions are on the scale of a thousandth of a millimeter and are not visible in the connective structure

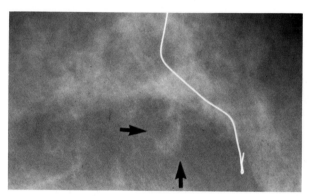

Fig. **9 Diagnosis of a reduced lesion during screening mammography:** benign appearance. Surgery after localization with a thread revealed adenocarcinoma (arrows)

years. They can be either typical or atypical and are generally plurifocal and bilateral. After many years, hyperplasia changes into one or several foci of cancer. Only this type of mastopathy should be described as a histologic high risk, necessitating cytohistologic typing. Plurifocal typing of the breast carried out bilaterally makes preventive or curative surgery, or hormonal therapy, possible. Recent studies have emphasized the role of high-risk mastopathy (5, 13, 15) and the consequent new prospects for "early diagnosis of breast cancer".

Percutaneous puncture in the breast is not limited to non-palpable, radiologically visible lesions, but extends to tissue characterization in a high-risk mastopathy. The breast is an organ connected with sexuality and a certain publicity, and the image of it reflected in our society no longer allows mutilating or defiguring surgical treatment. Today, diagnostic imaging favors surgical treatment with only minor esthetic consequences. The indications for tissue typing of a high-risk mastopathy should be broadened,

and biopsy should not be restricted to suspect circumscribed lesions, but applied to larger tissue areas, which are for the most part beyond clinical palpation (Fig. 8). Puncture of a non-palpable nodule in the breast is in fact rare in everyday practice. Surgical biopsy after previous mammographic localization is generally indicated (Fig. 9). Recent statistics from the Cancer Center and the University Department of Radiology in Montpellier have shown the low percentage of infraclinical breast cancers discovered in everyday practice: 0.4% out of 8,000 radiological examinations. This is probably due to the absence of a screening survey for breast cancer in France, and explains the tendency to perform surgical biopsy after radiologic localization of a lesion in the breast.

In breasts with a radiographically dense structure, localization of a suspect nodule turns out to be impossible. Under these circumstances, tissue typing is beneficial, all the more so because the risk of a false negative cytologic or histologic result cannot be avoided but is hard to accept, considering the

Table **3** Bilateral and plurifocal histologic typing by surgery: 33 patients. Research Group in Breast Pathology, Montpellier (GERPAM)	No hyperplasia	Epithelial hyperplasia		Cancer	
		Adenosis	Atypical	With epithelial hyperplasia in the other breast	Without epithelial hyperplasia
	6	18	3	6	0

reduced number of infraclinical breast cancers (Table **3**). On the other hand, surgery makes simultaneous diagnosis, treatment and plurifocal histologic typing of breast tissue during the same operation possible. We recommend that suspect isolated infraclinical lesions in the breast may be beneficially treated by surgical excision following localization. Histologic typing of a lesion is indicated in various clinical circumstances, which are mainly determined by the mammographic appearance (microcalcifications, fibrosis).

Breasts with fibrous and connective tissue changes, commonly called nodular fibrous mastitis, are common. No imaging method is able at the moment to detect epithelial hyperplasia and epithelial neoplastic changes within these breasts. Clinical and radiographic changes occur in particular age groups and types of patients. The histologic risk of cancerous transformation has to be known, indicating the surgical typing (Fig. **10**).

Calcifications in the breast can be suspicious for cancer according to their size, morphology, number and clustered arrangement. When they are diffuse, of the so-called benign type, located in several zones in one or both breasts, they may be located in the fibrous tissue, or may be intraductal, intra-epithelial or both (16, 17, 18). Calcifications correspond to an atypical lobular ductal hyperplasia and represent a high-risk area. Zones of dense fibrosis can also be present. These reflect an intense reaction in the breast tissue, and are mainly diffuse, but sometimes localized, mimicking circumscribed lesions. They sometimes accompany a hyperplasia of the same type as that seen with calcifications. These areas must also be screened for associated epithelial hyperplasia. In some patients, typing is required in multiple zones and in both breasts (Fig. **11**). Surgical incision is performed either around the nipple or in the subglandular groove.

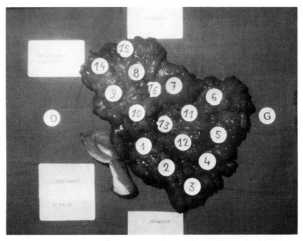

Fig. **10 Histologic typing of the entire right breast** in a patient aged 42. 32 samples were taken, showing: lobular hyperplasia and adenosis in 32 samples; lobular and regular ductal hyperplasia and foci of atypical lobular hyperplasia in 7 samples; regular adenosis in 9 samples; lobular and ductal hyperplasia in 5 samples; and atypical lobular hyperplasia in 4 samples. D: right; G: left

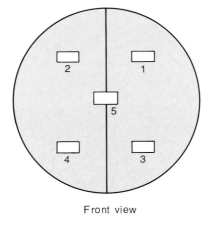
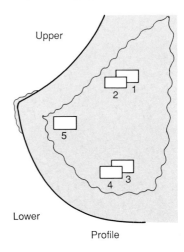

Fig. **11 Histologic plurifocal cell typing in the breast.**
5 samples, 1 in each quadrant and 1 in the retroareolar area

Front view

Upper

Lower

Profile

The entire gland can be reversed, with no surgical scar being visible later. By this approach (subcutaneous mastectomy and reconstruction), multiple foci of ductal and lobular cellular atypia are revealed. Close follow-up and hormonal therapy is indispensable in these patients.

This plurifocal surgical histologic typing is indicated according to the epidemiology, clinical findings and imaging, including factors such as age, family history, number of pregnancies, late menopause, hyperestrogenic impregnation, benign mastopathy (clinical or radiologic), large breasts, dense breasts, carcinophobia, and previously established epithelial hyperplasia.

References

1. Berger SM, Curcio BM, Gershoncohen J, Isard HJ. Mammographic localization of unsuspected breast cancer. AJR 1966;96:1046.
2. Bertin F, Contesso G, Lasser P, Mouriesse H, Rouesse J, Sarrazin D. Drill-biopsie et tru-cut préthérapeutiques. Paris: J.M.T. Conseil, 1981.
3. Colin C, Gordenne W. Evaluation du risque de cancer mammaire. In: Proceedings of the International Symposium of Senology. Liège: Mardaga 1985:376.
4. Dood G, Fry K, Delany W. Pre-operative localization of occult carcinoma of the breast. In: Nealon TF, ed. Management of the patient with cancer. Philadelphia: Saunders 1965:88.
5. Dupont WD, Page DL. Risk factors for breast cancer in women with proliferative breast disease. N Engl J Med 1985;312:147.
6. Duvauferrier R, Ramee A, Guibert JL, eds. Radiologie et échographie interventionnelles; vol 1. Montpellier: Axone, 1986:291–311.
7. Egan JF, Sayler CB, Goodman MJ. A technic for localizing occult breast lesions. CA 1976;26:32.
8. Fallenius AG, Skoog LK, Svane GE, Auer GU. Cytophotometrical and biochemical characterization of non-palpable mammographically detected mammary adenocarcinomas. Cytometry 1984;5:426.
9. Frankl G, Rosenfeld DD. Xeroradiographic detection of occult breast cancer. Cancer 1975;35:542–548.
10. Marc J, Homer MD. Nonpalpable breast lesion localization using a curved-end retractable wire. Radiology 1985;157:259.
11. Jensen SR, Lutteneggert TJ. Wire localization of non palpable breast lesions. Radiology 1979;132:484.
12. Kalisher L. An improved needle for the localization of non palpable lesions. Radiology 1978;128:815.
13. Lamarque JL, ed. Le sein: radiodiagnostic clinique. Paris: Medsi 1981:520.
14. Lamarque JL, ed. An atlas of the breast: clinical radiodiagnosis. London: Wolfe, 1984:528.
15. Lamarque JL. Confrontation anatomo-pathologique – Méthodologie du radiodiagnostic précoce des cancers du sein. In: Proceedings of the International Symposium of Senology. Liège: Mardaga, 1985:376.
16. Lamarque JL, Rodière MJ, Fontaine A, Pasqual J, Chardon F, Fournier A, Bruel JM, Senac JP, Laval-Jeantet M, Laval-Jeantet AM. Approche anatomo-histologique de la radio-anatomie mammaire. J Radiol. 1976;57:753.
17. Lamarque JL, Rodière MJ, Bisciglia HD. Pourquoi, quand et comment opérer les micro-calcifications dites suspectes? Bordeaux: 32e Assises Nationales de la Société Française de Gynécologie, 1985.
18. Lamarque JL, Rodière MJ, Baldet P, Boulet P. Mariotti J, Boubals E, Barriere A, Djoukhadar A. Existe-t-il des regroupements pathognomoniques des calcifications en mammographie? Senologia 1980;5:91.
19. Mulhow A. A device for precision needle biopsy of the breast at mammography. AJR 1974;121:843–845.
20. Nordenstrom B. New instruments for biopsy. Radiology 1975;117:474–475.
21. Nordenstrom B, Zajicek J. Stereotaxis needle biopsy and preoperative indication of non palpable mammary lesions. Acta Cytol. (Baltimore) 1977;21:350–351.
22. Nordenstrom B, Ryden H, Svane GE. Breast. In: Zornoza J, ed. Percutaneous needle biopsy. Baltimore: Williams and Wilkins 1981:43.
23. Rosato FE, Thomas J. Operative management of non palpable lesions detected by mammography. Surg. Gynecol Obstet 1973;137:491.
24. Sayler C, Egan JF, Raines JR, Goodman MJ. Mammographic screening. JAMA 1977;238:872.
25. Svane GE. A stereotaxic clinique for preoperative marking of non palpable breast lesions. Acta Radiol [Diagn] (Stockh) 1983;24:145.
26. Svane GE. Stereotaxic needle biopsy of non palpable breast lesions: a clinical and radiologic follow-up. Acta Radiol [Diagn] (Stockh) 1983;24:385.
27. Svane GE, Silverswand C. Stereotaxic needle biopsy non palpable breast lesions: cytologic and histopathologic findings. Acta Radiol [Diagn] (Stockh) 1983;24:283.
28. Theratt B, Appelman H, Dow R, O'Rourke T. Percutaneous needle localization of clustered mammary microcalcifications prior to biopsy. AJR 1974;21:839.

Abdominal Biopsy

R. C. Otto, R. F. Dondelinger and J. C. Kurdziel

Introduction

The rapid development of modern section imaging techniques such as US, CT and, more recently, MRI, has greatly expanded the spectrum of diagnostic modalities in the space of a few years. At present, it is still difficult to predict with any accuracy to what extent MRI will one day complement, enhance or completely replace other methods of examining the thorax and abdomen.

When the application of both US and CT had become an established routine in hospitals, it was soon realized that, although numerous disease foci could be detected, their nosological interpretation frequently remained obscure. For example, although a growth could be identified in the liver, it was impossible with either of these methods to ascertain whether it was a metastasis, a benign capillary hemangioma or the focus of an infection.

Even the application of angiography frequently fails to provide any conclusive information about the lesion in such cases, that is, if it is at all possible to reveal that it is space-occupying. Only if tumor vessels are manifested does a malignant growth strongly suggest itself. Even then, however, histologic examination remains indispensable. Prior histologic confirmation of the findings is obligatory, especially when aggressive therapeutic measures, for example chemotherapy, are called for. Although precise analysis of the histologic structure of a pathologic space-occupying lesion may not be imperative in all cases, its malignant character must be substantiated with at least cytologic proof. This is necessary in order to make a decision rejecting surgery in favor of radiotherapy or chemotherapy (105). A conclusive diagnosis can nowadays be made on the basis of just a few cells or aggregates of cells. This method, which dates back to a concept from the 1930s (31, 87), has now advanced to such a degree that it renders many diagnostic procedures, particulary exploratory surgery, unnecessary.

Guidance Modalities

There are various methods of percutaneous biopsy with constant visual supervision to obtain samples for the analysis of the cellular structure of a lesion, or for bacteriologic examination of body fluids. These methods may be classified as shown in Table **1**, and include:

– Fluoroscopy guidance
– US guidance
– Combined US and fluoroscopy guidance
– CT guidance
– MRI guidance

Large palpable abdominal tumors could theoretically be diagnosed by a percutaneous bedside biopsy, but it is common practice to perform percutaneous sampling with the aid of one or a combination of several imaging modalities (156), which allows better localization and full diagnosis of the components of the lesion, and avoids complications which could result from inadvertent puncture of vascular structures.

Fluoroscopy

Uniplanar and biplanar fluoroscopy is used, in combination with various selective opacifications as a guidance method for percutaneous biopsy of the gastrointestinal tract (41, 62, 84, 113, 152), the bile ducts (Fig. **1**) and the pancreatic duct, and the urinary system (117). Fluoroscopy is also used in combination with angiography (45, 145) and lymphangiography (46). Radiolucent handles have been described which accommodate one ore more types of needles allowing the operator's hands to be kept outside the primary beam (17, 125). Opacification of small-caliber structures such as the choledochus, the pancreatic duct, or the ureter, allows precise percutaneous biopsy even if they are not dilated and if a mass is not radiologically clear (41, 84).

Ultrasonography

Biopsy with US guidance represents the most important method of performing needle biopsy under visual control on soft tissue organs and circumscribed growths. Whereas only compound ultrasonography devices were previously available, more efficient real-time methods can be used nowadays that allow the full biopsy procedure to be observed in its entirety. Consequently, this interventional method must be rated very highly in terms of its diagnostic value and very low in terms of risk to the patient. Biopsy under US guidance under real-time conditions was developed in Zurich with a centrally perforated transducer because none of the other techniques then in use had proven totally satisfactory (110).

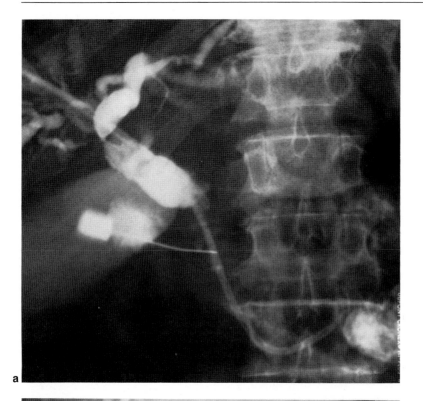

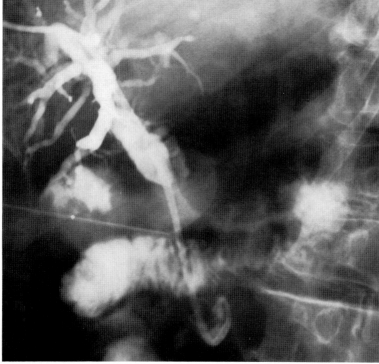

Fig. **1a, b   Percutaneous fine-needle biopsy guided by biplanar fluoroscopy.** Opacification of the biliary drainage catheter determines the level of obstruction: cholangiocarcinoma

Table **1** Guidance modalities for percutaneous biopsy	Fluoroscopy	Lung: focal lesions	Cytology, bacteriology
		Retroperitoneal lymph nodes (after lymphangiography)	Cytology
		Ureter, choledochus, pancreatic duct (after contrast medium injection)	Cytology
		Kidney (after contrast medium injection)	Biopsy
	Computed tomography	Focal lesions in the brain, vertebral canal, thorax and abdomen; in the extremities and cervical region (if not detectable sonographically)	Cytology, bacteriology (biopsy)
	Ultrasonography	Focal lesions in the soft tissue organs in the abdomen, in the extremities and cervical region; certain intrathoracic space-occupying lesions	Cytology, bacteriology
		Generalized parenchymal transformations in liver and kidneys (e.g. cirrhosis, glomerulonephritis, etc.)	Biopsy
		Certain malignant tumors (e.g. lymphoma, carcinoid)	Biopsy (cytology)

Techniques of Percutaneous Biopsy Using the Centrally Perforated Ultrasonography Transducer

When an obscure space-occupying lesion has been detected in an organ deep within the body, the line of sighting – this corresponds to a darker line running through the centre of the monitor image, and is produced by the absence of crystals in the transducer core – is trained on this find. The biopsy needle, which is characterized by a distinct echo, is then advanced along the line of sight all the way to the suspected pathologic space-occupying lesion. The end of the needle can be difficult to recognize in a hyperechoic lesion. The wedge-shaped groove of the centrally perforated ultrasonography transducer permits a slight angular shift of the needle, should this be necessary due to respiratory movements in the lesion in question. Attention must be paid during the biopsy to keeping the ultrasonography transducer in the longitudinal axis of the body so that the tip of the needle remains visible even during respiratory movements. Although the procedure usually takes no more than a few seconds, for psychological reasons, however, the patient ist permitted shallow respiration at the moment of aspiration. The great advantage of biopsy using the centrally-perforated transducer (Fig. **2**) is that the shortest puncture route is taken and that even highly flexible needles, like the Chiba needle, can be easily manipulated towards the region of interest. This is sometimes a problem when doing oblique punctures. Relatively rigid, larger-

bore needles are required if puncturing obliquely past the transducer, so that the needle cannot be deflected away from the puncture plane and into the

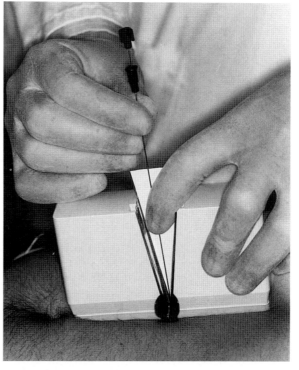

Fig. **2 Centrally perforated linear transducer** with a fine needle

Table **2** Percutaneous diagnostic and therapeutic measures in which ultrasonography guidance is preferable

Instrument	Purpose of puncture
Fine needle (Chiba)	Cytology Bacteriology
Injection of contrast medium using a fine needle under radiologic supervision	Visualization of a cavity system (bile ducts, anterograde pyelography, cystography, visualization of abscesses, discharging cysts and pseudocysts)
Cutting biopsy cannula	Histologic investigation of parenchymal transformation of an organ
Drainage catheter	Nephrostomy, intermittent/permanent Drainage of bile ducts, intermittend/permanent Suprapubic bladder fistula Percutaneous stomach fistula Abscess drainage

depth of the tissue. Inevitably, this also increases the puncture route. This method is recommended for use only in certain exigencies such as amniocentesis and for transvesical extraction of oocytes from the ovary.

Indications

Real-time biopsy using the centrally-perforated transducer has been performed on over 4000 patients in Zurich already, and has proved very successful, both in fine-needle biopsy to obtain tissue for histologic examination and to inject contrast media into hollow systems, and also for certain methods of interventional therapy (Table **2**). This method has undergone numerous modifications in the meantime, but the basic principle of application remains the same.

Combined US and Fluoroscopy Guidance

Interventional diagnosis with US guidance is also performed in combination with conventional radiologic methods, particularly for antegrade pyelography, as in the case of obstruction in the lower ureter which cannot be positively identified using retrograde pyelography (Fig. **3**) and to reveal indeterminate biliary obstruction. For this purpose, a fine-needle puncture of the urinary or biliary system is carried out on the X-ray table with US guidance. As soon as communication with the outside is indicated by the flow of urine or bile, contrast medium is carefully injected under fluoroscopy guidance. This technique of investigation with combined US and fluoroscopy guidance has two major advantages: no anesthesia is required, and the risk of infection is virtually eliminated. In addition to this, percutaneous cholangiography can also be performed on an out-patient basis if the puncture is transhepatic, since extravasation can be avoided with great certainty. Anterograde pyelography and visualization of cysts is done analagously. US-guided percutaneous pancreatography is another application of this technique (Fig. **4**). The evaluation of the pancreatic duct provides important information for planning pancreatic surgery. This examination should be reserved, however, for patients in whom retrograde endoscopic pancreatography has remained unsuccessful (91).

Furthermore, certain therapeutic measures with US and radiologic guidance are possible, such as the drainage of bile ducts in obstructive jaundice, drainage of abscesses, and nephrostomy.

Computed Tomography

Following its introduction, CT was employed for guiding the biopsy needle to the focus of interest. For biopsy guidance, CT is more time-consuming (Table **3**). Nevertheless, certain indications exist for this technique.

Localizing certain tumors using US alone may be difficult. Despite its known drawbacks (Table **3**), CT

Table **3** Biopsy with ultrasound and computed tomography guidance

Advantages		Disadvantages	
Ultrasound	Computed tomography	Ultrasound	Computed tomography
Quick	Good, objective image	Subjective	Slow
No exposure to X-rays	Small lesions can be aspirated, e.g. lymph nodes	Gas and skeleton not penetrable	Time-consuming
Permanent visual supervision	Gas or skeleton do not impede visibility	Difficult to objectify	No permanent visual supervision
Simple repeat examination		Problem areas (e.g. presacral region)	Exposure to X-rays
			Postintervention follow up more difficult and expensive

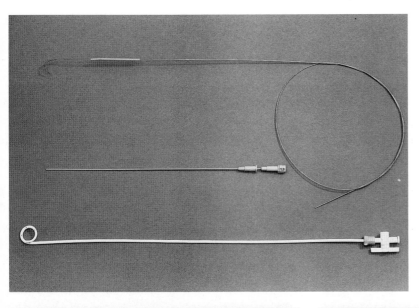

Fig. **3a** **Drainage set** for percutaneous nephrostomy

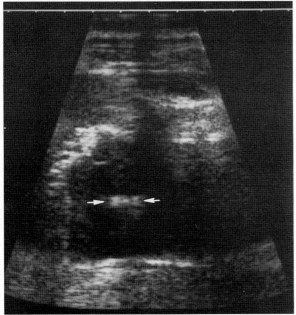

Fig. **3b Percutaneous US-guided puncture of the dilated renal pelvis.** The tip of the needle is indicated by arrows. The dark central line corresponds to the line of sight

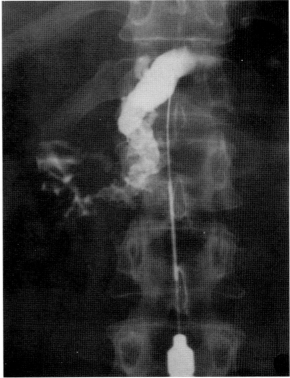

Fig. **4 Percutaneous US-guided opacification of the pancreatic duct,** after failure of endoscopic pancreatography: chronic pancreatitis. (Courtesy of D. Matter M.D., Strasbourg)

should be used for biopsy guidance in cases in which the outcome of cytologic and histologic examinations has a direct impact on the patient and alters the course of his treatment. CT is indicated as a guidance method for percutaneous biopsy whenever other imaging modalities have failed (116). As a rule, a lesion should be biopsied as soon as it has been clearly documented, provided that easy access is possible and that the operator is familiar with the type of procedure. It is false policy to take the

patient back to the US room when a lesion has been evidenced on CT, or to send patients to CT when biopsy could have been performed in combination with a previous US examination. Some lesions are more regularly approached with CT control and the aid of stereotaxic devices, such as lesions in the brain

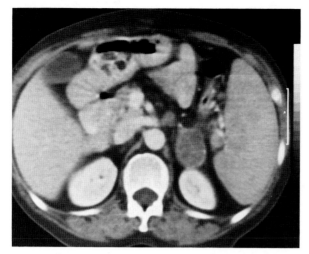

Fig. **5a**   **Patient with chronic lymphatic leukemia** presenting with a 4 cm solid mass in the left adrenal

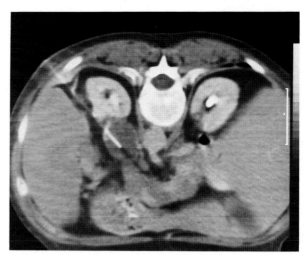

Fig. **5b**   **CT-guided percutaneous biopsy** by an extrasplenic approach: lymphoid infiltration

(14, 78, 99, 104, 118, 126, 140) and in the vertebral canal (1, 56, 72). Lesions located in the adrenals (Fig. **5**), in the posterior pelvis (2, 68) (Fig. **6**), small lymph nodes (77), lesions in the bone (42), head and neck lesions (43) are often best biopsied with CT control. Occasionally, breast lesions are punctured with CT (69). The CT guidance method can also be applied to children (143). Other interventional procedures such as percutaneous abscess drainage, infiltration of nervous structures, and implantation of radioactive seeds are successfully performed with CT guidance (75).

Indications

Indications for CT-guided biopsy are listed in Table **4**.

Table **4**   Main indications for computed tomography guidance

---

Brain
Orbit
Vertebral canal
Lesion originating from bone
Adrenal (small)
Lymph node
Posterior pelvis
Obesity, gas, ileus, surgery, drains
Pancreas (small)
Vascular lesion to be excluded
Failure of ultrasound or fluoroscopy
Interintestinal
Mediastinum
Apex of lung
Posterior sulcus
Operated lung
Complex thoracic lesion

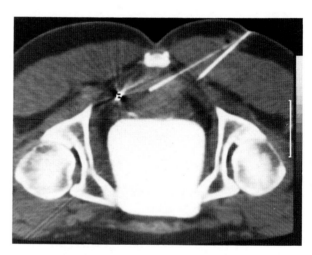

Fig. **6**   **Tumor mass in the posterior pelvis** one year following surgery for rectal carcinoma. Percutaneous CT-guided biopsy by a posterior approach. Notice redirection of the needle to the target: tumor recurrence

Reduction in the scanning and reconstruction time with recently-developed CT units has largely favored the spread of interventional procedures guided by this technique. CT is now used as often as other imaging modalities for percutaneous tissue sampling and other interventional techniques.

It has been stated that it is false policy not to use CT as a guidance method, when percutaneous biopsy has become an integrated part of imaging (10). Since the initial description of percutaneous biopsy guidance by CT (49), the number of contributions in the literature are convincing proof of the usefulness of this technique.

Technical Imperatives

Some technical imperatives have to be emphasized (29, 30, 75):

- The diameter of the gantry has to be large enough to admit the patient together with a stiff needle or a trocar.
- A light system inside the gantry is indispensable, indicating the precise level of the slice which has been selected to perform the guided puncture.
- The scanning time and reconstruction time of the CT image should not exceed a few seconds, in order to shorten the procedure. This is of extreme importance in lung biopsy and when the patient is less cooperative.
- The total irradiation dose can be reduced during CT control of a percutaneous procedure. The images do not need the same quality as that required for diagnostic examination (48).
- When a TV screen is placed inside the CT room, the radiologist can review the slices without having to leave the patient alone.
- When the patient is moved outside the gantry, the distance the table is moved should be indicated with precision on the table itself and also be readable by the operator on the console.
- The table has to be moved from the operator's console and from the table itself with millimeter precision.
- It should be possible to review any CT image at any moment of the procedure without time loss.
- A venous line has to be placed. This allows contrast medium to be reinjected during the procedure (48).

Advantages and Limitations of CT Guidance

Accuracy of anatomical display is the basic advantage of CT. Any anatomical structure can be precisely recognized, whatever the morphotype of the patient, and the anatomical compartment considered. Gas does not alter the image quality. Vascular structures can be recognized after intravenous bolus enhancement, and puncturing them is avoided. The degree of vascularity of a lesion is estimated prior to puncture. Fatty components and necrotic areas can be recognized, and the puncture can be directed to those parts of the lesion which are considered most specific. The entry point of the needle and the needle pathway can be planned on the images, and the distance from the skin to the target and the angulation of the needle can be measured. When the procedure has to be repeated, it can be performed in identical conditions. All steps of the procedure are documented, and potential complications are anticipated or documented at the end of the procedure. CT images inspire high medical confidence among referring physicians. The use of CT as a guidance method for interventional procedures is limited by the fact that imaging control is discontinuous. It is cumbersome to obtain slices in another plane than the axial one. The patient has to be more cooperative than with other imaging modalities, immobility and apnea during scanning are mandatory. The patient is moved in and out of the gantry during the procedure, which is more time-consuming than with US or fluoroscopy guidance. Particular problems arising during CT control are the partial volume effect, which makes it difficult to hit a lesion with a reduced diameter and in a deep location. Some lesions

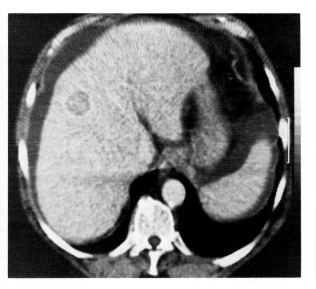

Fig. 7a **After contrast enhancement, CT shows a 3 cm hypodense lesion** in the liver in a patient with cirrhosis

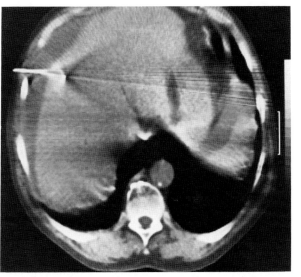

Fig. 7b **CT-guided biopsy.** The lesion has turned rapidly isodense after enhancement: hepatocarcinoma

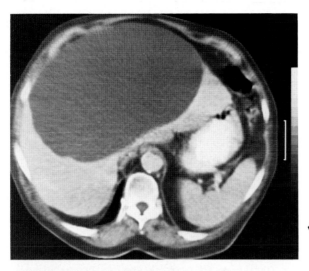

located in solid parenchyma (liver, spleen, kidney) may turn rapidly isodense after initial enhancement (Fig. **7**) and are no longer identifiable on late control scans. Multilocular cystic lesions may look perfectly homogenous, as CT is unable to confirm thin septae within such a lesion (Fig. **8**).

◀ Fig. **8a** **Homogenous cystic lesion in the liver** shown on CT. US showed septae within the lesion only after partial percutaneous aspiration

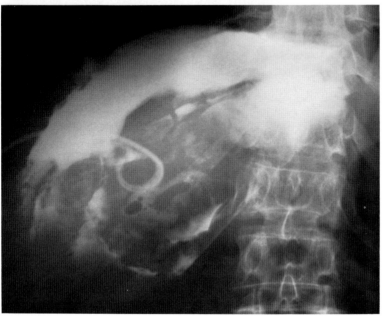

Fig. **8b** **Percutaneous opacification of the cystic lesion** showed multiple septae. Histology of a septum removed percutaneously confirmed cystadenocarcinoma

Technique

A detailed CT examination of the region is performed prior to percutaneous biopsy. This examination gives indications on the nature of the lesion, its vascularity, necrosis, and specific components. The level of percutaneous access to the lesion is determined in such a way that no great vessels and no lung parenchyma are interposed. As long as fine-gauge needles are used, other anatomical structures such as the bowel can be traversed, although not with cutting needles. Whenever possible, especially when a lesion is in a deep location, the needle pathway should be perpendicular or parallel to the table. The puncture route should be as short as possible. When a hypervascular lesion bulging under the capsule is punctured, normal parenchyma should remain interposed between the capsule and the lesion, minimizing bleeding through the capsular leak. The entry point on the skin is marked with a metallic pointer which is placed perpendicular on the selected slice level (Fig. **9**) and is identified as a point on the control slice (Fig. **16a**). The intersection of the selected slice level and the skin marker determines the entry point. Local anesthetic can be used. Care must be taken not to inject it into the target, because of the risk of cellular degradation. A small incision at the skin can be made with a blade so that a fine-gauge needle is not diverted from its course while traversing the skin. When puncture of the colon is unavoidable, the cytologist has to be informed, as components of the bacterial flora can contaminate cytologic smears. When the wall of the stomach is punctured by a fine

needle and repeated puncture (Fig. **6**). When the needle has been inserted in a strict axial plane, its entire length can be visualized within one slice (Fig. **10a**). The needle tip should be documented inside the target. The tip of the needle is recognized by a distal shadow due to the partial volume effect. When the biopsy is completed, a control scan is obtained when sampling has been performed in a critical area, in order to detect infraclinical complications like a pneumothorax. When the lesion cannot be reached by a perpendicular percutaneous approach (subphrenic, posterior pelvis), an oblique approach has to be chosen. When the needle is introduced in an oblique axial plane, it is not evident on a single slice as a whole (Fig. **10b, c**). The gantry can be angled if the obliquity of the needle is only slight (20 degrees), in order to identify the entire length of the needle. Otherwise, multiple slices are necessary in order to follow the progress of the needle in depth to the target. A profile digital radiograph can be performed when the needle is in place showing the inclination of the needle and allowing adjustment of the oblique axial plane in order to identify the needle along its entire length (149). Most abdominal intraperitoneal lesions are biopsied by a percutaneous anterior or anterolateral approach, the patient remaining in a supine position. In the past, determination of the selected axial slice in which puncture should be performed was achieved using a skin grid marker (23, 56). On actual CT units, a light reference system facilitates identification of the selected slice level when the patient is placed in the gantry. A light guidance system using intersecting laser beams providing precise guidance, including compound angles, has been described (39). A belt device placed on the abdomen of the patient may be helpful in determining the optimal point for skin puncture (64). Angulation of the needle can also be calculated by simple methods (6). Most lesions can be approached free hand. Stereotaxis devices are indispensable for carrying out percutaneous biopsy of the brain, but are rarely required in the body (107, 148). Combined use of a respiratory gating device is not applied routinely (70). Lesions that are located in the midline retroperitoneum are either approached anteriorly or by a posterior paraspinal approach, the patient lying prone (Fig. **11**). Renal or pararenal lesions are biopsied laterally or by a posterior puncture. The more cephalad-located adrenals may be hidden by the posterior pleural sulcus. They are biopsied anteriorly or posteriorly (9, 60, 86, 122), or by a transhepatic (120) or a transsplenic puncture. The patient can also be placed in lateral decubitus (61) facilitating a posterior extrapleural puncture. Pelvic lesions are biopsied anteriorly when they are in a lateral or anterior location to the urinary bladder (144). When in a deep location, a parallel approach to the iliac bone is helpful (119). Transcystic fine-needle biopsy makes

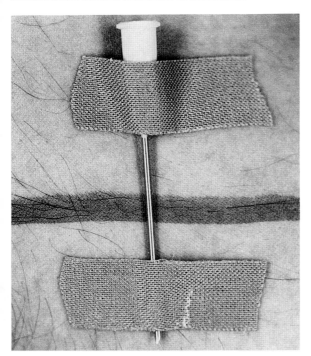

Fig. 9 Metallic needle placed on the patient's skin to determine the entry point for percutaneous computed tomography-guided biopsy

CT-guided biopsy

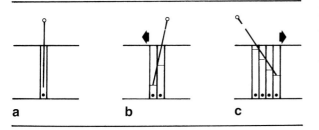

a   b   c

Fig. 10a The needle inserted parallel to the slice, and contained within the slice thickness, is visualized in its entire length on a simple CT image (cf. Fig. **11b**). **b, c** When the needle in inserted oblique to the CT slice, only a part of its length is visualized on one CT image (cf. Fig. **14b**)

gauge needle, its course can be deviated. All vascular and nervous structures which are identified are avoided whenever possible during puncture. It is recommended that organs or anatomical compartments that are not involved with the lesion or the spontaneous spread of the disease should not be traversed by the needle. This is of extreme importance for infected fluid collections and highly malignant tumors.

Control scans document the progression of the needle in depth to the target. An incorrect angulation of the needle is changed by withdrawal of the

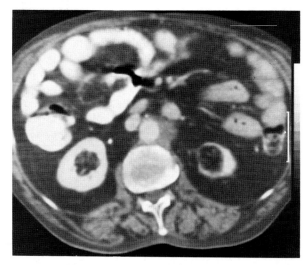

Fig. **11a   CT shows a 2 cm residual mass,** adjacent to the abdominal aorta, after chemotherapy for retroperitoneal lymph node metastases of a non-seminomatous tumor of the left testis

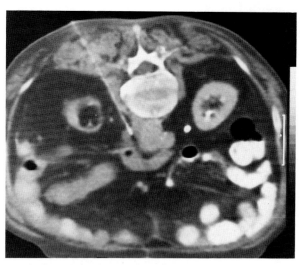

Fig. **11b   CT-guided percutaneous biopsy** confirmed fibroblasts without tumor cells

it possible to reach lesions in the posterior pelvis by an anterior pathway (136). A posterolateral transgluteal approach is indicated for puncture of presacral lesions or when larger needles are used (2, 115).

The coaxial technique consists in introducing a larger needle through the skin and the abdominal wall. When the needle is pointing to the lesion, a small-gauge needle is introduced coaxially in depth, and sampling can be repeated by introducing the inner needle several times (52). The modified coaxial technique is used when a deeply located lesion is difficult to reach. A small-gauge needle is first placed in the lesion. Then, the hub of the needle is removed and a larger gauge needle is placed over the first needle (92, 146). The tandem technique (36) consists in placing multiple identical needles parallel to the first needle inside the lesion. This technique also allows multiple sampling without repeating the guidance procedure after the first needle is placed (100). A triangular technique has been described to reach lesions which are situated high under the diaphragm and which cannot be reached in an axial plane without traversing the pleura, the lung and the diaphragm. The technique is based on the Pythagorean theorem, and is especially useful when large-bore needles or drainage catheters must be inserted (44, 147).

Injecting a small amount of diluted contrast medium after percutaneous sampling documents the biopsy site on a control slice (137). Injecting carbon dioxide through the percutaneous needle moves the bowel or the urinary bladder out of the intended path of the needle, creating a larger cleavage plane (50). When a pseudo-mass such as a non-opacified bowel loop after surgery, is present, a percutaneous opacification after aspiration of intestinal fluid delineates the mass and allows pseudotumoral bowel loops to be visualized (63).

MRI

Percutaneous MRI-guided biopsy has been described previously, but the precise value of the technique needs further evaluation (83, 101). Localization grids such as those formerly used in CT have been described (54). Steotactic guided biopsy is possible (141). The stainless-steel needles are visible on MRI, giving similar artifacts than those seen on CT (101).

Needles

Cytology

We generally use fine needles with a submillimeter diameter, including the "Chiba" model (106), for cytologic examination and to obtain material for bacteriologic preparation. The classic Chiba needle has been slightly modified and has a mandrin ground in. It is approximately 0.7 mm in diameter, and is suitable for removing cells from all regions of the body. As this disposable needle is very flexible, it has no trouble adapting itself to breathing movements in the inner organs, thus preventing the rupture of a capsule if it is stuck in far enough. Moreover, the US image of its tip is very distinct, especially if the mandrin is slightly retracted. The same instrument is also ideal for injecting contrast media under radiologic guidance into hollow organs, e. g. into the bile ducts.

Careful handling and processing of the material obtained for cytologic investigation is extremely important; it must be smeared and fixed immediately. The entire process of injecting the material onto the slide from the needle and fixing it in a Delauney solution should be completed within a few seconds, to prevent the cellular substance from becoming desiccated. The syringe and the needle can be rinsed with heparin to prevent early clotting of the cellular material. Sprays are used for fixation, but some cytologists are of the opinion that they do not allow optimal fixation. With the wet fixation method using the Delauney solution followed by staining, an initial assessment can be made just 10 minutes after tissue removal; it thus has a considerable edge not only over all other methods of fixation but also over histologic preparation of tissue. Fine-needle aspiration is particularly well-suited for examination of undefined circumscribed space-occupying lesions within parenchymal organs or at their periphery. Small-gauge needles, 20 G, are even able to produce sufficient cytologic material for the diagnosis of lesions such as hepatic hemangioma and adenoma (4). Cytologic diagnosis of a benign lesion should be considered with extreme caution, as other areas of the tumor may contain coexisting carcinoma. Another of its applications is for the examination of enlarged lymph nodes, such as those of the retroperitoneum, if malignant lymphoma or metastases are suspected. Finally, abscesses can be punctured and the sample, which often appears very viscous, passed on for bacteriologic examination. Material recovered with the Chiba needle is unsuitable for histologic examination.

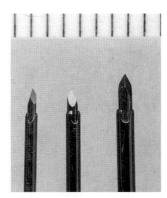

Fig. **12a Cutting biopsy cannula with mandrin,** designed by R. C. OTTO. Top: millimeter scale

Histology

In addition to the standard biopsy needles, in particular the Tru-cut needle which was used, formerly in frequent use, we have developed in Zurich another instrument for removing histologic tissue samples (Fig. **12a**). The outer diameter of this cutting biopsy cannula is just under or over 1 mm, making it much finer than other histology needles (Fig. **12b**). The principle employed here is to cut out tissue, but this is coupled with the principle of intensive aspiration as used with cytology needles (112). Due to the special configuration of the needle, injury to the larger vessels in the organ can generally be avoided. The tip of the cutting biopsy cannula has 2 notches with sharpened edges which punch out little cylinders when rotated clockwise in the tissue. The advantage of the cannula is that tissue can be removed in sufficient quantities to achieve reliable pathohistologic diagnosis, while the risk to the patient is drastically reduced. The cutting biopsy cannula is particularly well-suited to the removal of tissue samples from the kidney and the liver. In

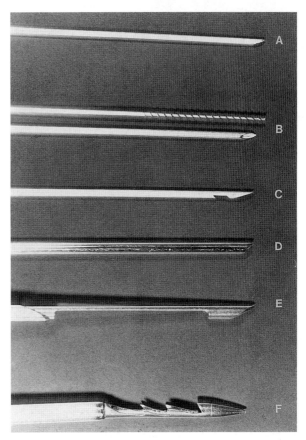

Fig. **12b** Different needles used for percutaneous tissue sampling:
A   Chiba needle (22 G)
B   Rotex screw needle (0.8 mm)
C   Westcott needle (20 G)
D   Menghini needle (14 G)
E   Tru-cut needle
F   Reinhardt needle

generalized diseases such as glomerulonephritis, accurate micromorphological analysis is often the key to therapy. As in the case of the Chiba needle, the tip is also clearly visible in the tissue, so that only that region of the kidney which is really of interest is actually reached, that is, the cortex and the peripheral medulla. Puncture of the renal pelvis is thus avoided (Fig. **13**). Another significant advantage of using the thin cutting biopsy cannula is the fact that the procedure can be performed on outpatients both in the kidney and the liver. The cutting biopsy cannula also permits tumor biopsy (58). However, if sophisticated cytologic laboratory facilities are available, there is usually no need for histologic

examination. The primary application of the cutting biopsy cannula is otherwise confined to biopsy in generalized diseases of parenchymal organs and of the thyroid, and to the removal of tissue in certain skeletal disorders. Clinical experience (51, 114), and laboratory experiments (5) comparing different types of needles have shown that large-bore needles produce quantitatively and qualitatively superior tissue samples than fine needles. Other small-bore needles with an acute bevel angle are superior to flat bevelled needles with an identical gauge (5), suggesting that the design of the biopsy needles influences results (79). Needles with multiple holes, and half-wall needles, give fragments for histologic assessment (121). Other small-gauge needles with a modified design are also able to produce histologic samples (142, 151) and may avoid the necessity of using larger needles. Each operator should use the needles which he thinks best suit his technique and give acceptable samples according to the cystologist or pathologist examining the material. One should not rely on one single type of needle. The present trend is to use larger needles (10). Curved needles allowing redirection can be used with fluoroscopy control and when a lesion is hidden by bone (18, 59) but are unsuitable for US and CT control. Using needle hub rotation, the curved needle can be redirected to the target (97).

When lymphoma is suspected, cytologic smears are not sufficient to establish a precise diagnosis, especially for subclassification of Hodgkin lymphoma (67). 22 G cutting needles give cytologic and histologic samples, but are still insufficient for the diagnosis of lymphoma (67). 14 G Tru cut needles can be safely used in the retroperitoneum. Sufficient tissue has to be obtained for immunotyping (33, 58, 66) (Fig. **14**). In the liver, the Menghini needle or

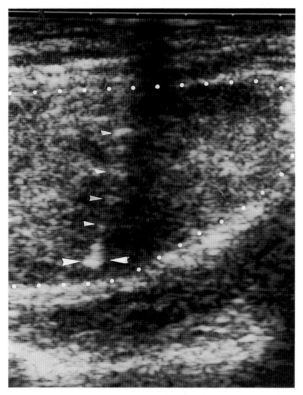

Fig. **13 Percutaneous punch biopsy of the inferior pole of the kidney.** The needle is located in the cortex (arrowheads), the kidney outlined by dots

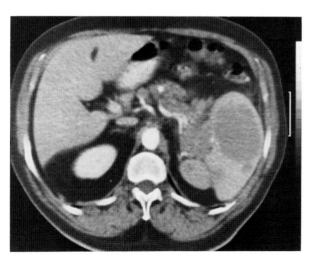

Fig. **14a   Tumor mass in the spleen** and the splenic hilum not dissociated from the tail of the pancreas

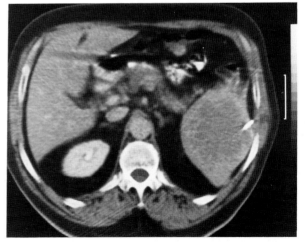

Fig. **14b   CT-guided biopsy of the spleen** with a punch biopsy needle: malignant non-Hodgkin lymphoma

large-gauge cutting needles can be safely used with imaging guidance. For the diagnosis of well-differentiated hepatocarcinoma, it is useful to take a specimen of the non-affected liver parenchyma, allowing histologic comparison. To begin with, an on-site microscope in the CT suite was thought to be indispensable (57) together with a rapid stain technique, obviating further unnecessary passes into the lesion (73). Immediate examination of smears is unpracticable, however, because of the large number of non-planned biopsies that are performed every day. When aspiration biopsy is performed, a 10 ml continuous suction should be employed. Maintenance of suction obtains a large sample. Aspiration of blood cells does not confuse the cytopathologic interpretation (65). Inclusion cytology is routinely recommended when possible, and permits easier preparation and interpretation of special stains compared with smear cytology (82). Other authors suggest routine multiple passes to ensure the recovery of diagnostic material (47).

Four passes are suggested in the pancreas (38, 85, 102), two passes in other organs, but more than ten passes expose the patient to risks of complications and malignant seeding. In addition, immediate cytologic assessment does not alter the accuracy, although it provides educational benefits (95).

Results

A comparison was made of the results from biopsies made under US and CT guidance on a selected group of patients in the past few years. It showed that in 84% to over 93% of the cases, specific material was able to be obtained for cytologic analysis. The failure rate amounted to only a few percent, and was primarily due to the simultaneous aspiration of blood, which makes it harder to identify tumor cells. In addition to this, aspiration of tissue characteristic of the tumor is sometimes a problem in tumors which are heavily fibrotic or in sarcoma. In Table 5, the main factors affecting the accuracy of percutaneous biopsy are listed. Table 6 shows the biopsy sites with CT guidance in a consecutive non-selected group of 415 patients, in whom 448 percutaneous procedures were performed. In this series, sensitivity was 86.6%, specificity 98.6%, and accuracy 90%.

Table 7 shows the results of tissue specimens from different organs obtained with US guidance. More

Table 5   Main factors influencing the accuracy of percutaneous biopsy

Quality of the guidance system
Expected information from tissue sampling
Anatomical location of the lesion
Operator expertise
Biopsy instrument
Number of samples
Patient cooperation
Cooperation with the cytologist or pathologist

Table 6   Biopsy sites with CT guidance in 415 patients. 448 percutaneous procedures were performed

Liver	85	Ovary	11
Lung	66	Extrapleural	8
Kidney	65	Adrenal	7
Intraperitoneal	43	Spleen	6
Pelvis	35	Spine	6
Pancreas	34	Paraspinal	5
Retroperitoneal	30	Neck	4
Mediastinum	18	Others	9
Pleura	16		

Table 7   Results of fine-needle aspiration biopsy with ultrasonography guidance

Organ	Total	Biopsies with specific local tissue suitable for evaluation		Suspected or definite malignancy	
	n	n	%	n	%
Liver	469	417	88.9	337	80.8
Pancreas	131	114	87.0	89	78.1
Retroperitoneal space-occupying lesions	168	155	92.3	144	92.9
Spleen	7	6		4	
Kidneys	112	96	85.7	84	87.5
Stomach, colon	35	28	80.0	24	85.7
Intrathoracic space-occupying lesions (without discharge)	69	59	85.5	41	69.5
Total	991	875	(= 88.3)	723	(= 82.6) 73.0
Total, including repeat biopsies	991	893	(= 90.1)	737	(= 82.5) 74.4

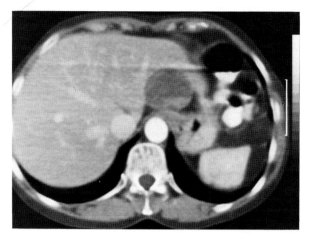

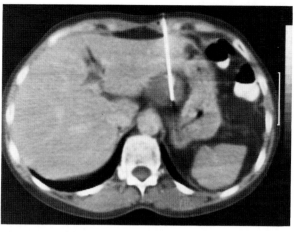

Fig. **15a   CT shows a 4 cm subhepatic solid mass** suggestive of an adenopathy

Fig. **15b   Percutaneous   transhepatic   CT-guided biopsy** disclosed caseum; cultures remained negative. No tumor cells

recent studies have produced similar results. All aspiration results were confirmed by additional examinations, by surgery, biopsy or autopsy, or by the subsequent course of the disease. No false-positive results were observed. Malignant growth was diagnosed in 74.4% of the cases. The assessment "not representative" or "not unequivocally malignant" which emerged for 11.7% of all patients presents some problems.

Repeating fine-needle biopsy in 31 patients in whom it was initially not diagnostic produced malignant findings in a further 14 patients. In 4 cases, the cellular substance provided no clues of malignancy, and with another 13 patients, no conclusive cytological diagnosis of their underlying disorder could be established.

Judging fine-needle biopsy for the purpose of removing cytologic material on the basis of these results, it may be stated that a malignant growth was suspected in over ⅘ of all patients, but that a malignant tumor was confirmed in only ¾ of the patients. In evaluating the information obtained by section imaging – whether US or CT – the investigator obviously tends to overinterpret it, and frequently suspects malignant growths where there are non (Fig. 15). Guided puncture with the fine needle is able to compensate for the weaknesses of the method and is therefore indicated in an ever-growing number of cases. Even with MRI, it is impossible in many cases to make an unequivocal diagnosis of whether a lesion is malignant or benign. The assessment of growths in the liver – hemangioma or metastasis? – is therefore often speculative, and a definite diagnostic differentiation between carcinoma and adenoma of the prostate is impossible in almost 30% of cases with prostatic hypertrophy.

Only in 8% of all patients was a benign tumor assumed right from the beginning and later also confirmed by cytologic information (e. g. abscess, capillary hemangioma, anticoagulant bleeding of the psoas, pancreatic pseudocysts, etc. (Fig. 16). Aspiration of ascites and pleural effusion was not included in this evaluation.

Diagnostic uncertainty with negative biopsy results can be illustrated by the example of liver hemangioma. The US findings are ambiguous, and on some occasions a malignant tumor cannot be ruled out with CT. Often, only blood is sampled, so that one cannot be certain that the sample is really representative. This uncertainty can be overcome by adopting the "harpooning" puncture, with which the endothelial cells needed for proof of a benign growth can be removed (112). Since fine-needle biopsy, if performed correctly, poses only a minimal and manageable risk to the patient, even the occasionally "superfluous" biopsy of a lesion later diagnosed as being benign seems justified, since numerous malignant tumors can be detected in a minimally invasive manner. Two absolute contra-indications for percutaneous biopsy should be kept in mind: functioning pheochromocytoma (19) and hemophilic pseudotumor.

The past few years have shown that other researchers have also achieved similarly positive results with fine-needle biopsy. Reviewing results obtained with percutaneous biopsy in the literature, an accuracy of 83% to 98% is obtained in the liver (12, 53, 88, 90, 139, 155, 156), 60% to 90% in the pancreas (12, 28, 55, 98, 130), over 90% in the kidney and in the adrenals (9, 86). Certain variations in the results can be attributed in part to differences in experience at various cytologic laboratories. Particularly simple and rewarding is the aspiration of an abscess, where it is sometimes difficult, using US and CT to differentiate between a necrotic disintegrating tumor or a solid space-occupying growth.

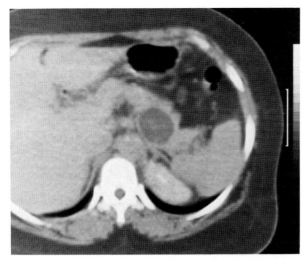

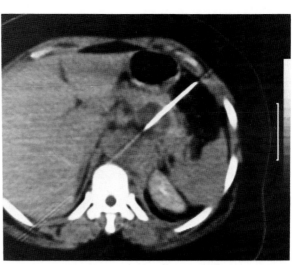

Fig. **16a   CT shows a well-defined 3 cm cystic mass in the pancreas.** The entry point for percutaneous approach is marked on the skin by a metallic pointer

Fig. **16b   Percutaneous CT-guided aspiration.** A retroperitoneal hematoma occurred during aspiration

It has been shown in a prospective study that percutaneous biopsy contributed significantly to the diagnosis in 75%, confused the diagnosis in 3%, and altered therapeutic plans in 32% (13). For the diagnosis of lymphoma, a diagnostic specimen is obtained with a cutting needle in 94% (33), and a definitive diagnosis in over 50% (66). Histologic subtyping is not established with confidence on the basis of cytologic smears alone. A distinct mass is easier to biopsy than moderately enlarged lymph nodes. The diagnosis of non-Hodgkin lymphoma is more easily established than for Hodgkin disease. It is still often difficult to establish the scleronodular type, or to ascertain recurrent Hodgkin disease following radiotherapy. Although to begin with, with lack of experience, it seemed that CT gave better results than US (38) for instance in pancreatic biopsy, both modalities are used in most departments, not necessarily by the same radiologist. A combination of methods should be used. Results depend on the number of passes (47, 52), and not significantly on the guidance modality.

Fine-needle biopsy to remove tissue for cytologic analysis is also inadequate in the case of generalized parenchymal transformation of the liver, or as in glomerulonephritis. Fine-punch biopsy with the cutting biopsy cannula is an invaluable aid in such cases (109). Despite its fine-bore outer diameter, it allows cylinders of tissue to be removed that can be examined to provide definite histological diagnosis.

Table **8** shows the initial findings for those patients who underwent biopsies using both the Tru-cut needle and the new cutting biopsy cannula. There is evidently no appreciable difference which might be of relevance for the final diagnosis. On the other hand, a significant reduction in the usual rate of

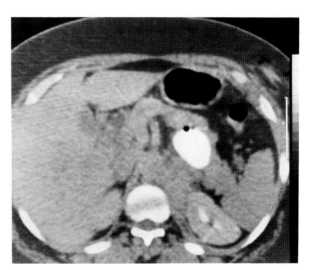

Fig. **16c   Opacification through the aspiration needle** confirms a unilocular cystic lesion with a regular wall. No tumor cells. Pancreatic cystadenoma was confirmed at surgery

Table **8**   Results of renal biopsy

	Cutting biopsy cannula	Tru-cut
No. of patients	57	61
Glomeruli	11 + 8	16 + 11
Electron microscopy	83%	86%
Immunofluorescence	52%	65%
Total informative	94%	94%
Optimum	75%	77%

complications (15, 129) has been observed in work with over 200 patients on whom biopsy was performed on the kidney. This can undoubtedly be ascribed not only to the new instrument, but also to the feasibility of permanent US supervision during and after the procedure. No operation or nephrectomy was therefore needed in any of these cases. In the meantime, this needle has been used for biopsy on a large number of transplanted kidney, on some even several times within a few weeks, without causing any complications.

Complications

Significant complications arising in percutaneous biopsies in the abdomen are rare, and require emergency surgery only in exceptional circumstances. Most side-effects are managed conservatively or by other interventional techniques, e. g. embolization for persistent bleeding, percutaneous aspiration of a fluid collection. Potential complications are listed in Table **9**.

A review of 11,700 patients who underwent percutaneous abdominal biopsy from 1969 to 1982 using 20–23 gauge needles disclosed a mortality rate of 0.008% and a rate of major complications of 0.05%. The total complication rate was 0.55% (80).

Another study on 63,180 patients (133) showed an overall complication rate of 0.16% : 4 deaths were due to hemorrhage in 3 patients and secondary to pancreatitis in another patient. The most significant complications were bleeding, bile leakage and infection. Seeding of malignancy along the needle tract was seen in 0.005%. Deeply-located, intraparenchymal lesions which are difficult to reach are more prone to complications than extraparenchymal and superficial lesions which are easy to hit. The risk of hemorrhage is extremely low in fine-needle biopsies, provided that they are performed only under the following conditions: a Quick's value of 50%, a

Table **9**   Potential complications following abdominal percutaneous fine-needle Biopsy

Discomfort	Arteriovenous fistula
Pain	Pneumothorax
Fever	Hemoperitoneum
Viral infection?	Pneumoperitoneum
Hypotension	Pleural effusion
Vagal reaction	Ascites
Shock	Cholangitis
Hematuria	Peritonitis
Hematoma	Septicemia
Urinoma	Abscess
Biloma	Pancreatitis
Lymphorrhea	Hemorrhage
Pseudoaneurysm	Metastases
Thrombosis	Death

thrombocyte count of no less than 80,000 per mm^3 (131) and normal bleeding time. Only rupture of the capsule of a solid organ, especially if it is marked by circumscribed or generalized changes, poses a certain risk. If the needle is inserted too shallowly, it can cut into the organ capsule like a knife when the patient takes a sudden deep breath, thus causing severe bleeding, e. g. of a hemangioma located at the surface. Oblique puncture through the still-healthy part of the organ is therefore strongly recommended (112). Even hepatic hemangiomas can be biopsied percutaneously, and a specific histologic diagnosis can be achieved (25). As their appearance is non-specific on US and CT (40) in a significant number of cases, puncture of these lesions is unavoidable. When a highly hypervascular liver tumor is biopsied, a plastic sheath can be left inplace enabling repeated biopsy through the sheath, minimizing hemorrhagic complications. The percutaneous tract is embolized with gelfoam before removal (21).

Experimental work in animals has shown that repeated puncture of hollow and solid viscera before and during operative control did not involve serious hemorrhagic complications necessitating blood transfusion (22, 45). Bleeding episodes are rare even after biopsy of hypervascular tumors. Even in the case of multiple biopsies of the pancreas, the surgeons were unable, in an operation immediately afterward, to identify the puncture route with any certainty. On occasion, a small flake of fibrin was thought to be detected on the transverse colon that could be taken for a fresh scar. Experiments with animals have also shown that it is relatively difficult to hit the small visceral vessels with the comparatively dull Chiba needle. Instead, these vessels tend to be pushed aside. Large vessels, such as the vena cava, can be punctured deliberately to prove septic thrombosis (96).

Fortunately, we did not observe any of the heavy bleeding of the varices often encountered by surgeons in the epigastric region after accidental perforation (in the case of patients with cirrhosis, for example). The primary reason for this may perhaps be the fact that we perform biopsy with the abdomen closed, so that the prevalent pressure conditions are different from those during surgery.

Use of larger needles or cutting needles does not significantly increase the complication rate in solid organs like the liver (53, 90, 114, 127), in comparison with fine-gauge needles, when imaging guidance directs the needle properly to the target. Percutaneous blind biopsy however, carries a more significant complication rate when larger needles are used (93, 154). Use of a cutting biopsy cannula is relatively simple. As a matter of fact, this instrument provides some assurance that larger vessels within the parenchyma will not be cut, thereby reducing the risk of hemorrhage. In all other invasive procedures, even when introducing drainage tubes, a lot depends on the instruments being correctly placed. Nor have we observed any cases of severe hemorrhaging here which would have necessitated surgery. Nevertheless, drainage of the biliary system should always be undertaken in preparation for surgery because extravasating bile, coupled with peritonitis, is a grave threat. The tendency of the exposed kidney to bleed after biopsy is macromorphologically similar in larger-bore needles and resembles that of the spleen. The fact that hemorrhage seems less severe after percutaneous biopsy is probably due to the different pressure conditions prevailing in an unopened cavity. Systematic angiographic control after liver biopsy or renal biopsy may reveal a certain number of occult abnormalities, such as arteriovenous fistulae or false aneurysms, which resolve spontaneously (24, 94).

As anticipated, the experience of the operator performing the biopsy is more crucial to low-risk work than the choice of needle, although studies with animals have revealed a certain relationship between the use of diverse types and bores of needles and a corresponding difference in hemorrhaging tendency (111). Immediate cytologic assessment diminishes the number of needle passes necessary to achieve a diagnosis, but does not necessarily change the complication rate (94). One point that demands special attention in liver biopsy, even when working with the Chiba needle, is the threat of hypotension associated with brachycardia, leading perhaps even to cardiac arrest. This phenomenon has been adequately described in a number of treatises (7, 11, 27, 35, 138). We have observed this condition in 3 patients within the past few years, and in one case it was very critical. Vagal reaction classically may follow puncture of intraperitoneal organs, but is also seen after percutaneous biopsy of the kidneys. Prolonged vagal tonus should not be confused with hypovolemic shock secondary to major bleeding (9).

It is often impossible to avoid perforating the stomach and intestine on the way to areas of the body lying deeper down, such as the retroperitoneum. This is generally of no consequence and causes little discomfort to the patient. No extrusion of intestinal contents from the site of perforation and no bleeding has been observed in experiments with animals. Fever, chills, bacteremia or generalized sepsis can be after traversing the bowel, especially distal parts of the gastrointestinal tract (38) during pelvic biopsy (89), or when a septic cavity (128) or the obstructed biliary or urinary system are punctured without immediate drainage being assured (80, 81). Puncture of an intraparenchymal hemolymphangioma can be followed by significant fistula of lymphatic fluid (26). Death occurring after percutaneous fine-needle biopsy is extremely rare. Fatal necrotizing pancreatitis has been described (34), but this was consequent to puncture of the normal pancreas.

Imaging techniques have to be used extensively to guide the needle puncture to the tumor tissue in the pancreas, which can be biopsied without significant risk of acute pancreatitis (by contrast with the normal gland). A sudden increase in blood pressure may be observed after puncture of an intermittently secreting pheochromocytoma. As these tumors can be in an ectopic extra-adrenal location, care must be taken in patients with suspicion of pheochromocytoma (19).

Dissemination of tumor cells, either spreading locally or seeding distant from the primary tumor, is an inherent risk in all biopsies, especially when using larger needles. This danger is extremely low in fine-needle biopsy (8, 32, 153) and is rarely to be feared in punch biopsies, although it can be observed from time to time (3, 76, 132). Several cases have been reported following percutaneous biopsy of hepatocellular carcinoma (108), of renal carcinoma (16), and of pancreatic carcinoma (20, 37, 123, 134). Malignant tumors of the ovary can be biopsied without significant risk of malignant seeding (71). A large number of needle passes may favor malignant spread. The needle tract can be excised when surgery is performed in high-grade malignant tumors (133). Metastasis following fine-needle biopsy alone does not affect the fatal course of a malignant disorder (37, 74, 135).

As a rule, spontaneous elimination of tumor cells is probably an earlier and more frequent occurrence than the appearance of metastases. The likelihood that tumor cells will disseminate, and that peripheral tumor embolisms will occur, is known to be influenced on the one hand by the diameter of the tumor, at an exponential rate (133); on the other hand, tumor cells can already be confirmed in bone biopsies while the carcinoma is still at an early stage and skeleton scintigraphy does not yet reveal any lesions. It is now known that fine-needle biopsy is in no way detrimental to the long-term survival rate (8), particularly in two intensively researched types of tumor – carcinoma of the breast and of the kidney (124, 150). Experimental animal work has not shown increased metastatic spread after fan-shaped fine-needle biopsy of Walker carcinosarcoma compared to a control group (103).

Conclusions

Imaging-guided percutaneous procedures for diagnosis and therapy in hospitals have gained considerable ground in a short time. In many patients, it is the carefully guided removal of small samples of tissue that makes possible definitive cytologic or histologic diagnosis of a focus detected earlier. It is already the case that decisions regarding patient management are frequently made based solely on the results of this basic examination.

The unique advantages of this method, the fact that the procedures can be performed quickly in the out-patients department, and that the risk involved is negligible, have encouraged its widespread adoption.

The future influence of other, more recent technologies, such as computer-assisted sonography and MRI, which promise to provide even more sophisticated tools for non-invasive diagnosis, remains to be seen. At the present time, it can be confidently assumed that biopsy guided by imaging techniques, with subsequent evaluation by pathologists or cytologists of the samples removed, will remain a primary and essential measure preceding more invasive forms of intervention.

References

1. Adapon AD, Legada BD Jr, Lim EVA. Silao JV Jr, Dalmacio-Cruz A. CT guided closed biopsy of the spine. J Comput Assist Tomogr 1981;5:73–78.
2. Adler OB, Engel A. CT guided transgluteal fine needle aspiration biopsy. Eur. J Radiol. 1987;7:101.
3. Allen IW, Honeckmann CC. Subcutaneous metastasis following needle biopsy of the pleura. J Am Osteopath Assoc 1974;73:522.
4. Alspaugh JP, Bernardino ME, Sewell CW, Sones PJ, Berkman WA, Price RB. CT directed hepatic biopsies: increased diagnostic accuracy with low patient risk. J Comput Assist Tomogr. 1983;7:1012.
5. Andriole JG, Haaga JR, Adams PB, Nunez C. Biopsy needle characteristics assessed in the laboratory. Radiology 1983;148:659.
6. Axel L. Simple method for performing oblique CT guided needle biopsies. AJR 1984;143:341.
7. Barrett GM. Hypotension after percutaneous liver biopsy. Lancet 1974;I:624.
8. Berg JW, Robbinson GF. A late look at the safety of aspiration biopsy. Cancer 1962;15:826.
9. Berkman WA, Bernardino ME, Sewell CW, Price RB, Sones PJ Jr. The computed tomography-guided adrenal biopsy: an alternative to surgery in adrenals mass diagnosis. Cancer 1984;53:2098.
10. Bernardino ME. Percutaneous biopsy. AJR 1984;142:41.
11. Bigongiari LR, Linshaw MA, Stapleton FB. Vagal hypotension after percutaneous biopsy: possible confusion with hypovolemic shock. Urol Radiol 1980;1:217.
12. Braun B, Dormeyer HH. Ultrasonically guided fine needle aspiration biopsy of hepatic and pancreatic space occupying lesions and percutaneous abscess drainage. Klin Wochenschr. 1981;59:707.
13. Bret PM, Fond A, Casola G, Bretagnolle M, Germain-Lacour MJ, Bret P, Labadie M. Buffard P. Abdominal lesions: a prospective study of clinical efficacy of percutaneous fine needle biopsy. Radiology 1986;159:345.
14. Brown RA. A stereotaxic head frame for use with CT body scanners. Invest Radiol 1978;14:300.
15. Buchborn R, Eigler J, Renner E. Klinische Wertigkeit der Nierenbiopsie. Internist (Berl) 1970;11:383.
16. Bush WH, Burnett LL, Gibbons RP. Needle tract seeding of renal cell carcinoma. AJR 1977;129:725.
17. Cardella JF, Young AT, Hunter DW, Castaneda-Zuniga WR, Amplatz K. New universal radiolucent handle. Radiology 1985;155:531.
18. Carrasco CH, Wallace S, Charnsangavej C. Aspiration biopsy: use of a curved needle. Radiology 1985;155:254.
19. Casola G, Nicolet V, van Sonnenberg E, Withers C, Bretagnolle M, Saba RM, Bret P. Unsuspected pheochromocytoma: risk of blood pressure alterations during percutaneous adrenal biopsy. Radiology 1986;159:733.
20. Caturelli E, Rapaccini GL, Anti M, Fabiano A, Fedeli G. Malignant seeding after fine needle aspiration biopsy of the pancreas. Diagn Imag Clin Med 1985;54:88.
21. Chuang VP, Alspaugh JP. Sheath needle for liver biopsy in high risk patients. Radiology 1988;166:261.
22. Coel MN, Niwayama G. Safety of percutaneous fine needle pancreatic biopsy: a porcine model. Invest Radiol 1978;13:547.
23. Costello P, Dusxlak EJ, Clouse ME. CT guided biopsy: a simplified approach. J Comput Assist Tomogr 1982;6:40.
24. Cremniter D, Chatel A, Bigot JM, Lacombe P, Helenon C. Angiographic abnormalities following needle biopsy of the liver. J Radiol 1978;59:33.
25. Cronan JJ, Esparza AR, Dorfman GS, Ridlen MS, Paolella LP. Cavernous hemangioma of the liver: role of percutaneous biopsy. Radiology 1988;166:135.
26. Damascelli B, Spagnoli I, Garragnati F, Ceglia E, Milella M, Masciadri N. Massive lymphorrhoea after fine needle biopsy of the cystic haemolymphangioma of the liver. Eur J Radiol 1984;4:107.
27. De Ford JW. Acute transient hypotension following percutaneous liver biopsy. Lancet 1974;I:741.
28. Dickey JE, Haaga JR, Stellato TA, et al. Evaluation of computed tomography guided percutaneous biopsy of the pancreas. Radiology 1987;103:586.
29. Dondelinger RF. CT guided percutaneous biopsy. J Belge Radiol 1982;65:227.
30. Dondelinger RF. Interventional CT. Radiol J CEPUR 1984;4:3.
31. Dudgeon LS, Barrett NR. The examination of fresh tissues by the wet-film method. Br J Surg 1934;22:4.
32. Engzell U, Esposti PL, Rubio C. Investigation on tumour spread in connection with aspiration biopsy. Acta Radiol [Diagn] (Stockh) 1971;10:385.
33. Erwin BC, Brynes RK, Chan WC, Keller JW, Phillips VM, Gedgaudas-McClees RK, Torres WE, Bernardino ME. Percutaneous needle biopsy in the diagnosis and classification of lymphoma. Cancer 1986;57:1074.
34. Evans WK, Ho CS, McLoughlin MJ, Tao LC. Fatal necrotizing pancreatitis after fine needle aspiration biopsy of a pancreas. Radiology 1981;141:61.
35. Falchuk KR. Hypotension after percutaneous liver biopsy. Lancet 1974;I:624.
36. Ferrucci JT Jr, Wittenberg J. CT biopsy of abdominal tumors: aids for lesion localization. Radiology 1978;129:739.
37. Ferrucci JR Jr, Wittenberg J, Margolies MN, Carey RW. Malignant seeding of the tract after thin needle aspiration biopsy. Radiology 1979;130:345.
38. Ferrucci JT Jr, Wittenberg J, Mueller PR, Simeone JF, Harbin WP, Kirkpatrick RH, Taft PD. Diagnosis of abdominal malignancy by radiologic fine needle aspiration biopsy. AJR 1980;134:323.
39. Frederick PR, Brown TH, Miller MH, Bahr AL, Taylor KH. A light-guidance system to be used for CT-guided biopsy. Radiology 1985;154:535.
40. Freeny PC, Marks WM. Hepatic hemangioma: dynamic bolus CT. AJR 1986;147:711.
41. Gadziala N, Doherty FJ. Percutaneous fine needle aspiration biopsy of the pancreas. Radiology 1982;143:573.
42. Gatenby RA, Mulhern CB Jr, Moldofsky PJ. Computed tomography guided thin needle biopsy of small lytic bone lesions. Skeletal Radiol 1984;11:289.
43. Gatenby RA, Mulhern CB Jr, Richter MP, Moldofsky PJ. CT-guided biopsy for the detection and staging of tumors of the head and neck. AJNR 1984;5:287–289.
44. Gerzof SG. Triangulation: indirect CT guidance for abscess drainage. AJR 1981;137:1080.
45. Goldstein HM, Zornoza J, Wallace S, Anderson JH, Bree RL, Samuel BI, Lukeman J. Percutaneous fine needle aspiration biopsy of pancreatic and other abdominal masses. Radiology 1977;123:319.
46. Gothlin JH. Post-lymphographic percutaneous fine needle biopsy of lymph nodes guided by fluoroscopy. Radiology 1976;120:205.
47. Gothlin JH, Gadeholt G. Percutaneous fine needle biopsy of abdominal and pelvic lesions. Eur J Radiol 1986;6:288.
48. Haaga JR. New techniques for CT guided biopsies. AJR 1979;133:633.
49. Haaga JR, Alfidi RJ. Precise biopsy localization by computed tomography. Radiology 1976;118:603.

50. Haaga JR, Beale SM. Use of CO_2 to move structures as an aid to percutaneous procedures. Radiology 1986;161:829.

51. Haaga JR. Lipuma JP. Bryan PJ. Balsara VJ. Cohen AM. Clinical comparison of small and large caliber cutting needles for biopsy. Radiology 1983;146:665–667.

52. Haaga JR, Reich NE, Havrilla TR, Alfidi RJ. Interventional CT scanning. Radiol Clin North Am 1977;15:449–456.

53. Haaga JR, Vanek J. Computed tomographic guided liver biopsy using the Menghini needle. Radiology 1979;133:405.

54. Hajec PC, Gylys-Morin VM, Stavas J, van Sonnenberg E. Localization grid for MR-guided biopsy. Radiology 1987;163:825.

55. Hall-Craggs MA, Lees WR. Fine needle aspiration biopsy: pancreatic and biliary tumors. AJR 1986;147:399.

56. Hammerschlag SB, Wolpert SM, Carter BL. Computed tomography of the spinal canal. Radiology 1976;121:361.

57. Harter LP, Moss AA, Goldberg H, Gross H. CT guided fine needle aspirations for diagnosis of benign and malignant disease. AJR 1983;140:303.

58. Hauenstein KH, Wimmer B, Freudenberg N. Cutting biopsy needle for the histological diagnosis of abdominal and retroperitoneal masses sonographically or CT aided puncture. RöFo 1985;143:96.

59. Hawkins IF, Caridi JG. Curved stylus for redirection of fine needle guide. Radiology 1984;151:530.

60. Heaston DK, Handel DB, Ashton PR, Korobkin M. Narrow gauge needle aspiration of solid adrenal masses. AJR 1982;138:1143–1148.

61. Heiberg, E, Wolverson MK. Ipsilateral decubitus position for percutaneous CT guided adrenal biopsy. J Comput Assist Tomogr 1985;9:217.

62. Ho CS, McLoughlin MJ, McHattie JD, Tao LC. Percutaneous fine needle aspiration biopsy of the pancreas following endoscopic retrograde cholangiopancreatography. Radiology 1977;125:351.

63. Hoddick WK, Demas BE, Moss AA. CT guided percutaneous bowel loopogram. AJR 1984;143:1098.

64. Hruby W, Muschik H. Belt device for simplified CT guided puncture and biopsy: a technical note. Cardiovasc Intervent Radiol 1987;10:301.

65. Hueftle MG, Haaga JR. Effect of suction on biopsy sample size. AJR 1986;147:1014.

66. Husband JE, Golding SJ. The role of computed tomography guided needle biopsy in an oncology service. Clin Radiol 1983;34:255.

67. Isler RJ. Ferrucci JT Jr, Wittenberg J, Mueller PR, Simeone JF, van Sonnenberg E, Hall DA. Tissue core biopsy of abdominal tumors with a 22 gauge cutting needle. AJR 1981;136:725.

68. Jaques PF, Staab E, Richey W, Photopoulos G, Swanton M. CT-assisted pelvic and abdominal aspiration biopsies in gynecological malignancy. Radiology 1978;128:651.

69. Jewell WR, Thomas JH, Chang CHJ. Computed tomographic mammography directed biopsy of the breast. Surg Gynecol Obstet 1983;157:75.

70. Jones KR. A respiratory monitor for use with body CT scanning and other imaging techniques. Br J Radiol 1982;55:530.

71. Karlsson S, Persson PH. Angiography, ultrasound and fine needle aspiration biopsy in the evaluation of gynecologic tumors. Acta Radiol [Diagn] (Stockh) 1979;20:779.

72. Kattapuram SV, Rosenthal D. Percutaneous biopsy of the cervical spine using CT guidance. AJR 1987;149:539.

73. Kidd R, Freeny PC, Bartha M. Single pass fine-needle aspiration biopsy. AJR 1979;133:333.

74. Kline TS, Neal HS. Needle biopsy: a pilote study. JAMA 1973;224:1143.

75. Kurdziel JC, Dondelinger RF. Ponction sous tomodensitométrie: technique, indications, résultats. Encycl. Méd. chir. (Paris, France) Radiodiagnostic IV/33680 A 10, 9, 1987. 10 pp.

76. Labardini MM, Nesbit RM. Perineal extension of adenocarcinoma of the prostatic gland after punch biopsy. J Urol 1967;97:891.

77. Laval-Jeantet M, Flandrin G, Frija J, Buy JN, Segui S, Valensi F, Martin-Bouyer Y. Computed tomography guidance of needle puncture for biopsy in haematology. J Radiol 1985;66:575.

78. Leksell L, Jernberg B. Stereotaxis and tomography: a technical note. Acta Neurochir (Wien) 1980;52:1.

79. Lieberman RP, Hafez GR, Crummy AB. Histology from aspiration biopsy: Turner needle experience. AJR 1982;138:561.

80. Livraghi R, Damascelli B, Lombardi C, Spagnoli I. Risk in fine needle abdominal biopsy. J Clin Ultrasound 1983;11:77.

81. Livraghi T, Lombardi C, Mascia G. Bile peritonitis: another complication after fine needle biopsy. Diagn Imag Clin Med 1983;52:33.

82. Livraghi T, Pilotti S, Ravetto C, Sangalli G, Solbiati L. Inclusion-cytology versus smear-cytology in fine needle abdominal biopsy. Eur J Radiol 1985;5:111.

83. Lufkin RB, Peresi LM, Hanafee WN. New needle for MR-guided aspiration cytology of the head and neck. AJR 1987;149:380.

84. Lunderquist A. Biopsy of the pancreas under radiological guidance. In: Anacker H, Gullotta U, Rupp N, eds. Percutaneous biopsy and therapeutic vascular occlusion. Stuttgart: Thieme 1980:43.

85. Luning M, Kursawe R, Schopke W, Lorenz D, Menzel A, Hoppe E, Meyer R. CT guided percutaneous fine needle biopsy of the pancreas. Eur J Radiol 1985;5:104.

86. Luning M, Neuser D, Kursawe R, Potschke R. CT guided percutaneous fine needle biopsy in the diagnosis of small adrenal tumors. Eur J Radiol. 1983;3:358.

87. Martin HE, Ellis EB. Biopsy by needle puncture and aspiration. Ann Surg 1930;92:169.

88. Martino CR, Haaga JR. Percutaneous biopsy of the liver. Semin Intervent Radiol 1985;2:245.

89. Martino CR, Haaga JR, Bryan PJ. Secondary infection of an endometrioma following fine needle aspiration. Radiology 1984;151:53.

90. Martino CR, Haaga JR, Bryan PJ, Lipuma JP, El Yousef SJ, Alfidi R. CT-guided liver biopsies: eight years experience. Radiology 1984;152:755.

91. Matter D, Spinelli G, Warter P. Ultrasonically guided percutaneous pancreatography. J Clin Ultrasound 1983;11:401.

92. McGahan JP. Percutaneous biopsy and drainage procedures in the abdomen using a modified coaxial technique. Radiology 1984;153:257.

93. McLoughlin MJ, Ho CS, Langer B, McHattie J, Tao LC. Fine needle aspiration biopsies of malignant lesions in and around the pancreas. Cancer 1978;41:2413.

94. Meng CH, Elkin M. Immediate angiographic manifestations of iatrogenic renal injury due to percutaneous renal biopsy. Radiology 1971;100:335.

95. Miller DA, Carrasco CH, Katz RL, Cramer FM, Wallace S, Charnsangavej C. Fine needle aspiration biopsy: the role of immediate cytologic assessment. AJR 1986;147:155.

96. Miner DG, Cohan RH, Davis WK. CT guided percutaneous aspiration of septic thrombosis of the inferior vena cava. AJR 1987;148:1213.

97. Mirfakhraee M, Gerlock AJ, Giyanani VL, Sadree A. Thin spinal or biopsy needle guidance. Radiology 1985;154:240.

98. Mitty HA, Efremidis SG, Yeh HC. Impact of fine needle biopsy on management of patients with carcinom of the pancreas. AJR 1981;137:1119.

99. Moran CJ, Naidich TP, Marchoski JA. CT guided placement in the central nervous system: results in 146 consecutive patients. AJR 1984;143:861.

100. Morettin LB, Brown RW, Amparo EG, Matteson R. Multiple simultaneous percutaneous needle biopsy technique for masses of the abdomen and peritoneum. Eur J Radiol 1987;7:98.

101. Mueller PR, Stark DD, Simeone JF, Saini S, Butch RJ, Edelman RR, Wittenberg J, Ferrucci JT. MR-guided aspiration biopsy: needle design and clinical trials. Radiology 1986;161:605.

102. Mueller PR, Wittenberg J, Ferrucci JT Jr. Fine needle aspiration biopsy of abdominal masses. Semin Roentgenol 1981;16:152.

103. Muhlberger G, Gottschalk A, Gericke D. Needle biopsy and metastasis investigations in rats. Radiologe 1983;23:185.

104. Mundinger F, Birg W, Klar M. Computer-assisted stereotaxic brain operations by means including computerized axial tomography. Appl Neurophysiol 1978;41:169.

105. Murrel DS, Melcher DH. Role of aspiration cytology in a radiotherapy and oncology center. Clin Radiol 1982;33:337.

106. Ohto M, Ono T, Tsuchiya Y. Saisho H, eds. Cholangiography and pancreatography. Tokyo: Igaku Shoin, 1979:10.

107. Onik G, Costello P, Cosman E, Wells T Jr, Goldberg H, Moss A, Kane R, Clouse ME, Hoddick W, Moore S, Demas B. CT body stereotaxis: an aid for CT guided biopsies. AJR 1986;146:163.

108. Onodera H, Oikawa M, Abe M. Cutaneous seeding of hepatocellular carcinoma after fine needle aspiration biopsy. J Ultrasound Med 1987;6:273.

109. Otto RC. Sonographische Feinnadelpunktion: Indikation und Ergebnisse. Dtsch Ärztebl 1984;81:3573.

110. Otto R, Deyhle P. Guided puncture under real-time sonographic control Radiology 1980;134:784.

111. Otto R, Weihe W, Burger HR. Zur Beurteilung der ultraschallgezielten Feinnadelpunktion: experimentelle Untersuchungen am Hund. DTW 1984;91:178.

112. Otto R, Wellauer J, eds. Ultraschallgeführte Biopsie. Berlin: Springer, 1985:86.

113. Owman I, Idvall I. Percutaneous fine needle biopsy guided by barium examinations of the GI tract. Gastrointest Radiol 1982;7:327.

114. Pagani JJ. Biopsy of focal hepatic lesions: comparison of 18 and 22 gauge needles. Radiology 1983;147:673.

115. Pardes JG, Schneider M, Koizumi J, Engel IA. Auh YH, Rubenstein W. Percutaneous needle biopsy of deep pelvic masses: posterior approach. Cardiovasc Intervent Radiol 1986;9:65.

116. Pelaez JC, Hill MC, Dach JL, Isikoff B, Morse B. Abdominal aspiration biopsies: sonographic versus computed tomographic guidance. JAMA 1983;250:2663.

117. Pereiras RV, Neuers A, Kunhardt B, Troner M, Hutson D, Barkin JS, Viamonte M. Fluoroscopically guided thin needle aspiration biopsy of the abdomen and the retroperitoneum. AJR 1978;131:197.

118. Perry JH, Rosenbaum AE, Lunsford LD, Swink CA, Zorub DS. Computed tomography guided stereotaxic surgery: conception and development of a new stereotactic methodology. Neurosurgery 1980;7:376.

119. Philips VM, Bernardino ME. The parallel iliac approach: a safe and accurate technique for deep pelvic node biopsy. J Comput Assist Tomogr 1984;8:237.

120. Price RB, Bernardino ME, Berkmann WA, Sones PJ Jr, Torres WE. Biopsy of the right adrenal gland by the transhepatic approach. Radiology 1983;148:566.

121. Quin D. New needle for puncture biopsy. AJR 1986;147:543.

122. Quinn SF, van Sonnenberg GE, Casola G, Wittich GR, Neff CC. Interventional radiology of the spleen. Radiology 1986;161:289.

123. Rashleigh-Belcher HJC, Russel RCG, Lees WR. Cutaneous seeding of pancreatic carcinoma by fine needle aspiration biopsy. Br J Radiol 1986;59:182.

124. Robbins GF, Brothers JH, Eberhart WF, Quan S. Is aspiration biopsy of brest cancer dangerous to the patient? Cancer 1954;7:774.

125. Rusnak B, Castaneda-Zuniga WR, Kotula F, Herrera M, Amplatz K. Radiolucent handle for percutaneous puncture under continuous fluorosocopic monitoring. Radiology 1981;141:538.

126. Savolaine ER, Greenblatt SH, Rayport M. Computed tomography guided intracranial biopsy and cyst aspiration: accumulated experience in 60 patients. J Comput Assist Tomogr 1987;11:221.

127. Schlolaut KH, Lackner K, von Uexkull-Guldenbrand V, Nicolas V, Vogel J. Results and complications of percutaneous CT guided biopsies using a wide lumen needle. RöFo 1987;147:25.

128. Schnyder PA, Candardjis G, Anderegg A. Peritonitis secondary to thin needle aspiration biopsy of abscess. AJR 1381; 137:1271.

129. Schutterle G, Fritsch H. Tödliche Komplikationen nach Nierenblindpunktion. Med Klin 1965;60:184.

130. Schwerk WB, Schmitz-Moormann P. Sonographisch gezielte perkutane transperitoneale Aspirationsbiopsie raumfordern-

der Pankreasprozesse. Dtsch Med Wochenschr 1980; 105:1019.

131. Sharma P, MacDonald GB, Banaji M. The risk of bleeding after percutaneous liver biopsy: relation to platelet count. J Clin Gastroenterol 1982;4:451.

132. Sinner WN, Zajicek J. Implantation metastasis after percutaneous transthoracic needle aspiration biopsy. Acta Radiol [Diagn] (Stockh) 1976;17:473.

133. Smith EH. The hazards of fine needle aspiration biopsy. Ultrasound Med Biol. 1984;10:629–634.

134. Smith FP, MacDonald JS, Schein S, Ornitz RD. Cutaneous seeding of pancreatic cancer by skinny needle aspiration biopsy. Arch Intern Med 1980;140:855.

135. Spratt JS, Donegan WL. Cancer of the breast. Philadelphia: Saunders 1967.

136. Steiner E, Mueller PR, Simeone JF. Transcystic biopsy: a new approach to posterior pelvic lesions. AJR 1987;149:93.

137. Stephenson TF, Mehnert PJ, Marx AJ, Boger JN, Roth-Moyo L, Balaji MR, Nadaraja N. Evaluation of contrast markers for CT aspiration biopsy. AJR 1979;133:1097.

138. Sullivan S, Watson WS. Acute transient hypotension as complication of percutaneous liver biopsy. Lancet 1974;i:389.

139. Sundaram M, Wolverson MK, Heiberg E, Pilla T, Vas WG, Shields JB. Utility of CT-guided abdominal aspiration procedures. AJR 1982;139:1111.

140. Thomas DGT, Anderson RE, Du Boulay GH. CT-directed stereotactic surgery with the Brown-Roberts-Wells (BRW) system. J Neurol Neurosurg Psychiatry 1983;46:369.

141. Thomas DGT, Davis CH, Ingram S, Olney JS, Young IR, Bydder GM. Stereotactic biopsy of the brain under MR imaging control. AJNR 1986;7:161.

142. Torp-Pedersen S, Juul N, Vyberg M. Histological sampling with a 23 gauge modified Menghini needle. Br J Radiol 1984;57:151.

143. Towbin RB, Strife JL. Percutaneous aspiration, drainage and biopsies in children. Radiology 1985;157:81–85.

144. Triller J, Kraft R, Marincek B. Computer tomographic aided fine needle biopsy of pelvic tumours. RöFo 1982;137:422.

145. Tylen U, Arnesgo B, Lundberg LG, Lunderquist A. Percutaneous biopsy of carcinoma of the pancreas guided by angiography. Surg Gynecol Obstet 1976;142:737.

146. Van Sonnenberg E, Lin AS, Casola G, Nakamoto SK, Wing VW, Cubberly DA. Removable hub needle system for coaxial biopsy of small difficult lesions. Radiology 1984;152: 226.

147. Van Sonnenberg E, Wittenberg J, Ferrucci JT Jr, Mueller PR, Simeone JF. Triangulation method for percutaneous needle guidance: the angled approach to upper abdominal masses. AJR 1981;137:757.

148. Vock P, Fuchs WA, Haertel M. Puncture of the abdomen under CT control. In Anacker H, Gullotta U, Rupp N, eds. Percutaneous biopsy and therapeutic vascular occlusion. Stuttgart: Thieme 1980:50.

149. Vogelzang RL, Matalon TA, Neiman HL, Sakovicz BA. Lateral scan radiograph in CT-guided aspiration biopsy. AJR 1983;140:164.

150. Von Schreeb T, Arner O, Skovsted G. Renal adenocarcinoma: is there a risk of spreading tumor cells in diagnostic puncture? Scand J Urol Nephrol 1967;1: 270.

151. Wittenberg J, Mueller PR, Ferrucci JT Jr, et al. Percutaneous core biopsy of abdominal tumors using 22 gauge needles: further observations. AJR 1982;139:75.

152. Yandow DR, Matallana RH. Gas contrast guided needle biopsy of the head of the pancreas. Radiology 1980;137:543.

153. Yankaskas BC, Staab EV, Craven MB. Delayed complications from fine needle biopsies of solid masses of the abdomen. Invest Radiol 1986;21:325.

154. Zamscheck W, Klausenstock O. Liver biopsy: the risk of needle biopsy. N Engl J Med 1953;249:1062.

155. Zornoza J. Needle biopsy of metastases. Radiol Clin North Am 1982;20:569.

156. Zornoza J, Wallace S, Ordonez N, Lukeman J. Fine needle aspiration biopsy of the liver. AJR 1980;134:331.

Percutaneous Lymph Node Biopsy

J. H. Göthlin

Aspiration of lymph nodes for diagnostic purposes was reported in 1904 in the diagnosis of try-panosomiasis (14), and in 1914 in an attempt to diagnose neoplastic (25) and infectious diseases (5).

Para-aortic lymph node biopsies with a paravascular approach were reported in 1968 (22) and 1969 (19). Both a translumbar and a paravascular approach were reported in 1972 (16). These examinations had a low yield and a high complication rate. The first report of a transperitoneal approach with a technique still used today appeared in 1976 (8). Guiding modalities today include fluoroscopy US and CT.

Guidance Modalities

Fluoroscopy

Lymphography is necessary to make the lymph nodes identifiable. Apart from premedication (which is not deemed necessary by all examiners), the patient requires no special preparation for the procedure. Premedication will vary from patient to patient, depending on their anxiety, cooperation, and general physical status. A recommended standard premedication consists of 0.5 mg atropine and 5 to 10 mg of diazepam administered 10 minutes before the start of the procedure (8, 9). Pain-sensitive patients may require 10 mg of morphine in addition.

The patients are preferably supine. Biplane fluoroscopy is desirable but not mandatory. The lymph nodes to be biopsied are identified and the overlying skin is sterilized. Local anesthetic is infiltrated down to the node, but not into it, to avoid distortion of the cytologic picture. An entrance needle may be useful, especially in obese patients, for a more accurate course of the biopsy needle and to facilitate repeat punctures. The biopsy needle with an outer diameter of 0.6 to 1.2 mm (fine needles) is directed toward the node, or the suspect part of it. A pair of forceps may be used to avoid direct radiation to the fingers. The shutters used should be as small as possible. A subtle resistance followed by a slight "give" is often felt when the needle penetrates the capsule. A mandrin may be of use, to stiffen, Chiba needles, for example. The needle position is verified by biplane fluoroscopy, oblique to the patient, or by fluoroscopic monitoring of the movement of the lymph node in unison with the movement of the needle tip.

Aspiration is performed with a syringe, 10 to 12 ml, while the tip of the needle is moved up and down 0.1 to 0.5 cm under maximal suction. A Franzén handle facilitates the procedure (7). If blood appears in the syringe, the procedure should be stopped. After release of the suction pressure, the needle is removed and smears are immediately plated onto glass slides, fixed, and cytologically examined. It is preferable to have the patient wait on the radiographic table with the entrance needle in place until the preliminary results of the cytologic examination are obtained (20). If the initial specimens are unsatisfactory, repeat puncture may then be performed immediately.

Ultrasonography

Usually only large lymph nodes are identified and biopsied (Fig. 1a, b). Premedication is not as common when using US as when using fluoroscopy, but the time factor is probably the main reason. The use of a biopsy probe or biopsy attachment is recommended. Sterilization is the same as for fluoroscopy. The needle is preferably monitored with real-time scanning. The procedure generally resembles that using fluoroscopy.

Computed Tomography

Lymph nodes as small as 3 to 4 mm can occasionally be identified. Premedication is the same as for fluoroscopy. A scan section is obtained through the desired lymph node and the section is marked on the skin with an ink pen. Distances to palpable or visible landmarks, the most suitable needle route, and the depth from the skin to the node center can be determined from the monitor image. The latter distance should be marked with a piece of tape on the needle. Grids for marking the entrance point are advocated but they are time-consuming and do not add to the accuracy of the procedure.

The needle is inserted and one or more control scan(s) obtained (Fig. 2). Often the needle is in correct position, but occasionally an adjustment is necessary. The procedure follows that for fluoroscopy. CT is the most time-consuming of the guiding modalities.

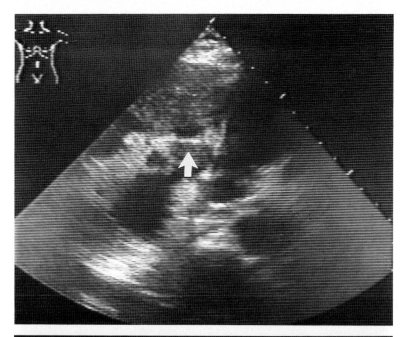

Fig. **1a** Enlarged lymph node seen with US (arrow pointing to center)

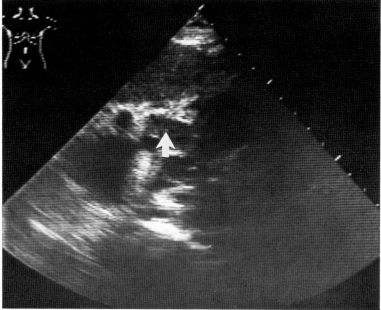

Fig. 1**b** Needle barely seen with tip inside the node (arrow). Lymph nodes are not easy to biopsy with US because they are often far away from the skin and surrounded by echo-rich fat tissue, making the needle difficult to see. Teflon-coated needles are easier to visualize with US than other needles

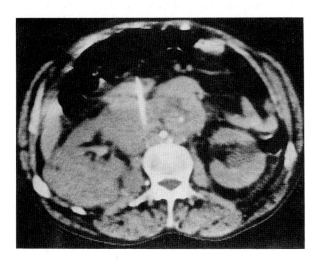

Fig. **2** Male with anaplastic teratoma of the right testicle. Lymphography not definitely positive, high periaortic lymph nodes not being well contrasted. CT revealed right-sided peri-aortic lymph nodes and CT-guided biopsy was performed. Cytology: malignant teratoma cells and lymphatic cells in various stages of maturity

Needles

Various needles are recommended for abdominal biopsies (1, 15, 23). For lymph nodes, needle references are few. Needles with outer diameters varying from 0.9 to 1.2 mm are suitable for most purposes, for example, metastatic disease, whereas thinner needles may be optimal in lymphomas (9).

Specimen Handling

The preparation of lymph node biopsy specimens varies from cytologist to cytologist and specific recommendations have been detailed in the Chapter by Labadie and Liaras. That immediate cytologic assessment is of value is indisputable (20) but it is not available in all examination facilities.

Clinical Indications

The main indications are:

- Verification or exclusion of equivocal findings (malignant, benign, normal)
- Verification or exclusion of lymph node involvement by general lymphatic disease
- Staging of Hodgkin and non-Hodgkin lymphomas
- Staging of genitourinary and gastrointestinal tumors in both males and females
- Obtaining specimens for tissue typing
- Monitoring the effectiveness of treatment of a disease involving the lymph nodes

In a more general framework, since percutaneous transperitoneal biopsy of lymph nodes offers significant cost benefits, since it is associated with good patient tolerance, low morbidity, and few complications, and since the procedure is relatively simple to perform with various guiding modalities, it should be considered and used in the following circumstances. It may be utilized to obviate the need for a more complicated, time-consuming, and sometimes major diagnostic technique. When time is an important element in the management of a patient's disease, biopsy of lymph nodes should be preferred to corresponding surgical diagnostic measures, since the latter often require hospitalization and are invariably more time consuming. Since the diagnosis in most instances is obtained at the initial biopsy procedure (immediate cytologic reporting), correct treatment may be instituted in an optimal time period in the disease process of the patient. Since the biopsy may be performed on an out-patient basis, hospitalization for diagnostic purposes will be avoided. When surgical procedures are neither justified nor possible, as in the case of very sick or debilitated patients who require a diagnostic procedure but cannot withstand a general anesthetic or a major surgical procedure, percutaneous biopsy will usually provide the correct diagnosis. On the other hand, the percutaneous biopsy will eliminate some diagnostic possibilites, thus allowing the subsequent investigation to be simpler and better oriented to the few remaining disease choices. Since the lymph nodes often are not removed, the effectiveness of treatment may be monitored by repeat biopsy of the abnormal nodes. This type of follow-up is not available if the total specimen has been previously removed, as would occur with a surgical procedure. Likewise, an early relapse of the disease process can be documented by percutaneous biopsy, provided the nodes are still present.

No major complications and no deaths have been reported from lymph node biopsy (11). Contamination of the desired specimen tissue by cells from traversed organs such as the bowel does not disturb the cytologic diagnosis (8).

Results

Retroperitoneal Biopsies in General

The results in verifying or excluding metastatic disease in equivocal findings at lymphography are good, with an accuracy of up to 95% (10). The results are improving with increasing experience with biopsy techniques. False-negative results are not uncommon, but false-positive results are rare (4, 11).

Cervical and Ovarian Carcinomas

US-directed percutaneous aspiration biopsy of peri-aortic lymph nodes in recurrence of cervical carcinoma has been mentioned (3). After lymphography, percutaneous biopsy of retroperitoneal lymph nodes in 129 patients with carcinoma of the cervix showed an overall accuracy of 68%, a sensitivity of 58%, and a specificity of 100%. The predictive value of a negative test was only 42%, but the predictive value of a positive test was 100% (6).

Using CT and fine-needle aspiration biopsy, 67% of patients with tumor-bearing lymph nodes were adequately evaluated (2).

Prostate and Urinary Bladder

The importance of staging prostatic carcinoma has been stressed in several publications (13). Negative lymphograms in clinically low-grade prostatic carcinoma but with positive lymph nodes by fine-needle biopsy have been reported in 15 to 20% (12, 13, 24). In 136 nodal chains of 26 patients with clinically localized carcinoma of the prostate and in 14 patients with bladder cancer, fine-needle aspiration biopsy had an overall accuracy of 97.5%, a sensitivity of 94%, and a specificity of 100% verified by lymphadenectomy (17). No false-positive results have been reported. Even negative aspirates may be accepted as definitive in excluding the presence of metastatic disease, and biopsy is mandatory before treatment of prostatic carcinoma (17). Percutaneous biopsy has an even more prominent role in accurately staging and selecting patients with bladder cancer for radical cystectomy and may result in sparing patients unnecessary radical surgery (Fig. **3, 4**).

Penile Carcinoma

Biopsy of regional lymph nodes visualized at pedal and penile lymphography has fruitfully been used for staging penile carcinoma. The technique used has been the same as for prostatic and bladder carcinomas (18).

Malignant Lymphoma

It is more difficult to obtain reliable results in staging or typing malignant lymphoma than metastatic disease. Correct diagnosis for staging purposes has been reported in 44% (26) and 57% (9). However, the results when aspirating palpable lymph nodes are not much better (21). Percutaneous biopsy of lymph nodes in malignant lymphoma has not gained wide acceptance.

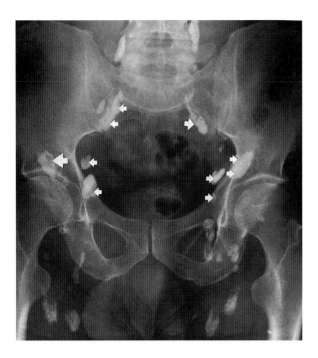

Fig. **3** Prostatic carcinoma, clinically stage 1 (Flock's classification). Large arrowheads show lymph nodes with metastatic involvement; small arrowheads show normal lymph nodes at percutaneous biopsy

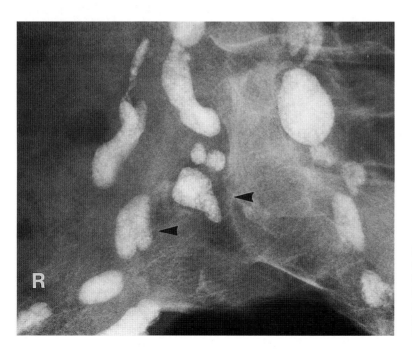

Fig. **4** Carcinoma of the urinary bladder, clinically stage B1 (Jewett's classification). Lymphography demonstrates completely normal lymph nodes in all sites. Cytology after percutaneous biopsy disclosed metastases in two nodes (arrows)

References

1. Andriole JG, Haaga, JR, Adams RB, Nunez C. Biopsy needle characteristics assessed in the laboratory. Radiology 1983;148:659.
2. Bandy LC, Clarke-Pearson DL, Silverman PM, Creasman WT. Computed tomography in evaluation of extrapelvic lymphadenopathy in carcinoma of the cervix. Obstet Gynecol 1985;65:73.
3. Berkowitz RS, Leavitt T Jr, Knapp RC. Ultrasound-directed percutaneous aspiration biopsy of periaortic lymph nodes in recurrence of cervical carcinoma. Am J Obstet Gynecol 1978;131:906.
4. Betsill WL Jr, Hajdu SI. Percutaneous aspiration biopsy of lymph nodes. Am J Clin Pathol 1980;73:471.
5. Chatard JA, Guthrie CG. Human trypanosomiasis: report of a case observed in Baltimore. Am J Trop Dis Prevent Med 1914;1:493.
6. Edeiken-Monroe, BS, Zornoza J. Carcinoma of the cervix: percutaneous lymph node aspiration biopsy. AJR 1982;138:655.
7. Franzén S, Giertz G, Zajicek H. Cytological diagnosis of prostatic tumours by transrectal aspiration biopsy: a preliminary report. Br J Urol 1960;32:193.
8. Göthlin JH. Post-lymphographic percutaneous fine needle biopsy of lymph nodes guided by fluoroscopy. Radiology 1976;120:205.
9. Göthlin JH. Percutaneous transperitoneal fluoroscopy-guided fine needle biopsy of lymph nodes. Acta Radiol [Diagn] (Stockh) 1979;20:660.
10. Göthlin JH, Macintosh PK. Interventional radiology in the assessment of the retroperitoneal lymph nodes. Radiol Clin North Am 1979;17:461.
11. Göthlin JH, Rupp N, Rothenberger KH, Macintosh PK. Percutaneous biopsy of retroperitoneal lymph nodes: a multicentric study. Eur J Radiol 1981;1:46.
12. Göthlin JH, Høiem L. Percutaneous fine needle biopsy of radiographically normal lymph nodes in the staging of prostatic carcinoma. Radiology 1981;141:351.
13. Göthlin JH. Prostatic carcinoma: staging with percutaneous lymph node biopsy. Bull Cancer (Paris) 1985;72:462.
14. Grieg ED, Gray AC. Lymphatic glands in sleeping sickness. Br Med J 1904;1:1252.
15. Innes DJ, Feldman PS. Comparison of diagnostic results obtained by fine needle aspiration cytology and tru-cut or open biopsies. Acta Cytol (Baltimore) 1983;27:350.
16. Keinert K. Erfahrungen mit der zytologischen Punktion lymphographisch angefärbter Lymphknoten in verschiedenen Regionen. Radiol Diagn (Berl) 1972;5:680.
17. Luciani L, Piscioli F, Menichelli E, Pusiol T. The value and role of percutaneous pelvic lymph node aspiration biopsy in definitive staging of prostatic and bladder carcinoma. Eur. Urol 1983;9:216.
18. Luciani L, Piscioli F, Scappini P, Pusiol T. Value and role of percutaneous regional node aspiration cytology in the management of penile carcinoma. Eur Urol 1984;10:294.
19. Lüning M, Romaniuk PA. Technik der paravasalen Punktion kontrastierter iliakaler Lymphknoten nach Rüttiman. Radiol Diagn (Berl) 1969;10:361.
20. Miller DA, Carrasco CH, Katz RL, Cramer FM, Wallace S, Charansangavej C. Fine-needle aspiration biopsy: the role of immediate cytologic assessment. AJR 1986;147:155.
21. Qizilbash AH, Elavathil LJ, Chen V, Young JEM, Archibald SD. Aspiration biopsy cytology of lymph nodes in malignant lymphoma. Diagn Cytopathol 1985;1:18.
22. Rüttiman A. Iliac lymph node aspiration biopsy through paravascular approach: Preliminary report. Radiology 1968;90:150.
23. Torp-Pedersen S, Juul N, Vyberg M. Histological sampling with a 23 gauge modified Menghini needle. Br J Radiol 1984;57:152.
24. Wajsman Z, Gamaro M, Park JJ, Beckely S, Pontes JE. Tansabdominal fine needle aspiration of retroperitoneal lymph nodes in staging of genitourinary tract cancer (correlation with lymphography and lymph node dissection findings). J Urol 1982;128:1238.
25. Ward GR, ed. Bedside haematology. Philadelphia: Saunders, 1914:130.
26. Zornoza J, Jonsson K, Wallace S, Lukeman JM. Fine needle aspiration biopsy of retroperitoneal lymph nodes and abdominal masses. An updated report. Radiology 1977;125:87.

Bone Biopsy

C. H. Carrasco, C. Charnsangavej, W. R. Richli and S. Wallace

Percutaneous skeletal needle biopsy was used initially for aspiration of bone marrow elements (42), wich remained the main area of interest until the 1930s when the initial experiences with aspiration biopsy of skeletal neoplasms were reported (9, 29). The uses of percutaneous needle biopsy have since been extended to the diagnosis of osteomyelitis and, to a lesser extent, to the evaluation of metabolic bone diseases (6, 7, 24, 34). This method of tissue acquisition has now gained wide acceptance and is routine in many medical centers.

Percutaneous needle biopsy, also known as closed biopsy, has many advantages over a surgical or open biopsy. For example, irradiation or chemotherapy can be instituted immediately after the biopsy without waiting for a large incision to heal. Resection of the needle tract is easier than en bloc resection of an incisional wound. There is minimal damage to normal tissues and possibly a decreased risk of tumor dissemination. The insult to the structural integrity of the bone is lessened, thus decreasing the risk of pathologic fracture. The complications associated with a surgical procedure and general anesthesia are avoided. Finally, the costs of this procedure are considerably less than those of an open biopsy.

Needles

The choice of instruments is determined by the experience of the operator, the need of a specimen for cytologic or histopathologic examination, the location of the lesion, and the integrity of the overlying cortical bone.

A stylet or a trocar is a common feature of the needles used for percutaneous biopsy. Thin-walled needles ranging in caliber from 18 to 23 gauge suffice for collection of material for cytologic examination. The needles with the more acute bevel angles and the Franzen trephine types will yield the best samples (3).

The Travenol Tru-Cut needle is used for biopsy of soft tissue and yields a sample measuring approximately 2×20 mm. In our experience, this needle provides the best histologic specimens and is the one most frequently used in suspected primary skeletal neoplasms.

The large-caliber trephine needles are used for perforation of cortical bone and acquisition of tissue for histologic examination. These needles frequently produce crushing artifacts, rendering compact bone useless for diagnosis, and so several instruments have been described that attempt to avoid these artifacts (19, 44).

Guidance Modalities

Conventional radiographs of the site to be biopsied are usually adequate for location and for election of the route of approach. CT and MRI are useful when the lesion is not adequately demonstrated by conventional radiography, particularly in flat bones and the spine. US helps to define the extra-osseous component of tumors but is seldom necessary for biopsy. Radionuclide bone scans may aid in the location of lesions not yet apparent by the other imaging modalities (10) (Fig. 1).

Technique

Selection of Needle Path

The anatomic relationships of the lesion have to be considered carefully to avoid damaging adjacent vascular, neural, and visceral structures. The long bones of the extremities are usually approached anteriorly or laterally because of the location of the large neurovascular bundles. In the pelvis, the approach to the pubis is anterior; the iliac wings, the ischia, and the sacrum are biopsied from a posterior approach. A posterolateral approach is used for biopsy of the vertebral bodies, transverse processes, and pedicles, whereas a posterior approach is used for the spinous processes and laminae.

The needle should be introduced along the long axis of the lesion to obtain the greatest quantity of tissue. This is particularly important in thin or flat bones, such as the ribs and pubis (Fig. 2), where a perpendicular approach risks damaging underlying structures. In addition, if surgical resection is contemplated, the biopsy tract should be within the planned incision.

Positioning and Preparation of Patient

Ideally, the biopsy needle should course through the shortest path from the skin surface to the target lesion while remaining parallel to the axis of the x-ray beam. The more the needle is angled in rela-

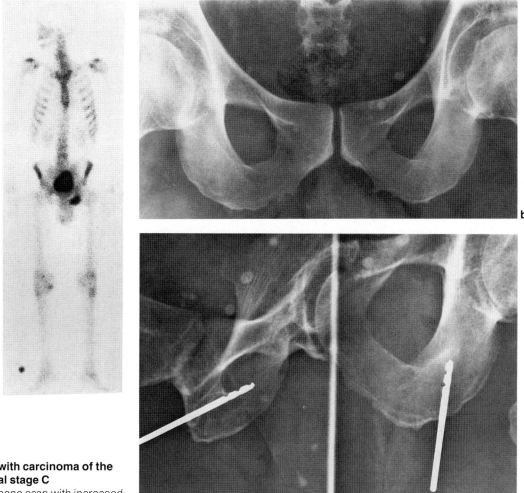

Fig. 1 **Patient with carcinoma of the prostate, clinical stage C**
a Radionuclide bone scan with increased uptake in the left ischium
b Plain radiograph does not demonstrate a lesion in the area of increased uptake
c Transgluteal biopsy using a drill for intramedullary aspiration was positive for adenocarcinoma

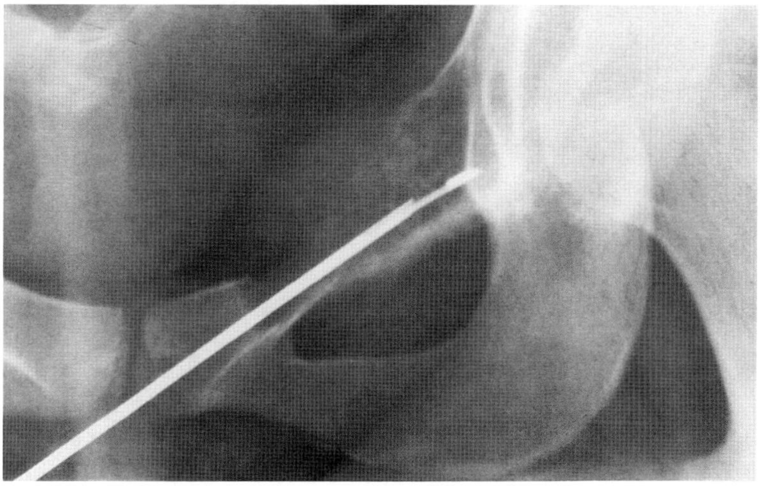

Fig. 2 **Lytic lesion of the superior ramus of the pubis; aneurysmal bone cyst was suspected radiographically.**
Percutaneous biopsy with a Tru-Cut needle inserted along the length of the lesion did not demonstrate malignancy. The radiologic diagnosis was confirmed by curettage

tion to the x-ray beam, the more difficult it is to maintain control of its tip. The ability to angle the fluoroscopy unit permits better needle control because it allows one to maintain the axis of the x-ray beam parallel to the needle in most situations. However, when this facility is not available, the patient can usually be positioned to meet this requirement.

After the patient has been positioned, the skin directly overlying the lesion is marked with indelible ink. Except in children and in adults undergoing biopsy of the upper cervical spine, the biopsy is usually performed under local anesthesia. The area is then prepared and draped. Under fluoroscopic observation, a local anesthetic (1% lidocaine) is infiltrated generously through the planned needle path, including the periosteum. Adequate anesthesia will result in a relatively painless biopsy.

Most skeletal diseases for which biopsy is indicated arise in the medullary cavity, from which they may destroy the cortex and become extra-osseous. Samples should be obtained from the extra-osseous soft tissue component when the lesion extends be-

yond the confines of bone. Entirely intra-osseous lesions require perforation of the cortex for biopsy of the underlying tumor. In blastic processes, tissue should be acquired from the least dense area of the lesion (5); compact bone, because of its hypocellularity, is of little diagnostic value in neoplastic disease, and special efforts to obtain a core of it are not warranted.

Perforation of the Cortex

The intact cortex can be perforated with one of the large trephine needles or a hand drill. When a trephine needle is used, the outer cannula and the inner pointed obturator are advanced to the surface of the bone. The obturator is exchanged for the trephine needle while maintaining the outer cannula firmly anchored on the bone surface. The cortex is perforated by rotating the trephine needle clockwise, and the tissue collected within the needle is removed with the aid of a blunt obturator. A hand drill attached to the hub of the trephine by means of an adapter will facilitate the procedure (25). Once the lesion has been reached, a Tru-Cut needle may be used for acquisition of tumor samples.

When a solid drill bit with a hand drill is used to perforate the cortex (8), it is advanced to the cortical surface under fluoroscopic observation, and drilling is performed while maintaining steady pressure. A sudden loss in resistance, usually accompanied by pain, indicates entry into the lesion or the medullary cavity. The cortical orifice should be of sufficient size to allow easy passage of the biopsy needle. When the cortex has been reduced to a thin shell, drilling is not necessary, since a small amount of pressure allows penetration of a biopsy needle into the lesion (Fig. 3).

Sampling

We prefer the Tru-Cut needle for acquisition of soft tissue specimens because we feel it provides the best samples, both quantitatively and qualitatively, compared with other needles of similar caliber. Under fluoroscopic observation, the needle in the closed position is introduced as far as the periphery of the lesion. A specimen is obtained by pushing the slotted inner component forward while keeping the outer cannula stationary. The cannula is then advanced over the inner component, trapping a small cylinder of tissue in the slot of the inner component.

Thin-walled needles ranging in caliber from 18 to 23 G are used to obtain samples for cytologic study. The needle is advanced into the lesion, the inner stylet is removed, and aspiration with a 10 or 20 ml syringe is performed while the needle is moved through short excursions within the lesion. Rarely, structures interposed between the skin puncture site

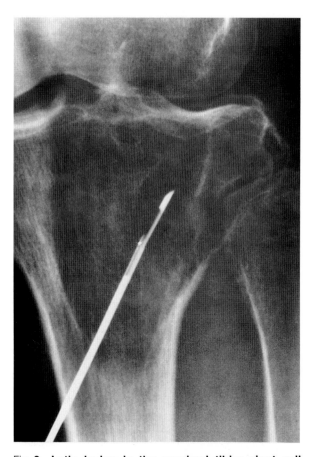

Fig. 3   Lytic lesion in the proximal tibia; giant cell tumor was suspected radiographically. Tru-Cut needle inserted into the lesion without the aid of a drill. Percutaneous biopsy confirmed the clinical diagnosis and excluded malignancy. The tumor was subsequently curetted

and the target lesion may make it difficult to obtain a sample. Curving the tip of a thin-walled needle can be used to circumvent the interposed structure and thus gain access to the lesion.

Spinal Biopsy Technique

Open biopsy of the vertebral column usually is a major surgical procedure; however, percutaneous needle biopsy can be performed with minimal risk, under local anesthesia, and on an out-patient basis. The entire length of the spinal column is accessible to percutaneous biopsy, and various techniques have been described over the last four decades (17, 20, 26, 27, 35, 37, 43, 50).

Cervical Spine. The technique for biopsy of the cervical spine differs from that used for the remainder of the vertebral column (38). The first three segments are biopsied through an anterior transpharyngeal approach with the patient supine and under general anesthesia with transnasal intubation. A mouth opener is applied once the patient is anesthesized. Under fluorosocopic observation, a thin-walled spinal needle is introduced into the body of the segment in question, and aspiration biopsy is performed in the usual manner.

The bodies of the lower cervical segments, including the first thoracic vertebra, are biopsied under local anesthesia through a lateral approach with the patient in the lateral decubitus position. The skin should be punctured behind the posterior margin of the sternocleidomastoid muscle to avoid the neurovascular bundle. We prefer to use needles 18 G or smaller for biopsy of the bodies of the cervical spine and the first thoracic vertebra. Thin-walled spinal or Franzen trephine type needles will usually be adequate; however, penetration through an intact cortex may not be possible with the smaller-gauge needles.

Thoracic Spine. Biopsy of the bodies of the thoracic spine is complicated somewhat by the proximity of the pleura and lung parenchyma which, however, can usually be avoided with adequate patient positioning. The prone oblique position (27, 35) facilitates the procedure considerably.

Thus, the patient initially is placed in the decubitus position contralateral to the side of the greatest vertebral body involvement. The pleural reflection is identified under fluoroscopy, and the patient is slowly turned toward the prone oblique position until the vertebral body is projected behind the pleural reflection. In this manner, a window is made available for the safe introduction of the biopsy instrument, with the pleural reflection lying anteriorly and the spinal canal posteriorly. When tube angulation is possible, it is used to provide optimal visibility of the structure to be biopsied.

Additional cephalocaudal angulation of the fluoroscopy unit is helpful to avoid adjacent transverse processes and ribs.

Lumbar Spine. The presence of relatively large paraspinal musculature facilitates biopsy of the lower thoracic and lumbar segments. The procedure is also performed with the patient in the prone oblique position. Sacral lesions are usually biopsied through a direct posterior approach.

For vertebral biopsies with an intact or sclerotic cortex, we usually use one of the larger trephine needles, such as a 14 cm Ackermann needle. Once the cortex has been perforated with the trephine needle, additional samples may be obtained with a Tru-Cut or a spinal-type needle introduced through the outer cannula of the trephine instrument.

Indications

Metastatic Disease. The principal indication for percutaneous biopsy is the diagnosis of metastatic disease. Skeletal metastases occur frequently in cancer patients, and most can be diagnosed with confidence on the basis of the radiographic features alone. However, a cytologic diagnosis is required in the following cases: apparent skeletal metastases that are in disagreement with the clinical stage of the disease; a positive radionuclide bone scan that cannot be elucidated by other imaging modalities in a patient with a known primary neoplasm; an atypical radiographic presentation, such as osteolytic lesions in a patient with prostatic carcinoma; skeletal metastases that would have different prognostic and therapeutic implications, depending on their site of origin in patients with more than one primary neoplasm; radiographically stable metastases, to determine the presence of viable cells that will affect the decision to continue therapy; and the presence of skeletal metastases without an obvious site of origin, since a biopsy may simplify the search for the primary lesion (16).

Primary Bone Tumors. The initial evaluation of patients with suspected primary skeletal neoplasms should be performed by a team comprising the pathologist, orthopedic surgeon, oncologist, and radiologist, all of whom should be familiar with the management of patients with these types of tumors. If referral of the patient is contemplated, this should be done before biopsy, since related complications are probably more likely in the referring institution than in the treating center (28).

Percutaneous needle biopsy in the diagnosis of primary skeletal neoplasms has not been as well accepted as that for metastatic disease. It is generally believed that larger quantities of tissue than those obtained by needle biopsy were required for the correct histologic diagnosis and that, since most of these lesions require surgical treatment, they were best diagnosed by an open biopsy. However, some primary skeletal neoplasms are managed with preoperative chemotherapy to downstage the tumor for limb salvage procedures and to attempt to identify a potentially effective postoperative adjuvant chemotherapeutic regimen. Percutaneous needle biopsy in these patients allows initiation of therapy without the delay incurred by the healing of a large wound (31). We also believe that wound contamination is much less likely to follow percutaneous needle biopsy than an open biopsy.

As a general rule, lesions that are obviously benign by radiologic criteria or have characteristic features do not require biopsy. Cartilagenous tumors are difficult to grade by needle biopsy; thus, when their diagnosis is apparent radiologically, they should be excised completely (1).

Percutaneous needle biopsy is also of value in the diagnosis of inflammatory lesions, including suspected osteomyelitis. In patients with eosinophilic granuloma, biopsy is used in conjunction with intralesional injection of methylprednisolone, which induces healing in nearly all patients (33).

Contra-Indications

There are no absolute contra-indications for percutaneous skeletal biopsies. A relative contra-indication is any uncorrectable bleeding diathesis. As with any other procedure, the risks of the biopsy must be weighed against the risks of initiating therapy without a specific diagnosis (22).

Complications

There are few complications associated with percutaneous needle biopsy of skeletal lesions. Pain is the most frequent side effect and is usually secondary to inadequate local anesthesia or negative pressure and manipulations within the medullary canal. A review of the literature reported a complication rate of 0.2% (32). Severe neurologic damage and paraplegia were among the most serious complications reported (4, 21, 28, 30, 32, 40, 45). Pneumothorax may occur with biopsies involving structures adjacent to the lungs (1, 4, 5, 12, 21, 23, 32). Hemorrhage is a rare complication (18, 36) that may occur in patients with coagulopathies or when large vessels are lacerated by the biopsy instrument. Tuberculous sinus tracts secondary to biopsy of tuberculous spondylitis have been reported (4, 12). Rarely, tumor contamination of the biopsy tract occurs.

Results

The diagnostic accuracy of percutaneous skeletal biopsies in most of the larger series reported has been around 80%, with a range of 50 to 94% (1, 8,

11, 13, 14, 15, 28, 32, 39, 41, 46, 47, 49). An overall diagnostic accuracy of 78.6% was reported in a series of 178 patients with primary skeletal tumors who underwent percutaneous needle biopsy at our institution (5). Needle biopsy was more accurate in the malignant neoplasms (83%) than in the benign tumors (64.2%). The accuracy in osteosarcomas was 78%, in giant cell tumors, 88%, in Ewing's sarcoma, 95%, and in spindle cell sarcomas, 87%. The principal reason for a nondiagnostic biopsy was the presence of blastic tumors (17 of 35 patients). Cystic lesions and faulty technique were believed to be the reasons for failure in the remaining patients.

In suspected infectious diseases of the skeleton, particularly in tuberculous spondylitis, the incidence of positive bacterial cultures has been generally low in comparison to the incidence of positive diagnosis made based on the histopathologic features of the biopsy specimen (2, 4, 21, 32, 39, 48).

Conclusions

Percutaneous needle biopsy of the skeleton is a safe, accurate, economical, and relatively painless method of obtaining tissue for histologic, cytologic, or bacteriologic diagnosis of skeletal lesions. The procedure can be repeated when needed with minimal morbidity and does not preclude a subsequent surgical biopsy.

It should be emphasized that the diagnostic accuracy of the procedure depends in large part on the experience of the cytopathologist. In primary bone tumors, the participation of a pathologist familiar with these diseases and interested in the examination of small specimens is of the utmost importance.

References

1. Akerman M, Berg NO, Persson BM. Fine needle aspiration biopsy in the evaluation of tumor-like lesions of bone. Acta Orthop Scand 1976;47:129–136.
2. Ambrose GB, Alpert M, Neer CS. Vertrebral body biopsy. JAMA 1966;197:619–622.
3. Andriole JG, Haaga JR, Adams RB, Nunez C. Biopsy needle characteristics assessed in the laboratory. Radiology 1983;148:659–662.
4. Armstrong P, Chalmers AH, Green G, Irving JD. Needle aspiration/biopsy of the spine in suspected disc space infection. Br J Radiol 1978;51:333–337.
5. Ayala AG, Zornoza J. Primary bone tumors: percutaneous needle biopsy: radiologic-pathologic study of 222 biopsies. Radiology 1983;149:675–679.
6. Baud CA, Lagier R, Boivin G, Boillat MA. Value of the bone biopsy in the diagnosis of industrial fluorosis. Virchows Arch [A] 1978;383:283–297.
7. Beck JS, Nordin BEC. Histological assessment of osteoporosis by iliac crest biopsy. J Pathol Bacteriol 1960;80:391.
8. Cohen, MA, Zornoza J, Finkelstein JB. Percutaneous needle biopsy of long-bone lesions facilitated by the use of a hand drill. Radiology 1981;139:750–751.
9. Coley BL, Sharp GS, Ellis EB. Diagnosis of bone tumors by aspiration. Am J Surg 1931;13:215–224.

10. Collins JD, Bassett L, Main GD, Kagan C. Percutaneous biopsy following positive bone scans. Radiology 1979;132:439–442.
11. Cramer LE, Kuhn C, Stein AH. Needle biopsy of bone. Surg Gynecol Obstet 1964;118:1253–1256.
12. Debnam JW, Staple TW. Needle biopsy of bone. Radiol Clin North Am 1975;13:157–164.
13. Debnam JW, Staple TW. Trephine bone biopsy by radiologists: results of 73 procedures. Radiology 1975;116:607–609.
14. Deeley TJ. The drill biopsy of bone lesions. Clin Radiol 1972;23:536–540.
15. DeSantos LA, Wallace S, Murray JA, Lukeman JM. Percutaneous needle biopsy of bone in the cancer patient. AJR 1978;130:641–649.
16. DeSantos LA, Zornoza J. Bone and soft tissue. In: Zornoza J, ed. Percutaneous needle biopsy. Baltimore: Williams and Wilkins, 1981:141–178.
17. Ellis F. Needle biopsy in the clinical diagnosis of tumors. Br J Surg 1947;34:240–261.
18. Fisher WB. Hazard in bone-marrow biopsy. N Engl J Med 1971;285:804.
19. Fornasier VL, Vilaghy MI. The results of bone biopsy with a new instrument. Am J Clin Pathol 1973;60:570–573.
20. Frankel CJ. Aspiration biopsy of the spine. J Bone Joint Surg [Am] 1954;36:69–84.
21. Gladstein MO, Grantham SA. Closed skeletal biopsy. Clin Orthop 1974;103:75–79.
22. Goodrich JA, Difiore RJ, Tippens JK. Analysis of bone biopsies. Am Surg 1983;49:594–598.
23. Hanafee WN, Tobin PL. Closed bone biopsy by a radiologist. Radiology 1969;92:605–606.
24. Hulth AG, Nilsson BE, Westlin NE, Wiklund PE. Bone biopsy in women with spinal osteoporosis. Acta Med Scand 1979;206:205–206.
25. Kattapuram SV, Rosenthal DI, Phillips WC. Trephine biopsy of the skeleton with the aid of a hand drill. Radiology 1984;152:231.
26. Kendall PH. Needle biopsy of the vertebral bodies. Ann Phys Med 1960;5:236–242.
27. Laredo J-D, Bard M. Thoracic spine: percutaneous trephine biopsy. Radiology 1986;160:485–489.
28. Mankin HJ, Lange TA, Spanier SS. The hazards of biopsy in patients with malignant primary bone and soft-tissue tumors. J Bone Joint Surg [Am] 1982;64:1121–1127.
29. Martin HE, Ellis EB. Biopsy by needle puncture and aspiration. Ann Surg 1930;92:169–181.
30. McLaughlin RE, Miller WR, Miller CW. Quadriparesis after needle aspiration of the cervical spine: report of a case. J Bone Joint Surg [Am] 1976;58:1167–1168.
31. Moore TM, Meyers MH, Patzakis MJ, Terry R, Harvey JP. Closed biopsy of musculoskeletal lesions. J Bone Joint Surg [Am] 1979;61:375–380.
32. Murphy WA, Destouet JM, Gilula LA. Percutaneous skeletal biopsy 1981: a procedure for radiologists-results, review, and recommendations. Radiology 1981;139:545–549.
33. Nauert C, Zornoza, J, Ayala A, Harle TS. Eosinophilic granuloma of bone: diagnosis and management. Skeletal Radiol 1983;10:227–235.
34. Nilsson BE, Wiklund P-E. Iliac crest biopsy in the diagnosis of metabolic bone disease: a method study. Acta Med Scand 1983;213:151–155.
35. Nordenstrom B. Percutaneous biopsy of vertebrae and ribs. Acta Radiol [Diagn] (Stockh) 1971;11:113–131.
36. Ottolenghi CE. Diagnosis of orthopedic lesions by aspiration biopsy: results of 1061 punctures. J Bone Joint Surg 1955;37:443–464.
37. Ottolenghi CE. Aspiration biopsy of the spine: technique for the thoracic spine and results of twenty-eight biopsies in this region, and over-all results of 1050 biopsies of other spinal segments. J Bone Joint Surg [Am] 1969;51:1531–1544.
38. Ottolenghi CE, Schajowicz F, De Schant FA. Aspiration biopsy of the cervical spine: technique and results in thirty-four cases. J Bone Joint Surg [Am] 1965;46:715–733.
39. Pepe RC, Lalli AF. Percutaneous aspiration bone biopsy by fluoroscopic guidance. Cleve Clin Q 1976;43:77–83.
40. Ramgopal V, Geller M. Iatrogenic Klebsiella meningitis following closed needle biopsy of the lumbar spine: report of a case and review of literature. Wis Med J 1977;76:41–42.
41. Schajowicz F, Derqui JC. Puncture biopsy in lesions of the locomotor system: review of results in 4050 cases, including 941 vertebral punctures. Cancer 1968;21:531–548.
42. Seyfarth C. Die Sternum-Trepanation: eine einfache Methode zur diagnostischen Entnahme von Knochenmark bei Lebenden. Dtsch Med Wochenschr 1923;49:180.
43. Siffert RS, Arkin AM. Trephine biopsy of bone with special reference to the lumbar vertebral bodies. J Bone Joint Surg [Am] 1949;31:146–149.
44. Smirnov AN, Baranov AE. Trephine for iliac crest biopsy. Lancet 1971;i:1353–1354.
45. Stahl DC, Jacobs B. Diagnosis of obscure lesions of the skeleton: evaluation of biopsy methods. JAMA 1967;201:229–231.
46. Stormby N, Akerman M. Cytodiagnosis of bone lesions by means of fine needle aspiration biopsy. Acta Cytol (Baltimore) 1973;17:166–172.
47. Synder RE, Coley BL. Further studies on the diagnosis of bone tumors by aspiration biopsy. Surg Gynecol Obstet 1945;80:517–522.
48. Tehranzadeh J, Freiberger RH, Ghelman B. Closed skeletal needle biopsy: review of 120 cases. AJR 1983;140:113–115.
49. Thommesen P, Frederiken P. Fine needle aspiration biopsy of bone lesions: clinical value. Acta Orthop Scand 1976;47:137–143.
50. Valls J, Ottolenghi CE, Schajowicz F. Aspiration biopsy in diagnosis of lesions of vertebral bodies. JAMA 1948;136:376–383.

Economic Considerations

M. Dicato, J. Freilinger, R. F. Dondelinger, and J. C. Kurdziel

Interventional radiology (IR) procedures have become widely available over the past few years and their indications now extend into most medical subspecialties. In oncology, percutaneous biopsies compare favorably with conventional procedures as far as sensitivity and specificity are concerned (2).

Staging, by itself, is poorly standardized except in lymphoma patients, and especially in Hodgkin disease, where a finer tuning of therapy is done according to disease stage. The method of staging is traditionally cumbersome, but markedly simplified with CT-guided IR procedures, which prompted us to do a cost study. Since the latter techniques are, in addition, very sparing of the patient and simple, a prospective randomized study could not be done for ethical reasons (e. g., lung biopsy versus thoracotomy).

In a first step, only lymphoma patients were studied from a cost point of view because of the more or less standardized and generally accepted method. Thereafter, the cost study was continued comparing standard procedures to the IR counterpart (e. g., thoracotomy versus percutaneous CT-guided fine needle sampling), rather than comparing histologic entities (lymphoma versus lung cancer). The method of sampling, IR or surgery, was determined by the treating physician.

Methods

Calculation of cost is done from hospital bills. All numbers given include medical fees. For the interventional procedures, there is no difference in billing as far as different anatomic regions (thoracic, abdominal, pelvic) are concerned. Major radiologic equipment is state subsidized, sometimes up to 80% of real investment cost. This is included in the calculation. Amortization of this type of equipment is calculated over 5 or 10 years, depending on the degree of sophistication and on the expected technical evolution. All calculations given include equipment, disposables, personnel, and physician costs.

For hospitalization cost, calculations are also done from hospital bills. The numbers given underestimate real cost, because hospitalization is not entirely covered by patient or health insurance. The deficit is compensated for (one and sometimes several years) later by price adjustments. Other means

of financial compensation through indirect subsidization by state sources could not be accounted for. It is stressed that in Luxembourg, hospitalization cost is disproportionately low as far as room and board go. Daily rates in 1986 were 2,434 francs (about $ 61).

Expenses of any kind (medications, laboratory tests, x-ray, physiotherapy, etc.) are calculated separately, added in the billing, and included in our cost study.

However, the discrepancy between out-patient and hospitalization cost is such that refinements to increase the already tremendous difference are not considered important in proving the point. Medical fees are controlled and represent 15 to 20% of the total cost for hospitalized patients and 25 to 30% for out-patient procedures. In general, procedures and bills can be divided into thoracic, abdominal, pelvic, and other (skeletal, breast, etc).

Of 120 patients with lymphoma, 99 were evaluable from a cost point of view. In lymphoma, and especially in Hodgkin disease, standard staging includes physical examinations, hematologic and biochemical blood tests, urinanalysis, chest radiograph, electrocardiogram, abdominal US, or total body CT. For exclusion of reticulo-endothelial disease at least one and often two iliac crest bone marrow biopsies are required. If this testing is negative, the question comes up of abdominal disease and splenectomy, since most patients present with supradiaphragmatic disease. This work-up is done on all patients.

Abdominal nodes or masses and liver involvement are readily biopsied percutaneously and most often in an out-patient setting. Since progression of disease is orderly in Hodgkin lymphoma and involvement of nodes below L2 are usually not visible without lymphangiography, this latter procedure is often done. In addition, the architectural pattern of unenlarged but involved nodes can help improve the staging. However, in non-Hodgkin lymphoma, about 50% of patients have lymph node involvement not visible on lymphangiography but on abdominal CT and practically all involved nodes are also enlarged as a rule (1) (Table 1).

At initial staging (Table 2), 20 of 32 Hodgkin lymphoma patients were staged conventionally, and of these two thoracotomies were required. Of 13 IR-CT staged patients two showed progression from stage II to stage IV disease.

Table **1** Infradiaphragmatic involvement encountered at staging laparotomy in previously untreated patients

	Hodgkin disease (%)	Non-Hodgkin lymphoma (%)
Para-aortic nodes	25	49
Mesenteric nodes	4	51
Spleen	37	40
Liver	8	14
Bone marrow	3	20
Kidneys	1	4
Gastrointestinal tract	0	8 adult 18 child

Table **2** Patient data at initial staging

	No.	Results
Hodgkin		
Conventionally	20	2 thoracotomies
CT	13	2 progressions of stage II to IV
Total	33	
Non-Hodgkin		
Conventionally	28	1 thoracotomy 2 laparatomy
CT	38	7 progressions of staging (5 thoracic, 2 abdominal)
Total	66	

In 66 non-Hodgkin lymphoma patients, 28 were staged conventionally and of these one thoracotomy and two laparotomies were required, and of 38 non-Hodgkin patients, seven progressions of staging were noted, five thoracic and two abdominal.

Interestingly enough, at standard restaging of lymphoma patients (Table **3**), 18% had been classified as complete remission and were found to have measurable histologically proved disease by IR staging.

Results

These data show that IR restaging of lymphoma patients improves diagnoses and requires also additional therapy in a substantial number of patients otherwise misjudged to be in complete remission.

Some of the patients showing an abnormal lymphangiogram were subjected to percutaneous lymph node biopsies to secure a histologic rather than a radiologic staging. The results of IR-guided techniques compare favorably from a medical point of view. Suffice it to say that the data given improve diagnostic yields, at least in lymphoma, in our

Table **3** Restaging by CT*

	Hodgkin (n = 33)	Non-Hodgkin (n = 45)	Total (n = 78)
Mediastinal	1	1	2
Lung	3	1	4
Liver		1	1
Abdominal mass		5	5
Abdominal nodes	1	1	2
	5 (15%)	9 (20%)	14 (18%)

* There were 78 procedures (some patients were staged several times) with 14 (18%) results of "occult" disease.

experience. The diagnostic results are extensively discussed in the previous chapters for other diseases. Overall, there is a 10- to 30-fold decrease in cost each time the procedures applied avoid hospitalization (Table **4**). Overall the cost results are shown on table **4** and are for 1986 expenses.

Table **4** Comparative costs for standard hospital versus interventional radiology procedures

Staging and biopsy	No. procedures	Average cost			IR/standard ratio
		Flux	Standard deviation	US$*	
IR procedures					
One setting	178	12,000	670	300	1
Two settings	18	18,200	2,900	455	
Anatomic sites+					
Thorax	16	570,000	112,500	14,250	1/47
Abdomen	36	460,800	72,600	11,500	1/38
Pelvis	22	418,000	61,800	10,450	1/34
Bone	12	367,000	66,000	9,175	1/30

* 1 US$ = 40 Flux
+ Standard hospital procedure.

Continuing our cost study by anatomic regions (thorax, abdomen, pelvis, bone, and others) showed similar results and therefore the tabulation shown is not broken down by histologic classification. For comparability, charges are given in addition to the local currency of Luxembourg francs (Flux and also in US dollars (1 $ = 40 Flux).

In view of the general trend of decreasing financial means and increasing expenditure, cost reduction has become a major issue of health care. IR procedures show a definite improvement of quality of care and are more tolerable for the patient. In addition, tremendous financial savings are achieved compared with standard procedures.

As with most medical techniques, the availability of a procedure implies the risk of overutilization, demand following offer and not necessarily the other way round, this being the only caveat. However, the major savings introduced by IR techniques are due to the fact that hospitalization is decreased by at least a factor of ten. Hospitalization being the largest share of the expenses in staging or treating patients, the financial gain is not in the evaluation of the cost of procedure details (number of films, price of material, or even price of heavy equipment), but resides in the mere question: Can the patient be managed without hospitalization? If this is feasable, a 10- to 30-fold cost decrease can be expected for that particular patient.

In view of the disease-related group payment system, incentives and pressures to introduce IR techniques in all medical specialties, such as those described in this book, will be obvious.

Apart from these considerations, the patient's interests have not been dealt with but seem obvious also (out-patient tissue sampling of a lung lesion with staging by total body CT in a 30- to 40-minute procedure, rather than 10-day hospitalization for a thoracotomy with convalescence, out of work time, discomfort, etc.). The cost of the latter items is certainly also important but could not be ascertained in our study.

Conclusions

In conclusion, IR techniques are preferable for the patient and economical, and should become standard medical practice. We believe that, allowing for some exceptions, there is no justification for continuing standard practices when IR techniques have been proved to give similiar and often better results.

References

1. Castellino RA, Marglin SI. Imaging of abdominal and pelvic lymph nodes. Invest Radiol 1982;17:433–443.
2. Dondelinger RF, Kurdziel J-C, Dicato M. Interventional computed tomography in oncology; vol. 2 Budapest: 14th International Cancer Congress, 1986:K-31, 2198.

Venous Blood Sampling by Percutaneous Catheterization

Systemic Veins

R. Sörensen

All hormone-secreting organs (except those draining into the portal system) have their effluent veins draining into the inferior or superior vena cava or its branches. These veins can be catheterized percutaneously and venous samples can be taken to study glandular secretion directly. Demonstration of a gradient between glandular effluent hormone levels and peripheral concentrations establishes secretion. Thus, gradients serve as semiquantitative estimates of momentary secretory activity of the organ. This method is, however, associated with significant errors: the calculation of secretion rates without determination of actual glandular blood flow during the procedure is problematic; knowledge about intraglandular hormone metabolism remains limited; the variable influences of premedication, stress, and application of contrast media on secretion can lead to inaccuracy; and the problems related to correct identification of the glandular veins and the accurate placement of the catheter result in admixture of the samplings (134–136). Nevertheless, this method provides useful qualitative information on hormone secretions.

Renal Veins

Bilateral selective renal vein blood sampling and calculation of the plasma renin activity (PRA) is performed in patients with hypertension in the presence of a renal artery stenosis (RAS). In unilateral disease PRA serves as an estimate of the hemodynamic significance of a stenosis in view of the curability of the hypertension after a revascularization procedure (54, 75, 114, 119, 137, 138, 155).

Renin is produced in the juxtaglomerular cells of the renal arterioles. Baroreceptors, macula densa cells of the distal tubule, and autonomic nervous activities regulate the release of renin and react to volume, pressure, plasma sodium, vascular tone, increased angiotensin II, and changes in plasma potassium and aldosterone. Renin secretion is stimulated by orthostasis, vasodilators, and angiotensin-converting enzyme inhibitors, and is inhibited by beta-adrenergic blockers, clonidin, and alpha-methyl-dihydrophenyl-alanin. These drugs should be discontinued before the sampling procedure (35).

Anatomy

Both renal veins join the inferior vena cava at the level of the second lumbar vetebra. In 28% of the cases multiple veins are present, which usually communicate. In 2% a single vein has two separate draining veins when entering the inferior vena cava (118). In 5 to 17% the right gonadal vein enters the right renal vein (3, 12, 71).

On the left side, the adrenal and the gonadal veins join the renal vein. In 3% the renal vein crosses the aorta posteriorly instead of anteriorly (76) and enters the inferior vena cava as low as the iliac bifurcation. Circumaortic venous rings are found in 17%, (11), (Fig. 1). Another variation is a left persistent inferior vena cava (3%), which joins the left renal vein before it drains into the right inferior vena cava (77). Renal vein valves (3%) do not interfere with sampling (12).

Technique

For correct laboratory results, a standard protocol is essential. The patient should be in a supine position for at least 2 hours. All antihypertensive drugs are to be discontinued 10 days before the examination. If this ist not possible, at least beta-adrenergic blocking agents and angiotensin-converting enzyme inhibitors must be eliminated. Treatment with a long-acting diuretic agent makes the difference between renin secretion of the normal compared with the abnormal side more evident (114, 119).

Catheterization of the renal veins is done by the transfemoral approach. It is performed under local anesthesia with a femorovisceral catheter (cobra shaped, side hole 1 mm from the tip). An injection of contrast media identifies the position of the catheter tip. Eight to 10 ml of blood are withdrawn distal to the orifices of the adrenal and gonadal veins on the left side. The right renal vein has no contribution of blood from another vein. As a variation, however, the right gonadal vein might drain into the right renal vein in 5 to 11% of cases (3, 12, 71).

The PRA is determined in both renal veins and in the peripheral blood.

If RAS is present on one side and the renal vein renin ratio is greater than 1.5:1.0 ng/ml/hour between the diseased and the normal kidney, the stenosis is hemodynamically significant and there will be a favorable response to a revascularization procedure

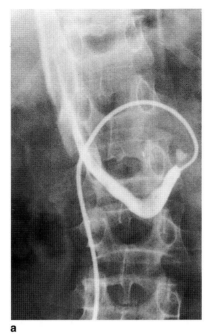
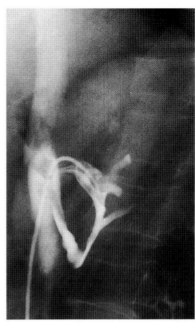

Fig. 1 Circumaortic renal collar.
a anterior – posterior projection. The catheter marks the superior portion of the venous ring.
b lateral projection. The inferior portion of the venous ring passes retro-aortal

a   b

in respect to the hypertension. If the ratio of the contralateral renal vein renin to the peripheral renin is less than 1.3:1.0, small vessel disease of the renal artery without a stenosis is unlikely (91, 144). The specificity of the method for the prediction to cure a patient's hypertension is 90 to 100% according to Vaughan et al. (155), and the sensitivity is 74%.

Indications

Bilateral renal vein sampling for determination of PRA is one method of estimating the significance of RAS in hypertensive patients. RAS however, occurs also in patients with normal blood pressure or in the presence of essential hypertension. Those cases will not benefit from a revascularization procedure. If patients with unilateral RAS have biochemical signs of renal insufficiency, both kidneys are contributing to the increase in PRA and there will be no cure of the hypertension. The predictive value of the method is thus limited.

Adrenal Veins

Selective venous sampling of adrenal veins with or without phlebography is performed to locate hormone-producing tumors (adrenal cortex, adrenal medulla), if they are too small to be diagnosed by noninvasive imaging techniques, or to verify the source of excessive hormone production of a tumor incidentally detected by CT, US, or MRI (120).

Technique

To catheterize adrenal veins and to perform selective sampling a femorovisceral catheter (cobra shaped, size 5 to 7 Fr with a side hole 1 mm from the tip) is used (74, 134). To avoid iatrogenic suppression of adrenal hormone output, no premedication is given. The tip of the catheter is guided to the orifice of both veins and three samples (8 to 10 ml) are taken at 5- to 10-minute intervals to compensate for episodic variations in hormone secretion (65).

To calculate gradients, samples from an iliac vein or a peripheral vein are taken simultaneously. Control of the position of the tip of the catheter (fluoroscopic control) is obtained with no more than 0.5 ml of a nonionic contrast material, which is injected gently. Routinely, 5000 U of heparin are given to avoid thrombus formation. Retrograde venography is only performed if there is clinical suspicion of a hormone active tumor to verify the side of hormone excess, of if the lesion cannot be seen by any other method.

Contrast Media

Retrograde injection of contrast media into a small vein of the adrenal gland induces a change of the secretory activity of the gland. This is dependent on the amount being injected. Although venography (3 to 6 ml) causes extremely high elevation of adrenal vein cortisol levels (Fig. **2**), the injection of minute volumes of contrast media (less than 0.5 ml) has no significant effect on adrenal steroid release. Catheterization itself causes only little stress. Peripheral cortisol during the procedure before ve-

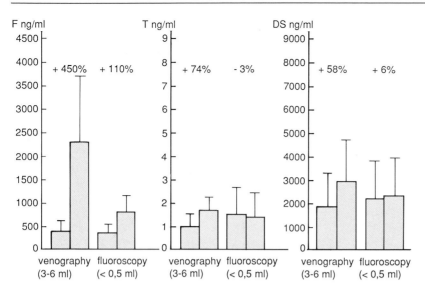

Fig. **2   Effects of contrast media on adrenal steroid release in nine patients with hyperandrogenism.** F: cortisol; T: testosterone; DHEAS: dehydroepiandrosterone sulfate. The percentage values denote the mean changes of adrenal vein steroid levels induced

nography was not significantly different ($p > 0.05$) from a normal outpatient control group in a study conducted by Moltz et al. (Fig. **3**), (106–108). Contrast media should be used with extreme care. Blood samples from adrenal veins should be drawn before the contrast injection (134, 136).

Severe side effects, such as thrombosis of the adrenal vein, iliac vein, or femoral vein, hemorrhage and infarction of the adrenal gland followed by ne-

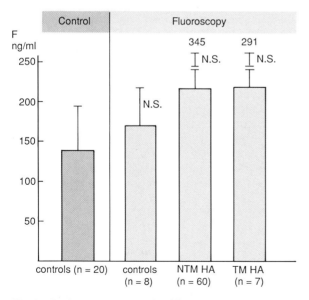

Fig. **3   Peripheral cortisol (F) levels during the catheterization procedure of 75 women in comparison with a control group of normal out-patients** (n = 20). Cortisol levels of the volunteers, nontumorous, and tumorous patients show no significant differences. NTM HA = nontumorous hyperandrogenism; TM HA = tumorous hyperandrogenism

crosis and adrenal insufficiency, are almost always related to contrast agents and occur in 0.1 to 5% of cases reported (9, 16, 38, 44, 49, 57, 83, 104). Minor reactions include extravasation of contrast media without sequelae, small hematomas at the puncture site, and allergic skin reactions. Most of the complications can be avoided if nonionic contrast media are used (4, 57).

Hyperaldosteronism (Conn's syndrome)

In humans, the most potent and predominant mineralo-corticoid is aldosterone, accounting for 50 to 60% of activity, with cortisol providing 30 to 40% and cortisone and others less than 10% (7, 35, 37, 154). It acts on the distal renal tubule to promote reabsorption of sodium and secretion of potassium and hydrogen ions. Hyperproduction of mineralocorticoids leads to sodium retention and hypertension accompanied by potassium depletion. In normal humans, angiotensin II regulates aldosterone secretion. In idiopathic hyperaldosteronism the situation is comparable. Aldosterone-producing adenomas, however, do not react to angiotensin II, but to ACTH (51). Among patients with adenomas, hypokalemia is expected in 90% or more, if repeated samples are taken while the patient is on a low salt diet. In 70 to 80% of the cases an adenoma is the cause of the symptoms. Two percent of the adenomas are bilateral. Twenty to 30% of patients are considered to have idiopathic hyperaldosteronism (18, 45, 46, 89, 161, 162), and less than 1% of all hypertensive patients are found to have an aldosteronoma of the adrenal gland (8, 13, 14, 23, 28, 69, 81, 147–149).

The accuracy of CT and US is 60 to 90% (36, 42, 61, 66, 67, 81, 101, 105, 124, 127, 170). Adenomas smaller than 1 cm in diameter are difficult to diagnose. False-positive diagnoses, however, are rare. It is not always possible to distinguish between small adenomas and bilateral nodular hyperplasia (18, 53, 59, 60, 100, 101, 147, 161, 162, 168). Nodules are common in the normal adrenal gland. They are usually not hormone active. Phlebography of the gland can demonstrate a nodule by showing displacement of parenchymal veins. The accuracy of this examination is 50 to 80%. Small adenomas are easily overlooked and bilateral hyperplasia is difficult to diagnose, because in the presence of hyperplasia the adrenal glands can be normal in size and shape (18, 27, 100, 161, 162). Selective bilateral catheterization of the adrenal veins in combination with blood sampling for aldosterone concentration provides a highly specific test. Its accuracy is described as being between 75 and 100%.

Hypercortisolism (Cushing's syndrome)

There are different forms of hypercortisolism: increased secretion of adrenocorticotropic hormone (ACTH); increased secretion of cortisol by tumors of the adrenal cortex (adenomas, carcinomas); ectopic ACTH production.

In 75% of patients with endogenous Cushing's syndrome, a micro-adenoma of the pituitary gland is diagnosed, and 25% are found to have either an adenoma of the adrenal cortex, or show signs of ectopic ACTH production by a malignant tumor (68). The ectopic ACTH syndrome is the result of excessive production of ACTH or precursors of ACTH of nonpituitary origin (small cell carcinoma of the bronchus, tumors of neuroectodermal tissue, thymomas, islet cell tumors of the pancreas, carcinomas of the lung, medullary thyroid cancer, pheochromocytomas) (6, 68, 122).

If a Chushing's syndrome is diagnosed biochemically, the source of excess hormones has to be located before treatment. Patients with pituitary hypercortisolism usually show, in 40 to 50% of the cases, suppression of 17-ketosteroids in their urine after dexamethasone. If a micro-adenoma of the pituitary gland can be seen on a conventional tomogram, or on CT, this will be most likely the source of hormone production. Dexamethasone does not suppress urine 17-ketosteroids in patients with ectopic ACTH production. The exception is a carcinoid tumor of the lung (81). To distinguish ectopic ACTH production from autonomous functioning adenomas of the adrenal cortex, plasma ACTH levels are measured. In patients with adenomas of the adrenal cortex, ACTH is suppressed evenly. In patients with ectopic ACTH production, normal and high ACTH levels are found in the plasma. CT of the adrenals will reveal the tumor. Hormone active tumors of the adrenal gland are usually small. If they exceed a diameter of 7 cm, they are most likely malignant

(24). If noninvasive imaging techniques cannot find the source of increased hormone secretion, selective and venous sampling is necessary.

Carcinoma of the Adrenal Gland

Malignant lesions of the adrenal gland can have signs of hormone overproduction. Patients with increased cortisol levels without an increase in androgen production are more likely to have an adenoma. Androgen excess-dehydroepiandrosterone, (DHEA), dehydroepiandrosterone sulfate (DHEAS), androstenedione, testosterone occurs more likely in malignant lesions (15, 88). They can be found by conducting peripheral blood samples by radioimmunoassay (RIA) and by analyzing metabolites of DHEA and DHEAS that are excreted in the urine (17-ketosteroids).

The hormone production of carcinomas of the adrenal cortex cannot be suppressed by dexamethasone or stimulated by ACTH. CT usually gives the diagnosis of a larger lesion. Carcinomas of the adrenal gland rarely are an indication for venous blood sampling.

Hypercatecholaminism (Pheochromocytomas)

Pheochromocytomas are tumors of the adrenal medulla. Their excessive and fluctuating production of catecholamine produces hypertension. They are found in 0.1% of the hypertensive population (10, 146, 152, 153). It is important to diagnose these tumors; they are a vital threat to the patient (hypertensive crisis) and they are curable by surgery. Less than 5% are malignant. Extra-adrenal pheochromocytomas (paragangliomas) are more likely to be malignant (103). Pheochromocytomas can be part of familial or nonfamilial multiple endocrine neoplasia syndrome (MEN II, MEN III) (10, 22, 26, 30, 62, 87, 132, 142). They are found wherever chromaffin cells are located, within the sympathetic ganglia and most likely in the adrenal medulla (90%). Extra-adrenal tumors are found from the carotid bifurcation to the urinary bladder, most of them within the paravertebral ganglia or the organ of Zuckerkandl at the aortic bifurcation. The second most common location of extra-adrenal tumors is the mediastinum. Multiple lesions occur in 10%. Bilateral adrenal tumors are found in familial MEN syndrome (87). Bilateral hyperplasia of the medulla is probably the precursor of pheochromocytomas (30). Most of the tumors produce norepinephrine and many produce epinephrine in addition.

Clinical symptoms are usually related to catecholamine release and include headache, palpitations, anxiety, and hot flushes (17, 19, 93). The symptoms appear paroxysmally and are combined with hypertension. The episodes usually last only a few minutes, but sometimes they continue for hours.

Measurements of catecholamines, total metane-phrine, vanillylmandelic acid in the urine are routine examinations to establish the diagnosis (26).

The lesion usually can be diagnosed by CT and US, if it is not smaller than 1 cm in diameter (143, 165, 169). Extra-adrenal tumors may be visualized by scintigraphy with iodine-131-m-iodobenzylguanidin, (50).

Arteriography and venography should be done only if patients are treated with phenoxybenzamine before the procedure, in order to prevent the provo-cation of a hypertensive crisis. Aortography with subtraction and venous blood sampling from all branches of the superior and inferior vena cava (Fig. 4) can be helpful to locate the tumor.

Incidentomas

Incidentomas are small adrenal nodules, 1 to 3 cm in diameter diagnosed by CT, MRI, or US incidentally

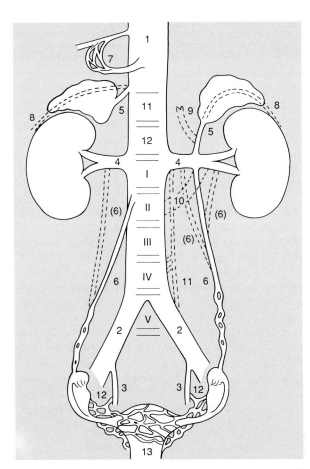

Fig. 4 The most common communications and anomalies of the female adrenal and ovarian system.
(1) inferior vena cava, (2) common iliac vein, (3) internal iliac vein, (4) renal vein, (5) adrenal vein, (6) ovarian vein, (7) hepatic vein, (8) capsular vein, (9) inferior phrenic vein, (10) retro-aortic renal collar, (11) ascending lumbar vein, (12) ovarian venous plexus, (13) uterine plexus

(133). Those lesions are relatively common and patients should be evaluated biochemically. If they are found to be hormone active, venous sampling should verify the diagnosis and be followed by surgery (24, 55). If they are not hormone producing, a follow-up CT 3 months later can determine growth. If there has been no change in size, no further therapy is necessary.

Adrenal Veins: Ovarian Veins, Female Hyperandrogenemia

Of all female endocrinopathies, hyperandrogenemia is the most common. The differentiation between normal, nontumorous, and tumorous conditions is necessary for medical management. Hyperan-drogenemia without tumor is usually due to increased hormone production by the ovaries or the adrenal glands. In rare instances it is caused by androgen-producing tumors. Multiple methods have been tried to locate the source of excess androgen production: however, most of these techniques proved to be unreliable (71–73, 95, 96, 99, 106–108, 139). Despite the fact that CT and US show improved quality of resolution, detection of ovarian and adrenal tumors remains difficult if their sizes are smaller than the size of the glands (2, 52, 104).

Anatomy

Knowledge of the anatomy of the veins and their variations is essential to the correct placement of the catheter tip into the orifice of ovarian and adrenal effluents (123) (Fig. **4**).

Left Adrenal Vein

The left adrenal vein drains into the left renal vein. The purity of the effluent hormone is influenced by the contribution of venous blood from the inferior phrenic vein, renal capsular veins, communicating veins of the renal vein, ureteral veins, veins of the epidural and paravertebral plexus, and by anasto-moses to the ovarian vein. Duplication of the adrenal vein is rarely seen. The inferior phrenic vein joins the left adrenal vein. Selective sampling of this vein should be avoided (Fig. **5**).

Right Adrenal Vein

The right adrenal vein is smaller than the left, and drains directly into the inferior vena cava. There are usually anastomoses from renal capsular veins, epidural and intervertebral veins, connections to the renal, hepatic, inferior phrenic, and ureteral veins. The differentiation between adrenal and small hepat-ic veins can be difficult. Lecky et al. (85) have given a table with roentgen signs to distinguish both veins (Table **1**).

Fig. **5** **Left adrenal vein:** most common communications.
a Catheterization of the adrenal vein: inferior phrenic vein (1 arrow) with venous valve; renal vein (2 arrows); capsular vein (3 arrows)
b Catheterization of the inferior phrenic vein: only a small amount of contrast medium is seen in the proximal adrenal vein (arrow). Sampling has been without cortisol, indicating that blood was not taken from the adrenal vein

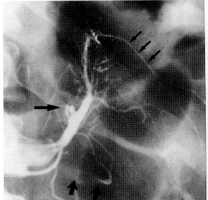
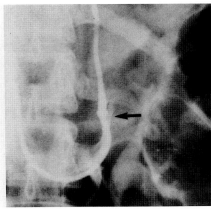

a   b

Left Ovarian Vein

The left ovarian vein drains into the left renal vein just oposite to the adrenal vein. Multiple venous connections give an admixture to the samples. Contributing veins are the internal iliac veins, parietal abdominal veins, ascending lumbar veins, small renal veins, veins of the sacral plexus with connections to the oposite side, ureteral veins, renal capsular veins, veins from the epidural and paravertebral plexus, inferior mesenteric veins, and gluteal veins (Fig. **6**).

Table **1** Differentiation between right adrenal veins and hepatic veins

	Right adrenal veins	Hepatic veins
Vena caval location of veins orifice	Posterolateral or posterior	Lateral or anterolateral (rarely posterior)
Angle of veins from inferior vena cava	Acute (sharply angulates)	Commonly less sharp; nearly straight
Contrast reflux into other hepatic veins	Rare	Common
Contour ends at visible liver edge	Never	Common
Contour corresponds to adrenal configuration	Common	Rare but may simulate adrenal
Suprarenal "capping" of kidney	Frequent	Rare .
Persistent tissue "blush"	Rare (exception, extravasation)	Common
Patient discomfort and pressure	Common	Very rare (? never)
Aspiration of blood sample	Difficult	Usually easy
Color of blood sample	Brighter red	Darker
Cortisol content related to inferior vena cava sample	Higher (exception, hypofunction)	Lower

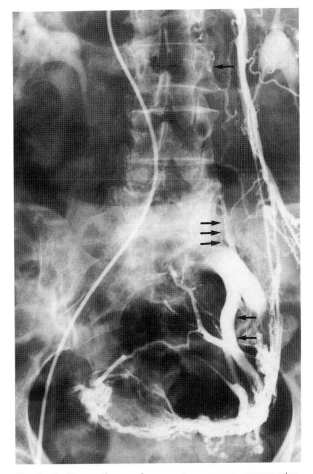

Fig. **6** **Left ovarian vein:** most common communications. Epidural veins (1 arrow) internal iliac veins (2 arrows) ascending lumbar veins (3 arrows)

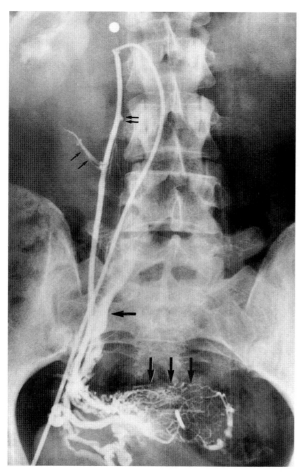

Fig. **7 Right ovarian vein:** most common venous communications. Uterine plexus (3 arrows) with communications to the left side; parietal vein (2 arrows); internal iliac vein (1 arrow)

The ascending lumbar vein can have a direct connection to the renal vein in 9%, or drain into the inferior portion of a retro-aortic renal collar (11, 47). There may be venous valves; however these do not affect the sampling procedure.

Right Ovarian Vein

The right ovarian vein drains directly into the inferior vena cava up to 5 cm below the orifice of the right renal vein. There are various contributing veins to this vessel. They originate from the uterine plexus, which has anastomoses to the ovarian vein of the oposite side, and from parietal, iliac, peridural, renal, ascending lumbar, ureteral and renal capsular veins (Fig. **7**). In 5 to 11% the right ovarian vein drains into the right renal vein (12). Despite these variations creating an admixture of the samplings of all four veins, gradients between glandular effluent levels and peripheral concentrations serve as semi-quantitative estimates of momentary secretory activity of the gland (Table **3**) (134–136).

Technique

For four-vessel venous sampling, the best catheterization results were observed using a femorovisceral catheter (cobra shaped, side hole at the tip). This catheter can be turned into six different shapes inside of the inferior vena cava (Fig. **8**) according to the angles of the inflowing veins (21, 41, 43, 75, 134–136, 160, 163, 164).

Table **2** reflects the method-related data representing the accuracy of the catheterization technique. The catheterization should be performed according to a strict protocol during the early follicular phase (days 3 to 7) between 8 and 10 a.m. to reduce interference from cyclic and circadian variations of androgen secretion. In order to avoid iatrogenic suppression of adrenal steroid output, no premedication should be administered.

Hormone Analysis

The following steroids are to be determined by direct RIA: DHEAS, 17-α-hydroxyprogesterone, cortisol, testosterone, dihydrotestosterone, δ-4-androstenedione. Table **3** demonstrates the results of peripheral, ovarian, and adrenal vein hormone analysis of testosterone, DHEAS, and cortisol of normal women, nontumorous patients, and patients

Table **2** Accuracy of catheterization of adrenal and ovarian veins in 75 women	Normal volunteers (n = 8)	Patients without tumors (n = 60)	Patient with tumors (n = 7)	Total (n = 75) No.	%
Left ovarian vein	8	36	6	50	67
Right ovarian vein	7	47	5	59	79
Left adrenal vein	8	58	7	73	97
Right adrenal vein	6	49	7	62	83

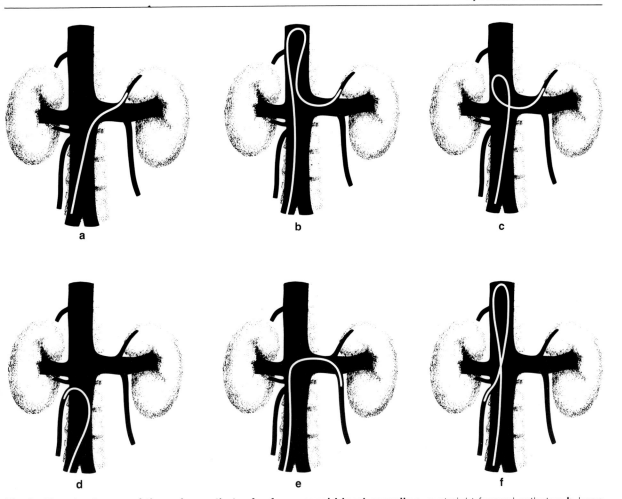

Fig. 8 **The six shapes of the cobra catheter for four-vessel blood sampling: a** straight forward catheter; **b** large loop, **c** short twisted loop, **d** short bend, **e** long bend, **f** large twisted loop

Table **3** Results of peripheral, ovarian, and adrenal vein hormone analysis of testosterone, dehydro-epiandrosterone sulfate, and cortisol

	Normal volunteers (n = 8)	Patients without tumors (n = 60)	Patients with tumors (n = 7)
Testosterone (ng/ml)			
Peripheral	0.36 ± 0.16*	0.68 ± 0.43*	1.3 − 10.7[+]
OPG	0.03 ± 0.09	0.4 ± 1.15	2.9 − 6.6
APG	0.48 ± 0.57	0.88 ± 1.33	0 − 2.3
DHEAS (ng/ml)			
Peripheral	1860 ± 850	3137 ± 1774	960 − 3050
OPG	191 ± 72	288 ± 523	0 − 290
APG	706 ± 824	854 ± 1223	0 − 1970
Cortisol (ng/ml)			
Peripheral	170 ± 50	216 ± 121	113 − 340
OPG	38 ± 11	35 ± 47	0 − 50
APG	610 ± 1329	1252 ± 2032	0 − 3790

* Mean ± SD. [+] Range.
OPG: ovarian/peripheral gradient; APG: adrenal/peripheral gradient

with tumors. A considerable overlap of individual steroid levels and gradients for testosterone and DHEAS is observed between androgenized and normal women (107).

The ovarian-peripheral gradient for testosterone must be at least 2.7 ng/ml to diagnose a hormone active tumor. In addition, selective catheterization is clinically helpful not only to differentiate between tumorous and nontumorous, but also between ovarian, adrenal, and mixed ovarian-adrenal hyperandrogenism (106–108, 134–136).

Androgen Secretion in Normal Women

In a study of normal women Moltz et al (108) determined the normal range of secretions. Random catheterization of the four glandular veins revealed no significant differences between the respective effluent concentrations of both the left and the right side. Ovaries have parallel androgen secretion during the early follicular phase; the same applies to the adrenal glands. Nonparallel hormone production is to be expected in the presence of preovulatory follicles or a corpus luteum (166). Dissimilar adrenal values may result from unpredictable pulsing (40, 112). The problems of data interpretation due to the episodic, circadian, and cyclic variations can be overcome by serial sampling and uniform timing of the procedure.

Nontumorous hyperandrogenemia

The ranges of concentration of testosterone and DHEAS in the peripheral as well as in the four glandular effluents overlap considerably in healthy and androgenized women. However, the mean values of all steroids in the peripheral blood are significantly elevated in women with non-neoplastic hyperandrogenemia as a group (107).

The differentiation between ovarian, adrenal, and combined hyperandrogenemia of non-neoplastic origin is calculated on the basis of catheterization studies in healthy women (108). Combined hypersecretion (41%) is the most frequent cause; purely ovarian (27%) or adrenal overproduction (12%) is identified less often; normal androgen output occurs in 20% of the patients. The relative incidence of ovarian or adrenal involvement in the etiology of non-neoplastic hyperandrogenemia is still under discussion (1, 25, 79, 80, 95–97, 156).

Polycystic Ovaries (Stein-Leventhal Syndrome)

Polycystic ovary (PCO) syndrome, thickened whitish cortex of the ovary combined with subcapsular cysts and gross enlargement of the organ, is now believed to be an individual response to androgen hypersecretion (141). The result of selective venous catheterization, sampling, and analysis of gradients reveals com-

bined ovarian-adrenal androgen overproduction in 21% and 12% of patients with PCO, respectively (56, 82, 110, 130, 140, 151). The percentage incidence of elevated ovarian/peripheral and adrenal/peripheral gradients (OPG, APG) does not deviate substantially from those found in a group of patients with nontumorous hyperandrogenemia. Gradient evaluation of the individual patient, however, showed that glandular hypersecretion of at least one androgen was present in 80%.

Ovarian Hyperthecosis

Hyperthecosis has been reported to be a tumorlike disease separate from PCO and characterized by pathognomonic histologic findings (78). The investigation after gradient analysis of all androgens has demonstrated a purely ovarian hypersecretion in six and an additional significant adrenal contribution in four patients (129). As in PCO, the cause of the condition is under discussion. Hyperthecosis most likely represents, as in PCO, an individual response to androgen overproduction.

Tumorous Hyperandrogenemia

Androgen-secreting ovarian and adrenal neoplasms may be the cause of virilism and related symptoms. Standardized bilateral ovarian or adrenal catheterization can locate the site of overproduction (Table **4**) (58, 90, 92, 102, 106, 109, 131, 150, 157). Before catheterization, peripheral testosterone levels should be in the tumor range (testosterone more than 1.5 ng/ml; DHEAS more than 6700 ng/ml). If the analysis of gradients after selective localization shows unilateral elevation of more than 2.7 ng/ml for testosterone, surgical exploration is indicated.

Selective catheterization is at the present time the most sensitive method for preoperative identification of an androgen-secreting neoplasm. The pathophysiologic mechanism of glandular androgen hypersecretion must be regarded as a continuous process without distinct boundaries between normal and non-tumorous conditions, as is the case in the PCO syndrome and hyperthecosis of the ovaries versus neoplastic disease.

Inferior Petrosal Sinus Sampling

Selective catheterization and bilateral inferior petrosal sinus venous sampling is performed in patients with clinically and biochemically suspected hormone-secreting micro-adenomas of the pituitary gland, if the source of excess hormone production is unknown, and cannot be localized by noninvasive imaging techniques. The hormone levels of the effluent veins of the pituitary gland and the calculation of gradients between selective and peripheral blood samples will

Table **4** Catheterization and pathologic results of seven patients with tumorous hyperandrogenism

Pt.	Age (yr)	Tp*	DHEAS$_p$*	Tov/tm*	Topg/tm*	Tumor (cm)	Histologic findings
1	26	5.7	600	16.6	5.9	0.6	Sertoli-Leydig
2	57	2.79	1730	10.4	6.6	1.5	Lipid cell
3	65	2.23	2630	4.7	3.4	1.0	Lipid cell
4	37	3.76	2640	5.0	2.9	1.5	Leydig cell
5	64	1.51	1850	4.7	2.7	2.2	Sertoli-Leydig
6	42	8.67	1290	(5.1)$^+$	?	1.0	Leydig cell
7	64	3.85	1400	8.1	4.2	1.8	Lipid cell

* Tp: peripheral testosterone; DHEAS$_p$: peripheral dehydroepiandrosterone sulfate; Tov/tm: testosterone level in the ovarian vein draining the tumor; Topg: ovarian-peripheral vein gradient of testosterone of the side of the tumor. All in ng/ml.
$^+$ Subselective sampling.

localize the side of the abnormality and distinguish pituitary-dependent hormone production from ectopic disease. The indications for the procedure are demonstrated in Table **5** (31, 32).

Anatomy

The anterior lobe of the pituitary gland, where most of the adenomas are located, is drained by the cavernous sinuses. These are interconnected by venous channels across the sella turcica. A network of veins cover the surface of the pituitary gland and drain laterally either into the intercavernous sinuses of directly into the cavernous sinus. They receive small veins from the anterior lobe of the gland. Thus, each half of the lobe drains into the corresponding side by the inferior petrosal sinus. A midline adenoma will theoretically have its effluents draining into the right and left inferior petrosal sinus equally, but this has not yet been found clinically (Fig. **9**) (33).

Technique

The procedure is carried out under local anesthesia by the percutaneous transfemoral approach using a 5 Fr catheter with a side hole close to its tip. Using a vascular sheath is advantageous in obese persons. The catheter is advanced under fluoroscopy through the right atrium into the right and the left internal jugular vein up to the base of the skull, and its tip is directed anteriorly and medially. If the direction of the X-ray beam is anteroposterior, the patients chin should be tilted upward as far as possible. In this projection the tip of the catheter can be seen fluoroscopically just below the maxillary sinuses (Fig. **10**). Pain in the ear that arises from the sensitive periostium of the jugular fossa occurs if the catheter is too high. If it is advanced too far, the tip will enter clival branches and pituitary effluents will be missed. Simple engagement of the catheter tip at the orifice of

Table **5** Inferior petrosal sinus sampling: Indications

Hypersecretion of ACTH
  Pituitary
  Ectopic
Hyperplasia of the adrenals
Hypersecretion of prolactin
Hypersecretion of thyrotropin

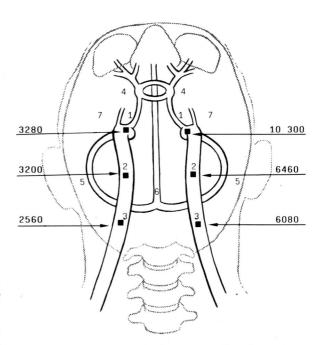

Fig. **9 Inferior petrosal sinus sampling for microadenomas of the pituitary gland. 1** inferior petrosal sinus, **2** jugular vein – middle, **3** jugular vein – proximal, **4** cavernous/intercavernous sinuses, **5** sigmoid sinus, **6** occipital sinus, **7** superior petrosal sinus ■ Prolactin levels in μU/ml/h of an infertile 35-year-old male patient with a left-sided prolactinoma of the pituitary gland

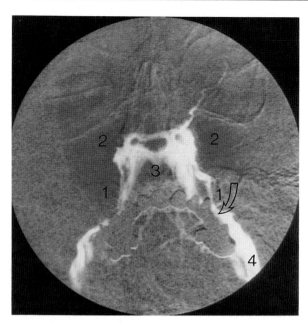

Fig. 10 Inferior petrosal sinus sampling for micro-adenomas of the pituitary gland. Digital subtraction angiography: contrast media is injected into the left inferior petrosal sinus. The tip of the catheter is marked (arrow). **1** inferior petrosal sinus, **2** maxillary sinus, **3** intercavernous sinuses, **4** jugular vein

the inferior petrosal sinus is adequate for sampling. A retrograde injection of diluted non-ionic contrast media is made, and digital subtraction images are taken thereafter to identify the position of the catheter. The pituitary gland reacts with increased hormone secretion to forceful angiography. Gentle retrograde venography should fill the ipsilateral cavernous sinus and the petrosal sinus of the opposite side immediately (31, 94, 128) (Fig. 10). Samples are taken either simultaneously from both sides using two catheters or with one catheter three times consecutively and separately on each side. An interval of 5 to 10 minutes between samplings will overcome pulsating hormone secretions.

Results

There are not yet enough experiences reported in the literature to give exact figures of the value of inferior petrosal sinus sampling (31, 32, 115, 128). The origin of an increased secretion of ACTH with clinical signs of Cushing's syndrome can be central (pituitary) or peripheral (carcinoma of the lung, pheochromocytoma, thymoma, carcinoma of the thyroid gland, carcinoid tumor, etc.; 5, 6, 48, 70, 84, 86, 98, 113, 117, 126, 145, 159, 167). A dexamethasone suppression test is one method of distinguishing central from ectopic hormone production, because ACTH-pro-

ducing pituitary tumors can be suppressed. Selective sampling usually locates the site of excessive hormone release.

Complications

Complications during or after inferior petrosal sinus sampling have not been reported yet. There are, however, reports of complications after contrast phlebography of the cavernous sinus, the veins of the base of the skull, and of the orbital veins, due to perforation of venous structures and thrombus formation (20, 63, 64, 128, 158). Gentle handling of the catheter by a skilled angiographer as well as the advantage of digital radiography with diluted non-ionic contrast media will avoid side effects.

Selective sampling of the inferior petrosal sinus is a useful method for locating micro-adenomas of the pituitary gland or ectopic hormone production not detectable by noninvasive imaging modalities. The side of tumor growth can be determined before surgical intervention to preserve pituitary function.

Thyroid Veins: Hyperparathyroidism

With the increase in spatial resolution of noninvasive imaging systems, venous sampling of parathormone-producing tumors is confined to the localization of ectopic parathyroid tissue. This ist most likely found in the mediastinum. When hypercalcemia has recurred after surgery, and US, CT, and MRI cannot find the mass lesion, selective sampling is the method of choice.

Anatomy

The parathyroid glands drain into the jugular and brachiocephalic veins via the superior, middle, and inferior thyroid veins (33, 34). The inferior thyroid veins can form a common trunk that drains into the left brachiocephalic vein at its superior aspect. Opposite to the thyroid trunk, the thymic veins enter the left brachiocephalic vein. The orifice of the azygos vein is found at the posterior wall of the superior vena cava. The right superior intercostal vein and the mediastinal veins are drained by the azygos system.

Technique

The technique is similar to that for sampling of the inferior petrosal sinus and has been described in the previous section. Samples are taken selectively from the superior, middle, and inferior thyroid veins, as well as from the jugular, subclavian, brachiocephalic, azygos, thymic, superior intercostal, and mediastinal veins (Fig. **11**) for determination of parathormone levels.

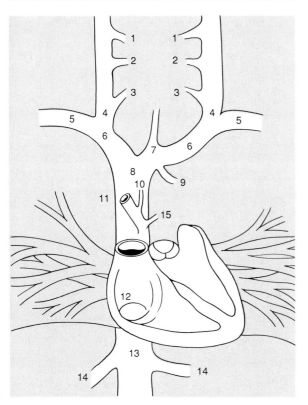

Fig. 11 Venous sampling for hyperparathyroidism.
1 superior thyroid vein, **2** middle thyroid vein, **3** inferior thyroid vein, **4** internal jugular vein, **5** subclavian vein, **6** brachiocephalic vein, **7** inferior thyroid trunk, **8** superior vena cava, **9** thymic vein, **10** superior intercostal vein, **11** azygos vein, **12** right atrium, **13** inferior vena cava, **14** renal vein, **15** mediastinal veins

Results

Mediastinal masses of parathyroid tissue occur in about 20% of cases examined for hyperparathyroidsm (111). The accuracy of the sampling technique in predicting the site of hormone excess ranges from 50 to 90%, according to published reports (29, 39, 116, 121, 125).

References

1. Abraham GE, Manlimos FS, The role of the adrenal cortex in hirsutism. In: James VHT, Serio M, Giusti G, Martini L, eds. The endocrine function of the human adrenal cortex. London: Academic Press, 1978:325.
2. Abrams HL, Siegelman SS, Adams DF, Sanders R, Finberg HJ, Hessel SJ, McNeil BJ. Computed tomography versus ultrasound of the adrenal gland: a prospective study. Radiology 1982;143:121.
3. Ahlberg NE, Bartley O, Chikedel N. Anatomic and roentgenographic study of communications of the renal vein in patients with and without renal carcinoma. Scand J Urol Nephrol 1967;1:43.
4. Almen T. Angiography with metrizamid. Acta Radiol [Diagn] (Stockh) 1977;355 (suppl) 419.
5. Aron DC, Tyrell JB, Fitzgerald PA, Findling JW, Forsham PH. Cushing syndrome: problems in diagnosis. Medicine (Baltimore) 1981;60:25.
6. Azzopardi J, Williams E. Pathology of nonendocrine tumors associated with Cushing syndrome. Cancer 1968;22:274.
7. Banks WA, Kastin AJ, Biglieri EG, Ruiz AE. Primary adrenal hyperplasia: a new subset of primary hyperaldosteronism. J Clin Endocrinol Metab 1984;3:783.
8. Battle DC, Kurtzman NA. Syndromes of aldosterone deficiency and excess. Med. Clin North Am 1983;67:879.
9. Bayliss RS, Edwards DM, Starer F. Complications of adrenal venography. Br J Radiol 1970;43:531.
10. Beard CM, Sheps SG, Kurland LT, Carney JA, Lie JT. Occurence of pheochromocytoma in Rochester, Minnesota 1950 through 1979. Mayo Clin Proc 1983;58:802.
11. Beckmann CF, Abrams HL. Circumaortic venous ring: incidence and significance. AJR 1979;132:561.
12. Beckmann CF, Abrams HL. Renal venography: anatomy, technique, applications, analysis of 132 venograms and a review of the literature. Cardiovasc Intervent Radiol 1980;3:45.
13. Beevers DG, Nelson CS, Padfield PL, et al. The prevalence of hypertension in an unselected population, and the frequency of abnormalities of potassium, angiotensin II and aldosterone in hypertensive subjects. Acta Clin Belg 1974;29:276.
14. Berglund G, Andersson O, Wilhelmsen L. Prevalence of primary and secondary hypertension: studies in a random population sample. Br Med J 1976;2:554.
15. Bertagna C, Orth D. Clinical and laboratory findings and results of therapy in 58 patients with adrenocortical tumors admitted to a medical center. Am J Med 1981;71:855.
16. Bookstein JJ, Conn J, Reuter SR. Intraadrenal hemorrhage as a complication of adrenal venography in primary aldosteronism. Radiology 1968;90:778.
17. Bravo EL. Pheochromocytoma. Primary Care 1983;10:75.
18. Bravo EL, Tarazi RC, Dustan HP, Fovad FM, Textor SC, Gifford RW, Vidt DG. The changing clinical spectrum of primary aldosteronism. Am J Med 1983;74:641.
19. Bray GA, De Quattro V, Fisher AA, et al. Catecholamines: a symposium. California Med 1972;117:32.
20. Brismar G, Brismar J, Cronquist S. Complications of orbital and skull base phlebography. Acta Radiol [Diagn] (Stockh) 1976;17:274.
21. Buvat J, L'Hermine C, Sailly F, Quandalle P, Houcke M, Racadot A. Cathéterisme sélectif combiné des veines ovariennes et surrénaliennes pour dosages hormonaux dans 25 cas de virilisme pilaire. J. Gynécol Obstét Biol Reprod (Paris) 1980;9:621.
22. Carney JH, Go VLW, Sizeniore GW, Hayles HB. Alimentary tract ganglioneuromatosis: a major component of the syndrome of multiple endocrine neoplasia type 2b. N Engl J Med. 1976;295:1287.
23. Conn JW, Knopf RF, Nesbit RM. Clinical characteristics of primary aldosteronism from an analysis of 145 cases. Am J. Surg 1964;107:159.
24. Copeland P. The incidentally discovered adrenal mass. Ann Intern Med 1983;98:940.
25. Cruikshank DP, Chapler FK, Yannone ME. Differential adrenal and ovarian suppression. Obstet Gynecol 1971;38:724.
26. Cryer PE. Physiology and pathophysiology of the human sympathoadrenal neuroendocrine system. N Engl J Med 1980;303:436.
27. Davidson JK, Morley P, Hurley GD, Holford MGH. Adrenal venography and ultrasound in the investigation of the adrenal gland: an analysis of 58 cases. Br J Radiol 1975;48:435.
28. Davies DL, Beevers DG, Brown JJ, Cumming AMM, Morton JJ, Robertson JIS, Titterington M, Tree M. Aldosterone and its stimuli in normal and hypertensive man: are essential hypertension and primary hyperaldosteronism without tumour the same condition? J Endocrinol 1979;81:79.
29. Davies DR, Ives DR, Shaw DG, Thomas BM, Watson L. Selective venous catheterization and radioimmunoassay of parathyroid hormone in the diagnosis and localization of parathyroid tumors. Lancet 1973;i:1079.
30. De Lellis RH, Wolfe HJ, Gagel RF, et al. Adrenal medullary hyperplasia. Am J Pathol 1976;83:177.

31. Doppmann JL, Oldfield E, Krudy AG, et al. Petrosal sinus sampling for Cushing's syndrome: anatomical and technical considerations. Radiology 1984;150:99.

32. Doppmann JL, Krudy AG, Girton ME, Oldfield EH. Basilar venous plexus of the posterior fossa: a potential source of error in petrosal sinus sampling. Radiology 1985;155:375.

33. Doppman JL. Parathyroid angiography In: Abrams HL, ed. Abrams angiography. Boston: Little, Brown, 1983:977.

34. Doppmann JL, Hammond WG. The anatomic basis of parathyroid venous sampling. Radiology 1970;95: 603.

35. Drury PL, Al-Pujaili EAS, Edwards CRW. The renin-angiotensin-aldosterone system. In: O'Riordan JLH, ed. Recent advances in endocrinology and metabolism; vol 2. Edinburgh: Churchill Livingstone, 1982:157.

36. Dunnick NR, Schaner EG, Doppman JL, Strott CA, Gill JR, Javadpour N. Computed tomography of adrenal tumors. AJR 1979;132:43.

37. Drury PL. Disorders of mineralocorticoid activity. Clin Endocrinol Metab 1985;14: 175.

38. Eagan RT, Page MI. Adrenal insufficiency following bilateral adrenal venography. JAMA 1971;215:115.

39. Eisenberg H, Palotta J, Sherwood LM. Selective arteriography, venography and venous hormone assay in diagnosis and localization of parathyroid lesions. Am J Med 1974; 56:810.

40. Eisenberg H. Radiologic techniques in tumor localization. In: De Groot LJ, Cahill GF Jr, Odwell WD, Martini L, Potts JT Jr, Nelson DH, Steinberg E, Winegard AJ, eds. Endocrinology; vol 3. New York: Grune and Stratton, 1979:2125.

41. El-Sherief MA, Hemmingsson A. Difficulties encountered in the examination of the adrenal glands. Ann Radiol 1979;22:414.

42. Elie G, Le Treut A, Dilhuydy MH, Brueneton JN, Calabet A. Computed tomography examination of the adrenal tumors in adults. J Radiol 1980;61:597.

43. Farber M, Millian VG, Turksoy RN, Mitchell GW. Diagnostic evaluation of hirsutism in women by selective bilateral adrenal and ovarian venous catheterization. Fertil Steril 1978;30:283.

44. Fellermann H, Dalakos TG. Remission of Cushing's syndrome after unilateral adrenal and ovarian venous catheterization. Fertil Steril 1978;30:283.

45. Ferriss JB, Beevers DG, Brown JJ, Davies DL, Fraser R, Lever AF, Mason P, Neville AM, Robertson JIS. Clinical, biochemical and pathological features of low-renin (primary) hyperaldosteronism. Am Heart J 1978;95:375.

46. Ferriss JB, Brown JJ, Fraser R, Lever AF, Robertson JIS. Primary aldosterone excess: Conn's syndrome and similar disorders. In: Robertson JIS, ed. Handbook of hypertension; vol 2. Amsterdam: Elsevier, 1983:132.

47. Field S, Saxton H. Venous abnormalities complicating left adrenal catheterization. Br J Radiol 1974;47:219.

48. Findling JW, Aron DC, Tyrell JB, Shinsako JH, Fitzgerald PA, Norma D, Wilson CB, Forsham PH. Selective venous sampling for ACTH in Cushing's disease. Ann Intern Med 1981;94:647.

49. Fisher CE, Turner FA, Horton R. Remission of primary hyperaldosteronism after adrenal venography. N Engl J Med 1971;285:334.

50. Francis IR, Glazer GM, Shapiro B, Sisson JC, Gross BH. Complementary roles of CT and I-MIBG scintigraphy in diagnosing pheochromocytoma. AJR 1983;141:719.

51. Fraser R, Beretta-Piccooli C, Brown JJ, et al. Response of aldosterone and 18-hydroxycorticosterone to angiotensin II in normal subjects and patients with essential hypertension, Conn's syndrome and non-tumorous hyperaldosteronism. Hypertension 1981;3 (suppl 1):187.

52. Gabrilove JL, Niccolis GL, Mitty HA. Virilizing adrenocortical adenoma by selective adrenal venography. Am J Obstet Gynecol 1976;125:180.

53. Geisinger MA, Zeich MG, Bravo EL, et al. Primary hyperaldosteronism: comparison of CT, adrenal venography and venous sampling. AJR 1983;141:299.

54. Geyskes GG, Puylaert CBAJ, Oei HY, Dorhout Mees EJ. Follow-up study of 70 patients with the renal artery stenosis treated by percutaneous transluminal dilatation. Br Med J 1983;287:333.

55. Glaser H, Weyman P, Sagel S, Levitt R, McClennan B. Nonfunctioning adrenal masses: incidental discovery on computed tomography. AJR 1982;139:81.

56. Goldzieher JW. Polycystic ovarian disease. Fertil Steril 1981;35:371.

57. Gottlob R. Über die lokalen Kontrastmittelschäden bei der Angiographie. Med Welt 1965;34:1893.

58. Granoff AB, Abraham GE. Peripheral and adrenal venous levels of steroids in a patient with virilizing adrenal adenoma. Obstet Gynecol 1979;53:111.

59. Gross MD, Shapiro B, Gretkin RJ, Freitas JE. Scintigraphic localization of adrenal lesions in primary aldosteronism. Am J Med 1984;77:839.

60. Guerin CK, Wahner HW, Gorman CA, Carpenter PC, Sheedy PF. Computed tomographic scanning versus radioisotope imaging in adrenocortical diagnosis. Am J Med 1983;75:653.

61. Haertel M, Probst P, Bollmann J, Zingg E, Fuchs WA. Computertomographische Nebennierendiagnostik. RöFo 1980;132:31.

62. Hamilton BP, Landsberg RJ. Measurement of urinary epinephrine in screening for pheochromocytoma in multiple endocrine neoplasia type II. Am J Med 1978;65:1027.

63. Hanafee WN. Orbital venography. Radiol Clin North Am 1982;10:63.

64. Hanafee W, Rosen LM, Weidner W, Wilson GH. Venography of the cavernous sinus, orbital veins, and basal venous plexus. Radiology 1965;84:751.

65. Hellman L, Nakada F, Curti J, Weitzman ED, Kream J, Rioffwarg H, Ellman S, Fukushima DK, Gallagher TF. Cortisol is secreted episodically by normal man. J Clin Endocrinol Metab 1970;30:411.

66. Hofer B, Triller J, Haertel M. Sonographisch-phlebographische Diagnostik der Nebenniere. RöFo 1978;129:686.

67. Hübener KH, Grehn ST, Schulze K. Indikation zur computertomographischen Nebennierenuntersuchung: Leistungsfähigkeit, Stellenwert und Differentialdiagnostik. RöFo 1980;132:37.

68. Huff TA. Clinical syndromes related to disorders of adrenocorticotropic hormones. In: Allen M, Mahesh V, eds. The pituitary: a current review. New York: Academic Press, 1977:153.

69. Hug MS, Pfaff M, Jaspersen D, Zicker JR, Kirschner MA. Concurrence of aldosterone, androgen, and cortisol secretion in adrenal venous effluents. J Clin Endocrinol Metab 1976;42:230.

70. Imura H, Matsukura S, Yamamoto H, Hirata Y, Nakai Y, Endo J, Tanaka A, Nakamura M. Studies of ectopic ACTH-producing tumors, II: clinical and biochemical features of 30 cases. Cancer 1975;35:1430.

71. Jacobs JB. Selective gonadal venography. Radiology 1969;92:885.

72. Judd HL, Spore WW, Talner LB, Rigg LA, Yen SSC, Benirschke K. Preoperative localization of a testosterone-secreting ovarian tumor by retrograde venous catheterization and selective sampling. Am J Obstet Gynecol 1974;120:91.

73. Kable WT, Yussman AA. Testosterone secreting adrenal adenoma. Fertil Steril 1979;32:610.

74. Kadir S. Loop catheter technique: a simple, rapid method for left adrenal vein catheterization. AJR 1980;131:31.

75. Kadir S, Athanasoulis CA. Renin determination in the management of renovascular hypertension. In: Athanasoulis CA, Pfister RC, Greene RE, Roberson GH, eds. Interventional radiology. Philadelphia: Saunders, 1982:299–310.

76. Kahn PC. Adrenal venography. In: Abrams HL, ed. Abrams angiography. Boston: Little, Brown 1974:941.

77. Kahn PC. Selective venography of the branches. In: Feris EJ, Hipona FA eds. Venography of the inferior vena cava and its branches. Huntington: Kiefer, 1973:154.

78. Karam K, Hajj S. Hyperthecosis syndrome. Acta Obstet Gynecol Scand 1979;58:73.

79. Kirschner MA, Jacobs JB. Combined ovarian and adrenal vein catheterization to determine the sites of androgen overproduction in hirsute women. J Clin Endocrinol Metab 1971;33:199.

80. Kirschner MA, Zucker IR, Jespersen D. Idiopathic hirsutism: an ovarian abnormality. N Engl J Med 1976;294:637.

81. Korobkin M, White EA, Kressel HY, Moss AA. Computed tomography in the diagnosis of adrenal disease. AJR 1979;132:231.

82. Korth-Schütz S, Levine LS, Merkatz LR, New MI. An unusual case of Cushing's syndrome, hilus cell tumor, and polycystic ovaries. J Clin Endocrinol Metab 1974;38:794.

83. Lamarque JL, Bruel LM, Lopez P, Michel JL, Rouanet JP, Senac JP, Bruno C, Roquefeuil C. Les complications de l'angiographie surrenalienne. Ann Radiol (Paris) 1979;22:401.

84. Lambers SWJ, de Jong FH, Birkenhäger JC. Evaluation of diagnostic and differential diagnostic tests in Cushing's syndrome. Neth J Med 1977;20:267.

85. Lecky JW, Wolfman NT, Modic CW. Current concepts of adrenal venography. Radiol Clin North Am 1976;14:309.

86. Liddle GW, Nicholson WE, Island DP, Orth DN, Abe K, Lowder SC. Clinical and laboratory studies of ectopic humoral syndromes. Recent Prog Horm Res 1969;25:283.

87. Lips KJM, Veer JVDS, Struyvenberg A, Alleman A, Leo JR, Wittebol P, Minder WH, Kooiker CJ, Geerdink RA, Van Waes PFGM, Hackeng WHL. Bilateral occurrence of pheochromocytoma in patients with the multiple endocrine neoplasia type 2a (Sipple's syndrome). Am J Med 1981;70:1051.

88. Lipsett M, Hertz R, Ross G. Clinical and pathophysiologic aspects of adrenocortical carcinoma. Am J Med 1963;35:374.

89. Lundt JO, Nielsen MD, Giese J, Gammelgaard PA, Hasner W, Hesse B, Tonnesen KH. Localization of aldosterone-producing tumors in primary aldosteronism by adrenal and renal vein catheterization. Acta Med Scand 1980;207:345.

90. Mack E, Sarto GE, Grummy AB, Carlson IH, Curet LB, Wu J. Virilizing adrenal angioneuroma. JAMA 1978;239:2273.

91. Marks LS, Maxwell MH. Renal vein renin: value and limitations in the prediction of operative results. Urol Clin North Am 1975;2:311.

92. Mandel FP, Voet RL, Weiland AJ, Judd H. Steroid secretion by masculinizing and "feminizing" hilus cell tumors. J Clin Endocrinol Metab 1981;52:779.

93. Manger WM, Gifford RW. Hypertension secondary to pheochromocytoma. Bull NY Acad Med 1982;58:139.

94. Manni A, Latshow RF, Page R, Santen RJ. Simultaneous bilateral venous sampling for adrenocorticotropin in pituitary dependent Cushing's disease: evidence for lateralization of pituitary venous drainage. J Clin Endocrinol Metab 1983;57:1070.

95. Maroulis GB, Lindstrom R, Abraham GE, Marshall JR. Testosterone and dihydrotestosterone secretion by the adrenal and ovary in hirsute patients. Endocrine Society Meeting, 1975:abstract 471:286.

96. Maroulis GB, Abraham GB. Concentration of androgens and cortisol in the various zones of the human adrenal cortex. In: Genazzani A, Thijssen JHH, Siiteri P, eds. Adrenal androgens. New York: Raven, 1980:49.

97. Maroulis GB. Evaluation of hirsutism and hyperandrogenemia. Fertil Steril 1981;36:273.

98. Mason AMS, Ratcliffe JG, Buckle RM, Mason AS. ACTH secretion by bronchial carcinoid tumors. Clin Endocrinol 1972;1:3.

99. Matthews JI, Feriss BL, Chertow BS, Howard WB. Adrenal adenoma with variable response to dexamethasone suppression and metyapone stimulation. J Clin Endocrinol Metab 1972;34:902–906.

100. McAreavey D, Brown JJ, Cumming AMM, Davidson JK, Duncan JG, Fraser R, Lever AF, Meek D, Robertson JIS. Preoperative localization of aldosterone-secreting adrenal adenomas. Clin Endocrinol 1981;15:593.

101. Meek DR, Duncan JG, McAreavey D. Computed tomography in the localization of aldosterone-secreting adrenal adenomas. Br J Radiol 1981;54:1039.

102. Meldrum DR, Abraham GE. Peripheral and ovarian venous concentrations of various steroid hormones in virilizing ovarian tumors. Obstet Gynecol 1979;53:36.

103. Melicow MM. One hundred cases of pheochromocytoma (107 tumors) at the Columbia-Presbyterian medical center. Cancer 1977;40:1987.

104. Mitty HA, Yeh HC, eds. Radiology of the adrenals with sonography and CT. Philadelphia: Saunders, 1982:56f.

105. Mödder UR, Lang R, Rosenberg J, Friedmann G. Computed tomography in the diagnosis of adrenal disease. Dtsch Med Wochenschr 1980;105:478.

106. Moltz L, Pickartz H, Sörensen R, Schwartz U, Hammerstein J. Ovarian and adrenal vein steroids in seven patients with androgen-secreting ovarian neoplasms: selective catheterization findings. Fertil Steril 1984;42:585.

107. Moltz L, Schwartz U, Sörensen R, Pickartz H, Hammerstein J. Ovarian and adrenal vein steroids in patients with nonneoplastic hyperandrogenism: selective catheterization findings. Fertil Steril 1984;42:69.

108. Moltz L, Sörensen R, Römmler A, Schwartz U, Hammerstein J. Ovarian and adrenal vein steroids in healthy women with ovulatory cycles: selective catheterization findings. J Steroid Biochem 1984;20:901.

109. Moltz L, Pickartz H, Sörensen R, Schwartz U, Hammerstein J. Sertoli-Leydig cell tumor and pregnancy: clinical, endocrine radiologic and electron microscopic findings. Arch Gynecol 1983;233:295.

110. Moltz L, Sörensen R, Römmler A, Schwartz U, Hammerstein J. Polyzystische Ovarien: eigenständiges Krankheitsbild oder unspezifisches Symptom? Geburtshilfe Frauenheilkd 1985;45:107.

111. Nathaniels EK, Nathaniels HM, Wang C. Mediastinal parathyroid tumors: a clinical and pathological study of 84 cases. Ann Surg 1970;171:165.

112. Nicolis GL, Babich AM, Mitty HA, Gabrilove LJ. Observation on the cortisol content of human adrenal venous blood. J Clin Endocrinol Metab 1974;38:638.

113. Northop G, Baldwin D, Farber LP, Schwartz TB. Dexamethasone suppression of urinary 17-hydroxycorticoids in a patient with an ACTH-producing bronchial adenoma. Presbyterian-St Lukes Med Bull 1970;9:43.

114. Oelkers W, Holze C, Molzahn M, Sörensen R. Renin, renin-substrate and angiotensin II concentration in renal venous blood. Contrib Nephrol 1976;3:150.

115. Oldfield EH, Chorous GP, Schulte HL, et al. Preoperative lateralization of ACTH-secreting pituitary microadenomas by bilateral and simultaneous inferior petrosal venous sinus sampling. N Engl J Med 1985;312:100.

116. O'Riordan JLH, Kendall BE, Woodland JS. Preoperative localization of parathyroid tumors. Lancet 1971;ii:1172.

117. O'Riordan JLH, Blanshard GP, Moxham A, Nabarro JDN. Corticotropin-secreting carcinomas. Q J Med 1966; 35:137.

118. Pick JW, Anson BH. Renal vascular pedicle: an anatomic study of 430 body halves. J Urol 1940;44:411.

119. Pickering TG, Sos TA, Vaughan ED, Case DB, Sealey JE, Harshfield GA, Laragh JH. Predictive value and changes of renin secretion in hypertensive patients with unilateral renovascular disease undergoing sucessful renal angioplasty. Am J Med 1984;76:398.

120. Pouliadis G, ed. Röntgenologische Diagnostik der Nebennieren. Stuttgart: Thieme 1980.

121. Powell D, Murray TM, Pollard JJ, Cope O, Wang C, Potts JT. Parathyroid localization using venous and radioimmunoassay. Arch Intern Med 1973;131:645.

122. Ratcliffe J, Knight R, Besser G. Tumor and plasma ACTH concentration in patients with and without the ectopic ACTH syndrome. Clin Endocrinol 1972;1:27.

123. Rossi P, Passariello R, Simonetti G, Rovighi L, Crecco M. Arterial and venous system of the adrenal glands: anatomical considerations. Ann Radiol (Paris) 1979;22:372.

124. Sample WF. Adrenal ultrasonography. Radiology 1978;127:461.

125. Satava RM, Beatrires DH, Scholz DH. Success rate of cervical exploration to hyperparathyroidism. Arch Surg 1975;110:625.

126. Schaaf M, Corriggan DF, Whaley RA, Czerwinski CL, Earll JM. Jugular-vein-sampling of ACTH. (letter to the editor). N Engl J Med 1977; 297:730.

127. Scherer K, Mischke W. Wertigkeit der Ultraschalluntersuchungen bei Tumoren und Hyperplasien der Nebenniere. RöFo 1978;128:609.

128. Schied H, Strack T, Günther R, Hey O, Küstner E, Krause B, Kahaly G, Thelen M, Beyer J. Selektive Blutentnahme aus

dem Sinus petrosus inferior mit digitaler Subtraktionsangiographie. RöFo 1986;144:627.

129. Schwartz U, Moltz L, Pickartz H, Sörensen R, Römmler A. Die Hyperthekose: eine tumorähnliche Ovarialveränderung bei androgenisierten Frauen. Geburtshilfe Frauenheilkd 1986;46:391–397.

130. Schwartz U, Moltz L, Hammerstein J. Die hyperandrogenämische Ovarialinsuffizienz. Gynäkologe 1981;14:119.

131. Scully RE. Ovarian tumors with endocrine manifestations. In: De Groot LJ, Cahill GF Jr, Odell WD, Martini L, Potts JJT, Nelson DH, Steinberger E, Winegard AJ, eds. Endocrinology; vol 3. New York: Grune and Stratton, 1979:1473.

132. Shea SD, Tse TF, Clutter WE, Cryer PE. The human sympathochromaffin system. Am J Physiol 1984;247:E 380.

133. Siegelmann S, Fishman E, Gatwood O, Goldman S. CT of the adrenal gland. In: Siegelmann S, Gatwood O, Goldmann S, eds. Computed tomography of the kidney and adrenals. Edinburgh: Churchill Livingstone, 1984:223

134. Sörensen R, Moltz L, Schwartz U. Technical difficulties of venous blood sampling in the differential diagnosis of female hyperandrogenism. Cardiovasc Intervent Radiol 1986;9:75.

135. Sörensen R, Moltz L. Technical aspects and anatomical difficulties of adrenal and gonadal phlebography and blood sampling. Amsterdam: Excerpta Medica 1980, (International congress series 550:78).

136. Sörensen R, Moltz L. Diagnostik bei progredientem Hirsutismus: Kathetertechnik und Ergebnisse. RöFo 1981;135:257.

137. Sos TA, Vaughan ED, Pickering TG, Case DB, Sniderman KB, Sealey J, Laragh JH. Diagnosis of renal vascular hypertension and evaluation of "surgical" curability. Urol Radiol 1982;3:199.

138. Sos TA, Pickering TG, Sniderman KW, Saddekni S, Case DB, Silane MF, Vaughan ED, Laragh JH. Percutaneous transluminal renal angioplasty in renovascular hypertension due to atheroma or fibromuscular-dysplasia. N Engl J Med 1983;290:274.

139. Stahl NL, Tesslink CR, Beauchamps G, Greenblatt RB. Serum testosterone levels in hirsute women: a comparison of adrenal, ovarian and peripheral vein values. Obstet Gynecol 1973;41:650.

140. Stahl NL, Teeslink CR, Greenblatt RB. Ovarian, adrenal and peripheral testosterone levels in the polycystic ovary syndrome. Am J Obstet Gynecol 1973;117:194.

141. Stein IF, Leventhal ML. Amenorrhea associated with bilateral polycystic ovaries. Am J Obstet Gynecol 1935;29:181.

142. Steiner AL, Goodman AD, Powers SR. Study of a kindred with pheochromocytoma, medullary thyroid carcinoma, hyperparathyroidism and Cushing's disease: multiple endocrine neoplasia, type 2. Medicine (Baltimore) 1968;47:371.

143. Stewart BH, Bravo EL, Haga J, Meaney TF, Tarazi RC. Localization of pheochromocytoma by computed tomography. N Engl J Med 1978;299:460.

144. Stockigt JR, Noakes CA, Collins RD, Schambelan M, Biglieri EG. Renal vein renin in various forms of renal hypertension. Lancet 1972;i:1194.

145. Strott CA, Nugent CA, Tyler FH. Cushing's syndrome caused by bronchial adenomas. Am J Med 1968;44:97.

146. Sutton H, Wyeth P, Allen AP, Thurtle OA, Hames TK, Cawley MID, Ackery D. Disseminated malignant pheochromocytoma: localization with iodine-131-labeled meta-iodobenzylguanidine. Br Med J 1982;285:1153.

147. Swales JD. Primary aldosteronism: how hard should we look? Br Med J 1983;287:702.

148. Tait JF, Tait SAS. Recent perspectives on the history of adrenal cortex. J Endocrinol 1979;83:3.

149. Thibonnier M, Sassano P, Dufloux MA, Plouin PF, Corvol P, Menard J. Test diagnostique simple de l'hyperaldosteronisme. Presse Med 1983;12:1461.

150. Trost BN, Koenig MP, Zimmermann A, Zachmann M, Müller J. Virilization of a post-menopausal woman by a testosterone secreting Leydig cell type adrenal adenoma. Acta Endocrinol (Copenh) 1981;98:274.

151. Tzingounis VA, Aksu MF, Natrajan PK, Greenblatt RB. The significance of adrenal and ovarian catheterization in patients with polycystic ovary syndrome. Int J Gynaecol Obstet 1979;17:78.

152. Valk TW, Frager MS, Gross MD, Sisson JC, Wieland DM, Swanson DP, Manager TJ, Beierwaltes WH. Spectrum of pheochromocytoma in multiple endocrine neoplasia: a scintigraphic portrayal using 131-I-metaiodobenzylguanidine. Ann Intern Med 1981;94:762.

153. Van Heerden JA, Sheps SG, Hamberger B, Sheedy PF, Poston JG, Remine W. Pheochromocytoma: current status and changing trends. Surgery 1982;91:367.

154. Vaughan NJA, Jowett TP, Slater JDH, Wiggins RC, Lightman SL, Ma JTC, Payne NN. The diagnosis of primary hyperaldosteronism. Lancet 1981;i:120.

155. Vaughan ED, Bühler FR, Laragh JH, Sealey JE, Baer L, Bard RH. Renovascular hypertension: renin measurement to indicate hypersecretion and contralateral suppression, estimate renal plasma flow, and score for surgical curability. Am J Med 1973;55:402.

156. Vermeulen A, Rubens R. Adrenal virilism. In: James VHT, ed. The adrenal gland. New York: Raven 1979:259.

157. Vermeulen A. Androgen secretion by adrenal and gonads. In: Mahesh VB, Greenblatt RB, eds. Hirsutism and virilism. Bristol: Wright, 1983:17.

158. Waga S, Kikuchi H, Handa J, Handa W. Carvernous sinus venography. AJR 1970;109:130.

159. Wahl TO, Kyner JL. Source of ACTH in Cushing's disease. N Engl J Med 1979;300:679.

160. Waltman AC, Courney WR, Athanasoulis CA. Techniques for left gastric artery catheterization. Radiology 1973;109:732.

161. Weinberger MH. Primary aldosteronism: diagnosis and differentiation of subtypes. Ann Intern Med 1984;100:300.

162. Weinberger MH, Grim CE, Hollifield JW, Kem DC, Ganguly A, Kramer NS, Yune HY, Wellman H, Donohue JP. Primary aldosteronism: diagnosis, localization and treatment. Ann Intern Med 1979;90:386.

163. Weinheimer B, Oertel G, Leppla W, Blaise H, Bette L. Die diagnostische Bedeutung der Nebennierenvenenkatheterisierung. Helv Med Acta 1963;30:482.

164. Weinheimer B, Oertel G, Leppla W, Blaise H, Bette L. Plasma steroid concentration of adrenal venous blood from women with and without hirsutism. Amsterdam: Excerpta Medica 1966. (International congress series 101:36.)

165. Welch TJ, Sheedy PFII, van Heerden JA, Sheps SG, Hattery RR, Stephens DH. Pheochromocytoma: value of computed tomography. Radiology 1983;148:501.

166. Wenk AC, White RI, Migeon CJ, Hsu TH, Barnes HV, Jones GS. Differential ovarian and adrenal vein catheterization. Am J Obstet Gynecol 1976;125:1000.

167. Werder KV, Scriba PC. Jugular-vein-sampling of ACTH (letter to the editor). N Engl Med J 1977;297:730.

168. White EA, Schambelan M, Rost CR, Biglieri EG, Moss AA, Korobkin M. Use of computed tomography in diagnosing the cause of primary aldosteronism. N Engl J Med 1980;303:1503.

169. Wilms G, Baert A, Marchal G, Goddeeris P. Computed tomography of the normal adrenal glands: correlative study with autopsy specimens. J Comput Assist Tomogr 1979;3:467.

170. Yeh HC. Sonography of the adrenal glands: normal glands and small masses. AJR 1980;135:1167.

Portal Venous System

G. P. Feltrin, R. Passariello, D. Miotto, and S. Pedrazzoli

Introduction

The clinical introduction of portal venous sampling began with Ingemansson et al. in 1975 (11) with the localization of insulinomas. The need to identify pancreatic endocrine tumors preoperatively is emphasized by the frequent inability of surgery to locate them. The first preoperative investigation consists of pancreatic arteriography. But very small tumors cannot be localized by arteriography, although those larger than 1 cm, and well-vascularized tumors such as glucagonomas and VIPomas, can usually be identified (2, 8, 13, 23, 26, 30, 32). Smaller tumors such as insulinomas and gastrinomas can often not be visualized, even when arteriography can show their hepatic metastases when present.

CT has the same dimension-related difficulties, and for this reason technical changes to improve detectability by CT have been proposed which would increase the density by dynamic scanning after a contrast bolus (14, 27). US does not offer extensive preoperative diagnostic prospects; its intraoperative applications (3, 9), when preoperative localization has already been established, are of much greater interest. When the tumor is neither visible nor palpable ("occult adenoma"), the surgical dilemma can be solved at laparotomy with a true "blind" pancreatic resection. For preoperative visualization, experience with digital angiography and MRI is still too limited to be evaluated with any accuracy (1, 10, 29).

In the last ten years, transhepatic portal sampling (THPS) has been used in several centers (4, 7, 10, 26), chiefly because other procedures frequently were unsuccessful. At the beginning of our experience, we systematically submitted almost all patients to THPS who were suspected of having a functioning pancreatic tumor. Recently, however, we have restricted its application to selected cases. In this chapter, we discuss the indications for the procedure and methods of application which will ensure that the best use is made of it.

Technique

About 130 patients were studied for pancreatic intestinal hyperendocrine syndrome at the university radiology departments in Padua and Rome between 1976 and 1988. All of them underwent arteriography and some of them were also examined using CT. CT was also used with the dynamic scan technique on a group of 32 of them (27). Transhepatic catheterization was applied in 76, and the results are presented in Table 1.

Table 1   Results of transhepatic portal sampling in 76 cases of functioning islet cell tumors

Tumors	Correct		Erroneous		Not proved	
	Localized	Diffuse	False localization	No localization	Localized	Diffuse
Insulinomas (n = 41)	29	3	4	5	–	–
	32/41 (78.0%)		9/41 (22.0%)			
Gastrinomas (n = 33*)	16	3	3	2	2[+]	7[‡]
	19/24 (79.2%)		5/24 (20.8%)			
Glucagonoma (n = 1)	1					
PPoma (n = 1*)	1					
76[§]	53/67 (79.1%)		14/67 (20.9%)		9	

* Diffuse hypergastrinism in the same patient
[+] Both and [‡] 4 patients underwent total gastrectomy; 3 patients not operated (medical treatment)
[§] 3 more patients: retained antrum syndrome

THPS is performed by introducing a needle with a plastic sheath into the patient's right side, usually at the level of the ninth intercostal space. When the sheath is correctly positioned in the portal trunk, the catheter is substituted through the sheath for another one without side-holes. The catheter tip is straight for catheterization of samples from the splenic, superior mesenteric, and portal veins or gently curved for selective introduction into the pancreatic veins. Before beginning the sampling in the main venous trunks and the selectively catheterized pancreatic veins, phlebography is performed to depict the whole venous tree of the pancreas and the main portal afferents in detail. Each sample consists of 4–5 ml of blood for the radioimmunoassay, and care is taken to number the samples and record the catheter position for each sample. This method has been reported previously (20). In the portal peripancreatic trunks we try to obtain at least 2 series of samples in two successive withdrawals.

In the early patients, embolization with fibrin was used in the parenchymal tract at the moment of withdrawal from the hepatic parenchyma to avoid possible significant hemorrhaging. Later, this precaution was shown to be superfluous and was dropped without any complications being observed.

Results

For *insulinomas* THPS results were evaluated on the basis of verification at surgery or at autopsy. We assessed the existence of secreting tumors in a pancreatic part, or insulin overproduction due to diffuse β-cell hyperplasia or nesidioblastosis, as positive results. Negative results were defined as the over-looking of tumors found subsequently at surgery, or their incorrect localization (Table 1).

Classification is more complex for the *Zollinger-Ellison syndrome:* positive results correspond to correct localization of gastrinomas confirmed at surgery. In the case of metastatic tumors, diffusely high values were also classified as positive results. Even 2 high values, one on the left and the other on the right of the superior mesenteric vein were considered as indicating diffuse pathology, corresponding to gastrin hypersecretion, as in diffuse β-cell hyperplasia. In two of our cases, the presence of gastrin-secreting cells in peripancreatic lymph nodes was shown (Fig. 1). These were considered to be diffuse hypersecretions similar to those in hypergastrinemia persisting after the removal of a preoperatively localized gastrinoma, because an occult gastrinoma had certainly been left. On the basis of diffusely high values of gastrin, some patients (3 cases) were not operated on, but were treated medically instead, and 4 underwent total gastrectomy as gastrinomas were not found at surgery (Fig. 2). These 7 cases of diffuse hypersecretion were assumed to be correctly localized, even though not strictly demonstrated. In fact, only an accurate serial search for the tumor in the part of the pancreas indicated by THPS and resected can be considered reliable. Nevertheless, diffusely high values in the pancreatic area were always assumed to be correct results, because pancreatic resection would have been unsuccessful (total pancreatectomy for a serial search for the gastrinoma could not be carried out). Negative results were false localizations (3 patients, surgically proved) or over-looked adenomas which were subsequently removed (2 patients).

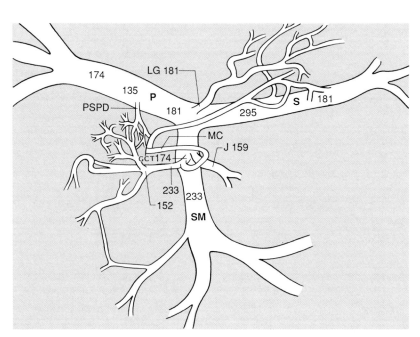

Fig. 1   Zollinger-Ellison syndrome. The samples indicate diffuse oversecretion of gastrin (values are expressed in pg/ml). Gastrinoma was not found at surgery. A left pancreatectomy was carried out, and multiple nodules of gastrin-secreting cells were found in the pancreatic specimen. Gastrin was also found in the peripancreatic and hepatic hilus lymph nodes (10 000–50 000 pg/g of tissue). GCT: gastrocolic trunk; LG: Left gastric vein; MC: middle colic vein; P: portal vein; PSPD: posterior superior pancreaticoduodenal vein; S: splenic vein; SM: superior mesenteric vein

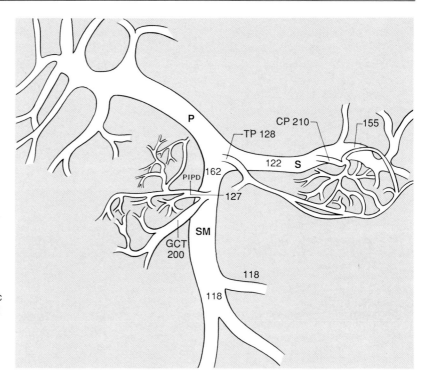

Fig. 2   Zollinger-Ellison syndrome with diffuse gastrin oversecretion. Gastrin values (pg/ml) are elevated both in selective samples and in the peripancreatic trunks. Primary tumor was not found; a total gastrectomy was carried out. CP: caudal pancreatic vein; GCT: gastrocolic trunk; P: portal vein; PIPD: posterior inferior pancreaticoduodenal vein; S: splenic vein; SM: superior mesenteric vein; TP: transverse pancreatic vein

Unverified cases included: patients with diffusely high gastrin values who were not operated on (3 cases) or underwent total gastrectomy (4 cases); and patients operated on in whom a tumor was not palpable at the site indicated by THPS (2 cases).

Evaluation of Hormonal Level

The highest hormonal values of the samples are interpreted differently by various groups of researchers (5, 19, 21, 22, 31). We took the average of the values of all samples as a reference value. Among them, the value that showed a hormonal activity 2 SD higher than average was considered significant and taken as the peak. This criterion was useful both for cases with generally low hormonal values, and for those with high values. It can also be considered to be of use for the various APUDoma (amine precursor uptake and decarboxylation) syndromes. The high number of samples usually required reduced the possibility of false positives and false negatives results.

Hypersecretions were correctly localized in 53 out of 67 proved cases (79.1%), while incorrect values were obtained in 14 (20.9%). These results are similar in the two most frequent syndromes: the values for correct localization were 78.0% for insulinomas and 79.1% for gastrinomas (Table 1, 3).

As previously stated, 2 peaks, on the left and on the right of the superior mesenteric vein, suggest diffuse hypersecretion and thus hyperplasia or nesidioblastosis. This was observed in 3 cases of hyperinsulinism, all confirmed after partial pancreatectomy. Similar findings were seen in 3 patients with hypergastrinism (Fig. 1). It is necessary to recognize hypersecretion on one or the other side of the superior mesenteric vein in order to guide surgical resection, which can then be performed not "blindly", as was previously the case but on the exact part of pancreas which contains a nonpalpable tumor.

Table **2**   Arteriography results in 56 patients with hyperinsulinism. 41 underwent transhepatic portal sampling

Correct	21	37.5%
Negative	33	62.5%
False positive	2	

Table **3**   Arteriography results in 39 patients with hypergastrinism. 33 underwent transhepatic portal sampling

THPS results (n = 33)		%
Correct: localized	16	78.8
diffuse	10+	
Erroneous: not localized	2	21.2
false localization	5±	
Arteriography results (n = 39)		
Correct	10	25.6
Negative	26	66.7
False positive	3	7.7
Hepatic metastasis	5/5	

+ 7 not verified; ± 2 not verified

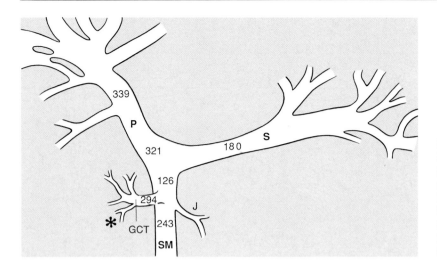

Fig. **3 Gastrinoma (0.9 cm) in the head of pancreas** (∗) Transhepatic portal sampling indicates the tumor site correctly. The sample from the head of the pancreas (GCT) confirms the peripancreatic trunk values (pg/ml). GCT: gastrocolic trunk; P: portal vein; S: splenic vein; SM: superior mesenteric vein

Correct Results

All patients in whom *correct localization,* that is demonstration of the unique site of hypersecretion (Fig. **3**) was achieved, underwent surgical intervention which confirmed the THPS results. Among these there were also 2 patients with hypergastrinism whose hormonal values were only high in the suprahepatic veins, not in the portal area, and in whom the tumor was shown to be in the liver only.

Diffuse hypersecretion was found in 3 patients with hyperinsulinism and in 10 with hypergastrinism. In the hyperinsulinism patients, THPS was confirmed at surgery: there were 2 β-cell hyperplasias and 1 nesidioblastosis. Of the 10 patients with diffuse gastrin hypersecretion, 3 had their THPS results confirmed at surgery: multiple adenomas (1 patient) and gastrin-secreting cells in lymphnode metastases were found (2 patients) (Fig. **1**). In 4 other cases, the primary tumor was not found, and patients underwent total gastrectomy (Fig. **2**). The other 3 patients were not submitted to surgery, since peaks both at the right and at the left side of the superior mesenteric vein were present. In these patients, medical treatment was of value.

Erroneous Results

Incorrect THPS values were obtained in 16 cases (only 14 proved).

Wrongly localized values (false positives), that is peaks indicating a location which proved to be incorrect, occurred in 9 cases: 4 insulinomas and 5 gastrinomas. In 2 of them, the adenoma was found elsewhere. In 2 other cases, a diffuse pathology was claimed (1 β-cell hyperplasia and 1 gastrin-secreting tumor with lymph node metastases). In 3 cases, no tumors were found either at surgery or autopsy at the sites indicated by THPS or at other sites, all of them accurately checked. These 7 cases could thus be

classified as false positives. The last 2 patients were submitted to gastrectomy alone, and an accurate search for tumor was not made.

Non-localized THPS values: in the other 7 cases of incorrect indication, the THPS results were treated as failures since, due to the absence of peaks, the values did not allow localization of a tumor which was subsequently found and removed in 6 (4 insulinomas and 2 gastrinomas), while in 1 case the missed localization was caused by anti-insulin antibodies.

THPS after Stimulation

In some patients, 3 with hyperinsulinism and 6 with hypergastrinism, the sampling was repeated after stimulation with arginin (2 patients), glucose (1 patient), secretin (5 patients), and bombesin (1 patient). In 4 patients, THPS results confirmed the high peaks previously obtained, in 3 patients they did not confirm the first results, and in the last 2 of the stimulated 9 cases, one stimulated by secretin and the other by arginin, THPS did not provide localization either before or after stimulation, and thus did not constitute a diagnostic improvement.

Suprahepatic Sampling

Suprahepatic vein catheterization was systematically performed in the early patients (7 with hyperinsulinism and 6 with hypergastrinism). All of them had correct THPS results, and increased values in the suprahepatic veins were only obtained in 2 cases of hypergastrinism, confirming the existence of gastrin-secreting hepatic tumors in both hepatic lobes (1 case) or in the right one only (1 case). In at least one of these patients, the absence of tumor in the pancreas, and low levels of gastrin in the pancreatic and peripancreatic samples suggested the presence of a primary hepatic gastrinoma. This was confirmed by

Table **4** Ability of selective pancreatic sampling to localize functioning endocrine tumors and confirm or exclude the pancreatic head. Correct results/number of samples; percentage of positive values given in brackets

Pathology	Peripancreatic main trunks	PSPD or ASPD	GCT or PIPD
Insulinomas	24/41 (58.5)	15/20 (75.0)	31/34 (91.2)
Zollinger-Ellison syndrome	18/24 (75.0)	7/11 (63.6)	13/20 (65.0)
Glucagonoma	1/1	1/1	
PPoma	1/1		
Total	44/67 (65.7)	23/32 (71.9)	44/54 (81.5)
Only APUDomas (non-metastatized)			
Head (confirmed)	13/30 (43.3)	14/18 (77.8)	19/26 (73.1)
Body and tail (head excluded)	22/25 (88.0)	5/7 (71.4)	20/21 (95.2)

the return of gastrin values to normal after resection. The other patient received clinical benefit from a gastrectomy. These 2 were therefore classified as having correctly localized THPS values.

Evaluation of Selective Samples from the Pancreatic Veins

The accuracy of samples taken in the peripancreatic trunks and selectively in the pancreatic veins is summarized in Table **4** according to the final result of each catheterization. As can be seen, the best results are given by samples from the gastrocolic trunk or posterior inferior pancreaticoduodenal vein, with 44 positives out of 54 (81.5%). The accuracy of samples from the posterior superior and anterior superior pancreaticoduodenal veins, with 23 positives out of 32 (71.9%), is slightly lower. All these values must be compared with the positive results from the peripancreatic trunks, which were 44 cases out of 67 (65.7%).

But with regard to accurate localizing values for the resected tumors, the effectiveness of selective samplings is as follows: to confirm the presence of tumor in the head of the pancreas, (Fig. **3**), gastrocolic trunk and posterior superior pancreaticoduodenal samples gave useful results in 73.0% and 77.7% of cases respectively, compared with the peripancreatic trunks, in which values were correct in only 43.3%. For adenomas situated in the body (Fig. **4**) or tail of the pancreas, samples from the peripancreatic trunks were correct in 88.0%, while

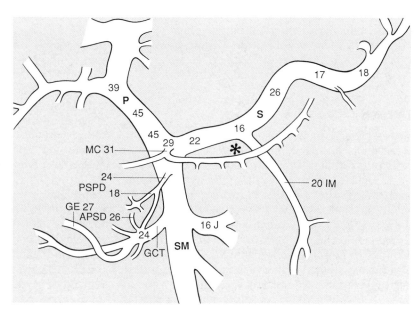

Fig. **4** **Insulinoma (1 × 0.5 cm) in the body of pancreas** (∗). Insulin oversecretion determines the peaks (μU/ml) in the portal vein very distally from the tumor site. Localization in the head of the pancreas is excluded by the PSPD, ASPD, and GCT samples. ASPD: anterior superior pancreaticoduodenal vein; GCT: gastrocolic trunk; GE: gastroepiploic vein; IM: inferior mesenteric vein; J: jejunal vein; MC: middle colic vein; P: portal vein; PSPD: posterior superior pancreaticoduodenal vein; S: splenic vein; SM: superior mesenteric vein

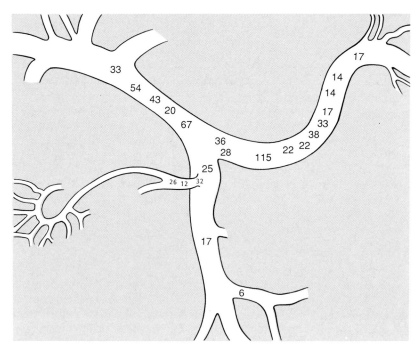

Fig. **5** **Hyperinsulinism.**
Transhepatic portal sampling indicates
hypersecretion in the left pancreas. A
partial pancreatectomy (body and tail)
guided by transhepatic portal
sampling was performed, and insulin
dropped to normal. The tumor was not
found in the pancreatic specimen.
Hormonal values are expressed in
pg/ml

selective samples exluded the head as the seat of the
tumor (Figs. **4** und **5**) in 71.4% when the sample was
taken from the posterior superior pancreaticoduodenal vein, and in 95.2% when it was taken from
the gastrocolic trunk.

Complications

When necessary, blood volume substitution can be
performed after THPS, as the total amount of blood
taken is often relevant not only to the number of
samples but also to the losses from the sheath during
the catheter substitution, and also for other outside
losses (wash-outs). It is also possible that the gallbladder may be punctured during the search for the
portal trunk. This may result in a choleperitoneum
which in turn may require urgent surgery. This
occurred in 1 patient not belonging to this series.

Current Trends

The accuracy of traditional arteriography in the
localization of functioning pancreatic tumors has
serious limitations (Tables **2, 3**). Varied results have
been reported in the literature, usually no better
than 80% (16, 17, 25); in particular, we observed
significant limitations with Zollinger-Ellison syndrome. The use of CT, especially with dynamic scan
technique, certainly improves the diagnostic possibilities of non-invasive techniques. The 77.0% of
insulinomas studied with dynamic scan were in fact
correctly visualized in a study carried out by one of
us (19). However, this procedure cannot be consid-

ered adequate for the study of these pathologies, as
is clear, not so much from the absolute value of its
accuracy, but by the fact that its accuracy is dependent on the size of the tumor. In this series, only
tumors with a diameter equal to or greater than 2 cm
could be recognized, and all false negatives had a
diameter less than that. Nevertheless, we cannot
ignore the fact that most tumors with a diameter over
2 cm would probably have been found at surgery
without preoperative localization. The most important problem thus concerns the difficulty of recognition during surgery, both with pancreatic exposure
and accurate palpation. US is advantageous if used
intraoperatively, but not in the preoperative phase
(9, 10, 14, 18, 28). On the other hand, the smallest
non-palpable tumors, among which all forms of diffuse islet cell hyperplasia and particularly Zollinger-
Ellison syndrome sustained by diffuse pathologies
must be included, maintain the need for indication
before any surgical approach. The frequent occurrence of interventions that end in a blind pancreatectomy is a serious question for all surgeons. We
should not only obtain morphologic information
about the pathology, but also an overall functional
definition of the hormonal disorder. Sometimes,
being able to recognize a diffuse hypersecretion
preoperatively suggests the advisability of medical
therapy rather than surgery, although the latter has
some indication in nesidioblastosis.

When Ingemansson et al. showed the potential of
THPS in localizing the site of a tumor, this technique
seemed to be the unique final possibility of achieving
an accurate preoperative diagnosis. For this reason

as a first step in our study, THPS was performed in all cases of hyperinsulinism and Zollinger-Ellison syndrome. However, as the technique is highly invasive and involves discomfort to the patient and difficulties for the operator, it can still not yet be proposed for all tumors. Both CT and arteriography have problems of interpretation due to false positive results, so that they are only suitable for preoperative diagnosis when their results correspond. However, in some cases, confirmation by THPS must be obtained. In our experience, for instance, a large mass at the jejunocolic junction recognized by arteriography and CT could well have been taken as an ectopic gastrinoma, but was in fact inflammatory, and a tumor was not found at surgery. In another patient with Zollinger-Ellison syndrome, a well-vascularized mass, seen with CT and arteriography at the head of the pancreas, was recognized as a Protein Precursor (PPoma) after surgical resection, but the patient remained hypergastrinemic. These situations, like diffuse hyperplasia, justify the need for THPS, which is therefore indicated in the following types of hyperinsulinism and hypergastrinism: tumors seen neither with arteriography nor CT; tumors seen by only one of these, with the other one negative.

Other more unusual pancreatic hypersecretion such as glucagonomas and VIPomas, have no valid indication for THPS, because they are usually well-vascularized and large. The only glucagonoma in our experience was well-visualized by arteriography.

THPS was valid, with correct tumor localization, in 78.0% of insulinomas and 79.1% of gastrinomas. These positive results are good mainly because diffuse hypersecretions are also included that cannot be diagnosed with CT and arteriography. This differs from what Günther et al. asserted (10). Among the erroneous results, false positives are of considerable importance. These are the cases in which localized hypersecretion was not subsequently confirmed at the same site. The criterion of choice in attributing validity to hormonal peaks is thus very important. Restrictive criteria tend to increase false negatives, while broader ones tend to increase false positives (22). Unfortunately, in insulinomas, we had a large number of non-localized tumors, nearly all of them with low insulin values. These were the first in our experience, and were connected with a small number of samples being taken. For this reason we are sure that the validity of THPS depends primarily on as high a number of samples as possible being taken from the largest possible number of veins (never less than 15). The only 2 missed gastrinomas were among the 24 cases proved by surgery. But it is possible that if all patients had been operated on, we would have had more missed localizations even among the gastrinomas. In fact the clinical characteristics of this type of tumor are significantly different from those of

insulinoma: the presence of diffusely high values, or the absence of peaks, rather than a guided resection of half of the pancreas (left or right) and the following accurate search for the tumor, indicate a gastrectomy. THPS thus plays a crucial role in the therapeutic decision (4). Indications for surgery are therefore slightly different for gastrinomas, due to clinical factors. However, a group of 10 out of 33 patients with Zollinger-Ellison syndrome (30.3%) with diffusely high values does not seem to be of negligible importance, even though it was impossible to obtain recovery through surgery (gastrinomas present a high incidence of metastatic diffusions not only at the liver, but frequently also in lymph nodes (Fig. **1**).

Among unproved cases, 6 were treated with total gastrectomy (Table **1**), without an actual verification of the presence of tumor at the indicated pancreatic level, as organ exploration was only done by palpation. When negative, this maneuver cannot be accepted as demonstrating the absence of tumor, as gastrinomas are often not palpable and may be so small that they are only found by serial section of the part of the pancreas removed, or when they are on the duodenal wall or surface of the pancreas. 3 of our gastrinomas had a diameter of 1–3 mm (Fig. **6**).

Significance of Selective Pancreatic Sampling

It has been questioned whether sampling should be carried out in the peripancreatic trunks alone or also selectively from the pancreatic veins (4, 15, 24). The impossibility of selectively catheterizing all or most of the veins of the body and tail of the pancreas reduced the problem to sampling from the veins of the head of the pancreas. This is almost always possible with the gastrocolic trunk and often also with the pancreatic veins that converge on it, while it is less frequently possible to catheterize the posterior superior pancreaticoduodenal vein, which usually drains alone into the portal vein. This portal outlet is sometimes missed, because the vein itself drains more proximally, at the portal trunk bifurcation or in the right branch, too proximally with respect to the point of entrance of the catheter into the portal vein (Fig. **7**).

Angiographic demonstration of an anomalous anatomic situation was possible by injecting selectively from the gastrocolic trunk into the posterior inferior or posterior anterior pancreaticoduodenal veins, which indicate the configuration of the superior pancreaticoduodenal vein through an anastomotic network. Catheterization of the veins of the head of the pancreas represents the correct exploration of at least one of the two halves of the pancreas, which can then be resected not blindly, but following the THPS indications, even when the tumor is not easy to find by palpation at the site indicated (6).

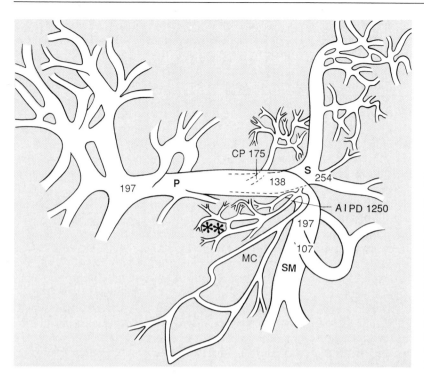

Fig. 6 **Zollinger-Ellison syndrome.** Two gastrinomas (0.2–0.1 cm) in the duodenal wall (∗). The superior mesenteric vein is retracted on the left due to a previous intervention (partial gastrectomy). Transhepatic portal sampling correctly indicates the site of the tumor only in samples from the head of the pancreas. No peaks were found in the peripancreatic trunks. AIPD: anterior inferior pancreaticoduodenal vein; CP: caudal pancreatic vein; MC: middle colic vein; P: portal vein; S: splenic vein; SM: superior mesenteric vein

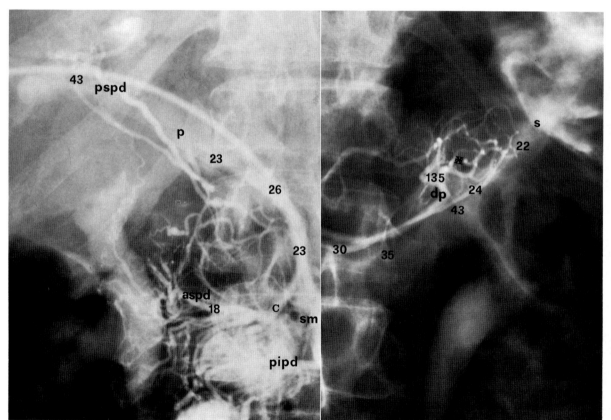

Fig. 7 **Insulinoma (1 cm) in the tail of the pancreas** (∗). Left: phlebography of the anterior superior pancreaticoduodenal vein shows the posterior inferior and posterior superior pancreaticoduodenal veins, which drain very proximally in the portal vein (P) at its bifurcation. Right: phlebography of the dorsal pancreatic vein. The values of the insulin concentration (μU/ml) in some samples are reported. The value in the anterior superior pancreaticoduodenal rules out a location in the head of the pancreas. The dorsal pancreatic vein values confirm a localized insulinoma, while the peripancreatic samples show no peaks. Arteriography and computed tomography were negative. ASPD: anterior superior pancreaticoduodenal vein; C: catheter; DP: dorsal pancreatic vein; PIPD: posterior inferior pancreaticoduodenal vein; PSPD: posterior superior pancreaticoduodenal vein; S: splenic vein; SM: superior mesenteric vein

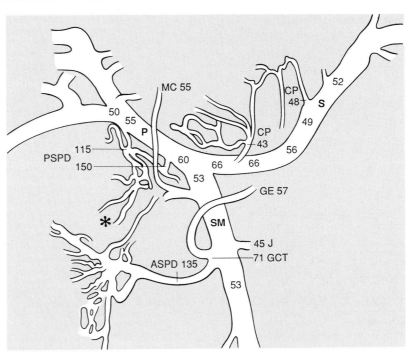

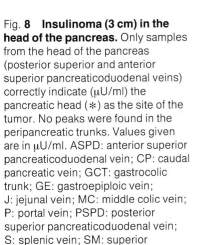

Fig. **8 Insulinoma (3 cm) in the head of the pancreas.** Only samples from the head of the pancreas (posterior superior and anterior superior pancreaticoduodenal veins) correctly indicate (µU/ml) the pancreatic head (∗) as the site of the tumor. No peaks were found in the peripancreatic trunks. Values given are in µU/ml. ASPD: anterior superior pancreaticoduodenal vein; CP: caudal pancreatic vein; GCT: gastrocolic trunk; GE: gastroepiploic vein; J: jejunal vein; MC: middle colic vein; P: portal vein; PSPD: posterior superior pancreaticoduodenal vein; S: splenic vein; SM: superior mesenteric vein

Thus, the possibility of deciding on tumor removal intraoperatively, even when neither palpation nor US are capable of indicating it exactly is supported by the certainty that THPS suggests a body and tail resection (Fig. **5**) or a cephalic duodenopancreatectomy, as the treatment of choice. This perspective gives a choice other than blind pancreatectomy that was performed for many years in similar circumstances, and cannot be justified today without a transhepatic investigation. For this reason, in our experience the values in the peripancreatic veins must be validated, with confirmation or exclusion of the pancreatic head as the tumor site. The peripancreatic trunks gave localizing results in 44 out of 67 patients (65.7%), while samples from the posterior superior pancreaticoduodenal vein and gastrolic trunk were correct in 71.8% and 81.4% respectively. These percentages were obtained from the combined confirmation and exclusion ability of the three groups of samples and only refer to the tumors localized and later identified (Table **4**).

Low positive values in the peripancreatic trunks have to be explained by an incomplete mixing of the hormone-rich blood when it converges in the main trunk. The laminar portal flow gives complete mixing only distally (4, 12). So differing from the experiences of Cho et al. (4), we expected that higher possibilities of erroneous results in the peripancreatic trunk samples would occur for pancreas head APUDomas (Figs **6, 8**). In fact, considering only the confirmation, tumors of the head of the pancreas were localized by peripancreatic trunk samples in

43.3%, by posterior superior pancreaticoduodenal vein samples in 77.7%, and by gastrocolic trunk samples in 73.0%. Conversely the ability to exlude the pancreatic head for tumors found elsewhere, was 88.0% for peripancreatic trunks, 95.2% for the gastrocolic trunk and 71.4% for the posterior superior pancreaticoduodenal vein samples.

Exclusion of the head of the pancreas could be obtained if insulin levels in the posterior superior pancreaticoduodenal samples were very low. But selective pancreas head blood from the posterior superior pancreaticoduodenal vein not diluted by portal non-pancreatic blood may contain normal insulin release from normal pancreatic tissue, and this would reduce the difference in hormonal measurements between the posterior superior pancreaticoduodenal vein values and the main trunk peaks in portions of the pancreas outside of the pancreas head.

In fact there were mistakes in 2 cases of insulinoma (1 in the pancreas body and 1 in the tail), where posterior superior pancreaticoduodenal values were elevated because during the sampling there was apparently an unforeseen insulin release. In any case, it is mandatory to catheterize one of the pancreas head veins, and not just the peripancreatic ones. However, selective sampling potentially reduces erroneous peripancreatic results, with an improvement in correct results from 65 to 81% (Table **4**), and is therefore highly recommended in THPS, contradicting the experience of Cho and co-workers (4).

Suprahepatic Sampling

Suprahepatic sampling should also be considered, to demonstrate the endocrine features of hepatic metastases detected by CT or US.

Sampling after Stimulation

With repetition of sampling after stimulation, the subsequent improvement of correct results we expected theoretically was not observed. Besides, it is quite hard to repeat all the samples at the same time as the induced stimulation. All stimulations were discontinued after our early studies. Conversely, sampling repetition was subsequently performed in order to obtain more selective and more serial samples from the peripancreatic trunks.

Conclusions

In conclusion, the best indications for THPS are:

Insulinomas. When arteriography or CT, or both, are negative; in the case of an unfruitful search for nonpalpable tumors by intraoperative US, THPS-guided partial pancreatectomy must be considered; in patients previously unsuccessfully operated.

Gastrinomas. In all patients, for the high incidence of diffuse hypersecretion (10 cases out of 33, 30.3%, 3 proved and 7 not strictly verified at surgery). Under these circumstances, location and removal of a tumor correctly visualized by arteriography or CT does not assure recovery. The difficulties of the examination are compensated for by the possible avoidance of intervention when medical therapy is appropriate, or by a simplification of it through total gastrectomy.

In the less common cases of glucagonomas and other APUDomas, easy to localize through CT or arteriography, THPS is usually not indicated. For APUDomas, digital arteriography or MRI do not represent an alternative diagnostic method, as their use in this respect needs to be tested further.

References

1. Baert AL, De Somer FM, Wilms GE. Value of intravenous digital subtraction angiography to demonstrate hypervascular endocrine tumors: report of two cases. Cardiovasc Intervent Radiol 1984;7:193–195.
2. Breatnach ES, Han SY, Rahatzad MT, Stanley RJ. CT evaluation of glucagonomas. J Comput Assist Tomogr 1985;9:25–29.
3. Charboneau JW, James EM, van Herdeen JA, Grant CS, Sheedy PF. Intraoperative real-time ultrasonographic localization of pancreatic insulinoma: initial experience. J Ultrasound Med 1983;2:251–254.
4. Cho KJ, Vinik AI, Thompson NW, Shields JJ, Porter DJ, Brady TM, Cadavid G, Fajans SS. Localization of the source of hyperinsulinism: percutaneous transhepatic portal and pancreatic vein catheterization with hormone assay. AJR 1982;139:237–245.
5. Dagget PR, Kurtz AB, Morris DV, Goodburn EA, LeQuesne LP, Nabarro JDN. Is preoperative localization of insulinomas necessary? Lancet 1981;i:483–486.
6. Doppman JL, Brennan MF, Dunnick NR, Kahn CR, Gorden P. The role of pancreatic venous sampling in the localization of occult insulinomas. Radiology 1981;138:557–562.
7. Feltrin GP, Passariello R, Miotto D, Pedrazzoli S, Sintich V, Rossi P, Simonetti G. Transhepatic portal catheterization (TPC) in the management of pancreatic apudomas. In: Abdomen and gastrointestinal tract. Proceedings of the 15th International Congress of Radiology, Brussels. Luxemburg: Interimages, 1984:232–243.
8. Fulton RE, Sheedy PF II, McIlrath DC, Ferris DO. Preoperative angiographic localization of insulin-producing tumors of the pancreas. AJR 1975;123:367–377.
9. Günther RW, Klose KJ, Rückert K, Kuhn FP, Beyer J, Klotter HJ, Cordes U. Islet-cell tumors: detection of small lesions with computed tomography and ultrasound. Radiology 1983;148:485–488
10. Günter RW, Klose KJ, Rückert K, Kuhn FP, Klotter HJ. Localization of small islet-cell tumors: preoperative ultrasound, computed tomography, arteriography, digital subtraction angiography, and pancreatic venous sampling. Gastrointest Radiol 1985;10:145–152.
11. Ingemansson S, Lunderquist A, Lunderquist I, Lovdahl R, Tiblin S. Portal and pancreatic vein catheterization with radioimmunologic determination of insulin. Surg Gynecol Obstet 1975;141:705–711.
12. Ingemansson S. Invited commentary. World J Surg 1984;8:581–582.
13. Korobkin MT, Palubinskas AJ, Glickman MG. Pitfalls in arteriography of islet cell tumors of the pancreas. Radiology 1971;100:319–328.
14. Krudy AG, Doppman JL, Jensen RT, Norton JA, Collen MJ, Gardner JD, McArthur K, Gorden P. Localization of islet-cell tumors by dynamic CT: comparison with plain CT, arteriography, sonography, and venous sampling. AJR 1984; 143:585–589.
15. Lunderquist A, Ericcson M, Ingemansson S, Larsson LI, Reichardt W. Selective pancreatic vein catheterization for hormone assay in endocrine tumors of the pancreas. Cardiovasc Radiol 1978;1:117–124.
16. Von Luska G, Zick R, Otten G, Mitzkat HJ. Perkutantranshepatische Pfortadersondierung (PTP) zur Diagnostik hormonproduzierender Tumoren im Splanchnikusgebiet. RöFo 1981;135:566–571.
17. Madsen B, Hansen ES. Correlation between angiographic diagnosis and histology of pancreatic insulinomas. Br J Radiol 1970;43:185–192.
18. Norton JA, Sigel B, Baker AR. Localization of an occult insulinoma by intraoperative ultrasonography. Surgery 1985;97:381–384.
19. Passariello R, Feltrin GP, Miotto D, Pedrazzoli S, Rossi P, Simonetti G. Transhepatic portal catheterization with pancreatic venous sampling versus angiography in the localization of pancreatic functioning tumors. Front Eur Radiol 1982;1:51–69.
20. Pedrazzoli S, Feltrin GP, Dodi G, Miotto D, Pasquali C, Cevese PG. Usefulness of transhepatic portal catheterization in the treatment of insulinomas. Br J Surg 1980;67:557–561.
21. Pedrazzoli S, Feltrin G. Ruolo del cateterismo transepatico dell'albero portale nella localizzazione degli insulinomi. In: Biliotti GC, ed. Iperinsulinismo. Padova: Piccin, 1985: 217–232.
22. Pedrazzoli S, Pasquali C, Miotto D, Feltrin GP, Petrin P. Transhepatic portal sampling (THPS) for preoperative localization of insulinomas. Surg Gynecol Obstet 1987;165:101–106.
23. Pistolesi GF, Frasson F, Fugazzola C, Taddei GT, Caresano A. Angiographic diagnosis of endocrine tumors of the pancreas. Radiol Clin (Basel) 1977;46:401–421.
24. Reichardt W, Ingemansson S. Selective vein catheterization for hormone assay in endocrine tumors of the pancreas. Acta Radiol [Diagn] (Stockh.) 1980;21:177–187.
25. Robins JM, Bookstein JJ, Oberman HA, Fajans JJ. Selective angiography in localizing islet cell tumor of the pancreas. Radiology 1973;106:525–528.
26. Roche A, Raisonnier AC, Gillon-Savouret MC. Pancreatic venous sampling in localizing insulinomas and gastrinomas: procedure and results in 55 cases. Radiology 1982; 145:621–627.

27. Rossi P, Baert A, Passariello R, Simonetti G, Pavone P, Tempesta P. CT of functioning tumors of the pancreas. AJR 1985;144:57–60.
28. Shawker TH, Doppman JL, Dunnick NR, McCarthy DM. Ultrasonic investigation of pancreatic islet-cell tumors. J Ultrasound Med 1982;1:193–200.
29. Stark DV, Moss AA, Goldberg HI, Deveney CW. CT of pancreatic islet cell tumors. Radiology 1984;150:491–494.
30. Stefanini P, Carboni M, Patrassi N, Basoli A. Beta islet cell tumors of the pancreas: results of a study on 1067 cases. Surgery 1974;75:579–609.
31. Tseng Hsien-chiu, Yao Chong-zheng, Zhong Shou-xian, Zhang Jian-xi, Zhu Yu. Percutaneous transhepatic portal vein catheterization for localization of insulinoma. World J Surg 1984;8:575–582.
32. Wawrukiewicz AS, Rosch J, Keller FS, Lieberman DA. Glucagonoma and its angiographic diagnosis. Cardiovasc Intervent Radiol 1982;5:318–324.

Percutaneous Management of Fluid Collections

Percutaneous Drainage Technique

S. G. Gerzof

Three developments have combined to allow the development of drainage of abdominal abscesses: effective antibiotics, sectional imaging for guidance, and atraumatic catheter introduction techniques. CT and US now demonstrate the anatomy for planning safe aspiration routes and experience has shown that abscesses can be aspirated without fear of dire consequences.

The application of sectional imaging to guide percutaneous needle procedures was introduced by Holm (15) who described the use of US as a guide for percutaneous puncture in 1972, and established it as a routine technique in 1973 (16). In 1974, Smith reported the first series of abdominal abscesses which were diagnosed by ultrasonically guided percutaneous aspiration (24). By 1976, Haaga described the value of CT for precise localization of biopsies (13) and then for detection and aspiration of abscesses (14). In 1977, Gronvall combined ultrasound guidance and needle aspiration, and reported the application of the Seldinger technique for introduction of indwelling catheters into the abdominal abscess (12). In none of these reports was there a case of significant septicemia, rupture of an abscess, or dissemination of sepsis.

By 1978, Gerzof was advocating percutaneous catheter drainage as a routine treatment of choice for abscesses (4), and by 1979 was beginning to challenge the results of operative drainage (5). Despite the initial guarded response from surgeons (27), percutaneous catheter drainage has now been acknowledged to be "one of the great advances in abdominal surgery in the past few years" (28).

Pathophysiology of Percutaneous Drainage

Abscesses are well-defined fluid masses composed of necrotic debris, leukocytes, bacteria, and fluid exudate. The abscess wall is a well-defined structure composed of fibrin, inflammatory cells, and dilated blood vessels, which acts as a physiologic and mechanical barrier to contain the infection. By the time the radiologist identifies a formed abscess, the wall has already organized. Percutaneous drainage maintains the integrity of the abscess wall as a barrier preventing dissemination of sepsis. This is done by the introduction of a drainage catheter with decompression and evacuation of pus as atraumatically as possible.

Abscesses are space-occupying lesions which have greater internal pressure than the surrounding structures. As a result, they exercise a right of domain and displace surrounding structures (Fig. 1). As abscesses expand, they often lie against the parietal peritoneum. Thus, abscesses usually create safe percutaneous routes for diagnostic aspiration and insertion of indwelling catheters. Because the abscess walls are pliable and their contents are fluid, as soon as the abscess is decompressed by the catheter, the walls collapse so that there is no residual mass.

US Characteristics of Abscesses

The ultrasound characteristics of abscesses (3, 6, 17, 18, 20, 22) include: a well-defined, oval, round, or elliptical mass with an anechoic or hypoechoic fluid center and good through-transmission of sound; a moderately echogenic fluid mass, caused by floating debris; a highly echogenic mass caused by cholesterol and lipoprotein aggregates, as well as debris; a well-defined mass with a fluid-fluid level caused by layering of internal debris; a fluid mass with multiple areas of highly echogenic foci caused by small gas bubbles and an air-fluid level within the abscess which can be seen only by transmission of the ultrasound beam from a point below the level of the fluid level (6–11). These ultrasound characteristics are so widely variable as to be quite non-specific. Because of the limitations of ultrasound (reflection by bone, operator-dependency, non-transmission by gas), and the difficulty of performing adequate examinations in the postoperative abdomen (open wounds, suture lines, stomas, and postoperative ileus), we prefer CT as the primary diagnostic modality for abscess detection.

CT Characteristics of Abscesses

The CT signs of abscesses have been well described (2, 4, 5, 19, 21). They usually appear as well-defined, relatively low-attenuation fluid masses which displace rather than infiltrate surrounding structures (Fig. 1). They usually have a low (0-20 Hounsfield units) attenuation, but may have a higher attenuation if there has been hemorrhage or tissue necrosis. Abscesses usually have a well-defined higher attenu-

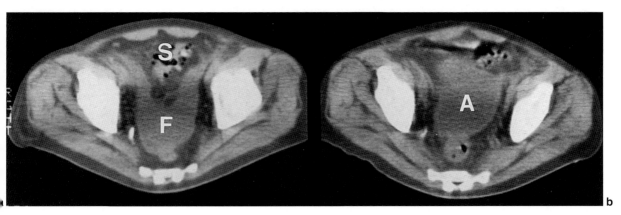

Fig. **1**   **Pelvic fluid evolving into an abscess**
a Free fluid (F) fills the pelvis and conforms to its peritoneal space. The sigmoid colon (S) indents the fluid anteriorly
b After infection developed three weeks later, the infected fluid has formed an abscess (A) with thicker, high-attenuation, convex walls. The abscess now exerts right of domain over the sigmoid, which it displaces anteriorly

ation wall which enhances variably with intravenous iodinated contrast. We have termed this the "rind sign" (4), and, although non-specific, it is commonly found in abscesses. It is due to luxury perfusion of the dilated inflammatory vessels in the abscess wall. CT demonstrates both the mottled pattern of inappropriate gas bubbles as well as well-defined air-fluid levels. In dealing with extraluminal, inappropriate gas, CT has the advantage over ultrasound, because it can visualize the normal bowel and define the extraluminal gas as inappropriate.

Differential Diagnoses

None of the CT and ultrasound signs are specific for abscess. This is particularly true in the postoperative abdomen, where a variety of intra-abdominal and retroperitoneal fluid collections must be considered. The differential diagnoses include postoperative fluid collections such as bilomas, lymphoceles, urinomas, seromas, and hematomas, as well as simple cysts of any origin, pancreatic pseudocysts, and dilated fluid-filled loops of bowel. Because these varieties of fluid collections cannot be distinguished from one another, and because of the importance of correct diagnosis for instituting proper therapy, definitive diagnosis should be made by needle aspiration. If a fluid-filled loop of bowel is considered, delayed scanning, or scanning in the prone or decubitus position may allow contrast and gas to enter that structure and identify its enteric origin.

Methodology

Percutaneous drainage of abscesses has five steps:
- Detection
- Route planning
- Diagnostic aspiration
- Catheter insertion
- Catheter management

Detection

Because of the advantages of CT, we emphasize its use in detection and route planning. Our routine protocol for CT detection of intra-abdominal abscesses consists of the sequence of 1 cm scans at 2 cm intervals extending from the symphysis pubis to the diaphragm. To identify the stomach and small bowel, 500 ml of 2% gastrografin is given orally over one hour prior to scanning. Since the colon is usually easily identified, rectally administered contrast is seldom necessary except when an appendiceal, perirectal or pericolic diverticular abscess is suspected. In this case, we perform a water-soluble iodinated contrast enema with fluoroscopy prior to CT, rather than giving the contrast enema on the CT scanner. This allows direct fluoroscopic control of the contrast, and decreases the potential for perforation. Intravenous contrast is given to better delineate the abscess wall from surrounding structures.

Route Planning

Once a suspected abscess is detected on the scans, a safe percutaneous access route must be planned. This is usually the shortest direct route from the skin to the abscess. However, oblique approaches are often necessary to avoid nearby vital structures. CT is the ideal modality for route planning, since it simultaneously demonstrates the abscess, major vessels, and loops of bowel, and is not blocked by overlying bone or bowel gas.

Three parameters should be determined to define the drainage route: the cutaneous entry site, the center of the abscess, and the distance and angle between them. Once this route is defined, the radiologist should attempt to follow it as closely as possible with the aspiration needle.

Diagnostic Aspiration

After the route has been planned, aspiration is performed. We measure the angle of entry from the CT scan and transfer this angle to the arms of a goniometer (a plastic variable angle measurer) to be used as a guide during the procedure. We also measure the exact distance from the skin to the abscess. This distance is then transferred to the aspiration needle with a sterile needle stop. After informed consent, and after routine preparation and draping of the skin, local anesthesia is obtained with 5 ml of 2% lignocaine. A 4 mm incision is made with a #11 scalpel blade.

We recommend a 20-gauge Teflon sleeve needle for diagnostic aspiration. We prefer it to the 22-gauge fine needle, since the lumen of the latter is often too small to aspirate viscous pus. We do occasionally use a 22-gauge needle when the route is uncertain or when bowel might be traversed.

The needle is then positioned exactly over the route planned from the CT scan. We have an assistant visually sighting across the goniometer to indicate appropriate corrections when significant angulation is required. The needle is then advanced along the route in a single motion.

A 5 ml sample of fluid is aspirated and sent for immediate Gram stain and aerobic, anaerobic, and fungal cultures. Air should be expelled from the transport syringe so that it does not interfere with anaerobic culture. If the fluid collection is sterile, we aspirate it entirely and remove the needle.

Techniques for Catheter Insertion

There are a variety of commercially available catheters now available for percutaneous drainage. Most are variations of either a modified Seldinger technique or a Trocar catheter technique.

The Seldinger technique uses a 0.035 guide wire inserted through the Teflon sleeve of the aspiration needle, followed by a dilator and then an 8 Fr pigtail catheter (Fig. 2). This is probably the smallest size one can use to effectively drain an abscess, but with multiple side-holes, this is usually sufficient. The Seldinger technique has the advantage that the pigtail catheter follows the exact predetermined course of the guidewire so that the final catheter has followed the diagnostic needle pathway exactly. It is limited to relatively small catheters, however. The Trocar technique uses a larger central stylet positioned within a 10–16 Fr catheter (Fig. 3). This allows insertion of larger catheters, but does require a second needle (Trocar) insertion after the diagnostic needle is removed.

The choice of catheter technique should depend on the location of the abscess and the relative safety of the route as determined by the "access window". The access window is conceived of as a 3-dimensional cone, the apex of which is the cutaneous entry site, and whose sides are defined by the surrounding structures which must be avoided. Thus, a small, deep abscess with little visceral displacement has a narrow cone and access window; a large, superficial abscess with marked visceral displacement has a wide cone and access window. With narrow access windows, it is best to use a Seldinger-type system to avoid a second Trocar pass. Typically, this occurs deep in the pelvis or mid-abdomen, parenchymal abscesses, or when the drainage route passes close to vital structures such as the mesenteric vessels or

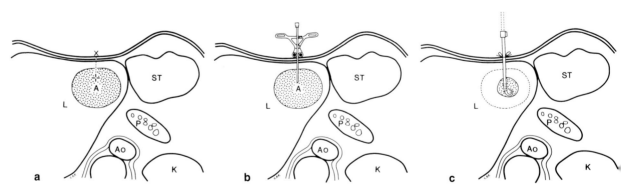

Fig. 2 Modified Seldinger technique

a Transverse diagram shows a 5 cm abscess (A) in the left lobe of the liver (L). The cursor marks indicate the cutaneous entry site, angle, and depth
b A 20-gauge Teflon sleeve needle with a needle stop is inserted over the planned route shown in (A)
c After the insertion of a J guide wire, an 8 Fr dilator is passed over the guide wire. An 8 Fr pigtail catheter is then inserted over the guide wire and advanced until it engages the far wall. The abscess is evacuated by manual syringe suction, and the catheter is sutured securely to the skin

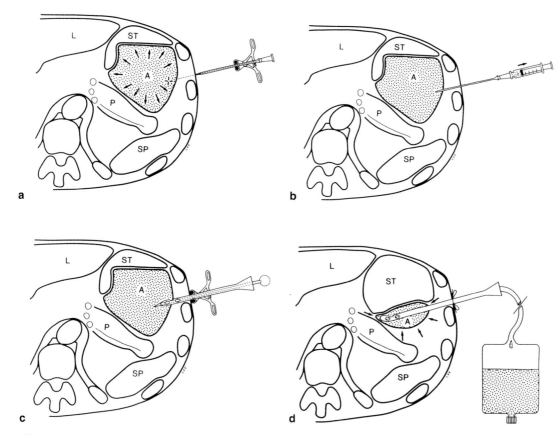

Fig. 3   Trocar technique
a A lesser sac abscess (A) displaces the stomach (ST) ventrad. The splenic flexure is displaced caudad, and therefore is not seen. Thus the abscess has provided itself with a safe percutaneous drainage route (dotted line and electronic cursor mark). With the aspiration needle in position, the depth to the near side of the abscess has been transposed to the aspiration needle with a rubber-shod clamp. P = pancreas; SP = spleen
b After the aspiration needle is inserted in a single pass over the planned route, a small sample of material is aspirated for an immediate Gram stain
c Trocar catheter is inserted in a single motion into the abscess over the preselected route
d After removal of the clamp, a central stylet is held fixed in position while the outer catheter is gently advanced over the stylet. The catheter should slide easily until a slight resistance indicates that it has engaged the far wall. During this maneuver, the central stylet functions like a guide wire. Note that care must be taken not to advance the cutting edge of the stylet deeper than the near wall of the abscess. Doing so may perforate the far wall. The stylet is then removed, and the abscess is manually evacuated by syringe suction. The catheter is sutured securely to the skin and connected to closed biliary bag drainage. With the decrease in mass effect (arrows), the surrounding structures return to a normal position and close the percutaneous access window. The catheter must now be protected against inadvertently falling out, since reinsertion may be impossible

loops of bowel. When there is a wide access window, the Trocar system can be used more safely. Thus, we tend to use Trocar catheters for large abscesses in contact with the parietal peritoneum.

To avoid intraperitoneal leakage of pus, all of the side holes should be seated within the abscess cavity. In small abscesses (less than 4 cm), the small, flexible 8 Fr pigtail catheter is recommended, since it can easily coil within the small space.

Catheter Management

After insertion of either drainage catheter, the abscess should be aspirated completely by manual syringe suction. Unilocular abscesses usually collapse immediately without any significant residual fluid. When the cavity has emptied, the free flow of pus suddenly stops. At this point, a slight bloody tinge to the purulent fluid is noted. This indicates suction on the vascular abscess wall, and syringe suction should cease. The total volume of the aspirate should be measured and compared to that estimated from the scan. If a gross discrepancy is found, a repeat scan is indicated to rule out an undrained loculation, since this may require a second drainage catheter. If a second loculation is found, it should be drained at that time, since the patient would remain at risk for septic complications.

To prevent accidental removal, we recommend two or three 1-0 silk sutures carefully tied to the skin. We discourage internal retention devices (Foley balloon or Cope loop) within the abscess cavity itself. If forcible traction is accidentally applied to such a catheter, this may avulse the wall of the abscess and cause serious hemorrhage or wide dissemination of pus (23).

For collection of drainage fluid, we advocate use of a biliary drainage bag supported by a belt around the patient's waist, in similar fashion to drainage of the biliary tree. The free portion of the catheter between the skin sutures and the bag should be carefully taped to the skin to provide further support. The bag should not be strapped to the lower leg as is common for urine collection bags, since this will place traction on the catheter and gradually pull it out. One should be aware that dressing changes by ward personnel may radically alter these supports, and we suggest that they be checked frequently.

Lavage of the abscess cavity has been advocated by some, but we do not endorse this as a routine (1, 25). Since most pus is thin enough to drain through even small catheters, we feel that lavage is unnecessary. Additionally, lavage may have potentially serious complications. In our experience, lavage has caused rupture of abscesses, precipitating emergency operations and at least one death (11). Although lavage may possibly decrease the duration of treatment, we do not feel it is justified as a routine. However, when very thick pus is encountered, small lavage aliquots of 10–15 ml of saline may be useful. In this case, we recommend the lavage be performed under close fluoroscopic control with only small volumes and low pressures by a radiologist who is thoroughly familiar with the case. Recent use of thrombolytic agents has been described for lysis of infected hematomas with good success (26). There still may be risk for rupture or intravasation into dilated friable veins. If contrast is noted in such periabscessal veins, one should anticipate that there may be intravasation of pus as well, and the patient should be treated for impending septicemia (11).

Surgeons have traditionally recommended dependent or gravitational positioning of their drainage catheters. However, we find such positioning to be unnecessary. Most percutaneous catheters are placed anteriorly and experience has shown they drain well against gravity. Because both the abscess wall and the abdominal wall remain intact, they transmit increases in intra-abdominal pressure (patient motion, respiration) to any residual abscess fluid, forcing it out of the drainage catheter. Even when the initial pus is very thick, as soon as the pressure in the abscess is relieved, the ensuing exudate produced by the abscess wall is very thin and drains easily.

The patient's temperature, white blood cell count, and daily drainage volumes, should be recorded to evaluate resolution of the abscess. Most patients become afebrile within 48 h, but it may take 7–10 days for the leukocytosis to return to normal. The first 72 h of drainage are the most important for determining adequacy of drainage. If clinical signs of sepsis persist beyond 24–48 h, percutaneous drainage may not have been sufficient. We then strongly advocate a repeat CT scan rather than abscessograms or exploration, to rule out an undrained residuum.

The catheter is removed when the temperature and white blood cell count have returned to normal and when daily drainage volumes decrease to less than 5–10 ml. A final CT scan is generally unnecessary, but may be used to confirm resolution in complex cases.

References

1. Aeder MI, Wellman JL, Haaga JR, Hau T. Role of surgical and percutaneous drainage in the treatment of abdominal abscesses. Arch Surg 1983;118:273–280.
2. Callen PW. Computed tomographic evaluation of abdominal and pelvic abscesses. Radiology 1979;131:171–175.
3. David PL, Filly RA, Goerke J. Echogenicity caused by sterile microbubbles in a protein-lipid emulsion. J Clin Ultrasound 1981;9:249–252.
4. Gerzof SG, Robbins AH, Birkett DH. Computed tomography in the diagnosis and management of abdominal abscesses. Gastrointest Radiol 1978;3:387–394.
5. Gerzof SG, Robbins AH, Birkett DH, Johnson WC, Pugatch RD, Vincent ME. Percutaneous catheter drainage of abdominal abscesses guided by ultrasound and computed tomography. AJR 1979;133:1–8.
6. Gerzof SG, Robbins AH, Johnson WC, Birkett DH, Nabseth DC. Percutaneous catheter drainage of abdominal abscesses: a five-year experience. N Engl J Med 1981;305:653–657.
7. Gerzof SG. Triangulation for indirect CT guidance. AJR 1981;137:1808–1881.
8. Gerzof SG, Gale ME. Computed tomography and ultrasonography for diagnosis and treatment of renal and retroperitoneal abscesses. Radiol Clin North Am 1982;9:185–192.
9. Gerzof SG, Johnson WC, Robbins AH et al. Percutaneous drainage of infected pancreatic pseudocysts. Arch Surg 1984;119:888–893.
10. Gerzof SG. Pancreatic fluid and abscess aspiration and drainage. Semin Intervent Radiol 1985;2:294–303.
11. Gerzof SG. Results and clinical correlations of percutaneous abscess drainage. In: RSNA, ed. Categorical course on interventional radiology. 1985:173–178.
12. Gronvall J, Gronvall S, Hegedus V. Ultrasound guided drainage of fluid-containing masses using angiographic catheterization techniques. AJR 1977;129:997–1002.
13. Haaga JR, Alfidi RJ. Precise biopsy localization by computed tomography. Radiology 1976;118:603–607.
14. Haaga JR, Alfidi RJ, Cooperman AM, Havrilla TR, Meaney TF, Ockner SA, Stiff P, Silver S. Definitive treatment of a large pyogenic liver abscess with CT guidance. Cleve Clin Q 1976;43:85–88.
15. Holm HH, Kristensen JK, Rasmussen SN, Northeved A, Barlebo H. Ultrasound as guide in percutaneous puncture technique. Ultrasonics 1972;10:83–86.

16. Holm HH, Rasmussen SN, Kristensen JK. Ultrasonically guided percutaneous puncture technique. J Clin Ultrasound 1973;1:27–31.

17. Jensen F, Pedersen JF. The value of ultrasonic scanning in the diagnosis of intra-abdominal abscesses and hematomas. Surg Gynecol Obstet 1974;139:326–328.

18. Kressel HY, Filly RA. Ultrasonic appearance of gas-containing abscesses in the abdomen. AJR 1978;130:71.

19. Koehler PR, Moss AA. Diagnosis of intra-abdominal and pelvic abscesses by computerized tomography. JAMA 1980;244:49–52.

20. Maklad NF, Doust BD, Baum JK. Ultrasonic diagnosis of postoperative intra-abdominal abscess. Radiology 1974;113:417–422.

21. Roche J. Effectiveness of computed tomography in the diagnosis of intra-abdominal abscess. Med J Aust 1981;2:85–88.

22. Schwerk WB, Durr HK. Ultrasound gray scale patterns and guided aspiration puncture of abdominal abscesses. J Clin Ultrasound 1981;9:389–396.

23. Shaver RW, Hawkins IF Jr, Sang J. Percutaneous cholecystostomy. AJR 1982;138:1133–1135.

24. Smith EH, Bartrum RJ Jr. Ultrasonically guided percutaneous aspiration of abscesses. AJR 1974;122:308–312.

25. Van Sonnenberg E, Wittich GR, Casola G, Neff C, Hoyt DB, Polansky AD, Keightley A. Periappendiceal abscess: percutaneous drainage. Radiology 1987;163:23–26.

26. Vogelzang RL, Tobin RS, Burstein S, Anschuetz SL, Marzano M, Kozlowski JM. Transcatheter intracavitary fibrinolysis of infected extravascular hematomas. AJR 1987;148:378–380.

27. Welch CE. Editorial: catheter drainage of abdominal abscesses. N Engl Med 1981;305:694–695.

28. Welch CE, Malt RA. Abdominal surgery. N Engl J Med 1983;308:753–760.

Intraperitoneal Fluid Collections

J. C. Kurdziel and R. F. Dondelinger

Diagnosis

Intraperitoneal abscesses may defy clinical diagnosis. They are associated with significant morbidity and mortality (47) when they remain undetected or insufficiently characterized. They can occur in any anatomic site or peritoneal organ, and have multiple causes. The limited diagnostic value of clinical evaluation and plain film radiographs (50, 65) has led to a widespread use of sophisticated imaging techniques, including 67^{Ga} scintigraphy, ^{111}Indium leukocyte scintigraphy, US and CT. Delay in diagnosing abdominal abscess is not acceptable, as it is a major factor in morbidity and mortality (114). When symptoms suggesting an abdominal abscess are present, and especially if there are clinical localizing signs, we use CT as the imaging modality of choice (75, 111) because of its higher diagnostic sensitivity (50, 113, 167) and the exquisite anatomical display it offers for the planning of the percutaneous access route. It allows aspiration or drainage, or both (49, 50, 66–74, 87–93, 112, 158–160, 162, 209–212), even when further placement of the catheter requires fluoroscopy (46) in addition. Radionuclide imaging is a useful adjunct for screening when there are no localizing signs, and in case of occult sepsis or fever of unknown origin. If positive, it can direct further imaging with CT or US.

Technical Considerations

Percutaneous aspiration and drainage is performed with US or CT control, according to the technique described in the previous chapter. A 5 Fr Teflon trocar is used for initial aspiration of fluid. Complications do not occur, due to the larger size of this trocar in comparison with the 20–22 G needles usually advocated (71, 143–145). The advantages are the ability to sample viscous pus and the possibility of using the 5 Fr catheter to perform secondary drainage with the angiographic technique, thus avoiding a second puncture of the cavity. When the need for drainage is foreseen from the clinical background and imaging, we prefer the trocar technique with a 9 Fr pigtail catheter or a 14 Fr straight catheter (213) when safe percutaneous access is possible. This avoids repeated passages of dilators along the drainage tract, with potential spillage of pus, which may favor infection to the drainage tract and subcutaneous abscess formation. These are uncomfortable for the patient, and generally do not resolve until the drainage material has been removed. Efficient suture of the catheter to the skin is mandatory to prevent withdrawal, a potentially severe complication. Self-retaining devices or catheters should not be used, as they carry a risk of catheter withdrawal and abscess wall disrupture. Catheter patency is guaranted by 2 to 4 daily gentle injections of 5 ml of saline in the catheter. Irrigation of the abscess cavity is no longer performed in our experience, as it has led to significant complications (50) and prolonged the duration of drainage. The efficiency of the injection of antibiotics or mucolytic agents (216) into the abscess cavity has not been proved (41), although a positive liquefying effect on the pus can be anticipated (216). Although the use of gentle suction has been advocated (57), gravity-dependent drainage is usually sufficient.

Sinograms, or imaging of the drained abscess cavity, are only performed when the clinical course is not favorable: this may involve persistent fever after 2 days of drainage, the occurrence of septic shock, persistent leukocytosis, or modification of the drainage output, increasing or changing its aspect. The drainage is stopped, and the catheter is withdrawn 2 days after the drainage decreases to 5–10 ml, with a disappearance of fever and normalization of leukocytosis.

Indications

Any intraperitoneal fluid collection which is clinically or morphologically significant should be evacuated. When no leukocytes are evidenced, and the Gram stain is negative on the initial aspirated fluid, no drainage is required, except to prevent recurrence when a large sterile fluid collection is present or fistulized (i.e. biloma). A small drain (8–9 Fr) is generally adequate, except for recent hematomas. These often enlarge during their development due to hyperosmolarity, resulting in a fluid accumulation in the cavity that makes them easier to aspirate after several weeks. Most intraparenchymal hematomas are post-traumatic and often resolve spontaneously (Fig. 1), as in the case of hemoperitoneum. If they persist or enlarge, single or multiple aspirations are generally curative (Fig. 2). When the patient has clinical evidence of a peritoneal abscess, drainage is

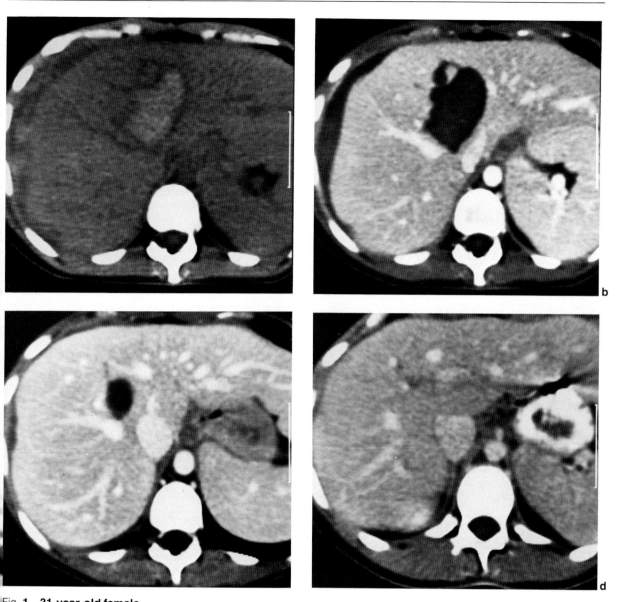

Fig. 1   31-year-old female

a   Initial CT after multiple organ trauma shows a hyperdense liver hematoma and perihepatic hemoperitoneum
b   Initial CT after intravenous contrast better delineates the hematoma, which appears hypodense
c   Control CT, 2 months after trauma, shows partial resolution of the hematoma, which appears liquefied
d   Control CT, 6 months after trauma, shows complete resolution. No percutaneous treatment was required

necessary in almost all patients. Parenchymal abscesses are drained when they are multiple, suspected to be secondary to a persistent underlying disease, or develop in an immunocompromised patient. A solitary parenchymal abscess may resolve after single or multiple aspirations when the organ is well vascularized, allowing diffusion of systemic antibiotherapy.

Contra-Indications

In the initial experience with percutaneous drainage of peritoneal abscesses, complex situations (multiloculated, fistulized, multiple abscesses) were considered as a contra-indication for percutaneous treatment. Overall experience in the literature (73, 214–215, 227) and our personal prospective experience (50) indicate that complex abscesses can be drained percutaneously with good results, although they may require more attention during treatment (50, 214, 227) (Fig. **3**).

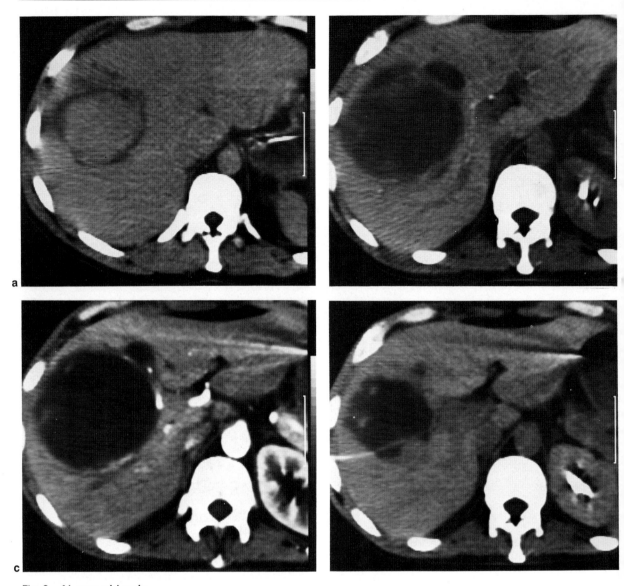

Fig. 2   **41-year-old male**
a Initial CT after multiple organ trauma shows a hyperdense liver hematoma with a hypodense peripheral ring
b Control CT, 1 month after trauma, shows decreased density of the lesion and enlargement
c Control CT, 2 months after trauma, shows a liquefied hematoma with persistent enlargement, requiring percutaneous treatment
d Control CT during aspiration of the 400 ml hematoma with a 5 Fr Teflon catheter. A second aspiration was performed 1 month later for a residual 60 ml fluid collection. Neither recurrence nor complication occurred

Relative contra-indications are the absence of an anatomical window for the percutaneous approach, a non-cooperative patient, and coagulation disorders (23). Patient mobilization, eventual sedation, and temporary correction of coagulation parameters, allow a percutaneous approach to almost any fluid collection in the peritoneal cavity or organs. Even interloop abscesses can be punctured, as a safe access can very often be found for catheter insertion (Fig. **4**), and once the catheter is in the abdomen, any corrections necessary can be made to the route of drainage to reach the abscess (30). Failure to define an appropriate route to a peritoneal cavity abscess is exceptional (<1%). Infected hematomas, previously considered as a contra-indication, can be treated efficiently by using fibrinolytic agents in addition. Necrotized superinfected tumors should be recognized with proper imaging and should not be drained.

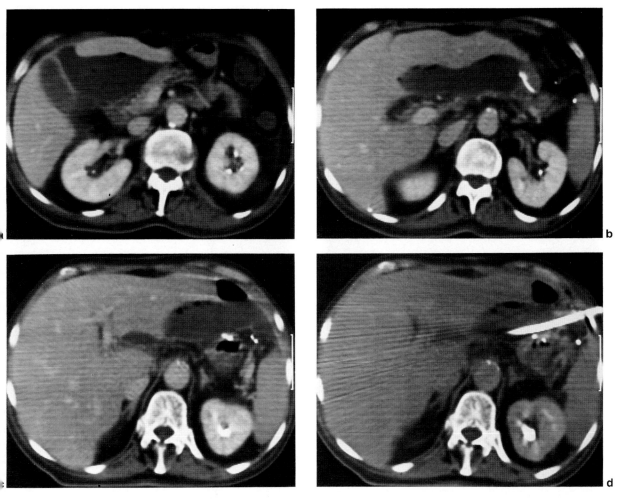

Fig. **3a–f** **76-year-old male.** Left subhepatic abscess, 7 days after gastric surgery, extending from the interlobar fissure (**a**) through the interhepatogastric compartment (**b**) to the left subphrenic space, where a loculation is evidenced (**c**). Percutaneous drainage was performed with a 14 Fr sump catheter, using the trocar technique (**d**). Initial abscessogram shows the extent of the cavity

Peritoneal Cavity Fluid Collections

Abscesses in the abdomen are most frequently found in intraperitoneal locations. They usually result from complications of surgery, or insufficiently treated peritonitis (34). Abscesses of the peritoneal cavity are the most common postoperative complication after trauma (61). Most of them are pyogenic with participation of any micro-organism from the gastrointestinal flora. Abscesses resulting from candidiasis can occur after violation of the gastrointestinal tract mucosa associated with predisposing factors such as CVP catheters, broad-spectrum antibiotics, parenteral alimentation, α-H2-blockers/antacids, malnutrition, alcoholism, steroids and chemotherapy (2).

Infectious Spread in the Peritoneal Cavity

Modern imaging modalities allow earlier diagnosis and a more localized treatment of intraperitoneal fluid collections. They require a proper understanding of the anatomy of the peritoneal cavity. Although cross-section anatomy of the abdomen is well-known, a knowledge of the peritoneal cavity compartments allows, besides topographic diagnosis of the lesion, an approach to the potential source of the infection through an understanding of the spread of infectious processes. This basic knowledge is essential before any attempt to aspirate or drain a peritoneal fluid collection. Peritoneal compartments have been well documented (20, 21, 117, 148, 151, 153, 224, 225) and are illustrated in Figure **5**. This information allows intraperitoneal abscesses to be classified according to their topography (Table **1**). Infectious spread in the peritoneal cavity is deter-

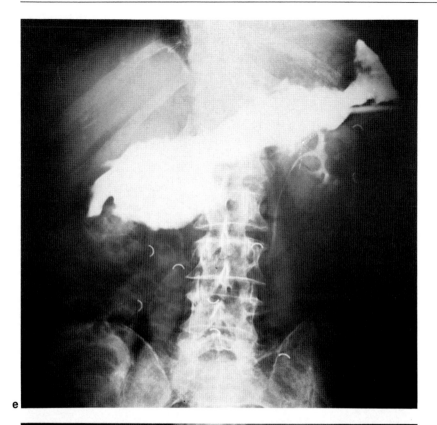

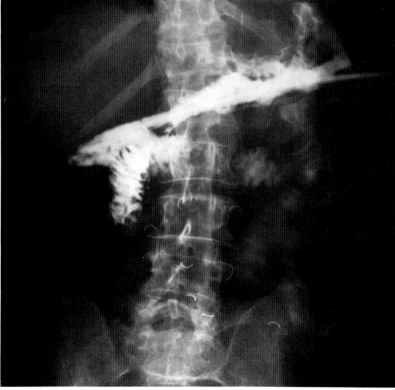

Fig. 3 (**e**) with no evidence of fistula. Due to an increase in the drainage return, an abscessogram was performed after 1 week which showed an enteric fistula (**f**). Drainage was continued for 2 weeks, and cured the fistula

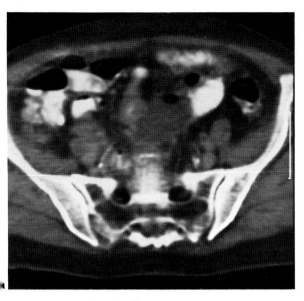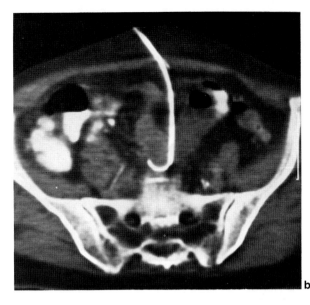

Fig. 4   77-year-old female

a   Interloop abscess after sigmoid diverticulitis, deeply located

b   Percutaneous drainage was performed using a 9 Fr pigtail catheter with the tandem trocar technique. After oblique insertion of the catheter/trocar in the peritoneal cavity through a safe access window (parallel to the needle used for local anesthesia), the catheter/trocar was pulled into a vertical position to reach the abscess cavity. Final positioning of the catheter was performed with a guide wire under fluoroscopy control

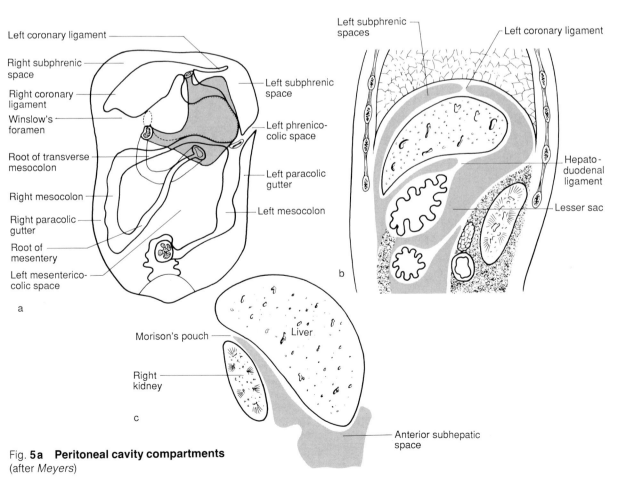

Fig. **5a   Peritoneal cavity compartments**
(after *Meyers*)

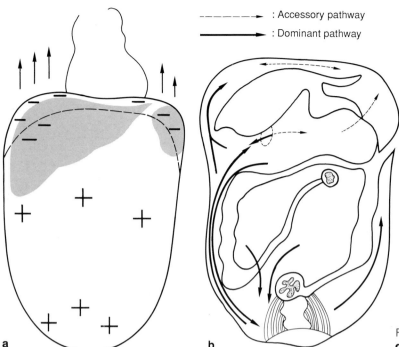

- - - - - - -→ : Accessory pathway

──────────────→ : Dominant pathway

a

b

Fig. **6a, b Peritoneal cavity pressure gradients** and pathways of fluid spread

Table **1** Anatomic and radiological classification of intraperitoneal abscesses. According to Meyers (151)

Supramesocolic space	Inframesocolic space
Right subphrenic	Pelvis
Anterior	Laterovesical fossae
Posterior	Pouch of Douglas
Right subhepatic	Right paracolic
Anterior	Left paracolic
Posterior	
Left subphrenic	Right mesentericocolic
Left subhepatic	Left mesentericocolic

mined by the site, nature and speed of infected fluid in the peritoneal cavity, peritoneal compartmentalization, secondary pyogenic membrane formation, gravity, gradients of intra-abdominal pressure, and the patient's position (117, 148–150). Intra-abdominal pressure (Fig. **6a**) is an important factor influencing the extent of infectious processes in the peritoneal cavity. Diaphragm movement during respiration and abdominal wall movements are responsible for lower hydrostatic pressure in the subphrenic spaces as compared to all the other compartments (7, 52, 174). These pressure gradients are responsible for the ascending migration of fluids in the peritoneal cavity. After laparotomy, these pressure gradients are temporarily compromised by the patient's difficulty in moving the diaphragm and

abdominal wall (186). The preferential pathways of infectious spread in the peritoneal cavity, according to anatomical and inflammatory compartmentalization, determine the planning of the access route (Fig. **6b**). The dynamics of fluids in the peritoneal cavity have been described on the basis of peritoneography studies (150). Fluids originating from the inframesocolic spaces always flow into the pelvic recesses due to gravity. This explains the frequency of residual pelvic abscesses after peritonitis. They extend afterwards to the paracolic gutters because of pressure gradients, mainly to the right, and then to the right subhepatic space due to gravity. The hepatorenal fossa (Morison's pouch) represents the most frequent site of infectious spread from the inframesocolic compartment (Fig. **5b**), prior to the right subphrenic space. Abscess formation in the anterior right subhepatic space is unusual. Instead, the infection spreads around the inferior border of the liver to the right subphrenic space, via the laterohepatic spaces. The formation of pyogenic membranes can restrict the infection to Morison's pouch. Extension to the subphrenic space depends on the speed and volume of the fluid and the virulence of the microorganism causing the infection. Abscesses that are located in the right subphrenic space are always secondary to Morison's pouch abscesses, and may be associated with them. A right subphrenic abscess may be diagnosed by US or CT without evidence of suppuration in the hepatorenal fossa, only non-visible residual inflammatory adhesions being present. The dynamics of intraperitoneal fluid explain the prevalence of right subhepatic, Morison's pouch and subphrenic abscesses, especially in series with predominantly appendiceal abscesses (4, 5, 117, 171, 172). Left subphrenic abscesses are generally secondary to infected fluid accumulation from an organ situated in the left upper quadrant. Abscess formation in the left subhepatic space (between the liver and stomach) is unusual, and results from an interhepatogastric membrane formation, generally after manipulation of the lesser omentum (biliary or pyloric surgery). Anastomotic leakage is an increasing cause of left subphrenic abscess formation. Large left subphrenic abscesses may have two pathways of extension: over the midline behind the border of the falciform ligament to the right subphrenic space, or to the pelvis via the left paracolic gutter, with potential ascent to the right subphrenic space via the right paracolic gutter. An extension of infection from the left paracolic gutter to the left subphrenic space has been considered exceptional when the phrenicocolic ligament is intact (148). Such spread can, however, easily occur (132) after surgical manipulations (148). Lesser sac abscesses are mainly secondary to pathology in an adjacent organ, as the foramen of Winslow is rapidly closed by pyogenic membranes. Contamination from the peritoneal cavity is, however, possible when the spread of infection occurs before the foramen is closed by inflammatory processes.

When percutaneous treatment of an intraperitoneal fluid collection is planned, special attention should be given to immediate access to the infected or sterile fluid collection, as previous surgical reports have emphasized a significant difference in the morbidity and mortality with a directed extraserous approach in comparison with a transperitoneal approach. The latter carries a high risk of infectious spread to previously uncontaminated compartments (Table 2) (12, 19, 152, 172, 192).

The determination of the percutaneous access route is therefore based on anatomic concepts and the necessity:

of an extraserous approach with direct puncture of the peritoneal abscess;

of transgressing none, or a minimal number, of the sterile peritoneal compartments when an extraserous approach is not feasible;

of not transgressing any of the intraperitoneal organs or vessels, or the gastrointestinal tract, when these are not affected by the pathological process.

of placing the catheter tip in the most dependent part of the cavity, or in a position where the greatest negative pressure is expected, to benefit from pressure gradients for pus evacuation during respiration.

Encapsulated abscesses in the peritoneal cavity have a low risk of infectious dissemination when drained percutaneously and treated with further adapted systemic antibiotherapy. A direct approach to the cavity is a definite guarantee of avoiding septic dissemination. CT allows a directed puncture to the single peritoneal compartment containing the abscess in about 91% of patients (50). 9% of the abscesses are reached by transgressing one compartment which is not affected by the infectious process. Secondary infection of that compartment never occurs (50). Although no significant problems occurred in cases where non-infected, or even pathological, organs were transgressed by the drainage catheter (142), such an approach is, at the very least, not indispensable, and all efforts should be made to achieve an ideal anatomical approach to the lesion.

Bacteriology

The bacteriology of peritoneal abscesses was previously dominated by *E. coli*, *Staphylococcus aureus* and some streptococci from the aerobic groups. Other Gram-negative bacteria from the aerobic groups are now being cultured with increasing frequency: *Klebsiella* spp., *Enterobacter* spp., *Proteus* spp. and *Pseudomonas* spp. Progress in culturing anaerobes has demonstrated the increasing presence of Gram-negative anaerobic bacteria such as *Cocci* and *Clostridia* which are present in the gastrointestinal tract (134, 155) (Table 3). Almost all intraperitoneal abscesses are polymicrobial, associating an "obligatory anaerobe" with a "facultative aerobe". This association is necessary to produce an experimental abscess (222). Proper methods of culturing anaerobes should diminish the incidence of single bacteria disclosed in intraperitoneal abscesses, provided that sampling has been cautious (134). Although the efficient treatment of one synergic

Table 2 Extraperitoneal (EP) versus transperitoneal (TP) surgical drainage	Author	Patients n	Drainage EP	TP	Mortality (%) EP	TP
	Berens (12)	160	103	57	21	30
	Bonfils-Roberts (19)	101	–	–	20	–
	Miller (152)	48	–	48	–	37.5
	Ochsner (172)	1693	–	–	13	41
	Sherman (192)	96	70	22	18	36

Table **3**   Incidence of different anaerobes in the normal human flora

	Gram negative		Gram positive	
	Anaerobes Cocci	Anaroves Bacillis	Clostridia	Anaerobes Non-spurule
Oral cavity	+ + + +	+ + +	rare	+ +
Intestine	+ + +	+ + + +	+ + +	+ + +

bacterium may be curative, the best results are obtained when combined antibiotherapy is used for polymicrobial abscesses. Good targetting of systemic antibiotics to the micro-organisms responsible for abscess formation is a key to the success of percutaneous treatment.

Subphrenic Abscess

Subphrenic abscesses are secondary to intra- or transperitoneal surgery, biliary obstruction or fistula, low-output hollow viscous perforation (ulcer, Crohn's disease) trauma, pancreatitis, and hematogenous or lymphatic spread from distant sites (29, 94, 100). Nearly all of them occur after operations for bowel perforation. They are most frequent in men during the third and fifth decades of life (220). The causal lesion originates from the peritoneal cavity, and the most frequent pathway of infection is directly through the peritoneal compartments, or by lymphatic drainage. Subphrenic abscesses predominate on the right side. Left subphrenic abscesses are tending to develop with the same frequency as on the right, especially since appendiceal or diverticular abscesses are seen with decreasing frequency. Post-traumatic subphrenic abscesses in younger patients are becoming more frequent (190). Simultaneous subphrenic and subhepatic abscesses, or bilateral abscesses, are seen in about 20% of patients (190).

Mortality after surgical treatment of subphrenic abscesses ranges from 13–43% (44, 172, 229). Patients who are not drained have a mortality close to 100% (9, 172). Patients over 50 years old, or with an underlying disease, have a higher mortality. Despite a lower morbidity and mortality with an extraserous surgical approach to subphrenic abscesses, the risk associated with leaving a simultaneous abscess undrained was the major reason for favoring transperitoneal drainage in most surgical experiences (12, 19, 24, 152, 172, 192). Early surgery has reduced the overall mortality of subphrenic abscesses. Progress in imaging has reduced the risk of a missed simultaneous abscess, and reduced the diagnostic delay from 32 to 14 days, with a reduction in surgical mortality to 17–28% (190, 206). An aggressive early approach is essential to improve the prognosis. Percutaneous drainage of subphrenic abscesses can be performed with US or CT control (67, 70, 91, 162, 207). US has the advantage that the diaphragm can be defined easily, in such a way that the percutaneous access route can be kept subdiaphragmatic (69, 162, 207). The lateral extent of subphrenic abscesses often allows axial puncture of the abscess with CT control, and secondary placement of the drain in the upper portion of the subphrenic space over a guide wire with fluoroscopy control (Fig. **7**). In specific cases, a "triangulation" approach (68, 209) can be used. Percutaneous drainage of subphrenic abscesses is performed with direct access to the infected space (Fig. **8**). Early radiographically guided procedures were performed according to the surgical dictum that an extraperitoneal and extrapleural approach was necessary (70, 209, 212). The most important technical consideration is avoidance of contamination of the pleura and lung. Accidental transgression of the pleural recess, which occurs in 2.6% of intercostal punctures (168), can be avoided by an access route that is caudal to the 10th rib laterally and 7th rib anteriorly. The triangulation method is associated with a 0.8% risk of diaphragmatic perforation (211). Both complications are accompanied by pleural contamination and a risk of empyema, which can also be treated percutaneously, as described in the last chapter of this section. In patients with a subphrenic collection, the inferior extent of the pleural reflection may be obliterated due to an inflammatory reaction to the adjacent subphrenic abscess. Consequently, transgression through this space may be safe. Empyema developed with that route in our prospective study (50) in 4% of patients. In most cases, a low subcostal approach is safe, easy and practical. But in patients in whom a subcostal angulation is not possible, an intercostal puncture provides a viable, though more risky, alternative. Multiloculated subphrenic abscesses may require multiple drains. Bilateral abscesses are drained separately and respond as well as unilateral abscesses do (Fig. **9**). Subphrenic abscesses associated with mediastinal abscess or empyema are efficiently treated with percutaneous drainage, when the drainage of the mediastinal and pleural abscesses is performed with separate drains (28). Isolated drainage of a subphrenic abscess associated with a bronchobiliary fistula may result in healing of both the abscess and the fistula (39). Drainage is usually performed with a

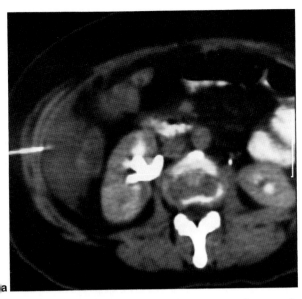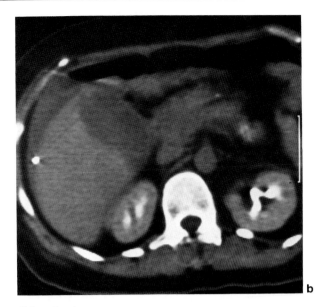

Fig. **7 49-year-old female.** Right subphrenic abscess after partial gastrectomy
a Lateral extent of the abscess down to the right paracolic gutter allows safe access to the cavity
b Positioning of the catheter upwards, in the right subphrenic space, is performed with a guide wire, pulled during CT scanning. Final positioning is performed under fluoroscopy control

large catheter (14–22 Fr) (50, 207), depending on the viscosity of the pus. Subphrenic abscesses commonly drain readily, and may resolve completely in a period ranging from 1–3 weeks, with a mean of 10 days (162). Duration of drainage is somewhat longer for subphrenic abscesses than for other peritoneal locations. The major reason is a high rate of fistulization of the small bowel, and communication with the bile ducts in up to 30% (162), requiring a prolonged drainage over several weeks until the fistula closes. One other reason for prolonged drainage is that subphrenic abscesses occupy "potential" intra-peritoneal spaces that may not heal as readily as vascularized spaces (i.e. the liver) (162). A search for a leak should be performed if the drainage output increases or changes its aspect. Careful opacification of the cavity can demonstrate the leak that should be treated. An overall success rate of 85% (162) to 87% (207) is achieved. Temporary drainage is performed in 8% (207) to 10% (162). Failure to achieve a complete cure of subphrenic abscess by percutaneous drainage occurs in 5% (207) to 10% (162) of cases. It is predictable, and depends on the presence of multiple non-contiguous collections that require the insertion of additional drains, and the cause of the collection (i.e. perforated ulcer or gallbladder, Crohn's disease) requiring surgery to cure the primary problem. Early assessment of the clinical and biological response to drainage is mandatory in order to perform any additional procedure before the patient's condition is impaired, increasing the risk for multi-organ failure, which is the major factor in mortality.

Mortality rates of 2% (162) to 5% (207) have been documented. They compare favorably with the surgical results. In the past 4 years, no patients with a subphrenic abscess have died after percutaneous drainage in our experience; our initial failures were due to the use of catheters that were too small (7–8 Fr). Follow-up of the drainage and the criteria for removing it are the same as for any abdominal abscess.

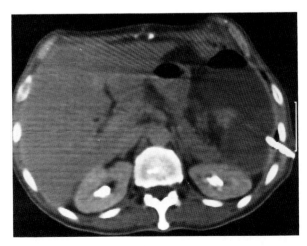

Fig. **8 53-year-old male.** Left subphrenic abscess after splenectomy. Direct percutaneous access is possible using a left posterolateral approach, with the trocar technique and a 14 Fr sump drainage catheter

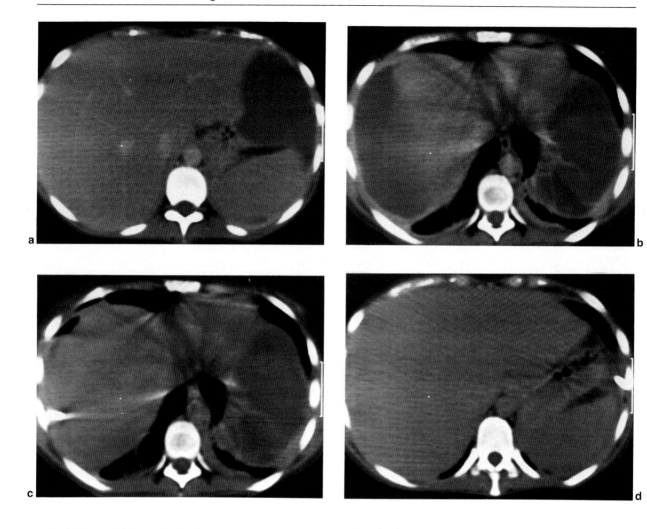

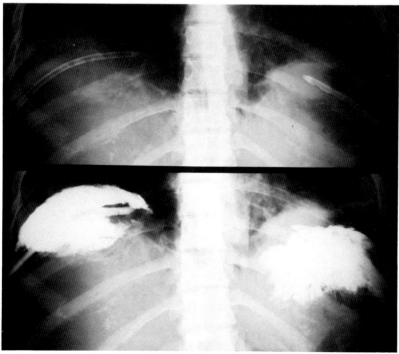

Fig. 9 31-year-old female. Bilateral subphrenic abscess after hysterectomy

a Lower extent of left subphrenic abscess

b Bilateral abscesses. Pyogenic membranes in the left subphrenic space

c After drainage of the right subphrenic abscess with a 14 Fr straight sump catheter, with the angiographic technique

d After drainage of the left subphrenic abscess with a second 14 Fr straight sump catheter, with the trocar technique

e Conventional anteroposterior view of the upper abdomen demonstrates correct positioning of both catheters. The abscessogram demonstrates the extent of both cavities. Successful drainage was achieved within 17 days

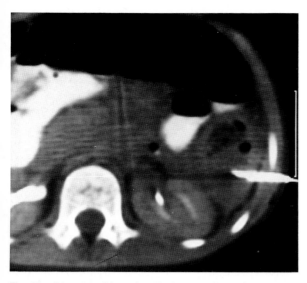

Fig. **10** **11-year-old male.** Drainage of a left paracolic gutter abscess, which developed 8 days after appendectomy

Paracolic Gutter Abscess

These are rare, and almost always secondary to appendiceal infection (Fig. **10**), diverticulitis, or Crohn's disease. The diagnosis is easy, and percutaneous drainage can be performed with direct access to the cavity. They respond to drainage administered with similar attention to the drain, and to the end of drainage criteria, as well as any peritoneal abscess does.

Interloop Abscess

Because of the location of these abscesses, diagnosis requires the use of CT (30, 67, 70, 91) with opacification of the bowel loops, to increase diagnostic accuracy. CT is indispensable in planning the best percutaneous access route, in order to avoid perforation of a hollow viscus. A safe route can almost always be found, and advancing the puncture material often displaces a loop that may be interposed rather than transgressing it (Fig. **4**). If an interloop abscess develops after surgery and a surgical drain is already present, catheterization of the drain is easy, and allows better repositioning or replacement by a large-bore catheter. When an enteric fistula is present, the tip of the catheter should be placed at the site of the leakage to control the enteric fistula and thereby reduce the volume of the abscess (141).

Associated anabolic treatment may help to cure the fistula. High-output fistulae, which have an associated mortality of 25% (196), may require more complete management (141). Several months of treatment may be required. Only rarely, when the enteric fistula is still present, is surgical correction

necessary once the patient's general condition has improved.

Abscess from Crohn's Disease

Crohn's disease is a chronic transmural inflammatory process of the digestive tract complicated by the formation of sinus tracts, fistulae and abscesses. Since the original report in 1932 of an abdominal abscess associated with regional enteritis (38), this complication has been reported in 12–28% of adult patients (56, 81, 83, 163, 199) and 3–10% of children or adolescents (17, 204). The mean time from the diagnosis of Crohn's disease to the formation of an abdominal abscess ranges in adults from 8–10 years (122, 163), but delays of 2–5 years only have been reported in children and adolescents (17, 204). Abscess formation occurs more often in previously operated patients (163, 199), and is usually related to a perforated and usually stenotic segment of bowel. Postsurgical abscesses may develop in 16–20% of patients (83, 199), and are secondary to anastomotic leaks, which are a notorious problem with Crohn's disease, and an important reason to limit surgery. The major problem with Crohn's disease is the difficulty in establishing the diagnosis of abscess. The usual diagnostic signs may be altered or absent as a result of steroid intake, and even when present, may be attributed to an exacerbation of regional enteritis rather than to an abscess (30). CT is excellent for detecting these abscesses in differentiating matted loops of bowel from abscesses (53, 63, 232); it is superior to barium studies in demonstrating mesenteric abscesses, enterovesical and enterocutaneous fistulae, and fistulae to the iliopsoas muscle and to the sacrum. Barium studies are superior to CT in demonstrating enteroenteric fistulae, sinus tracts, strictures, postsurgical anatomy, and the relation of recurrence to anastomosis (173). Most abscesses are located in the right lower quadrant (Fig. **11**) and the iliopsoas muscle, adjacent to thickened diseased bowel, and may extend to other peritoneal compartments.

The classical treatment for spontaneous Crohn abscesses has been surgery, consisting of abscess drainage followed by a second operation for resection of diseased bowel (83, 122). Surgical drainage alone has been the usual treatment for postoperative abscesses. However, postoperative recurrence ranges from 40–90%, and 70–90% of patients with Crohn's disease will undergo surgery during their lifetime (11, 60, 81, 82, 133). Therefore, avoiding an operation for abscess drainage is welcome.

Percutaneous drainage of abscesses related to Crohn's disease can be performed easily when CT control is used in order to avoid traversing adjacent bowel. A success rate of 100% has been reported (30). A limited number of patients (20%) may need

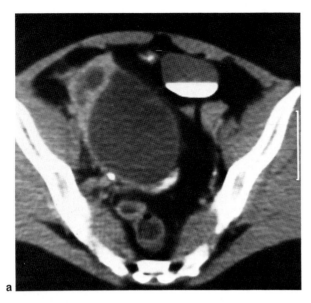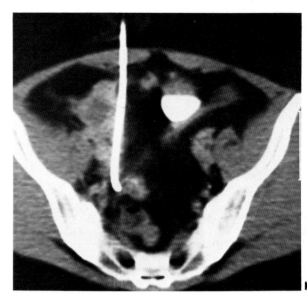

Fig. 11   32-year-old female
a Peritoneal cavity abscess related to Crohn's disease, displacing bowel and bladder (contrast-urine level)
b Same patient after insertion of a 9 Fr pigtail drainage catheter with the trocar technique and aspiration of 230 ml of pus. After 18 days of drainage, the catheter was removed. No surgery was performed, and no recurrence had occurred up to 6 months after the procedure

secondary bowel resection when fistulization persists after several weeks of drainage (30). No attempt to control the fistula should be made with interventional radiological techniques on diseased bowel (129). Preoperative temporary percutaneous abscess drainage is beneficial, since the patient can be rendered non-septic, with improved nutritional status and a non-infected operative field. A single one-stage operation for diseased bowel resection can then be performed, rather than a multiple-stage procedure. Concomitant adjunctive medical therapy, including total parenteral nutrition (196) and administration of antibiotics, should help to heal the underlying diseased bowel in most patients. Despite the high frequency of fistulae associated with regional enteritis, no iatrogenic cutaneous fistulae along the catheter path should occur (30). Potential complications, attention to the drain and criteria for ending drainage, are the same as for any percutaneous abscess drainage.

Liver Fluid Collections

Liver Abscess

Pyogenic liver abscesses have a frequency ranging from 0.29% to 0.5% in large autopsy series (105). The number of reported pyogenic abscesses in the radiological literature in the 1980s is more significant than that reported in the surgical literature before. The true incidence of liver abscess is unknown (178). It has not changed significantly in the past 50 or 60 years. The number of reports is increasing because of the widespread use of US and CT as primary diagnostic modalities. Pyogenic liver abscesses were associated with a 100% mortality during the pre-antibiotic era; surgical management allowed a reduction in the mortality to 70–90% (3, 118). Recent surgical reports still show an overall cumulative mortality of 55–65%, which was reduced to 34% with adequate drainage. The surgical mortality is 8–15% when a single abscess is present (118, 178). Only multiple abscesses have a 20% mortality (101). The factors causing liver abscesses have changed, mainly due to the extensive and more selective use of antibiotics (8). The involvement of a higher proportion of the older population (178), and associated systemic disorders (diabetes, alcoholism, immunosuppression, malignancy, cirrhosis) (105) are the most significant changes observed.

Sources of infection. Liver abscesses are due to the contamination of the liver parenchyma by bacteria from a biliary, portal or arterial source. They may also be secondary to trauma, surgery, contiguous spread, or may develop within a pre-existing lesion or after an interventional radiological procedure.

Bile ducts. Suppurative cholangitis can develop either with or without biliary obstruction, the former being the most frequent. Stagnation of bile is mainly due to stone obstruction or to biliary strictures of benign or malignant origin. Stagnant bile is infected by Gram-negative and anaerobic bacteria (105). Ascending   cholangitis   first   generates   direct peripheral biliary extension, and suppuration occurs later on in the liver, with pylephlebitis involving the portal radicles, which may be responsible for the irregular contours, and with multilocular or multiple abscesses evidenced on US or CT (138) (Fig. **12**). These abscesses represented 51% of the cases reported by Pitt and Zuidema (178).

Portal vein. The incidence of liver abscesses secondary to portal vein pylephlebitis associated with appendicitis was 34.2% in Ochsner's review (172).

Diverticulitis, infected hemorrhoids, benign or malignant ulcerations of the gastrointestinal tract, colitis, and pancreatic or splenic infection are well-known potential causes of liver abscesses by the portal route. The widespread use of antibiotics has markedly reduced the incidence of such abscesses, which currently account for about 1% of cases (8).

Hepatic artery. Any pathology that induces septicemic bacteriema can lead to hematogenous spread of infection in the liver and single or multiple abscess

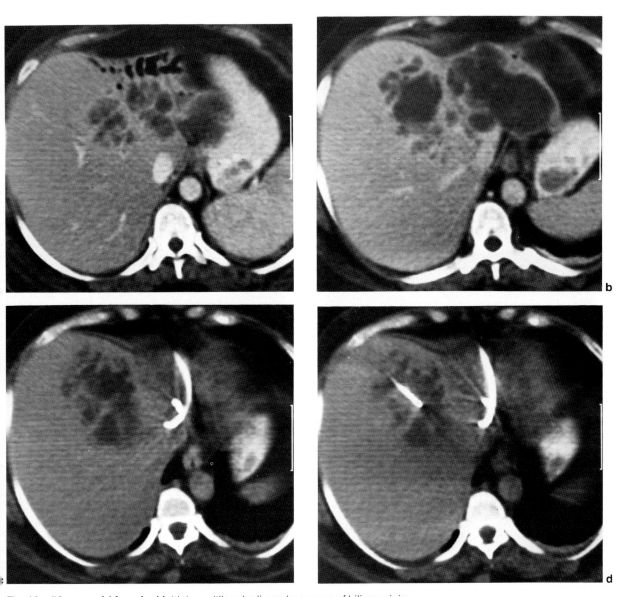

Fig. **12**   **52-year-old female.** Multiple multilocular liver abscesses of biliary origin
   a Multiseptated abscess of the left lobe and dilated bile ducts due to reflux in the left biliary tree after bilioenteric anastomosis
   b Almost total replacement of the left lobe of the liver by an abscess cavity
   c After insertion of a 9 Fr pigtail catheter in the left cavity with the angiographic technique
   d Aspiration of a second infected cavity in segment IV, which was also drained with a 9 Fr pigtail catheter. Temporary drainage was achieved after 3 weeks. Left hepatotectomy was performed later on, after one recurrence which was successfully treated percutaneously

formation. Such abscesses have been reported after furunculosis, parotitis, upper airways infections, endocarditis, bronchiectasis and osteomyelitis. This route of spread has been reported as a probable cause of 5–40% of liver abscesses (105).

Direct extension via contiguous spread. Infection can extend in the liver parenchyma from adjacent infectious pockets, especially from the gallbladder in case of cholangitis, even without perforation, but also from subphrenic abscess, infected peritoneal fluid from gastrointestinal perforation, pancreatic infec-

tion, and even empyema. Bacterial invasion can occur directly by capsular injury, or along lymphatic channels that penetrate the capsule (Fig. **13**).

Trauma or iatrogenic causes. Hematoma, contusion, laceration, and tissue devitalization after blunt or penetrating trauma to the liver, are potential sites for abscess formation (110, 226). Abscess may be responsible for 10% (105, 172) to 20% (189) of deaths after hepatic trauma, and it may occur as a non-fatal complication in an additional 4–30% of survivors (189).

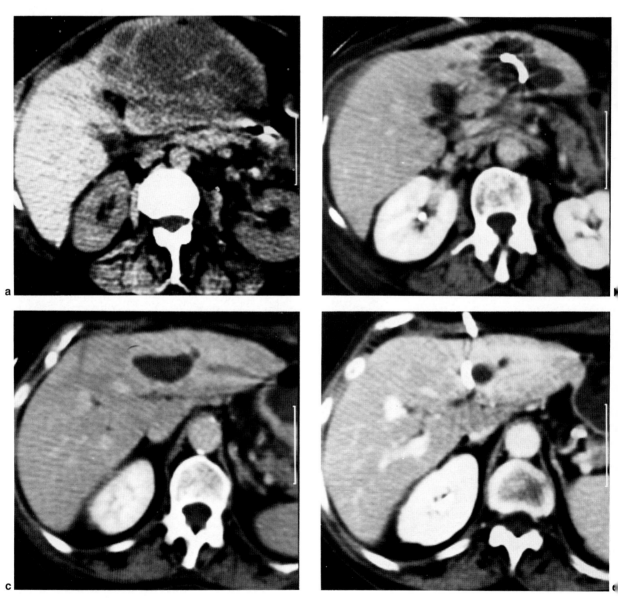

Fig. **13**   **66-year-old female.** Left liver lobe abscess after perforation of a gastric ulcer
a Large septated abscess of the left lobe of the liver
b Abscess cavity aspiration of 700 ml of thick pus through a 9 Fr pigtail catheter inserted with the trocar technique
c A more cranial CT slice shows a residual cavity
d Second cavity after insertion of a 9 Fr pigtail catheter with the angiographic technique and aspiration of 30 ml of pus

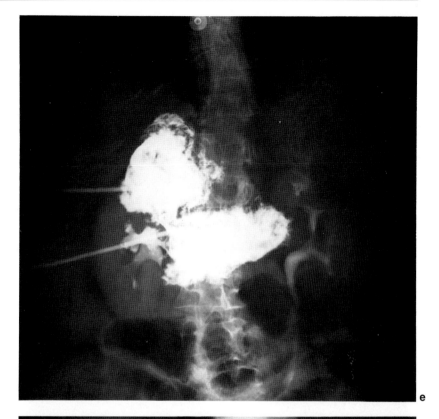

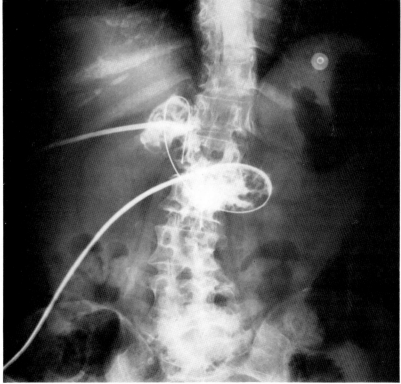

Fig. **13**
e Abscessogram showing both cavities of the left lobe of the liver
f Insertion of a guide wire in the lower catheter demonstrates communication of both cavities after 10 days of drainage. The upper catheter was removed and the lower left in place for 3 days, allowing complete recovery of the patient

Interventional radiology. Interventional techniques in the biliary system rarely account for the formation of an abscess if careful manipulation and proper antibiotherapy are used (97). Abscess complications have been reported (180) following embolization, chemotherapy or chemoembolization. Direct arterial injection of a micro-organism is always possible, and infarction following embolization may favor bacterial proliferation. A strictly aseptic technique is mandatory, as is control of portal vein patency. Some authors, however, recommend prophylactic antibiotherapy, as systematic portal bacteremia may be present (180). Direct access to the portal vein also requires cautious manipulation.

Cryptogenic and unusual causes. Cryptogenic liver abscesses represented 17% of cases in the review by Ochsner (172). Today, approximately 5% of liver abscesses have no evident cause, and are considered as cryptogenic (8). Most of them may be due to portal contamination from a non-evidenced cause, or hematogenous spread of anaerobic micro-organisms. Unusual causes include retrograde infection from the subhepatic veins or foreign bodies, peliosis hepatis (208) and Crohn's disease (201).

Pyogenic Liver Abscess

Pyogenic liver abscesses can be single or multiple. Multiple abscesses have an incidence of 45.5% (172) to 71% (178). Single abscesses are considered to involve mostly the right lobe of the liver. The current explanation is the preferential streaming of the superior mesenteric vein flow to the right lobe, whereas the stream from the inferior mesenteric vein and splenic vein is directed to the left lobe (123, 138). However, this does not explain the higher incidence of right lobe abscesses of arterial origin. Navarro (164) considers that pylephlebitis more often leads to a single abscess, whereas abscesses with a biliary origin are multiple.

Secondary liver abscesses can develop on preexisting lesions as benign cysts, hepatomas or any necrotizing tumor. They have the same clinical manifestations as primary pyogenic abscesses; their diagnosis may be difficult with imaging modalities, as the primary lesion may be missed.

Liver abscesses secondary to portal vein contamination contain intestinal flora (Table **2**). Before the antibiotic era, *E. coli* and streptococcus spp., especially from the *Enterococcus* and *viridans* groups, were predominant. More recently, Gram-negative anaerobic bacteria have been encountered with increasing frequency due to improvements in sampling and culture techniques (139). They may account for at least 50% of liver abscesses (3).

Subcapsular Liver Abscess

These generally develop from a pre-existing subcapsular hematoma or biloma, which is secondary to blunt or penetrating trauma, surgery (Fig. **14**), or interventional procedures such as biopsy or percutaneous biliary manipulation. Their exact frequency, previously unknown, was 30% of the hepatic abscesses treated in our experience (50).

Amebic Abscess

The liver represents the most frequent location of non-enteric complications of amebiasis (1–25%). More than half of the patients have no evidence of previous diarrhea or amebiasis in the stools at the time of diagnosis of the liver abscess. Despite the lower incidence of *Entamoeba histolytica* in European and North American countries, endemic areas are evidenced, and the incidence of the disease is increasing with migration phenomena and international travel. Amebic abscesses generally occur in the right lobe of the liver and are mostly unique (8). Potential complications are pleural or retroperitoneal rupture, pericarditis, rupture in the colon or in the biliary tree, and hematogenous spread to the brain. The clinical signs are generally more insidious than those for pyogenic abscesses. Secondary superinfection by pyogenic bacteria is possible.

Therapeutic Strategy for Liver Abscess

Due to the bad prognosis of liver abscesses in the absence of treatment, all efforts at rapid diagnosis and treatment should be made before the clinical signs become prominent and prior to major complications such as bacteremia, intraperitoneal or pericardial rupture, subphrenic abscess or metastatic spread.

Surgical treatment has for a long time been the only therapeutic alternative (3, 118, 139). The development of the treatment of liver abscesses can be summarized by two dates. The first was 1938, when Ochsner (172) stated that the treatment of solitary pyogenic liver abscesses needed incision and drainage, the absolute surgical objective being total avoidance even of minimal contamination to the pleural or peritoneal cavity. For that reason, he considered puncture of liver abscesses hazardous due to the potential risk of peritonitis. No alternative to that approach existed prior to the introduction of antibiotics. Nowadays, any potential seeding of bacteria in the peritoneal cavity at the time of removal of drainage material can be controlled. The second date is 1953, when MacFadzean (138) demonstrated that percutaneous aspiration in combination with antibiotherapy had an excellent prognosis in pyogenic liver abscesses.

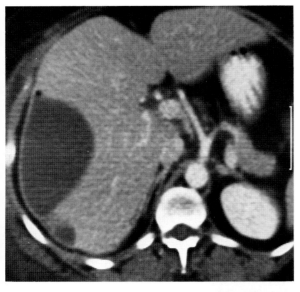

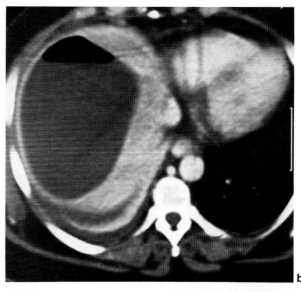

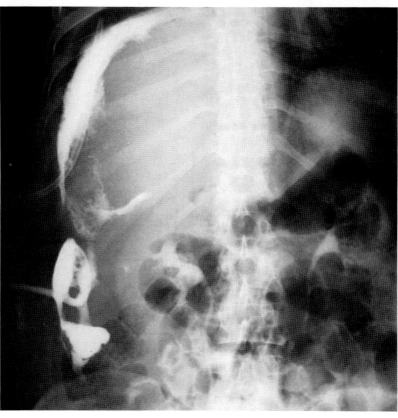

Fig. **14**   **44-year-old female.**
Subcapsular liver abscess
developed two years after
cholecystectomy complicated by
subcapsular hematoma
a Lower extent of the abscess,
showing a gas bubble.
A loculation is visible in the
dependent part of the
subcapsular space
b Upper extent of the abscess with
fluid-air level. Associated pleural
effusion
c Abscessogram performed after
positioning, with fluoroscopy
control, of a 14 Fr straight sump
catheter in the upper cavity and a
9 Fr pigtail in the lower cavity.
Presence of a fistula with the right
mesocolon, which required
3 weeks of drainage to cure the
patient

Fluoroscopy (138) and angiography (170) were used at first to guide the procedure. Modern imaging modalities, including US and CT, allow diagnosis in a shorter period of time (181) and explain the recent introduction of percutaneous treatment as the therapeutic procedure of choice, because of the precision in localizing the lesion (15, 27). A combination with immediate aspiration with 22 G to 5 Fr needles at the time of diagnosis allows specific antibiotherapy with little delay. If necessary, immediate drainage with 8–9 Fr pigtail catheters allows treatment to be started at the time of diagnosis. This strategy, speeding up diagnosis and therapy, results in a dramatic reduction of the mortality.

One further advantage of modern imaging modalities is the demonstration of multiple abscesses, which are no longer an autopsy discovery (Fig. **12**). A multilocular abscess may require puncture of the loculations to determine whether they are communicating (15, 84). A sophisticated approach such as this is not possible at surgery. Multiple abscesses may be a specific indication for percutaneous treatment, which avoids the extensive parenchymatous dissection that is necessary during surgical investigation, even with peroperative US (221, 231). Progress in imaging suggests that multilocular abscesses may have communicating loculations, finally converging into a larger single cavity, according to the theory first stated by Ochsner (172).

Puncture of suspicious intrahepatic lesions is also necessary for the differential diagnosis of an abscess and a necrotized tumor (146, 230). The diagnostic difficulty is increased by the variable aspects of liver abscesses on CT (96), especially after surgery (98). Some authors have suggested that percutaneous treatment of liver abscesses should be limited to patients with a poor operative risk (145). Other researchers consider the potential risk of peritonitis following percutaneous treatment to be too high to use it as a definitive treatment in a stable patient. Such a complication has never been reported in the radiological literature (23, 49, 50, 138, 143, 214). Antiobiotherapy associated with the percutaneous approach to liver abscesses may be responsible for the non-occurrence of this potential complication. Most authors suggest complete evacuation of the purulent content of the abscess. The mean volume of parenchymatous abscesses may vary greatly, from only a few milliliters to 2–31. Some reports have suggested that complete evacuation of pus is not necessary when specific antibiotics can be given on the basis of a diagnostic aspiration, allowing complete recovery of the patient (16, 43, 103, 205). However, once a needle or a small catheter has been introduced into the cavity, aspiration of the max-imum amount of pus seems logical, as such a procedure can only facilitate and accelerate the patient's recovery, with a positive impact on the length of hospital stay. The mean hospital stay in the surgical literature is 40 days, compared to 21 days with percutaneous treatment and systemic antibiotherapy. Liver abscesses have the best prognosis, particularly those treated with percutaneous techniques when punctured with US or CT control. Parenchymatous abscesses respond to percutaneous treatment as well as subcapsular abscesses do. The latter are more regularly drained than aspirated. When a biliary fistula is evidenced, prolonged drainage allows closure in most cases, and further treatment (biliary drainage, surgery) is only rarely required. Percutaneous diagnosis and treatment of pyogenic liver abscesses should be considered as the first choice when a suspicious image is evidenced on US or CT, as complete cure is achieved in 76% (115) to 100% (13, 138, 212) of cases (Table **4**). When an underlying causal disease persists, this should be treated in a second intention, in order to prevent recurrence of the abscess. Septic complications and bleeding at the time of drainage are exceptional. The mortality associated with percutaneous treatment of liver abscesses is less than 5%, which compares very favorably with the surgical literature. It is generally due to prolonged sepsis with multi-organ failure, and stresses the need for early diagnosis and treatment.

Cystic Liver Disease

Benign biliary cysts in the liver do not require percutaneous treatment, but might be aspirated for differential diagnosis with a necrotic or cystic tumor. Polycystic liver disease cannot be treated by a percutaneous approach. However, in these patients, some cysts may be complicated by hemorrhage or enlarge dramatically and become clinically signifi-

Table **4**   Percutaneous radiologically guided treatment of liver abscess

Author	n	Radiologic guidance	Aspiration	Drainage	Success n	%	Failure
McFadzean (1954)	13	X-ray	14	–	14	100	
Martin (1981)	7	CT: 1; US: 6	2	5	5	100	
Berger (1982)	15	US	15	–	15	100	
Kuligowska (1982)	12	US	–	12	10	83	1
Van Sonnenberg (1982)	10	US/CT	–	10	10	100	
Herbert (1982)	10	US: 9	10	–	9	90	1 (died)
Dahnert (1983)	17	US, CT	–	17	14	82	3
Johnson (1985)	21	US, CT	–	21	16	76	5
Mathieu (1988)	24	CT: 20; US: 4	6	18	21	87	3 (died)
Total	130	46 (36%)	83 (63%)	114	(88%)	13 (10%)	

cant. Percutaneous aspiration or drainage with US or CT control allows symptomatic treatment by decompression of the liver capsula and avoids surgery, which does not either cure the primary disease.

Hydatic and Echinococcal Cyst

Percutaneous puncture of hepatic *Echinococcus* disease is still feared because of the standard surgical recommendations to avoid an approach that may induce an anaphylactic shock and contamination from liver scolices spilling into the peritoneal cavity (10, 176, 182–184). But the potential risk of either anaphylactic shock or peritoneal seeding as a result of percutaneous drainage has been poorly quantified (203). Although anaphylactic shock from ruptured echinococcal cysts is documented, its exact frequency and pathophysiology have not been well detailed (99, 184, 187). Cases of intentional or accidental puncture of *Echinococcus* cysts have been documented without complications (59, 106, 136) when complete aspiration is performed to reduce intracystic pressure such that no residual leakage occurs (106). No spillage from a cavity content occurs with percutaneous aspiration or drainage of fluids and abscesses as long as the trocar technique is used. Echinococcal cysts have been successfully treated percutaneously in the thorax (119) and the liver (22, 156, 161). Complete aspiration of the cavity content and lavage of the cavity through the catheter with 30% hypertonic saline and 0.5% silver nitrate solution has been advocated (161, 176, 182, 183), as well as irrigation of the cavity with 0.5% silver nitrate solution every 3 days until laboratory evaluation of the returns from irrigation demonstrates no evidence of liver scolices. No signs of peritoneal spillage were observed in 13 patients treated by Bret (22), and a mild allergic reaction with temporary pruritus was observed in 2 patients. No recurrences developed during follow-up. Associated biliary fistulae and pyogenic superinfection can be treated by percutaneous drainage. Although open surgical drainage is considered the treatment of choice for *Echinococcus* liver disease (120), the safety and efficacy of elective percutaneous radiologically guided drainage has been demonstrated, and may at least serve as an alternative form of therapy for patients who have undergone several operations and those who are at poor surgical risk.

Biloma

Bilomas were initially considered as an encapsulated extrahepatic collection of bile (80); their current definition includes intrahepatic bile collections located outside the bile ducts (127). Bilomas can be solitary or multiple; they result from bile duct ruptures, and may occur following liver or biliary surgery, liver transplantation, nonsurgical iatrogenic causes – percutaneous transhepatic cholangiography (PTC) (130), biliary drainage, liver biopsy, endoscopic retrograde cholangiopancreatography (ERCP) (54) – trauma, or any cause of focal hepatic infarction associated with formation of a bile leak. The size and location of bilomas depends on the cause of bile duct rupture, the size and rate of bile leakage, and the rate of bile reabsorption by the peritoneum (77). Gallbladder rupture more often leads to generalized peritonitis due to the abrupt release of concentrated and often infected bile in the peritoneal cavity (35, 107). Slow leakage of unconcentrated bile generally results in encapsulated extraductal bile, forming a localized biloma (77).

Bilomas are generally confined to the upper two-thirds of the abdomen, and especially to the right abdomen, as the extraductal bile collects slowly and follows anatomical pathways. Most bilomas are fluid collections, but there may be complicated forms containing blood, inflammatory infiltrates or bacteria, leading to fluid draw into the biloma from an increase of oncotic pressure due to the presence of degenerating proteins (217). CT is the optimal examination to identify, localize and demonstrate the regional anatomy of a biloma more precisely than US. The differential diagnosis includes all potential peritoneal fluid collections. Clinical history, anatomy and location of the lesion, and clear greenish bile obtained by aspiration, are helpful distinguishing features.

Previously, bilomas were all drained surgically (107). The appropriate treatment for most bilomas is drainage, although small-sized bilomas may resolve spontaneously (217).

Percutaneous drainage using pigtail catheters has proved its effectiveness in the treatment of bilomas (127, 158, 217, 218). Percutaneous drainage is almost invariably successful, and often obviates the need for surgery (Fig. **15**). In case of persistent active bile leakage, endoscopic or percutaneous biliary drainage is mandatory, as described in the chapter on management of benign biliary disease below.

Spleen

Splenic abscesses are rare. They are generally secondary to hematogenous contamination. The initial infectious site may be cutaneous, in the upper airways, osseous, endometrial, endocardiac, or in any other organ. Occasionally, infection may be due to direct spread from an adjacent organ (pancreas), or by direct inoculation in the postoperative or post-traumatic patient. Other reported causes include splenic infarction due to ischemia secondary to hemoglobinopathy, non-penetrating trauma, or arterial transcatheter embolization (167). Conservative management of a traumatized spleen with subcapsular hematoma may lead to abscess formation (191). Postembolization abscesses have also been reported,

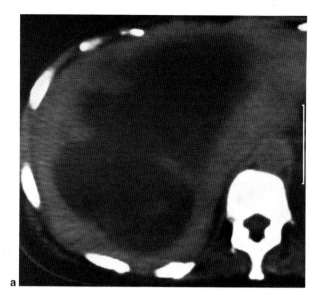

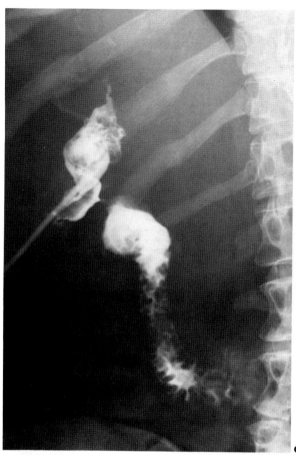

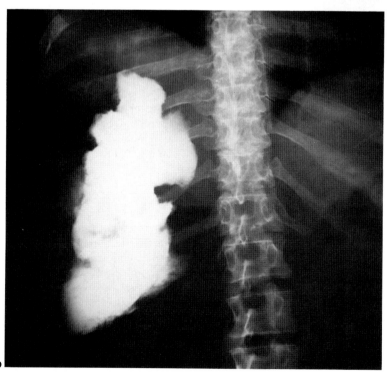

Fig. **15**   **49-year-old female.** Previous history of a severe multiple organ trauma with grade IV liver trauma treated by percutaneous embolization, without surgery

a CT scan 3 months after trauma shows a large fluid collection in the liver. Percutaneous aspiration demonstrated an infected biloma which was drained with a 9 Fr pigtail catheter

b Opacification of the cavity after aspiration of 2.6 l of brownish fluid demonstrates the extent of the biloma

c Final opacification after 4 months of drainage shows a minimal residual cavity with a duodenal fistula, which was cured with 2 additional weeks of drainage

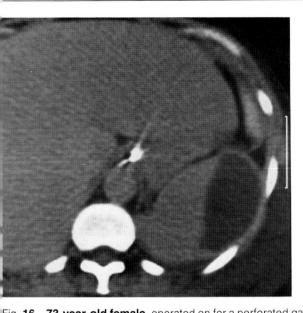 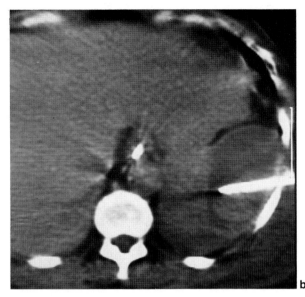

Fig. **16** **73-year-old female,** operated on for a perforated gastric ulcer two weeks previously
a CT scan of the spleen shows a 7 cm large subcapsular fluid collection not evidenced at surgery
b Percutaneous drainage with a 14 Fr sump catheter demonstrates an abscess due to *Candida,* that was efficiently treated percutaneously after 29 days of drainage

making preventive antibiotics and partial procedures a necessity (175, 198). Other factors such as hepatomegaly and portal hypertension may play a role in the formation of abscess by promoting venous stasis and reflux. Nelken (167) compared the literature before and after 1978, and demonstrated that splenic abscesses are now diagnosed, earlier, with a higher proportion of immunocompromised patients (24%) due to increasing use of steroids and chemotherapeutic agents. The diagnosis of fungal splenic abscesses, almost unheard-of before 1978, has increased to 26% of patients. The diagnostic sensitivity of CT (96%) was shown to be superior to US and to gallium, indium, and technetium-99m liver and spleen scans in 170 patients (167). The diagnosis of splenic abscess is often not considered, due to its rarity and the presence of predisposing conditions which obscure its clinical presentation. Fever and left upper quadrant abdominal tenderness are the most frequent clinical findings (202). Splenic abscesses carry a mortality of 80% to 100% if un-

treated (121). Splenectomy is the surgical treatment for these lesions. Postsplenectomy infections are well documented in the literature (188), and the mortality after operation for splenic abscesses varies from 13–30% (4, 44, 58, 188). Conservative surgical treatment of the spleen (splenotomy) and selected antibiotics have been advocated as improvements in the management (18). CT allows precise diagnosis of splenic abscesses or fluid collections (126) that may not be evidenced at laparotomy and surgical palpation (157). We have observed such a case with negative laparotomy and secondary successful percutaneous aspiration confirming the diagnosis (Fig. **16**). The vascularity and relative inaccessibility of the spleen (surrounding pleura and lung, splenic flexure of the colon) have produced some reluctance towards interventional procedures in that organ. A few reports (Table **5**) discuss the percutaneous approach to splenic fluid collections, including abscesses, and reflect both the infrequency of these lesions and the prevailing attitude that they require

Table **5** Splenic abscess: percutaneous treatment	Author		Success		Complications
		n	n	%	
	Quinn (1986)	9	7	78	1 pleural effusion
	Berkmann (1983)	2	2	100	
	Lerner (1984)	4	3	75	
	Total	15	12	80	

surgery (32, 131, 193). Splenic abscesses can, however, be drained percutaneously (14, 137, 147). The access route is left antero- or posterolateral, depending on the location and extent of the abscess; only one peritoneal compartment is transgressed by the aspiration or drainage material. The benefits of conservative treatment of the spleen and the absence of major surgery and postoperative risks make the attempt to treat splenic fluid collections percutaneously a preferable initial approach to the problem. Further experience is necessary to evaluate the treatment of splenic abscesses by single aspiration and selective antibiotherapy in the same way as for the liver. The risk of bleeding is minor, and should not be considered as a contra-indication when clotting parameters have been checked and corrected if necessary. Even a major hemorrhage can be controlled by arterial embolization prior to eventual surgery.

Failure of percutaneous aspiration and drainage of a pyogenic splenic abscess may be secondary to the presence of an underlying disease in the spleen that may require splenectomy. It appears that multiple small fungal abscesses can be treated with antifungal therapy alone (104, 167). Collected fungal abscesses respond to percutaneous treatment as well as pyogenic abscesses do (Fig. 16). Rupture in the left subphrenic space requires drainage of both the splenic and subphrenic abscess, and may even allow healing of an associated splenobronchial fistula (166). Neither bleeding complications nor mortality have been documented. A sterile pleural effusion occurred in one patient (179) (Table 5).

State of the Art

Percutaneous imaging-guided treatment of abdominal abscesses has been considered as the most important progress in abdominal surgery in the past decade (223). However, percutaneous abscess drainage is not the single factor that has improved the clinical outcome.

The causes of death with surgical treatment of abdominal abscesses have been well documented (45, 64, 177); they include multi-organ failure prior to treatment, multiple abscesses, some specific topographic sites for abscess formation (subphrenic, pelvis, subhepatic, lesser omentum and retroperitoneum), diagnostic delay, recurrent or persistent abscesses, and age over 50–60 years (36). Multiorgan failure present before drainage is associated with a significant increase in mortality (44, 64, 169). The lower incidence of predrainage multi-organ failure in recent studies seems to be a consequence of progress in resuscitation, the development of newer antibiotics, and a better understanding of the role of anaerobic bacteria in the pathogenesis of intra-abdominal infection. Sepsis does not seem to cause

organ failure per se, and is more likely to be due to the mediators of inflammation (45). The lower incidence of predrainage multi-organ failure currently observed is presumably also a consequence of earlier detection of abdominal abscesses.

Diagnostic delay has been considered another major determinant of the outcome and mortality of abdominal abscesses (64, 206). Considering diagnostic delay to be the time period separating the causal factor for abscess formation (when identified) from the diagnosis with CT and treatment, delays of 13 days have been observed for peritoneal abscesses, 38 days for retroperitoneal abscesses, and 48 days for pelvic abscesses in our prospective experience. These diagnostic delays are less than those reported in the surgical literature, which often exceed one month, expressed as the time interval between the onset of clinical signs and diagnosis (12). Progress in imaging is the major factor that reduces the diagnostic delay in abdominal abscesses. CT is the most sensitive and specific test for detection and localization of abdominal abscesses, with a specificity and sensitivity exceeding 90% (6, 25, 26, 45, 48, 111, 124, 125, 140, 154, 185, 228). Difficulties may be encountered in diagnosing an abscess with enteric communication (102) or in differentiating it from a necrotized tumor in the liver. US is slightly less sensitive and not as specific (48, 111). US rarely adds any information to CT (51), which should therefore be rapidly available when the problem of diagnosis and localization of an abdominal abscess has been raised. Ruling out an abdominal abscess is in our institution, considered as grounds for a CT scan on the same day as the examination is requested. US may be useful if bedside diagnosis and drainage is required (37) or as a guidance modality for some specific sites (162, 207). Scintigraphy is not well adapted to the requirements for rapid, specific and precise topographic diagnosis (55). Mortality increases when initial drainage fails, and decreases when the abscess is localized preoperatively and surgery is directed to the abscess (42, 78) as opposed to general abdominal exploration. A higher proportion of successful precise localizations of abscesses before drainage increases the chances of successful drainage at the initial attempt, and is therefore considered as a major factor in the improvement of the outcome for these patients (24, 45, 185).

Multiple and complex abscesses are still considered a contra-indication to percutaneous drainage by some authors (45, 135, 116). Our prospective study on initial percutaneous drainage in all cases of abdominal abscesses, including 50% multiple or complex (fistulized, multilocular) abscesses, demonstrated little difference in the clinical outcome when compared to unilocular abscesses (50). A success rate of 88% is achieved with percutaneous drainage of simple unilocular abscesses, and of 63% for com-

Table **6**   Percutaneous (PD) versus surgical (SD) drainage

Author	Drainage	Patients n	Success %	Compli- cations %	Mortality %	Drainage duration (days)
Aeder (1983)	PD	10	69	15	23	–
	SD	31	–	56	37	–
Brolin (1984)	PD	24	92	8	–	12
	SD	24	87	21	12	21
Glass (1984)	PD	15	47	6	–	–
	SD	44	88	23	–	–
Johnson (1981)	PD	27	89	4	11	17
	SD	43	70	16	21	29
Lurie (1987)	PD	29	80	–	17	–
	SD	60	81	–	17	–
Olak (1986)	PD	27	70	41	11	31
	SD	27	85	30	7	16
Moessner (1986)	PD	21	75	–	13	27
	SD	25	64	60	16	34
Deveney (1988)	PD	29	72	–	21	36
	SD	37	78	–	22	33
Total	PD	182	78.5	10	13	30
	SD	291	76.5	22	16.5	33

plex abscesses, with an associated mortality of 33% in the complex cases in which subsequent surgery was necessary (50). An overall success rate of 70% is expected when all the patients are included for percutaneous drainage (50), which is consistent with other reports (74). Multiple or complex abscesses may require temporary drainage (215) in 11% of cases of peritoneal abscesses and in 36% in the retroperitoneum. Depending on the cause of the abscess, secondary surgical treatment may be necessary (i.e. repair of an anastomotic leak) when no interventional treatment is considered (i.e. diversion of a high-output enteric fistula, biliary drainage, prolongation of the percutaneous drainage). Successful treatment of abscesses caused by biliary, small bowel and gastric fistulae, as well as anastomotic leaks, have been reported (74, 141, 144, 219), and make percutaneous drainage a reasonable first choice therapy in such cases (Figs. **3, 12, 15**). Surgery is always possible as a second choice, and is then performed in a non-infected operative field, which may allow one-stage surgery in most cases of diverticulitis (Fig. **4**) or Crohn's disease.

Many non-randomized studies have compared percutaneous drainage with surgical drainage (Table **6**). Considerable variations between the studies can be seen, but both modalities are actually considered equivalent in terms of initial drainage success, morbidity, mortality and length of hospital stay, when simultaneous groups of patients are considered (1, 76, 95, 116). Several reports indicate that percutaneous drainage may be better for specific sites, such as subphrenic abscesses (45, 162, 207). Surgical drainage and percutaneous drainage are both operator-dependent, and different institutions may exhibit variable results according to experience. The choice of a localized percutaneous or surgical treatment should therefore be determined on the basis of operator experience and poor surgical risk, as the complication rates, around 10%, are lower with percutaneous drainage (50).

Some anatomic sites have been considered to carry a high mortality risk (64). A comparison of the mortality for different abdominal areas resulting from surgical drainage and percutaneous drainage indicated a lower mortality with percutaneous drainage (Table **7**) (Fig. **3**).

Recurrent or persistent abscesses are also associated with high surgical mortality (4, 64, 94, 128, 152, 192) because of relaparotomy, a potential decrease of immunity, an initial inadequate drainage and therefore prolonged sepsis. A mortality of 50% has been reported after surgical treatment of recurrent abscesses. Only 20% of patients with recurrent abscess died after a second percutaneous drainage in our prospective experience, which makes this treatment a primary therapeutic choice in this setting. Abscesses which persist after percutaneous treatment should be operated on, as surgical debridement may in such cases be the only way to cure the patient.

Table **7**   Mortality in relation to the abscess site

Abscess site	Mortality (%)	
	Surgical drainage (Fry 1980)	Percutaneous drainage (author's series)
Subphrenic	28	22
Pelvis	31	20
Subhepatic	52	40
Lesser sac	69	–

In our prospective study, all of the patients with persistent abscesses were not adequately drained at surgery either, and they invariably died.

Conclusion

Percutaneous drainage is the reasonable initial treatment for abdominal abscesses (31, 33, 40, 62, 79, 85, 86, 108, 109, 194, 195, 197, 200). Early diagnosis and successful drainage, adequate antibiotherapy and resuscitation are the first objectives to be achieved when a patient presents with an abdominal abscess. An early assessment of the clinical response (48 h), management of the causal disease, with the choice between interventional and surgical procedures and an unsuccessful initial drainage requiring surgical debridement, are the most important factors that should determine whether the patient will be operated on or not. The absence of a safe access route should be the single actual determinant for initial surgery in a patient with abdominal abscesses. Superinfected tumors should be recognized and should not be treated. A septic venous thrombosis requires surgical treatment. Residual fluid collections in the peritoneal cavity are normally observed up to 12 days after surgery and should only be drained or aspirated if they become clinically significant or enlarge (165).

Hematomas should be observed with imaging. Their spontaneous development is to resolve after fluid drainage, due to their higher osmolarity. Aspiration should be performed if they become clinically significant, enlarge or persist after several months.

References

1. Aeder MI, Wellmann JL, Haaga JR, Hau T. Role of surgical and percutaneous drainage in the treatment of abdominal abscesses. Arch Surg 1983;118:273.
2. Alden SM, Frank E, Flancbaum L. Abdominal candidiasis in surgical patients. Am Surg 1989;55:45.
3. Altemeier WA, Schowengerdt CG, Whiteley DH. Abscesses of the liver: surgical considerations. Arch Surg 1970;101:258.
4. Altemeier WA, Culbertson WR, Fullen WD, Shook CD. Intra-abdominal abscesses. Am J Surg 1973;125:70.
5. Altemeier WA, Culbertson WR, Fidler JP. Giant horseshoe intraabdominal abscess. Ann Surg 1979;181:716.
6. Aronberg DJ, Stanley RJ, Levitt RG. Evaluation of abdominal abscess with computed tomography. J Comput Assist Tomogr 1978;2:384.
7. Autio V. The spread of intraperitoneal infection: studies with roentgen contrast medium. Acta Chir Scand (Suppl) 1964;321:1.
8. Balasegaram M. Management of hepatic abscess. Curr Prob Surg 1981;18:3.
9. Barnard HL. Surgical aspects of subphrenic spaces. Br Med J 1908;1:371.
10. Belli L, Del Favero E, Marni A, Romani F. Resection versus pericystectomy in the treatment of hydatidosis of the liver. Am J Surg 1983;145:239.
11. Bensoussan AL, Letourneau JN, Morin CC, Blanchard H. Surgical treatment of Crohn's disease. Can J Surg 1982;25:515.
12. Berens JJ, Gray HK, Dockerty MB. Subphrenic abscess. Surg Gynecol Obstet 1953;96:463.
13. Berger LA, Osborne DR. Treatment of pyogenic liver abscesses by percutaneous needle aspiration. Lancet 1982;i:132.
14. Berkman WA, Harris SA Jr, Bernardino ME. Nonsurgical drainage of splenic abscess. AJR 1983;141:395.
15. Bernardino ME, Berkman WA, Plemmons M, Sones PJ, Price RB, Casarella WJ. Percutaneous drainage of multiseptated hepatic abscess. J Comput Assist Tomogr 1984;8:38.
16. Bertoli D, Del Poggio P, Mazzolari M, Randone G. Management of liver abscesses. Lancet 1982;i:743.
17. Biller JA, Grand RJ, Harris BH. Abdominal abscesses in adolescents with Crohn's disease. J Pediatr Surg 1987;22:873.
18. Bonavina L, Rubaltelli L, Meleca A, Sandei F, Bardini R. Splenic abscess: the rationale for selective nonsurgical treatment. Ital J Surg Sci 1986;16:191.
19. Bonfils-Roberts EA, Barone JE, Nealon TF Jr. Treatment of subphrenic abscess. Surg Clin North Am 1975;55:1361.
20. Boyd TP. The anatomy and pathology of the subphrenic spaces. Surg Clin North Am 1958;38:619.
21. Boyd TP. The subphrenic spaces and the emperor's new robes. N Engl J Med 1966;275:911.
22. Bret PM, Fond A, Bretagnolle M, Valette PJ, Thiesse P, Lambert R, Labadie M. Percutaneous aspiration and drainage of hydatid cysts in the liver. Radiology 1988;168:617.
23. Brolin RE, Nosher JL, Leiman S, Lee WS, Greco RS. Percutaneous catheter versus open surgical drainage in the treatment of abdominal abscesses. Am Surg 1984;50:102.
24. Butler JA, Huang J, Wilson SE. Repeated laparotomy for postoperative intra-abdominal sepsis: an analysis of outcome predictors. Arch Surg 1987;122:702.
25. Bydder GM, Kreel L. Attenuation values of fluid collections within the abdomen. J Comput Assist Tomogr 1980;4:145.
26. Callen PW. Computed tomographic evaluation of abdominal and pelvic abscesses. Radiology 1979;131:171.
27. Callen PW, Filly RA, Marcus FS. Ultrasonography and computed tomography in the evaluation of hepatic microabscesses in the immunosuppressed patient. Radiology 1980;136:433.
28. Carrol CL, Jeffrey RB Jr, Federle MP, Vernacchi FS. CT evaluation of mediastinal infections. J Comput Assist Tomogr 1987;11:449.
29. Casley-Smith JR. The lymphatic system in inflammation. In: Grant PW, McCluskey RT, eds. The inflammatory process. 2nd ed. New York; Academic Press, 1973:161.
30. Casola G, Van Sonnenberg E, Neff CC, Saba RM, Withers C, Emarine CW. Abscesses in Crohn disease: percutaneous drainage. Radiology 1987;163:19.
31. Chalmers TC. Percutaneous catheter drainage of abdominal abscesses. N Engl J Med 1982;306:107.
32. Chun CH, Ralf MF, Contreras L, et al. Splenic abscess. Medicine (Baltimore) 1980;59:50.
33. Clark RA, Towbin R. Abscess drainage with CT and ultrasound guidance. Radiol Clin North Am 1983;21:445.
34. Condon RE. Peritonitis and intra-abdominal abscesses. In: Schwartz SI, ed. Principles of surgery. New York; McGraw-Hill, 1979:1397.

35. Conn JH, Chavez CM, Fain WR. Bile peritonitis: an experimental and clinical study. Am Surg 1970;36:219.

36. Connell TR, Stephens DH, Carlson HC, Brown ML. Upper abdominal abscess: a continuing and deadly problem. AJR 1980;134:759.

37. Crass, JR, Karl R. Bedside drainage of abscesses with sonographic guidance in the desperately ill patient. AJR 1982;139:183.

38. Crohn B, Ginzburg L, Oppenheimer G. Regional ileitis. JAMA 1932;99:1325.

39. Cropper LD Jr, Gold RE, Roberts LK. Bronchiobiliary fistula: management with percutaneous catheter drainage of a subphrenic abscess. J Trauma 1982;22:68.

40. Dahnert W, Gunther R, Klose K, Gamstatter G. Ergebnisse der perkutanen Abszessdrainagetherapie. RöFo 1983;139:400.

41. Dawson SL, Mueller PR, Ferrucci JT Jr. Mucomyst for abscesses: a clinical comment. Radiology 1984;151:342.

42. Deck KB, Berne TV. Selective management of subphrenic abscesses. Arch Surg 1979;114:1165.

43. Decock KM, Bhatt KM, Bhatt SM, Eeftinck-Schattenkerk JKM, Kager PA, Shah MV, Ogaga TO, Rees PH. Management of liver abscesses. Lancet 1982;i:743.

44. De Cosse JJ, Poulin TL, Fox PS, Condon RE. Subphrenic abscess. Surg Gynecol Obstet 1974;138:841.

45. Deveney CW, Lurie K, Deveney KE. Improved treatment of intra-abdominal abscess: a result of improved localization, drainage, and patient care, not technique. Arch Surg 1988;123:1126.

46. Dixon GD. Combined CT and fluoroscopic guidance for liver abscess drainage. AJR 1980;135:397.

47. Doberneck RC, Mittelman J. Reappraisal of the problems of intraabdominal abscess. Surg Gynecol Obstet 1982;154:875.

48. Dobrin PB, Gully PH, Grenlee HB, et al. Radiologic diagnosis of an intra-abdominal abscess. Arch Surg 1986;121:41.

49. Dondelinger R, Meoli S, Kurdziel JC. Aspiration et drainage percutanes des collections thoraciques et abdominales sous contrôle tomodensitométrique. J Radiol 1982;63:75.

50. Dondelinger RF, De Baets P, Kurdziel JC. Percutaneous aspiration and drainage of abdominal abscesses under X-ray computed tomography control: prospective study apropos of 63 cases. Ann Radiol 1987;30:373.

51. Doust BD, Thompson R. Ultrasonography of abdominal fluid collections. Gastrointest Radiol 1978;3:273.

52. Drye JC. Intraperitoneal pressure in the human. Surg Gynecol Obstet 1948;87:472.

53. Dubbins PA. Ultrasound demonstration of bowel wall thickness in inflammatory bowel disease. Clin Radiol 1984;35:227.

54. Dupas JL, Mancheron H, Sevenet F, Delamarre J, Delcenserie R, Capron JP. Hepatic subcapsular biloma: an unusual complication of endoscopic retrograde cholangiopancreatography. Gastroenterology 1988;94:1225.

55. Ebright JR, Soin JS, Manoli RS. The gallium scan: problems and misuse in examination of patients with suspected infection. Arch Int Med 1982;142:246.

56. Edwards H. Crohn's disease: an inquiry into its nature and consequences. Ann Roy Coll Surg 1969;44:121.

57. Edwards KC, Katzen BT, Woods C. Continuous gentle suction apparatus for abscess drainage. Radiology 1982;145:137.

58. Eraklis AJ, Filler RM. Splenectomy in childhood: a review of 1413 cases. J Pediatr Surg 1972;7:382.

59. Ertan A, Sahin B, Kandilci U, Acikalin T, Cumhur T, Danisoglu V. The mechanism of cholestasis from hepatic hydatid cysts. J Clin Gastroenterol 1983;5:437.

60. Farmer RG, Hawk WA, Turnbull RB Jr. Indications for surgery in Crohn's disease: analysis of 500 cases. Gastroenterology 1976;71:245.

61. Feliciano DV, Burch JM, Spjut-Patrinely V, Mattox RL, Jordan GL Jr. Abdominal gunshot wounds: an urban trauma center's experience with 300 consecutive patients. Ann Surg 1988;208:362.

62. Ferrucci JT Jr, Van Sonnenberg E. Intra-abdominal abscess: radiological diagnosis and treatment. JAMA 1981;246:2728.

63. Frager DH, Goldman M, Beneventano TC. Computed tomography in Crohn disease. J Comput Assist Tomogr 1983;7:819.

64. Fry DE, Garrison RN, Heitsch RC, Calhoun K, Polk HC. Determinants of death in patients with intraabdominal abscess. Surgery 1980;88:517.

65. Gagliardi PD, Hoffer PB, Rosenfield AT. Correlative imaging in abdominal infection: an algorithmic approach using nuclear medicine, ultrasound, and computed tomography. Semin Nucl Med 1988;18:320.

66. Gerzof SG, Robbins AH, Birkett DH. Computed tomography in the diagnosis and management of abdominal abscesses. Gastrointest Radiol 1978;3:287.

67. Gerzof SG, Robbins AH, Birkett DH, Johnson WC, Pugatch RD, Vincent ME. Percutaneous catheter drainage of abdominal abscesses guided by ultrasound and computed tomography. AJR 1979;133:1.

68. Gerzof SG. Triangulation: indirect CT guidance for abscess drainage. AJR 1981;137:1080.

69. Gerzof SG. Ultrasound in the search for abdominal abscesses. Clin Diag Ultrasound 1981;7:101.

70. Gerzof SG, Robbins AH, Johnson WC, Birkett DH, Nabseth DC. Percutaneous catheter drainage of abdominal abscesses: a five-year experience. N Engl J Med 1981;305:653.

71. Gerzof SG. Guided percutaneous catheter drainage of abdominal abscesses. In: Athanasoulis CA, Pfister RC, Greene RE, eds. Interventional radiology. Philadelphia: WB Saunders, 1982:557.

72. Gerzof SG. Surgical and computerized tomography guided drainage of intraabdominal abscess. Am J Surg 1984;147:426.

73. Gerzof SG, Johnson WC. Radiologic aspects of diagnosis and treatment of abdominal abscesses. Surg Clin North Am 1984;64:53.

74. Gerzof SG, Johnson WC, Robbins AH, et al. Expanded criteria for percutaneous abscess drainage. Arch Surg 1985;120:227.

75. Gerzof SG, Oates ME. Imaging techniques for infections in the surgical patient. Surg Clin North Am 1988;68:147.

76. Glass CA, Cohn I Jr. Drainage of intraabdominal abscesses: a comparison of surgical and computerized tomography guided catheter drainage. Am J Surg 1984;147:315.

77. Glenn F. Complications following operations upon the biliary tract. In: Hardy JD, ed. Management of surgical complications. Philadelphia: WB Saunders, 1975:501.

78. Glick PL, Pellegrini CA, Stein S, et al. Abdominal abscess: a surgical strategy. Arch Surg 1983;118:646.

79. Gobien RP, Young JWR, Curry NS, Gobien BS, Valicenti JF, Reines HD. Computed tomographic guidance of percutaneous needle aspiration and drainage of abdominal abscess. J Comput Assist Tomogr 1982;6:127.

80. Gould L, Patel A. Ultrasound detection of extrahepatic encapsulated bile: "biloma". AJR 1979;132:1014.

81. Greenstein AJ, Sachar DB, Pasternak BS. Reoperation and recurrence in Crohn's colitis and ileocolitis: crude and cumulative rates. N Engl J Med 1975;293:685.

82. Greenstein AJ, Meyers S, Sher L, Heimann T, Aufses AH. Surgery and its sequelae in Crohn's colitis and ileocolitis. Arch Surg 1981;116:285.

83. Greenstein AJ, Sachar DB, Greenstein RJ, Janovitz HD, Aufses AH Jr. Intraabdominal abscess in Crohn's (ileo)colitis. Am J Surg 1982;143:727.

84. Greenwood LH, Collins TL, Yrizarry JM. Percutaneous management of multiple liver abscesses. AJR 1982;139:390.

85. Gronvall J, Gronvall S, Hegedus V. Ultrasound-guided drainage of fluid-containing masses using angiographic catheterization techniques. AJR 1977;129:997.

86. Gronvall S, Gammelgaard J, Haubek A, Holm HH. Drainage of abdominal abscesses guided by sonography. AJR 1982;138:527.

87. Haaga JR, Alfidi RJ, Coopermann AM, Havrilla TR, Meaney TF, Ockner SA, Stiff P, Silber S. Definitive treatment of a large pyogenic liver abscess with CT guidance. Cleveland Clin Q 1976;43:85.

88. Haaga JR, Alfidi RJ, Havrilla TR, Cooperman AM, Seidelmann FE, Reich NE, Weinstein AJ, Meaney TF. CT detection and aspiration of abdominal abscesses. AJR 1977;128:465.

89. Haaga JR, Reich NE, Havrilla TR, Alfidi RJ. Interventional CT scanning. Radiol Clin North Am 1977;15:449.

90. Haaga JR, George C, Weinstein AJ, Cooperman AM. New interventional techniques in the diagnosis and management of inflammatory disease within the abdomen. Radiol Clin North Am 1979;17:485.

91. Haaga JR, Weinstein AJ. CT-guided percutaneous aspiration and drainage of abscesses. AJR 1980;135:1187.

92. Haaga JR, Alfidi RJ, Weinstein A. Percutaneous catheter drainage of abdominal abscesses. N Engl J Med 1982;306:106.

93. Hajek PC, Kumpan W, Inhof H, Riedl P, Salomonowitz E. Fully CT-guided percutaneous abscess drainage. Ann Radiol 1986;29:255.

94. Halasz NA. Subphrenic abscess: myths and facts. JAMA 1970;214:724.

95. Halasz NA, Van Sonnenberg E. Drainage of intraabdominal abscesses: tactics and choices. Am J Surg 1983;146:112.

96. Halvorsen RA, Korobkin M, Foster WL, Silverman PM, Thompson WM. The variable CT appearance of hepatic abscesses. AJR 1984;141:941.

97. Hamlin JA, Friedman M, Stein MG, Bray JF. Percutaneous biliary drainage: complications of 118 consecutive catheterizations. Radiology 1986;158:199.

98. Haney PJ, Whitley NO, Brotman S, Cunat JS, Whitley J. Liver injury and complications in the postoperative trauma patient: CT evaluation. AJR 1982;139:271.

99. Hankins J, Werner D, Kobout E. Surgical treatment of ruptured and unruptured hydatid cysts of the lung. Ann Surg 1968;167:336.

100. Harley HRS. Subphrenic abscess, with particular reference to the spread of infection: Hunterian lecture. Ann Roy Coll Surg 1955;17:201.

101. Hau T, Hartmann E. Pathologie, Diagnose und Therapie der Leberabszesse. Zentralbl Chir 1987;112:529.

102. Heavey LR, Glazer GM, Francis IR, Fugenshuch D, Jasinski R. Abscesses with enteric communication: a potential pitfall in computed tomography. J Comput Assist Tomogr 1987;11:470.

103. Herbert DA, Rothman J, Simmons F, Fogel DA, Wilson S, Ruskin J. Pyogenic liver abscesses: successful non-surgical therapy. Lancet 1982;i:134.

104. Helton WS, Carrico CJ, Zaveruha PA, Schaller R. Diagnosis and treatment of splenic fungal abscesses in the immunosuppressed patient. Arch Surg 1986;121:580.

105. Hiatt JR, Williams RA, Wilson SE. Intra-abdominal abscess: etiology and pathogenesis. Semin ultrasound 1984;4:71.

106. Hira PR, Lindberg LG, Francis I, Schweiki H, Shaheen Y, Leven H. Diagnosis of cystic hydatid disease: role of aspiration cytology. Lancet 1988;ii:655.

107. Hogan WJ, Dodds WJ, Geenen JE. Motor function of the biliary-duct system. In: Christensen J, Wingate DL, eds. A guide to gastrointestinal motility. London: Wright, 1983:157.

108. Holm HH, Kristensen JK, Rasmussen SN, Northved A, Barlebo H. Ultrasound as guide in percutaneous puncture technique. Ultrasonics 1972;10:83.

109. Holm HH, Pedersen JF, Kristensen JK, Rasmussen SN, Hancke S, Jensen F. Ultrasonically guided percutaneous puncture. Radiol Clin North Am 1975;13:493.

110. Ivatury HR, Zuboski R, Psarras P, Nallathambi M, Rohman M, Stahl WM. Intra-abdominal abscess after penetrating abdominal trauma. J Trauma 1988;28:1238.

111. Jasinski RW, Glazer GM, Francis IR, Harkness RL. CT and ultrasound in abscess detection at specific anatomic sites: a study of 198 patients. Comput Radiol 1987;11:41.

112. Jeffrey RB, Federle MP, Goodman PC. Computed tomography of the lesser peritoneal sac. Radiology 1981;141:117.

113. Jeffrey RB, Federle MP, Laing FC. Computed tomography of silent abdominal abscesses. J Comput Assist Tomogr 1984;8:67.

114. Johnson DJ, Tonnesen AS. The abdomen as a source of occult sepsis. Gastroenterol Clin North Am 1988;17:419.

115. Johnson RD, Mueller PR, Ferrucci JT Jr, Dawson SL, Butch RJ, Papanicolaou N, Van Sonnenberg E, Simeone JF, Wittenberg J. Pecutaneous drainage of pyogenic liver abscesses. AJR 1985;144:463.

116. Johnson WC, Gerzof SG, Robbins AH, Nabseth DC. Treatment of abdominal abscesses: comparative evaluation of operative drainage versus percutaneous catheter drainage guided by computed tomography or ultrasound. Ann Surg 1981;194:510.

117. Jorulf H. Roentgen diagnosis of intraperitoneal fluid: a physical, anatomic, and clinical investigation. Acta Radiol (Suppl) 1975;343.

118. Joseph WL, Kahn AM, Longmire WP Jr. Pyogenic liver abscess. Am J Surg 1968;115:63.

119. Kandil S, Boubekeur M, Taouagh BS, Dahmache H. Traitement par ponction-vidange transpariétale du kyste hydatique pulmonaire à localisation périphérique. Chirurgie 1986;112:255.

120. Karavias D, Panagopoulos C, Vagianos C, Vagenas C, Rathosis S, Androulakis J. Infected echinococcal cyst: a common cause of pyogenic hepatic abscess. Ups J Med Sci 1988;93:289.

121. Karlson KB, Fankuchen EI, Casarella WJ. Percutaneous abscess drainage. Surg Gynecol Obstet 1982;154:44.

122. Keighley MR, Eastwood D, Ambrose NS, Allan RN, Burdon DW. Incidence and microbiology of abdominal and pelvic abscess in Crohn's disease. Gastroenterology 1982;83:1271.

123. Kinney TD, Ferrebee JW. Hepatic abscess: factors determining its location. Arch Pathol 1948;45:41.

124. Kleinhaus U, Goldsher D, Kaftori JK. Computed tomographic diagnosis of abdominal abscesses. Radiology 1982;22:230.

125. Koehler PR, Moss AA. Diagnosis of intra-abdominal and pelvic abscesses by computerized tomography. JAMA 1980;244:49.

126. Korobkin M, Moss AA, Callen PW, De Martini WJ, Kaiser JA. Computed tomography of subcapsular splenic hematoma. Radiology 1978;129:441.

127. Kuligowska E, Schlesinger A, Miller KB, Lee VW, Grosso D. Bilomas: a new approach to their diagnosis and treatment. Gastrointest Radiol 1983;8:237.

128. Kune GA. Life-threatening surgical infection: its development and prediction. Ann Roy Coll Surg 1978;60:92.

129. Lambiase RE, Cronan JJ, Dorfman GS, Paolella LP, Haas RA. Postoperative abscesses with enteric communication: percutaneous treatment. Radiology 1989;171:497.

130. Lawson TL. Chronic subcapsular hepatic bile abscess: a rare complication of percutaneous transhepatic cholangiography. Am J Gastroenterol 1974;61:383.

131. Linos DA, Nagorney DM, McIlrath CE. Splenic abscess: the importance of early diagnosis. Mayo Clinic Proc 1983;58:261.

132. Livingston EM. A clinical study of the abdominal cavity and peritoneum. New York: Hoeber, 1932.

133. Lock MR, Farmer RG, Fazio VW, Jagelman DG, Lavery IC, Weakley FL. Recurrence and reoperation for Crohn's disease: the role of disease location in prognosis. N Engl J Med 1981;304:1586.

134. Lorber B, Swenson RM. The bacteriology of intra-abdominal infections. Surg Clin North Am 1975;55:1349.

135. Lurie K, Plzak L, Deveney CW. Intraabdominal abscess in the 1980s. Surg Clin North Am 1987;67:621.

136. McCorkell SJ. Unintended percutaneous aspiration of pulmonary echinococcal cysts. AJR 1984;143:123.

137. MacErlean DP, Gibney RG. Radiological management of abdominal abscess. J Roy Soc Med 1983;76:256.

138. MacFadzean AJS, Chang KPS, Wong CC. Solitary pyogenic abscess of liver treated by closed aspiration and antibiotics: a report of 14 consecutive cases with recovery. Br J Surg 1954;41:141.

139. MacDonald MI. Pyogenic liver abscess: diagnosis, bacteriology and treatment. Eur J Clin Microbiol 1984;3:506.

140. Machiedo GW, Suval WD. Detection of sepsis in the postoperative patient. Surg Clin North Am 1988;68:215.

141. McLean GK, Mackie JA, Freiman DB, Ring EJ. Enterocutaneous fistulae: interventional radiologic management. AJR 1982;138:615.

142. Manco LG. Percutaneous drainage of a left subphrenic abscess through a polycystic liver. JCU 1984;12:222.

143. Martin EC, Karlson KB, Fankuchen EI, Cooperman A, Casarella WJ. Percutaneous drainage in the management of hepatic abscesses. Surg Clin North Am 1981;61:157.

144. Martin EC, Karlson KB, Fankuchen EI, Cooperman A, Casarella WJ. Percutaneous drainage of postoperative intraabdominal abscesses. AJR 1982;138:13.

145. Martin EC, Fankuchen EI, Neff RA. Percutaneous drainage of abscesses: a report of 100 patients. Clin Radiol 1984;35:9.

146. Mathieu D, Vasile N, Fagniez PL, Segui S, Grably D, Larde D. Dynamic CT features of hepatic abscesses. Radiology 1985;154:749.

147. Meyer P, Huber O, Mirescu D, Rohner A. Le drainage percutané sous scanner des collections intra-abdominales. Schweiz Med Wochenschr 1984;114:721.

148. Meyers MA. Roentgen significance of the phrenicocolic ligament. Radiology 1970;95:539.

149. Meyers MA. The spread and localization of acute intraperitoneal effusions. Radiology 1970;95:547.

150. Meyers MA. Peritoneography: normal and pathologic anatomy. AJR 1973;117:353.

151. Meyers MA. Dynamic radiology of the abdomen. Berlin: Springer, 1976.

152. Miller WT, Talman EA. Subphrenic abscess. AJR 1967;101:961.

153. Mitchell GAG. The spread of acute intraperitoneal effusions. Br J Surg 1940;28:291.

154. Moir C, Robins RE. Role of ultrasonography, gallium scanning, and computed tomography in the diagnosis of intraabdominal abscess. Am J Surg 1982;143:582.

155. Moore-Gillon JC, Eykyn SJ, Phillips I. Microbiology of pyogenic abscesses. Br Med J 1981;238:8199.

156. Morris DL. Hepatic echinococcal cyst: successful percutaneous drainage (letter). Radiology 1986;159:567.

157. Moss ML, Kirschner LP, Peereboom G, Ferris RA. CT demonstration of a splenic abscess not evident at surgery. AJR 1980;135:159.

158. Mueller PR, Ferrucci JT Jr, Simeone JF, Cronan JJ, Wittenberg J, Neff CC, Van Sonnenberg E. Detection and drainage of bilomas: special considerations. AJR 1983;140:715.

159. Mueller PR, Simeone JF. Intraabdominal abscesses: diagnosis by sonography and computed tomography. Radiol Clin North Am 1983;21:425.

160. Mueller PR, Van Sonnenberg E, Ferrucci JT Jr. Percutaneous drainage of 250 abdominal abscesses and fluid collections, part II: current procedural concepts. Radiology 1984;151:343.

161. Mueller PR, Dawson SL, Ferrucci JT Jr, Nardi GL. Hepatic echinococcal cyst: successful percutaneous drainage. Radiology 1985;155:627.

162. Mueller PR, Simeone JF, Butch RJ, Saini S, Stafford SA, Vici LG, Soto-Rivera C, Ferrucci JT Jr. Percutaneous drainage of subphrenic abscess: a review of 62 patients. AJR 1986;147:1237.

163. Nagler S, Poticha S. Intra-abdominal abscess in regional enteritis. Am J Surg 1979;137:350.

164. Navarro C, Clam DJ. Perforated diverticulum of the terminal ileum: a previously unreported cause of suppurative pylephlebitis and multiple hepatic abscesses. Dig Dis Sci 1984;29:171.

165. Neff CC, Simeone JF, Ferrucci JT Jr, Mueller PR, Wittenberg J. The occurence of fluid collections following routine abdominal surgical procedures: sonographic survey in asymptomatic postoperative patients. Radiology 1983;146:463.

166. Neff CC. Splenobronchial fistula: interventional radiologic management. Gastrointest Radiol 1987;12:197.

167. Nelken N, Ignatius J, Skinner M, Christensen N. Changing clinical spectrum of splenic abscess: a multicenter study and review of the literature. Am J Surg 1987;154:27.

168. Nichols DM, Cooperberg PL, Golding RH, Burhenne HJ. The safe intercostal approach? Pleural complications in abdominal interventional radiology. AJR 1984;141:1013.

169. Norton LW. Does drainage of intraabdominal pus reverse multiple organ failure? Am J Surg 1985;149:347.

170. Novy SB, Wallace S, Goldman AM, Ben Menachem Y. Pyogenic liver abscess: angiographic diagnosis and treatment by closed aspiration. AJR 1974;121:388.

171. Ochsner A, Graves AM. Subphrenic abscess: an analysis of 3372 collected and personal cases. Ann Surg 1933;98:961.

172. Ochsner A, De Bakey M. Subphrenic abscess: collective review and an analysis of 3608 collected and personal cases. Int Abstr. Surg 1938;66:426.

173. Orel SG, Rubesin SE, Jones B, Fishman EK, Bayless TM, Siegelman SS. Computed tomography vs. barium studies in the acutely symptomatic patient with Crohn disease. J Comput Assist Tomogr 1987;11:1009.

174. Overholt RH. Intraperitoneal pressure. Arch Surg 1931;22:691.

175. Owman T, Lunderquist A, Alwmark A, Bjorjesson B. Embolization of the spleen for treatment of splenomegaly and hypersplenism in patients with portal hypertension. Invest Rad 1979;14:457.

176. Pissiotis CA, Wander JV, Condon RE. Surgical treatment of hydatid disease. Arch Surg 1972;104:454.

177. Pitcher WD, Musher DM. Critical importance of early diagnosis and treatment of intraabdominal infection. Arch Surg 1982;117:328.

178. Pitt HA, Zuidema GD. Factors influencing mortality in the treatment of pyogenic hepatic abscess. Surg Gynecol Obstet 1975;140:228.

179. Quinn SF, Van Sonnenberg E, Casola G, Wittich GR, Neff CC. Interventional radiology in the spleen. Radiology 1986;161:289.

180. Roche A, Musset D, Kraiem C, Aguilar K. L'embolisation artérielle en pathologie tumorale. Ann Radiol 1985;28:148.

181. Rubinson HA, Isikoff MB, Hill MC. Diagnostic imaging of hepatic abscesses: a retrospective analysis. AJR 1980;135:735.

182. Rutledge R, Benson M, Thomas CG Jr. A technique for drainage, irrigation and sterilization of intrahepatic echinococcal cysts. Surg Rounds 1984;2:56.

183. Saidi F, Nazarian I. Surgical treatment of hydatid cysts by freezing of cyst wall and instillation of 0.5% silver nitrate solution. N Engl J Med 1971;284:1346.

184. Saidi F. Hydatid cysts of the liver. In: F Saidi Ed. Surgery of hydatid disease. Philadelphia: WB Saunders, 1976:60

185. Saini S, Kellum J, O'Leary MP, et al. Improved localization and survival in patients with intraabdominal abscesses. Am J Surg 1983;145:136.

186. Salkin D. Intra-abdominal pressure and its regulation. Am Rev Tuberculosis 1934;30:436.

187. Schiller CF. Complications of echinococcus cyst rupture. JAMA 1966;195:158.

188. Schwartz PE, Sterioff S, Mucha P, Melton LJ, Offord KP. Postsplenectomy sepsis and mortality in adults. JAMA 1982;18:2279.

189. Scott CM, Grasberger RC, Heeran TF, Williams LF, Hirsch EF. Intraabdominal sepsis after hepatic trauma. Am J Surg 1988;55:284.

190. Serrano A, Dahl EP, Rubin RH, Ferrucci JT Jr, Mueller PR, Malt RA. Eclectic drainage of subphrenic abscesses. Arch Surg 1984;119:942.

191. Shah HR, Cue JI, Boyd CM, Cone JB. Solitary splenic abscess: a new complication of splenic salvage treated by percutaneous drainage. J Trauma 1987;27:337.

192. Sherman NJ, Davis JR, Jesseph JE. Subphrenic abscess: a continuing hazard. Am J Surg 1969;117:117.

193. Simson JNL. Solitary abscess of the spleen. J Surg 1980;67:106.

194. Smith EH, Bartrum RJ Jr. Ultrasonically guided percutaneous aspiration of abscesses. AJR 1974;122:308.

195. Snyder SK, Hahn HH. Diagnosis and treatment of intraabdominal abscess in critically ill patients. Surg Clin North Am 1982;62:229.

196. Soeter PB, Ebeid AM, Fischer JE. Review of 404 patients with gastrointestinal fistulas. Ann Surg 1979;190:189.

197. Sones PJ. Percutaneous drainage of abdominal abscesses. AJR 1984;142:35.

198. Spigos DG, Jonasson O, Mozes M, Capek V. Partial splenic embolization in the treatment of hypersplenism. AJR 1979;132:777.

199. Steinberg DM, Cooke WT, Alexander-Williams J. Abscess and fistulae in Crohn's disease. Gut 1973;14:865.

200. Stephenson TF, Guzzetta LR, Tagulinao OA. CT-guided Seldinger catheter drainage of a hepatic abscess. AJR 1978;131:323.

201. Teague M, Raddour LM, Wruble LD. Liver abscess: a harbinger of Crohn's disease. Am J Gastroenterol 1988;83:1412.
202. Teich S, Oliver GC, Canter JW. The early diagnosis of splenic abscess. Am Surg 1986;52:303.
203. Terpstra OT, Van Vroonhoven TJ, Muller H. An unexpected complication of a liver biopsy. Br JSurg 1977;64:436.
204. Teufel M, Meyer-Hohnloser H, Morcke EH, Stubig U, Niessen KH. Nachuntersuchungen bei 60 Kindern mit Colitis ulcerosa und Morbus Crohn. Monatsschr. Kinderheilkd 1988;136:378.
205. Thomas CT, Berk SL, Thomas E. Management of liver abscesses. Lancet 1982;i:742.
206. Trunet P. Computed tomography and postlaparotomy abscesses. Intensive Cave Med 1982;8:193.
207. Van Gansbeke D, Matos C, Gelin M, Muller P, Salcman C, Devière J, Struyven J. Percutaneous drainage of subphrenic abscesses. Br J Radiol 1989;62:127.
208. Van Schil P, Mortelmans L, Schoofs E, Bourgeois N, Van Hee R, Vaneerdeweg W, Vereycken H, Heytens L. Peliosis hepatis associated with liver and retroperitoneal abscesses. Digestion 1988;41:55.
209. Van Sonnenberg E, Wittenberg J, Ferrucci JT Jr, Mueller PR, Simeone JF. Triangulation method for percutaneous needle guidance: the angled approach to upper abdominal masses. AJR 1981;137:757.
210. Van Sonnenberg E, Wittenberg J, Mueller PR. Percutaneous abscess drainage. In: Ferrucci JT Jr, Wittenberg J, eds. Interventional radiology of the abdomen. Baltimore: Williams and Wilkins 1981:157.
211. Van Sonnenberg E, Ferrucci JT Jr, Mueller PR, Wittenberg J, Simeone JF. Percutaneous drainage of abscesses and fluid collections: technique, results and applications. Radiology 1982;142:1.
212. Van Sonnenberg E, Ferrucci JT Jr, Mueller PR, Wittenberg J, Simeone JF, Malt RA. Percutaneous radiographically guided catheter drainage of abdominal abscesses. JAMA 1982;247:190.
213. Van Sonnenberg E, Mueller PR, Ferrucci JT Jr, Neff CC, Simeone JF, Wittenberg J. Sump catheter for percutaneous abscess and fluid drainage by trocar or Seldinger technique. AJR 1982;139:613.
214. Van Sonnenberg E, Mueller PR, Ferrucci JT Jr. Percutaneous drainage of 250 abdominal abscesses and fluid collections. part I: results, failures and complications. Radiology 1984;151:337.
215. Van Sonnenberg E, Wing VW, Casola G, Coons HG, Nakamoto SK, Mueller PR, Ferrucci JT Jr, Halasz NA, Simeone JF. Temporizing effect of percutaneous drainage of complicated abscesses in critically ill patients. AJR 1984;142:821.
216. Van Waes PFGM, Feldberg MAM, Mali WPTM, Ruijs SHJ, Eenhoorn PC, Buijs PHO, Kruis FJ, Ramos LRM. Management of loculated abscesses that are difficult to drain: a new approach. Radiology 1983;147:57.
217. Vazquez JL, Thorsen MK, Dodds WJ, Quiroz FA, Martinez ML, Lawson TL, Stewart ET, Foley WD. Evaluation and treatment of intraabdominal bilomas. AJR 1985;144:933.
218. Vujic I, Brock JG. Biloma: aspiration for diagnosis and treatment. Gastrointest Radiol 1982;7:251.
219. Walters R, Herman CM, Neff R, et al. Percutaneous drainage of abscesses in the postoperative abdomen that is difficult to explore. Am J Surg 1985;149:623.
220. Wang SMS, Wilson SE. Subphrenic abscess: the new epidemiology. Arch Surg 1977;112:934.
221. Weed TE, Merrit CRB, Bowen JC. Surgical management of multiple hepatic abscesses using US for sequential evaluation. South Med J 1982;75:1270.
222. Weinstein WN, Onderdonk AD, Bartlett JG, Gorbach SL. Experimental intra-abdominal abscesses in rats: development of an experimental model. Infect Immunol 1974;10:1250.
223. Welch CE, Malt RA. Abdominal surgery, part III. N Engl J Med 1983;308:753.
224. Whalen JP, Bierny JP. Classification of perihepatic abscesses. Radiology 1969;92:1427.
225. Whalen JP. Radiology of the abdomen: anatomic basis. Philadelphia; Lea and Febiger 1976.
226. Whitley NO, Shatney CH. Diagnosis of abdominal abscesses in patients with major trauma: the use of computed tomography. Radiology 1983;147:179.
227. Wittich GR, Van Sonnenberg E, Karnel F, Casola G, Kumpan W, Jantsh H, Herold C, Schurawitzki H. Percutaneous drainage of complicated abscesses and fluid collections. Radiology 1987;27:216.
228. Wolverson MK, Jagannadharao B, Sundaram M, Joyce PF, Riaz MA, Shields JB. CT as a primary diagnostic method in evaluating intra-abdominal abscess. AJR 1979;133:1089.
229. Wooler AH. Subphrenic abscess. Thorax 1956;11:211.
230. Wooten WB, Bernardino ME, Goldstein HM. Computed tomography of necrotic hepatic metastases. AJR 1978;131:839.
231. Yaremchuck MJ, Kane R, Cady B. Ultrasound-guided catheter localization of intrahepatic abscesses: an aid in open surgical drainage. Surgery 1982;91:482.
232. Yeh HC, Rabinowitz JG. Granulomatous enterocolitis: findings by ultrasonography and computed tomography. Radiology 1983;149:253.

Retroperitoneal and Pelvic Fluid Collections

S. G. Gerzof

Retroperitoneal Abscess

Retroperitoneal abscesses may present diagnostic problems because they frequently do not present with the localizing signs found in intraperitoneal abscesses (1). In the past, many were recognized only if clinical suspicion was high because of previous instrumentation or surgery. Frequently, spontaneous retroperitoneal abscesses were discovered only at autopsy. The need for prompt diagnosis and treatment has been emphasized in the surgical literature (1, 26, 27). In one series, all patients with untreated retroperitoneal or renal abscesses died, whereas 84% of those diagnosed and treated survived. Our experience indicates that retroperitoneal abscesses are similar to intraperitoneal abscesses in their response to percutaneous drainage.

Retroperitoneal abscesses can occur in any of the three major spaces defined by the posterior peritoneum, the anterior and posterior reflections of Gerota's fascia, and the posterior extension of the transversalis fascia (20). The anterior pararenal space is the most anterior of these, lying between the posterior peritoneum and Gerota's fascia. We term it the "GI space" because it contains the retroperitoneal portions of the colon and duodenum as well as the pancreas. Most abscesses in this space are enteric in origin, resulting from pancreatitis, diverticulitis, or ulcer perforation (50).

Perinephric Abscess (Fig. 1)

The perinephric space lies between the anterior and posterior leaves of Gerota's fascia and contains the kidneys and adrenals surrounded by perinephric fat (20). Prior to antibiotics, the most common cause of perinephric abscesses was urinary tract infection (26, 28). Surgery, instrumentation and penetrating trauma of the genitourinary tract now accounts for the majority of these. As in the past, most primary perinephric abscesses originate from a renal abscess which has perforated into the perinephric space.

Renal Abscess

Most renal abscesses originate from infections occurring within a pre-existent renal cyst, or from progression of parenchymal infection with suppurative necrosis (17, 25). They are usually well-defined, low-attenuation masses easily seen within the parenchyma of the kidney, particularly after intravenous contrast enhancement (5, 11, 17). Needle aspiration is diagnostic, and percutaneous drainage can be

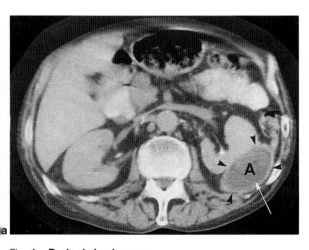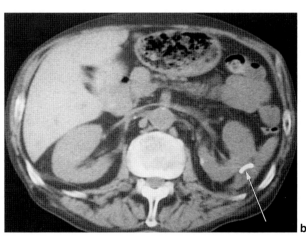

Fig. **1** **Perinehric abscess**
a CT scan ahows an elliptical left perinephric abscess (A) with a well-defined "rind sign" (arrowheads) compressing and displacing the left kidney anteriorly. The arrow indicates the posterolateral retroperitoneal route for percutaneous drainage
b A follow-up scan shows the tip of an 8 Fr pigtail catheter (arrow) in the collapsed abscess cavity

effected with Seldinger introduction of an 8 Fr pigtail catheter. Small catheters are preferred, since most renal abscesses are relatively small and often remain intraparenchymal in location. The percutaneous approach should always be posterior or posterolateral across the lumbodorsal fascia, to avoid the peritoneal cavity. The catheter should enter opposite the renal hilus, since this is the least vascular area of the cortex.

When renal abscesses perforate into the retroperitoneal space, they form perinephric abscesses, as in Fig. 1. Perinephric abscesses may remain localized around the kidney, or may extend into the psoas muscle. When performing CT scans for perinephric abscess, the scan sequence should extend far enough to exclude distant location, since they may dissect widely cephalad and caudad in the perinephric space.

Psoas and Iliopsoas Abscess

Iliopsoas abscesses are usually secondary to adjacent inflammatory processes: vertebral osteomyelitis, diverticulitis, appendicitis, iliac adenitis, and renal and perinephric abscesses (27). They are somewhat different from intraperitoneal abscesses, since they develop within the belly of a muscle. They have potential to dissect widely, extending along the fascial planes of the muscle. Unlike intraperitoneal abscesses, they tend to have internal septae (Fig. 2). The septae are not caused by the abscess itself, but rather represent the normal fascia of the muscle which persist. Ultimately, the septae will undergo septic necrosis. However, because of this tendency for loculation, multiple catheters are often required.

Both the psoas and iliacus muscle bundles and fascia are oriented in cephalocaudad direction as they merge to form a single muscle bundle (21). The

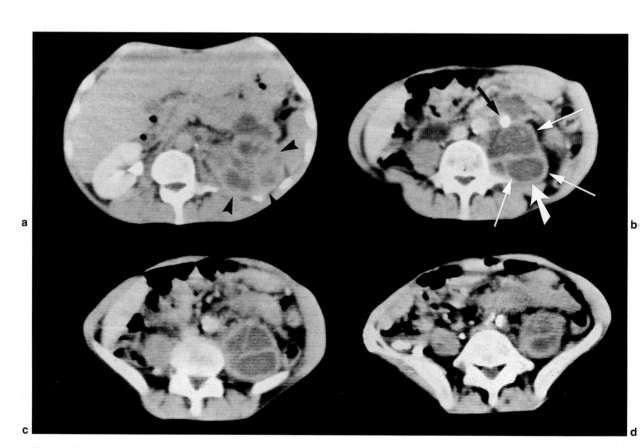

Fig. 2 **Psoas abscess from ruptured ureteral calculus**
a Scan of the upper abdomen shows a pyonephrosis of the left kidney (arrowheads)
b A large left ureteral calculus (black arrow) has obstructed and perforated the left ureter, with dissection into the psoas muscle causing a psoas abscess (white arrows). Note the dense, well-formed septae within the psoas abscess. The large white arrow indicates the site for needle aspiration
c, d The abscess extends well below the level of the iliac crest on these lower scans. These apparent septae are the preexistent fascia extending cephalocaudad throughout the length of the muscle. They have not yet undergone septic necrosis, and now appear as septations. It is important to show the full extent of a psoas abscess prior to either percutaneous or operative drainage, to avoid leaving an undrained loculus

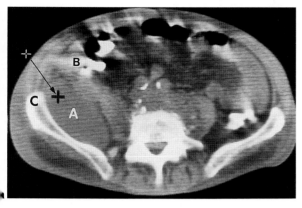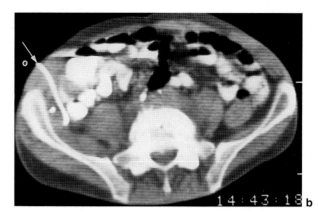

Fig. 3   Iliac fossa abscess
a There is an elliptical abscess (A) in the iliacus muscle. The proposed drainage route (black arrow) extends between the cursors, and must be planned to pass anterior to the anterior iliac crest (C), but posterior to the contrast-filled bowel (B)
b Post-drainage CT scan shows an 8 Fr pigtail catheter (arrow) in good position. The previously displaced bowel has now returned to normal position

psoas originates from the transverse processes and lateral aspects of the vertebral bodies, whereas the iliacus muscle arises from the inner aspect of the iliac bone. They are covered by a shared fascial sheath, so there is a potential path for spread of infection between the two muscles. Thus, infection may dissect along the length of either muscle (Fig. 2). It may present either in the upper abdomen at the level of the diaphragmatic crus, or may dissect caudad to present below the inguinal ligament, where the muscles form a common tendon.

On CT scan, these abscesses appear similar to abscesses in other locations, but may have a slightly higher attenuation because of muscle necrosis. Contrast enhancement is helpful to visualize the septations (Fig. 2). Percutaneous access to iliopsoas abscesses can usually be obtained in three ways: posterolaterally, through the lumbodorsal fascia (Fig. 2b); from a point just anterior to the iliac crest (Fig. 3); and from below the inguinal ligament upwards, if the abscess presents in this location.

The posterolateral approach is similar to renal and perinephric abscesses (Fig. 1). The anterior iliac crest approach requires CT guidance, with opacification of the bowel and an angled route between the bowel and the iliac crest. There is usually at least a narrow access window in this location where the needle can be directed anterior to the iliac crest but posterior to the bowel (Fig. 3). A flexible 8 Fr pigtail catheter is usually recommended here, because it can be directed cephalad or caudad and advanced the full length of the abscess to provide better drainage. When fluctuance can be palpated below the inguinal ligament and needle aspiration yields pus in this location, this catheter can be inserted at this point and directed cephalad. When multiple catheters are inserted, each should be numbered, and the amount of drainage recorded individually, since the loculations may not intercommunicate.

Pelvic Abscess

Pelvic abscesses are similar to intraperitoneal abscesses in the upper abdomen (CT appearance, absence of loculation), except that their location requires meticulous route planning to avoid surrounding structures such as bladder, rectum, major vessels and nerves, and loops of sigmoid colon and small bowel. This can be somewhat difficult because of the complex anatomy of the encircling bony pelvis. Using CT for guidance, safe approaches to pelvic abscesses can be found via the lower anterior abdominal wall (Fig. 4), posteriorly through the sciatic notch (Fig. 5), from the perineum angling cephalad, from above the iliac crest downward into the pelvis using triangulation, and transrectally.

Anterior Approach (Fig. 4)

The anterior approach is the easiest access to the pelvis. Unfortunately, it can be used only for large pelvic abscesses which displace small bowel loops cephalad so that the abscess lies in contact with the anterior abdominal wall. This creates an access window caudad to the loops of bowel and cephalad to the urinary bladder. When using this approach, the bladder should be identified and avoided. If the bladder is distended, it should be controlled with a Foley catheter.

When the abscess is entered via the anterior abdominal wall, the catheter should be advanced so that its terminal side holes are positioned as deep as

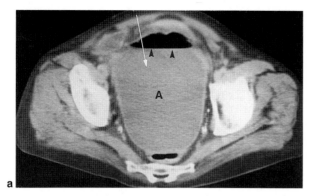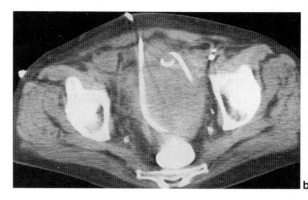

a   b

Fig. 4   Anterior approach to pelvic abscess
a There is a large pelvic abscess (A) with an air-fluid level (arrowheads) which has displaced the small bowel cephalad (therefore not seen on this scan) so as to lie in contact with the anterior abdominal wall. The proposed drainage route (white arrow) crosses the peritoneum below the small bowel and above the bladder
b CT scan immediately post-drainage. The pigtail tip has allowed the catheter to coil safely within the abscess rather than perforate the far wall. The catheter can then be repositioned so that its side-holes lie in the cul-de-sac

possible in the pelvis. We have accomplished this using the 8 Fr pigtail/Seldinger technique. Its pigtail coil reforms as soon as it slides off the guide wire, while its flexibility allows it to coil within the abscess, preventing perforation of the abscess wall. This approach certainly does not provide "dependent" drainage. On the contrary, it requires antigravitational drainage. However, our experience shows no difficulty in many cases of drainage of pus from this direction. We believe that, while dependant drainage may be important for operative drainage of abscesses, it may not apply to percutaneous drainage. In the closed abdomen, intra-abdominal pressure is transmitted to the walls of the abscess. This usually provides sufficient pressure to expel any residual pus through the catheter.

Transsciatic Notch Approach (Fig. 5)

When an abscess is small and lies deep in the pelvis, it may not be approachable anteriorly. However, using CT, there may be an access route through the greater sciatic notch (22). CT localization, guidance and monitoring is the best imaging modality for this route, and is best performed in the prone position. Transgluteal needle aspiration then becomes relatively simple.

The sciatic nerve often cannot be well seen on CT, but runs craniocaudad from medial to lateral across the sciatic notch close to the ischial spine. The further caudad one goes, the further laterally it lies. The needle path should be placed as close to the sacrum as possible to avoid this major nerve. In patients who have unilateral leg amputation, we have

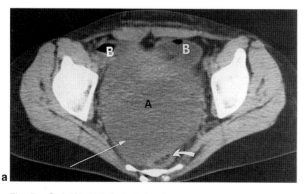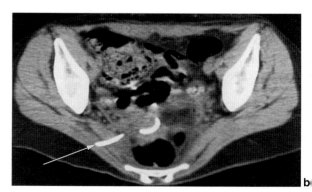

a   b

Fig. 5   Sciatic notch approach
a This large pelvic abscess (A) has small bowel (B) interposed between it and the anterior abdominal wall. The proposed transsciatic approach was made on the right side because the rectum (curved arrow) was displaced to the left. The long white arrow indicates the transsciatic drainage route
b Follow-up CT scan shows a pigtail catheter (arrow) in position, with no residual fluid. (Courtesy of Dr. Charles Munn, New England Baptist Hospital, Boston, MA)

used the ipsilateral sciatic notch to avoid damage to the nerves of the remaining leg.

Transrectal Approach

The transrectal approach is an example of percutaneous drainage following a well-established operative drainage route. One traditional surgical route for drainage of deep pelvic abscesses requires transrectal palpation of a fluctuant mass lying against the anterior wall of the rectum. Under general anesthesia, a needle is first passed transrectally into the mass. When pus is confirmed, a Kelly clamp is forced into the abscess to establish drainage through the rectal wall, and a Penrose drain is then inserted.

There were several problems with this approach: uncertainty whether the palpated fluid collection was infected or sterile; the danger that it might become infected by transrectal needle aspiration if it were sterile, and the uncertainty whether there was sufficient cephalad displacement of the small bowel to prevent its damage by this relatively blind approach. With CT, one can ascertain the displacement of the bowel loops, although we still rely on clinical signs to indicate the probability of infection. Needle aspiration is performed with a fine (22-gauge) needle, and if pus is obtained, a Trocar technique is used to insert a small catheter. This procedure is usually performed with the surgeon in the operating room, using general anesthesia. In both the transgluteal and transrectal approaches, the catheter may be uncomfortable, and prevention of dislodgment may be a problem in management. Restriction in ambulation may be advisable.

Transperineal Approach

In patients who have had the rectum resected, abscesses may develop deep in the pelvis without small bowel displacement. Catheters can be inserted from the perineum upwards, because the rectum is absent. Confirmation by fine-needle aspiration followed by 8 Fr pigtail catheters is recommended here. This approach may also be used for ischiorectal fossa abscesses when the rectum is present. It simply demands a pararectal approach laterally. In this procedure, the patient is placed in the prone position, and localization is determined by CT. Because the rectum may suddenly fill with gas, a rectal tube is recommended.

Triangulation Guidance (Fig. 6)

Triangulation is a method of guidance which is usually used in the upper abdomen to avoid the diaphragm when approaching the subphrenic space from below upwards (9). Its principles, however, can easily be applied to pelvic abscesses when approaching them from the iliac crest downward. This approach is applicable only for mid-pelvic abscesses which are not deep enough for a transsciatic approach, and which lie behind loops of bowel and major vessels, precluding an anterior approach.

In Fig. **6a**, needle aspiration and catheter placement were obtained on the first pass. With some practice, accuracy can be achieved. When using triangulation, we recommend that an exact diagram of the triangle be drawn and that the entry angle and depth be determined from the diagram rather than by use of trigonometry or the Pythagorean theorem (Fig. **6c**). This not only prevents mathematical errors in derivation of square roots, but also provides an exact diagram which can be used to ensure thath the path of the needle exactly parallels the hypotenuse of the diagram.

Appendiceal Abscess (Fig. 7)

The diagnosis of appendicitis is usually based on a synthesis of clinical history, abdominal examination, and laboratory results. When the findings are characteristic for acute appendicitis or for peritonitis due to appendiceal perforation, prompt operation is indicated, and there is little need for radiologic imaging. However, in some patients, the diagnosis is uncertain, and CT is the diagnostic imaging modality of choice. In patients with a palpable right lower quadrant mass, the differential diagnosis includes periappendiceal abscess and periappendiceal phlegmon (2). An abscess is a well-formed collection of fluid which can be drained either operatively or percutaneously. A phlegmon is a solid inflammatory soft tissue mass with little or no drainable fluid. This is an important distinction, since appendiceal phlegmons usually respond to antibiotic therapy and do not require emergency surgery, while appendiceal abscesses require some form of drainage. CT can select those patients with well-formed periappendiceal abscesses for either percutaneous catheter drainage or early operative drainage.

Management of these right lower quadrant masses remains controversial: choices range from immediate exploration to a trial of non-operative management with antibiotics. The problem is the clinical inability to distinguish abscess from phlegmon. CT is ideal for this distinction (7). Appendiceal abscesses have the same appearance as abscesses in other areas of the abdomen, although there is a higher incidence of gas, because of the communication with the appendiceal lumen. CT also can assess the extent of periappendiceal inflammation by defining any extensions of inflammation in the cul-de-sac or retroperitoneum. In patients with a periappendiceal phlegmon, we recommend antibiotics with close clinical and CT follow-up. For patients with an appendiceal abscess, we recommend percutaneous drainage (8, 29).

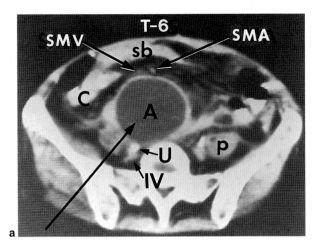

Fig. 6   Triangulation for CT guidance

a Triangulation is used to get around structures interposed within the axial CT plane. This pelvic abscess (A) is surrounded by cecum (C), small bowel (sb), mesenteric vessels (SMA,SMV), and the iliac bone posteriorly. U = ureter; IV = iliac vessels

b, c Drawing a right triangle with the sides representing the distance of the abscess from the skin in the axial CT plane (a) and the distance of the skin entry site above the CT plane (b), one can draw a life-size triangle and measure the hypotenuse (c), which is the actual distance of the needle from the skin to the abscess, as well as the entry angle (curved arrow) directly from the triangle. This avoids the use of either trigonometry of the Pythagorean theorem, with possible mathematical error. In this case, side a was 11 cm side b was 8 cm, and side c measured 13.5 cm, with an entry angle of 55 degrees caudad angulation. Using this approach, successful needle aspiration was performed in the plane of the long arrow in Fig. **6a** passing between the ureter and iliac vessels and the cecum. Needle placement was successful at the first pass

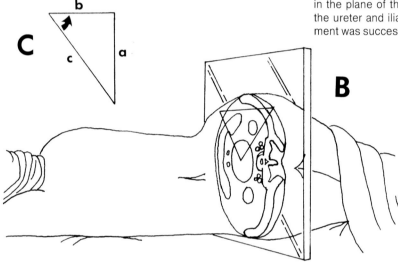

We prefer the Seldinger technique with an 8 Fr pigtail catheter, because of the close proximity to loops of bowel. A large amount of oral contrast should be given prior to the CT scan to be sure to identify the entire small bowel and ascending colon. A route should be planned which avoids the small bowel and colon. Otherwise the procedure is performed as in other locations. Close clinical and CT follow up is suggested to assure complete resolution and to exclude enteric fistulae.

Internal appendectomy can then be performed electively at the discretion of the surgeon. We have not performed internal appendectomy in 2 of our patients, because they were poor operative risks, and have not encountered recurrent appendicitis (16).

Diverticular Abscess (Fig. 8)

Diverticular abscesses are similar to appendiceal abscesses in several ways: they are usually located in the pelvis; they are of enteric origin and have similar bacteriology; they may go through a phase of pericolic phlegmon before progressing to frank abscess formation; the clinical differentiation between the mass effect of a phlegmon and an abscess is difficult; they may drain spontaneously into the bowel at their point of origin.

Diverticular abscesses differ significantly, however, in that they often require colonic resection for cure, whereas appendiceal abscesses do not (24). Thus, traditional operative management has often been a three-stage resection (abscess drainage with proximal colostomy, resection of the involved segment, and delayed closure of the colostomy), with three separate admissions over a six-month period. Although the three-stage operation decreases operative mortality, it has a prolonged morbidity. This has encouraged a search for elective one-stage resection with anastomosis. Percutaneous drainage is a management scheme which provides immediate decompression and control of sepsis in acutely ill patients, and permits an elective one-stage procedure (resection and primary anastomosis) during the same hospitalization (12).

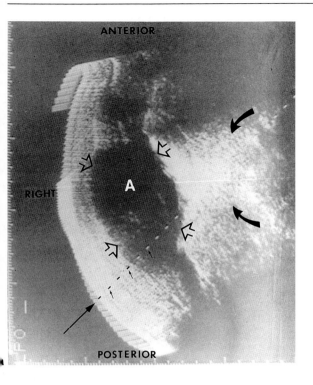

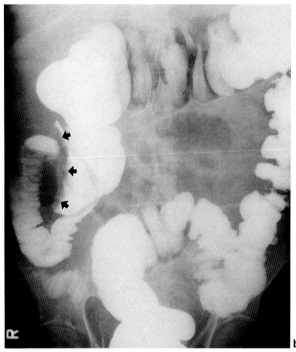

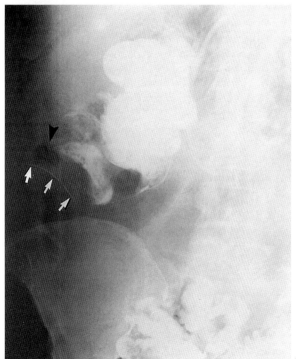

Fig. 7 Percutaneous drainage of appendiceal abscess

a Sonogram of right flank shows an oval 5 × 10 cm, relatively anechoic abscess (A) 4 cm deep to skin posterolaterally in the right lower quadrant. The long arrow and sonographic marker demonstrate the site and angle of the planned drainage route via the preferable retroperitoneal pathway. Sonographic markers at 1 cm intervals indicate the depth of the abscess

b Barium enema examination. Lateral compression and anteromedial displacement of the cecum by an extrinsic mass. The appendix is not visualized

c Radiograph immediately after percutaneous drainage. Trocar catheter (arrowheads) in the abscess. After initial drainage of 750 ml, there is decreased mass effect on the cecum, which has returned to its normal position

The CT findings in acute diverticulitis include bowel wall thickening with the presence of diverticula but no evidence of pericolic inflammation; a phlegmon with inflammation in the mesenteric fat, but no evidence of drainable fluid; frank abscess formation, where an extraluminal low-density fluid mass is seen; evidence of peritonitis, either with free intraperitoneal gas or fluid; obstruction of the colon or adjacent small bowel; and fistula formation to the abscess, to small bowel or to the bladder (15). These abscesses may be in immediate pericolic location, or somewhat removed in other areas of the pelvis. In one series of 43 cases, a frank pericolic abscess was identified in 35% (15).

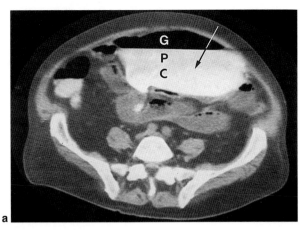
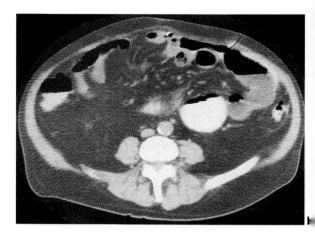

Fig. 8 Diverticular abscess
a A CT scan of the mid-pelvis shows a diverticular abscess with a "parfait sign", that is, layering of gas (G), pus (P) and contrast (C). This diverticular abscess is in contact with the anterior abdominal wall and can be drained at the site of the long white arrow
b A follow-up CT scan several days later shows almost complete resolution of the diverticular abscess. The patient later had an elective one-stage sigmoid colectomy

For suspected diverticulitis, CT scans should be performed at 1 cm intervals through the pelvis or other area of concern. Orally administered contrast should be used as in appendicitis. Rectally administered contrast should never be instilled while the patient is on the CT scanner, since it is without fluoroscopic control.

In many respects, the CT scan and contrast enema are complementary rather than competitive procedures. When there is free communication between the colon and the diverticular abscess, the abscess may fill with contrast. If one interprets a series of CT scans alone, one may mistake the contrast-filled abscess for the lumen of the bowel and completely overlook it. Our preference is a water-soluble contrast enema (Gastrografin) to image the lumen of the bowel and detect extravasation or fistula formation, followed immediately by CT scan to image the thickness of the bowel wall, the abscess, and any areas of pericolic phlegmon which cannot be seen on contrast enema.

Because the underlying colon pathology usually requires operative resection, percutaneous drainage of diverticular abscesses should be viewed as a preoperative temporizing measure to allow definitive single stage resection within one to three weeks of drainage. The importance of CT-guided percutaneous drainage lies in its ability to avoid the morbidity of a three-stage procedure and allow a one-stage resection with end-to-end anastomosis.

Pancreatic Drainage

When the pancreas becomes inflamed, it can create three different inflammatory masses: pseudocysts, fluid collections, and phlegmons. Each of these entities can be sterile or infected (10). CT is the imaging modality of choice to determine whether these pancreatic inflammatory masses are low-density fluid or higher-attenuation phlegmon. When these occur during acute pancreatitis, patients often exhibit a toxic reaction, with fever and leukocytosis, so that they appear septic. Unfortunately, because of the inflammatory nature of these pancreatic masses, they will be positive on [67]gallium and [111]indium-labeled leukocyte scans, whether they are sterile or infected. Guided needle aspiration of these fluid collections and phlegmons is the only method of determining whether they are infected or sterile.

Pancreatic Fluid Collections

Pancreatic fluid collections are acute collections of fluid which may accumulate within or outside the pancreatic capsule. Their incidence varies with the severity of pancreatitis, but is greater than 50% in cases of severe pancreatitis. They have a low-attenuation fluid center, and well-defined but somewhat irregular margins. They are usually transient, and tend to resolve spontaneously. However, they may persist and develop into pancreatic pseudocysts. They are usually sterile, since if they do become infected, they tend to change shape, round up and develop convex margins. Discovered at this stage, they are then termed infected pseudocysts.

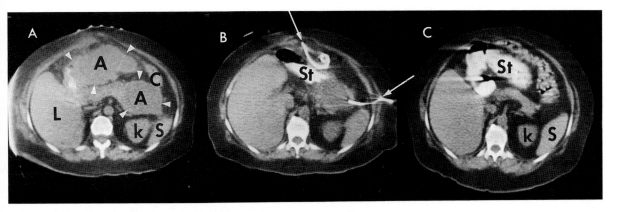

Fig. 9   Percutaneous drainage of infected pancreatic pseudocysts

a A CT scan of the upper abdomen, revealing two well-defined masses (A, arrowheads) arising from the anterior and the lateral aspects of the pancreas. Cephalad displacement of the stomach out of the scan plane and anterior displacement of the colon (C) allowed safe percutaneous access anteriorly and laterally. Diagnostic needle aspirations from each yielded pus. Percutaneous catheter drainages were performed. Liver: L, kidney: k, spleen: S

b A CT scan 24 h later, with the two catheters in place (white arrows). Note how the pigtail tip promotes coiling within the anterior abscess, and prevents perforation of the far wall. The tip of the lateral catheter extends out of the CT plane and is not shown. The stomach (ST) has returned to its normal position. The patient's temperature became normal within 24 h. The catheters were removed after 15 and 22 days

c A follow-up CT scan seven months later, confirming complete resolution

Pseudocyst

Pseudocysts are focal, well-defined inflammatory pancreatic fluid collections, either intrapancreatic or extrapancreatic. If they persist, they develop a fibrous capsule, and establish themselves as space-occupying masses. They have a characteristic round or oval configuration with a well-defined, higher-attenuation wall. This wall enhances significantly with intravenous contrast, because of the dilated inflamed vessels in its wall. On ultrasound, pseudocysts appear as round or oval, echo-free cystic masses with good through-transmission of sound and relatively smooth walls. Dependent layering of echoes caused by necrotic debris is often seen. Because of their mass effect, they displace surrounding structures, providing safe routes for percutaneous aspiration. Needle aspiration is indicated to differentiate sterile from infected pseudocysts. CT-scan localization is mandatory to identify and avoid the bowel, since needle transpassage of bowel may easily infect a previously sterile pseudocyst. We prefer needle aspiration with a 20-gauge Teflon sleeve needle, since this allows aspiration of even the viscous fluid frequently found in pseudocysts. This also provides access for percutaneous catheter insertion by a modified Seldinger technique if the Gram stain shows that the pseudocyst is infected.

Infected Pseudocyst (Fig. 9)

Infected pancreatic pseudocysts are curable by percutaneous catheter drainage combined with antibiotics (10). The drainage route is chosen depending on the location of the pseudocyst. The 8 Fr pigtail catheter (Seldinger technique) is our choice. Frequently there will be comunication between the pseudocyst and the pancreatic duct demonstrated by sinogram. In our experience, this has not prevented resolution of infected pseudocysts. We believe that infection changes the wall of the pseudocyst in some fashion such that there is a much higher resolution rate for infected pseudocysts than there is for sterile pseudocysts.

Sterile Pseudocyst

The role of simple aspiration and drainage of sterile pseudocysts is not established at present. It does seem to be a promising alternative to operative drainage. Hancke was the first to report 14 patients with simple pseudocyst aspirations (13). Most of those pseudocysts recurred, but two resolved. Others have reported variable success with this method, but most pseudocysts have required multiple aspirations (3, 6, 19). Overall, we estimate that about 20% of pseudocysts may resolve with a single aspiration. Higher resolution rates occur with repeat aspirations. Because the CT-guided procedure appears to be so safe and atraumatic, we believe that percutaneous needle aspiration of sterile pseudocysts is indicated whenever there is a safe access route and should precede the decision to operate wherever possible. Thus, only those pseudocysts which have recurred would then require surgery. In thish fashion, perhaps 20% of patients could be spared surgery by a single aspiration, and up to 50% of patients could be spared surgery by repeated aspirations.

An alternative to simple needle aspiration of pseudocysts is indwelling catheter drainage. We have been successful in 8 of 12 such cases, and others are now reporting good results with new techniques for this procedure (4, 14, 23). However, there is a higher incidence of infection when indwelling catheters are used. Two of our cases subsequently developed infection within the pseudocyst, and we no longer recommend this as a routine.

Pancreatic Phlegmon (Fig. 10)

The term "phlegmon" refers to a solid inflammatory mass with ill-defined margins which has not undergone central necrosis and has no definable fluid center. It tends to infiltrate surrounding structures, and only displaces them secondarily. Because of their solid inflammatory nature, they yield only a few drops to a few ml of fluid on diagnostic needle aspiration. When they infiltrate the retroperitoneum widely, pancreatic phlegmons usually incite a significant toxic response with marked abdominal pain, distension, high fever and leukocytosis. This toxic reaction occurs whether they are sterile (severe pancreatitis) or infected (pancreatic abscess). A sterile phlegmon may become infected and evolve into a pancreatic abscess.

The role of percutaneous aspiration of pancreatic phlegmons is twofold: diagnosis of infection as soon as possible to provide optimal antibiotic therapy and early surgery; prevention of unnecessary exploration for a suspected pancreatic abscess which is in fact a sterile phlegmon. The rationale for this is the fact that pancreatic abscesses require operative debridement, whereas sterile phlegmons usually improve without surgery. Exploratory surgery simply to exclude infection in a pancreatic phlegmon may be unnecessary, and may infect a previously sterile phlegmon, further jeopardizing the patient. Further, the survival in pancreatic abscesses decreases with delay in diagnosis. Therefore, the aspiration should be performed as soon as the question of infection is raised.

Needle aspiration of phlegmons should be performed with meticulous technique to avoid transpassage of bowel, since it is an ideal culture medium and is easily infected by bacteria introduced by a needle passing through the colon.

References

1. Altemeier WA, Alexander JW. Retroperitoneal abscess. Arch Surg 1961;83:512.
2. Barakos JA, Jeffrey RB Jr, Federle MP, Wing VW, Laing FC, Hightower DR. CT in the management of periappendiceal abscess. Radiology 1986;146:1161–1164.
3. Barkin JS, Smith FR, Pereiras R Jr. Therapeutic percutaneous aspiration of pancreatic pseudocysts. Dig Dis Sci 1981;26:585–586.
4. Bernardino ME, Amerson JR. Percutaneous gastrocystostomy: a new approach to pancreatic pseudocyst drainage. AJR 1984;143:1096–1097.
5. Conrad MR, Sanders RC, Mascardo AD. Perinephric abscess aspiration using ultrasound guidance. AJR 1977;128:459.
6. Colhoun E, Murphy JJ, MacErlean DP. Percutaneous drainage of pancreatic pseudocysts. Br J Surg 1984;71:131–132.
7. Gale ME, Birnbaum S, Gerzof SG, Sloan G, Johnson WC, Robbins AH. CT appearance of appendicitis and its local complications. J Comput Assist Tomogr 9 1985;9:34–37.
8. Gerzof SG, Robbins AH, Birkett DH, Johnson WC, Pugatch RD, Vincent ME. Percutaneous catheter drainage of abdominal abscesses guided by ultrasound and computed tomography. AJR 1979;133:1–8.
9. Gerzof SG. Triangulation for indirect CT guidance. AJR 1981;137:1808–1881.
10. Gerzof SG. Pancreatic fluid and abscess aspiration and drainage. Sem Intervent Radiol 1985;2:294–303.
11. Goldman SM, Minkin SD, Naraval DC et al. Renal carbuncle: the use of ultrasound in its diagnosis and treatment. J Urol 1977;118:525.
12. Greco RS, Kamath C, Nosher JL. Percutaneous drainage of peridiverticular abscess followed by primary sigmoidoscopy. Dis Colon Rectum 1982;25:53–55.
13. Hancke S, Pedersen JF. Percutaneous puncture of pancreatic cysts guided by ultrasound. Surg Gynecol Obstet 1976;142:551–552.
14. Ho CS, Taylor B. Percutaneous transgastric drainage for pancreatic pseudocyst. AJR 1984;143:623–625.
15. Hulnick DH, Megibow AJ, Balthazar EJ, Naidich DP, Bosniak MA. Computed tomography in the evaluation of diverticulitis. Radiology 1984;152:491–495.
16. Johnson WC, Gerzof SG. Appendiceal abscess: operative drainage or percutaneous drainage? Infect Surg 1984;May:367–369.
17. Laing FC, Jacobs RP. Value of ultrasonography in the detection of retroperitoneal inflammatory masses. Radiology 1977;123:169.

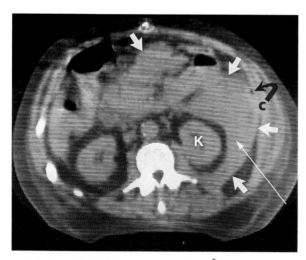

Fig. 10 **Pancreatic phlegmon.** There is a phlegmon in the anterior perirenal space dissecting around the left kidney (K) in this patient with known pancreatitis, fever, and leukocytosis. Diagnostic needle aspiration is the only modality which can determine whether this pancreatic phlegmon is infected or sterile. Needle aspiration over the route of the white arrow was planned to avoid the colon (curved arrow, C), and yielded many leukocytes and bacteria. Because phlegmons are solid and not amenable to percutaneous drainage, the patient was referred for surgery

18. Lee JKT, McClennan BL, Melson GL, Stanley RJ. Acute focal bacterial nephritis: emphasis on gray scale sonography and computed tomography. AJR 1980;135:87.

19. MacErlean DP, Bryan PJ, Murphy JJ. Pancreatic pseudocyst: management by ultrasonically guided aspiration. Gastrointest Radiol 1980;5:255–257.

20. Meyers MD. Dynamic radiology of the abdomen. New York: Springer 1976;139.

21. Mueller PR, Ferrucci JT Jr, Wittenbeg J, Simeone JF, Butch RJ. Iliopsoas abscess: treatment by CT-guided percutaneous catheter drainage. AJR 1983;142:359–362.

22. Mueller PR. Abscesses: special entities and access routes. American Roentgen Ray Society Syllabus in Interventional Radiology, 1985:163–171.

23. Peng SY, Chi YG, Peng SG. Sequential external and internal drainage of pancreatic pseudocyst. Br J Surg 1984;71:317.

24. Rodkey GV, Wlech CE. Changing patterns in the surgical treatment of diverticular disease. Ann Surg 1984;200:466–478.

25. Rosenfield AT, Glickman MG, Taylor KJW, Crade M, Hodson J. Acute focal bacterial nephritis (acute lobar nephronia). Radiology 1979;132:553.

26. Salvatierra O Jr, Bucklew WB, Morrow JW. Perinephric abscess: a report of 71 cases. J Urol 1967;98:296.

27. Stevenson EOS, Ozeran RS. Retroperitoneal space abscesses. Surg Gynecol Obstet 1969;128:1202.

28. Truesdale BH, Rous SN, Nelson RP. Perinephric abscess: a review of 26 cases. J Urol 1977;118:910.

29. Van Sonnenberg E, Wittich GR, Casola G, Neff CC, Hoyt DB, Polansky AD, Keightley A. Periappendiceal abscess: percutaneous drainage. Radiology 1987;163:23–26.

Percutaneous Drainage of Thoracic Fluid Collections

R. F. Dondelinger and J. C. Kurdziel

While percutaneous aspiration and drainage of fluid collections in the abdomen has rapidly become an established therapeutic technique, collections located in the thorax have received less attention. Thoracic fluid collections are located in the pleural space, the pericardium, the lung and the mediastinum. Percutaneous aspiration of these fluid collections is first indicated as a diagnostic procedure: cytologic, bacteriologic and chemical analyses are routinely obtained. When fluid is aspirated, demonstrating the presence of malignant cells, exudative or transudative fluid, blood, lymph, infected clear fluid or pus can be demonstrated. Percutaneous catheter drainage is the logical therapeutic extension of diagnostic aspiration.

Imaging Modalities

Thoracic fluid collections can be aspirated and drained percutaneously with fluoroscopic, US, and CT control.

Fluoroscopy

Fluoroscopy is the basic method of guiding aspiration of a pleural effusion, even of a small amount. Free pleural fluid is distinguished from encapsulated pockets, which remain unchanged when the patient is moved. Fluoroscopic control is not an optimal modality for guiding the insertion of a drainage catheter when the amount of pleural fluid is reduced, when it is located in the subpulmonary pleural space, or when anatomical distortion of the thoracic cage is present. During percutaneous drainage, fluoroscopy gives useful information on the pleural contact of a pulmonary abscess, its lobar topography, and the fluid-air level within a cavity. Large amounts of pleural fluid are drained with the patient placed in a posterior oblique position with the involved side up, the puncture being performed posterolaterally. Fluoroscopy is of little use for percutaneous aspiration, or for drainage of pericardial and mediastinal fluid collections. However, when a drainage catheter has been inserted percutaneously in a pleural empyema or in a pulmonary abscess with US or CT control, definitive adjustment of the position of the catheter tip is best achieved with fluoroscopy control. Uniplanar fluoroscopy is usually sufficient.

Ultrasonography

Real-time ultrasonography is used to guide percutaneous aspiration and catheter insertion into pleural and pericardial fluid collections, and is particularly useful when free fluid is present in small amounts. Changes in the location of the pleural fluid can be followed with respiratory movements and during changes in the patient's position. US monitoring allows the patient to be turned to a particular position which best evidences the pleural fluid collection in an intercostal space. Parasternal and paravertebral approaches remain difficult with US, however, due to the interposition of bone structures. Aspiration of minimal amounts of pleural fluid can be performed while the patient is in a sitting position. US is particularly useful for percutaneous diagnostic aspirations, due to the rapidity of the procedure. US is not useful for a percutaneous approach to collections situated in the lung parenchyma without a pleural contact, and those that are located in the mediastinum.

Computed Tomography

Computed tomography is a superb imaging modality for the guidance of percutaneous aspiration and drainage of thoracic fluid collections, since all anatomical structures, chest wall, pleural cavity, pleural fissures, lung, and mediastinum are depicted simultaneously. Despite these advantages, it is not always possible to differentiate a pulmonary abscess from an empyema or a bronchopleural fistula (54). In many circumstances, catheters can be inserted with the patient remaining in the comfortable supine position which he will also adopt in bed after the procedure. Fluid, necrotic tissue, normal mediastinal vascular structures, and potential pseudoaneurysms within the wall of a lung abscess, are seen after intravenous contrast enhancement before percutaneous drainage is attempted. Contact of a pulmonary cavity with the pleura is shown, and this determines the optimal percutaneous entry point. CT is particularly useful for planning percutaneous drainage of mediastinal and multiple encapsulated pleural collections which need multiple drainage catheters. Since pleural fissures are recognized with CT, a lung abscess can be drained without transgressing fissure planes, which would expose the patient to the risk of spread of infection to another lobe or to the fissure itself. Percutaneous CT-guided puncture and drainage of thoracic fluid collections may be difficult at the level of the apex of the lung and under the scapula, especially when puncture is performed with the patient holding his arms above his head. The catheter can kink, or cause discomfort or pain, limiting shoulder movement when inserted too close to the scapula. The patient can be placed to facilitate catheter insertion in an oblique or lateral decubitus, or in a prone position. CT even shows a minimal pneumothorax, a pneumomediastinum, or an alveolar filling, on control slices during the procedure. The precise relationship between the cutaneous entry point of the catheter and the ribs is not always precisely determined with CT.

Drainage Technique

In the percutaneous treatment of abdominal fluid collections, the diameter of the drainage catheter should be adapted to the content of the collection and the viscosity of the fluid to be drained.

When debris and viscous pus are present, large drainage tubes with multiple side-holes should be used for adequate drainage. On the other hand, small, flexible catheters are better tolerated by the patient (59). These are sufficient to drain water-like fluid, and are also more easily inserted in encapsulated pleural pockets and in pulmonary or mediastinal cavities when they are reduced in diameter. When catheters with multiple side-holes are used, care must be taken that the side-holes are not situated in the thoracic wall, in the normal lung, or in the pleural space during drainage of a lung abscess.

Large pleural effusions and pulmonary collections with close pleural contact are usually drained with the trocar technique (48). The percutaneous access must be planned so as to avoid any risk to vital thoracic structures. The tandem technique can be used, with the drainage catheter being inserted parallel to the small, Teflon-sheathed needle which is widely used for diagnostic aspiration.

The angiographic technique is recommended for encapsulated pleural collections, for pulmonary cavities without a large pleural contact, and for mediastinal collections situated in a critical area in the vicinity of the heart and large mediastinal vessels.

The risk of spread of infection is increased with the angiographic technique, which requires several exchanges of dilators or guide wires. When the angiographic technique is used, once the guide wire has been curled in the cavity with US or CT control, the catheter insertion can either be finished with CT alone or with fluoroscopy control. The continuous control provided by fluoroscopy is very helpful. The cavity is outlined by one or several curls of the guide wire. Perforation with the guide wire of the wall of a pulmonary abscess or of a mediastinal collection

should be avoided. Only guide wires with a soft tip and a curve should be used in the thorax. Particular care must be taken in the thorax when a stiff Lunderquist guide wire is used for drainage of an empyema limited by a thick pleural wall, in order to avoid perforation of the pleura, of the wall of a lung abscess, or of mediastinal vascular structures.

Biplanar control chest X-rays should be obtained in all cases before the patient is discharged from the radiology department, in order to ascertain the optimal position of the drainage catheter in an upright position. Pleural and pulmonary drainage catheters are connected to a continuous water-seal suction after initial decompression of the cavity. Daily control X-rays are indispensable, and should be obtained when drainage is interrupted, or when the patient's clinical course is not satisfactory. Drainage catheters retracted within the thorax can be removed percutaneously with fluoroscopy control, using methods derived from percutaneous nephrolithotomy (29). Appropriate systemic antibiotic therapy is mandatory during catheter drainage of thoracic fluid collections.

Indications and Results

Pleural Effusion and Empyema

Cytology, chemical and bacteriological analyses of pleural fluid determine the diagnosis in many pathological conditions. Pleural taps are usually performed at the patient's bedside, but difficulties arise when the amount of pleural effusion is reduced, when the effusion is encapsulated, or when the patient shows marked changes in the thoracic anatomy. Diagnostic aspiration of a pleural effusion is easily performed with US control, but very small amounts can also be aspirated with CT, even in a supine position. Encapsulated pleural fluid is reached by the shortest transthoracic approach. Small-gauge Teflon-sheathed needles are atraumatic, and adequate for diagnostic aspiration. Insertion of a pleural drainage catheter is indicated for therapeutic purposes, for treatment of a persistent or recurrent malignant pleural effusion, of encapsulated fluid pockets, hemothorax, and empyema. A pleural effusion can be efficiently drained with small-bore catheters of 14 G (9) to 7 Fr (34), with a technical success rate of about 95% (9, 34). A drainage catheter can also be left in place for the pleural instillation of drugs in cancer patients. Repetitive malignant pleural effusions can be treated with transcatheter fibrin glue (20), or injection of tetracycline or bleomycin. In some patients with malignant pleural effusions and underlying chronic interstitial lung disease, the pleural cavity does not collapse after drainage of pleural fluid, and fluid reaccumulates (34). Massive hemothorax occurring after chest trauma and compressing the underlying lung should be drained. In this condition, either large chest tubes have to be inserted in the appropriate position, or else multiple catheters, when a pneumothorax is associated with it.

The treatment of pleural empyema is the most satisfactory. Primarily, imaging-guided drainage is indicated to avoid chest tube failure (48). Treatment with closed chest tube drainage using large bore pleural tubes (24–30 Fr) can fail in 35% of patients (55), due to improper catheter positioning and adequate function, or to residual undrained pleural pockets. Placement of a thoracostomy tube carries a non-negligible mortality rate of 5% (47). The appearance of an empyema is not always pathognomonic on US and CT. Suggestive signs are the presence of air bubbles, diffuse thickening of the pleura, tension, and encapsulation. Pleural empyema is mainly unilateral (54) and consecutive to a pre-existing pulmonary or mediastinal infection, or an infection of the chest wall. It results from the spread of a subdiaphragmatic abscess or occurs as a complication of trauma. Thoracic surgery, contamination of the pleura during percutaneous drainage of a lung abscess or an abdominal abscess, and repeated puncture or drainage of pleural effusions, may be at

Table **1**   Percutaneous drainage of thoracic fluid collections

Reference	No. of patients	Location of fluid collection	Imaging guidance modality	Size of drainage catheter	Duration of drainage	Clinical success (%)	Complications
Van Sonnenberg 1984 (54)	17	Empyema	CT (59%) US (41%)	8.3–12 Fr		88	Bacteremia (1 patient)
Westcott 1985 (59)	12	Empyema	Fluoroscopy	8–10 Fr	1–7 days	83	–
O'Moore 1987 (34)	17	Empyema	US	12 Fr		88	–
Vasile 1987 (56)	11	Empyema	CT	7–9 Fr	3–7 days	73	–
Silverman 1988 (48)	43	Empyema	US (70%) CT (18%) Fluoroscopy (12%)	8.3–12 Fr	7–45 days	72	–
Vainrub 1978 (52)	3	Lung abscess	Fluoroscopy	16–18 Fr		100	–
Aronberg 1979 (2)	1	Lung abscess	Fluoroscopy	8 Fr	2 weeks	100	–
Keller 1982 (19)	1	Lung abscess	Fluoroscopy	9 Fr	Several weeks	100	–
Lorenzo 1985 (22)	5	Lung abscess	Fluoroscopy	18-gauge Teflon sheath needle	Aspiration	100	–
Rami-Porta 1985 (37)	13	Lung abscess	–	Repeat aspiration 5–30 Fr	15 days	100	–
Yellin 1985 (62)	7	Lung abscess	Fluoroscopy	–	15 days	100	–
Parker 1987 (35)	6	Lung abscess	Fluoroscopy	10 Fr	–	100	Pneumothorax (1 patient)
Rice 1987 (40)	11	Lung abscess	Fluoroscopy	–	–	73	–
Gobien 1984 (17)	6	Mediastinal abscess	CT and Fluoroscopy	8.3–12 Fr	5–91 days (mean: 35)	83	–
Meranze 1987 (26)	8	Mediastinal abscess	Fluoroscopy	8.3–12 Fr	2–4 weeks	88	–

CT: computed tomography; US: ultrasonography

the origin of an empyema. 50% of patients with empyema have coexisting pneumonia (48), but other causes (malignant lung tumors, thoracic surgery, pleuroscopy, trauma) are seen more frequently. When pus is aspirated during diagnostic aspiration, one or several pleural drainage catheters are inserted. Multiple catheters may be required in 92% of empyemas (59), while in other reports they are only necessary in 23% of patients (48). Attempts are made to drain the empyema as completely as possible. The diameter of pleural catheters is adapted to the viscosity of the fluid, and varies from 7–24 Fr. Technical success is obtained in almost all cases (53, 54, 59).

Clinical success is achieved in 72–88% of patients (48, 54, 56, 59) (Table 1). The results of percutaneous drainage of pleural empyema probably depend on the stage of the disease. Small-bore catheters may be sufficient in the early exudative phase, but the fibrinopurulent phase needs standard drainage catheters, and during the chronic phase, large tubes are required. Percutaneous catheter drainage is most efficient in the acute and subacute phase of an empyema (Fig. 1). Irrigation and lavage of the pleural cavity can be performed (48) when viscous material is present. Small satellite pleural fluid pockets can be aspirated on one or several occasions, without placing a drainage catheter, while the main empyema is drained by a dependent drainage. The duration of pleural drainage is variable, usually about one week or less (48, 56, 59).

Failure of percutaneous catheter drainage of empyema can occur in 18% of cases, and is related to the viscosity of the pus and thick debris obstructing

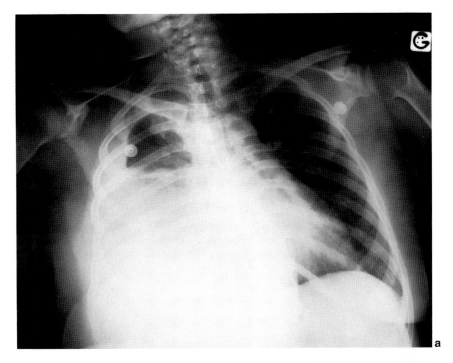

a

Fig. **1a–c Percutaneous drainage of a pleural empyema.** 37-year-old female with endocarditis localized on the tricuspid valve. Multiple septic pulmonary emboli complicated by a pleural empyema
a Chest X-ray demonstrates an extensive right pleural effusion
b Thoracic CT: an air-fluid level is seen inside the right pleural empyema. Percutaneous drainage with a 14 Fr catheter: 1000 ml of pus were drained. Culture reveals β-*streptococcus pyogenes* (group F), Bacteroides, and Peptostreptococcus. Duration of drainage: 12 days

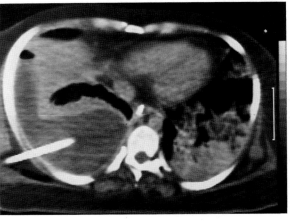

b

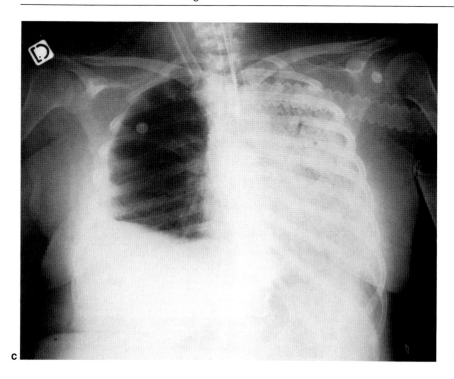

c

Fig. **1c**   Regression of the right pleural empyema after withdrawal of the drainage catheter. Massive pneumonia of the left lung. Patient cured after medical treatment

the usual drainage catheters, and to non-dependent drainage (59). An empyema confined to the subpulmonary pleural space may be difficult to reach with a percutaneous drainage catheter (59). Recurrences of adequately drained empyemas are seen, and require repetition of drainage. When a severe pleural tickening is present, limiting the empyema, the pleural cavity collapses only slowly during drainage, and continuous suction has to be applied (Fig. **2**). Failure to obliterate the pleural cavity can occur in 5% (34) to 12% (54) of patients. When the pleural cavity does not collapse after adequate percutaneous drainage, transcatheter injection of a sclerosing agent may be necessary (54). Pleural thickening limiting a long-standing empyema can be so extensive that transpleural introduction of a drainage catheter turns out to be impossible (56). Pleural decortication may be indicated (48), either because of inefficient drainage, or following percutaneous treatment of the empyema. Communication with the bronchial system, the esophagus, or a subdiaphragmatic abscess, should be ruled out by cautious intrapleural injection of contrast medium after adequate drainage. Undiagnosed pleural or pulmonary tumors can be biopsied percutaneously after the pleural fluid has been removed (54).

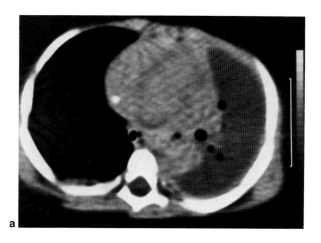

a

Fig. **2a–e**   **Two-year-old child:** pneumonia of the left lung complicated by a left pleural empyema, drained percutaneously
a CT shows a massive left pleural effusion, with gas bubbles and slight retraction of the left hemithorax

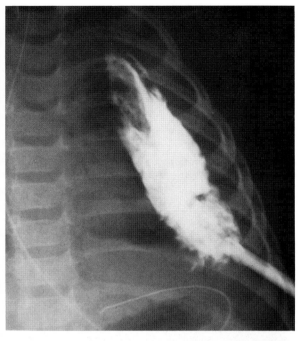

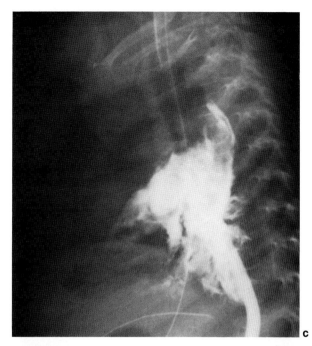

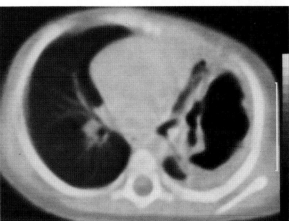

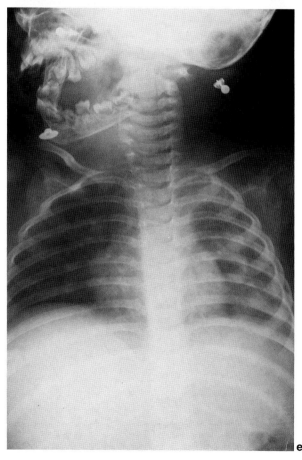

b and **c** CT-guided drainage of the left pleural empyema. An 8 Fr catheter placed initially is exchanged for a 14 Fr catheter, allowing adequate drainage: 30 ml of pus was aspirated. *Staphylococcus aureus, Streptococcus salivarius,* and *Haemophilus influenzae* are cultured from the pus. Opacification of the drainage catheter shows a pleural cavity with irregular margins and pleural thickening

d CT shows, after 12 days of successful percutaneous drainage, a persistent pleural cavity that has not collapsed. Extensive thickening of the left pleura is present

e Chest X-ray: further collapse of the left pleural cavity one week after drainage. Pleural decortication was not necessary

Lung Abscess

Pyogenic lung abscesses occur less often nowadays than in the past, due to early recognition, progress in antibiotic treatment (4, 8), and more efficient treatment of the predisposing pathologic conditions. The disease occurs rarely in children, less than 50 cases being reported in 20 years (22). Lung abscesses most commonly develop in patients whose general condition is debilitated by cancer, alcoholism, denutrition, diabetes mellitus, and immunodeficient disease. They either have a hematogenous origin, including bacterial endocarditis, or result from infection of a pre-existing pulmonary cavity (bulla, pneumatocele,

tuberculosis, fungus), or they complicate a bacterial pneumonia with or without bronchial obstruction by tumor, mucus plug or foreign body (2, 8, 13, 46) (Fig. 3). Pulmonary infarction and necrotic tumors can also result in pulmonary abscess. A pulmonary abscess can develop following any type of thoracic surgery. Other facilitating associations are chronic obstructive pulmonary disease and steroid therapy (52), general anesthesia, epilepsy, stroke or esophageal motility disorders ending in aspiration pneumonia. Pulmonary infections caused by Klebsiella and Pseudomonas are the ones most prone to lung necrosis (19, 36, 39). Bacteriological blood and sputum analysis may be negative, especially in chil-

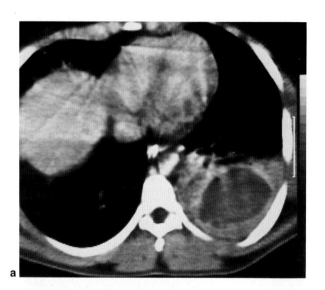

a

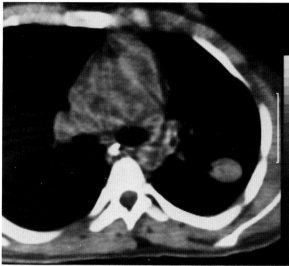

c

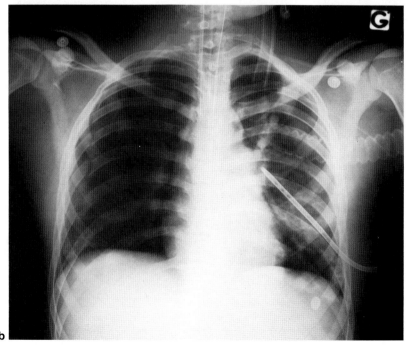

b

Fig. 3 **Twenty-year-old male** who had sustained a severe blunt trauma to the thorax
a CT of the thorax shows filling of a pre-existing pneumatocele of the left lung. The pneumatocele shows an air bubble, and is surrounded by pulmonary consolidation
b Percutaneous CT-guided drainage of the infected pneumatocele with a 14 Fr catheter. *Serratia marescens. Staphylococcus aureus* and *Peptostreptococcus magnus* are cultured from the drained pus Chest X-ray shows resolution of the filled lung cavity.
c CT shows a residual left pulmonary nodule with solid densities after 5 days of percutaneous drainage. The patient was cured

dren (22). Pulmonary abscesses with a hematogenous origin are more likely to be located in a subpleural position, while abscesses which spread from an upper airway infection develop in the posterior lung segments. Medical treatment usually resolves lung abscesses by systemic antibiotic therapy (4, 8, 14, 15, 44). A small number of pulmonary abscesses are resistant to medical treatment, postural and bronchoscopic drainage. In large surgical series, surgery was required in addition to antibiotic treatment in 17–21% (8, 13). Failure of medical treatment may be related partly to the size (3, 8, 57) rather than to the location of the abscess (3, 8). Before the advent of antibiotics, surgical drainage of lung abscesses was indicated (32, 33). After the introduction of antibiotics, patients with a persistent lung abscess resistant to medical therapy underwent surgery (8, 16). Lobectomy was used for a long time (8, 13, 16, 49), although at the same time abdominal abscesses were drained surgically without parenchymal resection. The surgical risk remains high when pulmonary resection is performed in debilitated patients (8). Surgical technique has changed over the years from lobectomy to limited wedge resection and open surgical transthoracic abscess drainage without parenchymal resection (16, 28, 32, 33, 50, 52, 58). Percutaneous surgical drainage of lung abscesses has a 3% mortality rate, which is lower than that for percutaneous drainage of abdominal abscesses, and a high success rate of 85–90% (11, 28, 32). Nowadays, the diagnosis of a pulmonary abscess is easily made in most circumstances, by a combination of the radiological appearance and the clinical background. US and CT confirm the diagnosis by suggestive signs, but bullae filled with fluid do not necessarily correspond to a lung abscess. A percutaneous diagnostic aspiration with a small-caliber needle can precede percutaneous drainage in doubtful cases, as for fluid collections located in the abdomen. A small lung abscess presenting as a lung nodule, or a lung abscess in children, is aspirated by a diagnostic transthoracic puncture, and does not need drainage for cure (22). In most circumstances, repeated percutaneous aspiration (37) should be replaced by percutaneous catheter placement. Mechanical ventilation is not a contra-indication to percutaneous abscess drainage (40). Percutaneous fluoroscopy-guided drainage of lung abscesses was first described for the treatment of tuberculous cavities, and later for pyogenic abscesses (18, 31). It is now indicated when medical treatment, repetitive bronchoscopy, and postural changes have failed (2, 6, 19, 22, 35, 37, 52, 62), and seems to be an adequate alternative to surgical drainage (50, 58) or to endoscopic transbronchial drainage (10, 18, 24, 41, 42, 43). Endoscopic transbronchial placement of a catheter inside a lung abscess can be monitored with fluoroscopy control. Permanent drainage is less comfortable for the patient than a percutaneous catheter. The bronchial bacterial contamination of the opposite lung is also a high risk with this technique (38). Lung abscesses are often located in the periphery of the lung, and they usually do not break the barrier of the lobar fissure. Contact with the pleura is usually present and extensive pleural symphyses are established, preventing the lung from collapsing when the percutaneous route is planned in such a way that normal lung parenchyma is not crossed by the catheter. Empyema following pleural contamination is unlikely to occur in these circumstances during percutaneous drainage. The transthoracic catheter should be inserted in such a way that a dependent drainage is achieved, as for empyemas. In our experience, when a lung abscess is shown radiologically with great precision, and a transthoracic route is planned without any particular risk, the trocard technique is preferred. The time of the procedure is reduced, and the percutaneous manipulation shortened, in comparison with the angiographic technique. The diameter of the catheter should be adapted to the viscosity of the pus and the contents of the infected cavity, as for empyema. Generally, small-bore catheters (35) varying from 7–14 Fr, are adequate for drainage of most lung abscesses. A flexible catheter, or one with a pigtail configuration, can be curled inside the cavity, allowing dependent drainage when sufficient side-holes are present (19). The drainage catheter is sutured to the skin, and connected to a waterseal aspiration. Pulmonary abscesses have a more or less thick wall, and do not always collapse rapidly after aspiration. Aspiration and drainage should be progressive, in order to avoid rupture of vessels incorporated in the wall of the abscess or located nearby. These vessels may be overstretched and rupture during a too rapid shrinkage of the cavity, provoking catastrophic bleeding. Lavage of a lung abscess can be dangerous, due to bronchogenic spread of the pus. Opacification of the abscess cavity through the drainage catheter does not add significant information in most cases. When it is performed, reflux in the bronchial system should be avoided (Fig. 4). A non-water-soluble contrast agent should be used to avoid massive alveolar edema (54). Patency of the drainage catheter can be checked daily by injecting minimal amounts of saline. When secondary fungus disease, complicating a pre-existing tuberculous cavity, is diagnosed, specific medication (amphotericin B) can be instilled percutaneously.

Percutaneous drainage of a lung abscess should be monitored by daily chest radiographs, and the patient should initially be placed in the intensive care unit for surveillance.

Results are usually good, cure being obtained in almost all cases without complications (22, 35, 37) (Table 1). The duration of drainage is variable, with closure of the cavity after 4–5 weeks (52). Surgery

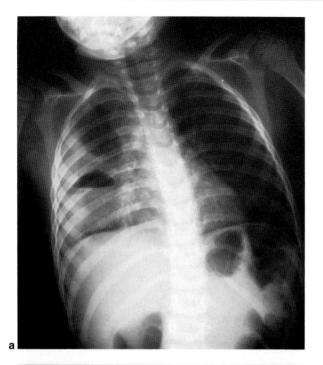

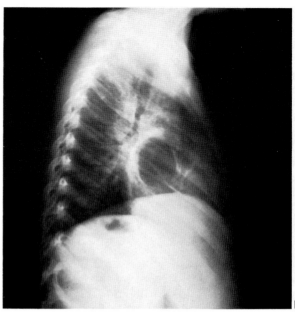

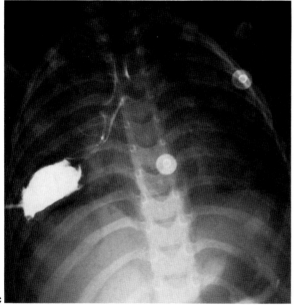

Fig. **4** **Four-year-old child** with a lung abscess following pneumonia of the right lung. No regression with medical treatment
a, b Chest X-ray shows a cavity with an air-fluid level in the right middle lobe
c Percutaneous abscess drainage with an 8 Fr pigtail catheter. A cautious transcatheter injection of contrast medium demonstrates a communication between the abscess and the bronchial system. Cure after short abscess drainage

remains indicated only in the presence of extensive necrosis of lung parenchyma and life-threatening hemorrhage (58) which cannot be efficiently managed by embolization.

Mediastinal Abscess

Mediastinal abscesses result from circumscribed mediastinitis. The prognosis is extremely poor when there is a delay in recognizing the disease (17, 26), but diagnosis is nowadays rapidly established with opacification of the esophagus and with CT, especially when a water-density collection is visible in the mediastinum. Most purulent collections which occur in the mediastinum result from penetrating trauma, either to the thoracic wall or from perforation of the esophagus. The esophagus either ruptures spontaneously (cancer, corrosion, ulceration, breakdown of surgical anastomoses, protracted vomiting) (26), or following endoscopic perforation using rigid endoscopes, laser therapy or endoscopic resection or bouginage (23). Extensive thoracic surgery can be followed by mediastinal abscess formation, or more rarely, a pulmonary or pleural infection can spread to the mediastinum.

Mediastinal abscesses can be located in any compartment of the mediastinum, according to the source of infection. CT is by far the most useful modality for diagnosis and for guiding percutaneous treatment. Abscesses located in the anterior mediastinum are drained by a parasternal approach, those located in the posterior and middle compartment most frequently by an extrapleural paravertebral approach, as used for percutaneous mediastinal biopsy (60) or sympathetic nerve block (12) (Fig. 5). Large mediastinal vessels and the heart are easily avoided by the catheter when recognized by intravenous injection of contrast medium. When necessary, multiple catheters are inserted, either on both sides of the thoracic spine or the sternum, or in the upper and lower parts of the mediastinum. There is a tendency to apply conservative treatment to esophageal perforation (1, 5, 27). When a tear of the esophagus is evidenced, an endoesophageal bypass can be inserted together with an endoesophageal (7, 26) or percutaneous (17) drainage catheter placed at the site of perforation. For transesophageal insertion of a drainage catheter, the nasogastric catheter is placed through the esophageal tear in the mediastinal abscess, under endoscopic and fluoroscopic control, especially when no safe percutaneous extrapleural approach to the mediastinal abscess can be defined. The drainage catheters are connected to a water-seal aspiration. The upper abdomen should always be examined to rule out subdiaphragmatic suppuration. As suppurative mediastinitis and mediastinal abscesses are a severe condition, occurring often in moribund patients, there are no large series of surgical or percutaneous drainage available (7, 17, 26). Surgery is not considered in most instances due to the extremely poor general condition of the patient, and percutaneous drainage is often the only treatment compatible with the patient's clinical status (17).

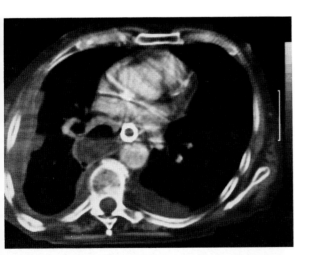

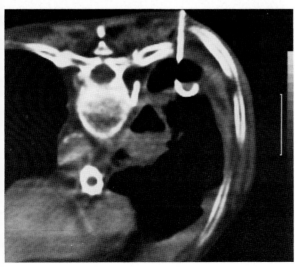

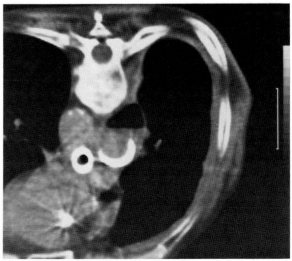

Fig. **5a–e Sixty-five-year-old male** with cancer of the esophagus. Perforation of the esophagus occurred during endoscopic placement of a Celestin prosthesis
a CT shows a mediastinal collection with an air-fluid level, situated close to the esophagus. Notice the Celestin tube in the esophagus
b CT-guided drainage of a sterile left pleural effusion with an 8 Fr pigtail catheter. Not the paravertebral insertion of the 8 Fr pigtail catheter into the mediastinal abscess
c CT shows the extremity of the 8 Fr pigtail catheter in the mediastinal abscess. *Staphylococcus epidermidis, Streptococcus faecalis* and *Streptococcus milleri* are cultured from the abscess content. Duration of drainage until closure of the esophageal tear: 35 days

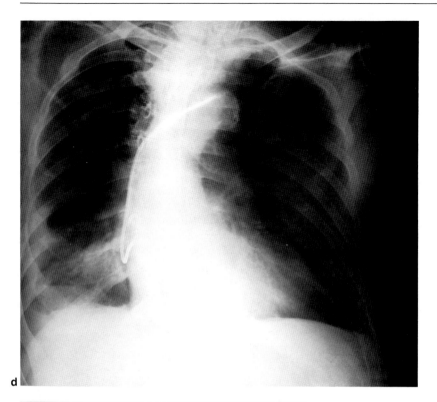

d

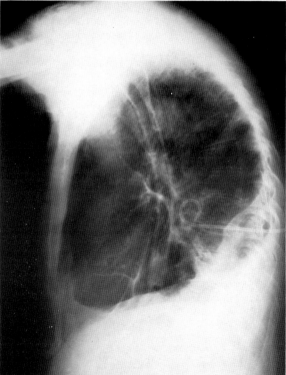

e

Fig. 5d, e Anteroposterior and lateral chest X-rays showing position of the percutaneous mediastinal abscess drainage catheter. The patient died suddenly 1 week after withdrawal of the catheter

Among 6 mediastinal abscesses reported (17), percutaneous treatment was successful in 5. The average duration of drainage is much longer than for empyema or lung abscesses (35 days), and even longer when an esophageal tear is responsible. In another report of 8 patients treated by a nasogastric transesophageal catheter, 7 patients were cured after 2 to 4 weeks of drainage (26) (Table 1).

As for abscesses located in the abdomen, no cure can be obtained when the cause of infection persists (tumor with superinfection, infected vascular graft).

Cysts developing from the thoracic duct (30), non-infected mediastinal bronchogenic cysts (21, 43) and pancreatic pseudocysts (61) extending to the mediastinum, are distinguished from a purulent fluid (45) content by percutaneous diagnostic aspiration. Pseudocysts are treated either by percutaneous or by a transbronchial or transesophageal aspiration, but they can also regress spontaneously (25).

Personal Experience

We have treated thoracic fluid collections with percutaneous drainage in 24 patients. The patients were 21 males and 3 females, aged 2 to 77 years, with a mean age of 47. Seven patients had a pulmonary abscess, which was located in the right lower lobe in 4, in the right middle lobe in 1, and in the left lower lobe in 2. Fourteen patients had a pleural empyema, located at the right side in 10 patients and at the left in 4 patients, while 2 patients had a post-traumatic sterile hemothorax. One patient had a mediastinal abscess due to perforation of the esophagus during bouginage for malignant obstruction. Twelve patients were assisted by mechanical ventilation during the course of their disease. In one patient with endocarditis, empyema spread from septic pulmonary emboli. Two patients had undergone previous cardiac surgery, one had had brain surgery, bone marrow aplasia was present in one patient, one patient had an infected post-traumatic pneumatocele, and one patient had tuberculosis. Two patients had pleural empyemas complicating right or left subphrenic abscesses. Four patients died from the underlying disease after catheter withdrawal following successful treatment of a lung abscess. Two patients died from the underlying disease following successful treatment of an empyema, and one following treatment of a mediastinal abscess.

Most patients were treated with single drainage catheters with computed tomography as a guidance modality. The trocar technique was used in 15 patients. All catheters were correctly placed at the first attempt, allowing adequate drainage.

The drainage catheters used varied in size from 8–24 Fr. Drainage catheters of 16–24 Fr were preferred for treatment of empyema, while 8–14 Fr catheters were inserted for treatment of pulmonary

abscesses. The germs most frequently identified by bacteriology were *Streptococcus faecalis*, *E. coli*, *Staphylococcus aureus* and *Bacteroides fragilis*. No specific bacterium was found. The volume of pus aspirated during the initial drainage varied from 10 to 1500 ml (mean 340). The mean drainage duration for empyema and lung abscess was 12 days (with a range of 6 days to 3 months). The patient presenting an empyema complicating a postoperative right subphrenic abscess with a pleural fistula underwent drainage for 3 months.

The seven pulmonary abscesses were successfully cured with percutaneous drainage alone. All exept one empyema, which recurred, were cured by percutaneous catheter treatment. The patient with a mediastinal abscess died from esophageal cancer after catheter withdrawal. No side-effects complicating the disease were noticed during percutaneous drainage.

Complications

Complications following percutaneous drainage of thoracic fluid collections guided by imaging techniques are rare (2, 17, 22, 28, 48, 51, 52, 54, 56, 59). Most of them result from inadequate technique during introduction of the drainage catheter. A large-bore catheter can create active bleeding from an intercostal artery by lacerating the vascular nervous bundle in the intercostal space, resulting in a hemothorax or a chest wall hematoma.

When the percutaneous drainage catheter establishes a communication between a lung abscess and the pleura, spread of infection from the lung to the pleural space can produce a secondary empyema or a bronchopleural fistula. However, extensive pleural adhesions usually prevent the occurrence of an empyema during drainage of a lung abscess. With inadequate guidance during catheter placement, the catheter may be introduced subdiaphragmatically into the spleen or liver, but these complications are more likely to occur when imaging guidance is not used. When the trocar technique is used, the lung parenchyma can be lacerated, producing a pulmonary infarction. Significant, life-threatening hemorrhage can be observed during rupture of the abscess cavity itself. Theoretically, a mediastinal catheter can erode mediastinal vessels and the trachea. However, no major complications have been observed in the series published. Bacteremia and hemoptysis may occur during catheter introduction. Pneumothorax is a potentially frequent complication when the lung parenchyma is crossed by a large catheter, but it should not occur during drainage of pleural fluid, and most pulmonary abscesses also present a contact with the pleura. Small pneumothoraces have been observed during pleural drainage under fluoroscopic guidance with a small catheter in 6% (9); using one or multiple 7 Fr catheters and with sonographic guidance, a rate of pneumothoraces as high as 25% has occurred (34). Pneumothoraces can be treated with a small-bore drainage catheter (9 Fr) connected to a Heimlich valve. A chylothorax may rarely be observed. A sinus tract from the pleura through the chest wall may persist when the patient has undergone previous irradiation (2). Minor complications include asymptomatic subcutaneous emphysema (59), local skin infection at the entry point of the catheter, and discomfort during deep breathing. When large drainage catheters are used, analgesics may be required, favoring the use of smaller catheters, which are better tolerated by the patient (59). Rib erosion, catheter leak, bending, obstruction, and leakage are other possible complications.

References

1. Anderson OJ, Glustra PE. Nonoperative management of contained esophageal perforation. Arch Surg 1981;116:1214.
2. Aronberg DJ, Sagel SS, Jost RG, Lee JI. Percutaneous drainage of lung abscess. AJR 1979;132:282.
3. Barnett TB, Herring CL. Lung abscess: initial and late results of medical therapy. Arch Intern Med 1971;127:217.
4. Bartlett JG, Gorbach SL, Tally FP, Friegold SM. Bacteriology and treatment of primary lung abscess. Am Rev Respir Dis 1974;109:510.
5. Brown RH, Cohen PJ. Nonsurgical management of spontaneous esophageal perforation. JAMA 1978;240:140.
6. Cameron EW, Whitton ID. Percutaneous drainage in the treatment of Klebsiella pneumoniae lung abscess. Thorax 1977;32:673.
7. Chang AE, Schwarz W, Ring EJ, Rosate EF. Transluminal catheter drainage of an esophageal disruption: an adjunct to nonoperative management. Surg Gastroenterol 1982;1:135.
8. Chidi CC, Mendelsohn HJ. Lung abscess: a study of the results of 90 consecutive cases. J Thorac Cardiovasc Surg 1974;68:168.
9. Collins JD, Byrd SE, Bassett LW. Thoracentesis under fluoroscopic control. JAMA 1977;237:2751.
10. Connors JP, Roper CL, Ferguson TB. Transbronchial catheterization of pulmonary abscesses. Ann Thorac Surg 1975;19:254.
11. Delarue NC, Pearson FG, Nelems JH, Cooper JD. Lung abscess: surgical implications. Can J Surg 1980;23:297.
12. Dondelinger RF, Kurdziel JC. Percutaneous phenol block of the upper thoracic sympathetic chain with computed tomography guidance. Acta Radiol 1987;28:511.
13. Estrera AS, Platt MR, Mills LJ, Shaw RR. Primary lung abscess. J Thorac Cardiovasc Surg 1980;79:275.
14. Fifer WR, Husebye K, Chedister C, Miller M. Primary lung abscess: analysis of therapy and results of 55 cases. Arch Intern Med 1961;107:668.
15. Finegold SM. Necrotizing pneumonias and lung abscess. In: Hoeprich PD. ed. Infectious diseases. Hagerstown, MD: Harper und Row, 1972:339.
16. Glover RP, Clagett OT. Pulmonary resection for abscess of lung. Surg Gynecol Obstet 1948;86:385.
17. Gobien RP, Stanley JH, Gobien BS, Vujic I, Pass HI. Percutaneous catheter aspiration and drainage of suspected mediastinal abscesses. Radiology 1984;51:69.
18. Groff DB, Marquis J. Treatment of lung abscess by transbronchial catheter drainage. Radiology 1973;107:61.
19. Keller FS, Rosch J, Barker AF, Dotter CT. Percutaneous interventional catheter therapy for lesions of the chest and lungs. Chest 1982;81:407.
20. Kreuser ED, Seifried E, Hartmann R, Schreml W, Rasche H. Therapy of malignant pleural effusion by fibrin glueing. Tumor Diagn Therap 1984;5:55.
21. Kuhlman JE, Fishmann EK, Wang KP, Zerhouni EA, Siegelman SS. Mediastinal cysts: diagnosis by CT and needle aspiration. AJR 1988;150:75.
22. Lorenzo RL, Bradford BF, Black J, Smith CD. Lung abscesses in children: diagnostic and therapeutic needle aspiration. Radiology 1985;157:79.
23. Mandel SR, Boyd D, Jaques PF, Mandell V, Staab E. Drainage of hepatic, intraabdominal and mediastinal abscesses guided by computerized axial tomography. Am J Surg 1983;145:120.
24. Marquis J. Treatment of lung abscess by transbronchial catheter drainage. Radiology 1973;107:61.
25. Martin KW, Siegel MJ, Chesna E. Spontaneous resolution of mediastinal cysts. AJR 1988;150:1131.
26. Meranze SG, Leveen RF, Burke DR, Cope C, McLean GK. Transesophageal drainage of mediastinal abscesses. Radiology 1987;165:395.
27. Michel L, Grillo HC, Malt RA. Operative and nonoperative management of esophageal perforations. Ann Surg 1981;194:57.
28. Monaldi V. Endocavitary aspiration in treatment of lung abscess. Chest 1956;29:193.
29. Monsein LH, Woodside JR, Dhillon JS. Percutaneous removal of thoracostomy tubes. Radiology 1987;165:743.
30. Morettin LB, Allen TE. Thoracic duct cyst: diagnosis with needle aspiration. Radiology 1986;161:437.
31. Morris JF, Okies JE. Enterococcal lung abscess: medical and surgical therapy. Chest 1974;65:688.
32. Neuhof H, Touroff ASW. Acute putrid abscess of the lung: hyperacute variety. J Thorac Surg 1942;12:98.
33. Neuhof H, Touroff AS, Aufses AH. The surgical treatment by drainage of subacute and chronic putrid abscess of the lung. Ann Surg 1941;113:209.
34. O'Moore PV, Mueller PR, Simeone JF, Saini S, Butch RJ, Hahn PF, Steiner E, Stark DD, Ferrucci JT Jr. Sonographic guidance in diagnostic and therapeutic interventions in the pleural space. AJR 1987;149:1.
35. Parker LA, Melton JW, Delany DJ. Percutaneous small bore catheter drainage in the management of lung abscesses. Chest 1987;92:213.
36. Pierce AK, Sanford JP. Aerobic gram-negative bacillary pneumonias. Am Rev Respir Dis 1974;110:647.
37. Rami-Porta R, Bravo-Bravo JL, Alix-Trueba A, Serrano-Munoz F. Percutaneous drainage of lung abscess. J Thorac Cardiovasc Surg 1985;89:314.
38. Reeder GS, Gracey DR. Aspiration of intrathoracic abscess: resultant acute ventilatory failure. JAMA 1978;240:1156.
39. Renner RR, Coccaro AP, Heitzman RE, Dailey ET, Markarian B. Pseudomonas pneumonia: a prototype of hospital-based infection. Radiology 1972;105:555.
40. Rice TW, Ginsberg RJ, Todd TRJ. Tube drainage of lung abscesses. Ann Thorac Surg 1987;44:356.
41. Rowe LD, Keane WM, Japek BW, Atkins JP Jr. Transbronchial drainage of pulmonary abscesses with the flexible fiberoptic bronchoscope. Laryngoscope 1979;89:122.
42. Schmitt GS, Ohar JM, Kanter KR. Indwelling transbronchial catheter drainage of pulmonary abscess. Ann Thorac Surg 1988;45:43.
43. Schwarz AR, Fishman EK, Wang KP. Diagnosis and treatment of a bronchogenic cyst using transbronchial needle aspiration. Thorax 1986;41:326.
44. Schweppe HI, Knowles JH, Kane L. Lung abscess: an analysis of the Massachusetts General Hospital cases from 1943 through 1956. N Engl J Med 1961;265:1039.
45. Semelka RC, Greenberg HM. Percutaneous drainage of an infected mediastinal pseudocyst. Can Assoc Radiol 1987;38:54.
46. Shafron RD, Tate CF Jr. Lung abscess: a five-year evaluation. Chest 1968;54:12.
47. Sherman MM, Subramanian V, Berger RL. Management of thoracic empyema. Am J Surg 1977;133:474.
48. Silverman SG, Mueller PR, Saini S, Hahn PF, Simeone JF, Forman BH, Steiner E, Ferrucci JT. Thoracic empyema: man-

agement with image-guided catheter drainage. Radiology 1988;169:5.

49. Skinner DB, Myerowitz PD. Recent advances in the management of thoracic surgical infections. Ann Thorac Surg 1981;31:191.

50. Snow N, Lucas A, Horrigan TP. Utility of pneumonotomy in the treatment of cavitary lung disease. Chest 1985;87:731.

51. Stavas J, Van Sonnenberg E, Casola G. Percutaneous drainage of infected and non-infected thoracic fluid collections. J Thorac Imag 1987;2:80.

52. Vainrub B, Husher DM, Guinn GA, Young EJ, Septimus EJ, Travis LL. Percutaneous drainage of lung abscess. Am Rev Respir Dis 1978;117:153.

53. Van Sonnenberg E, Ferrucci JT Jr, Mueller PR, Wittenberg J, Simeone JF. Percutaneous drainage of abscesses and fluid collections: technique, results, and applications. Radiology 1982;142:1.

54. Van Sonnenberg E, Nakamoto SK, Mueller PR, Casola G, Neff CC, Friedman PJ, Ferrucci JT, Simeone JF. CT and ultrasound-guided catheter drainage of empyemas after chest-tube failure. Radiology 1984;151:349.

55. Varkey B, Rose HD, Kutty Kesavan CP, Politis J. Empyema thoracis during a ten-year period. Arch Intern Med 1981;141:1771.

56. Vasile N, De Hys C, Mathieu D, Anglade MC, Brun-Buisson C, Lemaire F. CT and percutaneous drainage of thoracic empyema or abscesses in critically ill patients. J Belge Radiol 1987;70:515.

57. Weiss W. Cavity behavior in acute primary non-specific lung abscess. Am Rev Respir Dis 1973;108:1273.

58. Weissbeg D. Percutaneous drainage of lung abscess. J Thorac Cardiovasc Surg 1984;87:308.

59. Westcott JL. Percutaneous catheter drainage of pleural effusion and empyema. AJR 1985;144:1189.

60. Williams RA, Haaga JR, Karagiannis E. CT-guided paravertebral biopsy of the mediastinum. J Comput Assist Tomogr 1984;8:575.

61. Wittich GR, Karnel F, Schurawitzki H, Jantsch H. Percutaneous drainage of mediastinal pseudocysts. Radiology 1988;167:51.

62. Yellin A, Yellin EO, Lierman Y. Percutaneous tube drainage: the treatment of choice for refractory lung abscess. Ann Thorac Surg 1985;39:266.

Endoscopic and Percutaneous Management of Biliary Disease

Endoscopic Procedures

M. Cremer, M. Delhaye, and J. Devière

Twenty years ago, the advent of duodenoscopy, allowing for cannulation of the papilla (40), opened new fields of endoscopic diagnosis and therapy in biliary-pancreatic diseases. Endoscopic retrograde cholangiopancreatography (ERCP) has been shown to be the most accurate and reliable method for the diagnosis of diseases involving the biliary and pancreatic ducts (8).

Endoscopic sphincterotomy (ES), which is now 15 years old (4, 34), became the treatment of choice for common bile duct (CBD) stones after cholecystectomy, even with the gallbladder in situ. It also allowed a non-surgical approach to the management of benign and malignant strictures and fistulas of the biliary tree. This endoscopic approach to the biliary tract has decreased the complications of surgery in acute clinical situations (cholangitis, pancreatitis), and in the elderly.

Cannulation of the Main Papilla

ERCP is indicated for patients with obstructive jaundice or cholestasis for which the clinical data, laboratory and ultrasonic findings suggest any type of benign or malignant obstruction of the extrahepatic biliary tree. In our medico-surgical gastroenterology department, we also found it tremendously beneficial to assess the integrity of the CBD preoperatively in patients presenting with acute cholecystitis. This diagnostic approach should only be taken if one is prepared to carry out therapeutic biliary drainage.

For patients with suspected pancreatic disease, ERCP is the only method available which provides a precise diagnosis of the abnormalities of the pancreatic ducts in association with therapeutic procedures. Endoscopic pancreatic sphincterotomy is now extensively performed in combination with shock wave lithotripsy in order to extract pancreatic calculi, or, on its own, to stent the main pancreatic duct in patients with painful chronic pancreatitis. Cystoduodenostomy is a new associated procedure which could replace surgery when cysts or pseudocysts protrude into the duodenal wall or are visible behind the posterior wall of the stomach.

Opacification of the biliary and pancreatic ducts is obtained by injecting contrast medium via a 5 or 6 Fr catheter with a metal tip introduced into the orifice of the papilla of Vater. The metal tip has the advantage of being visible on fluoroscopy, allowing successful deep cannulation, even in patients with a tortuous papilla.

The universal catheter, used in all circumstances, has the following characteristics:

– a metal tip, preferably diabolo or conic, for easier insertion into difficult papillas
– Teflon coating, with a proximal guide wire providing rigidity for easier handling
– an external diameter of 5 or 6 Fr which
– allows for the passage of a 0.035 inch guide wire with various tips (straight, J type, sigmoid type), which
– allows one to push a 10 Fr stent over it.

It is usually easier to fill the pancreatic duct than the biliary tree because of the "natural" direction of the catheter coming out of the scope. One can often obtain successful opacification of the biliary tree by bending the catheter from below, allowing for proper entrance via the papilla (Fig. 1). If this fails, a soft needle catheter (19) introduced between 11 and 12 o'clock increases the success rate of cholangiography up to 98%. The most difficult papilla is the normal papilla; deep cannulation of the CBD is easier in patients with CBD stones and in acute cholangitis, where there is a bulging fold behind the papilla. In the case of papillary tumors, it is also difficult to locate and cannulate the papilla because the orifice is often eccentric, and its surface can bleed during the cannulation procedure.

The duodenoscopes presently used for diagnostic purposes have an operative channel of 3.2 mm (fiberscope Olympus JFIT 20) or 2.8 mm (videoduodenoscope Olympus JFV 10), and an outer diameter of 12.0 and 12.5 mm respectively. For children up to 2 years old and for patients with duodenal strictures, a more flexible and thinner duodenoscope is used (Olympus JF B4, outer diameter: 10.5 mm). Moreover, ERCP is feasible in infants from birth using a pediatric duodenoscope with an outer diameter of 8.5 mm (Olympus PJF) but still with an elevator to guide the catheter adequately in both directions in the biliary or pancreatic duct. Sedation with midazolam and meperidine facilitate cannulation and therapeutic procedures in adults, while general anesthesia is necessary for children and infants.

The endoscope has to be straightened by rotation after reaching the proximal duodenum, the patient

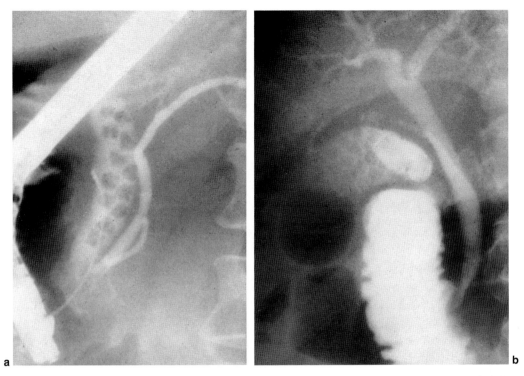

Fig. **1** **Male, 65 years old.** CBD and gallbladder stones of similar size. **a** Deep cannulation after bending the catheter from below. **b** Complete clearance of the common bile duct after endoscopic sphincterotomy and removal of the calculi

being in the left lateral prone position. The "short scope" position allows for easy access to the papilla, even when located around a diverticulum. Control of the tip of the instrument and catheters (and other devices) introduced into the papilla is easier than with the "long scope" position that was used many years ago, which was called the "japanese position".

The same method is used for patients with a Billroth I gastrectomy, but deep cannulation is more difficult. For patients with a Billroth II gastrectomy (Fig. **2**), the main problem is to reach the afferent loop: this is achieved by bending the tip of the endoscope into the orifice of the afferent loop, and then pushing the scope under fluoroscopy, with the patient lying on his back. In patients with large gastric stumps or long precolic afferent loops, selective filling of the loop with contrast medium via a catheter introduced as deeply as possible with a biliary J type of guide wire increases the success rate in reaching the afferent loop.

Most experts prefer lateral-viewing duodenoscopes to forward-viewing scopes, because selective cannulation is easier by maneuvering the elevator. In our experiences, in difficult cases, the success rate in reaching the afferent loop was not increased when using a forward-viewing scope.

In our series, we had a successful cannulation rate of 60% of patients during the early period (1971–1979), and a 78% success rate in the later period (1980–1985), corresponding to the advent of the new large viewing field duodenoscopes of the fourth generation. The success rate for selective cholangiography was also slightly lower than the success rate of pancreatography, but it has recently been improved by the use of straight and even sigmoid catheters.

Cannulation of the Accessory Papilla

In patients with pancreas divisum (present in about 7% of the population) and choledochal strictures, it is necessary to search for possible abnormalities of the dorsal main pancreatic duct in order to differentiate between chronic pancreatitis and carcinoma of the pancreas. Cannulation of the accessory papilla is performed with a needle catheter, which provided a success rate of 93% in our series (15).

Diagnosis of Obstructive Jaundice

For the last 18 years, ERCP has been shown to be the most effective method of diagnosis in cases of obstructive jaundice, and even for patients presenting with a cholestatic syndrome. In a series of 2600 patients presenting with obstructive jaundice and referred to us for ERCP, the spectrum and fre-

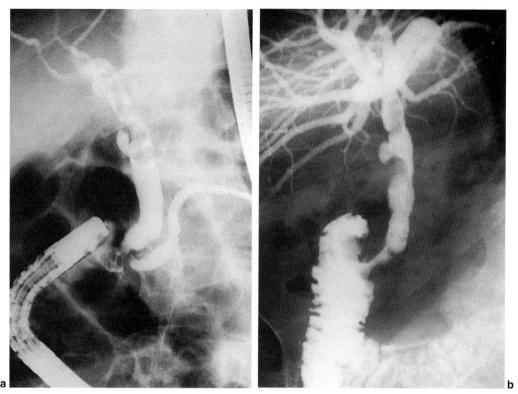

Fig. 2   Male, 71 years old. Billroth II gastrectomy; choledocholithiasis after cholecystectomy
a Endoscopic sphincterotomy
b Perfused nasobiliary catheter after 24 h, showing residual stones

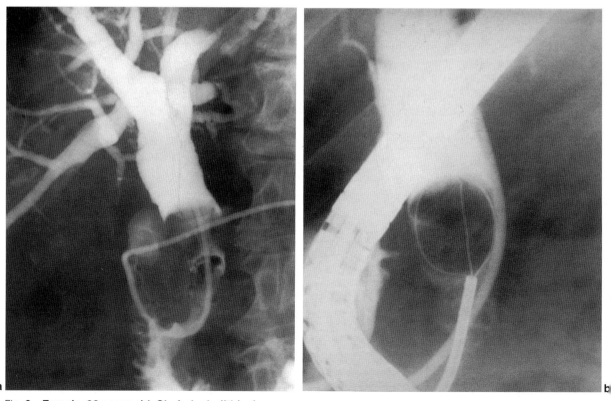

Fig. 3   Female, 88 years old. Choledocholithiasis
a Large stone and nasobiliary catheter
b Attempt at endoscopic mechanical lithotripsy with the Wilson-Cook lithotriptor

Fig. **4** **Female, 82 years old. Previous cholecystec-** ▶
tomy. Common bile duct stones and benign papillary
stricture, with a dilated common bile duct. Malignancy
was excluded after endoscopic sphincterotomy, repeated
biopsies performed 1 week afterward, and after follow-up

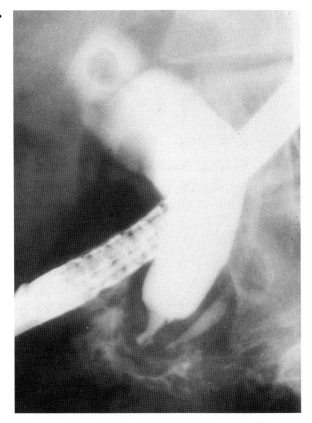

Fig. **5** **Female, 52 years old. Previous cholecystec-**
tomy, and choledochoduodenostomy for a relapse of
common bile duct stones
a Intrahepatic duct stones without any stricture of the
biliary tract
b, c After removal of the gallstones, dormia baskets, maneuvered with a forward-viewing gastroscope, were introduced into the choledochoduodenostomy
▼

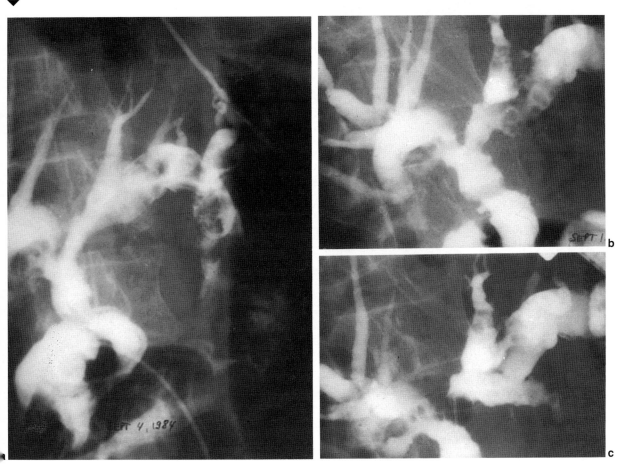

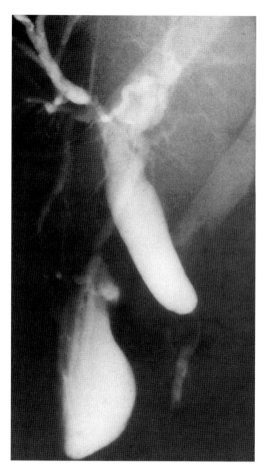

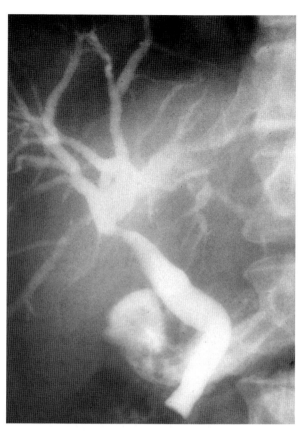

Fig. **6**   **Male, 17 years old. Fluctuant obstructive jaun-dice. Carcinoma of the head of the pancreas:** a dilated common bile duct above an abrupt stricture of the intrapan-creatic common bile duct. No dilation of the gallbladder or the intrahepatic bile ducts

Fig. **7**   **Female, 76 years old. Gallbladder stones on US. Gallbladder carcinoma** involving the common bile duct: non-symmetrical stricture and cystic duct not visible

quency of the various differential diagnoses observed in Belgium was:

– Choledocholithiasis (55%), which is most often associated with a dilation of the common bile duct (Figs. **3** and **4**), most of the patients having the gallbladder in situ. In Western countries, in-trahepatic gallstones are quite rare (about 3% of patients with gallstones) (Fig. **5**).

– A malignant stricture of the biliary tree was found in 26% of patients with jaundice, most often due to pancreatic cancer (Fig. **6**), but also due to common bile duct carcinomas, gallbladder car-cinomas (Fig. **7**), metastasis (Fig. **8**), and papillary carcinoma (Fig. **9**).

– The diagnosis of intrahepatic cholestasis was ap-plied to 9% of patients in whom no abnormalities were found in the entire biliary tract.

– In 6%, cholestatic jaundice and cholestasis with-out jaundice were due to a choledochal stricture from chronic pancreatitis involving the head of the pancreas.

– In 2% of the referred patients, a stricture of the CBD, often located near the bifurcation, was found, occurring up to 20 years after cholecystec-tomy.

– The remaining 2% of patients had several rare causes of obstructive jaundice, such as sclerosing cholangitis (which is very difficult to differentiate from Klatskin tumor) (Fig. **10**).

Hyperlipasemia and hyperamylasemia are usually observed in patients who have undergone ERCP. However, acute pancreatitis is uncommon. It can occur with repeated injections of contrast medium when attempting selective cannulation of the biliary

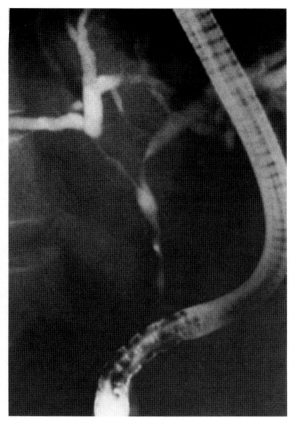

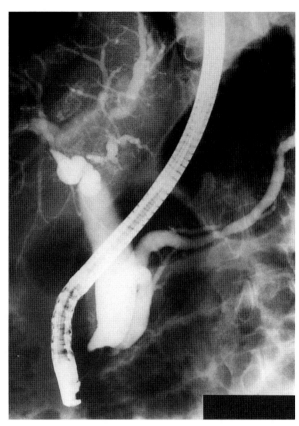

Fig. **8 Female, 76 years old. Hilar metastasis with a type II stricture** involving both left and right hepatic ducts

Fig. **9 Female, 74 years old. Papillary carcinoma** with both biliary and pancreatic ducts dilated: irregular shape of the distal common bile duct

tree, especially when the ERCP room is not equipped with a high-resolution X-ray monitor and amplifier. This complication can be avoided by injecting non-ionic or isotonic iodine contrast material. Careful studies have shown that the use of this type of contrast has decreased the occurrence of pancreatitis after ERCP.

One complication of ERCP is iatrogenic cholangitis. It can be avoided by using sterile equipment and by refusing cannulation if one is not prepared to drain the biliary tree.

Endoscopic Sphincterotomy

Endoscopic sphincterotomy was first described in 1974 by a German (4) and a Japanese group (34) almost simultaneously. The indications for endo-scopic sphincterotomy depend on patient selection and are summarized in Table **1** with the percentages of patients referred to our center between 1970 and 1983. The selection of referred patients in the last years has changed; indications for the stenting of malignant strictures and endoscopic management in chronic calcified pancreatitis have increased. Preoperative sphincterotomy for common bile duct stones has decreased the mortality related to choledochotomy and to other surgical procedures (T-tube drainage or choledochoduodenostomy) which sometimes have severe late complications (CBD strictures and newly formed stones).

Techniques of Sphincterotomy

Endoscopes and Accessories. Both diagnostic (Olympus JF1T 20 or JFV 10) and therapeutic

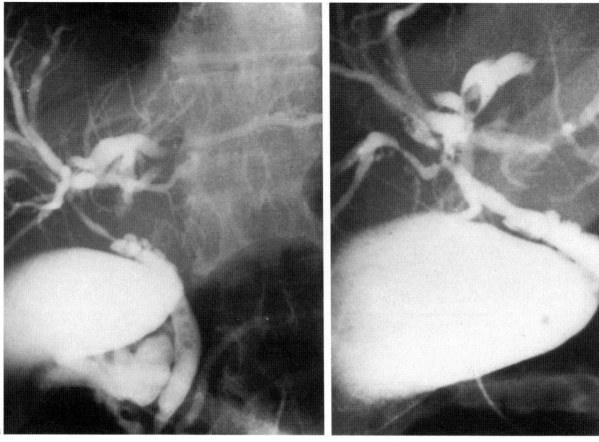

Fig. **10a, b   Female, 81 years old. Relapse of acute cholangitis. Sclerosing cholangitis** involving the common bile duct and intrahepatic ducts, with a stone visible in the left hepatic duct. Management with dilation, nasobiliary perfusion, and intermittent stenting

Table **1**   Indications for endoscopic sphincterotomy

1. CBD stones with gallbladder stones (51%).
2. CBD stones after cholecystectomy (27%).
3. CBD stones with gallbladder in situ without calculi (6.4%).
4. Papillary carcinoma (5.6%).
5. Malignant strictures of the biliary tree, allowing for the proper insertion of stents (4%).
6. Retained CBD stones with a T tube in place (4%).
7. Chronic pancreatitis with further extraction of stones, or dilation of the accessory pancreatic duct with pancreatic stents (1%).
8. Benign papillary stenosis (1%).
9. Postsurgical benign strictures before dilation (Fig. **11**) and/or stenting (4%).
10. Postsurgical fistulas (Fig. **12**).
11. Choledochocele (Figs. **13, 14**) or congenital choledochal cyst type III, which should not be confused with diverticula of the lower CBD (Figs. **15, 16**).

(Olympus TJF 10 or TJFV 10) duodenoscopes, with an outer diameter of 13.6 mm, are available to perform endoscopic sphincterotomy. In our opinion, the safest sphincterotome is the "proximal short sphincterotome" (Fig. **17**). It includes:

– A metal tip, which is easier to introduce into the papilla, because it can be followed on fluoroscopy during insertion; it also provides the medical and legal proof that the sphincterotome is actually in the CBD.
– A long nose (50 mm) free of any wire, to assure stability within the CBD during belching, vomiting or bleeding. This classical sphincterotome allows for coagulation of a bleeding site on the papilla (even when endoscopic vision is impaired by blood flow) by setting the diathermic wire of the sphincterotome on reference marks in fluoroscopy. A shorter nose (15–30 mm) is sometimes necessary

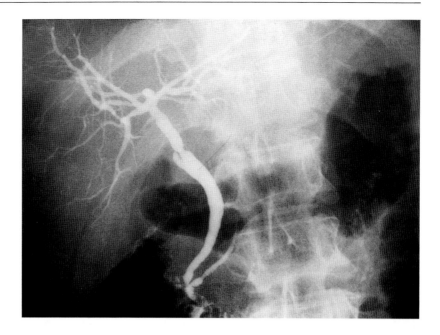

Fig. **11   Female, 54 years old.**
Postcholecystectomy stenosis
close to the cystic duct

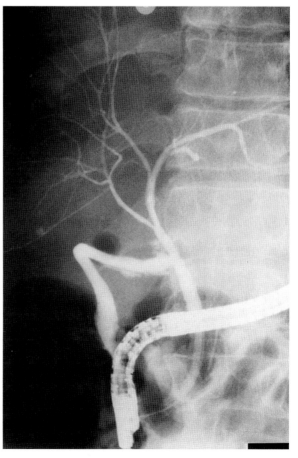

when a low stricture hinders the progression of the tip of the sphincterotome into the duct.

– A short cutting wire (20 mm), which avoids too large an initial incision. A radiopaque ring is present on the distal side of the wire. With the 30 mm cutting wires delivered by most manufacturers, there are 2 possibilities, neither of which is acceptable: either making a dangerously large incision in the papilla, or cutting both the papilla and the endoscope itself.

Some other sphincterotomes have been developed for special circumstances:

– After difficult deep cannulation of the CBD, it is possible to save some time by pushing the sphincterotome on a guide wire that has been left in place within the diagnostic catheter: this is the reason why each diagnostic catheter must allow for the insertion of a guide wire of 0.035 inches.

Fig. **12   Male, 56 years old. Biliary fistula after removal of the T-tube.** Small common bile duct. Healing followed endoscopic sphincterotomy

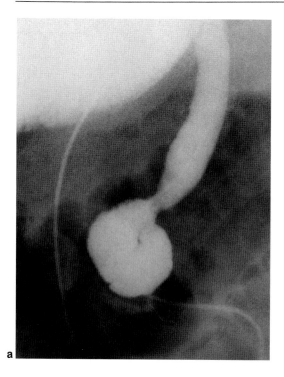

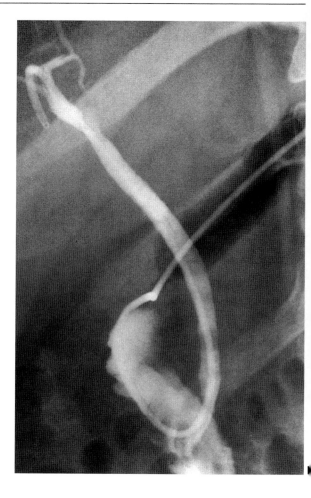

a

Fig. **13 Male, 45 years old. Choledochocele.** Acute cholecystitis and cholangitis, without gallstones
a Choledochocele with a nasobiliary catheter in place
b Cholangiography through a nasobiliary catheter after endoscopic sphincterotomy: healing without any further management

– The precut papillotome (10) or "minipapillotome", allowing one to cut the roof of the papilla to facilitate further selective cannulation with a standard papillotome. However, it has been shown that complications such as perforation or pancreatitis have occurred more often in this situation than with standard sphincterotomes,
– A diathermic needle was developed by Olympus in 1976. It is a 0.65 mm needle catheter allowing for puncture of the duodenal wall and further injection of contrast (Fig. **18**). This has occasionally been used to create an endoscopic choledochoduodenostomy on a bulging fold behind the papilla after failure of cannulation. In Billroth II patients, it has also been used carefully after failure of insertion of the "inverted sigmoid sphincterotome" (10).
The fine-needle knife papillotome was developed later (30). This consists of a Teflon catheter carrying a 0.2 mm stainless steel wire which extends up to 5 mm out of the catheter. This knife has been widely used by Huibregtse (19.2% of patients prior to endoscopic insertion of the stent, and 14.5% of patients prior to biliary stone removal)

to carry out a 5–6 mm incision from the orifice up to the roof of the papilla at 11 o'clock. It is certainly useful, but one must be extremely careful to avoid complications with this method.
– The Sohma or "push type" sphincterotome is an elliptical diathermic loop which is pushed into the papilla from below to above, while the classical "Classen" "full type" sphincterotome used in Western Europe is an arched, tracted papillotome (4, 5).
– For Billroth II gastrectomy, inverted sphincterotomes (10, 49) are useful to cut the papilla in the appropriate direction at 6 o'clock (in stead of 12 o'clock in the normal anatomy) (Fig. **19**).

The sphincterotomy must be performed through the distal third of the diathermic wire, step by step, with progression from outside to inside the sphincter, using the scope itself with the right hand to bend the wire appropriately up to the roof of the papilla. The size of the ES must be adapted to the anatomy of the duct: large incisions for large CBDs (except for patients with prepapillary strictures), and small cuts for smaller ducts or flat papilla.

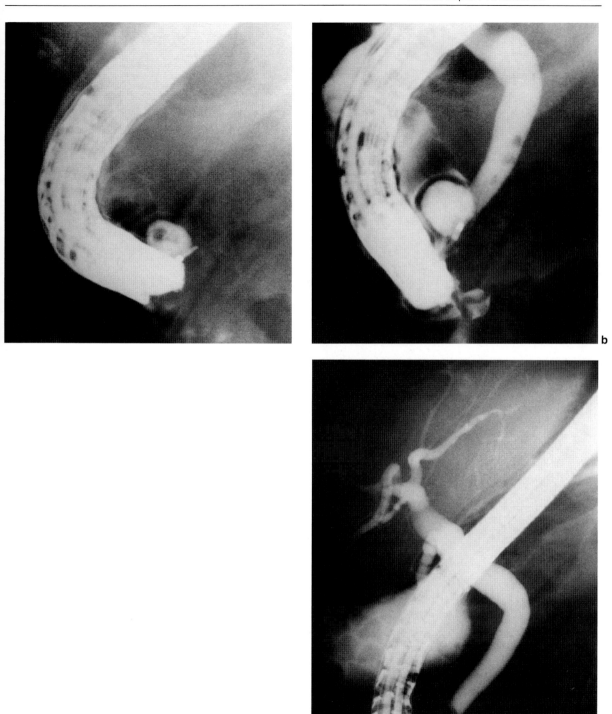

Fig. **14a–c   Female, 80 years old. Choledochocele** with gallstones flushed upstream by the contrast injection, and gallbladder stones. Healed after endoscopic sphincterotomy

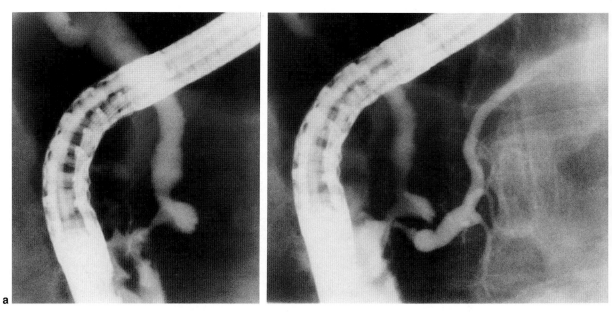

Fig. **15a, b   Male, 64 years old. Incidental discovery of a non-symptomatic diverticulum** of the lower common bile duct

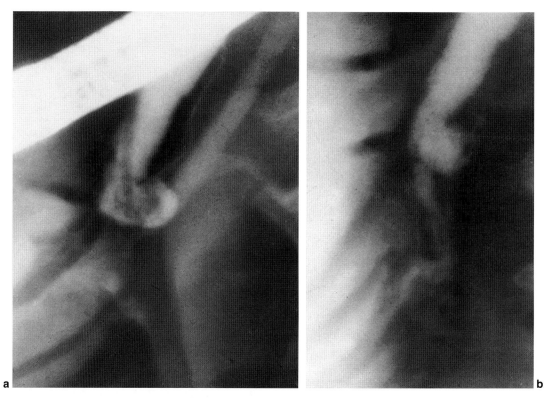

Fig. **16   Male, 81 years old, presenting with relapse attacks of acute pancreatitis**
a Diverticulum of the lower common bile duct, containing a solitary gallstone, without stones in the gallbladder
b Healing after endoscopic sphincterotomy and removal of the stone

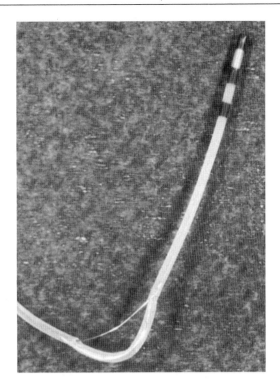

Fig. **17 Proximal short sphincterotome** with a metal tip,
a 50 mm-long nose, and a 20 mm wire

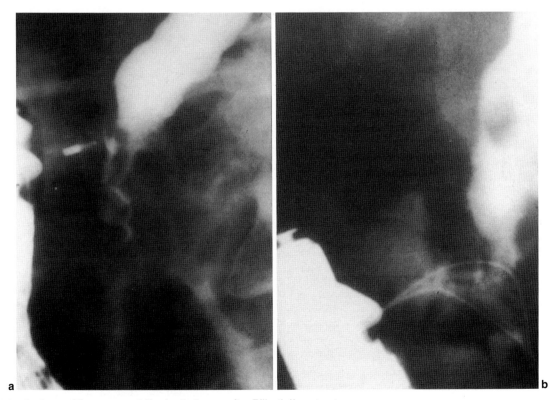

a

b

Fig. **18 Patient with common bile duct stones** after Billroth II gastrectomy
a Puncture of the bulging duodenal fold
b Further insertion of the classical sphincterotome, cutting from 6 to 12 o' clock

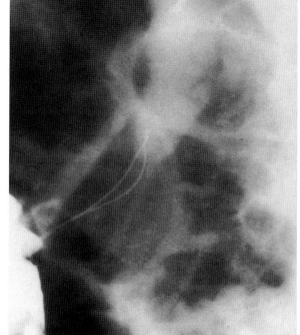

Fig. **19   Patient with Billroth II gastrectomy and gallstones in a dilated duct.** The inverted sphincterotome (**a**)
is inserted and turned spontaneously with the cutting wire
in the appropriate position

The success rate of ES reaches nearly 100% when
using all the tricks available with a wide range of
accessory devices and when working with an experienced team (gastroenterologist, radiologist and assistant nurses) and with high-definition of color pictures
(Olympus duodenoscopes), as well as high-definition
fluoroscopy. Furthermore, what is impossible to do
with surgery and dangerous to do with the percutaneous approach, can be done with therapeutic ERCP:
in patients with unsuccessful filling of the biliary tree,
it is possible to start again on the same patient after
24 h or better after 48 h, or one can refer difficult
patients to centers which have the most sophisticated
equipment.

To avoid iatrogenic cholangitis in patients with
biliary obstruction, antibiotics must be given where
successful cannulation is not carried out, and adequate biliary drainage has therefore not been
achieved. Given all of these conditions, the success
rate in ES reaches 99,5%, which is even higher than
the success rate for selective cannulation of the biliary tree.

Complications of ES

Early complications of ES have decreased in recent
years (Table **2**). It should be stressed that most
complications are related to technical mistakes.

To prevent cholangitis, it is mandatory to perfuse
the bile duct via a nasobiliary catheter for each
patient, even if "complete" stone extraction has been
performed. This is also necessary after sphincterotomy for papillary carcinoma and so-called
benign papillary stenosis. Perfusion can prevent the
impaction of any residual stones, and blood clotting
within the duct; these sequelae are often followed by
ascending cholangitis. Bleeding can always be
avoided by performing ES step by step, looking at
each mm of cut to see whether coagulation is needed
on its edges.

Acute pancreatitis occurs most often after excessive injection of contrast medium into the pancreatic
ducts. It can also be related to excessive use of
coagulation current during sphincterotomy.

Our policy is to cut the first 5 mm with a pure
cutting current, and to follow the sphincterotomy
using a blended current up to the top of the cut, i. e.
8–15 mm, depending on the diameter of the common
bile duct and the shape of the papilla.

Table **2** Percentage of complications following endoscopic sphincterotomy according to international (Madrid) and European inquiries

	Madrid, 1978 (4122 cases)	First series, 1974–1980 (3014 cases)	Later series, 1980–1982 (1473 cases)	Mortality rate from complications
Bleeding	2.8	2.6	1.4	13
Cholangitis	2.0	2.4	1.3	18
Pancreatitis	1.3	1.3	0.8	21
Perforation	0.8	1.3	0.7	14
Basket impaction		0.7	0.2	0
Total complications	7.5	7.9	4.4	
Mortality rate	1.1	1.3	0.6	

As a general rule, the width of the distal CBD determines the size of the cut needed; the wider the CBD, the larger the cut.

Retroperitoneal perforation (Fig. **20**) is the result of cutting at an incorrect angle (20); it can be avoided by turning the position of the diathermic wire from 11 to 12 o'clock.

The impaction of a stone and its basket is not yet a complication: it is the first step of mechanical lithotripsy. It should be emphasized that pancreatitis and perforation are more frequently observed when using special tricks such as precuts or punctures and in patients in whom benign papillary stenosis is suspected. Finally, it should be stressed that every patient in whom cholangitis is suspected, or who has had previous ERCP with unsuccessful drainage, must have broad-spectrum antibiotic therapy before any endoscopic or percutaneous transhepatic maneuvers are undertaken.

The late complications of ES have been investigated by Buset via an international inquiry (Table **3**) (3). Newly formed stones occur in 3.8%. Cholangitis "sine materia" is an inconclusive diagnosis, probably related either to non-visible material in the common duct at the time of ERCP, or to restenosis of the CBD. In all of these cases, no surgery is necessary, because most of the stones can be extracted without recutting.

Extraction of Stones

After ES, extraction of stones is attempted immediately with Fogarty catheters for medium or small-sized stones (Fig. **21**), or with a Dormia basket for larger stones (Fig. **22**). The passage of a balloon is useful to calibrate the effective size of the sphincterotomy precisely. The extraction of stones is attempted with the Dormia basket when the size of the stone is larger than the effective measurable size of the orifice after ES (8) (Fig. **22**).

Table **3** Percentage of late complications following endoscopic sphincterotomy: international inquiry (1888 patients)

Newly-formed common bile duct stones	3.8
Cholangitis "sine materia"	1.3
Papillary stenosis	0.8
Liver abscess	0.05

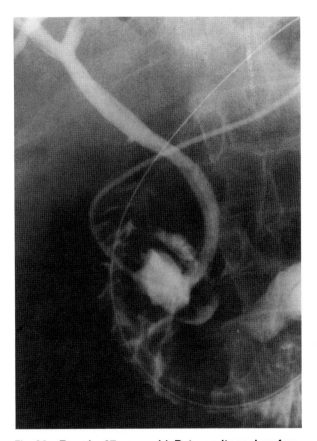

Fig. **20 Female, 67 years old. Retroperitoneal perforation** after endoscopic sphincterotomy of a paradiverticular papilla. Notice the leakage of contrast between the lower common bile duct and the duodenum. Nasobiliary catheter drainage

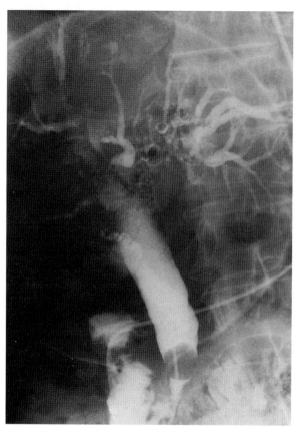

Fig. **21** **Fogarty catheter, used to extract stones after endoscopic sphincterotomy** and to calibrate the size of the sphincterotomy

The results of ES in 2 series (11) have been compared with the Mazzariello-Burhenne method using external maneuvers with the T-tube (Table **4**). The success rate is similar in both methods, but there is a lower complication rate with ES for CBD stones without the T tube in situ.

Complete clearance of the CBD after ES for cholecystectomized patients is not as successful as for those with the T-tube in place (Table **5**); these results have been improving in the last years with the advent of lithotripsy.

Lithotripsy

If the stone is too large to pass the sphincter, *mechanical* lithotripsy must be performed (8, 25, 44, 53), using either the Atkinson system (esophageal stent insertor) (Fig. **22**) or the more sophisticated Wilson-Cook lithotriptor (Fig. **3**).

After failure of mechanical lithotripsy (Fig. **23**), endoscopic lithotripsy may be proposed, using the forward-viewing baby scope inserted into a mother duodenoscope with an operative channel of 5.5 mm.

Endoscopic electrohydraulic lithotripsy has been successful when the baby scope can reach the stone directly. Endoscopic laser lithotripsy using a dye pulsed laser or a neodynium: YAG laser has been shown to be useful for ureteral stones. This method is now being applied to CBD stones.

Another non-endoscopic method, and therefore more comfortable, is *extracorporeal shock-wave lithotripsy* (ESWL) with which a few centers now have good experience (45, 46). ESWL for CBD stones has been successful in 19 out of 20 patients in our experience, using the Lithostar. Compared to endoscopic lithotripsy (except for the mechanical principle, which may always follow ES), ESWL seems to be the method of choice for the future due to its efficiency and the fact that it is much less invasive for giant stones and with elderly patients.

Endoscopic Management of Malignancies

Papillary Carcinoma

The first type of patients to benefit from preoperative decompression of the bile ducts were those with papillary carcinoma. Once cannulation is achieved, it is easy to insert the sphincterotome, and to carry out an incision as large as the tumor in order to reach the non-infiltrated choledochoduodenal wall.

Significantly more coagulation current is necessary to avoid bleeding, which is more frequent than in benign papillary stenosis. Stenting is only useful after deep infiltration of the lower CBD, which is observed in pancreatic carcinoma, or in patients with peripapillary carcinoma and further infiltration of

Table **4**   Comparison of the two methods of non-surgical extraction of common bile duct stones with the T tube in place

	No. of authors	No. of patients	Percentage success	Percentage morbidity	Percentage mortality
External maneuvers with the T tube	6	1841	95	6.6	0.3
Endoscopic sphincterotomy	2	270	99	5.0	0

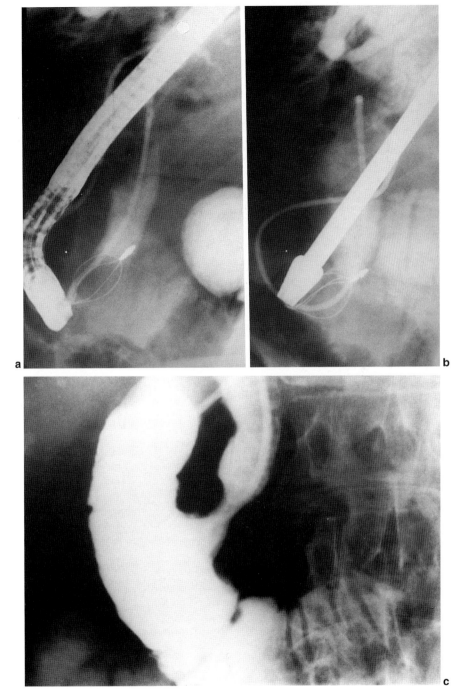

Fig. **22** **Female, 88 years old.**
Choledocholithiasis
a Impacted stone in the dormia
basket
b Lithotripsy with the Atkinson
system
c Appraisal of the size of the
sphincterotomy after successful
lithotripsy and extraction of
fragments

Table **5**   Results of endoscopic sphincterotomy for common bile duct stones after biliary surgery

	Without T-tube	With T-tube
Successful endoscopic sphincterotomy	99.5%	100%
Success of extraction	97.2%	98%
Total success rate	96,7%	98%

the pancreas, months or years after the initial sphincterotomy for instance.

The assessment of local and metastatic tumor spread is carried out in the days following sphincterotomy. Curative duodenopancreatectomy (which has the best prognosis in all biliopancreatic tumors) is performed after 2 or 3 weeks on patients in good clinical condition. Patients up to 82 years old have undergone duodenopancreatectomy in our depart-

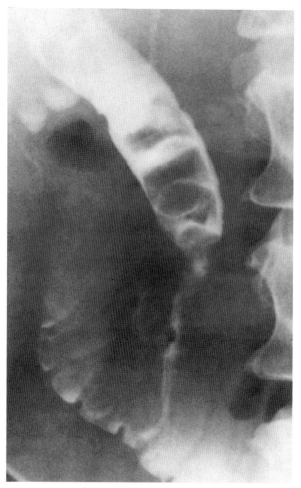

Fig. **23   Male, 68 years old. Multiple large common bile
duct stones** with downward, narrowed long choledochal
sphincter after endoscopic sphincterotomy. Indication for
lithotripsy

ment, with the mortality rate decreasing to 2% over
the last 10 years. However, the main difference
between "surgical" and "medical" patients is one of
age. Patients treated with ES alone were on average
16 years older than patients who underwent curative
surgery (Table **6**).

Table **6**   Management of papillary tumors. Series at the
Hôpital Erasme, Brussels, 1976–1987

	Patients	Average age
ES alone	66	83
ES + Whipple	22	67
ES + local resection	3	
ES + bypass	3	
Whipple only	1	
Total patients	95	

ES: endoscopic sphincterotomy

Stenting of the Bile Ducts

Endoscopic internal biliary drainage (EIBD) was
first described by Soehendra in 1979 (50). Thanks to
the development of accessories, and the advent in
1981 of the "Jumboscope" (operative duodenoscope
Olympus TJF, 3.7 mm), with a larger operative channel, EIBD has become the method of choice for
the non-surgical treatment of biliary strictures (26,
33, 37, 54). Although the endoscopic technique of
duodenoscopy and cannulation appears to be slightly
more difficult than doing a needle puncture of the
liver, access to strictures of the CBD and even of the
confluence is easier using the anatomical route of the
CBD than after introducing a guide wire through any
peripheral intrahepatic duct.

Another reason why the endoscopic route is now
preferred to percutaneous transhepatic cholangiographic drainage is the fact that complications are
less frequent and less severe (52).

EIBD can be proposed for malignant or benign
stricture of the biliary tree.

EIBD is an alternative to surgery. It can, in some
instances, offer results at least as good as those for
surgery, with less morbidity and mortality; however,
the specific indications for each technique still have
to be defined. As ES is now the first-choice technique for the treatment of CBD stones. EIBD is the
best treatment for high-risk patients with associated
diseases, and also for those with malignant unresectable tumors.

The choice between elective surgery and endoscopy is less clear for patients who are in excellent
clinical condition, and for those with benign strictures. Surgery, is, of course, at this point, the only
curative method for malignant resectable tumors.

Technique of Stenting

Materials. Although the standard duodenoscope
(Olympus JF1T 20 or JFV10) can make the procedure easier, in some difficult cannulation cases, Jum-
boscopes (fiberscope TJF10 or videoscope TJFV10)
can often be used during the entire procedure (for
instance, in the new operative duodenoscope TJFV
10, a special gutter in the elevator stabilizes small
catheters).

Sterilization of the duodenoscopes is mandatory
between each successive examination, Glutaral-
dehyde (Cidex) is used to perfuse all the channels of
the scope by means of an automatic endoscope disin-
fector.

The most frequently used prostheses in our per-
sonal experience were (Fig. **24**) the short, bent
C-shaped stent for strictures of the middle and lower
third of the CBD (BCCC), and the long sigmoid
C-shaped one for strictures of the confluence
(BSLC). Both of these stents have an external

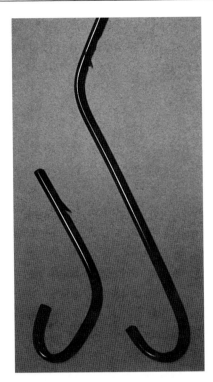

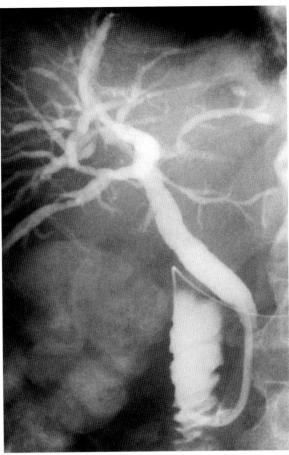

Fig. **24** **Stents:** BCCC (left) and BSLC for hilar strictures (right)

Fig. **25** **Male, 82 years old. Pancreatic head car-▶ cinoma.** BCCC stent in place, with nasobiliary catheter

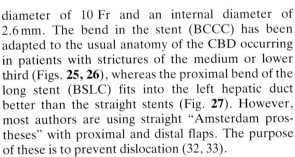

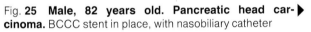

diameter of 10 Fr and an internal diameter of 2.6 mm. The bend in the stent (BCCC) has been adapted to the usual anatomy of the CBD occurring in patients with strictures of the medium or lower third (Figs. **25, 26**), whereas the proximal bend of the long stent (BSLC) fits into the left hepatic duct better than the straight stents (Fig. **27**). However, most authors are using straight "Amsterdam prostheses" with proximal and distal flaps. The purpose of these is to prevent dislocation (32, 33).

In vitro studies (36) with stents have shown that multiple holes decrease the bile flow compared to single tubes without holes. Despite the fact that only a few cases of duodenal perforation are reported with this straight stent, the C-shape of our stents has been proposed for prevention of duodenal ulceration and upward dislocation.

Insertion Procedure. After an ERCP has been performed for diagnostic purposes and to provide anatomical information, a papillotomy is carried out to facilitate the insertion of one or more large stents. This is also to prevent the theoretical risk of acute pancreatitis due to partial obstruction of the papilla by the stent.

A 6 Fr polyethylene radiopaque catheter with a distal metal ring, together with its guide wire, is introduced into the CBD. The metal guide wire, the tip of which is flexible and atraumatic, is maneuvered across the narrowed segment. Once the stricture is passed, the catheter is advanced over the guide wire; the stent is then guided over it and positioned with the help of a push catheter and the pulling of the flexed endoscope.

If possible, another nasobiliary catheter is inserted beyond the stent and perfused for one or two days with normal saline to prevent early clogging of the stent by debris and mucus which accumulate above the stent when it is passed through the stenosis. Aerobilia and an immediate decrease in the diameter of the bile ducts, along with a sufficient passage of contrast medium through the stent into the duodenum, afford the best radiological proof of adequate drainage. In addition, definitive proof that the stent is properly positioned can be provided by control cholangiography (Fig. **28**).

In cases of very tight strictures, insertion of the push catheter alone over the guiding catheter is attempted first. If it does not reach the stricture, a dilation is performed with a biliary bougie or with a

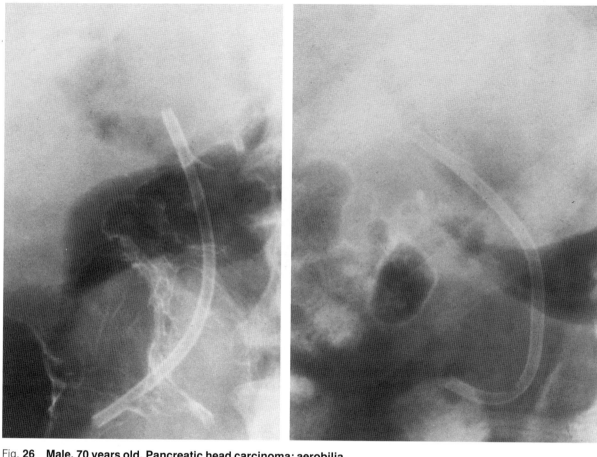

Fig. 26 Male, 70 years old. Pancreatic head carcinoma; aerobilia.
a "Straight" stent, with 2 flaps and the proximal tip impacted into the wall of the common bile duct, which remains dilated
b After replacement with a BCCC stent, which fits the bend of the common bile duct better, drainage has improved and dilation of CBD has disappeared

Fig. 28 Female, 73 years old. Invasive gallbladder carcinoma 1 year after cholecystectomy ▶
a Irregular hilar stricture with intrahepatic duct dilation
b Control cholangiography after 2 days of stenting, showing the stent in an appropriate position and a decrease in bile duct dilation

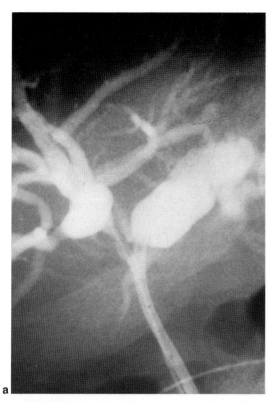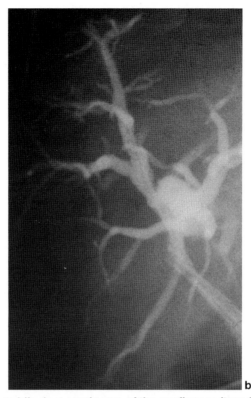

Fig. 27   Male, 76 years old, with obstructive jaundice due to bile duct carcinoma of the confluence (type II)
a Straight stent in the left hepatic duct and nasobiliary catheter in the right hepatic duct
b Dislocation of the stent in spite of a proximal flap being present

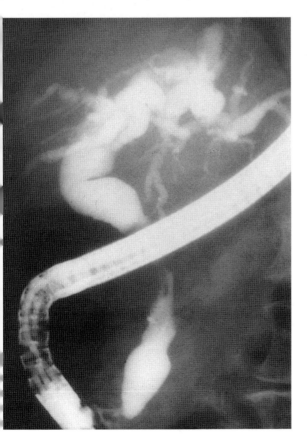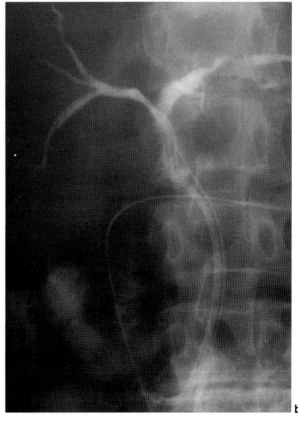

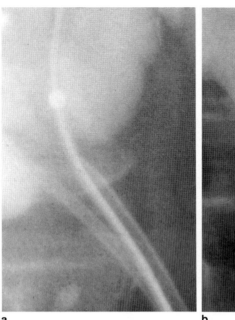
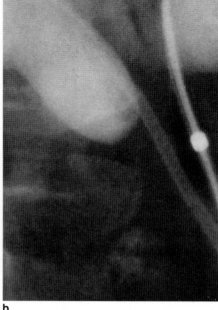

a   b

Fig. **29   Female, 68 years old. Gallbladder carcinoma involving the confluence (type II)**
a Nasobiliary catheter drainage in the right hepatic duct and attempted dilation of the stricture of the left hepatic duct
b Dilation of the left hepatic duct with a banana balloon catheter

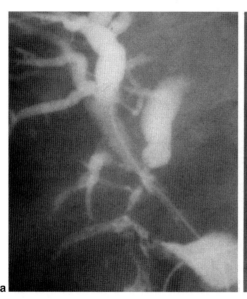
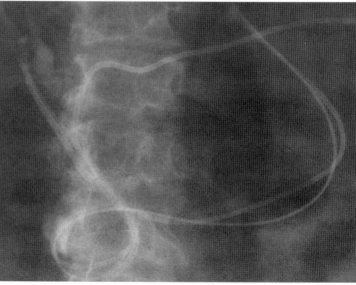

a

Fig. **30   Female, 75 years old. Invasive gallbladder carcinoma of the confluence (type II)**
a Nasobiliary catheter in the right hepatic duct
b Two nasobiliary catheters in the right side, and a percutaneous epigastric transhepatic Ring-Lunderquist catheter through the left hepatic duct

balloon catheter (Fig. **29**). Antibiotics are given systematically in cases of incomplete drainage. When the stricture involves the bifurcation, the same procedure is repeated for the second stent, but the left hepatic duct is always stented first. If the second stent cannot be placed by the endoscopic route (this occurs in 25% of patients with bifurcation tumor types II or III), the percutaneousendoscopic method is used. After percutaneous puncture using a Lun-

derquist P.T.C. needle, a metal guide wire is pushed through the stricture, followed by a Ring-Lunderquist internal-external catheter (Fig. **30**).

Either immediately, or more often in a second procedure, another long guide wire is threaded into the Ring-Lunderquist catheter, and retrieved in the large 4.2 mm channel duodenoscope with the help of a snare. Using this guide wire, a transpapillary stent can be passed easily through the stricture via the endoscope. The guide wire is then removed under fluoroscopic control, and an external catheter is left alongside the stent for the next 24 h.

Stenting in Benign Conditions

Benign strictures of the CBD which can benefit from EIBD include postoperative biliary strictures (with or without stones), choledochal strictures occurring in patients with chronic pancreatitis, certain situations in primary sclerosing cholangitis, and inoperable patients with unextractable gallstones. Since the advent of endoscopic and extracorporeal shock-wave lithotripsy (ESWL), failures in stone extraction have basically ceased to occur.

Stenting multiple strictures of the common bile duct as well as the left and right hepatic ducts in septic patients with primary sclerosing cholangitis is difficult and unsatisfactory. Perfusion through a nasobiliary catheter sometimes helps to resolve sepsis. However, multiple endoscopic manipulations produce a high risk of septic complications in these patients, making liver transplantation the preferred treatment.

For biliary strictures occurring after cholecystectomy and choledochotomy, or for patients with chronic pancreatitis, EIBD was at first reserved for patients unfit for surgery. Because of the morbidity and mortality of surgery, especially for patients without dilation of the intrahepatic biliary tree, EIBD has become an accepted method of permanent dilation using single and then multiple stents. In these cases, EIBD can be curative.

The results of these two indications will be analyzed. In patients with biliary iatrogenic or post-traumatic leakage, the place of ES, stenting, and drainage with naso-biliary tubes, will be discussed.

Treatment of Postoperative Bile Duct Strictures.
This complication occurs in about 0.25% of patients who undergo cholecystectomy (57). In most patients, it is probably due to immediate and unrecognized surgical trauma (Fig. 31).

Clinical manifestations can occur months or even years after cholecystectomy, and include cholestasis with or without jaundice, relapsing acute cholangitis, and biliary fistulas. The surgical treatment of these patients consists of a hepatico-jejunostomy or even sometimes end-to-end bile duct anastomosis. The morbidity of this treatment reaches 20%, and mortality remains around 5%, even in experienced surgical departments (24, 57). Moreover, relapsing strictures are frequent (up to 30%), necessitating repeated operations with an even higher risk than the first operation. Some endoscopic experts have experienced successful endoscopic dilation of such strictures (23), but long-term follow-up of these patients is not yet available. The stenting procedure is even more difficult than in malignant strictures, due to the

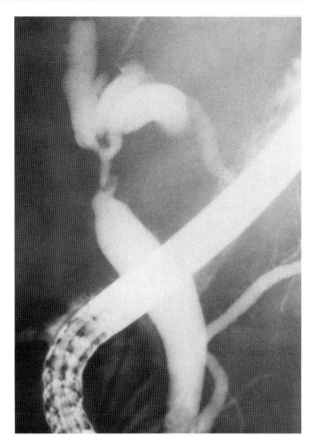

Fig. **31   Post-cholecystectomy stricture of the confluence**

fibrotic nature of the stricture. Multiple dilations are usually necessary prior to the successful threading of the stent through the stricture. Huibregtse (29) reports excellent immediate results, with resolution of jaundice and cholangitis, in 100% of patients successfully treated. The long-term follow-up in his series was also good in 70% of the cases, and the complications which occurred in the remaining 24% of patients (newly formed stones proximal to the stents, cholangitis due to stent blockage) were successfully treated by replacement of the stent.

However, after an average follow-up of two years, only one third of the patients were free of symptoms without a stent in place. What remains questionable is whether or not stenting can properly and definitively dilate the stricture, and what is the optimal duration of stenting.

In our experience, sufficient dilation is achieved after one to two years, and recurrent strictures occur in less than 20% of patients. If these results are confirmed in the future, EIBD would become a good alternative to surgery in terms of immediate and long-term results, with lower morbidity and mortality.

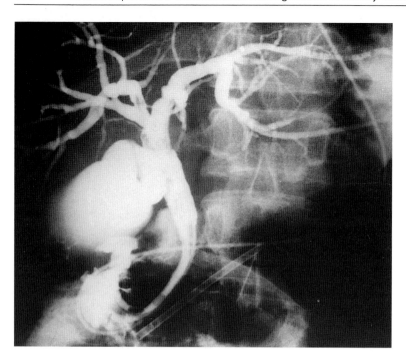

Fig. **32   Male, 56 years old. Chronic calcified pancreatitis.** Double endoscopic sphincterotomy and stenting of both biliary and pancreatic ducts

Stenting of CBD Strictures in Chronic Pancreatitis. CBD strictures occur in 10–20% of patients with chronic pancreatitis (1). Treatment is indicated in cases of persistent cholestasis or jaundice which present a risk of recurrent cholangitis and further secondary biliary cirrhosis (Fig. **32**). Due to the morbidity of surgery and the development of endoscopic management in chronic pancreatitis (13, 31), we have treated patients with CBD strictures and jaundice for this indication. We did not observe procedure-related mortality. While the results are encouraging in terms of the immediate resolution of jaundice or cholangitis, the long-term follow-up is disappointing. Among the 25 patients treated, only 3 are free of symptoms without a stent in place after a mean follow-up of 3 years. The problem in chronic pancreatitis is that relapsing stenosis seems to be the rule and, unlike in postoperative stenosis, dilation of the stenosis is transient. This is probably associated with the fibrotic process which involves the head of the pancreas itself, and not the CBD alone. Moreover it is possible that the presence of the stent itself in the CBD can provoke sclerosing changes in the duct as well.

Treatment of Biliary Leakage. Bile leakage and internal or external fistulas are most often complications of biliary surgery (24, 28). In a few cases, they occur after external trauma (18). Commonly, they occur postoperatively due to residual stones or strictures of the CBD; more recently, they have developed after transplantation with end-to-end hepaticocholedochal anastomoses. In some instances, they are probably related to ischemia from an unrecognized lesion of an arterial vessel around the CBD.

ES alone provides adequate treatment of residual stones and of patients with benign papillary stenosis together with a fistula (29, 47). However, therapeutic endoscopy now also has a major place even in the management of patients with inadvertent damage to the common or intrahepatic bile ducts, with ischemic lesions without strictures, or with posttraumatic leakage.

If bile duct or cystic stump leakage occurs, it can create external fistulas or subhepatic collections, leading to abscess formation, peritonitis and sepsis. ES is indicated in all cases, even in the absence of obstructring stones or strictures. It causes a reduction of pressure in the CBD from 8 cm H_2O to the level of the intraduodenal pressure (-2 cm H_2O), and provides preferential drainage downstream to the duodenum while healing the fistula. This treatment is effective in more than 90% of cases in our experience. However, most fistulas heal with stricture formation, and prevention of this by inserting a stent (56, 18), and even two prostheses if the fistula is located near the bifurcation, is recommended.

Stenting in Malignant Strictures

EIBD can be proposed as a palliative treatment for unresectable tumors or for patients unfit for surgery. It has also been proposed as a preoperative treatment of jaundice caused by resectable tumors, because the mortality and morbidity of biliary surgery in patients with deep jaundice result partly from associated metabolic disturbances.

These disturbances are reversible after biliary drainage, which can subsequently improve the patient's clinical status. Also, some retrospective studies promoting preoperative percutaneous transhepatic drainage have observed a reduction in operative mortality (22, 41, 42). Prospective randomized trials have never shown any benefit from percutaneous transhepatic drainage, probably because of the complications related to the technique (27, 43).

EIBD, by inserting stents through the papilla, avoids the complications of liver puncture (for instance, bile leakage into the peritoneum), but prospective randomized trials are not yet available to demonstrate the real benefits of preoperative EIBD. Lygidakis (38) showed reduced morbidity and mortality for patients with malignant strictures of the common bile duct who had a stent placed preoperatively. In our personal experience of preoperative drainage for pancreatic cancer (16), we did not find significant differences with regard to the mortality rate (which was low) or in the rate of postoperative complications.

However, preoperative drainage in the same session of diagnostic ERCP has two main advantages: iatrogenic cholangitis, which occurs in most patients with biliary strictures, can be avoided by immediate drainage or early surgery; once the internal biliary drainage is achieved, the physician has some time to decide whether or not surgery is indicated and whether it has a chance of being curative; if not, preoperative drainage becomes the definitive palliative treatment, which shortens the hospital stay.

With regard to palliative treatment in different kinds of tumors, it is important to decide upon the best indications for surgical management; this selection of patients leads to reduced postoperative morbidity and mortality.

Pancreatic cancer is the most frequently encountered cause of malignant obstructive jaundice. Surgery is considered as curative in only 10% of these patients (21, 51). Bypass surgery has a very high mortality rate (up to 50%), especially in the elderly and in patients with extensive metastatic disease (51). EIBD is the technique of choice for palliative treatment in these patients, with a success rate of about 95% in experienced centers; the procedure-related mortality is less than 5%. Patients in good clinical condition are better candidates for surgery, which offers the best evaluation of resectability, with less morbidity than for poor-risk patients (at the present time).

The results of series of EIBD for pancreatic cancer cannot be compared with surgical series, because most patients treated by endoscopy are not surgical candidates. One prospective study (48) has been done in the palliative management of unresectable carcinoma of the pancreas. Although not statistically significant because of the small sample size (51 patients), the 70-day mortality for EIBD (8%) was less than for surgery (25%). The unresolved problem is the definition of patient groups for which surgery or stenting appears to be the best treatment.

It is our impression that treatment of pancreatic cancer (16) will become a medical-surgical field. EIBD, by offering a safe palliative treatment for all patients, allows one to reserve surgery for selective indications, such as patients with resectable tumors or patients in excellent clinical condition. This selection will certainly improve the surgical results and the overall morbidity and mortality for this disease.

Gallbladder Cancer. Invasive gallbladder cancer almost never allows curative surgery. Surgical bypass procedures are often difficult in these situations (14), and EIBD is a good alternative. As this tumor most often involves the mid-CBD (Fig. 33), the results of EIBD can be compared with those obtained in pancreatic cancer. In our department, the survival rate (159 days) of 47 patients treated by endoscopy was at least comparable with that of 16 patients treated by surgery (135 days), although surgical candidates were younger and in better clinical condition prior to treatment. Because we know that most of these tumors rapidly entered into the confluence, we presently always attempt to insert 2 endoprostheses, even before the bifurcation becomes involved (Fig. **34**).

Hilar Tumors. These tumors include cholangiocarcinoma, gallbladder carcinoma, or metastases to the confluence. They are extremely difficult to manage either by surgery (2, 35) or by endoscopy (17). The rate of infectious complications following EIBD is unacceptable when only partial drainage of these tumors is obtained. However, only a small minority of these patients are candidates for extensive surgery, and the percutaneous route also has a high complication rate. It is for this reason that we attempt aggressive treatment, which consists of draining both hepatic lobes in patients with type II and III strictures. In some cases, it is necessary to use the associated percutaneous route to thread a guide wire through the stenosis, and to introduce the stent endoscopically, through the papilla. This technique has allowed for a reduction in the 30-day mortality and in the complications of EIBD in hilar tumors. Stenting hilar tumors is therefore an acceptable palliative method only if complete drainage can be obtained.

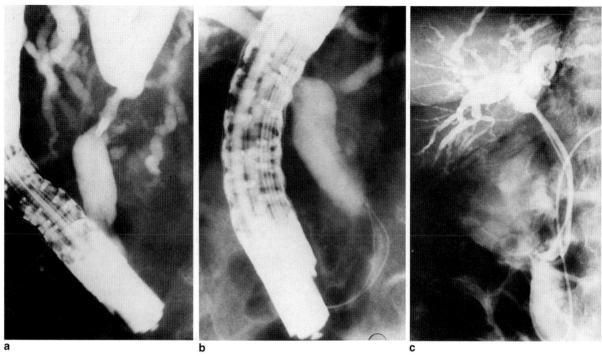

a　　　　　　　　　　　　**b**　　　　　　　　　　　　**c**

Fig. **33**　**Female, 82 years old. Gallbladder carcinoma.**
a Catheter inserted in the stricture. Large dilation of the CBD above stricture　　**b** Proximal short sphincterotome inserted
c Stenting with the BSLC: cholangiography through the nasobiliary catheter

Early Complications of Endoprosthesis Placement

Acute cholangitis is the most important procedure-related complication of EIBD, and is mainly responsible for the mortality observed (Table 7). Careful disinfection of the endoscopes between each examination, and the use of sterile devices, are man-datory, but this cannot prevent the contamination of bile ducts by gut or oral bacteria.

In tumors of the CBD, cholangitis is often related to clogging or dislodgment of the stent, and usually to incomplete drainage. In hilar tumors, cholangitis is related to inadequate drainage of some hepatic lobes or segments (Table 8).

Table **7**　Percentage of early complications of endoscopic internal biliary drainage in relation to the location of the stricture

	Lower third	Middle third	Hilus type I	Hilus types II and III
Cholangitis	13	10	10	30
30-day mortality	1	1	0	17

Table **8**　Results of endoscopic internal biliary drainage in patients with cancer

	Success rate (%)	Morbidity (%)	30-day mortality (%)	Mean survival (months)
Pancreas	95	10	2	8
Gallbladder or hilus type I	92	12	3	7
Hilar tumors involving both hepatic ducts	89 (67)*	17	8	6

* 67% by endoscopic route only

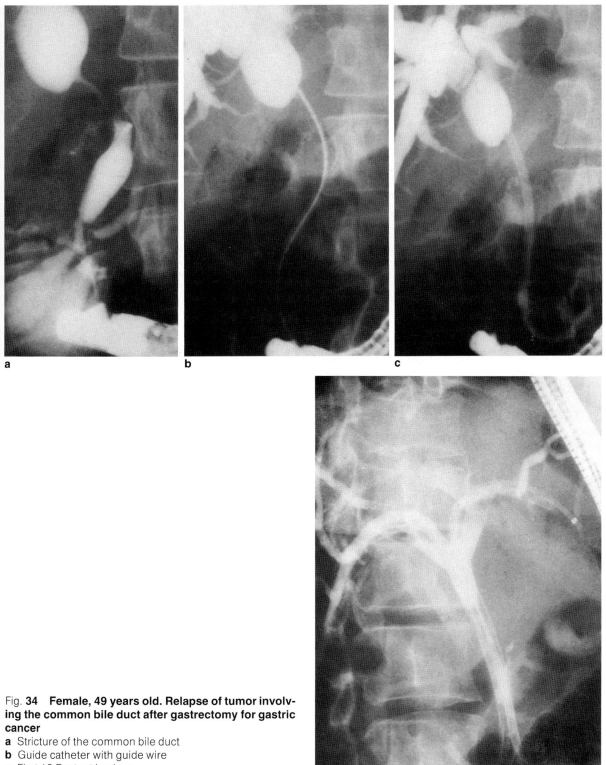

Fig. 34   **Female, 49 years old. Relapse of tumor involving the common bile duct after gastrectomy for gastric cancer**
a Stricture of the common bile duct
b Guide catheter with guide wire
c First 10 Fr stent in place
d After relapsing jaundice, stenting with 3 BSLCs

To reduce the rate of sepsis, 2 main rules have to be followed:

– Once the bile ducts have been injected with contrast medium and a stricture is demonstrated, drainage becomes a medical emergency. Most cases of cholangitis occur in patients in whom multiple attempts at stenting are necessary. The clinician must be able to place a stent, if possible, during the same session.
– In cases of tumors involving the confluence, if a single stent is sufficient to reduce bilirubin, the risk of cholangitis remains until complete drainage is achieved. Drainage must therefore be performed immediately.

Late Complications of Endoprosthesis Placement

Clogging of the stent with cholangitis, or a recurrence of jaundice, or both, is the most frequent late complication (Table **9**). It occurs, in our experience, between 10 days and 12 months after stent placement, with a mean of about 5 months. Clogging is not avoidable, but must be recognized quickly; treatment of it is simple, consisting of replacing the stent. At present, no methods or materials are available to prevent this clogging. Cleaning of clogged stents is contraindicated, because it can precipitate cholangitis, and is quickly followed by reobstruction of the stent.

The use of large stents (10 to 12 Fr) has reduced the frequency of clogging, probably because the time the stent takes to become completely obstructed is somewhat longer. Many patients with EIBD die at home with fever or a relapse of jaundice due to unrecognized obstruction of the stent. The general practitioner must be advised that treatment of this complication is easy, in contrast to the percutaneous technique, and that this complication will occur systematically in cases with prolonged survival. Recent experience (personal observations) suggests that the use of multiple large stents (up to 4) may decrease the occurrence of cholestasis relapses.

Conclusion

The development of modern duodenoscopic techniques has produced a major improvement in the management of benign and malignant diseases of the biliary tract. The diagnostic approach is now combined with immediate therapy, to reduce complications to a minimum and to increase the comfort of the patient. The endoscopic and percutaneous transhepatic approach to the biliary tree is now well delineated (Table **10**), and combined techniques have improved the success rate in the treatment of difficult or multiple strictures.

Table **9**   Percentage of late complications of endoscopic internal biliary drainage (400 cases)

Clogging	37
Dislodgment	3
Cholecystitis	1
Duodenal stenosis (pancreatic cancer)	5

Table **10**   Indications for various drainage procedures in non-surgical management of the biliary tree

Endoscopic internal biliary drainage:
All situations in which the papilla is accessible

Percutaneousendoscopy route:
After failure of – selective cannulation
                – endoscopic sphincterotomy
                – passage through the stenosis

Percutaneous route:
When the papilla is not accessible – hepaticojejunostomy
                                 – duodenal stenosis
                                 – esojejunostomy
                                 – some Billroth II
                                   gastrectomies

ES allows one to avoid surgical reoperation in patients with a relapse of lithiasis, or residual lithiasis, following cholecystectomy. It allows cholangitis and jaundice to settle before a simple cholecystectomy. Moreover, ES has considerably reduced the mortality and morbidity among elderly and poor-risk patients with stone diseases.

Thanks to new developments (mechanical or extracorporeal shock wave lithotripsy), the success rate of stone extraction now approaches around 99%. It is probable that, within a few years, surgery for stones of the CBD will completely disappear, as will T-tube drainage after cholecystectomy for gallstones.

Palliative treatment of neoplastic stenoses considerably improves the quality of life in inoperable patients. For patients in good condition, it is an alternative which permits a better selection of patients suitable for possible curative surgery.

Further developments in the use of multiple large removable stents and expandable, permanent Gianturco or wallstents, as alredy used with the percutaneous route, may make the non-surgical management of biliary strictures possible. If surgeons and gastroenterologists work together as a team with radiologists, it will probably improve surgical and endoscopic results in general.

References

1. Amman RW, Akovbiantz A, Lorgiader F, Schueller G. Course and outcome of chronic pancreatitis. Gastroenterology 1984;86:820–828.

2. Bismuth H, Corlette MB. Intrahepatic cholangio anastomosis in carcinoma of the hilus of the liver. Surg Gynecol Obstet 1975;140:170–178.

3. Buset M, Dunham F, Gulbis A, Royazis M, Jeanmart J, Toussaint J, Cremer M. Complications tardives de l'endoscopie diagnostique et opératoire des voies bilio-pancréatiques. Acta Gastroenterol Belg 1981;44:396–403.

4. Classen M, Demling L. Endoskopische Sphinkterotomie der Papilla Vateri und Steinextraktion aus dem Ductus Choledochus. Dtsch Med Wochenschr 1974;99:469.

5. Classen M, Demling L. EPT – 10 years on. In: Proceedings. International Conference, Erlangen 1983. Stuttgart: Thieme, 1984.

6. Classen M, Hagenmuller F. Biliary drainage. Endoscopy 1983;15:221–229.

7. Cotton PB. ERCP: Progress report. Gut 1977;18:316–341.

8. Cotton PB. Endoscopic management of bile duct stones (apples and oranges). Gut, 1984;25:587–597.

9. Cremer M, Engelholm L.: La cholangiowirsungographie endoscopique dans le diagnostic des ictères obstructifs. Acta Gastroenterol Belg 1973;36:642–675.

10. Cremer M, Gulbis A, Toussaint J, de Toeuf J, Van Laethem A. Endoscopic papillotomy in Belgium. In: Demling L, Classen M, eds. Endoscopic sphincterotomy of the papilla of Vater: International Workshop, Munich, March 1976. Stuttgart: Thieme, 1978:83–90.

11. Cremer M, Liguory C, Costamagna G, Buset M, de Toeuf J. Le traitement non-chirurgical de la lithiase résiduelle de la voie biliaire principale. Actualités digestives médico-chirurgicales, 1984.

12. Cremer M, Toussaint J, Dunham F, de Toeuf J. ERCP in the diagnosis and management of papillary tumors. In Bartelheimer H, Schreiber HW, Ossenberg FW, eds. Die Franken Gallenwege. Cologne: Verlag Gerhard Witztrock, 1979:153–159.

13. Cremer M, Toussaint J, Dunham F. Endoscopic management of chronic pancreatitis. Gastrointest Endosc 1980;26:65–69.

14. Cubertafond P, Gainant A. Les cancers des voies biliaires extra-hépatiques. Paris: Monographie de l'Association Française de Chirurgie, 1988:44–57.

15. Delhaye M, Engelholm L, Cremer M. Pancreas divisum: congenital anatomic variant or anomaly? Gastroenterology 1985;89:951–958.

16. Devière J, Baize M, Gelin M, Buset M, Des Marez B, de Toeuf J, Lambilliotte JP, Cremer M. Traitement du cancer de la tête du pancréas. Acta Gastroenterol Belg 1987;40:137–146.

17. Devière J, Baize M, de Toeuf J, Cremer M. Long-term follow-up of patients with hilar malignant stricture treated by endoscopic internal biliary drainage. Gastrointest Endosc 1988;34:95–101.

18. Devière J, Van Gansbeke D, Ansay J, de Toeuf J, Cremer M. Endoscopic management of a posttraumatic biliary fistula. Endoscopy 1987;19:136–139.

19. Dunham F, Deltenre M, Jeanmart J, Toussaint J, Cremer M. Special catheters for ERCP. Endoscopy 1981;13:81–83.

20. Dunham F, Bourgeois N, Gelin M, Cremer M. Retroperitoneal perforations following endoscopic sphincterotomy: clinical cause and management. Endoscopy, 1982;14:92

21. Fedusca N, Bert T, Lurdenauer S. Results of palliative operations for carcinoma of the pancreas. Arch Surg 1971;103:330–334.

22. Ferrucci JT, Mueller PR, Harbin WP. Percutaneous transhepatic biliary drainage: technique, results and applications. Radiology 1980;135:1–13.

23. Geenen JE. Balloon dilatation of bile duct strictures. In: Classen M, Geenen J, Kawai K, eds. Non-surgical biliary drainage. Berlin: Springer,1984:105–108.

24. Glenn F. Iatrogenic injury to the biliary ductal system. Surg Gynecol Obstet 1978;146:430–434.

25. Gosch H, Stalte M, Walz V. Endoscopic lithotripsy in the common bile duct. Endoscopy 1977;9:95–98.

26. Hagenmuller F. Results of endoscopic bilioduodenal drainage in malignant bile duct stenoses. In: Classen M, Greenen J, Kawai K, eds. Non-surgical biliary drainage. Berlin: Springer 1984:93–104.

27. Hatfield ARW, Tobras R, Teiblauche J, Girdwood AH, Fataar S, Harrier-Jauls R, Kemoff L, Marks LN: Preoperative external biliary drainage in obstructive jaundice: a prospective controlled trial. Lancet 1982;ii:896–898.

28. Hillus TM, Westbrook KL, Coldwell FT, Read RC. Surgical injury of the common bile duct. Am J Surg 1977;134:712–716.

29. Huibregtse K, Katau RM, Tytgat GNJ. Endoscopic treatment of postoperative biliary strictures. Endoscopy 1986;18:133–137.

30. Huibregtse K, Katau RM, Tytgat GNJ. Precut papillotomy via fine-needle knife papillotome: a safe and effective technique. Gastrointest Endosc 1986;32:403–405.

31. Huibregtse F, Schneider B, Vrij AA, Tytgat GNJ. Endoscopic pancreatic drainage in chronic pancreatitis. Gastrointest Endosc 1988;34:9–15.

32. Huibregtse K, Tytgat GNJ. Palliative treatment of obstructive jaundice by transpapillary introduction of a large-bore bile duct endoprosthesis. Gut 1982;23:371–375.

33. Huibregtse K, Tytgat GNJ. Endoscopic placement of biliary prostheses. In: Salmon PR, ed. Gastrointestinal endoscopy: advances in diagnosis and therapy. London: Chapman and Hall, 1984:219–23.

34. Kawai K, Akasaka Y, Murakami K, Tada M, Nakajima M. Endoscopic sphincterotomy of the ampulla of Vater. Gastrointest Endosc 1974;20:148–151.

35. Launois B, Campion JP, Brissot P. Carcinoma of the hepatic hilus: surgical management and the case for resection. Am Surg 1979;190:151–153.

36. Leung JWC, Del Favero G, Cotton PB. Endoscopic biliary prosthesis: a comparison of materials. Gastrointest Endosc 1985;32:93–95.

37. Liguory C, Meduri B, Canard JM, Fritsch J, Liberato M, Ingrosso M. Endoscopie transpapillaire des cancers sténosants de la voie biliaire principale avec des endoprothèses de 3.2 mm. Abstracts du IVe Symposium International d'Endoscopie Digestive, 10–11 mai, Paris, 1984

38. Lygidakis N, Van der Heyde M, Lubbers M. Evaluation of preoperative biliary drainage in surgical management of pancreatic head carcinoma. Acta Chir Scan 1982;148:613–619.

39. Lux G, Ell C, Hochberger J, Muller D, Demling L. The first successful endoscopic retrograde laser lithotripsy of common bile duct stones in man using pulsed neodymium: YAG laser. Endoscopy 1987;19:144–145.

40. McCune WS, Shorb PE, Moscovitz H. Endoscopic cannulation of the ampulla of Vater: a preliminary report. Ann Surg 1968;167:752–756.

41. Nakayama T, Ikeda A, Okuda K. Percutaneous transhepatic drainage of the biliary tract. Gastroenterology 1978; 74:554–559.

42. Norlander A, Kolin B, Sundklad R: Effect of percutaneous transhepatic drainage upon liver function and postoperative mortality. Surg Gynecol Obstet 1982;155:161–166.

43. Pitt HA, Games AS, Lois JF. Does preoperative percutaneous biliary drainage reduce operative risk or increase hospital cost? Am Surg 1985;201:545–553.

44. Riemann JF, Demling L. Lithotripsy of bile duct stones. Endoscopy 1983;15:191–196.

45. Sauerbruch T, Delius M, Paumgartner G, Holl J, Wess O, Weber W, Hepp W, Brendel W. Fragmentation of gallstones by extracorporeal shock waves. N Engl J. Med 1986; 314:818–822.

46. Sauerbruch T, Holl J, Sackmann M, et al. Treatment of bile duct stones by extracorporeal shock waves. SSEM, Ultrasound CTMR, 1987;8:155–161.

47. Sauerbruch T, Weinzierl M, Holl J, Protschke T. Treatment of postoperative bile fistulas by internal endoscopic biliary drainage. Gastroenterology 1986;90:1998–2003.

48. Shepherd HA, Royle G, Ross AP, Diba A, Arthur M, Colin-Jones D. Endoscopic biliary endoprosthesis in the palliation of malignant obstruction of the distal common bile duct: a randomized trial. Br. J. Surg 1988;75:1166

49. Soehendra N, Kempeneers I, Reynders-Frederix V. Ein neues Papillotom für den Billroth II Magen. Dtsch Med Wochenschr 1980;105:362.
50. Soehendra N, Reynders-Frederix V. Palliative bile duct drainage: a new endoscopic method of introducing a transpapillary drain. Endoscopy 1980;12:8–11.
51. Sorr MG, Cameron JL: Surgical palliation of unresectable carcinoma of the pancreas. World J Surg 1984;8:906–918.
52. Stanley J, Gobien RP, Cunningham J, Andriole J. Biliary decompression: an institutional comparison of percutaneous and endoscopic methods. Radiology 1986;158:195–197.
53. Staritz M. Mechanical gallstone lithotripsy. Endoscopy 1983;15:316–318.
54. Tytgat GNJ, Bartelsman JFWM, Den Hartog Jager WA et al. Upper intestinal and biliary tract endoprosthesis. Dig Dis Sci 1986;31:57–76.
55. Van Heerden JA, Remme WH, Werland LM, McIllroth DC, Ilstrup DM. Total pancreatectomy for ductal adenocarcinoma of the pancreas. Am J Surg 1981;147:308–319.
56. Van Steenbergen W, Haemers A, Pelemans W, Vanwing J, Verbeken E, Fevery J. Postoperative biliocutaneous fistula: successful treatment by insertion of an endoprosthesis. Endoscopy 1987;19:34–36.
57. Warren KW, Jefferson MF. Prevention and repair of strictures of the intrahepatic ducts. Surg Clin North Am 1973;53:1169–1191.

Percutaneous Transhepatic Cholangiography and Percutaneous Biliary Drainage

J. Hoevels

Percutaneous Transhepatic Cholangiography

The first report of the radiologic visualization of the biliary tract in cadavers and a limited number of patients was published by Burckhardt and Müller (9). After percutaneous transhepatic puncture of the gallbladder from an intercostal lateral approach, the injection of contrast medium resulted in demonstration of the gallbladder and the biliary ducts. The needles used by these investigators had an outer diameter ranging from 0.5 to 0.8 mm. Huard et al. (41) described the percutaneous transhepatic puncture of dilated intrahepatic bile ducts combined with injection of Lipiodol for diagnostic cholangiography (41). When Carter and Saypol (12) and Leger et al. (50) 15 years later published their experiences with percutaneous transhepatic cholangiography (PTC) using water-soluble contrast media, they initiated an era of increasing application of this diagnostic method for disorders involving the biliary duct system.

During the following years, numerous investigations regarding the indications, techniques, results, and complications of PTC were published (7, 8, 20, 22. 26, 49, 63, 77, 80, 82, 90). In these reports a variety of different methodologic details were described, mainly concerning the caliber and length of the puncture needle, which was used with or without a stylet and a catheter sheath; the site of the needle entry into the liver parenchyma; the direction of the puncture; and the number of puncture trials. Wheras Glenn et al. (22) used a needle with an outer diameter of 0.81 mm, until 1975 in most clinical centers PTC was performed with a large sheathed needle with an outer diameter ranging between 1.0 mm and 1.6 mm. Generally, an aspirating technique was applied, i. e., the contrast medium was not injected unless bile was aspirated, indicating that the tip of the needle or catheter had entered a bile duct.

The latest and apparently the most essential technical refinement was published by the Japanese investigators Ohto et al. (68, 69) and Tsuchiya (88). They advocated PTC with a fine needle with an outer diameter of 0.7 mm and injection of contrast medium into the liver parenchyma during retraction of the needle to facilitate the demonstration of dilated as well as nondilated intrahepatic bile ducts. The usefulness of fine-needle PTC in the diagnosis of biliary duct disorders was documented in larger series by Ariyama et al. (2) and Okuda et al. (70). In recent years the value and safety of this method was further confirmed by investigators outside Japan (4, 17, 19, 21, 24, 25, 31, 34, 40, 42, 62, 74). The fine-needle method has generally been accepted as the standard procedure for percutaneous transhepatic visualization of the biliary system.

Indications

Ultrasonography and computed tomography are the primary diagnostic methods for visualizing the bile ducts in patients with suspicion of cholestatic jaundice. When noninvasive procedures confirm the extrahepatic cholestasis but fail to define the exact site or cause of the obstructing lesion, PTC or endoscopic retrograde cholangiography (ERC) is the next step to demonstrate the biliary system in greater detail and to evaluate further the cause of the jaundice. If successfully performed, both methods may demonstrate: whether or not extrahepatic cholestasis is present; the site of the obstruction; and in the majority of cases the probable cause of the obstruction. PTC compared with ERC is less time-consuming, technically simpler, less costly, and with less patient distress. The endoscopic examination of the duodenum and the papilla of Vater, including histologic and cytologic diagnosis, and the combined access to the biliary and pancreatic duct systems are the major advantages of endoscopic retrograde cholangiopancreatography.

In the majority of cases PTC and ERC are equally suitable for visualization of biliary duct disorders. However, because of a higher success rate and the ease of performance, fine-needle PTC may be advocated as the primary invasive diagnostic method in patients with suspected extrahepatic cholestasis. PTC is indispensable for demonstration of the biliary system before surgical intervention, if ERC fails or provides doubtful information; ERC is not feasible because of a bilidigestive anastomosis; and ERC does not show the bile ducts proximal to an obstruction and fails to outline the length of an occluded or strictured segment of the extrahepatic bile ducts. Because of the risk of complications, PTC is not to be performed, if suspicion that cystic echinococcal disease or a hypervascular tumor of the liver is present. In patients with extrahepatic cholestasis, ERC should be considered under these circumstances. Fine-needle PTC is not contra-indicated in patients with purulent cholangitis and abscesses of the liver, provided transhepatic biliary drainage is performed after the diagnostic procedure.

Technique

Before PTC, the coagulation parameters are controlled. Fine-needle PTC should only be performed with a platelet count greater than $60 \times 10^9/liter$. The partial thromboplastin time should be less than 45 seconds and the prothrombin time should be no more than 3 seconds prolonged over control. In patients with disorders of the clotting function, fine-needle PTC and subsequent drainage procedures have to be postponed until adequate corrective measures have been accomplished. For premedication, 50 mg meperidine and 0.5 mg atropine are given intramuscularly.

The examination is performed with the patient supine. After antiseptic skin preparation and sterile draping, local anesthesia of the skin, the subcutaneous tissue, and the intercostal musculature is given. From the right midaxillary line below the costophrenic angle, a 15 cm needle (outside diameter [OD], 0.7 mm) with stylet is inserted and directed

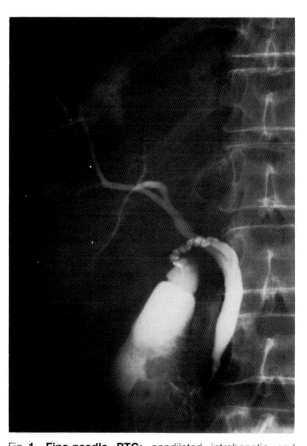

Fig. **1** **Fine-needle PTC:** nondilated intrahepatic and extrahepatic bile ducts. Stones in gallbladder. Free flow of contrast medium to duodenum

under fluoroscopic guidance parallel to the table top into the central part of the liver approximately 2 to 3 cm cranially to the estimated location of the hilus of the liver. The flexibility of the puncture needle enables the patient to breathe normally throughout the procedure.

The insertion of the needle, however, is facilitated when the patient holds his breath in a midrespiratory position. The puncture is performed neither from a particular intercostal space, nor is the needle directed toward a particular vertebra as a possible landmark. The site and the direction of the puncture are chosen depending on the fluoroscopically estimated position of the hilus of the liver, the size of the liver, and its position according to the actual respiratory phase. Puncture of the gallbladder and the extrahepatic bile ducts should be avoided because of an increased risk of bile leakage when extrahepatic cholestasis is present. The stylet is removed and a flexible polyethylene tube is attached to the fine needle. During continuous injection of small amounts of contrast medium (iopromid, 300 mg I/ml) into the parenchyma of the liver, the needle is slowly withdrawn under fluoroscopic control toward the periphery of the liver.

Accidental puncture of intrahepatic arteries or veins is recognized by the vascular ramification pattern and the rapid clearance of contrast medium. When the tip of the needle enters a bile duct and free flow of contrast medium through nondilated ducts to the duodenum is present, the needle is removed after radiographic demonstration of the findings (Fig. **1**). In case of biliary duct dilation a sufficient amount of contrast medium (20 to 60 ml) is injected to demonstrate the intrahepatic and extrahepatic bile ducts and to visualize the site and the appearance of the obstruction (Fig. **2**). Aspiration of bile before the injection of contrast medium is limited by the size of the needle. Overfilling of the biliary system with contrast medium has to be avoided because this may result in sepsis due to leakage of possibly infected bile into the blood circulation. The needle is withdrawn and films are taken for diagnostic purposes in anteroposterior and both oblique projections. It is rare that the semierect position is necessary for visualization of the extrahepatic bile ducts.

If a bile duct is not entered during withdrawal of the needle, the needle is reinserted with a slightly different puncture direction. To minimize the damage to the liver capsule during repeated puncture attempts, the needle is not completely withdrawn from the liver before reinsertion. The puncture might be repeated up to 12 times before the examination is abandoned. Forced respiration in the course of fine-needle PTC has to be avoided because this may result in tears of the liver capsule, increasing the possibility of intraperitoneal hemorrhage and bile leakage.

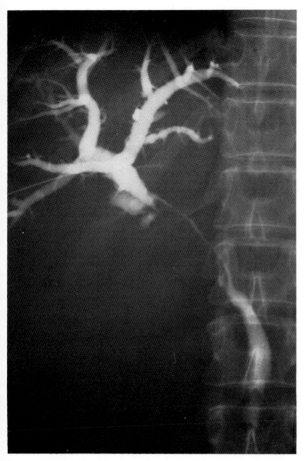

Fig. 2 **A 52-year-old patient with extrahepatic biliary tumor.** Fine-needle PTC: stricture of common hepatic duct and retroduodenal segment of common bile duct. Dilation of intrahepatic bile ducts

Complications

Sepsis, cholangitis, biliary peritonitis, and hemorrhage are the most frequent complications after fine-needle PTC and have been communicated by various investigators (42, 48, 70, 74, 77). In a comprehensive analysis based on a multi-institutional review of the experience with the fine-needle technique for transhepatic cholangiography Harbin et al. (31) ascertained the incidence and types of complications. Serious complications occurred in 3.4% of 2005 cases (31). Twenty-eight patients (1.4%) experienced sepsis. Bile leakage was discovered at surgery in 29 patients (1.45%), all of whom had extrahepatic biliary duct obstruction. In 13 of these patients biliary peritonitis developed, requiring emergency surgery in four. Intraperitoneal hemorrhage was reported in seven patients (0.35%) not necessitating surgical intervention.

In a study on the risks of fine-needle PTC by Kreek and Balint (48), 33 (10.2%) of 322 patients had a total of 43 major complications. Death followed the procedure in three cases (0.9%). Emergency surgery was required in 11 cases (3.4%). Bleeding occurred in 13 patients (4.0%). Sepsis occurred in ten patients (3.1%) and bile leakage or peritonitis occurred in six patients (1.9%). These figures are considerably lower when compared with the rate of complications after fine needle PTC reported by Juler et al. (44). These investigators noted bile leakage in 12 patients (40%), sepsis in seven (23.3%) and mortality due to intraperitoneal bleeding in one (3.3%) of a total of 30 patients. Benjamin et al. (4) reported on two cases of septicemia after fine-needle PTC, one of them fatal. Apparently, reflux of infected bile into the blood circulation occurs secondary to increased intraductal pressure after the injection of contrast medium. Ariyama et al. (2) observed no relationship between the number of puncture attempts and subsequent complications. In the series of 314 examinations reported by Okuda et al. (70) emergency surgery was performed in one patient for biliary peritonitis. The low frequency of bile leakage and biliary peritonitis appears to be attributable to the lateral access resulting in a long puncture tract and to the fine diameter and the flexibility of the puncture needle.

Fine-needle puncture of the extrahepatic bile ducts or of the gallbladder in patients with extrahepatic cholestasis implies a high risk of bile leakage and may necessitate surgical intervention. Controversial opinions exist regarding the need for surgery if an obstructing lesion has been verified by fine-needle PTC. Whereas Ariyama et al. (2) and Okuda et al. (70) pointed out that a surgical procedure may be postponed after fine-needle PTC, Jain et al. (42) advocated surgical intervention within 24 hours. Intraperitoneal hemorrhage after fine-needle PTC seems to be a very rare occurrence in patients with normal coagulation parameters. According to clinical studies, arteriovenous fistulas and pseudoaneurysms after puncture of the liver for a biopsy or PTC seem to heal spontaneously within weeks to months. A large subcapsular hematoma complicating fine-needle PTC with subsequent surgical intervention was reported by Zilly et al. (91). The true incidence, however, of subcapsular hematoma and intrahepatic vascular lesions remains unknown due to lack of clinical relevance.

Clinical Significance

Various investigators have reported demonstration of biliary ducts with fine-needle PTC from 94 to 100% of patients with extrahepatic cholestasis (4, 17, 21, 31, 42, 74). In patients with nondilated bile ducts, visualization of the biliary tract has been achieved in 50 to 95% of cases (4, 17, 21, 42, 74). The different results may reflect a different attitude toward the number of puncture attempts, varying from 1 to 12 needle passes through the liver. The 100% success rate reported by several workers documents that fine-needle PTC is a very reliable method for demonstration of extrahepatic biliary duct obstruction. From the experiences of others, however, reporting a success rate less than 100%, it is evident that biliary duct obstruction cannot be ruled out with certainty by failing to opacify the bile ducts. Apparently, the rate of successful visualization of dilated and non-dilated biliary ducts increases with an increasing number of puncture trials and approaches 100% in patients with extrahepatic cholestasis when 10 to 12 needle passes are performed.

Percutaneous Transhepatic Biliary Drainage

An overwhelming number of publications on the percutaneous transhepatic approach to the bile ducts dealt mainly with its diagnostic aspects. Leger et al. (50), however, as early as 1952, described a combination of diagnostic transhepatic access to the biliary system with preoperative external bile drainage in extrahepatic cholestasis caused by a malignant tumor. Subsequently, various techniques have been described for bile drainage by percutaneous transhepatic intubation of the bile ducts, mainly in patients with malignant tumors and extrahepatic cholestasis (10, 27, 28, 30, 33, 43, 45, 54, 58, 60, 63, 64, 73, 86, 89). More recently the therapeutic efficacy of bile drainage via a nonsurgically introduced catheter has been further improved. By manipulation of a guide wire and a drainage catheter through the obstructing lesion, combined internal and external bile flow is made possible (5, 6, 13, 16, 18, 19, 27, 35, 36, 55, 58, 61, 62, 73, 76, 78, 83, 87).

Indications

Transhepatic biliary drainage in the vast majority of cases is performed in patients with malignant obstruction of the extrahepatic bile ducts. When jaundice is caused by extrahepatic cholestasis because of a malignant tumor, death will result in the majority of cases from hepatic failure due to progressive biliary obstruction rather than from massive neoplastic invasion of the liver or tumor spread to extrahepatic sites. It is therefore essential to establish effective bile duct decompression in these cases. The main benefits of well-functioning drainage of the biliary tract are marked recovery of the liver parenchyma, relief of severe pruritus, and improvement of the general condition of the patient. As an alternative to surgical decompression as a first step in a two-stage procedure, decrease of cholestasis can be achieved by temporary preoperative nonsurgical percutaneous transhepatic catheterization of the bile ducts. A decrease of operative morbidity and mortality secondary to preoperative transhepatic bile duct decompression in patients with extrahepatic cholestasis has been reported (14, 23, 27, 32, 64, 81). Other investigators observed no significant difference in postoperative complications and mortality between patients treated with preoperative transhepatic bile drainage and jaundiced patients operated on without prior drainage (33, 38, 67). Pitt et al. (75) pointed out eight different factors related to surgical complications in the jaundiced patient. Total serum bilirubin values above 170 μmol/liter (10 mg/dl) were regarded as one of these risk factors. When all eight factors were present, the operative mortality reached 100%.

The age and general condition of the jaundiced patient or the site of the tumor may preclude operative bile duct decompression. Relief of biliary obstruction by nonsurgical procedures should, therefore, be considered as an alternative form of palliative therapy. In recent years increasing experience with palliative bile drainage through a percutaneous transhepatic catheter has been collected (5, 15, 18, 30, 35, 36, 55, 62, 76, 78, 83). When the diagnostic workup has shown a cytologically verified malignant bile duct obstruction, patients who may be suited for permanent palliative nonsurgical biliary duct drainage via a transhepatic catheter or via an endoprosthesis, including those with:

- A prohibitively high operative risk
- A tumor that is nonresectable, as demonstrated by ultrasonography, computed tomography, and angiography
- Metastases to the liver or to distant organs
- A metastatic tumor obstructing the extrahepatic bile ducts
- A primary bile duct tumor involving the confluence of the hepatic ducts and the intrahepatic biliary radicles

In addition, nonsurgical biliary drainage should be offered to patients not belonging to the previous groups when an operative bilidigestive anastomosis is not feasible for technical reasons. It must be emphasized, however, that patients in the final stage of tumor disease from the medical and ethical points of view are not suitable candidates for transhepatic biliary drainage procedures.

Benign strictures secondary to pancreatitis may indicate temporary preoperative biliary drainage when severe jaundice is present (38, 89). Temporary internal bile drainage for relief of obstructive jaundice without subsequent surgical intervention has been reported in patients with pancreatitis (30).

Long-term postoperative stenting of a bilibiliary anastomosis may also be performed with a transhepatically inserted catheter. Relief of postoperative leakage from a damaged bile duct or a bilidigestive anastomosis may be handled by temporary transhepatic biliary tract drainage. In patients with a benign stricture involving the biliary ducts in the hilus of the liver, long-term transhepatic intubation for biliary decompression and relief of cholestatic symptoms may be an alternative when an attempt at surgical repair is unsuccessful (35). These indications will be discussed in a separate chapter.

Inflammatory lesions involving the ductal structures within the hepatoduodenal ligament and large stones causing long-standing jaundice and impairment of the function of the liver may motivate preoperative bile drainage in selected patients (35, 36). Transhepatic biliary drainage as a valuable emergency treatment in patients with suppurative cholangitis and sepsis complicating biliary duct obstructions has been described (38, 45, 64). Biliary drainage can be performed with equal effectiveness via a transhepatic catheter or via an endoprosthesis. Preoperatively, a catheter for external drainage is preferred by most investigators. For palliative treatment, it is more advantageous to achieve combined internal and external drainage via a catheter or internal drainage via an endoprosthesis. If internal decompression is performed, no loss of water, bile acids, and electrolytes occurs (85). The drainage catheter should be changed after 2 to 3 months to avoid drainage malfunction because of incrustation and sludge within the tube.

Technique

The diagnostic and therapeutic transhepatic procedures are performed in two stages, necessitating two punctures of the intrahepatic biliary tract. Fine-needle PTC as the first step facilitates fluoroscopically directed puncture and catheterization of a bile duct most suited for subsequent introduction of a drainage catheter or an endoprosthesis. An intrahepatic bile duct randomly punctured in fine-needle PTC may be disadvantageous for subsequent introduction of a drainage tube.

Following immediately after fine-needle PTC, additional local anesthesia is given to the skin, intercostal muscles, and around the intercostal nerve. The opacified duct system is punctured from the right midaxillary line with a 20 cm mandrin sheathed with a radiopaque polyethylene catheter, OD 1.6 mm; inside diameter (ID) 1.0 mm; under biplane fluoroscopic control if available. Penetration of the pleural sinus should be avoided. An attempt is made to puncture a peripheral bile duct of the right lobe of the liver. This will result in a long intraductal course of the drainage catheter, reducing the risks of catheter dislodgement and intrahepatic vascular lesions. If the puncture of a peripheral bile duct fails, a centrally located bile duct is punctured. When repeated puncture attempts are necessary, the catheter is not completely removed from the liver before renewed insertion of the mandrin, to minimize the trauma to the capsule of the liver. In most cases no more than two to four puncture trials are necessary. On rare occasions, if only one-plane fluoroscopy is available, up to ten passes of the sheathed mandrin are required before a bile duct suitable for catheterization is entered. During fluoroscopy, the puncture of a bile duct can be observed. The tip of the mandrin dislodges the opacified duct slightly before the duct is intentionally perforated by the sheathed mandrin. The mandrin is removed and the catheter is gradually withdrawn until bile is aspirated freely. A guide wire (0.9 mm) with a soft, slightly curved tip is introduced into the bile duct and manipulated toward the site of the obstruction (Fig. **3a**). The catheter is advanced into the same position (Fig. **3b**). In most cases the guide wire can be manipulated through the stricture, even if complete obstruction is suggested, by gently rotating the curved tip (Fig. **3e**). This is achieved by circular torque of the external part of the guide wire (Fig. **4**). With the tip of the guide wire is in the duodenum, the catheter can easily be pushed into the same position. Aspiration of bile from the dilated ductal system reduces the risk of bilivenous or bililymphatic reflux and facilitates the manipulation of the guide wire and the catheter through the obstructed segment of the extrahepatic ducts. The guide wire is removed and exchanged for an extremely rigid guide wire with a 10 cm flexible segment at its tip (47). The puncture catheter is removed and exchanged for the drainage catheter (OD 2.8 mm; ID 1.4 mm), which is manipulated over the guide wire through the obstruction. This procedure is painful and necessitates additional intravenous administration of analgesics.

Combined internal and external bile drainage is rendered possible by multiple side holes in the catheter proximal and distal to the site of obstruction (Figs. **3f, 5, 6**). The holes are made according to the pathologic findings in the individual case. Taking care to avoid any kinking, the catheter is sutured to the skin and connected to a collecting bag.

If the obstruction cannot be passed by the guide wire, a catheter should be left in place in an intrahepatic or preferably an extrahepatic bile duct, depending on the site of the obstruction (Fig. **3c**). After 2 to 3 days of external drainage and daily irrigation with saline, it is often possible to advance the guide wire and the catheter through the obstruction. If attempts to pass the obstruction are unsuccessful, external drainage has to be performed. To obtain a stable position of the catheter, its tip should be manipulated into a major bile radicle and advanced as peripherally as possible (Fig. **3d**). Catheter segments with side holes should not be placed in the parenchyma of the liver because this may result in a communication between the lumen of the catheter

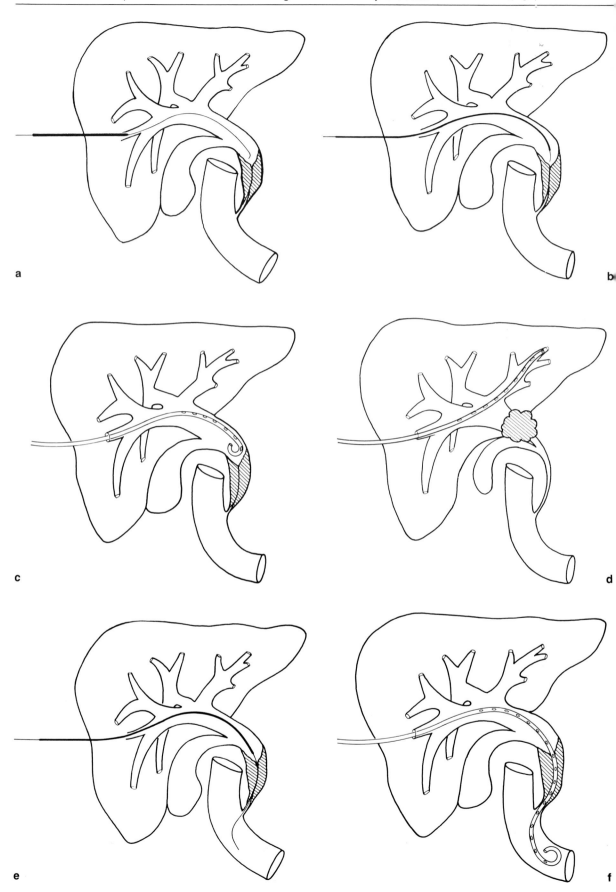

Fig. 3a–f Percutaneous transhepatic biliary drainage (PTBD)
a Puncture catheter with tip in intrahepatic bile duct. Guide wire inserted through catheter with slightly curved tip proximal to tumor obstruction of extrahepatic bile ducts (Reproduced with permission from Röntgenpraxis 38: 81, 1985)
b Puncture catheter advanced into extrahepatic bile ducts
c Drainage catheter with curved tip and multiple side holes inserted into extrahepatic bile ducts close to tumor obstruction (Reproduced with permission from Röntgenpraxis 38: 81, 1985)
d Drainage catheter with multiple side holes inserted into intrahepatic bile ducts. Tip of catheter advanced into bile duct of left liver lobe (Reproduced with permission from Röntgenpraxis 38: 81, 1985)
e Puncture catheter advanced into extrahepatic bile ducts. Guide wire passed through obstructed bile duct segment with tip in duodenum (Reproduced with permission from Röntgenpraxis 38: 81, 1985)
f Drainage catheter manipulated through tumor obstruction. Side holes for internal drainage proximal and distal to site of obstruction (Reproduced with permission from Röntgenpraxis 38: 81, 1985)

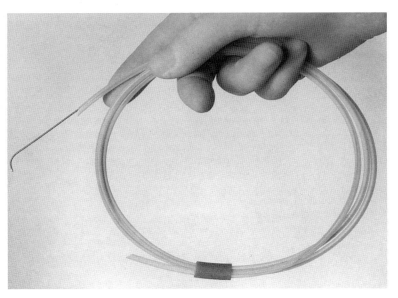

Fig. **4 Circular torque of external part of J-shaped guide wire** (Reproduced with permission from Langenbecks Arch. Chir. 354: 55, 1981)

and hepatic vessels, causing hemobilia or leakage of bile, possibly infected, into the blood circulation. In addition to drainage of the bile ducts of the right lobe of the liver, decompression of the bile ducts of the left lobe can be performed when the obstructive lesion involves the confluence of the hepatic ducts (43, 62). The bile ducts of the left lobe of the liver are punctured and catheterized from the epigastrium (Fig. **7a, b**).

If partial catheter dislodgement occurs, the position of the catheter can easily be readjusted with a guide wire and a more stable position is achieved by pushing it further distally to the obstruction. When total dislodgement of the catheter occurs, reinsertion should be attempted immediately. After injection of contrast medium through the puncture hole in the skin, the tract through the liver to the bile ducts may be visualized to allow a guide wire to be manipulated through the canal for introduction of a new drainage catheter. If this fails, the puncture procedure has to be repeated as already described. Regardless of the amount of bile drained externally, the catheter must be flushed with saline at least once a day. The external drainage is blocked when the amount of bile drained externally has decreased below 1 dl/24hours. Serum alkaline phosphatase and serum bilirubin are checked regularly for detection of cholestasis, indicating insufficient drainage by the indwelling catheter. When a large volume of bile is drained externally, appropriate measures have to be taken to restore the loss of water, electrolytes, and bile acids.

Cytologic confirmation of the diagnosis of a malignant lesion obstructing the extrahepatic biliary tract can be obtained by fluoroscopically directed fine needle aspiration biopsy from the area of the biliary duct obstruction.

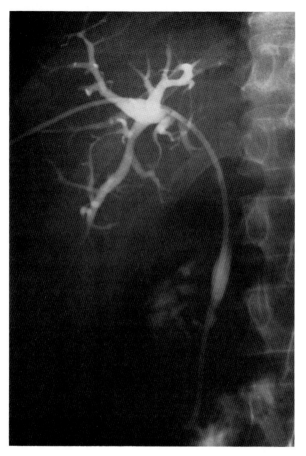

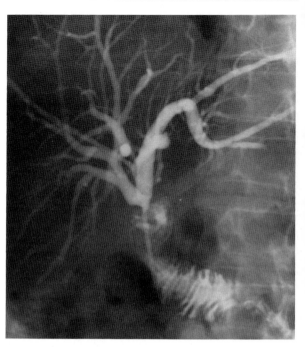

Fig. **6   A 64-year-old patient with extrahepatic chole-stasis secondary to edema at site of hepatico-jejunos-tomy.** Catheter for internal and external bile drainage was passed through anastomosis into the jejunum (Reproduced with permission from Hoevels et al. [35])

Fig. **5   A 50-year-old patient with obstructive chole-stasis due to nonresectable tumor of head of pan-creas.** For internal and external drainage, the catheter was manipulated through obstructed segment of common hepatic and common bile ducts. Curved tip of catheter is in duodenum

Table **1**   Complications of trans-hepatic biliary drainage proce-dures in 250 patients*

Type of complication	No.	Surgical intervention	Fatal outcome
Intraperitoneal hemorrhage	5	–	3
Cholangitis	65	–	–
Cholangitis with sepsis	15	–	5
Biliary peritonitis	12	7	–
Intrapleural bile leakage	2	–	–
Abscess	6	6	–
Perforation of duodenum	6	5	–
Dislocation or occlusion of drain-age catheter or endoprosthesis	20/34	–	–
Excessive fluid loss via drainage catheter	4	–	–

* Reprinted with permission from Hoevels (39)

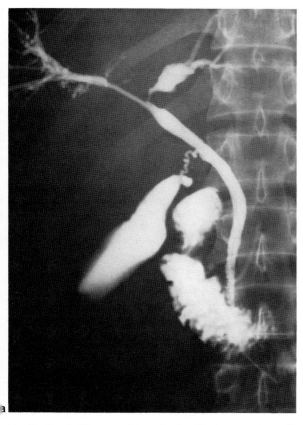
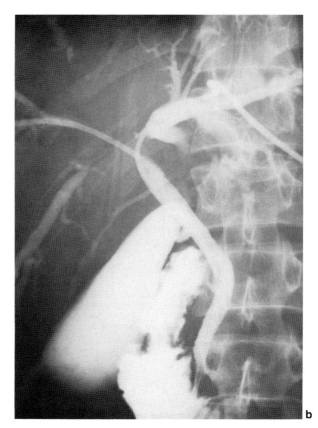

Fig. **7a, b** **A 39-year-old patient with tumor at confluence of hepatic ducts.** Infiltration of liver in porta hepatis (Reproduced with permission from Fortschr. Röntgenstr. 131: 140, 1979)
a Tumor obstruction passed by catheter with tip in duodenum. Multiple side holes proximal and distal to obstruction warrant internal decompression and drainage of bile duct system of one segment of right liver lobe. Tumor stricture of left hepatic duct occurred close to hepatic confluence
b For decompression and drainage, separate catheter placed in dilated bile duct of left liver lobe with ventral approach. Tip of catheter is in distal segment of common bile duct. Side holes proximal and distal to tumor stricture of left hepatic duct facilitate internal drainage

Complications

Percutaneous transhepatic biliary decompression is highly invasive, and a variety of procedure-related complications (Table **1**) are on record (1, 3, 5, 11, 29, 30, 33, 37, 39, 43, 51, 56, 61, 65–67, 76, 85, 89). The possible damage to the hepatic blood vessels by the puncture needle and the drainage catheter or by the endoprosthesis with subsequent formation of pseudoaneurysms and communications between the hepatic arteries, hepatic and portal veins, and the biliary tract (Table **2**; Figs. **8a, b, 9**) was angiographically demonstrated by various investigators (33, 52, 54, 57, 59, 72, 76, 79, 84). Death after intra-abdominal hemorrhage or massive hemobilia has been reported (37, 61). If severe arterial hemorrhage occurs, this can be handled either by surgical ligation or by transcatheter occlusion of the hepatic artery. The transcatheter treatment is to be preferred, since by this means the damaged arterial branch can be

occluded selectively (39, 57, 59, 84). Ligation or occlusion of the main hepatic artery in the jaundiced patient may result in liver failure.

Table **2** Intrahepatic vascular lesions in 83 patients with nonsurgical percutaneous transhepatic bile duct intubation*

Type of lesion	No. cases
Aneurysm of intrahepatic artery	14[+][±]
Hematoma	7
Arterioportal venous fistula	6
Arteriohepatic venous fistula	1[±]

[+] In two patients the aneurysm was surrounded by a hematoma.

[±] In one patient an arteriohepatic venous fistula was present adjacent to an aneurysm.

* Reprinted with permission from Hoevels and Nilsson (37)

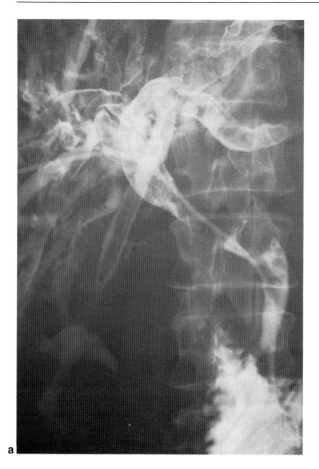

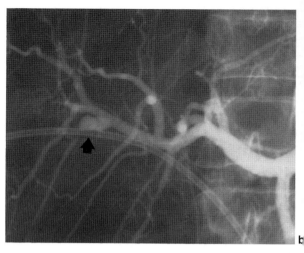

Fig. **8   A 59-year-old patient with carcinoma of the gallbladder infiltrating hepatoduodenal ligament.** Palliative bile drainage through a transhepatic catheter (Reproduced with permission from Hoevels and Nilsson [37])

a Percutaneous   transhepatic   cholangiography through an indwelling drainage catheter reveals extensive casting of biliary ducts by blood clots due to hemobilia
b Hepatic angiography demonstrates large aneurysm adjacent to drainage catheter in central part of right liver lobe (arrow)

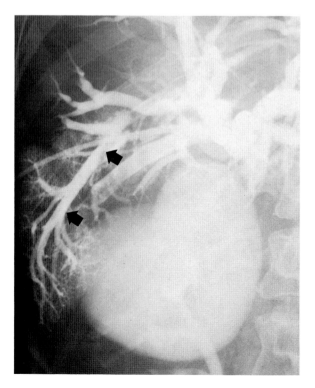

Fig. **9   A 43-year-old patient with extrahepatic cholestasis secondary to nonresectable tumor in hepatoduodenal ligament.** Percutaneous transhepatic cholangiography through transhepatic drainage catheter shows communication between bile ducts and intrahepatic portal vein branch (arrows) (Reproduced with permission from Hoevels et al. [35])

Slight to moderate bleeding into the biliary tract during the intubation procedure is not a rare occurrence and does not indicate a serious complication in the vast majority of cases (11, 29, 61). Intraductal blood clots may obstruct the biliary tract for a period of 1 to 3 days until the clots are dissolved. Transgression of the pleural space may cause a pneumothorax and a bilipleural fistula (5, 11, 39, 61, 64). Malignant pleural effusion secondary to transhepatic biliary drainage may occur (1). Müller et al. (61) communicated a fatal complication in a patient with severe emphysema who sustained a pneumothorax and bilious pleural effusion. A case of sudden death from multiple pulmonary bile emboli after biliary drainage was reported by Armelin et al. (3). Fever, chills, and hypotension indicating sepsis may develop during or after the procedure (5, 39, 61). Acute pancreatitis with fatal outcome secondary to transhepatic biliary intubation for internal drainage has been described by Luska and Poser (53). Episodes of cholangitis have been reported in patients with long-term transhepatic biliary drainage (5, 11, 18, 30, 39, 51, 61). Cholangitis as a main cause of fatal outcome in patients with palliative transhepatic biliary drainage has been described (11, 29, 30). Seeding of neoplasm along the tract of a transhepatic drainage tube is on record (35, 46, 71).

Clinical Significance

For patients undergoing preoperative decompression, external drainage as a short-term solution of extrahepatic biliary obstruction is the optimal procedure if internal drainage fails. Provided a stable position of the external drainage catheter has been achieved, the volume of bile drained during 24 hours ranges approximately between 500 and 1200 ml. In single cases up to 2000 ml of bile may drain during the first 24 hours after biliary duct decompression. The volume of drained bile varies greatly from patient to patient and is not correlated to the degree of jaundice. In the early drainage period the decrease of the serum bilirubin value averages 2 mg/dl serum during 24 hours. A drainage period of 1 to 2 weeks reduces the serum bilirubin level significantly (14, 18, 30, 36). Whereas only a small number of patients reach normal values, the majority of patients experience a decrease of the serum bilirubin to slightly or moderately elevated levels. However, decrease of serum bilirubin is not a reliable criterion of improved liver function. Japanese investigators have demonstrated that a drainage period of 4 to 6 weeks seems to be necessary for improvement of mitochondrial respiratory function and ketogenesis, indicating recovery of the hepatocytes from cholestasis. It was also observed that the degree of recovery after relief of biliary obstruction depended on both the duration of obstruction and the period after biliary decompression (47).

Several groups of investigators have reported that temporary transhepatic biliary drainage before surgery for obstructive jaundice might the followed by recovery of liver funtion, thus reducing the perioperative and postoperative morbidity and mortality (14, 27, 30, 32). Nakayama et al. (64) concluded that preoperative biliary decompression to a bilirubin level less than 86 µmol/liter decreased the operative mortality from 28 to 8% in patients with cancer undergoing radical or palliative surgery. In a recently published prospective randomized controlled clinical trial, Hatfield et al. (33) have demonstrated that the justification for the routine use of preoperative biliary drainage must be questioned. For long-term palliative treatment, combined internal and external drainage is preferable. When the internal bile flow is not impeded, the volume of bile drained externally via the catheter ranges between approximately 1 and 2 dl/24 hours. Increasing external bile flow indicates malfunction of the internal limb of the catheter passing through the biliary duct obstruction. Forced flushing with 10 to 20 ml of saline or passing a guide wire for cleaning the catheter may restore internal bile drainage. If this fails, it is advisable to replace the drainage catheter by a new one using the guide wire technique.

The passage of a catheter through the obstructing lesion of the external bile ducts is possible in approximately 70 to 80% of cases. In the remainder of patients external drainage for palliative decompression has to be performed. Both methods have proved effective in accomplishing relief of extrahepatic cholestasis in the majority of patients. Müller et al. (61) analyzed 200 consecutive percutaneous biliary drainage procedures, and successful drainage was achieved in 188 (94%). Internal drainage was performed in 144 (72%) and external catheter drainage in 44 (22%) instances.

There are, however, some shortcomings involved in these methods, especially with regard to long-term palliative treatment. The drainage may be interrupted by spontaneous catheter dislodgement or infection of the biliary duct system through the external catheter. External leakage of ascitic fluid or bile around the percutaneous transhepatic catheter and inflammation and pain at the puncture site may be further disadvantages of the procedure. Furthermore, the knowledge that the catheter and the collecting bag must be worn permanently may constitute a severe psychologic strain for the patient. These obvious disadvantages are avoidable when internal biliary drainage is performed through a transhepatically or endoscopically inserted endoprosthesis.

References

1. Anschuetz SL, Vogelzang RL. Malignant pleural effusion: a complication of transhepatic biliary drainage. AJR 1986;146:1165.
2. Ariyama J, Shirakabe H, Ohashï K, Roberts GM. Experience with percutaneous transhepatic cholangiography using the Japanese needle. Gastrointest Radiol 1978;2:359.
3. Armellin GM, Smith RC, Faithfull GR. Pulmonary bile emboli following percutaneous cholangiography and biliary drainage. Pathology 1981;13:615.
4. Benjamin IS, Allison MEM, Moule B, Blumgart LH. The early use of fine-needle percutaneous transhepatic cholangiography in an approach to the diagnosis of jaundice in a surgical unit. Br J Surg 1978;65:92.
5. Berquist TH, May GR, Johnson CM, Adson MA, Thistle JL. Percutaneous biliary decompression: internal and external drainage in 50 patients. AJR 1981;136:901.
6. Burcharth F, Nielbo N. Percutaneous cholangiography with selective catheterization of the common bile duct. AJR 1976;127:409.
7. Burcharth F, Christiansen L, Efsen F, Nielbo N, Stage P. Percutaneous transhepatic cholangiography in diagnostic evaluation of 160 jaundiced patients: results of an improved technique. Am J Surg 1977;133:559.
8. Burcharth F, Kam-Hansen L. Obstructive jaundice in pancreatitis investigated by percutaneous transhepatic cholangiography. Scand J Gastroenterol 1978;13:589.
9. Burckhardt H, Müller W. Versuche über die Punktion der Gallenblase und ihre Röntgendarstellung. Dtsch Chir 1921;162:168.
10. Caridi JG, Hawkins IF Jr, Hawkins MC. Single-step placement of a self-retaining "accordion" catheter. AJR 1984;143:337.
11. Carrasco CH, Zornoza J, Bechtel WJ. Malignant biliary obstruction: complications of percutaneous biliary drainage. Radiology 1984;152:343.
12. Carter RF, Saypol GM. Transabdominal cholangiography. JAMA 1952;148:253.
13. Cope C. Use of crossed-limb loop anchor for percutaneous biliary bypass. AJR 1982;138:974.
14. Denning DA, Ellison EC, Carey LC. Preoperative percutaneous transhepatic biliary decompression lowers operative morbidity in patients with obstructive jaundice. Am J Surg 1981;141:61.
15. Dooley JS, Dick R, Olney J, Sherlock S. Non-surgical treatment of biliary obstruction. Lancet 1979;ii:1040.
16. Druy EM, Melville GE. Obstructed hepatic duct bifurcation: decompression via single percutaneous tract. AJR 1984;143:73.
17. Ferrucci JT Jr, Wittenberg J, Sarno RA, Dreyfuss JR. Fine needle transhepatic cholangiography: a new approach to obstructive jaundice. AJR 1976;127:403.
18. Ferrucci JT Jr, Mueller PR, Harbin WP. Percutaneous transhepatic biliary drainage: technique, results and applications. Radiology 1980;135:1.
19. Ferrucci JT Jr, Mueller PR. Interventional radiology of the biliary tract. Gastroenterology 1982;82:974.
20. Flemma RJ, Shingleton WW. Clinical experience with percutaneous transhepatic cholangiography: experience with 107 cases. Am J Surg 1966;111:13.
21. Fraser GM, Cruikshank JG, Sumerling MD, Buist TAS. Percutaneous transhepatic cholangiography with the Chiba needle. Clin Radiol 1978;29:101.
22. Glenn F, Evans JA, Mujahed Z, Thorbjarnarson B. Percutaneous transhepatic cholangiography. Ann Surg 1962;156:451.
23. Gobien RP, Stanley JH, Soucek CD, Anderson MC, Vujic I, Gobien BS. Routine preoperative biliary drainage: effect on management of obstructive jaundice. Radiology 1984;152:353.
24. Gold RP, Casarella WJ, Stern G, Seaman WB. Transhepatic cholangiography: the radiological method of choice in suspected obstructive jaundice. Radiology 1979;133:39.
25. Gold RP, Price JB. Thin needle cholangiography as the primary method for the evaluation of the biliary-enteric anastomosis. Radiology 1980;136:309.

26. Göthlin J, Tranberg KG. Complications of percutaneous transhepatic cholangiography (PTC). AJR 1973;117:426.
27. Gundry SR, Strodel WE, Knol JA, Eckhauser FE, Thompson NW. Efficacy of preoperative biliary tract decompression in patients with obstructive jaundice. Arch Surg 1984;119:703.
28. Günther RW, Dähnert W. Self-retaining small-looped catheter for narrow bile ducts in high common bile duct obstruction. Eur J Radiol 1985;5:81.
29. Hamlin JA, Friedman M, Stein MG, Bray JF. Percutaneous biliary drainage: complications of 118 consecutive catheterizations. Radiology 1986;158:199.
30. Hansson JA, Hoevels J, Simert G, Tylén U, Vang J. Clinical aspects of nonsurgical percutaneous transhepatic bile drainage in obstructive lesions of the extrahepatic bile ducts. Ann Surg 1979;189:58.
31. Harbin WP, Mueller PR, Ferrucci J Jr. Transhepatic cholangiography: complications and use patterns of the fine-needle technique. Radiology 1980;135:15.
32. Hatfield ARW, Murray RS. Preoperative biliary drainage in patients with obstructive jaundice. S Afr Med J 1981;60:737.
33. Hatfield ARW, Tobias R, Terblanche J, Girdwood AH, Fataar S, Harries-Jones R, Kernoff L, Marks IN. Preoperative external biliary drainage in obstructive jaundice. Lancet 1982;ii:896.
34. Hinde GDB, Smith PM, Craven JL. Percutaneous cholangiography with the Okuda needle. Gut 1977;18:610.
35. Hoevels J, Lunderquist A, Ihse I. Perkutane transhepatische Intubation der Gallengänge zur kombinierten inneren und äußeren Drainage bei extrahepatischer Cholestase. RöFo 1978;129:533.
36. Hoevels J, Lunderquist A, Ihse I. Percutaneous transhepatic intubation of bile ducts for combined internal-external drainage in preoperative and palliative treatment of obstructive jaundice. Gastrointest Radiol 1978;3:23.
37. Hoevels J, Nilsson U. Intrahepatic vascular lesions following nonsurgical percutaneous transhepatic bile duct intubation. Gastrointest Radiol 1980;5:127.
38. Hoevels J, Hoffmeister A. Preoperative transhepatic biliary drainage. Ann Radiol (Paris) 1984;27:361.
39. Hoevels J. Complications of percutaneous transhepatic biliary drainage. Ann Radiol (Paris) 1986;29:148.
40. Holst Pedersen J, Gammelgaard J, Haubek A, Hancke S, Jensen LI, Burcharth F. Ultrasonic localization of the porta hepatis prior to percutaneous transhepatic cholangiography. RöFo 1982;136:260.
41. Huard P, Do-Xuan-Hop: La ponction transhépatique des canaux biliaires. Bull Soc Med Chir Indochine 1937;15:1090.
42. Jain S, Long RG, Scott J, Dick R, Sherlock S. Percutaneous transhepatic cholangiography using the "Chiba" needle: 80 cases. Br J Radiol 1977;50:175.
43. Jaques PF, Mandell VS, Delany DJ, Nath PH. Percutaneous transhepatic biliary drainage: advantages of left-lobe subxiphoid approach. Radiology 1982;145:534.
44. Juler GL, Conroy RM, Fuelleman RW. Bile leakage following percutaneous transhepatic cholangiography with the Chiba needle. Arch Surg 1977;112:954.
45. Kadir S, Baassiri A, Barth KH, Kaufman SL, Cameron JL, White RI Jr. Percutaneous biliary drainage in the management of biliary sepsis. AJR 1982;138:25.
46. Kim WS, Barth KH, Zinner M. Seeding of pancreatic carcinoma along the transhepatic catheter tract. Radiology 1982;143:427.
47. Koyama K, Takagi Y, Ito K, Sato T. Experimental and clincial studies on the effect of biliary drainage in obstructive jaundice. Am J Surg 1981;142:293.
48. Kreek MJ, Balint JA. "Skinny needle" cholangiography: results of a pilot study of a voluntary prospective method for gathering risk data on new procedures. Gastroenterology 1980;78:598.
49. Lang E. Percutaneous transhepatic cholangiography. Radiology 1974;112:283.
50. Leger L, Zara et Arvay M. Cholangiographie et drainage biliaire par ponction trans-hépatique. Presse Med 1952;42:936.
51. Lois JF, Gomes AS, Grace PA, Deutsch LS, Pitt HA. Risks of percutaneous transhepatic drainage in patients with cholangitis. AJR 1987;148:367.

52. Lunderquist A, Lunderquist M, Owman T. Guide wire for percutaneous transhepatic cholangiography. Radiology 1979;132:228.
53. Luska G, Poser H. Acute pancreatitis in obstructive jaundice following combined internal and external percutaneous transhepatic bile duct drainage (PTBD). Eur J Radiol 1983;3:112.
54. Makuuchi M, Bandai Y, Ito T, Watanabe G, Wada T, Abe H, Muroi T. Ultrasonically guided percutaneous transhepatic bile drainage. Radiology 1980;136:165.
55. McLean GK, Ring EJ, Freiman DB. Therapeutic alternatives in the treatment of intrahepatic biliary obstruction. Radiology 1982;145:289.
56. McPherson GAD, Benjamin IS, Nathanson B, Blenkharn IB, Bowley NB, Blumgart LH. Advantages and disadvantages of percutaneous transhepatic biliary drainage as part of a staged approach to obstructive jaundice. Gut 1981;22:427.
57. Mitchell SE, Shuman LS, Kaufman SL, Chang R, Kadir S, Kinnison ML, White RI Jr. Biliary catheter drainage complicated by hemobilia: treatment by balloon embolotherapy. Radiology 1985;157:645.
58. Molnar W, Stockum AE. Relief of obstructive jaundice through percutaneous transhepatic catheter: a new therapeutic method. AJR 1974;122:356.
59. Monden M, Okamura J, Kobayashi N, Shibata N, Horikawa S, Fujimoto T, Kosaki G, Kuroda C, Uchida H. Hemobilia after percutaneous transhepatic biliary drainage. Arch Surg 1980;115:161.
60. Mori K, Misumi A, Sugiyama M, Okabe M, Matsuoka T, Ishii J, Akagi M. Percutaneous transhepatic bile drainage. Ann Surg 1977;185:111.
61. Mueller PR, van Sonnenberg E, Ferrucci JT Jr. Percutaneous biliary drainage: technical and catheter-related problems in 200 procedures. AJR 1982;138:17.
62. Mueller PR, Ferrucci JJ Jr, van Sonnenberg E, Warshaw AL, Simeone JF, Cronan JL, Neff CC, Butch RJ. Obstruction of the left hepatic duct: diagnosis and treatment by selective fine-needle cholangiography and percutaneous biliary drainage. Radiology 1982;145:297.
63. Mujahed Z, Evans JA. Percutaneous transhepatic cholangiography. Radiol Clin North Am 1966;4:535.
64. Nakayama T, Ikeda A, Okuda K. Percutaneous transhepatic drainage of the biliary tract: technique and results in 104 cases. Gastroenterology 1978;74:554.
65. Neff CC, Mueller PR, Ferrucci JT Jr, Dawson SL, Wittenberg J, Simeone JF, Butch RJ, Papanicolaou N. Serious complications following transgression of the pleural space in drainage procedures. Radiology 1984;152:335.
66. Nilsson U, Evander A, Ihse I, Lunderquist A, Mocibob A. Percutaneous transhepatic cholangiography and drainage: risks and complications. Acta Radiol [Diagn] (Stockh) 1983;24:433.
67. Norlander A, Kalin B, Sundblad R. Effect of percutaneous transhepatic drainage upon liver function and postoperative mortality. Surg Gynecol Obstet 1982;155:161.
68. Ohto M, Tsuchiya Y. Medical cholangiography: technique and cases. (In Japanese.) Medicina 1969;6:735.
69. Ohto M, Ohno T, Tsuchiya Y, Saisho H. Percutaneous transhepatic cholangiography. (In Japanese.) Tokyo: Igaku Shoin, 1973.
70. Okuda K, Tanikawa K, Emura T, Kuratomi S, Jinnouchi S, Urabe K, Sumikoshi T, Kanda Y, Fukuyama Y, Musha H, Mori H, Shimokawa Y, Yakushiji F, Matsuura Y. Nonsurgical, percutaneous transhepatic cholangiography: diagnostic significance in medical problems of the liver. Am J Dig Dis 1974;19:21.
71. Olega JA, Ring EJ, Freiman DB, McLean GK, Rosen RJ. Extension of neoplasm along the tract of a transhepatic tube. AJR 1980;135:841.
72. Ott DJ, Gelfand DW. Complications of gastrointestinal procedures, II: complications related to biliary tract studies. Gastrointest Radiol 1981;6:47.
73. Passariello R, Pavone P, Rossi P, Simonetti G, Modini C, Lasagni RP, Manella P, Gazzaniga GM, Paolini RM, Iaccarino V, Feltrin G, Roversi R, Mallarini G. Percutaneous biliary drainage in neoplastic jaundice: statistical data from a computerized multicenter investigation. Acta Radiol [Diagn] (Stockh) 1985;26:681.
74. Pereiras R Jr, Chiprut RO, Greenwald RA, Schiff ER. Percutaneous transhepatic cholangiography with the "skinny" needle: a rapid, simple, and accurate method in the diagnosis of cholestasis. Ann Intern Med 1977;86:562.
75. Pitt HA, Cameron JL, Postier RG, Gadacz TR. Factors affecting mortality in biliary tract surgery. Am J Surg 1981;141:66.
76. Pollock TW, Ring ER, Oleaga JA, Freiman DB, Mullen JL, Rosato EF. Percutaneous decompression of benign and malignant biliary obstruction. Arch Surg 1979;114:148.
77. Redeker AG, Karvountzis GG, Richman RH, Horisawa M. Percutaneous transhepatic cholangiography: an improved technique. JAMA 1975;231:386.
78. Ring EJ, Oleaga JA, Freiman DB, Husted JW, Lunderquist A. Therapeutic applications of catheter cholangiography. Radiology 1978;128:333.
79. Rosen RJ, Rothberg M. Transhepatic embolization of hepatic artery pseudoaneurysm following biliary drainage. Radiology 1982;145:532.
80. Shaldon S, Barber KM, Young WB. Percutaneous transhepatic cholangiography: a modified technique. Gastroenterology 1962;42:371.
81. Schwarz W, Rosen RJ, Fitts WT Jr, Mackie JA, Oleaga JA, Freiman DB, McLean GK, Ring EJ. Percutaneous transhepatic drainage preoperatively for benign biliary strictures. Surg Gynecol Obstet 1981;152:466.
82. Seldinger SI. Percutaneous transhepatic cholangiography. Acta Radiol [Suppl] (Stockh) 1966;253.
83. Smale BF, Ring EJ, Freiman DB, Oleaga JA, Reichman R, Mullen JL, Rosato EF. Successful long-term percutaneous decompression of the biliary tract. Am J Surg 1981;141:73.
84. Sniderman KW, Morse SS, Rapoport S, Ross GR. Hemobilia following transhepatic biliary drainage: occlusion of an hepatoportal fistula by balloon tamponade. Radiology 1985;154:827.
85. Taber DS, Stroehlein JR, Zornoza J. Work in progress: hypotension and high-volume biliary excretion following external percutaneous transhepatic biliary drainage. Radiology 1982;145:639.
86. Takada T, Hanyu F, Kobayashi S, Uchida Y. Percutaneous transhepatic cholangial drainage: direct approach under fluoroscopic control. J Surg Oncol 1976;8:83.
87. Takada T, Uchida Y, Yasuda H, Kobayashi S, Sakakibara N, Hanyu F. Conversion of percutaneous transhepatic cholangiodrainage to internal drainage in obstructive jaundice. Jpn J Surg 1977;7:10.
88. Tsuchiya Y. A new safe method of percutaneous transhepatic cholangiography. (In Japanese.) Jpn J Gastroenterol 1969;63:438.
89. Tylén U, Hoevels J, Vang J. Percutaneous transhepatic cholangiography with external drainage of obstructive biliary lesions. Surg Gynecol Obstet 1977;144:13.
90. Wiechel KL. Percutaneous transhepatic cholangiography: technique and application. Acta Chir Scand [Suppl] 1964;330.
91. Zilly W, Liehr H, Hümmer N. Chiba-needle percutaneous cholangiography: a method without risk to the patient? Endoscopy 1980;12:12.

Biliary Endoprostheses in Malignant Obstruction

R. F. Dondelinger and J. C. Kurdziel

Indications

As preoperative percutaneous biliary drainage is no longer considered a major therapeutic adjunct prior to curative surgery, except in selected cases (5, 44, 51), most percutaneous biliary drainage procedures are performed in malignant disease in order to place a permanent biliary endoprosthesis or to create an access for intraductal irradiation, as described in the chapter by Nunnerley and Karani below.

Most of these patient have a limited life expectancy. Their hospital stay should be reduced, and they should be freed as early as possible from percutaneous tubes and fluid-collecting bags. Besides the psychological trauma related to a percutaneous drainage catheter, several complications may occur: high volume external bile loss, skin infection at the puncture site, bile leakage around the catheter, fracturing of the catheter, rib erosion, hemobilia of arterial and portal origin caused by displacement of the proximal side ports of the catheter into the liver parenchyma, inadvertent dislodgment or withdrawal of an inadequately fixed catheter, spread of malignant cells to the skin along the percutaneous catheter (52), and finally cholangitis following high-pressure rinsing of the tube. These complications can be largely obviated by placing an endoprosthesis.

In recent years, introduction of a biliary stent has become a routine therapeutic alternative to surgery in the palliation of biliary obstruction due to malignant disease. Pretherapeutic staging of the malignancy must have proved that the patient has no chance of being cured by surgical resection. Patients with slowly progressive malignant disease should be considered potential candidates for surgical palliation. Although surgery has a higher perioperative mortality rate, especially for tumors situated at the liver hilum (4, 38) compared with percutaneous and endoscopic stenting, long-term comfort is improved, as all the problems connected with an endoprosthesis are avoided. When a nonoperative palliative treatment is considered, a definitive diagnosis must be established by all means, and only an irrefutable cytologic or histologic diagnosis of malignancy is accepted prior to palliation. Endoscopic cannulation of the bile ducts represents the favored approach (16, 17, 63), as detailed above by Cremer and Delhaye, and carries a low periprocedural morbidity rate. However, the endoscopic route for placing a large-bore endoprosthesis may fail in 9%, 25% and 60% if the obstruction is located at the pancreatic, mid-choledochal and hilar levels, respectively (41). Huibregtse (31) succeeded only in 40 out of 253 (16%) of cases in placing a second endoprosthesis endoscopically in patients with malignant obstruction at the liver hilum. In case of endoscopic failure, either a combined endoscopic-percutaneous approach (13, 26, 40, 42, 55, 64) or an exclusively percutaneous stent positioning remains mandatory, particularly if an extensive or tight stenosis is present, or if the biliary obstruction is located at the level of the liver hilum, with intrahepatic tumor growth, requiring more than one tube to restore correct bile flow.

The advantages of endoprostheses compared to naso-biliary or percutaneous internal catheter drainage include a diminished risk of biliary infection spreading through the catheter, a reduction in hydroelectrolytic imbalance caused by external fluid loss, increased comfort, and psychological tolerance by the patient. Only those patients with malignant disease who are not preterminal and who have improved clinically and biologically after catheter drainage without significant complications should be considered candidates for percutaneous insertion of an endoprosthesis.

Technique

Since the first description of percutaneous placement of a biliary endoprosthesis (56) (Fig. 1) many attempts have been made to define the optimal configuration of biliary stents. They should be easy to insert, removable, function over an extended period, and should induce a minimal number of complications during placement and once they have been abandoned in the biliary system. A large number of home-made and commercially available devices with variable consistencies (Teflon, polyethylene, polyurethane, Silicone, Percuflex), and variable diameters and shapes have been described in the literature without, any particular model being able to lay claim to general approval (7, 10, 11, 14, 15, 21, 27, 28, 32, 33, 34, 57, 65). As bile flow is slow, 5 Fr prostheses should be large enough to assure efficient permanent functioning, but the tendency of bile to form sludge and incrustations renders a diameter of 10–12 Fr mandatory to maintain a long patency. There is no evidence that larger prostheses of 14–24 Fr show a

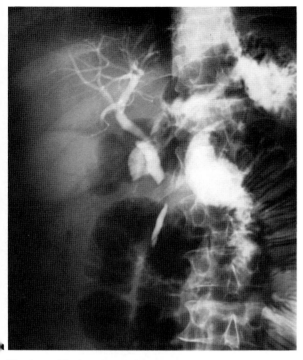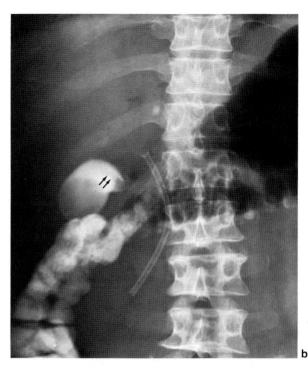

Fig. **1** **a Cholangiocarcinoma** causing a short obstruction of the middle third of the choledochus. **b** Percutaneous insertion of a 12 Fr prosthesis (Pereiras) with a flared upper end and rings. Residual blood clots in the gallbladder (arrows)

significantly improved patency rate in malignant obstruction.

Large prostheses increase trauma to the liver and expose the patient to complications such as the formation of a pseudoaneurysm, arteriobiliary or portobiliary fistulae, intrahepatic or perihepatic biloma, hematoma or abscess, pleural effusion, and ascites or thrombus of an arterial or a major portal branch by compression from the catheter.

It is possible to overcome complications due to the transhepatic approach when the combined transhepatic-endoscopic procedure is used. This technique is mainly applied today when endoscopic insertion of the prosthesis has failed. The obstructed intrahepatic biliary system is entered percutaneously with a 5 Fr catheter, which is negotiated with a guide wire through the papilla. This is possible in most cases even when obstruction at the lower choledochus renders endoscopic cannulation difficult.

The guide wire, when protruding through the papilla, is caught by the endoscope and brought out through the mouth. In this manner a transhepatic-peroral communication is established with the guide wire, and a large-bore endoprosthesis can be pushed over the guide wire orally. When the prosthesis is in the correct position, the guide wire is removed.

Expandable metallic stents are also available (Gianturco stents, Wallstents) (Fig. **2, 3**) (11, 14,

34). They are introduced through a 7 or 12 Fr catheter in their collapsed state. They expand when released, and may open up to 10 mm and maintain permanent expansion of the bile ducts. Unfortunately, these stents, in spite of their large diameter, do not stay open indefinitely, and become obstructed due to sludge or tumor ingrowth, shortening after release (Wallstents), inadequate placement, and too short purchase or displacement, particularly when severe anatomical distorsion is present. These stents cannot be removed when obstruction occurs, as they are rapidly incorporated into the wall of the bile ducts. Balloon expandable polymer-coated stents are under investigation in animal models (2). The coating should minimize intraluminal tumor proliferation, but hyperplasia of the biliary mucosa still persists.

We used 12 and 16 Fr endoprostheses adapted from commercially available polyethylene standard drainage catheters. Internal bile drainage is a prerequisite before an endoprosthesis can be inserted percutaneously. Complete opacification of the obstructed biliary tree must be obtained before drainage. Multiple fine-needle cholangiographies may be required in obstruction at the hilum to demonstrate all the obstructed intrahepatic territories. They should be adequately drained, although this may be impossible when massive tumor invasion above the bifurcation is present. On the

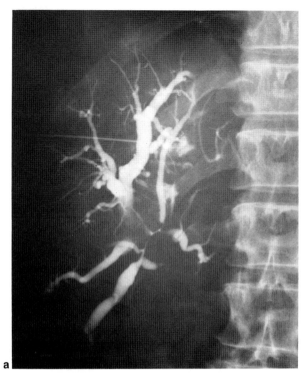
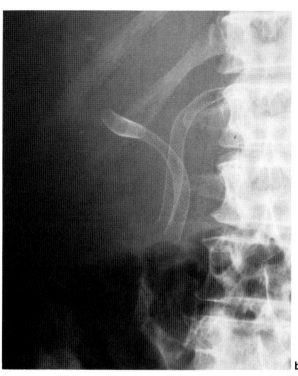

Fig. **2   a Metastatic spread from a uterine carcinoma to the liver hilum.** PTC shows a Bismuth type III obstruction.
b Percutaneous insertion of 2 expandable metallic prostheses (Wallstent), draining both lobes of the liver

other hand, these cases are more often selected for percutaneous biliary drainage today, as endoscopists can achieve correct stenting at the lower and middle third of the choledochus but tend to fail at the level of the hilum. An 8 or 12 Fr catheter is placed during the initial percutaneous drainage, and left in place for 24 or 48 h. Clotting disorders should be checked and corrected before each percutaneous manipulation. During that period, the transhepatic tract will mature and be lined out with granulation tissue in a few days, which minimizes the risk of bleeding and infection when the catheter is exchanged for the endoprosthesis. Introduction of the prosthesis is facilitated, and almost painless for the patient, when a two-step procedure is used. Decompression of the biliary system, and clearing of blood clots, debris and bacteria from the bile ducts during adequate previous drainage, prevents complications occuring when the endoprosthesis is placed.

Furthermore, during the initial percutaneous drainage period, responders can be separated from those patients whose serum bilirubin level does not decrease in spite of correct bile drainage. If the patient's clinical course is uneventful, and adequate bile drainage is achieved, the 12 Fr catheter is changed for a permanent endoprosthesis in a similar way to the description given by Coons (15). The optimal length of the endoprosthesis is determined from radiographs according to the individual biliary anatomy, the extent of obstruction, and the site of the catheter's entry point into the intrahepatic bile ducts, in such a way that the endoprosthesis will largely cover the extent of the obstruction. Then the catheter is retrieved over a Lunderquist guide wire (43), and the prosthesis is cut to the desired length from the distal end of the catheter. Proximal side ports are added to the endoprosthesis with a hole punch or a Menghini needle (19), when necessary. The prosthesis is then correctly positioned over the stiff guide wire by pushing it with the remaining proximal end of the catheter. The distal end of the prosthesis is advanced into the duodenum (20). The side ports, which are distributed through the whole length of the wall of the endoprosthesis, should allow bile to enter the lumen of the prosthesis from intrahepatic radicles. The proximal end of the endoprosthesis is attached to a suture thread, which is fixed subcutaneously onto a 1 cm rod in a similar way to other devices (46), preventing downward displacement. The thread can also be used to correct placement of the stent by retracting its proximal end (53). If obstruction of the endoprosthesis is suspected, a percutaneous skinny-needle cholangiography can be performed by puncturing the close

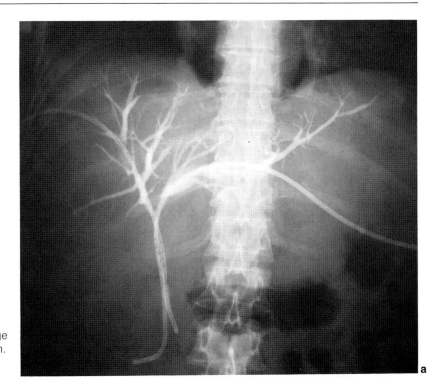

Fig. 3   a Cholangiocarcinoma involving the liver hilum.
Percutaneous biliary catheter drainage of both lobes of the liver for six month. The patient was reluctant to have an endoprosthesis placed.

environment around the endoprosthesis. Contrast medium will still flow through one or several unobstructed side-holes inside the endoprosthesis, and the patency of the lumen can easily be controlled. The endoprosthesis can also be rinsed by percutaneous flushing with saline through the side-holes before intraluminal incrustations lead to complete obstruction (23). On the other hand, side-holes which are too clustered may weaken the wall of the endoprosthesis and make its introduction through a resistent stenosis difficult. The retention suture (6), or a simple snare (35), can be used to remove a clogged endoprosthesis percutaneously. Also, it is theoretically possible to recatheterize the proximal end of an obstructed or displaced prosthesis, by a percutaneous approach although this is not always easy. When successful catheterization is possible, a balloon catheter can be placed inside the prosthesis. When the balloon is inflated below or inside the prosthesis, its position can be corrected by pulling or pushing on the balloon catheter. Sludge can be dislodged by the same movements (30).

The patient should be discharged from the hospital rapidly after the prosthesis has been placed.

A minority of patients or their relatives prefer to keep a percutaneous drainage catheter and take care of it in an obsessional manner. They are reluctant to accept the prosthesis when they are told that the procedure eventually has to be repeated, when occlusion occurs, or when they see the stent as the end of palliation or even as an abandonment.

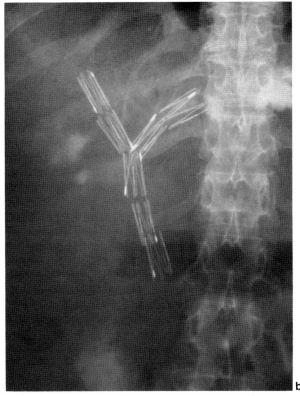

b When the patient became preterminal and unable to take care of her catheters, expandable metallic stents (Gianturco) were placed and functioned until the patient died two months later

Results and Complications

Placement of an endoprosthesis is only rarely unsuccessful once internal drainage has been established (Fig. **4**). We observed an overall success rate in establishing internal drainage in 89% of 178 patients, a result confirmed by others (1, 9, 15, 18, 21, 36, 39, 47). It is interesting to notice that the same success rate has been obtained in 40 consecutive patients with obstruction at the liver hilum, and 80% of patients showing a Bismuth type II or III obstruction (3). In this group of patients, at least two drainage catheters are required, sometimes three or four.

Once the initial internal catheter has been placed through the papilla, it is unusual that placement of the endoprosthesis fails. A tight stricture can be dilated, with a balloon catheter facilitating passage of the prosthesis.

The aim of biliary drainage is to drain functional liver parenchyma. In patients with obstruction at the hilum, atrophy and hypertrophy of different liver lobes or segments therefore has to be considered, and anatomic variants of the intrahepatic bile ducts as well, before planning the insertion of multiple prostheses (Fig. **5**). In many instances, tumor infiltration at the liver hilum predominates around the right hepatic duct. Selective drainage of the left lobe alone often reduces jaundice and pruritus (48) significantly. The most dramatic complications related

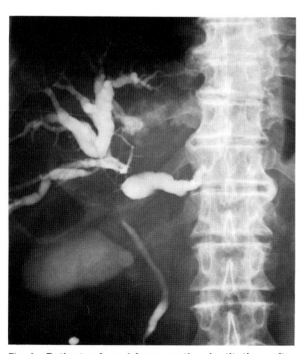

Fig. **4** **Patient referred from another institution, after percutaneous placement of a biliary prosthesis was attempted under general anesthesia, without internal drainage being established.** The prosthesis is located in the liver parenchyma above the obstructed hilum

to percutaneous catheterization of the biliary system occur during the initial drainage procedure. Death has been reported in 1.5% (49, 50) to 5.6% (12) of patients. Clinically significant complications which may overshadow percutaneous biliary drainage are largely detailed in the literature, and occur in 8 to 11% (49, 50), requiring conservative or radiological management (embolization of a pseudoaneurysm, drainage of a biloma, hematoma or abscess), and on rare occasions only surgical cure. The 30-day mortality rate after placement of an endoprosthesis in patients with malignant obstruction was 27% in our experience, and 56% in nonselected patients with obstruction at the liver hilum presenting a Bismuth type II or III obstruction. In the literature, a mortality rate of 25.9% to 31.5% has been reported (22). Most patients die due to advanced malignant disease or biliary sepsis. Introduction of an endoprosthesis is thought to be a relatively harmless procedure, bearing only a small additional risk once the drainage catheter has been correctly positioned in the bile ducts and left for several days, although a complication rate of 13% has been observed (15). In accordance with the local facilities and the expertise of the radiologist, the benefits for the patient resulting from percutaneous stenting should be weighed against the risks of complications in each individual situation. A certain number of patients with far advanced disease and a poor prognosis should not be considered for the percutaneous procedure when endoscopic intubation of the biliary stenosis has been unsuccessful. The combined percutaneous-peroral approach should be largely applied when close cooperation between radiologists and endoscopists is available. When the prosthesis can be inserted through a T-tube tract, the complication rate is minimal, even when a large-bore stent is used (61).

Data on complications which may ensue from insertion of an endoprosthesis are scanty, but such complications seem to be only rarely lifethreatening, if the introduction of the endoprosthesis is not attempted during the initial percutaneous drainage procedure. Clogging of the endoprosthesis is the most common complication. Serume bilirubin and alkaline phosphatase will rise after partial or complete obstruction of the stent. Cholangitis, intrahepatic abscess, perihepatic biloma or bile ascites, and external bile fistula emerging through the percutaneous transhepatic drainage tract, and biliary pleural effusion may develop. Patients with a clogged endoprosthesis should be attended to without delay, and the correct biliary drainage should be reestablished as soon as possible. Medical treatment with mucolytic drugs has not been proved efficient in reducing incrustation and sludge formation inside the prosthesis.

As many patients die after a short period of only a few months despite biliary drainage, the patency rate

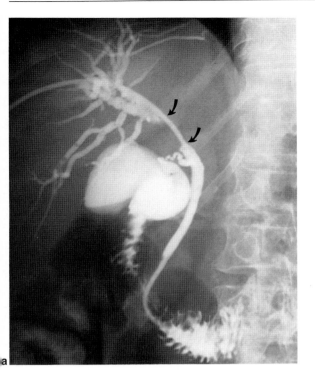

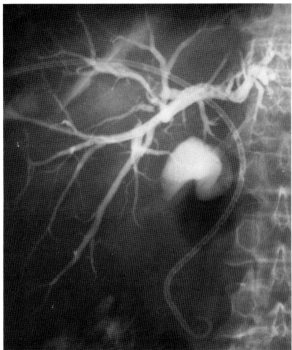

of biliary endoprostheses is difficult to evaluate. In our experience, the 12 or 16 Fr endoprostheses clogged in 18.3% of the cases after a mean functioning period of 16.2 weeks (20). Other reports claim a functioning period of 24 weeks and more (58). Obstruction is still too frequent an event, despite the more regular use of 14 and 16 Fr prostheses (54, 60). In large series (36, 47), about 6–23% of prostheses obstruct due to sludge, food impaction, migration and kinking of the prosthesis, intraluminal tumor growth through the side ports, or overgrowth at the ends of the stents when the prosthesis selected is short for the length of the occlusion. In vitro studies have shown that too many side ports create a turbulent bile flow inside the endoprosthesis, which may impair correct drainage (57), and that Teflon endoprostheses have a higher incrustation rate compared to polyethylene and polyurethane (37). The use of large silicone stents with a diameter of 28 Fr has been advocated (33), but percutaneous insertion of large-bore prostheses may become extremely difficult and painful for the patients, necessitating heavy sedation or even general anesthesia. It is essential to keep the initial percutaneous drainage procedure and the insertion of a first prosthesis as patient-friendly as possible, to avoid refusal of further procedures by the patient when obstruction of the stent occurs during follow-up. Most authors have found that a large inner diameter of the endoprosthesis, above 10 Fr guarantees free bile flow and a long patency rate for the stent (12, 15, 28, 29, 49, 58, 59). An increase in the inner diameter of the drainage catheter from 10 to 12 Fr leads to a reduction in cholangitis

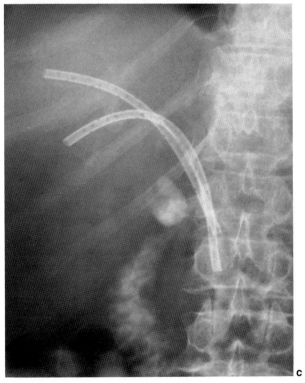

Fig. 5   **a Cholangiocarcinoma at the liver hilum causing a Bismuth type II obstruction.** An initial percutaneous catheter only drains the quadrate lobe of the liver. **b** A second percutaneous catheter drains the right lobe of the liver and shows atrophy of the lateral segment of the left lobe. **c** Two 12 Fr prostheses are inserted, draining the entire functional liver parenchyma. The atrophic part of the left lobe was not drained

from 63% to 11% (49). There is an obvious tendency to prefer large-bore endoprostheses, not only for the percutaneous but also for the endoscopic route, where damage to the liver parenchyma is not expected (26, 32). Only a few reports emphasize that endoprostheses with a smaller diameter may do equally well for long-term biliary drainage (7, 25). Even the more recently available expandable metallic stents occluded rapidly (in 33% of patients in our experience) when an intraluminal tumor was present. The unavoidable obstruction of the stents has generated pessimistic attitudes toward the usefulness of biliary drainage in malignant obstruction (45). Inadequate bile drainage and increased ductal pressure are followed by recurrent episodes of cholangitis, which are observed in almost all patients after a drainage period of four months (24). It is thought that patients with repeated cholangitis must be experiencing at least a temporarily impaired bile flow, or persistent biliary obstruction in a segment or lobe.

Transpapillary positioning of an endoprosthesis is controversial (Fig. **6**). It seems that the transpapillary position of the endoprosthesis, and the potential interaction between bile salts, duodenal fluid and the material the endoprosthesis is made of, favor early clogging. The sharp, stiff distal end of most of the short, rigid models may irritate the duodenal mucosa and lead to hemorrhage or even perforation when inserted through the papilla. A transpapillary position is unavoidable in bridging an occlusion situated at the level of the lower choledochus and the ampulla. Blockage of the pancreatic duct by the

endoprosthesis in unusual, and clinically significant pancreatitis is an exception after transpapillary stenting, even if multiple prostheses are placed through the papilla side by side. Some authors recommend a systematic suprapapillary position for the endoprosthesis (25). Micro-organisms are cultured from the bile in 94% if the drainage catheter has entered the duodenum, compared to 61% if its distal end remains in the choledochus below the obstruction (50). The presence of a foreign body in the choledochus is invariably followed by deposition of a glycoprotein on the wall of the prosthesis, and subsequent bacterial growth. Most of our patients with a transpapillary stent showed biological and mild to moderate clinical signs of cholangitis during follow-up. Catheters or prostheses with bound antibiotics have been designed (66), but prevention of bile infection or a significant reduction in cholangitis with these has yet to be proved. When the prosthesis has been placed in a transpapillary position, obstruction often starts from the intraduodenal portion, and debris from food are found at removal.

The main advantage of the transpapillary position for the endoprosthesis is to ensure endoscopic access to its distal end, allowing positional correction, withdrawal of the prosthesis, and rinsing of its lumen by catheterization through the distal intraduodenal holes (54). In order to maintain endoscopic access to a prosthesis placed in a suprapapillary position, a filament is fixed at its distal end protruding in the duodenum.

Spontaneous displacement of large-bore endoprostheses is rare when they are fixed under the skin

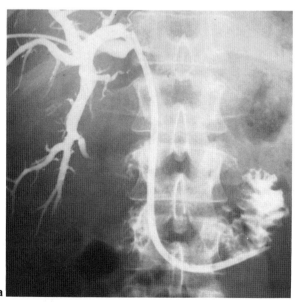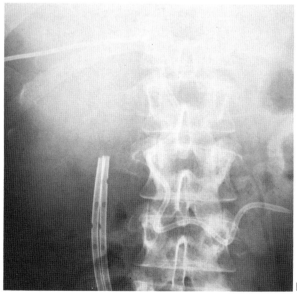

a

b

Fig. **6**   **a Cholangiocarcinoma at the liver hilum.** A 12 Fr Carey-Coons prosthesis was placed percutaneously. **b** The 12 Fr prosthesis obstructed, and was pushed through the papilla. A second 12 Fr prosthesis was placed, but migrated distally. A spiral-shaped stent was then placed, and also obstructed. (Courtesy of Dr. A. Adams, Hammersmith Hospital, London)

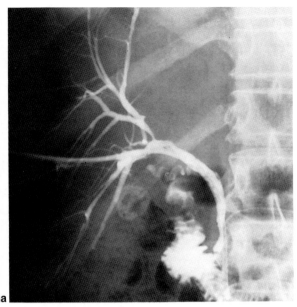
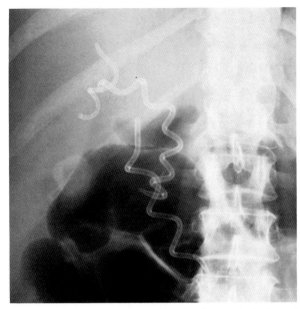

Fig. **7** **a Advanced cholangiocarcinoma with Bismuth type III** obstruction at the liver hilum. **b** Three spiral-shaped stents allowed adequate drainage of the obstructed intrahepatic radicles. (Courtesy of Dr. A. Adams, Hammersmith Hospital, London)

and placed through the papilla. A dislocation rate of 4% (8) to 6% and 40% (27) has been reported in the literature.

Adding ridges, pigtails, loops, hooks (32) collapsible mushrooms (65), screws (10), a spiral-shaped design for intrahepatic stenting (67) (Fig. **7**), flares or barbs (28, 56), or incorporating Hydrogel rings in the wall of the prosthesis (62), reduces the risk of displacement and illustrates the imaginative capacity of interventional radiologists.

Conclusion

Percutaneous placement of a biliary prosthesis is still an alternative to endoscopic insertion in the palliative management of malignant obstruction, carrying an acceptable complication rate in experienced hands. The combined peroral-percutaneous method minimizes trauma to the liver. Many patients who undergo an exclusive percutaneous transhepatic approach show obstruction at the liver hilum and are technically difficult to treat, requiring two or more tubes. Patient selection becomes critical, and overtreatment is a risk in patients with very limited survival. Large-bore prostheses have gained acceptance. Transpapillary positioning is still controversial. Obstruction of the stents is the major drawback, and has not yet been solved.

References

1. Ahlstrom H, Lorelius LE, Jacobson G. Inoperable biliary obstruction treated with percutaneously placed endoprosthesis. Acta Chir Scand 1986;152:301.

2. Alvarado R, Palmaz JC, Garcia OJ, Tio FO, Rees CR. Evaluation of polymer-coated balloon-expandable stents in bile ducts. Radiology 1989;170:975.
3. Bismuth H, Corlette MB. Intrahepatic cholangioenteric anastomosis in carcinoma of the hilus of the liver. Surg Gynecol Obstet 1975;140:170.
4. Blumgart LH, Benjamin IS, Hadjis NS, Bearzley R. Surgical approaches to cholangiocarcinoma at confluence of hepatic ducts. Lancet 1981;i:66.
5. Bonnel D, Ferrucci JT Jr, Mueller PR, Lacaine F. Comparison of surgical and radiological decompression in malignant biliary obstruction: a study using multivariate risk factor analysis. Radiology 1984;152:347.
6. Brown AS, Mueller PR, Ferrucci JT. Transhepatic removal of obstructed Carey-Coons biliary endoprosthesis. Radiology 1986;159:555.
7. Burcharth F. A new endoprosthesis for nonoperative intubation of the biliary tract in malignant obstructive jaundice. Surg Gynecol Obstet 1978;146:76.
8. Burcharth F. Nonsurgical drainage of the biliary tract. Semin Liver Dis 1982;2:75.
9. Burcharth F, Efsen F, Christiansen LA, Hancke S, Jensen LI, Nielson OU, Pedersen JH, Pedersen G. Nonsurgical internal biliary drainage by endoprosthesis. Surg Gynecol Obstet 1981;153:857.
10. Burcharth F, Jorgensen P, Nielsen H, Mygind T. A new transhepatic endoprosthesis to prevent dislodgement. Röfo 2096;145:214.
11. Carrasco CH, Wallace S, Charnsangavej C, Richli W, Wright KC, Fanning T, Gianturco C. Expandable biliary endoprosthesis: an experimental study. AJR 1985;145:1279.
12. Carrasco CH, Zornozua J, Bechtel WJ. Malignant biliary obstruction: complications of percutaneous biliary drainage. Radiology 1984;152:343.
13. Cohen H, Quinn M. Antegrade assistance for retrograde sphincterotomy using a new sphincterotome. Gastrointest Endosc 1986;32:405.
14. Coons HG. Self-expanding stainless steel biliary stents. Radiology 1989;170:979.
15. Coons HG, Carey PH. Large bore long biliary endoprosthesis (biliary stents) for improved drainage. Radiology 1983;148:89.
16. Cotton PB. Duodenoscopic placement of biliary prostheses to relieve malignant obstructive jaundice. Br J Surg 1982;69:501.

17. Cotton PB. Endoscopic methods for relief of malignant obstructive jaundice. World J Surg 1984;8:854.
18. Dick R, Platts A, Gilford J, Reddy K, Duncan IJ. The Carey-Coons percutaneous biliary endoprosthesis: a three-centre experience in 87 patients. Clin Radiol 1987;38:175.
19. Dondelinger R. L'aiguille de Menghini: un dispositif simple pour percer des orifices lateraux dans les cathéters de drainage biliaire percutané. J Radiol 1982;63:131.
20. Dondelinger RF, Kurdziel JC. Biliary and urinary prostheses derived from percutaneous biliary drainage catheters. J Belge Radiol 1984;67:37.
21. Dooley JS, Dick R, George P, Kirk PM, Hobbs KEF, Sherlock S. Percutaneous transhepatic endoprosthesis for bile duct obstruction. Gastroenterology 1984;86:905.
22. Ferrucci JT Jr, Mueller PR, Harbin WP. Percutaneous transhepatic biliary drainage. Radiology 1980;135:1.
23. Gibson RN. Biliary endoprosthesis blockage: clearance using a 22-gauge needle (technical note). AJR 1986;147:404.
24. Hansson JA, Hoevels J, Simert G, Tylén U, Vang J. Clinical aspects of nonsurgical percutaneous transhepatic bile drainage in obstructive lesions of the extrahepatic bile ducts. Ann Surg 1979;189:58.
25. Hellekant C, Jonsson K, Genell S. Percutaneopus internal drainage in obstructive jaundice. AJR 1980;134:661.
26. Herlan RK Jr, Ring EJ, Pogany AC, Jeffrey RB Jr. Biliary endoprostheses: insertion using a combined peroral-transhepatic method. Radiology 1984;150:828.
27. Hoevels J, Ihse I. Percutaneous transhepatic insertion of a permanent endoprosthesis in obstructive lesions of the extrahepatic bile ducts. Gastrointest Radiol 1979;4:367.
28. Hoevels J, Lunderquist A, Ihse I. Perkutane transhepatische Intubation der Gallengänge zur kombinierten inneren und äußeren Drainage bei extrahepatischer Cholestase. Röfo 1978;129:533.
29. Hoevels J, Lunderquist A, Owman I, Ihse I. A large-bore Teflon endoprosthesis with side holes for nonoperative decompression of the biliary tract in malignant obstructive jaundice. Gastrointest Radiol 1980;5:361.
30. Honickman SP, Mueller PR, Ferrucci JT Jr, Van Sonnenberg E, Kopans DB. Malpositioned biliary endoprosthesis: retrieval using a vascular balloon catheter. Radiology 1982;144:423.
31. Huibregtse K. Endoscopic biliary and pancreatic drainage. Stuttgart: Thieme, 1988:104.
32. Huibregtse K, Haverkamp HJ, Tytgat GN. Transpapillary positioning of a large 3.2 mm biliary endoprosthesis. Endoscopy 1981;13:217.
33. Iaccarino V, Niola R, Porta E. Silicone biliary stents. AJR 1987;148:741.
34. Irving D, Adams A, Dick R, Dondelinger RF, Lunderquist A, Roche A. Gianturco expandable metallic biliary stents: results of a European trial. Radiology 1989;172:390.
35. Kadir S, Kauffmann GW. Technical note: percutaneous transhepatic removal of biliary endoprosthesis using a snare. Cardiovasc Intervent Radiol 1988;11:39.
36. Lammer J, Neumayer K. Biliary drainage endoprostheses: experience with 201 placements. Radiology 1986;159:625.
37. Lammer J, Stoffler G, Petek WW, Hofler H. In vitro long-term perfusion of different materials for biliary endoprostheses. Invest Radiol 1986;21:329.
38. Launois B, Campion J, Brissot P, Gosselin M. Carcinoma of the hepatic hilus: surgical management and the case for resection. Ann Surg 1979;190:151.
39. Leung JWC, Emery R, Cotton PB, Russell RCG, Vallon AG, Mason RR. Management of malignant obstructive jaundice at the Middlesex Hospital. Br J Surg 1983;70:584.
40. Leyman P, Barthelme G, Kurdziel JC, Dondelinger RF. Combined percutaneous and endoscopic procedures in the biliary system. J Belge Radiol 1987;70:311.
41. Liguory C, Meduri B, Canard JM, Di Giulio E. Intubation endoscopique transpapillaire des obstructions malignes de la voie biliaire principale: premiers résultats avec les endoprothèses de gros calibre (3.2 mm). Gastroenterol Clin Biol 1983;7:125A.
42. Long WB, Schwarz W, Ring EJ. Endoscopic sphincterotomy assisted by antegrade catheterization. Gastrointest Endosc 1984;30:36.
43. Lunderquist A, Lunderquist M, Owman T. Guide wire for percutaneous transhepatic cholangiography. Radiology 1979;132:228.
44. McPherson GAD, Benjamin IS, Hodgson HJF, Bowley NB, Allison DJ, Blumgart LH. Preoperative percutaneous transhepatic biliary drainage: the results of a controlled trial. Br J Surg 1984;71:371.
45. Mendez G Jr, Russell E, Lepage JR, Guerra JJ, Posniak RA, Trefler M. Abandonment of endoprosthetic drainage technique in malignant biliary obstruction. AJR 1984;143:617.
46. Miskowiak J, Mygind T, Baden H, Burcharth F. Biliary endoprosthesis secured by a subcutaneous button to prevent dislocation. AJR 1982;139:1019.
47. Mueller PR, Ferrucci JT Jr, Teplick SK, Van Sonnenberg E, Haskin PH, Butch RJ, Papanicolaou N. Biliary stent endoprosthesis: analysis of complications in 113 patients. Radiology 1985;156:637.
48. Mueller PR, Ferrucci JT Jr, Van Sonnenberg E, Warshaw AL, Simeone JF, Cronan JJ, Neff CC, Butch RJ. Obstruction of the left hepatic duct: diagnosis and treatment by selective fine-needle cholangiography and percutaneous biliary drainage. Radiology 1982;145:297.
49. Mueller PR, Van Sonnenberg E, Ferrucci JT Jr. Percutaneous biliary drainage: technical and catheter-related problems in 200 procedures. AJR 1982;138:17.
50. Nilson U, Evander A, Ihse I, Lunderquist A, Mocibob A. Percutaneous transhepatic cholangiography and drainage: risks and complications. Acta Radiol 1983;24:433.
51. Norlander A, Kalin B, Sundblad R. Effect of percutaneous transhepatic drainage upon liver function and postoperative mortality. Surg Gynecol Obstet 1982;155:161.
52. Oleaga JA, Ring EJ, Freiman DB, McLean GK, Rosen RJ. Extension of neoplasm along the tract of a transhepatic tube. AJR 1980;135:841.
53. Owman T, Lunderquist A. Sling retraction for proximal placement of percutaneous transhepatic biliary endoprosthesis. Radiology 1983;146:228.
54. Palmaz JC, Burbige EJ. Removable biliary endoprosthesis. AJR 1983;140:812.
55. Passi RB, Rankin RM. The transhepatic approach to a failed endoscopic sphincterotomy. Gastrointest Endosc 1986;32:221.
56. Pereiras RV, Rheingold OJ, Hutson D, Mejia D, Viamonte M, Chiprut RO, Schiff ER. Relief of malignant obstructive jaundice by percutaneous insertion of a permanent prosthesis in the biliary tree. Ann Int Med 1978;89:589.
57. Rey JF, Maupetit P, Greff M. Experimental study of biliary endoprosthesis efficiency. Endoscopy 1985;17:145.
58. Ring EJ, Kerlan RK Jr. Interventional biliary radiology. AJR 1984;142:31.
59. Ring EJ, Olega JA, Freiman DB, Husted JW, Lunderquist A. Therapeutic applications of catheter cholangiography. Radiology 1978;128:333.
60. Ring EJ, Schwarz W, McLean GK, Freiman DB. A simple, indwelling biliary endoprosthesis made from common available catheter materials. AJR 1982;139:615.
61. Sammon JK, Teplick SK, Haskin PH. Insertion of a large-caliber biliary endoprosthesis via the T-tube tract (technical note). AJR 1986;147:164.
62. Silander T, Thor K. A "nondislodgeable" endoprosthesis for nonsurgical drainage of the biliary tract. Ann Surg 1985;201:323.
63. Soehendra N, Reynders-Frederix V. Palliative bile duct drainage: a new endoscopic method of introducing a transpapillary drain. Endoscopy 1980;12:8.
64. Tanaka M, Matsumoto S, Ikeda S, Miyazaki K, Yamauchi S. Endoscopic sphincterotomy in patients with difficult cannulation: use of an antegrade guide. Endoscopy 1986;18:87.
65. Teplick SK, Haskin PH, Goldstein RC, Goodman LR, Pavlides CA, Corvasce JM, Frank EB. A new biliary endoprosthesis. AJR 1983;141:799.
66. Trooskin SZ, Donetz AP, Harvey RA, Greco RS. Prevention of catheter sepsis by antibiotic bonding. Surgery 1985;97:547.
67. Yeung EYC, Adam A, Gibson RN, Benjamin IS, Allison DJ. Spiral-shaped biliary endoprosthesis: initial study. Radiology 1988;168:365.

Percutaneous Irradiation in the Bile Ducts

H. B. Nunnerley and J. Karani

Accurate preoperative diagnosis in patients with obstructive jaundice is now more frequent. This is because of the development of the newer radiologic techniques of US, CT and PTC with guided needle biopsy techniques. Consequently, cholangiocarcinoma involving the hepatic ducts is now diagnosed preoperatively with increasing frequency (10). This allows for consideration of the most appropriate therapy for the patient. Curative surgery may not be possible in a large number of patients. Palliative therapy to relieve jaundice either at laparotomy or percutaneously, is, therefore, necessary. This may then be combined with local radiotherapy using an iridium-192 wire. Our studies indicate that this technique is successful in palliating symptoms and results in improved survival (6).

Pathology and Etiology

Cholangiocarcinoma, first described by Klatskin (7), develops at a relatively young age, with one-third of patients presenting under the age of 50 years (14) and with a male predisposition. Sclerosing cholangitis and choledochal cysts have been recognized as predisposing factors. Cholangiocarcinoma has also been described in association with inflammatory bowel disease in the absence of preexisting sclerosing cholangitis or pericholangitis and has followed successful total colectomy for the primary bowel abnormality (14).

Histologically, the tumors are characterized by a marked scirrhous reaction with clumps of carcinoma cells surrounded by fibrous tissue, resulting in a neoplastic stricture. The tumors are slow growing and spread into the liver parenchyma with local invasion of the hepatic arteries and portal vein. It is this feature that limits surgical resectability. The tumor has to be distinguished from peripheral cholangiocarcinoma arising from small intrahepatic ductules. The tumors are distinct in their clinical presentation and course with the peripheral type only complicated by jaundice at a later stage, whereas in extrahepatic or hilar cholangiocarcinoma biliary obstruction is usually an early presenting feature. Rarely, a papilliferous growth may occur, expanding the hepatic ducts (13). Distant lymphatic or blood-borne metastatic spread is not a major feature, occurring in only 12% of patients at presentation (14).

Clinical Features

Patients generally present with features of biliary obstruction, with pruritus, pale stools, and dark urine. Accompanying features of weight loss, weakness, diarrhea, and anorexia may be present. Spontaneous fluctuations with anicteric periods may occur, and it is this factor that probably results in the long period from onset of symptoms to diagnosis, being of the order of 4 to 6 months (2, 14). Clinical signs of portal hypertension may be present if there has been preexisting liver disease or if there has been neoplastic involvement of the portal venous system.

Biochemical investigations confirm an obstructive picture with elevation of bilirubin and alkaline phosphatase concentrations predominantly, and this may be accompanied by hypoalbuminemia, particularly with prolonged jaundice.

Radiologic Investigation and Findings

US will confirm the presence of dilation of the intrahepatic biliary system and delineate the level of the obstruction. The site of the tumor may be demonstrable as an area of high reflectivity, its echocharacteristics reflecting the fibrous nature of the tumor.

CT may similarly map the extent of local parenchyma involvement, its relation to the portal vein, and assess the presence of lobe atrophy, an important feature if radical surgery is considered. Arterioportography will delineate any involvement of the hepatic arteries or portal vein, with encasement as the significant radiologic sign. The tumors are avascular, so other angiographic features of malignancy are not present generally.

PTC is the principal diagnostic technique. Both endoscopic and percutaneous cholangiography may be necessary in fully mapping the biliary system proximal and distal to the stricture. Dilated ducts and the site of the malignant stricture will be demonstrated in more than 90% of patients (14). Separate puncture of the ducts within the left and right lobes may be necessary to fill all the occluded biliary segments. In our experience, there are areas where confirmation of the diagnosis may be difficult. Firstly, in patients with long-standing sclerosing cholangitis the cholangiographic pattern of the concomitant neoplastic stricture may be indistinguishable from that of the multiple benign strictures of the preexisting disease. Solitary inflammatory strictures, although less common, may also produce similar appearance and highlights the necessity for histologic confirmation before treatment is instituted.

Metastatic nodal spread and local invasion from a gallbladder carcinoma are also diagnostic differentials, but these should be differentiated from cholangiocarcinoma by other imaging investigations.

Early tissue diagnosis may be a problem, for even at initial laparotomy the mass may be overlooked in 30 to 60% of patients (15). In the past some investigators have advocated that the diagnosis may have to be based on clinical and radiologic criteria alone (12). However, fine-needle aspiration may be diagnostic in more than 50% of patients (2). It is now our policy to perform fine-needle aspiration biopsy under US or fluoroscopic control after cholangiography. Cytologic assessment of brushings carried out percutaneously or endoscopically may provide an alternative method of obtaining a tissue diagnosis, but this is unproved as yet. Even with this approach, there will still be patients for whom histologic confirmation will only be obtained at surgery or autopsy.

Treatment

Despite the techniques for diagnosing cholangiocarcinoma and the low biologic activity of the tumor, the prognosis for these patients remains poor, with a survival of 2 months if untreated. The only chance of cure lies in radical hepatic resection or liver transplantation. Even with an aggressive surgical approach as advocated by Blumgart et al. (2) with staging by preoperative cholangiography and indirect portography, resection was contraindicated in up to 68% of patients. The cholangiographic and angiographic criteria precluding surgery are bilateral extension beyond the second order ducts or the presence of involvement of the main portal vein by tumor. A further 10 to 12% of patients will either be unfit for major radical hepatic resection or the tumor will be irresectable at laparotomy with preoperative staging underestimating the extent of the disease. This overall resectability rate of 10 to 12% is in accordance with other series (1, 5). Although hepatic resection is potentially curative, one-third of patients develop, and die from tumor recurrence within 2 years, and it is this factor that also limits the success of liver transplantation (3, 9). Excluding those patients for whom transplantation is considered appropriate, up to 80% of patients will require palliative therapy.

Biliary decompression alone, whether carried out at laparotomy or percutaneously, results in an improved survival of about 8.5 months (2, 8, 14). Operative cholangioenteric anastomosis or U-tube insertion may be associated with a mortality as high as 35% (8). Without treatment, death generally occurs within 3 months with development of recurrent cholangitis, sepsis and hepatic failure secondary to biliary obstruction.

The combination of biliary drainage with internal radiotherapy with iridium-192 wire has been used since 1978 as a palliative procedure. Internal biliary drainage with an exteriorized tube is established either at laparotomy with placement of a transhepatic tube or alternatively with percutaneous biliary drainage as the primary procedure with placement of a Ring-Lunderquist catheter (4, 11). In a recent series of 30 patients reported from King's College Hospital (6), 21 patients had undergone laparotomy as the initial procedure, but 14 of these patients required subsequent percutaneous drainage to achieve full decompression of other occluded major biliary segments.

Preparation and Placement of Iridium Wire

A 120 cm long 0.35 mm diameter angiographic guide wire is prepared by removing the central core and using this to advance a 5 cm length of nylon thread down the inside channel to the tip of the guide wire. This ensures that the tip of the guide wire remains flexible during insertion. The core is again removed and an appropriate length of iridium equivalent to the length of the tumor on the cholangiogram is prepared. This is designed to deliver a radiation dose between 4000 and 5000 cGy over about 48 hours at a point 0.5 cm from the wire. This is calculated using standard Paterson-Parkes tables. The length of iridium is then advanced to the level of the nylon stop with the flexible core and fixed in position (Figs. 1–5). Iridium-192 wire is marketed as a 3 mm-diameter flexible wire in 50 cm lengths by Amersham International. It consists of an active platinum alloy within a 0.1 mm platinum sheath. The platinum sheath shields all beta radiation. Consequently, the wire is virtually a pure gamma emitter with an energy level of 300 to 600 keV (mean, 400 keV).

The loaded guide wire is then positioned under fluoroscopic control through the exteriorized limb of the biliary tube so that the active iridium is within the main bulk of the tumor. Protective lead screens are placed around the patient during treatment, nursing and medical personnel being monitored with pocket dosimeters.

After irradiation, internal drainage is maintained with a Ring-Lunderquist catheter or alternatively an indwelling endoprosthesis. Those patients with exteriorized catheters are instructed on daily irrigation of the tube and returned to the hospital electively for replacement of the tube at about 3 monthly intervals, to prevent blockage by debris or tumor. This necessitates a 24-hour hospital admission and antibiotic course for the procedure.

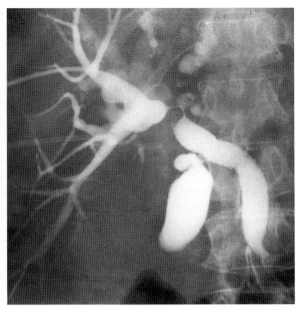

Fig. 1 **Cholangiogram demonstrating a tight stricture at the hilum** involving the right and left hepatic ducts. External biliary drainage has been established percutaneously

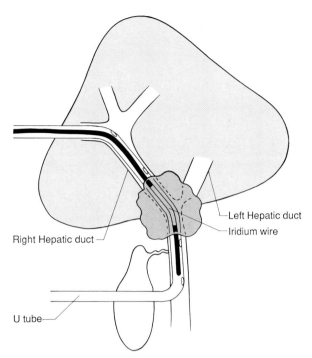

Fig. 4 **Technique for positioning loaded guide wire** within the tumor to deliver radiation

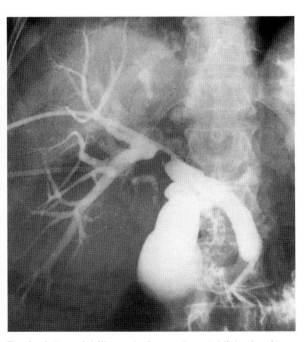

Fig. 2 **Internal biliary drainage** is established using a Ring-Lunderquist catheter following passage of a guide wire through the cholangiocarcinoma

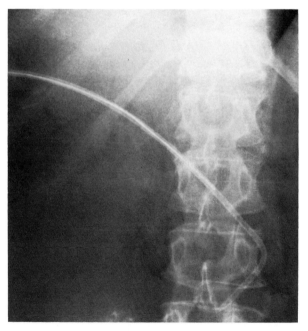

Fig. 5 **The active iridium wire** advanced to the level of the tumor and secured in position under screening control

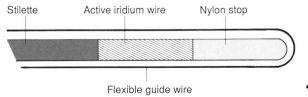

Fig. 3 **Loaded guide wire**

Results

This technique of after-loading interstitial radiotherapy provides a high dose of radiation to the area around the wire with rapid tail off beyond this area, thus limiting radiation damage to surrounding organs. Although improved survival has been reported in patients with transhepatic U tubes and external beam radiotherapy (13), this may be complicated by radiation damage to adjacent structures, with development of hemorrhagic gastritis, radiation hepatitis, and duodenal obstruction. It also requires long-term out-patient attendance. Complications related to this technique are those of placement of biliary tubes with septic cholangitis, the major problem arising in up to 40% of patients, but this can be limited and electively treated with antibiotic therapy. In our series (6) two patients have developed mucoceles of the gallbladder, secondary to cystic duct obstruction by the tumor and one of these patients required surgery because of duodenal obstruction 3 years after initial therapy. One patient developed a fistula to the small bowel, but at post-mortem this was shown to be due to tumor progression and not as a consequence of the radiation.

In a recent published analysis of this treatment (6) we have studied 30 patients with hilar cholangiocarcinoma whom we have followed over a 6-year period. There were 19 men and 11 women with a mean age of 51.9 years (range, 25 to 69). Of the 30 patients, 21 have survived for more than 1 year and five for more than 2 years. The overall mean survival was 16.8 months, which compares favorably with the small group of patients in whom radical surgery was performed and is certainly far better than cholangioenteric bypass surgery or percutaneous drainage alone, with a doubling of the mean survival rate. Of note is that at 6 years after presentation, the first patient treated in this series is alive and well with a histologically proved tumor, with another two patients still alive after 4 years. The mean survival in the patients who have died was 13.1 months (range, 1 to 42) and 23.2 months in the patients alive at the time of analysis. Although histologic confirmation of tumor was not obtained in all cases, the mean survival was 19.1 months in the selected group with positive histologic findings and 9.3 months in the seven patients without histologic confirmation. Nineteen patients died from effects of tumor progression

with further biliary obstruction. Autopsy examinations carried out in six of these patients showed evidence of extrahepatic tumor dissemination.

These figures would indicate that this combination of treatment results in effective palliation and improved survival for a relatively young group of patients for whom treatment options may be limited. It should be advocated as a further maneuver that may be instituted in those patients for whom hepatic surgery is not possible.

References

1. Akwari OE, Kelly KA. Surgical treatment of adenocarcinoma: location: junction of the right, left and common hepatic biliary ducts. Arch Surg 1979;114:22.
2. Blumgart LH, Benjamin IS, Hadjis NS, Beasley R. Surgical approaches to cholangiocarcinoma at confluence of hepatic ducts. Lancet 1984;i:66–70.
3. Calne RY. Liver transplantation for liver cancer. World J Surg 1982;6:76–80.
4. Hoevels J, Lunderquist A, Ihse K. Percutaneous transhepatic intubation of bile ducts for combined internal/external drainage in preoperative and palliative treatment of obstructive jaundice. Gastrointest Radiol 1978;3:23–31.
5. Incuye AA, Whelan TJ. Carcinoma of the extrahepatic biliary ducts: a 10 year experience in Hawaii. J Surg 1978;136:90.
6. Karani J, Fletcher M, Brinkley D, Dawson JL, Williams R, Nunnerley H. Internal biliary drainage and local radiotherapy with Iridium-192 wire in treatment of hilar cholangiocarcinoma. Clin Radiol 1985;36:603–606.
7. Klatskin G. Adenocarcinoma of the hepatic duct at its bifurcation within the porta hepatis: an unusual tumor with distinctive clinical and pathological features. Am J Med 1965;38:241–256.
8. Launois B, Campion JP, Brissot P, Gosselin M. Carcinoma of the hepatic hilus: surgical management and the case for resection. Ann Surg 1979;190:151–157.
9. MacDougall BRD, Williams R. Indications for and results of liver transplantation. In Calne RY, ed. Liver Surgery. Padua: Piccin, 1982: 187–194.
10. Malchow-Muller A, Matzen P, Bjerregaard B. Causes and characteristics of 500 consecutive cases of jaundice. Scand J Gastroenterol 1981;16:1–6.
11. Ring EJ, Husted JW, Oleaga JA. A multihole catheter for maintaining long term percutaneous antegrade biliary drainage. Radiology 1979;132:752–754.
12. Terblanche J, Saunder SJ, Louw JH. Prolonged palliation in carcinoma of the main hepatic duct junction. Surgery 1972;7:720–731.
13. Terblanche J, Saunder SJ, Louw JH. U-tube drainage in the palliative therapy of carcinoma of the main hepatic duct junction. Surg Clin North Am 1973;53:1245–1255.
14. Wheeler PG, Dawson JL, Nunnerley H, Brinkley D, Laws J. Newer techniques in the diagnosis and treatment of proximal bile duct carcinoma: an analysis of 41 consecutive patients. Q J Med 1981;50:247–259.
15. Whelton MS, Petrelli M, George P, Young WB, Sherlock S. Carcinoma at the junction of the main hepatic ducts. Q J Med 1969;38:211–230.

Percutaneous Management of Benign Disease in the Bile Ducts

R. F. Dondelinger and J. C. Kurdziel

Dilation of Benign Biliary Strictures

Indications

Benign strictures in the extrahepatic bile duct mainly result from surgical trauma during routine biliary surgery (13, 53, 111, 154, 155). Most patients presenting with a benign stenosis of the choledochus have been operated for biliary calculi (95%) (13, 53). The choledochus can be damaged when cholecystectomy has been rendered difficult, due to extensive inflammation extending from cholecystitis, to gallstones impacted in the gallbladder neck, to a too short cystic duct or to an aberrant course of the cystic artery or bile duct. The main bile duct can also be damaged during other surgical procedures, such as gastrectomy or duodenopancreatectomy. The mechanism of biliary stricture of the choledochus following surgery is explained by ischemia following dissection of the porta hepatis, attempts to control bleeding during operation, and surgical repair of choledochal damage which has occurred during a complicated operation (84, 103, 130, 154). When the main bile duct has been injured during surgery, immediate hepaticojejunostomy produces less secondary anastomotic stenoses than repair (72), but benign strictures (15–40%) also develop at the anastomotic site of a choledochoenterostomy (113, 154) (Fig. 1a), a choledochoduodenostomy, or on surgical drains. These strictures are also often treated surgically at a first attempt (42, 111, 119, 129), but a recurrence rate of 14–22% is observed (111, 113, 156). Patients referred for radiological management are those who have already undergone multiple operations. More rarely encountered causes of

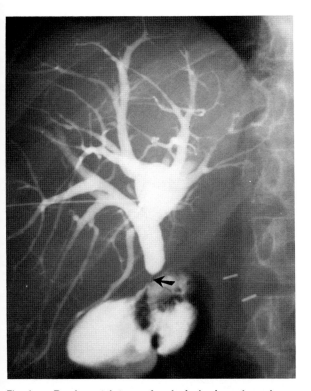

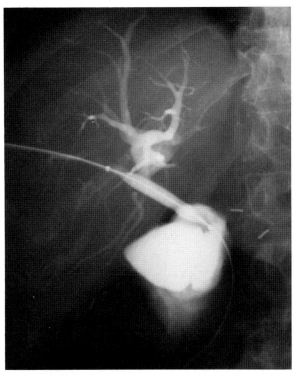

Fig. 1 **a Benign stricture of a choledochoenterostomy performed during a technically difficult cholecystectomy.** Repeated episodes of cholangitis. PTC evidences a tight stenosis at the anastomosis (arrow) and moderately enlarged intrahepatic bile ducts

b Transhepatic balloon dilation (8 mm) of the anastomotic stricture

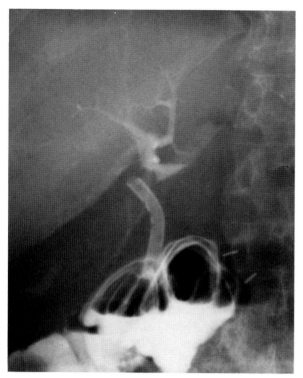

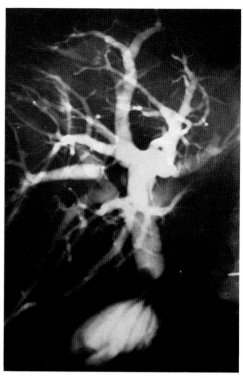

Fig. **1 c**   **A short 16 Fr endoprosthesis is left in place** at the site of the stricture for permanent calibration

d Two years later, the patient experienced episodes of cholangitis again. The 16 Fr biliary stent has migrated into the jejunum. A tight anastomotic stricture is evidenced, with a small translucent gallstone above the stenosis

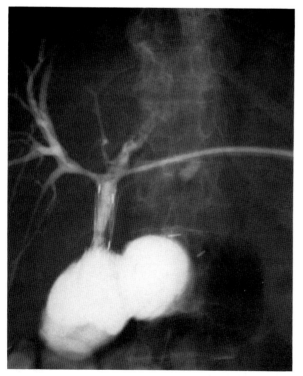

e The benign stricture was dilated again through a left transhepatic approach, the stone was pushed into the jejunum through the anastomosis, and expandable metallic Gianturco stents (1 cm) were placed at the anastomotic junction

benign biliary strictures include blunt or penetrating abdominal trauma, infection, sclerosing cholangitis, postirradiation fibrosis, and congenital strictures. The intrahepatic bile ducts can be affected as well, especially by the spread of inflammatory disease, and strictures can follow erosion of the intrahepatic bile ducts by gallstones. Two entities are mainly responsible for strictures of the intrahepatic bile ducts: sclerosing cholangitis, which is in fact a pseudo-benign disease during the course of which multifocal strictures develop in the intra- and extrahepatic bile ducts, and oriental cholangiohepatitis. Although diffuse stenotic lesions are present in both diseases, patients may exhibit one or several high-grade strictures, which significantly reduce bile flow. These strictures can be selected for percutaneous treatment (91, 102). Strictures of the main bile duct resulting from chronic pancreatitis or dilation of the papilla (25) are considered only in particular circumstances (99).

A stricture of the bile ducts is strongly suspected if the patient develops progressive obstructive jaundice, cholangitis or sepsis and pain in the right upper quadrant of the abdomen, in the early phase after surgery. The presence of a surgical tube, or of a biliary-cutaneous fistula, renders the patient asymptomatic (161).

When the stricture stays for a long time, liver tests are abnormal and progressive liver failure, biliary cirrhosis, and portal hypertension develop (14%) (10).

It is therefore important to treat these patients rapidly before liver function is impaired. If left untreated, operative mortality during late surgical correction rises to 27%, compared to an operative mortality of 3.2% if a stricture repair alone is performed in normal conditions (10). A history of bile fistula, multiple operations, postoperative abscess or infected wound or drain, favors the formation of biliary strictures. Longstanding biliary obstruction is followed by lobar or segmental atrophy of the liver parenchyma, itself followed by compensatory hypertrophy, making surgical repair of a stricture at the liver hilum difficult due to marked anatomical changes.

Technique

Burhenne (15) reported the first dilation of a benign biliary stricture through the T-tube, and Molnar (97) gave the first transhepatic description. The basic principle of percutaneous treatment is to break the fibrous scar and to keep the bile duct open in the long term. A percutaneous biliary drainage should be established first. Surgical stents, if present, will be removed. A malignant stenosis should be excluded by all means, including imaging, bile cytology, biopsy and transhepatic cholangioscopy (51). Bile should be cultured, and infection within the biliary system must be treated with intravenous antibiotics before other manipulations through the percutaneous drainage catheter are planned. Percutaneous access to the biliary system may be difficult in patients with longstanding biliary obstruction, when the liver is atrophic, the bile ducts are crowded around the liver hilum, and when the patient shows already uncorrectable coagulation defects due to liver failure. Previous surgical fixation of the jejunal Roux-en-Y limb of choledochojejunostomy or hepaticojejunostomy to the abdominal wall eliminates the need for a transhepatic approach to the bile ducts (26, 63). Radiological procedures are possible by percutaneous puncture of the afferent jejunal limb. In the same way, if a T-tube or U-tube is in place, the procedure can be performed through this approach (15, 64, 99, 160). The surgical tubes can be removed once a secure percutaneous access to the bile ducts has been established. Percutaneous dilation of a stricture should be considered after several days of drainage and extraction of residual gallstones. Culture of bile has to be sterile when dilation is performed. As dilation of the bile ducts is always particularly painful, adequate sedation is necessary, including general anesthesia in pain-sensitive patients.

Some tight strictures cannot be traversed with a balloon catheter (99). The stricture can be recanalized with a stiff needle, creating a new channel allowing bile flow (54), or with an everting balloon catheter (4). Standard angioplasty balloon catheters are mainly used for dilation of benign biliary strictures (47, 86, 87, 89, 91, 97, 102, 120, 137, 162) (Fig. **1b**). Usually the diameter of the balloon chosen for a stricture located above the bifurcation is 5–8 mm, in the common bile duct 6–10 mm. As in transluminal angioplasty, comparison with the diameter of adjacent normal segments of bile ducts is advisible. Variable dilation techniques are used, either 3–5 inflations of the balloon at low (4–6 atm) or high pressure (10 to 20 atm), varying from 30 s to several minutes, until no residual deformity is seen on the balloon during inflation. Prolonged dilation with inflation of the balloon for 8–12 h has been advocated (32, 120, 122). Precise positioning of the balloon catheter at the level of the stricture is achieved when a 22 G needle has been introduced percutaneously during opacification and serves as a marker. When the percutaneous catheter can be mobilized through the area of stricture with the inflated balloon, a good result is achieved. The effect of dilation can be checked by manometry during perfusion of bile ducts with variable flow (147). After dilation is completed, a percutaneous biliary drainage catheter is replaced for permanent access, calibration of the stenosis and repeat dilation (86, 97, 99, 120, 160, 161, 162). Large catheters should be used (12–16 Fr), which can remain in place for a long period of time, although the value of catheter calibration is not generally admitted (63, 111, 113, 118, 120). In order to avoid a protruding percutaneous catheter, an internal biliary stent can be placed (Fig. **1c**). This stent will calibrate the stenosed bile duct, and maintains the lumen open after dilation. The indwelling stent can be left in place for a long period, varying from 3–12 months; stenting should cover a longer period (1 year) for treatment of a primary stricture than after dilation of a stricture of a bilioenteric anastomosis (6 months) (120). Indwelling stents, may, however migrate, occlude or become a source of infection (Fig. **1d**). For treatment of strictures at the bifurcation, bilateral transhepatic dilation and stents are necessary (91). Expandable metallic stents have been used (Figs. **1e, 2d**). These short stents can be difficult to position correctly at a stenosed hepaticojejunostomy. The permanent force of expansion of the prosthesis should guarantee opening of the strictured zone. Retrievable expandable stents which could stay in place for days or weeks are under investigation.

Strictures of biliary enteric anastomoses can also be treated by percutaneous electrocautery (55) using a 5 Fr papillotome.

Results

Surgical repair of benign biliary strictures has a success rate of near 80% (111, 113, 119, 155), but carries a morbidity rate of 25% and a mortality rate of 4–13% (42, 147, 153), with a mean of 8.3% (152) according, to the variable impairment of liver function described above. Results of percutaneous treatment are variable, due to the lack of therapeutic standardization and the variable selection of patients. Patients retained for percutaneous treatment have often had one or more surgical attempts at repair, and may show bad prognostic criteria such as cirrhosis, portal hypertension, liver failure, and lobar atrophy. It seems that the best results are obtained after treatment of biliary enteric anastomoses (63, 89, 104, 134, 150, 160, 162), even after a follow-up of 5 years (89). A longer interval between initial trauma and correction of stricture favors optimal results (161). Better results are also achieved in short diaphragmatic strictures compared to longer, eccentric stenoses. In general, in primary ductal strictures, a success rate of 67–87% (120, 161) is obtained, and in biliary enteric anastomoses, a sucess rate of 72–86% is observed (99, 120, 161), but results are difficult to assess, as most reports contain only a restricted number of patients (86, 89, 120, 137, 162) and only a few studies contain a sufficiently large number of patients with an extended follow-up period (102, 161). In sclerosing cholangitis, a re-stricture rate of 42% (102) to 58% (99) is reported. Strictures caused by chronic pancreatitis do not respond well to balloon dilation alone, but are more amenable to radiological treatment with an expandable prosthesis (Fig. 2). No significant complication should occur during dilatation itself once the percutaneous biliary drainage is established and the bile is sterile.

Management of Biliary Fistulae

Indications

Extravasation of bile may occur through a leak situated in the intrahepatic bile ducts, the choledochus or in the gallbladder. A biliary fistula is present when continuous loss of bile lasts for days or weeks. A temporary bile leakage of a small amount around the liver usually follows percutaneous manipulations of the bile ducts, but is rarely clinically significant (73). Permanent extravasation of bile creates either an external biliary-cutaneous fistula, or bile accumulates in the liver parenchyma, under the capsule, in the perihepatic spaces, in the pleura or spreads through the peritoneal cavity (70). When bile collects, a biloma is formed (73, 136, 151). Collected bile has a high risk of abscess formation. As long as the collection of bile remains in communication with the bile ducts through a persistent leak, its volume will increase, and recurrence of the collection is common, despite percutaneous aspiration or drainage. Obstruction of the bile ducts is often responsible for a persistent leakage of bile. A rise in pressure in the biliary system may be due to the presence of gallstones, malignant or benign strictures, chronic pancreatitis, accidental ligation or transection of the choledochus, or a clogged endoprosthesis. Even a small leakage may be responsible for the formation of a biloma, which in return compresses the bile duct and increases the leakage (116). Many causes are responsible for bile leakage itself: traumatic laceration, which often occurs at the level of the liver hilum, peroperative damage, or laceration occurring during percutaneous transhepatic cholangiography, postoperative bile leakage following early removal or drop of a T-tube, external or intrahepatic fistula following resection of liver parenchyma, erosion of intrahepatic bile ducts by an abscess or hematoma, and inadequate healing of a biliary-enteric anastomosis (70, 116, 136, 162). Anomalous bile ducts draining a part of the right lobe of the liver directly into the cystic duct or the choledochus are exposed to accidental ligation or injury during cholecystectomy if they are not recognized before or during surgery (135). A poor general condition and hypoalbuminea favor postoperative bile leakage. The resulting external biliary-cutaneous fistula may be well tolerated for a long time when loss of bile remains moderate. Internal bile leakage, however, may induce chronic bile peritonitis (136), or acute signs suggestive of abdominal abscess, cholangitis or general sepsis. Patients may become rapidly critically ill, half of them are jaundiced, and a metabolic acidosis may follow permanent bile leakage in the most debilitated patients (70). Treatment is difficult, as surgery carries a significant number of potential complications due to the patients' bad general condition, infection, technical difficulties and intricate problems.

Technique

Precise radiological demonstration of the site of bile leakage is necessary for efficient treatment. Cholescintigraphy and US are able to disclose bile leakage (157), but the biliary system has to be entirely opacified by the retrograde or percutaneous transhepatic approach (Fig. 3a, b). The basic principle of conservative treatment of bile fistulae is to transform an uncontrolled fistulous tract in a controlled catheter tract, or to favor bile diversion away from the leakage point by bridging the point of leakage with a catheter and favoring healing (Fig. 3c). Endoscopic retrograde opacification of the bile ducts may be performed first in order to demonstrate the point of leakage and to evidence the cause of the underlying biliary obstruction. A stent bridging the fistula may also be introduced endoscopically (123). Percutaneous transhepatic cholangiography and drainage (68,

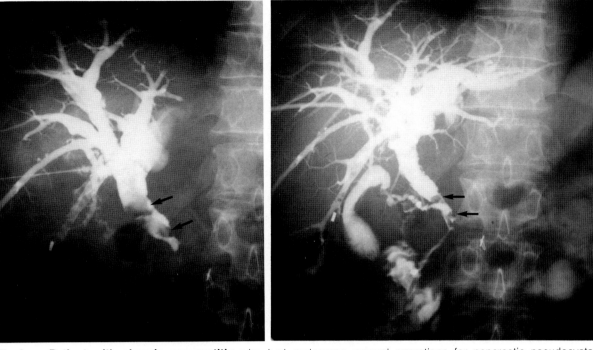

Fig. **2** **a Patient with chronic pancreatitis** who had undergone several operations for pancreatic pseudocysts, presenting with obstructive jaundice and cholangitis. PTC confirms compression of the choledochus by pancreatitis and several gallstones in the dilated choledochus (arrows)
b Transhepatic infusion of MTBE in the choledochus reduces significantly the size of the gallstones (arrows) after one session of treatment (100 ml MTBE, 1 h); narrowing of the distal choledochus by pancreatic compression is evidenced

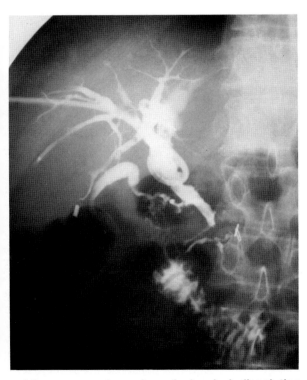

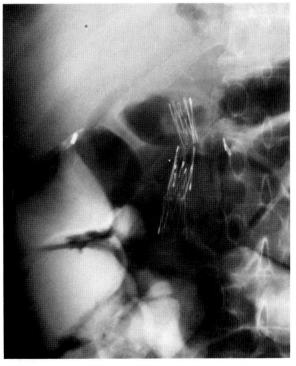

c After a second session of chemical dissolution (100 ml MTBE, 1 h), complete resolution of the choledochal stones is achieved

d Three expandable metallic Gianturco stents are placed in the narrowed distal choledochus. Good expansion of the biliary stents is shown on the control radiograph. The patient has been free of symptoms since 16 months

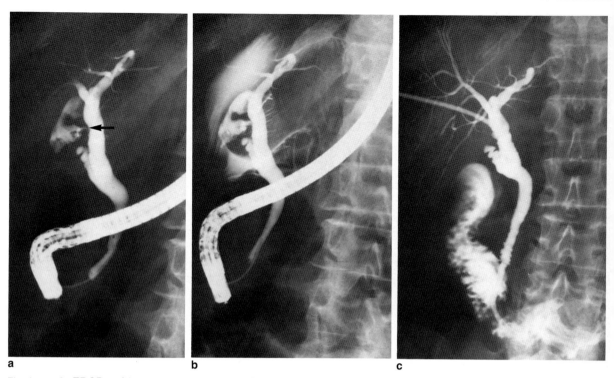

a   b   c

Fig. 3 **a, b ERCP evidences a biliary leak from the choledochus** (arrow) resulting from trauma during cholecystectomy
c After 3 weeks of percutaneous transhepatic biliary drainage with an 8 Fr catheter, healing of the biliary fistula is
achieved

57, 162) remains a diagnostic alternative, but is technically more difficult, since the intrahepatic bile
ducts are not, or are only moderately, dilated in
many cases. The transhepatic route is the preferred
modality if leakage is situated in the intrahepatic bile
ducts. A T-tube tract or a biliary-cutaneous sinus can
also be recatheterized and serve for subsequent
introduction of a biliary drainage catheter (Fig. **4**). A
coexisting obstruction of the bile ducts can be treated
on the same occasion through the transhepatic catheter by dilation of a benign stricture, or dissolution or
extraction of residual gallstones. When an internal
duodenal biliary drainage catheter has been placed,
combined internal and external drainage should be
maintained in order to avoid any rise of pressure in
the biliary system. During a long drainage period,
output of bile must be compensated for (70). Side-
holes in the drainage catheter located at the site of
the bile leakage are not relevant. In some patients
with malignant disease, an endoprosthesis bridging
the leakage point can be inserted for definitive treatment of the fistula and the underlying malignant
tumoral obstruction. In patients with benign disease,
catheter bile drainage has to be continued until closure of the leakage has been documented radiographically. The mean duration of drainage before
closure of a bile leakage is 3–4 weeks (70). Control

opacifications should be performed with care, avoiding any rise of pressure in the biliary system or
massive extravasation of contrast medium. Surgery
can be completely avoided when treatment of the
fistula and its eventual cause have been successfully
achieved.

Fig. **4   a Opacification through the T-drain** shows the ▶
extracholedochal position of its tip, bile drainage through
the surgical subhepatic drain, and a 10 mm residual gallstone (arrow) in the distal choledochus
**b The choledochus is catheterized through the
T-tube,** with two guide wires: one is left in the duodenum
for permanent access, the other remains in the
choledochus and allows introduction of a 6 Fr catheter and
Dormia baskets
**c The gallstone (arrow) is trapped in the Dormia bas-
ket** (arrow) before extraction through the T-tube sinus tract
d An 8 Fr biliary drainage catheter is kept in place for
several days. Control opacification shows no residual
choledochal stone

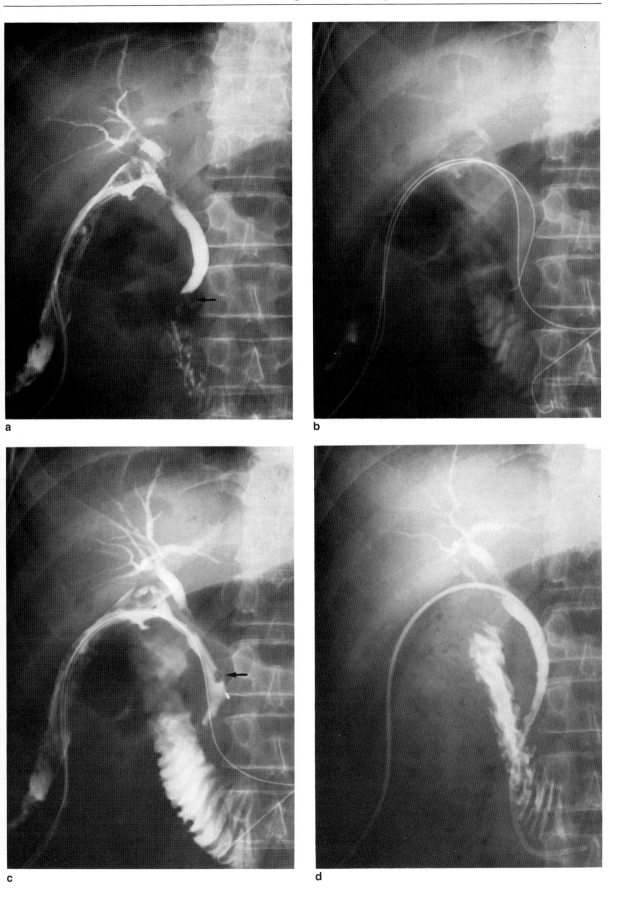

a

b

c

d

Results

Surgical repair of a biliary fistula carries a success rate of 60–90% (38), but also a complication rate of 25% and a mortality rate of 13% (153) or 50–75% if acute obstructive cholangitis is present (11, 37, 106). Results of non-surgical percutaneous management of biliary fistulae are scant in the literature, as most of the patients present with other underlying problems such as benign strictures or residual stones or intra- or perihepatic abscess or biloma (68, 70, 73, 116). Usually, a simple biliary leak closes by catheter drainage in almost all cases (107, 162). In situations with variable complexity, the success rate in healing the bile fistula depends on the underlying disease and on the possibilities of simple percutaneous management.

Residual Gallstones

Percutaneous Manipulation through the T-Tube Tract

Indications

Residual gallstones in the main bile duct following cholecystectomy may occur in 1.4% (131) to 4% (124, 127) of patients. An incidence as high as 8% (131) has been reported. Routine preoperative imaging of the bile ducts, peroperative cholangiography, choledochal manometry and choledocoscopy during cholecystectomy, should reduce the incidence of residual choledochal stones to a minimum. The diagnosis of retained stones is established during the postoperative period by opacification of the surgically placed T-tube. Reoperation on the extrahepatic bile ducts for residual gallstones carries a higher morbidity and mortality than cholecystectomy, demanding a simple non-surgical alternative of extraction of residual calculi.

Technique

Mondet reported percutaneous extraction of choledochal stones though the T-tube tract (98). Mazariello (92, 93, 95) and other authors (24, 80) reported extraction with a rigid forceps following dilation of the T-tube tract. The forceps has different curves for variable choledochal configurations. Its jaws open in the bile duct without increase of the diameter of the forceps in the sinus tract. Occasional reports on non-surgical removal of residual gallstones through the T-tube have been published (74, 83).

Percutaneous extraction of residual gallstones with Dormia baskets, which are routinely used in the ureter, has occasionally been reported (41, 48, 76, 78, 159). Bean (7, 8) described a procedure protocol using preshaped angiographic catheters and tip-deflecting guide wires. Burhenne (14, 16, 17, 19, 21, 22) defined the principles of the technique under fluoroscopy using a steerable catheter and special Dormia baskets.

The diagnosis of residual choledochal gallstones is established by opacification through the T-tube using diluted contrast medium in order to detect calculi of a reduced diameter (Fig. **4a**). When a single stone is present and the procedure is believed to be simple and rapid, prophylactic antibiotherapy is not necessary, but may become very important in other, more complicated, situations. The patient can remain during the procedure in a semi-erect position, which helps to differentiate air bubbles from stones in the choledochus, prevents their upward migration, and facilitates disimpaction of intrahepatic stones. Most often, non-calcified stones are present. Precise documentation of the number, size and shape of the gallstones is mandatory. The T-tube is catheterized with a flexible guide wire, which is pushed through the papilla rather than placed in the intrahepatic bile ducts, where it may slip out during the procedure. The T-tube is removed. Maturing of the T-tube over several weeks is not indispensable in performing the procedure (33). A Fr 12 or Fr 14 sheath is placed over the guide wire through the sinus tract, and the end of the sheath is positioned near the entry to the choledochus. The sinus tract can be dilated with rigid dilators or balloon catheters.

A second guide wire is inserted through the sheath in the choledochus, allowing introduction of a 6 Fr catheter with either a straight or a curved tip (Fig. **4b**). Dormia baskets of different shapes and sizes for varying sizes of calculi are manipulated through the 6 Fr catheter (Fig. **4c**). The surgically placed T-tube should come out of the right side of the choledochus and leave the skin under the liver in as straight a course as possible. The course of the T-tube may deviate due to anatomical changes, particularly hepatomegaly. A right lateral position of the T-tube allows optimal fluoroscopy control in a frontal view, and limits irradiation to the hands of the operator. When the T-drain comes out of the anterior wall of the abdomen, fluoroscopy control is less easy, and irradiation to the operator's hands is increased. The Dormia basket is selected according to the size of the calculus to be extracted. It should be larger than the stone to be extracted. The basket is moved up and down in the choledochus and rotated. As soon as the calculus is caught in the basket, the basket is closed by pulling it against the tip of the catheter. The catheter and the Dormia basket with the trapped calculus are retrieved percutaneously through the sinus tract. When multiple stones or severe angulation of the choledochus are present, opening of the Dormia basket can become difficult. Efforts should be made to advance the catheter beyond the most distal stone. Careful manipulation avoids the calculus slipping out of the basket when leaving the choledochus. When the diameter of the stone is superior to the caliber of the T-tube, the entry to the choledochus and the sinus tract should be dilated before extraction. Repeated advancement of the Dormia basket through the papilla should be performed with extreme caution, as the mucosa of the papilla can be trapped in the basket, and removal of the basket becomes traumatic or even impossible. Calculi of less than 5 mm, or fragments resulting from mechanical lithotripsy, are eventually pushed through the papilla when caught in the basket (21, 30). Gallstones with a diameter from 5–10 mm and more are extracted, and pushing through the papilla without previous sphincterotomy or balloon dilation is not attempted. Suction of stone fragments can be performed (81). Cholesterolic stones are soft, and can be fragmented when compressed in the basket or during removal. When the stone is crushed, a percutaneous dilation of the papilla with a 10 mm balloon catheter can be performed. Flushing the choledochus with saline allows antegrade passage of stone fragments. When the catheter with the Dormia basket has been withdrawn, repeat access to the choledochus is achieved over the permanent intraduodenal guide wire. The introducer sheath is replaced over the duodenal guide wire, and another guide wire, together with the catheter, is again inserted in the choledochus through the sheath, allowing reintroduction of Dormia baskets through the catheter.

When gallstones are flushed back during manipulation at the hilar bifurcation or in the intrahepatic bile ducts, the guide wire and the catheter are directed upwards, and intrahepatic stones are either extracted with baskets or pulled back in the choledochus with a balloon catheter. This is usually easy to perform. When stone extraction becomes difficult, or causes too much discomfort to the patient, or when the procedure becomes too long when multiple stones are present, or bleeding occurs, a large 12–16 Fr biliary drainage catheter is left in place, with the tip in a transpapillary position, and a second session is scheduled. A T-tube can also be replaced, with each limb passing over a separate guide wire (61). The transpapillary catheter widens the papilla and allows rapid passage of small stone fragments during the next session (Fig. **4d**).

Results

Percutaneous extraction of retained choledochal gallstones through the T-tube is particularly rewarding, due to the relative simplicity and high success rate of the procedure. Radiographic clearing of the bile ducts is achieved with the technique described by Burhenne in 78–99% of patients (22, 33, 44, 50, 58). The use of non-steerable, preshaped angiographic catheters assured a success rate of 75% (7, 8). Maz-

zariello, using rigid forceps, obtained a similar success rate to the use of a steerable catheter and baskets (92, 95).

Complications

Complications following percutaneous extraction of residual choledochal gallstones through the T-tube are rare, accounting for a morbidity rate of 4–6% (20, 22, 50). Discomfort and pain during the procedure vary with the number and the size of stones, with the degree of complication, and with the length of the procedure. The main complications (0.5–1.5%) (20, 22) include fever, episodes of cholangitis or pancreatitis, vasovagal reactions, nausea, vomiting, and formation of a subhepatic biloma. False passage of the guide wire and catheter and rupture of the T-drain are usually only minor incidents. Perforation of the sinus tract is without significant consequences (20), and only rarely results in bile peritonitis (50). Hemorrhage is avoided when manipulations are performed through a maturated sinus tract. Pancreatitis seems to be the most significant complication, as it resulted in one reported death (114).

Pancreatitis is due to intense manipulation of the papilla and formation of edema, or to massive reflux of the contrast medium into the pancreatic duct during attempts to flush large stones. Perforation of the duodenal wall with the guide wire or the Dormia basket is another potential complication.

Diarrhea may follow massive injection of contrast medium in the bile ducts.

Percutaneous Transhepatic Manipulation

Indications

When a surgical tube is not present to give immediate access to the bile ducts, endoscopic sphincterotomy and extraction is considered the primary treatment for residual choledochal gallstones before percutaneous manipulation is attempted. Endoscopic extraction of choledochal stones is successful in 96–99%, as shown here in the chapter by Cremer above. The percutaneous transhepatic approach is valuable when ERCP has failed (30) due to technical difficulties, previous surgery with no access to the papilla or the extrahepatic bile duct, or due to a tight stenosis which prevents catheterization of the extrahepatic bile duct above the stricture and makes transpapillary extraction of gallstones impossible. Retained stones have to be treated during, or even before, balloon dilation of a benign biliary stricture when infection is present, and always prior to the insertion of an endoprosthesis. When the percutaneous transhepatic route has been chosen for these treatments, residual stones can be managed by the same approach. Intrahepatic gallstones in combina-

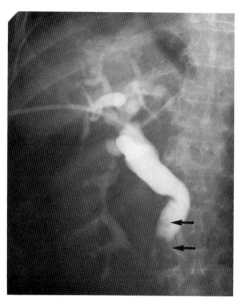

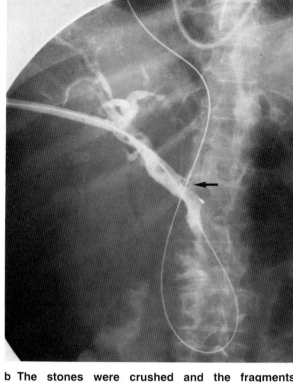

Fig. 5 a Patient presenting with obstructive jaundice and cholangitis. ERCP failed due to intrathoracic hernia of the stomach. PTC evidenced two radiolucent gallstones (arrows) in the distal choledochus. Local transhepatic infusion of MTBE failed

b The stones were crushed and the fragments extracted with Dormia baskets through the transhepatic approach. Notice an 18 Fr transhepatic working sheath, a guide wire kept in the duodenum (stomach situated in the thorax) and a stone fragment (arrow) caught in the Dormia basket

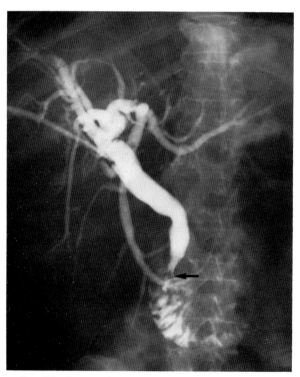

c A residual stone fragment (arrow) is flushed through the papilla

tion with oriental cholangiohepatitis represent a bad indication for endoscopic management, due to the location and number of the stones (71, 109, 146). After failure of gallstone extraction through the T-tube, or when the T-tube has fallen out and access to the bile duct cannot be re-established through the sinus tract, the percutaneous transhepatic approach still represents an alternative to endoscopy. Some patients refuse repeat ERCP and feel the transhepatic approach to be less uncomfortable.

Technique

However, the transhepatic access limits the possibilities of percutaneous extraction of gallstones. As with the procedure performed through the T-tube, small calculi with a diameter of up to 5 mm are readily evacuated through the papilla, with or without previous balloon dilation of the sphincter. Intravenous injection of glucagon, or intracholedochal injection of 1% lidocaine, facilitate relaxation of the sphincter and passage of calculi. Antegrade dilation of the papilla (23, 25) (Fig. **6d**), and even sphincterotomy, can be performed by an antegrade approach, even through the cystic duct, when percutaneous access to the gallbladder is possible (90). Larger calculi of more than 1 cm in diameter pass easily through a biliary-enteric anastomosis after balloon dilation, but generally, transhepatic extraction of stones through the liver parenchyma is traumatic, and restricted by the diameter of the transhepatic catheter or sheath. Transhepatic removal of gall-stones is documented through the literature only in a few reports (43, 56, 59). Permanent access to the bile ducts during the procedure has to be preserved either by placement of an introducer sheath or by leaving a guide wire in the duodenum or in the intrahepatic bile ducts (Fig. **5a, b**). Placing a sheath through the liver parenchyma lowers the risk of catheter bending,

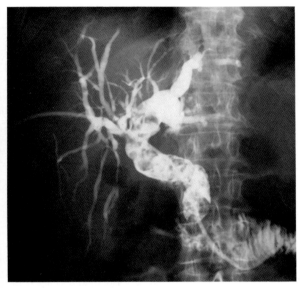

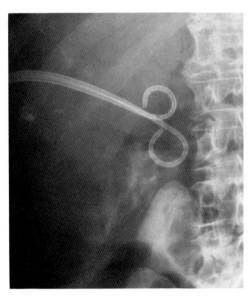

Fig. **6a–e** **a Multiple choledochal stones** following cholecystectomy performed 10 years before are confirmed by PTC and PBD. ERCP failed

b Two pigtail catheters are inserted percutaneously in the proximal choledochus for dissolution with MTBE. No significant effect was obtained

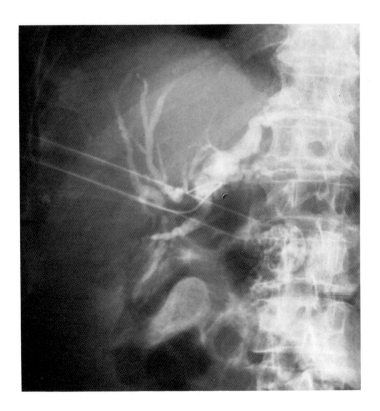

c Stones are extracted through a 30 Fr transhepatic sheath with flexible forceps and endoscopic control over several sessions

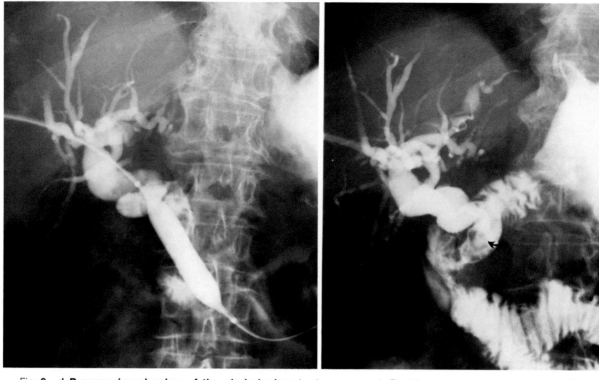

Fig. **6   d Progressive clearing of the choledochus** is demonstrated. Residual stones (arrow) remain in the lower choledochus. Balloon dilation (12 mm) of the papilla is performed, allowing transpapillary flushing of the residual stones

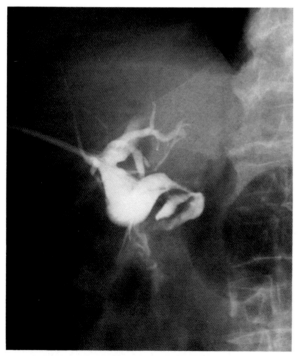

e Complete clearing of the bile ducts is achieved at the conclusion of treatment

is more comfortable for the patient during catheter exchange, and allows contrast medium injection during the procedure when a one-way flow valve is present (30). A working sheath of up to 30 Fr (Fig. **6c**) as used for percutaneous extraction of renal stones can be placed through the liver parenchyma after previous dilation of the tract and allows transhepatic extraction of large 1 cm stones. Strong mechanical lithotriptors, as used endoscopically, can be easily introduced transhepatically to crush hard, resistant stones (35). The instruments are more easily manipulated through the transhepatic approach than through the sharply angulated T-tube tract. Direct vision of the biliary system is achieved by the introduction of flexible endoscopes (27). An angiographic catheter can be introduced into the bile ducts to flush out small and multiple calculi or stone fragments, which flow back through the sheath. In order to obtain a straight access to the biliary system, a percutaneous approach to the right lobe of the liver is advocated. Residual stones may be trapped in a long cystic remnant duct, or in a choledochal diverticulum. Fogarty balloons (14, 69, 132), occlusion balloon catheters (96), and angioplasty balloon catheters (24, 40) can be used through the T-tube tract (96) and transhepatically, to push stones through the papilla, to disimpact stones in the papilla, to calibrate the papilla, and to extract stones from the intrahepatic bile ducts by pulling the catheter with the inflated balloon.

Two balloon catheters can be used to dislodge and fragment retained stones (3). The cystic duct may be catheterized itself percutaneously and stones can be flushed out or pushed in to the choledochus. Extraction of gallstones with a Dormia basket can be difficult when gallstones are fixed in a sharply angulated segment of the choledochus. In order to minimize trauma caused to the choledochus, papilla and duodenum, a basket with a flexible-tipped guide can be used (28, 30). When multiple stones are present, several sessions of extraction are necessary as with manipulations through a T-tube. The procedure must be performed in several steps, and may last as long as one month, with a mean of 10 days (30) (Fig. **6**). A large sheath (30 Fr) can be reintroduced each time. During the interval, a biliary drainage catheter is left in place, and adequate bile drainage is preserved, preventing cholangitis, edema of the papilla, and pancreatitis (30). Flushing the bile ducts with saline or other substances should be performed with caution in the intrahepatic bile ducts (Fig. **5c**). Pressure should not rise beyond 30 cm of water, in order to prevent bacteremia and septic shock. Once a secure transhepatic access to the bile ducts has been achieved without significant complications (pleural effusion, intrahepatic, perihepatic or subcapsular collection, hemobilia, infection), repeat access with repeat dilation of the liver parenchyma is possible, and reintroduction of a large sheath does not add to the complications by repetition of the procedure. When hemobilia is present, during the initial approach, further manipulation should be delayed, and a drainage catheter kept in place for several days. The large sheath should be placed in the proximal part of the common bile duct, forcing calculi reflux in the sheath during flushing. Intrahepatic stones are difficult to treat, and often necessitate a bilateral transhepatic access. Distal retrograde catheterization of the left intrahepatic bile ducts is easier to perform from the right transhepatic approach with a tip deflector than the reverse.

Results

There are no consistent figures on the success rate of percutaneous transhepatic extraction of intrahepatic or extrahepatic gallstones, as indications are rare due to progress of ERCP, and only isolated reports are found in the literature (29, 36, 43–45, 56, 58, 112, 118) except for Asian contributions reporting a significant number of cases of oriental cholangiohepatitis (109), where a success rate of 68% in the retrieval of intrahepatic stones is observed. The transhepatic approach remains an option in comparison with surgery, as reoperation on the bile ducts carries a mortality as high as 6.5% (12).

Complications

Complications following percutaneous transhepatic gallstone manipulation result from trauma to the liver parenchyma during catheter or sheath insertion and exchange, and from repeat catheterization of the bile ducts and manipulation of the gallstones, especially through the papilla, with various devices. A complication rate as high as 21% (30) may be observed, including all potential complications associated with PTC and PBD, and more specifically procedure-related complications such as gallstone ileus, pancreatitis, choledochal or duodenal perforation, and entrapment of the Dormia basket with a stone in the choledochus or the duodenum, or the empty Dormia basket trapped in the duodenal or papillary mucosa, requiring at least complementary endoscopy, if not surgery. Manipulation of an inflated balloon in the bile ducts can create mucosal stripping, although this complication has not been documented. The trauma caused by large introducer sheaths and Dormia baskets can lead, by creating hemorrhage, pressure and infections, to scar strictures.

Additional Methods of Gallstone Extraction

Mechanical Fragmentation

In addition to the basic technique of gallstone extraction, either transhepatically or through the T-drain using Dormia baskets and rigid or flexible forceps, other devices have been used, including ultrasonic lithotripsy (5), a small wire ultrasound drill (6), laser (105), electrohydraulic lithotripsy (18, 75, 88), a pulverization wire, and cholangioscopy (101).

All of these complementary techniques are helpful as adjuncts to achieve fragmentation of retained gallstones, which are too large, impacted, or hard to be crushed, or which are resistant to chemical dissolution.

Chemical Dissolution

Chemical dissolution of choledochal or intrahepatic gallstones with local infusion is indicated when stones are too large to be extracted mechanically, when no direct access to the bile ducts is present, when stones are too numerous, or when extraction through the T-drain or through the liver seems to be risky, or has failed with these approaches or endoscopically.

Among the various substances tried, including saline, sodium dehydrocholate, heparin (49, 141), chloroform and ether, two are used in clinical practice:

- Mono-octanoin is a cholesterol solvent (46, 59, 62, 65, 77, 79, 133, 138, 141, 142, 144) composed of 70% glyceryl mono-octanoin, 30% glyceryl 1–2 dioctanoate and elements of glyceryl trioctanoate and octanoic acid. Mono-octanoin emulsifies with bile, and must be applied at a temperature of between 20 and 50 degrees C to avoid solidification.
- Methyl-tertiary-butyl ether (MTBE) is also a cholesterol solvent (1, 2, 34, 66, 148), which evaporates at 55°C.

Both substances dissolve cholesterol stones containing at least 40% of cholesterol (125). Gallstones showing a predominant calcium composition are unsuitable for chemical dissolution. Radiopaque stones have a 50% success rate of dissolution by chemical solvents (141). Smaller stones are more easily dissolved than large ones. The effect of dissolution may be incomplete, ending in a reduction of size only, which allows subsequent stone extraction.

Mono-octanoin is generally infused at a rate of 5 ml/h for several hours per day, by an automatic pump. The dissolution effect is rather slow, and treatment may last several days, up to 2 or 4 weeks, according to the number, size and composition of the stones.

MTBE has a more rapid dissolution effect, estimated to be up to 50 times faster (1, 140) than mono-octanoin. Complete dissolution can be achieved in one or several sessions of 1 h each, during which MTBE is infused by injections of 10 ml which are reaspirated each time (Fig. **2a–c**). 100 ml can be injected per session. Glass syringes should be used, as plastic may be dissolved by MTBE. The dissolution effect can be appreciated immediately during reaspiration of the solvent, which shows small particles in suspension when effective dissolution is in progress. When one or several stones are present in the choledochus, a pigtail catheter should be used, with its tip curved around the stone, allowing optimal contact between the stone and the solvent. When multiple stones have to be dissolved the smaller ones can be extracted either through the T-tube or transhepatically, and a test in vitro and chemical analysis determine the presence of cholesterolic stones which can be dissolved. Prior to treatment, the calcium content of the calculi can be appreciated with CT. Particularly when using a rapid treatment sequence with MTBE, evacuation of the solvent through the normal papilla or a previous sphincterotomy can be slowed down by placing a balloon catheter in the distal choledochus, or even a double-balloon catheter trapping a choledochal stone immersed in MTBE. When treatment lasts for days or weeks, a second biliary drainage catheter besides the infusion catheter is useful (Fig. **6b**).

When dissolution is performed through a T-drain, a small infusion catheter has to be placed either through the upper limb or the lower limb of the drain, according to the location of the stones. Stones situated above the T-drain will not be reached by the solvent when injected through the T-drain itself, because of a preferential downward flow.

Clinical results indicate a larger use of mono-octanoin, but the drawback of this solvent is the long perfusion time over several weeks. Complete dissolution of retained stones has been reported in 26% only of cases in a large series (108), but an overall success rate of 75% (62, 77, 133, 139, 142, 145) is accepted.

Using MTBE, a similar success rate of 75% (140) is reported. When chemical dissolution is combined with mechanical extraction, a success rate of 90–100% is obtained (59, 67).

Complications following chemical dissolution include bile colic, nausea, vomiting, diarrhea, somnolence, duodenal ulceration (62, 143), dyspnea, facial flushing (58) and choledochomalacia (31).

Percutaneous Cholecystostomy

Indications

Percutaneous cholecystostomy is an alternative emergency procedure to surgical cholecystostomy (52, 85, 128, 158), which is indicated mainly in poor-risk patients presenting with acute cholecystitis, gallbladder empyema or cholangitis (39, 60, 110, 115, 126). Cholecystectomy can in all cases be postponed when the patient has improved after gallbladder drainage.

Percutaneous opacification of the gallbladder, with or without catheter drainage, is indicated, when a limited gallbladder tumor has to be ruled out and transhepatic and endoscopic opacification have failed, or when the biliary tree itself cannot be opacified (39, 110, 126).

Percutaneous drainage is established for decompression of acute cholecystitis, either due to gallstones or when acalculous cholecystitis is present, as in stress situations. This latter indication is best suited to percutaneous decompression of the gallbladder, as relief of bile stasis until the cystic duct is patent again is therapeutic, and secondary cholecystectomy is not required (100).

Percutaneous decompression of the gallbladder may be indicated in selected cases of pancreatitis, with sudden gallbladder distension and probable biliary sepsis.

In rare circumstances, the percutaneous access to the gallbladder can be used to reach the main bile duct for biliary stricture dilation, antegrade cholangioscopy, antegrade sphincteroplasty (90), or stone removal (22, 50, 94).

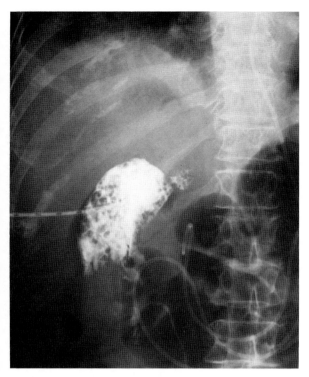

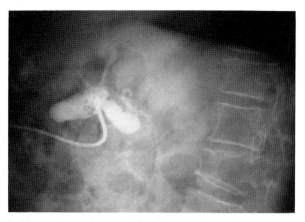

b The catheter inserted by the transhepatic approach enters the gallbladder in the middle (profile view)

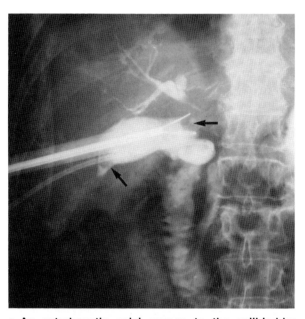

Fig. **7a–e Acute cholecystitis. a** Choledochal gall-stones were evacuated through endoscopic sphincterotomy. Percutaneous transhepatic gallbladder drainage with an 8 Fr pigtail catheter was performed. Multiple gall-stones are present

c An extrahepatic axial access to the gallbladder allows better extraction of large gallstones (arrows) with a forceps through a 30 Fr sheath. Notice that the pigtail catheter is kept in place, avoiding intraperitoneal biliary leakage

When acute cholecystitis is due to gallstones, percutaneous extraction or dissolution (142, 149) of the stones can be attempted. Only cholesterol stones respond to chemical dissolution with MTBE or mono-octanoin with variable results, as in the choledochus. Attempts are under investigation to defunctionalize the gallbladder by various techniques, including injection of ethanol into it (121) and closure of the cystic duct with electrocoagulation (9).

Technique

The gallbladder is best punctured with US- or CT-guided imaging by a percutaneous anterolateral approach through the liver parenchyma, entering the gallbladder through the hepatic aspect, which is not directly open to the peritoneal cavity (Fig. **7a**). The risk of diffuse bile peritonitis is thus limited and the risk of puncture in the cystic artery and vein is not relevant. When the gallbladder is clearly shown by US or CT and percutaneous transhepatic puncture is secure, the trocar technique is preferred for drainage, as bile leakage is minimized, manipulation of the gallbladder is reduced, and bile can be aspirated as soon as the catheter has entered its lumen.

The tandem technique can also be used for percutaneous drainage when cholecystography has been performed through a fine-gauge needle.

The angiographic technique can be used through a 5 Fr catheter or Chiba needle after dilation of the percutaneous and transhepatic tract before definitive catheter exchange.

The usual percutaneous approach is anterolateral, the catheter entering the gallbladder in the middle (Fig. **7b**). This approach is not always adequate for percutaneous stone extraction, antegrade catheterization of the cystic duct, or endoscopic inspection of the gallbladder (Fig. **7d**). When optimal decompres-

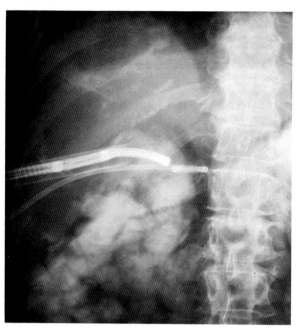

d Percutaneous endoscopy of the gallbladder confirms that no residual stones are present

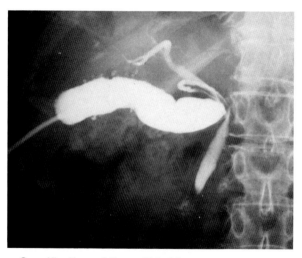

e Opacification of the gallbladder at the conclusion of treatment confirms the patency of the cystic duct

sion of the gallbladder has been obtained through an initial drainage catheter, the bottom of the gallbladder can be punctured without risk, without a transhepatic route, allowing better working access along the long axis of the gallbladder (Fig. **7c**). A pigtail or accordion-type catheter should always be placed in the gallbladder, preventing displacement and severe bile leakage (Fig. **7d**).

Complications

When proper technique is used, complications accompanying percutaneous cholecystostomy are few. Biliary leakage from a distended gallbladder is prevented by rapid aspiration as soon as the gallbladder has been entered with a needle or a catheter. A single-step drainage is therefore preferable to percutaneous cholecystostomy (82). Bile extravasation can lead to peritonitis, septic shock and death, especially in debilitated patients who undergo this procedure (126). Vagal reactions, as seen during percutaneous biopsy in the abdomen can be observed (148), and may be prevented by adequate premedication.

References

1. Allen MJ, Borody TJ, Bugliosi TF, May GR, La Russo NF, Thistle JL. Cholelitholysis using methyl-tertiary-butyl ether. Gastroenterology 1985;88:122.
2. Allen MJ, Borody TJ, Bugliosi TF, May GR, La Russo NF, Thistle JL. Rapid dissolution of gallstones by methyl-tertiary-butyl ether. N Engl J Med 1985;312:217.
3. Alspaugh JP, Chuang VP, Martin LG, McGarity WC. A dual-balloon technique for nonoperative removal of retained biliary stones. Cardiovasc Intervent Radiol 1986;9:161.
4. Alspaugh JP, Martin LG, Chuang VP. Everting balloon catheter in the biliary tree: a technical note. Cardiovasc Intervent Radiol 1986;9:164.
5. Bean W, Daughtry JD, Rodan BA, Mullin, D. Ultrasonic lithotripsy of retained common bile duct stone. AJR 1986;144:1275.
6. Bean WJ, Davies H, Barnes F. Ultrasonic fragmentation of retained common bile duct stones. JCU 1977;5:188.
7. Bean WJ, Smith SL, Calonje MA. Percutaneous removal of residual biliary tract stones. Radiology 1974;113:1.
8. Bean WJ, Smith SL, Mahorner HR. Equipment for nonoperative removal of biliary tract stones. Radiology 1973;107:452.
9. Becker CD, Quenville NF, Burhenne HJ. Gallbladder ablation through radiologic intervention: an experimental alternative to cholecystectomy. Radiology 1989;171:235.
10. Blumgart LH, Kelley CJ, Benjamin IS. Benign bile duct stricture following cholecystectomy: critical factors in management. Br J Surg 1984;71:836.
11. Boey JH, Way LW. Acute cholangitis. Ann Surg 1980;191:264.
12. Bordley HIV, Whitte TT. Causes for 340 reoperations on the extrahepatic bile ducts. Ann Surg 1970;189:442.
13. Braasch JW, Bolton JS, Rossi RL. A technique of biliary tract reconstruction with complete follow-up in 44 consecutive cases. Ann Surg 1981;194:635.
14. Burhenne HJ. The technique of biliary duct stone extraction Radiology 1974;113:567.
15. Burhenne HJ. Dilatation of biliary tract strictures: a new roentgenologic technique. Radiol Clin North Am 1975;44:153.
16. Burhenne HJ. Nonoperative retained biliary tract stone extraction. AJR 1973;117:388.
17. Burhenne HJ. The technique of biliary duct stone extraction: experience with 126 cases. Radiology 1974:133:567.
18. Burhenne HJ. Electrohydraulic fragmentation of retained common bile duct stones. Radiology 1975;117:721.
19. Burhenne HJ. Extracting retained biliary tract stones without reoperation. Comtemp Surg 1975;7:24.
20. Burhenne HJ. Complications of nonoperative extraction of retained common duct stones. Am J Surg 1976;131:260.
21. Burhenne HJ. Nonoperative instrument extraction of retained bile duct stones. World J Surg 1978;2:439.

22. Burhenne HJ. Percutaneous extraction of retained biliary tract stones: 661 patients. AJR 1980;134:888.

23. Burhenne HJ, Morris DC. Biliary stricture dilatation: use of the Grüntzig balloon catheter. Can Assoc Radiol J 1980;31:196.

24. Caprini JA, Thorpe CJ, Fotopoulos JP. Results of nonsurgical treatment of retained biliary calculi. Surg Gynecol Obstet 1980;151:630.

25. Centola C, Jander H, Stauffer A, Russinovich NAE. Balloon dilatation of the papilla of Vater to allow biliary stone passage. AJR 1981;136:613.

26. Chen HH, Zhang WH, Wang SS. Twenty-two year experience with the diagnosis and treatment of intrahepatic calculi. Surg Gynecol Obstet 1984;159:519.

27. Choi TK, Lee MJR, Lui R, Fok M, Wong J. Postoperative flexible choledoscopy for residual primary intrahepatic stones. Ann Surg 1986;203:260.

28. Clouse ME. Dormia basket modifications for percutaneous transhepatic common bile duct stone removal. AJR 1983;140:395.

29. Clouse ME, Falchuk KR. Percutaneous transhepatic removal of common duct stones. Gastroenterology 1983;85:815.

30. Clouse ME, Stokes KR, Lee RGL, Falchuk KR. Bile duct stones: percutaneous transhepatic removal. Radiology 1986;160:525.

31. Crabtree TS, Dykstra R, Kelly J, Preshaw RM. Necrotizing choledochomalacia after use of mono-octanoin to dissolve bile duct stones. Can J Surg 1982;25:644.

32. Cragg AH, Kotula F, Castaneda-Zuniga WR, Amplatz K. A simple mechanical device for inflation of dilating balloons. Radiology 1983;147:273.

33. Dähnert W, Günther R, Schmidt HD, Staritz M, Thelen M. Entfernen zurückgelassener Gallengangskonkremente durch den T-Drainkanal. RöFo 1984;141:63.

34. Di Padova C, Padova F, Montorsi W, Tritapepe R. Methyl-tertiary-butyl ether fails to dissolve retained radiolucent common bile duct stones. Gastroenterology 1986;91:1296.

35. Demling L, Seuberth K, Riemann JF. A mechanical lithotriptor. Endoscopy 1982;14:100.

36. Dotter CT, Bilbao MK, Katon RM. Percutaneous transhepatic gallstones removal by needle tract. Radiology 1979;133:242.

37. Dow RW, Lindenauer SM. Acute obstructive suppurative cholangitis. Ann Surg 1969;169:272.

38. Dunphy JE. Injury to the common bile duct. In: Hardy JD, ed. Rhoads textbook of surgery: principles and practice. 5th ed. Philadelphia: Lippincott, 1977:994.

39. Elyaderani M, Gabriele OF. Percutaneous cholecystostomy and cholangiography in patients with obstructive jaundice. Radiology 1979;130:601.

40. Fataar S, Bassiony H, Abou-Neema T. The percutaneous „stretch and push" technique for removing retained biliary calculi. Br J Radiol 1982;55:456.

41. Fenessy JJ, You YD. A method for the expulsion of stones retained in the common bile duct. AJR 1970;110:256.

42. Fernandez M. Trend of benign strictures of the biliary ducts. World J Surg 1980;4:479.

43. Fernstrom I, Delin NA, Sunblad R. Percutaneous transhepatic extraction of common bile duct stones. Surg Gynecol Obstet 1981;143:405.

44. Ferrucci JT Jr, Mueller PR. Postoperative instrumentation of the biliary tract. In: Ferrucci JT Jr, Wittenberg J, ed. Interventional radiology of the abdomen, Baltimore: Williams and Wilkins, 1981:11,35,95.

45. Ferrucci JT Jr, Mueller PR, Harbin WP. Percutaneous transhepatic biliary drainage: techniques, results, applications. Radiology 1980;135:1.

46. Gadacz TR. Efficacy of Capmul and the dissolution of biliary stones. J Surg Res 1979;26:378.

47. Gallacher DJ, Kadir S, Kauffman SL, Mitchell SE, Kinnison ML, Chang R, Adam P, White RI, Cameron JL. Nonoperative management of benign postoperative biliary strictures. Radiology 1985;156:625.

48. Galloway SJ, Casarella WJ, Seaman WB. The non-operative treatment of retained stones in the common bile duct. Surg Gynecol Obst 1973;137:55.

49. Gardner B, Dennis CR, Patti J. Current status of heparin dissolution of gallstones. Am J Surg 1975;130:239.

50. Garrow DG. The removal of retained biliary tract stones: report of 105 cases. Br J. Radiol 1977;50:777.

51. Gazzaniga GM, Faggioni A, Bondanza G, Gogolo L, Filauro M, Pastorino G. Percutaneous transhepatic cholangioscopy. Int Surg 1983;68:357.

52. Glenn F. Cholecystostomy in the high-risk patient with biliary tract disease. Am Surg 1977;195:185.

53. Glenn F. Iatrogenic injuries to the biliary duct system. Surg Gynecol Obstet 1978;146:430.

54. Günther RW. Transhepatic transcatheter puncture of an occluded biliary intestinal anastomosis for recanalization. Radiology 1985;155:249.

55. Günther RW, Klose KJ, Schmidt HD. Work in progress: percutaneous transhepatic electrocutting of stenoses after hepaticojejunostomy. Radiology 1983;146:355.

56. Günther R, Klose K, Schmidt HD, Staritz M. Perkutane transhepatische Zertrümmerung von Gallensteinen und Fragmentextraktion. RöFo 1983;139:256.

57. Hansson JA, Hoevels J, Simert G, Tylén U, Vang J. Clinical aspects of nonsurgical percutaneous transhepatic bile drainage in obstructive lesions of the extrahepatic bile ducts. Ann Surg 1979;189:58.

58. Haskin PH, Teplick SK. Percutaneous management of biliary stones. Sem Intervent Radiol 1985;2:81.

59. Haskin PH, Teplick SK, Gambescia RA, Zitomer N, Pavlides CA. Percutaneous transhepatic removal of a common bile duct stone after mono-octanoin infusion. Radiology 1984;151:247.

60. Hawkins IF. Percutaneous cholecystostomy. Sem Intervent Radiol 1985;2:97.

61. Herrera M, Coleman CC, Castaneda WR, Amplatz K. New T-tubes. AJR 1984;142:102.

62. Hofmann AF, Schmack B, Thistle JL, Babayan VK. Clinical experience with mono-octanoin for dissolution of bile duct stones: an uncontrolled multicenter trial. Dig Dis Sci 1981;26:954.

63. Hutson DG, Russell E, Schiff E, Levi JJ, Jeffers L, Zeppa R. Balloon dilatation of biliary strictures through a choledocho-jejuno-cutaneous fistula. Ann Surg 1984;199:637.

64. Jakimowicz JJ, Mak B, Carol EJ, Van Baalen JM. Postoperative choledochoscopy. Arch Surg 1983;118:810.

65. Jarrett LN, Bell GD, Balfour TW, Knapp DR, Rose DH. Intraductal infusion of mono-octanoin: experience in 24 patients with retained common duct stones Lanct 1981;i:68.

66. Juliani G, Gandini G, Gabasio S, Bonardi L, Fascetti E, Gremo L. Colelitolisi chimica transcutanea con metil-ter-butil etere (MTBE) Radiol Med 1985;71:569.

67. Juliani E, Bonardi L, Cesarini F, Gabasio S, Regge D, Righi D, Gandini G. Colelitolisi con metil-ter-butil etere (MTBE) della calcolosi colesterinica dei dotti biliari. In: Lupatelli L, Barzi F, eds. Moderne metodiche d'imaging del fegato e delle vie biliari. Perugia: Benucci, 1989:375.

68. Kadir S, Baassiri A, Barth KH, Kaufman SL, Cameron JL, White RI Jr. Percutaneous biliary drainage in the management of biliary sepsis. AJR 1982;138:25.

69. Kaufman SL, Harrington DP, Barth KH, White RI Jr, Cameron JL. Nonoperative retrieval of impacted intrahepatic biliary stones using the Fogarty balloon catheter. Radiology 1979;133:803.

70. Kaufman SL, Kadir S, Mitchell SE, Kinnison ML, Cameron JL, White RI Jr. Percutaneous transhepatic biliary drainage for bile leaks and fistulae. AJR 1985;144:1055.

71. Kerlan RK Jr, Progany C, Goldberg HI, Ring EJ. Radiologic intervention in oriental cholangiohepatitis. AJR 1985;145:809.

72. Kitahama A, Elliott LF, Overby J, Webb WR. The extrahepatic biliary tract injury. Ann Surg 1982;196:536.

73. Kuligowska E, Schlesinger A, Miller KB, Lee VW, Grosso D. Bilomas: a new approach to their diagnosis and treatment. Gastrointest Radiol 1983;8:237.

74. Lamis PA, Letton AH, Wilson JP. Retained common duct stones: a new nonoperative technique for treatment. Surgery 1969;66:291.

75. Lear JL, Ring EA, Macoviak JA, Baum S. Percutaneous transhepatic electrohydraulic lithotripsy. Radiology 1984;150:589.

76. Leary JB, Parshall WA. Percutaneous common duct stone extraction. Radiology 1972;105:452.

77. Leuschner U, Wurbs D, Landgraf H. Dissolution of biliary stones with mono-octanoin. Lancet 1979;ii:103.

78. Light W. Extraction of residual biliary calculi in the X-ray department. Can Ass Radiol J 1974;24:209.

79. Mack E, Patzer EM, Crummy AB, Hofmann AF, Babayan VK. Retained biliary tract stones. Arch Surg 1981;116:341.

80. Magarey CJ. Non-surgical removal of retained biliary calculi. Lancet 1971;i:1044.

81. Magill HL, Baker CRF Jr. A simple catheter suction technique for nonoperative retrieval of a retained common bile duct stone. Radiology 1982;142:788.

82. McGahan JP, Philips HE, Nyland T, Tillman P. Sonographically-guided percutaneous cholecystostomy performed in dogs and pigs. Radiology 1983;149:841.

83. Mahornet H, Bean WJ. Removal of a residual stone from the common bile duct without surgery. Ann Surg 1971;173:857.

84. Maingot R. Surgical aspects of non-malignant strictures of the bile ducts with special reference to post-operative stricture. Proc R Soc Med 1960;53:545.

85. Malmstrom P, Olssom AM. Cholecystostomy for acute cholecystitis. Am J Surg 1973;126:397.

86. Martin EC, Karlson KB, Fankuchen EI, Mattern RF, Casarella WJ. Percutaneous transhepatic dilatation of intrahepatic biliary strictures. AJR 1980;135:837.

87. Martin EC, Fankuchen EI, Schultz RW, Casarella WJ. Percutaneous dilatation in primary sclerosing cholangitis: two experiences. AJR 1981;137:603.

88. Martin EC, Wolff M, Neff RA, Casarella WJ. Use of electrohydraulic lithotriptor in the biliary tree of dogs. Radiology 1981;139:215.

89. Martin FC, Fankuchen EI, Laffey KJ, Sibley RE. Percutaneous management of benign biliary disease Gastrointest Radiol 1984;9:207.

90. Mason RR, Shorvon PJ, Cotton PB. Percutaneous descending biliary sphincterotomy with a choledoscope passed through the cystic duct after cholecystostomy. Br J Radiol 1982;55:595.

91. May GR, Bender CE, Larusso NF, Wiesner RH. Nonoperative dilatation of dominant strictures in primary sclerosing cholangitis. AJR 1985;145:1061.

92. Mazzariello R. Removal of residual biliary tract calculi treated without operation. Surgery 1970;67:566.

93. Mazzariello R. Review of 220 cases of residual biliary tract calculi treated without operation: an eight-year study. Surgery 1973;73:299.

94. Mazzariello RM. Transcholecystic extraction of residual calculi in the common bile duct. Surgery 1974;75:338.

95. Mazzariello RM. A fourteen-year experience with nonoperative instrument extraction of retained bile duct stones. World J Surg 1978;2:447.

96. Meranze SG, Stein EJ, Burke DR, Hartz WH, McLean GK. Removal of retained common bile duct stones with angiographic occlusion balloons. AJR 1986;146:383.

97. Molnar W, Stockum A. Transhepatic dilatation of choledocho-enterostomy strictures. Radiology 1978;129:59.

98. Mondet A. Tecnia de la extraccion: incruenta de las calculos en la litiasis residuale de coledoco. Bol Soc Cirurg (Buenos Aires) 1962;46:278.

99. Moore AV, Illescas FF, Mills SR, et al. Percutaneous dilatation of benign strictures. Radiology 1987;163:625.

100. Moore EE, Kelly GL, Driver T, Eiseman B. Reassessment of simple cholecystostomy. Arch Surg 1979;114:515.

101. Moss JP, Whelan JG Jr, Powel RW et al. Postoperative choledocoscopy via the T-tube tract. JAMA 1976;236:278.

102. Mueller PR, Van Sonnenberg E, Ferrucci JT, Weyman PJ, Butch RJ, Malt RA, Burhenne HJ. Biliary stricture dilatation: multicenter review of clinical management in 73 patients. Radiology 1986;160:17.

103. Northover JM, Terblanche J. A new look at the arterial supply of the bile duct in man and its surgical implications. Br J Surg 1979;66:379.

104. Oleaga JA, McLean GK, Freiman DB, Ring EJ. Interventional biliary radiology. In: Ring EJ, McLean GK, eds. Interventional radiology: principles and techniques. Boston: Little, Brown, 1981:245.

105. Orii K, Ozaki A, Takase Y, Iwasaki Y. Lithotomy of intrahepatic and choledochal stones with YAG-laser. Surg Gynecol Obstet 1983;156:485.

106. Ostermiller W Jr, Thompson RJ Jr, Carter R, Hinshaw DB. Acute obstructive cholangitis. Arch Surg 1965;90:392.

107. Palestrant AM, Vine HS, Sacks BA, Weinstein M, Ellison H. Nonoperative drainage of fluid collections following operations on the biliary tract. Surg Gynecol Obstet 1983;156:305.

108. Palmer KR, Hofmann AF. Intraductal mono-octanoin for the direct dissolution of bile duct stones: experience in 343 patients. Gut 1986;27:196.

109. Park JH, Choi BI, Han MC, Sung KB, Choo IW, Kim CW. Percutaneous removal of residual intrahepatic stones. Radiology 1987;163:619.

110. Pearse DM, Hawkins IF Jr, Shaver R, Vogel S. Percutaneous cholecystostomy in acute cholecystitis and common duct obstruction. Radiology 1984;152:365.

111. Pellegrini CA, Thomas MJ, Way LW. Recurrent biliary stricture: patterns of recurrence and outcome of surgical therapy. Am J Surg 1984;147:175.

112. Perez MR, Oleaga J, Freiman DB, McLean GL, Ring EJ. Removal of a distal common bile duct stone through percutaneous transhepatic catheterization. Arch Surg 1979;114:107.

113. Pitt H, Miyamoto T, Parapatis S, Tomkins W, Longmire WP. Factors influencing outcome in patients with postoperative biliary strictures. Am J Surg 1982;144:14.

114. Polack EP, Fainsinger MH, Bonnano SV. A death following complications of roentgenologic nonoperative manipulations of common bile duct calculi. Radiology 1977;123:585.

115. Radder RW. Ultrasonically guided percutaneous catheter drainage for gallbladder empyema. Diagn Imaging 1980;49:330.

116. Rovere J. Bile leakage following T-tube removal. Radiology 1982;144:267.

117. Runge D, Gebhardt J, Burmeister W, Wurbs D. Mechanische Lithotripsie von Gallengangsteinen. Dtsch Med Wochenschr 1985;110:1981.

118. Russel R, Hutson DG, Guerra JJ, Nunez D, Yrizarry JM, Schiff E. Dilatation of biliary strictures through a stomatized jejunal limb. Acta Radiol 1985;26:283.

119. Saber K, El Manaialawi M. Repair of bile duct injuries. World J Surg 1984;1:82.

120. Salomonowitz E, Castaneda-Zuniga WR, Lund G, Cragg AH, Hunter DW, Coleman CC, Amplatz K. Balloon dilatation of benign biliary strictures. Radiology 1984;151:613.

121. Salomonowitz E, Frick MP, Simmons RL. Obliteration of the gallbladder without formal cholecystectomy. Arch Surg 1984;119:725.

122. Salomonowitz E, Kotula F, Coleman CC, Hunter DW, Castaneda-Zuniga WR, Amplatz K. Balloon-inflation device: the inflation helix. Radiology 1984;150:587.

123. Sauerbruch T, Weinzierl M, Holl J, Pratschke E. Treatment of postoperative bile fistulae by internal endoscopic biliary drainage. Gastroenterology 1986;90:1998.

124. Seif RM. Routine operative cholangiography: a critical appraisal. Am J Surg 1977;134:566.

125. Sharp KW, Gadacz TR. Selection of patients for dissolution of retained common duct stones with mono-octanoin. Ann Surg 1982;196:137.

126. Shaver FW, Hawkins IF, Soong J. Percutaneous cholecystostomy. AJR 1982;138:1133.

127. Shore JM. A modern approach to managing common duct stones. Contemp Surg 1976;9:13.

128. Skillings JC, Kumai C, Hinshaw JR. Cholecystostomy: a place in modern biliary surgery? Am J Surg 1980;139:865.

129. Smith R. Hepaticojejunostomy with transhepatic intubation: a technique for very high strictures of hepatic ducts. Br J Surg 1964;51:186.

130. Smith R. Obstruction of the bile duct. Br J Surg 1979;66:69.

131. Smith SW, Engel C, Averbrook B, Longmire WP Jr. Problems of retained and recurrent common bile duct stones. JAMA 1957;164:321.

132. Smith PL, Mirza FH. Percutaneous removal of a biliary stone impacted in a cystic duct remnant. Radiology 1981;140:240.
133. Steinhagen RM, Pertsemlidis D. Mono-octanoin dissolution of retained biliary stones in high risk patients. Am J Gastroenterol 1983;78:756.
134. Stringer R. Cathéter à ballonets d'angioplastie de Grüntzig dans le traitement des sténoses de la voie biliaire. Ann Radiol 1984;27:125.
135. Sussman SK, Hall FM, Elboim CM. Radiographic assessment of anomalous bile ducts. Gastrointest Radiol 1986;11:269.
136. Taormina V, McLean GK. Chronic bile peritonitis with progressive bile ascites: a complication of percutaneous biliary drainage. Cardiovasc Intervent Radiol 1985;8:103.
137. Teplick SK, Goldstein RC, Richardson PA, Haskin PH, Wilson AR, Corvasce JM, Ring EJ, Wolferth CC Jr. Percutaneous transhepatic choledochoplasty and dilatation of choledochoenterostomy strictures. JAMA 1980;244:1240.
138. Teplick SK, Haskin PH. Mono-octanoin perfusion for in vivo dissolution of biliary stones. Radiology 1984;153:379.
139. Teplick SK, Haskin PH. In vivo dissolution of biliary stones by perfusion with mono-octanoin: a series of 11 patients. Radiology 1984;153:735.
140. Teplick SK, Haskin PH, Goldstein RC, Corvasce JM, Frank EB, Sammon JK, Hofman AF. Common bile duct stone dissolution with methyl-tertiary-butyl ether: experience with three patients. AJR 1987;148:372.
141. Teplick SK, Pavlides CA, Goodman LR, Babayan VK. In vitro dissolution of gallstones: comparison of mono-octanoin, sodium dehydrocholate, heparin and saline. AJR 1982;138:271.
142. Thistle JL, Carlson G, Hofmann AF, La Russo NF, Mac Carty RL, Flynn GL, Higuchi WI, Babayan VK. Mono-octanoin: a dissolution agent for retained cholesterol bile duct stones: physical properties and clinical applications. Gastroenterology 1980;78:1016.
143. Train JS, Dan SJ, Cohen LB, Mitty HA. Duodenal ulceration associated with mono-octanoin infusion. AJR 1983;141:557.
144. Tritapepe R, Di Padova C, Pozzoli M, Rovagnati P, Montorsi W. The treatment of retained biliary stones with mono-octanoin: report of 16 patients. Am J Gastroenterol 1984;79:710.
145. Uribe M, Uscanga L, Farka S, Ganjurjo JL, Lagarriga J, Ortiz JH. Dissolution of cholesterol ductal stones in the biliary tree with medium chain glycerides. Dig Dis Sci 1981;26:636.
146. Van Sonnenberg E, Casola G, Cubberley DA, Halasz NA, Cabrera OA, Wittich GR, Mattrey RF, Scheible FW. Oriental cholangiohepatitis: diagnostic imaging and interventional management. AJR 1986;146:327.
147. Van Sonnenberg E, Ferrucci JT, Neff CC, Mueller PR, Simeone JF, Wittenberg J. Biliary pressure: manometric and perfusion studies at percutaneous transhepatic cholangiography and perfusion biliary drainage. Radiology 1983;148:41.
148. Van Sonnenberg E, Wing VW, Pollard JW, Casola G. Life threatening vagal reactions associated with percutaneous cholecystostomy. Radiology 1984;151:377.
149. Van Sonnenberg E, Wittich GR, Casola G, Princenthal RA, Hofmann AF, Keightley A, Wing VW. Diagnostic and therapeutic percutaneous gallbladder procedures. Radiology 1986;160:23.
150. Vogel SB, Howard R, Caridi J, Hawkins IF Jr. Evaluation of percutaneous transhepatic balloon dilatation of benign biliary strictures in high risk patients. Am J Surg 1985;149:73.
151. Vujic I, Brock JG. Biloma: aspiration for diagnosis and treatment. Gastrointest Radiol 1982;7:251.
152. Warren KW, Christophi C, Armendariz R. The evolution and current perspectives of the treatment of benign bile duct strictures: a review. Surg Gastroenterol 1982;1:141.
153. Warren KW, Jefferson MF. Prevention and repair of strictures of the extrahepatic bile ducts. Surg Clin North Am 1973;53:1169.
154. Warren KW, McDonald WM. Facts and fiction regarding strictures of the extrahepatic bile ducts. Ann Surg 1964;159:996.
155. Warren KW, Mountain JC, Midell AI. Management of strictures of the biliary tract. Surg Clin North Am 1971;51:711.
156. Way LW, Dunphy JE. Biliary stricture. Am J Surg 1972;124:287.
157. Weismann HS, Chun KJ, Frank M, Koenigsberg M, Milstein DM, Freeman LM. Demonstration of traumatic bile leakage with cholescintigraphy and ultrasonography. AJR 1979;133:843.
158. Welch JP, Malt RA. Outcome of cholecystostomy. Surg Gynecol Obstet 1972;135:717.
159. Wendth AJ, Lieberman RC, Alpert M. Nonsurgical removal of a retained common bile duct calculus. Radiology 1972;103:207.
160. Weyman PJ, Balfe DM. Percutaneous dilatation of biliary strictures. Sem Intervent Radiol 1985;2:50.
161. Williams HJ Jr, Bender CE, May GR. Benign postoperative biliary strictures: dilatation with fluoroscopic guidance. Radiology 1987;163:629.
162. Zuidema GD, Cameron JL, Sitzmann JV, Kadir S, Smith GN, Kaufman SL, White RI Jr. Percutaneous transhepatic management of complex biliary problems. Ann Surg 1983;197:584.

Endoscopic and Percutaneous Management of Urinary Disease

Percutaneous Nephrostomy

W. Hruby

History

In 1896, only one year after the discovery of X-rays, Haschek and Lindenthal first depicted arteries in cadavers and thereby laid the foundation for interventional radiology. It took another 35 years until the first publications on invasive diagnostic interventions on the living human being were published.

In 1931 Dos Santos et al. and Forssmann described the first experience with arterial and venous angiography. These techniques, which were primarily limited to the diagnostic evaluation of the vascular system, formed the basis for developing instruments and puncturing devices, which were soon to be adapted for other purposes and organs.

In 1954 Wickbom (44) first utilized percutaneous puncture of the renal pelvis for antegrade pyelography, and Weens used this technique systematically in the diagnosis of outflow obstruction.

In 1955 Goodwin and Casey (17) were the first to use percutaneous nephrostomy as a therapeutic approach for draining obstructed kidneys and gaining surgical access to the renal collecting system. Inadequate surgical instruments and poor imaging equipment prevented an immediate breakthrough, and it was not until high-resolution image intensifying systems and gray-scale B-mode sonography became widely available that percutaneous nephrostomy was integrated into routine uroradiology.

In 1976 Fernström and Johannson (14) first systematically utilized this approach for removing renal and ureteral calculi. Improved puncture devices, in particular the three-part coaxial puncture needle by Günther et al. (19), facilitated the procedure significantly, and within 5 years it became the technique of choice for draining obstructed kidneys (2, 4, 11–13, 20, 26, 38, 41–43, 45–47).

From November 1979 until now, 3100 percutaneous nephrostomies have been performed at our institute either for diagnostic or therapeutic reasons. In 80% percutaneous nephrostomies served for subsequent percutaneous stone manipulations (24).

Indications

Percutaneous nephrostomy is primarily used to drain the renal pelvis or ureter, fluid collections being within the renal parenchyma or the perirenal space.

Table 1 Indications for percutaneous nephrostomy

Drainage
Antegrade stent placement
Percutaneous nephrolithotripsy
Percutaneous litholysis
Percutaneous pyelolysis
Abscess drainage
Pre- and postoperative manipulations of ureteral lesions

The nephrostomy tract serves for a variety of percutaneous manipulations, such as antegrade stenting of the ureter, endo-urologic stone removal, percutaneous pyelolysis, percutaneous chemolitholysis, abscess drainage, pre- and postoperative manipulations of ureteral lesions, and for treatment of lesions within the collecting system or the ureter (8, 22, 26, 30, 31, 34, 39, 42) (Table 1).

Technique

The success of percutaneous nephrostomy mainly depends on the correct position of the tube, which must provide a straight tract to a calyx, yet should avoid significant trauma to the kidney and perirenal structures.

The situation differs from the requirements for simple drainage of obstructed kidneys, since the collecting system of stone-bearing kidneys is usually not dilated. The tract must also be adapted to the specific anatomic situation. Special techniques and materials have been developed to meet these demands. Special reference is given to difficult anatomic situations that frequently result in failure in inexperienced hands.

Preoperative diagnosis is usually based on an intravenous excretory urogram and renal sonography. The nephrostomy tract is routinely established in the angiography suite with an undertable tube and availability of biplane fluoroscopy or a C-arm.

Percutaneous nephrostomies have to be placed either in the oblique or prone position: we prefer the latter (8, 26, 36, 37, 45). Regardless of the position, respiration may be embarrassed significantly in patients with cardiorespiratory insufficiency (Fig. 1).

The patient is positioned prone and non-ionic contrast material (iopamidol 370, 1 ml/kg body weight) and 10 mg diazepam are administered

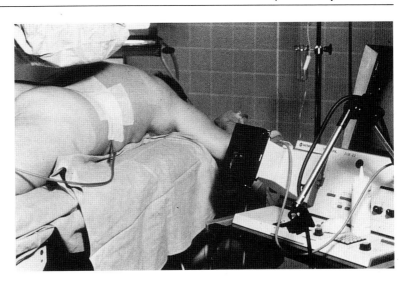

Fig. **1   Prone position for percutaneous nephrostomy**

intravenously. Using a real-time ultrasound scanner with a linear or sector transducer, the kidney and perirenal space are inspected for precise localization and for defining the collecting system, the parenchyma, the paracolic gutter, and the pleura. The ideal approach to a lower pole calyx is in the direction from the lateral convexity of the kidney through the thickest possible parenchymal margin, which can readily be delineated sonographically (Fig. **2**). Definitive puncture is performed under fluoroscopic guidance because sonographic control alone has proved to be insufficient in our experience; approximately 75% of the renal units we treated had a nondilated collecting system, and the lower pole calyx could only be depicted adequately after contrast medium was administered.

Ultrasound guidance with biopsy transducer is used only in nonfunctioning kidneys (Fig. **3**). In patients in whom endo-urologic procedures follow the nephrostomy in one step, the collecting system is delineated with contrast material through a ureter catheter. We do not use balloon ureter catheters to overdistend the collecting system (27).

The puncture site is marked after an orientating ultrasound examination. The flank is prepared and draped as for standard surgery. If the patient is not under anesthesia, the puncture site is anesthesized with 15 ml 1% mepivacaine hydrochloride 50 mg. Puncture is routinely performed below the 12th rib and as far posteriorly and laterally as possible. The most secure access and best approach is through a posterior lower pole calyx.

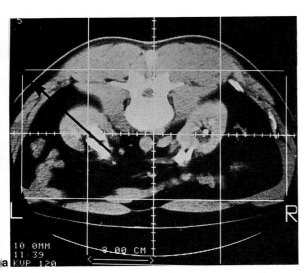
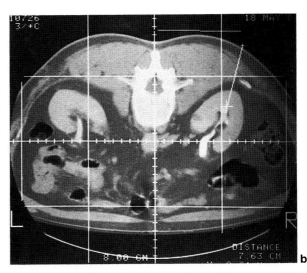

Fig. **2a, b   Computed tomography demonstrates the ideal puncture site** for entrance through the thickest possible parenchymal margin through a posterior calyx

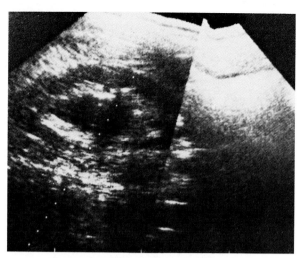

Fig. 3 Hydronephrotic non-functioning kidney with viscous pus: ultrasound guidance

Anatomic Considerations

Under normal conditions, the posterior and lateral margins of both kidneys lie immediately subjacent to the lateral abdominal wall, the posterior leaf of Gerota's fascia, the perirenal fat, the fibrous capsule of the kidney, and the renal parenchyma. With the exception of the pleura in the posterior costodiaphragmatic recess, which overlaps the anterior pole of the kidney, and the colon, which is in close contact with the medial, anterior aspect of the kidneys, there are no adjacent organs liable to be injured. Although on transverse and sagittal cross-sections the pancreas, spleen, liver, and adrenal glands are shown to be in close proximity to the kidney, they are never interposed between the posterior aspect of the kidney and the abdominal wall. In a series of more than 3100 patients subjected to percutaneous nephrostomy we never experienced an injury to these organs, and only once did a lesion of an aberrant bile duct occur (24).

The lower line of the pleura usually crosses the 12th rib at the lateral border of the erector spinae, so that the part of the 12th rib posterior to this point lies above the line of the pleura. If the puncture is performed at a point below the 12th rib and approximately two fingerbreadths lateral to the lateral border of the erector spinae, that is, approximately along the posterior axillary line, pleural lesions are reliably avoided. With a supracostal puncture, there is, of course, an increased likelihood of opening the pleura and causing a pneumo- or hydrothorax and even urinary extravasation into the chest.

The relationship of the 12th rib to the collecting system shows considerable individual variation and is influenced by the respiratory movement of the organ and its mobility. Wickham et al. (45, 46) investigated the position of the various calyces in relation to the 12th rib on excretory urograms taken at maximum aspiration with the patient supine: 80% of the lower pole calyces of the right kidney were positioned below the 12th rib, but only 42% of the middle and 20% of the upper calyces. The left kidney was usually slightly higher, with 78% of the lower pole calyces, 30% of the middle, and only 15% of the upper pole calyces in a subcostal position. In women the middle calyces on the right were slightly lower than in men. The figures clearly demonstrate that a lower pole calyx will be the routine area of entry into the collecting system unless specific problems, such as a stone in an upper pole calyx, inaccessible by any other approach, justify the higher risk of a supracostal puncture.

The position of the colon is easily defined by sonography, which is routinely performed immediately before the puncture for delineating the direction of the optimum tract. Problems only occur with extremely mobile kidneys, which with the patient in the prone position may drop medially to the colon.

In the classic type of kidney with a true renal pelvis the anterior and posterior calyces are arranged in angles of 70 degrees and 20 degrees to the coronal plane of the kidney (29). On a standard urogram, the anterior calyces will therefore appear as the lateral extensions of the collecting system with the typical cuplike structures, whereas the posterior calyces will be easily seen in an orthotopic projection due to the overlying pelvis (8, 26, 38, 39, 45). The posterior calyces are more easily identified from lateral oblique views or by sonography from a lateral oblique view. The latter technique also delineates the position of the pleura and the colon. Computed tomography, of course, is unsurpassed in showing the morphologic details of the kidney, stone, and perirenal structures in difficult pathologic situations.

The renal artery and vein and most of their major branches are anterior to the renal pelvis and, therefore, almost opposite to the point of entry into the kidney. First-order branches that overlie the hilum include the renal pelvis in the anterior and posterior aspect. Direct puncture of the renal pelvis can expose the patient to significant bleeding.

Once the collecting system is punctured and the needle is not advanced further, there is little risk of damaging larger vessels. The posterior segmental artery feeding the posterior segment between the apical and basilar segments of the kidney lies posterior to the pelvis, but usually crosses it at the level of the upper pole infundibulum and then courses downward parallel to the hilar rim. It crosses the direction of the nephrostomy tract and may be injured if the kidney is punctured too medially. The lower pole segmental artery supplies the basilar segment either with the major vessel anterior to the pelvis or with anterior and posterior branches on both sides. They tend to be close to the lower pole

b

Fig. **4a, b** **Entrance of the needle through the papilla** in correlation to the renal vessels

infundibulum and may also be traumatized when the collecting system is punctured too medially or the needle is advanced too far anteriorly.

The arterial supply of the kidney is arranged segmentally, with no collaterals between major vessels. The distribution of the various segments varies greatly, but within the peripheral cortex the feeding interlobular arteries run in a strictly radial direction along the columns of Bertin. When approaching the papilla as peripherally as possible directly from the convexity of the kidney, major arteries are rarely encountered and this approach has been used widely for the multiple radial nephrostomy technique. The same approach through the cusp of the papilla is therefore also the entry point of choice for percutaneous nephrostomy to minimize bleeding (Fig. **4**). With the blunt dilation techniques, the risk of lesions to the vascular system can be significantly avoided.

Puncture Technique

Since ultrasound screening has already provided the information necessary for determining the optimum angle and the point of entry in the skin and the collecting system, a nephrostomy is established under fluoroscopic control using a fine-needle technique and a commercially available nephrostomy set (7, 8, 13, 19, 26, 38, 39).

A three-part coaxial needle set consisting of an outer blunt cannula and an inner 22 G beveled needle and a stylet is advanced through the abdominal wall to the fibrous capsule of the kidney (3, 19). The collecting system is punctured with the fine needle only when the correct position is obtained.

Successful puncture is ascertained by urine dripping from the needle after the stylet is withdrawn or by the injection of diluted contrast media into the collecting system.

If the collecting system is not dilated and urine does not drip from the needle, it is better to insert a 0.035 J guide wire through the outer cannula, after removing the inner needle. The guide wire should be directed into an upper pole calyx. Then the cannula is removed and the tract dilated progressively with fascial dilators from 8 to 16 Fr. A 14 Fr polyurethane nephrostomy tube with an open end and one side hole is introduced into the tract. If the tube is too soft, a similar polyvinyl tube may be stiffened by freezing in a commercial deep freezer. In addition the guide wire can be stabilized with a 7.8 Fr angiographic catheter, so that the system is used as a coaxial system.

Alternatively, dilation over 10 Fr can also be performed using a 0.035 Lunderquist exchange guide wire with a 5 cm floppy J tip. For simple drainage purposes, a 7.2 or 7.8 Fr straight tube with five side holes or a pigtail catheter does not cause difficulty when exchanging it for other instruments, if further manipulations are planned.

The 14 Fr nephrostomy tube can be used for drainage in staged procedures. To avoid tube dislocation from respiratory movement, it should be advanced as far into the collecting system as possible. A tube of this diameter could obstruct the ureter, so that it is best directed into an upper pole calyx. It provides good drainage with little risk of kinking or clotting and admits a variety of guide wires or coaxial catheter systems for further manipulation (Figs. **5–12**).

In a one-stage percutaneous nephrolithotripsy, a J guide wire and a Lunderquist guide wire are inserted directly through the tube; the former serves as a safety guide wire in case the tract is lost, the latter for further tract dilation (1, 6, 7, 28, 33).

This system is also used for manipulations down the ureter. The tract is dilated to the final size with the Lunderquist wire and the other guide wire is used

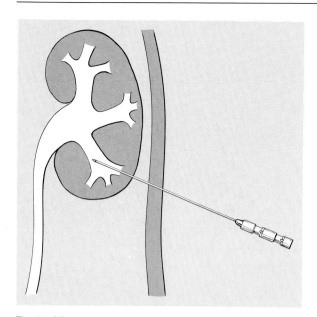

Fig. **5** **Ultrasound or fluoroscopy guidance of percutaneous puncture** of the intrarenal urinary system

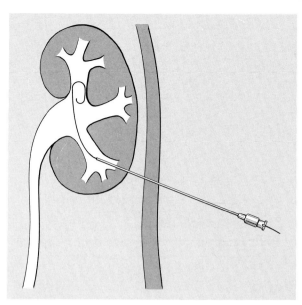

Fig. **6** **Remove the stylet and inner beveled needle; insert the J portion of the guide wire**

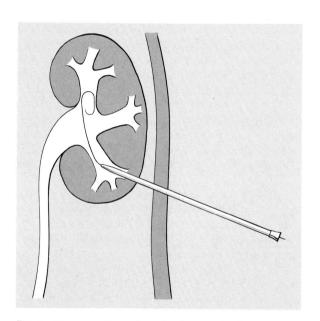

Fig. **7** **Remove the outer blunt cannula. Progressing from 8 to 16 Fr, insert the dilators over the guide wire**

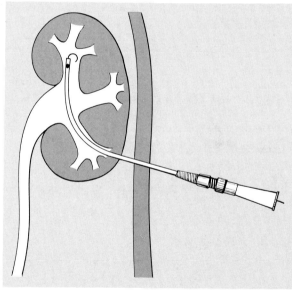

Fig. **8** **Insert the frozen nephrostomy catheter** (Catheter is frozen to give stiffness during insertion)

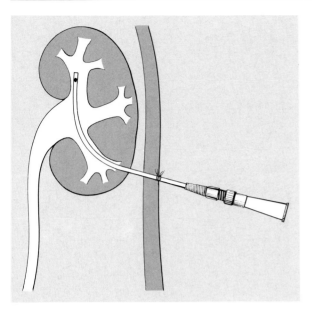

Fig. 9   **Suture the catheter to the skin**

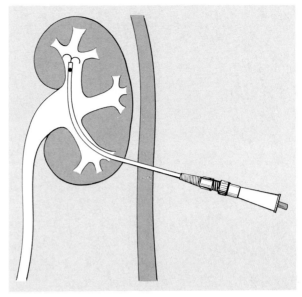

Fig. 10   **If stone manipulations or ureteral manipulations are done through the nephrostomy tract in one session, insert the Lunderquist guide wire through the nephrostomy catheter.** Further manipulation and dilation will take place over the stiff guide wire

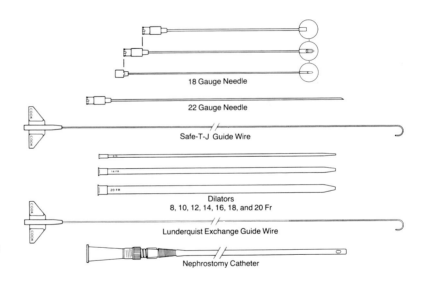

Fig. 11   **Percutaneous nephrostomy set** (Hruby, Marberger)

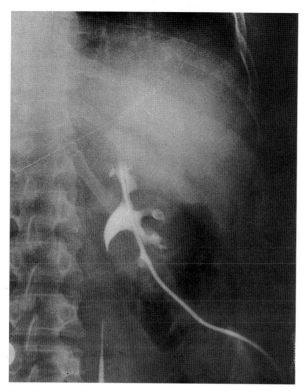

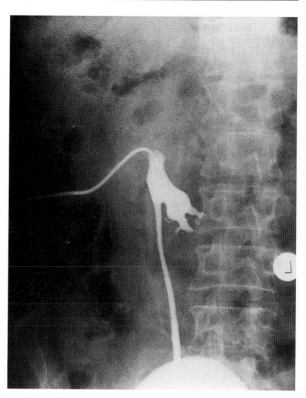

Fig. **12**   **Percutaneous nephrostomy:** ideal entrance and good position of the tube in the upper pole calyx

Fig. **13b**   **Nephrotomogram** in a horseshoe kidney

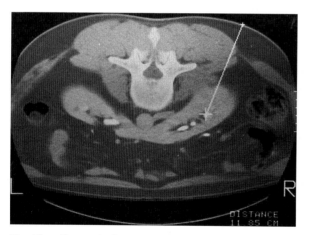

Fig. **13a**   **Computed tomography** shows entrance to a horseshoe kidney

cases computed tomography can provide the information necessary for puncturing the correct calyx (Fig. **13**).

Dilation may be difficult in mobile kidneys (Fig. **14a–e**) because they tend to move when dilators are forced through the fibrous capsule. The coaxial system, a Lunderquist guide wire – 7.8 Fangiocatheter – and a frozen 14 Fr nephrostomy tube, will usually solve the problem and further dilation can be performed with metal telescope dilators (1, 7). Nephrostomy catheters have a greater tendency to dislocate from mobile kidneys. In this situation they can be stabilized with an angiocatheter left within them as a coaxial system.

within the ureter. It is then quite simple to place a thin 6 Fr tube into the collecting system as a safety nephrostomy during further manipulations.

Special Problems

In malformed kidneys orientation by sonography and fluoroscopy may be insufficient to delineate the optimal point of entry into the collecting system. In such

Risks and Complications and Their Treatment

The risks of the procedure are, of course, mainly influenced by the patient. Age is an important factor. We have treated patients from 3 days to 92 years old.

Naturally, the procedure per se does not differ decisively, but in infancy the tube has to be placed under general anesthesia. The risks are therefore mainly connected with the risks of general anesthesia. Likewise, the risks of manipulating extremely old patients increase as do all surgical risks.

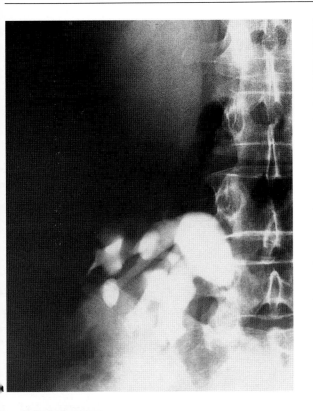

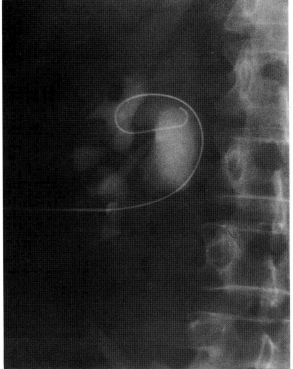

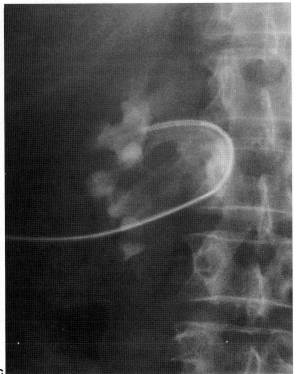

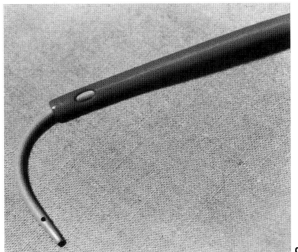

Fig. **14 a Mobile kidney:** intravenous pyelography in upright position
b, c Placement of a coaxial nephrostomy system
d   Coaxial system: angiographic catheter (7.2 Fr) placed through a 14 Fr tube
e   Possible coaxial systems through a 14 Fr tube

Anatomic factors influence success and risks of the procedure. Extremely obese patients and those with scoliosis, significant emphysema, and hepatomegaly are more difficult to treat. Extremely mobile kidneys may be pushed away with the tip of the needle during puncture, rendering penetration difficult, and dilation of the tract may fail for the same reason (8, 9, 15, 16, 21, 38, 39, 46) (Table 2).

Relative Risks

Based on our experience, we consider the following factors to be relative risks for percutaneous nephrostomy (Table 3): hypertension, vascular malformation, bleeding disorders, endotoxic shock in septicemia with highly viscous pus, and subcortical abscess. With pyonephrosis, any surgical manipulation and therefore, of course, percutaneous puncture as well, may result in septicemia and possibly endotoxic shock.

Patients with significant azotemia almost always also have clotting disorders and are, therefore, particularly prone to hemorrhage problems. The physician establishing the percutaneous nephrostomy must be aware of these problems, and be prepared to treat the potential complications. He must – and this is most important – also weigh the indications for a percutaneous nephrostomy against the potential complications. However, establishing urinary drainage is frequently the only lifeline a patient has, and in view of the many vital indications for emergency percutaneous procedures, the potential risks outlined must truly be considered minimal (8–10, 18, 20, 22, 31, 32, 35–37, 39).

In 3100 patients treated with percutaneous nephrostomy, we experienced seven complications requiring surgical intervention; a complication rate of 0.25% (Table 4).

Problems During Manipulation

More annoying in everyday practice are complications not requiring surgical intervention, but endangering the success of urinary drainage (Table 5). Kinking of the guide wire during the early phase of dilation may result in loss of the tract, in particular with very mobile kidneys and excessive retroperitoneal obesity. By using semirigid Teflon dilators, this can usually be overcome, but occasionally it may require that use of a rigid telescope dilator over a guide wire (1, 6–9, 13, 18, 25, 39, 40, 46).

Temporary hemorrhage is usually rapidly controlled by forced diuresis or insertion of a thicker tube. If this fails, we usually just stop up the drain for a short period. Larger lumen drains are usually easy to insert with the same coaxial technique if neccessary and the elasticity of the drain can be reduced by deep freezing it. Extravasation looks terrifying, but provided

Table 2 Aggravating factors for percutaneous nephrostomy

Anatomic factors: obesity, kyphoscoliosis, gibbosity, emphysema, hepatomegaly
Mobile kidney
Malformed kidney
Age

Table 3 Relative risks for percutaneous nephrostomy

Systolic blood pressure more than 190 mmHg
Bleeding disorders
Intrarenal vascular malformations

Table 4 Complications requiring surgical intervention in 3100 patients

Bleeding (intercostal artery)	1
Endotoxic shock	1
Urinoma	1
Bile duct perforation	1
Parenchymal bleeding (multiple arteriovenous malformations)	1

Table 5 Problems during manipulation

Kinking of the guide wire
Problems during insertion
Temporary hemorrhage
Extravasation
Perirenal hematoma
Intermittent hematuria
Renal colic

Table 6 Complications

Surgical intervention	0.17%
Arteriovenous aneurysms	0.22%
Mortality	0.03%
Total	3100

the kidney is drained by a good nephrostomy, it practically always remains without sequelae.

Perirenal hematomas have not been a problem in our series. An intermittent hematuria occurs occasionally, but rarely causes problems. In seven patients in 3100 percutaneous renal manipulations we have observed intermittent hematuria for a longer period, so that an angiographic examination was indicated. All showed aneurysms, which were treated successfully with superselective embolization in the same session with angiography. One patient with a solitary kidney and multiple arteriovenous malformations died (Table 6).

Pain is a very decisive factor, because the patient judges the procedure from this factor alone. The therapy is with pain-relief drugs.

Tube Problems: Clotting

Initially, when we used many of the multiple thin nephrostomy sets available, we experienced a significant rate of problems of kinking, clogging, and dislocation (5, 40). Since we now routinely use large-lumen standard surgical nephrostomy tubes, we have significantly reduced this complication. When we routinely used a 14 Fr nephrostomy tube with the dilation technique, we very rarely failed to insert it at the first puncture. In addition to excellent drainage this larger tube offers excellent access to the collecting system for any additional manipulation. However, we do not place it down the ureter because this could obstruct the ureter and potentially even cause strictures. We very carefully place the tube from the lower pole calyx into an upper pole calyx to have an adequate length of the tube within the collecting systems to prevent dislocation from respiratory movement.

The nursing staff is trained to monitor the nephrostomy tube and the urine bag connected to it. With insufficient drainage of urine, the tube is immediately irrigated with saline and, if this does not improve drainage, the position of the tube should routinely be controlled with a guide wire inserted down it, rather than with contrast. If the tube is dislocated, this is immediately indicated by the position of the guide wire, and the field is not camouflaged with contrast for any additional manipulation that may be neccessary. If the drain has to be exchanged or its position improved, this can usually be performed over the guide wire.

With long-term drainage for palliative reasons and therefore permanent nephrostomy tracts, urine may occasionally leak along the tube. Increasing the diameter of the tubes slightly can prevent this problem. Balloon catheters tend to obstruct parts of the collecting system and are therefore not recommended.

Mallecot-type catheters are difficult to change, particularly when they are incrusted, and therefore we do not use them either.

Treatment

There was only one fatality in our series and 0.17% experienced complications requiring surgical intervention that were attributable to establishing and dilating the tract. In two patients the kidney was explored because of hemorrhage directly after nephrostomy. Bleeding parenchymal vessels in the area of the nephrostomy tract were ligated during exploration. In two other cases hemorrhage occurred before nephrostomy was completed. In one patient, a severed intercostal artery was ligated and in the other patient a peripheral interlobar artery was occluded by superselective embolization with Gelfoam. Seven patients required blood transfusions. Frequently, brisk venous bleeding was observed when the 14 Fr nephrostomy tube was reinserted, and occasionally a major vein was opacified when contrast medium was injected into the collecting system. We rarely resorted to insertion of large tubes for compressing the tract, because this measure only promotes late hemorrhage and prolonged drainage of urine from the tract after tube removal. In seven patients, arteriovenous aneurysms were the cause of intermittent hematuria and were treated with superselective embolization.

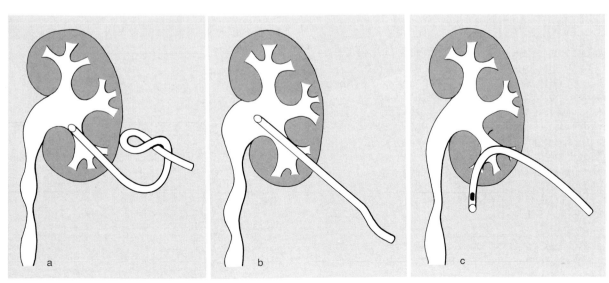

Fig. **15a–c**   **Tube kinking and dislocation**

In the first 100 patients tube problems, such as dislocation and kinking, required reinterventions in 14% (Fig. **15a–c**). Changing to larger caliber tubes rather than thin pigtail catheters reduced this to less than 1%. Nevertheless, tube dislocation remains an annoying complication, because even with a coaxial system allowance for respiratory movement cannot always be made with very mobile kidneys. Dislocated tubes are not removed, but the tract through the abdominal wall is re-used, and only the intraparenchymal tract is re-established. The best way to avoid the problem overall, is to reduce the drainage time as much as possible.

The final nephrotomogram at the end of percutaneous nephrostomy rarely shows extravasation. When the kidney is drained correctly, with a properly positioned nephrostomy tube and saline is used as irrigation fluid, even extensive extrarenal fluid collections can disappear within hours. Two large urinomas requiring surgical drainage in this series were seen early in our experience. They resulted from multiple perforation of the collecting system of obstructed kidneys without properly draining the kidneys subsequently; currently, we would manage this patient percutaneously.

Perirenal hematomas are not problematic. In 62 patients, evaluated by computed tomography 12 months after percutaneous nephrostomy, only one patient was found to have significant fatty degeneration of the psoas muscle suggestive of a rather extensive perirenal hematoma. Overall perirenal scarring was minimal, and in 79% of kidneys no alterations were observed (8, 23, 28, 46).

Clinical Significance

The applicability of percutaneous nephrostomy depends on establishing percutaneous access, and this is directly related to the radiologist's experience. With the standardized approach and equipment outlined here, we were able to manage a wide spectrum of difficult urologic problems and approximately 90% of all renal calculi requiring surgical treatment. Using wide caliber tubes advanced into an upper pole calyx significantly reduces tube complications while establishing the tract. Modifications of the dilation technique, in particular the use of a variety of coaxial systems combined with metal telescope dilators, permitted more precise tract placement and dilation. Multiple tracts were subsequently established more liberally for further manipulations, so that today we feel secure in puncturing any calyx directly.

This has extended the scope of the technique to treatment of multiple calyceal stones and branched staghorn calculi and as therapy to be used in combination with extracorporeal shock wave lithotripsy.

Parallel to the refinement of the technique, we have also become more liberal in treating patients with relative risks. Extreme obesity and spinal or thoracic deformity may render the percutaneous nephrostomy considerably more difficult, but this is also true for open surgery. In one patient with severe spinal deformity from myelomeningocele, in whom percutaneous treatment was denied, a kidney was practically completely shielded by the pleura. In patients in whom we used the intercostal access when puncturing an upper pole calyx, we have experienced no complications such as pneumo- or hydrothorax.

Hypertension in excess of 190/110 mmHg is considered a contra-indication to percutaneous nephrostomy but, with proper treatment of the blood pressure, hypertension has not been an exclusion factor.

Frequently, acute infection and obstruction require emergency drainage. A 14 Fr nephrostomy tube is far superior to a ureteral catheter in draining highly viscous purulent urine.

Although we have successfully treated azotemic patients with abnormal blood clotting factors, bleeding disorders are at the present time still considered relative contra-indications. Renal vascular malformation in particular arterial aneurysms, represent an absolute contra-indication.

A wide spectrum of surgical indications are becoming indications for percutaneous nephrostomy, since it is safer for the patient. The complication rate is lower, and there are almost no limiting factors for the procedure itself.

References

1. Alken P. Teleskopbougierset zur perkutanen Nephrostomie. Aktuel Urol 1981;12:216–219.
2. Babcock JR Jr, Shkolnik A, Cook WA. Ultrasound guided percutaneous nephrostomy in the pediatric patient. J Urol 1979;121:327–329.
3. Baltaxe HA, Mitty HA, Pollack HM. Multipurpose coaxial needle used for percutaneous nephrostomy. Radiology 1984;153:259.
4. Barbaric ZL. Percutaneous nephrostomy for urinary tract obstruction. Radiology 1984;143:803.
5. Baron RL, McClennan BL. Replacing the occluded percutaneous nephrostomy catheter. Radiology 1981;141:824.
6. Casal GL. Fascial dilator for percutaneous drainage procedures. Radiology 1985;155:833.
7. Clayman RV, Castaneda-Zuniga WR, Hunter DW, Miller RP, Lange PH, Amplatz K. Rapid balloon dilatation of the nephrostomy tract for nephrolithotomy. Radiology 1983;147:884.
8. Clayman RV, Castaneda-Zuniga WR. Techniques. In: Clayman RV, çd. Endourology. Minneapolis: 1984.
9. Cronan JJ, Dorman GS, Amis ES Jr, Denny DF. Retroperitoneal hemorrhage after percutaneous nephrostomy. AJR 1985;144:801.
10. Cronan JJ, Amis ES Jr, Dorman GS. Percutaneous drainage of renal abscesses. AJR 1984;142:351.
11. Dretler SP, Pfister RC, Newhouse JH. Renal stone dissolution via percutaneous nephrostomy. N Engl J Med 1979; 300:341–343.
12. Dubuisson RL, Eichelberger RP, Jones TB. Simple modification of real-time section sonography to monitor percutaneous nephrostomy. Radiology 1983;146:232.

13. Elyaderani MK, Dorn JS, Gabriele OF. Percutaneous nephrostomy utilizing a pigtail catheter: new technique. Radiology 1979;132:750.
14. Fernstroem I, Johannson B. Percutaneous nephrolithotomy: a new extraction technique. Scand J Urol Nephrol 1976; 10:257–259.
15. Gavant ML, Gold RE, Church JC. Delayed rupture of renal pseudoaneurysm: complication of percutaneous nephrostomy. AJR 1982;138:948.
16. Gonzalez-Serva L, Weinerth JL, Glenn JF. Minimal mortality of renal surgery. Urology 1977;9:253–255.
17. Goodwin WE, Casey WC. Percutaneous trocar nephrostomy in hydronephrosis. JAMA 1955;157:891–894.
18. Gray RR, St Louis EL, Grosman H. Failure in placement of trocar mounted catheters. J Can Assoc Radiol 1986;37:102.
19. Guenther R, Alken P, Altwein JE. Percutaneous nephrostomy using a fine needle puncture set. Radiology 1979;132:228–230.
20. Gypser G, Kratochvil K, Schreyer H, Justich E. Percutaneous nephropyelostomy: indications and technique. RÖFO 1979;131:529–531.
21. Harris RD, Walther PC. Renal arterial injury associated with percutaneous nephrostomy. Radiology 1984;153:272.
22. Hildell JG, Aspelin P, Sigfussion B. Percutaneous nephrostomy: aspects on clinical application. Acta Radiol [Diagn] (Stockh) 1980;21:485–490.
23. Hruby W, Marberger M. Late sequelae of percutaneous nephrostomy: work in progress. Radiology 1984;152:383.
24. Hruby W, Marberger M. Safety of percutaneous nephrostomy: a report about 500 patients with variety of indication. Bordeaux: European Congress of Radiology, 1983.
25. Hruby W, Marberger M, Stackl W. Perkutane renale Eingriffe versus Operation. Kongreßband. Wien: Van-Swieten-Tagung, 1985.
26. Hruby W, Stackl W, Marberger M. Perkutane Nephrostomie: Indikation, Technik und Ergebnisse. In: Kratochwil A, Reinold E, eds. Ultraschalldiagnostik '81: Radiologisches Drei-Länder-Treffen Graz. Stuttgart: Thieme, 1982.
27. Hunter DW, Salomonowitz E, Castaneda-Zuniga WR, Young AT, Mercado S, Amplatz K. Carbon dioxide as a lighter-than-urine contrast medium for percutaneous nephrostomy. Radiology 1984;152:211.
28. Ivancev K, Ekelund L, Jonsson N. Morphologic changes following nephrostomy track dilatation: experimental investigation in the pig. Acta Radiol [Diagn] (Stockh) 1986;27:123.
29. Kaye KW. Renal anatomy for endourologic stone removal. J Urol 1972;44:246.
30. Lang EK. Diagnosis and management of ureteral fistulas by percutaneous nephrostomy and antegrade stent catheter. Radiology 1981;138:311.
31. Lang EK, Price ET. Redefinitions of indications for percutaneous nephrostomy. Radiology 1983;147:419.
32. LeRoy AJ, Williams HJ Jr, Bender CE, Segura JW, Patterson DE, Benson RC. Colon perforation following percutaneous nephrostomy and renal calculus removal. Radiology 1985;155:83.
33. LeRoy AJ, May GR, Segura JW, Patterson DE, Mc Cough PF. Rapid dilatation of percutaneous nephrostomy tracks. AJR 1984;142:355.
34. Levy JM, Potter WM, Stegman CJ. New catheter system for permanent percutaneous nephrostomy (Abstract). Radiology 1980;134:570.
35. LiPuma JP, Haaga JR, Bryan PJ, Resnick SJ, El Yousef LP, Caldamone A. Percutaneous nephrostomy in neonates and infants. J Urol 1984;132:722–724.
36. Maillet PJ, Pelle-Francoz D, Laville M, Gay F, Pinet A. Nondilated obstructive acute renal failure: diagnostic procedures and therapeutic management. Radiology 1986;160:659.
37. Naidich JB, Rackson ME, Mossey RT, Stein HL. Nondilated obstructive uropathy: percutaneous nephrostomy performed to reverse renal failure. Radiology 1986;160:653.
38. Newhouse JH, Pfister RC. Percutaneous catheterization of the kidney and perinephric space: trocar technique. Urol Radiol 1981;2:157–164.
39. Pfister RC, Newhouse JH, Yoder IC. Percutaneous Interventional Uroradiologic Procedures: Principles and Experience. In: Athanasoulis CA, Pfister RC, Greene RC, Roberson GH, eds. Interventional Radiology. Philadelphia: Saunders, 1982:400–520.
40. Pollack HM, Banner MP. Replacing blocked or dislodged percutaneous nephrostomy and ureteral stent catheters. Radiology 1982;145:203.
41. Sadlowski RW, Finney RP, Branch WT, Rosenthal NS, Sharpe JR. New technique for percutaneous nephrostomy under ultrasound guidance. J Urol 1979;121:559–561.
42. Saxton HM. Percutaneous nephrostomy technique. Urol Radiol 1981;2:131–139.
43. Schilling A, Goettinger H, Marx FJ, Schueller J, Bauer HW. New technique for percutaneous nephropyelostomy. J Urol 1981;125:475–476.
44. Wickbom I. Pyelography after direct puncture of the renal pelvis. Acta Radiol [Diagn] (Stockh) 1954;41:505–512.
45. Wickham JE, Kellet M. Percutaneous nephrolithotomy. Br J Urol 1981;53,297.
46. Wickham JE, Miller RA, eds. Percutaneous renal surgery. Edinburgh: Churchill Livingstone, 1983.
47. Zegel HG, Banner MP, Goldberg BB, Arger PH, Mulhern C, Kurtz A, Dubbins P, Coleman B, Koolpe H. Percutaneous nephrostomy: comparison of sonographic and fluoroscopic guidance. AJR 1981;137:925.

Endoscopic and Percutaneous Management of Ureteral Strictures and Fistulas

A. N. Dardenne and P. J. Van Cangh

Since the introduction of percutaneous nephrostomy, a variety of pyeloureteral procedures have been developed. They include stone retrieval and percutaneous lithotripsy, dilation of ureteral strictures, and treatment of urinary tract fistulas by temporary catheterization (15, 20). Similar procedures using the retrograde, cystoureteroscopic route have correlatively developed and have become valuable interventional procedures.

This chapter reviews the technique of antegrade and retrograde ureteral stent insertion and placement of catheters for balloon dilation via these two routes. Ureteral stenting is principally advocated in the management of ureteral obstruction and fistulas (3), whereas balloon dilation is essentially used for the treatment of some ureteral strictures.

In these applications, the accuracy of the nephrostomy procedure is fundamental for antegrade ureteral stent placement (8). The route for access to the ureter, indeed, requires selecting a mid or upper pole calyx (8), and selection of the proper calyx for entry requires a particularly accurate determination technique, since the calyces may be minimally distented or there may be no calicectasis at all, even in patients with obstructive uropathy (18).

Ureteral Stenting

Initially, stents were often placed prophylactically to prevent stricture formation and extravasation of urine during surgical procedures involving the ureters. Ureteral stenting is presently used as a nonsurgical therapeutic procedure (7, 13, 15, 19, 20).

Two types of ureteral stents are being used: external and indwelling. In external stenting (Fig. 1), the proximal end of the stent emerges at the skin surface via the nephrostomy tract; this end of the stent is accessible externally and may possibly be obstructed. Once placed in the ureter, the distal end lies in the bladder and has a pigtail shape. Indwelling ureteral stents (endoprostheses) have a double-pigtail shape. They cannulate the ureter over its whole length and have no external emergence. Retrograde insertion is the most common placement procedure. The main advantage of internal ureteral stents is that they make collecting bags unnecessary, thereby improving the patient's comfort. A major drawback is that cystoscopy is necessary for the exchange or removal of such stents.

Indications

Usual indications for ureteral stents. Ureteral stenting is a procedure used to re-establish or improve drainage from kidney to the bladder, to provide a pathway for drainage of urine across a compromised ureteral segment, to prevent leakage of urine into the retroperitoneal space, to provide a pathway for the growth of uroepithelium to bridge a defect, and to prevent formation of a tight ureteral stricture during the healing phase (13).It is thus mainly used with ureteral obstruction, whether it be secondary to intraluminal blockage, edema, periureteral fibrosis, or malignant encasement (2, 8).

In patients with benign stenosis, such as retroperitoneal fibrosis, ureteral stenting may be considered while awaiting the therapeutic effects of corticotherapy or to permit postponement of surgical intervention until better conditions are reached. In the patients presenting an increased risk, internal ureteral stenting may be definitively preferred to surgical ureterolysis (15, 20).

In patients with malignant strictures, ureteral stenting may maintain drainage in supravesical obstruction while radiation or chemotherapy is being applied (3).

With percutaneous lithotripsy and stone retrieval techniques, the urothelium can be damaged. Placement of a ureteral stent until the edema subsides and small fragments have passed is therefore the complementary technique of choice (8). Ureteral stents are also placed as an adjunct to external calculus therapy (extracorporeal shock wave lithotripsy), during chemical infusions and after manipulation, to maintain drainage (2, 8).

Specific indications for external ureteral stents. Due to external exposure, these catheters are best suited to short-term use (8). External stents are mainly advocated for the management of ureteral fistulas, a condition always difficult to treat (16, 19). Most of these fistulas are iatrogenic and result from surgical interventions in the gynecologic, urologic, or colorectal sphere, or follow kidney transplantation or urologic endoscopy (in particular retrograde or percutaneous ureteroscopy) (8, 16, 20).

Contra-indications

Contra-indications for ureteral stenting are similar to those of nephrostomy. However, it must be stated

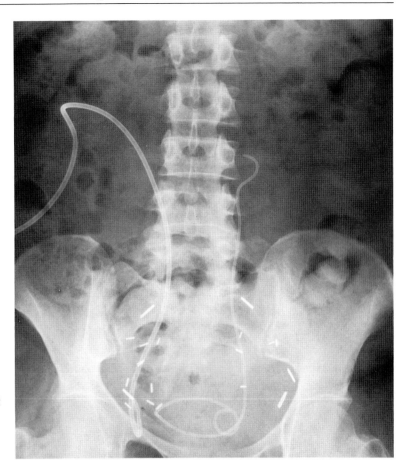

Fig. 1 **Right external stent in a patient with urinary tract fistula after gynecologic surgery.** Partial downward migration of a left internal ureteral stent is shown

that there is presently no formal contra-indication to nephrostomy (15), although it is important that infection be under control before catheter and guide manipulation, and if a percutaneous nephrostomy must be placed for access, bleeding disorders are a relative contra-indication (8).

No specific contra-indication to the placement of ureteral stents has been reported; yet the procedure is limited by the possibility of by-passing a stricture and restoring ureteral continuity within the fistulas (19).

Another consideration before placing a stent is whether there is distal outlet obstruction at either the bladder or the intestinal conduit: a functioning indwelling stent would be rendered useless if outlet obstruction existed (8, 10).

Finally, in the patients with advanced neoplasm and in poor general condition for whom no future therapeutic step is planned, urinary diversion would only result in time-limited, uncomfortable, and expensive life prolongation. In such cases, when anuria is documented, the decision to remove the obstacle, whatever the procedure, should be discussed (15).

Routes of Access

For external stent placement, the percutaneous route is practically the most common method. For internal stents, if cystoscopy is necessary for other reasons, retrograde placement is the logical choice (8). However, retrograde placement may be impossible (14). If cystoscopy is not necessary for other reasons, the antegrade approach is desirable because it avoids operating room expenses and anesthesia. Moreover, in most cases of obstruction, the antegrade approach is usually preferred because the proximal dilation enhances catheter and guide wire manipulations (8). In fact, in some cases, it is not uncommon for one approach to be impossible and subsequently for the other method to proceed smoothly (8).

In the treatment of fistulas, the choice between antegrade and retrograde placement varies in each case, based on the course of the ureter in relation to the fistulous tract, but the classic retrograde approach has a high failure rate (8, 16).

After ureterointestinal diversion, the antegrade approach is usually required (8).

Sometimes a combined approach using the nephrostomy track for access and retrieval of the guide wire or catheter via the bladder or ileostomy permits dual access to the ureteral problem. This approach can be used to position stents in difficult cases (8).

Material

We usually use drainage catheters of 5 to 10 Fr in diameter.

Besides the nephrostomy equipment, the necessary external drainage set consists of a 0.035 or 0.038 (145 cm) guide wire, a stiffer 120 cm Lunderquist control wire, and a 50 cm J-shaped ureteral catheter (5, 19, 20). This external stent catheter can be custom-made by converting angiographic pigtail catheters: additional side holes are cut into the catheter at a level anticipated to be located in such a way as not to be located at the level of a urinary tract fistula (13, 19, 20).

Indwelling stent insertion sets consist of a 145 cm guide wire, a 120 cm Lunderquist wire, and a double-J stent. Appropriate length for the stent is determined by ureteral size. The body of the stent and the pigtails have multiple side holes. A complementary 30 to 40 cm pusher guide is necessary. Antegrade catheterization additionally requires a nephrostomy set (19, 20). The catheter positioner or pusher is a short straight non-tapered catheter supplied with the stent sets necessary to push the indwelling catheters into position (8). The guide wire should be long enough to extend beyond the combined length of the stent catheter and pusher (8). Sometimes a positioning thread retractor is attached to the proximal end of the double J (8).

For the antegrade insertion of ureteral stents, some technical refinements have been proposed. A dilating introducer sheath has been advocated. The insertion set consists of a 9 Fr, 45 cm long, Teflon peel-away sheath with an inner dilating introducer tapered from 9 to 5 Fr over its distal 5 cm (6). Another refinement is a modified internal stent. The body of the stent and proximal pigtail are 7.5 Fr in diameter. The distal pigtail end is tapered to 5 Fr diameter to be more pliable and thus minimize bladder irritation (9).

It remains controversial whether silicone or polyethylene stents are less prone to encrustation (8). Some investigators advocate preferential use of silicone stents, which are more comfortable, more flexible, less prone to encrustation, and have a better biocompatibility (6). In fact, the soft silicone catheters are now usually reserved for intra-operative or uncomplicated retrograde placement (8). The increased flexibility of silicone, indeed, increases friction and causes the stent to buckle like an accordion over the guide wire when attempting to pass areas of tight stenosis; reports of antegrade placement silicone catheters in the literature describe dual control with pulling the stent into position (6, 8). Sterile mineral oil as a lubricant is sometimes needed

to overcome the friction that exists between the guide wire and the silicone catheter. Polyethylene and polyurethane catheters are currently used more than silicone or Silastic, mainly for antegrade placement when torque control is important (1). Nevertheless polyethylene, a relatively stiff material, may cause bladder irritation in some patients and is thought by some investigators to be prone to premature encrustation. Continual bathing in urine causes depolymerization of polyethylene, which leads to increased brittleness and a tendency toward breakage (6).

Polyurethane seems generally to be the material of choice. It is softer, more pliable, and has better memory characteristics than polyethylene; unlike silicone, it has only minor frictional resistance (8, 9, 13). However, polyurethane, like polyethylene, has surface characteristics that may promote premature encrustation (6).

Technique

The following section essentially concentrates on antegrade placement of ureteral stents. Provided there is some adaptation, similar manipulations may be used for retrograde stent placement.

Preoperative tranquilizer and analgesic administration is desirable. Intravenous injection is advised, because it allows medication monitoring during the procedure (19). The patient is placed in the prone position (8, 20). The contrast media used to opacify the ureter during manipulations should be diluted so that the guide wire and catheter are not obscured (8).

Introduction is performed via the nephrostomy track and the ureter is cannulated using a 6.5 Fr 65 cm polyethylene end-hole angiographic catheter with a slightly curved tip to aid in manipulation and with a variety of guide wires (0.035 or 0.038 inch straight or 3 mm J guide wire) in order to pass the obstacle (stenotic or fistulous area). Negotiation of the strictures must be achieved softly and carefully (1, 2, 8, 17, 19, 20).

Once the stenotic or fistulous segment has been traversed, the guide wire is advanced until it reaches the bladder, where a sufficient coil is obtained to secure resistance (19). The insertion catheter is then removed and replaced on the guide wire by the stent catheter. Adequate position is achieved when the distal end coil reforms within the bladder, that is, when the distal pigtail extends at least 1.5 cm beyond the ureterovesical junction (13).

If the pigtail catheter will not pass a stenotic segment, a nephrostomy catheter should be left in the renal pelvis; a delay of 5 to 14 days sometimes solves the problem, because the edema subsides and the ureter becomes less redundant after decompression (8). At times, because of the presence of a fistulous track or an otherwise compromised lumen, or if the ureter is nearly or completely interrupted, passage is accomplished most easily with a 25 G floppy-tipped guide wire. After this guide wire has been advanced into the distal ureteral segment, the 0.025 inch wire is exchanged for a 0.032 inch wire, and finally a 0.035 or 0.038 inch wire (2, 13).

A pushing catheter is introduced over the wire and used to advance the stent to the bladder until the proximal end reaches the renal pelvis. The guide wire is then removed, resulting in both J-shaped ends of the stent recoiling within the bladder and renal pelvis (19). The guide wire is always removed before the pusher (8).

If placement of the stent is too distal, correction can be made via the safety thread attached to the proximal end and side holes of the stent catheter (6, 8). If placement is too proximal, cystoscopic adjustment is necessary (8).

For catheter dilation of ureteral stenoses, if a large stent catheter cannot be placed initially, progressively larger stents are passed over a period of days to weeks until a 10 Fr catheter can be placed. This catheter should be left in situ for 4 to 8 weeks (1). Long Teflon fascial dilators up to 10 Fr in size may also be useful (2, 8). Alternatively, if the stenosis is too tight, it could be dilated with an angioplasty balloon (9).

Placement of a stent through a tight ureteral stenosis may be difficult: a stiff guide wire may allow the double-pigtail catheter to follow more easily and prevent buckling in the soft tissues or renal pelvis. The passage can also be facilitated if the guide wire can be controlled at both ends. This can be done by the endoscopist who can retrieve the guide wire in the bladder (2, 8, 17). Another possibility is to place a straight red, rubber end-hole urethral catheter with its tip at the junction of the bladder and urethra. The curved vascular catheter is advanced and rotated so that its tip engages the urethral catheter (17).

In patients with fistulas, an external stent (usually 9 Fr) is provided with multiple drainage holes, except at the level of the fistula (2, 16).

At times, separation of the ureteral segments may be aggravated by a retroperitoneal urinoma or hematoma that tends to separate, angulate, and splay these segments. Percutaneous aspiration of the urinoma will reduce the separation and splaying and therefore facilitate passage of the guide wire across the partially dehiscent ureter. If the ureter is severed completely, re-entry into the distal segment is not possible (13). However, entry into the bladder from a distal segment of the ureter can be accomplished provided the distance to the bladder is short and there are no interposed structures. This can be done by perforating the wall of the bladder with a stylet guide wire (transseptal perforating guide wire) under fluoroscopic guidance (13). In another technique, an electrocautery cutting current is applied to the rigid end of a standard angiographic guide wire under fluoroscopy until the tip passes into the bladder (11).

In patients with ureterointestinal anastomosis, retrograde access to the ureter through endoscopy is usually the easiest route. Following the antegrade route, dual access naturally occurs when the guide wire reaches the intestinal conduit (8). The guide wire is usually easily found by sweeping the finger in a circular motion in the conduit. Rarely, forceps or endoscopy is required to retrieve the guide wire (8, 20).

In internal ureteral stenting, the use of a sheath may facilitate transrenal insertion of a ureteral stent: a 8, 9, or 10 Fr introducer sheath has proved useful to facilitate entry of the stent into the calyceal system (2, 6, 9).

The required stent catheter length can be estimated from the radiographs, allowing for magnification. The 25 to 26 cm long stent catheter is usually acceptable for most average adults. Exact length can be measured by grasping or bending twice the external portion of a guide wire at the hub of the guiding catheter external to the patient: first when the guide wire end is positioned approximately 1 cm beyond the ureterovesical junction or in the middle portion of the bladder, second when the guide wire is withdrawn in the middle portion of the renal pelvis at least 1 cm above the ureteropelvic junction. The distance from where the wire is grasped to the hub of the catheter is the correct length for the stent (2, 8).

Follow-up

Surveillance of the patency of external stents may be achieved by direct inspection. Besides, the percutaneous route enables easy stent exchange (19). The follow-up of internal stents requires intravenous urography or cystography. Besides, cystoscopy is necessary for removal of the stents (19).

In all patients, a nephrostogram is obtained 1 day after stent placement to monitor position and, if relevant, patency (2). In patients with strictures and internal stents, the nephrostomy tube is removed at that time (2). Normally, we stent ureteral strictures for 12 to 16 weeks (4).

In patients with urinary tract fistulas, percutaneous treatment can often be performed on an outpatient basis, the patient simply being hospitalized for a few days for removal of the stent (16). External stents are usually kept in place for 1 to 12 weeks, according to the size of the fistula, its cause and site, and above all the possible observation of modifications in the periureteral tissues (neoplasm or irradiation) (15, 20). Follow-up is performed approximately every 20 days to assure continued healing (2, 16). If necessary, the external stent may be converted at any time to a nephrostomy tube, exchanged for an identical stent, or replaced by a double-pigtail catheter (16).

When a fistula appears to have complete-ly, the stent is exchanged for 2 to 3 days for a simple nephrostomy tube, and, finally, if renal function is stable and the patient is asymptomatic, the nephro-stomy tube is removed (2, 16). Should residual stenosis occur, secondary dilation with an angio-plasty balloon catheter may be performed (16).

Results

The major causes of failure include excessive ureter tortuosity, excessively severe or impassable strictures or fistulas after total ureteral dehiscence, and loss of substance (19, 20). For pyeloureteral fistulas, per-cutaneous nephrostomy is generally sufficient. How-ever, an external ureteral stent not only allows for drying but also contributes to the closure of the fistula in the best conditions (16).

The antegrade percutaneous approach ist able to bypass the fistula site in 90% of cases (16).

Success rate for the treatment of fistulas is around 70 to 80% although secondary stenosis may develop in 15% (15, 16). Early treatment is important: the success rate reaches 82% with early treatment but decreases to 33% when efficient treatment is initi-ated after more than 1 month (16).

Fistulas subsequent to endourology appear to have the best results after immediate repair by the percutaneous route (16). The same good results are obtained after ureterointestinal reimplantation owing to dehiscence of the anastomosis (16).

The success rate of the treatment of ureteric fistulas complicating inflammatory disease, or radia-tion therapy, or surgery in patients with pelvic neo-plasms, proved much lower (13). In a series of such fistulas a success rate less than 50% was obtained (16). The urine leakage compounds the problem with ureteral and periureteral fibrosis. The success rate is lower in patients with fistula in transplanted kidneys (20). However, the severity and difficulty of surgical treatment are so great that they justify an attempt at percutaneous treatment despite its low success rate (16).

Complications

Besides the complications associated with the place-ment of stent catheters, the major complication of external stenting is infection (20). Patients who undergo transplants are immunocompromised and they are treated routinely with antibiotics before and after the nephrostomy is performed (4).

The main complications resulting from the use of internal stents most frequently include occlusion, upward migration (rare), downward migration (more common), breakage, encrustation, renal pelvic per-foration, erosion through the ureteral wall into the blood vessels or bowel, or death (14, 20). Occlusion mainly occurs in patients with long malignant stric-

tures, generally in the first 10 days after placement (2).

Ureteral Dilations

Initially developed for use in the blood vessels, bal-loon catheters have become important tools for treating stenoses in other organs (1). Successful dila-tion of ureteral stenoses, without the need for inter-nal stenting or subsequent nephrostomy drainage, will minimize morbidity and significantly reduce costs (3, 7).

Indications

It may be worthwhile to attempt balloon dilation of all benign ureteral strictures before relegating patients to additional surgery or chronic indwelling ureteral stents that must be periodically changed cystoscopically (1).

One of the most commonly involved sites is the pelvic ureter, in particular in ureterovesical anasto-moses (Fig. 2) (19). Generally speaking, short, mem-brane-like strictures of the distal ureters are more likely to respond to balloon inflation than are long, fusiform strictures (1).

Excellent indications for balloon dilation are strictures after ureterotomy, ureterovesical, or ureteroileal anastomosis (Bricker procedure) (Fig. 3) (15). Patients with recent, benign, cicatricial, traumatic, or postoperative strictures may also benefit from the procedure (8, 15, 20). Attemps at dilation have also been made with tuberculous stric-tures (20). Certain strictures of the lumbar ureter after therapeutic radiology have also been reported to respond to dilation (15, 20). However, inflamma-tory cicatricial strictures appear to be less responsive, due to reactional fibrosis (20).

In patients with kidney transplant, dilation can only be achieved in the short strictures that are usually located in the anastomotic area (19, 20).

Contra-indications

Old, densely fibrotic strictures and strictures second-ary to ischemia do not respond to dilation, and strictures that present years after ureteroneocysto-stomy are unlikely to respond to dilation (8).

Dilation by itself seems to have little place in the palliation of malignant encasement; balloon dilation risks intravascular dissemination of tumor cells (3). For ureteroileostomy strictures, dilation after pelvic exenteration for malignant gynecologic diseases usually fails due to ureteral ischemia associated with radical hysterectomy or high-dose radiotherapy (1, 8).

Ureteropelvic junction obstructions are better managed by endoscopic lysis (3).

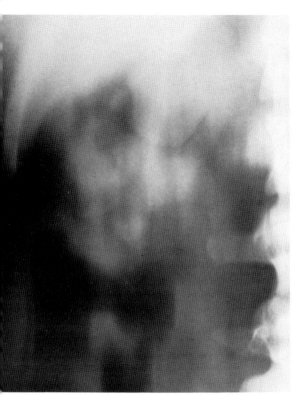

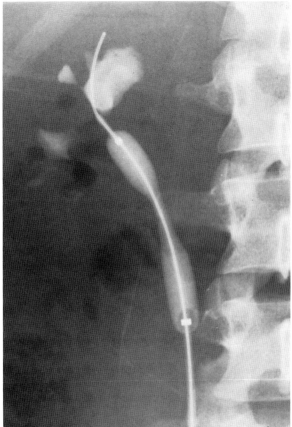

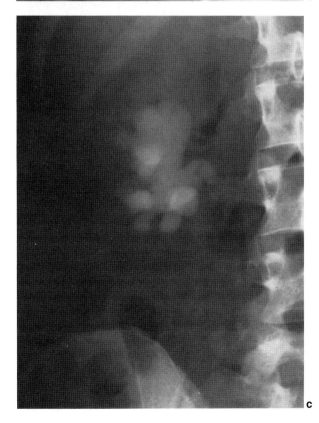

Fig. 2 **Dilation of an inflammatory stenosis of the right pyeloureteral junction after percutaneous removal of a staghorn stone**
a Urographic aspect before treatment showing very poor opacification and dilation of the pelvis and calices
b Balloon catheter in situ during treatment
c Control intravenous pyelogram demonstrating good opacification of the calices

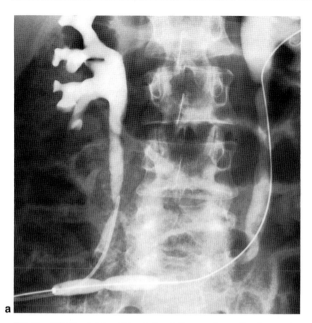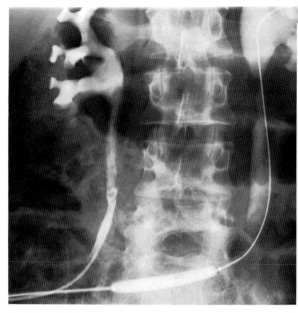

Fig. 3   **Dilation of a stenosis of the uretero-ileal anastomosis after a Bricker procedure**
a Aspect during dilation
b Dilation is completed: the waist aspect of the balloon has disappeared

In patients who have undergone kidney transplantation, extensive strictures are a poor indication. Such fusiform strictures are due to ischemic necrosis and attempts at dilation are rather discouraging (19, 20).

Material

Besides the insertion set used for the placement of internal or external ureteral stents, a balloon catheter of varying length is required (5, 20). A frequently used balloon catheter is a 7 Fr catheter with a reinforced polyethylene balloon, 4 mm in diameter and 3 to 4 cm long. A 5 Fr catheter with a similar balloon is used for very tight strictures. The 7 Fr catheter accomodates a standard 0.038 inch (0.96) wire, the 5 Fr catheter requires a smaller guide wire (1).

Routes of Access

In women, dilation and stenting in retrograde fashion, without anesthesia, may seem preferable with distal ureteral strictures. Nevertheless, generally speaking, the drawback of not having percutaneous access to the collecting system to obtain follow-up studies easily and the greater ease with which larger catheters can be passed through the intramural ureter in antegrade fashion limit the number and efficacy of retrograde dilations per urethra (1).

Moreover, to correct forming strictures, external stent catheters greatly facilitate exchange of catheters, introduction of larger lumen catheters, and intermittent transluminal dilations (13).

Balloon dilation can also be used during percutaneous endoureteral manipulations initially performed for another purpose (e.g., percutaneous extraction of calculi).

Technique

Before embarking on balloon dilation, accurate evaluation of the stenotic segment and the condition of the ureter beneath the stricture is mandatory (20). A 6 Fr end hole catheter is passed down the ureter to the stricture, and contrast material is injected to document its appearance and length (1). As in the placement of ureteral stents, the major problem to overcome is crossing the stricture (20).

A guide wire is manipulated into either the bladder or a bowel conduit (1). Lunderquist torque guide wire exchanges can facilitate passage of both a 7 Fr balloon catheter and a larger stent catheter after dilation (1).

The radiopaque markers on the balloon are centered over the stricture, and the balloon is distended with dilute contrast material with a 5 ml syringe. Pressure is maintained for 2 to 10 minutes, until fully expanded or until the balloon waist disappears (1, 12, 19). For the newer reinforced polyethylene balloons, a mechanical hand injector can be used to generate pressures of up to 17 atm (1).

When passing either a balloon or stent catheter across a tight ureteral stricture in patients who have had ureteroileostomies, it is helpful to advance a guide wire through the ileal conduit and retrieve its distal end from the stoma (1).

Follow-Up

After balloon dilation, the ureter is stented for a week with a usually 9 or 10 Fr external (or internal) stent. With an internal stent, absence of a drainage catheter in the kidney thereby limits non-invasive follow-up evaluation to excretory urography (1).

When removed, the ureteral stent is replaced with a nephrostomy catheter. About 48 hours later, an antegrade pyelogram is performed. If drainage is adequate, nephrostomy is capped for a week. If the patient remains asymptomatic, the catheter is uncapped and both renal pelvis pressure and residual urine are measured. Normal limits (pressure: < 12 to 15 cm H_2O; residual urine: < 10 ml for a nondilated collecting system). If these measurements are equivocal or slightly elevated, a formal upper tract urodynamic study (a Whitaker test) is performed in conjunction with the nephrostogram. In uncertain or obviously unsatisfactory cases, the dilation procedure may systematically be repeated (1, 19, 20). In the patients undergoing repeat dilations for tuberculous strictures, a regimen of triple antitubercular chemotherapy is installed. The dilation is repeated weekly or biweekly at first, then monthly or bimonthly until the upper tract has stabilized (3).

Results

The cause and duration of a ureteral stricture are major determinants of the outcome of dilation therapy (1). Strictures detected soon after surgical procedures for benign conditions seem to have the best prognosis for successful dilation (3, 7, 20). Ureteropelvic junction obstruction after unsuccessful surgery may be an exception (3). In strictured ureteroileal anastomoses, the success rate varies between 40 and 68% (1, 3). The results obtained in strictures of longer duration are irregular (3). The 60% success rate reported in tuberculous strictures using multiple dilations suggests that persistence may ultimately have led to success in some of the postoperative failures (3).

The poorest results are obtained in patients with ureteral strictures resulting from devitalization after renal transplantation, ureteral surgery, and localized radiotherapy (20). Equally bad results are obtained in female patients presenting with ureteral strictures after radical hysterectomy and who had preoperative radiation or ureteral stripping that whould have impaired blood supply (3). Strictures that follow radical hysterectomy are thus usually not amenable to treatment by dilation. However, stenting of a ureteral fistula that develops after radical hysterectomy, followed shortly thereafter by prophylactic balloon dilation of the ureter at the former fistula site, may prevent stricture formation, whereas a simple indwelling stent probably will not (1).

Some ureters may appear satisfactorily dilated after removal of the ureteral stent only to recontract within a few days. An occasional one will recontract months to years after successful dilation (1).

Complications

The specific complication of balloon dilation of ureteral stricture is partial ureteral rupture (Fig. 4) which has to be treated by nephrostomy and ureteral stenting (1).

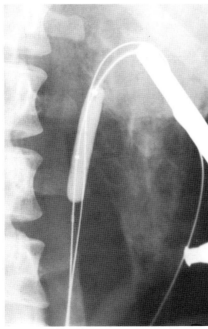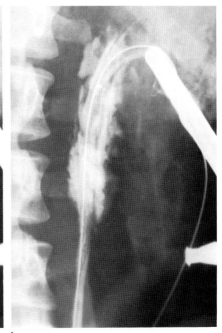

Fig. **4 Ureteral rupture after dilation through the nephrostomy track**
a Aspect of the balloon completely dilated
b Injected contrast media showing periureteral extravasation

a   b

References

1. Banner MP, Pollack HM. Dilatation of ureteral stenoses: techniques and experience in 44 patients. AJR 1984;143:789–793.
2. Bettmann MA, Perlmutt L, Finkelstein J, Meyerovitz MF, Richie JP. Percutaneous placement of soft, indwelling ureteral stent. Radiology 1985;157:817–818.
3. Bigongiari LR. Transluminal dilatation of ureteral strictures. In: Lang EK, ed. Percutaneous and interventional urology and radiology. Berlin: Springer 1986:113–118.
4. Cardella JF, Hunter DW, Hulbert J, Young AT, Castaneda-Zuniga WR, Amplatz K. Obstructed calycocystectomy site in association with a transplanted kidney: percutaneous management. Radiology 1985;156:67–68.
5. Cardella JF, Kotula F, Hunter DW, Young AT, Castaneda-Zuniga WR, Amplatz K. Very stiff guide wire with a floppy tip. Radiology 1985;156:837.
6. Druy EM. A dilating introducer-sheath for the antegrade insertion of ureteral stents. AJR 1985;145:1274–1276.
7. El-Mahrouky A, Ford KK, van Moore A, Shore N, King LR. Balloon dilatation of ureteral strictures in dogs. J Urol 1984;131:582–586.
8. Fritzsche PJ. Antegrade and retrograde ureteral stenting. In: Lang EK, ed. Percutaneous and interventional urology and radiology. Berlin: Springer 1986:91–111.
9. Hackethorn JC, Boren SR, Dotter CT, Rösch J. Antegrade internal ureteral stenting: a technical refinement. Radiology 1985;156:827–828.
10. Hoffer FA, Lebowitz RL. Intermittent hydronephrosis: a unique feature of ureteropelvic junction obstruction caused by a crossing renal vessel. Radiology 1985;156:655–658.
11. Horowitz MI, Feigenbaum LA. Transcatheter electrocautery as a aid in the percutaneous insertion of a ureteral stent. J Urol 1984;132:111–112.
12. Johnson CD, Oke EJ, Dunnick NR, van Moore A, Braun SD, Newman GE, Perlmutt L, King LR. Percutaneous balloon dilatation of ureteral strictures. AJR 1987;148:181–184.
13. Lang EK. Antegrade ureteral stenting for dehiscence, strictures and fistulae. AJR 1984;143:795–801.
14. Leroy JA, Williams HJ, Segura JW, Patterson DE, Benson RC. Indwelling ureteral stents: percutaneous management of complications. Radiology 1986;158:219–222.
15. Maillet PJ, Pelle-Francoz D, Pinet A. Nephrostomies et dérivations internes percutanées: technique et résultats: a propos de 130 cas. J Radiol 1984;65:343–353.
16. Maillet PJ, Pelle-Francoz D, Leriche A, Leclercq R, Demiaux C. Fistulas of the upper urinary tract: percutaneous management. J Urol 1987;138:1382–1385.
17. Mitty HA. Ureteral stenting facilitated by antegrade transurethral passage of guide wire. AJR 1984;142:831–832.
18. Naidich JB, Rackson ME, Mossey RT, Stein HL. Nondilated obstructive uropathy: percutaneous nephrostomy performed to reverse renal failure. Radiology 1986;160:653–657.
19. Pelle-Francoz D, Maillet PJ, Pinet A. Techniques sur les voies excrétrices urinaires. In: Duvauferrier R, Ramée A, Guibert JL, eds. Imagerie interventionnelle en pathologie urologique: problèmes particuliers. Montpellier: Axone 1986:572–577.
20. Pinet A, Maillet PJ, Pelle-Francoz D, Finas B. Radiologie urinaire d'intervention sur les cavités excrétrices. Encyclop. Méd Chir (Paris) [Radiodiagnostic] 1987;5:34350 A10.

Endoscopic Management of Stones in the Urinary Tract

P. J. Van Cangh and A. N. Dardenne

The vast majority of urinary concretions will be eliminated spontaneously due to their small size. Up to the size of 4 mm, 90% of the lower ureteral and 80% of the upper ureteral stones will pass spontaneously. Conversely, of the stones measuring between 4 and 6 mm in diameter, only 50% of the lower ureteral and 20% of the upper ureteral stones will pass unimpeded (37). Although anecdotal reports of spontaneous expulsion are frequent, larger stones necessitate interventional maneuvers more frequently according to their size and the duration of symptoms (46).

Open surgical operations and blind manipulations are well established procedures with a high percentage of success and a well-known morbidity (9, 10, 14, 15). The need for more precise and less traumatic procedures has promoted the development of manipulations under direct vision, i.e., ureteroscopy.

We will review the technique and the present status of ureteroscopy in ureteral stone management. Other diagnostic and therapeutic aspects of ureteroscopy, or other endourologic procedures for ureteral stones will not be discussed. Recent advances in extracorporeal shock wave lithotripsy (ESWL), endourology, and pulsed-dye laser technology (47) are rapidly modifying the field at the present time (32).

History of Ureteroscopy

Anecdotal reports of endoscopic viewing of grossly dilated ureters appeared shortly after the development of effective cystoscopy. The routine use of a pediatric cystoscope was reported in 1978 (17, 28). Pérez Castro and Martinez-Pineiro (38) reported the first series of patients managed successfully with a specially designed rigid ureteronephroscope. An important technical step was accomplished by Bichler et al. (4) with the development of an offset optic lens and a straight operating channel allowing the passage of rigid instruments.

Ureteroscopy was initially designed as a transurethral or *retrograde* procedure; later, however, concomitantly with the development of percutaneous renal surgery, it was also performed as an *antegrade* prodecure (19).

In the beginning, ureteroscopy was limited to observation and simple manipulations. Application of electrohydraulic and ultrasonic stone disintegra-

tion in the ureter was investigated early (16, 40); it became a safe procedure as soon as it could be performed under direct vision (4, 19, 30, 48).

Flexible ureteroscopes were considered early in the history of ureteroscopy, and improved models are appearing regularly on the market (1, 2, 6). With a few exceptions, they have not gained widespread popularity (7). A technical incongruity persists between the imperatives of a small diameter and simultaneous adequate irrigation, working, and viewing capabilities.

The present development of a fine and effective flexible laser fiber might reverse that trend in the near future and motivate further development of flexible endoscopes (2).

Instrumentation

A detailed comparative description of available instruments is beyond the scope of this review. The interested reader is referred to the pertinent literature (29, 34).

Technique

Although the "easy" ureteral stone can be managed under intravenous sedation, the procedure usually requires adequate anesthesia. In addition to the usual factors influencing the choice of the type and level of anesthesia, the position and size of the stone should be taken into consideration. Moreover, the need for adjuvant procedures such as percutaneous nephrostomy and antegrade ureteroscopy can be anticipated and will influence the decision. A purposely designed uroradiologic table greatly facilitates the procedure, because it allows simultaneous excellent lithotomy positioning, easy fluoroscopy, and radiography during the procedure. Wide-spectrum antibiotics are administered at the beginning of the operation. The entire procedure is performed through a 23.5 Fr cystoscope sheath that allows the passage of all instruments and dilators as well as permanent decompression of the bladder. We prefer to start with the insertion of a 150 cm long soft tip guide wire into the ureter and under fluoroscopic control usually negotiate the passage of the wire above the stone into the renal pelvis (Fig. **1a**). Precurved angiographic catheters and guide wires of

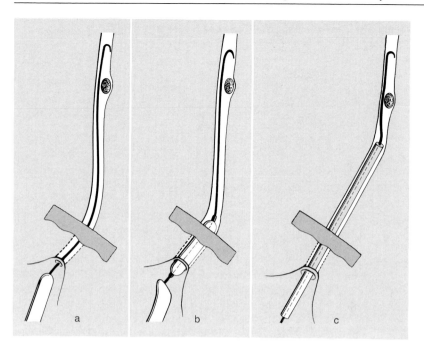

Fig. 1   Schematic drawing of retrograde ureteroscopy
a Insertion of a J-shaped guide wire above the stone
b Balloon dilation of the ureteral orifice
c Introduction of scope via the guide wire

various configurations can be exchanged over the initial wire and greatly facilitate this step.

Introduction of the scope into the ureter can be achieved with several techniques. Direct insertion of the ureteroscope together with an additional ureteral

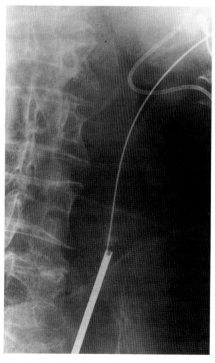

Fig. 2   Guide wire and ureteroscope are shown in place

catheter in the instrument channel can be accomplished with an elegant twisting maneuver. In our experience this is only possible in about 50% of the cases, and we therefore prefer to use an angioplasty balloon introduced over the initial guide wire. The balloon should be of sufficient length to provide one-step dilation of the ureteral orifice and intramural ureter (Fig. **1b**). Diluted contrast medium injected into the balloon allows for fluoroscopic monitoring of the dilation process. A significant waist type of image is usually seen at the site of the orifice, and it is important for easy introduction of the scope to ascertain that no constricted portion remains.

Alternative techniques of ureteral dilation exist. Insertion of a ureteral catheter for 24 to 48 hours will soften the ureter and facilitate the passage and the progression of the ureteroscope. Various guided and nonguided rigid and plastic dilators can be used according to individual experience and preference (13, 29). We have found the simplicity and the speed of the angioplasty balloon difficult to surpass.

The ureteroscope is inserted over the guide wire, which is directed to exit through the side channel of the sheath. This permits further manipulation through the working channel, with the guide wire remaining in place (Figs. **1c, 2**). It is noteworthy that the procedure is more difficult to perform in men, especially those with an enlarged prostate or a urethral stricture. Previous ureteral or radical pelvic surgery tends to decrease the mobility of the pelvic ureter and therefore complicate the procedure. In women, the presence of pelvic floor descensus can

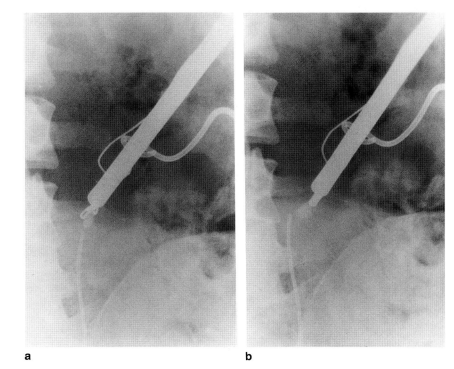

Fig. **3 Antegrade
ureteroscopy: manipulation
of the stone**
a Grasping forceps
b Ultrasonic lithotripsy

a   **b**

complicate the procedure; an intravaginal sponge stick is useful to correct the inclination of the intramural ureter.

The passage of the ureteroscope above the iliac vessels is usually possible, but may be difficult and dangerous. When it appears that the stone is impacted in the proximal ureter, the use of antegrade ureteroscopy is preferable: it is much safer to manage the problem from above through the proximally dilated ureter (19, 41). In that case, a percutaneous nephrostomy is performed, taking care to enter the collecting system via a middle or superior calyx. The track is dilated, the nephroscope is introduced, and the ureteropelvic junction is identified. It is often possible to reach a proximal ureteral stone with the nephroscope itself (Fig. **3a, b**). Alternatively, the (short) rigid ureteroscope or the flexible ureteronephroscope is introduced through the sheath of the nephroscope and manipulated downward following the path already traveled by the stone (Fig. **4a–c**). Direct vision provides precise control over the manipulations of an impacted stone and transforms an otherwise risky blind extraction into a safe procedure.

Small stones can be extracted directly with a variety of grasping instruments or baskets (Fig. **5**). Larger stones necessitate fragmentation. Ultrasonic lithotripsy has been found to be adequate for this purpose when performed under direct vision and in short application sequences to avoid thermal damage to the ureteral wall (4, 19, 22) (Fig. **6**). Alternatively, electrohydraulic lithotripsy can be successful; it has

the additional advantage, that it can be performed through a flexible instrument that is sometimes easier to manipulate down a convoluted ureter (18). It is, however, more dangerous than ultrasonic lithotripsy, and direct visual control is imperative to avoid severe damage to the ureteral wall (48). Larger stone fragments can be removed through the ureteroscope sheath; this can be facilitated by the use of a "ureteral access system," which allows multiple reinsertions of the instruments (36). Smaller fragments may be left in situ to be eliminated spontaneously.

Postoperative Drainage

In simple procedures on the lower ureter it is usually not necessary to drain the system. In case of prolonged manipulations or management of proximal ureteric stones, postoperative drainage is very helpful (41). It is indispensable in case of ureteric perforation or extravasation. We and others (31) use a double-J stent in almost every case, since it considerably reduces postoperative pain. The use of a nylon thread exiting via the urethral meatus simplifies the removal of the stent. A ureteral catheter may also be used as a cheaper drainage alternative (12, 20). When a nephrostomy has been established, concomitantly with ureteroscopy, a stent through the ureteral orifice is needed to avoid stenosis of the manipulated defunctionalized ureter (27).

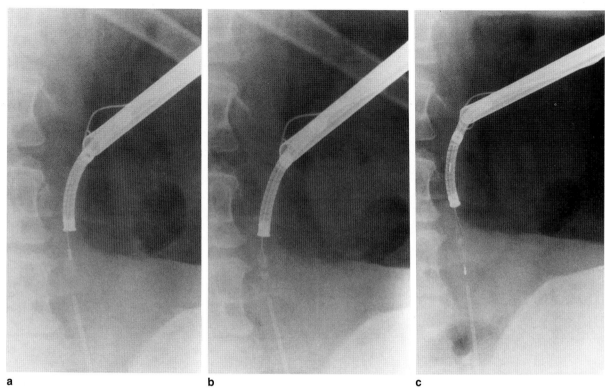

a   b   c

Fig. 4   **Management of a large ureteral calculus by antegrade flexible ureteronephroscopy**
a **Fragmentation** with the electrohydraulic probe
b **Extraction** of fragments with flexible tripod forceps
c **Dormia basket** is used to capture the last fragment

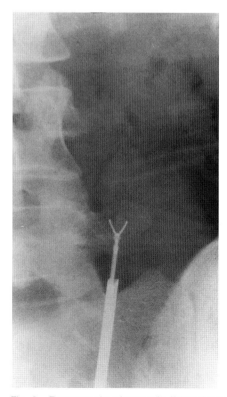

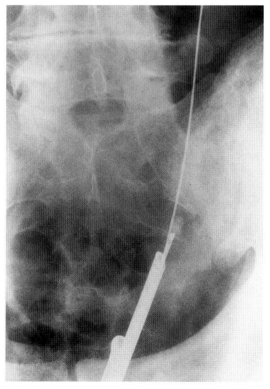

Fig. 6   **Retrograde ultrasonic lithotripsy of distal ureteral calculus**

Fig. 5   **Direct retrograde extraction of small ureteral calculus**

Results

Results of 2755 cases published in the English and French literature (8, 11, 12, 19, 20, 22, 23, 27, 29, 31, 42, 43, 45, 49) or as recent congress abstracts (American Urological Association, 81st annual meeting, May 18–22, 1986, New York; European Association of Urology, 7th Congress, June 26–28, 1986, Budapest; 80e Congrès, Association Française d'Urologie, 19–21 nov. 1986, Paris) are summarized in Table **1**. As with any new technological development, a "learning curve" is to be expected: with experience, results improve and complications diminish (45, 49).

Presently, overall success for ureteral stones managed by ureteroscopy is about 85%; it remains higher for lower ureteral stones. When a decided endourologic attitude is adopted, combination of retrograde and antegrade techniques improves the results considerably. Several studies report close to 100% success using that approach. Our personal experience over the last 4 years with more than 200 patients with ureteral calculi confirms those latter results.

The average duration of hospitalization for successful cases is 3 days, which is significantly shorter than for ureterolithotomy.

When retrograde ureteroscopy fails to remove the stone, the rate of subsequent open ureterolithotomy reflects the preferences of the physician in the selection of the therapeutic strategy. Some will proceed immediately to open operation and report a 15% rate of lithotomy (13); others favor further endoscopic or extracorporeal manipulations and report an open procedure rate of only 0 to 5% (19, 27).

Complications

Ureteroscopy is a difficult and a potentially dangerous procedure (Table **2**) (5, 24). It is imperative that sufficient time be allowed for the procedure, since hurried and rough handling is the surest way to experience complications (20).

Early or Perioperative

Major complications occur in 2 to 8% of the published series (8, 44). They include mainly ureteral perforation or false passage and ureteral avulsion or disruption. The rate of immediate or delayed surgery for ureteroscopy complications approximates 2 to 3% (11).

Minor complications occur in 5 to 15% of the cases, and include fever, flank pain, sepsis, and unwanted mobilization of the stone. Stone expulsion through the wall of the ureter can occur with forceful maneuvers, but apparently does not produce severe side-effects (49). Displacement of the stone into the renal pelvis is a frustrating experience, and is

Table **1**   Results of ureteroscopy

	Success rate (%)
Overall	50–100
Lower ureteral stones	85–100
Upper ureteral stones	
Retrograde ureteroscopy only	25– 62
Combined with antegrade ureteroscopy and/or ESWL	80–100

Table **2**   Complications

	%
Perforation	3
Avulsion	< 1
Stricture	< 1
Reflux	< 1

theoretically a failure of the procedure. It is, however, an excellent preparation for percutaneous extraction or ESWL. Minor extravasation when looked for routinely occurs in 28% of the cases (20).

Late Complications

The precise rate of stricture formation after ureteroscopy is not yet known. Weinberg et al. (49) reviewed 941 cases performed in 28 centers and found less than 1% stricture formation. One study revealed no increased stricture rate after a 20-month period in 42 patients (43); the same investigators found no evidence of an increased rate of urinary tract infection or hypertension. Others have found no evidence for the development of late complications by clinical and imaging studies performed up to 24 months after ureteroscopy (8, 11, 20). In our series, 50 patients had a postoperative intravenous urogram more than one year after operation; no patient had a significant lesion requiring operative intervention.

The occurrence of vesicoureteral reflux has not been routinely investigated (29). One study has reported the presence of low-grade sterile reflux in 2 out of 42 patients studied 2 years post-ureteroscopy (43).

Most of the late complications can be managed conservatively by endourologic techniques (11, 23).

Present Strategy for Ureteral Stones

The development of endourology and ESWL is changing the current approach to ureteral calculi (11, 25, 27, 32, 35, 39, 42).

Lower Ureteral Stones (below the Iliac Vessels)

Blind manipulations, such as with a Dormia basket, remain valuable procedures for small ureteral calculi. Ureteroscopy is, however, a more precise and therefore less dangerous procedure and has replaced most of the indications for the use of a basket. Larger stones can also be approached and fragmented under direct vision.

Recently, ESWL with a modified positioning of the patient has been used with success for lower ureteral stones (33).

Upper Ureteral Stones (above the Iliac Vessels)

ESWL can be used for upper ureteral stones with or without ureteral catheterization (39). The rate of success is not as high as in cases of renal stones (11, 35). The insertion of a ureteral stent alongside the stone before ESWL, although adding to the morbidity of the procedure, increases the success rate of treatment (11). When a ureteral catheter is inserted, it is preferable to try to place the stone in the renal pelvis for further management by either percutaneous nephrostomy (so-called "push-pull") or ESWL (so-called "push-bang") technique (20, 26). Retrograde stone flushing is facilitated by occlusion of the ureteral lumen distally by a specially designed large-size double-lumen or ballon-equipped catheter (3, 21, 23).

When there is acute obstruction or sepsis, or when the stone is resisting ESWL, antegrade ureteroscopy as described above is the procedure of choice.

Open ureterolithotomy is now only required in 0 to 7.5% of ureteral calculi (11, 19, 20).

Ureteral obstruction by compacted fragments produced by ESWL of large-size calculi ("Steinstrasse") presents a difficult management problem. Ureteroscopy is the preferred treatment of that complication, although one-session ureteroscopy is successful in only 50 to 60% of the cases. The insertion of a double J stent before ESWL is therefore recommended, because it is a useful prevention of Steinstrasse formation.

Conclusion

Ureteroscopy has acquired an important place in the management of ureteral stones. Direct vision is indeed the key to safe manipulations of stones in the confined ureteral lumen. Ureteroscopy has changed forever the attitude toward ureteral calculi. It has invalidated the old dictum prohibiting closed manipulations for large ureteric stones or those located above the iliac vessels. Using either the retrograde and antegrade routes, or both, almost any stone can be visualized, safely manipulated or fragmented, and removed.

The place of ureteroscopy in the armamentarium for ureteric stone management depends on the urologist's preference and familiarity with the technique. The procedure is now safe and effective; its future will depend on the development and availability of other technologies, such as ESWL and pulsed-dye laser (47). No single technique is able to solve every stone problem; ideally, all techniques should be available and interchangeable according to each individual patient and stone requirement.

References

1. Bagley DH, Huffman JL, Lyon ES. Combined rigid and flexible ureteropyeloscopy. J Urol 1983;130:243.
2. Bagley DH. Flexible ureteropyeloscopy with modular, "disposable" endoscope. Urology 1987;29:296–300.
3. Beckman CF, Roth RA. Use of retrograde occlusion balloon catheters in percutaneous removal of renal calculi. Urology 1985;25:277.
4. Bichler K-H, Erdmann D, Schmitz-Moormann P, Halim S. Operatives Ureterorenoskop für Ultraschallanwendung und Steinextraktion. Urologe [A] 1984;23:99–104.
5. Biester R, Gillenwater JY. Complications following ureteroscopy. J Urol 1986;136:380–382.
6. Bush IM, Goldberg E, Javadpour N, Chakrobortty H, Morelli F. Ureteroscopy and renoscopy: a preliminary report. Chicago Med School 1970;30:46.
7. Bush IM, Sadoughi N, John T, Bush J, Solanki H, Cohen E, Guinan P, Burlington IL. Experience and complications with 600 flexible fiberoptic ureterorenoscopic examinations. J Urol 1985;133:216A.
8. Carter SSC, Cox R, Wickham JEA. Complications associated with ureteroscopy. Br J Urol 1986;58:625–628.
9. Constantian HM. Management of ureteral calculi: series of 574 cases with special emphasis on use of Davis loop extractor. J Urol 1974;112:33.
10. Drach GW. Stone manipulation: modern usage and occasional mishaps. Urology 1978;12:286–289.
11. Dretler SP, Keating MA, Riley J. An algorithm for the management of ureteral calculi. J Urol 1986;136:1190–1193.
12. El-Kappany H, Gaballah MA, Ghoneim MA. Rigid ureteroscopy for the treatment of ureteric calculi: experience in 120 cases. Br J Urol 1986;58:499–503.
13. Ford TF, Parkinson CM, Wickham JEA. Clinical and experimental evaluation of ureteric dilatation. Br J Urol 1984;56:460–463.
14. Fox M, Pyrah LN, Raper FP. Management of ureteric stone: a review of 292 cases. Br J Urol 1965;37:660–670.
15. Furlow WL, Bucchiere JJ. The surgical fate of ureteral calculi: review of the Mayo Clinic experience. J Urol 1976;116:559–562.
16. Goodfriend R. Ultrasonic and electrohydraulic lithotripsy of ureteral calculi. Urology 1984;23:5–8.
17. Godman TM. Ureteroscopy with a pediatric cystoscope in adults. Urology 1977;9:394.
18. Green DF, Lytton B. Early experience with direct vision electrohydraulic lithotripsy of ureteral calculi. J Urol 1985;133:767–770.
19. Gumpinger R, Miller K, Fuchs G, Eisenberger F. Antegrade ureteroscopy for stone removal. Eur Urol 1985;11:199–202.
20. Hosking DH, Ramsey EW. Rigid transurethral ureteroscopy. Br. J Urol 1986;58:621–624.
21. Hulbert JC, Reddy PK, Hunter DW, Young AT, Castaneda-Zuniga WR, Amplatz K, Lange PH. Percutaneous management of ureteral calculi facilitated by retrograde flushing with carbon dioxide or diluted radiopaque dye. J Urol 1985;134:29–32.
22. Huffman JL, Lyon ES, Bagley DH. Transurethral ureteropyeloscopy. In: Bagley DH, Huffman JL, Lyon ES, eds. Urologic endoscopy: a manual and atlas. Boston: Little, Brown 1985:185–206.

23. Kahn RI. Endourological treatment of ureteral calculi. J Urol 1986;135:239–243.
24. Kaufman JJ. Ureteral injury from ureteroscopic stone manipulation. Urology 1984;23:267–269.
25. Keating MA, Heney NM, Young HH, Kerr WS, O'Leary MP, Dretler SP. Ureteroscopy: the initial experience. J Urol 1986;135:689–693.
26. Kellet MJ, Wickham JE, Payne SR. Combined retrograde and antegrade manipulations for percutaneous nephrolithotomy of ureteral calculi: "push-pull" technique. Urology 1985;25:391–392.
27. Lingeman JE, Sonda LP, Kahnoski RJ, Coury TA, Newman DM, Mosbaugh PG, Mertz JHO, Steele RE, Frank B. Ureteral stone management: emerging concepts. Br J Urol 1986;135:1172–1174.
28. Lyon ES, Banno JJ, Schoenberg WH. Transurethral ureteroscopy in men using juvenile cystoscopy equipment. J Urol 1979;122:152–153.
29. Lyon ES, Huffman JL, Bagley DH. Ureteroscopy and ureteropyeloscopy. Urology 1984;23 (suppl):29–36.
30. Marberger M. Disintegration of renal and ureteral calculi with ultrasound. Urol Clin North Am 1983;10:729.
31. Marberger M. Die endoskopische Behandlung des Uretersteins. Urologe [A] 1984;23:308–316.
32. Miller K, Fuchs G, Rassweiler J, Eisenberger F. Treatment of ureteral stone disease: the role of ESWL and endourology. World J Urol 1985;3:53–57.
33. Miller RA, Bubeck JR, Hautmann R. Extracorporeal shock wave lithotripsy of distal ureteral calculi. Eur Urol 1986;12:305–307.
34. Miller RA, Ramsay JWA, Crocker PR, Carter S, Eardley I, Whitfield HN, Wickham JEA. Ureterorenal endoscopy: which instrument, what cost? Br J Urol 1986;58:610–616.
35. Mueller SC, Wilbert D, Thueroff JW, Alken P. Extracorporeal shock wave lithotripsy of ureteral stones: clinical experience and experimental findings. J Urol 1986;135:831–834.
36. Newman RC, Hunter PT, Hawkins IF, Finlayson B. The ureteral access system: a review of the immediate results in 43 cases. J Urol 1987;137:380–383.
37. O'Flynn JD. The treatment of ureteric stones: report on 1120 patients. Br J Urol 1980;52:436–438.
38. Pérez-Castro Ellendt E, Martinez-Pineiro JA. Ureteral and renal endoscopy. Eur Urol 1982;8:117–120.
39. Rassweiler J, Lutz K, Gumpinger R, Eisenberger F. Efficacy of in situ extracorporeal shock wave lithotripsy for upper ureteral calculi. Eur Urol 1986;12:377–386.
40. Reuter HJ, Kern E. Electronic lithotripsy of ureteral calculi. J Urol 1973;110:181–183.
41. Smith AD. Percutaneous ureteral surgery and stenting. Urology 1984;23 (suppl):37–42.
42. Sonda LP, Frank B. Ureteral stone management: emerging concepts. J Urol 1986;135:257A.
43. Stackl W, Marberger M. Late sequelae of the management of ureteral calculi with the ureterorenoscope. J Urol 1986;136:386–389.
44. Thomas R, Ulker EU. Rigid ureteroscopy: pitfalls and remedies. J Urol 1986;135:256A.
45. Vallancien G, Veillon B, Charton M, Brisset JM. Technique, échecs et complications de l'extraction des calculs de l'uretère par urétéroscopie rigide. Ann Urol 1985;19:228–232.
46. Walsh A. An aggressive approach to stones in the lower ureter. Br J Urol 1974;46:11–14.
47. Watson GM, Wickham JE. Initial experience with a pulsed-dye laser for ureteric calculi. Lancet 1986;i:1357–1358.
48. Webb DR, Fitzpatrick JM. Experimental ureterolithotripsy. World J Urol 1985;3:33–35.
49. Weinberg JJ, Ansong K, Smith AD. Complications of ureteroscopy in relation to experience: report of survey and author experience. J Urol 1987;137:384–385.

Percutaneous Management of Stones in the Urinary Tract

T. P. Smith and W. R. Castaneda-Zuniga

Percutaneous nephrolithotomy began clinically some 10 years prior to this writing (26). At approximately the same time, extracorporeal shockwave lithotripsy (ESWL) was also being developed (16). Percutaneous nephrolithotomy rapidly gained in clinical popularity and became the main method of stone removal (2, 11, 13, 20, 24, 50, 59). It proved to be as successful as open surgical removal, with less morbidity postoperatively, and was often superior in economic terms (3,7). During its life span, the development of better equipment, including improved endoscopes, led to its continued growth. However, in the last few years, percutaneous procedures have seen a rapid decline, with the steady increase in the use of extracorporeal methods (62, 63). Like percutaneous procedures in comparison with open lithotomy, ESWL is more cost-effective, causes less patient morbidity, and has ever-increasing success rates when compared to percutaneous methods (8). ESWL is now available on a worldwide basis, with well-deserved clinical acceptance. It is now considered the primary mode of therapy for the majority of upper urinary tract calculi (17, 27). Although continued technical developments will inevitably improve extracorporeal methods, percutaneous stone removal will continue to be an alternative method of therapy in selected situations. Therefore, percutaneous techniques must remain in the armamentarium of the interventional radiologist and urologist. Difficulty arises in that the more easily removed pelvic stones will rarely be approached percutaneously, leaving difficult and involved cases such as staghorn calculi and strictured systems for percutaneous removal, either on its own or in combination with extracorporeal methods. The technique of percutaneous stone removal must therefore remain extremely fine-tuned if success is to be achieved.

This chapter discusses the basic approach to percutaneous stone removal. The basic principles are presented with easier stone cases, and the more difficult types are considered in detail in the hope of presenting information which is useful and up-to-date in the rapidly changing field of nephrolithotomy.

Patient Selection

The indications for nephrolithotomy are that the urinary stone is causing symptoms, obstruction, is a source of infection, or has the potential to cause any of these. In patients with purely asymptomatic stones, some believe the stones should not be removed. However, surgical literature has demonstrated irreversible renal parenchymal damage if the stones are left in place, particularly large stones such as staghorn calculi (52, 60). Therefore, nephrolithotomy, by whatever method, should be a decision carefully made which is individualized to each patient. Once such a decision to remove the calculus is made, percutaneous nephrolithotomy is indicated in any patient with renal or ureteral stones necessitating surgical intervention. There are no absolute contra-indications to percutaneous nephrolithotomy other than medical conditions which preclude any intervention. The relative contra-indications include an uncorrectable bleeding diathesis, active untreated infection or sepsis, extreme obesity (as the instrumentation may not be of sufficient length to facilitate stone removal), severe kyphoscoliosis precluding an adequate approach, and urinary and anatomical defects requiring surgical correction.

Patient preparation, of course, is essential. The patient should be informed of the possible complications, the chance of unsuccessful stone removal, and the possibility of long-term nephrostomy drainage. Preoperative laboratory work is essentially the same as for any invasive procedure. An intravenous pyelogram is helpful in determining the renal collecting system anatomy as well as stone position. Oblique views are essential for localization of possible percutaneous entry sites.

Anesthesia

Percutaneous nephrolithotomy is best performed either under general tracheal anesthesia or lumbar extradural anesthesia. Local anesthesia (1% Lidocaine) with intravenous narcotic augmentation can be used, but local anesthesia is difficult for tracts requiring large degrees of dilation. This is especially true for deep tissues, particularly at the level of the renal capsule. A 22 gauge needle can be passed along the line of entry for the injection of local anesthesia. A Tuohy-Borst adapter can be attached to the initial dilator to inject local anesthesia into the deep tissues. This assures anesthesia along the site of entry. Percutaneous stone removal is certainly not without pain. A comfortable, quiet patient is essential to the success of the procedure. The overall choice of anesthesia should be carefully evaluated and individualized to the patient (47).

Patient Positioning

A Foley catheter is always inserted prior to positioning the patient. Positioning of the patient is extremely important for proper access (19, 20). The patient is usually placed in a prone oblique position with the affected side elevated approximately 30 degrees (Fig. **1**). If a C-arm arrangement is used, the patient can remain in a completely prone position and all needed angulation accomplished with the fluoroscopic unit. Patient or C-arm positioning allows a posterolateral approach to the kidney. Such an approach provides better fixation of the drainage catheters, is less likely to injure pelvic vessels (6, 28), as the area of least vascularity is transgressed, and results in improved patient comfort postoperatively. The patient is draped so as to control spillage of irrigant solutions, as such solutions are needed for endoscopic visualization. If the room is not equipped for drainage of irrigant solutions, drapes with collection arrangements connecting to suction can be purchased and function well.

Opacification of the Collecting System

Once the patient is positioned on the fluoroscopic table, the collecting system must first be visualized. This is important both for the puncture and to observe any change in the position of the renal stone since prior studies. Since most renal stones are radiopaque, the stone itself can be used fluoroscopically as a guide to the collecting system location for the initial puncture. One must be aware, however, that a change in stone position could have occurred since prior diagnostic studies. Intravenous contrast material can be used if the stone is not obstructing. US can also visualize the collecting system for the initial puncture. In addition, a widely dilated system can be easily approached without prior opacification. In all of these methods, a fine neddle (22 gauge Chiba) is first advanced into the collecting system for the injection of positive contrast material. Alternatively, a retrograde ureteral catheter has proved to be advantageous, particularly when a non-obstructing stone is present. Once the catheter has been cystoscopically placed in the upper ureter, contrast material can be injected at will with excellent visualization of the pelvis (Fig. **2**). After skinny needle or retrograde ureteral catheter placement and injection of positive contrast, carbon dioxide can be easily injected by the same route. As the patient is in a prone position, this will visualize the posterior calyces (31, 34, 35, 56). If a C-arm fluoroscopic unit is not utilized, the patient often needs to be repositioned for the definitive, posterolateral access. Dislodgment of the fine needle can be avoided by placing a 3 Fr catheter in the renal collecting system over an 0.018 guide wire placed directly through the initial fine neddle. Such a catheter is small and therefore causes little damage, regardless of its entry site, and provides stable, continued access to the renal collecting system throughout the procedure.

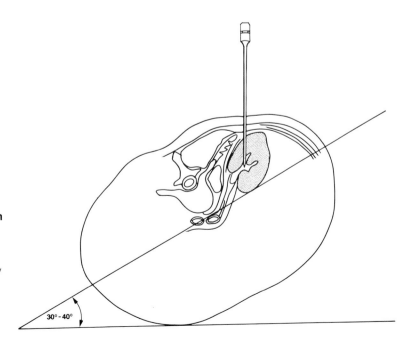

Fig. **1** **Sagittal image of a patient in an oblique view at 30 degrees.** The needle has been placed via a posterior calyx. This allows a straight placement of the needle into the kidney through a relatively avascular area. The patient can also remain flat on the table, with a C-arm apparatus being used for rotational purposes

30° - 40°

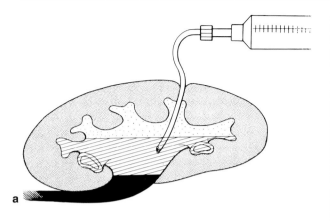
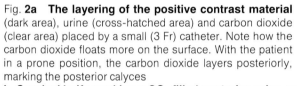
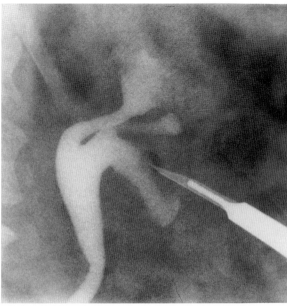

Fig. **2a** **The layering of the positive contrast material** (dark area), urine (cross-hatched area) and carbon dioxide (clear area) placed by a small (3 Fr) catheter. Note how the carbon dioxide floats more on the surface. With the patient in a prone position, the carbon dioxide layers posteriorly, marking the posterior calyces

b **Surgical knife marking a CO_2-filled posterior calyx,** seen as a rounded lucent area. This provides an excellent target for puncture into the posterior collecting system

Approaches

Once the collecting system is well opacified, the site of the stone can be determined by obliquing the patient or the fluoroscopic unit, given a C-arm type of apparatus, and by comparison with prior radiographic studies. Selection of the proper site of approach is critical to the success of percutaneous nephrolithotomy (19). The access must be planned in such a manner as to be safe, facilitate adequate tract dilation, allow appropriate instruments to reach the stone or stones, and provide for placement of adequate drainage catheters (20). For a safe definitive entry into the kidney, the site on the skin must be chosen so as to facilitate a posterolateral approach. A direct posterior puncture often transgresses the thick paraspinal muscles and makes tract dilation difficult. A puncture directed more than thirty degrees from the sagittal plane increases the chances of passing through the organs of the retroperitoneum. If in doubt, computed tomography (CT) examination or ultrasound guidance may prove helpful in localizing a tract. In addition, the puncture must be made inferior enough to avoid the pleural space.

When considering the approach for percutaneous nephrolithotomy, the method of removal must be an initial consideration (45, 49) (Fig. **3**). It is always best to have a relatively straight path to the stone, as many of the percutaneous instruments for removal are rigid. For small pelvic stones, a posterior calyx in the mid- or lower pole is usually punctured. For larger pelvic stones and staghorn calculi (1, 36, 64), a

posterior calyx is punctured in the middle or lower pole, which facilitates passage of the guide wire into the ureter. Passing the guide wire around a staghorn calculus can prove to be difficult, as can tract dilation. The retrograde catheter is often helpful in that it distends the renal pelvis upon injection of contrast material. During puncture onto a staghorn calculus, the definitive 18 gauge needle is often used to push the stone for a distance of a few millimeters to allow the guide wire to enter the renal pelvis. Calyceal

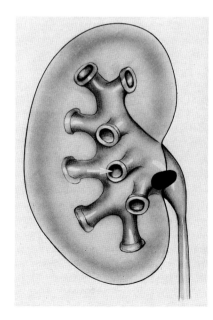

Fig. **3a**

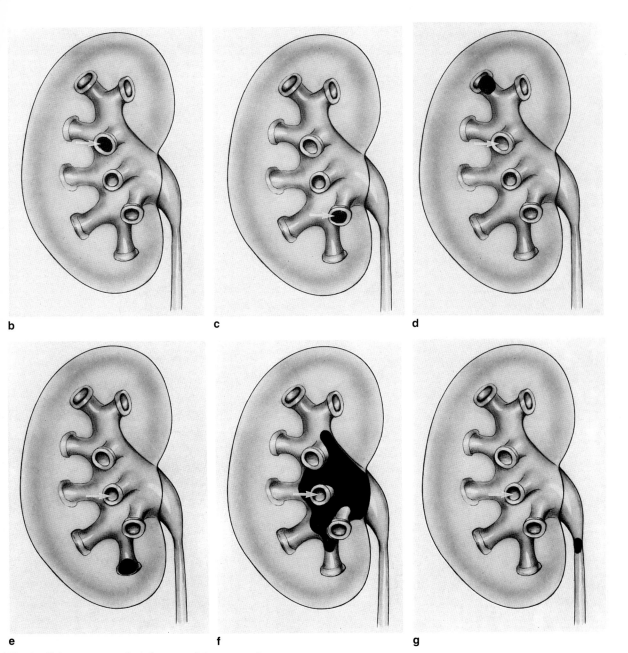

Fig. 3 Urinary stone sites for possible removal

a Pelvic stone. The arrow indicates a midpole calyceal access which would be ideal for stone removal. With pelvic stones, several posterior calyceal accesses can prove successful

b Posterior midpole stone. The ideal access, indicated by the arrow, would be directly onto the stone

c Posterior lower calyceal stone. Access can be directly onto the stone, as indicated by the arrow, but a midpole access using flexible instrumentation is also a possibility

d Upper pole stone. Access can be directly onto the stone, if it is located in a posterior calyx. This will often require an intercostal approach. If the stone is located in an anterior calyx, a distal site of access, as indicated here by the arrow, is necessary. With distal access, rigid instrumentation may be used if a straight enough approach to the infundibulum can be achieved. If not, flexible instrumentation must be used

e Anterior lower pole stone. Access in this case must be from a posteriorly-located calyx which would allow instrumentation to reach the lower pole. As with the upper pole, if a straight enough access can be obtained, rigid instrumentation may be used. However, as can be seen in this case, access into the posterior calyces (arrow) will require flexible instrumentation

f Staghorn calculus. Access to a staghorn calculus is best achieved to remove the largest stone volume. This is best approached either from the lower or the midpole, as indicated by the arrow. This allows a large amount of debulking, with possible extracorporeal shockwave lithotripsy to follow. When done entirely by a percutaneous route, multiple access sites are often needed

g Ureteral stone. In the event of an isolated ureteral stone, the ideal access should simply be to place catheters down the ureter. This is best achieved from a midpole calyx, as shown here (arrow). However, multiple access sites can be available

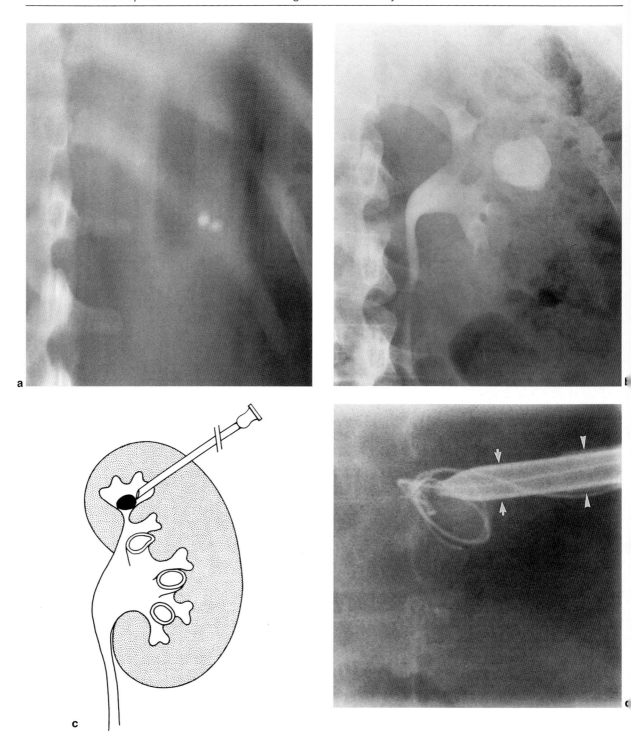

Fig. **4   Stone removal from a calyceal diverticulum**
a   Plain tomographic image demonstrating two radiopaque calculi
b   Intravenous pyelogram demonstrating a calyceal diverticulum in the region of the stones
c   Direct needle puncture into the diverticulum containing the stone
d   The guide wire has been coiled within the calyceal diverticulum. From this point, the wire is usually placed through the neck of the diverticulum into the renal pelvis and down the ureter if possible. However, if this cannot be accomplished, as in this case, direct dilation to the level of the diverticulum can be obtained. Note the large dilator (arrows) with the accompanying Teflon sheath (arrowheads)

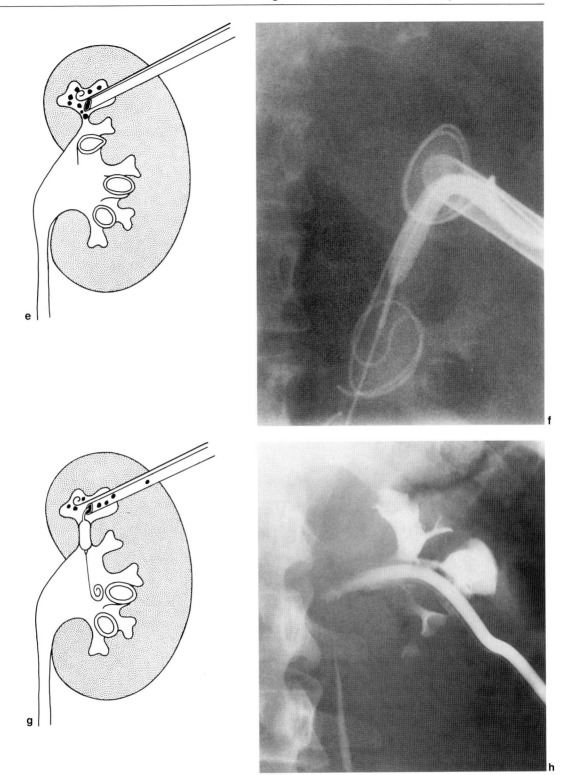

Fig. **4**
e A sheath with a disintegrated stone following placement of the lithotriptor
f Guide wires are present in the diverticulum, renal pelvis, and down the ureter. A balloon catheter has been placed via the working sheath across the neck of the diverticulum for dilation
g Balloon dilation of the neck of the diverticulum
h Nephrostogram with a catheter stenting the neck of the diverticulum. Stenting of the neck of the diverticulum is recommended for at least several weeks following dilation

stones can be approached in one of two ways, depending upon the location of the calyx (4, 5). The direct approach involves puncturing the calyx which contains the stone. This is the preferred technique for isolated mid- and lower pole posterior calyceal stones, where the puncture is usually made just medial to the retained calculus, usually at the level of the calyceal–infundibular junction. This traps the stone between the puncture site and the tract, and does not displace the stone into the renal pelvis. For upper pole posterior calyceal stones, a direct puncture onto the stone is made whenever possible. For high-lying kidneys, an approach from the lower pole becomes necessary. This limits removal to flexible instrumentation. For isolated anterior calyceal stones, a direct puncture on the stone traverses a large amount of renal tissue. In addition, a difficult turn is often created as the guide wires are placed in the renal pelvis. The indirect puncture often proves to be more favorable for anterior calyces. This involves puncture onto the posterior calyx which provides as straight as possible a pathway to the anterior calyx containing the stones. Upper pole anterior calyceal stones can often be approached through a lower pole posterior calyx. Often by virtue of a slightly cephalad-oriented tract, even rigid instruments can be passed from the lower pole posterior calyx across the renal pelvis to the stone-

containing upper pole calyx without great difficulty. Likewise, mid- and lower pole anterior calyceal stones are probably best approached via a posterior, midpole calyx. Again, removal by rigid instrumentation across the renal pelvis is possible. A slightly caudad-oriented tract may be helpful to straighten the path to the lower pole.

A different problem arises when the stones are contained in a calyx with a stenotic infundibulum or within a diverticulum (29, 39) (Fig. **4a, b**). If posterior in location, the mandatory approach is directly onto the stone (Fig. **4c**). There is little risk of displacing the fragments into the renal pelvis past the neck of the diverticulum or the stenotic infundibulum. Once a guide wire is coiled within the pocket containing the stone, it is directed through the neck of the infundibulum or diverticulum and into the renal pelvis, or down the ureter, for safety (Fig. **4d–h**). If the diverticulum or stenotic infundibulum occur anteriorly, an opposite posterior calyx can be entered, the neck of the diverticulum or stenotic infundibulum balloon dilated or cut via a cautery, and the stone removed (Fig. **5a–d**). In addition, high anterior stones can likewise be removed after dilating or cutting, but are best approached from a mid- or lower pole posterior calyx.

Ureteral stones are best approached via a posterior calyx so as to facilitate easy access down the

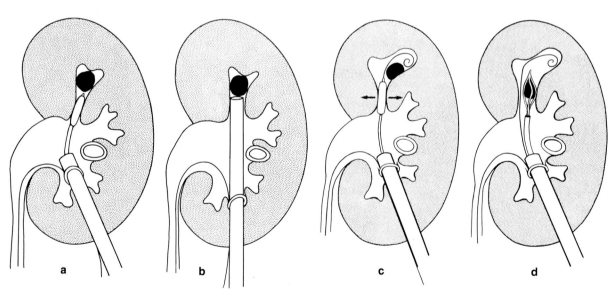

Fig. **5   Approach to a diverticular stone without direct puncture**
a Puncture is carried out in a posterior lower pole calyx providing access to the upper pole infundibulum. Following placement of the working sheath and maneuvering a guide wire to this point, the neck of the diverticulum can be adequately dilated with a balloon catheter. Alternatively, this can be incised endoscopically
b Removal of the stone can then be accomplished using a lithotriptor. This depends on the access for the rigid endoscope, as well as on the stone size, for adequate removal via the working sheath
c, d Alternatively, following balloon dilation of the neck of the diverticulum, basketing of the stone can be accomplished. Note the safety wire in the calyx

ureter, usually best achieved from a midpole approach. Upper pole approaches can be dangerously high in location. Lower pole approaches may result in buckling of guide wires and catheters in the renal pelvis during ureteral manipulations.

For a combination of stones, each approach must be tailored to the particular situation and may even involve multiple entry sites.

Puncture

The definitive puncture of a posterior calyx is usually made with an 18 gauge needle. This can be easily guided by a radiolucent handle (54). The patient or the C-arm apparatus should be positioned in such a way that the needle is passed in a perfectly tangential manner to the desired calyx in a parallel orientation to the associated infundibulum. A posterior calyx is chosen by the injection of carbon dioxide as described previously. The posterior calyceal puncture avoids the highly vascular region of the renal pelvis and, in addition, traverses the least possible renal parenchyma.

Once the puncture is made with the 18 gauge needle its exact position can be verified by the parallax effect of a C-arm, or an aspiration and contrast injection if the C-arm is not available. After the renal collecting system is properly engaged, a floppy guide wire is easily passed into the renal pelvis. The tract is subsequently dilated (22) with standard rigid dilators to at least 7 Fr, where a form of guiding catheter such as a cobra catheter can be advanced to position the guide wire in a safe location. Depending upon the stone location, the guide wire is most often placed down the ureter if possible. If not, placement in a calyx distant from the stone is best. It is often best at this point to exchange the softer floppy guide wire for a stiffening guide wire (10). Such a guide wire resists buckling outside the renal collecting system during the ensuing tract dilation. The tract is subsequently dilated with fascial dilators up to approximately 10–12 Fr. At this point, a catheter of sufficient lumen to accommodate a second guide wire is placed over the original guide wire, and the second guide wire is placed again in a distant location such as down the ureter or into a non-adjacent calyx for safety (Fig. 6a). This safety wire can be covered with a soft 5 Fr catheter, such as a Kifa catheter, to prevent dislodgment. Once sutured into place, the outside portion can be coiled on the patient out of the way of the working field. Such a safety wire guarantees easy re-access to the collecting system or ureter should the initial working sheath be lost during manipulation.

Continued tract dilation can now be accomplished using graduated fascial dilators (Fig. 6b). Two main varieties are available, either rigid metal dilators or semirigid, polyurethane types (55). Both types are placed over the stiffening guide wire, which is usually supported by an 8 Fr catheter. Careful fluoroscopic monitoring of dilator placement is critical. Despite the stiffening wire and protective catheter, the guide wire can easily be kinked if a straight approach is not maintained (Fig. 6c). Each dilator is best advanced using steady pressure and turning motions. Care must be taken, if rigid, fascial dilators are used, not to buckle the guide wire within the renal pelvis, which can easily be perforated (Fig. 6d). Multiple dilations, increasing progressively by 2 Fr size dilators, are carried out until the tract reaches the desired size. Multiple, graduated dilators are effective but are obviously slow, requiring many exchanges. Alternatively, a high-pressure balloon catheter can easily be inserted into the 10–12 Fr tract over the guide wire and can effectively dilate the tract by a single inflation (Fig. 6e). This is obviously a much more rapid process than multiple graduated dilators. The size of tract dilation depends upon the instrumentation used, as well as the planned method of stone removal. Most rigid endoscopic instruments require a 30 Fr internal diameter working sheath. However, flexible endoscopic instruments, as well as baskets and snares for fluoroscopic stone removal, require lesser-sized sheaths.

The greatest barriers to tract dilation include the skin entry site, subcutaneous fascial tissues, and the renal capsule. Both the skin site and the subcutaneous fascial tissues can easily be incised with a surgical knife. The renal capsule therefore becomes the major emphasis of tract dilation. The final dilation step consists of a fascial-type dilator which is surrounded by the tapered working sheath of the desired internal diameter. This is then advanced into the renal pelvis over the fascial dilator, and left in place. The purpose of the working sheath is to provide a smooth tract for access to the kidney and to protect the retroperitoneum from the irrigant solutions needed in endoscopic procedures. The sheath is usually thin-walled and made of Teflon. Its tip is slightly tapered for ease of placement. To prevent laceration, care must be taken never to advance the sheath without its proper tapered fascial dilator. The dilator should first be placed at the desired location, and the Teflon sheath then advanced to that point using gentle turning motions and fixing the rigid fascial dilator in place.

Special Puncture Techniques

An intercostal puncture (above the 12th rib) may become necessary for direct access to the upper and middle poles, especially in high-lying kidneys (48). A subcostal approach to a high-lying kidney results in too cephalad an approach for successful calculus removal. Also, the shape of the renal pelvis, such as a bifid system with a stone in the upper system, may

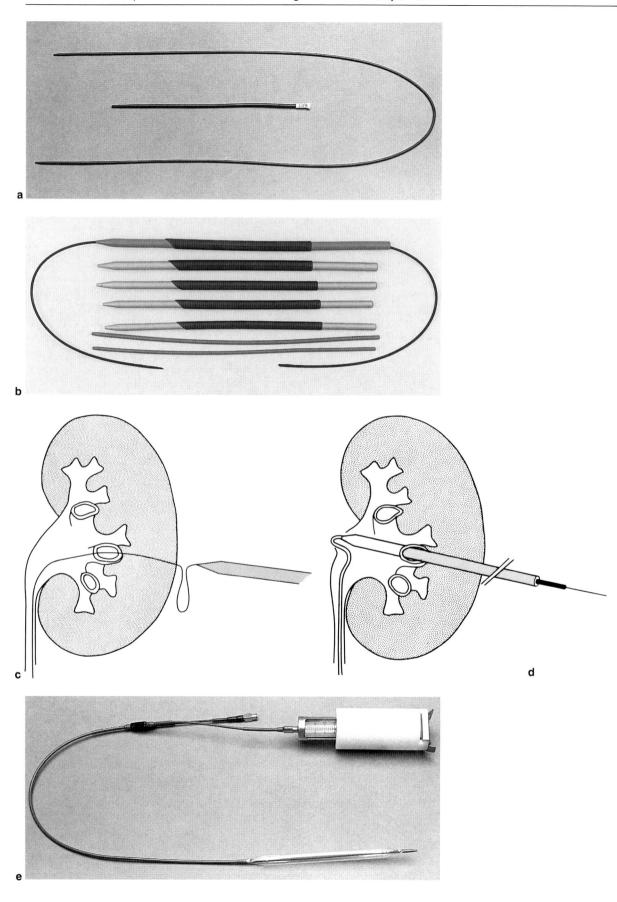

make an intercostal approach a prerequisite to successful stone removal. It is likely that most intercostal punctures traverse the pleural space. Accumulations of fluid occur with intercostal punctures in approximately 30% of cases (65). These are usually small. Larger effusions have, however, occurred. These are best avoided by maintaining the position of the working sheath. Intercostal punctures should always be over the rib, not just under the rib, as major vessels can be lacerated, leading to bleeding. A pneumothorax is possible with punctures through the pleural space, either due to air from the tract or a lacerated lung. This has, however, proven to be very rare. Overall, although not without risks, the intercostal approach has proven invaluable in selected cases.

Double punctures are necessary for staghorn calculi or multiple calculi when the initial access cannot completely eliminate stones in the collecting system. Flexible nephroscopy helps to eliminate the need for such punctures, but particularly in duplex-type collecting systems, branched calculi, and multiple widespread stones, more than a single access can be mandatory (38). It is in such difficult cases that prior planning as to the best mode of therapy should be applied. Either an antegrade, retrograde, or extracorporeal approach, or a combination of these, may be necessary. A form of double puncture, the "Y-puncture" (44) simply involves puncturing an adjacent calyx through the existing tract, so that the patient has only one skin entry site. A "needle-push" puncture involves a direct needle stick onto the stone, which is then pushed by the needle into a more desired location for removal (Fig. 7). This is usually applied to upper-pole calyceal stones, which can be pushed into the renal pelvis and a lower-pole, more desirable tract can be formed.

Stone Removal

Stones are removed percutaneously using direct vision by endoscopy or by fluoroscopy.

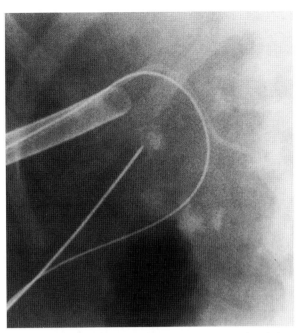

Fig. **7** **"Needle-push" technique.** A working sheath has been placed in the upper pole. In addition, a lower pole approach was previously made. Note the through-and-through wire. A needle has been placed on the midpole calculus. This was subsequently pushed into the renal pelvis for easy removal. The needle-push technique represents an alternative to insertion of another working sheath

Urologic Instrumentation

Nephroscopes come in either rigid or flexible varieties. The rigid scope has the advantage of easier control, although it requires a somewhat larger tract. Through the rigid scope, the ultrasonic lithotriptor can be advanced. This disintegrates the calculus by ultrasonic energy. In addition, a large variety of baskets, snares, and graspers can also be advanced through the rigid scope. In order to use the rigid nephroscope, the tract to the calculus must be relatively straight (Fig. **8**).

◀ Fig. **6a** **6–11 Fr coaxial dilating system.** The 6 Fr catheter is easily passed over the guide wire. The 11 Fr catheter can subsequently be passed over the guide wire and 6 Fr catheter. Upon removal of the 6 Fr catheter, two wires can easily be placed through the lumen of the 11 Fr catheter, resulting in the desired "working" and "safety" wires
b Graduated polyurethane dilators. Note the darker sheaths surrounding the dilators. These represent the working sheaths
c Kinking of the guide wire just outside the renal capsule when placing the dilators. This can be avoided by optimum tension on the wire, slow turning motions with steady pressure for advancement, and constant fluoroscopic monitoring. A stiffening wire also helps to prevent kinking
d Buckling of the guidewire within the renal pelvis resulting in perforation of the renal pelvis. The larger dilators should not be forced around curves, and care must be taken when advancing these dilators, regardless of their position
e High-pressure balloon with inflation handle. High-pressure balloons are now available on short shafts which can easily dilate nephrostomy tracts with a single inflation

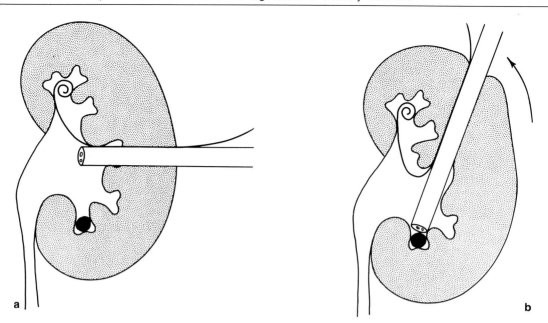

Fig. **8a**   **Rigid endoscopic removal of a lower pole calculus** via a midpole approach
b Note how the rigid scope can be slowly moved medially and advanced to the level of the stone. This circumvented a direct lower pole puncture. This can be quite useful if more than one stone is present in the collecting system

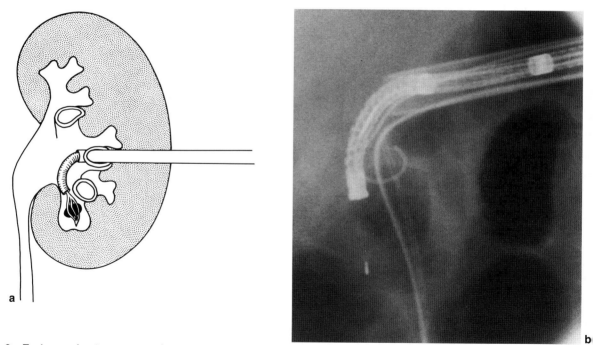

Fig. **9**   **Endoscopic stone removal**
a Basketing of a lower pole stone using the flexible endoscope from a midpole approach. Note the ease with which a stone not at the site of access can be grasped using the flexible scope
b The basket has been placed in the upper ureter via the flexible endoscope. The stone has been engaged for removal through the working sheath
c Basketing of an upper ureteral stone using the flexible endoscope
d, e Grasping of a ureteral stone using the alligator-type grasper via the flexible endoscope. In all of these cases, the stones are removed intact

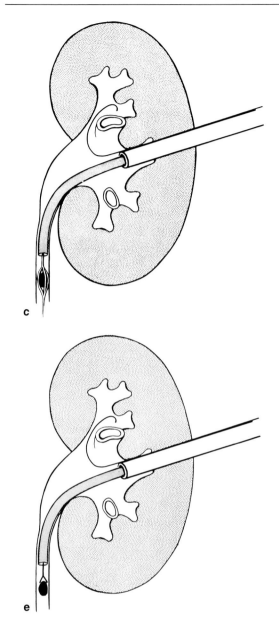

c

e

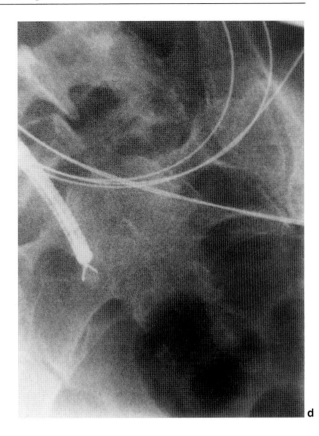

d

Fig. **9c–e**

Calculi smaller than 1 cm are probably best re-moved directly through the Teflon sheath using the scopes and graspers or baskets. Calculi larger than 1 cm may be pulled through the sheath, depending upon the shape of the stone. However, in general, the stone usually needs to be disintegrated by intro-ducing of the ultrasonic probe. The probe is passed through the rigid scope onto the stone. Disintegra-tion begins along the periphery, gradually decreasing the stone size. Particles are removed as they disinte-grate, using constant suction and continuous irrigant flow. On rare occasions, the probe alone can be placed under fluoroscopic control onto the stone when the rigid scope cannot be advanced to the level of the stone. The ultrasonic probe does not damage the mucosa, and can therefore be done safely so long as the probe is not forced into the mucosa, risking perforation.

Flexible endoscopes have a smaller shaft, and can be used to approach distant calyces or the ureter. The flexible endoscope can accommodate baskets and grasping forceps, as well as other accessories, such as snares (Fig. **9a**). Endoscopic removal in the ureter can be accomplished either in an antegrade or retrograde manner. The antegrade approach depends upon the use of the flexible endoscope and its ability to pass down the ureter to the stone (Fig. **9b–e**). Such flexible endoscopy has significantly improved the success of ureteral stone removal. Removing lower ureteral stones in the antegrade manner can only be accomplished by fluoroscopic means, due to the length of the endoscopes. If endoscopic procedures are desired, a retrograde approach via the bladder is commonly used. The termination of most percutaneous stone removals involves placement of the flexible scope to visualize the entire collecting system as much as possible to find any remaining calculi, particularly in dependent calyces. Any small residual fragments can be removed via the flexible scope with baskets or graspers. It is emphasized that the flexible scope is somewhat difficult to maneuver without an experienced endoscopist.

Irrigant solutions are a must throughout the endoscopic portion of the examination for optimum visualization. Clot from the initial tract dilation can be removed using the graspers through the endoscopes, also aiding visualization.

Fluoroscopic Instrumentation

Stone extraction under fluoroscopic visualization has the advantage of being both simple and rapid if it is successful. Also, the stone is usually removed without fragmentation (21). The largest limitation is stone size. The stones must be of adequate size to be easily seen fluoroscopically, and yet small enough (under 1 cm) to be easily removed through a percutaneous tract.

Very small stones in the renal pelvis can be removed, or moved to a more favorable location, by flushing and aspirating in a large renal pelvis (12). This is particularly useful for removing small stone fragments after ultrasonic disintegration. A large Teflon sheath is placed in the renal pelvis. A large-bore plastic syringe is attached directly to the sheath, and 30% contrast material is gently injected under fluoroscopic visualization. Once the pelvis is filled, the contrast is forcefully aspirated, removing small stones. It is essential that a balloon catheter be placed in the upper ureter to prevent dislodgment of renal stones into the ureter. The balloon catheter can be placed antegrade, usually beside the working sheath. Alternatively, the balloon catheter can be placed retrograde, and the same catheter also used for the initial contrast injection for collecting system visualization. Although smaller angioplasty balloons will suffice, smaller, less expensive wedge arterial balloons slip easily over small guide wires and are quite atraumatic to the urothelium. More forceful injections can be performed via the retrograde catheter, and aspiration accomplished with a bulb-type syringe through the large Teflon working sheath. Contrast is injected at a rate of from 5 ml per second to up to 25 ml per second using a power injector. Aspiration occurs simultaneously. Stones in the ureter can be moved to the renal pelvis in a similar fashion by flushing contrast or carbon dioxide via the ureteral catheter below the level of the stone (66). In this case, the balloon-type catheter is, of course, not essential. Once the stone has been dislodged to the pelvis, its removal becomes much simpler. If the stone cannot be removed by flushing once in the renal pelvis, more conventional endoscopic removal can be undertaken. Stones can be flushed from calyces using 24–26 Fr Red Robinson catheters, which are placed via the nephrostomy tract to the calyx containing the stone. Forceful injections by hand dislodge the stones, and allow them to be flushed into the renal pelvis for easier removal. Smaller catheters, such as Cobra catheters, which are easier to manipulate, can be placed more easily in distal calyces. Injections by hand through these catheters can dislodge small stones, and can be useful after ultrasonic lithotripsy. However, injections forceful enough to remove lodged calculi are difficult through such small catheters, and the resulting small jets of contrast can be damaging to the urothelium.

Grasping techniques using fluoroscopic guidance can be divided basically into: baskets and snares, flexible forceps, and rigid forceps.

Baskets are relatively atraumatic, and can be used for removal of stones both in the collecting system and in the entire ureter (Fig. 10). However, all baskets have limited maneuverability. Several types of basket are commercially available, including three- and four-wire baskets in varying sizes (Fig. 10a). The size of the basket should be carefully chosen. The basket itself must be large enough to accommodate the stone easily, yet small enough to

Fig. **10a** **A variety of baskets.** Baskets come in many designs and sizes; a careful selection should be made depending ▶ upon the site and size of the stone to be removed

b, c   A basket is placed via the working sheath. Once the stone is engaged by to-and-fro and twisting motions, the stone is directly removed through the working sheath. Note the safety catheter down the ureter

d The basket can also be guided fluoroscopically into sites remote from the initial access. Here, a stone is being removed from a lower pole calyx via a midpole approach. Basketing of calyceal stones can be difficult, as it is difficult to get beyond the stone with the basket, and the calyx offers a restricted area, hampering complete basket opening

e Flexible alligator forceps can also be used to remove small stones, particularly away from the site of access, as indicated here

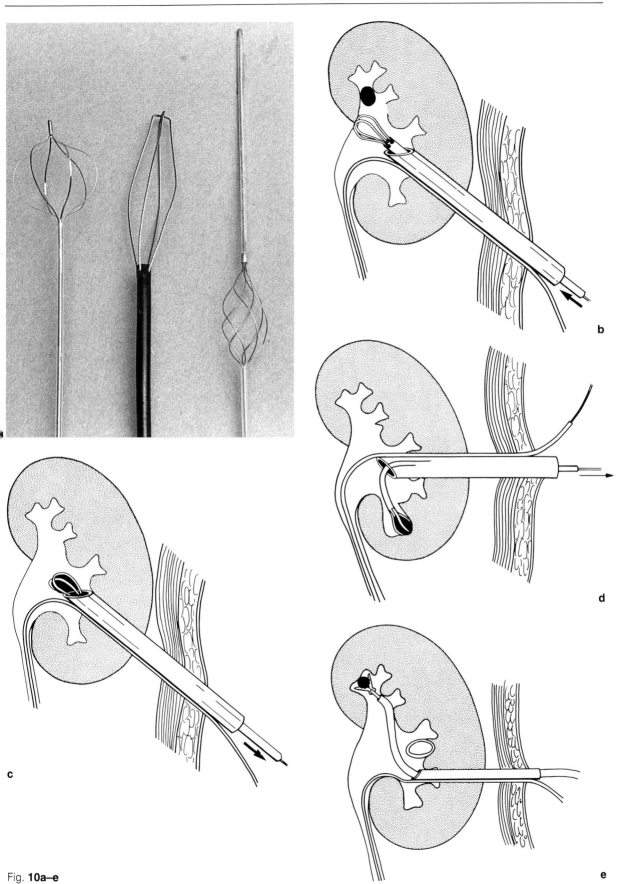

Fig. **10a–e**

open fully when placed in the region of the stone. Basket designs also vary from those with no end wire to those with long end wires. The end wire allows one to make multiple attempts at engaging the stone, if it is missed at the first attempt, by simply re-advancing the basket, so long as the end wire remains past the stone in a safe location throughout the initial attempt. The wire then serves simply to lead the basket safely past the stone for another retrieval attempt. The basket itself is enclosed within a sheath, and the entire complex is advanced through the working sheath. The basket sheath itself can often be advanced over a guide wire which has been steered to the correct location. Once the guide wire is removed, the basket can then be advanced through its own sheath. The basket is gently exposed by pulling its housing sheath back. The basket can then be spun, coupled with a to-and-fro motion, in an attempt to lodge the stone inside the wire struts. Once the stone is lodged in the basket, its housing sheath can then be gently advanced to snug the stone tightly into position. The whole complex is subsequently removed through the Teflon working sheath. Calyceal stones are difficult to remove by basketing, because the basket cannot be passed beyond the stone if a separate calyx is chosen for access. In

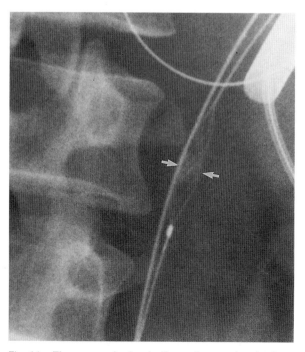

Fig. **11** **Fluoroscopic basketing of a ureteral stone** (arrows). Note that in this case the basket has the long guide wire which avoids the need to reinsert a separate wire with each attempt. The stone was successfully engaged despite a safety wire being in place. In many cases, the safety wire hampers complete basket opening, and must be removed

addition, due to the smallness of a calyx, the basket may fail to open fully, severely limiting its usefulness. Baskets are most useful for extracting stones in the ureter (Fig. 11). When a stone lodges in the upper ureter, it rapidly develops a sleeve of granulation tissue which makes it inaccessible to removal by instruments. The stone can sometimes be loosened by prying with a torque control catheter, such as a Cobra catheter, prior to basketing. The failure rate of attempted stone removal from the upper ureter is most likely due to the damaged and irritated mucosa which tightly entraps the stone. Aside from dislodging the stone, the most difficult portion of the procedure is opening the basket fully. A safety wire past the basket also tends to prevent free opening. Several baskets have been developed with stiffer wires and balloon-type designs to facilitate basket opening within the edematous ureter. However, a definitive solution has not yet been achieved. In addition, basketing can cause spasm in the ureter when trying to remove ureteral stones. This is best treated with 10 ml of 1% Lidocaine infused slowly directly into the ureter. Despite the difficulties encountered, basketing has proved to be quite successful for ureteral stone extraction (30).

Flexible forceps most often consist of alligator-type graspers, and are only useful for stones up to about 4 mm in size. The 7 Fr alligator forceps can be introduced through a 13 Fr steerable catheter. Once the catheter is in place, the graspers are advanced to the end of the catheter, the catheter subsequently withdrawn, and the jaws snugged into place around the stone. Movement of the forceps, particularly in the open position without replacement of the catheter over the forceps, can result in damage to the urothelium and possibly perforation of the collecting system or ureter. Flexible forceps have proved useful in removing small calyceal stones in areas in which baskets or snares cannot be advanced and would not fully open in such small areas. Similarly, the ureter presents a small area for baskets to open fully and forceps can be used successfully here as well. Opening the graspers in the ureter must be done carefully to avoid damage to the ureteral wall.

Rigid forceps such as the Randall and Mazariello–Caprini forceps are useful for direct stone removal when the stone lies within a direct path from the working sheath, mostly in the renal pelvis (Fig. **12a**). The forceps have a grooved border so that they can be advanced over a guide wire to the correct location (Fig. **12b**). This prevents false passages and possible perforation. Rigid forceps cannot be used through Teflon working sheaths, as such sheaths prevent opening. Rigid forceps are thus introduced through dilated soft-tissue tracts. Once in the collecting system, the position of the forceps has to be determined either by biplane fluoroscopy or parallax effect using a C-arm. If biplane fluoroscopy or a

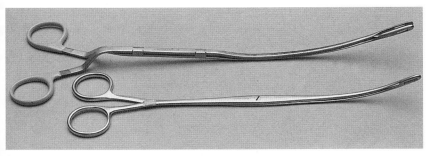

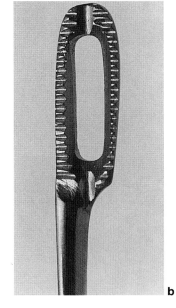

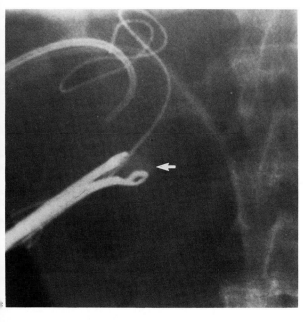

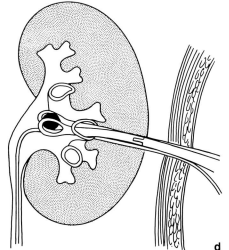

Fig. **12a   Mazariello-Caprini** (above) and (below) **Randall forceps.** Note that the Mazariello-Caprini do not open with a scissors action, and can therefore be placed through smaller tracts

b   A close-up shows the grooved portion of the forceps' end which allows it to be placed safely over a guide wire

c, d   Grasping of a stone using the forceps. Note that the guide wire lies beyond the stone (arrow) in order to place the forceps safely in the renal pelvis at the level of the stone. It is only when the forceps are in place can they be safely opened. Monitoring in multiple views either using biplane fluoroscopy, a C-arm apparatus, or patient positioning, is critical for safe and effective stone removal

C-arm are not available, of the rotation patient is necessary to determine the exact relationship of the forceps to the stone. Once in the correct location, the forceps are gently opened, and the stone is entrapped (Fig. **12c, d**). Randall forceps open in a conventional scissor action and thus need a well-dilated, relatively short tract. However, the Mazariello–Caprini forceps have a rotational-type attachment of the two arms, which upon opening prevents the shaft from enlarging greatly. Therefore, the Mazariello–Caprini forceps can be used even through long soft-tissue tracts. Both the Randall and Mazariello-Caprini forceps, as well as other designs, can be purchased in a variety of curvatures. Rigid forceps

can be used in the upper ureter depending on the size and position of the upper ureter, which would ideally be enlarged in the face of an obstructing calculus. Like the alligator-type graspers, the rigid forceps cannot be advanced in an open position or moved haphazardly, due to marked damage to the urothelium and possible perforation of the renal collecting structures. The rigid forceps have the advantage of excellent control, and are very useful in selected cases. Impacted ureteral stones must always be removed carefully, no matter which technique is used. Ureteral tears or avulsion can occur if too much force is used in pulling out impacted ureteral stones.

Drainage after Stone Removal

Once the stones have been removed percutaneously, drainage catheters are left in place. The catheters serve not only to drain the renal pelvis, but also to tamponade bleeding, prevent dissection of urine into the perirenal spaces and beyond, and to provide further access to the kidney if necessary.

In most patients, a catheter is placed with its tip in the renal pelvis. The catheter size depends upon the initial size of the working sheath, and is usually not less than 8 Fr smaller. In addition, a second catheter is virtually always left in place over the initial safety wire. This is most often a wire which is down the ureter, and a small catheter such as a 5 Fr Kifa is left at least in the distal ureter. This allows easy and safe access to the kidney, and preserves the integrity of the collecting system should a second procedure be attempted. A variety of drainage catheters are available, varying mostly in their mechanisms of retention. The larger catheter within the renal pelvis is most often a Foley or Council type catheter. This can be placed over a guide wire stiffened somewhat by a Teflon dilator or 7 Fr catheter. Once in place, the balloon can be slightly inflated (1–2 ml) and snugged back along the opening. This ensures both the stability of the catheter and minimal leakage of blood or urine back along the nephrostomy tract. If a stone has been removed from the ureter or there is significant trauma in the region of the ureteropelvic junction, a catheter of at least the same size as the native ureter should be advanced down the ureter to its distal portion or within the bladder. This allows excellent drainage of urine to the bladder, as well as providing a stent for ureteral healing. Catheters must be adequately fixed in place to prevent dislodgment. Most tubes should be sutured at the skin as well as bandaged.

Irrigation of the catheters with 5 ml of normal saline every 2–4 h is usually only necessary in the first 24 h. Dressing changes should be carried out for tract leakage during the first 24 h. If bleeding or leakage from the tract is excessive, this is best treated by placement of a larger catheter to tamponade the tract.

The length of time the catheter should remain within the collecting system depends upon a number of factors, including the expected degree of damage to the urothelium, continued bleeding, presence of antegrade flow to the bladder, and the need for ureteral stenting. In procedures involving only the renal collecting system, in the absence of residual fragments requiring a second procedure, most catheters can be removed within one week. The initial nephrostogram should be performed approximately 48 h post procedure, the catheter being to external drainage up to this time. In addition, plain films and tomography are useful for determination of retained calculi. If none are present or are coincidental, and there is good flow to the bladder on nephrostogram, a trial of internal drainage is warranted. Internal drainage is performed simply by clamping the catheter. In the absence of leakage or flank pain, the catheter can be removed in approximately 24 h. Most tracts leak up to 48 h in decreasing amounts, as the tract closes. Persistent ureteral edema is best treated by allowing the patient to be discharged with the catheter in place. Close monitoring with nephrostograms on an out-patient basis is used to determine the best time for discontinuing the catheter. Following ureteral stone removal, particularly with procedures which are complicated and inevitably result in a moderate amount of trauma to the ureter, stenting may be required for a number of weeks or even months. However, in this instance, an internal–external ureteral stent with side-holes in the renal pelvis and bladder can be placed, eliminating the need for a drainage bag. If longer intervals of ureteral stenting are required, entirely internal (double J) ureteral stents can be placed, depending upon patient preference (9).

Success of Stone Removal

The success of percutaneous renal stone removal depends on multiple factors, including the number and size of stones, the location of the stones, renal anatomical variations, and the experience of the interventional team. Percutaneous stone removal has success rates of 98–99% in experienced hands (50, 60). Success always means removal of the "targeted" stone. However, residual fragments may or may not persist. Retained fragments occur in 1–21% of cases (23, 37, 50, 59). The number of retained fragments depends upon the size of the initial stone, its location, and the experience and diligence of the interventional team.

Staghorn calculi managed percutaneously are notorious for requiring multiple procedures and resulting in retained stone fragments (1, 64). From 80–100% require a second procedure. From 40–48% require more than one entry site. Residual fragments are reported to be present in 32–40% of cases at the time of patient discharge. In addition, 40–50% complication rates have been reported, bleeding requiring transfusion being the most common complication.

Calyceal stones, including diverticuli and stenotic infundibuli, have up to a 100% success rate (38, 51). Up to 90% can be rendered stone-free after a single procedure. However, if stones in other locations are present, more than one approach is virtually always needed. A complication rate of around 8% has been reported, with bleeding requiring transfusion being the most common complication (5).

Ureteral stones have success rates of 88–100% (30, 50, 59). However, with the diligence required for 100% success rates, the serious complication rate was 11%, including ureteral avulsion, fistula formation, and bleeding.

The level of experience with percutaneous stone removal greatly affects the success of the procedure and the number of complications. Once adequate experience has been achieved, the success rates increase, with an accompanying decrease in both major and minor complications (37).

Complications

The number of both acute and long-term complications from percutaneous nephrolithotomy has proved to be surprisingly low, around 3%, excluding retained fragments (18, 23, 37, 41, 42, 50, 59). Complications most often listed consist of bleeding, perforation of the collecting system, infection, abdominal organ perforation, obstruction to renal outflow, and death.

Some degree of hemorrhage is a common complication (6). It is usually well-controlled after placement of the working sheath. If bleeding is severe, the dilated tract can be tamponaded with a dilating balloon. Bleeding usually ceases within 15 min. If bleeding does not significantly stop with the balloon or the working sheath, the procedure can be terminated at this point, and a large catheter placed for a longer interval of time. If bleeding is severe and cannot be tamponaded, arteriographic embolization, in as selective a manner as possible, becomes the treatment of choice. Hemorrhage requiring transfusion ranges from 8% to as little as 0.43% of cases (37, 50). The most common value reported is usually 3% (23, 59). Arteriovenous fistula formation requiring intervention has also occurred, usually the result of a medially-placed puncture into the renal pelvis (18).

Perforation of the collecting system can be quite common, reported in up to 5% of cases (41). Once perforation is recognized, the procedure should most likely be terminated, catheters placed across the area of perforation (particularly if it is in the ureter) and the procedure reinitiated at a separate sitting. Virtually all procedures result in a degree of extravasation at the tract. This usually resolves without incident. Leakage along the tract often occurs during the 24 h period immediately after the procedure, and is usually only incidental. However, urinoma formation is the potential major complication, occurring in up to 1.7% of cases (37).

If irrigant fluid extravasates, large fluid collections can be formed. Normal saline solutions are most often used as irrigants, except when electrocautery devices are needed for additional endosurgical procedures (58). Normal saline is the most physiologic solution available. Significant intraperitoneal leakages usually occur when there is a renal pelvic perforation with a rent also created in the peritoneum. If renal function is compromised, or if the amount of fluid is massive, electrolyte disturbances follow, although this is unusual, reported in only 0.03% to 1.3% of cases (23, 37). Percutaneous abdominal drainage is necessary immediately, as well as physiologic stabilization.

Extravasation into the pleural cavity also occurs rarely. As in the abdomen, drainage is the key to treatment, and a chest tube must be placed immediately. Pneumothorax is an unusual complication, usually resulting from high punctures. The rate of pneumothorax, with or without hydrothorax, ranges from 0.2% to 0.75%, being less than 1% in all reports (23, 37, 41, 50).

Infection can be a very serious complication. Obstructed patients with an infected pelvis must be drained initially and treated with antibiotics before stone removal should be attempted. All patients must be monitored post procedure for signs of sepsis. Although this is a rare complication (15), sepsis has been reported in up to 0.8% of cases (41).

Perforation of the colon and adjacent retroperitoneal organs occurs in approximately 0.2% of cases (23, 37, 41). Perirenal abscess formation occurred in nearly 1% of a large series, although the overall rates drastically decreased with the experience of the individuals involved (37).

Deaths have occurred from percutaneous nephrolithotomy, but the numbers are small. In two series, there were no deaths (23, 50). In one large series, the rate was only 0.046%, with hemorrhage and infection being the most common causes (37).

Obstruction of renal outflow after stone removal is common, but is not often considered a true complication. In the absence of prior ureteral obstruction, such as stricturing, the usual causes are edema, blood clots, and residual or retained stone fragments. Edema usually subsides in 48–72 h, as do most blood clots. Retained fragments may pass spontaneously, depending on their size and the condition of the ureter, but may need to be retrieved either endoscopically or by fluoroscopic techniques. The frequency of retained fragments has been discussed previously. It should be noted, however, that in many cases the retained fragments were judged to be only incidental and were left in place intentionally.

Dislodgment of percutaneous drainage tubes is not considered in most figures for complication rates. Dislodgment of drainage tubes depends on multiple factors, not the least of which is patient cooperation. In one series, tube dislodgment requiring replacement occurred in 45% of the cases (50). Although this number would appear quite high, it serves to illustrate the need for excellent post-procedural care.

Percutaneous Techniques and Extracorporeal Shock Wave Lithotripsy

ESWL has become the primary mode of treatment in patients with renal calculi (8). Upper ureteral calculi are now treated primarily with retrograde catheterization, either alongside the stone or by dislodgment of the stone back into the renal pelvis, with the patient subsequently being subjected to extracorporeal methods (46). As ESWL techniques cannot be used when the stone is obscured by the bony pelvis, transurethral ureteroscopic removal of small calculi in the distal ureter has become commonplace and is widely accepted.

Patients for percutaneous stone removal now fall into a category where these newer methods have not proved successful. The largest group of these patients are those with large stone volumes, such as staghorn or branched calculi (14). To manage such patients with extracorporeal methods would require multiple procedures. Large stones have been shown to have a greater complication rate in ESWL when compared to smaller stones (33). In addition, nearly 30% of patients with stones over 2.5 cm require percutaneous nephrostomy after attempted extracorporeal methods (37). Patients with obstruction to infundibuli, the ureteropelvic junction, or the ureter itself, cannot pass stone fragments following ESWL, and therefore are preferably treated with percutaneous techniques. In addition, areas of stenosis can be treated percutaneously either by balloon dilation or endopyelotomy techniques (40). The same type of situation exists when stones are present in calyceal diverticuli. If the patient is known to have cystine calculi, these may very well be best removed percutaneously, as such stones may fragment poorly with the extracorporeal units (32). Most extracorporeal lithotriptors have both height and weight limitations, and large patients are therefore often managed percutaneously.

The combination of ESWL and percutaneous techniques is very useful for large stone volumes (32). A single percutaneous tract can be created to remove a large bulk of the stone, with ESWL to follow. Such patients do not require a second percutaneous tract, and can be rendered stone-free by extracorporeal methods. In addition, percutaneous catheters provide an alternative route for urine and stone debris drainage. Pulsating jets of flush solution via percutaneous catheters have been shown to wash out the slush of retained fragments *(Steinstrasse)* with great success (61). Infected systems should always be drained prior to ESWL, and percutaneous methods can eventually be applied, if needed, once access is gained.

ESWL is not without its own complications, demonstrating subcapsular hematomas in nearly 15% of cases under CT (57). However, its complication rates do not exceed those of percutaneous methods (25, 43, 53). ESWL is overall a safe, effective method of stone removal which should be applied in all cases possible. The role of percutaneous removal is more that of an alternative and supportive measure in selected cases. Possibly ESWL may take the same road if even less hazardous, easier methods are developed in the future.

References

1. Adams GW, Oke EJ, Dunnick NR, Carson CC. Percutaneous lithotripsy of staghorn calculi. AJR 1985;145:803–807.
2. Alken P. Percutaneous ultrasonic destruction of renal calculi. Urol Clin North Am 1982;9:145–151.
3. Brannen GE, Bush WH. Percutaneous ultrasonic vs. surgical removal of kidney stones. Surg Gynecol Obstet 1985;161:473–478.
4. Bush WH, Brannen GE. Percutaneous removal of calyceal calculi. AJR 1985;144:139–142.
5. Brannen GE, Bush WH, Lewis GP. Calyceal calculi. J Urol 1986;135:1142–1145.
6. Brodel M. The intrinsic blood-vessels of the kidney and their significance in nephrotomy. Johns Hopkins Hosp Bull 1901;118:10–13.
7. Brown MW, Carson CC, Dunnick NR, Weinerth JL. Comparison of the cost and morbidity of percutaneous and open flank procedures. J Urol 1986;135:1150–1152.
8. Bush WH, Gibbons RP, Lewis GP, Brannen GE. Impact of extracorporeal shock wave lithotripsy on percutaneous stone procedures. AJR 1986;147:89–93.
9. Cardella JF, Castaneda-Zuniga WR, Hunter DW, Hulbert JC, Amplatz K. Urine-compatible polymer for long-term ureteral stenting. Radiology 1986;161:313–318.
10. Cardella JF, Kotula F, Hunter DW, Young AT, Castaneda-Zuniga WR, Amplatz K. Very stiff guidewire with a floppy tip. Radiology 1985;156:837.
11. Castaneda-Zuniga WR, Clayman R, Smith A, Rusnak B, Herrera M, Amplatz K. Nephrostolithotomy: percutaneous techniques for urinary calculus removal AJR 1982;139:721–726.
12. Castaneda-Zuniga WR, Coleman CC, Hunter DW, Castaneda F, Young AT, Amplatz K. Flushing techniques for the removal of retained urinary stones. Semin Intervent Radiol 1984;1:56–59.
13. Castaneda-Zuniga WR, Miller RP, Amplatz K. Percutaneous removal of kidney stones. Urol Clin North Am 1982;9:113–119.
14. Charig CR, Webb DR, Payne SR, Wickham JEA. Comparison of treatment of renal calculi by open surgery, percutaneous nephrolithotomy, extracorporeal shockwave lithotripsy. Br Med J 1986;292:879–882.
15. Charton M, Vallancien G, Veillon B, Brisset JM. Urinary tract infection in percutaneous surgery for renal calculi. J Urol 1986;135:15–17.
16. Chussy C, Eisenberger F, Wanner K, et al. Use of shockwaves for the destruction of renal calculi without direct contact. Urol Res 1976;4:181.
17. Chaussy C, Schmiedt E, Jocham D, Schuller J, Brandl H, Liedl B. Extracorporeal shock wave lithotripsy for treatment of urolithiasis. Urology 1984;23:59–66.
18. Clayman RV, Surya V, Hunter DW, Castaneda WR, Miller RP, Coleman CC, Amplatz K, Lange PH. Renal vascular complications associated with the percutaneous removal of renal calculi. J Urol 1984;132:228–230.
19. Coleman CC, Castaneda-Zuniga WR, Kimura Y, Miller RP, Young AT, Castaneda F, Lange P, Clayman RV, Reddy P, Hunter DW, Amplatz K. A systematic approach to puncture-site selection for percutaneous urinary tract stone removal. Semin Intervent Radiol 1984;1:42–49.

20. Coleman CC, Castaneda-Zuniga WR, Miller R, Lange P, Clayman R, Reddy P, Hunter DW, Hulbert JC, Salomonowitz E, Lund G, Amplatz K. A logical approach to renal stone removal. AJR 1984;143:609–615.

21. Coleman CC, Kimura Y, Castaneda F, Young AT, Castaneda-Zuniga WR, Hunter DW, Amplatz K. Fluoroscopically guided techniques for renal and ureteral stone removal. Semin Intervent Radiol 1984;1:63–69.

22. Coleman CC, Kimura Y, Castaneda-Zuniga WR, Hunter DW, Young AT, Castaneda F, Clayman RV, Lange P, Amplatz K. Dilatation of nephrostomy tracts for percutaneous renal stone removal. Semin Intervent Radiol 1984;1:50–55.

23. Dunnick NR, Carson CC, Braun SD, Miller GA, Cohen R, Degesys GE, Illescas FF, Newman GE, Weinert H. Complications of percutaneous nephrostolithotomy. Radiology 1985;157:51–55.

24. Dunnick NR, Carson CC, Moore AV, Ford K, Miller GA, Braun SD, Newman GE, Weinert JL. Percutaneous approach to nephrolithiasis. AJR 1985;144:451–455.

25. Ekelund L, Lindstedt E, Lundquist SB, Sundin T, White T. Studies on renal damage from percutaneous nephrolitholapaxy. J Urol 1986;135:682–685.

26. Fernstrom I, Johansson B. Percutaneous pyelolithotomy, a new extraction technique. Scand J Urol Nephrol 1976;10:257–259.

27. Grantham JR, Miller MR, Kaude JV, Finlayson B, Hunter PT, Newman RC. Renal stone disease treated with extracorporeal shock wave lithotripsy: short-term observations in 100 patients. Radiology 1986;158:203–206.

28. Graves FT. The anatomy of the intrarenal arteries and its application to segmental resection of the kidney. Br J Surg 1954;42:132–139.

29. Hulbert JC, Reddy PK, Hunter DW, Castaneda-Zuniga WR, Amplatz K, Lange PH. Percutaneous techniques for the management of calyceal diverticula containing calculi. J Urol 1986;135:225–227.

30. Hunter DW, Castaneda-Zuniga WR, Young AT, Cardella J, Lund G, Rysavy JA, Hulbert J, Lange P, Reddy P, Amplatz K. Percutaneous removal of ureteral calculi: clinical and experimental results. Radiology 1985;156:341–348.

31. Hunter DW, Salomonowitz E, Castaneda-Zuniga WR, Young A, Mercado S, Amplatz K. Carbon dioxide as a lighter-than-urine contrast medium for percutaneous nephrostomy. Radiology 1984;152:211–212.

32. Kanoski RJ, Lingeman JE, Coury TA, Steele RE, Mosbaugh PG. Combined percutaneous and extracorporeal shock wave lithotripsy for staghorn calculi: an alternative to anatrophic nephrolithotomy. J Urol 1986;135:679–681.

33. Kaude JV, Williams CM, Millner MR, Scott KN, Finlayson B. Renal morphology and function immediately after extracorporeal shock-wave lithotripsy. AJR 1985;145:305–313.

34. Kaye KW. Renal anatomy for endourologic stone removal. J Urol 1983;130:647–648.

35. Kaye KW, Goldberg ME. Applied anatomy of the kidney and ureter. Urol Clin North Am 1982;9:3–13.

36. Kerlan RK, Kahn RK, Laberge JM, Pogany AC, Ring EJ. Percutaneous removal of renal staghorn calculi. AJR 1985;145:797–801.

37. Lange EK. Percutaneous nephrostolithotomy and lithotripsy: a multi-institutional survey of complications. Radiology 1987;162:25–30.

38. Lange EK, Glorioso LW. Multiple percutaneous access routes to multiple calculi, calculi in calyceal diverticula, and staghorn calculi. Radiology 1986;158:211–214.

39. Lange PH, Reddy PK, Hulbert JC, Clayman RV, Castaneda-Zuniga WR, Miller RP, Coleman CC, Amplatz K. Percutaneous removal of calyceal and other "inaccessible" stones: instruments and techniques. J Urol 1984;132:439–442.

40. Lee WJ, Badlani GH, Smith AD. Percutaneous nephrostomy for endopyelotomy. AJR 1987;148:189–192.

41. Lee WJ, Smith AD, Cubelli V, Badlani GH, Lewin B, Vernace F, Cantos E. Complications of percutaneous nephrolithotomy. AJR 1987;148:177–180.

42. Marberger M, Stackl W, Hruby W, Kroiss A. Late sequelae of ultrasonic lithotripsy of renal calculi. J Urol 1985;133:170–173.

43. Mayo ME, Krieger JN, Rudd TG. Effect of percutaneous nephrostolithotomy on renal function. J Urol 1985;133:167–169.

44. Mercado S, Hunter DW, Castaneda-Zuniga WR, Amplatz K, Young AT, Cardella JF, Lange PH, Hulbert JC, Reddy P. The double puncture: an effective percutaneous technique for removing complex, multiple renal calculi. Radiology 1986;158:207–209.

45. Meyers MA. The extraperitoneal spaces: normal and pathologic anatomy. In: Meyers MA, ed. Dyanamic radiology of the abdomen: normal and pathologic anatomy. Berlin: Springer 1976:113–194.

46. Mueller SC, Wilbert D, Thueroff JW, Alken P. Extracorporeal shock wave lithotripsy of ureteral stones: clinical experience and experimental findings. J Urol 1986;135:831–834.

47. Peterson GN, Krieger JN, Glauber DT. Anaesthetic experience with percutaneous lithotripsy: a review of potential and actual complications. Anaesthesia 1985;40:460–464.

48. Picus D, Weyman PJ, Clayman RV, McClennan BL. Intercostal-space nephrostomy for percutaneous stone removal. AJR 1986;147:393–397.

49. Pollack HM, Banner MP. Percutaneous extraction of renal and ureteral calculi: technical considerations. AJR 1984;143:778–784.

50. Reddy PK, Hulbert JC, Lange PH, Clayman RV, Marcuzzi A, Lapointe S, Miller RP, Hunter DW, Castaneda-Zuniga WR, Amplatz K. Percutaneous removal of renal and ureteral calculi: experience with 400 cases. J Urol 1985;134:662–665.

51. Reddy PK, Lange PH, Hulbert JC, Clamyn RV, Breen JF, Hunter DW, Coleman CC, Castaneda-Zuniga WR, Amplatz K. Percutaneous removal of calyceal and other "inaccessible" stones: results. J Urol 1984;132:443–447.

52. Rous SN, Turner WR. Retrospective study of 95 patients with staghorn calculus disease. J Urol 1977;118:902–904.

53. Rubin JI, Arger PH, Pollack HM, Banner MP, Coleman BG, Mintz MC, van Arsdalen KN. Kidney changes after extracorporeal shock wave lithotripsy: CT evaluation. Radiology 1987;162:21–24.

54. Rusnak B, Castancda-Zuniga WR, Kotula F, Herrera M, Amplatz K. Radiolucent handle for percutaneous punctures under continuous fluoroscopic monitoring. Radiology 1981;141:538.

55. Rusnick B, Castaneda-Zuniga WR, Kotula F, Herrera M, Amplatz K. An improved dilator system for percutaneous nephrostomies. Radiology 1982;144:174.

56. Salomonowitz E, Castaneda-Zuniga WR, Lange PH, Cragg AH, Lund G, Hunter DW, Coleman CC, Amplatz K. Percutaneous stone removal: use of carbon dioxide as contrast material. Radiology 1984;150:833–834.

57. Schiff RG, Lee WJ, Eshghi M, Moskowitz GW, Levy LM, Smith AD. Morphologic and functional changes in the kidney after percutaneous nephrostolithotomy. AJR 1986;147:283–286.

58. Schultz RE, Hanno PM, Wien AJ, Levine RM, Pollack HM, van Arsdalen KN. Percutaneous ultrasonic lithotripsy: choice of irrigant. J Urol 1983;130:858–860.

59. Segura JW, Patterson DE, LeRoy AJ, Williams HJ, Barrett DM, Benson RC, May GR, Bender CE. Percutaneous removal of kidney stones: review of 1000 cases. J Urol 1985;134:1077–1081.

60. Singh M, Chapman R, Tresidder GC, Blandy J. The fate of the unoperated staghorn calculus. Br J Urol 1973;45:581–585.

61. Tegtmeyer CJ, Kellum CD, Jenkins A, Gillenwater JY, Way WG, Barr J, Perous G, Springer R, Lippert MC, Wyker AW. Extracorporeal shockwave lithotripsy: interventional radiologic solutions to associated problems. Radiology 1986;161:587–592.

62. Webb DR, McNicholas TA, Whitfield HN, Wickham JEA. Extracorporeal shockwave lithotripsy, endourology, and open surgery: the management and follow-up of 200 patients with urinary calculi. Ann Coll Surg Engl 1985;67:337–340.

63. Webb DR, Payne SR, Wickham JEA. Extracorporeal shock-wave lithotripsy and percutaneous renal surgery: comparisons, combinations, and conclusions. Br J Urol 1986;58:1–5.

64. Young AT, Hulbert JC, Cardella JF, Hunter DW, Castaneda-Zuniga WR, Reddy P, Amplatz K. Percutaneous nephrostolithotomy: application to staghorn calculi. AJR 1985;145:1265–1269.

65. Young AT, Hunter DW, Castaneda-Zuniga WR, Hulbert JC, Lange P, Reddy P, Mercado S, Amplatz K. Percutaneous extraction of urinary calculi: use of the intercostal approach. Radiology 1985;154:633–638.

66. Young AT, Hunter DW, Lange P, Lund GB, Castaneda-Zuniga WR, Hulbert JC, Mercado S, Cardella JF, Amplatz K. The CO_2 flush: a new technique for percutaneous extraction of ureteral calculi. Radiology 1985;154:828.

Therapeutic Angiographic Techniques

Angiographic Embolization Techniques

V. P. Chuang

"Getting there is half the fun."

This old adage very properly describes the joy of visceral angiography. In the majority of the embolization procedures, "getting there" is more than half the fun and challenge. There are many ways to do visceral angiography. In this chapter, I shall briefly describe the basic techniques of arterial catheterization that I have used in more than 1000 embolizations. It is my philosophy to select the safest and simplest method whenever possible (1, 2).

Catheter Selection

Torque control and radiopacity are important in catheter material selection. A catheter with a good memory for shape is another major factor in selection. Finally, a proper inner lumen for embolization material to pass through is very important. Generally, I use two groups of catheters, 5 and 6.5 Fr. Both accept 0.035 inch (0.9 mm) and 0.038 inch (1.0 mm) guide wires. Some 5 Fr catheters only accept 0.035 or 0.032 inch guide wires and are unsuitable for Gianturco coil embolization. The 5 Fr polyethylene catheter with an extrathin wall that can accommodate a 0.038 inch guide wire is preferable, since the Gianturco coils and other coaxial systems can be applied without limitation. Because of its extrathin wall, the 5 Fr catheter is more flexible and less traumatic. However, poorer torque control, catheter memory, and radiopacity are its limitations.

The 6.5 Fr torque-control catheter is more radiopaque because of the wiremesh reinforcement of the catheter wall. It has better torque control. Its increased rigidity makes the passing of the catheter into the smaller artery more traumatic than a 5 Fr catheter. In younger patients or easier procedures, a 5 Fr catheter is the first choice. In older patients with more tortuous arteries, the 6.5 Fr catheter with its improved torque control and radiopacity is preferable.

Catheter Curves

Many different catheter curves with various names have been described. However, there are many similarities between catheters with different names; a Headhunter I, for example, is similar to a cobra curve or a double-renal curve. This can be simplified as follows: a catheter can have *a single curve* to turn in one direction, or it can turn twice toward the same direction (a *double curve*), or toward opposite directions (a *reverse curve*) (Fig. 1). However, if the first curve is 90 degrees to the second curve in a double or reverse curve, it becomes a hepatic or splenic curve of Rösch (4) (Fig. 1e). More rarely, a catheter can turn three times or more, as in the loop method. Thus, the catheter curves are best summarized using descriptive terms such as the following:

– Single (or simple) curve (Fig. 1a)
– Double curve (Fig. 1d): Double renal curve, cobra curve, femoral renal curve, and femoral celiac curve
– Reverse curve (Fig. 1b): Mikkaelson curve, Rösch left gastric curve, shepherd's crook, Simmons sidewinder curve, etc.
– Triple curve (Fig. 1c): when a double-curve catheter is turned into a loop as in the loop method, it becomes a triple curve. Using the tailored catheter curve principle, a triple curve of all shapes that fits arterial anatomy becomes very useful for superselective catheterization of small peripheral arteries.

The terminology for various portions of a catheter in this chapter include: "body" for the main or straight portion of the catheter, "t" for the catheter tip, and "a," "b," and "c" for the first, second, and third curves. The length of the catheter between different curves is described as ta, ab, bc segment, etc. (Fig. 1).

The most commonly used catheters for visceral angiography are five sizes of single curve (Fig. 2) and seven sizes of reverse curve (Fig. 3) in a 6.5 Fr torque-control catheter.

A simple-curve catheter is the routine catheter for selective celiac, superior mesenteric, and renal arteriograms. A "rule of 110" is applied to select the different catheter length of A (28 mm), B (25 mm), C (22 mm), D (18 mm), and E (13 mm) for various size patients (Fig. 2).

The rule of 110 states that both the length of the catheter tip (ta segment) and the width of the catheter curve should be 10% longer than the width of the abdominal aorta at the level of the branch artery to be catheterized (Fig. 2). When this principle is applied to the selection of the proper size of catheter for the celiac or superior mesenteric artery, it has the following advantages: it can enter the artery with the catheter curve a in either open or closed position; it does not scratch the aortic wall too much; it

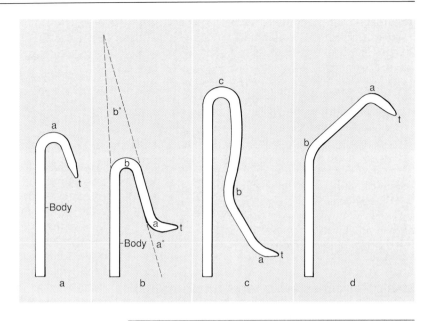

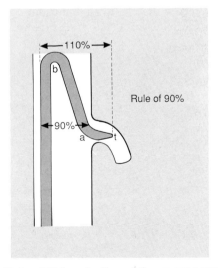

Fig. **1 Catheter curves and terminologies**
a Simple curve
b Reverse curve
c Triple curve
d Double curve
e Hepatic left and splenic right curve (of Rösch)

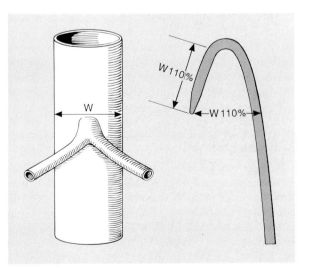

Fig. **2 Rule of 110 for single-curve selection.** The length of ta segment and the distance from the tip (t) to the catheter body should be approximately 10% wider than the width (W) of the abdominal aorta

Fig. **3 Rule of 90 in selection of the reverse curve.** The b curve is formed to make the distance from the primary curve a to the body of the catheter 90% of the width of the aorta. From the catheter tip t to the catheter body, it becomes 110% of the aortic width minimizes the catheter recoil during contrast medium injection (because the ta segment is 10% longer than the aortic width); and it increases the chance of hepatic or splenic artery catheterization (see Method I for hepatic artery catheterization), which usually follows celiac arteriogram.

In forming the reverse-curve catheter, a "rule of 90" is used. The rule is defined as forming curve a to 90% of the width of the aorta (slightly smaller than the width of the aorta). The ta segment adds another 20% of the width of the aorta. Thus, from the body of the catheter to the tip is again 110% of the aortic width, as in the single-curve catheters (Fig. 3). This principle is important in selecting a short reverse-curve catheter for the celiac, splenic, hepatic, and left gastric arteriograms.

Basic Principles in Visceral Angiography

Catheter–guide wire compatibility. Most guide wires from various manufacturers look alike externally. Because of different methods of internal construction, however, their clinical applications can be vastly different. For visceral angiography, a guide wire with a J tip of 2 to 3 mm radius, a short soft tip of 3 to 4 cm length, and a gradual transition zone from the soft to the rigid segment is most important. The rigidity of a guide wire should match that of a catheter. For the 6.5 Fr torque-control catheter, the stainless steel, fixed core guide wire is more useful than the Teflon movable core guide wire of the same configuration from the same company. This is due to the abrupt transition of the soft to rigid segment in the movable core guide wire.

Tailored catheter curve. A catheter with one or multiple curves that matches the anatomy of the artery to be catheterized can enter the artery auto-

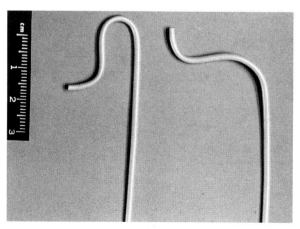

Fig. 4   Modification of the reverse curve (left) to the left gastric curve (right) by altering the b curve from near 180 to 90 degrees

matically and sit in it securely. This principle is very frequently applied in the catheterization and infusion of the left gastric and gastroduodenal arteries.

Three-dimensional vision. All angiographies as well as radiographs display 3-dimensional anatomy in two dimensions. Most arteries, e.g., abdominal aorta, renal, hepatic, and splenic arteries, are parallel to the plane of the x-ray film, and are thus not foreshortened very much on the films. Certain arteries, however, such as the celiac trunk and the first portion of the superior mesenteric artery, are typically foreshortened on the frontal projection. When a catheter enters the celiac artery, the angiographer, by knowing the length of the ta segment of the catheter and by pulling the catheter gently in and out of the artery, can get a feel for the length of the celiac trunk which will assist in planning the next step for superselective catheterization of the left gastric, hepatic, and splenic arteries. In more difficult cases, an oblique view might be necessary to get the exact anatomy.

Modification of the catheter curves. Every catheter curve (or angle) and every catheter segment (e.g., ta and ab segments in a double-curve catheter) can be modified to fit a specific patient or artery. The modification of a 2 cm reverse curve to a left gastric curve is an example (Fig. 4).

Superselective Catheterization Technique for the Hepatic Arteries

For practical purposes, superselective catheterization is defined as placing a catheter beyond the first order of artery from its takeoff in the aorta. The techniques in the catheterization of the common, proper, right, and left hepatic arteries are summarized here briefly, proceeding from the easiest to the more difficult. These techniques can be applied to all other visceral arteries, such as the left gastric and splenic arteries.

Method 1: Single-Curve Catheter Pushing Over Guide Wire Method

Following routine celiac angiography with a single-curve catheter, a J (3 mm radius), or tight J (2 mm radius) guide wire is advanced into the hepatic arteries (Fig. 5a). After the rigid part of the guide wire is well seated in the hepatic artery, the single-curve catheter is advanced over the guide wire into the hepatic artery (Fig. 5b). This simple maneuver requires that the flexible segment of the tip of the guide wire be short (3 to 4 cm), so that the rigid part may be advanced well into the artery (Fig. 5a). If a guide wire with a long flexible tip (e.g., a movable-core or a Bentson guide wire) is used in a similar

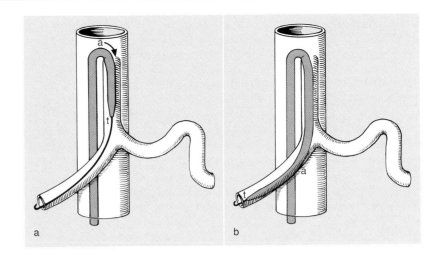

Fig. 5 Single-curve catheter pushing over guide wire method

a Place the catheter as deeply as possible in the celiac artery. Advance a tight J guide wire as far as possible in the hepatic artery. The transition zone, i.e., the rigid segment of the guide wire (arrow) is inside the hepatic artery

b The catheter is pushed over the guide wire

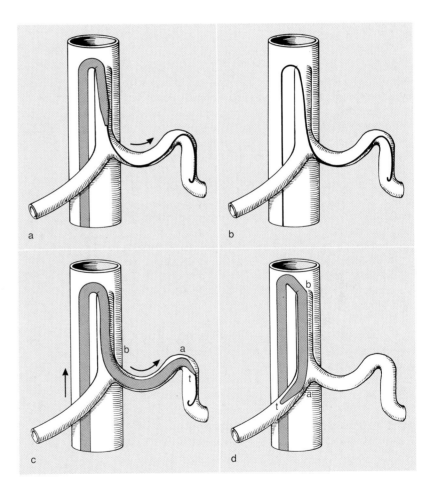

Fig. 6 Catheter exchange method using tailored curve

fashion, the flexible part of the guide wire cannot carry the catheter into the periphery of the artery. Thus, a guide wire with a long flexible tip is of little value in this method. The catheter–guide wire compatibility principle is very important here.

The success rate of this method is proportional to the length (ta segment) of the catheter inside the celiac trunk. A single-curve catheter selected according to the rule of 110 has a much longer ta segment than that of a double- or cobra-curve catheter; thus, the single-curve catheter has a greater success rate for subsequent superselective hepatic or splenic artery catheterization. This is why it is chosen for routine visceral angiography. Another benefit of a longer ta segment in the celiac artery is that the catheter is less likely to recoil during contrast medium injection for celiac arteriography.

Method 2: Catheter Exchange Method Using Hepatic-Curve Catheter

A new catheter with a tailored configuration is exchanged for the initial catheter for catheterization of an artery that cannot be reached by a guide wire passed through the initial catheter. If the splenic artery is larger than the hepatic artery, a J-tip guide wire often enters the splenic artery preferentially. The guide wire should then be advanced far into the splenic artery (Fig. **6a**) and the initial single-curve catheter exchanged with a hepatic-curve catheter into the splenic artery. The guide wire is fixed with one hand and the catheter alone is gradually removed a few centimeters at a time with the other hand until it is totally removed (Fig. **6**). With the tip of the guide wire carefully maintained in a stationary position within the splenic artery, the hepatic-curve catheter (Fig. **1e**) is introduced over the guide wire into the splenic artery beyond the celiac bifurcation (Fig. **6c**). After the wire is removed, the catheter is withdrawn gradually from the splenic artery until curve b is located in the aorta. Since the ta segment points to the right in relation to the b curve in this catheter, the ta segment frequently pops into the common hepatic artery (Fig. **6d**) automatically at this time. A gentle counterclockwise rotation also can assist the ta segment to move into the common hepatic artery.

During this maneuver, attention should be paid to the formation and adjustment of the ta segment, the ab segment, and the angles of curves a and b. If the ab segment equals the length of the celiac trunk, the ta segment will turn into the common hepatic artery easily. The secondary curve b is used to assist and direct the primary curve a (Figs. **1e, 6d**). The ta segment should not be too long when compared with the width of the celiac trunk, otherwise its turning from the splenic artery to the common hepatic artery can be restricted by the narrower celiac lumen.

Method 3: Hepatic-Curve Catheter and Catheter–Guide Wire Piggyback Method

If the celiac anatomy is known from a previous arteriogram, a hepatic-curve catheter can be used initially for common hepatic artery catheterization. When this catheter is introduced into the aorta, its curve b is open, and, therefore, it is advanced to the aortic arch and usually rotated clockwise to resume its hepatic-curve configuration (i.e., to close the curve b).

At the celiac level, the hepatic-curve catheter is turned so that the catheter body is to the right, the ab segment is to the patient's left, and the catheter tip,

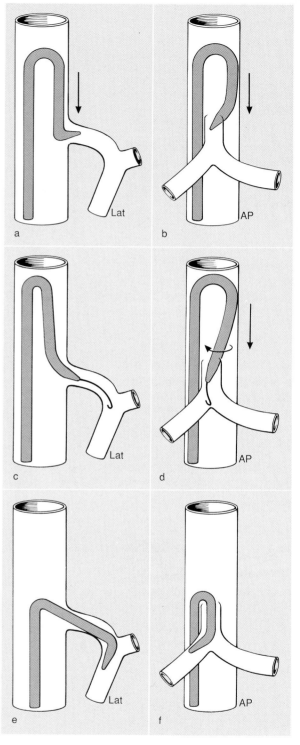

Fig. **7a–f   Hepatic curve catheter and catheter–guide wire piggyback method**

ta segment, is directed anteriorly toward the celiac artery (Fig. **7a, b**). With the catheter tip in the celiac artery, a J or C guide wire is inserted barely beyond the catheter tip, and the catheter–guide wire combi-

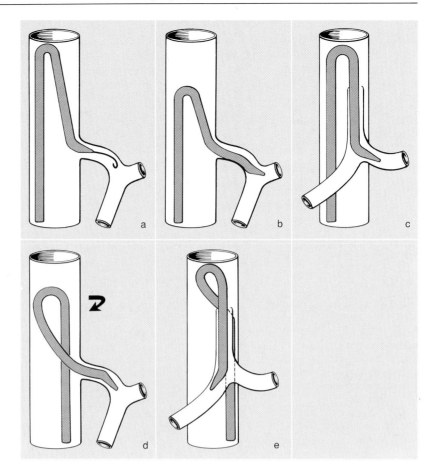

Fig. **8 Long reverse-curve catheter and figure-of-eight method. a, b, d** lateral view; **c, e** frontal view

nation is gradually pulled down and into the celiac trunk. This maneuver, in which the guide wire helps to avoid intimal injury by the catheter tip, is called the catheter–guide wire piggyback method. The length of the flexible part of the guide wire should be longer than the tab segment, so that when the wire is introduced beyond the catheter tip, it does not significantly alter the catheter configuration (curve b) (Fig. **7c**). As the tip of the catheter is being pulled down toward the celiac bifurcation, the catheter is turned counterclockwise gradually so that its tip slides easily into the common hepatic artery (Fig. **7c–e**). The catheter–guide wire piggyback method greatly facilitates the downward movement of a hepatic-, splenic-, or reverse-curve catheter into a caudad-directed aortic branch and significantly decreases the incidence of intimal injury.

Method 4: Long Reverse-Curve Catheter and Figure-of-Eight Method

In a very long downward course of the celiac artery, a long reverse-curve catheter becomes very useful. The ab segment is selected to match the length of the celiac trunk and common hepatic artery. With this

catheter, the reverse curve is re-formed in one of several sites: the thoracic arch, the descending thoracic aorta with the use of a guide wire deflector, and the abdominal aortic bifurcation, where the catheter is deflected into the opposite common iliac artery.

After the reverse curve is re-formed, the catheter tip is placed into the orifice of the celiac artery and the catheter is gradually pulled down to the bifurcation of the celiac trunk (Fig. **8a–c**). If the catheter catches on the anterior wall of the celiac trunk or enters the left gastric artery, the catheter-guide wire piggyback method is applied using a Bentson guide wire (the long soft tip of the guide wire matches the long ab segment of the catheter).

When the catheter tip is at the celiac bifurcation, there is equal opportunity for the catheter tip to catch either the common hepatic or splenic artery. If the catheter body is rotated counterclockwise, the catheter curve b and the catheter body, which are in the aorta, should turn to the left, while its tip (ta segment), which is inside the celiac trunk, turns to the right facing the common hepatic artery (Fig. **9**). The catheter then can be pulled down gently to the common hepatic and proper hepatic artery. The

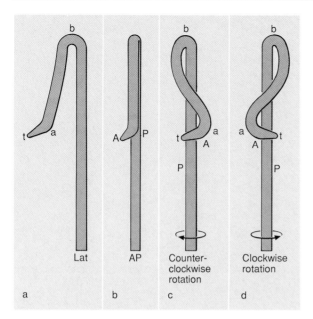

Fig. 9 **The formation of a figure-of-eight in long reverse-curve catheter.** A: anterior. P: posterior

a, b Lateral and frontal view of the catheter

c Counterclockwise rotation of the catheter with ta segment at celiac bifurcation. The ta segment points to the right (or hepatic artery)

d Clockwise rotation of the same. The ta segment point to the left (or splenic artery)

pulling of the catheter down to the proper hepatic artery should be monitored fluoroscopically with repeated small injections of contrast material or with a Bentson guide wire in place (the piggyback method). For the splenic artery, the reverse maneuver can be performed, that is, the catheter body is rotated clockwise. In this method, the long reverse catheter is rotated into a figure-of-eight configuration so that its tip is directed toward either the hepatic or the splenic artery (Fig. **9**).

A short reverse-curve (2.5 cm) catheter also can be used for catheterization of the hepatic or splenic arteries. If the celiac trunk is about 2 cm long, the short reverse-curve catheter can be rotated to the right or left to catheterize the hepatic or splenic arteries directly, without forming the figure-of-eight configuration. However, there are two drawbacks to this short reverse-curve catheter. First, it is not as stable as a hepatic-curve catheter for long-term infusion in the common hepatic artery, but it is acceptable for a diagnostic study. Secondly, it cannot be easily advanced further into the proper hepatic artery because of its shorter ab segment.

Method 5: Catheter-Deflecting Method

When a short single-curve or a double-curve catheter is used with a guide wire-deflector apparatus, the angle of the catheter tip should have a gentle curve (angle a) and its ta segment should be short (1 cm) to minimize intimal injury. A straight catheter also can be used. The configuration of the tip also should be selected or adjusted to match the artery to be catheterized.

If the celiac artery is to be catheterized, the distal 2 to 3 cm of the catheter should be deflected anteriorly. The catheter tip is then advanced to the celiac trunk for about 1 to 2 cm to reach the celiac bifurcation, while the deflector wire remains at the celiac orifice. If the common hepatic artery is to be selected, the catheter is rotated clockwise so that the trunk of the catheter is in the right posterior and the ab segment forms an arc to the left anterior of the aorta and its tip (ta segment) points to the right (Fig. **10a, b**). When the splenic artery is to be catheterized, a counterclockwise rotation directs the catheter tip to the left (Fig. **10c**).

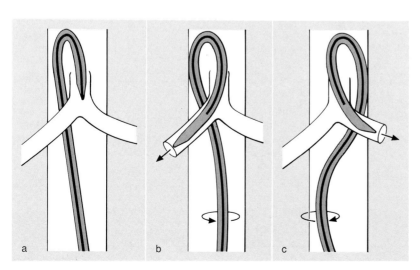

Fig. **10 Catheter-deflecting method**

a The catheter is brought to the celiac bifurcation by deflector wire

b A clockwise turn directs the catheter tip toward the right (hepatic artery)

c A counterclockwise turn directs the catheter tip toward the left (splenic artery)

The catheter is advanced continuously over the deflector wire until its tip is about 4 to 3 cm within the common hepatic artery. The deflecting procedure is best terminated at this time. The catheter position is checked with contrast medium and a safer, conventional guide wire (SCF) is used to advance the catheter, as in Method 1. A catheter can be deflected far into the desired artery, especially if the common and proper hepatic arteries are relatively large in diameter and form a very smooth arc with the celiac trunk.

Method 6: Loop (or Triple-Curve) Method

The loop method was initially described by Waltman et al. (6, 7) for left gastric artery catheterization, and was subsequently applied to the catheterization of most other visceral arteries. The formation of the loop can be facilitated when the curve b of a double-curve catheter is overbent from an angle of 45 degrees into 135 degrees. A loop is readily formed in the contralateral common iliac (Fig. **11a–d**) or superior mesenteric artery. Once the loop is created, the tertiary curve (c) becomes the fulcrum of the catheter, thus, a triple-curve catheter. It is preferable that the distance between the b and c curves be more than 5 cm, so that the tertiary curve c remains within the aorta during manipulation. It should be stressed that curve c is not present in the initial catheter and is formed at a random point in the catheter body. The loop functions similarly to a long reverse-curve (6 to 8 cm) catheter. The tip (ta segment) of a triple curve catheter can be turned easily to the right or left in a manner similar to the figure-of-eight method already described, and the "loop" is thus similar to a long reverse-curve with an ab segment of 5 cm or longer.

Left Gastric Artery Catheterization

Following the celiac arteriogram, a reverse-curve catheter is chosen so that its ab segment approximates the length (generally 1 to 2 cm) from the aorta

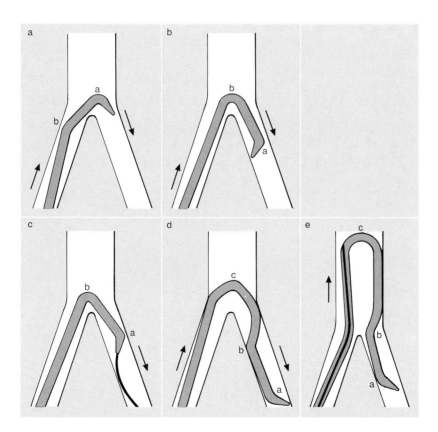

Fig. 11   Formation of a triple curve from a double-curve catheter in the iliac arteries
a The ta segment of a modified double-curve catheter is placed in the opposite common iliac artery
b When the catheter is pushed forward, the ab segment advances into the opposite iliac artery (the modified b curve facilitates this maneuver)
c A J guide wire is passed distally
d The catheter is advanced over the guide wire so that the b curve is at least 5 cm or more from the bifurcation
e The guide wire is pulled back to the ipsilateral iliac artery and the catheter and guide wire as a unit are advanced into the abdominal aorta to create a c curve (and a triple curve)

to the origin of the left gastric artery. A guide wire (generally, a stainless steel fixed coil guide wire with a 2 or 3 mm J tip) is advanced to the hepatic or splenic artery. With the guide wire fixed in place, the new catheter with tailored left gastric curve (Fig. **12a, b**) is advanced into the hepatic or splenic artery and the guide wire is removed (Fig. **12c**). The catheter is gradually withdrawn to the celiac bifurcation and a very small amount of the contrast medium is intermittently injected under fluoroscopy. When the b curve is in the aorta, it directs the ta segment to point anteriorly and superiorly. The tip (t) of the catheter can only pop into the left gastric artery (Fig. **12d**) when the catheter is continuously pulled back for a few millimeters. This manipulation is similar to Method 2 of hepatic artery catheterization. Three-dimensional thinking is very important in the selection and tailoring of a left gastric-curve catheter.

Renal Artery Catheterization

In an average patient, for whom a B single curve is ideal for the celiac and superior mesenteric arteries, a C single curve (one size smaller) is probably ideal for the renal artery. This is because the abdominal aorta is narrower at the renal level. The renal flow is also slower than in the celiac or superior mesenteric artery and requires a smaller injection rate (thus, less catheter recoiling).

When renal arterial embolization is contemplated, a 2.5 or 3 cm reverse-curve catheter is chosen so that the catheter can be more deeply seated to avoid regurgitation of the embolization materials.

The position of the first bifurcation of the renal artery, the size of the catheter (5 vs 6.5 Fr), and the previous experience of the angiographer with specific catheter curves and the embolization materials frequently determine whether the exchange of a single-curve for a reverse-curve catheter is necessary.

Inferior Mesenteric Artery Catheterization

The inferior mesenteric artery takes off from the left anterior aspect of the abdominal aorta at the mid L3 to mid L4 level. Since its first few centimeters can be obscured by the abdominal aorta itself, rotation of the patient or imaging tube into a slight (10 to 15 degrees) left posterior oblique position usually projects the inferior mesenteric artery in profile with the aorta.

A small single-curve catheter (D or E) frequently catches the inferior mesenteric artery easily. An alternative method is a 2 or 2.5 cm reverse-curve catheter; its ta segment enters the orifice of the inferior mesenteric artery without much difficulty. If the catheter needs to be seated more securely, the catheter-guide wire piggyback method (using a Bentson wire) is the best way to avoid spasm of the artery.

Lumbar Artery Catheterization

The lumbar artery originates at the mid posterior wall of the aorta, its main trunk, approximately 2.5 cm in length, goes laterally and horizontally until the edge of the lumbar vertebrae. Its second position turns posteriorly abruptly and divides into dorsal and

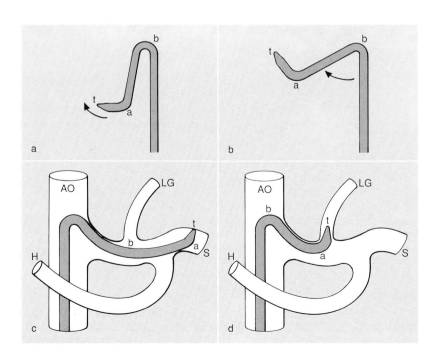

Fig. **12 Left gastric artery catheterization**
a A 2 or 2.5 cm reverse curve
b The curve b is open to fit the anatomy of the iliac and left gastric arteries
c, d See text for details

spinal branches. For embolization, it is best to have the catheter seated securely in the distal half of the horizontal segment. The double-curve catheter can select the lumbar artery easily. With a modified double curve, it can be advanced into the lumbar artery deeply, especially with the assistance of a guide wire (5).

An alternative method is to use a small reverse curve (2.5 cm) catheter to select the origin of the lumbar artery. A guide wire with soft and straight tip (typically, a Bentson guide wire) is advanced beyond the catheter tip, and the catheter and guide wire as a unit are pulled into the lumbar artery (the catheter-guide wire piggyback method). In this method, it is preferable that the tip of the catheter is not advanced beyond the horizontal portion of the lumbar artery. Otherwise, the catheter shape and the arterial anatomy become misfit and arterial spasm tends to occur. Do not violate the tailored catheter curve principle, if possible!

Inferior Phrenic Artery Catheterization

The inferior phrenic artery is important in the diagnosis and treatment of the primary and metastatic adrenal tumors, upper gastrointestinal hemorrhage, and hepatic tumors.

The inferior phrenic artery originates in the midanterior aspect of the aorta, immediately proximal to the origin of the celiac artery. It courses superiorly and laterally to supply the upper portion of the adrenal glands and the inferior aspect of both hemidiaphragms. The catheterization techniques are similar to the lumbar artery using either a double-curve or reverse-curve catheter.

Midsacral Artery Catheterization

Embryologically, the middle, or median, sacral artery is a continuation of the abdominal aorta. It descends to the surface of the last lumbar vertebra and along the frontal midline of the sacrum to the upper part of the coccyx. At the sacral level, it anastomoses with the lateral sacral arteries, of which there may be one to four on each side. The terminal branches of the middle sacral artery form a network of small arteries that pass through the mesorectum to supply the posterior surface of the rectum. This artery is important in the treatment of lower gastrointestinal bleeding, rectal tumor, sacral tumor, and recurrent pelvic tumors.

Since the middle sacral artery is usually small, selective catheterization depends on a thorough understanding of its precise location and its relationship to the aortic bifurcation. A 5 or 6.5 Fr catheter with a 2.5 cm reverse curve is commonly used. Since the artery is small, the soft tip of the guide wire should be extended beyond the tip of the catheter before pulling the catheter into the middle sacral artery (catheter-guide wire piggyback method), thereby significantly lessening arterial spasm and trauma (3). In patients with a large sacral tumor, the middle sacral artery is usually large, so that its catheterization can be accomplished with the catheter alone.

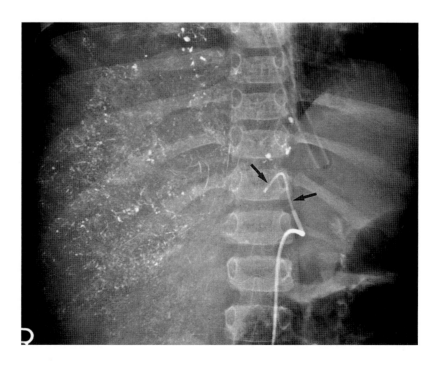

Fig. 13 **Hepatoma of right lobe and medial segment.** The right lobe is huge and has displaced the hepatic artery across the midline. The right hepatic artery was embolized with Ivalon and Ethiodol 5 days previously. A 0.038 inch open-end guide wire catheterizes the midhepatic artery for second embolization and spares the lateral segment

Coaxial Systems

A coaxial catheter system can be very useful when an artery is very small, very tortuous, or very difficult to reach with conventional catheterization techniques. Four coaxial systems are commercially available: 3 Fr Teflon catheter; Cope-Eisenberg coaxial system, a 4 Fr inner catheter, a 7 Fr outer catheter, and a torque-control guide wire; open-end guide wire in two sizes, 0.035 inch and 0.038 inch; Tracker-18 infusion catheter, 2.7 to 3 Fr catheter accepting a 0.018 inch or smaller torquable guide wire.

The coaxial catheter or guide wire can be utilized for infusion chemotherapy or arterial embolization. For arterial embolization, small particles less than 250 μm can be used, e.g., Ivalon particles, 150 to 250 μm, and Angiostat collagen, 20 to 200 μm. A superselective midhepatic embolization in Figure **13** illustrates the usefulness of the coaxial system.

References

1. Chuang VP. Basic rule in catheter selection for visceral angiography. AJR 1981;136:432–433.
2. Chuang VP, Soo CS, Carrasco CH, Wallace S. Superselective catheterization technique in hepatic angiography. AJR 1983;141:803–811.
3. Kudo S, Chuang VP, Wallace S, Bechtel W, Mir S. Middle sacral arteriography: diagnostic and therapeutic implications. Radiology 1984;151:65–67.
4. Rösch J, Grollman JH. Superselective arteriography in the diagnosis of abdominal pathology: technical considerations. Radiology 1969;92:1008.
5. Soo CS, Wallace S, Chuang VP, Carrasco CH, Phillies G. Lumbar artery embolization in cancer patients. Radiology 1982; 145:655–659.
6. Waltman AC, Courey WR, Athanasoulis CA, Baum S. Technique for left gastric artery catheterization. Radiology 1973;109:732–734.
7. Waltman AC. Catheter systems used in therapeutic angiography and methods of superselective vessel catheterization. In: Athanasoulis CA, Pfister RC, Green R, Roberson GH, eds. Interventional radiology. Philadelphia: Saunders, 1982:14–21.

Embolization Materials

D. Novak

For transcatheter arterial embolization (intra-arterial occlusion, transcatheter occlusive therapy, endovascular therapy, thrombotherapy, embolotherapy, thromboembolotherapy), a wide choice of embolization materials (embolic agents, occlusive agents, embolizing substances) is available (Table 1).

A large amount of clinical and experimental information about embolic agents has been collected. Our current knowledge about particular embolizing agents is based on empirical clinical applications, as well as on experimental data, including gross pathology and histopathological findings. Embolizing substances can be classified as following: according to their chemical and physical properties: resorbable or non-resorbable, particulate or liquid substances; according to the duration of occlusion: temporary, intermediate or long-acting occluding agents; according to the level of occlusion: proximal or peripheral embolizing materials.

The ideal embolic agent would have the following characteristics: reliable occlusion of both the primary and collateral vessels; non-toxicity, and no adverse reaction of the adjacent tissue structures; painless and safe embolization, with a low failure and recurrence rate; easy application; universal availability at low cost.

In general, the search for a new embolizing agent results from the cumbersome nature of the embolizing procedure, inadvertent reflux leading to embolization of non-target organs, and the relatively high frequency of incomplete embolization. Factors that determine the selection of an embolizing substance are: the pathovascular nature, site and hemodynamic status of the lesion to be embolized; the aims of the transcatheter occlusive therapy, either preoperative, palliative or definitive; the systemic and local effects of embolization, and potential complications; the availability and cost of the embolic material; e) the practicability of injection, and lack of technical difficulties; the personal experience of the interventional radiologist.

There is no single embolization material that can be used optimally for embolotherapy in all clinical conditions. Because of the variety of clinical conditions, the therapeutic aims of the embolization procedure are also various. Familiarity with all available embolization materials is therefore essential for the appropriate use of each substance. It is a challenge to the intelligence, clinical judgment and experience of the interventional radiologist to choose the best possible embolic agent in order to treat the patient in an optimal way.

In this chapter, the physical, chemical and biological properties of embolization substances are defined. The preparation of agents and embolization techniques are summarized. Recommended catheters are mentioned. Advantages and disadvantages of the embolic material are discussed, and basic

Table 1 Embolization materials

Particulate materials

Autologous materials
 Native and modified blood clot
 Tissue fragments: muscle, fat, dura, fascia lata

Resorbable materials
 Gelfoam: gelatine sponge
 Oxycel: oxidized cellulose
 Avitene: microfibrillar collagen
 Tachotop: of collagen flocculi
 Ethibloc: occlusion gel

Nonresorbable materials
 Ivalon: polyvinyl alcohol (PVA)
 Silicone spheres
 Plastic and metallic pellets and spheres

Liquid materials
 Bucrylate: isobutyl-2-cyanoacrylate (IBCA)
 Silicone
 Absolute ethanol
 Sclerosing agents
 Hot contrast medium
 Hypertonic glucose solution
 Barium sulfate

Mechanical devices
 Stainless steel coils

Balloon catheter systems
 Non-detachable balloon catheters
 Calibrated-leak balloon catheter systems

Detachable balloon catheter systems
 Latex detachable balloons (Serbinenko, Debrun)
 Silastic detachable balloons (DeCaprio, Hieshima)

Experimental embolizing agents

Chemoembolization agents

Electrocoagulation (electrothrombosis)

Labeling of embolizing substances with contrast agents

Table **2** Chronology of the development and application of embolizing agents

Year	Reference	Embolizing agent	Application
1930	Brooks (11)	Muscle tissue	Treatment of carotid cavernous fistula
1937	Hampy and Gardner (63)	Muscle tissue	Cavernous fistula with pulsating exophthalmos
1966	Luessenhof (98, 99)	Silicone spheres	Cerebral arteriovenous malformations
1968	Doppman (43)	Autologous clot	Spinal cord arteriovenous malformation
1971	Djindjian (41)	Fragments of muscle	Angioma embolization
1971	Doppman (45)	Silicone rubber	Experimental transcatheter embolization
1972	Rosch (118)	Autologous clot	Gastrointestinal bleeding
1972	Kricheff (87)	Silastic spheres	Arteriovenous malformation
1973	Djindjian (40)	Gelfoam	Embolotherapy in neuroradiology
1973	Tadavarthy (122)	Polyvinyl alcohol	Renal tumors
1974	Serbinenko (119)	Detachable balloons	Cerebral lesions
1975	Gianturco, Anderson and Wallace (57)	Stainless steel coils	Occlusion in hypernephroma, bleeding tumors
1975	Dotter (46)	Bucrylate	Selective arterial occlusion
1975	Hilal (67–69)	Low-viscosity silicone	Embolization of lesions of the head and spine
1975	Kerber (80)	Bucrylate	Intracranial arteriovenous malformations
1976	Kerber (81)	Calibrated-leak balloon	Occlusive catheter therapy
1977	Barth (2)	Autologous clot oxycel, Gelfoam	Transcatheter embolization
1978	Debrun (34)	Detachable balloons	Treatment of cerebral vascular lesions
1978	Castaneda-Zuniga (21)	Polyvinyl alcohol	Occlusion therapy, long term effects
1980	Ellman (52)	Absolute ethanol	Renal infarction
1984	Becker (5)	Absolute ethanol	Renal cell carcinoma

experimental and histopathological data are analyzed. The most frequent clinical applications are cited. In addition, the chronology of the development and application of embolizing substances is described (Table **2**).

Particulate Materials

Autologous Materials

Native and modified blood clot. Autologous blood clot was one of the first embolic materials used. The blood clot was prepared from about 20–50 ml of the patient's blood. The formation of a suitable clot was promoted by the addition of 3–5 drops of a thrombin solution. The clot was sectioned into 4×8 or 2×3 mm slices, which were loaded into a syringe filled with contrast agent. The blood clot was easily injected through a catheter. This fact and the prompt availability are a distinct advantage of using blood clot compared with other embolizing materials. Embolization with blood clots leads to vessel occlusion for 24–48 h. The clot lysis occurs from 3–24 h after embolization (2). Lysis can be delayed by mixing the blood clot with Amicar (ε-aminocaproic acid). The main disadvantage of embolization with blood clots is the unpredictable duration of occlusion. Gelfoam and other particulate materials have largely replaced autologous blood clots for transcatheter embolization. The use of blood clots as an embolic agent has now been practically abandoned.

Tissue fragments: muscle, fat, dura, fascia lata. Biological materials such as muscle slips, subcutaneous and fibrous tissue, fat tissue, dura and fascia lata were used at the time when embolization was a surgical procedure (11, 91). The surgical exposure of an artery was connected with an incision in order to obtain tissue material. With the advent of percutaneous catheter embolization, the use of such biological embolizing materials became obsolete.

Resorbable Materials

Gelfoam: gelatine sponge. Gelfoam is a resorbable gelatine sponge, and is still the most widely-used embolic material. Gelatine sponge is relatively easy to use and is readily available at low cost. Usually Gelfoam is packaged in sterile sheets that are cut into strips and pledgets in various sizes, e.g. 2×5 mm, 3×5 mm, $3 \times 3 \times 30$ mm (Fig. **1**). Powdered form Gelfoam is also available, e.g. for distal vessel occlusion in case of hemorrhage in the gastrointestinal tract. Gelfoam powder may be mixed with water-soluble contrast agent, and used for distal embolization of arteries of less than 1 mm in diameter. Gelfoam particles could be combined with a sclerosing agent, e.g. sodium tetradecyl sulfate (Sotradecol) in order to enhance thrombus formation. All sizes of Gelfoam are injected through conventional standard angiographic catheters. It is important to place the catheter tip at the most distal point in the vascular network leading to the lesion. Embolization could be started with small fragments of Gelfoam powder in order to occlude small end-arteries. For more proximal occlusion, pledgets of increasing sizes are used. Usually, large Gelfoam pledgets are injected individually. The moistened Gelfoam is rolled into a cigar-shaped plug, which is placed directly into the hub of the catheter or stopcock. The technique mostly used in embolization with Gelfoam can be summarized as follows:

– Gelfoam strips are cut into fragments, e.g. $2 \times 3 \times 5$ mm
– the strips are manually compressed into cylinders approximately 1 mm in diameter
– the fragments are inserted in dry form into the tip of a saline-filled syringe
– the syringe is connected to the catheter stopcock, and the embolus is gently injected
– the use of balloon catheters for embolization with Gelfoam particles is strongly advocated.

Gelfoam acts as a matrix for the formation of the thrombus. Its embolus produces vascular spasm, and also causes platelet agglutination and rapid clot for-

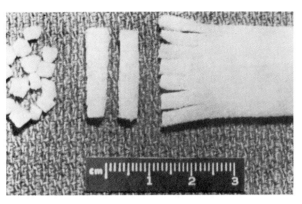

Fig. **1** **A Gelfoam sheet** cut into strips and small square pieces

mation. Inflammatory changes of the wall of the vessels are also reported. The occlusion produced by Gelfoam is not permanent, and partial recanalization occurs between 21 and 23 days, with complete recanalization after 30–35 days (2). Gelfoam has no long-term toxicity.

Clinical applications. Gelfoam is used to embolize various lesions. For instance, the goal of Gelfoam embolization in neuroradiology is to render a difficult surgical case more feasible, but also to provide definitive treatment (8). Embolization of lesions of the head, neck and spine, including the spinal cord, constitutes the major part of embolotherapy in neuroradiology. Gelfoam is used for transcatheter embolization of bronchial arteries in the treatment of massive hemoptysis. Arterial embolization in epistaxis is very successful (32). For partial splenic embolization, Gelfoam particles are mixed with a solution of 50,000 units of penicillin and 12 mg of gentamicin. Renal tumors have been embolized with Gelfoam, and also with Spongostan (50, 51), which is similar to Gelfoam and consists of 99% gelatine.

Oxycel: oxidized cellulose. Oxidized cellulose is a hemostatic agent. Clotting is induced by promotion of platelet aggregation. Oxycel, a gauze-like material, also creates a matrix for the deposition of fibrin. Oxycel is mixed with the patient's own blood in vitro in order to obtain a solid Oxycel clot, which is then cut into small pledgets. The embolization procedure is the same as that for autologous blood clot or Gelfoam. Oxycel pledgets are not injected as smoothly as blood clots. Oxycel embolization is of intermediate duration, because the embolus is usually resorbed within 30 days. A mild transient vasculitis caused by Oxycel is reported (2). It has no significant advantages over Gelfoam, and has practically been abandoned as an embolizing material.

Avitene: microfibrillar collagen. Avitene is microfibrillar bovine collagen. Suspensions and slurries of Avitene are achieved by mixing it with water-soluble contrast agents in a container. Low viscosity suspensions and slurries can be readily injected through catheters as small as 3 Fr placed in a superselective position. Usually an amount of 0.5 to 1.0 ml of Avitene suspension is injected to achieve peripheral embolization. This is a distinct advantage of Avitene over particulate embolizing agents (38). Avitene emboli dimensions range from 200 microns (fibres) to 1 × 1 cm (clumps of particles). Distal embolization with Avitene is also combined with proximal embolization using a coil or a detachable balloon. Apart from its mechanical occlusion of vessels, Avitene also serves as matrix for fibrin deposition and embolus formation. It produces a severe granulomatous arteritis mostly at the level of the arterioles, and leads to intensive and extensive tissue infarction. Following intra-arterial injection of Avitene, the thrombosis of small arteries is present for up to 3 months. The large vessels may recanalize in a shorter period of time, e.g. in about 2 weeks (76).

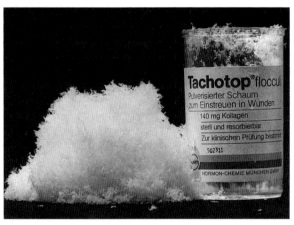

Fig. 2   **Tachotop flocculi,** a preparation from equine collagene

Clinical applications. Avitene is a suitable embolizing agent for preoperative occlusion of highly vascularized renal tumors, as well as vascular tumors of the head and neck. Avitene has been used for embolotherapy in hemobilia, and for occlusion of arteriovenous malformations. The use of Avitene is contra-indicated in embolization of gastrointestinal lesions, because of the danger of an extensive infarction. Also, caution is required in the embolization of pelvic processes to avoid unintentional occlusion of the blood supply to the sciatic nerve.

Tachotop: collagen flocculi. Tachotop flocculi are prepared from equine collagen. The basic material is isolated frome equine connective tissue. The collagen foam is transformed into tufts (Fig. **2**) of various sizes, ranging from 1.8–4 mm and from 3–7 mm. Tachotop flocculi can be suspended in saline or in a water-soluble contrast medium. Radiopaque collagen flocculi can be injected smoothly through standard angiographic and balloon catheters due to Tachotop's favorable lubricating properties. The material can be used for distal as well as proximal embolization. Thrombotic occlusion of segmental and subsegmental intrarenal arteries has been found 7 weeks after renal embolization.

Clinical applications. Tachotop has been used for preoperative and palliative embolization of malignant renal tumors (113), for the embolization of urinary bladder malignancies, and for renal ablation in patients with malignant renal hypertension.

Ethibloc: occlusion gel. Ethibloc is a viscous emulsion of zein, sodium amidotrizoate tetrahydrate, oleum papaveris and propylene glycol. The emulsion is made radiopaque by adding a water-soluble contrast medium. Ethibloc is available in a volume of 7.5 ml in a ready-to-inject syringe (Fig. **3**). The emulsion can be injected through a standard angiographic catheter, but the use of a balloon catheter to prevent

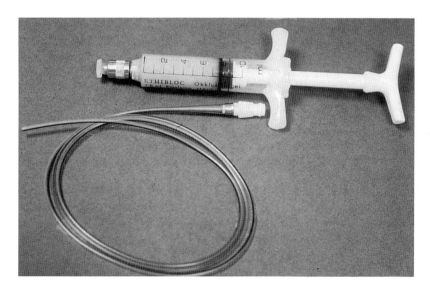

Fig. **3**   **Ethibloc occlusion gel**
in a ready-to-inject syringe

retrograde flow of the emulsion is recommended (106, 132). Ethibloc emulsion precipitates after contact with blood and other ionic agents within 5 min. The precipitate forms a semi-solid embolus. The embolization is basically a mechanical occlusion (77, 78). Ethibloc is biodegradable within 30 days after injection. Recanalization of occluded renal arteries after 4 weeks has been reported (129).

Clinical applications. Ethibloc has been used for preoperative embolization of renal tumors (15).

Non-Resorbable Materials

Ivalon: polyvinyl alcohol (PVA). This is a plastic sponge material available in blocks, sheets, spheres and particles. PVA is also available in radiopaque form by the addition of 60% barium sulfate or tantalum powder. PVA is dried in the compressed state, but re-expands when dampened. This unique property of PVA allows smaller particles to be used in the dried state in order to occlude much larger vessels. Various methods of preparation of PVA emboli before injection have been described (72, 75, 143). From a compressed PVA sheet, plugs of proper size are cut using a cork bore, or shavings are produced from a PVA block using a saw blade, or precut particles are used (65). The particles thus obtained are separated by sieve in order to obtain emboli of the predetermined uniform size. PVA particles have been available in various size ranges including, 149–250, 250–590 and 590–1000 µ. Particulate polyvinyl alcohol (PVA) sponge prepared by a blender technique shows two types of particles: large particles (> 50 µ) with irregular shapes and short, jagged edges, and smaller particles (2–50 µ). The embolization using PVA particles, pledgets or shavings is carried out in a manner similar to that for Gelfoam particles. Particulate PVA of the appropriate size is suspended in a tuberculin syringe filled with saline. The PVA is first injected into the catheter and then propelled into the artery using a second saline-filled tuberculin syringe. Passing the suspension between two syringes through a partially closed stopcock to break up the aggregates has been suggested (84). Better dispersion of the particles has been achieved by washing, blending and filtering PVA (7). After sterilization, the mixture is stored in jars filled with sterile water. Before the use of the suspension for embolization, the water must be decanted and the PVA particles resuspended in a contrast medium (122). A method has been developed to prepare a suspension of the PVA particles in contrast medium that can be stored ready for use without additional preparation (121). The non-radiopaque particles are best suspended with diluted contrast medium, allowing fluoroscopic observation during injection. Suspension of the PVA particles is facilitated using a glucose solution or low-molecular dextran. Com-

pressed PVA has a greater tendency to lodge permanently in the catheter. For embolization with PVA particles of any type, non-tapered catheters are recommended. The disadvantage of embolization with PVA is the difficulty of delivering it through small catheters. PVA particles can also be delivered into vessels by means of a wire. PVA plugs of different size and length are compressed around a stainless steel wire. The plugs are delivered through the catheter, and can be extended at the preselected site, beyond the catheter tip. After the PVA plug has re-expanded, it is stripped off against the catheter tip. PVA is physiologically inert, and the PVA embolus causes only minimal inflammatory changes in the artery itself. Embolization is primary a mechanical occlusion of the vessel lumen by PVA particles, but vessel occlusion is permanent. Long-term examinations showed a complete organization of the PVA thrombus (21).

Clinical applications. PVA embolization has a broad application spectrum in different clinical situations (25). The use of small calibrated particles of polyvinyl alcohol (150–250 µ) permits occlusion of the nidus of the spinal intramedullary arteriovenous malformation, with preservation of the anterior spinal artery and the normal central spinal arteries. PVA is used for arterial embolization of epistaxis. PVA and Gelfoam are also recommended as a synergystic mixture for therapeutic embolization (70). Polyvinyl alcohol foam mixed with Gelfoam is used to embolize intramedullary arteriovenous malformations of the spinal cord.

Silicone spheres. Silicone spheres impregnated with barium sulfate are available in sizes from 0.5–3.0 mm. Like all silicone preparations, silicone spheres are non-resorbable, but biocompatible. They are used to embolize arteriovenous malformations, carotid cavernous sinus fistulas, and juvenile angiofibromas (93).

Plastic and metallic pellets and spheres. Different spheres with uniform and exact particle size have been used for embolization of head and neck lesions. Included in this group are: acrylic spheres, methylmethacrylate spheres, Sephadex particles and polystyrene microspheres. Polystyrene microspheres have a nominal mean size of 50 ± 10 µ and 200 ± 25 µ. This particulate embolizing material has been used for distal hepatic artery embolization in pigs in order to study the development of collateral circulation.

Dextran microspheres have two different size ranges: 40–150 µ and 100–300 µ. Dextran microspheres can be injected through 2 Fr catheters, calibrated-leak balloons, and open-ended guide wires (39). Dextran microspheres enlarge by about 30–50% after suspension in normal saline. Microspheres remain in suspension in an equal mixture of normal saline and contrast agent.

Clinical applications. Dextran microspheres have been used to embolize meningioma, dural arteriovenous malformations, renal tumors, bone metastases, multiple myeloma, peripheral angioma. Metallic embolic particles, stainless steel pellets, metal fillings and steel balls have also been used in experimental and clinical embolization.

Liquid Materials

Isobutyl-2-cyanoacrylate (Bucrylate). This liquid embolizing agent (Fig. **4**) is classified as an investigational device by the U. S. Food and Drug Administration. Bucrylate is also classified as a suspect carcinogen and limited to life-threatening indications

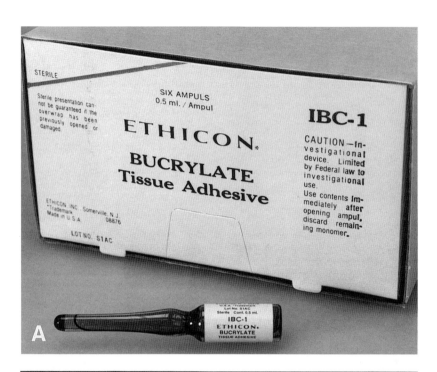

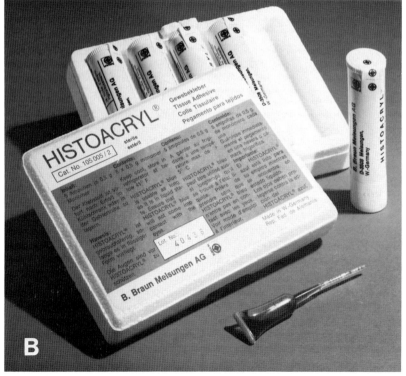

Fig. **4   Isobutyl-2-cyano-acrylate** in the form (A) Bucrylate and (B) Histoacryl

only. Isobutyl-2-cyanoacrylate (IBCA) is known as a tissue adhesive. IBCA polymerizes almost instantaneously by an anionic mechanism following contact with the blood or another ionized medium. The initiation of polymerization can be inhibited with the addition of small amounts of glacial acetic acid (3.7%–7.1% by volume). By this means polymerization time is prolonged from 2.3 s to 7.8 s (31). Bucrylate may be made radiopaque by mixing it with ethiodol, iophendylate (Pantopaque) or tantalum powder. The polymerization time of Bucrylate is prolonged in proportion to the volume of contrast agent added. Usually a concentration of 20–30% iophendylate results in sufficient radiopacity of the bucrylate (108). Bucrylate is then visible under fluoroscopy during injection, and on post-embolization X-rays (109). The mixture of Bucrylate and contrast agent also allows the best possible control during embolization. The safest and most effective embolization with Bucrylate is achieved using a coaxial or coaxial-balloon catheter system (Fig. **18**). The inner and outer catheters are perfused with a dextrane solution in order to prevent polymerization of Bucrylate before delivery at the site of the desired embolization (58). Usually, a coaxial catheter system with an inner catheter of 3.6 Fr and an outer catheter of 7.0 Fr are used (106). The use of coaxial catheter systems has definite advantages. In case of occlusion of the inner catheter owing to a premature polymerization of Bucrylate, it can be easily replaced. Also, using a coaxial catheter system, the inner catheter can be removed as soon as possible in order to prevent "gluing" of the catheter. Using an outer balloon catheter, slowing of blood flow or stasis "in situ" is achieved. Reflux of Bucrylate is prevented, and embolization of larger vessels is better controlled. Following embolization with Bucrylate, a mild histiocytic giant cell reaction which evolved into end-state sclerotic arteritis, was found to develop in animal experiments (30). Similar reactions were found in human trials (55).

Clinical applications. Bucrylate has been used to embolize renal tumors (18, 19, 61, 107, 109) and cerebral arteriovenous malformations (35, 80, 81, 82); in the occlusive therapy of genitourinary abnormalities (54, 55); in splenic embolization (60); for occlusion of renal arteriovenous fistulae (85); in spermatic vein embolization (88, 89, 90), and in obliteration of the left gastric vein and esophageal varices (96).

Silicone. Silicone rubber mixture consists of a medical-grade preparation of the Silastic elastomer 382 (Dimethylpolysiloxane), and silicone fluid 360. Both components are mixed in varying proportions in order to achieve the desired viscosity. There are basically two silicone mixtures available for transcatheter embolization (68, 69). The most commonly used mixture consists of 4 ml Dow Corning elastomer 382, 30 ml silicone fluid with a viscosity of 20 cp, and 0.5 ml of cross-linker (tetraethylsilicate). Secondly a low-viscosity silicone mixture is obtained using a silicone fluid with a viscosity of 5 cp (68, 69). Silicone rubber mixture is a biocompatible embolizing substance, used for permanent and complete casting of the vascular bed. The total vulcanization time is regulated by using different concentrations of catalysts, i.e. stannous octoate (Dow Corning catalyst M), and a cross-linker of colinker tetraethyl silicate. In this way, the vulcanization time, i.e. the time needed to change silicone from a liquid to a solid rubber substance, can be predetermined to last from less than a minute up to 20 min. Silicone mixture, and the catalyst, in separate containers, are steam autoclaved before use for embolization. The vulcanization time should be assessed prior to embolization by taking a sample of the mixture and stirring it within a vial (58). Silicone is easily made radiopaque by adding tantalum powder, zirconium dioxide, or iophendylate (68, 108, 110). Safe embolization is achieved by using a double-lumen balloon catheter or a coaxial balloon catheter. Low-viscosity silicone allows superselective embolization, because it can be injected through catheters as small as 1.0 Fr (68). In order to ensure the safest injection, a selective catheter position is recommended. Also, a complete vascular bed casting should be achieved, in order to prevent the distal migration of silicone plugs. This is important, because the silicone rubber has no adhesive properties, and does not react with tissue. Extensive experimental studies have been performed to evaluate local and systemic responses to silicone (58). Animal and human studies have shown that silicone has less toxicity than any other foreign material placed in the living body (45). Silicone is essentially histopathologically inert. It is not phagocytized or metabolized, and it has no antigenic or carcinogenic properties. Advantages of silicone which should be mentioned are: its lack of toxicity, the fact that radiopacity is easy to achieve, that injection through catheters as small as 1.0 Fr is possible, that vulcanization time can be assessed prior to the injection. The disadvantages are: that injection may be difficult using relatively highly viscous material, and that total occlusion of small vessels may cause organ infarction (58).

Clinical applications. Silicone mixtures have been used for embolization in various clinical situations (6, 68, 69). Silicone has been used for organ ablation (45), embolotherapy of extracranial vascular tumors (68, 69), and dural malformations (68). Low viscosity silicone mixtures have been used for the occlusion of spinal cord malformations and neoplasms of the spine (43, 67, 68, 69).

Absolute ethanol. The efficacy of intra-arterial ethanol as an embolizing agent has been demonstrated experimentally and clinically (48–53). Intra-arterial transcatheter injection of absolute ethanol produces permanent vascular occlusion and organ or tumor infarction. Ethanol causes vascular occlusion that is more peripheral than with most occlusive agents (92). Following ethanol injection, arterial blood flow in the injected vascular bed is significantly slowed, probably because of arterial spasm and rapid occlusion of smaller peripheral vessels. Reflux is likely to occur at this point if further amounts of ethanol are injected. The use of balloon occlusion catheters is therefore of the utmost importance to prevent reflux. Injection of ethanol through a balloon occlusion catheter is now universally accepted (48–51). The main benefits of balloon occlusion are the interruption of local blood flow, with the resultant prolonged contact between the ethanol and the endothelium, and prevention of inadvertent ethanol reflux. An additional benefit of the use of balloon catheters is the reduction in the amount of ethanol needed to achieve total occlusion (61). An amount of 8–18 ml (average 12.9 ml) is needed for complete occlusion of a renal artery (62). A suitable mixture of non-ionic contrast agent and ethanol – without diluting the ethanol – helps to control the embolization procedure better (5). The advantages of ethanol are: its universal availability and minimal cost, ease of administration, lack of toxicity, low complication rate when injected through an inflated balloon catheter. The main mechanism of action of intra-arterial ethanol is damage to the endothelium and activation of the coagulation systems (14). Ethanol produces complete infarction of the target organ or tumor. Infarction is attributed both to the denaturation of tissue protein and vascular thrombosis due to the endothelial damage (5). Recanalization of ethanol-injected vessels failed to occur in animal experiments (92).

Clinical applications. Ethanol as an intra-arterial embolizing agent has been used successfully for infarction of renal tumors (47, 48, 50, 51, 52, 53, 114). For renal ablation, a dose of 0.2 ml/kg body weight of absolute ethanol (99% ethyl alcohol) is normally used. Ethanol is injected through a balloon catheter inflated in the mid-portion of the renal artery. The balloon beyond the origin of the inferior adrenal and gonadal arteries is kept inflated for 2 minutes after the injection of ethanol (62). The renal vein concentration of ethanol was measured during embolization of renal cell carcinoma in patients (62), and varied from trace amounts to 0.79%. It has been concluded from this that the concentration of ethanol in the renal vein remains sufficiently low as to be negligible when proper balloon occlusion is used (62). Renal ablation (medical nephrectomy) with ethanol is used in patients with uncontrollable hypertension (37, 104). Ethanol is useful in obliterating esophageal varices (79). An ethanol dose of 0.4 ml/kg body weight is normally used. Ethanol is also used

for percutaneous transhepatic sclerosis of esophageal varices (5, 79, 142). Bronchial artery embolization to control severe hemoptysis has been performed using ethanol (103). Transcatheter splenectomy using ethanol has also been performed (101). Ethanol is also an effective sclerosing agent for spermatic vein occlusion. Embolization of an arteriovenous malformation of the extremity with ethanol via a direct percutaneous puncture has also been mentioned (141). Ablation of the adrenals with ethanol seems to be ineffective (44).

Sclerosing agents. Sclerosing agents currently in use are: *Sodium tetradecyl sulfate* (Sotradecol), a synthetic anionic detergent available as a 1% or 3% aqueous solution. The solution contains 2% benzyl alcohol as an anesthetic agent. *Sodium morrhuate* (Varicocid), a sodium salt of the fatty acids of cod liver oil. This sclerosant is available as a 5% solution with the addition of 3% benzyl alcohol as an anesthetic. *Polidocanol* (Aethoxysklerosol). This sclerosant is used in 3–4% solution, but also in combination with Bucrylate (88, 116). Indications and injection techniques for sclerosants in the sclerotherapy of the spermatic veins have been described (88, 89, 90, 115, 116, 120, 144).

Hot contrast medium. Hot contrast medium as a venous occlusion substance was first used experimentally in superficial veins and in spermatic veins (117). It has also been injected for renal ablation (29). Hot contrast medium used for "thermal sclerotherapy" of spermatic veins effectively occludes the primary vein and collaterals (71). Injecting it is painful, however, and this represents the major drawback of the method. The internal jugular approach is advocated as the most reliable method of injection (71). An introduction sheath should be used in the neck to prevent a hematoma forming. The catheter tip should be positioned in the pelvic portion of the spermatic vein. For the occlusion of the left spermatic vein, a modified 7 Fr headhunter catheter is used (71).

Hypertonic glucose solution. Hypertonic glucose solution has been used for the obliteration of esophageal varices.

Barium sulfate. Barium sulfate is used to make silicone spheres radiopaque. It is injected as a liquid embolizing agent into tumor vessels, leading to permanent occlusion. Histologic examination of the kidneys following embolization with barium sulfate showed infarcts and a granulomatous reaction (24). The long-term effects of intravascular injected barium sulfate are not known. Occlusion of the renal artery with barium sulfate has been reported in patients with end-stage renal disease.

Mechanical Devices

Coils. Stainless-steel coils were originally developed by Gianturco, Anderson and Wallace (1, 57, 130, 131). The Gianturco-Anderson-Wallace coils (GAW-coils) have undergone several important modifications that have simplified their delivery and improved their safety (28) (Figs. 5–9). The coils presently available (helix diameters of 3 mm, 5 mm, 8 mm, 10 mm, 12 mm and 15 mm) are injected, and pass through the standard angiographic catheters using a standard 0.038 guide wire. The minicoils are designed for delivery via a 5.0 Fr catheter (1), and can also be introduced using standard tapered cathe-

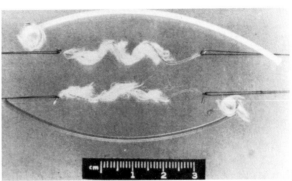

Fig. 5 **Various stainless steel coils. a** (left) Mini-coil and (right) original Gianturco coil and **b** more recent coils

b

Fig. 6 **Various occluding spring emboli**

Fig. 7 **Occluding spring emboli.** Giant coil (left), and "mini" coil (right)

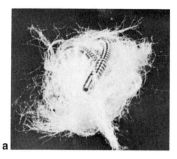
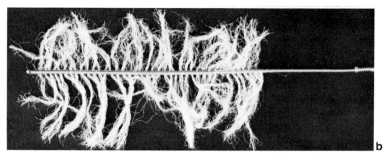

Fig. **8** **Stainless steel coil. a** Coiled embolus and **b** extended embolus

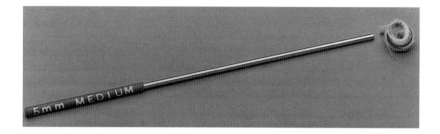

Fig. **9** **Occluding spring embolus** with loading cartridge

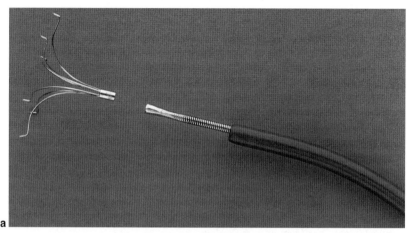

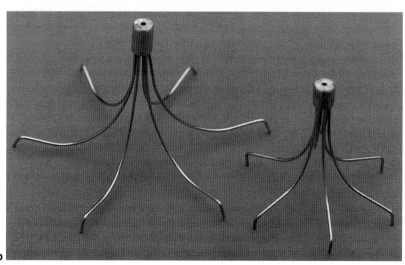

Fig. **10** **Amplatz vascular obstructing device. a** With Teflon guiding catheter, positioning guide wire, and "spider". **b** "Spiders" of 9 and 13 mm

ters (28). Standard coils are received from the manufacturer in a sheath. Placement in the catheter is also made easier. The introduction sheath is placed in the hub of the catheter, and the coil is slid into the catheter with an appropriate guide wire. Following this, the coil is advanced to a point at which the catheter begins to curve. The coil is then extruded from the catheter with a guide wire. The coil reforms and lodges in situ. Based on the angiographic findings, a coil with a diameter as close as possible to that of the vessels to be occluded is chosen. The choice of the appropriate coil size is important. A coil that is too large will elongate rather than assume the proper shape. On the other hand, the using too small a coil leads to peripheral rather than the desired proximal occlusion.

Embolization using coils is sometimes associated with technical problems. Coils may become wedged in the catheter. Wool or Dacron strands may become impacted and stick in the tip of the catheter. The coil may be extruded, but not the tail. With the withdrawal of the catheter, the coil may also be withdrawn. The catheter may recoil before complete delivery is achieved. The coil may extend into larger arteries, e.g. the aorta. Coils may pass through large arteriovenous malformations or fistulas and embolize the pulmonary vascular bed. Injecting the coil too forcefully into a renal artery may result in embolization of the contralateral renal artery.

Coils of different lengths and diameters can be home-made from standard guide wires. Usually, wool, silk or Dacron threads are tied along the coil at certain intervals in order to provide thrombogenicity (Fig. 6). To embolize large arteriovenous malformations and fistulas, large coils with barbs or stainless steel "spider" umbrellas are recommended (20, 22, 23, 94, 95) (Fig. 10). Also, several additional coils can be introduced for the formation of a large coil embolus network (26, 27). Other embolic materials, such as silk, are injected in combination with coils. Silk induces an inflammatory and foreign-body reaction. In this way a permanent occlusion is achieved. The silk tufts ("streamers") can be made by using silk threads, wedging them into a small piece of hypodermic tubing. In order to minimize the risk of coil dislodgment into normal peripheral vessels, the "coil-in-coil" technique of vascular embolization is proposed (17). Two coils of different sizes are used. A large coil is introduced into the artery, followed by a smaller coil, which is delivered into the lumen of the first coil. The "packing" the vessel with two coils in a row has advantages for the occlusion of short, anomalous arteries (17). Coils have also been modified to include a screw-on attachment for the delivery wire, which allows safe, accurate placement (95). Currently, 2 mm coils formed from 0.025 guide wires are available (100). All of these occlusion coils incorporate strands of Dacron, which act as a nidus for the formation of thrombus, producing a permanent occlusion of the vessel (3, 100). Gross pathology and histological examinations of specimens after embolization using coils with wool strands showed extensive inflammatory changes in the occluded arteries and periadventitial tissue. An organized thrombus was found on the proximal and distal end of the coil (3). A permanent occlusion was also found following embolization with coils having silk as well as Dacron strands.

Clinical applications. GAW (Gianturco-Anderson-Wallace) coils are the fastest, easiest and least expensive way of producing large vessel occlusion. Coils are a consistent and reliable device for permanent occlusion of larger vessels. They can be placed precisely in the desired position serving as an internal vessel ligature. Coils have been used successfully to embolize renal arteries, arteriovenous malformations and fistulas (10, 56, 64), post-traumatic arteriovenous fistulas and post-biopsy renal fistulas, gastric and esophageal varices and spermatic veins with varicocele (9). In patients with post-traumatic arteriovenous fistulas with high blood flow, or in patients with coagulopathy, the pretreatment of coils with thrombin solution ensures prompt and effective occlusion of the large target vessels (100).

Balloon Catheter Systems

Non-detachable balloon catheters. These are used for occlusion arteriography and phlebography; for injection of particulate and liquid embolization materials; for preoperative occlusion; for treatment of hemorrhage; for occlusion of unclippable internal carotid artery aneurysms (106, 132). Non-detachable balloon catheters may have only one lumen (Fogarty balloon catheter) or a double-lumen design (106, 132).

Calibrated-leak balloon catheter systems. A calibrated-leak balloon catheter has been developed, the balloon measuring less than 1 mm in diameter (81–83, 86). A balloon with a small leak is permanently fixed on the tip of the catheter. Keeping the balloon sufficiently inflated, a contrast agent or liquid embolic material (e.g. Bucrylate) can be delivered. The balloon is flow-directed, and can reach the distal region of the vascular bed. Debrun uses a latex balloon with a leak. The latex balloon is attached to the end of a small Teflon or polyethylene catheter (34, 36).

Detachable Balloon Catheter Systems

Serbinenko was the first to use a detachable balloon for superselective angiography and for the embolization of neurovascular arteriovenous malformations (119). Debrun has developed a coaxial catheter system and detachable latex balloons for the treatment of neurovascular malformations (33, 34). Mini-balloons have been introduced in cardiovascular interventional radiology by a group of radiologists at Johns Hopkins Hospital, Baltimore (133–138). Silastic detachable balloons have also been introduced (66) (Figs. **11–18**).

The Debrun detachable balloon system consists of 3 coaxial catheters: the 2 Fr Teflon catheter (catheter A), 110 cm long with a latex balloon on the tip; the 5 Fr radiopaque polyethylene catheter (catheter B), 100 cm long; the 9 Fr thin-walled non-tapered polyethylene catheter (catheter C), 80 or 90 cm long (33,

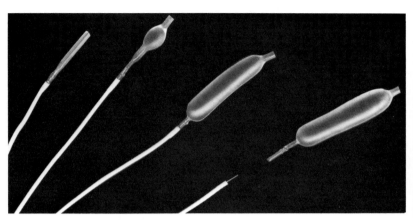

Fig. **11   Detachable balloons.** Balloon filling and detachment

Fig. **12   2 mm and 1 mm mini-balloons**

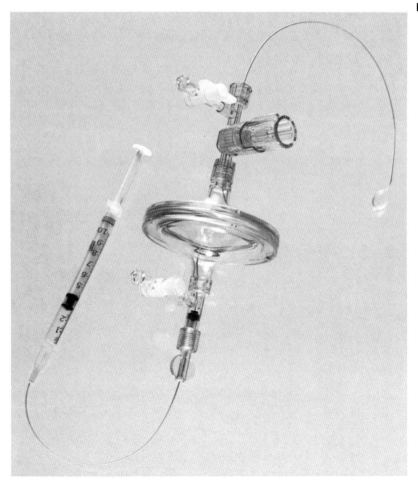

Fig. **13   Mini-balloon catheter delivery system**

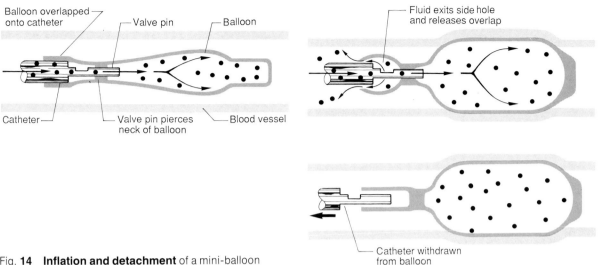

Balloon overlapped onto catheter — Valve pin — Balloon

Catheter — Valve pin pierces neck of balloon — Blood vessel

Fluid exits side hole and releases overlap

Catheter withdrawn from balloon

Fig. 14 Inflation and detachment of a mini-balloon

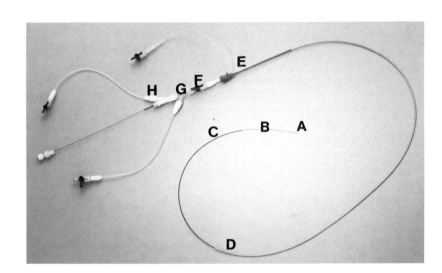

Fig. 15 Embolization set with Debrun's detachable balloon, consisting of: (A) balloon, (B) 2 Fr carrier catheter, (C) 3 Fr coaxial catheter, (D) 9 Fr guiding catheter, (E) introducer sheath, (F) two-way stopcock, (G) transparent lambda connector, and (H) lambda (Tuohy-Borst)

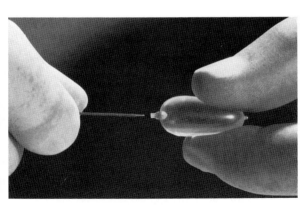

Fig. 16 Mounting of the gold valve balloon on the carrier catheter

Fig. 17 Gold valve balloon ▶

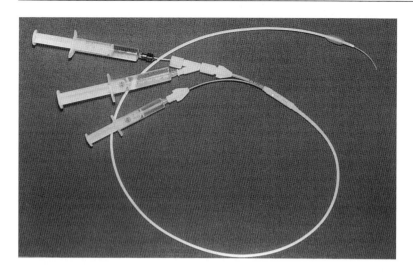

Fig. **18   Coaxial balloon catheter system** for embolization with liquid embolization substances

34). Debrun uses two basic types of detachable latex balloon. The type I balloon is held on the catheter tip by only a narrow portion of the sleeve. This balloon does not require a second coaxial catheter for detachment. The type II balloon is not self-sealing. It can be filled with contrast medium or a liquid polymerizing substance. The type II balloon is firmly tied to the tip of a Teflon catheter (0.4 mm ID, and 0.6 mm OD) with an elastic latex thread. In order to detach this type of balloon, a second coaxial catheter (catheter B) is needed. Debrun's detachable balloon catheters can have either a single lumen or a double lumen.

The technique of balloon preparation, introduction and injection of contrast medium and liquid embolization materials has been described (33–36). To introduce a 1 mm mini-balloon, a 5 Fr or 6.5 Fr non-tapered polyethylene catheter ("Cobra" and "Sidewinder" types) is used (133–138). The mini-balloon is attached to a 2 Fr bismuth-loaded polyurethane catheter. The outer catheter is introduced through a 7.0 Fr percutaneously-placed sheath. To introduce a 2 mm mini-balloon, a thin-walled 9 Fr polyethylene introducer catheter is used. The 1 mm balloon can be inflated to a maximum diameter of 4 mm, and the 2 mm balloon can be distended to 8 mm in diameter. Only iso-osmotic contrast agents are used as balloon fillers. The application of mini-balloons can be described as follows: the balloon catheter is loaded into a coiling chamber through a coaxial catheter valve. The coiling chamber ensures safe injection of the balloon catheter. The proximal catheter is anchored to a Tuohy-Borst adapter to prevent unintentional introduction of the whole balloon catheter. The bolus injection of saline through the side arm of the coaxial catheter valve propels the balloon catheter through the vessel. Usually, the balloon catheter comes to a halt beyond the desired site of occlusion. The balloon catheter is pulled back to its final position under fluoroscopy. At this point, the balloon is filled with an iso-osmotic contrast medium solution. The total amount of contrast agent for a 1 × 5 mm uninflated balloon is 0.6 ml, and for a 2 × 7 mm balloon, the maximum volume is 2.2 ml. A test injection of contrast agent through the introducer catheter shows whether the balloon is occluding the vessel completely. Now the balloon is detached. The final position of the balloon is checked by the aid of a post-occlusion angiogram (133–138).

Clinical applications. Embolotherapy using detachable balloons is basically performed in the following clinical situations: hemorrhage; preoperative occlusion of vascular neoplasms; treatment of vascular malformations (16, 105, 123, 124, 126, 127, 128, 133, 135–138). Detachable balloons were used in the occlusion of traumatic carotidcavernous fistulas, vertebral fistulas, cerebral dural and facial arteriovenous malformations, unclippable aneurysms, some meningiomas and glioblastomas, and in the treatment of intractable epistaxis and hemorrhage in cases of Rendu-Osler-Weber disease (34, 35, 133–138). Detachable balloons are also applied in the occlusion of spermatic veins in varicocele, and in the obliteration of pulmonary, renal and splenic arteriovenous malformations (133–138). Detachable mini-balloons have also been used for embolotherapy in patients with hemobilia as a complication of biliary catheter drainage (102).

Experimental Embolizing Agents

There is a long list of substances which have been tested as potential embolizing agents (42, 109–111). Polyurethane has been studied for vessel occlusion (42, 109–111) Polyurethane is a solvent-free, two-component vulcanizing substance, consisting of a

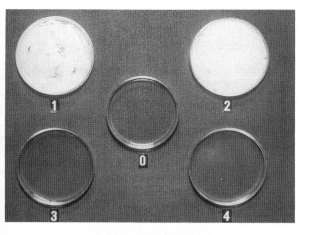

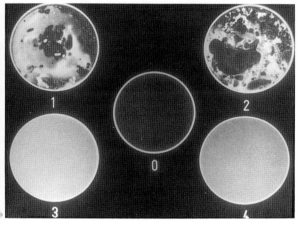

Fig. **19 Labeling polyurethane with contrast agents.**
a Photograph and **b** Roentgenogram. 0 = control, 1 =
meglumine ioxaglamate, 2 = iohexol, 3 = Pantopaque, 4 =
Lipiodol

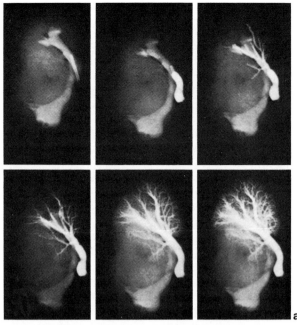

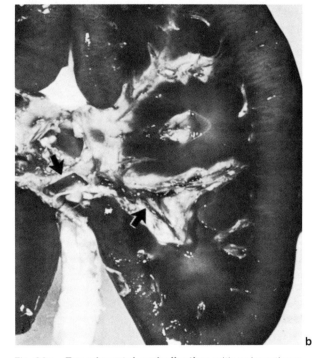

Fig. **20a Experimental embolization** with polyurethane
labeled with Pantopaque on kidney model **b** Kidney specimen following embolization

mixture of component I (a mixture of different
aliphatic polyetherpolyols), and component II (an
aliphatic isocyanate). A mixture of 20 g of component I and 8.4 g of component II, with stannous
octate as a catalyst, has been used experimentally.
Polyurethane is promising as a liquid "long-term"
embolizing substance. Radiopacity is readily
achieved with Pantopaque (Fig. **19**). The working
and vulcanization times are proportional to the concentration of the catalyst. Intra-arterial injection of
polyurethane leads to complete and permanent
occlusion of the vascular bed (Fig. **20**).

Vilan 500 has also been used experimentally to
occlude the renal artery (112); it is a partly-hydroly-
zed polyvinyl acetate in 95% alcohol.

Chemoembolization Agents

Chemoembolization is a combination of the intra-
arterial infusion of a chemotherapeutic agent with
intra-arterial embolization (4, 73, 74). The potential

therapeutic effect is considered to be a function of
microinfarction and prolonged drug release. The
advantage of chemoembolization is decreased systemic toxicity of chemotherapy (4, 73). Chemoembolization with mitomycin C microcapsules is the
best-known procedure.

Electrocoagulation (Electrothrombosis)

Transcatheter electrocoagulation (TCEC) is a technique of producing blood clots in vivo. TCEC has been experimentally developed and also used clinically (12, 13, 125).

A steel guide wire anode is extended through the selectively placed catheter at the site of the desired occlusion. A constant current is applied with a neutral electrode attached to the body. The coagulation of blood occurs at the anode site. The intimal damage to the vessel produced by the anode is probably caused by a marked decrease in pH at the electrode tip. The main advantages of TCEC are that the site of occlusion can be precisely determined, the extent of the occlusion is controllable, and occlusion is possible despite heparinization or thrombocytopenia. Also there is no risk of reflux or non-target embolization (59). The disadvantage of TCEC is the considerable amount of time (30–60 min) needed to achieve occlusion. There are also difficulties in positioning the anode precisely at the desired site of occlusion. Another disadvantage is that the stainless steel anode undergoes electrolysis and occasionally breaks off.

Clinical applications. TCEC has been applied in the treatment of arteriovenous malformations, to control hemorrhage, and in the infarction of vascular tumors (12, 59, 125).

Labeling Embolizing Substances with Contrast Agents

The aim of labeling or tagging embolization materials is to achieve the safest injection under fluoroscopy control, and simplified follow-up control of embolization sequelae using post-embolization roentgenograms while the embolizing substance is still radiopaque (58, 108, 110).

The embolization materials are made radiopaque with the following contrast agents: water-soluble iodinated contrast agents; oily contrast agents; tantalum powder and tantalum oxide powder; barium sulfate; zirconium dioxide. Solid biological embolization materials, e.g. Gelfoam, Tachotop, or Avitene have been successfully labeled with all water-soluble iodinated contrast agents (e.g. Lipiodol, Duroliopaque), but the most stable solution is achieved with Pantopaque (106). A concentration of 20–30% Pantopaque results in sufficient radiopacity in Bucrylate. Pantopaque delays the speed of polymerization of Bucrylate (58), and it reacts with tissue and tends to promote thrombosis. Silicone mixture and polyurethane are labeled with tantalum powder or tantalum oxide powder as well as with Pantopaque and zirconium dioxide. A concentration of 20–30% of contrast medium is needed.

References

1. Anderson JH, Wallace S, Gianturco C, Gerson LP. "Mini" Gianturco stainless-steel coils for transcatheter vascular occlusion. Radiology 1979;132:301.
2. Barth KH, Strandberg JD, White RI Jr. Long term follow-up of transcatheter embolization with autologous clot, oxycel and gelfoam in domestic swine. Invest Radiol 1977;12:3.
3. Barth KH, Strandberg JD, Kaufman SL, White RI Jr. Chronic vascular reactions to steel coil occlusion devices. AJR 1978;131:455.
4. Bechtel W, Wright KC, Wallace S, Mosier B, Mosier D, Mir S, Kudo S. An experimental evaluation of microcapsules for arterial chemoembolization. Radiology 1986;161:601.
5. Becker GJ, Holden RW, Klatte EC. Therapeutic embolization with absolute ethanol. Semin Intervent Radiol 1984;1:118.
6. Berenstein A. Flow-controlled silicone fluid embolization. AJR 1980;134:1213.
7. Berenstein A, Graeb DA. Convenient preparation of ready-to-use particles in polyvinyl alcohol foam suspension for embolization. Radiology 1982;145:846.
8. Berenstein A, Russel EJ. Gelatin sponge in therapeutic neuroradiology. Radiology 1981;141:105.
9. Berkman WA, Price RB, Wheatley JK, Fajman WA, Sones PJ, Casaralla WJ. Varicoceles: a coaxial coil occlusion system. Radiology 1984;151:73.
10. Braun IF, Hoffman JC Jr, William J, Casarella J, Davis PC. Use of coils for transcatheter carotid occlusion. AJNR 1985; 6:953.
11. Brooks B. The treatment of traumatic arterio-venous fistula. South Med J 1930;23:100.
12. Brunelle F. Electric transcatheter vascular obliteration: electrothrombosis, electrocoagulation. Front Eur Radiol 1982;1:101.
13. Brunelle F, Kunstlinger F, Quillard J. Endovascular electrocoagulation with a bipolar and alternating currents: a follow-up study in dogs. Radiology 1983;148:113.
14. Buchta K, Sands J, Rosenkrantz H, Roche WD. Early mechanism of action of arterially infused alcohol U.S.P. in renal devitalization. Radiology 1982;145:45.
15. Bucheler E, Hupe W, Kosterhalfen H, Altensaehr E, Erbe W. Neue Substanz zur therapeutischen Embolisation von Nierentumoren. Rö Fo 1978;128:599.
16. Burrows PE, Rosenberg HC, Chuang HS. Diffuse hepatic hemangiomas: percutaneous transcatheter embolization with detachable silicone balloons. Radiology 1985;156:85.
17. Butto F, Hunter DW, Castaneda-Zuniga WR, Amplatz K. Coil-in-coil technique for vascular embolization. Radiology 1986;554.
18. Carmignani G, Belgrano E, Puppo P, Giuliani L. Cyanoacrylates in transcatheter renal embolization. Acta Radiol [Diagn] (Stockh) 1978;19:49.
19. Carrasco CH, Charnsangavej C, Wallace S. Transcatheter embolization of neoplasms. Semin Intervent Radiol 1984;1:146.
20. Castaneda-Zuniga WR, Galliani CA, Rysavy J. "Spiderlon": new device for simple, fast arterial and venous occlusion. AJR 1981;136:637.
21. Castaneda-Zuniga WR, Sanchez R, Amplatz K. Experimental observations on short and long-term effects of arterial occlusion with ivalon. Radiology 1978;126:783.
22. Castaneda-Zuniga WR, Tadavarthy SM, Galliani CA, Laerum F, Schwarten DE, Amplatz K. Experimental venous occlusion with stainless steel spiders. Radiology 1981;141:238.
23. Castaneda-Zuniga WR, Tadavarthy SM, Gonzales R, Rysavy J, Amplatz K. Single barbed stainless steel coils for venous occlusion: a simple but useful modification. Invest Radiol 1982; 17: 186.
24. Cho, KJ, Ensminger WD, Shields JJ, Adams DF. Selective tissue ablation by therapeutic pharmacoangiography. In: Abrams HL, ed. Vascular and interventional radiology; vol 3. 3rd ed. Boston: Little, Brown, 1983;2175.
25. Chuang VP, Soo CS, Wallace S. Ivalon embolization in abdominal neoplasms. AJR 1981;136:729.

26. Chuang VP, Szwarc I. The coil baffle in the experimental occlusion of large vascular structure. Radiology 1982;143:25.

27. Chuang VP, Wallace S. Current status of transcatheter management of neoplasms. Cardiovasc Intervent Radiol 1980;3:256.

28. Chuang VP, Wallace S, Gianturco C. A new improved coil for tapered-tip catheter for arterial occlusion. Radiology 1980;135:507.

29. Cragg AH, Rosel P, Rysavy JA. Renal ablation using hot contrast medium: an experimental study. Radiology 1983;148:683.

30. Cromwell LD, Freeny PC, Kerber CW, Kunz LL, Harris AB, Shaw CM. Histologic analysis of tissue response to bucrylate-pantopaque mixture. AJR 1986;147:627.

31. Cromwell LD, Kerber CW. Modification of cyanoacrylate for therapeutic embolization: preliminary experience. AJR 1979;132:799.

32. Davis KR. Embolization of epistaxis and juvenile nasopharyngeal angiofibromas. AJR 1987;148:209.

33. Debrun G, Fox A, Drake C, Peerless S, Girvin J, Ferguson G. Giant unclippable aneurysms: treatment with detachable balloons. AJNR 1981; 2:167.

34. Debrun G, Lacour P, Caron JP, Hurth M, Comoy J, Keravel Y. Detachable balloon and calibrated-leak balloon techniques in the treatment of cerebral vascular lesions. J Neurosurg 1978;49:635.

35. Debrun G, Vinuela FV, Fox AJ, Drake GG. Embolization of cerebral arteriovenous malformations with bucrylate: experience in 46 cases. J Neurosurg 1982;56:615.

36. Debrun, G, Vinuela FV, Fox AJ, Kan S. Two different calibrated-leak balloons: experimental work and applications in humans. AJNR 1982;3:407.

37. Denny DF, Perlmutt LM, Bettmann MA. Percutaneous recanalization of an occluded renal artery and delayed ethanol ablation of the kidney resulting in control of hypertension. Radiology 1984;151:381.

38. Diamond NG, Casarella WJ, Bachman DM, Wolff M. Microfibrillar collagen hemostat: a new transcatheter embolization agent. Radiology 1979;133:775.

39. Dion JE, Rankin RN, Vinuela FV, Fox AJ, Wallace AC, Mervart M. Dextran microsphere embolization: experimental and clinical experience with radiologic-pathologic correlation: work in progress. Radiology 1986;160:717.

40. Djindjian R, Cophignon J, Rey A, Theron J, Merland JJ, Houdart R. Superselective arteriography embolization by the femoral route in neuroradiology: study of 60 cases. Neuroradiology 1973;6:132.

41. Djindjian R, Houdart R, Cophignon J, Hurth M, Comoy J. Premiers essais d'embolisation par voie fémorale de fragments de muscle dans un cas d'angiome medullaire et dans un cas d'angiome alimenté par la carotide externe. Rev Neurol (Paris) 1971;125:119.

42. Doppman JL, Aven W, Bowman RL, Word LL, Girton M. A rapidly polymerizing polyurethane for transcatheter embolization. Cardiovasc Intervent Radiol 1978;1:109.

43. Doppman JL, Dichiro G, Ommaya A. Obliteration of spinal-cord arteriovenous malformation by percutaneous embolization. Lancet 1968;i:447.

44. Doppman JL, Girton M. Adrenal ablation by retrograde venous ethanol injection: an ineffective and dangerous procedure. Radiology 1984;150:667.

45. Doppman JL, Zapol W, Pierce J. Transcatheter embolization with a silicone rubber preparation: experimental observations Invest Radiol 1971;6:304.

46. Dotter CT, Goldman ML, Rösch J. Instant selective arterial occlusion with isobutyl-2-cyanoacrylate. Radiology 1975;114:227.

47. Earthman WJ, Mazer MJ, Winfield AC. Angiomyolipomas in tuberous sclerosis: subselective embolotherapy with alcohol, with longterm follow-up study. Radiology 1986;160:437.

48. Ekelund L, Ek A, Forsberg L, Honkaas S, Henrikson H, Kalland T, Boijsen E. Occlusion of renal arterial tumor supply with absolute ethanol: experience with 20 cases. Acta Radiol [Diagn] (Stockh) 1984;25:195.

49. Ekelund L, Jonsson N, Treugut H. Transcatheter obliteration of the renal artery by ethanol injection: experimental results. Cardiovasc Intervent Radiol 1981;4:1.

50. Ekelund L, Karp W, Mansson W, Olson AM. Palliative embolization of renal tumors: follow-up in 19 cases. Urol Radiol 1981;3:13.

51. Ekelund L, Mansson W, Olson AM, Stigson L. Palliative embolization of arterial renal tumour supply: results in 10 cases. Acta Radiol [Diagn] (Stockh) 1979;20:323.

52. Ellman BA, Green CE, Eigenbrodt E, Garriot JC, Curry TS. Renal infarction with absolute ethanol. Invest Radiol 1980;15:318.

53. Ellman BA, Parkhill BJ, Curry TS III, Marcus PB, Peters PC. Ablation of renal tumours with absolute ethanol: a new technique. Radiology 1981;141:619.

54. Freeny PC, Bush WH, Kidd R. Transcatheter occlusive therapy of genito-urinary abnormalities using isobutyl-2-cyanoacrylate (bucrylate). AJR 1979;133:647.

55. Freeny PC, Mennemeyer R, Kidd CR, Bush WH. Long-term radiographic-pathologic follow-up of patients treated with visceral transcatheter occlusion using isobutyl-2-cyanoacrylate. Radiology 1979;132:51.

56. Fuhrman BP, Bass JL, Castaneda-Zuniga W, Amplatz K, Lock JE. Coil embolization of congenital thoracic vascular anomalies in infants and children. Circulation 1984;70:285.

57. Gianturco C, Anderson JH, Wallace S. Mechanical devices for arterial occlusion. AJR 1975;124:428.

58. Goldman ML. Bucrylate, silicones and ivalon as agents for intravascular embolization. In Abrams HL, ed. Vascular and interventional radiology; vol 3. 3rd ed. Boston: Little, Brown, 1983:2191.

59. Greenfield AJ. Transcatheter vessel occlusion: methods and materials. In: Athanasoulis CA, Pfister RC, Greene RE, Roberson GH, eds. Interventional radiology. Philadelphia: Saunders, 1982:40.

60. Günther R, Bohl J, Klose K, Anger J. Transkatheterembolisierung der Milz mit Butyl-2-Cyanoacrylat: experimentelle Ergebnisse und klinische Anwendung. RöFo 1980; 133:158.

61. Günther R, Schubert U, Bohl J, Georgi M, Marberger M. Transcatheter embolization of the kidney with butyl-2-cyanocrylate: experimental and clinical results. Cardiovasc Radiol 1978;1:101.

62. Haapanen AA, Dean PB. Renal vein ethanol concentration during ablation of renal cell carcinoma. Cardiovasc Intervent Radiol 1986;9:205.

63. Hamby WB, Gardner WJ. Treatment of pulsating exopthalmos with report of two cases. Arch Surg 1933;37:676.

64. Han SS, Parry CE, Simeone FA. Embolization of dural arteriovenous malformations using Gianturco coils. AJNR 1982;3:341.

65. Herrera M, Rysavy J, Kotula F, Rusnak B, Castaneda-Zuniga WR, Amplatz K. Ivalon shavings: technical considerations of a new embolic agent. Radiology 1982;144:638.

66. Hieshima GB, Grinnel VS, Mehringer CM. A detachable balloon for therapeutic transcatheter occlusions. Radiology 1981;138:227.

67. Hilal SK. Endovascular treatment of arteriovenous malformations of the central nervous system. In: Wilson CB, Stein BM eds. Intracranial arteriovenous malformations. Baltimore: Williams and Wilkins, 1984:259.

68. Hilal SK, Sane P, Mawad ME, Michelsen WJ. Therapeutic interventional radiologic procedures in neuroradiology. In Abrams HL, ed. Abrams angiography: vascular and interventional radiology; vol 3. 3rd ed. Boston, Little Brown, 1983:2223–2255.

69. Hilal SK, Sane P, Michelson WJ, Kosseim A. The embolization of vascular malformations of the spinal cord with low-viscosity silicone-rubber. Neuroradiology 1978;16:430.

70. Horton JA, Marano GD, Kerber CW, Jenkins JJ, Davis S. Polyvinyl alcohol foam-gelfoam for therapeutic embolization: a synergistic mixture. AJNR 1983;4:143.

71. Hunter DW, Castaneda-Zuniga WR, Coleman CC, Young A, Mercado S, Cardella J, Amplatz K. Spermatic vein embolization with hot contrast medium or detachable balloons. Semin Intervent Radiold 1984;1:163.

72. Jack CR Jr, Forbes G, Dewanjee MK, Brown ML, Earnest F. Polyvinyl alcohol sponge for embolotherapy: particle size and morphology. AJNR 1985;6:595.

73. Kato T, Namoto R, Mori H, Takahashi M, Tamakawa Y. Transcatheter arterial chemoembolization of renal cell carcinoma with microencapsulated mitomycin C. J Urol 1981;125:19.

74. Kato T, Nemoto R, Mori H, Takahashi M, Tamokawa Y, Havada M. Arterial chemoembolization with microencapsulated anticancer drug JAMA 1981;245:1123.

75. Kaufman SL. Simplified method of transcatheter embolization with polyvinyl alcohol foam (ivalon). AJR 1979;132:853.

76. Kaufman SL, Strandberg JO, Dumbarta KH, White RI Jr. Transcatheter embolization with microfibrillar collagen in swine. Invest Radiol 1978;13:200.

77. Kauffmann GW, Rassweiler J, Richter G, Hanenstein KH, Rohrbach R, Friedburg H. Capillary embolization by ethibloc: a new embolization concept tested in dog kidney. AJR 1981;137:1163.

78. Kauffmann GW, Richter G, Rassweiler J, Rohrbach R. New topics in embolization: effects of central, peripheral, or capillary type of occlusion in animal models simulating tumor embolization. Front Eur Radiol 1982;1:71.

79. Keller FS, Rösch J, Dotter CT. Transhepatic obliteration of gastroesophageal varices with absolute ethanol. Radiology 1983;146:615.

80. Kerber CW. Intracranial cyanoacrylate: a new catheter therapy for arteriovenous malformations. Invest Radiol 1975;10:536.

81. Kerber CW. Balloon catheter with a calibrated leak: a new system for superselective angiography and occlusive catheter therapy. Radiology 1976;120:547.

82. Kerber CW. Flow-controlled therapeutic embolization: a physiologic and safe technique. AJNR 1980;1:77.

83. Kerber CW, Bank WO, Cromwell LD. Calibrated leak balloon microcatheter: a device for arterial exploration and occlusive therapy. AJR 1979;132:207.

84. Kerber CW, Bank WO, Horton JA. Polyvinyl alcohol foam: prepackaged emboli for therapeutic embolization. AJR 1978;130:1193.

85. Kerber CW, Freeney PC, Cromwell LD, Margolis MT. Cyanoacrylate occlusion of a renal arteriovenous fistula. AJR 1977;128:663.

86. Kerber CW, Heilman CB. New calibrated-leak microcatheters for cyanoacrylate embolization and chemotherapy. AJNR 1985;6:434

87. Kricheff IS, Berenstein A. Simplified solid-particle embolization with a new introducer. Radiology 1979;131:794.

88. Kumpan W, Riedl P, Bliem J, Hajek PC, Salomonowitz E. Cyanoacrylate in spermatic vein embolization. Semin Intervent Radiol 1984;1:170.

89. Kunnen M. Neue Technik zur Embolisation der Vena spermatica interna: intravenöser Gewebekleber. RöFo 1980;133:625.

90. Kunnen M. Non-surgical curve of varicocele by embolization with isobutyl-2-cyanoacrylate. Ann Radiol (Paris) 1981;24:406.

91. Lang ER, Buch PC. Treatment of carotid-cavernous fistula by muscle embolization alone: the Brooks method. J Neurosurg 1965;22:387.

92. Latschaw RF, Pearlman RL, Schaitkin BM, Griffith JW, Weidner WA. Intraarterial ethanol as a long-term occlusive agent in renal, hepatic and gastrosplenic arteries in pigs. Cardiovasc Intervent Radiol 1985;8:24.

93. Longacre JJ, Unterthiner RA. Treatment of facial hemangioma by intravascular embolization with silicone spheres: case report. Plast Reconstr Surg 1972;50:618.

94. Lund G, Cragg AH, Rysavy JA. Detachable stainless-steel spider: a new device for vessel occlusion. Radiology 1983;148:567.

95. Lund G, Rysavy JA, Kotula F, Castaneda-Zuniga WR, Amplatz K. Detachable steel spring coils for vessel occlusion. Radiology 1985;155:530.

96. Lunderquist A, Borjesson B. Isobutyl-2-cyanoacrylate (bucrylate) in obliteration of gastric coronary vein and esophageal varices. AJR 1978;130:1.

97. Lunderquist A, Ericsson M, Nobin A, Sanden G. Gelfoam powder embolization of the hepatic artery in liver metastases of carcinoid tumors. Radiology 1982;22:65.

98. Luessenhof AJ. Artificial embolization of inoperable arteriovenous malformations. In: Pia MW, Gleave JRW, Grote E, Zierski J, eds. Cerebral angiomas. Berlin: Springer, 1975.

99. Luessenhof AJ, Spence WT. Artificial embolization of cerebral arteries: report of use in a case of arteriovenous malformation. JAMA 1960;172:1153.

100. McLean GK, Stein EJ, Burke DR, Meranze SG. Steel occlusion coils: pretreatment with thrombin. Radiology 1986;158:549.

101. Mineau DE, Miller FJ Jr, Lee RG, Nakashima EN, Nelson JA. Experimental transcatheter splenectomy using absolute ethanol. Radiology 1982;142:355.

102. Mitchell SE, Shuman L, Kaufman SL, Chang R, Kadir S, Kinnison M, White RI Jr. Biliary catheter drainage complicated by hemobilia: treatment by balloon embolotherapy. Radiology 1985;157:645.

103. Naar CA, Soong J, Clore F, Hawkins IF. Control of massive hemoptysis by bronchial artery embolization with absolute alcohol. AJR 1983;140:271.

104. Nanni GS, Hawkins IF, Orak JK. Control of hypertension by ethanol renal ablation. Radiology 1983;148:51.

105. Norman D, Newton TM, Edwards MS, De Caprio V. Carotid-cavernous fistula: closure with detachable silicone balloons. Radiology 1983; 149:149.

106. Novak D. Coaxial and balloon catheters in tumor embolization: experimental results and follow-up studies. In: Veiga-Pires JA, Martins de Silva M, Oliva L, eds. Interventional radiology. Amsterdam: Excerpta Medica, 1980: 302–308.

107. Novak D. Transkatheter-Embolisation von Nierentumoren. In: Loose KE, Loose DA, eds. Gefäss-Patient-Therapie. Baden-Baden: Witzstrock, 1980:232.

108. Novak D. Labeling of embolizing substances with contrast agents. In: Amiel M, ed. Contrast media in radiology. Berlin: Springer, 1982:237.

109. Novak D. Transcatheter renal tumor embolization with liquid acrylates, silicones and polyurethanes. In: Jeanmart L, ed. Urogenital tract. Proceedings of the 15th International Congress of Radiology. Luxembourg: Interimages, 1983:144.

110. Novak D, Weber J, Wieners H, Zabel G. New liquid and semiliquid embolizing substances for tumor embolization: an experimental study. Ann Radiol (Paris) 1981;24:428.

111. Novak D, Wieners H, Rueckner R. Applicability of liquid radiopaque polyurethane for transcatheter embolization. Cardiovasc Intervent Radiol 1983;6:133.

112. Peregrin JH, Kaspar M, Haco M, Vanecek R, Belan A. New occlusive agent for therapeutic embolization tested in dogs. Cardiovasc Intervent Radiol 1984;7:97.

113. Powischer G, Wolf GA, Syre G. Kidney embolization with collagen flocks in malignant renal hypertension. In: Anacker H, Gullotta U, Rupp N, eds. Percutaneous biopsy and therapeutic vascular occlusion. Stuttgart: Thieme, 1980: 169.

114. Rabe FE, Yune HY, Richmond BD, Klatte EC. Renal tumor infarction with absolute ethanol. AJR 1982;139:1139.

115. Richter EI, Zeitler E, Seyferth W. Phlebography and sclerotherapy of the spermatic veins. Semin Intervent Radiol 1984;1:175.

116. Riedl P, Kumpan N, Maier U, Stackl W, Lunglmayr G. Long-term results after sclerotherapy of the spermatic vein in patients with varicocele. Cardiovasc Intervent Radiol 1985;8:46.

117. Rholl KS, Rysavy JA, Vlodaver Z, Cragg AH, Castaneda-Zuniga WR, Amplatz K. Spermatic vein obliteration using hot contrast medium in dogs. Radiology 1983;148:85.

118. Rösch J, Dotter CT, Brown MI. Selective arterial embolization: a new method for control of acute gastrointestinal bleeding. Radiology 1972;102:303.

119. Serbinenko FA. Balloon catheterization and occlusion of major cerebral vessels. J Neurosurg 1974;41:125.

120. Seyferth W, Jecht E, Zeitler E. Percutaneous sclerotherapy of varicocele. Radiology 1981;139:335.

121. Szwarc IA, Carrasco CH, Wallace S, Richli W. Radiopaque suspension of polyvinyl alcohol foam for embolization. AJR 1986;146:591.

122. Tadavarthy SM, Coleman CC, Hunter D, Castaneda-Zuniga WR, Amplatz K. Polyvinyl alcohol (ivalon) as an embolizing agent. Semin Intervent Radiol 1984;1:101.

123. Taki W, Handa H, Miyake H, Kobayashi A, Yanekawa Y, Yamamura K, Suzuki M, Ikada Y. New detachable balloon technique for traumatic carotid-cavernous sinus fistulae. AJNR 1985;6:961.

124. Terry PB, Barth KH, Kaufman SL, White RI Jr. Balloon embolization for treatment of pulmonary arterio-venous fistulas. N Engl J Med 1980;302:1189.

125. Thompson WM, Johnsrude IS. Vessel occlusion with transcatheter elelctrocoagulation. Cardiovasc Intervent. Radiol 1980; 3:244.

126. Tomsick TA, Ball JB. Balloons and coils: aids in particulate/liquid head-neck embolization. AJNR 1985;6:598.

127. Tubman D. Balloon catheter systems in interventional vascular radiology. Semin Intervent Radiol 1984;1:110.

128. Uflacker R, Lima RS, Ribas GC, Piske RL. Carotid-cavernous fistulas: embolization through the superior opthalmic vein approach. Radiology 1986;159:175.

129. Vlahos L, Karatzas G, Papaharalambous N, Pontifex GR. Percutaneous arterial embolization in kidneys of dogs: a comparative study of eight different materials. Br J Radiol 1980;53:289.

130. Wallace S, Chuang VP, Anderson JH, Gianturco C. Steel coil embolus and its therapeutic applications. In Abrams HL, ed. Vascular and interventional radiology; vol 3. 3rd ed. Boston: Little, Brown, 1983:2151.

131. Wallace S, Gianturco C, Anderson JH, Goldstein HM, Davis JL, Bree RL. Therapeutic vascular occlusion utilizing steel coil technique: clinical applications. AJR 1976;127:381.

132. Weber J, Novak D. Occlusion arteriography: diagnostic and therapeutic applicability of balloon catheters. Cardiovasc Intervent Radiol 1980;3:81.

133. White RI Jr. Embolotherapy with detachable balloons. In Abrams HL, ed. Abrams angiography: vascular and interventional radiology; vol 3. 3rd ed. Boston: Little, Brown, 1983:2211–2222.

134. White RI Jr. Embolotherapy in vascular disease. AJR 1984;142:27.

135. White RI Jr, Barth KH, Kaufman SL, Decaprio V, Strandberg JD. Therapeutic embolization with detachable balloons. Cardiovasc Intervent Radiol 1980;3:229.

136. White RI Jr, Kaufman SL, Barth KH, Decaprio V, Strandberg JD. Therapeutic embolization with detachable silicone balloons. JAMA 1979;241:1257.

137. White RI Jr, Kaufman SL, Barth KH, Decaprio V, Strandberg JD. Embolotherapy with detachable silicone balloons: technique and clinical results. Radiology 1979;131:619.

138. White RI Jr, Kaufman SL, Barth KH, Kadir S, Smyth JW, Walsh PC. Occlusion of varicoceles with detachable balloons. Radiology 1981;139:327.

139. White RI Jr, Strandberg JD, Cross GS, Barth KH. Therapeutic embolization with long-term occluding agents and their effects on embolized tissues. Radiology 1977;125:677.

140. Widrich WC, Robbins AH, Nabseth DC. Transhepatic embolization of varices. Cardiovasc Intervent Radiol 1980;3:298.

141. Yakes WF, Pevsner P, Reed M, Donohue H, Ghaed N. Serial embolizations of an extremity arteriovenous malformation with alcohol via direct percutaneous puncture. AJR 1986;146:1038.

142. Yune HY, Klatte EC, Richmond BD, Olson EW, Becker GJ, Strickler SA. Ethanol thrombotherapy of esophageal varices: further experience. AJR 1985;144:1049.

143. Zollikofer C, Castaneda-Zuniga WR, Galliani C. Therapeutic blockage of arteries using compressed ivalon. Radiology 1980;136:635.

144. Zeitler E, Jecht E, Richter EI, Seyferth W. Selective sclerotherapy of the internal spermatic vein in patients with varicoceles. Cardiovasc Intervent Radiol 1980;3:166.

Complications of Arterial Embolization

D. Novak

Complications directly related to arterial emboliza-tion are described and analyzed in this chapter. Complications of embolization are generally caused by: ischemia, infarction and inflammation of the embolized organ (e.g. organ necrosis and abscess formation, necrosis of the gallbladder); reflux or "passing through" of the embolization material, with unintentional occlusion of a non-target vessel (e.g. peripheral ischemia and gangrene, lung embolism, spinal cord infarction); sequelae of the embolizing procedure (e.g. thrombosis, hemorrhage, retro-peritoneal phlegmon, hepatic and/or renal insuf-ficiency).

Included in the evaluation are post-embolization ileus, pneumonia, pancreatitis, pleural effusion, renal and cardiac failure.

Excluded from it are: side-effects due to the em-bolization technique, embolizing material and con-trast agent (e.g. "gluing" of bucrylate to the tip of the catheter, partial delivery of a coil, contrast medium allergy, etc.); symptoms of the "post-embolization syndrome" (e.g. pain, fever, nausea, vomiting etc.)

Major post-embolization complications are usual-ly caused by: incomplete angiographic demonstra-tion and inadequate analysis of the vascular supply to the lesion and the surrounding collaterals before embolization; use of inappropriate embolization material; choice of inadequate catheters and insuf-ficient selective catheterization; further injection of embolizing material after stasis of local blood flow is reached; rapid injection of too a large quantity of embolizing agent. The published data on the complications of intra-arterial embolization are very inconsistent because usually only data from one institution or one working group are evaluated.

Data Collection and Statistical Evaluation

Data collected concerning intra-arterial embolization and post-embolization complications include a total of 12,822 patients (Table 1). All relevant data, including indications for embolization and the use of embolization material, as well as detailed descrip-tions of the complications of embolization, were collected from a total of 301 different institutions. The data were gathered from a special questionnaire filled out by 81 different working groups, or collected from 220 publications published between January 1975 and June 1987 (Figs. 1, 2).

The frequency of complications in intra-arterial embolization is shown in Fig. 2. An overall complica-tion rate of 3.8% and a fatality rate of 0.9% was found (Table 1).

The complication and fatality rates differ from one embolized vascular area to another. The compli-cations encountered after intra-arterial embolization of each particular vascular area are summarized below.

Renal Embolization

Embolization of the renal artery was performed in a total of 2831 patients (1, 2, 11, 14, 25, 52, 71, 75, 77, 78, 82, 84, 102, 104, 113, 114, 121, 126, 131). Indica-tions for embolization and complication and fatality rates are indicated in Table 2. The most frequent complication is unintentional embolization of peripheral arteries of the lower extremities due to reflux or dislodgment of emboli (Fig. 3a). This com-plication was observed in 31 cases (32.6%). In 5 cases, ischemic gangrene of the leg or foot required amputation. In 26 out of 31 patients, embolectomy was performed.

Table 1 Arterial embolization: overall complication and mortalitiy rates

Origin of data	No. of patients	No. of compli-cations	Complication rate (%)	No. of deaths	Mortality rate (%)
Questionnaires n = 81	8796	220	2.5	58	0.7
Reports n = 220	4026	271	6.7	58	1.4
Total	12822	491	3.8	116	0.9

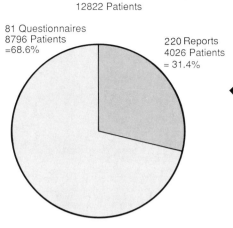

12822 Patients

81 Questionnaires
8796 Patients
=68.6%

220 Reports
4026 Patients
= 31.4%

◀ Fig. 1   **Origin of data on intra-arterial embolization in 12,822 patients:** an evaluation of 220 published reports and 81 questionnaires

Fig. 2   **Overall complication** ▶ **and mortality rates** following intra-arterial embolization in 12,822 patients

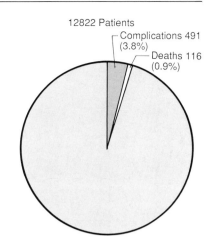

12822 Patients
Complications 491 (3.8%)
Deaths 116 (0.9%)

Some typical complications of renal embolization may be mentioned. Distal embolization and gangrene of the foot secondary to Gelfoam embolization of the renal artery was reported by Woodside et al. (134). In 19 patients with renal carcinoma undergoing palliative renal artery embolization, complications occurred in 2 cases (10%). In one patient, the reflux of bucrylate resulted in occlusion of the right external iliac artery. In another patient, the coil was dislodged into the femoral artery, requiring emergency embolectomy (36). Unintentional distal occlusion resulting in foot gangrene occurred in one dialysis patient after bilateral renal ablation with Gelfoam (11). In 6 patients undergoing preoperative renal artery embolization with subsequent nephrectomy, one case with distal migration of a Gianturco-Anderson-Wallace coil into the hypogastric artery, and one case with migration into the contralateral renal artery was observed. The coils were removed by arteriotomy (87). Migration of Gianturco-Anderson-Wallace coils was also reported by Tisnado et al. (116), Weber (127) and Klein et al. (58). A large aneurysm of the renal artery developed after occlusion of the renal artery with the Gianturco-Anderson-Wallace coil because of massive renal carcinoma

(111). Paraplegia due to occlusion of the spinal arteries with Gelfoam emboli following renal embolization was reported in one patient with dialysis cachexia (38). Other very frequent complications of renal embolization are: renal failure, renal abscess, colon infarction, spinal cord infarction, and pulmonary embolism (Fig. 3a).

Renal ablation with ethanol without using balloon catheters resulted in frequent complications. Infarction of the left colon following ethanol ablation of a renal tumor was observed (28, 78). One fatal complication was also reported after ethanol renal ablation in 13 children with end-stage kidney disease (39). In one patient, skin infarction in the lumbar region occurred after transcatheter embolotherapy of a hypernephroma with ethanol (118). Of 16 renal tumor infarctions with intra-arterial ethanol injection through a balloon catheter, only one complication – a perinephric abscess – was observed (92). Renal embolotherapy is the most frequently performed procedure (Fig. 7). Published complication rates varied between 10% and 20%. A mortality rate of about 3.0% was usually reported (62, 72). Lammer et al. (62) reported a complication rate of 9.9% (12 out of 121 patients), with a mortality of 3.3% (4 out of 121

Table **2**   Renal embolization and complications

Indications	No. of patients	No. of complications	Complication rate (%)	No. of deaths	Mortality rate (%)
Renal carcinoma	2769	88	3.2	18	0.7
End-stage renal disease	40	4	10.0	3	7.5
Bleeding after renal biopsy	14	1	7.1	–	–
Miscellaneous (angiomyo-lipoma, pyonephrosis)	8	2	25.0	–	–
Total	2831	95	3.4	21	0.7

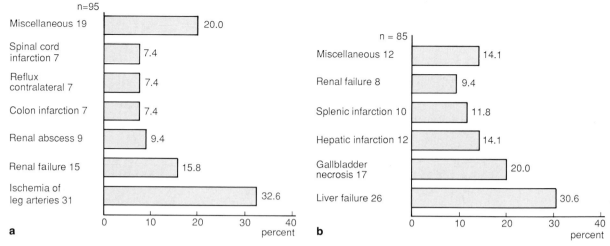

Fig. 3   **Frequency and type of complications** in **a** renal and **b** hepatic embolization

patients) following renal tumor embolization. The incidence of complications in palliative embolization was 20%, with a mortality of 7.3%. In preoperative embolization, the complication rate was 4.9%, with a mortality of 1.2%. The most commonly encountered complications were renal failure and unintentional embolization of non-target organs.

Marx et al. (72) reported serious side-effects in 20%, and death in 3%, after palliative embolization of inoperable renal carcinoma in 29 patients. Chuang et al. (25) and Wallace et al. (126) observed major complications in 3 out of 100 patients following renal embolization. Renal failure occurred with two patients and renal abscess in one patient. The most important reports about complications of renal embolotherapy are summarized in Table **3**.

Hepatic Embolization

Indications for hepatic embolization (22, 23, 31, 45, 91, 95, 110, 112, 135) are listed in Table **4**. The overall complication rate is 4.4% and the mortality rate is 1.9%. The most frequent complication is liver failure, in 26 out of 85 cases (30.6%), followed by necrosis of the gallbladder or gangrenous cholecystitis in 17 out of 85 patients (20%) (Fig. **3b**). Hepatic infarction or necrosis was encountered in 12 cases (14%). Inadvertent splenic infarction was observed in 11.8%, and renal failure in 9.4% (Fig. **3b**).

The most informative reports published may be summarized as follows: liver necrosis was reported by Jacob et al. (54), Stothert et al. (110), Trojanowski et al. (117), Sjoevall et al. (103). Prediction of early death following hepatic embolization is discussed by Powell-Tuck et al. (89). It was emphasized that the infarction or necrosis of the gallbladder is one of the most characteristic compli-

cations of hepatic embolization (27, 60, 80, 85). In order to avoid unnecessary embolization of the cystic artery during hepatic embolization, placement of the catheter tip distal to the origin of the cystic artery is recommended (85).

Splenic Embolization

The most frequent indication for splenic embolization (40, 59, 86, 88, 106, 129, 132) is hypersplenism. The overall complication rate, 48 out of 266 patients from 1975–1985, is 18.0%. The mortality rate is high, at 7.4%. An analysis of complication and mortality frequency in 42 patients undergoing embolization between 1975 and 1979 shows different results than in 224 patients in whom splenic embolotherapy was performed between 1980 and 1985 (Table **5**). The unacceptably high complication and mortality rate after splenic embolization has discredited the procedure. In the early phase of development of splenic embolotherapy the patients were probably overtreated. Total splenic necrosis and subsequent complications were often fatal (3, 18, 20, 46, 117, 122, 129).

The most frequent complications observed after splenic embolotherapy are: abscess, pneumonia, splenic necrosis, pleural effusion and splenic vein thrombosis (Fig. **4a**). A significant reduction in the complication and mortality rates is achieved by following the multi-stage protocol recommended by Spigos et al. (107, 108): only partial splenic embolization, strict aseptic technique, antibiotic prophylaxis and effective control of pain. Delcour et al. (32) strongly recommend peripheral embolization, with only a small portion (20–30%) of the splenic volume to be embolized. Reduction in the complication rate of splenic embolization is achieved by using a flexible

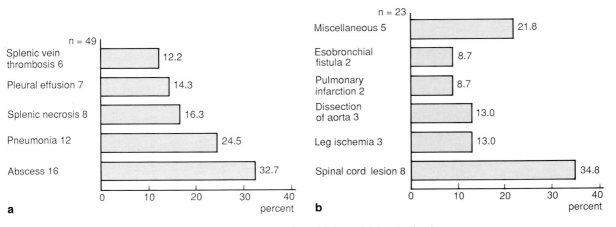

Fig. 4 **Frequency and type of complications** in **a** splenic and **b** bronchial embolization

Table **3**   Renal tumor embolization: Reported complications and
mortality rates (1980–1985)

No. of patients	Complication rate (%)	Fatality rate (%)	Publication
100	3 = 3%	1 = 1%	Wallace et al. 1981 (126)
19	2 = 10.5%	0	Ekelund et al. 1981 (36)
28	2 = 7.1%	2 = 7.1%	Teasdale et al. 1982 (113)
29	4 = 13.8%	2 = 6.9%	Marx et al. 1982 (72)
15	1 = 6.7%	0	Rabe 1982 (92)
121	12 = 9.9%	4 = 3.3%	Lammer et al. 1985 (62)
Total 312	24 = 7.7%	9 = 2.9%	

Table **4**   Hepatic embolization and complications

Indications	No. of patients	No. of compli-cations	Complication rate (%)	No. of deaths	Mortality rate (%)
Primary liver neoplasms	1872	76	4.0	35	1.9
Liver metastases	72	6	8.3	1	1.4
Liver hemangioma	6	1	16.7	1	16.7
Miscellaneous	4	2	50.0	1	25.0
Total	1954	85	4.4	38	1.9

Table **5**   Splenic embolization: patients, complications, deaths

Period	No. of patients	No. of compli-cations	Complication rate (%)	No. of deaths	Mortality rate (%)
1975–1985	266	48	18.0	19	7.1
1975–1979	42 (15.8%)	15	35.7	8	19.0
1980–1985	224 (84.2%)	33	14.7	11	4.9

flow-directed 5 Fr Swan-Ganz balloon catheter, with which it is possible to perform occlusion of the splenic artery beyond the origin of the pancreatic branches (73).

Gastrointestinal Embolization

Indications for embolization (12, 26, 44, 53, 68, 100) of the left gastric artery or the gastroduodenal artery (Fig. **5b**) are upper gastrointestinal bleeding (Table **6**). Embolization for lower intestinal bleeding was performed in 177 patients. The overall complication rate was 4.9%, and the mortality rate 1.3%. Embolotherapy of the left gastric artery was connected with several complications: gastric necrosis and infarction (15, 43, 90), duodenal mucosal necrosis, and abscess formation (12) were observed.

Pelvic Embolization

Indications for pelvic embolotherapy (8, 17, 21, 51, 63, 79) are: trauma, abdominal and pelvic hemorrhage, cancer of the urinary bladder, gynecological cancer, and bleeding (Table **7**). The overall complication rate is 5.0%, and the mortality rate is 0.4%. Complications and mortality rates for specific regions or organs are shown in Table **7**. Following

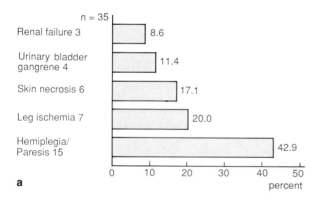

a

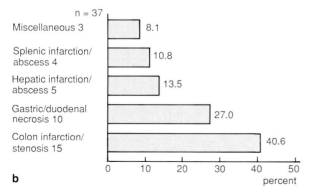

b

Fig. 5   **Frequency and type of complications** in **a** pelvic and **b** gastrointestinal embolization

pelvic embolization, hemiplegia and/or paresis were encountered in 15 patients out of 35 cases of post-embolization complications (42.9%). Leg ischemia was observed in 7 (20%), and skin necrosis in 6 patients (17.1%). Urinary bladder gangrene was found in 4 patients (11.4%) (Fig. **5a**). The most frequent complications reported in the literature following embolization of the urinary bladder were gangrene and necrosis (16, 51), bilateral paresis (33), and Brown-Sequard syndrome (42). Jander and Russinovich (55) collected 39 reports involving Gelfoam embolization in abdominal, retroperitoneal and pelvic hemorrhage in 188 patients. There were 5 embolization-related deaths (1.7%) and 7 other complications (2.4%). These involved 2 patients with gastric necrosis, 2 patients with lumbar muscle infarction, one splenic abscess, one spinal cord infarction and one colonic stricture. Ischemic necrosis of the transverse colon was found after transcatheter embolization of the middle colic artery for diverticular bleeding (101). Out of a total of 23 patients treated by embolotherapy with Gelfoam for lower gastrointestinal bleeding, acute colonic mucosal necrosis developed in 3 patients (96). A colonic stricture was found following embolization of the inferior mesenteric artery for diverticular bleeding (76). In another patient with angiodysplasia, bowel infarction resulted from therapeutic occlusion of the ileocolic artery (41). A cecal infarction was observed after embolization of the ileocolic artery because of massive bleeding (125). Out of 9 gynecological patients undergoing palliative embolization, one case of urinary bladder necrosis and abscess formation following occlusion of both hypogastric arteries with GAW coils was observed (99).

In 51 patients, 4 complications occurred following bilateral therapeutic occlusion of the hypogastric arteries in uncontrollable hematuria and gynecological bleeding (109). Embolization of the hypogastric artery for postoperative bleeding led to necrosis of the iliac bone (37). A vesicovaginal fistula developed secondary to hypogastric embolization with Gelfoam for massive vaginal bleeding (7). Extensive lower limb paresis developed in three patients with pelvic cancer following internal iliac artery embolization (49).

Bronchial and Pulmonary Embolization

The most frequent indications for this (4, 13, 50, 120, 130) are: massive hemoptysis caused by tuberculosis, bronchiectasis, pneumoconiosis, aspergillosis and bronchial carcinoma; arteriovenous lung malformation.

The overall complication rate in bronchial artery embolization in 846 patients with hemoptysis was 2.7% (Table **8**). The most serious complication of bronchial artery embolization is spinal cord ischemia

Table **6** Gastrointestinal embolization

Indication	No. of patients	No. of complications	Complication rate (%)	No. of deaths	Mortality rate (%)
Upper GI bleeding	573	22	3.8	10	1.7
Lower GI bleeding	177	15	8.5	–	–
Total	750	37	4.9	10	1.3

Table **7** Pelvic embolization and complications

Indications	No. of patients	No. of complications	Complication rate (%)	No. of deaths	Mortality rate (%)
Urinary bladder tumor and/or hemorrhage	396	20	5.1	3	0.8
Gynecological tumor and/or bleeding	239	6	2.5	–	–
Pelvic trauma	31	6	19.4	–	–
Arteriovenous malformations	27	3	11.1	–	–
Total	693	35	5.1	3	0.4

Table **8** Bronchial embolization

Indication	No. of patients	No. of complications	Complication rate (%)	Deaths
Hemoptysis	846	23	2.7	–

(94, 98, 119) (Fig. **4b**). Infarction of the spinal cord with resulting paraplegia following embolization because of hemoptysis was reported by Remy et al. (93, 94). Embolization of intercostal arteries to control massive hemoptysis in 3 patients led to spinal cord infarction in one case (123, 124). The risk of spinal cord damage as a complication of embolotherapy of the bronchial and pulmonary arteries is minimized by the use of digital subtraction angiography and diluted contrast material. Complete diagnostic angiography should precede embolotherapy (128). Proper catheter positioning and appropriate choice of embolization technique are important in avoiding complications (128). Complications can also be avoided by monitoring somatosensory-evoked potentials during embolotherapy (10, 47, 98).

Pulmonary embolization for arteriovenous fistulas was performed in 32 patients. Only 2 complications (inadvertent occlusion of peripheral arteries) were observed.

Embolization in Neuroradiology

Indications for embolization in neuroradiology (6, 19, 29, 30, 34, 35, 48, 56, 57, 61, 64, 66, 67, 69, 74, 105, 133) are listed in Table **9**. The overall complication rate is 6.7%, and the mortality rate 1.3%. Complications and mortality rates for specific regions of embolization are shown in Fig. **6**. The most

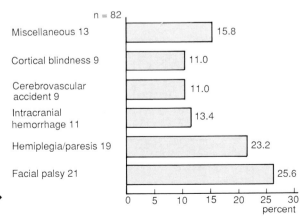

Fig. **6 Frequency and type of complications** following ▶ intra-arterial embolization in neuroradiology

Table **9**   Embolization in neuroradiology

Indications	No. of patients	No. of complications	Complication rate (%)	No. of deaths	Mortality rate (%)
Craniofacial arteriovenous malformations	584	40	6.8	9	1.5
Spinal arteriovenous malformations	78	5	6.4	1	1.3
Meningiomas	25	7	28.0	–	–
Cranial tumors	432	21	4.9	2	0.5
Angioma	23	2	8.7	–	–
Epistaxis	22	1	4.5	–	–
Carotid-cavernous fistulas	65	6	9.2	4	6.2
Total	1229	82	6.7	16	1.3

frequent complications are: facial palsy (25.6%) and hemiplegia or paresis (23.2%).

Specific complications reported are as follows: facial palsy following middle meningeal artery embolization for treatment of large sphenoid wing meningiomas was observed in 4 patients (9), and in 2 patients after embolotherapy of meningioma and epidermoid carcinoma (70). One patient showed signs of pulmonary embolism after embolization of a spinal arteriovenous malformation (9).

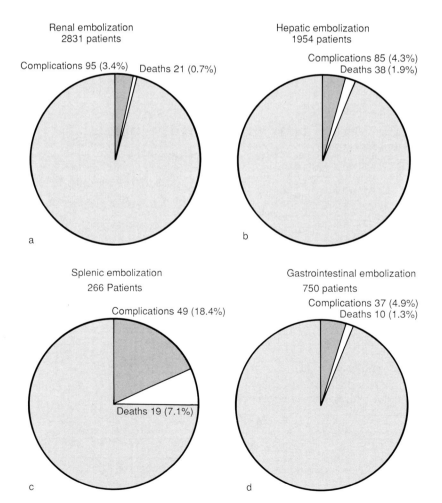

Renal embolization
2831 patients

Complications 95 (3.4%)   Deaths 21 (0.7%)

a

Hepatic embolization
1954 patients

Complications 85 (4.3%)
Deaths 38 (1.9%)

b

Splenic embolization
266 Patients

Complications 49 (18.4%)

Deaths 19 (7.1%)

c

Gastrointestinal embolization
750 patients

Complications 37 (4.9%)
Deaths 10 (1.3%)

d

Fig. **7   Overview of complications and mortality rates** following **a** renal, **b** hepatic, **c** splenic and **d** gastro-intestinal embolization

Table **10** Organ-specific overall complication and mortality rates

Embolization	No. of patients	No. of compli-cations	Complication rate (%)	No. of deaths	Mortality rate (%)
Renal	2831	95	3.4	21	0.7
Hepatic	1954	85	4.4	38	1.9
Splenic	266	49	18.4	19	7.1
Gastrointestinal	750	37	4.9	10	1.3
Pelvic	693	35	5.1	3	0.4
Bronchial	846	23	2.7	–	–
Neuroradiologic	1229	82	6.7	16	1.3

Development of multiple aneurysms at the embolization site after embolotherapy with Gelfoam of a large arteriovenous malformation of the scalp was observed (5). In 33 patients in whom carotid and vertebral fistulas were treated with balloon embolotherapy, 2 patients developed fatal complications due to unintentional occlusion of the internal carotid artery without adequate collateral circulation through the circle of Willis (97).

Conclusion

Complication and mortality rates of intra-arterial transcatheter embolotherapy (Figs. **7** and **8**, Table **10**) should be judged in comparison with the results of surgical treatment. The overall mortality for emergency surgery in upper gastrointestinal bleeding, for example, is approximately 30%, and in bleeding from colonic diverticula it is also 30% (55, 76).

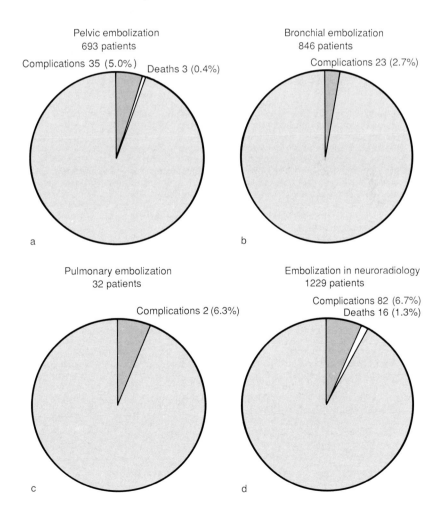

Pelvic embolization
693 patients
Complications 35 (5.0%)   Deaths 3 (0.4%)

a

Bronchial embolization
846 patients
Complications 23 (2.7%)

b

Pulmonary embolization
32 patients
Complications 2 (6.3%)

c

Embolization in neuroradiology
1229 patients
Complications 82 (6.7%)
Deaths 16 (1.3%)

d

Fig. **8 Overview of complications and mortality rates** following **a** pelvic, **b** bronchial, **c** pulmonary and **d** neuroradiological embolization

With increasing experience in embolization, the complication and mortality rates are significantly reduced. Chuang et al. (24) reported a complication rate of 0.6% after embolotherapy, with a total of 1200 coils. An increasing number of reports specify prevention of complications (10, 24, 47, 65, 81, 83, 98, 107, 108, 115).

To prevent complications following intra-arterial embolization, the following recommendations should be considered:

- superselective catheterization;
- use of balloon catheters;
- use of radiopaque embolization agents;
- injection of small quantities of embolizing material;
- finishing the injection when local blood flow stasis is observed;
- use of high-resolution equipment for accurate fluoroscopic control of the embolization procedure.

References

1. Almgard LE, Fernstrom J, Haverling M, Ljungquist A. Treatment of renal adenocarcinoma by embolic occlusion of the renal circulation. Br J Urol 1973;45:474.
2. Almgard LE, Slezak P. Treatment of renal adenocarcinoma by embolization: a follow-up of 38 cases. Eur Urol 1977;3:279.
3. Alwmark A, Bengmark S, Gullstrand P, Joelsson B, Lunderquist A, Owman T. Evaluation of splenic embolization in patients with portal hypertension and hypersplenism. Ann Surg 1982;196:518.
4. Arnaud A, Chauvin G, Girand R, Clement JP, Charpin J. L'embolisation des artères systémiques pulmonaires: techniques, indications, incidents et accidents. Rev Fr Malad Resp 1976;4:803.
5. Balsys R, Cross R. Multiple aneurysm formation as a complication of interventive angiography. Radiology 1978;126:91.
6. Barrow DL, Fleischer AS, Hoffman JC. Complications of detachable balloon catheter technique in the treatment of traumatic intracranial arteriovenous fistulas. J Neurosurg 1982;56:396.
7. Behnam K, Jarmolowski CR. Vesicovaginal fistulas following hypogastric embolization for control of intractable pelvic hemorrhage. J Reprod Med 1982;27:304.
8. Ben-Menachem Y, Handel SF, Thaggard A, Carnovale RL, Katragodda C, Glass TF. Therapeutic arterial embolization in trauma. J Trauma 1979;19:944.
9. Bentson J, Rand R, Calcaterra T, Lasjaunias P. Unexpected complications following therapeutic embolization. Neuroradiology 1978;16:420.
10. Berenstein A, Young W, Ransohoff J, Benjamin V, Merkin H. Somatosensory evoked potentials during spinal angiography and therapeutic transvascular embolization. J Neurosurg 1984;60:777.
11. Bergreen PW, Woodside J, Paster SB. Therapeutic renal infarction. J Urol 1977;118:372.
12. Bookstein JJ, Chlosta EM, Foley D, Walter JF. Transcatheter hemostasis of gastrointestinal bleeding using modified autogenous clot. Radiology 1974;113:277.
13. Bookstein JJ, Moser KM, Kalafer MF, Higgins CB, Davis GB, James W. The role of bronchial arteriography and therapeutic embolization in hemoptysis. Chest 1977;72:658.
14. Bracken RB, Johnson DE, Goldstein HN, Wallace S, Ayala AG. Percutaneous transfemoral renal artery occlusion in patients with renal carcinoma: preliminary report. Urology 1975;6:6.
15. Bradley EL, Goldman ML. Gastric infarction after therapeutic embolization. Surgery 1976;79:421.
16. Braf ZF, Koontz WW Jr. Gangrene of bladder: complication of hypogastric artery embolization. Urology 1977;9:670.
17. Bree RL, Goldstein HM, Wallace S. Transcatheter embolization of the iliac artery in the management of neoplasms of the pelvis. Surg Gynecol Obstet 1976;143:597.
18. Bücheler E, Thelen M, Schirmer G. Katheter-Embolisation der Milzarterien zum Stopp der akuten Varizenblutung. RöFo 1975;122:539.
19. Calcaterra TC, Rand RW, Bentson JR. Ischemic paralysis of the facial nerve: a possible etiologic factor in Bell's palsy. Laryngoscope 1976;86:92.
20. Castaneda-Zuniga WR, Hammerschmidt DE, Sanchez R, Amplatz K. Nonsurgical splenectomy. AJR 1977;129:805.
21. Choo YC, Cho KJ. Pelvic abscess complicating embolic therapy for control of bleeding cervical carcinoma and simultaneous radiation therapy. Obstet Gynecol 1980;55:765.
22. Chuang VP, Wallace S. Current status of transcatheter management of neoplasms. Cardiovasc Intervent Radiol 1980;3:256.
23. Chuang VP, Wallace S. Hepatic artery embolization in the treatment of hepatic neoplasms. Radiology 1981;140:51.
24. Chuang VP, Wallace S, Gianturco C, Soo CS. Complications of coil embolization: prevention and management. AJR 1981;137:809.
25. Chuang VP, Wallace S, Swanson DA. Technique and complications of renal carcinoma infarction. Urol Radiol 1981;2:223.
26. Chuang VP, Wallace S, Zornoza J, Davis IJ. Transcatheter arterial occlusion in the management of rectosigmoidal bleeding. Radiology 1979;133:605.
27. Coldwell DM, Hottenstein DW, Ricci JA, Wengert PA. Emphysematous cholecystitis as a complication of hepatic arterial embolization. Cardiovasc Intervent Radiol 1985;8:36.
28. Cox GG, Lee KR, Price HI, Gunter K, Noble MJ, Mebust WK. Colonic infarction following ethanol embolization of renal-cell carcinoma. Radiology 1982;145:343.
29. Davis KR. Embolization of epistaxis and juvenile nasopharyngeal angiofibromas. AJR 1987;148:209.
30. Debrun G, Vinuela F, Fox A, Drake CG. Embolization of cerebral arteriovenous malformations with bucrylate. J Neurosurg 1982;56:615.
31. Dejode LR, Nicholis RJ, Wright PL. Ischemic necrosis of the gallbladder following hepatic artery embolism. Br J Surg 1976;63:621.
32. Delcour C, Spiegl G, Brion JP, De Vaere S,. Struyven J. Complications in splenic embolization. Ann Radiol (Paris) 1982;25:453.
33. Diamond NG, Casarella WJ, Bachman DM, Wolff M. Microfibrillar collagen hemostat: a new transcatheter embolization agent. Radiology 1979;133:775.
34. Doppman JL, Di Chiro G, Ommaya AK. Percutaneous embolization of spinal cord arteriovenous malformations. J Neurosurg 1971;34:48.
35. Doyon D, Lasjaunias P, Merland JJ, Picard L, Theron J. Analysis of the complications of therapeutical angiography: review of 500 embolizations in the cranio-cephalic area. Neuroradiology 1978;16:48.
36. Ekelund L, Karp W, Mansson W, Olsson AM. Palliative embolization of renal tumors: follow-up in 19 cases. Urol Radiol 1981;3:13.
37. Feldman L, Greenfield AJ, Waltman AC, Novelline RA, van Breda A, Luers P, Athanasoulis CA. Transcatheter vessel occlusion: angiographic results versus clinical success. Radiology 1983;147:1.
38. Gang DL, Dole KB, Adelman LS. Spinal cord infarction following therapeutic renal artery embolization. JAMA 1977;237:2841.
39. Garel L, Mareschal JL, Gagnadoux MF, Pariente D, Guilbert M, Sauvegrain J. Fatal outcome after ethanol renal ablation in child with end-stage kidneys. AJR 1986;146:593.
40. Gerlock AJ Jr, MacDonell RC, Muhlethaler CA. Partial splenic embolization for hypersplenism in renal transplantation. AJR 1982;138:451.

41. Gerlock AJ Jr, Muhlethaler CA, Berger JL, Halter SA, O'Leary JP, Avant GR. Infarction after embolization of the ileocolic artery. Cardiovasc Intervent Radiol 1982;4:202.

42. Giuliani L, Carmignani G, Belgrano E, Puppo P. Gelatin foam and isobutyl-2-cyanoacrylate in the treatment of life-threatening bladder haemorrhage by selective transcatheter embolization of the internal iliac arteries. Br J Urol 1979;51:125.

43. Goldman ML, Land WC, Bradley EL, Anderson RT. Transcatheter therapeutic embolization in the management of massive upper gastro-intestinal bleeding. Radiology 1976;120:513.

44. Goldstein HM, Medellin H, Ben-Menachem Y, Wallace S. Transcatheter arterial embolization in the management of bleeding in the cancer patients. Radiology 1975;115:603.

45. Goldstein HM, Wallace S, Anderson JH, Bree RL, Gianturco C. Transcatheter occlusion of abdominal tumors. Radiology 1976;120:539.

46. Günther R, Bohl J, Klose K, Anger J. Transkatheterembolisierung der Milz mit Butyl-2-Cyanoacrylat. RöFo 1980;133:158.

47. Hacke W, Zeumer H, Berg-Dammer E. Monitoring of hemispheric or brainstem functions with neurophysiologic methods during interventional neuroradiology. AJNR 1983;4:382.

48. Handa J, Nakasu S, Matsuda I. Facial nerve palsy following therapeutic embolization. Surg Neurol 1981;14:377.

49. Hare WS, Holland CJ. Paresis following internal iliac artery embolization. Radiology 1983;146:47.

50. Helenon CH, Chatel A, Bigot JM, Brocard H. Fistule oesophago-bronchique gauche après embolisation bronchique. Nouv Presse Med 1977;6:4209.

51. Hietala SO. Urinary bladder necrosis following selective embolization of the internal iliac artery. Acta Radiol [Diagn] (Stockh) 1978;19:316.

52. Hlava A, Steinhart L, Navratil P. Intraluminal obliteration of the renal arteries in kidney tumors. Radiology 1976;121:323.

53. Hunt TH, Gelfand DW. Complications of gastrointestinal radiologic procedures, III: complications of diagnostic and interventional angiography. Gastrointest Radiol 1981;6:57.

54. Jacob ET, Shapira Z, Morag B, Rubinstein Z. Hepatic infarction and gallbladder necrosis complicating arterial embolization for bleeding duodenal ulcer. Dig Dis Sci 1979;24:482.

55. Jander HP, Russinovich NAE. Transcatheter Gelfoam embolization in abdominal, retroperitoneal, and pelvic haemorrhage. Radiology 1980;136:337.

56. Jones FD, Boone SC, Whaley RA. Intracranial hemorrhage following attempted embolization and removal of large arteriovenous malformations. Surg Neurol 1982;18:278.

57. Kaz Soong H, Newman A, Kumar AAJ. Branch artery occlusion: an unusual complication of external carotid embolization. Arch Ophthalmol 1982;100:1909.

58. Klein FA, Texter JH, Mendez-Picon G. Complications of the Gianturco coil in preoperative infarction of renal cell carcinoma. J Urol 1981;125:105.

59. Kumpe DA, Rumack CM, Pretorius DH, Stoecker TJ, Stellin GP. Partial splenic embolization in children with hypersplenism. Radiology 1985;155:357.

60. Kuroda C, Iwasaki M, Tanaka T. Gallbladder infarction following hepatic transcatheter arterial embolization. Radiology 1983;149:85.

61. Kvam DA, Michelsen WJ, Quest DO. Intracerebral hemorrhage as a complication of artificial embolization. Neurosurgery 1980;7:491.

62. Lammer J, Justich E, Schreyer H, Petteck R. Complications of renal tumor embolization. Cardiovasc Intervent Radiol 1985;8:31.

63. Lang EK. Transcatheter embolization of pelvic vessels in control of intractable hemorrhage. Radiology 1981;140:331.

64. Langford KH, Vitek JJ, Zeiger E. Migration of detachable mini-balloon from ICA causing occlusion of the MCA: case report. J Neurosurg 1983;58:430.

65. Lasjaunias P. Nasopharyngeal angiofibromas: hazards of embolization. Radiology 1980;136:119.

66. Lasjaunias P, Doyon D, Edouard A. Les paralysies faciales peripheriques post-embolisation: rapport sur un cas, discussion, prévention. Ann Otolaryngol Chir Cervicofac 1978;95:595.

67. Latchaw RE, Gold LH. Polyvinyl foam embolization of vascular and neoplastic lesions of the head, neck, and spine. Radiology 1979;131:669.

68. Lyonnet D, Pinet A. Hemorragies digestives: place et résultats de l'embolisation arterielle. Ann Radiol (Paris) 1981;24:413.

69. Manelfe C, Guiraud B, David J, Eymeri JC, Tremoulet M, Espagno J, Rascol A, Geraud J. Embolisation par cathétérisme des méningiomes intra-crâniens. Rev. Neurol (Paris) 1973;128:339.

70. Martin H, Martin C, Veyret C, Brunon J. Paralysie faciale post-embolisation: a propos de deux cas. Ann Otolaryngol Chir Cervicofac 1983;100:45.

71. Marx FJ, Chaussy C, Moser E. Grenzen und Gefahren der palliativen Embolisation inoperabler Nierentumoren. Urologe [A] 1982;21:206.

72. Marx FJ, Eisenberger F, Bassermann R. Komplikationen nach transfemoraler Nierentumorenembolisation: Übersicht und eigene Erfahrungen. Urologe [A] 1978;17:79.

73. Mazer M, Smith CW, Martin VN. Distal splenic artery embolization with a flow-directed balloon catheter. Radiology 1985;154:245.

74. McCormick WF, Kelly PJ, Sarwar M. Fatal paradoxical muscle embolization in traumatic carotid-cavernous fistula repair: case report. J Neurosurg 1976;44:513.

75. Milewski JB, Malewski AW, Malanowska S, Borkowski A, Skowronski IA, Tomankiewicz Z, Sawicka E. Spinal cord damage as a complication of renal artery embolization in patients with renal carcinoma. Int Urol Nephrol 1981;13:221.

76. Mitty HA, Efremidis S, Keller RJ. Colonic stricture after transcatheter embolization for diverticular bleeding. AJR 1979;133:519.

77. Mukamel E, Hadar H, Nissenkorn I. Servadio C. Widespread dissemination of gelfoam particles complicating occlusion of renal circulation. Urology 1979;14:194.

78. Mulligan BD, Espinosa GA. Bowel infarction: complication of ethanol ablation of a renal tumor. Cardiovasc Intervent Radiol 1983;6:55.

79. Nadalini Y, Positano N, Bruttini GP, Piccardo M, Fasce L. Complications arterielles au cours de deux embolisations thérapeutiques renovesicales. J Radiol 1980;61:111.

80. Nakamura H, Kondoh H. Emphysematous cholecystitis: complication of hepatic artery embolization. Cardiovasc Intervent Radiol 1986;9:152.

81. Novak D. Coaxial and balloon catheters in tumor embolization: experimental results and follow-up studies. In: Veiga-Pires JA, ed. Intervention radiology. Amsterdam: Excerpta Medica, 1980:302–308.

82. Novak D. Transkatheter-Embolisation von Nierentumoren. In: Loose KE, Loose DA, eds. Gefäß-Patient-Therapie. Baden-Baden: Witzstrock, 1980:232–236.

83. Novak D. Labeling of embolizing substances with contrast agents. In: Amiel M, ed. Contrast media in radiology. Berlin: Springer, 1982:237–240.

84. Novak D. Transcatheter renal tumor embolization with liquid acrylates, silicones and polyurethanes. In: Jeanmart L, ed. Urogenital tract. Proceedings of the 15th International Congress of Radiology. Luxembourg: Interimages, 1983:144–157.

85. Onodera H, Oikawa M, Abe M, Goto Y. Gallbladder necrosis after transcatheter hepatic arterial embolization: a technique to avoid this complication. Radiology 1984;152:209.

86. Owman T, Lunderquist A, Alwmark A, Borjesson B. Embolization of the spleen for treatment of splenomegaly and hypersplenism in patients with portal hypertension. Invest Radiol 1979;14:457.

87. Palmer T, Hall W, Venable D. Questionable value of renal arterial embolization before radical nephrectomy. South Med J 1982;75:1211.

88. Papadimitriou J, Tritakis C, Karatzas G, Papioannou A. Treatment of hypersplenism by embolus placement in the splenic artery. Lancet 1976;ii:1268.

89. Powel-Tuck J, McIvor J, Reynolds KW, Murray-Lyon JM. Prediction of early death after therapeutic hepatic arterial embolization. Br Med J 1984;288:1257.

90. Prochaska JM, Flye MW, Johnsrude JS. Left gastric artery embolization for control of gastric bleeding: a complication. Radiology 1973;107:521.

91. Pueyo J, Guzman A, Fernandez F, Garzia-Moran M, Medina MF, Faedo J, Rodrigo L, Jimenez JR. Liver abscess complicating embolization of focal nodular hyperplasia. AJR 1979;133:740.

92. Rabe FE, Yune HY, Richmond BD, Klatte EC. Renal tumor infarction with absolute ethanol. AJR 1982;139:1139.

93. Remy J, Arnaud A, Fardou H, Girand R, Voisin C. Treatment of hemoptysis by embolization of bronchial arteries. Radiology 1977;122:33.

94. Remy J, Marache P, Lemaitre L, Lafitte JJ, Tonnel AB, Voisin C. Accidents de l'embolisation dans le traitement des hémoptysies. Nouv Presse Med 1978;7:4306.

95. Roche A, Doyon D, Harry G, Weingarten A, Edouard A. L'embolisation artérielle hépatique: 35 cas. Nouv Presse Med 1978;7:633.

96. Rosenkrantz H, Bookstein J, Rosen RJ, Goff WB, Healy JF. Postembolic colonic infarction. Radiology 1982;142:47.

97. Scialfa G, Vaghi A, Valsecchi F, Bernardi L, Tonon C. Neuroradiological treatment of carotid and vertebral fistulas and intracavernous aneurysms. Neuroradiology 1982;24:13.

98. Schrodt JF, Becker GJ, Scott JA, Warren CH, Benenati SV. Bronchial artery embolization: monitoring with somatosensory evoked potentials. Radiology 1987;164:135.

99. Schuur KH, Bouma J. Palliative embolization in gynaecological patients. Eur J Radiol 1983;3:9.

100. Shapiro N, Brandt L, Sprayregan S, Mitsudo S, Glotzer P. Duodenal infarction after therapeutic Gelfoam embolization of a bleeding duodenal ulcer. Gastroenterology 1981;80:176.

101. Shenoy SS, Satchidanand S, Wesp EH. Colonic ischemic necrosis following therapeutic embolization. Gastrointest Radiol 1981;6:235.

102. Simunic S, Cecuk L, Bradic J, Gurtl R, Gabric Y, Klenkar M. Percutaneous transcatheter preoperative embolization of the renal artery. Lijec Vjesn 1982;104:479.

103. Sjoevall S, Hoevels J, Sundqvist K. Fatal outcome from emergency embolization of an intrahepatic aneurysm: a case report. Surgery 1980;87:347.

104. Skjennald A, Kilvmark B, Stenwig JT. Transcatheter embolization on the renal artery with bucrylate in renal carcinoma. Acta Radiol [Diagn] (Stockh) 1980;21:215.

105. Soong HK, Newman SA, Kumar AA. Branch artery occlusion: an unusual complication of external carotid embolization. Arch Ophthalmol 1982;100:1909.

106. Spigos DG. Severe complications following partial splenic embolization (letter). Br J Radiol 1982;55:320.

107. Spigos DG, Jonarson O, Mozes MF, Capek V. Partial splenic embolization in the treatment of hypersplenism. AJR 1979;132:777.

108. Spigos DG, Tan WS, Mozes MF, Pringle K, Iossifides I. Splenic embolization. Cardiovasc Intervent Radiol 1980;3:282.

109. Steinhart L, Hlava A, Navratil P, Svab J. Indications for obliteration of pelvic arteries in bleeding lesions of pelvic organs. In: Veiga-Pires JA, ed. Interventional radiology. Amsterdam: Excerpta Medica, 1980:111–117.

110. Stothert JC, Dubuque TJ Jr, Srivisal S. Massive hepatic necrosis following selective arterial embolization: case report. Mo Med 1979;76:489.

111. Struthers NW, Samu P, Chalvardjian A. Renal artery aneurysm: a complication of Gianturco coil embolization of renal adenocarcinoma. J Urol 1980;123:105.

112. Takayasu K, Moriyama N, Muramatsu Y, Suzuki M, Ishikawa T, Ushio K, Matsue H, Sasagawa M, Yamada T. Splenic infarction: a complication of transcatheter hepatic arterial embolization for liver malignancies. Radiology 1984;151:371.

113. Teasdale C, Kirk D, Jeans WD, Penry JB, Tribe CT, Slade N. Arterial embolization in renal carcinoma: a useful procedure? Br J Urol 1982;54:616.

114. Tegtmeyer CJ, Smith TH, Shaw A, Barwick KW, Kattwinkel J. Renal infarction: a complication of gelfoam embolization of hemangio-endothelioma of the liver. AJR 1977;128:305.

115. Theron J, Cosgrove R, Melanson D, Ethier R. Spinal arteriovenous malformations: advances in therapeutic embolization. Radiology 1986;158:163.

116. Tisnado J, Beachley MC, Cho SR, Amendola M. Peripheral embolization of a stainless steel coil. AJR 1979;133:324.

117. Trojanowski JQ, Harrist TJ, Athanasoulis CA, Greenfield AJ. Hepatic and splenic infarctions: complications of therapeutic transcatheter embolization. Am J Surg 1980;139:272.

118. Twomey BP, Wilkins RA, Mee AD. Skin necrosis: a complication of alcohol infarction of a hypernephroma. Cardiovasc Intervent Radiol 1985;8:202.

119. Uflacker R, Kaemmerer A, Neves CMC, Picon PD. Management of massive hemoptysis by bronchial artery embolization. Radiology 1983;146:627.

120. Uflacker R, Kaemmerer A, Picon P, Rizzon CFC, Neves CMC, Oliveira ESB, Oliveira MEM, Azavedo SNB, Ossanai R. Bronchial artery embolization in management of hemoptysis: technical aspects and longterm results. Radiology 1985;157:637.

121. Vlakos L, Giannopoulos A, Caridis G, Giannopoulos P, Benakis V, Dimopoulos C, Pontifex G. Transcatheter arterial embolization in the management of tumours of the urinary tract. Eur Urol 1978;4:106.

122. Vujic I, Lauver JW. Severe complications from partial splenic embolization in patients with liver failure. Br J Radiol 1981;54:492.

123. Vujic I, Pyle R, Parker E, Mithoefer J. Control of massive hemoptysis by embolization of intercostal arteries. Radiology 1980;137:617.

124. Vujic I, Pyle R, Hungerford GD, Griffin CN. Angiography and therapeutic blockade in the control of hemoptysis: the importance of nonbronchial systemic arteries. Radiology 1982;143:19.

125. Walker WJ, Goldin AG, Shaff MI, Allibone GW. Per catheter control of hemorrhage from the superior and inferior mesenteric arteries. Clin Radiol 1980;31:71.

126. Wallace S, Chuang VP, Swanson D, Bracken B, Hersh EM, Ayala A, Johnson D. Embolization of renal carcinoma. Radiology 1981;138:563.

127. Weber J. A complication with the Gianturco coil and its non-surgical management. Cardiovasc Intervent Radiol 1980;3:156.

128. White RI Jr, Lundell C. Prevention of complications during embolotherapy of the lung. Ann Radiol (Paris) 1984;27:310.

129. Wholey MH, Chamorro HA, Rao G, Chapman W. Splenic infarction and spontaneous rupture of the spleen after therapeutic embolization. Cardiovasc Radiol 1978;1:249.

130. Wholey MH, Chamorro HA, Rao G, Ford WB, Miller WH. Bronchial artery embolization for massive hemoptysis. JAMA 1976;236:2501.

131. Wirthlin LS, Gross WS, James TP, Sadiq S. Renal artery occlusion from migration of stainless steel coils. JAMA 1980;243:2064.

132. Witte CL, Ovitt TW, van Wyck DB, Witte MH, O'Mara RE, Woolfenden JM. Ischemic therapy in thrombocytopenia from hypersplenism. Arch Surg 1976;111:1115.

133. Wolpert SM, Stein BM. Factors governing the course of emboli in the therapeutic embolization of cerebral arteriovenous malformations. Radiology 1979;131:125.

134. Woodside J, Schwarz H, Bergreen P. Peripheral embolization complicating bilateral renal infarction with gelfoam. AJR 1976;126:1033.

135. Yamada R, Sato M, Kawabata M, Lakatsuka H, Nakamura K, Takashima S. Hepatic artery embolization in 120 patients with unresectable hepatoma. Radiology 1983;148:397–402.

Angiographic Management of Bleeding

Bronchial Bleeding

J. Rémy and M. Jardin

The treatment of hemoptysis includes medical, surgical, endobronchial, and endovascular therapy. In 1974 (39), we introduced endovascular treatment by bronchial artery embolization. The first results were published in 1977 (35), describing a cooperative study of the efficacy of bronchial artery occlusion. It became increasingly apparent that some bronchial bleeding could not be resolved by this treatment. Clinical studies showed that this resulted from bleeding originating from the pulmonary artery (37, 38) and from systemic non-bronchial arteries, which could also be treated by vaso-occlusion. In this chapter methods, indications, contra-indications, complications and results of endovascular treatment of hemoptysis will be described. In the terminology used, "bronchial arteries" denotes the systemic arteries originating from the descending aorta and with an intrapulmonary course accompanying the bronchi. "Ectopic bronchial arteries" also accompany the bronchi, but they have an ectopic origin. "Non-bronchial systemic arteries" enter the parenchyma via the pulmonary ligament or through the adherent pleura. Their course is not parallel to that of the bronchi.

Method

The method has been described in detail previously (31, 46). We will describe separately the embolization of the bronchial arteries, of the systemic non-bronchial arteries, and of the pulmonary arteries. Most technical considerations are common to the various arteries, whether they are of bronchial or of non-bronchial systemic origin.

Bronchial Artery Embolization

Localization of the bronchial artery requires anatomical and technical knowledge. In 80% of cases, the right bronchial artery arises from an intercostobronchial trunk, which forms an oblique angle of approximately 130 degrees with the descending aorta. The common trunk and both the right and left bronchial arteries often start perpendicularly to the axis of the aorta on its anterior aspect. In older subjects, the aorta undergoes an axial rotation which disorientates the ostia. Its lumen also becomes dilated. The curves of the catheter must therefore be adapted to the age of the patient. Generally speaking, it is easy during catheterization to distinguish the part of the aorta that is most easily studied from the part that constantly escapes exploration. The left intercostal arteries are frequently catheterized, because the orientation of the catheter is dictated by the aorta-iliac curves. In this case, the tip of catheter turns backwards. Attempts to direct it forward risk failure. Either the curve of the catheter has to be changed, or catheterization must be attempted through the opposite femoral artery. In many cases, it has been noted that right femoral catheterization leads to failure and left femoral catheterization is successful. In all cases, perseverance is required. On some occasions we are able to locate the abnormal artery only after three unsuccessful attempts spread out over several months of repeated hemoptysis.

Catheterization of the bronchial artery must be precise. If it is not selective, embolization material may flow back into the aorta. An unstable catheter may be displaced during embolization, and its tip may enter a nearby artery, such as an intercostal artery giving rise to an anterior spinal branch. If catheterization is too selective, significant arteries may be missed, such as a branch of a common bronchial trunk for the right and the left, or the intercostal branch of an intercostobronchial trunk. The latter error may be serious if the intercostal artery gives an anterior spinal artery that may not have been recognized (Fig. 1).

Location of Arterial Occlusion

Because of the presence of proximal anastomoses connecting the bronchial arteries to each other or to non-bronchial systemic arteries, arterial occlusion must not be too proximal. Preparation of the embolization material has to be adapted to the arterial diameter of the artery. An occlusion that is too proximal may be rapidly collateralized. This is why we recommend against the use of metal spirals, cyanoacrylate (19) or intravascular electrocoagula-

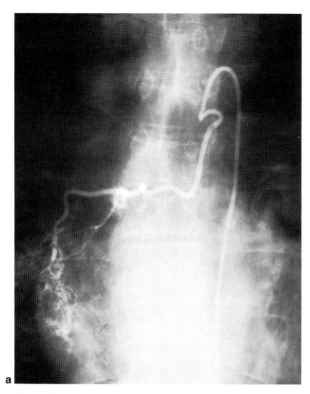
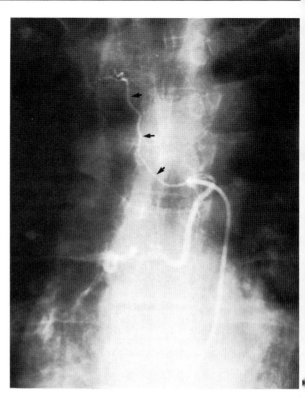

a

Fig. 1   Hemoptysis originating in the right inferior lobe in a case of coal miner's pneumoconiosis. a Selective catheterization shows the presence of a dilated and sinous right bronchial artery. Embolization is considered. After injecting 60 particles of lyophilized dura mater, the angiographic control (**b**) shows the displacement of the catheter from the right bronchial artery to the intercostobronchial trunk. The right superior intercostal artery (arrows) was totally ignored throughout the first part of the embolization. In the absence of a visible anterior spinal artery, embolization was pursued. Hemoptysis was stopped

tion. Another reason is that repeated embolization of the same artery must remain possible. Definitive proximal occlusion must not be the aim of the procedure. In 235 patients treated by embolization, we used cyanoacrylate in one case of iatrogenic communication that had occurred after bronchial biopsy between a bronchial artery, 3 mm in diameter, and a lobar bronchus. The whole material used previously (Gelfoam and dura mater) was removed in the blood aspirated from the bronchus, because of the large diameter of the bronchioarterial fistula.

Nor should embolization be too distal, as occurs when using absolute alcohol (30). Complications following necrosis, such as endobronchial rupture of a large pulmonary artery trunk, have been described previously (21). The ideal embolization material would be particles of approximatively 50 to 100 µ.

Which Arteriographic Abnormalities Should be Embolized?

No parallel can be drawn between arterial anomalies and hemoptysis. Considerable bronchial hypervascularization is not necessarily the cause of hemopty-

sis. Conversely, a bronchial artery that appears normal on the arteriogram can be the cause of massive hemoptysis. Highly vascularized abnormalities located in the periphery of the lung can escape nonselective opacification at low-dose injection. Even a normal-looking artery must be embolized if there is a topographical correspondence between the radiological abnormalities and endoscopy. A stenotic or amputated bronchial artery that gives rise to several abnormal branches must be embolized with fragments of sufficiently small dimensions to pass through the stenosis and penetrate the small abnormal branches.

Consequences of Bronchial Arterial Flow Diversion

Bronchial hypervascularization causes increased flow to the lesion. High bronchial arterial flow prevents opacification of all collaterals. On the other hand, embolization stops flow diversion. The consequences of this hemodynamic peculiarity are threefold: the arteriogram of the intercostobronchial trunk may not show the anterior spinal artery until the bronchial arterial flow slows down; the non-embolized collaterals of the bronchial arteries may break during angiographic controls following embolization. These breaks, probably of capillary origin, and to our knowledge rarely significant, lead to the appearance of pools of contrast medium which has extravasated into the mediastinum or into the wall of the aorta through its vaso vasorum. The latter should always be avoided, as extravasation in the aortic wall may lead to occlusion of the arterial ostium to be embolized, or of the origin of an intercostal artery giving off a spinal branch; anastomoses between the high-flow bronchial artery and other bronchial or non-bronchial systemic arteries may be ignored, because they are non-functional prior to embolization. They may become functional if embolization has been carried out too proximally to these anastomoses.

Correlation Between Hypervascularization and Embolization

Depending on the degree of arterial dilation and hypervascularization, experience enable one to estimate the number of fragments of embolization material of a given size necessary, and the time required to obtain occlusion. It is therefore possible to recognize an embolization that is too proximal and obtained too rapidly in relation to the number of fragments used (Fig. 2). This balance depends on three factors: bronchial arterial spasm, involuntary cruoric embolization, and agglutination of several fragments (13). These factors have in common the risk of the occlusion reopening too early, with subsequent recurrence of hemoptysis. If embolization materials of the same size are used for the same artery in a second session, a comparison can then be made between the small number of fragments used the first time and the large number necessary the second time.

Constricting Effect or Arresting Bronchial Artery Flow

As soon as surgical ligation of a bronchial artery has been performed, its diameter becomes much smaller (Fig. 3). This reduction can also be seen during embolization. This phenomenon probably explains the difficulties encountered in recatheterizing an embolized artery. An artery with no flow will not opacify from its ostium up to the occlusion unless it has been selectively catheterized.

Choice of Embolization Material

The choice of material must be dictated above all by the catheterization technique. If the artery is correctly catheterized and if there are no risks of aortic backflow, non-resorbable material is recommended. In most cases, we use lyophilized dura mater at the first attempt. The flow in the bronchial artery carries the fragments to the periphery (23). When bronchial flow is considerably slowed, contrast medium, even when injected at a low rate, flows back to the aorta. We then use Gelfoam, because its backflow into the aorta is probably less dangerous. Several varieties of embolization material can be used (24). The long-term effects of embolization material have been studied by angiography much more often than by pathological anatomy. Studies on Bucrylate (8) up to 7 years after embolization have shown that vessels embolized with Bucrylate remain permanently occluded; that acute inflammatory changes decrease and are replaced by an obliterating endarteritis, and that there are no signs of metaplasia.

Two years after occlusion, we have noted on histological specimens that the fragments of lyophilized dura mater were floating freely in the arterial lumen without any signs of thrombosis. Later angiographic controls reveal restitutio ad integrum. Return to the previous state can also be observed after using a non-resorbable material. In other cases, a repermeabilized artery, but with a smaller diameter, was observed, indicating that arterial flow is maintained, but reduced.

Combination of Treatments

As the diagnosis of abnormal arteries and occlusion may take several hours, it may be necessary to isolate the bleeding site with an endobronchial balloon catheter, which can be inserted under endoscopy control. However, if tracheobronchial flooding hinders endoscopy, the balloon can be inserted under fluoroscopy control. It is possible that bronchial occlusion with a balloon catheter could compress the submucosal bronchial flow, reduce hypervascularity, and block arterial embolization material, but we have never observed this. These risks are a reason for temporarily deflating the balloon.

The patient is almost always under medical treatment when embolization is considered. Embolization material may successfully cause occlusion of arteries which are constricted due to medical treatment. When the vasoconstriction resolves, however, the embolization may turn out to be incomplete. It is therefore recommended to maintain the patient under vasopressin if this treatment has been initiated previously. It is ideal to stop vasopressin 1–2 hours before embolization, if the condition of the patient allows. The combination of medical and endovascular or endobronchial treatments has cumulative advantages and disadvantages which the physician should be aware of.

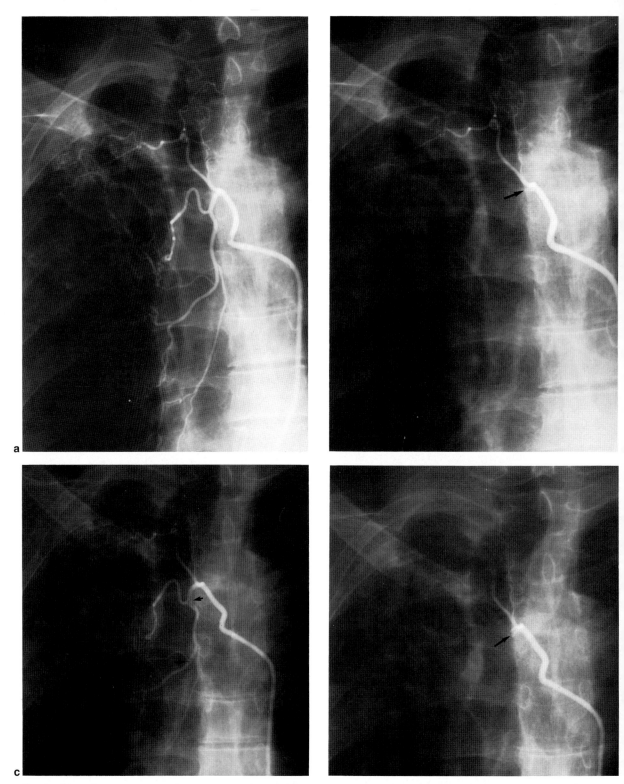

Fig. 2   Abundant and recurrent hemoptysis originating from the right superior lobe in a case of pulmonary tuberculosis. a Selective arteriography of the intercostobronchial trunk shows bronchial and perhaps mild intercostal hypervascularization in the right superior lobe. Complete occlusion of the right bronchial artery (**b**, arrow) is obtained with 15 fragments of lyophilized dura mater. Hemoptysis stopped, but rebleeding was present two days later. **c** Catheterization of the intercostobronchial trunk revealed permeation of the right bronchial trunk. It contained multiple defects (arrows) corresponding to the embolizing material introduced two days earlier. It is probable that the first embolization (**b**) caused either bronchial artery spasm, temporary agglutination of the embolizing material, or thrombus. Cessation of the spasm or

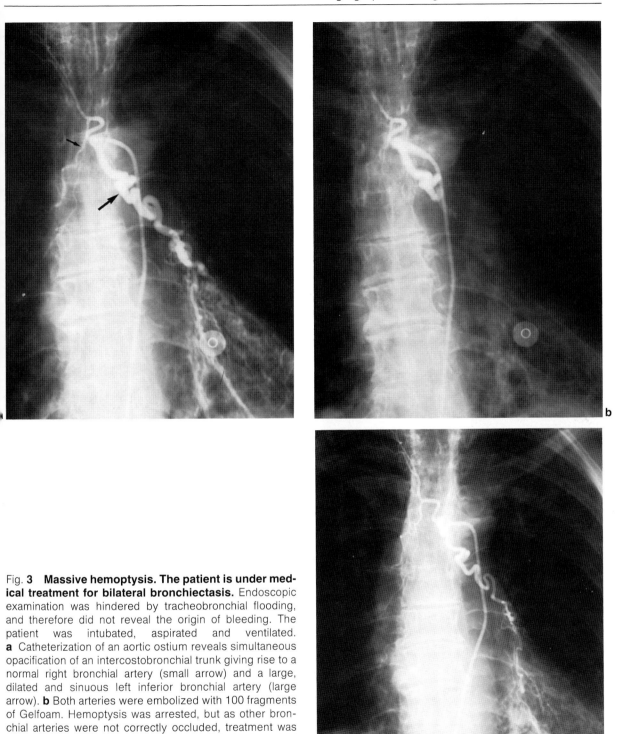

Fig. 3 **Massive hemoptysis. The patient is under medical treatment for bilateral bronchiectasis.** Endoscopic examination was hindered by tracheobronchial flooding, and therefore did not reveal the origin of bleeding. The patient was intubated, aspirated and ventilated. **a** Catheterization of an aortic ostium reveals simultaneous opacification of an intercostobronchial trunk giving rise to a normal right bronchial artery (small arrow) and a large, dilated and sinuous left inferior bronchial artery (large arrow). **b** Both arteries were embolized with 100 fragments of Gelfoam. Hemoptysis was arrested, but as other bronchial arteries were not correctly occluded, treatment was repeated two weeks later (**c**). The left inferior bronchial artery was repermeabilized, but showed a significantly smaller diameter

Fig. 2 (cont.)
lysis of the thrombus cused migration of the embolizing material. **d** A second embolization with 70 fragments of dura mater of the same size used in **b** arrested hemoptysis completely. Embolization that is too proximal or too rapidly obtained in relation to the number of fragments and size of the embolizing material used is probably ineffective

Systemic Non-Bronchial Embolization
(29, 45)

This procedure is derived from the study of the systemic non-bronchial vascularization of the lung. Non-bronchial arterial supply is minimal under normal conditions, but considerably developed in pathology. Three specific features will be detailed here: plurality of pedicles; anastomoses; and consequent difficulties in applying endovascular treatment.

Plurality of Pedicles

We stopped hemoptysis by selective embolization of intercostal, internal and external mammary, acromiothoracic, superior and inferior phrenic arteries and the arteries of the pulmonary ligament. The different causes and different localizations of the bleeding source must be discussed. Some are responsible for the considerable development of systemic vascularization in the lung.

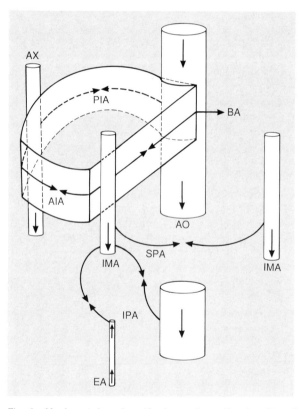

Fig. 4 **Horizontal and vertical anastomotic circuits of the internal mammary artery:** a radial transverse section through the lung closed in a semicircle of systemic vascularization. AX: Collaterals of the axillary artery; PIA: posterior intercostal artery; AIA: anterior intercostal artery; BA: bronchial artery; IMA: internal mammary artery; SPA: superior phrenic artery; IPA: inferior phrenic artery; EA: epigastric artery; AO: aorta

The two most frequent examples are bronchiectasies and intracavitary aspergilloma. With regard to localization, some diseases are distributed in the central part of the lung, such as the massive fibrous masses of coal miner's pneumoconiosis, while others are peripheral, against the pleural wall. Other diseases have resulted in complications such as pleural effusions and pleural symphysis, that cause, in turn, a systemic transpleural flow. The combination of a disease causing systemic hypervascularization and a contact with the pleura is found in intracavitary aspergilloma. Diseases can also be classified according to their location in the lung: in the apical, basal, anterior, posterior, medial or lateral areas. Each sector has its own transpleural vascularization. Apical diseases have the richest transpleural vascularization, resulting from identified vessels or other small branches of the subclavian and axillary arteries.

Anastomoses

Pleuropulmonary pathological conditions lead to anastomoses between the collateral or terminal branches of a vessel or to anastomoses between several vessels. These multiple anastomoses are not present in the normal state. The internal mammary artery (Fig. **4**) represents the systemic non-bronchial artery most often found to be abnormal in the arteriographic study of hemoptysis. It has anastomoses with the epigastric artery. Embolization of the internal mammary artery may be compensated for by the epigastric artery. The superior and inferior phrenic arteries are also anastomosed. The internal accessory mammary artery anastomoses the internal mammary artery to the homolateral anterior intercostal arteries. This anastomosis can be responsible for persistent flow after a proximal occlusion of the internal mammary artery. The internal mammary arteries are anastomosed to each other by retrosternal transverse anastomoses.

The anterior intercostal arteries that are branches of the internal mammary artery are anastomosed to the intercostal arteries in connection with the axillary artery. The anterior intercostal arteries are anastomosed to the posterior intercostal arteries that are branches of the thoracic aorta. These intercostal anastomoses circle the hemithorax. The internal mammary artery can be anastomosed with the homolateral bronchial artery.

It is not possible to describe all the anastomoses. The internal mammary artery is the most representative example, but others can also be described, such as an anastomosis between a common bronchial trunk and the left vertebral artery (10); anastomoses between the intercostobronchial artery and the intercostocervical trunk; an indirect anastomotic circuit between the left bronchial artery and the left internal mammary artery via the left inferior thyroid artery and the thyrobicervicoscapular trunk. From there, flow of contrast medium opacifies the left internal mammary artery, because the two vessels start from a common trunk. An anastomotic circuit between the intercostobronchial trunk and the right axillary artery, via a posterior intercostal artery connecting this trunk to a branch of the lateral thoracic or acromiothoracic artery (Fig. **5**). The only important point to remember is that these circuits are either discovered after embolization of the abnormal vessels, or are blocked by the embolization material. The radiologist must always look out for their occurrence.

Embolization of the Pulmonary Artery

The study of four particular references in the literature is especially informative. The reports of Auerbach (3) and Plessinger (34) contain magnificent descriptions of anatomopathological studies of pulmonary cavities resulting from tuberculosis in patients who died from massive hemoptysis, and in patients without hemoptysis but still with non-ruptured pulmonary arterial aneurysms. These authors describe the contact between the artery and the cavity, the rupture of the media, and the eccentric protrusion of the intima into the cavity. The rupture of the intima causes fatal hemoptysis. The studies of Middleton (28) and Davis (12) give a description of young adults who died from massive hemoptysis during pulmonary tuberculosis.

We have described (36, 37) the principles of treatment, and we may recall here some fundamental observations: endoscopic diagnosis of hemoptysis with a low flow of black blood is a sign of bleeding from a pulmonary artery; hemoptysis of red blood may correspond to systemic blood of either systemic or pulmonary arterial origin if the pulmonary artery is perfused by bronchopulmonary shunts; the occurrence of a so-called "alarm" hemoptysis during necrosis of lung parenchyma, even if minimal, should be considered as a sign of unfavorable prognosis. This complication calls for aggressive therapy. Fatal hemoptyses following a minimal hemoptysis by several hours or days have been described in cases of tuberculosis (28), pulmonary abscess with common pyogenic germs (40), intracavitary aspergillosis (22, 32), invasive aspergillosis (1, 4, 18) and mucormycosis (20). Hemoptysis in invasive aspergillosis, considered rare in 1980, is considered frequent in 1987. It occurs in 26% of leukemic patients after bone marrow aplasia (1). During the 48 h following aplasia, when an increase in granulocytes is noticed, scrutinizing the lungs for a cavity or an intracavitary nodule is mandatory. The occurrence of both these radiological signs in a leukemic patient emerging from bone marrow aplasia indicates a risk of massive hemoptysis. The history and the clinical, radiological

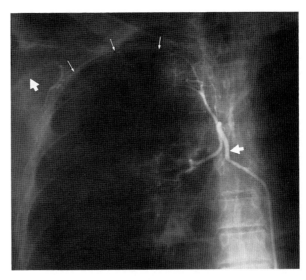

Fig. **5 Anastomosis between the intercostobronchial trunk** (large arrow) **and the right axillary artery** (large arrow) via the second posterior intercostal artery (small arrows). After occlusion of the intercostobronchial trunk, vascularization would persist via the right axillary artery

and anatomopathological signs are the same as for mucormycosis (20). The risk of hemorrhage from an intracavitary aspergilloma is high, and relapses are to be feared either during medical treatment, or during or immediately after surgical treatment. Statistically, this risk has been estimated to lie between 60% and 80%. Of the 85 cases reported by Jewkes (2), 7% died from hemoptysis after medical or surgical treatment.

According to Jewkes, bronchial embolization is an alternative to resection in severe hemoptysis, which is the most effective treatment, and to cavernostomy. In these various pathological conditions, a cavity in the lung may not be recognized if filled by hemorrhage. Limited bronchial bleeding may conceal far more abundant intracavitary bleeding. Systemic hypervascularization of the area around the cavity can be associated with an intracavitary pulmonary arterial pseudoaneurysm. Prophylactic treatment is justified (Fig. **6**). The wall of an erosive pseudoaneurysm of the pulmonary artery is very fragile. Intracavitary blood or aspergilloma may conceal an aneurysm. Angiography or CT should be performed to determine its presence following hemorrhage. We consider CT scanning to be a useful part of the pretherapeutic examination, establishing the relation between the cavity and the surrounding vessels. Above all, it makes identification of a Rasmussen aneurysm and its systemic or pulmonary arterial opacification possible. CT is also useful in follow-up of these lesions after endovascular treatment.

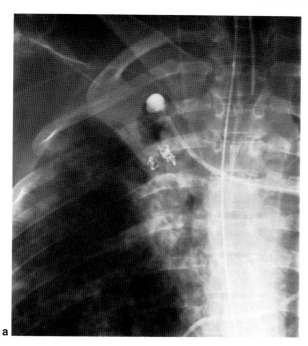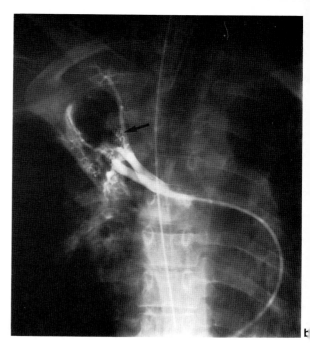

a
b

Fig. 6 **Massive hemoptysis that has caused anoxic cardiac arrest.** The patient was intubated, aspirated and ventilated. Large tuberculous cavity of the right superior lobe filled by a clot obstructing the right superior lobar bronchus. Initially, systemic arteriography revealed extensive pericavitary bronchial hypervascularization, which was embolized. Thereafter, and without any rebleeding having occurred, selective pulmonary arteriography revealed arterial branches in close contact with the cavity, treated by embolization. **a** Superselective angiography revealed a Rasmussen aneurysm at the superior pole of the cavity. **b** Its arterial pedicle was also obstructed with metal spirals (arrow). Even after effective bronchial embolization, the location of erosive pseudoaneurysms by CT or pulmonary angiography must be attempted when necrosis of the lung parenchyma is present

Pulmonary angiographic technique in a patient with a pulmonary arterial aneurysm depends on the fragility of the lesion. Excess injection pressure and too selective catheterization must be avoided. When the pedicle of the aneurysm is catheterized, the sack opacifies. The sack can either be drained by the pulmonary arterial flow, or it drains into the cavity. In order to identify contrast medium within the cavity, the catheter has to be maintained in an occlusive position. If the cavity fills with contrast medium, the pedicle must be occluded with a balloon or metal spirals. Any vessel can be eroded by a cavity: the pulmonary arteries, an intracavitary arteriovenous aneurysm (25), the bronchial arteries or non-bronchial systemic arteries (Fig. **7**). Even though it has not been described, so far as we know, erosive pseudoaneurysms must certainly also occur in pulmonary veins.

The aneurysms we have observed during angiographic treatment of hemoptysis, and their causes, are shown in Table **1.** Of 14 aneurysms, 12 were intracavitary erosive pseudoaneurysms; tuberculosis was present in 7 cases, aspergilloma in 1 case, invasive aspergillosis in one case and abscesses in 3 cases.

In one case an atheromatous aneurysm was present, which developed in the first centimeter of a highly-dilated bronchial artery in a patient with bronchiectasis (Fig. **8**). A traumatic intercostal pseudoaneurysm following attempts at transthoracic drainage of an intracavity aspergilloma has been observed. One of the erosive pseudoaneurysms had simultaneous bronchial and pulmonary perfusion (37, 38). Current indications for the occlusion of branches of the pulmonary artery in the treatment of hemoptysis are:

- erosive pulmonary artery pseudoaneurysm;
- erosive pulmonary arteriovenous pseudo-aneurysm;
- erosive hypothetic pulmonary venous pseudo-aneurysm;
- pulmonary vessels in contact with the wall of a necrotic cavity in the lung (tuberculosis, abscess);
- spontaneous or iatrogenic extravasation of contrast medium during angiography;
- persistence of a systemic-pulmonary shunt after systemic embolization (5) to reduce focal pulmonary hypertension;
- pulmonary vein obstruction.

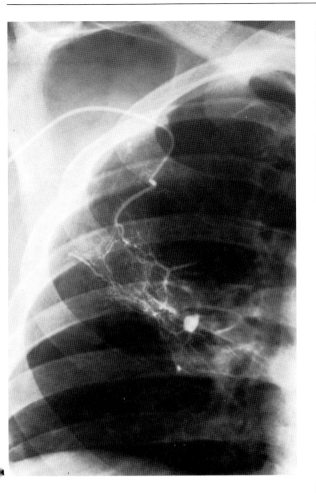

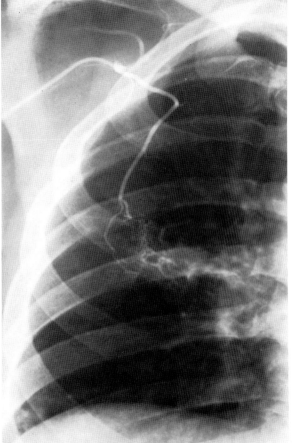

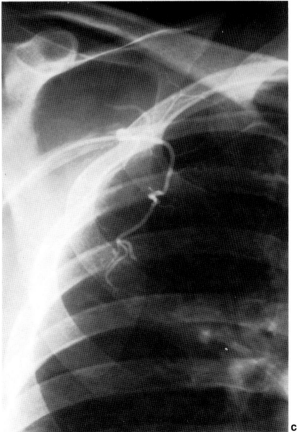

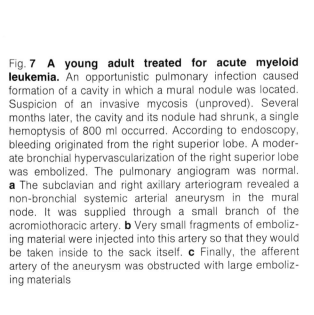

Fig. 7 **A young adult treated for acute myeloid leukemia.** An opportunistic pulmonary infection caused formation of a cavity in which a mural nodule was located. Suspicion of an invasive mycosis (unproved). Several months later, the cavity and its nodule had shrunk, a single hemoptysis of 800 ml occurred. According to endoscopy, bleeding originated from the right superior lobe. A moderate bronchial hypervascularization of the right superior lobe was embolized. The pulmonary angiogram was normal. **a** The subclavian and right axillary arteriogram revealed a non-bronchial systemic arterial aneurysm in the mural node. It was supplied through a small branch of the acromiothoracic artery. **b** Very small fragments of embolizing material were injected into this artery so that they would be taken inside to the sack itself. **c** Finally, the afferent artery of the aneurysm was obstructed with large embolizing materials

Table **1**   Aneurysms observed during angiographic treatment of hemoptysis and their causes

Etiology	Pedicle	Size (mm)	Treatment
Chronic cavitary tuberculosis	Posterior intercostal artery	10	Surgical
Chronic cavitary tuberculosis	Left bronchial artery	7	Bronchial embolization
Intracavitary aspergilloma	Right bronchial artery Subsegmental pulmonary artery	20	Bronchial and pulmonary arterial embolization
Chronic cavitary tuberculosis	Inferior pulmonary artery	70	Surgical
Chronic cavitary tuberculosis	Segmental pulmonary artery	15	Embolization
Recent cavitary tuberculosis	Right bronchial artery	2	Embolization
Intracavitary aspergilloma	Posterior intercostal artery (iatrogenic)	5	Embolization
Abscess	Subsegmental pulmonary artery	20	Embolization
Abscess	Subsegmental pulmonary artery	10	Embolization
Chronic cavitary tuberculosis	Subsegmental pulmonary artery	20	Embolization
Bronchiectasis	Common bronchial trunk	10	Embolization
Invasive aspergillosis	Acromiothoracic artery	7	Embolization
Abscess	Subsegmental pulmonary artery	5	Embolization
Recent cavitary tuberculosis	Subsegmental pulmonary artery	20	Embolization

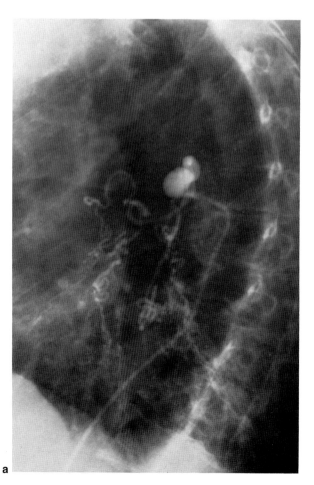

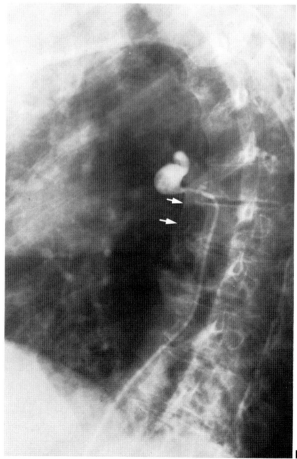

a   b

Bredin (5) believes that after bronchial embolization at the bleeding site, broncho-pulmonary, capillary and pre-capillary anastomoses continue to be perfused by the pulmonary artery. If the pressure gradient between the bronchial artery and the pulmonary artery is inverted after bronchial embolization, the antegrade pulmonary arterial flow may reappear at the bleeding site. This may, at least theoretically, explain the persistence of hemoptysis. We corroborate Bredin's hypothesis, because in three of the patients we injected during selective peripheral pulmonary angiography, systemic pulmonary anastomoses operated in the opposite direction, at least under the effect of the injection pressure in the catheter placed in the pulmonary artery (Fig. 9). Reduction of perfusion at the bleeding site may then be obtained by systemic or pulmonary artery occlusion.

Hemoptysis may appear at the site where pulmonary veins are obstructed. We have observed this complication on several occasions either during involvement of the left atrium and pulmonary veins by bronchial carcinoma, or after surgical correction of partially abnormal pulmonary return. The persistence of pulmonary arterial circulation in the territory of pulmonary vein obstruction or in the bronchial mucosa may explain these hemoptyses. Palliative treatment may be obtained by pulmonary artery occlusion at the bleeding site (Fig. 10).

Indications

Therapeutic indications for angiographic treatment of hemoptysis vary from one team to another. They are difficult to list, and depend on the extent of bleeding, risk of relapse of hemoptysis, and on respiratory function. The severity of hemoptysis should never be judged by the volume of blood expectorated, because a single massive hemoptysis of 1 l or more is compatible with a long survival in some cases (42); moderate hemoptysis can cause asphyxiation if respiratory function is seriously hampered before the bleeding episode; minimal hemoptysis can precede fatal hemoptysis by several hours or days;

and bronchial bleeding can be trapped in a cavity and only slightly exteriorized.

We know of no way of predicting the severity of the symptoms, but it does appear that some hemoptyses give reason to fear serious relapse. This is the case in lung necrosis, cavitary aspergilloma, and erosive pseudoaneurysms.

Preventive treatment does exist. We have used it in the following 4 cases: in bronchial biopsies carrying a risk of hemorrhage. This risk is predictable when endoscopy suggests a carcinoid tumor, or lesions described as angiomatous by endoscopy. This term probably covers different lesions, such as telangiectases in Rendu-Osler-Weber disease, submucosal venous flow replacing obstruction in a pulmonary vein, or bronchial hyperemia identical to that found in chronic obstructive disease of the lung. Intracavitary erosive aneurysms, regardless of their volume or etiology (11, 15, 16, 37, 38, 40); in hemorrhagic or hypervascularized tumor prior to laser therapy (2, 33); in a cavity with considerable systemic hypervascularization prior to percutaneous drainage (41). An interesting discussion on the risks of hemorrhage due to percutaneous drains was recently published by Mengoli (27).

For some indications, treatment by embolization may be attempted instead of surgery, when resection requires a disproportionate sacrifice of lung parenchyma in relation to the extent of the lesion, or when the preoperative diagnosis shows benign disease. Apart from these specific cases, treatment by embolization should be reserved for massive or repeated hemoptyses compromising the vital prognosis of the respiratory function in patients with temporary or permanent surgical contra-indications, and for whom medical treatment has proved ineffective. Surgical contra-indication may be only temporary and due to poor respiratory function, which in turn may be due to flooding of the alveoli. The most frequently-encountered causes in the literature (7, 17) and in our 235 observations (35) are active tuberculosis or sequelae, bronchiectasis, chronic bronchitis, coal miners' pneumoconiosis, and intracavitary aspergilloma.

◄ Fig. 8 **Same patient as in Figure 3. a** Aneurysm of the bronchial artery located in the common trunk. This common trunk does not correspond to the right and left bronchial arteries described in Figure 3. **b** It was embolized with fragments of lyophilized dura mater. Only the aneurysmal sack remained patent after embolization. It is probably an atheromatous aneurysm caused by extensive and long-standing hyperflow in the bronchial artery. Similar aneurysms are found in some congenital heart diseases. The aneurysm was too close to the descending aorta (arrows) to be embolized without risk. The respiratory function contraindicated surgery. It was hoped that the suppression of bronchial arterial flow by embolization would cause spontaneous thrombosis of the aneurysm. There was no relapse of hemoptysis between 1984 and 1987 in this patient

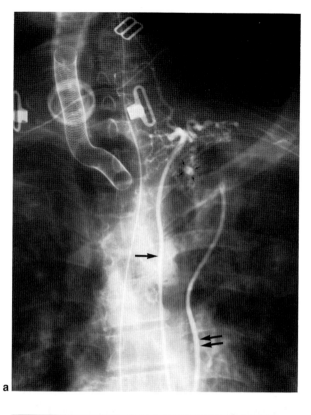

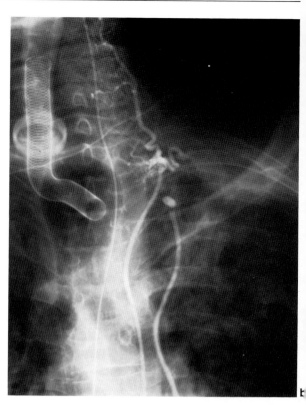

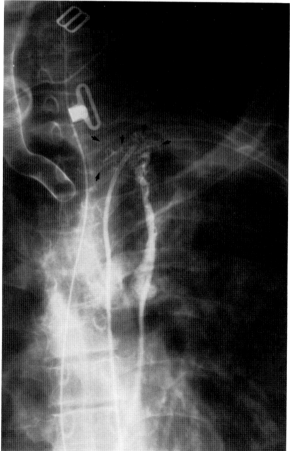

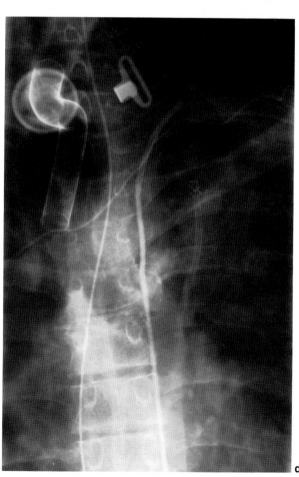

Contraindications

We will not stress general contra-indications to arteriography here, discussing only those that are specific to the treatment of hemoptysis.

The presence of an anterior spinal artery discovered during opacification of an intercostal artery is a contra-indication for embolization of this artery. This situation may arise during catheterization of an intercostobronchial trunk and of intercostal arteries. It may also be found during voluntary or involuntary embolization, when the embolization medium flows back into the aorta. Uflacker (43, 44) points out two cases in which this contra-indication was not respected, and no neurological complication occurred. We have made the same observation in two cases. Nonetheless, caution should be exercised and the spinal or related artery should be avoided in the absence of a hemoptysis which endangers the patient's life. If the vital prognosis is in question, occlusion should be performed with large embolization material blocks before it can reach the spinal artery.

Three specific situations should be mentioned: opacification of an anterior spinal artery only after the flow has been stopped in the bronchial artery that is a tributary of an intercostobronchial artery; the presence of an anterior spinal artery which is not seen during arteriography or digital subtraction angiography because of its very small diameter (45); and we have also observed a transient paraparesis several hours after embolization of the intercostobronchial trunk when the arterial blood pressure dropped. The Wada test (14) may help to avoid embolization of a right bronchial artery which is a branch of an intercostobronchial trunk participating in the medullar vascularization.

When acquired or congenital pulmonary artery obstruction is present, a bronchial and non-bronchial systemic flow develops. This flow may be suspected if antegrade systemic-pulmonary shunts are evidenced (6, 9, 26). The question might be asked as to whether this collateral flow can be obstructed without risk. We have encountered three possibilities: first, bronchial embolization of the post-embolic antegrade bronchopulmonary shunts without any complication (16); secondly, bronchial embolization of the post-embolic antegrade bronchopulmonary shunts followed by complications in 2 patients. In the first patient, a peripheral pulmonary nodule appeared, with a small homolateral pleural effusion, both of which resolved spontaneously. In the second patient, a pulmonary infarction with cavitation appeared several days after bronchial embolization. Thirdly, we observed bronchial embolization of non-postembolic antegrade bronchopulmonary shunts without complications. We believe that the ischemic risk involved in the occlusion of systemic arteries replacing a pulmonary artery obstruction should not be overlooked.

Role of Embolization in Understanding the Pathophysiological Mechanism of Hemoptysis

If hemoptysis is stopped by occlusion of a vessel, it could be reasonably believed that this vessel was responsible for the hemoptysis. However, the multiple anastomoses between the systemic and pulmonary vessels prevent one from drawing firm conclusions in such bleeding. If occlusion of a vessel stops hemorrhage, the angiogram may indicate the precise mechanism of the bleeding in selected cases only.

Fig. 9 **Massive hemoptysis orginating from the superior lobe** in a patient with pulmonary tuberculosis that had caused anoxic cardiac arrest. The patient was intubated, aspirated and ventilated. **a** Selective catheterization of the left cervicointercostal trunk starting from the thoracic aorta (large arrow) indicated pulmonary or pleural systemic hypervascularization of the medial part of the left apex. The presence of an aneurysm (small arrows) required exploration of a pulmonary arterial pedicle in the same region (large double arrow). **b** Embolization of the cervicointercostal trunk with 90 fragments of lyophilized dura mater stopped most of the systemic hypervascularization. The contrast medium was found stagnating in the aneurysm. The catheter in the pulmonary artery was then located under the aneurysm. **c** Pulmonary arterial injection during blocked catheterization opacified, in addition to the aneurysm, a great number of small branches (arrows) which correspond morphologically and topographically to those opacified by the cervicointercostal trunk (compare **a** and **c**). They are probably small abnormal systemic-pulmonary shunts following embolization of the cervicointercostal trunk (5). **d** In order to arrest the antegrade pulmonary arterial flow in the aneurysm and in these vessels, the pulmonary arterial branch was occluded next to the aneurysm, using metal spirals

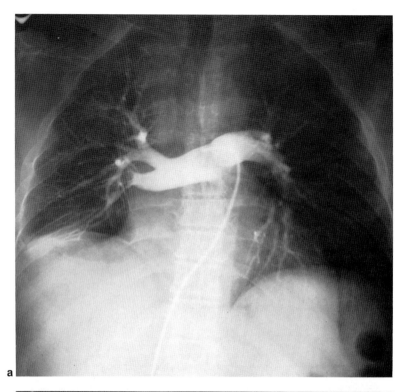

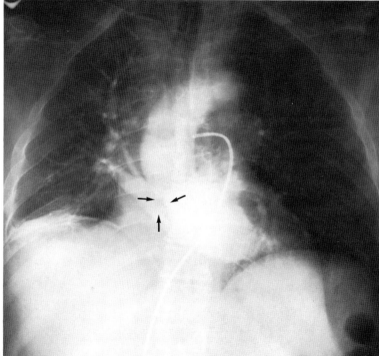

Fig. 10 **Inoperable bronchogenic carcinoma of the intermediate bronchus** involving the right inferior pulmonary vein and the left atrium. Hemoptysis of 150 to 200 ml per 24 hours for 10 days. **a** Pulmonary angiography revealed a tight stenosis of the right inferior pulmonary artery. **b** The venous phase (b) revealed a small filling defect in the right part of the left atrium. It corresponds to neoplastic involvement of the right inferior pulmonary vein (not opacified) propagated to the left atrium (proved by post-mortem examination).

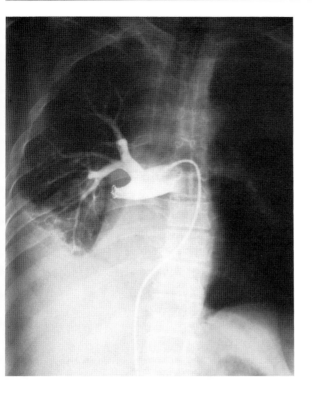

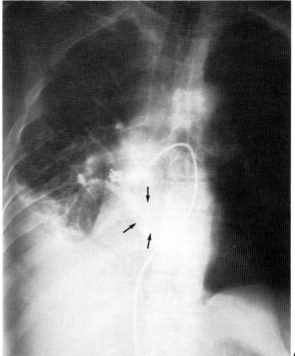

d

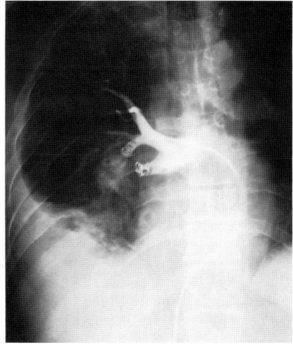

e

Fig. **10** (cont.)
c The right inferior artery was obstructed with three metal spirals. This occlusion immediately arrested hemoptysis for two months. **d** Rebleeding was studied by a second pulmonary angiography which revealed a reduction in the venous return in the right superior pulmonary vein, but extension of the neoplastic thrombus into the left atrium. **e** Hemoptysis was treated by vasoocclusion of a segmental branch of the anterior trunk of the right pulmonary artery. This second occlusion caused immediate arrest of hemoptysis until the patient's death two months later

Finally, two causes of hemorrhage may be combined in the same lesion. For example, a Rasmussen aneurysm may receive simultaneous bronchial and pulmonary artery perfusion (37), or the wall of a cavity may be perfused by bronchial hypervascularization, while the cavity contains an aneurysm perfused only by the pulmonary artery (Fig. **9**). Stopping hemoptysis by the occlusion of a single vessel does not exclude bleeding from another vessel if anastomoses are present. Arterial occlusion and cessation of bleeding may also be coincidental. Nonetheless, in the light of these restrictions, embolization makes it possible to describe three types of hemoptysis: those of bronchial arterial origin, non-bronchial arterial origin and pulmonary arterial origin.

Results

Between 1973 and 1986, we treated 235 patients by embolization. Of these, 144 were treated during hemoptysis or at the latest less than 6 h after arrest. We stopped bleeding in 101 out of 144 patients (70%). The year 1979 marks a turning point, as it corresponds to the moment when we started to study pulmonary flow in two indications: either because of the failure of bronchial embolization, or because of the presence of a necrotic cavity as a cause of hemoptysis (37).

The percentage of rebleeding after embolization is difficult to assess, as the 235 patients have to be divided into three categories: those treated by embolization alone, those in whom the causal disease was treated medically, and finally, those who underwent surgical resection of the hemorrhagic lesion after embolization. For the first group of patients, and for all etiologies combined, the percentage of relapse is about 50%.

Complications

Of the 235 patients treated by embolization of one or several bronchial, non-bronchial systemic or pulmonary arteries, we observed no complications linked with catheterization, even when repeated or prolonged. The complications we did find were due to the following causes: interruption of bronchial vascularization: pulmonary infarction, pleural fluid. Bronchial ischemia: bronchial necrosis with bronchoesophageal or bronchoarterial fistula (21) were reported. The necrosing role of absolute alcohol would appear to be considerable. We found no complications due to ischemia. Displacement of an atheromatous plaque or formation of thrombi around a catheter remaining several hours in the subclavian artery or in the aorta. We observed hemiplegia in 3 cases: one definitive, one resolved and one fatal because of ischemic damage to the cerebral trunk. Aortic backflow of the embolization mate-

rial: it can result in ischemic complications in the digestive tract or in the lower limbs. We only noted transient complications which resolved spontaneously. Anterior spinal ischemia. As we have already pointed out, this complication is to be feared, especially in occlusion of the intercostobronchial trunk. The medullar toxicity of contrast media must also be considered. Paraplegia resulting from a right superior pulmonary lobectomy is rarely a complication, although this lobectomy does result in an occlusion of the intercostobronchial artery near its origin. Embolization of this same vessel is probably not capable of causing spinal ischemia. For this reason, certain authors use large embolization materials in the presence of an anterior spinal artery (43, 44). Both cases of paraplegia which we observed occurred before the period of embolization, i.e. before 1973, out of a total of 350 bronchial angiograms carried out between 1967 and 1973.

References

1. Albelda SM, Talbot GH, Gerson SL, Miller WT, Cassileth PA. Pulmonary cavitation and massive hemoptysis in invasive pulmonary aspergillosis. Am Rev Respir Dis 1985;131:115–120.
2. Arabian A, Spagnolo SV. Laser therapy in patients with primary lung cancer. Chest 1984;86:519–523.
3. Auerbach O. Pathology and pathogenesis of pulmonary arterial aneurysm in tuberculosis cavities. Am Rev Tuberc 1939;39:99–115.
4. Borkin M, Arena FP, Brown AE, Armstrong D. Invasive aspergillosis with massive fatal hemoptysis in patients with neoplastic disease. Chest 1980;78:835–839.
5. Bredin CP, Richardson PR, King TKC, Sniderman KW, Sos TA, Smith JP. Treatment of massive hemoptysis by combined occlusion of pulmonary and bronchial arteries. Am Rev Respir Dis 1978;117:969–973.
6. Chitwood WR, Lyerly HK, Sabiston DC. Surgical management of chronic pulmonary embolism. Ann Surg 1985;201:11–25.
7. Conlan AA, Hurwitz SS, Krige L, Nicolaou N, Pool R. Massive hemoptysis. J Thorac Cardiovasc Surg 1983;85:120–124.
8. Cromwell LD, Freeny PC, Kerber CW, Kunz LL, Harris AB, Shaw CM. Histologic analysis of tissue response to bucrylate-pantopaque mixture. AJR 1986;147:627–631.
9. Dalen JE, Haffajee CI, Alpert JS, Howe JP, Ockene IS, Paraskos JA. Pulmonary embolism, pulmonary hemorrhage and pulmonary infarction. N Engl J Med 1977;296:1431–1435.
10. Darrason R, Revert R, Auderbert M, Remond A. Anastomose artérielle broncho-vertébrale: une anomalie rare. Ann Radiol (Paris) 1986;29:560–562.
11. Davidoff AB, Udoff EJ, Schonfeld SA. Intraaneurysmal embolization of a pulmonary artery aneurysm for control of hemoptysis. AJR 1984;142:1019–1020.
12. Davis CE, Carpenter JL, McAllister CK, Matthews J, Bush BA, Ognibene AJ. Tuberculosis: cause of death in antibiotic era. Chest 1985;88:726–729.
13. Dion JE, Rankin RN, Vinuela F, Fox AJ, Wallace AC, Mervart M. Dextrane microsphere embolization: experimental and clinical experience with radiologic-pathologic correlation. Radiology 1986;160:717–721.
14. Doppman JL, Girton M, Oldfield EH. Spinal Wada test. Radiology 1986;161:319–321.
15. Edelman RR, Johnson TS, Jhaveri HS, Kim D, Kasdon E, Frank HA, Simon M. Fatal hemoptysis resulting from erosion of a pulmonary artery in cavitary sarcoidosis. AJR 1985;145:37–38.

16. Ferris EJ. Pulmonary hemorrhage, vascular evaluation and interventional therapy. Chest 1981;80:710–714.
17. Garzon A, Cerruti MM, Golding ME. Exsanguinating hemoptysis. J Thorac Cardiovasc Surg 1982;84:829–833.
18. Gefter WB, Albelda SM, Talbot GH, Gerson SL, Cassileth PA, Miller WT. Invasive pulmonary aspergillosis and acute leukemia; limitations in the diagnostic utility of the air crescent sign. Radiology 1985;157:605–610.
19. Greiner P, Cornud F, Lacombe P, Viau F, Nahum H. Bronchial artery occlusion for severe hemoptysis: use of isobutyl-2-cyanoscrylate. AJR 1983;140:467–471.
20. Hoy J, Fainstein V. Mucormycosis. In Sarosi G, Davies SF, eds. Fungal diseases of the lung. Orlando: Grune and Stratton, 1986:191–203.
21. Ivanick MJ, Thorwarth W, Donohue J, Mandell V, Delany D, Jaques PF. Infarction of the left main-stem bronchus: a complication of bronchial artery embolization. AJR 1983;141:535–537.
22. Jewkes J, Kay PH, Paneth M, Citron KM. Pulmonary aspergilloma: analysis of prognosis in relation to haemoptysis and survey of treatment. Thorax 1983;38:572–578.
23. Kerber CW. Flow-controlled therapeutic embolization: a physiologic and safe technique. AJR 1980;134:557–561.
24. Kunstlinger F, Brunelle F, Chaumont P, Doyon D. Vascular occlusive agents. AJR 1981;136:151–156.
25. Lundell C, Finck E. Arteriovenous fistulas originating from Rassmussen aneurysms. AJR 1983;140:687–688.
26. Matsuda A. Bronchial arteriography in patients with pulmonary embolism. Chest 1984;85:767–773.
27. Mengoli L. Giant lung abscess treated by tube thoracostomy. J Thorac Cardiovasc Surg 1985;90:186–194.
28. Middleton JR, Sen P, Lange M, Salaki J, Kapila R, Louria DB. Death-producing hemoptysis in tuberculosis. Chest 1977;72:601–604.
29. Moore LB, McWey RE, Vujic I. Massive hemoptysis: control by embolization of the thyrocervical trunk. Radiology 1986;161:173–174.
30. Naar CA, Soong J, Clore F, Hawkins IF. Control of massive hemoptysis by bronchial artery embolization with absolute alcohol. AJR 1983;140:271–272.
31. Olson RR, Athanasoulis CA. Hemoptysis: treatment with transcatheter embolization of the bronchial arteries. In: Athanasoulis CA, Pfister RC, Greene R, Roberson GH, eds. Interventional radiology. 1st ed. Philadelphia: Saunders, 1982:196–202.
32. Pennington JE. Aspergillus. In Sarosi G, Davies SF, eds. Fungal diseases of the lung. Orlando: Grune and Stratton, 1986:175–189.
33. Personne C, Colchen A, Leroy M, Vourc'H G, Toty L. Indications and technique for endoscopic laser resections in bronchology. J Thorac Cardiovasc Surg 1986;91:710–715.
34. Plessinger VA, Jolly PN. Rasmussen's aneurysms and fatal hemorrhage in pulmonary tuberculosis. Am Rev Respir Dis 1949;60:589–603.
35. Remy J, Arnaud A, Fardou H, Giraud R, Voisin C. Treatment of hemoptysis by embolization of bronchial arteries. Radiology 1977;122:33–37.
36. Remy J, Lemaitre L. Management of severe hemoptysis by endovascular occlusion. Pract Cardiol 1983;9:117–122.
37. Remy J, Lemaitre L, Lafitte JJ, Vilain MO, Saint Michel J, Steenhouwer F. Massive hemoptysis of pulmonary arterial origin: diagnosis and treatment. AJR 1984;143:963–969.
38. Remy J, Smith M, Lemaitre L, Marache P, Fournier E. Treatment of massive hemoptysis by occlusion of a Rasmussen aneurysm. AJR 1980;135:605–606.
39. Remy J, Voisin C, Dupuis C, Beguery P, Tonnel AB, Denies JL, Douay B. Traitement des hémoptysies par embolisation de la circulation systémique. Ann Radiol (Paris) 1974;17:5–16.
40. Renie WA, Rodeheffer RJ, Mitchell S, Balke WC, White RI. Balloon embolization of a mycotic pulmonary artery aneurysm. Am Rev Respir Dis 1982;126:1107–1110.
41. Snow N, Lucas A, Horrigan TP. Utility of pneumonotomy in the treatment of cavitary lung disease. Chest 1985;87:731–734.
42. Stern RC, Wood RE, Boat TF, Matthews LW, Tucker AS, Doershuk CF. Treatment and prognosis of massive hemoptysis in cystic fibrosis. Am Rev Respir Dis 1978;117:825–828.
43. Uflacker R, Kaemmerer A, Neves C, Picon PD. Management of massive hemoptysis by bronchial artery embolization. Radiology 1983;146:627–634.
44. Uflacker R, Kaemmerer A, Picon PD, Rizzon CFC, Neves CMC, Oliveira MEM, Azevedo SNB, Ossanai R. Bronchial artery embolization in the management of hemoptysis: technical aspects and long-term results. Radiology 1985;157:637–644.
45. Vujic I, Pyle R, Parker E, Mithoefer J. Control of massive hemoptysis by embolization of intercostal arteries. Radiology 1980;137:617–620.
46. Wholey MH, Cooperstein LA. Embolization of bronchial arteries in patients with hemoptysis. In: Wilkins RA, Viamonte M, eds. Interventional Radiology. Oxford: Blackwell 1982:137–150.

Upper Gastrointestinal Bleeding

P. Rossi and P. Pavone

Angiography plays an important role in both diagnosis and treatment of upper gastrointestinal (GI) bleeding of arteriocapillary origin. Since the first demonstration of the sites of GI bleeding by Nusbaum and Baum in 1963 (22), the applications of angiography in GI bleeding have been well established in relation to other diagnostic and therapeutic techniques.

Actually, only a small number of patients presenting with upper GI bleeding will finally undergo angiography. This invasive procedure is, in fact, limited to patients in whom other methods have failed to show the site of bleeding or to stop it. In the majority of cases noninvasive procedures allow definitive control of the hemorrhage.

Gastric lavage, histamine (H2) receptor antagonists (cimetidine), bed rest, sedation, blood transfusions and volume replacement can be effective in 75% of the cases and stop bleeding (9). Endoscopy also has important applications for both diagnosis and treatment of upper GI bleeding and should be used before angiography (9).

Emergency angiography in cases not responding to conservative treatment should always be used with the purpose of demonstrating the site of GI bleeding and of performing interventional procedures in order to provide definitive control of the hemorrhage. Intra-arterial infusion of vasoconstricting drugs or transcatheter embolization are effective in this respect in a high percentage of cases (1, 37).

In this chapter we shall discuss the techniques and materials used for angiographic localization and control of upper GI bleeding with their relative therapeutic contributions according to specific anatomic sites and pathologic states.

Localization of the Site of Bleeding

Diagnostic Modalities

Patients presenting with GI bleeding should be submitted initially to gastric intubation. If the nasogastric aspirate is hemorrhagic, then an upper GI site of bleeding is strongly suspected and conservative therapeutic procedures are undertaken in order to attempt control of the hemorrhage. Upper GI bleeding may, in fact, be intermittent, and initial control can easily be obtained with such conservative trials (9).

If bleeding continues, exact localization of the bleeding site is required and further diagnostic procedures are to be programmed.

Barium studies should not be used as an initial attempt to localize the site of bleeding. Small superficial lesions are not detected with this modality, and the bleeding site could also originate from a point different from the eventual pathologic condition shown on the barium study (19). Moreover, the presence of contrast material in the bowel might disturb further diagnostic investigation with selective angiography.

Endoscopy performed by an experienced endoscopist may reveal the site of bleeding in up to 80% of patients (34). Presence of massive hemorrhage in the stomach, and uncooperative patients, can impair the results of endoscopy, and the GI bleeding site may not be observed (15, 31). Even if endoscopy has definitely shown the bleeding site, but no therapeutic intervention has been performed, angiography is required if bleeding continues (2).

Angiography is capable of detecting the bleeding site when performed with accurate technique and selective injection of contrast material. Due to the intermittent nature of upper GI bleeding episodes, it is important to document the presence of active bleeding immediately before performing angiography. A bleeding rate of at least 0.5 ml/min can be correctly identified with angiography (22). Angiography is therefore only indicated when a rapidly decreasing hematocrit after continuous blood replacement and evidence of bright red nasogastric aspirate are present (2, 9).

Angiographic Technique

The identification of the site of bleeding requires correct planning of the angiographic technique and a number of selective arterial injections (22).

The procedure can be started with a celiac injection if the upper origin of the GI bleeding has been shown by endoscopy or is suspected on the basis of the positive nasogastric aspirate. The celiac angiogram also plays a role in excluding the presence of undetected gastroesophageal varices, which can be the cause of venous bleeding.

Extravasation of contrast medium in the GI lumen can be detected after simple celiac injection. However, superselective studies are always required to confirm the diagnosis and to perform further therapeutic procedures.

The left gastric artery can be selectively catheterized using a cobra catheter, forming a loop into the mesenteric artery, or with a Simmons-I catheter. The selective injection may show a diffuse blush of contrast medium in the late angiographic phase, located in the region of the fundus. This is often related to the presence of intense edema due to gastric lavage and to the presence of the nasogastric tube. Only when no other areas of contrast medium extravasation are demonstrated can it be presumed, that the intense blush is related to hemorrhagic diffuse gastritis.

Selective studies of the left inferior phrenic artery may also be helpful in negative cases, since a few gastric branches of the fundus can originate from this artery. Intense parenchymal opacification of the adrenal glands is observed after such an injection and should not be mistaken for an area of extravasation.

The other arteries supplying the stomach should also be fully evaluated. A selective splenic arteriogram will opacify the area supplied by the short gastric arteries and the left gastroepiploic artery. Gastroduodenal artery injection has the purpose of opacifying the right gastroepiploic artery and to rule out bleeding originating from the pyloroduodenal region. Finally, selective hepatic artery opacification can show the right gastric artery and might visualize the origin of upper GI bleeding, when hematobilia is the cause, as occurs with hepatic artery aneurysm or laceration after liver biopsy (23).

A superior mesenteric artery study serves to visualize the inferior pancreatico-duodenal arcades, sometimes demonstrating hemorrhage not shown by a selective gastroduodenal study. The trunk of the panreaticoduodenal arcades can also be selectively catheterized and injected.

During this extensive angiographic diagnostic work up, care should be taken to identify anatomic variants. A left gastric artery originating directly from the aorta must be searched for if it is not visualized by celiac injection.

In patients after gastric resection the first two jejunal branches, originating from the superior mesenteric artery and supplying blood to the anastomosed jejunal loop, should be selectively injected.

Finally, if no definitive extravasation of contrast medium has been documented, as last attempt should be made with an aortographic study to identify the presence of an aorto-enteric fistula. When even this clinical entity has not been found, the catheter should not be removed. In fact, in some cases the initial arterial injection may fail to reveal a bleeding site that subsequent injections may demonstrate (29). The patient should, therefore, be taken to the intensive care unit, the vital signs and the gastric aspirate, should be supervised continuously, and selective examination should be restarted when hemorrhage has clearly recurred.

The catheter can be left selectively placed in the left gastric artery, when endoscopy has previously shown the gastric origin of the hemorrhage, in order to start a therapeutic trial with vasopressin infusion (16).

Angiographic Control of Upper Gastrointestinal Bleeding

Upper GI bleeding can be successfully controlled with angiographic techniques either with infusion of vasoconstrictive agents or with transcatheter embolization. The respective indication in each clinical setting will be discussed later; a comprehensive evaluation of these therapeutic techniques follows here.

Vasoconstrictive agents. Vasopressin is the most effective drug to attempt control of the hemorrhage. Its activity is due both to splanchnic vasoconstriction of arteries and to contraction of the smooth muscle of the GI tract. Vasopressin is an aqueous solution of the active hormone of the posterior pituitary gland, without oxytocic action (13, 28).

Other vasoconstrictive agents, such as epinephrine, prostaglandin F, and glypressin, have not proven to be so effective for this purpose. Their use has been tested experimentally, but they are no longer considered for clinical mesenteric vasoconstriction (30, 33).

Vasopressin, if infused intra-arterially through the catheter selectively placed in the artery supplying the hemorrhage demonstrates a higher efficacy than after intravenous infusion (6). Moreover, it seems that fewer side-effects are observed at the lower doses used intra-arterially. Side effects are related to general vasoconstriction caused by the drug. Hypertension and arrhythmias may affect the cardiovascular system, and myocardial infarctions have also been described (14). Peripheral vascular constriction may cause leg or foot gangrene, whereas its action on the visceral bed may cause bowel ischemia and infarction. The metabolic derangement, with hyponatremia, induced by the drug has caused episodes of cerebral edema. The true incidence of such complications is actually low. Athanasoulis (1) describes 41 major complications in 599 patients treated with intra-arterial and intravenous vasopressin.

Complications can be controlled simply by discontinuing therapy. Since the action of the drug is direct and immediate, early discontinuation of the drug can reverse the side effects. Such fast action of the drug allows early control of the hemorrhage in the majority of cases. The therapeutic protocol should include an early angiographic control 20 minutes after beginning the vasopressin infusion (1). The infusion ist initially carried out at a rate of 0.2 U/min. If after 20 minutes extravasation is no longer evident, infusion is continued at the same rate for 12 to 24 hours and reduced to one-half in the next 24 hours.

If control of the hemorrhage is not obtained after 20 minutes, the dose is increased to 0.4 U/min, and a follow-up done after 24 hours will indicate whether therapy is to be continued or a switch mode to embolization if no control of bleeding has been obtained.

Catheter dislodgment should also be checked if no control has been obtained initially (17). When selective catheterization of the branch supplying the bleeding site is not possible, infusion is performed in the celiac trunk or the superior mesenteric artery.

Efficacy of bleeding control with vasopressin for each application will be discussed later. Its application is mainly indicated to control bleeding of mucosal origin and not bleeding duodenal ulcer. Vasopressin infusion, however, does not prevent further therapy with embolization.

Arterial Embolization

Percutaneous transcatheter embolization of the artery with the bleeding site is an alternative therapeutic approach for reduction of arterial flow and control of the hemorrhage. The materials used for embolization are the same as those used in other vascular areae and for other purposes (such as blood flow reduction in tumors or arterio-venous malformations). Resorbable or not resorbable materials are used according to the bleeding site and the underlying disease. Also, the size of the artery to be occluded influences the choice of material.

Resorbable materials include autologous clot and Gelfoam (26). Non-resorbable materials include particulate emboli, such as polyvinyl alcohol foam or cyanoacrylic glues (10, 11) and mechanical devices such as coils (8) or detachable balloons (38).

Gelfoam is indicated for occluding arteries supplying bleeding of mucosal origin (25). Since there is little anatomic alteration of the layer of the gastric or bowel wall in these cases, the use of resorbable material may result in complete bleeding control, with restoration of the normal mucosal vascularization after resorption of the material in a few weeks.

Bleeding originating from extensive anatomic lesions, such as chronic ulcers, including the deeper layer of the bowel wall, or due to neoplastic growth or traumatic laceration of the bowel wall, need to be treated with non-resorbable material to avoid recanalization of the embolized vessels and recurrence of hemorrhage.

Either Gelfoam or polyvinyl alcohol are used in these instances to occlude the more peripheral vessels. The main branch is occluded near its origin with a larger device, such as a Gianturco type coil (8) or detachable balloon (38). Cyanoacrylic glues can also be used for this purpose (11). Extreme care should be taken with the glues to avoid back flow and sticking of the tip of the catheter to the glue or the arterial wall.

A few points should be stressed to enhance the results of transcatheter embolization and to reduce the number of potential complications. Gelfoam powder should be used in small pledgets (0.5 mm) to obtain peripheral embolization. Smaller sized pledgets or powder should not be used, to avoid complete occlusion of smaller mucosal arteries, preventing the development of collateral flow. Gastric infarction may develop after embolization with Gelfoam powder (32). More proximal occlusion of the supplying artery, after reduction of flow has been achieved, must be performed with larger sized particles. Emboli of Gelfoam can be cut manually for this purpose, 1 to 2 cm long and with a diameter of 1 to 1.5 mm, according to the caliber of the catheter. The advantage is that when flow becomes slower or in complete absence of flow in the embolized vessel, smaller Gelfoam particles may reflux and cause unwanted embolization. Hepatic artery occlusions found a few days after embolization of the gastroduodenal artery are caused by displaced Gelfoam particles from the embolized artery (32). Larger particles stay firmly in the arterial bed and are a more stable embolizing agent. Polyvinyl alcohol and glues have been extensively used for arterial embolization. However, they produce a definitive closure of the artery. Proximal definitive embolization must be performed with non-resorbable mechanical devices. For reasons of cost, ease of introduction, and reliability, Gianturco coils are more convenient than detachable balloons. The availability of different sizes allows occlusion of smaller caliber vessels as well as definitive occlusion of the larger branches, such as the gastroduodenal or the hepatic artery.

Since flow may still be present through the coil, it is extremely important to reduce the distal peripheral flow in the artery by means of small Gelfoam particles. Also, after detachment of the coil, it is advisable to inject a few Gelfoam pledgets in order to completely occlude the vessels. Multiple coils can also be used for this purpose.

Percutaneous embolization must be performed with extreme care in order to avoid possible complications, which include infarction of the embolized intestinal segment and incidental embolization of other areas in back flow of embolizing agents into the general circulation (32). The presence and further development of extensive collateral circulation of the bowel wall usually prevents the development of infarction. However, very peripheral embolization with smaller-sized materials or powder may completely occlude collateral circulation with infarction of the area, especially if used after perfusion with vasoconstrictive agents. Moreover, in the postoperative patient there are vascular alternations with surgical interruption of normally developed collateral vessels, and infarctions are more prone to develop in such cases after embolization.

Backflow of the embolized material can occur during the procedure. In the later phase, when reduction of flow is present, the material should be delivered very slowly in order to avoid reversal of flow with dislodgement of emboli into the general circulation. Although performed without problems for therapeutic purposes, hepatic artery embolization with development of infarction and abscess has been described after gastroduodenal embolization (32). The dislodgment of Gelfoam pledgets into the splenic artery may result in splenic infarction with abscess formation (32).

When coils are used, the danger of unintended embolization is lower. However, with the use of lager-sized coils, cases of attachment of the coil to the tip of the catheter with further detachment into a peripheral vessel during retrieval of the catheter have been described (3).

Control of Hemorrhage in Specific Sites

Esophageal Bleeding

Bleeding originating from the upper two-thirds of the esophagus cannot be controlled by angiographic means, because the direct aortic origin of the arterial branches supplying this area makes the procedure extremely difficult.

The lower third and the cardioesophageal junction are vascularized by branches of the inferior phrenic artery or the left gastric artery. Angiographic control of hemorrhage at these sites is, therefore, possible with vasopressin infusion or embolization for bleeding due to Mallory-Weiss tears or esophagitis (4, 20).

Bleeding of Gastric Origin

The therapeutic angiographic approach and results obtained differ according to the underlying pathologic condition (Fig. 1).

Superficial mucosal lesions. Minimal anatomic lesions of the gastric mucosa are often the cause of gastric bleeding, Stress ulcers, diffuse hemorrhagic gastritis, alcoholic gastritis and Mallory-Weiss tears are included in this group.

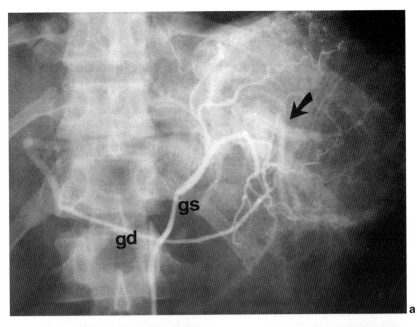

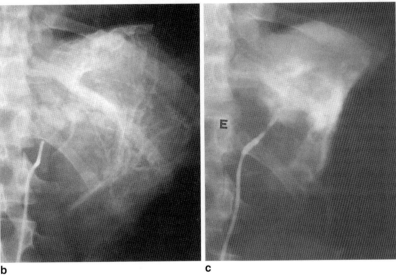

Fig. 1 **Acute upper gastro-intestinal bleeding of a gastric tumor in a 40-year-old inoperable patient.** Selective arteriography (**a, b**) of the left gastric artery (gs) shows a collection of extravasated contrast medium evident also in the later phase (**c**). After embolization there is complete occlusion of the left gastric artery. Hemorrhage was controlled by the embolization and did not recur through the right gastric artery (gd)

Vasopressin is highly effective if the bleeding originates from a single discrete point or if it is diffuse in nature. Selective infusion into the left gastric artery should be performed. Control of bleeding is obtained in 80 to 84% of patients (7, 12). However, lower rates of success (42%) have been described after infusion into the celiac trunk (7).

Recurrent bleeding rates of 18 and 25% have been documented after selective and nonselective infusion, respectively (7, 12).

Embolization should be used in case of recurrence, although it has also been proposed as the initial and only therapy in these patients (12, 26). However, occlusion of gastric vessels in patients who have undergone gastrojejunostomy may result in gastric infarction, and this therapy should be limited to those cases uncontrollable with vasopressin infusion (12, 24, 26).

Deeper mucosal and neoplastic lesions

In peptic ulcers, the anatomic lesions cannot always be controlled with vasopressin infusion alone, but it can be successful in a high percentage (80 to 84%) of cases (7, 12). However, due to chronic inflammatory changes, the gastric or duodenal wall may, in some cases, not completely respond to the vasoconstrictive agent. Moreover, erosion of a small to middle-sized artery is often the cause of the bleeding, and definitive occlusion of such a vessel is the recommended therapy in these instances (12, 26).

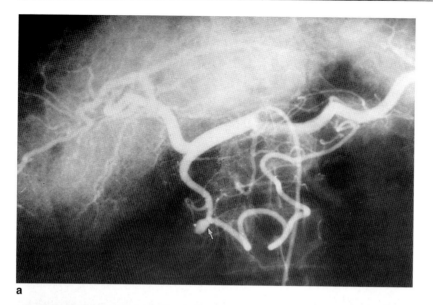

a

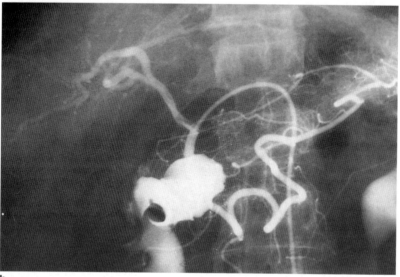

b

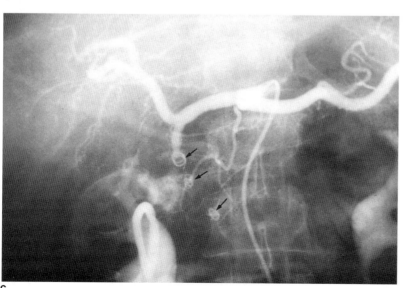

c

Fig. 2 **Acute upper gastrointestinal bleeding of duodenal origin in a 52-year-old patient** operated on three times for a bleeding ulcer without definitive control of hemorrhage.

a Injection of contrast medium in the celiac trunk shows only minimal alteration of the gastroduodenal artery (arrows).

b Only after selective injection in the latter vessel is large extravasation of contrast material into the duodenal lumen and outside of the bowel wall into a drainage catheter evident

c Embolization has been performed with three coils (arrows). The distal coil has been positioned in the vessel distally to the bleeding site, the medium at the level of the laceration, and the last at a more proximal level. Control injection of contrast material into the celiac trunk shows a complete occlusion of the vessel and definitive control of bleeding

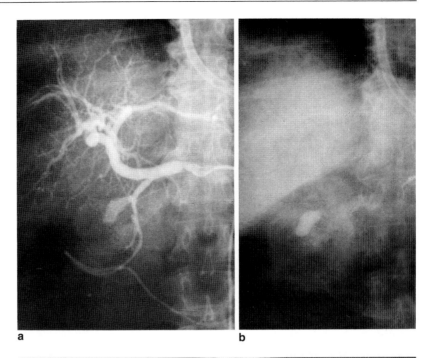

a   b

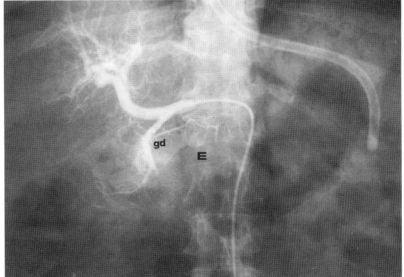

Fig. 3   **Gastrointestinal bleeding of duodenal origin in a 70-year-old woman** 10 days after operation on the biliary tree.
a Injection in the common hepatic artery
b An extravasation of contrast material is present lateral to the gastroduodenal artery and evident also in the later phase
c The gastroduodenal artery (gd) has been embolized and no further extravasation is evident. Note complete occlusion of the gastroduodenal artery after Gelfoam pledget embolization; no hepatic artery emboli are present

c

In hemorrhage due to a neoplastic lesion embolization is mandatory, since neoplastic vessels do not respond to vasoconstrictive agents. Of course, the procedure has a palliative purpose when surgery cannot be performed.

Bleeding of pyloroduodenal origin

The double blood supply to this anatomic area partially impairs the results of angiographic control. The bleeding can be due to a peptic ulcer not responding to medical therapy. A macroscopic arterial lesion, frequently located on the gastroduodenal artery or on one of its branches, is often the cause of the bleeding (Figs. **2, 3**). Embolization can therefore be indicated as a primary therapeutic modality (6, 12, 39). Vasopressin infusion has, in fact, been shown not to be very effective in this area, controlling the bleeding in 33% of cases, with recurrence rate of 31% (36).

Occlusion should be carried out with superselective embolization of the gastroduodenal artery, as peripheral as possible in order to avoid development of collateral circulation from the inferior pancreaticoduodenal arcades supplied by the superior mesenteric artery (Figs. **2, 3**). In many instances double occlusion is recommended: gastroduodenal artery and inferior pancreaticoduodenal artery, to prevent continuing bleeding from the arcade.

Definitive proximal occlusion of the gastroduodenal artery can be easily accomplished with mechanical devices, such as Gianturco coils (Fig. 2).

Postoperative bleeding

Upper GI bleeding may occur after total or partial gastrectomy in the immediate postoperative period or in a later phase. In the first case, slipped ligatures or indwelling tubes are the causes of the bleeding, whereas in the later phase the presence of anastomotic ulcers should be suspected (18, 27).

In both cases the diagnostic workup should include injection in the left gastric artery as well as in the jejunal branches supplying the jejunal side of the anastomosis. Detection of bleeding from one of the arteries indicates clearly which branch should be catheterized for angiographic control. More often, the jejunal arteries supply the contrast medium extravasation.

Vasopressin can be effective in these cases. However, when slipped ligatures or macroscopic arterial lesions are evident, embolization is the only effective procedure (18, 27).

Care should be taken not to perform embolization with Gelfoam powder or smaller particles, since previous surgery may prevent the development of collateral circulation and infarction may occur. The incidence of infarction is greater, when embolization of the left gastric artery is performed (12, 24, 26).

Upper gastrointestinal bleeding of other origins

A cirsoid aneurysm of a branch of the left gastric artery has been described by Athanasoulis (1) as an unusual cause of upper GI bleeding. Hemobilia can also present as upper GI bleeding (1). Traumatic hepatic artery laceration or ruptured aneurysm can be the underlying cause (21). Selective embolization of the hepatic artery branch supplying the lesion is the procedure of choice for definitive treatment (23, 29, 35).

Conclusion

Angiographic control of upper GI bleeding can be an effective therapeutic modality, when other noninvasive approaches have failed. Technical skill and good knowledge of the materials is required to increase success and limit the complication rate. The combined approach with vasopressin infusion and embolization can result in control of the hemorrhage in more than 90% of all cases (1).

References

1. Athanasoulis CA. Upper gastrointestinal bleeding of arteriocapillary origin. In: Athanasoulis CA, Pfister RC, Greene R, Roberson GH, eds. Interventional radiology; chapter 6. Philadelphia: Saunders 1982:55–89.
2. Athanasoulis CA. Severe upper gastrointestinal bleeding: diagnosis with arteriography. In: Barany FR, Torsoli A, eds. Gastrointestinal emergencies. Oxford: Pergamon 1977:153.
3. Chuang VP. Non-operative retrieval of Gianturco coils from abdominal aorta. AJR 1979;132:996–997.
4. Clark RA. Intra-arterial vasopressin infusion for treatment of Mallory-Weiss tears of the esophagogastric junction. AJR 1979;133:449–451.
5. Clark RA, Colley DP, Eggers FM. Acute arterial gastrointestinal haemorrhage: efficacy of transcatheter control. AJR 1981;136:1185–1189.
6. Davis, GB, Bookstein JJ, Coel MN. Advantage of intra-arterial over intravenous vasopressin infusion in gastrointestinal hemorrhage. AJR 1977;128:733.
7. Eckstein, MR, Kelemouridis V, Athanasoulis CA, Waltman AC, Feldman L, Van Breda A. Gastric bleeding: therapy with intra-arterial vasopressin and transcatheter embolization. Radiology 1984;152:643–646.
8. Gianturco C, Anderson JH, Wallace S. Mechanical devices for arterial occlusion. AJR 1975;124:428.
9. Gilbert DA, Silverstein FE, Auth DC. The nonsurgical management of acute non variceal upper gastrointestinal bleeding. In: Spaet T, ed. Progress in hemostasis and thrombosis; vol. 4. New York: Grune and Stratton, 1978:349.
10. Goldin AR. Control of duodenal haemorrhage with cyanoacrylate. Br J Radiol 1976;49:583.
11. Goldsman ML, Freeney PC, Tallman JM, Glombos JT, Bradley EL, Salam A, Dank T, Gordon IJ, Mennemeyer R. Transcatheter vascular occlusion therapy with isobutyl-2-cyanoacrylate (bucrylate) for control of massive upper gastrointestinal bleeding. Radiology 1978;129:41.
12. Gomes AS, Lois JF, McCoy RD. Angiographic treatment of gastrointestinal hemorrhage: comparison of vasopressin infusion and embolization. AJR 1986;146:1031–1037.
13. Goodman LS, Gilman A, eds. The pharmacological basis of therapeutics. 5th ed. New York: Macmillan, 1975:855.
14. Greenfield AJ, Waltman AC, Athanasoulis AC. Vasopressin in control of gastrointestinal haemorrhage: complications of selective intra-arterial versus systemic infusion. Gastroenterology 1979;76:1114.
15. Hoare AM. Comparative study between endoscopy and radiology in acute upper gastrointestinal haemorrhage. Br J Med 1975;1:27–30.
16. Kadir S, Athanasoulis CA. Angiographic management of gastrointestinal bleeding with vasopressin. RöFo 1977;127:111–119.
17. Kadir S, Athanasoulis CA. Catheter dislodgement: a cause of failure of intra-arterial vasopressin infusion to control gastrointestinal bleeding. Cardiovasc Radiol 1978;1:187.
18. Kerlan RK, Pogany AC, Burke DR, Ring EJ. Angiographic management of upper gastrointestinal bleeding. AJR 1986;147:1185–1188.
19. McCray RS, Martin F, Amir Ahmadi H. Erroneous diagnosis of hemorrhage from esophageal varices. Am J Dig Dis 1969;14:755.
20. Michal JA, Brody WR, Walter J, Wexler L. Transcatheter embolization of an esophageal artery for treatment of a bleeding esophageal ulcer. Radiology 1980;134:246.
21. Moreaux J, Bismuth M, Lagneau P. Les hemobilies postoperatoires par lesion arterielle pediculaire. Ann Chir 1966;20:368–375.
22. Nusbaum M, Baum S. Radiographic demonstration of unknown sites of gastrointestinal bleeding. Surg Forum 1963;14:374–375.
23. Perlberger R. Control of hemobilia by angiographic embolization. AJR 1977;128:672–673.
24. Prochaska JM, Flye MW, Johnsrude IS. Left gastric artery embolization for control of gastric bleeding: a complication. Radiology 1973;107:521–522.

25. Reuter RS, Chuang VP, Bree RL. Selective arterial embolization for control of massive upper gastrointestinal bleeding. AJR 1975;125:119.

26. Rösch J, Keller FS, Kozak B, Niles N, Dotter CT. Gelfoam powder embolization of gastric artery in treatment of massive small vessel gastric bleeding. Radiology 1984;151:365–370.

27. Rosenbaum A, Sigelman S, Sgrayregen S. The bleeding marginal ulcer: catheterization, diagnosis and therapy. AJR 1975;125:812.

28. Sherman LM, Shenoy SS, Cerra FB. Selective intra-arterial vasopressin: clinical efficacy and complications. Ann Surg 1979;298.

29. Sos TA, Lee JG, Wixson D, Sniderman KW. Intermittent bleeding from minute to minute in acute massive gastrointestinal hemorrhage: arteriographic demonstration. AJR 1978;131:1015–1017.

30. Steckel RJ, Ross G, Grollman JH. A potent drug combination for producing constriction of the superior mesenteric artery and its branches. Radiology 1968;91:579.

31. Steer ML, Silen W. Diagnostic procedures in gastrointestinal hemorrhage. N Engl J Med 1983;309:646–650.

32. Trojanowski JQ, Harrist TJ, Athanasoulis CA. Hepatic and splenic infarctions: complications of therapeutic transcatheter embolization. Am J Surg 1980;139:272.

33. Vosmick J, Dedlick AK, Mudler JL. Action of the triglycyl hemorrhage of vasopressin (Glypressin) in patients with liver cirrhosis and bleeding esophageal varices. Gastroenterology 1977;72:605.

34. Waldram R, Davis M, Nunnerly M. Emergency endoscopy and radiology in acute gastrointestinal haemorrhage in 50 patients with portal hypertension. Br Med J 1974;4:94.

35. Walter JF, Paaso BT, Cannon WB. Successful transcatheter control of massive hematobilia secondary to liver biopsy. AJR 1976;127:847–849.

36. Waltman AC, Greenfield AJ, Novellin RA, Athanasoulis CA. Pyloroduodenal bleeding and intra-arterial vasopressin: clinical results. AJR 1979;133:643–646.

37. Welch CA, Hedberg S. Gastrointestinal hemorrhage, part 1: general considerations of diagnosis and therapy. Adv Surg 1973;7:95.

38. White RJ, Ursic TA, Kaufman SL, Barth KH, Kim W, Gross GS. Therapeutic embolization with detachable balloons: physical factors influencing permanent occlusion. Radiology 1978;126:521.

39. White RJ, Giargiana FA, Bell W. Bleeding duodenal ulcer control: selective arterial embolization with autologous blood clot. JAMA 1974;229:456.

Lower Gastrointestinal Bleeding

J. Rösch

Lower gastrointestinal bleeding (LGIB) originates, in the majoritiy of patients, from lesions in the large bowel or small intestine. Up to 10% of patients with LGIB, however, have the bleeding source proximally to the ligament of Treitz, in the duodenum, stomach, or even in the esophagus (25). LGIB may be chronic and present with intermittent blood loss with positive fecal occult blood tests or melanotic stools and may cause chronic anemia. Acute LGIB often presents as single or recurrent episodes of massive hemorrhage requiring transfusions. Occasionally, the massive LGIB is continuous and results in significant hypovolemia and even exsanguination. The character of bloody stools depends on the length of time the blood remains in the bowel. Generally, a melanotic or tarry stool has its source in the small intestine, maroon stools, in the right colon, and red-blooded stools, in the left colon and rectum. With a fast bowel passage, however, fresh, red-colored stools may be caused by hemorrhage in the small intestine or even duodenum. LGIB can be caused by various bowel lesions. Diverticula, congenital arteriovenous malformation (AVM), acquired angiodysplasias, ischemia, inflammation, ulcerations, benign or malignant tumors, and iatrogenic injury such as polypectomy are among its more common causes (6, 25, 41, 46, 47). Aorto-enteric fistula, visceral artery aneurysm, small or large bowel varices, fecal disimpaction, hemobilia, or bleeding from the pancreas are some of its less common causes (31).

Angiographic techniques have been very useful in the management of LGIB. Since the first use of operative mesenteric arteriography in 1960 (27), angiography has become an important method in the diagnosis of chronic and acute LGIB (1). In the 1970 angiographic interventional techniques were introduced into the treatment of LGIB. Initially, selective, intra-arterial vasoconstrictive infusions were used for control of massive hemorrhage (3, 5, 37). Later, vascular occlusion by embolization was applied in selected patients to control massive LGIB, particularly in patients not responding to intra-arterial vasoconstrictive treatment (7, 12, 21).

Diagnosis

Techniques

In patients with possible bleeding from rectosigmoid or distal ileum, a Foley catheter should be placed in the bladder to prevent its filling with contrast medium, which may obscure sites of potential bleeding. We often select the left femoral artery for catheter introduction because it facilitates catheterization of the inferior mesenteric artery. Occasionally, we use a left axillary approach, particularly when superselective catheterization for embolization treatment is not possible from the femoral approach. In adult patients, we use a 6 Fr pigtail catheter for abdominal aortography and pelvic angiography. For selective angiography, we use 6 Fr Torcon visceral catheters preshaped according to the anatomy of the

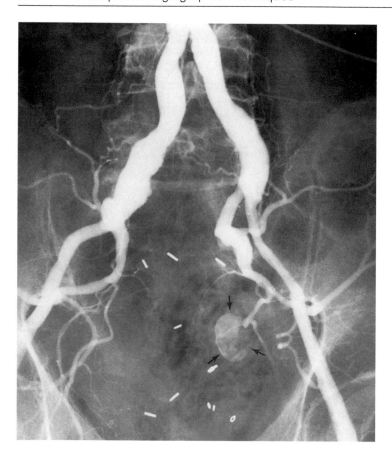

Fig. **1** **Acute bleeding from the rectal pouch** in a 61-year-old man with status postrectosigmoid carcinoma resection 5 years before this bleeding episode. Pelvic angiogram shows extravasation of contrast medium from a branch of the left hypogastric artery into the rectal pouch (arrows). The patient was treated surgically (the study was done in 1972)

individual vessels. For superselective catheterization, we use a long tapered tip (6 to 10 cm) 6 Fr Torcon catheter, a 5 Fr Torcon catheter introduced via a sheath, or a 3 Fr catheter coaxially introduced via a 6 Fr Torcon catheter. The 3 Fr catheter is manipulated with the help of a steering, platinum tip, 0.018 inch guide wire.

Abdominal aortography is performed only when an aorto-enteric fistula is suspected in patients with a history of aortic bypass surgery or aortic aneurysm. Aortograms are obtained in frontal and lateral projections, the latter demonstrating bleeding better, particularly if done in a prone position (34, 49). In patients with aorto-iliac grafts or an iliac aneurysm, aortography is complemented by pelvic angiography to exclude a leak at the distal anastomosis or aneurysmal rupture (23). Pelvic angiography is also an essential part of the study in patients after colectomy with residual rectal pouch and in pelvic malignancies, particularly those treated by radiation; their vascular bowel anatomy is usually grossly distorted, and they can bleed from the hypogastric arteries and their branches (14, 15) (Fig. **1**).

The majority of patients with LGIB, however, have only selective visceral studies. We usually perform the inferior mesenteric angiography first, and two injections are often needed to visualize the entire left colon from the splenic flexure to the rectum. If the study is negative, superior mesenteric angiography follows. In the case of a suspicious finding, superselective angiography of the area in question is performed, usually with a magnification technique to facilitate diagnosis of small lesions (Fig. **2**). When mesenteric angiograms are negative, celiac angiography is done. This not only helps to exclude bleeding from the stomach, duodenum, liver, and pancreas manifesting as LGIB, but also may visualize an accessory middle colic artery occasionally originating from the celiac artery, which may supply a bleeding site in the transverse colon (1). We perform 5-second contrast medium injections at a rate of 3 or 4 ml/s for inferior mesenteric arteriography and 7 to 9 ml/s for superior mesenteric and celiac arteriography. When pharmaco-angiography with the use of vasodilators is performed for better visualization of small vascular lesions, the injection rate is increased. We use tolazoline, usually 25 mg for the inferior mesenteric artery and 37.5 to 50 mg for the superior mesenteric artery injection. We dilute tolazoline in 10 cc of normal saline and inject it over 20 seconds. Angiography is done 30 seconds later. The injection rate of contrast medium is 4 to 5 ml/s for the inferior mesenteric and 9 to 12 ml/s for the superior mesenteric pharmaco-angiography. The first seven films are taken at a rate of one per second and are followed by seven films exposed every other

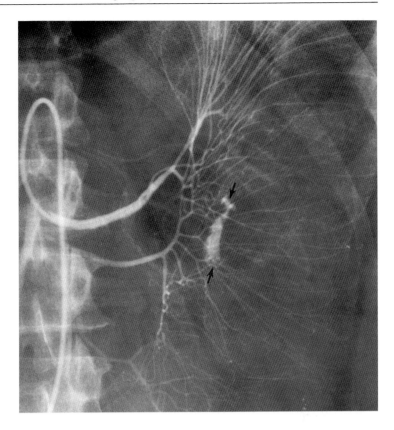

Fig. 2 **Acute bleeding from an ulcer** in a Roux-en-Y jejunal anastomosis in a 41-year-old man with sclerosing cholangitis and recent hepatojejunostomy. Superior mesenteric angiography was suggestive of active bleeding. Selective angiogram of a jejunal branch shows obvious extravasation of contrast medium into the jejunal lumen (arrows). Selective vasopressin infusion temporarily controlled the bleeding; the patient was stabilized and had elective surgery

second. In patients with portal hypertension, the filming is extended to 25 to 30 seconds.

We have used predominantly conventional large film angiography in the diagnosis of LGIB. Good results can also be obtained with digital subtraction angiography, particularly when increased peristalsis is not present. Digital substraction angiography is also very useful in interventional therapy, especially for studies during and after embolization to evaluate efficacy of the treatment.

The angiographer can also help the surgeon by facilitating exact localization of a bleeding site or vascular lesion at surgery by selective intraoperative mesenteric methylene blue injection (1). This is important mainly in lesions of the small intestine where exact intraoperative localization may be difficult (9). When a vascular lesion or active bleeding is found on a superior mesenteric angiogram, the 6 Fr catheter is advanced into the branch of the superior mesenteric artery supplying the segment of bowel containing the lesion. A 3 Fr catheter is then co-axially introduced through the 6 Fr catheter and advanced deep into the supplying artery close to the bowel wall. After magnification angiography confirms the position, both catheters are securely taped to the skin to prevent their dislodgment and are then perfused with heparinized saline. At surgery, 1 ml of methylene blue is injected through the small catheter

and the segmental bluish coloration of the small intestine exactly delineates the area of the lesion. This technique enables the surgeon to perform a selective, short-segment bowel resection (1).

Chronic Bleeding

In recurrent, low-grade rectal bleeding, angiography is of value in patients in whom other investigations, particularly barium studies and endoscopic examinations, failed to define the source of hemorrhage. Done on an elective basis, angiography is obtained to demonstrate a structural, vascular lesion in the bowel as a potential bleeding source. There is about a 45% chance of finding such a lesion, but the incidence of false-negative findings is high, about 13% (42). Use of pharmaco-angiography with vasodilators enhancing visualization of vascular lesions may decrease this high false-negative rate (44). Acquired angiodysplasias, congenital AVMs, and benign or malignant tumors are the most frequently found lesions. Angiography is particularly important in the diagnosis of lesions located in the small intestine, where they easily escape detection by other techniques. Visceral artery aneurysm, Meckel's diverticulum, or regional enteritis are among other causes of chronic LGIB.

Angiodysplasias or vascular ectasias are considered acquired lesions and are seen in the elderly, with a higher incidence in patients with aortic valvular disease (4, 6). They are often located in the cecum and ascending colon, but they may also occur in other parts of colon or small intestine (18). Angiodysplasias appear as small localized clusters of tangled arteries or vascular tufts with focal opacification of the bowel wall, 5 mm to 2 cm in size. They are often multiple and occasionally diffusely involve the cecum or a portion of the ascending colon (Fig. **3**). Angiodysplasias characteristically are supplied by slightly dilated arteries and show early drainage through dilated veins (4, 51). Angiographic findings of angiodysplasias are often difficult to document at surgery or examination of the resected specimen unless a special injection technique is used (1, 4).

AVMs of developmental origin can be localized in any portion of the bowel. They can be solitary lesions or part of a generalized vascular disorder such as Rendu-Osler-Weber syndrome (1, 32) (Fig. **4**).

Depending on the prevalence of their vascular structures, they have various angiographic appearances. They sometimes appear as multiple telangiectasias consisting of closely packed networks of minute vessels or small focal densities in the bowel wall. They are usually supplied by normal-sized vasa recta and do not exhibit early venous filling. Magnification angiography is helpful in their visualization. Cavernous hemangiomas occasionally occur in the bowel as clusters of vascular lakes supplied by an enlarged artery. When they exhibit early and dense venous drainage via an enlarged vein, they are called arteriovenous fistulas. Localized phlebectasias, which may present in the form of a few ectatic veins but more often as nets of enlarged veins, usually present a challenge to angiographic diagnosis. They show no arterial changes or only minimal arterial dilation and may not be obvious on a conventional study because of dilution of contrast medium in the

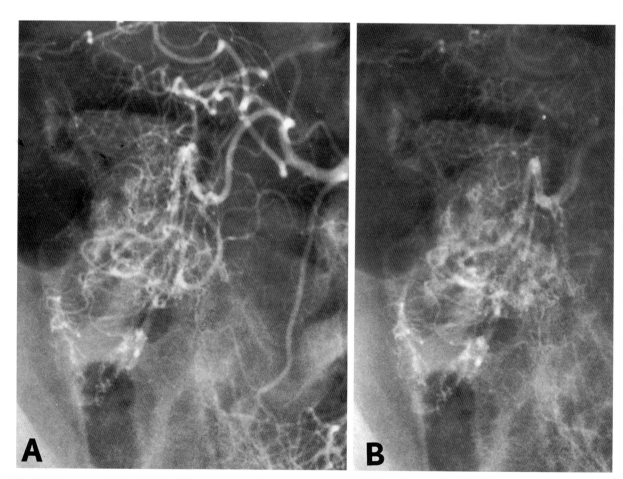

Fig. **3** **Large angiodysplasia of the cecum and ascending colon** in a 73-year-old woman causing recurrent low-grade rectal bleeding. The patient was treated surgically
A Close-up view of the arterial phase of superior mesenteric angiogram shows increased vascularity and multiple areas of tangled vessels in the cecum and ascending colon
B Parenchymal phase shows increased blush of the angiodysplastic area and dense filling of the draining veins

enlarged venous structures. Tolazoline pharmaco-angiography enhances their visualization and facilitates their diagnosis. Occasionally, diffuse venous angiomatosis is found involving a major portion of the bowel, such as the rectum or sigmoid colon. It consists of multiple vascular lakes, appearing in the late parenchymal and venous phase of the study.

Aneurysms of the visceral arteries may occasionally be the cause of chronic bleeding, particularly when localized close to the bowel lumen or inside the liver (hemobilia) or pancreas. However, even ruptured aneurysm of the splenic artery may cause LGIB (24). In patients with portal hypertension, varices are often seen in the mesentery close to the bowel wall, particularly at the sites of postsurgical adhesions. Their relationship to LGIB, however, is uncertain. If no other bleeding source is found to explain the recurrent rectal hemorrhage, a transhepatic portogram may be useful for detailed evaluation of the relationship of mesenteric varices to the bowel wall.

Tumors of the small intestine, particularly leiomyoma and leiomyosarcoma, present angiographically as hypervascular masses containing nets of irregular tumor vessels, tumor blush in the capillary phase and early dense filling of an enlarged draining vein or veins. Other tumors, such as carcinoid or melanoma, are less obvious. Carcinoid is usually diagnosed by its desmoplastic reaction in the mesentery causing irregularity and retraction of surrounding vessels. Melanoma of the small bowel may be hypervascular or present only by irregular encasement of surrounding vessels.

Acute Bleeding

In acute LGIB, angiography should be performed on an emergency basis when the patient is actively bleeding. Extravasation of contrast medium into the bowel lumen is the main finding to look for on angiograms. Finding of a hypervascular lesion, as described in chronic bleeding, is also important but is only suggestive of a potential bleeding source. Before angiography, patients should have digital rectal and proctosigmoidoscopic examinations to exclude an anal or rectal source of hemorrhage. Inferior mesenteric angiography can visualize hemorrhoids or rectal carcinoma; however, it is not

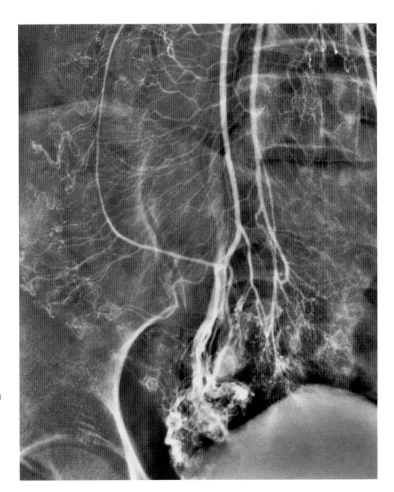

Fig. 4 **Large arteriovenous malformation of the terminal ileum and cecum and multiple telangiectasias of the ascending colon** in a 56-year-old woman with Rendu-Osler-Weber syndrome and recurrent LGIB. The patient also had multiple lung AVMs. The bowel AVM was treated surgically

the best and most economical way to diagnose the anorectal bleeding. However, when active rectal bleeding is found at proctoscopy, inferior mesenteric angiography can be useful for interventional control of the hemorrhage. Some gastroenterologists also perform colonoscopy, but in massive bleeding it may be difficult to perform and evaluate the study because of the presence of large amounts of blood in the colon. If performed, the finding of an approximate bleeding site helps to orient the angiographic search. Bleeding from a source in the upper gastrointestinal tract must always be excluded before angiography; aspiration of gastric content is helpful but endoscopy may be required to exclude a duodenal ulcer (6, 25).

Success of angiography in visualization of the site of hemorrhage by contrast medium extravasation

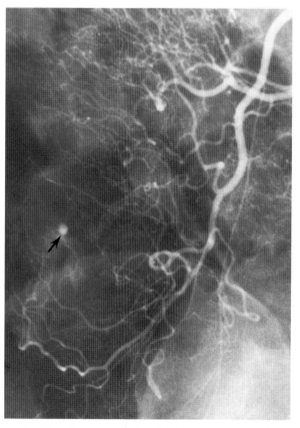

Fig. 5 **Recurrent, massive bleeding from a diverticulum in the ascending colon** in a 76-year-old man diagnosed with help of systemic heparinization. The patient had a negative angiographic study during his previous episode of active bleeding. When acute rectal hemorrhage recurred, he was given 6000 U of heparin intravenously. Follow-up superior mesenteric angiography showed active extravasation of contrast medium into a diverticular sac (arrow) with some spilling into the bowel lumen. Bleeding was controlled by selective infusion of vasopressin, and the patient was stabilized and had elective surgery

depends on proper timing of the examination; it has to be done during active bleeding at a rate greater than 0.5 ml/min. Patients with continuous massive rectal bleeding who are hemodynamically unstable are probably actively bleeding and should have angiography as the first study. In these patients angiography has shown an efficacy of visualization of extravasation in the range of 67 to 92% (1). In hemodynamically stable patients, activity of LGIB is much more difficult to assess, particularly when it originates from the small bowel or proximal colon. It is often intermittent in nature – from minute to minute (45) – and a bloody rectal discharge can continue for several hours after bleeding has actually stopped. Angiography performed solely on the basis of clinical criteria in hemodynamically stable patients has often been unrevealing, with an efficacy of between 30 to 40% (1, 36, 39). These patients should first be evaluated by radionuclide scanning for activity of bleeding. Technetium-labeled sulfur colloid or technetium-labeled red blood cells help to determine the state of hemorrhagic activity with higher sensitivity than angiography and can detect bleeding of as little as 0.1 ml/min. Active bleeding is demonstrated by the activity of extravasated scanning agent into the gut (19). If the radionuclide study is negative, the patient should be followed by sequential images to detect a temporarily ceased, intermittent bleeding. If the radionuclide scan is positive for active bleeding on either early or delayed images, angiography should be done without delay.

Efficacy of angiography in visualization of active bleeding in hemodynamically stable patients can be enhanced by several interventions that help to prolong, augment, or reactivate bleeding (38). In our experience, these interventions increased the diagnostic yield of angiography for demonstration of extravasation from 32 to 65%; moreover, they decreased the percentage of negative studies from 27 to 16% and the percentage of angiograms revealing only a vascular lesion as a possible bleeding source from 41 to 19% (39). Diagnostic interventions, however, should be used only in patients who constitute diagnostic and therapeutic dilemmas, in whom risk of prolonging or reactivating bleeding is outweighed by the potential diagnostic gains.

Anticoagulants, in particular heparin, are used first, with the objective of prolonging the existing bleeding until angiography can be performed (Fig. 5). We administer it intravenously at the time of angiography scheduling when the radionuclide scan indicates active bleeding – 1000 U of heparin per 10 kg body weight. After the study successfully demonstrates extravasation, protamine sulfate is given to neutralize the effects of heparin. Ten mg of protamine sulfate is sufficient to neutralize each 1000 U of heparin. The dose of protamine sulfate, however, should be decreased in proportion to the duration of he procedure, since heparin has a half-life of about 2 hours.

When angiography after heparin does not reveal extravasation or an obvious vascular lesion as the potential bleeding site, we proceed to a further interventional measure, use of the vasodilator tolazoline. This is aimed at augmentation of a low volume bleeding or reactivation of a recently ceased hemorrhage to a greater rate then 0.5 ml/min. Induced vasodilation opens constricted vessels at the bleeding site and, together with increased blood flow, can dislodge a soft fibrin plug in the bleeding vessel or vessels (Fig. 6). Selection of the site of tolazoline injection reflects the suspected level of bleeding. The superior mesenteric artery is most often injected because hemorrhage of the small intestine and right colon is difficult to diagnose without angiography (Fig. 7). The dose of tolazoline depends on the size of the catheterized vessel and the weight of the patient, and ranges from 25 to 50 mg. Tolazoline is injected over 20 seconds. Angiography follows 60 seconds later with increased volume and injection rate of contrast material.

Further interventional measures in the case of negative tolazoline angiography depend on the urgency of need for diagnosis. In most cases the catheter is left in the artery supplying the presumed bleeding area and the patient is returned to the ward. The indwelling catheter allows prompt repeat angiography when clinical evidence of active bleed-

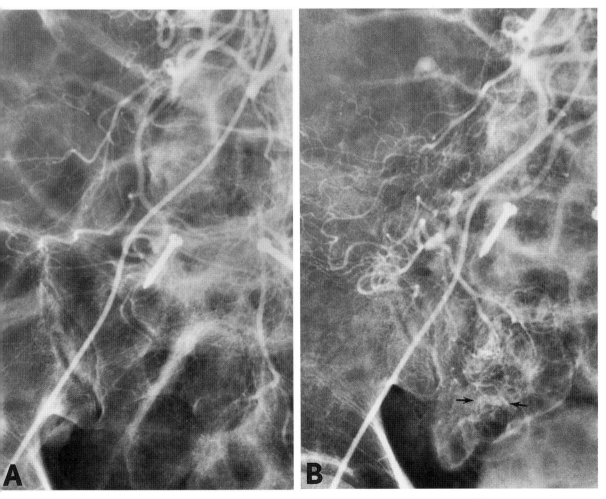

Fig. 6 Recurrent massive rectal hemorrhage from an angiodysplasia in the terminal ileum and cecum in a 70-year-old man diagnosed with use of heparin and tolazoline. The bleeding stopped with selective infusion of vasopressin, and the patient had elective surgery

A Superior mesenteric angiogram after heparin shows extensive vasoconstriction of the ileocolic artery branches and no angiodysplasia or extravasation

B Tolazoline pharmaco-angiogram, which was done after the patient had a large bowel movement of bloody stool, reveals enlarged ileocolic branches feeding several angiodysplastic areas in the terminal ileum and cecum and extravasation of contrast medium (arrows)

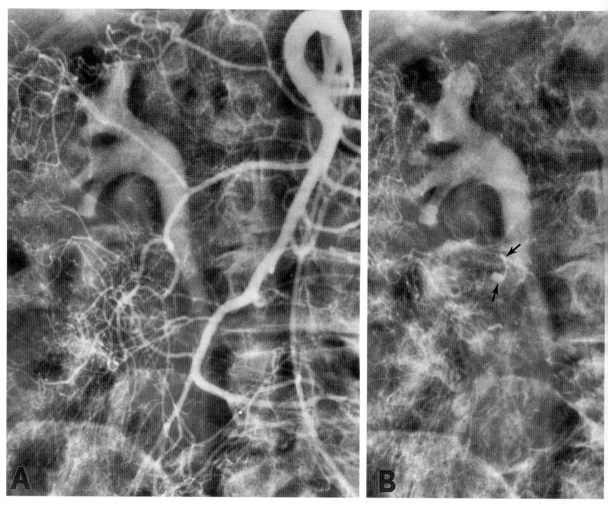

Fig. **7** **Acute bleeding from an ulcerated carcinoid tumor in the distal ileum** diagnosed with use of heparin and tolazoline. Superior mesenteric angiography after intravenous administration of 7500 U heparin was negative for active bleeding. Pharmaco-angiography performed after 50 mg of tolazoline revealed small extravasation of contrast medium (arrows) **A** Arterial phase **B** Parenchymal phase. The patient was treated surgically

ing recurs (Fig. **8**). The indwelling catheter is sometimes the only intervention in patients with severe underlying disease in whom use of heparin and tolazoline is contra-indicated (39). The catheter is left in the artery for 1 to 3 days, depending on the patient's clinical condition.

When the need for diagnosis is desperate, particularly when patients continue to bleed despite previous resective surgery for LGIB, use of fibrinolytic agents, streptokinase or preferably urokinase, is indicated to reactivate the bleeding (Fig. **9**). They are likely to reactivate bleeding that has recently ceased, no more than a few hours before the procedure. Their effectiveness decreases with the age of the hemostatic plug, and a short-term infusion will probably have no effect on an established, well-organized, hemostatic thrombus (38). Tolazoline

angiography is done after infusion of fibrinolytic agents, and the induced vasodilation and increased flow help to break up and dislodge the partially lysed thrombus and reactivate the bleeding. All decisions about the use of fibrinolytic agents have to be reached in conjunction with the referring gastroenterologist and surgeon, and blood for transfusions must be at hand for emergency needs. The fibrinolytic agent is infused selectively into the artery supplying the presumed bleeding site, usually the superior mesenteric, for 30 to 60 minutes. With streptokinase, we have used an initial bolus of 20000 to 40000 U, which was followed by infusion of 2000 to 4000 U/min, depending on the patient's weight. With urokinase, a dose of 20000 to 30000 U/min should be effective. These low-dose, short-term selective infusions usually do not cause a systemic

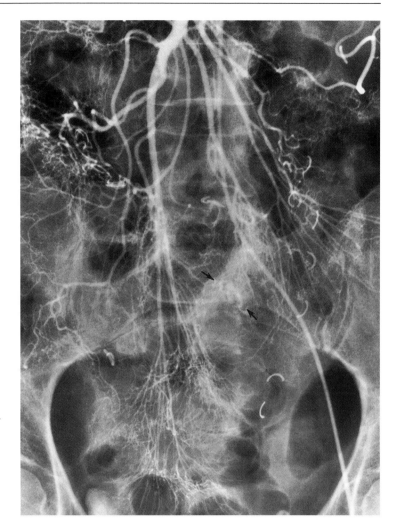

Fig. 8 **Acute bleeding from a lymphoma in the mid-ileum** in a 57-year-old woman diagnosed with use of an indwelling catheter. After a superior mesenteric angiographic study was negative for active bleeding, the catheter was left in place for 3 days. When the patient started to pass bloody stools again, a repeat study was done. It showed extravasation of contrast medium (arrows). The patient was treated surgically

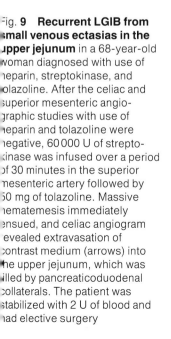
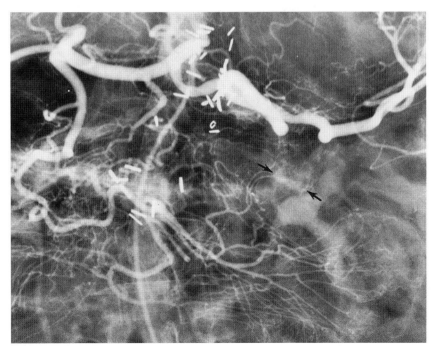

Fig. 9 **Recurrent LGIB from small venous ectasias in the upper jejunum** in a 68-year-old woman diagnosed with use of heparin, streptokinase, and tolazoline. After the celiac and superior mesenteric angiographic studies with use of heparin and tolazoline were negative, 60 000 U of streptokinase was infused over a period of 30 minutes in the superior mesenteric artery followed by 50 mg of tolazoline. Massive hematemesis immediately ensued, and celiac angiogram revealed extravasation of contrast medium (arrows) into the upper jejunum, which was filled by pancreaticoduodenal collaterals. The patient was stabilized with 2 U of blood and had elective surgery

thrombolytic effect with undesired remote bleeding; however, the induced bleeding may require corrective fluid replacement.

The diagnostic interventional measures have their contra-indications and carry certain risks. Use of heparin, tolazoline, and fibrinolytic agents is contra-indicated in patients with severe underlying disease combined with coagulopathy or impaired cardiac function. Tolazoline also should not be used in patients with hypotension. In patients with compromised renal function, the amount of contrast material has to be limited and the approach altered (39).

Contrast medium extravasation in LGIB is practically always at the arterial or arteriolocapillary level and appears early or later in the arterial phase of angiography and persists in the parenchymal and venous phases. With a large amount of blood or fluid in the involved bowel, it may become diluted and decrease in density or even disappear on later venous films. Its amount varies, depending on severity of bleeding, from barely visible extravasation to a massive pooling outlining or filling the lumen of the involved bowel, particulary in a brisk hemorrhage in the small intestine. Extravasations provoked by vasodilators and fibrinolytic agents are usually small and in a diagnostically borderline range (Fig. **7**). High-quality angiograms and careful evaluation are necessary not to overlook them. The majority of extravasations occur in a normal bowel and are easily diagnosed. Extravasation occurring in a pathologically changed bowel, as in a hypervascular wall due to inflammation or ischemia, angiodysplasia, AVM, or tumor may be difficult to differentiate from the underlying lesion. Late angiographic phases usually help; extravasation persists while filling of the underlying lesion disappears. Location of the extravasation is usually easy to establish by tracing the arterial branch feeding the bleeding point. With overlapping vessels of different portions of the bowel, it may be more difficult. It may happen in the hepatic flexure and low-positioned transverse colon where the right and middle colic arteries are superimposed over the inferior pancreaticoduodenal and jejunal arteries feeding the duodenum and the jejunum. In case of doubt, superselective angiography helps to find the exact site of hemorrhage.

The source of hemorrhage can be diagnosed only occasionally when bleeding originates from a hypervascular, well-defined lesion. Occasionally, a small rate diverticular bleeding also gives a characteristic picture of a well localized, rounded density by contrast medium filling of a diverticular sack (Fig. **5**). With major diverticular hemorrhage, contrast medium usually spills freely into the bowel lumen. In colonic diverticula, bleeding is more frequent and more severe from those localized in the right colon, even when more diverticula occur in the left colon

and sigmoid (1, 10). Postoperative bleeding is usually at the area of an anastomosis, particularly if metallic clips were used, and the area has to be well evaluated. With an aorto-enteric fistula, which most often occurs in the duodenum, the extravasation is seen only rarely and mainly on a lateral aortogram in the prone position (34, 35, 49). More often, however, only a pseudoaneurysm at the area of the graft anastomosis or a bulging aneurysm is seen (35, 49). Hemobilia, which has been occurring recently with increased incidence because of interventional percutaneous treatment of obstructive jaundice, often is manifested by hematemesis; with slow rate or intermittent hemorrhage, however, LGIB may be its only sign. With angiography a slow rate of hemorrhage into the biliary tract cannot be visualized and usually only indirect but diagnostically important findings such as intrahepatic pseudoaneurysm and arteriovenous or arterioportal fistula are obtained (29, 52). In bleeding from the pancreas, extravasation into the pancreatic duct is occasionally seen, but finding of a pseudoaneurysm or aneurysm of pancreatic vessels is also important for diagnosis.

Vasoconstrictive Therapy

Selective infusion of a vasoconstrictive agent into the artery supplying the bleeding site is the primary angiographic therapy for control of LGIB. Vasopressin, an aqueous solution of the pressor component of the posterior pituitary gland with significant antidiuretic properties, is presently the preferred choice of a vasoconstrictive agent. It causes contraction of the smooth muscle of the gastrointestinal tract and its vascular bed, especially of the capillaries, small arterioles, and venules. These effects are not antagonized by adrenergic blocking agents or prevented by vascular denervation. Vasopressin produces a significant and sustained reduction in splanchnic blood flow that is particularly intense in the areas where it is selectively infused. Vasopressin infusion has the best chance to control capillary, arteriolar, and small vessel bleeding in patients with normal hemocoagulation. Prolonged vasoconstriction enables formation of a stable clot at the area or areas of hemorrhage and control of the bleeding. In patients with a coagulopathy, usually temporary control only is achieved during infusion, and bleeding recurs after cessation of infusion. Vasopressin is also less effective in bleeding from larger arteries and vessels without smooth musculature, particularly those changed by tumor, inflammation, or abscess.

Vasopressin infusions should be considered for control of angiographically documented LGIB in all patients except those in whom it is contra-indicated. Clinically significant coronary artery disease, particularly recent myocardial infarction, advanced peripheral and cerebral vascular disease, congestive heart failure, and renal failure with fluid retention, are among the main contra-indications to vasopressin use. In patients with colonic diverticula, which represent the majority of LGIB in the elderly, vasopressin infusion can control hemorrhage in about 90% (1, 54). Bleeding recurs in only about 30% of patients, from hours to months after initial control (1); thus surgery can be prevented in more than half of patients with diverticular hemorrhage. Patients with lesions that have higher recurrence rates of rebleeding after infusion, such as major angiodysplasias, or with lesions that have to be treated surgically, such as large AVMs, can also profit from vasopressin infusions. The temporary control of

bleeding during infusion gives time to stabilize the patient so that surgery can be performed on an elective basis. If effective control of bleeding cannot be achieved by vasopressin infusion and the patient is not a surgical candidate, selective embolization of the bleeding artery should be considered.

Vasopressin is selectively infused into the artery supplying the bleeding point, usually the main trunk of the inferior or superior mesenteric artery (Fig. 10). In patients with an aberrant hepatic artery originating from the superior mesenteric, the infusion catheter has to be positioned beyond the origin of the aberrant artery to prevent loss of vasopressin to the liver. When a large ileocolic artery supplies bleeding in the distal ileum or cecum, the catheter

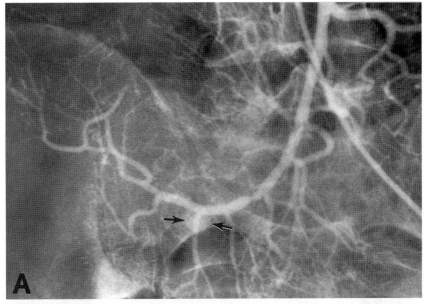

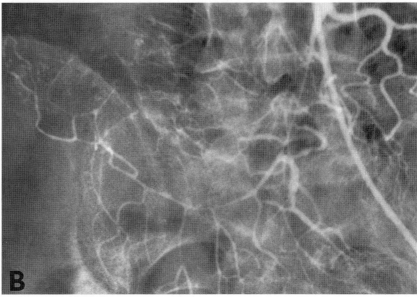

Fig. **10 Acute bleeding from an ileal ulcer** in a 64-year-old man with total colectomy successfully treated with selective vasopressin infusion
A Close-up view of mesenteric angiogram shows early extravasation in the ileum (arrows)
B Close-up view of angiogram done after 20-minute infusion of vasopressin at a rate of 0.3 U/min. shows extensive vasoconstriction and no extravasation. Infusion was continued for 24 hours at a rate of 0.2 U/min. No bleeding recurred, no surgery was necessary

can be advanced into a superselective position to achieve more localized effect. Direct jejunal artery infusion is preferable for bleeding control of a jejunal ulcer, particularly if it is at the site of a surgical anastomosis. In bleeding from an aberrant middle colic artery originating from the celiac artery, direct catheterization has to be achieved. In catheterization of these smaller vessels, the catheter has to be in a free position to allow adequate blood flow around it, otherwise infarction of the infused bowel can occur. In bleeding localized in the splenic flexure, which is supplied by both the inferior and superior mesenteric arteries, vasopressin infusion in one artery is not sufficient to control the bleeding, and a second catheter has to be introduced and used for simultaneous infusion of both mesenteric arteries. Vasopressin infusion, however, should not be used for control of hemobilia. After a short

vasoconstrictive effect, vasopressin causes paradoxical vasodilation of hepatic arterial vasculature with increased blood flow (2). Infusion of epinephrine is more effective for hepatic vasoconstriction, but selective embolization of the bleeding hepatic branch is usually the treatment of choice for hemobilia.

Vasopressin is diluted in normal saline or 5% dextrose into a $0.2\,\mu/ml$ concentration and is delivered with an arterial infusion pump. Infusion dose rate depends on the size of the catheterized artery. For the inferior mesenteric artery, the initial rate is 0.1 to $0.2\,\mu/min$ and for the superior mesenteric artery 0.2 to $0.3\,\mu/m$. An initial 20-minute test infusion is performed in the angiograph room and is followed by a repeat angiogram to assess the efficacy of the infusion. If no further bleeding is demonstrated and no excessive vasoconstriction is seen, the catheter is secured at the groin, and the infusion is

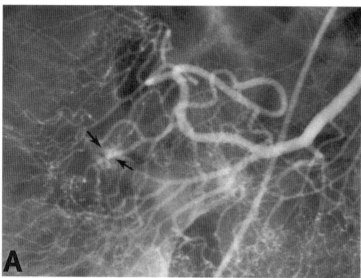

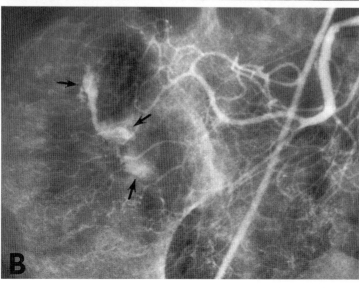

Fig. **11 Acute bleeding from an ulcer in the distal ileum** in a 61-year-old woman with Crohn's disease and colectomy not responding to vasoconstrictive infusion; surgical treatment was done
A Close-up view of selective ileal angiogram reveals extravasation of contrast medium (arrows)
B Close-up view of angiogram done after 20-minute selective infusion of vasopressin at a rate of 0.3 U/min. shows extensive vasoconstriction and significantly increased extravasation

continued in the intensive care unit. If bleeding persists after a 20-minute vasoconstrictive infusion, the vasopressin dose is increased, but no more than 0.3 µ/min for the inferior mesenteric and 0.4 µ/min for the superior mesenteric artery for a further 20-minute test infusion. Failure to control the bleeding using these high doses or absence of significant vasoconstrictive effect on follow-up angiograms indicates that safe vasoconstrictive control cannot be expected, and alternative therapeutic methods should be used (Fig. 11). With a good vasoconstrictive response on follow-up angiograms, infusion is continued at full dose rate for 12 to 24 hours, depending on the patient's condition and clinical response. The initial rate is then halved for the ensuing 24 hours and the infusion is discontinued if there is no clinical evidence of further bleeding. The catheter may be kept in place with a low volume 5% dextrose infusion for another 12 to 24 hours to be ready for repeat vasopressin infusion should the bleeding clinically recur.

During the first 20 minutes of vasopressin infusion, some patients may experience abdominal cramps or abdominal pain because of vasopressin-induced bowel contractions, which may result in a beneficial emptying of the bowel of the accumulated blood clots. The cramps and pain should subside in 30 minutes, and their persistence or later occurrence is indicative either of too high a dose rate or of dislodgment of the catheter tip and selective infusion into a small branch. A decreased infusion rate and check of the catheter position will help to define the cause of patient discomfort.

Selective mesenteric vasoconstrictive treatment is not without risk, and complications may result from the prolonged presence of an intravascular catheter or from the vasopressin infusion per se (1, 22, 54). Vascular spasm and thrombosis may occur at the puncture site of the femoral artery and result in leg ischemia; spasm and thrombosis of the infused artery or arteries may cause bowel infarction. Chest pain, cardiac arrhythmias, in particular bradycardia, and even myocardial infarction may occur. The antidiuretic effect of vasopressin may lead to decreased diuresis, edema, and hyponatremia. These complications have been reported mainly with prolonged use of superior mesenteric vasopressin infusions in cirrhotic patients for control of bleeding from gastroesophageal varices where infusions lasted for 5 to 10 days (17). With treatment of arterial bleeding, for which a relatively short-term infusion is normally used, the incidence of complications is substantially lower and can be expected in a range of 3 to 5%. It can be kept at a minimum by strict observance of contra-indications, limiting the time of intravascular catheter placement and keeping the dose rate of vasopressin at the lowest effective level.

Embolization Therapy

Embolization of the bleeding artery or arteries of the small intestine and large bowel has to be approached with much greater caution than that of the stomach and duodenum, where a multiple-vessel blood supply minimizes the risk of significant ischemic injury. The small intestine and large bowel, with the exception of the splenic flexure and distal rectum, are supplied by only one artery and have less collateral capacity than the stomach and duodenum. Small bowel collaterals consist of vascular arcades in the mesentery close to the bowel wall; there is usually a single arcade in the jejunum and several arcades in the ileum. Large bowel arteries are interconnected by branches in the mesentery, forming a marginal artery. Vasa recta of both the small intestine and large colon arise predominantly as single arteries and do not communicate directly. In the bowel wall, however, their branches anastomose and form rich intramural vascular networks, particularly at the level of submucosal arterioles. Because of the paucity of larger collaterals, embolization therapy of LGIB involves a significant risk of ischemic injury. Review of the reported cases indicates that this risk may range between 15 and 25% for embolization in the small intestine and 10 and 15% for the large bowel (8, 20, 22, 33, 40, 53). Ischemic injury may be acute and manifested by transmural necrosis and bowel infarction. Ischemic necrosis involving only mucosa may cause bowel stricture after healing (30). Risk of bowel injury, however, can be kept at a minimum by careful selection of patients and performance of the embolization procedure.

Embolization is usually used as a secondary angiographic intervention for control of massive LGIB after vasoconstrictive infusion failure and when the patient is not a good candidate for emergency surgery. Embolization, however, can easily be justified as a primary procedure for fast hemostasis when the patient is bleeding profusely, his condition is rapidly deteriorating, and large amounts of blood are necessary for stabilization. It should be considered particularly in lesions that respond poorly to vasoconstrictive treatment, such as bleeding from major AVMs or large vessels. In this situation, embolization may be a life-saving procedure replacing emergency surgery, which has high morbidity and mortality, particularly in elderly and debilitated patients. It allows stabilization of the patient, and with lesions requiring surgical removal, an elective operation can be performed with much less risk. In lesions amenable to medical treatment, embolization may be the definitive therapy. If bowel ischemia requiring surgery occurs, the operation is usually done on an improved, stabilized patient, and usually no more bowel has to be removed than would ordinarily be resected if surgery had been performed for the initial control of bleeding. Embolization may also be the only effective palliative treatment for control of bleeding from inoperable tumors, particularly when located in the rectum (14, 15).

Safety of the bowel embolization is closely related to the techniques used, and to decrease its risks, several rules should be followed.

The embolization has to be superselective and only the bleeding artery or its small feeder or feeders should be occluded. Direct catheterization and embolization of the bleeding artery is often possible in hypervascular lesions such as larger AVMs or angiodysplasias that have enlarged feeding arteries. Occasionally a nidus of this lesion may be directly

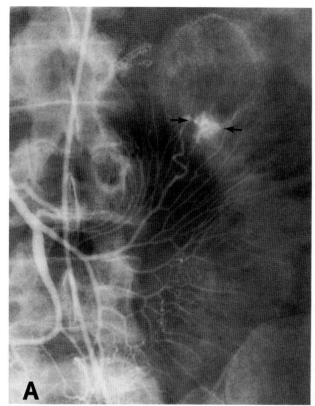

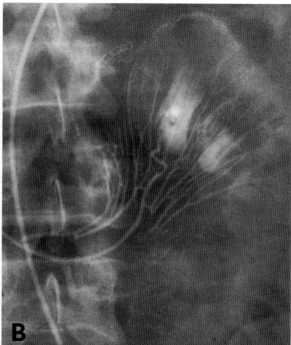

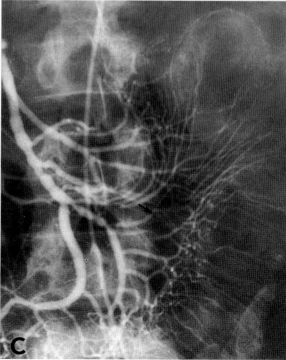

Fig. **12   Massive bleeding from a recent surgical anastomosis in the jejunum** in a 35-year-old man with hepatitis and coagulopathy. Bleeding was controlled for 2 days by selective infusion of vasopressin but recurred immediately after discontinuation of infusion. It was successfully treated by selective embolization. No complications developed

A Selective angiogram of a jejunoileal branch shows extravasation of contrast medium at the area of metallic clips (arrows)

B Selective angiogram of the bleeding artery using a long tapered 6 Fr Torcon catheter shows increased extravasation. The catheterized artery was occluded with one Gelfoam strip

C Follow-up angiogram shows occlusion of the embolized artery (arrow), absence of extravasation, and collateral filling of the embolized area. Postcatheterization spasm of the larger arteries is also present

catheterized and occluded. Embolization of lesions supplied by normal-sized artery or arteries is technically more demanding, but with use of long tapered 6 Fr Torcon catheters or 3 Fr coaxial catheters, a high degree of selective catheterization can usually be achieved (Fig. **12**). During catheterization, care has to be taken to minimize major spasm and avoid intimal dissection of vessels not supplying the bleeding site. Decreased flow to the nonembolized bowel diminishes chances of development of collaterals and increases the risks of significant bowel ischemia. If major spasm develops during catheterization, selective intra-arterial administration of small doses of nitroglycerin and a few minutes of waiting help to decrease or resolve it. Premedication with calcium antagonists may also be useful for prevention of the catheter-induced spasm.

Except in cases in which direct occlusion of a nidus of a hypervascular lesion is possible, **embolization should not be peripheral.** It should spare distal communicating arcades in the small intestine, the marginal artery in the large bowel, and intramural vascular networks. Only the distal intestinal branches and proximal communicating arcades should be occluded. The goal of embolization is to decrease the pulse pressure at the bleeding site and thus allow for spontaneous hemostasis. Such a type of embolization is safe and usually effective in patients with normal coagulation. In patients with coagulation defects, however, it may not be safe. Bleeding may continue from collateralization and a decision about more distal and less safe embolization has to be made on the basis of the patient's condition. Sometimes it is necessary to take a higher risk and manage complications later. In patients with bleeding from rectal lesions, particularly malignant tumors, embolization can be more aggressive (14, 15, 28). Because of dual supply of the rectum from the

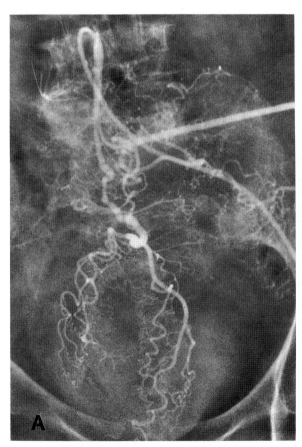
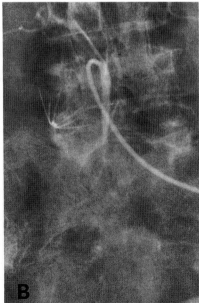

Fig. **13** **Recurrent massive rectal bleeding from uterine carcinoma invading the rectum and sigmoid colon** in a 74-year-old woman. Diffuse bleeding in rectum was seen at proctoscopy, and the patient, who was not a surgical candidate, was referred for angiographic treatment. Bleeding was controlled by embolization of the superior hemorrhoidal artery with Ivalon particles. No complication developed. The patient has a Mobin-Uddin filter in the right common iliac vein
A Inferior mesenteric angiogram reveals encasement of the superior hemorrhoidal artery and diffuse hypervascularity of the rectum and sigmoid colon. Catheter for embolization was placed below the origin of the large sigmoidal branch
B Follow-up angiogram after embolization shows occlusion of the superior hemorrhoidal artery. The large sigmoidal branch went into spasm during catheterization

inferior mesenteric and hypogastric arteries, the superior hemorrhoidal artery can be occluded with low risk of ischemic consequences (Fig. **13**).

The number of occluded vessels has to be kept to a minimum, and optimally only the bleeding artery should be occluded. After embolization of the catheterized vessel, the catheter is pulled back proximally and an angiogram obtained to document the distal vessel occlusion and absence or persistence of bleeding. With ongoing extravasation, another branch feeding the bleeding site should be catheterized and occluded, and a follow-up angiogram obtained. Embolization of more than one branch, however, increases the risk of ischemia and bowel infarction, and decisions about the number of branches to be occluded when bleeding persists on follow-up angiograms has to be made again, depending on the patient's condition and location of the bleeding lesion.

No vasopressin infusion should be done after embolization because it would impair chances of development of collateral circulation. Vasoconstrictive effect would add to the vascular compromise and increase the risk of bowel infarction. No definitive answer, however, can be drawn about the use of vasopressin infusion before embolization. Some of the reported bowel infarctions were after embolization preceded by vasopressin infusion (40, 53). Other embolizations were complication-free, even when done shortly after a vasoconstrictive infusion (7, 8, 21, 33). The majority of patients for embolization treatment of LGIB, however, will have had preceding ineffective vasopressin infusions. Common sense dictates waiting as long as possible after infusion until the effect of vasopressin disappears or substantially diminishes before embolization is performed. Not only will collateral circulation have a better chance to develop, but superselective catheterization will also be easier to perform than in constricted vessels highly sensitive to catheter and guide wire manipulation.

Choice of the proper occlusive material is critical for safety of embolization. Autogenous blood clot mixed with aminocaproic acid was explored in canines (13) and was used successfully in patients (8, 12). However, the clots have a tendency to fragment and migrate peripherally, and thus carry a risk of occlusion of the vasa recta and intramural vascular networks. For the majority of patients with LGIB, the material of choice has been surgical gelatin, Gelfoam, in particulate form (8, 11, 12, 14, 22, 33, 43, 53). Gelfoam powder has to be avoided for LGIB embolization because of its peripheral penetration and occlusion of vascular networks in the bowel wall. Particles of Gelfoam are easily delivered through 5 Fr and 6 Fr catheters and achieve a rapid and temporary vessel occlusion that persists from a few days to a few weeks. This is satisfactory for the majority of patients with LGIB. Particle size of Gelfoam for embolization depends on the diameter of the vessel to be occluded. We use small strips (torpedos) 2 to 3 mm in diameter and 3 to 5 mm in length, and inject one strip at a time. It is rolled into a cylinder, compressed, and inserted into the nozzle of a tuberculin syringe containing contrast medium. We inject the Gelfoam strip directly into the catheter without a stopcock and then use a 5 ml syringe filled with contrast medium to propel the strip through the catheter tip with the least force and slowest speed possible. In this way selective occlusion of the catheterized vessel can be achieved without Gelfoam particle passage into the periphery or its refluxing into another branch. Carefully injected contrast medium helps to check he degree of obstruction and the need for injection of more strips. Strict attention to aseptic technique is necessary because wetted Gelfoam shows rapid contamination.

With use of 3 Fr catheters and peripheral catheterization of vessels 1 to 2 mm in diameter where Gelfoam particles are difficult to inject, we use occlusive Gianturco mini-springcoils 2 mm in size. They can be easily and safely introduced through these small catheters and stay at the point of placement in a small artery. They result in an instantaneous, localized, permanent occlusion and favor development of peripheral collateral circulation. Cyanoacrylate tissue adhesive (Isobutyl-2-cyanoacrylate [IBC]) is another possible occlusive material that can be used with 3 Fr catheters. It causes an immediate, permanent, and, mixed with iophendylate, a controlled vessel occlusion. In my opinion, however, it should be used only as a last resort in patients with malignant diseases, particularly tumors, when other occlusive materials or devices are not suitable to use or have failed to occlude the lesion.

A long-term occlusive agent, polyvinyl alcohol (Ivalon) also has its place in embolization treatment of LGIB. It is suitable mainly for embolization of hypervascular lesions supplied by enlarged arteries when a catheter can be advanced close to or directly into the lesion. Delivered through 5 Fr or 6 Fr catheters as small (0.5 to 1 mm) particles or as larger (1 to 2 mm) plugs, it can directly occlude the vascular nidus of the lesion and result in long-term bleeding control (48, 50).

With bleeding from medium-sized vessels larger than 2 to 3 mm in diameter, which may happen with hemobilia and pancreatic bleeding, a 3 mm springcoils can be used for occlusion, if the bleeding vessel can be directly catheterized (52) (Fig. **14**). When direct catheterization is impossible, a small detachable balloon can be a useful occlusive device. Its location can be checked with contrast medium injection after being positioned, and it is not detached until it is lodged properly in the bleeding vessel (29).

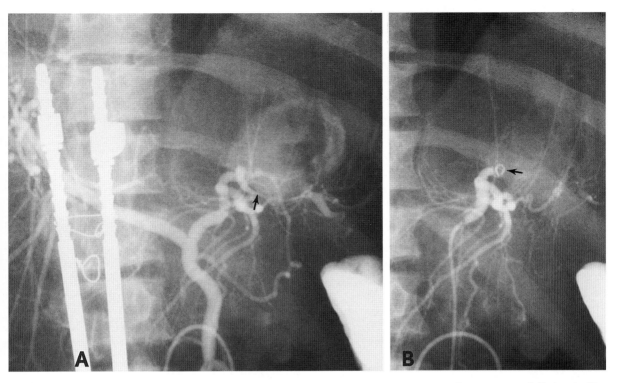

Fig. **14   Post-traumatic hemobilia in a 17-year-old male presenting with recurrent melena successfully treated by selective embolization; no complication developed**
A Close-up view of selective hepatic angiogram in a slightly oblique projection reveals a large (6 by 5 cm) pseudo-aneurysm in the left liver lobe originating from a third order branch (arrow).
B Selective left hepatic angiogram after occlusion of the involved branch with a 3 mm Gianturco springcoil (arrow) placed through a long tapered-tip 6 F Torcon catheter shows absence of aneurysm filling

Bleeding from a larger vessel, particularly from a hypogastric artery aneurysm perforating into the rectum, is best managed by a combination of occlusive devices and materials. Depending on the size of the aneurysm, various sizes of occlusive springcoils (5, 8, 12 mm) are placed directly into the aneurysmal sac or its feeding vessel. With a large aneurysm, multiple coilsprings often have to be used. Thrombin, particulate occlusive material (Gelfoam or Ivalon), or liquid polymer (IBC) can then be injected and interspersed between the springcoils to accelerate thrombus formation and thrombosis of the entire aneurysm or its feeder (Fig. **15**).

Bowel embolizations should be done with antibiotic coverage because of easy contamination of Gelfoam and presence of bowel bacteria, which can easily migrate across the ischemic bowel wall (22).

Successful occlusion of the bleeding vessel or vessels results in immediate cessation of bleeding and the patient's rapid stabilization. Bloody stools usually continue for a few hours because of the large amount of blood retained in the bowel from previous bleeding. With occlusion of a small-sized vessel, the patient usually does not have any significant discomfort or has only minor abdominal pain persisting for a few hours. With occlusion of a larger mesenteric branch or several branches supplying larger segments of bowel, discomfort and abdominal pain are usually significant, persist for a few days, and require narcotic medication. Localized ileus is sometimes present with abdominal distension. A febrile reaction and mild leukocytosis often occur, even with small vessel embolization; however, they need not be signs of bowel infarction. They can be caused by migration of bowel bacteria across the wall due to transient loss of integrity of ischemic bowel (22). All these symptoms should resolve in 2 to 4 days. If they persist, and particularly if they increase in intensity, the major complication of embolization, significant bowel ischemia and infarction, has to be considered. All decisions about embolization therapy of LGIB have to be made together with clinicians and surgeons. Surgeons should follow the patient after embolization as primary physicians and make decisions about the need for surgical intervention if complications of embolization develop.

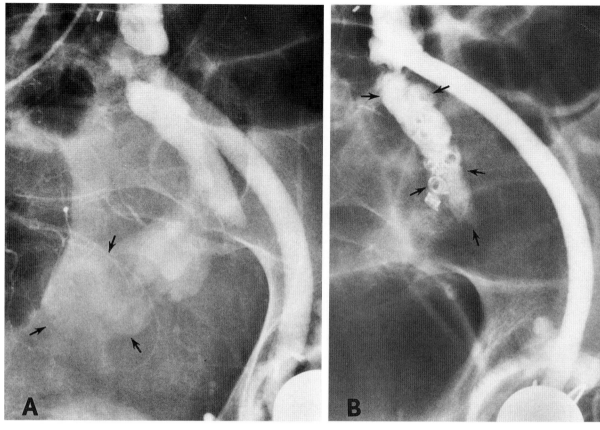

Fig. 15   Acute, recurrent rectal hemorrhage from a large aneurysm of the left hypogastric artery eroding into the rectum in a 78-year-old man with recent left common iliac-femoral graft. Ligation of the hypogastric artery was attempted at surgery with only partial success. Placement of multiple occlusive springcoils and large Gelfoam particles decreased bleeding, which was finally controlled by cast occlusion by tissue adhesive – IBC

A Late phase of pelvic angiogram reveals diffusely dilated left hypogastric artery entering into a large aneurysm from which contrast medium extravasates into the rectum (arrows)

B Follow-up common iliac angiogram shows a cast occlusion of the hypogastric artery with springcoils and tissue adhesive opacified by tantalum (arrows) and no filling of aneurysm

Conclusion

Diagnosis and catheter therapy of LGIB has been and will continue to be an important part of interventional angiographers' work. Even with refinement and wider use of endoscopic techniques, there will be much need for angiographic diagnosis for chronic, recurrent, and acute, massive bleeding. Angiography is particularly important for diagnosis of hemorrhage from lesions of the small intestine. Interventional diagnostic measures promise to improve significantly the diagnostic efficacy of emergency angiography in patients who constitute diagnostic dilemmas. Interventional therapeutic techniques have much to offer for the control of LGIB. Selective infusion of vasopressin is the primary technique for treatment of active hemorrhage and should be considered in all patients except where the use of vasopressin is contra-indicated. Embolization techniques are slowly gaining in popularity even when they carry a signifi-

cant risk of complications. Careful selection of patients and performance of the procedure, however, can decrease risks of embolization to an acceptable minimum, with gains outweighing risks of the treatment.

References

1. Athanasoulis CA. Lower gastrointestinal bleeding. In: Athanasoulis CA, Pfister RC, Greene RE, Roberson GH eds. Interventional radiology. Philadelphia: Saunders, 1982:115–148.
2. Barr JW, Lakin RC, Rösch J. Vasopressin and hepatic artery: effect of selective celiac infusion of vasopressin on the hepatic artery flow. Invest Radiol 1975;10:200.
3. Baum S, Nusbaum M. The control of gastrointestinal hemorrhage by selective mesenteric arterial infusion of vasopressin. Radiology 1971;98:497.
4. Baum S, Athanasoulis CA, Waltman AC, Galdabini J, Schapiro RH, Warshaw AL, Ottinger LW. Angiodysplasia of the right colon: a cause of gastrointestinal bleeding. AJR 1977;129:789.

5. Baum S. Angiography and the gastrointestinal bleeder. Radiology 1982;143:569.
6. Boley SJ, Brandt LJ, Frank MS. Severe lower intestinal bleeding: diagnosis and treatment. Clin Gastroenterol 1981;10:65.
7. Bookstein JJ, Naderi MJ, Walter JF. Transcatheter embolization for lower gastrointestinal bleeding. Radiology 1978;127:345.
8. Bookstein JJ. Angiographic diagnosis and transcatheter therapy and lower gastrointestinal bleeding. In Wilkins RA, Viamonte M, eds. Interventional radiology. Oxford: Blackwell, 1982:111–136.
9. Briley CA, Jackson DC, Johnsrude IS, Mills SR. Acute gastrointestinal hemorrhage of small-bowel origin. Radiology 1980;136:317.
10. Casarella WJ, Galloway SJ, Taxin RN, Follett DA, Pollock EJ, Seaman WB. "Lower" gastrointestinal tract hemorrhage: new concepts based on arteriography. AJR 1974;121:357.
11. Chalmers AG, Robinson PJ, Chapman AH. Embolisation in small bowel haemorrhage. Clin Radiol 1986;37:379.
12. Cho KJ, Reuter SR. Embolic control of superior mesenteric artery hemorrhage caused by abdominal abscesses. AJR 1977;128:1041.
13. Cho KJ, Schmidt RW, Lenz J. Effects of experimental embolization of superior mesenteric artery branch on the intestine. Invest Radiol 1979;14:207.
14. Chuang VP, Wallace S, Zornoza J, Davis LJ. Transcatheter arterial occlusion in the management of rectosigmoidal bleeding. Radiology 1979;133:605.
15. Chuang VP, Charnsangavej C, Carrasco H, Wallace S, Soo CS, Bechtel W, Strohlein J. Transcatheter treatment of gastrointestinal hemorrhage in cancer patients. J Intervent Radiol 1986;1:43.
16. Clark RA, Colley DP, Eggers FM. Acute arterial gastrointestinal hemorrhage: efficacy of transcatheter control. AJR 1981;136:1185.
17. Conn HO, Ramsby GR, Storer EH, Milton G, Mutchnick MG, Joshi PH, Phillips MM, Cohen GA, Fields GN, Petroski D. Intraarterial vasopressin in the treatment of upper gastrointestinal hemorrhage: a prospective, controlled clinical trial. Gastroenterology 1975;68:211.
18. Emanuel RB, Weiser MM, Shenoy SS, Satchidanand SK, Asirwatham J. Arteriovenous malformations as a cause of gastrointestinal bleeding: the importance of triple-vessel angiographic studies in diagnosis and prevention of rebleeding. J Clin Gastroenterol 1985;7:237.
19. Froelich JW, Winzelberg GG. Radionuclide detection of gastrointestinal hemorrhage. In: Athanasoulis CA, Pfister RC, Greene RE, Roberson GH, eds. Interventional radiology. Philadelphia: Saunders, 1982:149–156.
20. Gerlock AJ, Muhletaler CA, Berger JL, Halter SA, O'Leary JP, Avant GR. Infarction after embolization of the ileocolic artery. Cardiovasc Intervent Radiol 1981;4:202.
21. Goldberger LE, Bookstein JJ. Transcatheter embolization for treatment of diverticular hemorrhage. Radiology 1977;122:613.
22. Gomes AS, Lois JF, McCoy RD. Angiographic treatment of gastrointestinal hemorrhage: comparison of vasopressin infusion and embolization. AJR 1986;146:1031.
23. Husted J, Dempsey D. Angiographic management of arteriocolic fistulae. Cardiovasc Intervent Radiol 1986;9:158.
24. Koehler PR, Nelson JA, Berenson MM. Massive extra-enteric gastrointestinal bleeding: angiographic diagnosis. Radiology 1976;119:41.
25. Levinson SL, Powell DW, Callahan WT, Jones JD, Kinard HB, Jackson AL, Lapis JL, Drossman DA. A current approach to rectal bleeding. J Clin Gastroenterol 1981;3:9.
26. Lyonnet D, Pinet A. Hémorragies digestives graves. Ann Radiol (Paris) 1981;24:413.
27. Margulis AR, Heinbecker P, Bernard HR. Operative mesenteric arteriography in the search for the site in unexplained gastrointestinal hemorrhage. Surgery 1960;48:534.
28. Merland JJ, Thiébot J, Tubiana JM, Roche A. Angiography and emergency embolisation of digestive haemorrhages. J Belge Radiol 1978;61:83.
29. Mitchell SE, Shuman LS, Kaufman SL, Chang R, Kadir S, Kinnison ML, White RI. Biliary catheter drainage complicated by hemobilia: treatment by balloon embolotherapy. Radiology 1985;157:645.
30. Mitty HA, Efremidis S, Keller RJ. Colonic stricture after transcatheter embolization for diverticular bleeding. AJR 1979;133:519.
31. Naderi MJ, Bookstein JJ. Rectal bleeding secondary to fecal disimpaction: angiographic diagnosis and treatment. Radiology 1978;126:387.
32. Nyman U, Boijsen UN, Lindström C, Rosengren JE. Angiography in angiomatous lesions of the gastrointestinal tract. Acta Radiol [Diagn] (Stockh) 1980;21:21.
33. Palmaz JC, Walter JF, Cho KJ. Therapeutic embolization of the small-bowel arteries. Radiology 1984;152:377.
34. Pingoud EG, Pais SO. Usefulness of the prone position for aortography of aortic graft-intestinal fistulae. AJR 1979;132:836.
35. Pelz DM, Rankin RN. Alternate bleeding sites in suspected graft-enteric fistula. AJR 1981;136:707.
36. Rahn NH, Tishler JM, Han SY, Russinovich NA. Diagnostic and interventional angiography in acute gastrointestinal hemorrhage. Radiology 1982;143:361.
37. Rösch J, Dotter CT, Rose RW. Selective arterial infusions of vasoconstrictors in acute gastrointestinal bleeding. Radiology 1971;99:27.
38. Rösch J, Keller FS, Wawrukiewicz AS, Krippaehne WW, Dotter CT. Pharmacoangiography in the diagnosis of recurrent massive lower gastrointestinal bleeding. Radiology 1982;145:615.
39. Rösch J, Kozak BE, Keller FS, Dotter CT. Interventional angiography in the diagnosis of acute lower gastrointestinal bleeding. Eur J Radiol 1986;6:136.
40. Rosenkrantz H, Bookstein JJ, Rosen RJ, Goff WB, Healy JF. Postembolic colonic infarction. Radiology 1982;142:47.
41. Sanchez FW, Rogers JM, Vujic I, Chuang VP. Transcatheter control of postpolypectomy hemorrhage. Gastrointest Radiol 1986;11:254.
42. Sheedy PF, Fulton RE, Atwell DT. Angiographic evaluation of patients with chronic gastrointestinal bleeding. AJR 1975;123:338.
43. Sniderman KW, Franklin J, Sos TA. Successful transcatheter gelfoam embolization of a bleeding cecal vascular ectasia. AJR 1978;131:157.
44. Sniderman KW, Baxi RK, Saddekni S, Sos TA. Use of tolazoline enhanced superior mesenteric arteriography to improve opacification of a cecal vascular ectasia: a case report. Gastrointest Radiol 979;4:339.
45. Sos TA, Lee JG, Wixson D, Sniderman KW. Intermittent bleeding from minute to minute in acute massive gastrointestinal hemorrhage: arteriographic demonstration. AJR 1978;131:1015.
46. Spiegel RM, Schultz RW, Casarella WJ, Wolff M. Massive hemorrhage from jejunal diverticula. Radiology 1982;143:367.
47. Sutton D, Murfitt J, Howarth F. Gastrointestinal bleeding from large angiomas. Clin Radiol 1981;32:629.
48. Tadavarthy AM, Castaneda-Zuniga W, Zollikofer C, Nemer F, Barron J, Amplatz K. Angiodysplasia of the right colon treated by embolization with ivalon (polyvinyl alcohol). Cardiovasc Intervent Radiol 1981;4:39.
49. Thompson WM, Jackson DC, Johnsrude IS. Aortoenteric and paraprosthetic-enteric fistulas: radiologic findings. AJR 1976;127:235.
50. Tisnado J, Cho SR, Beachley MC, Margolius DA. Transcatheter embolization of angiodysplasia of the rectum. Acta Radiol [Diagn] (Stockh) 1985;26:677.
51. Vallee C, Legmann P, Favriel JM, Garnier T, Levesque M. Colonic angiodysplasia: clinical, endoscopic, arteriographic signs and histopathological correlations. Eur J Radiol 1984;4:258.
52. Vaughan R, Rösch J, Keller FS, Antonovic R. Treatment of hemobilia by transcatheter vascular occlusion. Eur J Radiol 1984;4:183.
53. Walker WJ, Goldin AR, Shaff MI, Allibone GW. Per catheter control of haemorrhage from the superior and inferior mesenteric arteries. Clin Radiol 1980;31:71.
54. Waltman AC. Transcatheter embolization versus vasopressin infusion for the control of arteriocapillary gastrointestinal bleeding. Cardiovasc Intervent Radiol 1980;3:289.

Bleeding from Gastroesophageal Varices

C. L'Herminé and P. Chastanet

Percutaneous transhepatic embolization (PTE) of gastroesophageal varices appeared to be a highly promising procedure for the management of hemorrhage in cirrhotic patients when first described by Lunderquist (9). This method was reported to control bleeding in 70 to 94% of patients, according to different investigators (1–7, 10–12, 14–17). However, neither portal hypertension nor hepatic insufficiency can be improved by PTE, and increasing experience demonstrated the efficacy of this procedure to be temporary. Recurrent bleeding occurred in 37 to 65% of patients within a few months after embolization. The results of long-term survival are difficult to evaluate in these patients, the prognosis depending mainly on the severity of associated hepatic failure. PTE was said to be difficult to perform, time consuming, carry a high radiation exposure, and have a significant rate of technical failures and complications. For these reasons, the disadvantages of PTE seemed significant compared with endoscopic sclerotherapy of esophageal varices and indications decreased substantially. The most pessimistic opinion about PTE was expressed by Sos (13), who claimed that this procedure neither reduced immediate and long-term mortality nor the incidence of rebleeding in patients with acute hemorrhage from gastroesophageal varices. Results of PTE are difficult to evaluate when relying on a too small and too heterogeneous group of patients, since the outcome depends mainly on the underlying liver disease, which may include a wide range of different conditions, according to the cause and the stage of the disease, the degree of hepatic failure, pathologic lesions of the liver parenchyma, and the rate of progression of the disease. Therefore, when performed on a small group of patients, most of them having end-stage liver disease, PTE is likely to provide only poor results, together with a high rate of technical failures and complications. However, as experience increases, technical difficulties can be overcome and results are evaluated on the basis of a large number of patients with a long enough follow-up. It appears that efficacy of PTE in providing control of acute variceal bleeding in cirrhotic patients is unquestionable. This is why, in the last 7 years, PTE has become and remains a routine procedure for the management of variceal bleeding in our department.

Technique

Percutaneous transhepatic portography is performed according to the method described by Lunderquist (9), which is easy in most cases, provided enough experience has been gained with this procedure. We have only little experience in the transjugular route, which we think more difficult to perform, more time-consuming for the operator, and more harmful for the patient than the transhepatic approach. After a mild premedication by clorazepate (25 to 50 mg) and atropine (0.25 mg), the liver is punctured with a 19 G Teflon-sheathed needle in a frontal plane situated 2 cm anteriorly to the midaxillary line. The puncture site is chosen as high as possible according to the depth of the lateral costophrenic sulcus, and the needle tip is directed toward the 11th thoracic vertebra while the patient is asked not to breathe.

The needle is then slowly withdrawn until reflux of blood indicates the location of its tip in a right portal branch or the distal portal vein itself. Several attempts are often necessary, because the orientation of the portal vein partly depends on the size of the liver. The greatest difficulties result from a markedly atrophic liver and massive ascites, mainly when associated with a deep pleural sulcus. The portal vein is then catheterized and the tip of the catheter selectively placed in the left gastric vein, which is usually the main vein draining gastroesophageal varices. Catheterization is usually easily achieved by using the Lunderquist guide wire, which permits the catheter to progress through a hard sclerotic liver and enter the gastric vein, although it may arise from the portal vein at a sharp angle. The stiff part of the guide wire can be slightly bent, and the smooth extremity as well, in order to conform as exactly as possible to the shape of the portal vein. When the left gastric vein cannot be catheterized directly, portography is performed to demonstrate the different pedicles draining the varices. However varices with reduced and low flow may not be evident by portography and may require selective catheterization. This condition is commonly encountered in patients referred for a second PTE after recurrent bleeding.

Selective left gastric phlebography is performed to evaluate the size, the anatomic display of the varices, and hepatofugal flow. Portal pressure is recorded (Fig. **1a**). Embolization is performed using either 0.5 to 2 cc of isobutyl-2-cyanoacrylate (IBC) mixed with an equal amount of ultrafluid Lipiodol or absolute ethanol and stainless steel coils. IBC was used during the first years, after injection of 20 to 80 cc of 66% hypertonic glucose, which permitted a decrease in hepatofugal flow through the varices. Although the venous obstruction resulting from this procedure was shown to be permanent in 80% of

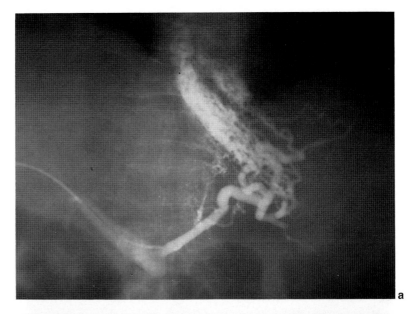

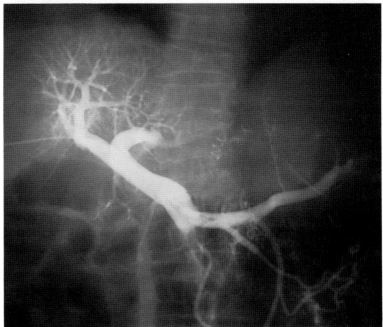

Fig. 1   **Child's class C, alcoholic cirrhosis treated by PTE** (10 ml of absolute ethanol and two stainless steel coils within the left gastric veins)
a Selective catheterization of the left gastric vein demonstrates the gastroesophageal varices, Portal pressure: 500 mm H_2O
b Portography after embolization shows obliteration of the varices and the lack of other pedicles. Follow-up: the bleeding was controlled and did not recur, but the patient died 4 months later from hepatic failure

patients, as demonstrated by angiography control, the use of IBC does not allow precise control of the site of obstruction and exposes the patient to the risk of reflux in the portal vein. This method has been abandoned since 1984, variceal obliteration being achieved by an injection of 20 to 25 cc of absolute ethanol, while occlusion of the venous stem is completed by stainless steel coils. Although absolute ethanol is probably the best sclerosing agent used for gastroesophageal varices so far, it is not suitable in unusual cases, when varices develop via a spontaneous high-flow portocaval anastomosis, since the ve-

nous tract uniting both venous systems is usually much shorter, wider, and with a higher flow rate than in the case of esophageal varices. This is the case in gastric varices, which may be associated with a spontaneous splenorenal anastomosis, found relatively frequently, together with intestinal and umbilical varices, which are an uncommon cause of bleeding (1.5%) (8). Therefore, obliteration of such varices must be done with steel coils or IBC, or both, according to each specific case.

Obstruction of large gastric varices often raises a difficult problem because the high hepatofugal flow

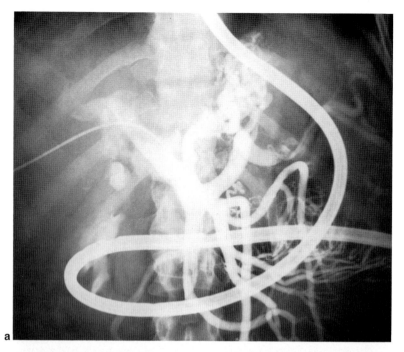

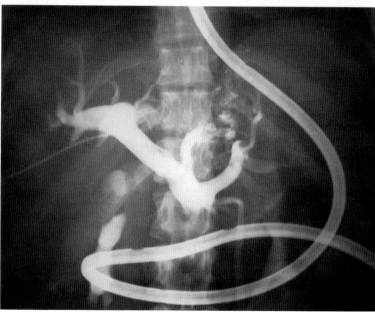

Fig. 2 **Alcoholic cirrhosis in a 42-year-old woman** (Child's class B)
a Portography (on Feb 17, 1983) shows hepatofugal flow through a widened left gastric vein and mesenteric veins. Portal pressure: 320 mm H_2O
b Portography after embolization of the left gastric vein with 1 ml of IBC mixed with Lipiodol. The left gastric vein is occluded, but a small accessory vein that was thought to be too small to be embolized remains patent. Follow-up: the bleeding was controlled and did not recur for 39 months

toward the left renal vein precludes the use of IBC. The varices are sometimes so large that they cannot be completely occluded with steel coils only. It is then still necessary to rely on IBC to achieve obstruction of such varices, but only after the hepatofugal flow has been slowed sufficiently with steel coils (Fig. **3**). After embolization, portography is performed with the tip of the catheter within the splenic vein in order to check obliteration of the left gastric vein and to detect other pedicles draining the varices that should be occluded as well (Fig. **1, 2**). The catheter is

then withdrawn. PTE is completed within less than 1 hour in most cases. Embolization of the transhepatic needle tract was advocated in order to decrease the risk of hemoperitoneum. This procedure has proved unnecessary and we have refrained form it for years without additional complications.

Since 1980, 482 cirrhotic patients have been treated by PTE, 50 of them undergoing several embolizations for recurrent bleeding. The procedure was performed twice in 44 patients and three times in 6 patients. In total, 538 PTEs were achieved success-

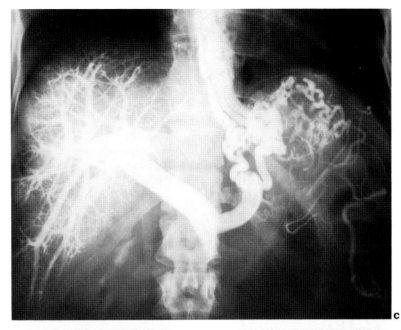

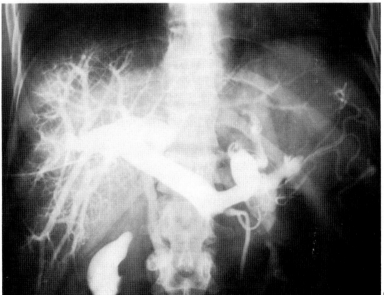

Fig. **2**
c Portography performed again 39 months later (on May 22, 1986) for recurrent bleeding. The left gastric vein remains occluded but new varices have developed through enlarged short gastric veins. Portal pressure: 260 mm H_2O
d Portography after embolization with 8 ml of absolute alcohol and two coils shows obstruction of varices and both short gastric veins. The bleeding was controlled and did not recur within a 3-month follow-up

fully in 482 patients. Although PTE is theoretically always feasible provided the portal vein is patent, some technical failures cannot be precluded resulting from difficulties in catheterization of either the portal vein or the gastric veins draining the varices. PTE failed in 55 out of 593 attempts, being successful 538 times. The technical failure rate is 9% on the whole series. However, it was higher when we started with PTE (15% in the 125 first attempts) and dropped to 6% since 1982. With increasing experience one can overcome most of the technical difficulties, so that

PTE has become easy, whereas it could be considered to have been relatively difficult at the beginning.

Results of PTE are evaluated on the basis of a group of 400 patients treated exclusively by PTE, 39 of them having undergone two or three embolizations for recurrent bleeding. The procedure was technically successful in 400 patients. Recurrent bleeding rate and survival rate are calculated according to the actuarial method. Of the 400 patients, 271 were males (68%) and 129 females (32%); 50 were

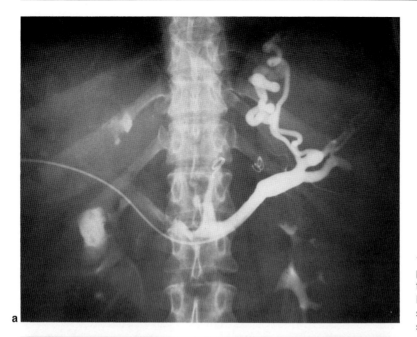

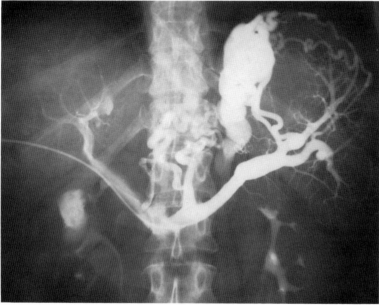

Fig. 3 **Alcoholic cirrhosis in a 47-year-old woman** (Child's class B, portal pressure: 400 mm H_2O) successfully treated by PTE 39 months earlier. Embolization of the left gastric vein and a short gastric vein was performed by stainless steel coils only because of a spontaneous high flow-rate splenorenal anastomosis
a, b Portography performed again 39 months later for recurrent bleeding due to gastric varices evident on fibroscopy. Visualization of the two coils in the previously embolized veins. The left gastric vein is recanalized and the splenorenal anastomosis is fed again through two short gastric veins arising from the splenic hilum and giving rise to large gastric varices. The left gastric vein is embolized with 20 ml of alcohol. Two coils are placed in one of the two veins feeding the varices, allowing the hepatofugal flow to be greatly decreased but not completely interrupted
c Plain film of the abdomen after the second PTE showing the coils in each of the three pedicles. Follow-up: bleeding stopped immediately but recurred 8 days later. A surgical portocaval shunt was performed

less than 40 years old (12.5%), 265 were between 40 and 60 years of age (66.25%), and 85 were more than 60 years old (21.25%).

Alcoholic cirrhosis was present in 90% and nonalcoholic cirrhosis in 10%. According to the classification of Child and Pugh, 142 patients belonged to group B (35.5%) and 258 patients to group C (64.5%). Because Child's class C is a heterogeneous group, it was subdivided into two parts, C1 and C2, according to whether the degree of hepatic failure was noted at 10, 11, 12 or 13, 14, 15. Thus, 171 patients belonged to the C1 group (43.6%) and 82 to the C2 group (20.9%). Two hundred ninety-seven

patients were actively bleeding at the time of embolization (74.25%), and PTE was performed as an elective procedure in 103 patients (25.75%).

Complications

When insignificant and inconspicuous complications are excluded, such as a small intrahepatic arterioportal fistula or subcapsular hematoma of the liver, main complications of PTE consist of hemoperitoneum, hemothorax, pulmonary embolism, and portal vein thrombosis. Neurologic, respiratory, and renal disturbances, a parietal or a subcapsular hematoma,

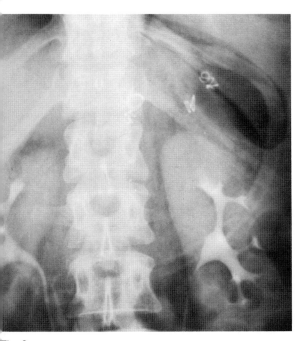

Fig. **3c**

and migration of embolic material into the portal vein or the left renal vein are rare and harmless complications.

Forty significant complications were encountered in 538 successful PTEs (7.4%), and 13 complications resulted in death (2.4%). Hemoperitoneum was relatively rare (seven cases). Some patients had severe coagulation deficits that should not be considered as a contra-indication to the transperitoneal puncture of the liver. Hemothorax and pneumothorax (eight cases) resulting from a puncture site located too cephalad should be avoided.

Pulmonary embolism occurred in five patients, resulting in death in three patients. Death occurred after embolization with IBC of varices connecting the portal and caval system through relatively short and high-flow pathways. One patient died immediately after embolization of large gastroesophageal varices with IBC. The cause of death was cerebral embolism, possibly related to an anastomosis between the portal vein and pulmonary veins, which is known to develop in cirrhosis occasionally. Embolization with absolute ethanol was responsible for transient convulsions and coma in one patient and respiratory distress in two patients.

Dislocation of the distal tip of the Lunderquist guide wire or migration of a stainless steel coil into the portal vein were encountered in three cases. Embolization with IBC of a high-flow spontaneous splenorenal anastomosis resulted in partial obstruction of the left renal vein in one case. The bleeding was controlled and the patient experienced no symptoms from this complication at a 6-month follow-up.

Portal vein thrombosis is an important point to be considered because, PTE might be thought to carry a high risk for this complication. Ten cases of portal vein thrombosis became evident by angiography in 482 patients treated with PTE. No conclusion about the true frequency of portal vein thrombosis can be drawn, because many cases remain undetected.

Eight cases of portal vein thrombosis were encountered in a group of 50 patients who underwent a transhepatic portography for recurrent bleeding after PTE. A rate of 16% portal vein thrombosis is similar to that previously reported (9). In three of eight patients who re-bled shortly after the procedure, portal vein thrombosis was due to a technical failure, such as reflux of IBC in the portal vein during embolization. Since embolization is performed with absolute ethanol and IBC is no longer used routinely, this complication is avoided.

When excluding these three cases, the rate of portal vein thrombosis decreases to 10%, or approximatively the same rate that is reported to occur spontaneously in cirrhosis. Shortly after PTE, two of the five remaining patients had undergone a surgical mesocaval shunt, which occluded so that portal vein thrombosis might have resulted from PTE or from surgery. In two other cases it was unlikely that PTE was responsible for portal vein thrombosis, since it was shown by portography performed 14 and 18 months later during a recurrent bleeding episode, whereas the bleeding was initially controlled by PTE. Therefore, once the risk of portal vein obstruction induced by IBC is avoided, PTE is unlikely to be responsible for a high risk of portal vein thrombosis, as previously stated by Lunderquist.

Finally two important points must be stressed concerning potential complications of PTE. Complications seem to occur more frequently or to turn out to be more severe in patients with end-stage liver disease and in cases when PTE is a life-saving procedure in an emergency situation.

The number of complications decreased progressively as experience increased. The complication rate dropped from 12.7% in 1980 and 7.1% in 1981 (9.6% on the 125 first procedures) to 5% since 1982. PTE can be considered as a relatively well-tolerated procedure, especially in view of the poor condition of most actively bleeding patients to whom it is usually proposed.

Results

Short-Term Results

PTE was performed as an emergency procedure in 297 actively bleeding patients, hemorrhage was either immediately life-threatening or uncontrolled for 24 to 48 hours by medical therapy and Sengstaken tube. Cessation of bleeding was observed in 245 patients (82.7%), the success rate being higher in Child's class B patients (93.8%) than in Child's class C (78%). The procedure failed to control bleeding in 52 patients, 90% of whom belonging to Child's C group. Some patients died within a few days of the procedure from recurrent bleeding or from liver failure, even though hemorrhage was initially successfully controlled. This early mortality rate must be taken into account in order to have a better evaluation of the efficacy of PTE. Of the 400 successfully embolized patients, 97 died within the first 10 days after the procedure (24.3%), the mortality rate depending greatly on the degree of liver failure, as demonstrated by Child's classification. Among these 97 patients, 11 belonged to Child's class B (7.7%), 49 to Child's class C1 (28%), and 37 to Child's class C2 (44.5%). Then-day survival rate was 75.8%, but decreased to 55.5% in Child's group C2 patients, most of whom had end-stage liver disease. On the other hand, 10-day survival rate was three times higher when PTE was successful in controlling the bleeding than in case of failure. Therefore, whatever the role of liver failure in early survival after embolization is, it can be demonstrated that control of bleeding plays a major role as well.

Long-Term Results

Late results of recurrent bleeding and patient survival have been evaluated on the basis of a group of 348 patients: PTE was performed as an elective procedure in 103, and as an emergency procedure in 245 who were actively bleeding. Results were estimated according to the actuarial method from the day of the embolization to 4 or 5 years every 6 months. Results show follow-up of all the patients in whom PTE was initially successful, including the 10 patients who died.

Recurrent Bleeding

Results of recurrent bleeding may be considered discouraging, since more than half of the patients rebled within the first 6 months, after PTE. Rate of recurrent bleeding was 55% at 6 months, 66% at 1 year, 81% at 2 years, and 92% at 3 years in 348 patients (Fig. 4). Rebleeding was more frequent in Child's group C (70, 75, 90 and 90%, respectively) than in Child's group B (38, 55, 71, and 85%, respectively) at least within the first 3 days after the procedure (Fig. 5). However, recurrent bleeding was less severe in about half of the cases and responded well to conservative treatment, so that survival rate appears more favorable.

Survival

Survival rate was 56% at 6 months, 48% at 1 year, 40% at 2 years, 32% at 3 years, and 26% at 5 years (Fig. 6). Survival was higher in Child's group B (79%, 59%, 48%) than in group C (42%, 27%, 16%) at 6 months, 2 years and 4 years (Fig. 7). Mortality rate was particularly high within 6 months in Child's class C (58%). Survival curves decreased more slowly, following a parallel course in both groups, survival rate remaining about 30% higher in Child's group B. Standard deviation of the curve varied from 3.5 to 4.5% in group C, from 3.5 to 6% at 4 years and 10% at 5 years in group B. The difference between both groups is statistically significant. Regarding Child's classification, the survival rate was significantly different according to whether the patients were classified as C1 or C2, at least within the first 2 years after PTE (Fig. 8). Six-month mortality rate was high in Child's group C2 (64%) compared with C1 (51%), so that in those patients with more severe liver failure the benefit from PTE may be considered questionable. It must be noted that all patients who

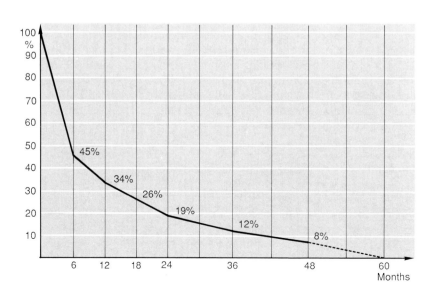

Fig. **4 Recurrent bleeding rate in 348 patients after PTE.** Actuarial percentage of patients who do not have recurrent bleeding. Standard deviation ranging from 4 to 4.5%

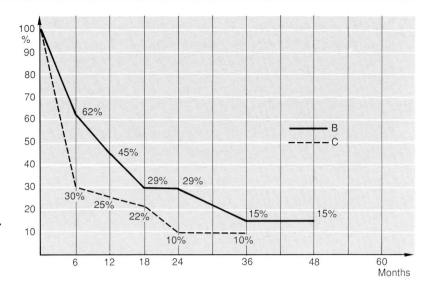

Fig. **5 Recurrent bleeding rate according to Child's classification.** Standard deviation ranging from 7 to 7.5% in Child's group B and from 4.5 to 5.5% in Child's group C

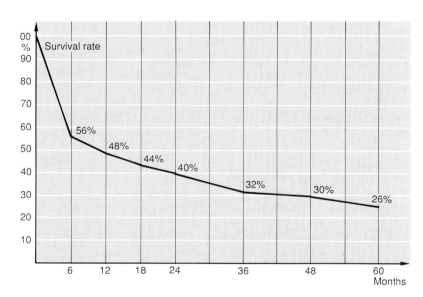

Fig. **6 Life-table analysis curve in the group of 348 patients whose bleeding was initially controlled after PTE.** Standard deviation ranging from 2.5 to 3.5% until 4 years, then 4.5% at 5 years

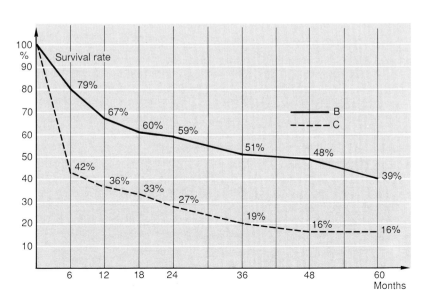

Fig. **7 Life-table analysis curve in the group of 348 patients whose bleeding was initially controlled after PTE,** according to Child's classification. Child's class B (standard deviation ranging from 4 to 6% until 4 years, then 10% at 5 years); Child's class C (standard deviation ranging from 3.5 to 4.5%)

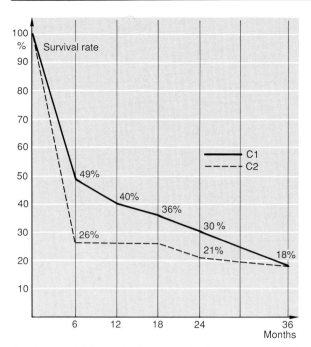

Fig. **8 Life-table analysis curve in the group of 348 patients whose bleeding was initially controlled after embolization.** Comparison between Child's classes C1 and C2. Child's class C1 (standard deviation ranging from 4 to 5.5%); Child's class 2 (standard deviation 5.5%)

survived at 6 month were alive at 18 months, while the survival rate was still 21% at 2 years and 18% at 3 years (standard deviation: 5.5%). It can be concluded that mortality rate after successful embolization predominates within the first 6 months after the procedure. It is higher in actively bleeding patients and as high as severity of liver failure with a particularly poor prognosis in patients belonging to Child's class C2. The role of liver failure is also demonstrated by the fact that among a group of 143 patients whose cause of death could be proved, 66 died from bleeding and 77 died from liver insufficiency or other causes without recurrent bleeding. Therefore, about half of the patients who died after successful PTE did not die from recurrent bleeding, this number increasing progressively with time. Whatever the role of liver failure in long-term survival, results indicate that about half of the patients were alive 1 year after successful PTE, one-third survived 3 years, and one-fourth, 5 years.

Although the results reported here permit an evaluation of the efficacy of PTE on bleeding and patient survival, they do not give an exact score of the total survival rate after PTE, the 52 patients with uncontrolled bleeding having been excluded. Total survival rate in 400 patients in whom PTE was successfully achieved whatever its initial result on bleeding was then a little lower: 49% at 6 months, 41% at 1 year, and 33% at 2 years (Fig. **9**). The difference between patients in Child's groups B and C is nearly the same as in the group of 348 patients, or even slightly greater, since the mortality rate is three times higher in patients with uncontrolled bleeding by PTE, and 90% of them belong to Child's class C (Figs. **10, 11**).

Conclusion

Provided enough experience has been gained, PTE is a safe and easy procedure that can be proposed routinely in all cases of variceal bleeding when the portal vein is patent. The technical success rate is 94%. The 6% complication rate is relatively low considering the poor condition of most patients. PTE is only a palliative method, which can improve neither portal hypertension nor hepatic failure, so that its limitations in achieving long-term control of bleeding or prolongation of life are obvious.

Efficacy in the control of acute bleeding is unquestionable (82.7%) and undoubtedly results in a decrease of early mortality (24.4% at 10 days). Long-term efficacy on patient survival is difficult to evaluate because it depends mainly on the severity of the liver failure. PTE is likely to improve patient survival by reducing the mortality rate due to recurrent bleeding, at least within the first 18 months after the procedure.

References

1. Bengmark S, Borjesson B, Hoenels J, Joelsson B, Lunderquist A, Owman T. Obliteration of esophageal varices by PTP. Ann Surg 1979;190:549–554.
2. Benner KG, Keefe EB, Keller SF, Rösch J. Clinical outcome of percutaneous transhepatic obliteration of esophageal varices. Gastroenterology 1983;85:146–153.
3. Cello JP, Crass R, Trurkey DD. Endoscopic sclerotherapy versus esophageal transsection in Child's class C patients with variceal hemorrhage: comparison with results of portocaval shunt: preliminary report. Surgery 1982;91:333–338.
4. Chuang VP, Lunderquist A, Herlinger H. Portal hypertension. In: Herlinger H, ed. Clinical radiology of the liver; part B. New York: Dekker 1985:645–713.
5. Franco D, D'Hubert E, Kunslinger F, Bismuth H. Valeur de l'embolisation transhépatique des varices oesophagiennes dans le traitement d'urgence des hémorragies digestives du cirrhotique. Gastroenterol Clin Biol 1980;4:921–922.
6. Hervieu C, Levade M, Pascal JB. Embolisation par voie transcutanée des varices oesophagiennes. Gastroenterol Clin Biol 1982;6:692–698.
7. Houssin D, Brunet AM, Brochard L, D'Hubert E, Ben Mansour A, Roche A, Bismuth H. Traitement des hémorragies incontrôlables dues aux varices oesophagiennes chez le cirrhotique. Presse Med 1986;15:509–513.
8. L'Hermine C, Chastanet P, Bonniere P, Gauthier P. Traitement par embolisation des varices intestinales et ombilicales au cours de l'hypertension portale. Sem Hôp Paris 1987;63:2650–2654.
9. Lunderquist A, Borjesson B, Owman T, Bengmark S. Isobutyl-2-cyanoacrylate (bucrylate) in obliteration of gastric coronary vein and esophageal varices. AJR 1978;130:1–6.

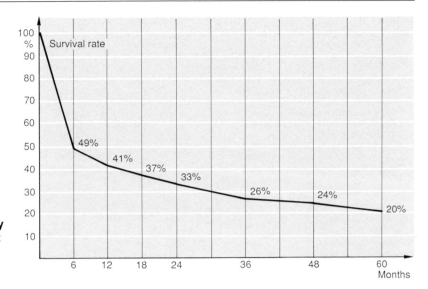

Fig. 9 **Life-table analysis curve in the group of 400 patients treated by PTE whatever the immediate result on bleeding** (standard deviation ranging from 2.5 to 4%)

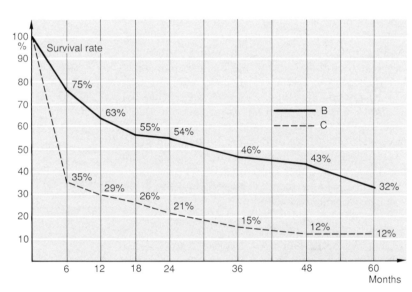

Fig. 10 **Life-table analysis curve in the group of 400 patients treated by PTE whatever the immediate result on bleeding,** according to Child's classification. Child's class B (standard deviation ranging from 4 to 6% until 4 years, then 10% at 5 years); Child's class C (standard deviation ranging from 4 to 5%)

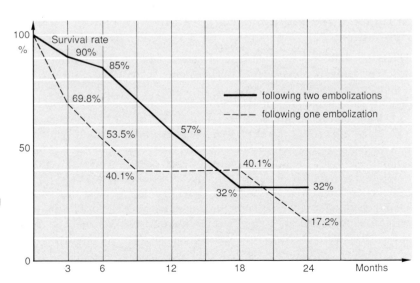

Fig. 11 **Actuarial survival curve in a group of 20 Child's class C1 patients undergoing a second embolization for recurrent bleeding** compared with another group of 73 Child's class C1 patients after one PTE. Standard deviation ranging from 7 to 11% in the first group and from 4 to 5% in the second

10. Novis BH, Duys P, Barbezat GO, Clain J, Bank S, Terblanche J. Fiberoptic endoscopy and the use of the Sengstaken tube in acute gastro-intestinal hemorrhage in patients with portal hypertension and varices. Gut 1976;17:258–263.
11. Ottinger LW, Noncure AC. Transthoracic ligation of bleeding esophageal varices in patients with intrahepatic portal obstruction. Ann Surg 1974;179:35–38.
12. Passariello R, Thau A, Rossi P, Lombardi M, Simonetti G, Stipa S. Control of gastroesophageal bleeding varices by percutaneous transhepatic portography. Surg Gynecol Obstet 1980;150:155–160.
13. Sos TA. Transhepatic portal venous embolization of varices: pros and cons. Radiology 1983;148:569–570.
14. Terblanche J, Northover JMA, Bornman P. A prospective controlled trial of sclerotherapy in the long-term management of patients after variceal bleeding. Surg Gynecol Obstet 1979;148:323–333.
15. Uflacker R. Percutaneous transhepatic obliteration of gastroesophageal varices using absolute alcohol. Radiology 1983;146:621–625.
16. Vinel JP, Scotto JM, Levade M, Teisseire R, Cassigneul J, Cales P, Voigt JJ, Pascal JP. Embolisation des varices oesophagiennes par voie transjugulaire dans les hémorragies digestives graves du cirrhotique. Gastroenterol Clin Biol 1985;9:814–818.
17. Widrich WC, Robbins AH, Nabseth DC. Transhepatic embolization of varices. Cardiovasc Intervent Radiol 1980;3:298–307.

Bleeding from Trauma

Y. Ben-Menachem

Angiographers have been contributing to the management of trauma, and in particular to control of hemorrhage, for well over a decade, evolving from use of autogenous clot (12, 38) to detachable balloons (16, 53). Both the numbers of patients and the severity of the injuries treated by angiographers are increasing (7, 26, 43) as demand by traumatologists rises (31, 35). The purpose of this chapter is to provide an overview of the subject on the basis of my experience and in light of the current literature. Some space will be devoted to discussion of wounding mechanisms and of some challenges posed by trauma; without understanding these, arterial trauma can be neither fully diagnosed nor successfully treated. Potential complications of angiographic hemostasis will be discussed within the subject matter of each body area.

Surgical or Angiographic Exploration and Hemostasis?

There is a wide variation in surgical accessibility of different body regions. Areas such as the pelvis, upper thigh, axilla, and parts of the neck have enough depth and anatomic complexity to make surgical exploration and hemostasis quite difficult and not without risk, even more so in the presence of hemorrhage or large hematomas. Against this background, and given the time consumed by each operation on large numbers of patients in busy emergency centers, exploration and hemostasis by angiography are excellent alternatives to surgery. Compared with surgical exploration, angiography is far less invasive and destructive, yet more accurate and comprehensive; similarly, angiographic control of hemorrhage is often easier, much more merciful to human tissue, and by far more cost-effective than an operation (5, 30).

Objectives and Indications

Clinical Objectives

The goals of angiography and embolization in trauma are: to remove the need for operations designed solely for control of hemorrhage; to stabilize patients in shock preoperatively; to permit postponement of a necessary operation pending completion of more urgent surgery on the same or another patient; to create a temporarily bloodless field for the surgeon; and to embolize pre emptively an injured but still nonbleeding artery that is deemed expendable.

It is, therefore, clear that hemorrhagic shock is not an absolute contra-indication to angiography. Indeed, in a significant number of cases, shock patients gain very much from angiography and embolization (7, 8, 45).

Rationale for Angiography and Embolization in Trauma

The indication for any radiologic procedure in trauma must take into account the following determinants: One must first diagnose and treat the most critical injuries; only direct evidence of injury or normalcy provides reliable diagnostic information and the radiologic modality that produces it is, by definition, the examination of choice; and for the diagnosis of critical injuries, one uses radiologic examinations in order to establish the indication for surgery; it is an error to attempt to establish indications for the radiologic examinations first.

Except where brain injuries determine patients' final disposition, vascular wounding almost always heads the list of critical injuries. Hemorrhage is the common denominator of most causes of death in trauma, and arterial injury is a leading cause of permanent disability in its survivors (5, 7). Therefore, unless the patient is in need of immediate surgery, the indication for exploratory angiography is absolute whenever a vascular injury is suspected, irrespective of symptoms.

The indication for angiographic hemostasis follows whenever the angiographer can control a hemorrhage at least as effectively and as safely as the surgeon can do it. Indeed, the strength of the indication for embolization in a particular region increases in direct proportion to the degree of difficulty and loss of functioning tissue inherent in the surgery of that region.

Diagnostic Angiography

Planning

The diagnostic angiogram must be individually designed for each patient according to the wounding capacity of the mechanism of injury, in order to identify every possible vascular injury. Thus, for example, the investigation of gunshot wounds must account for soft tissue trauma in a large area surrounding the residual wound tract. This is because the tissue in front of the nose of the moving bullet is accelerated forward at the velocity of the projectile and the tissue alongside it is displaced laterally by pressure waves, forming a temporary cavity that can attain a diameter 30 times the bullet's caliber. Having reached its maximum size, the temporary cavity collapses, then reexpands and contracts several times in diminishing amplitudes. The most serious tissue damage is inflicted as the cavity collapses, affecting all soft tissue components within its perimeter, most of them without ever coming into direct contact with the bullet (1, 2, 4). Hence the term "proximity injury."

Anesthesia

General anesthesia is highly desirable for angiography of multitrauma patients, children, and combative persons. Anesthesia permits the angiographer to work freely and with less risk or error on the well-monitored patient, saves time and contrast medium, creates a palpable gain of information, and allows greater success in embolization (4).

Performance

Angiography should be a formal, transcatheter study, on film series or digital matrix. The use of transarterial digital subtraction angiography (DSA) should be encouraged. Transarterial DSA reduces contrast medium usage and saves much time by virtue of its real-time image projection. Transarterial DSA is at least as good as film angiography in detection of hemorrhage, but probably not so for documentation of intimal tears (7). On the other hand, transvenous DSA is not recommended in trauma except in rare events when an arterial approach is impossible. Transvenous DSA adds a risk of contrast overload and cardiac injury and its images are noisy and of inferior quality. It is also time consuming and does not provide access to control of hemorrhage.

Portable, one-film angiography by needle must be discouraged: it restricts the investigation to the area of the artery supplied by the needle, increases the risk of missing an injury, does not permit dynamic assessment of the circulation, and offers no access to control of hemorrhage (4, 5).

The diagnostic angiogram, in addition to delineation of the injury, must document the primary and collateral arteries to the entire region under investigation, especially the alternative blood supply to the area perfused by the target artery. Multitrauma patients require comprehensive angiography of all injured regions. All bleeding points can then be assessed and prioritized simultaneously in order to avoid overlapping embolizations. The diagnostic study should, therefore, begin with a midstream, survey-angiogram of a wide area and not with selective arteriography.

The catheter used for the midstream study must be of a large enough caliber, and contrast medium should be injected in volumes and injection rates sufficient to opacify the entire area of interest, not forgetting that most trauma patients present with an abnormally high cardiac output. It is wise to work through an introducer sheath with a diaphragm, capable of accomodating different French sizes of catheters. It allows one to start with a large catheter for diagnosis and continue with a smaller one for selective angiography and embolization. Specially tapered catheters or coaxial catheter systems can be also used. It may be convenient to work through two access arteries.

Embolization

Principles

The method of hemostasis must be carefully tailored to the injury, subject to two important prerequisites, namely, that one must not experiment during emergencies or work too slowly with patients in shock, and that embolization must be highly selective in order to achieve hemostasis without unnecessary loss of tissue.

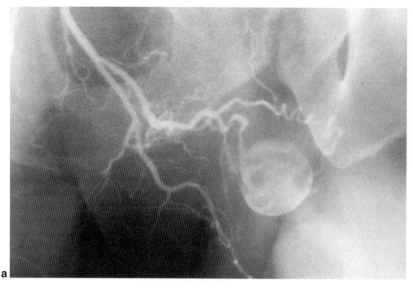

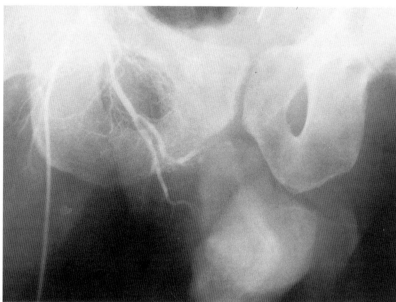

Fig. 1 **Selective, peripheral embolization. Accidental transection of the artery of the bulb of the penis during transendoscopic resection of a urethral stricture.**
a Hemorrhage from the transected artery into a false aneurysm. A surgical approach to this artery would have required perineal incision and exploration, with a serious risk of impotence secondary to surgical injury to local nerves. In contrast, selective embolization of the right internal pudendal artery with Gelfoam holds a better promise of preserved erectile function. Two Gelfoam torpedoes were injected into the internal pudendal artery
b Control study: Both penile and scrotal branches of the internal pudendal artery are occluded. Bleeding did not recur and erections remained normal. (Reprinted with permission from Slack, Inc.)

Although embolization should be as selective as possible, with isolation and occlusion of the injured artery alone (Fig. 1), this is not always possible or practical, as is the case in hemorrhage from multiple branches of a major artery (e.g., the hepatic or internal iliac). Separate, selective embolizations of each bleeding branch may be too slow to accomplish hemostasis and could aggravate the risk to a severely injured patient by unnecessarily prolonging the angiographic session. In such an event one should embolize the main artery in a single procedure, preferably using a method that occludes the first- and second-generation branches of the embolized artery and leaves the smaller, distal branches open to collateral blood flow. Such an embolization effectively controls the hemorrhage, but does not cause severe ischemia.

Overlapping embolizations must be avoided. Arteries such as the internal iliac and the ipsilateral deep femoral supply adjacent regions and are also each other's primary collateral routes. Their simultaneous embolization is likely to result in widespread tissue necrosis.

Access to the site of bleeding, and to the treatment of most arteriovenous fistulas (AVF), is transluminal arterial. However, in some AVFs this approach fails and the lesion can be accessed and treated through its venous component (19, 20, 40, 42).

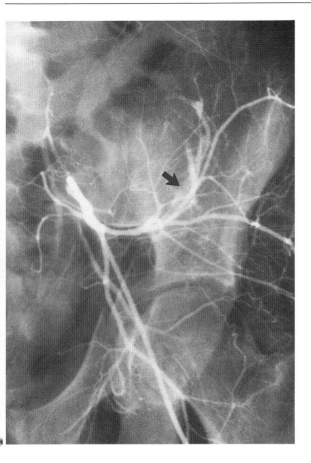

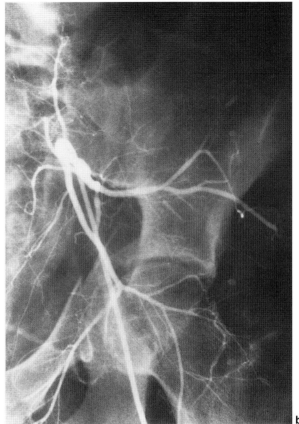

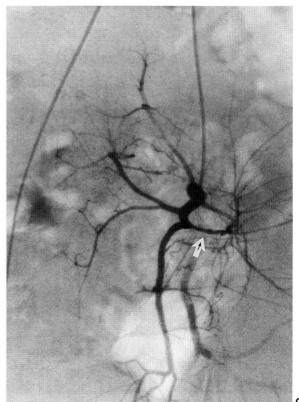

Fig. **2 Embolization with Gelfoam for temporary, long-term occlusion**

a Selective superior gluteal arteriogram. Traumatic arterio-venous fistula in a patient with pelvic fractures. Early appearance of the superior gluteal vein (arrows)

b Immediately after scatter embolization with Gelfoam pudding, there is obliteration of the fistula

c Follow up angiogram several months after embolization. The superior gluteal artery is almost completely recanalized (arrow). (Reprinted with permission from W. B. Saunders and from Williams and Wilkins)

Selection of a Catheter

A catheter is well suited for the procedure if it can easily reach the site of bleeding, anchor itself near that point, and safely deliver the occluding agent. A smooth, low-torque catheter is most likely to satisfy these requirements. As much as possible, the leading segment of the catheter should be shaped to resemble a tracing of the vascular anatomy of the target artery. Thus, once in place, the catheter is "comfortable" and does not readily shift or retract during the embolization. The catheter's inner diameter must be suited to the selected embolic agent. Whereas Gelfoam can be delivered through catheters of any size above 4 Fr, the inner diameter of a catheter used in coil delivery must be narrow enough so that the coil remains extended and the propelling guide wire does not pass beside the coil during delivery.

Selection of Occluding Agents

Occluding agents may be selected from among a variety of available materials (23), depending on the required duration of occlusion and the caliber of the bleeding artery. Except for powders, which tend to cause infarction, and destructive fluids, such as ethanol or phenol, angiographers are advised to opt for the embolic materials with which they are most experienced and have had the best rate of success.

In most instances the embolization should result in reversible arterial occlusion, so that when the injured region heals it will be perfused by its native artery rather than be dependent on collaterals. The long-term, reversible occlusion desirable for this purpose is best achieved by Gelfoam, whose intra-arterial life is limited to a few weeks (Fig. 2). Gelfoam can be injected either as a single torpedo or as pudding (a suspension of small Gelfoam pledgets in diluted contrast medium). Due to the risk of microemboli, Gelfoam must not be used in or near the central nervous system.

When permanent arterial occlusion is acceptable, and when the size of the arterial wound or its nearness to the central nervous system preclude the use of Gelfoam, steel coils are preferred. The correct size of the selected coil should allow it to rewind itself into a tight spiral in the artery without migrating beyond the chosen point of occlusion. A solitary coil is usually insufficient to occlude a medium-caliber vessel completely. A backup embolus of one or more Gelfoam torpedoes is then added. Additional coils may be necessary, also as a substitute for Gelfoam in arteries with connections to the central nervous system. In occluding a relatively wide artery, a coil too large to rewind completely can be placed initially; it will settle in the artery as a flat spiral into which smaller coils can be safely anchored. An added advantage to using coils lies with the possibility to pass a small catheter between the coil and the arterial wall soon after the embolization in order to embolize another branch of the artery.

Detachable balloons (DB) are most suitable for treatment of AVFs, especially in the central nervous system, by virtue of the ability to preserve the artery (16). However, work with detachable balloons is slow, complex, requires a high degree of expertise, and may be prohibitively expensive, and therefore less suitable than coils for routine management of traumatic hemorrhage.

Fixed occlusion balloon catheters provide effective short-term occlusion of a major artery until it can be surgically repaired (Fig. 3). Also, being a

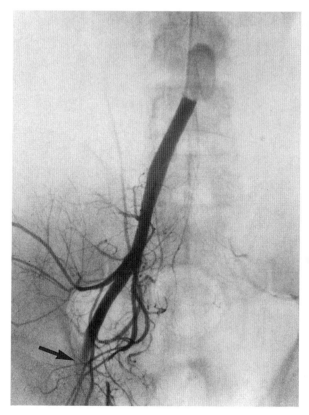

Fig. 3 **Preoperative hemostasis by occlusion balloon catheter.** The patient was admitted with hemorrhage from both groins after impalement by a forklift. He arrived at the angiography suite in pneumatic trousers that could not be released. A 100 cm long catheter with a fixed 27 mm balloon was introduced via left axillary access. The balloon was inflated in the aortic bifurcation and left in place for about 20 minutes. The pneumatic trousers were removed as soon as the balloon was inflated, and the patient ceased to bleed and became stable. After the angiograms, the patient left with the balloon in place for use as proximal control in the operating room. Illustrated is the right iliac angiogram through the balloon catheter. Blood flow into the common femoral artery (arrow) is much delayed in comparison with the normal filling of internal iliac artery branches. (Reprinted with permission from Slack, Inc. and from J. B. Lippincott)

palpable foreign body inside the artery, the balloon catheter can serve as a guide to the site of injury at the time of surgical exploration (4).

Limbs

Injuries

Two-thirds of the patients have penetrating trauma and these, except for an occasional iatrogenic injury, are divided evenly between stab wounds and injuries by firearms (5). Injuries are confined to one limb in roughly two-thirds of the patients. The remaining patients have sustained injuries in several regions or the whole body, resulting in a more complex clinical presentation and greater difficulty in localization of hemorrhage.

Anatomy

The anatomic complexity of the axilla and upper thigh make operative access difficult. Surgical explo-

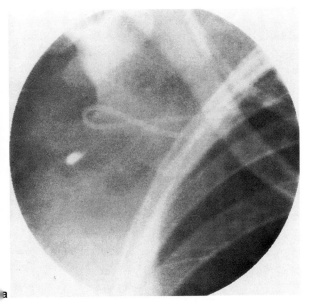

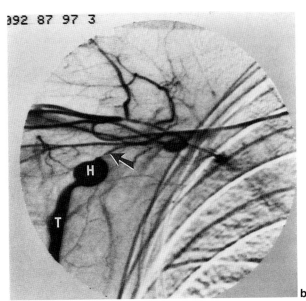

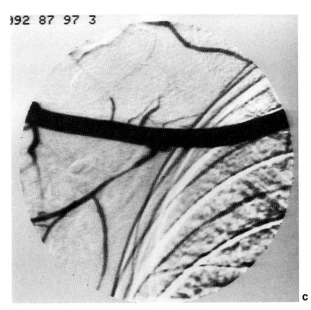

Fig. **4 Secure anchoring of a catheter for selective embolization.** The patient had a stab wound of the axilla 1 day before angiography. Several attempts at selective catheterization of the bleeding artery, using catheters of all commercially available configurations, have failed, because the hemorrhage is from the pectoral division of the thoracoacromial artery – a very short branch of the axillary artery with a slightly recurrent course – which does not offer a safe anchor to conventional catheters. A 5 F polyethylene, 100 cm long, catheter with an original H-1 curve configuration, was bent in hot saline over a 0.035 inch guide wire to reverse the direction of its distal 5 cm and form a leading curve of less than 8 mm diameter. The catheter was stabilized with a slightly bent, hard guide wire, placed proximal to the leading curve, and was easily and atraumatically advanced – blind end first – into the innominate-subclavian-axillary conduit; the guide wire was then replaced with a 5 mm J movable-core wire and the catheter was retracted until the wire – and then the catheter tip – entered and anchored itself in the thoracoacromial artery. A single 1 by 1 by 10 mm Gelfoam torpedo was injected slowly, producing complete occlusion

a The catheter, having been advanced blind end first is anchored in the thoracoacromial artery

b Preembolization study: Hemorrhage from the pectoral branch of the thoracoacromial artery (arrow) into a partially contained hematoma [H], and from it to the knife's wound tract [T]

c Postembolization study: the thoracoacromial artery is occluded, and bleeding has stopped. (Reprinted with permission from Slack, Inc. and from J. B. Lippincott)

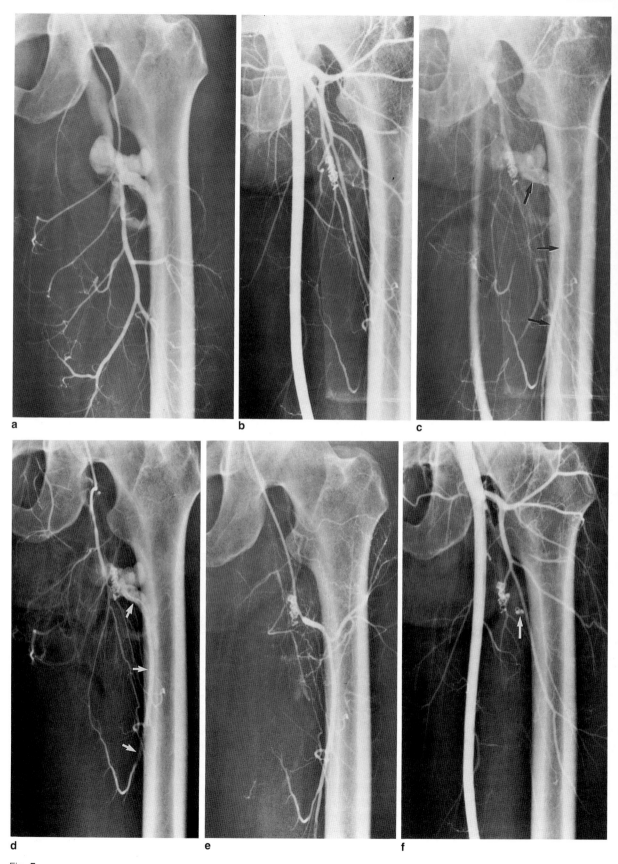

Fig. **5**

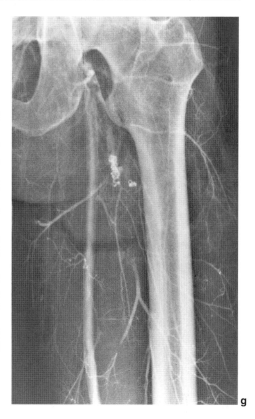

Fig. 5 Mid-course, segmental embolization of the left deep femoral artery, 2 weeks after a subgluteal stab wound

a Preembolization study: deep femoral arteriovenous fistula. The catheter tip is in a correct position at the fistula. Four coils were placed above, at, and below the fistula

b The early phase of the postembolization study shows that the main source of the AVF is occluded

c However, the late phase reveals an additional, retrograde tributary (arrows)

d Selective angiography of a proximal femoral branch shows that the tributary (arrows) is actually the first perforator, now with reversed blood flow from collaterals that cannot be embolized

e The coils have permitted careful manipulation of the catheter between themselves and the arterial wall, into the first perforator. Preembolization study confirms good catheter positioning. A solitary small coil was then placed

f Postembolization angiogram: the early phase shows the new coil in place (arrow), thrombosis of the proximal, branchless deep femoral artery, and elimination of the AVF

g The late phase of the study shows satisfactory collateral filling of the distal deep femoral branches. (Reprinted with permission from Slack, Inc.)

g

ration of these regions is unattractive, given the tedium of the operation and the increased risk of iatrogenic injury (19, 44). Injuries to branches of the deep femoral and axillary arteries are thus commonly treated by embolization (4, 9, 13, 19, 44, 53), although accessible distal injuries may be treated as well (13, 18, 19, 47).

Embolization

Small, peripheral branches can be selectively embolized with Gelfoam. Hemostasis is usually accomplished with placement of one Gelfoam torpedo of appropriate thickness and length through a well-positioned catheter (Fig. **4**) (4, 19).

Embolization of an AVF or an incomplete transection of the deep femoral artery must follow the rules of surgical management. The injured segment of the artery must be isolated from proximal and distal blood flow in a manner that will not affect collateral tissue perfusion. Occlusion of the injured segment can be accomplished by placing coils of suitable size above and below the injury, or throughout the length of the injured segment (Fig. **5**). When feasible, an AVF can be occluded by placement of a detachable balloon in the fistulous tract, thus preserving arterial patency (17).

In selected cases very distal or previously occluded arteries can be treated by direct percutaneous injection of thrombin (15).

Head and Neck

Injuries

The majority of injuries to the neck are penetrating. The ratio between blunt and penetrating trauma to the head and face varies according to the predominant type of violent trauma seen in different hospitals. Injuries to the neck must be surgically or angiographically explored, irrespective of symptoms, whenever there is penetration through the platysma (32). Angiography of head and face injuries is usually done for gross hemorrhage, or when there is a specific suspicion of arterial injury.

Anatomy

The region is anatomically very complex and must be divided into three separate areas of management – neck, face and scalp, and brain. The neck itself cannot be regarded as a single entity and is further divided into three zones, as proposed by Saletta et al. (39).

Zone I includes the thoracic outlet to the level of cricoid cartilage. Surgical access in this zone is free, although it often requires sternotomy. Injuries in Zone I often require emergency surgery for hemorrhage. However, about one-third of the patients are stable, may benefit from angiographic diagnosis, and some can be managed by temporary or permanent transcatheter occlusion (9, 37, 40).

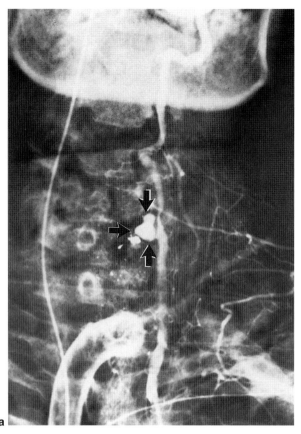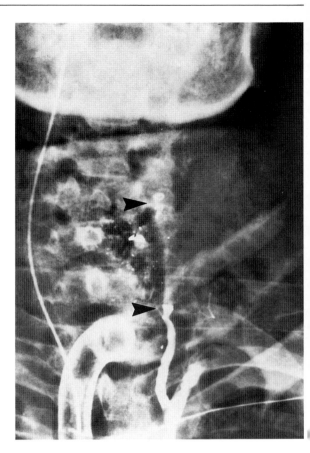

a

Fig. **6** **Trapping of an injured arterial segment by coils**
a Selective left vertebral arteriogram. Hemorrhage from a puncture wound of the left vertebral artery (between arrows)
b After embolization, the injured segment is effectively trapped by coils, placed above and below the bleeding site (arrowheads). (Reprinted with permission from Williams and Wilkins)

Zone II, between the cricoid cartilage and the angle of the mandible, offers free surgical access to all structures except the vertebral arteries, which are surrounded by bone and fascia – an anatomic environment that interferes with diagnosis of injuries and makes surgical access to the arteries extremely difficult. Exploration and management of vertebral artery trauma should therefore be angiographic (Fig. **6**) (6).

Zone III, from the mandibular angle up to and including the base of the skull, offers the surgeon, if at all, extremely difficult access. Its injuries must be explored angiographically and, when feasible, treated by transcatheter embolization (6, 40, 46).

Another deterrent to surgical exploration of the neck is added in the presence of an AVF that does not open directly into the internal jugular vein. In this event all venous plexuses of the neck may participate in draining the AVF, thus becoming acutely "arterialized." This adds a palpable risk of uncontrollable hemorrhage to surgery of the neck.

In the face, angiographic exploration and hemostasis should be preferred because, except for the most superficial structures, surgical access is difficult and the operation itself may be quite deforming (40).

Embolization

The vicinity of the central nervous system severely restricts the choice of occluding agents. Gelfoam and similar materials tend to fragment and embolize the distal microcirculation. Therefore, together with all powders and fluids, they must be avoided as much as possible and replaced by coils or detachable balloons (4).

The vertebral artery is usually expendable and can be embolized without risk of neurologic injury. In a small number of patients the contralateral vertebral artery is either hypoplastic, absent, or terminates in the posterior inferior cerebellar artery, in which case an attempt at surgical repair is necessary (6). Complete transections are embolized proximally (9, 29); if retrograde bleeding from the distal segment is documented, distal ligation may be needed (40, 46). Hemorrhage from a puncture wound is treated by distal and proximal deposition of coils (6) or by total segmental occlusion (10). The risk of delayed hemorrhage from an injured vertebral artery justifies preemptive embolization of this artery (6).

The external carotid artery and its main branches may be embolized with coils. Distal branches must usually be occluded by Gelfoam, a procedure calling for two protective measures: Firstly, the Gelfoam must be wet before cutting, to reduce the likelihood of microemboli, and, secondly, the Gelfoam must be delivered via an occlusion balloon catheter in order to avoid inadvertent retrograde embolization of the internal carotid artery. Because of the anatomic continuity of the external carotid circulation across the sagittal plane, effective control of hemorrhage from this artery may require bilateral embolizations (40).

The internal carotid artery is embolized very rarely, when surgical ligation is indicated but is difficult or impossible to perform, and then only if the embolization is judged not capable of further deteriorating the patient's neurologic status, or if a comprehensive and provocative study of the intracranial circulation and the circle of Willis proves that such an embolization is safe (40).

Other arteries, including the thyrocervical and costocervical and their branches, must be embolized with caution. Both arteries often supply significant branches to the spinal cord, and their compromise may result in quadriplegia (4).

Chest

Injuries

The most likely targets for embolization in chest trauma are the internal mammary arteries. The surgical alternative is their ligation via median sternotomy. These vessels are subject to wounding in both blunt and penetrating incidents. The intercostal arteries, lesser candidates for embolization, sustain injuries by fractured ribs in blunt trauma, by penetrating weapons, as well as by excessively traumatic insertion of trocars and thoracostomy tubes.

Embolization

The internal mammary artery is supported by an extensive array of collaterals throughout its course. When embolizing this artery, one must attempt to place the occluding agents between the site of injury and the collateral arteries immediately above and below it. Proximally, the internal mammary artery is usually tortuous and may not lend itself to easy, deep catheterization. In such an event, or in the presence of complete transection of the artery, coils, minicoils, Gelfoam, or detachable balloons may be advanced into the artery from above, with satisfactory results (40, 49). The success of this incomplete procedure probably stems from the occlusion of the primary blood flow in the artery and some degree of

spasm along the entire vessel secondary to the embolus, which between them diminish the blood flow in the artery to a rate that permits gradual, spontaneous cessation of bleeding.

Embolization of an intercostal artery calls for caution and meticulous catheter techniques in view of the risk of spinal cord infarction (4, 40, 50, 52). The catheter must be advanced as peripherally as possible. The occluding agents of choice are minicoils and detachable balloons.

Abdomen

Injuries

Trauma to the spleen and liver is the most common source of post-traumatic intra-abdominal bleeding. The spleen is injured primarily by blunt trauma; the liver is injured evenly from blunt and penetrating trauma as well as from an increasing incidence of percutaneous iatrogenic injuries. Past surgical traditions of diagnosis and management by peritoneal lavage and exploratory celiotomy with organ resection or repair have produced unacceptable ratios of nontherapeutic celiotomies and increased postsplenectomy morbidity and mortality (17). Radiologists were not actively involved in management of intra-abdominal hemorrhage until encouraged to do so by the current trends toward selective conservatism in management of abdominal trauma, which occurred in parallel with the establishment of diagnosis by CT and interventional vascular radiology (7, 17, 41) and which stress the equal importance of organ preservation and control of hemorrhage.

Embolization

Spleen. Whereas an occasional solitary bleeding vessel in the splenic periphery can be controlled by selective embolization of the individual branch, the technical objective of most embolizations of the spleen is to lower total splenic arterial pressure and blood flow to levels at which the hemorrhage is lessened and clot can form in the lacerations until bleeding subsequently stops. Such a procedure should preserve a functioning spleen and allow its healing (Fig. 7) (41). It is accomplished by deposition of a coil in the splenic artery at a point between the origins of the dorsal pancreatic and pancreatica magna arteries; more distal embolization is acceptable as long as the embolus remains in the main splenic artery. Collateral perfusion of the spleen continues via the short gastric, pancreatic, and gastroepiploic arteries, almost always with complete success of hemostasis as well as splenic preservation.

Splenic embolization may have to be avoided when the diagnostic angiogram shows loss of collateral arteries due to adjacent injuries or previous

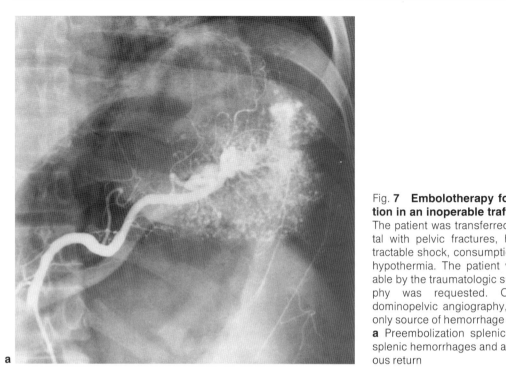

a

Fig. 7 **Embolotherapy for splenic preservation in an inoperable traffic accident patient.** The patient was transferred from another hospital with pelvic fractures, hemoperitoneum, intractable shock, consumption coagulopathy, and hypothermia. The patient was deemed inoperable by the traumatologic surgeon and angiography was requested. On exploratory abdominopelvic angiography, the spleen was the only source of hemorrhage
a Preembolization splenic angiogram: multiple splenic hemorrhages and a somewhat early venous return

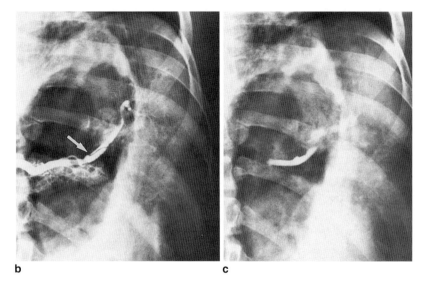

b   c

Fig. **7**
b, c During manipulation of the guide wire, an inadvertent dissection of the splenic artery was incurred (arrow in b). This was utilized as an anchoring site for a long Gelfoam torpedo to complete the occlusion. The control angiogram demonstrates very little flow into the spleen. After embolotherapy, the patient became stable and has subsequently recovered without requiring celiotomy

surgery, although conditions may exist that mandate its performance as a life-saving measure in lieu of celiotomy (Fig. **7**) (8), or as a temporary procedure to stabilize a patient in shock before surgery (7).

Liver. Embolization of the hepatic artery is required mostly as a postoperative intervention, either to reinforce surgical arterial hemostasis, occlude an intrahepatic AVF, or treat an extrahepatic postoperative complication (41).

Before embolization for hepatic arterial hemorrhage, the diagnostic angiogram must show patency of the portal vein and good portal flow into the liver.

A major embolization must not be done in their absence. A second precaution calls for placement of the embolizing catheter's tip distal to the origin of the cystic artery.

Selection of the occluding agent depends on the number of bleeding vessels and their location, and on the intensity of bleeding. Multiple peripheral bleeding vessels are best controlled by a slow scatter embolization of Gelfoam pudding. Coils should be avoided as much as possible: occlusion by coil is usually central and, as such, becomes a barrier against future embolizations.

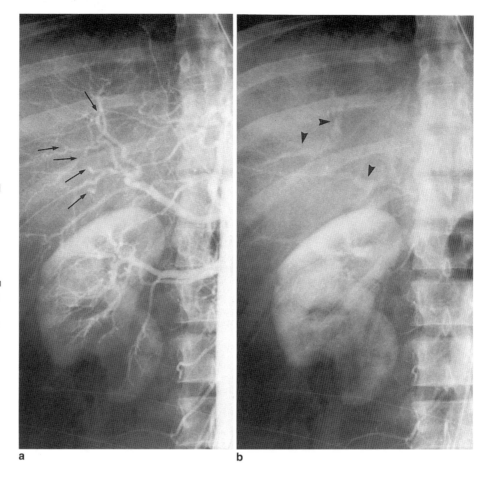

a   b

Fig. 8 **Evolution and subsequent embolotherapy of vascular injury in blunt hepatic trauma (caused by a fall of 7 m, landing supine on a railway line)**
a Admission angiogram, arterial phase. Several branches of the hepatic artery are spastic or amputated (arrows) – sign of a stellate fracture in the right lobe. There is also a south-pole fracture of the right kidney
b The capillary phase of the same study shows early appearance of peripheral portal vein branches in the same area (arrowheads), but without a clear demonstration of an AVF

Hepatic-portal AVF is a major cause of post-traumatic portal hypertension. It can form by transection of the portal triad by an intrahepatic fracture from blunt trauma or by a penetrating injury. Formation of the AVF may occur days or weeks after the incident, hence its absence on the admission angiogram (Fig. **8**). One should be alerted to the potential for delayed occurrence of an AVF whenever the admission angiogram shows nonbleeding transections of hepatic artery branches (Fig. **8a**). Close follow-up and repeat angiography are recommended. For embolization of a hepatic-hepatic or hepatic-portal AVF, coils are used, placed distal and proximal to a centrally located AVF (41) or proximal to a peripheral lesion (Fig. **8e**). Return of portal blood flow to normal can be documented immediately after embolization of a hepatic-portal AVF (Fig. **8f**).

Other Arteries. Post-traumatic hemorrhage from the gastric and mesenteric arteries is treated with the same methods as bleeding from nontraumatic causes. Occasionally, large arterial injuries call for temporary angiographic intervention, such as balloon occlusion of the superior mesenteric artery before and during surgery (4).

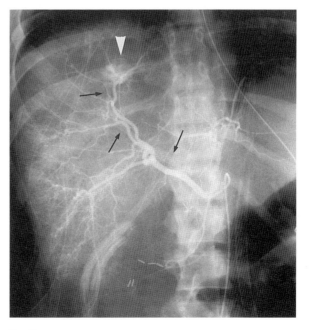

Fig. **8**
c Follow-up study 10 days later. There is now a fully developed hepatic AVF (arrowhead) with reversal of flow in the right portal vein (arrows)

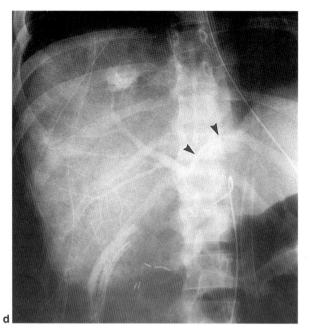

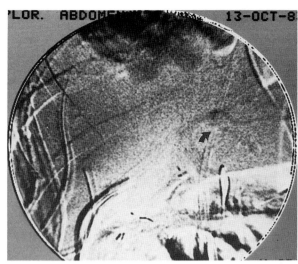

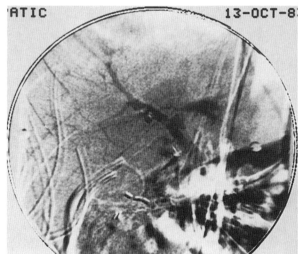

Fig. 8

d A later frame of the same study shows the perifistular hematoma in the right lobe, opacification of the right portal system, and retrograde flow into the left portal vein (arrowheads)

e The preembolization digital angiogram of the portal vein via superior mesenteric artery injection demonstrates that, due to the reversal of flow in the right intrahepatic portal vein, all portal venous return is shunted into the left lobe (arrow)

f After embolization of the right hepatic artery with one coil, a repeat digital angiogram demonstrates return to normal of the right portal blood flow

Extraperitoneum

Injuries

Penetrating renal trauma, divided evenly between iatrogenic injuries and street trauma, is the most common acute extraperitoneal injury. Second in frequency are blunt renal injuries, followed by blunt or penetrating street trauma to the lumbar arteries (20). Duodenal and pancreatic arterial hemorrhage is usually seen and treated as a postoperative complication. Embolizable hemorrhage from arteries such as the adrenal is extremely rare, as is angiographic management of inferior vena caval injuries (36).

Diagnosis

Intrarenal and extraperitoneal vascular injuries require an aggressive radiologic exploration because their clinical diagnosis is very difficult (7, 20). In blunt renal trauma or after injuries by firearms the kidneys must be investigated by CT and, if needed, followed by angiography. Renal stab wounds of any cause should undergo angiography (14, 20). (Excretory urography [intravenous pyelogram] is not necessary. It offers too little useful information about the kidneys and no information regarding the rest of the abdomen). The presence or absence of hematuria is irrelevant. Given the history of violent trauma to the flank or midabdomen, an investigation is needed to find the source of hematuria or equally to find why there is no hematuria.

Operative access to the lumbar arteries is difficult and can be mutilating, with particular threat to the ureter in a transabdominal approach and to the lumbar plexus in a surgical approach from any direction (20).

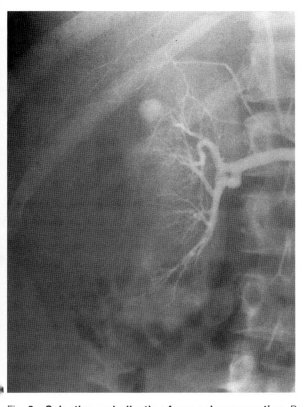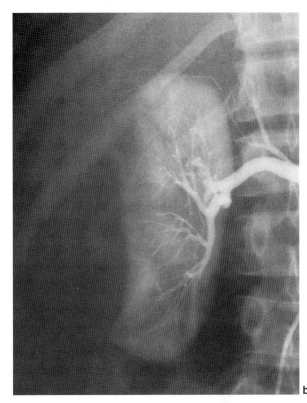

b

Fig. **9** **Selective embolization for renal preservation.** Persistent hematuria 4 weeks after a traffic accident
a Selective right renal angiography. A branch of the renal artery is bleeding into a false aneurysm. A large subcapsular hematoma causes deformation and compression of the renal parenchyma
b After embolization with Gelfoam, the injured artery is effectively occluded. Only a very small volume of renal parenchyma was infarcted. (Reprinted with permission from Slack, Inc.)

Embolization

Renal Artery. Gelfoam is the embolic agent of choice. Steel coils or detachable balloons may be used when necessary but should be reserved for the event of unsuccessful occlusion with Gelfoam (20). The embolization must be restricted to the bleeding branch alone, because the occlusion is irreversible and always results in infarction. However, despite the infarction, patients are not expected to develop postembolization hypertension (11). The success of an embolization is absolute when hemostasis is achieved without surgical intervention or widespread infarction (Fig. **9**). Rarely, in cases of massive and unremitting renal hemorrhage, angiographic ablation of a kidney is far more desirable than nephrectomy (7).

Early angiography and embolization of injured renal artery branches are essential: accumulation of intrarenal hematoma in a neglected injury creates an anatomic deformation that alters the course of renal artery branches and thus prevents selective catheterization and embolization (7, 20).

Lumbar Arteries. Great care must be taken to avoid damage to nerve roots, the cauda equina, or the spinal cord by inadvertent embolization of the spinal branches of the lumbar arteries, since these participate in the blood supply to the nerve roots and cauda equina (52); furthermore, the great anterior root artery of Adamkiewicz, which is sometimes the only ventral feeder to the lower cord, may take origin as low as L-3 (50).

A soft, small-caliber catheter should be advanced as peripherally as possible beyond the origin of the spinal branch. Gelfoam, usually the preferred occluding agent, should be wet before cutting and injected very carefully. A coil may be used if the arterial wound is too large to accomodate Gelfoam (20).

Pelvis

Injuries

The angiographer's primary concern is with pelvic ring disruptions from blunt trauma (8, 33). There is an occasional involvement in hemorrhage from penetrating injuries and postoperative complications (Fig. 1).

Because of the extremely violent force involved, pelvic fractures are almost always a part of a whole-body injury. They are usually complex and are often accompanied by tears in the perineum (28). Mortality from pelvic fracture is high and, in the absence of head injuries, is almost invariably from hemorrhage,

either by exsanguination soon after the impact or from late complications of hemorrhage (8, 21, 31).

Hemorrhagic shock is, therefore, not a contra-indication to angiography and embolization in pelvic ring disruption. Indeed, it is its strongest indication for angiography wherever equipment and personnel are immediately available.

Diagnosis of Hemorrhage in Pelvic Fractures

Three pelvic sources of hemorrhage (arterial, venous, and osseous) and three remote sources (abdomen, chest, and thighs) are potential contributors to shock in pelvic ring disruption. The intensity of bleeding, if any, from each source cannot be predicted by clinical or plain radiographic criteria (8, 27). However, arterial intrapelvic hemorrhage and severe arterial or parenchymal intra-abdominal bleeding are the most common causes of severe shock and, therefore, highest in priority for diagnosis and treatment.

Exploratory celiotomy is contra-indicated because is carries an inordinately high mortality rate in the presence of pelvic fractures (8, 25, 27, 31, 35, 48).

Patients with pelvic fractures should not be assessed by peritoneal lavage. Peritoneal tears occur very frequently with these injuries; the small quantities of blood that seep through them from extraperitoneal hematomas into the peritoneal cavity are responsible for a high rate of false-positive peritoneal lavage and, as a result, for unnecessary celiotomy (8, 27, 31, 35).

The diagnosis and management of abdominopelvic hemorrhage must, therefore, be angiographic. Furthermore, the urgency of angiography demands

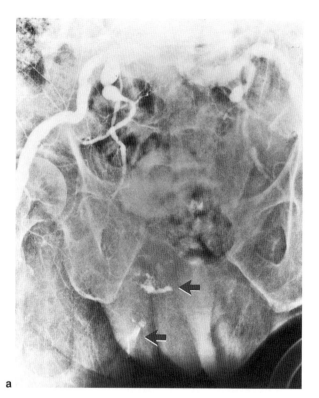

a

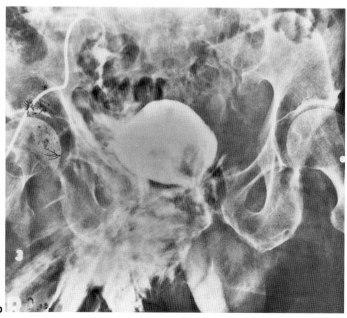

b

Fig. **10 Contrast studies of the urinary tract must not precede angiography. The patient is an 84-year-old man with open pelvic fractures** after an automobile pedestrian accident

a Several points of arterial hemorrhage are seen (arrows)

b After successful embolotherapy, rupture of the urethra was found on urethrography. Notice the spread of extravasated contrast medium directly into the perineum, where angiography has previously shown hemorrhage. Had urethrography been done first, it would have been impossible to diagnose and treat the hemorrhage. (Reprint with permission from Slack, Inc., W. B. Saunders, and Appleton-Century-Crofts)

that, except for the admission films of the chest, pelvis, and lateral C-spine, all other investigations be postponed until after angiography.

It is especially important not to allow intravenous pyelography and cystourethrography to be done before angiography, firstly, because urologic injuries are not life-threatening and, secondly, because if these examinations are positive, extravasated contrast medium will prevent diagnosis of arterial hemorrhage (Fig. **10**) (3, 8).

Nonangiographic Control of Hemorrhage

Reduction and fixation of the fractures is the best means of stopping intrapelvic venous and osseous hemorrhage. However, the surgeon cannot control pelvic arterial hemorrhage: operative ligation of the internal iliac arteries is ineffective and lethal (8, 26, 31, 35, 54) and should be replaced by angiographic hemostasis (8, 31, 35) in conjunction with open reduction and internal fixation of the pelvic fractures (22).

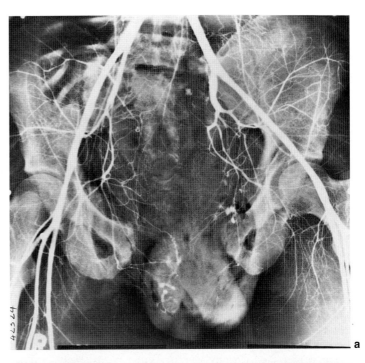

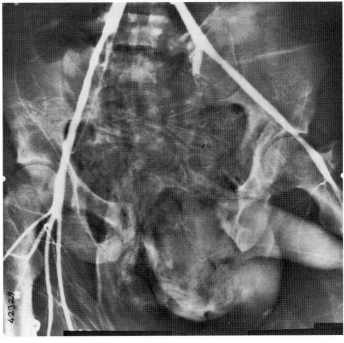

Fig. **11** **Bilateral scatter embolization. Open, unstable pelvic fractures after a traffic accident.** The patient was admitted in severe hemorrhagic shock and was taken immediately to the angiographic suite
a Pelvic arteriography shows multiple, bilateral arterial hemorrhages
b Both internal iliac arteries were embolized with Gelfoam pudding. Bleeding has stopped. After embolization, the following were performed on the angiography table: abdominal aortography, splenic arteriography, urethrography, cystography, and proctoscopy, all showing no injuries. The patient recovered without abdominal surgery. (Reprinted with permission from Slack, Inc., W. B. Saunders, and Appleton-Century-Corfts)

Embolization

It is desirable to embolize the bleeding artery alone by a single Gelfoam torpedo. However, the patient's condition may not permit the investment in time required for meticulous, superselective embolization, and the entire branch system of an internal iliac artery may have to be embolized with Gelfoam pudding (8). Hemorrhage from multiple branches should also be treated with Gelfoam pudding. This type of scatter embolization produces immediate and simultaneous proximal occlusion of all first- and second-generation branches of the internal iliac artery. Retrograde hemorrhage via primary collaterals is thus prevented, but perfusion of the injured area via secondary collaterals can continue. In extreme situations, bilateral internal iliac artery occlusion may be necessary as a life-saving measure (Fig. **11**).

Wide lacerations or transections of the internal iliacs or their divisions should be embolized by coil with Gelfoam backup. In certain patients occlusion by balloon catheter may be needed first. However, one must remember that the occlusion produced by coil or balloon is proximal, similar to a ligation of the internal iliac artery, leaving its branches open to continued hemorrhage through major collaterals (8, 26).

At this juncture one must be aware that it is a fallacy to think of embolization as the ultimate and definitive treatment. At the time of angiography a great many patients have coagulopathy and hypothermia, which, if not reversed, encourage collateral hemorrhage and thus nullify the effect of the embolization (8). Therefore, except for reduction and fixation of the fractured pelvis, if this was not done before angiography, surgery must be avoided and the patient treated supportively in an environment that allows restoration of normal body temperature and clotting activity.

The most common associated extrapelvic injury is to the spleen. Injuries to this organ should be diagnosed and, if necessary, embolized during the initial exploratory angiogram (Fig. **7**) (7, 8).

A risk of necrosis of the urinary bladder, and the uterus in the female, after an effective, bilateral embolization of the interna liliac arteries is a hypothetical possibility far outweighed by the threat of exsanguination. I am not aware of an occurrence of this complication in embolization for post-traumatic hemorrhage.

Injuries to the sacral plexus are very common in pelvic ring disruption. These, as well as perineal injuries, are the primary causes of impotence in these patients. It is, therefore, impossible to say whether or not embolization of the internal pudendal or internal iliac arteries in the male can lead to impotence (31). However, even if it does, weighing this risk against the risk of death, we assume that most patients are likely to opt for the former.

Conclusion

The importance of embolotherapy in the management of arterial hemorrhage is indisputable. The key to its success is rapid diagnosis. Unless a patient needs a life-saving operation, angiography and embolization should be performed preoperatively, often as a replacement for surgery, and always before execution of any diagnostic or therapeutic procedure that is not essential to save life.

Critical injuries must be suspected and pursued irrespective of clinical symptoms. The diagnostic angiogram should therefore be planned in light of the mechanism of injury and its wounding capacity, and without undue regard to obvious and therefore superficial injuries.

Embolotherapy should be planned and performed with care and expertise as a prelude to, or as a replacement for surgery, only when it is considered more beneficial to the patient than an operation and can be so executed.

Given that the purpose of angiography and embolotherapy is to diagnose and treat hemorrhage when other means cannot do so, then, in the appropirate setting, hemorrhagic shock cannot constitute a contra-indication to the transport of a patient to the angiographic suite.

References

1. Barach E, Tomlanovich M, Nowak R. Ballistics: a pathophysiologic examination of the wounding mechanisms of firearms, part 1. J Trauma 1986;26:225–235.
2. Barach E, Tomlanovich M, Nowak R. Ballistics: a pathophysiologic examination of the wounding mechanisms of firearms, part 2. J Trauma 1986;26:374–383.
3. Ben-Menachem Y. Logic and logistics of radiography, angiography,and angiographic intervention in massive blunt trauma. Radiol Clin North Am 1981;19:9–15.
4. Ben-Menachem Y, ed. Angiography in trauma: a work atlas. Philadelphia: Saunders 1981.
5. Ben-Menachem Y. Vascular injuries of the extremities: hazards of unnecessary delays in diagnosis. Orthopedics 1986;9:333–338.
6. Ben-Menachem Y, Fields WS, Cadavid G, Gomez LS, Anderson EC, Fisher RG. Vertebral artery trauma: transcatheter embolization. AJNR 1987;8:501.
7. Ben-Menachem Y, Handel SF, Ray RD, Childs TL III. Embolization procedures in trauma: a matter of urgency. Semin Intervent Radiol 1985;2:107–117.
8. Ben-Menachem Y, Handel SF, Ray RD, Childs TL III. Embolization procedures in trauma: the pelvis. Semin Intervent Radiol 1985;2:158–181.
9. Ben-Menachem Y, Handel SF, Thaggard A III, Carnovale RL, Katragadda C, Glass TF. Therapeutic arterial embolization in trauma. J Trauma 1979;19:944–952.
10. Bergsjordet B, Strother CM, Crummy AB, Levin AB. Vertebral artery embolization for control of massive hemorrhage. AJNR 1984;5:201–203.
11. Bertini JE Jr, Flechner SM, Miller P, Ben-Menachem Y, Fischer RP. The natural history of traumatic branch renal artery injury. J Urol 1986;135:228–230.
12. Chuang VP, Reuter SR, Walter J, Foley WD, Bookstein JJ. Control of renal hemorrhage by selective renal embolization. AJR 1975;125:300–306.
13. Clark RA, Gallant TE, Alexander ES. Angiographic management of traumatic arteriovenous fistulas: clinical results. Radiology 1983;147:9–13.

14. Cope C, Zeit RM. Pseudoaneurysms after nephrostomy. AJR 1982;139:255–261.
15. Cope C, Zeit RM. Coagulation of aneurysms by direct percutaneous thrombin injection. AJR 1986;147:383–387.
16. Debrun G, Lacour PP, Vinuela F, Fox A, Drake CG, Caron JP. Treatment of 54 traumatic carotid-cavernous fistulas. J Neurosurg 1981;55:678–692.
17. Debrun G, Legre J, Kasbarian M, Tapias PL, Caron JP. Endovascular occlusion of vertebral fistulae by detachable balloons with conservation of the vertebral blood flow. Radiology 1979;130:141–147.
18. Edwards H, Martin E, Nowygrod R. Nonoperative management of a traumatic peroneal artery false aneurysm. J Trauma 1982;22:323–326.
19. Fisher RG, Ben-Menachem Y. Embolization procedures in trauma: the extremities: acute lesions. Semin Intervent Radiol 1985;2:118–125.
20. Fisher RG, Ben-Menachem Y. Embolization procedures in trauma: the abdomen: extraperitoneal. Semin Intervent Radiol 1985;2:148–157.
21. Gilliland MD, Ward RE, Barton RM, Miller PW, Duke JH. Factors affecting mortality in pelvic fractures. J Trauma 1982;22:691–693.
22. Goldstein A, Phillips T, Sclafani SJA, Scalea T, Duncan A, Goldstein J, Panetta T, Shaftan G. Early open reduction and internal fixation of the disrupted pelvic ring. J Trauma 1985;26:325–333.
23. Greenfield AJ. Transcatheter vessel occlusion: methods and materials. In: Athanasoulis CA, Pfister RC, Greene RE, Roberson GH, eds. Interventional radiology. Philadelphia: Saunders 1982:40–54.
24. Hebeler RF, Ward RE, Miller PW, Ben-Menachem Y. The management of splenic injury. J Trauma 1982;22:492–495.
25. Hubbard SG, Bivins BA, Sachatello CR, Griffen WO Jr. Diagnostic errors with peritoneal lavage in patients with pelvic fractures. Arch Surg 1979;114:844–846.
26. Jander HP, Russinovich NAE. Transcatheter gelfoam embolization in abdominal, retroperitoneal, and pelvic hemorrhage. Radiology 1980;136:337–344.
27. Kam J, Jackson H, Ben-Menachem Y. Vascular injuries in blunt pelvic trauma. Radiol Clin North Am 1981;19:171–186.
28. Kane WJ. Fractures of the pelvis. In: Rockwood CA, Green DP, eds. Fractures. Philadelphia: Lippincott 1975:923–973.
29. Kobernick M, Carmody R. Vertebral artery transection from blunt trauma treated by embolization. J Trauma 1984;24:854–856.
30. Merion RM, Harness JK, Ramsburgh SR, Thompson NW. Selective management of penetrating neck trauma: cost implications. Arch Surg 1981;116:691–696.
31. Mucha P Jr, Farnell MB. Analysis of pelvic fracture management. J Trauma 1984;24:379–386.
32. Ordog GJ, Albin D, Wasserberger J, Schlater TL, Balasubramaniam S. 110 bullet wounds to the neck. J Trauma 1985;25:238–246.
33. Panetta T, Sclafani SJA, Goldstein AS, Phillips TF, Shaftan GW. Percutaneous transcatheter embolization for massive bleeding from pelvic fractures. J Trauma 1985;25:1021–1029.
34. Peck JJ, Berne TV. Posterior abdominal stab wounds. J Trauma 1981;21:298–306.
35. Peltier LF. Comments to the 43rd annual session of the American Association for the Surgery of Trauma, Chicago, Sept 29 to Oct 1, 1983. J Trauma 1984;24:385.
36. Ravikumar S, Stahl WM. Intraluminal balloon catheter occlusion for major vena cava injuries. J Trauma 1985;25:458–460.
37. Richardson A, Soo M, Fletcher JP. Percutaneous transluminal embolization of vertebral artery injury. Aust NZ J Surg 1984;54:361–363.
38. Ring EJ, Athanasoulis C, Waltman AC, Margolies MN, Baum S. Arteriographic management of hemorrhage following pelvic fracture. Radiology 1973;109:65–70.
39. Saletta JD, Lowe RJ, Lim LT, Delk S, Moss GS. Penetrating trauma of the neck. J Trauma 1976;16:579–587.
40. Sclafani SJA. Transcatheter control of arterial bleeding in the neck, mediastinum and chest. Semin Intervent Radiol 1985;2:130–138.
41. Sclafani SJA. Angiographic control of intraperitoneal hemorrhage caused by injuries to the liver and spleen. Semin Intervent Radiol 1985;2:139–147.
42. Sclafani SJA. Angiographic treatment of chronic post-traumatic arteriovenous fistulas of the extremities. Semin Intervent Radiol 1985;2:125–129.
43. Sclafani SJA, Cooper R, Shaftan GW, Goldstein AS, Glantz S, Gordon DH. Arterial trauma: diagnostic and therapeutic angiography. Radiology 1986;161:165–172.
44. Sclafani SJA, Shaftan GW. Transcatheter treatment of injuries to the profunda femoris artery. AJR 1982;138:463–466.
45. Sclafani SJA, Shaftan GW, Mitchell WG, Nayaranaswamy TS, McAuley J. Interventional radiology in trauma victims: analysis of 51 consecutive patients. J Trauma 1982;22:353–360.
46. Sclafani SJA, Panetta T, Goldstein AS, Phillips TS, Hotson G, Loh J, Shaftan GW. Management of arterial injuries caused by penetration of zone III of the neck. J Trauma 1985;25:871–881.
47. Shah PM, MacKey R, Babu SC, Kulkarni S, Clauss RH. Pseudoaneurysm of anterior tibial artery after occlusion from blunt trauma: non operative management. J Trauma 1985;25:656–658.
48. Shah R, Max MH, Flint LM Jr. Negative laparotomy: mortality and morbidity among 100 patients. Am Surg 1978;44:150–154.
49. Smith DC, Senac MO, Bailey LL. Embolotherapy of a ruptured internal mammary artery secondary to blunt chest trauma. J Trauma 1982;22:333–335.
50. Tveten L. Spinal cord vascularity, III: the spinal cord arteries in man. Acta Radiol [Diagn] (Stockh) 1976;17:257–273.
51. Uflacker R, Lima S, Ribas GC, Piske RL. Carotid-cavernous fistulas: embolization through the superior ophthalmic vein approach. Radiology 1986;159:175–179.
52. Walls EW. The blood vascular and lymphatic systems. In: Romanes GJ, ed. Cunningham's textbook of anatomy. 10th ed. London: Oxford University Press 1964:893–898.
53. White RI Jr, Barth KH, Kaufman SL, DeCaprio V, Strandberg JD. Therapeutic embolization with detachable balloons. Cardiovasc Intervent Radiol 1980;3:229–241.
54. Yellin AE, Lundell CJ, Fink EJ. Diagnosis and control of posttraumatic pelvic hemorrhage. Arch Surg 1983;118:1378–1383.

Embolization Techniques in the Brain, Head and Neck, and Spinal Cord

Embolization in the Brain

C. Manelfe, P. Lasjaunias, V. V. Halbach and A. S. Mark

The brain has remained one of the last territories in which therapeutic embolization has been used, because of the risk of cerebral ischemia and its devastating neurological consequences. The advances in superselective catheterization have allowed a better understanding of functional vascular anatomy (mainly the various vascular territories and the potential anastomoses between them). This improved knowledge of the angiographic anatomy was greatly helped by the improvement in catheterization equipment over the past ten years: microcatheters, balloons, propulsion chambers, non-ionic contrast media, and various other embolization materials.

While embolization of the external carotid artery has become widely accepted for treatment of vascular malformations and palliation of head and neck tumors, intracerebral embolization is still performed only in several highly specialized centers.

Historical Background

It appears that the first embolization was performed by Dawbarn in 1904 (18) for a malignant tumor in the territory of the external carotid artery after surgical exposure of the vessel; the embolization was performed with a mixture of paraffin and petroleum jelly. Brooks, in 1930, used autologous muscle in the internal carotid artery to occlude a post-traumatic carotid cavernous fistula (CCF) (12). In the 1960s and 1970s, several authors used endovascular occlusion in the treatment of certain arteriovenous malformations (AVMs) and CCFs (51, 73, 99). Djindjian in France, as early as 1971, developed and improved the technique of superselective embolization via the femoral route, and defined its main indications (26). As mentioned above, the first embolizations were performed in the territory of the external carotid artery because of the reduced risks of cerebral ischemia (27, 28, 49, 75, 76, 77, 78, 94).

Embolization in the internal carotid territory was first described by Luessenhop and Spence (72) in 1960 for treatment of a cerebral AVM. The embolization was performed with silastic spheres after sur-

gical exposure of the internal carotid artery. Advanced interventional radiology techniques in the internal carotid territory started in the early 1970s: Boulos et al. (11) treated cerebral AVMs that were considered inoperable using Teflon spheres introduced in the internal carotid artery; Prolo and Hambery (99), in 1971, treated a CCF using a Fogarty balloon. This pioneering work showed that embolization in the internal carotid artery was possible, but the indications for the technique remained infrequent (58, 93). As early as 1971, Serbinenko showed an original technique for closure of a CCF with preservation of the internal carotid artery (107). Later, he reported 300 cases of lesions treated by the endovascular route (CCFs, cerebral AVMs, and aneurysms) using detachable balloons (108). However, no technical details were given in these articles. Shortly after, Debrun et al. reported their own detachable balloon technique, and demonstrated their first results in the treatment of AVMs and aneurysms (19). Kerber, in the United States, introduced superselective catheterization of the intracerebral vessels using a calibrated-leak balloon microcatheter (55). This microcatheter allowed the injection of isobutyl-2-cyanoacrylate, a rapidly polymerizing plastic, into AVMs (4, 23, 56, 110, 124). Considerable technical improvements of the balloon microcatheters (silastic, latex, siltane, pursil), and of the propulsion devices, have been developed in the last five years (22, 82, 92, 102).

Anatomical and Clinical Considerations

The brain is particularly sensitive to ischemia, and its terminal vascularization explains the serious consequences of arterial spasm and distal emboli. This also explains why the femoral technique is preferred to the direct carotid puncture whenever technically feasible. Access to the intracerebral circulation via the carotid or vertebral arteries presents several problems, according to the type of lesion.

Access through the carotid siphon (CCFs or intracavernous aneurysms) is relatively easy, and was one of the first regions to be accessed with a Fogarty balloon (99). The technique of coaxial catheters with a detachable balloon allows adequate treatment of most intracavernous carotid lesions (19). The catheterization of the distal branches of the internal carotid artery requires use of a calibrated-leak balloon microcatheter. Only dilated vessels with increased flow (as seen in AVMs) may be easily accessed. It is usually not possible, in spite of the different attempts at magnetic guidance, to steer the catheter selectively in a specific vascular bifurcation; this usually requires the placement of a second balloon catheter (57).

The same considerations are true for the catheterization of the vertebrobasilar system. Due to the uniqueness of the basilar artery, the risk of ischemia is even greater at this level, with potentially devastating neurologic consequences. The femoral route is preferred to the axillary route. The curves of the vertebral artery, especially in its third segment in front of C1 and C2, may make the approach to low-flow lesions difficult. The posterior cerebral arteries can be catheterized through the vertebral arteries or, when a high-flow lesion such as an AVM is present, through the carotid and posterior communicating arteries.

Initially, endovascular embolization was considered only in patients with inoperable lesions who could not benefit from radiation therapy or any other treatment. With further technical improvements, the indications for endovascular treatment have been extended and now can be considered in: the definitive treatment of certain lesions, such as traumatic CCFs and intracavernous aneurysms, where the detachable balloon technique has completely transformed the treatment and prognosis of this lesion; in preparation for surgery, such as in certain AVMs; as a palliative technique when surgery is impossible.

It is important to remember that intracerebral lesions often have a vascular supply originating both from the internal carotid and/or vertebral artery, and from the external carotid artery (65). This is often the case for dural arteriovenous malformations at the skull base, or in the posterior fossa, where the embolization of the external carotid territory may produce a considerable decrease in the internal carotid or vertebral supply.

Technical Considerations

As mentioned earlier, most institutions use the femoral approach whenever possible. However, certain authors propose the use of axillary or direct carotid punctures (82). Intracranial embolization requires constant monitoring of the patient's neurologic status. The high risk of neurologic complications due to spasm or migration of the balloon or the embolic material makes general anesthesia unsuitable for this procedure. Neuroleptanalgesia is

the technique of choice, combining patient comfort and safety. It also allows neuropsychological tests to be performed prior to embolization in the functional cerebral territory. As mentioned earlier, there is a considerable risk during embolization from clot formation on the endovascular material. For this reason, most authors (23, 69, 95, 120) use full heparinization (clotting time 3 times that of the control) during the procedure. After the embolization is performed, the anticoagulation is reversed with protamine sulfate.

The type of material used (catheters, embolization material, etc.) varies according to specific indications (6, 7). We would only like to mention the invaluable role played by digital substraction angiography in the performance of therapeutic embolization. This technique has several advantages over conventional angiography: one can assess the position of the balloon and microcatheter in relation to the lesion and evaluate inflation and detachment of the balloon; considerable decrease in examination time; approximately 50% decrease in the amount of contrast used; use of smaller-sized catheters is possible.

Indications

Dural Arteriovenous Fistulas (DAVFs)

Classically considered to represent 10–15% of the intracranial AVMs (7% of supratentorial AVMs, 35% of posterior fossa AVMs), DAVFs are probably more frequent than previously thought (1, 50, 86). The average age of presentation is in the fifth decade, with an equal sex distribution. The clinical presentation depends not only on the site of the fistula, but also on its venous drainage, which is also a main prognostic factor determining the therapeutic approach (66).

Two anatomic and clinical types can be distinguished (13): DAVFs with venous drainage into a sinus present with pulsatile bruit, exophthalmos, or oculomotor palsy; DAVFs with cortical venous drainage can present with focal neurologic findings (seizures, motor deficit) or hemorrhagic complications (intracerebral, subarachnoid or subdural hematoma) (38, 63, 66).

Knowledge of the arterial vascularization of the meninges and its variations is extremely important in identifying the various pedicles supplying the DAVF; in assessing the type of venous drainage (into a sinus or into a cortical vein); in assessing the therapeutic possiblities: choice of catheter and embolization materials; and in assessing the risks of embolization (61, 62, 64, 67). This leads to a simple angiographic protocol, depending on the location of the malformation (Table 1). We will first consider the various

Table **1** Angiographic protocols

Region to explore: homolateral pedicles	Internal carotid artery (ICA)	Internal maxillary artery (IMA)	Middle meningeal artery (MMA)	Ascending pharyngeal artery (APA)	Occipital artery (OA)	Vertebral artery (VA)	Other pedicles
1) *Anterior cranial fossa*	AP L	AP	L				Contralateral ICA: AP Distal IMA: AP MMA: AP
2) *Cavernous sinus* * Anterior part (superior orbital fissure)	L	L	L	L			Contralateral ICA: AP IMA: AP MMA: AP
* Middle and posterior part	L	L	L	L	L ±	L	Contralateral ICA: AP APA: AP IMA: AP
3) *Tentorium and torcular*	L	L	L	L	L	L	Contralateral ICA: AP APA: AP
	AP		L	L	L	AP + L	MMA: AP APA: L OA: AP
4) *Lateral and sigmoid sinus*	L		L	L	L	AP + L	OA: AP
5) *Foramen magnum*	AP (±)		L (+)	L	L	AP + L	Contralateral APA: AP Contralateral OA: L

topographic locations and then the therapeutic approach to DAVFs.

Location and clinical presentation

DAVFs of the anterior cranial fossa (17, 32, 52, 71, 122). Most of these are located at the level of the cribriform plate of the ethmoid bone. Their vascularization originates from the anterior ethmoidal artery, branch of the ophthalmic artery, the frontal branch of the middle meningeal artery, or from the sphenopalatine branch of the internal maxillary artery. The venous drainage is most often into a frontal cortical vein, the superior sagittal sinus or towards an olfactory or basilar vein.

Subarachnoid hemorrhage is the commonest clinical presentation, often associated with subdural hematoma. Seizures, recurrent epistaxis, or visual field deficits are much more rare.

The treatment is essentially surgical, since only partial embolization is possible because of the predominant supply from the internal carotid artery. However, since the ethmoidal branches communicate at the level of the nasal cavity with the distal branches of the sphenopalatine artery, this artery may be used as a potential route of embolization. Thus, the embolization of the sphenopalatine artery

with Ivalon fragments may be performed after surgical ligation of the ethmoidal artery (63).

DAVFs of the cavernous region (5, 24, 29, 63, 74, 85, 86, 90, 97, 115, 119). Clinically, these present with exophthalmos, most often moderate in size, conjunctival hyperemia, and an intracranial bruit with unilateral or bilateral third or fourth cranial nerve palsy. According to their location, they can be separated into:

Anterior DAVFs close to the superior orbital fissure, which most often present with hemorrhagic events or seizures. The arterial supply originates from the internal maxillary, the anterior meningeal and middle meningeal arteries, and from meningeal branches of the internal carotid artery from the inferolateral trunk, penetrating the orbit via the superior orbital fissure and anastomosing with the ophthalmic artery (Fig. **1**). The venous drainage is both towards the sinus (superior ophthalmic vein), and cortical veins (temporal sylvian vein).

DAVFs of the cavernous sinus itself are the second commonest DAVFs after those of the transverse sinus. They occur mainly in women older than 50. Arterial hypertension is associated in almost 50% of the cases (5). Selective angiography demonstrates the exact type: external carotid artery to cavernous

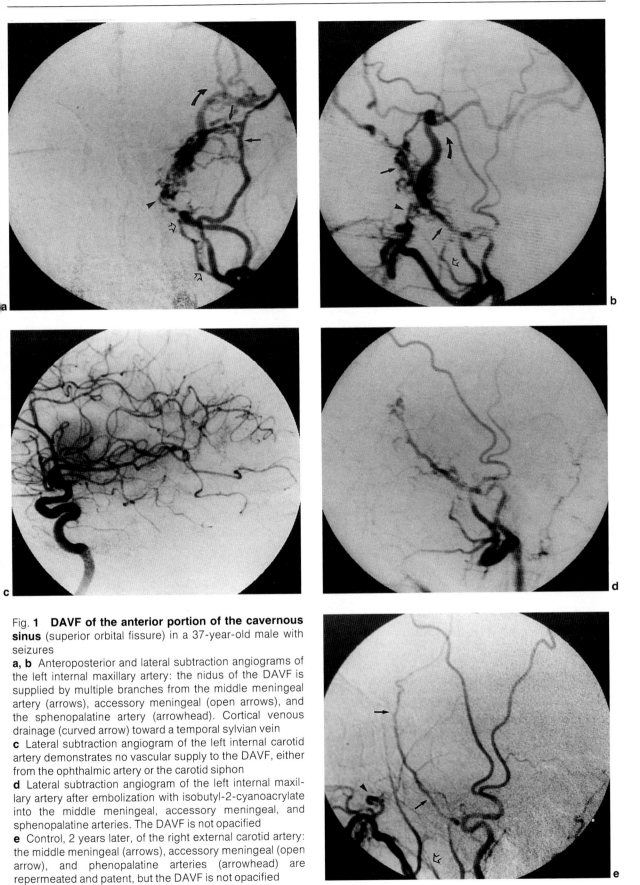

Fig. 1 DAVF of the anterior portion of the cavernous sinus (superior orbital fissure) in a 37-year-old male with seizures

a, b Anteroposterior and lateral subtraction angiograms of the left internal maxillary artery: the nidus of the DAVF is supplied by multiple branches from the middle meningeal artery (arrows), accessory meningeal (open arrows), and the sphenopalatine artery (arrowhead). Cortical venous drainage (curved arrow) toward a temporal sylvian vein

c Lateral subtraction angiogram of the left internal carotid artery demonstrates no vascular supply to the DAVF, either from the ophthalmic artery or the carotid siphon

d Lateral subtraction angiogram of the left internal maxillary artery after embolization with isobutyl-2-cyanoacrylate into the middle meningeal, accessory meningeal, and sphenopalatine arteries. The DAVF is not opacified

e Control, 2 years later, of the right external carotid artery: the middle meningeal (arrows), accessory meningeal (open arrow), and phenopalatine arteries (arrowhead) are repermeated and patent, but the DAVF is not opacified

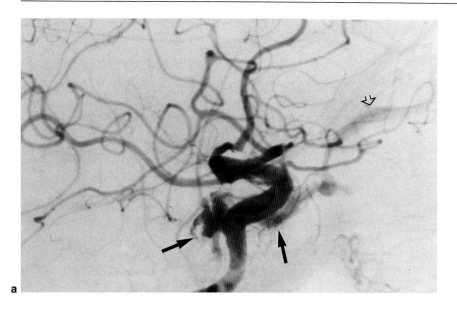

a

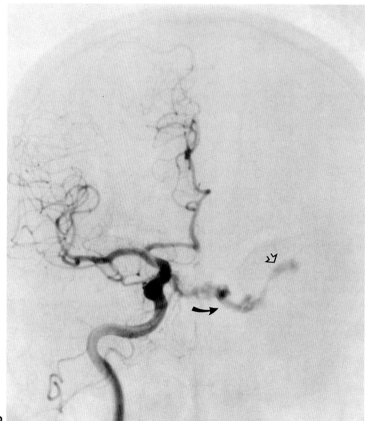

b

Fig. **2**   **DAVF of the cavernous sinus** in a
60-year-old male with moderate bilateral
proptosis, eye redness, and slight intracranial
tinnitus
a, b Lateral and anteroposterior subtraction
angiograms of the right internal carotid artery:
opacification of the cavernous sinus by
intracavernous clival branches (arrows). The
venous drainage crosses the midline through
anastomoses behind the dorsum sellae
(curved arrow) and opacifies the cavernous
sinus and superior ophthalmic vein (open
arrow) on the left side

sinus of mixed internal and external carotid to
cavernous sinus (Figs. **2, 3**).

The external carotid artery supply originates from
the internal maxillary artery (pterygoid branches),
the middle meningeal artery (cavernous branch), the
meningohypophyseal trunk, and the ascending
pharyngeal artery (neuromeningeal trunk and clival

branch). The internal carotid artery supply originates
mainly from the inferolateral trunk, which has a
reciprocal balance with the cavernous branches of
the homologous internal maxillary artery. The venous drainage is to the superior ophthalmic vein, the
superior and inferior petrosal sinuses (or both) and,
in cases of cortical venous drainage, towards the

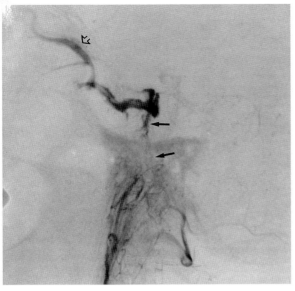

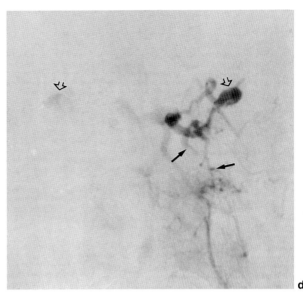

Fig. **2**
c, d Lateral and anteroposterior subtraction angiograms of the left ascending pharyngeal artery. The cavernous DAVF is opacified by clival branches (arrows) of the ascending pharyngeal artery, and drains into the superior ophthalmic veins (open arrows). Compare with **b.** The ascending pharyngeal artery was embolized with lyophilized dura-mater

Fig. **2**
e Lateral subtraction angiogram of the right external carotid artery. Faint opacification of the posterior part of the cavernous sinus and superior ophthalmic vein (open arrows) by the middle meningeal artery; this pedicle was embolized with lyophilized dura mater particles

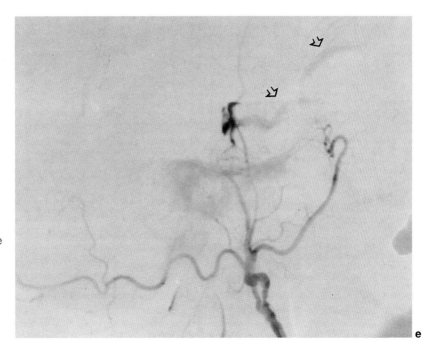

superficial sylvian veins. The presence of arterial anastomoses on each side of the sella between the two internal and external carotid systems requires bilateral and selective angiography.

Accurate identification of the type of DAVF and vascular supply is extremely important. Indeed, in patients with mixed fistulas (both external and internal carotid to cavernous sinus) the nidus may be obliterated via the external carotid artery without requiring embolization of the internal carotid artery. The placement of a detachable balloon in the internal carotid artery as a primary treatment is indeed contra-indicated in this type of mixed fistula. Balloon occlusion of the internal carotid artery must be con-

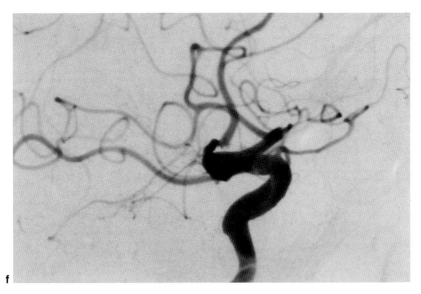

f

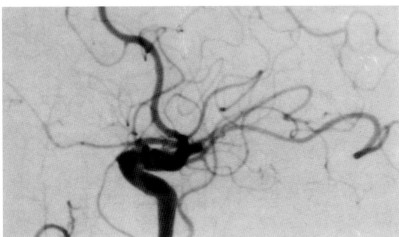

g

Fig. **2**
f, g Follow-up angiography one year after embolization. The patient is symptom-free. Lateral subtraction angiograms of the right and left internal carotid arteries: the DAVF is not opacified. Note the disappearance of the clival branches of the internal carotid artery (a) after embolization in the external carotid area alone

sidered in case of failure to embolize the external carotid supply and recurrence of symptoms.

DAVFs of the tentorial incisura and torcular (63, 109). These fistulas are rare, and are more common in men. Since the cerebellar and cerebral falx are not anatomic barriers to extradural vessels, angiographic exploration must be bilateral and include both the supra- and infratentorial vessels. Venous drainage of the fistula is usually mixed into the sinus and cortical veins. The clinical presentation includes papilledema, visual disturbances, seizures or intracranial bruit. Treatment is difficult, and the embolization is usually performed in several sessions.

DAVFs of the transverse sinus (30, 50, 63, 83, 84, 86, 88, 98, 112, 113). This is the commonest variety. A retroauricular bruit is present in at least 75% of patients. Headaches, papilledema, hemianopsia, seizures, intracerebral or subdural hemorrhage can be the presenting symptoms. The neurological findings

appear to correlate with venous hypertension. The hemorrhagic complications are more common when the venous drainage is into a cortical vein. Djindjian suggested an angiographic classification in three categories based on the pattern of venous drainage (30):

Type 1: Fistulas with venous drainage towards the internal jugular vein on the same side as the fistula;

Type 2: Fistulas with venous drainage into the contralateral sinus (Fig. **3**);

Type 3: Fistulas with cortical venous drainage.

This classification may represent three different stages of the evolution of a similar disease. The severity of the symptoms correlates with the severity of the venous occlusive disease.

The arterial supply is often multiple: occipital artery, middle meningeal artery (posterior branch), posterior auricular artery, and ascending pharyngeal

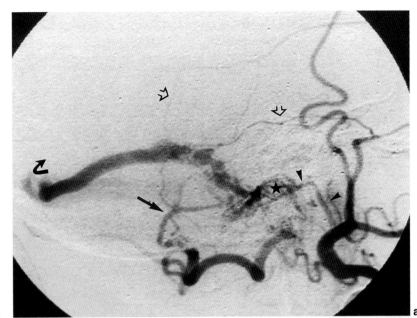

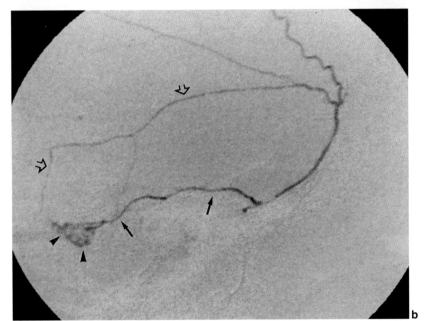

Fig. 3 **DAVF of the lateral sinus**
in a 60-year-old male with pulsatile
tinnitus
a Lateral subtraction angiogram of the
right external carotid artery. Dural
fistula of the lateral sinus supplied by
multiple pedicles arising from the
occipital artery (arrow), ascending
pharyngeal artery (arrowheads), and
posterior branches of the middle
meningeal artery (open arrows).
The right lateral sinus is partially
thrombosed in its sigmoid portion
(star), and venous drainage is toward
the opposite lateral sinus (curved
arrow) (Type II fistula)
b Lateral subtraction of superselective injection in the middle
meningeal artery through an open
guide wire. The nidus (arrow-heads)
of the DAVF is well demonstrated, and
supplied by the petrosal branch
(arrows) and by the inferior and
posterior branch (open arrows) of the
middle meningeal artery. This artery
was embolized with a mixture of 50%
IBCA and 50% Lipiodol with tantalum
powder

artery (jugular branch of the neuromeningeal trunk).
Supply from the internal carotid artery is noted in
30–40% of cases, originating from meningeal
branches along the clivus and the superior aspect of
the petrous bone. The vertebral artery supplies the
fistula in 20–30% of cases via inferior and posterior
meningeal branches.

Cortical venous drainage is seen in 25–40%. The
interruption of the transverse sinus proximal or distal
to the fistula is more frequent in Type 3 than in Type
2 and Type 1 (Type 1: 6 out of 26; Type 2: 15 out of
26; Type 3: 18 out of 19) (44, 98). Occlusion of the

transverse sinus is an almost constant finding in Type
3. Several hypotheses have tried to explain the
pathogenesis of these DAVFs. Currently it is thought
that these lesions are acquired by opening of
arteriovenous shunting after thrombophlebitis of the
transverse sinus. A history of hypertension, trauma,
or worsening during periods of hormonal stimulation
(pregnancy, menopause) are frequently encountered
(14, 63).

DAVFs of the foramen magnum. These are rare,
and can be mistaken for cervicobulbar AVMs. The

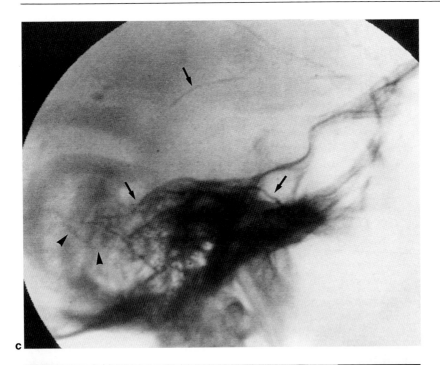

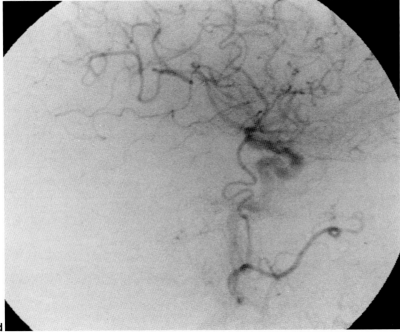

Fig. 3
c Lateral skull view after embolization. The radiopaque glue is well
visualized in the embolized vessels,
the petrosal and posterior branches of
the middle meningeal artery (arrows),
and in the nidus (arrowhead). N. B.:
The middle meningeal artery was the
only pedicle embolized, and no
embolization was performed in the
occipital or ascending pharyngeal
arteries
d Follow-up right common carotid
angiography one week after middle
meningeal artery embolization: lateral
subtraction, capillary phase. There is
no filling of the lateral sinus fistula and,
above all, no opacification from the
ascending pharyngeal and occipital
arteries

presenting symptoms may include cerebellar signs, subarachnoid hemorrhage, or, as in one of our patients, intractable hiccups. The supply from the external carotid artery via the hypoglossal branch of the neuromeningeal trunk of the ascending pharyngeal artery and of the occipital artery confirms the dural attachment of this malformation (Fig 4). If the anterior and posterior meningeal branches of the vertebral arteries and the external carotid branches share a common nidus, treatment of the fistula is only possible by embolization in the external carotid territory.

Treatment

The decision to treat or not to treat a DAVF depends upon the patient's clinical symptoms and the type of DAVF. 10–60% of spontaneous DAVFs may heal spontaneously (5, 33, 53); these are usually slow-

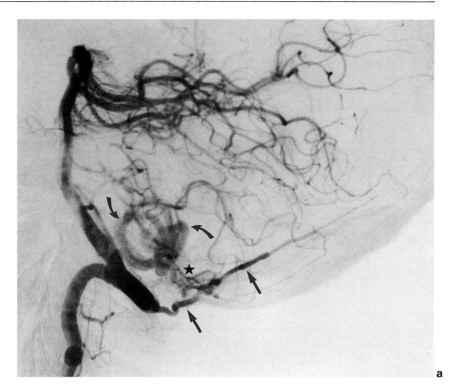

a

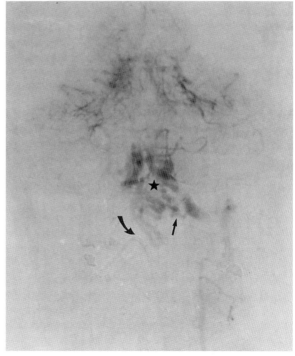

b

Fig. **4   DAVF of the foramen magnum** in a 55-year-old male with subarachnoid hemorrhage, cerebellar signs, and intractable hiccup

a, b Lateral subtraction angiogram of the left vertebral artery arterial phase and anteroposterior capillary phase. Early filling of posterior fossa veins close to the foramen magnum and medulla (curved arrows). Hypertrophy of the posterior meningeal artery (arrows) which supply tortuous vessels representing the nidus (star). There is no obvious supply of the vascular malformation by the posterior inferior cerebellar artery

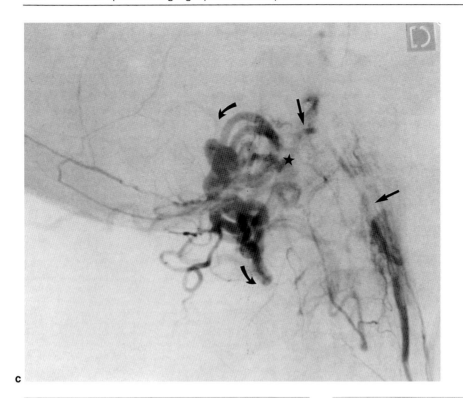

c

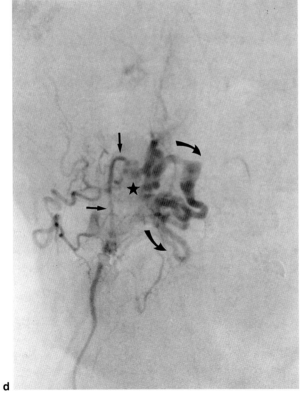

d

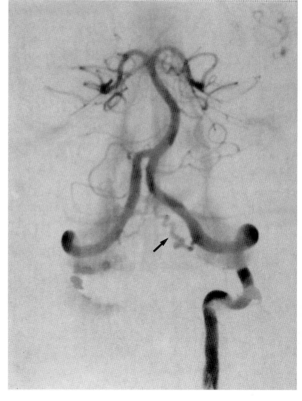

Fig. 4
c, d Lateral and anteroposterior subtraction angiogram of the right ascending pharyngeal artery. Hypertrophy of the neuromeningeal trunk (arrows) and early venous filling of the same veins as demonstrated on vertebral angiography (curved arrows). The nidus (star) is common with the vertebral artery (compare with b). The ascending pharyngeal artery was selectively embolized with duramater and Ivalon particles

e Control, 18 months later, of the left vertebral artery. The posterior meningeal branch (arrow) is present and patent, and there is no opacification of the fistula. Clinical cure

flowing fistulas. The closure occurs most commonly following arteriography.

The surgical treatment (direct approach or arterial ligation) is difficult technically and often clinically incomplete (112). Radiation therapy has been proposed for slow-flow fistulas (10). The aim of endovascular treatment is to obliterate the nidus between the meningeal vessels and the venous drainage completely. If the nidus can be totally obliterated by injection of the external carotid supply, the internal carotid and/or vertebral supply will spontaneously regress. Visual disturbances (progressive decrease of visual acuity, progressive exophthalmos, glaucoma or diplopia), intracranial hemorrhage, refractory seizures, and intolerable bruit are all strong indications for endovascular treatment. The technique depends upon: the ability to catheterize the supplying arteries selectively; the venous drainage (cortical vein or sinus); and the potential risks of the procedure (anastomoses and/or dangerous vessels).

DAVFs with cortical drainage are particularly prone to hemorrhage. In these patients, the use of a non-resorbable embolic material such as isobutyl-2-cyanoacrylate (IBCA) is recommended whenever possible. Particulate emboli such as Ivalon, lyophylized dura, or polypropylene microspheres are used for the initial treatment of DAVFs draining into a sinus.

Complications

Pain in the embolized territories is generally transient and easily controlled with appropriate medication. An inflammatory reaction in the orbit secondary to venous congestion may be seen after embolization of the DAVFs of the cavernous sinus. This may require treatment with corticosteroids and anticoagulants (63). A peripheral 7th nerve palsy can be seen after embolization of the middle meningeal artery, especially if the stylomastoid branch of the occipital artery has also been embolized. Paralysis of the 9th, 10th, 11th and 12th cranial nerve may occur after embolization of the ascending pharyngeal artery. These cranial nerve palsies can occur with any embolic material, but are more severe and permanent after embolization with IBCA. The risk of migration of the embolic material on the venous side with secondary venous hypertension is only seen in high-flow fistulas. This requires the use of a rapid polymerizing material such as IBCA. These iatrogenic venous thromboses rarely require treatment with anticoagulants.

Carotid Cavernous Fistulas

Carotid cavernous fistulas (CCFs) are spontaneous or acquired connections between the internal carotid artery and the cavernous sinus. Direct connections between the internal carotid artery and the cavernous sinus may occur as a consequence of trauma, ruptured intracavernous carotid aneurysms, collagen deficiency syndromes, arterial dissection, fibromuscular dysplasia, and direct surgical trauma (16, 25, 43).

Clinical Presentation

The most common presenting symptoms secondary to a CCF include retroorbital bruit, pulsating exophthalmos, conjunctival edema, headache, and ophthalmoplegia. CCFs can, however, produce massive epistaxis, fatal intracerebral hemorrhage, transient or permanent neurological deficits, and blindness.

The normal tributaries to the cavernous sinus include the superior and inferior ophthalmic veins, central retinal vein, and cortical veins draining into the sphenoparietal sinus. Normal venous drainage from the cavernous sinus includes the inferior and superior petrosal sinuses. The third, fourth, and fifth cranial nerves course through the cavernous sinus.

With the establishment of a direct connection between the internal carotid artery and cavernous sinus there is increased flow through the low resistance shunt. The turbulent blood flow accounts for the pulse-synchronous bruit. There is reversal of flow in the superior and inferior ophthalmic veins, causing these veins to be under higher pressure. The engorgement of the veins results in transudation of fluid to the soft tissues, proptosis, and pulsatile exophthalmos. The circular sinus connects the two cavernous sinuses and allows bilateral drainage and symptoms from a unilateral fistula. Hyperemia of the conjunctival vessels is a further reflection of the increased venous pressure. The incrased pressure in the superior ophthalmic veins diminishes the absorption of aqueous humor and results in increased intraocular pressure (glaucoma). The low resistance shunt into the fistula decreases arterial flow and pressure in the ophthalmic artery. Retinal perfusion pressure is a function of ophthalmic artery pressure minus superior ophthalmic vein pressure, divided by the intraocular pressure (103). When this pressure decreases sufficiently, retinal ischemia and blindness can result. Ischemic changes can occur at all levels of the ocular system. Corneal blebs, corneal opacities, pupillary paralysis, cataracts and retinal neoproliferative changes can all result from hypoxic effects secondary to a CCF (103). The pressure within the cavernous sinus can result in paralysis or paresis of the oculomotor nerves. Stretching of the sensitive dura lining of the cavernous sinus results in retroorbital headache.

If venous drainage is diverted into the cortical veins through the sphenoparietal sinus, venous hypertension can result in neurological dysfunction or hemorrhage (Fig. 5). If the initial basal skull

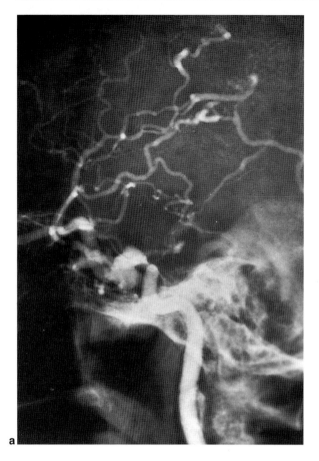

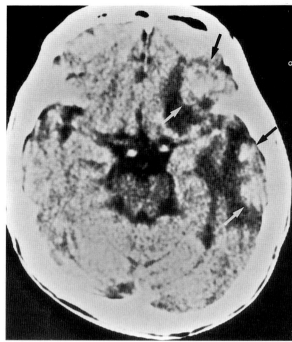

Fig. 5 **Post-traumatic carotid cavernous fistula** (CCF)
a Left internal carotid injection, lateral view, demonstrates
cortical venous drainage from a CCF without opacification
of the internal carotid artery
b Non-contrast CT demonstrates frontal and temporal
hemorrhages (arrows) secondary to the cortical venous
hypertension

fracture extends into the sphenoid sinus, massive epistaxis can occur.

Symptoms caused by CCFs are related to their size, duration, location, adequacy and route of venous drainage, and the presence of arterial and venous collaterals (66).

Treatment

Unfortunately the natural history of CCFs is not completely understood. Spontaneous closure has been documented by Seeger et al., as well as closure following diagnostic angiography (106). Angiographic findings and clinical signs and symptoms that herald a high-risk fistula, and therefore are indications for emergency therapy, have been identified (42). These include the presence of a large cavernous sinus varix or cortical venous drainage which has an increased risk of subarachnoid or intraparenchymal hemorrhage. Rapid or severe visual loss, progressive proptosis, increased intracranial pressure, and neurological deficits are also indications for emergency therapy.

Surgical and angiographic techniques which have been described for the closure of CCFs include carotid occlusion, trapping procedures, direct surgi-

cal exposure and closure, embolization with muscle, glue, thrombus, wires, and, more recently, detachable balloons (3, 8, 20, 31, 43, 54, 87, 89, 93, 99, 104, 105, 107). None of these therapies is without its risks, however.

In patients with less symptomatic fistulas, a trial of carotid compression may reduce or obliterate the fistula. In this therapy, the patients are instructed to compress their own carotid artery and jugular vein with the contralateral hand for a duration, beginning with ten seconds per compression, several times per hour. If tolerated, the duration of the compression is gradually increased to thirty seconds per compression. The first few compressions are monitored by a physician to observe for signs of hypotension or cerebral ischemia. The contralateral hand is utilized so that, if weakness develops without the patient knowing, the compressing hand falls away and the treatment is automatically terminated. Patients are instructed to watch carefully for signs of cerebral ischemia. During effective compression, the bruit is obliterated. The combination of diminished arterial inflow and increased venous outflow resistance promotes thrombosis within the fistula. The maximal effectiveness is usually within 4–6 weeks. Successful treatment is often accompanied by mild retroorbital pain secondary to the thrombosis (116). There are several contra-indications to this form of therapy, including patients with underlying carotid atherosclerosis. Patients who demonstrate cortical venous drainage from the fistula should not further aggravate their venous hypertension by intermittently compressing the jugular vein. Patients with clinical signs and symptoms with a poor prognosis, such as rapid visual decline or neurological deficit, deserve more rapid and agressive forms of therapy. Eight of the 48 patients (17%) treated by compression therapy have had complete resolution of their fistula (47). There have been no complications from this form of therapy.

Of the patients who have failed or are excluded from compression therapy, transvascular embolization is currently the treatment of choice. We initially perform a diagnostic angiogram including a 3-vessel study, with and without compression of the involved carotid artery over the catheter, to delineate the site and size of the fistula. Injection of the vertebral artery with simultaneous compression of the involved carotid artery can also help to delineate the fistula (81). Selective external carotid angiography is usually not needed, except to document the size of the superfical temporal artery if an external carotid-internal carotid bypass is necessary.

A transarterial approach is tried first with detachable balloons, and is successful in the majority of cases. The large flow into the cavernous sinus helps the balloon enter the fistula. The balloon is then inflated to a diameter greater than the caliber of the internal carotid artery to ensure that it does not enter the arterial circulation and, if it is in a satisfactory position, it is detached.

The detachable balloon technique results in closure of the fistula with preservation of the carotid flow in 90% of cases. In about 10%, the balloon does not enter the cavernous sinus, mainly because the orifice of the fistula is too small. In some cases the venous compartment of the fistula is too large, and cannot be occluded by a single balloon; complete occlusion of the fistula requires several balloons and carries the risk of oculomotor palsies by compression of the nerves in the cavernous sinus. In some cases, permanent occlusion of the internal carotid artery in front of the fistula by the balloon is the only possible treatment. Permanent occlusion of the internal carotid artery using a balloon is safer than arterial ligature.

A transvenous approach through the inferior petrosal sinus or superior ophthalmic vein and occlusion of the fistula with balloons, liquid adhesives, or coils may be successful (79). Rarely, both transarterial and transvenous approaches fail to alleviate the fistula, and surgical exposure, with direct puncture and embolization of the cavernous sinus, may be necessary.

Risks and Complications

If thrombus forms on the catheters, or the balloon prematurely detaches, a transient or permanent neurological deficit may develop. Cranial nerve palsy may develop or worsen when balloons are placed within the cavernous sinus, but is often transient (40, 54). Intracerebral hemorrhage and blindness can occur if the venous outflow pathways are occluded without occluding the fistula. Thrombosis can occur in the dilated superior ophthalmic vein following closure of the fistula, with transient worsening of symptoms (109). Post-traumatic fibrosis may result in narrowing and delayed occlusion of the carotid artery. If balloon deflation occurs within the cavernous sinus, a pseudoaneurysm may develop, and can present with symptoms similar to those of a cavernous aneurysm (pain, ophthalmoplegia and emboli).

Aneurysms

Clinical Presentation

Most giant aneurysms induce mass effects; ocular palsies are common with intracavernous aneurysms, and blindness is one of the most severe complications. Subarachnoid or intracerebral hemorrhage are rare in cases of intracavernous aneurysms.

Treatment

The optimal treatment of intracranial aneurysms is surgical clipping. For giant aneurysms, aneurysms in inaccessible locations (cavernous sinus, petrous carotid), aneurysms with a wide or absent neck, and patients with severe underlying diseases, surgical clipping may not be possible. For these unclippable aneurysms various treatments have been devised, including electrothrombosis, wrapping of the aneurysm, proximal ligation, or trapping procedures with ligatures, clamps, or, more recently, balloons (9, 21, 36, 39, 96, 114). Subsequent advances in technique and technology have permitted the treatment of intracranial aneurysms (46, 48, 101). In aneurysms with a definable neck a balloon can be negotiated into the aneurysm and detached, thus preserving parent artery flow. In aneurysms without a definite neck, proximal occlusion or trapping procedures can be performed with detachable balloons (36, 45).

Current indications for treatment include failed neurosurgical clipping, surgically inaccessible aneurysms, and patients who are not surgical candidates (poor clinical status or severe underlying diseases). As previously mentioned, the procedure is performed under local anesthesia and intravenous sedation to allow continuous neurological monitoring.

If the aneurysm has a definable neck, a silicone or latex balloon is navigated into the aneurysm, inflated to exclude the aneurysm from the cerebral circulation, and then detached (Fig. **6**). The balloon is filled

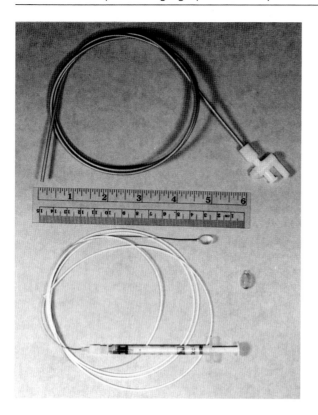

Fig. 6 **Equipment used at the University of California – San Francisco** for treatment of intracranial aneurysms includes silicone detachable balloons attached to a 2 Fr catheter

with a polymer to prevent aneurysm recanalization should the shell of the balloon deteriorate. If the aneurysm lacks a definable neck, a test occlusion of the parent artery is performed under systemic anticoagulation. If tolerated, a proximal occlusion or trapping procedure is performed. If test occlusion is not tolerated then bypass surgery to augment cerebral perfusion is done, followed by permanent occlusion if tolerated.

Most of the aneurysms treated by balloon occlusion are located in the cavernous carotid region. The location of the remainder of the aneurysms include carotid ophthalmic, supraclinoid, posterior communicating, carotid bifurcation, posterior inferior cerebellar artery origin, mid-basilar, basilar tip, and posterior cerebral artery (Fig. **7**). The parent artery can be preserved in about one third of the cases (45). Proximal ligation and trapping procedures are performed in the remainder. In patients who present with symptoms of mass effects related to the aneurysm, parent artery preservation by placing the balloon in the aneurysm or permanent occlusion are effective in the alleviation of mass effects (Fig. **8**) (60).

Complications

Neurological complications such as stroke can be related to ischemia, by compression of the parent vessel by the balloon inflated into the aneurysm; to distal emboli from the occluded artery or from the partially occluded aneurysmal sac; and to hemorrhage by aneurysm rupture. Neurological complications account for about 10% of patients treated by balloon; the remaining 90% have an excellent clinical outcome (45, 48).

Arteriovenous Malformations (AVMs)

Clinical Presentation

Arteriovenous malformations (AVMs) represent 1.5–2% of surgically proved intracranial masses (91). Men and women are involved with equal frequency. Approximately 2000 new cases in the United States, and 400 in France (40 in children) are diagnosed every year (34, 59, 91). AVMs are congenital anomalies, probably representing dysfunction of the development of the vascular system which leaves an arteriovenous communication without the usual interposition of a capillary bed (2, 73).

AVMs can be differentiated according to the type of vessels they involve. With time, secondary changes may be superimposed on the primary embryological defect: these changes may be progressive, secondary to the chronic arteriovenous shunting, or acute, producing sudden complications, such as acute hemorrhage. Regardless of the cause, these secondary changes will disturb the initial vascular architecture, making it more susceptible to further complications.

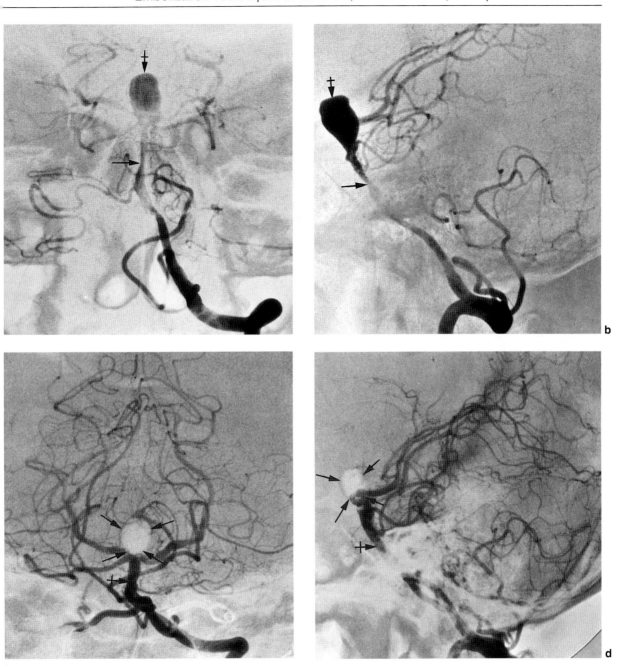

Fig. **7**   **Basilar tip aneurysm** in a 46-year-old male with a large subarachnoid hemorrhage
a, b Anteroposterior and lateral left vertebral angiograms demonstrate a distal basilar aneurysm (crossed arrow). There is associated vasospasm of the mid-basilar artery to a diameter of 1.5 mm (arrow). A balloon angioplasty was performed on the mid-basilar narrowing, and a single detachable balloon was navigated into the lumen of the aneurysm and detached
c, d Post-embolization left vertebral angiograms in Towne's and lateral view demonstrate obliteration of the aneurysm sac (arrow) and disappearance of basilar artery spasm (crossed arrow)

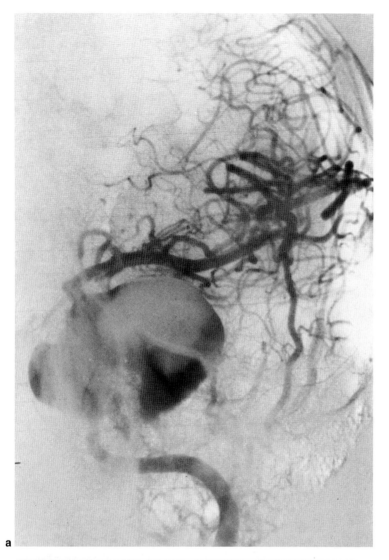

a

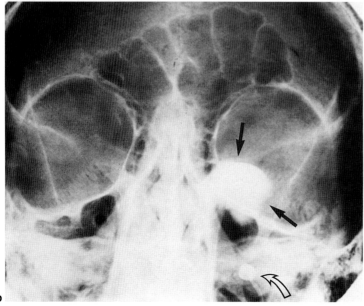

b

Fig. **8 Giant intracavernous aneurysm** in a 16-year-old patient with left complete ophthalmoplegia and subarachnoid hemorrhage
a Anteroposterior subtraction angiogram shows a giant intracavernous aneurysm
b Plain skull film with the balloon inflated in the intrapetrous portion of the internal carotid artery. Thrombase was perfused with the balloon inflated. The polygon of Willis was patent

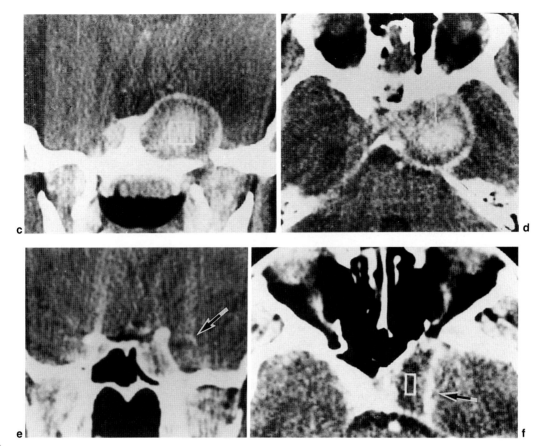

Fig. 8
c, d Coronal and axial CT enhanced sections immediately post balloon placement. Note the ring enhancement of the aneurysm and the mass effect
e, f 7 months after balloon occlusion of the internal carotid artery. Marked decreased of the mass effect related to aneurysm thrombosis (arrows). Clinical recovery

The vast majority (72–94%) of AVMs are supratentorial. 60–70% involve the cortex and the lateral ventricles, 15–20% the basal ganglia, and 10% the corpus callosum.

The most common clinical presentations are hemorrhage, seizures, focal neurological deficits or headaches. Hydrocephalus, intracranial bruit, heart failure, or mental retardation are rarer clinical presentations. A close correlation exists between the age of the patient at the time of the diagnosis of his AVMs and the risk of a major complication during his life, in particular a massive hemorrhage. The younger the patient, the higher the chances of a hemorrhage. The risk of hemorrhage in a patient who has never bled before is approximately 2–3% per year (37, 41). In other words, a patient has a 25% chance of having a first bleed in the 15 years which follow his initial diagnosis, a 25% chance of a rebleed within four years, and another 25% chance of a third bleed within one year. 100% of the children who have bled before age 15 have a second hemorrhage before age 25. The hemorrhage may be secondary to

the rupture of a draining vein, secondary to venous hypertension following thrombosis or stenosis of the venous outlet (59), or secondary to rupture of an arterial aneurysm in the nidus of the AVMs (70). These data result from the analysis of the natural history of untreated patients at a time when the diagnosis of AVM was made by angiography. Magnetic resonance imaging (MRI) has shown that evidence of chronic subclinical hemorrhage is noted in a large number of AVMs in asymptomatic patients. The difficulty of diagnosing a hemorrhage retrospectively from the patient's clinical history leads to different therapeutic approaches by various teams for the same patient or in similar clinical situations.

Indication for Endovascular Treatment

The treatment of AVMs includes surgery, therapeutic neuroangiography, and radiation therapy, either on their own or in combination. The initial endovascular treatment used free-flow embolization with

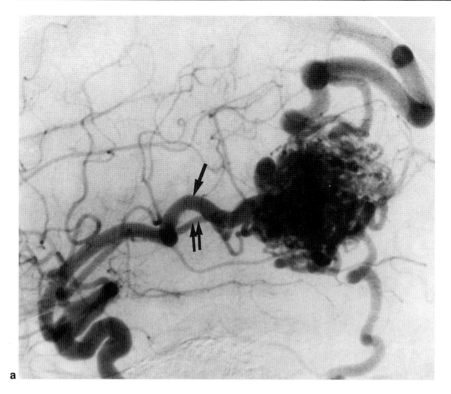

a

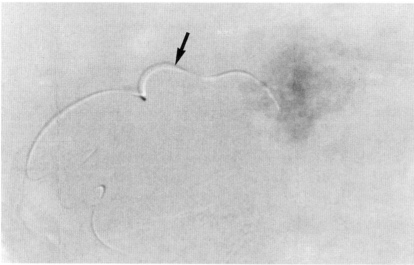

b

Fig. **9** **Left temporoparieto-occipital AVM** in a 24-year-old patient with subarachnoid hemorrhage
a Lateral subtraction angiogram of the left internal carotid artery demonstrates a large AVM involving the temporoparieto-occipital region. The AVM is supplied by 2 main pedicles (arrow and double arrows) from the middle cerebral artery
b, c Lateral superselective angiogram of the 2 pedicles (arrow and double arrows) with a microcatheter. Opacification of then idus of the AVM. The 2 pedicles were embolized with a mixture of IBCA, Lipiodol and tantalum powder

microspheres (11, 111, 123). The random distribution of the embolized material raises the possibility of embolizing normal brain parenchyma. This technique is used in large AVMs where the size of the supplying arteries is at least 4 times that of the adjacent normal vessels. In these patients, most of the blood is stolen by the AVM and thus, most of the embolic material ends up in the AVM. However, this technique is rarely curative in itself, since the whole malformation can rarely be embolized.

Advances in selective catheterization of the intracranial branches of the carotid artery have made possible the selective embolization of the nidus of the AVM with polymers such as isobutyl-2-cyanoacrylate (IBCA) (4, 15, 23, 69, 95, 118). Initially, this technique was limited to AVMs which could not be approached surgically (deep AVMs of the basal ganglia or brain stem) or as preoperative technique in large AVMs (Fig. **9**). The indications for endovascular treatment are still evolving. The treatment of the AVMs requires close collaboration between the neurosurgical and neuroradiology teams. Several clinical, anatomical, and hemodynamical considerations will lead to the decision to embolize an AVM.

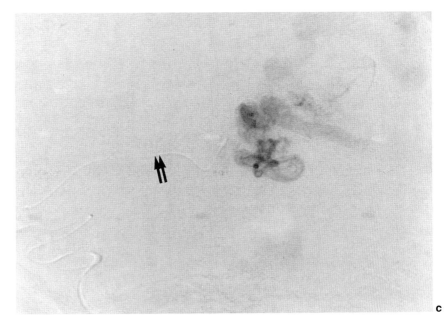

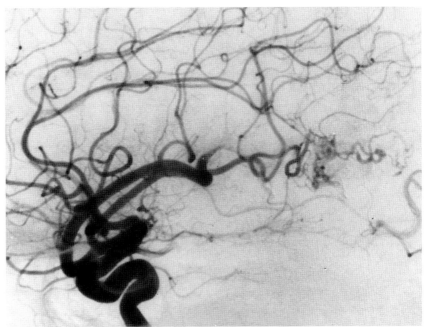

Fig. **9**
d Lateral subtraction angiogram after embolization, showing a marked decrease in the size of the AVM

Hemorrhage. A previous hemorrhage represents one of the main indications for endovascular treatment. The aim of the therapy is to obliterate the nidus of the AVM completely. However, complete cure is achieved in only 10% of patients (69, 95). The angiographic demonstration of aneurysms within the nidus, or signs of venous outflow obstruction (areas of narrowing along the draining vein, drainage towards a different territory than expected, obstruction of dural sinuses) are angiographic signs that put the patient at high risk of hemorrhage, and are indications for endovascular treatment (70). The

purpose of the endovascular treatment is to decrease the flow in the territory where the aneurysms were identified and to decrease the venous hypertension.

Other clinical symptoms (focal neurologic deficit, seizures, severe debilitating headaches). In addition to hemorrhage, both steal of a normal vascular supply and extension of the venous hypertension toward normal parenchyma can also lead to neurologic symptoms. These symptoms depend primarily upon the anatomic location of the AVM, the flow within the AVM (the higher the flow, the higher the vascular steal from the adjacent territory), and the type of venous drainage. The venous hypertension in the adjacent normal cortical veins can be diagnosed by noting the slow flow time in the AVM compared with the normal veins. Persistent cortical veins on the late phases of the arteriogram, drainage into a dural sinus far from the expected sign of drainage of the territory of the AVM, or drainage into the contralateral hemisphere, are signs of venous hypertension. The

progression of these neurologic symptoms is difficult to predict after endovascular treatment.

Technique

The endovascular treatment is performed, as mentioned earlier, under neuroleptanalgesia and full heparin therapy, with continuous monitoring of the patient's neurologic status. A microcatheter is introduced via a femoral puncture and advanced with a propulsion chamber. Careful study of the angioarchitecture of the AVM by hyperselective injection of the pedicles supplying the malformation is fundamental (68, 95, 120) (a) to the therapeutic choice of whether to embolize or not and (b) to the choice of the concentration of IBCA to inject.

An Amytal test is performed prior to the selective embolization: a positive Amytal test is a contraindication to embolization with IBCA; however, this test is not totally reliable, and false negatives have been described (95). Certain areas, such as AVMs in the area of the anterior choroidal artery, carry a high therapeutic risk. Conversely, AVMs located in the corpus callosum and behind the motor strip are less dangerous to embolize than those located anteriorly. Certain basal ganglia AVMs can be treated by embolization using a double approach, through the deep perforating branches and through the cortical branches (95).

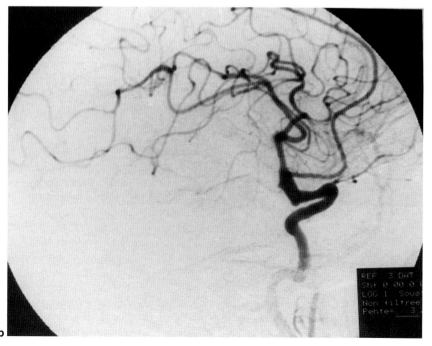

Fig. 10 **Large meningioma of the right sphenoid ridge**
a Lateral subtraction angiogram of the selective middle meningeal and **b** internal carotid arteries. The tumor is almost exclusively supplied by the anterior branch of the middle meningeal artery

Usually, 1–3 feeding arteries are embolized during each session depending upon the findings of the selective arteriogram. Depending upon the patient's tolerance and the morphological results, 1–3 sessions a year may be performed.

Only 10–15% of AVMs can be completely cured by endovascular treatment. While the angiographic appearance after embolization of nonsurgical AVMs may be good, the long-term results are still being evaluated (35, 69, 121).

Risks and Complications

Brain stem AVMs entail high therapeutic risks, but their natural evolution is usually dramatic. Currently, in good hands, the operative mortality of endovascular treatment is 1–2% and transient morbidity and permanent morbidity 4–5% (69, 95).

Miscellaneous

Various intracranial tumors, such as meningiomas or extracranial tumors of the head and neck, can also benefit from endovascular treatment.

Meningiomas

The goal of preoperative embolization of intracranial meningiomas is to facilitate their surgical removal by reducing tumor vascularity and decreasing blood loss during surgery. Embolization is performed during diagnostic angiography. The choice of embolic material depends upon the location and size of the tumor, the size of the feeding arteries, and the presence of potentially dangerous anastomoses between the external carotid and internal carotid vertebral artery, or arteries supplying the cranial nerves. Embolization is useful in large tumors with predominant external artery supply, in skull base meningiomas, in middle fossae and paracavernous lesions. Falcine and parasagittal meningiomas receiving blood supply from the opposite side, and posterior fossa meningiomas, are also helped by preoperative embolization (80) (Fig. **10**).

Skull Base Tumors with Intracranial Extension

Certain ENT tumors, such as glomus tumors or juvenile angiofibromas, may extend intracranially, making surgical resection of them extremely difficult. The supply of the external carotid artery can be embolized with various embolic materials. If the supply from the internal carotid artery (in its intrapetrous or intracavernous portion) is significant, the artery may be permanently occluded by a detachable balloon when the polygon of Willis is patent (100). Successfull embolization of the petrous and cavernous branches of the internal carotid artery can also be achieved with particles after temporary occlusion of the internal carotid artery (76, 117).

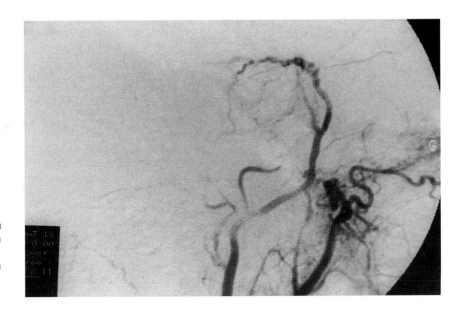

Fig. **10**
c After selective embolization in the middle meningeal artery with Ivalon particles (150 to 250 μ) the tumor blush disappears, with preservation of the main trunk of the middle meningeal artery

References

1. Aminoff MJ. Vascular anomalies in the intracranial dura mater. Brain 1973;96:601–612.
2. Andre JM, Picard L, Kissel P. Les dysplasies vasculaires systématisées. J Neuroradiol 1970;1:3–45.
3. Bank WO, Kerber CW, Drayer BP, Troost BT, Maroon JC. Carotid cavernous fistula: endarterial cyanoacrylate occlusion with preservation of carotid flow. J Neuroradiol 1978;5:279–285.
4. Bank WO, Kerber CW, Cromwell LD. Treatment of intracerebral arteriovenous malformations with IBCA: initial clinical experience. Radiology 1981;139:601–616.
5. Barrow DL, Spector RH, Braun IF, Landman JA, Tindall SC, Tindall GT. Classification and treatment of spontaneous carotid-cavernous sinus fistulas. J Neurosurg 1985;62:248–256.
6. Berenstein A, Kricheff II. Catheter and material selection for transarterial embolization: technical considerations, part. 1: catheters. Radiology 1979;132:619–631.
7. Berenstein A, Kricheff II. Catheter and material selection for transarterial embolization, part 2: materials. Radiology 1979;132:619–630.
8. Berenstein A, Kricheff II, Ransohoff J. Carotid cavernous fistulas. AJNR 1980;1:449–457.
9. Berenstein A, Ransohoff J, Kuppersmith M, Flamm E, Graeb D. Transvascular treatment of giant aneurysms of the cavernous carotid and vertebral arteries: functional investigation and embolization. Surg Neurol 1984;21:3–21.
10. Bitoh S, Hasegawa H, Fujiwara M, Nakao K. Irradiation of spontaneous carotid-cavernous fistulas. Surg Neurol 1982;17:282–286.
11. Boulos R, Kricheff II, Chase NE. Value of cerebral angiography in the embolization treatment of cerebral arteriovenous malformations. Radiology 1970;97:65–70.
12. Brooks B. Treatment of traumatic arteriovenous fistula. South Med J 1930;23:100–106.
13. Castaigne P, Bories J, Brunet P, Cassan JL, Meininger V, Merland JJ. Fistules artérioveineuses de la dure-mère: etude clinique et radiologique de 13 observations. Ann Med Interne (Paris) 1975;126:813–817.
14. Chaudhary MY, Sachdev VP, Weitzner I, Puljic S, Huang JP. Dural arteriovenous malformation of the major venous sinuses: an acquired lesion. AJNR 1982;3:13–19.
15. Cromwell LD, Harris BA. Treatment of cerebral arteriovenous malformations: a combined neurosurgical and neuroradiological approach. J Neurosurg 1980;52:705–708.
16. Dandy WE. Carotid cavernous aneurysms (pulsating exophthalmos). Zentralbl Neurochir 1937;2:77–113, 165–204.
17. Dardenne G. Dural arteriovenous anomaly fed by ethmoidal arteries. Surg Neurol 1978;10:384–388.
18. Dawbarn RHM. The starvation operation for malignancy in the external carotid area. JAMA 1904;17:792–795.
19. Debrun G, Lacour P, Caron JP, Hurth M, Comoy J, Keravel Y, Loisance D. Traitement des fistules arterio-veineuses et d'anévrysmes par ballon gonflable et largable. Nouv Presse Med 1975;4:2315–2318.
20. Debrun GM, Lacour P, Vinuela F. Treatment of 54 traumatic carotid-cavernous fistulas. J Neurosurg 1981;55:678–692.
21. Debrun G, Fox A, Drake C, Peerless S, Gervin J, Fergusson G. Giant unclippable aneurysms: treatment with detachable balloons. AJNR 1981;2:167–173.
22. Debrun G, Vinuela FV, Fox AJ, et al. Two different calibrated-leak balloons: experimental work and application in humans. AJNR 1982;3:407–411.
23. Debrun G, Vinuela F, Fox AJ, Drake G. Embolization of cerebral arteriovenous malformations with bycrylate: experience in 46 cases. J Neurosurg 1982;56:562–570.
24. De Keizer RJW. Spontaneous carotid cavernous fistulas. Neuro-Ophthalmology 1981;2:35–46.
25. Delens E. De la communication de la carotide interne et du sinus caverneux (anévrysme arterioveineux) [Thèse] (A. Parent). Paris: 1870.
26. Djindjian R, Houdart R, Cophignon J, Hurth M, Comoy J. Premiers essais d'embolisation par voie fémorale de fragments de muscle dans un cas d'angiome alimenté par la carotide externe. Rev Neurol 1971;125:119–130.
27. Djindjian R, Cophignon J, Theron J, Merland JJ, Houdart R. L'embolisation en neuroradiologie vasculaire: technique et indications à propos de 30 cas. Nouv Presse Med 1972;1:2153–2158.
28. Djindjian R, Cophignon J, Theron J, Merland JJ, Houdart R. Superselective arteriographic embolization by the femoral route in neuroradiology: study of 50 cases, III: embolization in craniocerebral pathology. Neuroradiology 1973;6:143–153.
29. Djindjian R, Manelfe C, Picard L. Fistules arterio-veineuses carotide externe-sinus caverneux: etude angiographique à propos de 6 observations et revue de la litterature. Neurochirurgie 1973;19:91–110.
30. Djindjian R, Merland JJ. Superselective arteriography of the external carotid artery: vol 1. Berlin: Springer 1978.
31. Dolenc V. Direct microsurgical repair of intracavernous vascular lesions. J Neurosurg 1983;58:824–831.
32. Doyon D, Metzger J. Malformations vasculaires dure-mériennes sus-tentorielles. Acta Radiol [Diagn] (Stockh) 1973;13:792–800.
33. Endo S, Hoshu K, Suzuki J. Spontaneous regression of posterior fossa dural arteriovenous malformations. J Neurosurg 1979;51:715–717.
34. Forster DMC, Steiner L, Hakanson S. Arteriovenous malformations of the brain: a long-term clinical study. J Neurosurg 1972;37:562–570.
35. Fox AJ, Girvin JP, Vinuela F, Drake CG. Rolandic arteriovenous malformations: improvement in limb function by IBC embolization. AJNR 1985;6:575–582.
36. Fox AJ, Vinuela F, Pelz DM, Peerless SJ, Ferguson GG, Drake CG, Debrun G. Use of detachable balloons for proximal artery occlusion in the treatment of unclippable aneurysms. J Neurosurg 1987;66:40–47.
37. Fults D, Kelly DL Jr. Natural history of arteriovenous malformations of the brain: a clinical study. Neurosurgery 1984;15:658–662.
38. Gaston A, Chiras J, Bourbotte G, Leger JM, Guibert-Tranier F, Merland JJ. Meningeal arteriovenous fistulae draining into cortical veins (31 cases). J Neuroradiol 1984;11:161–177.
39. Giannotta SL, McGillicuddy JE, Kindt GW. Gradual carotid artery occlusion in the treatment of inaccessible internal carotid artery aneurysm. Neurosurgey 1979;5:417–421.
40. Goto K, Hieshima GB, Higashida RT, Halbach VV, Bentson JR, Mehringer CM, Pribram H. Treatment of direct carotid cavernous sinus fistulae: various therapeutic approaches and results in 148 cases. Acta Radiol [Suppl] (Stockh) 1986;365:576–579.
41. Graf CJ, Perret GE, Torner JC. Bleeding from cerebral arteriovenous malformations as part of their natural history. J Neurosurg 1983;58:331–337.
42. Halbach VV, Hieshima GB, Higashida RT, Reicher M. Carotid cavernous fistulae: indications for urgent treatment. AJNR 1987;8:627–633.
43. Hamby WB. Carotid cavernous fistula; vol 1. Springfield: Thomas 1966.
44. Handa J, Yoneda S, Handa H. Venous sinus occlusion with a dural arteriovenous malformation of the posterior fossa. Surg Neurol 1975;4:433–437.
45. Hieshima GB, Higashida RT, Halbach VV, Cahan L, Goto K. Intravascular balloon embolization of a carotid-ophthalmic artery aneurysm with preservation of the parent vessel. AJNR 1986;7:916–918.
46. Hieshima GB, Higashida RT, Wapenski J, et al. Intravascular balloon embolization of a mid-basilar artery aneurysm. J Neurosurg 1987;66:124–127.
47. Higashida RT, Hieshima GB, Halbach VV, Bentson JR, Goto KG. Closure of carotid cavernous sinus fistulae by external compression of the carotid artery and jugular vein. Acta Radiol [Suppl] (Stockh) 1986;367:580–583.
48. Higashida RT, Hieshima GB, Halbach VV, Goto K, Dormandy B, Bell J, Cahan L, Bentson JR. Intravascular detachable balloon embolization of intracranial aneurysms: indications and techniques. Acta Radiol [Suppl] (Stockh) 1986;367:594–596.
49. Hilal SK, Michelsen JW. Therapeutic percutaneous emboli-

zation for extra-axial vascular lesions of the head, neck and spine. J Neurosurg 1975;43:275–287.

50. Houser OW, Baker HL Jr, Rhoton AL, Okazaki H. Intracranial dural arteriovenous malformations. Radiology 1972;105:55–64.

51. Ishimori S, Hattori M, Shibata Y, Shizawa H, Fujinaga R. Treatment of carotid-cavernous fistula by gelfoam embolization. J Neurosurg 1967;27:315–319.

52. Ito J, Kobayashi K, Tsuchida T, Soto S. Dural arteriovenous malformations of the base of the anterior cranial fossa. Neuroradiology 1983;24:149–154.

53. Kataoka K, Taneda M. Angiographic disappearance of multiple dural arteriovenous malformations. J Neurosurg 1984;60:1275–1278.

54. Kendall B. Results of treatment of arteriovenous fistulae with the Debrun technique AJNR 1983;4:405–408.

55. Kerber CW. Balloon catheter with a calibrated leak. Radiology 1976;12:547–550.

56. Kerber CW, Bank WO, Cromwell LD. Calibrated leak balloon microcatheter: a device for arterial exploration and occlusive therapy. AJR 1979;132:207–212.

57. Kerber CW, Bank WO, Manelfe C. Control and placement of intracranial microcatheters. AJNR 1980;1:157–159.

58. Kricheff II, Madayag M, Braunstein P. Transfemoral catheter embolization of cerebral and posterior fossa arteriovenous malformations. Radiology 1972;103:107–111.

59. Laine E, Jomin M, Clarisse J, Combelles G. Les malformations artério-veineuses cérébrales profondes: classification topographique, possibilités et résultats thérapeutiques à propos de 46 observations. Neurochirurgie 1981;27:147–160.

60. Lapresle J, Lasjaunias P, Verret JM, Dhaene T. Anévrysme géant de la carotide intracaverneuse compliqué d'hémorragie méningée: traitement en urgence par ballonnet occlusif et thrombose in situ. Nouv Presse Med 1979;8:3037–3040.

61. Lasjaunias P, ed. Cranio facial and upper cervical arteries: functional, clinical and angiographic aspects. Baltimore: Williams and Wilkins 1981.

62. Lasjaunias P, ed. Cranio facial and upper cervical arteries: collateral circulation and angiographic protocols. Baltimore: Williams and Wilkins 1983.

63. Lasjaunias P, Halimi P, Lopez-Ibor L, Sichez JP, Hurth M, De Tribolet N. Traitement endovasculaire des malformations vasculaires durales (MVD) pures "spontanées": revue de 23 cas explorés et traités entre mai 1980 et octobre 1983. Neurochirurgie 1983;30:207–223.

64. Lasjaunias P, Lopez-Ibor L, Abanou A, Halimi P. Radiological anatomy of the vascularization of cranial dural arteriovenous malformations. Anat Clin 1984;6:87–99.

65. Lasjaunias P, Berenstein A. Surgical neuroangiography. Functional anatomy of craniofacial arteries. 1 vol. Springer Verlag 1986.

66. Lasjaunias P, Ming C, Terbrugge K, Atul T. Neurological manifestations of intracranial dural arteriovenous malformations. J Neurosurg 1986;64:724–730.

67. Lasjaunias P, Berenstein A. Surgical neuroangiography; vol 2: Endovascular treatment of craniofacial lesions. Berlin: Springer 1987.

68. Lasjaunias P, Manelfe C, Chiu M. Angiographic architecture of intracranial AMVS and fistulas: pretherapeutic aspects. Neurosurg Rev 1986;9:253–263.

69. Lasjaunias P, Manelfe C, Terbrugge K, Lopez-Ibor L. Endovascular treatment of cerebral arteriovenous malformations. Neurosurg Rev 1986;9:265–275.

70. Lasjaunias P, Piske R, Terbrugge K, Willinsky R. Cerebral arteriovenous malformations (C. AVM) and associated arterial aneurysms (AA). Analysis of 101 C. AVM cases, with 37 AA in 23 patients. Acta Neurochir (Wien) 1988;91:29

71. Lepoire J, Montaut J, Bouchot M, Laxenaire M. Anevrysmes arterioveineux intrafrontaux vascularisés par l'artère ethmoïdale antérieure. Neurochirurgie 1963;2:159–165.

72. Luessenhop AJ, Spence WT. Artificial embolization of cerebral arteries: report of use in a case of arteriovenous malformation. JAMA 1960;172:1153–1155.

73. McCormick WF. Report on the cooperative study on intracranial aneurysms: the pathology of vascular ("arteriovenous") malformations. J Neurosurg 1966;24:807–816.

74. Mahaley MS Jr, Boone SC. External carotid cavernous fistula treated by arterial embolization. Case report. J Neurosurg 1974;40:110–114.

75. Manelfe C, Fardou H, David J, Combes PF. Embolisation thérapeutique par cathétérisme fémoral. Ann Radiol (Paris) 1974;17:571–592.

76. Manelfe C, Djindjian R, Picard L. Embolisation par cathétérisme fémoral des tumeurs irriguées par l'artère carotide externe. Acta Radiol [Suppl] (Stockh) 1975;347:175–186.

77. Manelfe C, Espagno J, Guiraud B, Tremoulet M, Geraud G, Rascol A. Therapeutic embolization of cranio-cerebral tumors. J Neuroradiol 1975;2:257–274.

78. Manelfe C, Picard L, Bonafe A, Roland J, Sancier A, l'Esperance G. Embolisations et occlusions par ballonnets dans les processus tumoraux: sept années d'expérience. Neuroradiology 1978;6:395–398.

79. Manelfe C, Berenstein A. Treatment of carotid cavernous fistulas by venous approach. J Neuroradiol 1980;7:13–21.

80. Manelfe C, Lasjauinias P, Ruscalleda J. Preoperative embolization of intracranial meningiomas. AJNR 1986;7:963–972.

81. Mehringer CM, Hieshima GB, Grinnell VS, Tsai F, Pribram HF. Improved localization of carotid cavernous fistula during angiography. AJNR 1982;3:82–84.

82. Merland JJ, Ruffenacht D. A detachable latex balloon with valve mechanism for the permanent occlusion of large brain arteriovenous fistulas of cerebral arteries. In: Valk J, ed. Neuroradiology. Amsterdam: Elsevier 1985.

83. Newton TH, Greitz T. Arteriovenous communication between the occipital artery and transverse sinus. Radiology 1966;87:824.

84. Newton TH, Weidner W, Greitz T. Dural arteriovenous malformations in the posterior fossa. Radiology 1968;90:27–35.

85. Newton TH, Hoyt WF. Dural arteriovenous shunts in the region of the cavernous sinus. Neuroradiology 1970;1:71–81.

86. Newton TH, Troost T. Arteriovenous malformations and fistulas. In: Newton T, Potts DG, eds. Radiology of the skull and brain. Saint Louis: Mosby 1974:2490–2565.

87. Norman D, Newton TH, Edwards MS. Carotid cavernous fistula: closure with detachable silicone balloons. Radiology 1983;149:149–159.

88. Obrador S, Suoto M, Silvela J. Clinical symptoms of arteriovenous malformations of the transverse-sigmoid sinus. J Neurol Neurosurg Psychiatry 1975;38:436–451.

89. Parkinson D. Carotid cavernous fistula: direct repair with preservation of the carotid artery. J Neurosurg 1973;38:99–106.

90. Peeters FLM, Kroger R. Dural and direct cavernous sinus fistulas. AJR 1979;132:599–606.

91. Perret G, Hishioka H. Arteriovenous malformations: an analysis of 545 cases of cranio-cerebral arteriovenous malformations and fistulae reported to the cooperative study. J Neurosurg 1966;25:467–490.

92. Pevsner PH, Doppman JL. Therapeutic embolization with a microballoon catheter system. AJNR 1980;1:171–180.

93. Picard L, Lepoire J, Montaut J, Hepner H, Roland J, Guyonnard JC. Endarterial occlusion of carotid cavernous sinus fistulae using a balloon-tipped catheter. Neuroradiology 1974;8:5–10.

94. Picard L, Manelfe C, Roland J, Treil J, Andre JM, de Ker Saint Gilly A, Morel C. Embolisations et occlusions par ballonnets dans les lésions vasculaires cranio-faciales: sept années d'expérience. Neuroradiology 1978;16:393–394.

95. Picard L, Moret J, Lepoire J. Traitement endovasculaire des angiomes artério-veineux intracérébraux. J Neuroradiol 1984;11:9–28.

96. Picard L, Bracard S, Moret J, Forlodou P, Giacobbe HL, Salinas M, Moret C, Per A, Roland J. Occlusions endovasculaires dans le territoire cranio-encéphalique. In: Duvauferrier R, Ramée A, Guibert JL, eds. Radiologie et echographie interventionnelles. Montpellier: Axone 1986: 111–125.

97. Picard L, Roland J, Bracard S, Lepoire J, Montaut J. Spontaneous dural fistulas: classifcation, diagnosis, endovascular treatment. In: Auer LW, Loew F, eds. Berlin: Springer 1983:317–323.

98. Piton J, Guilleux H, Guibert-Tranier F, Caille JM. Fistules du sinus latéral. J Neuroradiol 1983;11:143–159.
99. Prolo DJ, Hambery JW. Intraluminal occlusion of carotid cavernous sinus fistula with a balloon catheter. J Neurosurg 1971;35:237–242.
100. Riche MC, Cophignon J, Thurel C, George B, Hadjean E, Melki JP, Merland JJ. Embolization of the cavernous and petrous segments of the internal carotid artery in severe basilar skull and petrous bone lesions. J Neuroradiol 1981;8:301–316
101. Romodanov AP, Shcheglov VI. Intravascular occlusion of saccular aneurysms of the cerebral arteries by means of a detachable balloon. In: Krayenbühl H, et al., eds. Advances and technical standards in neurosurgery; vol 9. Wien: Springer 1982:25–49.
102. Ruffenacht D, Merland JJ. Superselective catheterization using very flexible, formed catheters. Acta Radiol [Suppl] (Stockh) 1986;367:600–602.
103. Sanders MD, Hoyt WF. Hypoxic ocular sequelae of carotid cavernous fistulae. Br J Ophthalmol 1969;53:82–97.
104. Scialfa G, Vaghi A, Valsecchi F, Bernardi L, Tonon C. Neuroradiological treatment of carotid and vertebral fistulas and intracavernous aneurysms: technical problems and results. Neuroradiology 1982;24:13–25.
105. Sedzimir CB, Occleshaw JV. Treatment of carotid cavernous fistula by muscle embolization and Jaeger's maneuver. J Neurosurg 1967;22:309–314.
106. Seeger JF, Gabrielsen TO, Gianotta S, Lotz P. Carotid cavernous sinus fistulae and venous thrombosis. AJNR 1982;1:141–148.
107. Serbinenko FA. Balloon occlusion of a cavernous portion of the carotid artery as a method of treating carotid cavitary anastomoses. Probl Neurosurg 1971;6:3–8.
108. Serbinenko AF. Balloon catheterization and occlusion of major cerebral vessels. J Neurosurg 1974;41:125–145.
109. Sergett RC, Grossman RT, Savino PT, et al. The syndrome of paradoxical worsening of dural cavernous sinus arteriovenous malformations. Ophthalmology 1987;94:205–212.
110. Spiegel SM, Vinuela F, Goldwasser JM, Fox AJ, Pelz DM. Adjusting the polymerization time of isobutyl-2-cyanoacrylate. AJNR 1986;7:109–112.
111. Stein BM, Wolpert SM. Arteriovenous malformations of the brain, II: current concepts and treatment. Arch Neurol 1980;37:69–75.
112. Sundt TM, Piepgras DG. The surgical approach to arteriovenous malformations of the lateral and sigmoid dural sinuses. J Neurosurg 1983;59:32–39.
113. Takeyawa SD, Holman BC. Roentgenologic diagnosis of anomalous communication between external carotid artery and intracranial veins. AJR 1965;95:822–825.
114. Taki W, Handa H, Yamagata S, Ishikawa M, Iwata H, Ikada Y. Balloon embolization of a giant aneurysm using a newly developed catheter. Surg Neurol 1979;12:363–365.
115. Taniguchi RM, Goree JA, Odom GL. Spontaneous carotid-cavernous shunts presenting diagnostic problems. J Neurosurg 1971;35:384–391.
116. Tsai FY, Hieshima GB, Mehringer CM, Grinnel V, Pribram HW. Delayed effects in the treatment of carotid cavernous fistulae. AJNR 1983;4:357–361.
117. Valavanis A. Preoperative embolization of the head and neck: indications, patient selection, goals and precautions. AJNR 1986;7:943–952.
118. Vinuela F, Fox AJ, Debrun G, Drake, CG, Peerless SJ, Girvin JP. Progressive thrombosis of brain arteriovenous malformations after embolization with IBCA. AJNR 1983;4:1233–1238.
119. Vinuela F, Fox AJ, Debrun G, Peerless SJ, Drake CG. Spontaneous carotid-cavernous fistulas: clinical, radiological, and therapeutic considerations: experience with 20 cases. J Neurosurg 1984;60:976–984.
120. Vinuela F, Fox AJ, Debrun G, Pelz D. Pre-embolization superselective angiography: role in the treatment of brain arteriovenous malformations with isobutyl-2-cyanoacrylate. AJNR 1984;5:765–769.
121. Vinuela F, Fox AJ, Pelz D, Debrun G. Angiographic follow-up of large cerebral AVMs incompletely embolized with isobutyl-2-cyanoacrylate AJNR 1986;7:919–925.
122. Waga S, Fujimoto K, Morikawa D, Morooka Y, Okada M. Dural arteriovenous malformations of the anterior fossa. Surg Neurol 1977;8:356–358.
123. Wolpert SM, Stein BM. Catheter embolization of intracranial arteriovenous malformations as an aid to surgical excision. Neuroradiology 1975;10:73–85.
124. Zanetti PH, Sherman FE. Experimental evaluation of tissue adhesive as an agent for the treatment of aneurysms and arteriovenous anomalies. J Neurosurg 1972;36:72–79.

Embolization Techniques in the Face and Neck

L. Picard, S. Bracard, H. L. Giacobbe, A. Per, J. Moret, and J. Roland

In 1904, Dawbarn (4) performed the first embolization in the world by injecting hot liquid wax into the external carotid of a patient presenting with a craniofacial tumor. Since then, the techniques of embolization have steadily improved, and indications for it have considerably expanded. However, facio-cranio-encephalic embolization really developed in the 1970s, thanks to the lift given by R. Djindjian, who founded the present French school of interventional neuroradiology (5, 6, 7, 8).

The considerable progress achieved over the last ten years is of course due to improvements in the material available for catheterization, as well as improved embologenic substances. However, the extensive work on microvascular anatomy which allowed a reduction of the risks and consequently improved the safety of these interventions must be given its due. However, certain indications are essentially of an esthetic nature, and the authors feel that the possible vital and functional risks involved render these indications unjustifiable. Patient safety requires a skilled and experienced neuroradiologist working with a team of critical care-anesthesiologists who themselves are perfectly familiar with, and trained for, these particular interventions.

Anatomy – Physiology – Hemodynamics

From an anatomical and physiological point of view, the cervicofacial vascular area represents a vast and complex domain. This is due to the existence of a large number of highly functional areas which are themselves in direct communication and also in multiple anastomotic communication with neighboring areas. The anastomoses not only develop vertically (labial, nasal, orbital, etc.) but also horizontally and especially transversally (14).

It should be recalled that no real medial boundary exists in the facial domain: any lesion which is lateralized can eventually be vascularized by contralateral vessels. This fact explains why arterial ligation, as once practiced for hemostasis of epistaxis, for example, can be ineffective. The development of embolization and the possibilities it offers are such that ligation now constitutes a therapeutic mistake. This is because it definitely blocks the approaches available for the only therapeutic option presenting a real physiopathologically-oriented action. Thus, it is easy to understand the need for surgical repermeabilization of a previously-ligated external carotid, to treat a complex arteriovenous malformation of the face.

Four distinct vascular systems are present:

- The external carotid system, whose branches essentially vascularize the craniofacial envelope, the oropharynx, part of the orbits and the auricular regions. In addition, it is responsible for the greater part of the meninges and part of the vascularization of the cranial nerves.
- The internal carotid system, which not only plays a role by way of the ophthalmic artery, but also by way of numerous vestigial branches coming from the carotid siphon. Their functional importance increases considerably as soon as a pathologic process develops in their vicinity.
- The vertebrobasilar system, by way of the segmental and muscular branches of both vertebral arteries. The wealth of anastomoses between the upper segmental branches of the vertebral arteries and the occipital arteries constitutes one of the most frequent causes of complications by erratic embolization in the external carotid area.
- The "proximal" subclavian system. This system corresponds to all the cervical branches of the subclavian arteries, which are also richly anastomosed with the vertebral arteries.

These distinct, adjoining systems, entangled without real partition, explain the fundamental notion of "hemodynamic balance" which regulates cervicofacial vascularization. With the exception of the auricular region, no other area can be considered as really being distal. This explains the fortunate rarity of necrotic complications, except for cases in which plastic embologenic substances are used.

Thus, the angiographic work-up should not only be localized to the vessels "theoretically" vascularizing the pathologic territory. It is advisable that the vessels vascularizing neighboring territories be explored as well. In this way, the neuroradiologist can choose the most effective and safest approach, and thus achieve the goal set by embolization. It is noteworthy that post-embolization follow-up angiographies of a lesion embolized using a given artery are of better quality if performed using a different artery vascularizing the same area. An example is the use of the facial artery to appraise a nasopharyngeal fibroma which has been embolized by way of the maxillary artery, allowing the eventual factor of vasospasm to be eliminated.

Technique

Approach

Without a doubt, the "gold standard" approach is via femoral catheterization, due to the frequent need for a bilateral approach and for obvious reasons of radioprotection. Direct puncture is only indicated in cases where the femoral approach is not possible, as in very elderly patients presenting with arterial stenosis. In some cases, the direct approach allows embolization to be completed by catheterization of a branch which is otherwise inaccessible by low femoral puncture. An axillary approach may also provide further remedy in particularly difficult cases.

Anesthesia and Critical Care

Anesthesiological Techniques

Either neuroleptanalgesia, which allows continuous evaluation of the patient's neurologic state, or general anesthesia with assisted ventilation, are available, and each has its supporters and its detractors. Our experience has been that each method has its proper indications. General anesthesia, when carried out by a suitable anesthesiological team, is in fact a "comfortable" method for both the patient and the operator. It also has the advantage of providing for deep analgesia and vasoplegia (using nitroprussiate-type drugs), thus helping to avoid vasospasm. However, because of their numerous parietal nerve fibers, the branches of the external carotid have a troublesome tendency to become spastic at the slightest "aggression". Such vasospasm has the double inconvenience of rendering embolization almost impossible, and especially of considerably increasing the risks of this therapy by favoring reflux of injected emboli into other possibly "dangerous" arteries. Neuroleptanalgesia, when correctly performed, also provides excellent results. This technique is not as serious, but has the inconvenience of providing lower quality subtraction because of patient movements which are often unavoidable. However, when the intervention involves a functionally important vessel (internal carotid, vertebral artery), neuroleptanalgesia allowing continuous peroperative neurologic surveillance is preferable to general anesthesia.

Surveillance of Selected Parameters

The risk of embolism is slight for interventions involving the external carotid and its branches. However, if catheterization is prolonged in an elderly or disabled patient, the risk of thromboembolism increases, and is such that substantial anticoagulant therapy using heparin can be of use. Heparin is used at a dose varying from 10 to 30 IU/kg/h. The amount of heparin prescribed is carefully accounted for, allowing quick neutralization using protamine sulfate if required.

Blood flow must also be monitored. In fact, the aim of embolization is to reach the lesion without obstructing the afferent pedicles. Ligation is problematic because it results in afferent vessel obstruction. With this in mind, it is useful that blood flow be increased while embolization is performed. This can be done artificially, by increasing arterial blood pressure using pharmacodynamic means. This explains why, contrary to certain opinions, it is preferable that embolization be performed with lower selectivity. In fact hyperselective embolization often results in the reduction of blood flow because of the mere presence of a catheter in a given vessel. This could explain the failure of certain embolizations, which result in "proximal pseudoligation".

Material

The material used for catheterization must be adapted to each individual case. However, it should be recalled that the best material is usually the finest (3 to 5 Fr), and that the use of guides, which are always traumatic, and sources of vasospasm should be avoided as much as possible. Among the numerous emboli available, preference should be given to solid microparticles calibrated according to the lesion to be treated. For reasons of cost-efficiency we tend to rely on dura mater, whereas Anglosaxon authors prefer Ivalon. Spongel (Gelfoam) has certain indications because of its malleability. At this time we are carrying out trials using powdered collagen with encouraging results. This is due to the distal character of the embolization. Fluid plastic substances which are secondarily polymerized, the "cyanoacrylates" in particular, should be contra-indicated, or

used only if absolutely necessary. This is because of the risk of skin necrosis associated with their use. Detachable balloons are of use in case of direct arteriovenous fistulas with a high blood flow rate.

Finally, the absolute necessity of subtraction techniques, whether "manual" or, preferably, digital, should be remembered. High-quality digital angiographic equipment affords an excellent margin of safety for intervention as well as making it quicker. Thus, the overall safety for the patient is further improved.

Indications

There are three basic indications for embolization therapy in the cervicofacial field. These are: tumors, vascular malformations, and hemorrhage.

Tumors

Many types of tumors can be treated using embolization. The aim varies, depending on whether the lesion is "operable" or not (15, 17, 22, 23, 25, 32).

Pre-Operative Embolization

Embolization is indicated in cases of hypervascularized tumor where excision is difficult or dangerous because of the risk of hemorrhage. This essentially applies to nasopharyngeal fibromas and chemodectomas.

Nasopharyngeal fibromas. Highly vascularized, these tumors usually develop in male adolescents. This hypervascularization explains the cataclysmic nature of peroperative hemorrhage by tumors which are not preoperatively embolized. Since these tumors are located paramedially, the selective preoperative angiographic work-up must systematically explore the internal carotid arteries, the ascending pharyngeal arteries, the internal maxillary arteries, and the facial arteries bilaterally (15, 17).

The choice of the best pedicle or pedicles to be used to reach the center of the tumor is based on the results of the angiographic work-up. Currently, the internal maxillary arteries and the ascending pharyngeal arteries are most often used (Fig. **1**).

Fig. **1**   **Recurring nasopharyngeal fibroma with intracavernous extension** in a 14-year-old male
a, b Frontal (a) and lateral (b) right internal carotid angiography. The intracavernous extension of this recurrence is clearly seen. Tumor revascularization reaches and surrounds the anteroinferior portions (C3 and C4) of the left carotid siphon
c, d Occlusion of the left carotid siphon is performed using a detachable balloon detached at C3 (dotted lines). The right contralateral carotid (c) and vertebrobasilar (d) follow-up angiographies show the excellent compensatory vascularization of the left hemisphere by way of the circle of Willis.

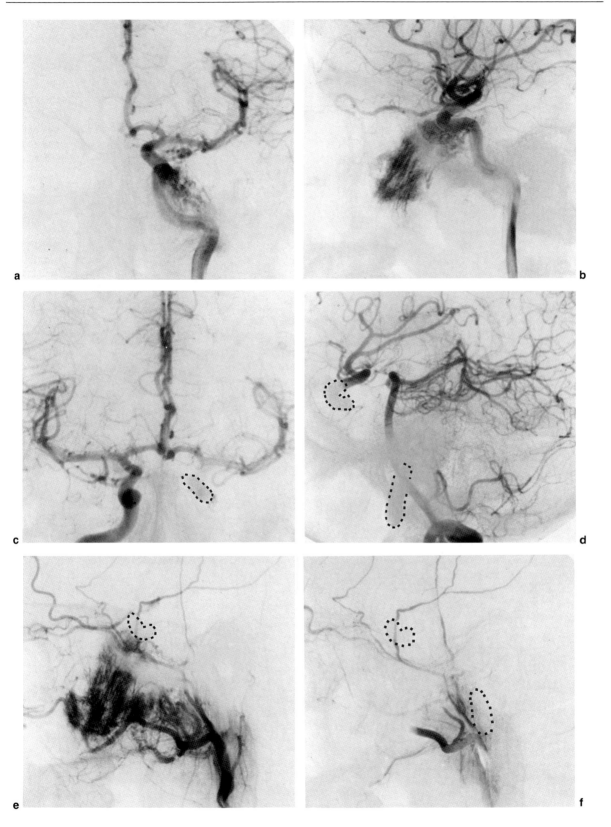

e, f Left maxillotemporal trunk (e) angiography following occlusion of the carotid siphon by a detachable balloon (dotted line) perfectly opacifies the complete tumoral process which can then be embolized using microparticles of dura. Post-embolization follow-up angiography (f) shows the quality of the embolization. Even though not hyperselective, the left middle meningeal and superficial temporal arteries are respected, and the tumor is no longer visible

Total occlusion of the internal carotid artery axis is only indicated in exceptional cases presenting with extension of the tumor by invasion of the base of the skull, particularly the cavernous sinus. These cases are generally due to tumor recurrence, and the therapeutic aim is the elimination of the vascularization supplied by the vestigial branches of the intracavernous carotid. An occlusion of this type can be performed using a detachable balloon and may be associated to an underlying embolization, the overall aim being to reach the parts of the tumor which depend on the vessels. In certain cases, it is only at this price that it is possible to obtain a cure in patients in whom tumor extension presents seemingly insurmountable surgical problems.

Chemodectomas or Paragangliomas. These tumors are grouped with the so-called neurocristopathies, which involve tissues derived from the neural crests. In addition, they belong to the amine precursor uptake and decarboxylation (APUD) system, which explains their multiple localizations. In the cervicofacial region they are mainly found at the tympanic glomus (ear drum case), the jugular glomus (jugular bulb, posterior jugular notch), the plexiform ganglion (pneumogastric nerve) and the glomus caroticum (carotid bifurcation) (9, 10, 13, 15, 16, 20).

Some of these tumors are characterized by a particularly slow and insidious clinical course. This explains why they are often discovered late in their development, at which time they are quite voluminous. This is especially true for chemodectomas of the jugular glomus, whose extension often poses difficult problems for the surgeon. Their symptomatology can be quite variable, depending on tumor location and extension. Furthermore, some symptoms are totally incomprehensible, since certain tumors of enormous size may be practically asymptomatic, whereas the opposite may be true of even very small tumors.

The angiographic work-up also varies according to tumor location. It is always bilateral, since multiple localization is not infrequent. The internal carotid, the vertebral, the internal maxillary, the ascending pharyngeal, the posterior auricular, and the occipital arteries should all undergo investigation.

Following the angiographic work-up, it is necessary for all the afferent pedicles, the venous drainage and the monocompartmental or multicompartmental character of the lesion to be determined (20). The angiographic presentation of these tumors is extremely characteristic. Tumor opacification in the form of patches of contrast which are relatively homogenous is rapid and early. Opacification visibility is prolonged, and venous drainage is multiple and well-individualized (Fig. 2). These lesions often bulge into the venous lumen; this is particularly true for the internal jugular vein.

This notion is very important, because a monocompartmental tumor could theoretically be completely embolized using a unique pedicle, whereas a multicompartmental tumor can never be completely embolized using the dominant pedicle. The endovascular approach requires embolization of at least two, if not more, pedicles. In principle, embolization of these tumors is preoperative, the aim being to facilitate surgical excision of the tumor, or make an otherwise impossible excision possible. Embolization is usually carried out using particles or secondarily polymerizable fluid plastics.

In some cases, tumor size and extension are such that excision, even after embolization, leads to vital and functional risks which are too grave. In such cases, isolated palliative embolization is sometimes indicated. Such embolizations may completely relieve or reduce certain troublesome clinical symptoms. These symptoms include tinnitus, facial paralysis or difficulties with swallowing. In any case, even when clinical improvement lasts several years, fol-

Fig. 2 **Lingual hemolymphangioma** in a 7-year-old child. The patient presented practically daily episodes of bleeding as well as intense pain which disturbed feeding. Partial glossectomy was foreseen

a Right lingual angiography before embolization. The hypervascularization of the hemolymphangioma is most obvious in the anterior two-thirds of the tongue, and is accompanied by an abnormally early venous return. Partial reflux of contrast into the internal maxillary artery can be noted

b Lateral right lingual follow-up angiography following embolization using microparticles of dura. The hemolymphangioma is no longer opacified, but the lingual artery is still permeable and so may be reutilized should the need arise

c Left angiography after right lingual arterial embolization. The opacification of the posterior portion of the tongue, the appearance of which is practically normal, can be seen

d Given the importance of the anastomoses formed between the right and left lingual arteries, complementary embolization was carried out systematically on the right lingual artery

e Clinical aspect of the tongue before embolization

f Clinical aspect of the tongue five years after embolization. The bothersome clinical symptoms have disappeared and glossectomy was avoided

low-up angiograms always show repermeabilization, the aspect being identical to that of pre-embolization angiography. This element in the natural history of these tumors is of particular interest, since it is rarely encountered so constantly in other pathological pro-cesses. As for the precise knowledge of the effects of such palliative embolizations on the clinical course of the tumor, it is impossible to ascertain, because the development is normally exceedingly slow. In many cases, embolization is so effective that it often leads

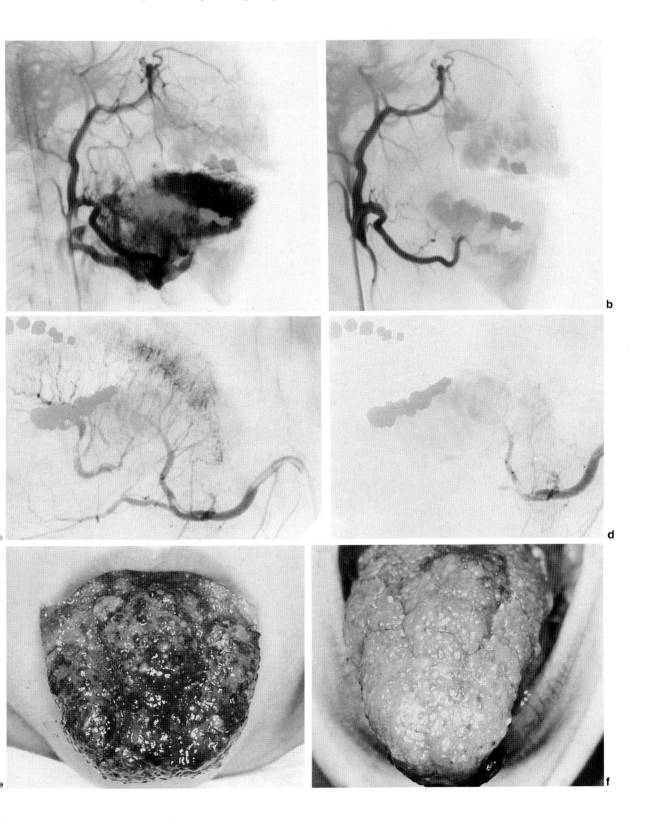

elderly patients, who are often poor surgical candidates, to interrupt the initial therapeutic protocol and refuse surgery which they no longer find necessary because they have the impression of being cured.

Other tumors. Preoperative embolization is therefore indicated for all hypervascularized tumors. For some teams, however, embolization now constitutes a systematic preoperative act prior to excision of even poorly-vascularized or avascular cervicofacial tumors. These embolizations can also concern tumors located in areas requiring precise dissection, to ensure that nerve structures are protected as much as possible (the buccofacial region, for example). Extensive malignant tumors which often require "extended vascular sacrifice" are also prime candidates for preoperative embolization. For instance, enlarged excision of cervicoparotid cancers might benefit from internal carotid occlusion by detachable balloon, associated with massive internal and external carotid embolization before surgery. After embolizations, the risk of hemorrhage or neurologic damage is avoided, in spite of the required sacrifice of an entire carotidojugular vascular axis.

Embolization of "Isolated" Tumors

These are not necessarily palliative embolizations indicated for relieving pain or hemostasis in patients presenting with malignant tumors. In some situations, the embolization may be so effective that functionally or esthetically damaging surgery is avoided altogether.

A good example of this is the various locations of hemolymphangiomas, particularly those located on the tongue. These lesions are more often classified as hamartomas than as vascular malformations. Their potential for blastic development can be quite capricious. They may undergo accelerated growth at times of infection, endocrine perturbation, psychological problems or trauma. Hemolymphangioma may stabilize, especially during puberty. On numerous occasions, sometimes after repeated embolization, tumor involution was noted, and prolonged stabilization compatible with a normal life was obtained (Fig. **2**).

Vascular Malformation

In approaching this section, we were at first asked to choose an appropriate system of classification. However, this could not be done whithout difficulty, considering the plethora of terms often used, each one bearing a different meaning depending on the different experts in this field, be they neuroradiologists, pediatricians, dermatologists, maxillofacial surgeons or internists. The problem is further complicated by the eventual inclusion of these malformations in the framework of systematized vascular angiodysplasia (1, 2, 12, 18, 19, 22, 24, 25, 26, 30, 31).

Whatever the case, the classic descriptive scheme (plane angioma, cavernous angioma, angiectasic angioma ...) has been superseded by a more dynamic classification which includes angiographic data. Immature angioma must no longer be separated from mature angioma.

Immature Angiomas

These are often hardly visible at birth, and develop during the first few weeks or months of life. These lesions tend to develop relatively quickly. This is of importance, since depending on their location, they may have serious consequences on the functional or vital prognosis. Clinically, these lesions tend to be apulsatile or only slightly pulsatile. In most cases, auscultation reveals no murmur. Angiographically, they present as expansive hypervascularized processes in the form of a "blush", which is most visible at the arteriolocapillary phase. Afferent arterial pedicles are usually not dilated, and arteriovenous shunts are either absent or of little importance. Immature angiomas should benefit from a conservative therapeutic approach, as they may undergo spontaneous regression in a large number of cases. This regression, which is sometimes incomplete, is often seen during the first 6 years of life. An episode of accelerated development can justify temporary corticoid therapy. In cases where the development is uncontrollable or dangerous, angiography and embolization, sometimes followed by surgical excision, are indicated (18, 19, 31) (Fig. **3**).

Mature Angiomas

The best classification for so-called mature angiomas appears to be one which takes the situation of the lesion in the vascular bed into account. This anatomic classification, however, should be modified using a hemodynamic classification distinguishing high blood flow malformations from low blood flow malformations (12, 28). Thus, it is possible to define three major malformative entities, depending on whether the lesion predominates in the arterial, capillary or venous system.

Malformations of the arterial system. These are quite numerous, and should be classified according to their anatomic characteristics, and perhaps according to the arteriovenous shunts they may be responsible for.

Arterial aneurysms. These represent the most elementary lesions. By contrast with those of the encephalic region, congenital aneurysms of the cervicofacial region are exceptional. In most cases, these lesions originate as a result of trauma (aneurysms of the cervical carotid following cervical

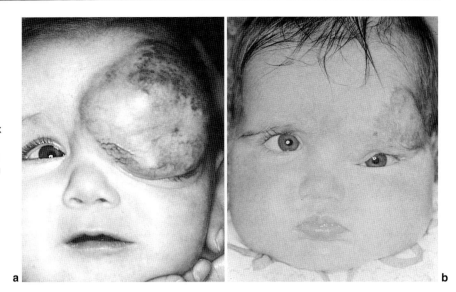

Fig. 3 **Immature-type orbitopalpebral angioma**
in a newborn

a Clinical aspect at the age of six months. Following an episode of accelerated growth, the angioma has led to a complete obstruction of the left eye. Thus a major functional problem has been created

b Following three months of corticotherapy, the angioma has considerably regressed, with reestablishment of ocular function

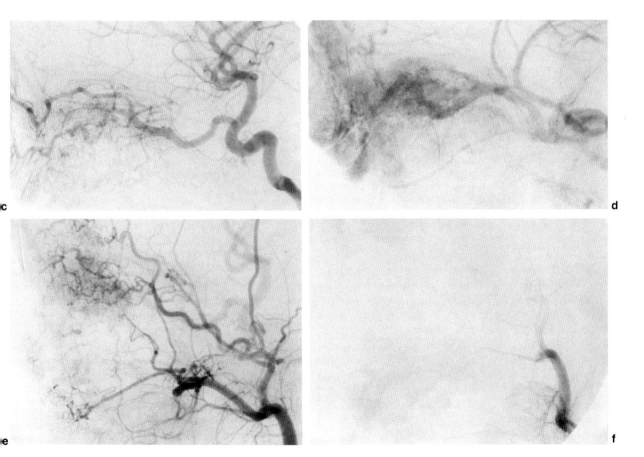

Fig. **3**

c, d Left internal carotid angiograph at arterial (c) and venous (d) phases. The ophthalmic artery opacifies the entire intraorbital portion of the malformation, which is unreachable using an endovascular approach without the possible risk of blindness

e Pre-embolization lateral left maxillotemporal angiography. Opacification of the entire palpebral and extraorbital portion of the malformation, which can then be partially embolized using microparticles of dura

f Follow-up angiography of the left maxillotemporal trunk following massive embolization using dura microparticles. This embolization was followed by the surgical excision of almost 80% of the malformation. The later clinical course was satisfactory

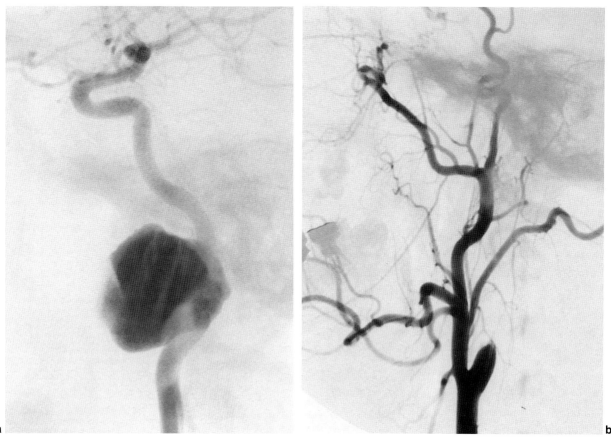

a   b

Fig. 4 **Post-traumatic aneurysm of the cervical carotid** treated by endovascular occlusion
a Lateral left carotid angioghraphy, showing a large aneurysm located at the prepetrous portion of the internal carotid
b Angiography of the left common carotid, following total occlusion of the internal carotid artery using a detachable balloon. Compensatory blood supply to the left hemisphere is ensured by the branches of the circle of Willis, which remained perfectly functional

trauma), or present as mycotic aneurysm, which may even present as giant aneurysm. Other presenting forms may be dysplasic lesions entering into a picture of systematized vascular angiodysplasia, such as those seen in the neurofibromatoses. Treatment of such aneurysms calls for either a direct surgical approach, or selective endovascular occlusion of the aneurysm by detachable balloon (Fig. **4**).

Direct arteriovenous fistulas. These lesions may be considered as true arterial leaks. In fact, they put the arterial and venous systems in direct communication. Whether they involve the carotid or vertebral vessels (Fig. **5**) or are congenital or acquired, the treatment of choice is to put a detachable balloon on the venous part of the lesion. In such cases the arterial axis involved is spared.

Arteriovenous Angiomas. These lesions are true "vascular tumors", whose development may be accelerated. Their blood flow rate tends to be extremely high. Clinically, they present as voluminous, or at times even monstrous tumefactions. They

are warm, hyperpulsatile, and at auscultation one may perceive a thrill and hear a murmur. The clinical course of these lesions is quite unpredictable, and an episode of accelerated growth may ensue as a result of trauma, surgery, hormonal imbalance or infection. The therapeutic strategy for these lesions should be carefully planned, but only after analysis of a complete and precise angiographic work-up. In some cases, embolization may successfully treat localized lesions or stabilize "inoperable" lesions. In most cases, embolization and surgical excision are combined. Due to the fact that the surgery required is at times mutilating, repeated embolization may allow time to be gained. This may be especially important during growth.

Capillary malformations. These include the so-called plane angiomas, which preferentially involve the teguments. Basically, these present as patches of more or less intensely-colored skin which vary from pink to deep purple, thus representing the classic

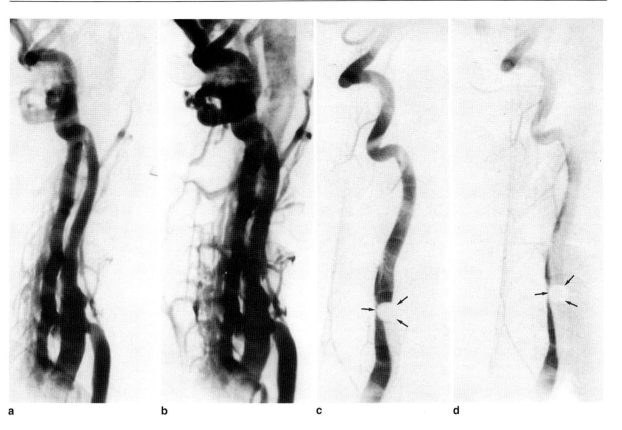

a   b   c   d

Fig. 5   **Spontaneous right vertebrovertebral fistula in an 18-year-old female**
a, b Lateral right vertebral angiography centered on the cervical region. Immediate and massive opacification of the vertebral vein as well as the epidural and cervical venous plexi can be seen
c, d Lateral right vertebral angiography, following occlusion of the fistula using a detachable balloon at the venous side. The balloon is easily seen at the level of C5/C6, where it bulges into the lumen of the vertebral artery, which remains perfectly permeable. On a radiograph taken a little later during the same seriography (d), the spinal vascularization is well visualized

"wine stain" lesion. Such lesions may be isolated or form part of an overall picture of Sturge-Weber-Krabbe's encephalotrigeminal angiomatosis. Embolization of such malformations is ineffective. Their management is limited to make-up for cosmetic purposes.

The cutaneous and mucous membrane capillary telangiectasias can be regrouped under one heading made up of various malformations which are essentially encountered in Rendu-Osler's angiomatosis (familial telangiectasia). At the level of the ENT mucous membranes, these telangiectasias are responsible for repeated distillating hemorrhages which may be cataclysmic. In some cases, embolization of the internal maxillary arteries using solid microparticles often provides excellent results in the control of hemorrhage in these patients (Fig. **6**). If such an embolization is not completely effective, complementary embolization of the facial arteries must sometimes be combined with it. Embolization should often be repeated in the years which follow.

This explains why it is advisable to preserve the afferent arterial axes at all costs, should their reuse be again necessary.

Venous malformations. All the lesions located downstream from the capillary system are regrouped under this heading. They may present as true varicosities or sometimes as cavernomas. The latter are constituted by large blood cavities limited by a thin fibrous wall which is lined by an endothelium. The cavernomas can be the site of thrombosis, which explains the onset of accelerated development or of calcification. These lesions may be isolated, or may form part of a systematic angiodysplasic syndrome such as Bean's "Blue Rubber Bled Naevi".

Given the situation of these lesions on the vascular bed, embolization therapy is frequently ineffective. This statement however, should be approached with an open mind, as our experience has shown that we were able to obtain surprising results following systematic embolization of all the arteries afferent to

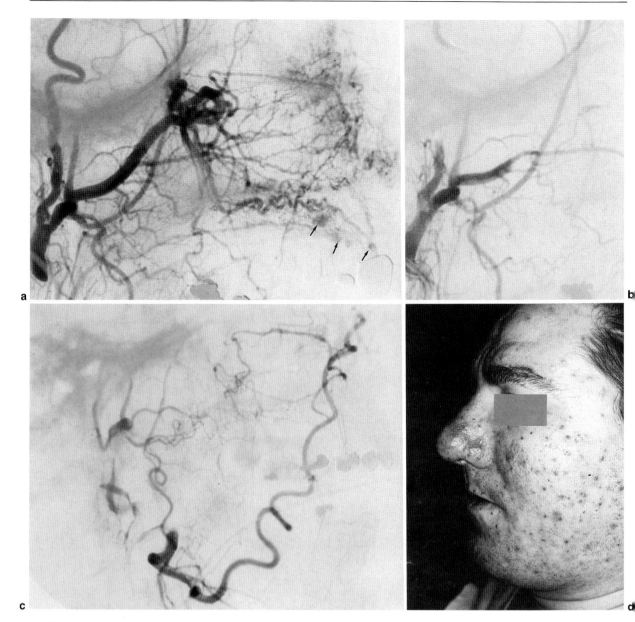

Fig. **6 Severe epistaxis during the clinical course of a case of Rendu-Osler's familial telangiectasic angiomatosis** in a 35-year-old male

a Lateral angiography of the right maxillotemporal trunk. The telangiectasic mass responsible for the epistaxis is seen clearly

b Lateral follow-up angiography of the right maxillotemporal trunk following embolization using dura microparticles. A good distal occlusion with conservation of the internal maxillary artery and the middle meningeal and deep temporal arteries can be seen

c Post-embolization lateral right facial artery angiography of the internal maxillary artery area. The excellent quality of the results obtained are confirmed by the continued permeability of the suborbital and sphenopalatine branches of the internal maxillary artery, whereas the telangiectasias are no longer opacified

d Clinical aspect of the patient, whose face is dotted by numerous cutaneous telangiectasias

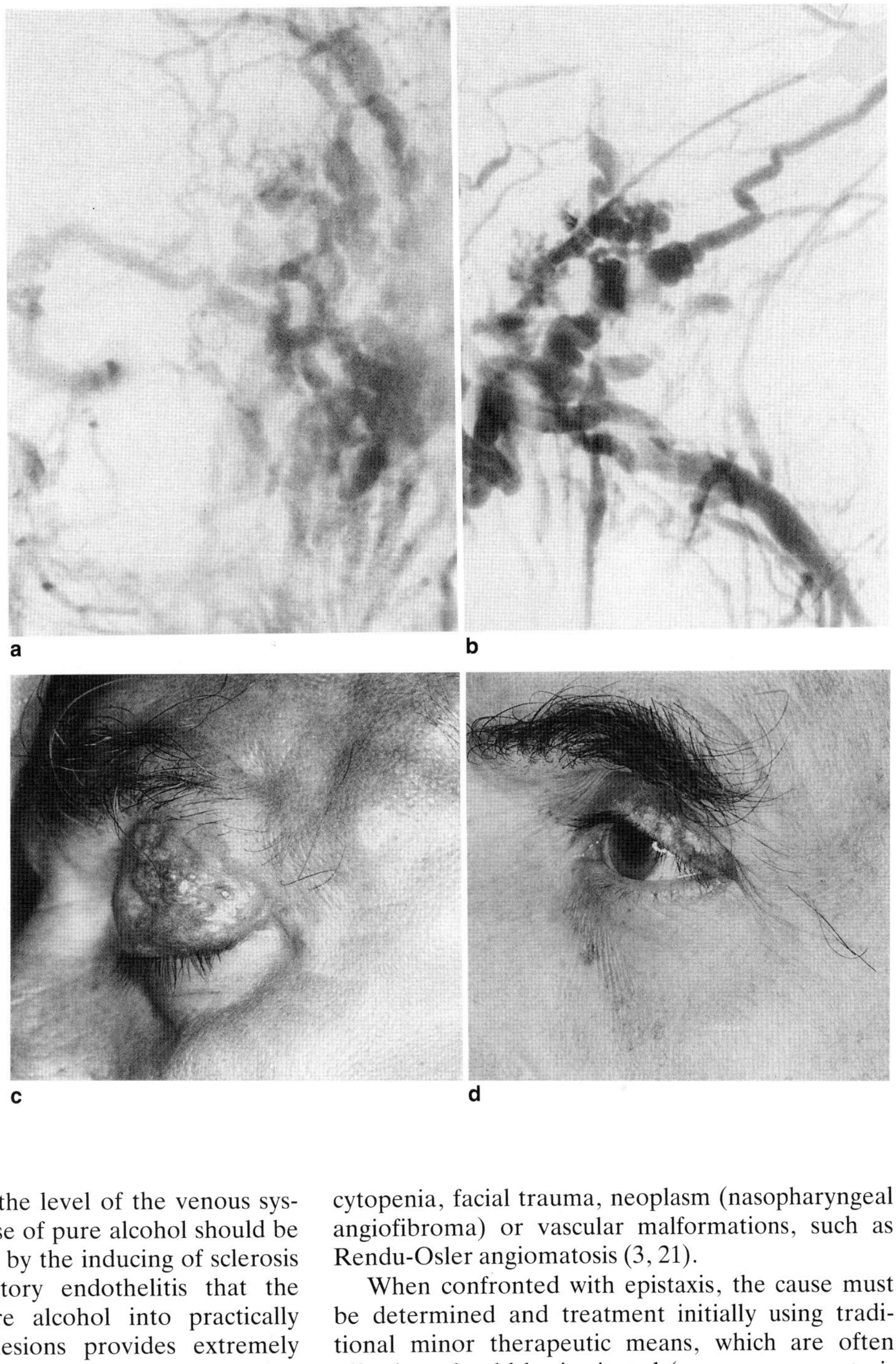

Fig. **7** **Orbitopalpebral venous dysplasia** in a 45-year-old male
a, b The venous malformation has such a low blood-flow rate that opacification by the injection into the afferent arteries of this territory is impossible. Opacification, seen here in frontal (a) and lateral (b) views, can only be obtained by direct puncture. This allows an injection of 2 ml of pure alcohol
c Clinical aspect before the injection of alcohol: the venous dilation is such that the eyelid cannot be opened
d Clinical aspect three months after alcohol injection: the eyelid can be opened normally. The frontal venous dilations have disappeared, while those of the eyelid are considerably diminished

a pathological area. At the level of the venous system, the endovascular use of pure alcohol should be underlined. It is, in fact, by the inducing of sclerosis secondary to inflammatory endothelitis that the direct injection of pure alcohol into practically closed-off endothelial lesions provides extremely interesting results (Fig. **7**). It is also in such cases that direct injection of Ethibloc may be of interest.

Hemorrhage

Embolization obviously represents a method of choice in the treatment of cervicofacial bleeding syndromes, particularly epistaxis. Epistaxis has numerous etiologies, and may be secondary to hypertensive crisis, anticoagulant therapy, hemopathies presenting with or without thrombo-

cytopenia, facial trauma, neoplasm (nasopharyngeal angiofibroma) or vascular malformations, such as Rendu-Osler angiomatosis (3, 21).

When confronted with epistaxis, the cause must be determined and treatment initially using traditional minor therapeutic means, which are often effective, should be instituted (compresses, cauterization).

In a second phase, if the earlier treatment options are ineffective, other possibly harmful or ineffective treatments such as proximal arterial ligation should be avoided, and embolization should be indicated without loss of time. For the authors, multiple blood transfusions prior to embolization, which in itself quickly resolves the therapeutic problems, are useless, costly and no without risk. Of course, once the indications for embolization have been confirmed, a pre-embolization angiographic work-up will be performed. Among the vessels explored will be the internal carotids, to study the ophthalmic arteries from which the ethmoidal arteries, which are sometimes involved in such pathologic processes, originate. The internal maxillary and sometimes the facial arteries may also undergo study (11, 27, 29).

The technique of endovascular occlusion depends on the nature of the causative lesions. If non-vascular lesions are apparent, the systematic embolization of the two internal maxillary arteries using microparticles often suffices to control bleeding. If this fails, embolization of the facial arteries may be a useful complement. Our experience has been that hemorrhage originating from the ethmoidal branches of the ophthalmic arteries is exceptional, as is the need for a surgical approach to these vessels to perform distal ligation. On the other hand, it is obvious that if an epistaxis originates from a tear in the cavernous sinus, with bleeding into the sphenoidal sinuses by way of a possible false aneurysm, only occlusion of the cavernous carotid or the aneurysm, using a detachable balloon, can resolve the problem.

Conclusion

The space reserved for such a chapter is too small to offer the possibility of describing the numerous indications for endovascular occlusion in the cervicofacial region. It is of the utmost importance that a precise analysis of the clinical and paraclinical data be undertaken before any valid indications are made. With this in mind, it should be recalled that a careful and complete physical examination which provides for possible classification of a given lesion within the framework of a regional angiomatosis (Bean's syndrome, Rendu-Osler familial telangiectasia, Sturge-Weber-Krabbe encephalotrigeminal angiomatosis, Klippel-Trenaunay-Weber syndrome, Bonnet Dechaume and Blanc's angiomatosis) is extremely important (1, 2, 3). Such a nosological appraisal is not merely speculative, as it allows better understanding of a given pathological process and prediction as to its clinical course, and consequently the necessary therapeutic decisions can be made.

Further criteria, patient age in particular, must also be taken into consideration. For example, if a small child under 6 years of age presents with an immature angioma without functional repercussions, one must know that the treatment of choice is therapeutic abstinence. In addition, the treatment of an angioma which could lead to problems requiring major plastic and reconstructive surgery, must in some cases be postponed and performed at the end of growth; whereas in other cases quick action may be required to avoid or diminish dysmorphism due to asymmetrical bone growth provoked by high blood-flow vascular malformations.

Once all these facts are taken into consideration, a precise therapeutic strategy should be established after consultation with the various specialists concerned with the problem. Once decided, this strategy must be clearly explained to the patient and family so that the possible constraints be understood and accepted. Sometimes it is very difficult for the parents of a child who presents a large immature angioma to agree to temporary therapeutic abstinence. Naturally they often prefer a quick "cure-all", even though the results risk being less than satisfying. Finally, it should be underlined that the therapeutic risks taken by a patient are directly attributable to the quality of the health-care team. Performing a good embolization with the smallest risk requires an experienced neuroradiologist working together with a capable anesthesiologist who is also perfectly "broken-in" concerning these types of interventions. It is only at this price that excellent results, which we could once hardly hope to obtain before the development of embolization techniques, can be had. The aim is not only the cure of a given lesion, but also preservation of the numerous anatomical and functional structures involved, not forgetting the importance of esthetic factors.

References

1. Andre JM, ed. Les dysplasies vasculaires systématisées. Paris: Expansion Scientifique Francaise 1973:566.
2. Andre JM, Picard L, Kissel P. Les angiodysplasies systématisées. J Neuroradiol 1974;1:3–45.
3. Andre JM, Picard L, Fays J, Kissel P. Angiomatose de Rendu-Osler: etude clinique et pathogénique, aspects angiographiques des localisations viscérales. J Neuroradiol 1974;1:233–256.
4. Dawbarn RHM. The starvation operation for malignancy in the external carotid area. JAMA 1904;17:792–795.
5. Djindjian R. Indications, contre-indications, accidents, incidents dans l'embolisation de la carotide externe. J Neuroradiol 1975;2:173–200.
6. Djindjian R, Merland JJ, eds. Superselective angiography of the external carotid artery. Berlin: Springer 1978.
7. Djindjian R, Picard L, Manelfe C, Merland JJ, Theron J. Développement de la neuroradiologie thérapeutique. Neuroradiology 1978;16:381–384.
8. Djindjian R, Theron J, Merland JJ. Embolisation dans les malformations et tumeurs cervico-thoraciques et rachidiennes. J Neuroradiol 1975;2:39–72.
9. Hilal SK, Michelsen JW. Therapeutic percutaneous embolization for extra-axial vascular lesions of the head, neck and spine. J Neurosurg. 1975;43:275–287.
10. Lacour P, Doyon D, Manelfe C, Picard L, Salisachs P, Schwaab G. L'embolisation artérielle thérapeutique dans les chémodectomes (tumeurs glomiques). J Neuroradiol 1975;2:275–287.
11. Lasjaunias P, Marsot-Dupuch K, Doyon D. Bases radio-anatomiques de l'embolisation artérielle au cours des épistaxis. J Neuroradiol 1979;6:45–52.
12. Lasjaunias P, Doyon D. Malformations vasculaires de la cavité buccale. J Neuroradiol 1980;7:243–270.
13. Lasjaunias P, Menu Y, Bonnel D, Doyon D. Paragangliomes non chromaffines de la tête et du cou. J Neuroradiol 1981;8:281–300.
14. Lasjaunias PL, ed. Crâniofacial and upper cervical arteries: functional, clinical and angiographic aspects. Baltimore: Williams andWilkins 1981.

15. Manelfe C, Djindjian R, Picard L. Embolisation par cathétérisme fémoral des tumeurs irriguées par l'artère carotide externe: a propos de 40 cas. Acta Radiol [Suppl] (Stockh) 1975;347:175–186.
16. Manelfe C, Doyon D, Guigicelli A. Apport de l'angiographie sélective de la carotide externe dans le diagnostic des tumeurs du glomus tympanique. Ann Otolaryngol Chir Cervicofac 1973;90:541–552.
17. Manelfe C, Picard L, Bonafe A, Roland J, Sancier A, l'Esperance G. Embolisation et occlusion par ballonnets dans les processus tumoraux: sept années d'expérience. Neuroradiologie 1978;16:395–398.
18. Merland JJ, Djindjian R. Technique et résultats de l'embolisation des angiomes du territoire carotidien externe. J Neuroradiol 1975;2:201–232.
19. Merland JJ, Tricot JF, Madjean E, Riche MC, Enjolras O. Les malformations vasculaires cervico-céphaliques: protocole actuel de traitement: a propos de 230 cas. Phlébologie 1980;33:95–103.
20. Moret J, Delvert JC, Lasjaunias P. Architecture vasculaire des tumeurs glomiques, tympanojugulaires: applications à l'angiographie thérapeutique. J Neuroradiol 1982;9:237–260.
21. Picard L, Andre JM, Djindjian R, Roland J, Manelfe C, Sigiel M, Wayoff M, Kissel P. Angiographie supersélective et embolisation des localisations ORL de l'angiomatose de Rendu-Osler. J Neuroradiol 1974;1:351–363.
22. Picard L, Andre JM, Roland J, Montaut J, Lepoire J, Arnould G, Kissel P. L'embolisation: intérêt et indictions en oto-neuro-ophtalmologie. Oto-Neuro-Ophtalmologie 1975;47:79–89.
23. Picard L, Andre JM, Roland J, Sigiel M, Lepoire J. L'occlusion endo-vasculaire thérapeutique dans les tumeurs crânio-faciales. Concours Méd. 1977;99:35,5078,5089.
24. Picard L, Andre JM, Roland J, Sigiel M, Montaut J,Lepoire J. L'embolisation dans les malformations vasculaires méningo-crânio-cutanées complexes. J Neuroradiol 1975;2:233–256.
25. Picard L, Bracard S, Moret J, Forlodou P, Giacobbe HL, Salinas M, Moret C, Per A, Roland J. Occlusions endo-vasculaires dans le territoire cranio-encéphalique. In: Duvauferrier R, Ramée A, Guibert JL, eds. Radiologie et échographie interventionelle. Montpellier: Axone 1986;1:111–125.
26. Picard L, Manelfe C, Roland J, Treil J, Andre JM, de Ker Saint Gilly A, Morel C. Embolisation et occlusions par ballonnets dans les lésions vasculaires crânio-faciales. Neuroradiologie 1978;16:393–394.
27. Picard L, Perrin C, Roland J, Dolisi B. Intérêt de l'embolisation dans les épistaxis graves post-traumatiques. Oto-Neuro-Ophtalmologie 1978;50:127–132.
28. Piton J, Grenier N, Kien P, Caille JM. Embolisation en territoire cervico-facial de l'adulte. In: Duvauferrier R, Ramée A, Guibert JL, eds. Radiologie et échographie interventionnelle. Montpellier: Axone 1986:1,127–138.
29. Riche MC, Chiras J, Melki JP, Merland JJ. Place de l'embolisation dans le traitement des épistaxis graves: a propos de 54 cas. J Neuroradiol 1979;6:207–220.
30. Riche MC, Hadjean E, Tricot JF, Henriquez C, Merland JJ. Les risques de la ligature de la carotide externe dans le traitement des angiodysplasies cervico-faciales. Ann Oto-Laryngol 1980;97:3–13.
31. Stricker M, Picard L. Les tumeurs vasculaires de la face. Encyclop Méd Chir (Paris) [Stomatologie] 1984;1:22062,E15.
32. Voigt K. Selective embolization with the catheter technique in neck and face. Ann Radiol (Paris) 1980;23:232–237.

Embolization Techniques in the Spinal Cord

J. J. Merland and D. Reizine

For the past 20 years, since the work of Djindjian (2) and Dichiro et al. (1), we have had a special interest in vascular malformations of the spinal cord. Successive changes have occurred in therapeutic capabilities, which may be chronologically schematized as follows:

– Until 1970: Surgical excision of the posterior spinal arteriovenous malformation or ligature of its radicular feeders was performed.
– 1970–1977: Two new types of treatment appeared: the development of microsurgical procedures with excision of some intramedullary arteriovenous malformations, located on the midline, via a posterior comissurotomy (7, 12, 13) and preoperative or palliative embolization of inoperable or partially excised lesions (4). However, excision remains difficult, it is partial in any case, and postoperative deficits may occur. In 1977, Djindjian et al. (3) desribed extramedullary arteriovenous fistulas.
– 1978–1985: This period brought the development of angiographic superselective technique, the use of nonresorbable particles, detachable microballoon systems, and isobutyl cyanoacrylate (5, 10).

It opened up the possibility of clinically controlled procedures under neuroleptanalgesia using new contrast media. Embolization of intramedullary arteriovenous malformations via the posterior and anterior spinal arteries is undertaken as a curative and exclusive treatment. The dural spinal arteriovenous fistula with medullary venous drainage is defined as a separate entity from the other intracanalicular arteriovenous malformations.
– Since 1985: new possibilities have occurred in selective catheterization and embolization thanks to the supple, thermoplastic microcatheters and new detachable microballoon systems.

During the last 10 years, 150 patients have been treated and they constitute the data source for this review.

Classification

Angiomatous malformations may be classified according to hemodynamic or anatomic considerations (Fig. 1) (11).

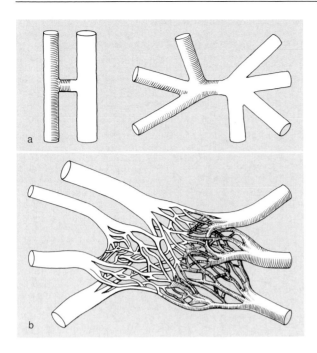

Fig. **1** **Hemodynamic classification of vascular malformations.** In an arteriovenous fistula (a), there is a single shunt between one or several arterial feeders and one or several draining veins. The shunts are multiple in an arteriovenous malformation (b)

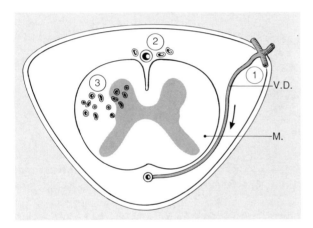

Fig. **2** **Anatomic classification of spinal cord malformations**
1. Extramedullary spinal dural fistula draining into the medullary veins. (V. D.: draining vein; m = medulla)
2. Intradural perimedullary arteriovenous fistula
3. Intramedullary arteriovenous malformation

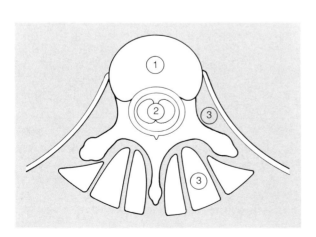

Fig. **3** **Metameric arteriovenous malformation,** including vertebral (1), medullary (2), and muscular (3) malformations

Hemodynamic Classification

The slow flow group includes venous, capillary, telangiectatic, and lymphatic types; until now, they have been very difficult to diagnose radiologically in the spinal cord and its canal.

The fast flow type includes arteriovenous fistulas and arteriovenous malformations. These are the only lesions that can actually be studied in the spinal canal.

Anatomic Classification

Intraspinal vascular malformations. Intramedullary arteriovenous malformations are partially or totally located in the spinal cord and have a nidus fed and drained by the medullary vessels (Fig. **2**).

Peri-extramedullary arteriovenous fistulas are situated on the surface of the cord. They are usually fed by the anterior spinal artery or by the posterior spinal artery, anterior and posterior spinal arteries, and some radicular arteries.

Extraretromedullary arteriovenous malformations are more or less extramedullary, fed by the posterior spinal artery, and seem to be rare.

Spinal-dural arteriovenous fistulas are an unusual and newly recognized entity. They are localized in the dura itself and drain exclusively through medullary veins. They have been incorrectly classified as retromedullary arteriovenous malformations for many years.

Epidural arteriovenous malformations are exceptional if they are localized; they may represent an epidural extension of a spinal hemangioma.

Spinal hemangiomas. Commonly located in the vertebral body, these may expand into the arch, the spinal canal, and the surrounding spaces. They may be of venous, capillary-venous, or arteriovenous type. The latter is exclusively seen in a metameric form.

Paraspinal arteriovenous malformation may be giant and sometimes may be associated with other spinal, epidural, and medullary locations.

Disseminated and metameric arteriovenous malformations. Disseminated arteriovenous malformations are usually associated with Osler-Weber-Rendu disease and may have brain or spinal cord locations. Multiple spinal hemangiomas may also occur, with or without other osseous hemangiomas.

Metameric arteriovenous malformations (Fig. **3**) may include cutaneous, muscular, visceral, spinal, dural, perimedullary, and medullary locations. Typically, they constitute the Cobb syndrome. They may involve one or more metameric segments and may extend to the limb, usually unilaterally at the cervical and lumbosacral segments.

Diagnosis and Therapy

The clinical symptoms may be variable: acute myelopathy, subarachnoid hemorrhage, or progressive myelopathy, with or without a neurologic level. Plain films are usually normal, but on occasion they show some bone erosion of the vertebral arch, body, or foramen, a spinal canal enlargement, or rarely calcifications. Before magnetic resonance imaging (MRI), the most important step was myelography. This examination may reveal vascular dilations on the surface of the cord or in the lumbosacral region. These dilations may be large or small, localized or diffuse. MRI has added to the diagnostic process (1); it is helpful if the malformation is intramedullary or has large perimedullary vascular dilations. However, it can be falsely negative if there are only minimal perimedullary vascular dilations, as are observed in dural arteriovenous malformations. Overall, myelography remains important for complete understanding of the abnormality, combined with plain films and myelotomography.

Spinal cord angiography remains the gold standard for the diagnosis of these lesions. First, we usually perform an aortic opacification to get an overview of the arteriovenous malformation and its potential components (spinal cord, intradural, dural, epidural, spinal, paraspinal, and metameric components). This may be obtained with bilateral retrograde simultaneous iliac injection opacifying the sacral, lumbar, and lower intercostal arteries, usually up to T-8, sometimes higher. Upper thoracic aortography may be indicated for lesions that are more superiorly located. Bilateral simultaneous retrograde brachial angiography is, in our experience, the best technique for an overview of cervical arteriovenous malformations. During these procedures, a Valsalva maneuver may be helpful to improve opacification of the intercostal arteries. As a second step, we perform a selective catheterization to show the feeders, the type of vascular malformation, its morphology, location, and extension, venous drainage, and hemodynamics.

The best therapeutic procedure can then be chosen according to the myelographic and angiographic data: surgery or embolization with particles, isobutyl cyanoacrylate or balloon methods. Each treatment has its own field of indication.

Spinal Dural Fistula with Medullary Venous Drainage

Recently identified as a separate entity (6, 8), this is a microscopic, direct arteriovenous fistula between one or several dural arterioles and a unique intradural vein (Fig. **4**). This arteriovenous fistula is located in the dura itself and its flow is very slow, which is the main reason why its diagnosis is difficult

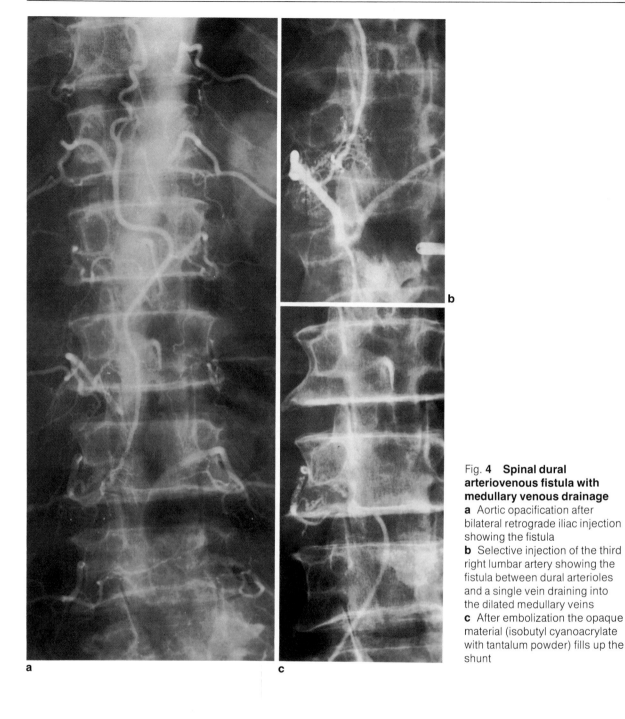

Fig. 4 **Spinal dural arteriovenous fistula with medullary venous drainage**
a Aortic opacification after bilateral retrograde iliac injection showing the fistula
b Selective injection of the third right lumbar artery showing the fistula between dural arterioles and a single vein draining into the dilated medullary veins
c After embolization the opaque material (isobutyl cyanoacrylate with tantalum powder) fills up the shunt

and, even now, too rare. Clinically, it is seen as a progressive myeloradiculopathy in patients, mostly men, 40 to 80 years old. Complete paraplegia occurs in 2 to 3 years, due to progressive venous stagnation with chronic medullary ischemia. An efficient treatment consists of occlusion of the dural arteriovenous fistula, either by surgery or embolization. The efficacy of either treatment is dependent on the duration of symptoms before their effective treatment.

Surgery

After a two-level laminectomy, opening the dura, and localizing the efferent draining vein, which is arterialized and dilated, the treatment consists of ligating this vein. The dura containing the shunt may be excised for pathologic study, although this does not afford any additional benefit to the patient and lengthens the duration of the procedure.

Embolization

This is performed under neuroleptanalgesia during angiography or as a separate, subsequent procedure. Because of the morphology of the arteriovenous fistula (small dural arterioles with 40 to 60 μm shunts that enter an ectatic vein), polymerizing material to fill the shunt and its venous part is required. This is to ensure that no recanalization can occur. The agent used is cyanoacrylate mixed with Lipiodol and tantalum powder in order to tailor the polymerization time to the structure to be occluded. This also enables us to visualize and control progression of isobutyl cyanoacrylate to the point of definitive cure and no further. A potential failure and risk must be kept in mind: occlusion of the dural arterial network, even in the area of the arteriovenous fistula itself, will open the way for an early or late recanalization. Occlusion of veins at the surface of the cord may occlude a functional medullary-venous channel and increase pressure in the remaining venous system, leading to further medullary veins that drain the arteriovenous fistula. These are also the veins that drain the cord itself. This drainage is very poor and may function solely through these ectatic vessels.

Indication for Surgery or Embolization

Our staff always consider embolization as the first treatment because of its noninvasiveness, efficiency, and safety if well-controlled. An anterior spinal artery fed from the same pedicle is the only contraindication. The procedure is impossible if selective catheterization of the feeder cannot be obtained. Either of these two conditions are indications for a surgical approach. A later indication would be unsuccessful embolization, which is suspected if the radiopaque agent has not entered the draining vein. In such a case there may be no clinical improvement, or even deterioration secondary to embolization.

Results

During the last 8 years, 63 patients have been treated at our institution, either by embolization (36 patients) or surgery (27 patients) or both. All of our patients have been treated with isobutyl cyanoacrylate, except three: one with Ethibloc, two with 100 to 250 μm Ivalon. Sixty-six percent have been cured with embolization. Failures have occurred due to materials different from isobutyl cyanoacrylate or proximal balloon occlusion. In one case, the patient became paraplegic immediately after embolization with Lipiodol and isobutyl cyanoacrylate without tantalum powder. We probably did not see the embolic agent entering the medullary veins themselves. In one case, surgery was unsuccessful as a secondary measure. In four surgical cases a transient deterioration occurred.

Clinical improvement is the rule after a few days or weeks, but always, except one case, within 3 months. The patient is followed clinically at 1, 3, and 6 months and then annually. The improvement usually continues over an 18-month period. If this is not the case, we ask the patient to have an angiographic examination after 6 weeks, 3 months, or later, according to his neurologic state. When possible, we perform myelography and angiography, studying the anterior spinal artery circulation time after 1 year, looking for the state of the myelographic vascular dilations and the reappearance of venous drainage, correlated to clinical improvement.

The neurologic improvement depends mainly on the illness duration before treatment. In our series, 80% have a significant improvement, initially and mainly in motor deficit, regaining ambulation in most cases. Sensory and sphincteric deficits improve over a longer time period but not to the same extent.

Because of its more simple procedure, in skilled hands, embolization is the treatment of choice for a dural spinal arteriovenous fistula. Since general anesthesia or opening of the dura is not performed, no clinical deterioration is expected. However, efficient embolization or surgical ligation of the draining vein has the same long-term results. The most important step is identifying the illness. Otherwise, the patient will rapidly become paraplegic, which is still the case for many patients. The inevitable deficits that occur, must encourage us to sharpen our clinical awareness and thereby identify instances of this curable disease.

Intradural Perimedullary Arteriovenous Fistula Fed by Radiculo-Medullary Arteries

Identified by Djindjian et al. (3), intradural perimedullary arteriovenous fistulas constitute a clinical, angiographic, and therapeutic entity. Their symptoms are a progressive radiculopathy or myelopathy occurring in young adults. 14 to 42 years old, spontaneously progressing to spinal transection within 7 to 9 years. These lesions are usually located at the conus or cauda equina. Plain films do not show any abnormality. Myelography often finds dilated vessels in the lumbar region around a conus of normal size, but in some cases the dilation may be minimal. We do not yet have any experience with MRI in these lesions. Spinal cord angiography is the key to diagnosis: it usually shows a dilated and tortuous anterior spinal artery entering a medullary vein through a unique, direct, and large shunt. This artery and vein may be dilated, even giant, and the venous drainage may simulate a malformation or the vessels may be normal in size and myelography may appear normal. In most cases, one may find other smaller feeders joining and indicating the point of arteriovenous fistula. At this point, we frequently observe a venous ectasia, thereby acting as an indicator for the location of the shunt.

Treatment

It may be surgical or embolic, depending on the type of fistula (Fig. **5**).

In type 1, the arteriovenous fistula is small, with a minimally dilated medullary feeder, and the flow may be very slow. Myelography may be normal and treatment is surgical.

In type 2, the arteriovenous fistula is larger, with evident dilation of the arterial feeder or feeders and draining veins. A venous ectasia is present at the point of the shunt and several feeders may be found. Treatment may be surgical, embolic, or both. A temporary balloon occlusion may help the surgeon during clippage of the shunt, when the origin of the anterior spinal artery is far from the point of the arteriovenous fistula.

In type 3 (Fig. **6**), the arteriovenous fistula is giant, but always unique: the flow is very fast and several main or secondary feeders are shown, but there is always a main feeder originating from the anterior or the posterior spinal artery. An ectatic dilation may exist at the point of the fistula, sometimes giant. Artery and vein or veins are tortuous and dilated and may be falsely diagnosed as an intramedullary arteriovenous malformation. The prognosis has been completely changed with balloon treatment. Surgical approach has a high risk of rupture, whereas entering a balloon is efficient and without great risk. These arteriovenous fistulas usually occur in the area of the conus and cauda equina. However, they may be found in any spinal canal location, in adults or children.

Intramedullary Arteriovenous Malformations

Surgery has greatly improved with microsurgery and posterior commissurotomy, but remains a difficult and dangerous procedure, even if preoperative embolization helps the neurosurgeon. Since 1977, embolization has become a curative procedure, due to the actual possibility of catheterization and permanent occlusive matertials. Because of the impossibility of knowing if the posterior spinal artery and anterior spinal artery feeders do or do not supply the normal cord, we believe that polymerizing agents must be used only in a few selected cases, particles remaining the best choice.

Clinically, intramedullary arteriovenous malformations are usually revealed in young patients, with hemorrhage, spinal cord deficit, or acute transection of the cord. Myelography is the first step for the diagnosis, but it will be progressively replaced by MRI. Both explorations are able to locate the lesion into the cord, partially or totally.

The main step remains spinal cord angiography. It is always better to have a general view of the lesion, which is sometimes extended to other spinal or extraspinal structures. For this reason, we prefer to do an aortography, then a selective opacification of the feeders, in anteroposterior and lateral views. Angiotomography remains very useful, to identify clearly the sulco-commissural arteries.

The main feeder of such malformations is the anterior spinal artery, but in most of the cases posterior spinal feeders participate. Venous drainage may be anterior or posterior, ascending or descending.

Neurologic exploration must clearly show the architecture of the arteriovenous malformation, with location, volume, and flow defining the criteria for treatment, either surgery or embolization, or both.

Surgery:

– Is there an anterior or a posterior venous drainage?
– Is the malformation in close contact with the anterior spinal artery or at some distance? Lateral angiotomography will answer this question.
– Is the arteriovenous malformation median or lateral? An anteroposterior view is necessary.
– Is it a well-defined mass or more or less scattered?

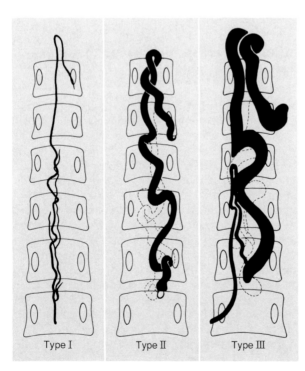

| Type I | Type II | Type III |

Fig. **5** **Extramedullary arteriovenous fistula fed by radicular arteries.** Diagram of the three types of intradural perimedullary arteriovenous fistulas

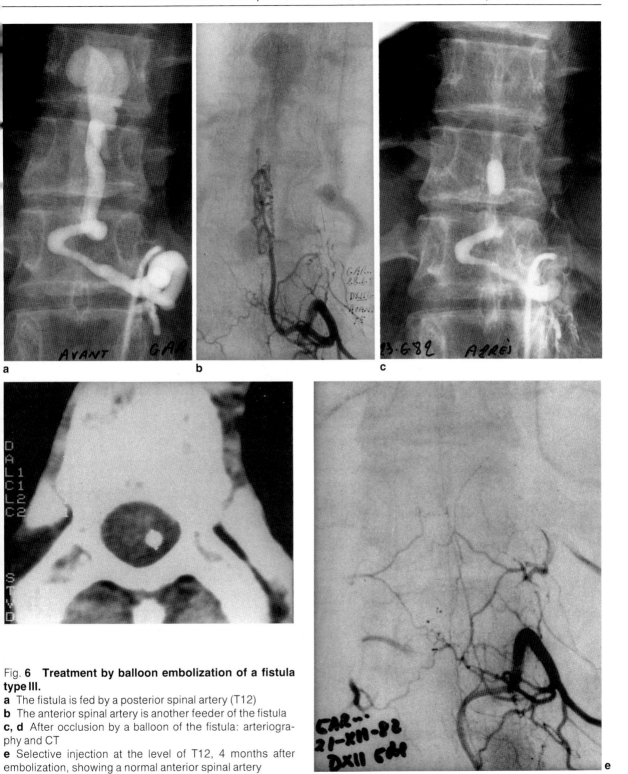

Fig. **6** **Treatment by balloon embolization of a fistula type III.**
a The fistula is fed by a posterior spinal artery (T12)
b The anterior spinal artery is another feeder of the fistula
c, d After occlusion by a balloon of the fistula: arteriography and CT
e Selective injection at the level of T12, 4 months after embolization, showing a normal anterior spinal artery

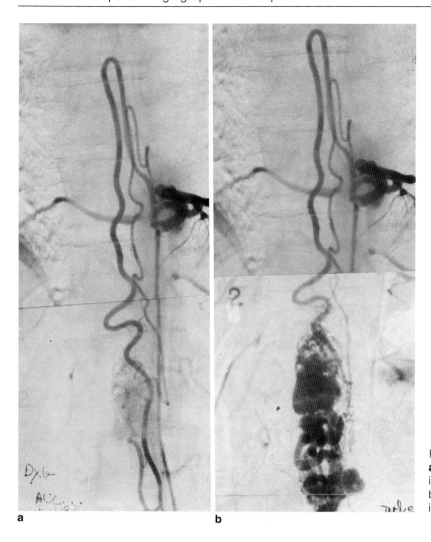

a   b

Fig. **7a, b Thoracic intramedullary arteriovenous malformation:** there is no arterial supply to the conus below the malformation. Embolization is contra-indicated

– Is there any large vascular lake that contributes to a mass effect?

Embolization of the anterior spinal artery component:

– Is the anterior spinal artery large, short and straight, or narrow, long, and sinuous?
– Does the anterior spinal artery end in an arteriovenous malformation?
– Is there a significant steal of flow entering the arteriovenous malformation?
– Are the shunts small or large, or both?
– Most of all, is the anterior spinal artery above and below the arteriovenous malformation fed by other sources and is the normal anterior spinal artery above and below connected to the arteriovenous malformation?

Having all this information, the therapeutic protocol can be proposed. Because of its ease of performance, safety, and efficacy, embolization is usually the first step of treatment, and in most of the cases the clinical and angiographic result is good enough to

become the only treatment. During follow-up, angiography will be performed after 6 months, 1 year, 2 years, and a new embolization or surgical exclusion of a remaining lesion may be undertaken.

In the dorsolumbar area, the main contra-indication for embolization is the lack of arterial supply to the conus below the arteriovenous malformation, or its arterial supply jointly coming from the arteriovenous malformation feeders themselves (9) (Fig. 7).

In the upper thoracic region, the anterior spinal artery supply may originate from the thoracic or the cervical area. Embolization must be very carefully performed because of the precariousness of the arterial supply to the cord in this area.

In the cervical area, anterior spinal artery feeders to the arteriovenous malformation are usually multiple: vertebral, deep cervical, upper intercostal, and vertebrobasilar junction. The most difficult is the treatment of upper cervical arteriovenous malformations or lower arteriovenous malformations with an anterior spinal artery supply from the vertebrobasilar junction. However, a supple microcatheter may

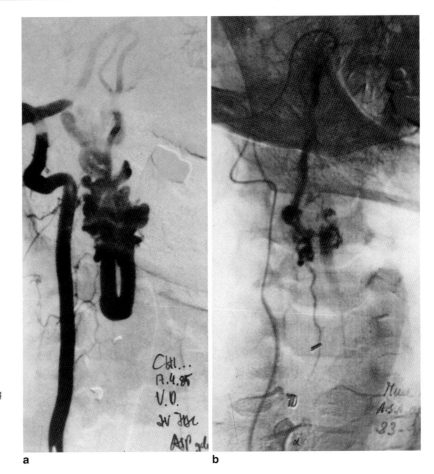

Fig. 8   Cervical intramedullary arteriovenous malformation.
a Fed by anterior and posterior radiculomedullary arteries originating from the vertebral arteries
b Selective injection of the anterior spinal artery after embolization with particles through a microcatheter

enter the lesion and offer new possibilities of treatment in previously desperate cases (Fig. **8**). In this area, embolization becomes the treatment of choice regarding the risk of surgery. Another way is to perform embolization while temporarily protecting the vertebral artery with a balloon occlusion.

In all of these territories, embolization with particles is the safest technique. In our experience, with regard to the contraindications previously described, side-effects are very rare, and improvement of cord deficit is the rule. However, because of possible secondary displacement of the particles or development of collateral circulation to a remaining arteriovenous malformation, follow-up angiography is needed after 6 and 12 months and later, according to angiographic findings. In very selected cases, polymerizing embolization may be proposed, especially in the territory of the posterior spinal artery and very rarely in the territory depending on the anterior spinal artery. We must know that the risk of complications with this material is difficult to foresee, even if the angiographic data are of good quality.

Later, new steps of treatment may be needed, according to the clinical state of the patient. In our experience, most of them are in good state and most are better than before treatment.

Metameric Arteriovenous Malformation

Very few cases have been previously published, but the recent review of our material (150 cases) has shown that one-third of the arteriovenous malformations of the cord had some extension outside: spinal arteriovenous malformation, epidural or radicular arteriovenous malformation, paraspinal, metameric, or cutaneous components. In such cases, the clinical symptoms may be closely related to these extensions, either due to the mass effect to the arterial steal, or to the increased venous pressure in the epidural veins or the medullary vein. The therapeutic decision is more difficult to take. However, surgery is much more hazardous, and embolization is generally the only treatment.

References

1. Dichiro G, Doppman JL, Dwyer AJ. Tumors and arteriovenous malformations of the spinal cord: assessment using MR. Radiology 1985;156:689–697.
2. Djindjian R, ed. Angiographie de la moelle épineuse. Paris: Masson 1970.
3. Djindjian M, Djindjian R, Rey A, Hurth M, Houdart R. Intradural extramedullary spinal arteriovenous malformations fed by the anterior spinal artery. Surg Neurol 1977;8:85–94.
4. Doppmann JL, di Chiro G, Ommaya A. Obliteration of spinal cord arteriovenous malformations by percutaneous embolization. Lancet 1968;11:477–479.
5. Guegen B, Merland JJ, Riche MC, Rey A. Vascular malformations of the spinal cord: intrathecal perimedullary arteriovenous fistulas fed by medullary arteries. Neurology 1987;37:969–979.
6. Kendall B, Logue V. Spinal epidural angiomatous malformations draining into intrathecal veins. Neuroradiology 1977;13:181–189.
7. Logue V. Angiomas of the spinal cord: review of the pathogenesis, clinical features and results of surgery. J Neurol Neurosurg Psychiatry 1979;42:1–11.
8. Merland JJ, Riche MC, Chiras J, Pariente D. Les fistules artérioveineuses intra-canalaires à drainage veineux médullaire. J Neuroradiol 1980;7:271–320.
9. Riche MC, Melki JP, Merland JJ. Embolization of spinal cord vascular malformations in the anterior spinal artery. AJNR 1983;4:378–381.
10. Riche MC, Scialfa G, Gueguen B, Merland JJ. Giant extramedullary arteriovenous fistula supplied by anterior spinal artery: treatment by detachable balloon. AJNR 1983;4:391–394.
11. Riche MC, Reizine D, Melki JP. Classification of spinal cord malformation. Radiat Med. 1985;3:17–24.
12. Symow L, Kuyama J. Kendall B. Dural arteriovenous malformations of the spine: clinical features and surgical results in 55 cases. J Neurosurg 1984;60:239–247.
13. Yazargil MG, Delong WB, Guarwaschicci JJ. Complete microsurgical exams of cervical extramedullary and intramedullary vascular malformations. Surg Neurol 1975;4:211–224.

Angiographic Management of Malignant Tumors in the Thorax, Abdomen and Bones

Lung Tumors

U. Tylén

The idea of treating inoperable lung tumors by regional infusion of cytostatic drugs is not new. Efforts were made in the early 1960s with nitrogen mustard, methotrexate, and similar drugs (1, 7, 15, 20, 24). The results, however, were poor, severe complications occurred (6, 18, 22, 23), and the treatment modality was abandoned. More recently, the development of new, more potent chemotherapeutic agents has promoted new efforts and optimistic results have been reported (21).

Anatomy

A prerequisite for regional treatment of a tumor is that it is vascularized and that a tumor-feeding artery can be identified and catheterized. The vascularization pattern of lung tumors depends on the location. It has been demonstrated by microangiographic investigations that bronchial carcinomas with central location are supplied by bronchial arteries. Metastases, as well as primary lung tumors located in the periphery of the lung parenchyma, on the other hand, are fed by the pulmonary artery. Primary lung tumors with peripheral site but still in close context with a bronchus may be supplied by both bronchial and pulmonary arteries (19). Supply from intercostal arteries is not seen unless there is tumor growth into the thoracic wall.

The anatomy of the bronchial arteries is rich in variations (2, 3). The arteries usually originate from the ventral or ventrolateral circumference of the aorta at the level of the fifth or sixth thoracic vertebrae. Origin at other levels of the aorta, however, often occurs. Aberrant origin, for example, from the internal mammary, thyrocervical (Fig. 1), phrenic, innominate, or left subclavian arteries is also common. Although the branching pattern varies, three patterns occur in more than two-thirds of the population (2) (Fig. 2):

I. One bronchial artery to each lung (17%).
II. One artery originating together with the third intercostal artery supplying the entire right lung, the left lung being supplied by two arteries, one to the upper lobe and one to the lower (27%).

Communication between left bronchial arteries and intercostal arteries is extremely rare (13).

III. A common trunk supplying the upper lobe of the left lung and the lower lobe of the right, the upper lobe of the right lung and the lower lobe of the left each being supplied by separate branches (17%).

The bronchial arteries may often give off branches to the spinal cord, the aorta, the esophagus, the trachea, and the heart. The existence of such branches is the cause of the complications reported. The branches may be very small and not always visible on the angiographic films. Their occurrence is

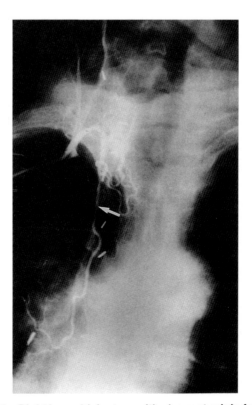

Fig. 1 **Right bronchial artery with aberrant origin from inferior thyroid artery** (arrow). Patient previously operated on for parathyroid adenoma

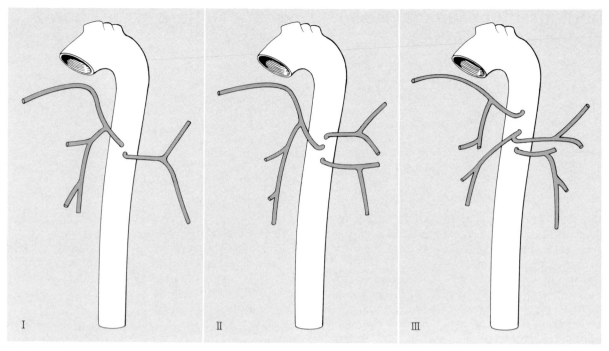

Fig. **2   Main variations of bronchial artery anatomy.** (After Botenga [2])

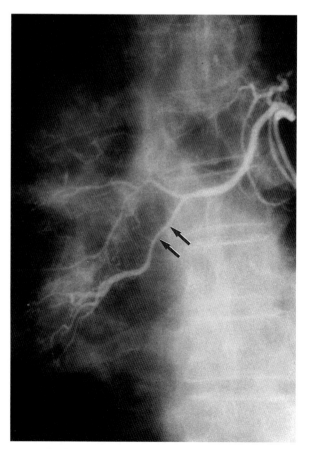

Fig. **3   Patient with squamous cell carcinoma of the right lung.** Encasement of widened bronchial artery (arrow) indicating malignant growth into mediastinum

important to bear in mind, however, when planning infusion of cytostatic drugs, so that the risk of side effects may be evaluated. It is recommended that cytostatic infusion be avoided should an anastomosis to the Adamkiewicz artery to the spinal cord be demonstrated.

Angiographic Technique

The variant anatomy with common occurrence of multiple tumor-supplying branches (14) as well as aberrant origin of arteries makes meticulous mapping of the arterial supply extremely important before the start of infusion therapy. The evaluation should also include angiography of intercostal arteries in the proximity of the tumor and sometimes also of the internal mammary artery. Blood supply from these arteries indicates tumor growth into the thoracic wall and precludes successful infusion therapy.

Catheterization of bronchial arteries is best done from the femoral artery. Most patients with lung cancer are older, and the aortic wall is arteriosclerotic. A 6 or 7 Fr catheter with good torque control and a cobra or shepherd's hook type curve is recommended (10). It is important that the tip of the catheter be thin so that blood flow is not obstructed. Use of non-ionic contrast media should be encouraged to minimize pain and risk of contrast-media-induced complications.

Films should be taken in anteroposterior and oblique projections. An aluminium wedge may be used to compensate for the large attenuation differences between mediastinum and the lung parenchyma. Film subtraction technique is of value for identification of small branches to the spinal cord. Digital subtraction technique may facilitate the examination, by reduction of examination time and use of less contrast medium. Whether the spatial resolution will be sufficient for revelation of small branches to the spinal cord remains to be discovered.

In addition to demonstrating the arterial anatomy, the angiography may also be used for staging of tumor growth and selection of patients for cytostatic treatment. Encasement of the bronchial artery or opacification of lymph nodes in the mediastinum thus indicates growth into the mediastinum, making the patient unsuitable for treatment (11) (Fig. 3). As previously mentioned, vascularization of the tumor from arteries to the thoracic wall points to the same fact.

Technique of Cytostatic Drug Infusion

The anatomy of the bronchial arteries makes positioning of a catheter for long-term infusion impossible. The use of cytostatics such as 5-fluorouracil is therefore less suitable. The most commonly used drug is mitomycin C, which may be given as a rapid infusion, after which the catheter is withdrawn.

Mitomycin is an antibiotic with an alkylating effect producing inhibition of DNA synthesis and mitotic activity (17). The effect is exerted on all fast-growing tissues. Its main side effect is myelosuppression.

For infusion in a bronchial artery 10 mg of mitomycin is diluted in 100 ml of saline and is infused at a rate of 5 to 7 ml/min. The position of the catheter should be checked periodically during the infusion. In the presence of multiple tumor-feeding arteries the dose may be divided according to the relative size of the supply. The arteries anastomose within the tumor, however, and this should not be critical. During the infusion, the patient may experience some irritation in the throat and an urge to cough but no other particular sensations. The catheter may, after cessation of the infusion, immediately be withdrawn. During the 3 to 4 days after the treatment, symptoms of bronchitis may occur and in a few patients some pain has been noted on swallowing. These local side effects are usually not severe but indicate vascular anastomoses between bronchial arteries and the trachea and esophagus. Due to the regional effect of the drug, no systemic side effects are usually registered, but the myelopoietic activity should be followed during the weeks after treatment. The treatment may be repeated three to four times with an interval of about 2 weeks.

Since the effect of cytostatic infusion in bronchial arteries is strictly regional, systemic therapy may be added. Hellekant and Svanberg (9) recommend the use of bleomycin or vincristine, the effects of which potentiate the effect of mitomycin C. Radiotherapy directed toward the tumor and mediastinum may also be used (4).

Indications

The indications for treatment have not been thoroughly investigated. Reports so far do not give details on patient selection, and randomized studies do not exist. Bronchial artery infusion of cytostatic drugs, however, is recommended as an adjuvant to systemic therapy in the palliation of patients with unresectable tumor. It is also recommended preoperatively in some patients with complicating diseases, e.g., obstructive lung disease or cardiac decompensation, to reduce tumor burden and convert a life-threatening pneumonectomy into a limited resection (5, 8). Recently, general preoperative treatment has been suggested as an adjuvant in an effort to improve the long-term results of surgery in lung cancer (5).

Results

The largest experience so far published, is from Ogata and Yoneyama (21) who in 1975 published a series of 431 patients treated with mitomycin C. The treatment was given preoperatively in the majority of patients and the results were good in 426 (21). Hellekant (12) reported his experiences from treatment of 35 patients, 27 with squamous cell carcinoma, seven with adenocarcinoma, and one with small cell carcinoma. Most patients had inoperable tumors and were treated with repeat infusions of mitomycin C, usually in combination with systemic cytostatic treatment. Reduction of tumor size, as evaluated by radiography and bronchoscopy, occurred in 19 of the patients. Remission occurred in all types of tumor. The best results, however, were obtained in poorly differentiated lesions (12). In five of his patients, who before treatment were considered inoperable, the tumor could be resected after treatment. Ekholm et al. (4) report similar experiences in 15 patients, 12 with squamous cell carcinoma and three with adenocarcinoma. In seven of the patients with squamous cell carcinoma, infusion treatment was combined with radiotherapy to the mediastinum. Tumor regression was noted in 11 of the patients (Fig. 4). The most marked reduction in the tumor size was recognized between the first and second treatment. In both series, marked regressive changes were evident in tumors examined histopathologically. Ekholm et al. (4) even report no viable tumor in three of their patients at autopsy.

Life expectancy in unresectable lung cancer is poor. So far, no evidence has been published sup-

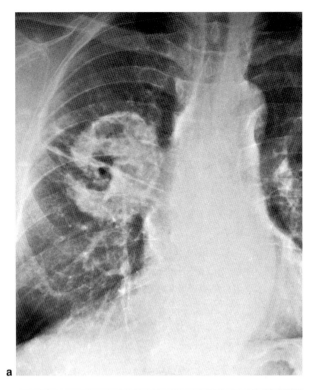

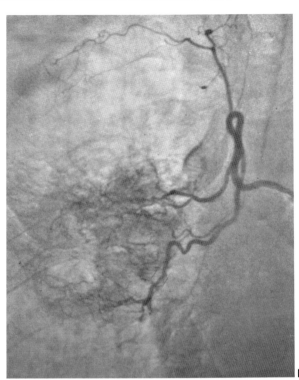

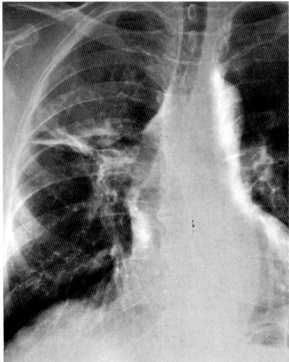

Fig. 4 Male aged 72 years with squamous cell carcinoma
a Large tumor with central necrosis
b Bronchial arteriography, subtraction film, Widened bronchial artery with abundant tumor vessels
c Marked regression of tumor size 2 months after cessation of infusion therapy consisting of 10 mg of mitomycin C at four treatments with 2-week intervals. Patient died 7 months later from hemoptysis

porting the fact that the addition of bronchial artery infusion of cytostatic drugs may change this. Whether preoperative treatment, as recommended by Ekholm et al. (5), may be of value remains to be proved.

Complications

In early attempts at bronchial artery infusion, severe complications were reported. Such complications included transverse myelitis, aortic rupture, and ulceration of the trachea and esophagus (16, 18, 22, 23). These complications contributed to the abandonment of the method. It has been supposed that the complications to a great part were caused by the drugs used at that time and that new drugs with better specificity would have decreased the risk. In the series of Hellekant et al. (8) the rule was slight fever and malaise. Chemical pneumonitis developed in two patients but no severe complications were registered (12). Ekholm et al. (4) on the other hand, who followed their 15 patients until death, report ulceration of the esophagus in two patients and tracheobronchial fistula in one. Skin necrosis occurred in an additional patient and chemical pneumonitis in one. Three patients died from hemoptysis, although no viable tumor was evident at autopsy in two of these patients (4). It may be claimed that radiotherapy to the mediastinum was given to some patients, but the complications occurred also in patients not given radiotherapy.

Future Developments

Published results of treatment of lung cancer with infusion of cytostatic drugs are not entirely positive. Although there are series from Japan including many patients with good therapeutic results, the number of published reports are few and the experiences still limited. The risk of severe complications makes the treatment modality potentially dangerous. This risk should be balanced against the fact that although tumor mass may be reduced by the infusions there is no proved prolongation of life. Infusion of cytostatic drugs in bronchial arteries in patients with lung cancer therefore should only be undertaken as part of a scientific protocol. Much basic research remains to be done on selection of patients, choice of drug and dose, proper treatment schedule, whether infusion should be combined with systemic therapy or radiation, and so on. The final role of the treatment modality then has to be settled in a randomized series.

References

1. Boijsen E, Dahlbäck O, Kugelberg J, Schüller H, Zsigmond M. Die Behandlung des inoperablen Bronchuskarzinoms mit Zytostaticainfusionen via A.A. bronchiales. Thoraxchir Vask Chir 1964;12:198–201.
2. Botenga ASJ, ed. Selective bronchial and intercostal arteriography. Leiden: Stenfert Kroese 1970.
3. Cauldwell EW, Siekert RG, Lininger RE, Anson BJ. The bronchial arteries: an anatomic study of 150 human cadavers. Surg Gynecol Obstet 1948;86:395.
4. Ekholm S, Albrechtsson U, Tylén U. Bronchial artery infusion of mitomycin-C in carcinoma of the lung. Cardiovasc Intervent Radiol 1983;6:86–96.
5. Ekholm S, Dahlbäck O, Tylén U. Preoperative treatment of squamous cell carcinoma of the lung with mitomycin-C in the bronchial artery. Eur J Radiol 1986;6:9–11.
6. Feigelson HH, Ravin HA. Transverse myelitis following selective bronchial arteriography. Radiology 1965;85:663–665.
7. Haller JD, Bron KM, Wholey MH, Poller S, Enerson DM. Selective bronchial artery catheterization for diagnostic and physiologic studies and chemotherapy for bronchogenic carcinoma. J Thorac Cardiovasc Surg 1965;51:143–152.
8. Hellekant C, Boijsen E, Svanberg L. Preoperative infusion of mitomycin-C in the bronchial artery in squamous cell carcinoma of the lung. Acta Radiol [Diagn] (Stockh) 1978;19:1045–1056.
9. Hellekant C, Svanberg L. Bronchial artery infusion of mitomycin-C in advanced bronchogenic carcinoma. Acta Radiol Oncol Radiat Phys Biol 1978;17:449–462.
10. Hellekant C. Bronchial angiography and intraarterial chemotherapy with mitomycin-C in bronchogenic carcinoma: anatomy, technique and complications. Acta Radiol [Diagn] (Stockh) 1979;20:478–496.
11. Hellekant C, Svanberg L. Bronchial angiography in the staging of bronchogenic carcinoma. Acta Radiol Oncol Radiat Phys Biol 1979;18:81–96.
12. Hellekant C. Bronchial angiography and intraarterial chemotherapy in lung carcinoma [Dissertation]. Malmö 1978.
13. Hellekant C, Tylén U. Left-side intercostobronchial trunk: a rare anomaly. AJR 1980;134:590–591.
14. Hellekant C, Jonsson K. Double blood supply of bronchogenic carcinoma from multiple arteries. Acta Radiol [Diagn] (Stockh) 1981;22:403–406.
15. Kahn PC, Paul RE, Rheinlander HF. Selective bronchial arteriography and intra-arterial chemotherapy in carcinoma of the lung. J Thorac Cardiovasc Surg 1965;50:640–645.
16. Kardien V, Symenonov A, Chankov I. Etiology, pathogenesis and presentation of spinal cord lesions in selective angiography of the bronchial and intercostal arteries. Radiology 1974;112:81–83.
17. Lown JW. The molecular mechanism of antitumor action of the mitomycins. In: Carter SK, Crooke ST, eds. Mitomycin-C: current status and new developments. New York: Academic Press 1979:5–26.
18. Mark JBD, Hockman RP, Carrington CB. Experimental bronchial arterial-infusions of mechlorethamine. J Thorac Cardiovasc Surg 1965;50:15–19.
19. Milne ENC. Circulation of primary and metastatic pulmonary neoplasms: a postmortem microangiographic study. AJR 1967;100:603–619.
20. Nordenström B. Selective catheterization with Tifocyl injection of bronchomediastinal arteries in bronchial carcinoma. Acta Radiol Ther Phys Biol 1966;4:298–304.
21. Ogata T, Yoneyama T. Regional arterial infusion therapy for lung tumour. (In Japanese.) Gan To Kagaku Ryoho (Cancer and Chemotherapy) 1975;921.
22. Remy J, Wallaert C, Voisin C, Gerney-Rieux C. Angiographie sélective des artères bronchiques. Presse Méd. 1968;76:729–732.
23. Steckel RJ, Doppman JL, Rolley RT, Martos EJ. Rupture of the aorta after mechlorethamine HCl infusion of a bronchial artery. JAMA 1967;199:936–939.
24. Tate CF, Viamonte M, Agnew JR. Bronchial artery perfusion with cytotoxic agents for bronchogenic carcinoma. Am Rev Respir Dis 1968;97:685–693.

Liver Tumors

C. Charnsangavej, C. H. Carrasco, W. R. Richli and S. Wallace

In Western countries, hepatic metastases are the most common malignant hepatic neoplasms, since the liver is the major organ most frequently involved by metastatic disease. It has been estimated that metastatic neoplasm to the liver is 20 times more common than primary hepatic malignancies, which are most common in Africa and Eastern countries. Despite advances in diagnostic imaging, malignant hepatic neoplasms, primary or secondary, are often diagnosed when they are beyond surgical resectability. Surgical resection remains the best treatment for the tumor confined to an anatomic segment or lobe of the liver. Unfortunately, only 10 to 15% of the patients are surgical candidates and when extended resection is contemplated, the morbidity of the procedure is still high.

The prognosis of the patients who have primary or secondary neoplasms of the liver is poor. One-half to two-thirds of the patients who die of cancer of the gastrointestinal tract, pancreas, breast, and ovary and one-third of the patients who die of lung and kidney cancers have liver metastases (1). The median survival period for patients with untreated liver metastases from colon carcinoma is 5 months, from the stomach, 2 months, and from the pancreas, 50 days (1, 6, 27). The 1-year survival rate for patients with metastatic carcinoma to the liver from all sites is 7% (44). For hepatocellular carcinoma, a median survival among untreated patients is approximately 75 days (27). The patient's survival from the time of diagnosis also depends on the stage of the disease, the volume of tumor, and the performance status. Patients with a performance status of Zubrod 0 had a median survival of 52 weeks, those with a Zubrod 1 or 2 performance status, 16 weeks, and those with a performance status of 3, a median survival of only 5 weeks (18). Because of this poor prognosis of nonresectable primary and secondary hepatic neoplasms, an aggressive therapeutic approach is justified. At the M. D. Anderson Hospital and Tumor Institute, transcatheter management of hepatic neoplasms, by infusion, embolization, or chemoembolization offers viable therapeutic alternatives.

The rationale for transcatheter management of hepatic neoplasms is based on the principle that most primary and secondary neoplasms of the liver receive their blood supply almost exclusively (90%) from the hepatic artery (9, 24). Approximately 75% of blood flow to the normal liver parenchyma is from the portal vein and 25% from the hepatic artery. Catheterization of the hepatic artery via a femoral artery or an axillary approach can be routinely performed under fluoroscopic guidance, thus providing an access for delivery of chemotherapeutic agents or embolic materials. The treatment delivered to the hepatic artery almost selectively affects the neoplasms.

Hepatic Artery Infusion Chemotherapy

The basic concept of hepatic artery infusion (HAI) of chemotherapy (HAIC) is to deliver a high dose of chemotherapeutic agents directly to the liver, since most of the blood supply to hepatic tumors, whether they are primary or metastatic lesions, is derived from the hepatic artery. When a catheter is placed in the hepatic artery for chemotherapy infusion, it is hoped that only the tumors will be selectively infused. However, the normal organs, such as the liver parenchyma, gallbladder, bile ducts, stomach, and duodenum, in the distribution of the hepatic artery may also be infused in addition to the tumors. Complications from local drug toxicity, including chemical hepatitis, chemical cholecystitis (12), sclerosing cholangitis (8, 25), and chemotherapy-induced gastroduodenal ulcerations (23, 26, 29), occur as a result of a malposition of the catheter or an unintentional or unavoidable infusion of these normal organs.

In order to achieve the maximum effect of chemotherapy and minimize the local complications of HAIC, the vascular anatomy and hemodynamics of the liver and its adjacent organs should be carefully evaluated before the infusion.

Radiologic Evaluation of the Hemodynamics and Anatomy of the Hepatic Artery

The anatomy and hemodynamics of the hepatic artery can be assessed before and after placement of the catheter by angiography, radionuclide flow study, and arterial contrast-enhanced CT. When the catheter is placed surgically, fluorescein is used to evaluate the distribution of flow in the liver and to exclude extrahepatic infusion.

Angiography. Selective hepatic arteriography is accomplished by the injection of contrast material at the rate of 3 to 6 ml/s for a total to 10 to 15 seconds, depending on the size of the liver, the vascularity of the tumors, and the position of the catheter. Because of this high injection rate, it does not truly reflect the distribution of the chemotherapy, which is usually infused at 50 to 200 ml/h. However, the gross direction of the blood flow in the common hepatic and gastroduodenal arteries can be demonstrated.

Radionuclide flow study. Radionuclide flow study has been used for the evaluation of the distribution of chemotherapy infusion after catheter placement in the hepatic artery. One to 5 mC. of technetium-99m-macroaggregated albumin (^{99m}Tc-MAA) in a volume of 0.5 to 1.0 ml is slowly infused by a mechanical pump into the catheter at the flow rate of 40 ml/h (7). The study can also be performed through a totally-implanted drug delivery system connected to a surgically placed catheter in the hepatic artery (51). ^{99m}Tc-MAA is slowly injected into the side port of the pump with a Huber needle over 1 to 2 minutes. Scintigraphy of the liver is obtained in the anterior and both lateral views.

Since the infusion rate in the radionuclide flow study is similar to the rate of chemotherapy infusion, the flow distribution as demonstrated by the radionuclide flow study reflects the distribution of chemotherapy. In addition, extrahepatic uptake and the presence of arteriovenous shunting can be easily recognized.

Arterial contrast-enhanced computed tomography. At our hospital CT of the liver was performed with contrast material delivered through the percutaneous catheter placed in the hepatic artery to compare the distribution of flow at the rate of 200 ml/h with that at 1 to 2 ml/s. Our preliminary data demonstrated that this technique can simulate the anatomic distribution of the infusion. The result was similar to that of Miller et al. (35) who used lipid soluble contrast material (EOE-13) infused into the hepatic artery.

Hemodynamic Considerations

The hemodynamics of HAIC can be evaluated in three categories: the delivery system, the extrahepatic circulation, and the intrahepatic circulation.

Delivery system. In general, chemotherapy infusion through a percutaneously-placed catheter is delivered by a mechanical infusion pump at the rate of 50 to 200 ml/h for 2 hours to as long as 7 days. The infusion catheter can also be placed surgically and connected to a totally-implanted pump. The pump consists of a chamber, automatically compressible by body temperature, which delivers the chemotherapeutic agents at the rate of 2 to 5 ml/day. Since most infusion systems deliver the infusate at a rate much slower than the arterial blood flow (50 to 200 ml/h versus 3 to 6 ml/s), laminar flow or streaming occurs, resulting in poor mixing of the infusate and the blood and an uneven distribution.

In an exprimental model by Wright et al. (49), ink was infused at a steady rate through a vascular catheter inserted into a transparent tube carrying water at a rate similar to that of arterial blood. The ink ran in discrete streams for 10 to 15 cm before mixing with the water. There were substantial differences in the concentrations of ink in the water collected at various distances from the catheter tip.

A similar situation is illustrated in Figure 1. When a catheter was placed in the proper hepatic artery, radionuclide flow study demonstrated the lack of infusion of the lateral segment of the left lobe. A pulsing device developed by Wright et al. (49) disrupted the steady stream, immediately mixed the infusate with the bloodstream, resulting in a better distribution. This has been applied in clinical use with an improvement of flow distribution in 19.3% of the 83 hepatic studies.

The infusion rate delivered by an implantable infusion pump is 2 to 5 ml/day. This flow rate has not been duplicated and evaluated by any imaging technique, since most radionuclide flow studies and CT scans performed through the side port of this pump are infused at 40 ml/h.

Hemodynamics of extrahepatic circulation. Extrahepatic circulation is defined as tributaries of the common hepatic, proper hepatic, right and left hepatic arteries, which supply the non-parenchymal portion of the liver and the organs adjacent to the liver. These vessels include the gastroduodenal artery, right gastric artery, supraduodenal artery, cystic and bile duct arteries, dorsal pancreatic artery, pancreaticoduodenal arcades, and common hepatic artery. Optimal catheter placement must consider the direction of blood flow in this extrahepatic circulation.

Under normal circumstances, the direction of blood flow in extraparenchymal vessels is in a hepatofugal direction to supply various organs in their distribution. Placement of the catheter should avoid the infusion of these extrahepatic vessels, since it may be associated with a high incidence of complications. For instance, the catheter should be placed in the proper hepatic artery rather than the common hepatic artery to avoid infusion of the gastroduodenal artery, which may result in chemotherapy-induced duodenal ulceration or pancreatitis.

When there is an increased demand for arterial blood supply to the liver due to various pathologic conditions, such as hypervascular neoplasms, arteriovenous shunting, cirrhosis, and portal hypertension and enlarged liver, the direction of blood flow in these vessels may reverse to a hepatopetal direction, acting as collateral supply to the liver. Placement of the catheter in the common hepatic artery for hepatic infusion is adequate in such circumstances. Extrahepatic infusion will not be at risk.

Celiac axis stenosis or compression by the median arcuate ligament is encountered in 10 to 15% of the patients. With celiac axis stenosis, the superior mesenteric artery provides blood supply to the liver, stomach, and spleen through the pancreatic vessels. There is a reversal of blood flow not only in the

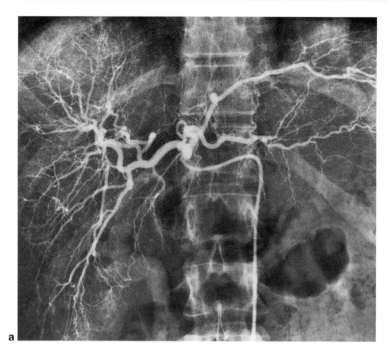

a

b

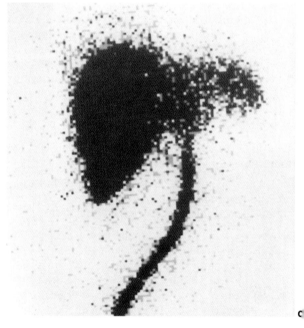

c

Fig. 1 Hepatic artery infusion chemotherapy
a Catheter is placed in the proper hepatic artery
b Radionuclide study demonstrates lack of perfusion of the left lobe in the distribution of the left hepatic artery
c With pulsatile pump, good distribution is now demonstrated

gastroduodenal artery, but also in the common hepatic artery to supply the stomach and the spleen. Placement of the catheter in the common hepatic artery will result in the infusion of the spleen. The proper hepatic artery must be catheterized for the infusion of the liver.

Hemodynamics of intrahepatic circulation. The hemodynamics of intrahepatic circulation incorporates the patterns of flow in the lobar or segmental distribution of the liver, and the uptake in the normal parenchyma and the tumor. The distribution of flow in the normal liver is presumably uniform in each lobe or segment. Changes in distribution occur in various disease states. Increasing flow may be associated with the vascularity of the tumor, arteriovenous shunting, cirrhosis and portal hypertension, portal vein occlusion, bile duct obstruction, and hepatic vein occlusion. On the other hand, a decrease in arterial blood flow may be caused by occlusion or encasement of the artery, avascular or necrotic tumors, and hypoplastic or atrophic liver.

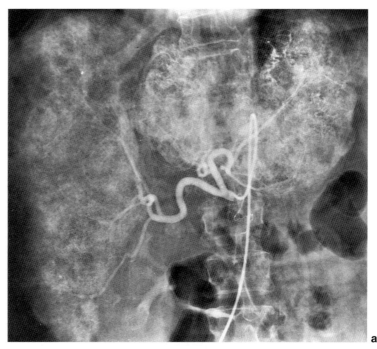

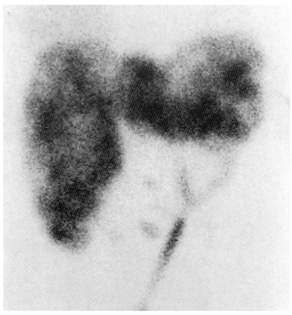

Fig. 2 **Hepatic artery infusion chemotherapy**
a Hypervascular tumors in both lobes
b The flow study demonstrates a good uptake in the tumor due to the hypervascularity

In a hypervascular tumor, increased arterial flow can be expected because the vascularity of the tumor acts as a sump. In the absence of arteriovenous shunting, there is direct delivery of chemotherapeutic agents to the tumor (Fig. 2). Although arteriovenous shunting increases flow, blood may be rapidly shunted away from the tumor to the systemic circulation or hepatic parenchyma, depending on the types of shunt, i.e., arteriohepatic venous or arterioportal venous shunt.

In hepatic cirrhosis with portal hypertension, de-spite an overall reduction in hepatic blood flow, there is an increase in hepatic arterial flow due to a decrease in portal venous flow. With presinusoidal block as in schistosomiasis, periportal fibrosis, and biliary cirrhosis, arterial flow to the sinusoids increases. Arterioportal shunts may develop at the level of the sinusoids (transsinusoidal) or in the wall of the portal vein (transvasal) in postsinusoidal or sinusoidal block in postnecrotic, Laennec's, and alcoholic cirrhosis. Since the fibrosis of cirrhosis may involve the liver asymmetrically with more promi-

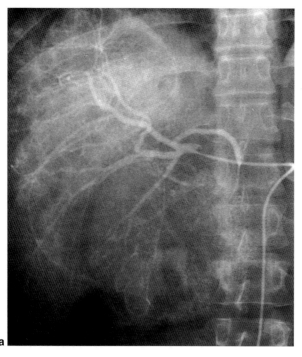

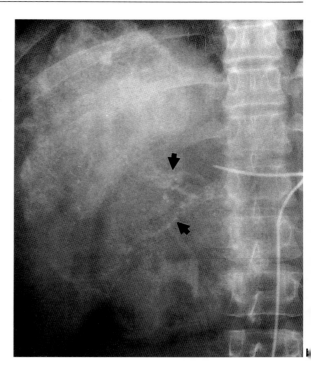

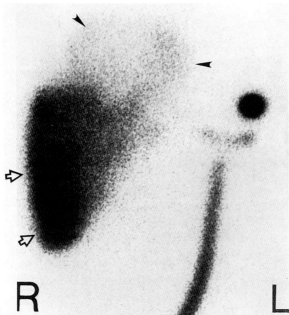

Fig. 3   **Hepatic artery infusion chemotherapy**
a Multiple hypervascular metastases from melanoma
b Occlusion of the right portal vein branches (arrows)
c Anterior view of the flow study. Despite hypervascularity of the tumor, the flow was diverted to the normal parenchyma (open arrows) in the right lobe away from the tumor (arrowheads)

nent shrinkage of the right lobe, differential flow in the hepatic artery may occur when intra-arterial chemotherapy infusion is delivered to patients with hepatic cirrhosis.

Portal venous occlusion has been observed in various hepatic neoplasms, especially primary hepatocellular carcinoma. Increased hepatic arterial supply in the distribution of the occluded portal vein may be beneficial during hepatic artery infusion chemotherapy, for the increased arterial flow may improve the distribution of chemotherapy to the tumors confined to the lobe or segment distal to the occluded portal vein. This may be a disadvantage if flow is delivered to the normal parenchyma, away from the tumors occupying the other lobe or segments (13) (Figs. **3, 4**).

Alterations in hepatic hemodynamics occur in hepatic veno-occlusive disease and have been demonstrated in both experimental animals and clinical experiences (21, 31). Increasing arterial flow

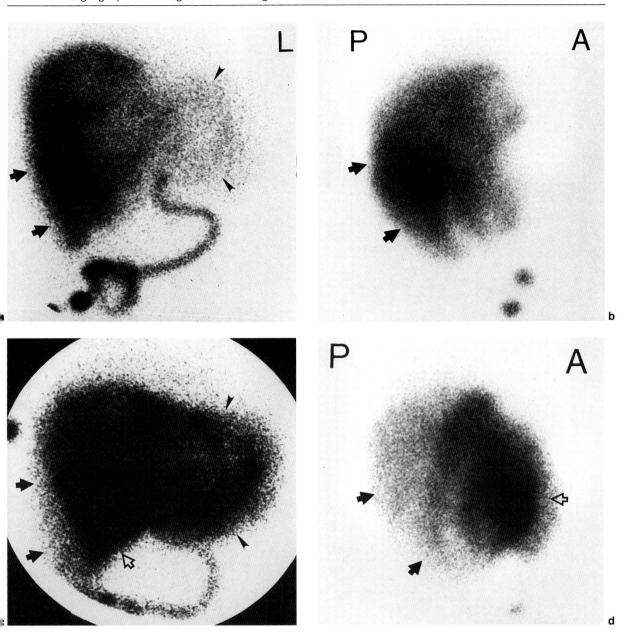

Fig. 4a, b Hepatic artery infusion chemotherapy. Flow study through the surgically placed catheter demonstrates predominant flow to the right lobe while the tumor is in the left lobe
c, d Six months later, there was a progression of the tumor. The flow study shows an increase in the flow toward the left lobe

with crowding of arterial branches, dense hepatogram due to congestion of the liver parenchyma, and retrograde flow in the portal vein may be observed. Similar changes can be demonstrated in radiation hepatitis. With tumor involvement or occlusion of the hepatic vein, increased arterial flow to the liver and stagnation of blood flow to the region with poor venous drainage can occur (Fig. 4).

In obstructive jaundice, a decrease in total hepatic blood flow with an increase in hepatic arterial blood flow and a decrease in portal blood flow have been documented (4, 39, 45). As a result, chemotherapy infusion should increase to the lobe or segment with obstructed bile ducts.

Anatomic Consideration

Variations of hepatic artery anatomy. There are at least 10 variations of the hepatic arterial anatomy, aberrant arteries arising directly from the aorta as

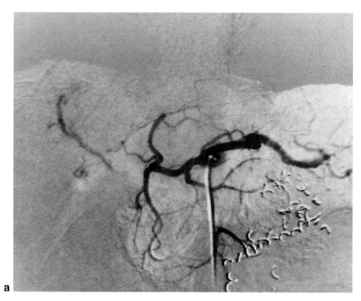

a

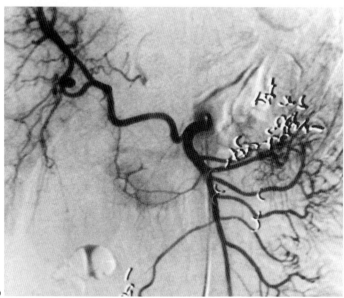

b

Fig. **5   Hepatic artery redistribution for HAIC**
a, b Celiac and superior mesenteric arteriograms demonstrate a type III anatomy: the right hepatic artery arises from the superior mesenteric artery

well as from the left gastric, gastroduodenal, and superior mesenteric occurring in approximately 45% of the general population (34), which become a significant obstacle to HAI.

A decrease in the size of the tumor in one lobe following HAI with a simultaneous increase in size in the noninfused lobe was observed repeatedly. Proximal occlusion of the aberrant vessels will lead to reconstruction of their territory through intrahepatic collaterals arising from the other hepatic artery (14, 16). Infusion of the latter artery will redistribute the flow throughout the entire liver (Fig. **5**).

Variations of extraparenchymal branches of the hepatic artery. Anatomic variations of the blood supply to the stomach, duodenum, gallbladder, bile duct, and pancreas are well established. These vessels may arise from the common hepatic, proper hepatic, lobar and segmental hepatic arteries. They should be identified in order to avoid unnecessary infusion of these organs. Purposeful occlusion of some of these arteries, whenever possible, can reduce the risk of complications, such as chemotherapy-induced gastroduodenal ulceration, pancreatitis, cholecystitis.

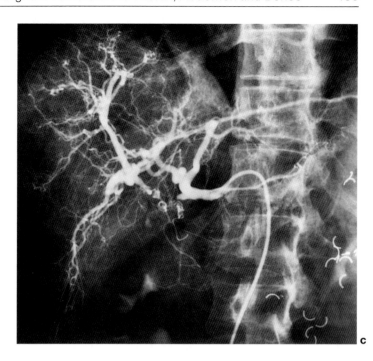

Fig. **5**
c The right hepatic and gastroduodenal arteries
are occluded by using stainless steel coils   **c**

Results of Hepatic Artery Infusion Chemotherapy

Metastatic Colorectal Carcinoma

The results of HAI were well evaluated in the management of hepatic metastases from colorectal carcinoma. In most reports, 5-fluorouracil or floxuridine was used for infusion through the catheter placed by a surgical or a percutaneous approach. The treatment schedules, dosage, and infusion techniques vary, depending on the experience of the oncologist, surgeon, or radiologist and the pharmacokinetic studies. The response rates, 32 to 88%, depend on different criteria, i.e., clinical examination, radionuclide study, carcinoembryonic antigen, or CT (5, 40, 42, 43, 46–48). HAIC provided a better response for hepatic tumors than systemic chemotherapy, but may be associated with higher incidence of local complications. However, despite effective control of hepatic tumors, extrahepatic metastases may develop, continue to progress, and cause death.

Our chemotherapy regimen consists of floxuridine at $100\,mg/m^2$ continuous infusion over 24 hours for 5 days and mitomycin C at 10 to $15\,mg/m^2$ infused over 2 hours on the first day. The treatment is repeated every 4 weeks for at least three cycles. In another regimen, mitomycin C is replaced by cisplatin at $100\,mg/m^2$ infused over 2 hours on the first day. The response criteria include a decrease in the tumor size by at least 50% evaluated by CT, angiography, and a significant decrease in carcinoembryonic antigen.

For the floxuridine and mitomycin C regimen, a response rate of 45% in 22 patients who had previously failed on systemic 5-fluorouracil and 61% in 33 previously untreated patients was accomplished (40, 43). The median survival from the initiation of HAIC was 8 months, and 15 months when associated with occlusion of the hepatic artery. A total response rate of 52% was found in 29 patients who were infused with floxuridine and cisplatin regimen.

Hepatocellular carcinoma. The intra-arterial regimen for hepatocellular carcinoma at our hospital consisted of a 5-day infusion of floxuridine (100 mg/ m^2 for each day), doxorubicin ($40\,mg/m^2$ for 2 hours on day 1), and mitomycin C ($10\,mg/m^2$ for 2 hours on day 2) (15, 41). The dose of doxorubicin can be reduced to $10\,mg/m^2$ when the patient is jaundiced. The treatment is repeated every 4 weeks. A response rate of 62% was achieved among 30 patients treated, with a median survival of 11.5 months.

Metastatic breast carcinoma. Several regimens have been used for HAIC in patients with hepatic metastases from carcinoma of the breast, but mostly as a second-line treatment after they have failed systemic chemotherapy. HAIC with cisplatin ($120\,mg/m^2$ at 4-week intervals) yielded a 19% response rate among 26 patients, with a median response period of more than 15 weeks and a median survical period of 11 months (20). Using a combination of cisplatin ($100\,mg/m^2$) and vinblastine ($1.7\,mg/m^2$ daily) a partial response rate of 33% (11 of 33 patients) was achieved. A similar median survival period of 11 months was observed.

Hepatic Artery Embolization

Materials

Different types of embolic materials can be used for embolization, depending on the indications of embolization. Proximal occlusion of the hepatic artery by stainless steel coils, Gelfoam segments, or silicone detachable balloons are useful for vascular redistribution of HAIC. Peripheral embolization with small particulate materials, sclerosing agents, or liquid polymers should be used for occlusion of the tumor vascular bed in order to create tumor necrosis or to control the hemorrhage.

Indications

Embolization as a primary treatment. Hepatic metastases from neuroendocrine tumors, including carcinoid tumors and islet cell tumors of the pancreas, respond dramatically to hepatic artery embolization. Some of these tumors secrete pharmacologically active amines or peptides, producing several well-described syndromes. Generally, they grow slowly and even after metastasizing they can be associated with long survival. Hepatic artery embolization offers significant palliation by reducing the tumor bulk, thus decreasing the production of these pharmacologically active substances.

Hepatic artery embolization can be useful in the treatment of certain complications of hepatic neoplasms. Spontaneous rupture and bleeding of tumors as well as bleeding secondary to diagnostic needle biopsy of the liver may require immediate intervention. Previously, surgical exploration and packing of bleeding sites or hepatic artery ligation was necessary to control the bleeding. Embolization of the hepatic artery using Ivalon and Gelfoam particles provides an alternative method to control the hemorhage and allow further definitive treatment. Arteriovenous shunting in hypervascular neoplasms, such as infantile hemangioendothelioma, metastatic hypernephroma, or primary hepatocellular carcinoma, may result in congestive heart failure. Embolization with Gelfoam cubes or segments or stainless steel coils disrupts high-flow arteriovenous shunting and can resolve congestive heart failure before further definitive treatment of the tumors.

Embolization after failure of chemotherapy. One of the most frequent indications for hepatic artery embolization at our hospital was failure of systemic chemotherapy or HAIC. HAIC remains the treatment of choice for many neoplasms, particularly when there is good evidence that they are sensitive to chemotherapy. Embolization is usually performed for tumors that demonstrate no further improvement or progression after chemotherapy.

Embolization as an adjunct to intraarterial chemotherapy. Two or more arteries supply the liver in approximately 45% of the population. Nonresectable hepatic neoplasms associated with a dual arterial supply requiring intra-arterial chemotherapy cannot be effectively infused by selective catheterization of only one artery. Placement of two or more catheters at one time is not practical. Occlusion of a replaced or accessory hepatic artery with a stainless steel coil (proximal occlusion) and catheter placement into the other artery, results in a vascular supply redistribution, which delivers the infused chemotherapeutic agents throughout the entire liver via the interlobar or intersegmental collaterals (Fig. 5).

Stainless steel coils or Gelfoam segments are used to occlude the proximal portion of the gastroduodenal artery to prevent reflux or infusion into the artery (Fig. 5). This is particularly beneficial for the patient who develops symptoms of gastritis or duodenal ulcer after intra-arterial chemotherapy. Documented flow reversal in the gastroduodenal artery renders embolization for symptomatic relief unnecessary.

Embolization for redistribution of the hepatic artery to assist HAIC was described in a previous section.

Results

From 1975 to 1983, 320 patients underwent hepatic artery embolization for the management of various hepatic neoplasms. Metastatic carcinoma of the colon, neuroendocrine tumors, melanoma, and leiomyosarcoma accounted for the majority of the patients (63.5%). Others included primary hepatocellular carcinoma, metastatic carcinoma of the breast, and hypernephroma. The majority of these patients (82%) had failed systemic chemotherapy, HAIC, or both. Embolization was performed using Gelfoam, Ivalon (Polyvinyl alcohol foam), absolute ethanol, or the combination of these materials.

Thirty-one patients (9.7%) died within 1 month of embolization and 38 patients (12%) were lost to follow-up after one embolization. The median survival time of the entire group of patients was 7 months. However, when the patients who died within 1 month and the patients lost to follow-up after one embolization were excluded, the median survival time was 10.5 months. One-year survival rate was 22%.

When the causes of death of the patients who died within 1 month after embolization were analyzed, 19 patients died from hepatic or hepatorenal failure. These patients were distinguished by the extent of their hepatic metastases, i.e., replacement of more than 50% of the liver by tumor, serum lactic dehydrogenase (LDH) levels above 425 mU/ml, serum glutamic oxaloacetic transaminase (SGOT) levels above 100 mU/ml, and bilirubin levels above 2 mg/dl. Embolization is contra-indicated in patients who fulfill all the criteria just listed. The remaining 12 patients died of other causes, such as gastrointestinal bleeding, sepsis, and progressive disease.

Complications

The most common complications encountered after hepatic artery embolization are grouped together and known as the postembolization syndrome. Fever and pain are the most prominent features seen in nearly every patient. The fever is low grade, varying from 100° to 102°F, and lasts from 2 to 7 days. The pain is located mostly in the right upper quadrant of the abdomen radiating to the back or shoulder, or in the upper midabdomen. It develops during embolization and usually lasts 5 to 7 days or at times as long as 3 weeks. The severity of the pain depends on the pain tolerance of the patient and the volume of the liver embolized. Nausea and vomiting are seen in approximately 50% of the patients, and are occasionally associated with abdominal distension in the first few days after embolization.

Pain und fever are attributed to ischemia of the neoplasms, the liver, and gallbladder produced by the vascular occlusion. Most patients, however, even those with gallbladder infarction, do not require surgical intervention but rather conservative management and close observation.

The postembolization syndrome is treated symptomatically. The severe pain during the first few days after embolization is usually controlled by intravenous analgesics; 50 to 75 mg of meperidine hydrochloride or 10 to 15 mg of morphine sulfate can be given every 3 to 4 hours as needed. Low-grade fever usually responds to aspirin, indomethacin, or acetaminophen. For nausea and vomiting, 5 to 10 mg of prochlorperazine can be administered intravenously or intramuscularly.

Liver function tests in patients after hepatic artery embolization demonstrate a marked but transient elevation of liver enzymes, particularly serum SGOT and LDH. The enzyme elevation can be as high as 10 to 20 times the preembolization level and lasts for 5 to 7 days. In most patients, the enzymes usually return to preembolization level within 10 days, but at times not until 3 weeks after embolization.

Liver abscess or acute emphysematous cholecystitis rarely occurs after hepatic artery embolization. More frequently, nonspecific gas formation is observed in the embolized tumors by CT, US, and occasionally on conventional radiographs. This gas formation may be the result of tumor necrosis and liquefaction, or the air introduced during embolization.

Hepatic Artery Embolization in Metastatic Neuroendocrine Tumors

The best results of hepatic artery embolization were observed in patients with metastatic neuroendocrine tumors to the liver (2, 10, 11, 30, 32, 33, 36). Of the 25 patients with malignant carcinoid syndrome who underwent embolization to palliate the symptoms of this syndrome, 23 could be evaluated. Twenty (87%) of the 23 patients responded to embolization with a median response duration of more than 11 months, one (4%) did not respond, and two (9%) died of complications from the embolization. The symptomatic responses correlated with a decrease in the extent of hepatic metastases and a decrease in the urine 5-hydroxyindolacetic acid values to a mean of 41% of pretreatment levels (10).

Of the 20 patients with symptoms from islet cell carcinoma metastatic to the liver, 16 (80%) achieved objective tumor regression after embolization. Sequential and periodic embolization is required for an effective palliation over prolonged periods of time.

Chemoembolization

The treatment of hepatic neoplasms by a combination of hepatic artery occlusion and regional chemotherapy has been investigated since 1970 (19, 22, 37). Based on the theory that hepatic artery ligation creates an incomplete tumor necrosis with viable tumor cells existing at the periphery of the lesion, local chemotherapy via intra-arterial or intraportal infusion may enhance the effectiveness of hepatic artery ligation. An improvement in response rate and mean survival has been demonstrated in comparison to hepatic artery ligation alone.

As an alternative to hepatic artery ligation, Aronsen et al. (3) and Dakhil et al. (17) used biodegradable starch microspheres injected through an infusion catheter placed in the hepatic artery supplying the tumor to create a temporary blockade of the arterial flow to decrease washout of drugs given immediately afterward and enhance the chemotherapy gradient. Biodegradable starch microspheres, specially formulated cross-linked starch spheres of 40 µm in diameter, cause an occlusion of small arterioles and are degraded by serum amylase with the half-life of 15 to 30 minutes in vitro. The chemotherapeutic agent acts only on the surrounding tissue and, thereby limits systemic side effects.

Chemoembolization, originally proposed by Kato et al. (28), is the simultaneous combination of intra-arterial chemotherapy and peripheral embolization of the arterial supply to a tumor. The chemotherapeutic agent, mitomycin, is encapsulated in ethylcellulose to make microcapsules of 225 µm in diameter. The microcapsules cause peripheral embolization of the tumor with local obstruction of blood flow creating tumor ischemia. According to Kato and associates, the ethylcellulose shell degrades and releases the encased drug into the surrounding tissues in a gradual and sustained manner. In addition to the slow release, there is an increase in contact time and local concentration of the chemotherapeutic agent. The ischemia of the endothelial cells may increase the permeability and result in the enhancement of chemotherapeutic effect.

Clinical experiences with chemoembolization in the management of primary hepatocellular carcinoma have been established in Japan (38, 50). Gelfoam particles, mixed with Lipiodol and various chemotherapeutic agents, such as mitomycin C,

Fig. 6 Ivalon and cisplatin for chemoembolization. The Ivalon suspension in contrast material is mixed with the powdered cisplatin

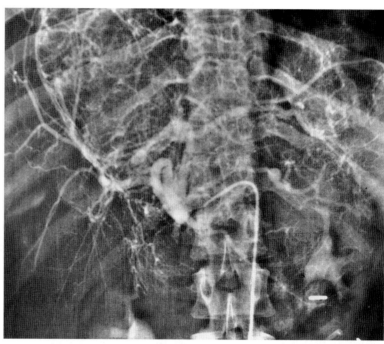

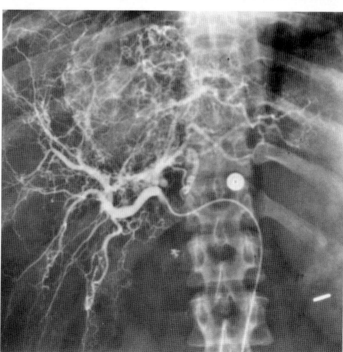

Fig. 7 Combined hepatic artery infusion and embolization in the management of hepatocellular carcinoma
a Before treatment
b After treatment

doxorubicin, cisplatin, and Lipiodol are used for hepatic embolization. At our hospital, the combination of Ivalon and cisplatin (Fig. **6**), has been most effective. At times, the hepatic artery is embolized and the catheter is left in place to be infused with chemotherapy in 24 to 28 hours when the radionuclide slow pattern demonstrates an adequate distribution.

Results

Hepatocellular carcinoma. Yamada et al. (50) reported on 120 patients with primary hepatocellular carcinoma treated by chemoembolization using Gelfoam and mitomycin C or doxorubicin (Fig. **7**), 1-, 2-, and 3-year cumulative survival rates were reported at 44, 29, and 15% respectively. Ohishi et al.

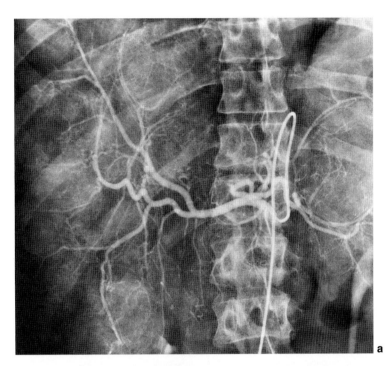

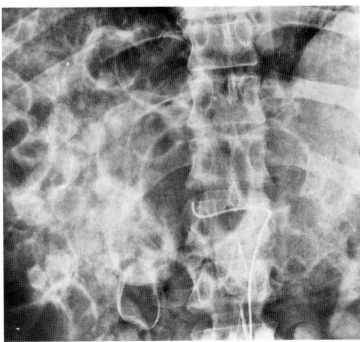

Fig. **8** **Chemoembolization for metastatic ocular melanoma**
a Proper hepatic arteriogram
b Postembolization, tumor now has low density

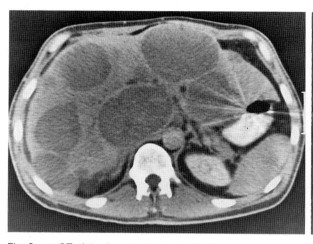

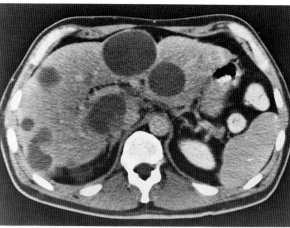

Fig. **8** **c** CT of the liver, before embolization

d CT of the liver, after embolization

(38) used Gelfoam with Lipiodol and mitomycin C or doxorubicin for hepatic artery embolization. They reported a 1-year survival rate of 69% among 97 patients treated. A significant decrease in serum α-fetoprotein was observed in 90% of the patients.

Ocular melanoma. At our hospital, 23 patients with ocular melanoma metastatic to the liver were embolized with Ivalon and cisplatin (Fig. **8**). Fourteen patients (61%) responded to the treatment with a median survival of 8 months and the longest survival of 41 months. The postembolization syndrome is more severe than hepatic artery embolization alone but can be controlled by intravenous analgesia.

References

1. Abrams HL, Spiro R, Goldstein N. Metastases in carcinoma: analysis of 1000 autopsied cases. Cancer 1950;3:74–85.
2. Allison DJ, Modlin IM, Jenkins WJ. Treatment of carcinoid liver metastases by hepatic artery embolization. Lancet 1977;ii:1323–1325.
3. Aronsen KF, Hellekant C, Holmberg J, Rothman U, Teder H. Controlled blocking of hepatic artery flow with enzymatically degradable microspheres combined with oncolytic drugs. Eur Surg Res 1979;11:99.
4. Aronsen KF, Nylander G, Ohlsson EG. Liver blood flow studies during and after various periods of total biliary obstruction in the dog. Acta Chir Scand 1969;135:55–59.
5. Balch CM, Urist MM, Soong SJ, McGregor M. A prospective phase 2 clinical trial of continuous FUDR regional chemotherapy for colorectal metastases to the liver using a totally implantable drug infusion pump. Ann Surg 1983;198:567–573.
6. Bengmark S, Hafstrom L. The natural history of primary and secondary malignant tumors of the liver, I: the prognosis for patients with hepatic metastases from colonic and rectal carcinoma by laparotomy. Cancer 1969;23:198–202.
7. Bledin AG, Kantarjian HM, Kim EE, Wallace S, Chuang VP, Patt YZ, Haynie TP. ^{99m}Tc-labeled macroaggregated albumin in intrahepatic arterial chemotherapy. AJR 1982;139:711–715.
8. Botet JF, Watson RC, Kemeny N, Daly JM, Yeh S. Cholangitis complicating intraarterial chemotherapy in liver metastasis. Radiology 1985;156:335–337.
9. Breedis C, Young G. The blood supply of neoplasms in the liver. Am J Pathol 1954;30:969–985.
10. Carrasco CH, Charnsangavej C, Ajani J, Samaan NA, Richli W, Wallace S. The carcinoid syndrome: palliation by hepatic artery embolization. AJR 1986;147:149–154.
11. Carrasco CH, Chuang VP, Wallace S. Apudomas metastatic to the liver: treatment by hepatic artery embolization. Radiology 1983;149:79–83.
12. Carrasco CH, Freeny PC, Chuang VP, Wallace S. Chemical cholecystitis associated with hepatic artery infusion chemotherapy. AJR 1983;141:703–706.
13. Charnsangavej C, Carrasco CH, Wallace S, Richli W. Hepatic arterial flow distribution in portal vein occlusion: its significance in hepatic artery infusion chemotherapy. Radiology 1987;165:71–73.
14. Charnsangavej C, Chuang VP, Wallace S, Soo CS, Bowers T. Angiographic classification of hepatic arterial collaterals. Radiology 1982;144:485–494.
15. Charnsangavej C, Chuang VP, Wallace S, Soo CS, Bowers T. Transcatheter management of primary carcinoma of the liver. Radiology 1983;147:51–55.
16. Chuang VP, Wallace S. Hepatic arterial redistribution for intra-arterial infusion of hepatic neoplasms. Radiology 1980;135:295–299.
17. Dakhil S, Ensminger W, Cho KJ, Niederhuber J, Doan K, Wheeler R. Improved regional selectivity of hepatic arterial BCNU with degradable microspheres. Cancer 1982;50:631–635.
18. Falkson G, McIntyre JM, Moertel CG, Johnson LA, Scherman RC. Primary liver cancer: an ECOG therapeutic trial. Cancer 1984;54:970–977.
19. Fortner JG, Mulcare RJ, Solis A, Watson RC, Golbey RB. Treatment of primary and secondary liver cancer by hepatic artery ligation and infusion chemotherapy. Ann Surg 1973;178:162.
20. Fraschini G, Fleishman G, Yap HY, Carrasco CH, Charnsangavej C, Patt YZ, Hortobagyi GN. Percutaneous hepatic arterial infusion of cisplatin for metastatic breast cancer. Cancer Treat Rep 1987;71:313–315.
21. Galloway S, Casarella WJ, Price JB. Unilobar veno-occlusive disease of the liver: angiographic demonstration of interhepatic competition simulating hepatoma. AJR 1973;119:89–94.
22. Guelessarian HP, Lawton LL, Condon RE. Hepatic artery ligation and cytotoxic infusion in treatment of liver metastases. Arch Surg 1972;105:280.
23. Hall DA, Clouse ME, Gramm HP. Gastroduodenal ulceration after hepatic artery infusion chemotherapy. AJR 1981;136:1216–1218.
24. Healey JE, Sheena KS. Vascular patterns in metastatic liver tumors. Surg Forum 1963;14:121–122.

25. Hohn DC, Melnick J, Stagg RJ, Altman D, Friedman M, Iguaffo R, Ferrell L, Lewis B. Biliary sclerosis in patients receiving hepatic arterial infusion of floxuridine. J Clin Oncol 1985;3:98–102.

26. Hohn DC, Stagg RJ, Price DC, Lewis RJ. Avoidance of gastroduodenal toxicity in patients receiving hepatic artery 5-fluoro-2¹-deoxyuridine. J Clin Oncol 1985;3:1257–1260.

27. Jaffe BM, Donegan WL, Watson F, Spratt JS. Factors influencing survival in patients with untreated hepatic metastases. Surg Gynecol Obstet 1968;127:1–11.

28. Kato L, Nemoto R, Mori H, Takahashi M, Tamakawa Y, Harada M. Arterial chemoembolization with microencapsulated anticancer drug. JAMA 1981;245:1123–1127.

29. Kemeny N, Daly J, Oderman P, Shike M, Hoo C, Petroni G, Geller N. Hepatic artery pump infusion: toxicity and results in patients with metastatic colorectal carcinoma. J Clin Oncol 1984;2:595–600.

30. Lunderquist A, Ericsson M, Nobin A, Sanden G. Gelfoam powder embolization of the carcinoid tumors. Radiology 1982;22:65–70.

31. Maguire R, Doppman JL. Angiographic abnormalities in partial Budd-Chiari syndrome. Radiology 1977;122:629–635.

32. Martensson H, Nobin A, Bengmark S, Lunderquist A, Owman T, Sanden G. Embolization of the liver in the management of metastatic carcinoid tumors. J Surg Oncol 1984;27:152–158.

33. Maton PN, Camilleri M, Griffin G, Allison DJ, Hodgson HJF, Chadwick VS. Role of hepatic arterial embolisation in the carcinoid syndrome. Br Med J 1983;287:932–935.

34. Michels NA, ed. Blood supply and anatomy of the upper abdominal organs. Philadelphia: Lippincott, 1955: 152–154, 256–259, 375.

35. Miller DL, Schneider PD, Gianola FJ, Willis M, Vermess M, Doppman JL. Assessment of perfusion patterns during hepatic artery infusion chemotherapy: EOE-13 CT and ⁹⁹ᵐTc-MAA scintigraphy. AJR 1984;143:827–831.

36. Mitty HA, Warner RRP, Newman LH, Train JS, Parnes IH. Control of carcinoid syndrome with hepatic artery embolization. Radiology 1985;155:623–626.

37. Murray-Lyon IM, Dawson JL, Parson VA, Holmes EC, Morton DL. Treatment artery and infusion of cytotoxic drugs. Lancet 1970;ii:172–175.

38. Ohishi H, Uchida H, Yoshimura H, Ohue S, Ueda J, Katsuraci M, Matsuo N, Hosoci Y. Hepatocellular carcinoma detected by iodized oil: use of anticancer agents. Radiology 1985;154:25–29.

39. Ohlsson EG, Rutherford RB, Boitnott JK, Haalehos MMP, Zuidema GD. Changes in portal circulation after billiary obstruction in dogs. Am J Surg 1970;120:16–22.

40. Patt YZ, Boddie AW Jr, Charnsangavej C, Ajani JA, Wallace S, Soski M, Claghorn L, Mavligit G. Hepatic artery infusion with floxuridine and cisplatin: overriding importance of antitumor effect versus degree of tumor burden as determinants of survival among patients with colorectal cancer. J Clin Oncol 1986;4:1356–1364.

41. Patt YZ, Charnsangavej C, Soski M, Mavligit GM. Regional arterial therapy in the management of primary liver neoplasms. In: Bottino JC, Opfell R, Muggia F, eds. Liver Cancer. The Hague: Nijhoff: 1985:263–273.

42. Patt YZ, Chuang VP, Wallace S, Mersh EM, Freireich EJ, Mavligit GM. The palliative role of hepatic arterial infusion and arterial occlusion in colorectal carcinoma metastatic to the liver. Lancet 1981;i:349–351.

43. Patt YZ, Mavligit GM, Chuang VP, Wallace S, Johnston S, Benjamin RS, Valdivieso M, Hersh EM. Percutaneous hepatic artery infusion of mitomycin C and floxuridine (FUDR): an effective treatment of metastatic colorectal carcinoma in the liver. Cancer 1980;46:261–265.

44. Rappaport AH, Burleson RL. Survival of patients treated with systemic fluorouracil for hepatic metastases. Surg Gynecol Obstet 1970;130:773.

45. Reuter SR, Chuang VP. The location of increased resistance to portal blood flow in obstruction jaundice. Invest Radiol 1976;11:54–59.

46. Shepard KV, Levin B, Karl RC, et al. Therapy for metastatic colorectal cancer with hepatic artery pump. J Clin Oncol 1985;3:161–169.

47. Sterchi JM. Hepatic artery infusion for metastatic neoplastic disease. Surg Gynecol Obstet 1985;160:477–489.

48. Weiss GR, Garnick MB, Osteen RT, et al. Long-term hepatic arterial infusion of 5-fluorodeoxyuridine for liver metastases using an implantable infusion pump. J Clin Oncol 1983;1:337–344.

49. Wright KC, Wallace S, Kim EE, Haynie T, Charnsangavej C, Carrasco H, Chuang VP, Gianturco C. Pulsed arterial infusions: chemotherapeutic implications. Cancer 1986;57:1952–1956.

50. Yamada R, Sato M, Kawabata M, Nakatsuka H, Nakamura K, Takashima S. Hepatic artery embolization in 120 patients with unresectable hepatoma. Radiology 1983;148:397–401.

51. Ziessman HA, Thrall JH, Yang PJ, Walker SC, Cozzi EA, Niederhuber JE, Cyves JW, Ensminger WD, Tuscan MC. Hepatic arterial perfusion scintigraphy with Tc-99m-MAA: use of a totally implanted drug delivery system. Radiology 1984;152:167–172.

Renal Tumors: Experimental Results

G. W. Kauffmann and G. M. Richter

The angio-occlusive approach to renal cancer is still a matter of controversy (31), especially among urologists. Looking back on a 10-year experience of clinical tumor embolization, a great variety of occlusion techniques produced only disappointing long-term results. Recurrence of hematuria was reported after various types of vascular occlusion, thus indicating that sometimes not even palliation was achievable (Table 1). Complete tumor necrosis was never reported. The therapeutic pitfalls are directly related to lack of influence on the fatal parasitic vascular supply in renal carcinoma. An experimental renal tumor of genuinely malignant character can be considered a suitable model of such a parasitic vascular supply, but most experimental work has been performed on normal organs (12, 32). Studies using tumor models are extremely rare (7, 25, 26). However, the establishment of an experimental renal tumor – with an angioarchitecture and biologic behavior resembling renal carcinoma as closely as possible – makes systematic evaluation of different occlusion types and materials possible.

Table **1**   Recurrence of hematuria in clinical renal tumor embolization

Reference	Embolization medium	No.
Hlava et al. (15)	Gelfoam	3/8
Steckenmesser et al. (29)	Muscle tissue	1/4
Marberger and Georgi (21)	Blood/thrombin	2/5
Haertl et al. (14)	Gelfoam	1/10
Frasson et al. (10)	Gelfoam	4/12
Mueller et al. (29)	Ivalon	7/12
Riedl and Flamm (27)	GAW coil*	2/8
MacErlean et al. (20)	GAW coil	1/1
Frasson et al. (11)	Gelfoam	13/13
Günther et al. (13)	Cyanoacrylate	1/2
Marx et al. (22)	Muscle tissue	3/11
Our cases	Gelfoam/GAW coil	2/29

* GAW: Gianturco-Anderson-Wallace.

Influence of Malignant Angioarchitecture on Embolization

The organization of the vascular supply of malignant tissue differs widely from that of normal or inflammatory tissue. The morphologic, morphometric, and rheologic differences can be summarized as follows:

– Caliber fluctuations, vascular avulsions, change of direction, and change in predominant vascular structure are essential features, whereas statistically the parameter "caliber fluctuation" is most characteristic in renal cell carcinoma (17).

– The rheologic situation in a tumor differs completely from that of a normal organ: in peripheral vessels, flow resistance might be 20-fold higher than in normal organs (30). This is also valid for richly vascularized tumors. On the other hand, there might be an extremely low vascular resistance in the vicinity of arteriovenous shunts. This exists in three-fourths of all renal tumors. Most often when shunts are not demonstrable angiographically, scintigraphy reveals shunt rates of 10 to 20% (1).

– Tumor tissue establishes a parasitic supply by enlargement of natural collaterals and by the production of "angiogenesis growth factor" of Folkman,

inducing true new vessels arising from the surrounding tissue. This is found in renal cell cancer already in T2 stages (4).

These morphologic features add to the disorganized and anarchic vascular pattern of tumors, which fundamentally influence the therapeutic efficacy of any vaso-occlusive treatment. Especially the combination of two extremes – a very high flow resistance in the periphery and a very low resistance in arteriovenous shunts – represent the most substantial problem for a homogeneous vascular occlusion. Total tumor necrosis can only be achieved if an embolization medium is directed to the core or to the nidus of the tumor, which means transporting it to the level of the capillaries. Another problem is the fact that tumor cell necrosis needs at least a 24-hour period of anoxia (6).

Principle of Capillary Embolization

According to the level of vascular occlusion within the kidney, three different types of embolization can be distinguished:

– *Central type:* occlusion of the main artery and proximal parts of segmental arteries.
– *Peripheral type:* occlusion of lobular or arcuate arteries.
– *Capillary type:* occlusion of arterioles and glomeruli.

Even in the normal kidney with few collaterals, total necrosis including the subcortical and hilar structures is only achieved by the capillary type of occlusion (16, 24, 25, 26). Thus, this capillary embolization concept is of essential importance for tumor embolization. Characteristics of embolization media used for capillary transportation are summarized in Table **2**.

The principle of capillary occlusion as derived from the normal kidney includes four important factors (16, 25):

– Correct quantity
– Correct quality
– Correct viscosity
– Homogeneous distribution

Table **2**   Characteristics of embolization media for capillary occlusion

	Viscosity at 37 °C (cps)	Radiodensity (mg l/ml)	Occlusion mechanism
Ethibloc	200	130	Precipitation
Tissue adhesive e. g., Bucrylate/Lipiodol	7	240	Polymerization
Alcohol	0.85	0	Endothelial damage Secondary thrombosis

In the following, the adaptation of these prerequisites to embolization of experimental malignant tissue is presented.

Experimental Tumors

During the last 6 years we established three different renal tumor models in Wistar rats for the evaluation of capillary embolization:

– Chemical induction of tumors (dimethyl-nitrosamine [DMN])
– Transparenchymal implantation of Walker sarcoma
– Transarterial implantation of Yoshida sarcoma cells

The method of DMN induction has been presented elsewhere (16, 25, 26). After a single intraperitoneal injection of 60 mg of DMN in female Wistar rats (100 g) mesenchymal and epithelial tumor types develop regularly during a period of 6 to 9 months. Their biologic behavior and angioarchitecture resemble those of renal cell carcinoma (16, 17, 25, 26). An exact overview of the entire material and results is given in Table 3.

These tumors were treated with central, peripheral, and capillary types of occlusion using ligation of the renal artery, Gelfoam powder suspended in contrast medium, the tissue adhesive bucrylate mixed with Lipiodol, and Ethibloc. The central occlusion type never achieved a total tumor necrosis and the peripheral type was effective only in T1 stages. The capillary embolization, however, showed a definitely higher therapeutic efficacy. This was valid only under the condition that the entire arterial compartment was primarily occluded, e.g., Ethibloc achieved a total tumor necrosis in three-fourths of T4 stages (Table 3).

The therapeutic efficacy of Ethibloc was statistically significantly higher than that of bucrylate, although both media were transported to the capillary level and the same quantities were used. The cause of this is less homogeneous transportation of bucrylate throughout the arterial compartment, which can be shown angiographically (Fig. 1) and microscopically. The non-homogeneous distribution has two causes: the low viscosity of bucrylate (Table 2) and a polymerization time that is pre-fixed for each individual embolization and depends on the volume ratio, e.g., bucrylate/Lipiodol. The low viscosity of bucrylate may lead to transvenous passage or even pulmonary embolism through arteriovenous shunts, especially if it is injected relatively fast. Capillary transportation is not guaranteed, however, if it is injected too slowly. Independent of injection speed, the preset polymerization time is valid throughout any vascular structure of the tumor. This represents a further cause for bucrylate being lost via arteriovenous shunts, while the entire arterial compartment is not filled completely.

The occlusion mechanism of Ethibloc is entirely different from all other embolization materials. It is not a chemical reaction such as polymerization, or a mechanical obstruction, as in particle embolization. Its principle of occlusion is based on a precipitation with gradual increase of viscosity until total hardening within the vessels occurs. Ethibloc is a highly saturated alcoholic solution of a corn protein and further ingredients (see Table 4). This corn protein, a zein, is not water soluble. If Ethibloc is injected into blood, its component alcohol diffuses. The precipitation of zein starts since alcohol is no longer availabe to keep the protein in solution. The speed of this reaction is dependent on the speed of solution of alcohol in blood. We found that pre-injection of a substance with a high osmotic pressure varies the kinetics of this physicochemical reaction (16, 24, 25).

Table 3   Treatment protocols and results in DMN-induced renal rat tumors

Material and animal groups

Control group:	glucose perfusion	8
Central occlusion:	ligation of renal artery	23
Peripheral occlusion:	Gelfoam powder	58
Capillary occlusion:	Bucrylate/Lipiodol 1 : 1	58
	Ethibloc/glucose	74
		221

Results of long-term groups (n = 122)

	Total necrosis	Growth delay	Tumor progression
Arterial ligation:			
Stage T1, T2	0/5	4/5	1/5
Stage T3, T4	0/19	0/19	19/19
Gelfoam powder:			
Stage T1, T2	3/3	0/3	0/3
Stage T3, T4	0/27	16/27	11/27
Bucrylate/Lipiodol:			
Stage T1, T2	4/4	0/4	0/4
Stage T3, T4	8/23	19/23	4/23
Ethibloc/glucose:			
Stage T1, T2	6/6	0/6	0/6
Stage T3, T4	17/28	11/28	0/28

Table 4   Composition of Ethibloc

1 ml of occlusion gel contains

210 mg zein, corn protein (an occlusive agent)
162 mg sodium amidotrizoate (contrast medium)
145 mg oleum papaveris, poppy seed oil (softener)
5 mg propylene glycol (bacteriostatic)

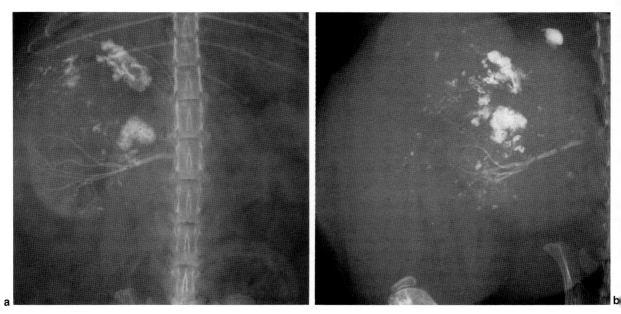

a   b

Fig. **1**   **Tumor progression in bucrylate embolization of DMN tumors.** Embolization of a T4 stage tumor with 0.21 ml
bucrylate/Lipiodol
a Non-homogeneous distribution of bucrylate
b Under-embolized area with rapid tumor progression within 3 weeks

Pre-injection of 40% glucose in a quantity corresponding to 20% of the entire embolization volume reduces the precipitation speed and guarantees capillary propagation. Amazingly, substantial venous propagation is not observed with Ethibloc under these conditions. The high osmotic power of 40% glucose slows down the dissolution of alcohol by its water-binding capacity. The volume of the venous compartment is five times that of the arterial compartment. Thus, the pre-injected 40% glucose is diluted adequately when passing from the arterial to the venous side. When Ethibloc reaches the venous compartment, precipitation must take place. This especially applies to arteriovenous shunts. Another reason for lack of venous propagation is the slow intra-arterial perfusion of Ethibloc because of its high viscosity.

This selective increase of viscosity in the area of arteriovenous shunts, together with hardening of the embolization medium, takes place when Ethibloc is still liquid in the rest of the arterial compartment. Thus, it is possible to establish a pressure that is high enough to overcome the high vascular peripheral resistance within the smallest tumor vessels. At the same time an impermissible risk of venous propagation via these arteriovenous shunts is avoided, at quantities of Ethibloc that were encountered with a high percentage of tumor necrosis (Table **3**, Fig. **2**).

These experimental data suggest that a medium with low and uncontrollable viscosity might be able to ablate a normal organ totally, but is not adaptable to the disorganized and anarchic vascular pattern of tumors. Especially if it is not able to occlude arteriovenous shunts selectively, it cannot fulfill the basic requirement of homogeneous capillary occlusion. This contributes to the high rate of pulmonary embolism.

In clinical studies, absolute alcohol is presented and used as a capillary occlusion medium (8, 9, 28). This substance has only been tested experimentally in normal organs, in which it proved sufficiently effective (9). In clinical renal tumor embolization some severe complications, such as mesenteric artery embolism, spinal cord injury, skin necrosis, and inferior vena cava thrombosis, were encountered (5, 8, 9, 19, 28). These complications seem to be closely related to the low viscosity of alcohol. Like tissue adhesives, its vascular transportation is not adaptable to the ill-defined rheologic situation within tumors. It may escape via arteriovenous shunts into central veins but also via the parasitic vascular supply into the surrounding healthy tissue, especially in T4 carcinomas.

We performed a pilot study in experimental renal tumors to evaluate the unpredictable behavior of alcohol and to compare its therapeutic efficacy to

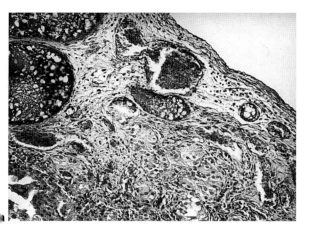

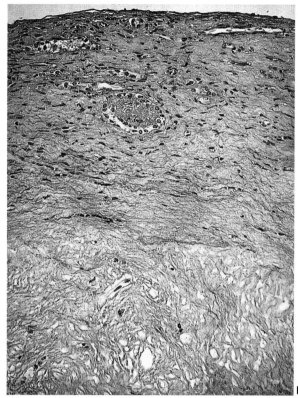

Fig. 2   Ethibloc embolization in DMN tumors
a Microscopic section of a subcortical tumor area: medium and small tumor sinusoids are completely occluded by Ethibloc (foamy dark material). In venous vessels no Ethibloc. (H & E, × 220)
b Microscopic section of a subcortical tumor area 6 weeks after embolization. Tumor tissue necrotized and organized by fibrous tissue. (H & E, × 120)

Ethibloc: we used the previously mentioned model based on transarterial implantation of Yoshida sarcoma. To our knowledge, this is the first time that it was possible to implant Yoshida sarcoma cells into the kidney transarterially, thus producing a valid tumor model. The implantation technique is briefly summarized as follows: Two groups of male Wistar rats (200 g) were kept under standard laboratory conditions: one for continuous passage of the ascitic form of Yoshida sarcoma, the other for the treatment protocols. Yoshida sarcoma cells were harvested on day 6 after intraperitoneal passage from rapidly developing hemorrhagic ascites of the animals under continuous passage. After surgical exposure of the aortic origin of the renal artery (under general anesthesia), a lymphographic cannula was introduced into the left renal artery via the contralateral aortic wall. The tip of the cannula was inserted as deeply as possible and secured by ligation to prevent reflux of tumor cells. After injection of 0.04 to 0.06 ml of ascites and withdrawal of the cannula, the aorta was compressed for 2 minutes.

Within 10 to 20 days, a moderately vascularized tumor developed within the kidney (Fig. 3). Most of the animals reach a T3 stage on the 15th day after implantation. Embolization is performed exclusively at that stage. Embolization volume was calculated from the volume of the surgically exposed tumor.

Embolization was performed with identical quantities of Ethibloc and alcohol following the same technique that has been published elsewhere (16, 25). Control groups underwent nephrectomy or received no treatment. Ethibloc produced complete tumor necrosis in 75% of animals without any complication, but alcohol achieved tumor necrosis only in 50% of animals; however, this was combined with a 10% rate of lethal pulmonary embolism (Figs. 4, 5). These results clearly demonstrate that the application of alcohol for capillary tumor embolization is dangerous and ineffective. If a homogeneous distribution throughout the entire arterial compartment is the goal, venous propagation is the logical consequence. This is documented very well in a clinical case (19). At the present time, we are preparing a study involving exact quantification of the venous shunting during quantitatively correct capillary embolization with alcohol.

Clinical Consequences

If intracorporeal nephrectomy or tumor ablation is required, it seems reasonable to adopt the concept of capillary embolization to occlude the entire tumor, including its nidus, primarily, and to cut off as much of the parasitic collaterals as possible. We think that our unsatisfactory results with central and peripheral

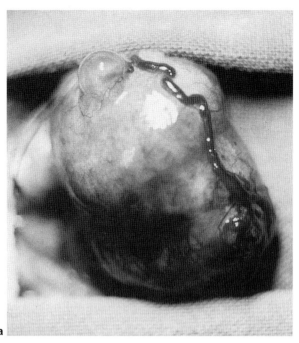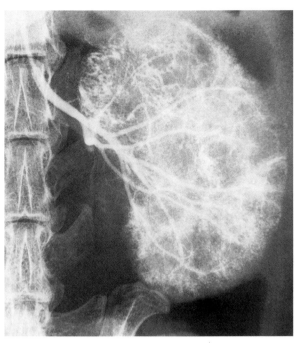

a

Fig. 3 Transarterially implanted Yoshida sarcoma in Wistar rat
a Macroscopic aspect on day 17. T3 stage with large collateral vessels
b Selective angiography of the same tumor, demonstrating the typical malignant vessels

Number of animals n = 17 -25

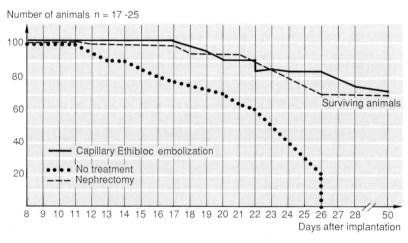

Capillary Ethibloc embolization
•••• No treatment
- - - Nephrectomy

Surviving animals

8 9 10 11 12 13 14 15 16 17 18 19 20 21 22 23 24 25 26 27 28   50
Days after implantation

Fig. 4 Survival data after capillary Ethibloc embolization of Yoshida sarcoma
The baseline in the figure shows data from control groups (nephrectomy; no treatment). Survival rate in capillary Ethibloc embolization identical to nephrectomy

Number of animals n = 17 - 25

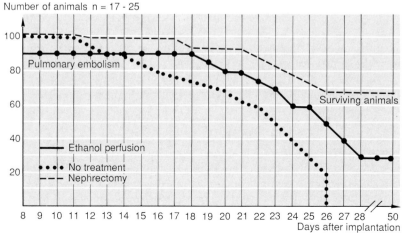

Pulmonary embolism

Ethanol perfusion
•••• No treatment
- - - Nephrectomy

Surviving animals

8 9 10 11 12 13 14 15 16 17 18 19 20 21 22 23 24 25 26 27 28   50
Days after implantation

Fig. 5 Survival data after ethanol perfusion of Yoshida sarcoma
The baseline shows data from control groups (nephrectomy, no treatment). Survival rate in ethanol embolization significantly worse ($p > 0.1$) than nephrectomy or Ethibloc (Fig. **4**). There were 35% long-term survivors, 10% lethal pulmonary embolism

types of occlusion in the DMN tumor model are comparable to clinical embolization using the same embolization types. This explains the clinical reality with incomplete tumor necrosis, including sometimes even poor palliative results. Table 1 shows the rate of recurrence of hematuria following several occlusion types.

Our experimental results imply that clinical Ethibloc embolization should abolish hematuria completely, reaching a maximum of therapeutic efficacy. The relatively high viscosity of Ethibloc requires a high injection pressure, but vascular resistance, combined with a slow rate of transportation, is in this way overcome.

We cannot recommend substances with low and unchangeable viscosity (3) for a capillary type of occlusion. On the other hand, we are able to present our own long-term results of clinical Ethibloc embolization in renal cell cancer: 80% of patients of T3 and T4 stage (41 of 50) had total tumor necrosis. CT studies never demonstrated local recurrences in those patients. Some of our patients had no metastases. The overall therapeutic efficacy of Ethibloc embolization was comparable to nephrectomy. In several patients with remote metastasis, we had a statistically relevant prolongation of survival time (18).

Another aspect occurs with the increasing use of chemoembolization (2): since only Ethibloc is homogeneously distributed throughout the tumor vessels, it seems to be the ideal carrier for a chemotherapeutic agent rather than for particles of any size. An experimental study with a combination of Ethibloc and various chemotherapeutic substances is under way in our department.

References

1. Barth KH, White RI, Marshal FF. Quantification of arteriovenous shunting in renal carcinoma. J Urol 1981;125:161–163.
2. Bechtel W, Wright KC, Wallace S, Mosier B, Mir S, Kudo S. An experimental evaluation of microcapsules of arterial chemoembolization. Radiology 1986;161:601–604.
3. Berenstein A, Kricheff II. Catheter and material selection for transarterial embolization: technical considerations, 2: materials. Radiology 1979;132:631–639.
4. Buist TAS. Parasitic arterial supply to intracapsular renal cell carcinoma. AJR 1974;120:653–659.
5. Cox GG, Lee KR, Price HI, Gunter K, Noble MJ, Mebust WK. Colonic infarction following ethanol embolization of renal cell carcinoma. Radiology 1982;145:343–345.
6. Denekamp J, Hill SA, Hobson B. Vascular occlusion and tumor cell death. Eur J Cancer Clin Oncol 1983;19:271–275.
7. Ekelund L, Jonsson JO. Angiography in dimethylintrosamine-induced rat renal tumors. Acta Radiol [Diagn] (Stockh) 1971;11:489–496.
8. Ellman BA, Parkhill BJ, Curry TS, Marcus PB, Peters PC. Ablation of renal tumors with absolute ethanol: a new technique. Radiology 1981;141:619–626.
9. Ellman BA, Green CE, Eigenbrodt E, Garriot JC, Curry TS. Renal infarction with absolute ethanol. Invest Radiol 1980;15:318–322.
10. Frasson F, Fugazzola C, Bianchi G, et al. Selective arterial embolization in renal tumors. Radiol Clin 1978;47:239–251.
11. Frasson F, Roversi RA, Simonetti G, Ziviello M. Embolization of renal tumors: a survey of the Italian experience: 282 patients. Ann Radiol 1981;24:396–399.
12. Günther R, Schubert U, Bohl J, Georgi M, Marberger M. Transcatheter embolization of the kidney with buthyl-2-cyanoacrylate: experimental and clinical results. Cardiovasc Radiol 1978;1:101–108.
13. Günther R, Klose K, Thelen M, Jacobi G. Superselektive Embolisationen mit Gewebekleber am Urogenitaltrakt. RöFo 1981;134:536–539.
14. Haertl M, Zaunbauer W, Zingg E. Die Katheterembolisation maligner urologischer Tumoren. Schweiz Med Wochenschr 1977;107:584–588.
15. Hlava A, Steinhart L, Navratil P. Intraluminal obliteration of the renal arteries in kidney tumors. Radiology 1976;121:323–329.
16. Kauffmann, GW, Richter GM, Rassweiler J, Rohrbach R. New topics in embolization. In: Baert AL, Boijsen E, Fuchs WA. Heuck FHW, eds. Frontiers of european radiology; vol 1. Berlin: Springer 1982:72–99.
17. Kauffmann GW, Strecker EP, Bammert J, Meyer P, Wenz W. Angiomorphometry in malignant tumors and inflammatory disease. Invest Radiol 1980;15:475–480.
18. Kauffmann GW, Richter GM. Palliative capillary embolization in renal carcinoma. Ann Radiol (Paris) 1986;29:205–207.
19. Löhr E. Vena-cava-Thrombose nach Alkohol-Embolisation. Radiologe 1985;25:381–382.
20. MacErlean DP, Owens AP, Bryan PJ. Hypernephroma embolization: is it worthwhile? Clin Radiol 1980;31:297–300.
21. Marberger M, Georgi M. Balloon occlusion of the renal artery in tumor nephrectomy. J Urol 1975;114:360–363.
22. Marx FJ, Chaussy CH, Moster E. Grenzen und Gefahren der palliativen Embolisation inoperabler Nierentumoren. Urologe [A] 1982;21:206–210.
23. Müller JHA, Engel D, Waigand J, Mebel M. Spätergebnisse nach palliativer Gefässembolisierung bei inoperablen Nierentumoren (vorläufige Mitteilung). Z Urol Nephrol 1978;71:481–490.
24. Rassweiler J, Kauffmann GW, Rohrbach R, Richter GM. Kapilläre Embolization, Teil 1: Verschluss des gesamten arteriellen Gefäss-Systems der gesunden Rattenniere. RöFo 1980;133:644–653.
25. Richter GM, Rohrbach R, Kauffmann GW, Rassweiler J. Kapilläre Embolisation, Teil 2: Verschluss des gesamten arteriellen Gefäss-Systems experimentell erzeugter Nierentumoren. RöFo 1981;135:85–97.
26. Richter GM, Rassweiler J, Kauffmann GW, Wenz W, Crawford DB. Experimental study of the effectiveness of capillary embolization using contrast-enhanced ethibloc. Invest Radiol 1984;19:36–44.
27. Riedl P, Flamm J. Kontrollangiographische Befunde nach palliativer Nierenarterienokklusion mit der GAW-(Gianturco-Anderson-Wallace-)Spirale. RöFo 1979;130:398–403.
28. Rosenkrantz H, Sands JP, Buchta KS, Healy JF, Kmet JP, Gerber F. Renal devitalization using 95% ethylalcohol. J Urol 1982;127:873–875.
29. Steckenmesser R, Bayindir S, Rothauge CF, Nöske K, Weidner W. Embolisation maligner Nierentumoren. RöFo 1976;125:251–257.
30. Vaupel P. Effect of hyperoxia, hypoxia and hypercapnia on O_2 supply of malignant tumors in situ. Bibl Anat 1977;15:288–290.
31. Wallace S, Chuang VP, Swanson DA, Bracken B, Hersh EM, Ayala A, Johnson D. Embolization of renal carcinoma: experience with 100 patients. Radiology 1981;138:563–570.
32. Wolf KJ. Therapeutische Embolisation von Organarterien: tierexperiementelle Untersuchungen, erste klinische Erfahrungen, Einführung eines neuen Embolisationsmaterials, Teil II. RöFo 1979;131:511–519.

Renal Tumors: Clinical Results

S. Wallace, C. Charnsangavej, C. H. Carrasco, W. R. Richli and D. Swanson

Transcatheter embolization of renal neoplasms was initially suggested by Lalli et al. in 1969 (18). In 1971 Lang, (19) using radioactive gold grains as embolic material, noted a decrease in the size of renal carcinoma in 20 patients. Almgard et al. in 1973 (1) reported encouraging results after autologous muscle tissue embolization of renal neoplasms.

At our institution, we have embolized primary renal carcinoma in more than 320 patients. The indications for transcatheter embolization of renal neoplasms are to control hemorrhage, polycythemia, hypercalcemia, congestive failure, and hypertension; preoperatively to facilitate surgical resection by decreasing blood and operating time; to inhibit tumor growth; to reduce tumor cell population, theoretically exposing the remaining neoplasm to a higher concentration of chemotherapy or immunotherapy; to relieve pain by decreasing tumor bulk; and, perhaps, to stimulate an immune response to the ischemic neoplasm (28–30, 34).

Technical Considerations

The renal artery is selectively catheterized with a 5 or 6.5 Fr catheter shaped to conform to the vessel. A reverse curve (sidewinder) configuration is frequently well suited for catheterization of the renal artery. In the event of an early bifurcation of the renal artery, each branch is selectively catheterized in preparation for embolization. The experience of the angiographer, the vascularity of the neoplasm, and the degree of shunting dictate the choice of embolic agents. Although recommended by many, we rarely use a balloon catheter for embolization. Blood flow assists in peripheral embolization and relative stasis of flow is the endpoint. In the presence of rapid arteriovenous shunting (opacification of the renal vein within the first second after the injection) it is safer to embolize with sclerosing agents or larger particles (Gelfoam 3 mm or greater). The tumor vessels even in the event of early shunting are seldom larger than 100 µm in diameter and can be occluded with any of the frequently used embolic materials. Attempts are made to occlude all parasitic blood supply to the neoplasm, whenever possible (Fig. 1).

Embolic Materials

The materials available for embolization include autologous clot and tissue; clot modified by thrombin, epsilon-aminocaproic acid (Amicar), and heat; absorbable gelatin sponge (Gelfoam); oxidized cellulose (Oxcel); polyvinyl alcohol foam (Ivalon); cyanoacrylates; silastic; resin and dextran microspheres (Dowex, Sephadex, and Spherex); Ethibloc; microfibrillar collagen hemostat (Avitene) and crosslinked collagen (Angiostat); sodium tetradecyl sulfate (Sotradecol); absolute ethanol; balloon catheters, and detachable balloons; and metallic devices such as brushes and stainless steel coils.

At the M. D. Anderson Hospital and Tumor Institute, embolization of renal carcinoma has been accomplished primarily with Gelfoam and steel coils (34). Ivalon and ethanol, alone or in combination, were also used. Ethiodol (ethyl ester of poppy seed oil containing iodine) or Bacille Calmette-Guérin (BCG) with Gelfoam and coils have been injected into the renal artery in an attempt to stimulate a nonspecific inflammatory reaction (27, 36). Interferon has also been infused into the renal artery (22).

Gelfoam. We prefer Gelfoam cubes (1 to 3 mm on a side) for peripheral renal artery embolization and stainless steel coils for central occlusion. For some reason, still to be determined, this combination has been more frequently associated with a reduction in size of the pulmonary metastases. Gelfoam provokes a nonspecific inflammatory response, which may be of some importance.

Eight to ten cubes of Gelfoam are loaded in a 1 ml tuberculin syringe that is then filled with contrast media and injected into the catheter. This is followed by an injection of 1 ml of contrast material to empty the catheter of particles. Embolization continues in the same fashion until flow slows and stasis is evident.

Ivalon. Ivalon particles (150 to 250 µm) are suspended in contrast material (10 mg Ivalon/ml Conray 60) (31). One ml of this combination is diluted further with contrast media in a 3 ml syringe. The catheter is irrigated with saline or contrast material injected with a 3 ml syringe after each injection of emboli. The occlusion of the peripheral vascular bed is heralded by stasis of the contrast material. Embolization is continued with Gelfoam strips until blood flow is almost at a standstill. Stainless steel coils are then deposited in the main renal artery to complete the occlusion.

Ethanol. A total of 0.5 ml/kg of absolute ethanol can be injected into the renal artery (12, 16, 31). The limitation is the systemic effect of alcohol. Alcohol is rendered radiopaque when the expected volume (15 to 30 ml) is dissolved in the lyophilized component of one vial of metrizamide, thereby maintaining the high concentration of alcohol. This sclerosing solu-

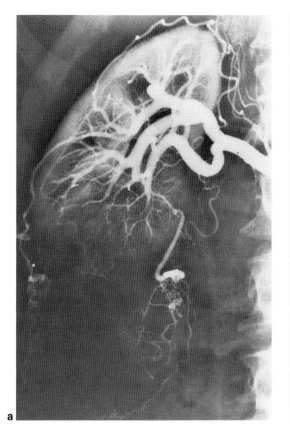

a

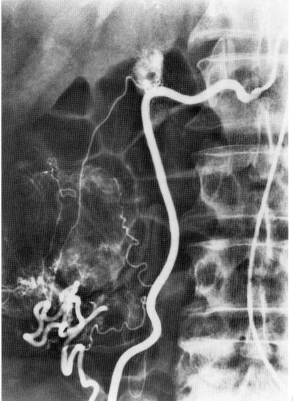

b

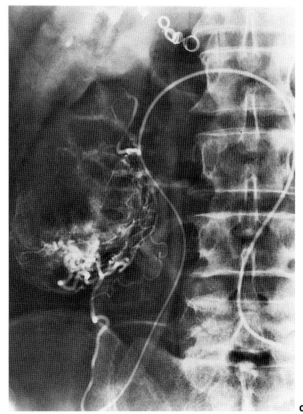

c

Fig. **1 Preoperative embolization of renal cell carcinoma**
a Right renal arteriogram
b Testicular arteriogram. Note stainless steel coil embolization of the right renal artery
c Embolization of testicular artery with Ivalon and Gelfoam

tion produces thrombosis of the renal vascular bed and infarction of the neoplasm and kidney.

A balloon catheter is used by many to increase the local concentration of alcohol and, therefore, increase the local effect, decrease the total dose necessary for infarction, and minimize the potential complications. Reflux into the inferior mesenteric artery has been reported to result in necrosis in the left colon. A 3 to 5 ml bolus is injected with the balloon occluding the vessel. After 3 to 5 minutes, the balloon is slowly deflated to allow more peripheral distribution of the alcohol. Stasis of flow is ascertained by the injection of contrast material. The sequence is repeated until stasis is accomplished.

We rarely use a balloon catheter for this purpose. We believe blood flow assists in the peripheral distribution of the sclerosing agent and also, in our opinion, decreases the possibility of reflux. The end point is the initial appearance of stasis. Repeated boluses of 2 to 3 ml of alcohol-metrizamide are injected, followed by similar boluses of contrast material. The total dose of absolute alcohol necessary for occlusion is higher when no balloon is used.

Severe pain accompanying the injection of alcohol can be decreased by the preliminary injection into the renal artery of lidocaine (2 to 3 ml, 2%). Epidural anesthesia requires more careful surveillance but is more effective. Once the transient pain during the injection of alcohol subsides, the postembolization pain is significantly less than with particulate matter and coils.

Sotradecol. A total dose of 10 to 15 ml has been adequate to produce sclerosis, thrombosis, occlusion, and infarction (7). This technique is similar to that with alcohol. Sodium tetradecyl sulfate (Sotradecol) or alcohol is especially useful with tumor extension into the renal vein or inferior vena cava.

Steel Coils. 3 mm, 5 mm, and 8 mm coils are available for embolization through a 5 to 6.5 Fr catheter tapered to an 0.038 inch wire (33). Steel coil occlusion is at times used alone for occlusion of the renal artery in the presence of rapid arteriovenous shunting (venous opacification in the first second after injection). Otherwise, coils are used after peripheral vascular bed occlusion. The size of the coil necessary for the occlusion can be determined by measurement of the opacified renal artery considering the 15 to 20% magnification. Multiple coils of the same or different sizes may be necessary, e.g., an 8 mm coil within which is placed a 5 mm coil, within which is placed a 3 mm coil. Gelfoam segments may be necessary to complete the obstruction. Steel coils should be placed far enough within the renal artery or its branches to allow easy clamping and transection. This is even more critical on the right because the right renal artery lies posterior to the inferior vena

cava. The urologist must be informed as to the number and position of the coils. This must be confirmed immediately after resection. If there is a question, radiographs should be exposed while the patient is still on the operating table. Oliguria in the immediate postoperative period must be investigated by a portable radiograph of the abdomen for the presence of a coil in the contralateral renal artery. Unintentional embolization with a coil must be investigated and usually treated as an emergency.

Chemo-embolization

This approach, proposed by Kato et al., is the combination of intra-arterial chemotherapy and peripheral embolization of the arterial supply to the tumor (15). A chemotherapeutic agent, mitomycin C, is incorporated in nondegradable ethyl cellulose microcapsules, 225 μm in diameter. These microcapsules are injected into the artery supplying the tumor to obstruct blood flow and create tumor ischemia. The combination of the ischemic effect on the tumor and the increase in contact time and local drug concentration may enhance the chemotherapeutic effect.

We have combined Ivalon or Gelfoam with mitomycin C, doxorubicin, dactinomycin, or cisplatin for chemo-embolization. In our laboratory, floxuridine and cisplatin have been encapsulated in cellulose polymers, mono- or diglycerides, waxes, and lactide polymers to form degradable and nondegradable particles of 100 μm in diameter for chemo-embolization (2, 37).

Gelfoam and Ethiodol. Particles of Gelfoam (1 to 3 mm) are suspended in Ethiodol (total of 5 to 10 ml), the ethyl ester of poppy seed oil containing iodine, in an attempt to increase the nonspecific inflammatory response. The larger arteries are occluded with Gelfoam strips and stainless steel coils.

Gelfoam and Bacille Calmette-Guérin. Organisms, 1×10^6 to 10^8 (Connaught BCG), are mixed with Gelfoam cubes and injected into the renal artery supplying the neoplasm. Contrast material (1 ml increments) is injected after each milliliter of this mixture. Gelfoam segments and stainless steel coils complete the embolization. A nephrectomy is performed usually after 2 weeks. This approach is an attempt to produce a nonspecific immune response (27, 36).

Ivalon and Cisplatin. 5 ml of Ivalon in a contrast material suspension is added to each 50 mg vial of powdered cisdiaminedichloroplatinum (cisplatin) so that each milliliter contains 10 mg Ivalon and 10 mg cisplatin (6, 31). A mixture of 100 to 150 mg Ivalon and 100 to 150 mg of cisplatin is the usual dose for a single embolic procedure. The patient is hydrated before embolization and 3% saline and mannitol are given to promote a diuresis and minimize renal toxicity on the normal kidney. The main renal artery remains patent to allow repeated episodes of Ivalon and cisplatin embolization at monthly intervals until complete occlusion.

Results

The approach to management of the primary renal carcinoma by renal artery embolization can be divided into three groups based on the extent of the disease (8, 14, 17, 28–30, 34).

Group I. This group consists of patients with regionally advanced tumors without metastases, stages I through III. When tumors are large (9 cm or greater in diameter), especially if hypervascular, dilated tortuous veins usually cover the surface of the neoplasm and the renal hilum. Regional lymph node metastases or tumor thrombus in the renal vein or inferior vena cava may impede access to the renal artery. Preoperative renal artery occlusion with resultant collapse of the veins facilitates the thrombectomy. In addition, the infarcted neoplasm and kidney become edematous, creating a more definable plane with the renal bed. These factors have reduced the blood loss and decreased operating time. Usually a delay of 24

hours to, preferably, 72 hours after embolization results in more optimal conditions for the operative procedure (Fig. **2**). For neoplasms less than 9 cm in diameter, it is not considered advisable as yet to subject the patient to the morbidity associated with embolization.

Group II. One hundred patients with locally resectable renal carcinoma and metastases, excluding brain and more recently liver, were treated according to a planned protocol of transcatheter embolization of the renal artery, a therapeutic delay of 4 to 7 days (median, 5 days), a radical nephrectomy, and medroxyprogesterone acetate (Depo-Provera), 400 mg intramuscularly twice a week (3, 24). The present analysis of these 100 patients followed for a minimum of 30 months or until death demonstrates that the benefit is for a highly selected group of patients with pulmonary metastases alone (28–30, 34).

Seven of the 100 patients demonstrated complete disappearance of all known metastatic disease. One patient remains alive without clinical evidence of recurrent disease 90 months after nephrectomy, and six had new metastatic lesions after intervals of 7 to 31 months (median, 13 months) and died of the disease. Survival times ranged from 14 to 90 months,

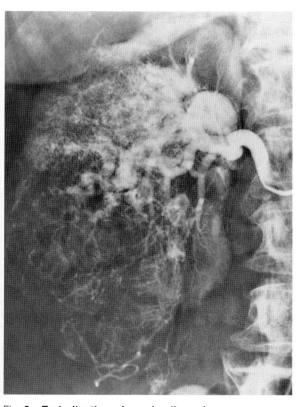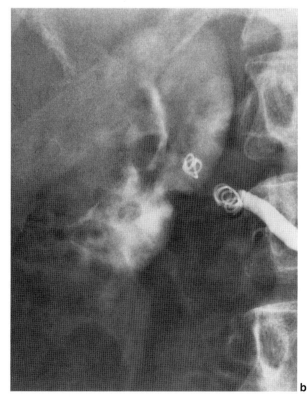

Fig. **2   Embolization of renal cell carcinoma**
a Right renal arteriogram. **b** Post embolization with Gelfoam and coils

with a median survival for the seven complete responders of 19 months.

Eight patients exhibited a partial response, a decrease of at least 50% in the product of the two maximum perpendicular diameters. Two remain alive at 30 and 36 months, the latter still without progression. In six of these eight patients, progression occurred in 5 to 29 months (median, 11 months) after the nephrectomy. Survival times ranged from 12 to 64 months (median, 21 months).

Thirteen of the 100 patients had stabilization for greater than one year. Progression occurred subsequently in eight patients, 13 to 28 months after nephrectomy (median, 18 months), but five patients remained stable and alive 31 to 70 months post nephrectomy. In all, seven patients remained alive at 31 to 70 months, and six have died at 17 to 62 months postnephrectomy (overall median survival, 36 months).

When the survival rate for these 28 patients (responders) is compared with the 72 other patients (nonresponders), the difference is significant. The expected median survival was 39.1 months with a 38% 5-year survival versus 8.4 months and no 5-year survivors. There is an apparent survival advantage for patients with pulmonary metastases only, who underwent infarction followed by nephrectomy when compared with those similar stage IV patients treated at our institution by nephrectomy without prior infarction. The median survival was more than doubled in the infarction and nephrectomy patients with pulmonary metastases only and the difference was statistically significant ($p = 0.017$). For patients with nonlung metastases (with or without concomitant lung metastases), there was no demonstrable improvement in survival rates in patients who underwent angioinfarction before nephrectomy. Nephrectomy after renal artery embolization was associated with a mortality of 2.7%.

Gelfoam and BCG. Objective regressions and improved survival times have been noted in patients with metastatic renal cell carcinoma treated by angioinfarction with inert materials and subsequent radical nephrectomy, but the responses to date have been limited and temporary. To evaluate whether infarcting with a biologically active agent might improve results, we treated 11 patients with advanced metastatic renal cell carcinoma by percutaneous arterial embolization of the primary tumor with Gelfoam particles soaked in Connaught BCG (10^6 to 10^8 organisms) and steel coils followed by radical nephrectomy 7 to 24 days later (27). Morbidity has been limited to pain, fever, and gastrointestinal complaints, all characteristic of angioinfarction without BCG. We have not seen systemic BCG disease; only one nephrectomy specimen had a positive culture for acid-fast organisms.

Recall skin tests, lymphocyte differentials, cellular toxicity, lymphoblastic response to mitogens, and monocyte adherence were performed serially on eight patients. The results were variable and failed to indicate whether or not there was an altered host immune status (21, 32).

Two patients achieved radiographic complete regression of all pulmonary metastases, one of whom remains alive without evidence of disease at 47 months. The other relapsed at 10 months but is still alive and well at 46 months despite slow progression of his lung nodules. One other patient remains alive at 48 months with stable disease in his lung and liver, although progression of his humeral metastasis required amputation. The other eight patients experienced progression and are dead of their disease. This study is experimental and the significance of the results are still to be determined.

Group III. Group III consists of patients treated by embolization alone, without nephrectomy. These patients were not candidates for surgery because of their general medical condition or extensive tumor involvement; metastases were frequently present in the liver or brain. We also included in this group patients with contralateral renal or diffuse abdominal metastases. We performed palliative infarction to control either gross hematuria, persistent flank pain, hypercalcemia, polycythemia, hypertension, or congestive failure. Treatment did not significantly prolong the survival period for patients in this group; the approach was primarily for palliation.

Sequential Embolization. More recently, patients with extensive metastatic disease negating nephrectomy were managed by sequential embolization of the renal carcinoma (Obrez) and the metastases using Ivalon or Ivalon and Cisplatin. The metastatic foci embolized include the liver, the adrenals and retroperitoneal lymph nodes. Our initial experience was favorable in that we believe palliation was related to the "debulking" procedure. The sequential nature of the embolization at 2- to 4-week intervals was well tolerated. Further embolization is performed at 3- to 6-month intervals as long as the supplying vessels are patent and the patient's clinical course warrants it.

Renal Carcinoma in a Solitary Kidney. Metastases to the residual kidney or a second primary carcinoma in the solitary kidney creates unique problems (25). Three patients with such clinical circumstances were treated by embolization at our institution. When the patient is a good operative risk, surgical resection of a localized lesion is the preferred approach. Transcatheter occlusion to control hematuria, hypertension, hypercalcemia, etc., may be considered if the neoplasm has replaced less than 50% of the kidney and is supplied by a single branch of the renal artery (Fig. **3**). Sequential renal artery embolization of a second renal neoplasm in the residual kidney used as

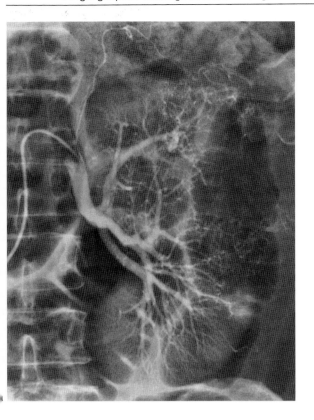

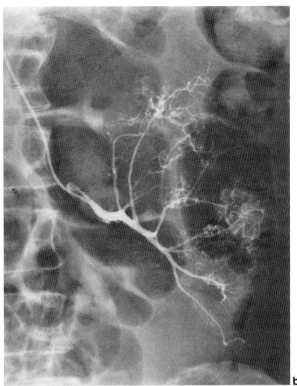

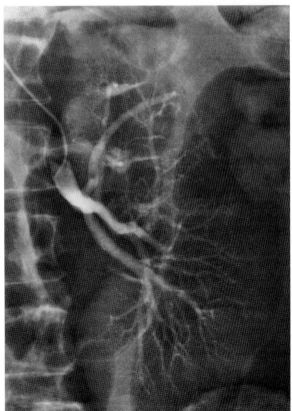

**Fig. 3 Segmental embolization for control of hema-
turia in a solitary kidney with hypernephroma**
a Left renal arteriogram
b Selective catheterization of a segmental branch of the
left renal artery
c Postembolization arteriogram

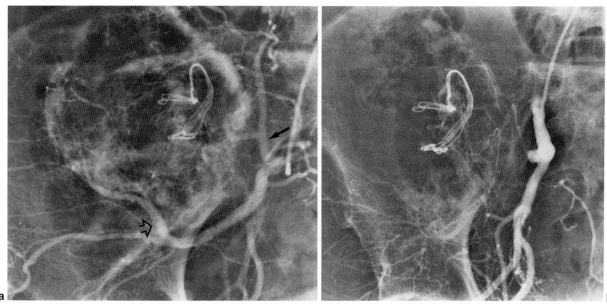

Fig. 4   Embolization of metastatic hypernephroma to the right ilium
a Right internal iliac arteriogram. The majority of the blood supply to the hypervascular tumor in the right ilium derives from the iliolumbar (arrow) and superior gluteal artery (open arrow)
b Right internal iliac arteriogram after embolization of the right iliolumbar and superior gluteal artery

the definitive treatment is illustrated in a patient who was not a surgical candidate. Embolization was carried out on four occasions over a 5½-year period with Gelfoam, Ivalon, steel coils, and alcohol. He is still alive and asymptomatic with tumor in the kidney. Two additional patients have been treated for hemorrhage and hypercalcemia in a similar fashion.

Renal Carcinoma with Impaired Renal Function. One patient with small kidneys and elevated blood urea nitrogen and creatinine levels experienced hematuria due to a carcinoma of the upper pole of the left kidney. The neoplasm occupied less than 50% of the kidney. The blood supply to the renal carcinoma was occluded, controlling the hemorrhage. The creatinine level was further elevated temporarily and fortunately returned to the preembolization level in one week.

Complications

Almost every patient treated by embolization of the renal artery experiences flank pain lasting 24 to 48 hours and requires narcotics for relief. Temperature up to 40°C frequently accompanies the pain and lasts as long as 5 days, but antibiotics are seldom needed. Anorexia, nausea, and vomiting may occur for 3 to 5 days, requiring symptomatic management. Paralytic ileus requires nasogastric suction and intravenous fluids. Hypertension occurs in many patients during embolization and lasts 2 to 4 hours. No patient has experienced persistent hypertension.

Major complications have been relatively few (28–30, 34). Renal failure occurred in two of our first 20 patients, in one of whom it was irreversible. This was believed to be related to the large volume of contrast material (300 ml) and to the infarction that was performed at the same time. These two events are now separated by at least 24 hours, without another episode of renal failure. Renal abscess complicated occlusion in one patient. Most patients have gas in the kidney and neoplasm presumably introduced during embolization or due to tumor necrosis. In the presence of a urinary infection or calculi, antibiotics are given before and after embolization.

Unintentional embolization with the gelatin sponge, polyvinyl alcohol foam particles, alcohol, and steel coils is always a potential complication. Loss of a coil can be managed with the use of a basket, Fogarty catheter, or surgery (9, 10, 13, 35). A balloon catheter will minimize alcohol reflux, which has been reported with resultant left colic necrosis (20). Errors are prevented by careful and meticulous attention to the techniques of embolization.

Metastases

Skeletal. Bone metastases from renal cell carcinoma occur in 30 to 45% of patients; the lumbar spine and pelvis are the most common sites. Radiation therapy is the preferred approach for managing these metastases. We have not undertaken embolization until at

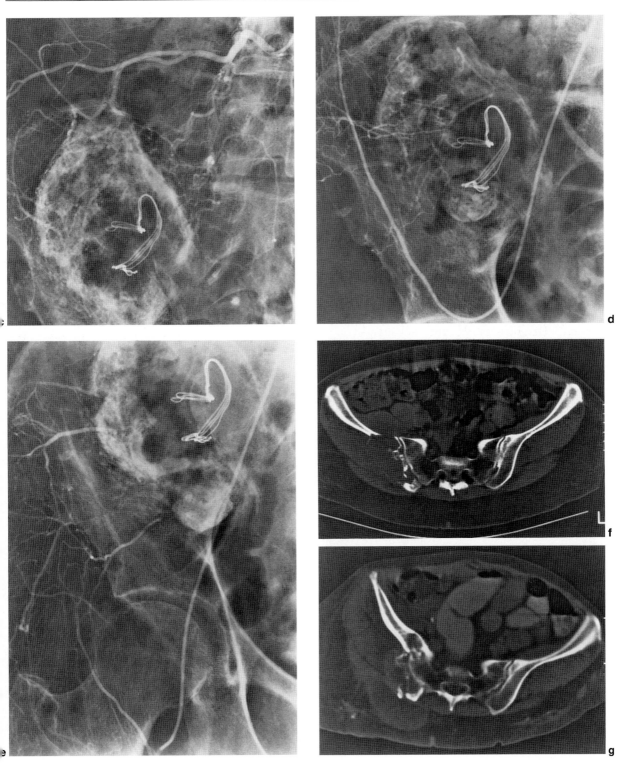

Fig. **4**
c Right fourth lumbar ateriogram
d Right deep iliac circumflex arteriogram
e Right superficial iliac circumflex arteriogram
Collateral arteries are embolized after the primary blood supply has been occluded. The patient responded to embolization with pain control for more than 6 months
f CT of the ilium before embolization
g CT after embolization

least 6 weeks after radiotherapy has been completed but has been unseccessful in controlling bone pain (Fig. **4**). Arterial occlusion of these usually hypervascular lesions has effectively alleviated pain in 21 patients (11, 26). The relief of symptoms began within 12 hours to several days after embolization and lasted from 1 to 6 months.

When a pathologic fracture occurs, or is impending, internal fixation is usually indicated to relieve pain and permit the patient to remain ambulatory. Surgical excision and prosthetic replacement should also be considered as treatment for intractable pain when the lesion is in an accessible site, usually at the end of the long bones. This is especially true when the bone lesion is solitary, because a patient with a single lesion can be expected to have a long disease-free interval.

Biopsy, open reduction and internal fixation, and resection are usually complicated by the hypervascularity of these lesions. Carpenter et al. (5) reported an average blood loss of 1500 to 3000 ml in such patients. Hemorrhage of this magnitude greatly increases the surgical difficulty as well as the operative risk. This problem can be controlled in the majority of patients by preoperative arterial occlusion. Preoperative embolization was considered to have been successful in six of eight patients so treated at our hospital (4). Their estimated blood loss at the time of surgery averaged 550 ml. In the remaining two patients, preoperative occlusion was not adequate and the blood losses were 3800 and 7000 ml. In one patient, the collateral vessels from the internal iliac artery to the neoplasm were neither identified nor occluded. In the other patient, multiple vessels from the superficial femoral artery supplied the neoplasm of the midshaft of the femur. These were not embolized for fear of jeopardizing the viability of the extremity.

Hepatic. Liver metastases from renal carcinoma are ominous and associated with a median survival of 3 months. Two approaches have been pursued: sequential hepatic embolization as well as renal embolization and nephrectomy and renal embolization and hepatic artery infusion with floxuridine, doxorubicin, mitomycin C, with or without cisplatin (FAMP). If the kidney has already been resected, we attempt either of these two approaches or a combination of both, i.e., sequential hepatic artery embolization with Ivalon or Ivalon with Cisplatin or hepatic artery infusion of FAMP. Thus far, the median survival time of six patients treated in this manner is 1 year; the longest survivor is still alive with disease 3 years after renal artery and hepatic artery embolization.

Other. The reported response rates for interferon in patients with metastatic renal carcinoma are approximately 20% (23). In an attempt to increase the

response, alpha interferon was infused intra-arterially in 12 patients. Up to 40×10^6 units were infused intra-arterially over a 30-minute period each day for 7 days. The renal, hepatic, internal mammary, and lumbar arteries were catheterized selectively and infused to treat renal cell carcinoma and metastases to the liver, mediastinum, and retroperitoneum. Fever, malaise, chills, nausea, vomiting, myalgia, diarrhea, dysgenesia, and cognitive dysfunction were mild and transient, as was leukopenia. Although the toxicity was tolerable, the response was less than dramatic (22).

References

1. Almgard LE, Fernstrom E, Haverling M, Ljungquist A. Treatment of renal adenocarcinoma by embolic occlusion of the renal circulation. Br J Urol 1973;45:474–479.
2. Bechtel W, Wright KC, Wallace S, Mosier B, Mosier D, Mir S, Kudo S. An experimental evaluation of microcapsules for arterial embolization. Radiology 1986;161:601–604.
3. Bloom HJG. Hormone treatment of renal tumors: experimental and clinical observations. In: Riches EW, ed. Tumors of the kidney and ureter. Edinburgh: Livingstone 1964:311–320.
4. Bowers TA, Murray JA, Charnsangavej C, Soo CS, Chuan VP, Wallace S. Bone metastases from renal carcinoma. J Bone Joint Surg [Am] 1982;64:749–754.
5. Carpenter PR, Ewing JW, Cook AJ, Kuster AH. Angiographic assessment and control of potential operative hemorrhage with pathologic fractures secondary to metastases. Clin Orthop 1977;123:6–8.
6. Carrasco CH, Wallace S, Charnsangavej C, Papadopoulos NEJ, Patt YZ, Mavligit GM. Treatment of hepatic metastases in ocular melanoma: embolization of the hepatic artery with polyvinyl sponge and cisplatin. JAMA 1986;255:3152–3154.
7. Cho KJ, Nishiyama RH, Shields JJ, McGormick JL, Forrest ME. Experimental renal infarcts. AJR 1981;136:493–496.
8. Christensen K, Dyreborg U, Andersen JF, Nissen HM. The value of transvascular embolization in the treatment of renal carcinoma. J Urol 1985;133:191–193.
9. Chuang VP. Nonoperative retrieval of Gianturco coils for abdominal aorta. AJR 1979;132:996–997.
10. Chuang VP, Wallace S, Gianturco C, Soo CS. Complications of coil embolization: prevention and management. AJR 1981;137:809–813.
11. Chuang VP, Wallace S, Swanson DA, Zornoza J, Handel SF, Schwarten DA, Murray J. Arterial occlusion in the management of pain from metastatic renal carcinoma. Radiology 1979;133:611–614.
12. Ellman BA, Green CE, Eigenbrodte E, Garriot JB, Curry TS. Renal infarction with absolute alcohol. Invest Radiol 1980;15:318–322.
13. Habighorst VLV, Kreutz W, Klug B, Sparwasser HH, Göbel EA. Spiralembolisation der Nierenarterie nach Gianturco. RöFo 1978;128:47–51.
14. Kaisary AV, Williams G, Riddle PR. The role of preoperative embolization in renal cell carcinoma. J Urol 1984;131:641–646.
15. Kato T, Nemoto R, Mori H, Takahashi M, Tamakawa Y. Transcatheter arterial chemoembolization of renal cell carcinoma with microencapsulated mitomycin C. J Urol 1981;125:19–24.
16. Klimberg I, Hunter P, Hawkins IF, Drylie DM, Wajsman Z. Preoperative angioinfarction of localized renal cell carcinoma using absolute ethanol. J Urol 1985;133:21–24.
17. Kurth KH, Cingualbre J, Oliver RTD, Schulman CC. Embolization and subsequent nephrectomy in metastatic renal cell carcinoma. World J Urol 1984;2:122–126.
18. Lalli AF, Peterson N, Bookstein JJ. Roentgen guided infarction of kidney and lung: a potential therapeutic technique. Radiology 1969;93:434–435.

19. Lang EK. Superselective arterial catheterization as a vehicle for delivering radioactive infarct particles to tumors. Radiology 1971;98:391–399.
20. Mulligan BD, Espinosa GD. Bowel infarction: a complication of ethanol ablation of a renal tumor. Cardiovasc Intervent Radiol 1983;6:55–57.
21. Nakano H, Nihira H, Toge T. Treatment of renal cancer patients by transcatheter embolization and its effects on lymphocyte proliferative responses. J Urol 1983;130:24–27.
22. Neidhart J, Tenney D, Quesada J, Charnsangavej C, Carrasco CH. Intra-arterial lymphoblastoid interferon (Wellferon; IFN alpha N) therapy renal cancer [Abstract]. American Society of Clinical Oncology, May, 1986.
23. Quesada JR, Trindade A, Swanson DA, Trindade A, Gutterman JU. Renal cell carcinoma: antitumor effects of leukocyte interferon. Cancer Res 1983;43:940–947.
24. Raghavaiah NV. Hormone treatment of advanced renal cell carcinoma. Urology 1982;19:123–126.
25. Soo CS, Chuang VP, Wallace S, Charnsangavej C, Bowers TA. Segmental renal artery embolization in solitary renal carcinoma. Urology 1981;18:420–423.
26. Soo CS, Chuang VP, Wallace S, Charnsangavej C. Interventional angiography in the treatment of metastases. Radiol Clin North Am 1982;20:591–600.
27. Swanson DA, McDonald M, Wallace S. Angioinfarction with BCG for metastatic renal carcinoma. Proceedings of the 78th annual meeting of the American Urologic Association (Abstract 529) 1983:224.
28. Swanson DA, Johnson DE, von Eschenbach AC, Chuang VP, Wallace S. Angioinfarction plus nephrectomy for metastatic renal cell carcinoma: a update. J Urol 1983;130:449–452.
29. Swanson DA, Wallace S. Current results of infarction-nephrectomy for advanced renal adenocarcinoma. In: De Kernion JB, Pavone-Macaluso M, eds. Tumors of the kidney: international perspective in urology; vol 13. Baltimore: Williams and Wilkins 1986:184–193.
30. Swanson DA, Wallace S. Surgery of metastatic renal carcinoma and use of renal infarction (Abstract). In: Status of treatment of metastatic renal cell carcinoma. International symposium, Vienna, March 1987.
31. Szwarc I, Carrasco CH, Wallace S, Richli W. Radiopaque suspension of polyvinyl alcohol foam for embolization. AJR 1986;146:591–592.
32. Tykka H, Oravisto KI, Lehtonen T, Sarna S, Tallberg T. Active specific immunotherapy of advanced renal-cell carcinoma. Eur Urol 1978;4:250–258.
33. Wallace S, Chuang VP, Anderson JH, Gianturco C. Steel coil embolus and its therapeutic applications. In: Abrams HL, ed. Abrams angiography. Boston: Little, Brown 1983:2151–2174.
34. Wallace S, Chuang VP, Swanson DA, Bracken B, Hersh EM, Ayala A, Johnson D. Embolization of renal carcinoma: experience with 100 patients. Radiology 1981;138:563–570.
35. Wirthlin LS, Gross WS, James TP, Sadiq S. Renal artery occlusion from migration of stainless steel coils. JAMA 1980;243:2064–2066.
36. Wright KC, Soo CS, Wallace S, McDonald MW, Ayala A. Experimental percutaneous renal embolization using BCG-saturated gelfoam. Cardiovasc Intervent Radiol 1982;5:260–263.
37. Wright KC, Wallace S, Mosier B, Mosier D. Microcapsules for arterial embolization: appearance and in vitro drug release characteristics. J. Microencapsul. 1988;5:13.

Genitourinary Tumors

S. Wallace, C. Charnsangavej, C. H. Carrasco and W. R. Richli

The internal iliac arteries, the blood supply to genitourinary viscera in the true pelvis, are readily approached after percutaneous puncture and catheterization of each femoral artery (Fig. 1). For adults, 5 and 6.5 Fr as well as 6.5 Fr tapered to 5 Fr polyethylene catheters are used. In older patients, a 6.5 Fr torque-controlled catheter is extremely helpful. 3.7 to 5 Fr catheters are preferred for smaller patients, especially women and children. The ipsilateral internal iliac artery is usually catheterized with a reversed-curve catheter configuration. Frequently, contralateral femoral artery puncture and passage over the aortic bifurcation with an accentuated cobra catheter configuration allows more selective catheterization of the anterior division of the internal iliac artery and its branches. On rare occasions, because of arteriosclerotic stenosis or occlusion of one femoral artery, two catheters (5 Fr) can be introduced from one side to both internal iliac arteries. The catheter tip may be left in the main trunk of the internal iliac artery for infusion of both the anterior and posterior divisions in order to treat disease that extends to the pelvic side walls. When the neoplasm is localized in the uterus (corpus and cervix), bladder, prostate, vagina, vulva, urethra, or penis and the immediately adjacent structures, selective catheterization of the anterior division or a specific branch of the anterior division may be necessary. Because of the variations in the distribution of the vascular supply originating from the internal iliac arteries and because of the necessity to increase flow to the neoplasm and decrease drug toxicity to the normal tissues, the superior and inferior gluteal branches may be occluded just beyond the pelvic brim with steel coils and Gelfoam segments (46) (Fig. 2).

An arteriogram is obtained to define the extent of disease and to verify catheter placement. Bilateral simultaneous injection of meglumine diatrizoate (60%), ioxaglate meglumine 39.3% and ioxaglate sodium 19.6% or non-ionic contrast material is accomplished through a Y adaptor at a rate of 5 to 7 ml/s for a total of 30 to 36 ml; 2 ml of 1% lidocaine is added to each 10 ml of diatrizoate to minimize the pain of injection. Rarely, either air or carbon dioxide may be injected into the bladder through a Foley catheter before arterial opacification. This allows better identification of tumor vascularity in the wall of the bladder. Pelvic genitourinary carcinomas are often hypovascular, and the angiographic diagnosis of the extent of the neoplasm is difficult. When the neoplasms are hypervascular, the diagnosis is more

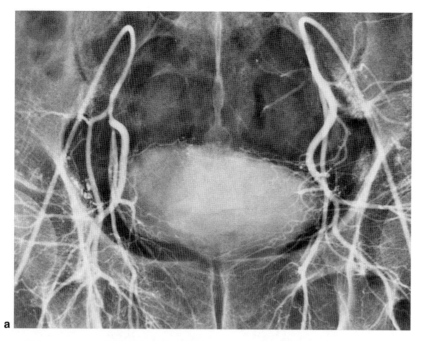

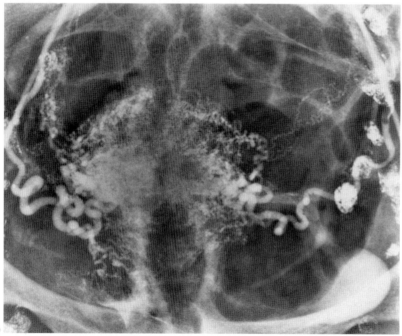

Fig. 1 **Internal iliac artery**
a Selective catheterization of the anterior division of each internal iliac artery
b Contralateral catheterization of each uterine artery originating from the anterior division of the internal iliac artery

readily established, but changes due to infection or radiation therapy are frequently superimposed and differentiation from neoplasms is difficult.

The catheters are fixed in place at the groin with sutures or plastic adhesive covered by gauze pads and attached to individual infusion pumps to ensure optimal delivery. To maintain catheter patency and to minimize vascular thrombosis, a solution of 250 ml of 0.9 N saline with 5000 U of heparin is infused at 50 ml/h into each vessel through two separate pumps until definitive therapy is instituted.

Catheter position is monitored in each patient shortly after placement to ensure the desired distribution of the chemotherapeutic agents. The injection of the radioisotope technetium-99m-macro-aggregated albumin (Fig. **2**) at the same rate (50 ml/h) as the infusion provides a more accurate evaluation of distribution when compared with the angiographic injection rate of 3 ml/s (11). The combination of the angiographic delineation of the anatomy and scintigraphy is used to determine the relative dosage to be delivered to each catheter

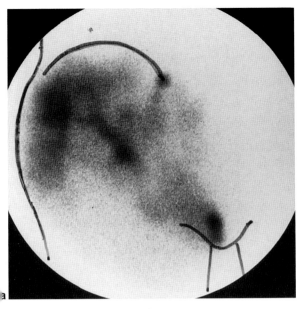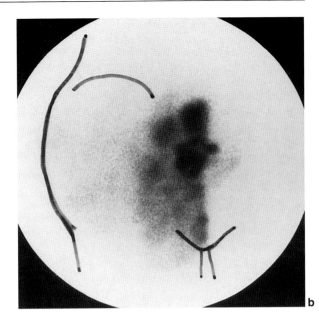

Fig. 2 Occlusion for infusion
a Scintigraphy after the injection of technetium-99m-macro-aggregated albumin through a catheter in the right internal iliac artery at the same rate as the infusion (50 ml/h). Note the distribution of flow to the buttocks
b Scintigraphy after the occlusion of the gluteal arteries. Blood flow is directed to the pelvic viscera

through the individual pumps. Because of the differential flow studies and the localization of the bulk of the tumor (palpation and radiologic studies), the agents are at times infused more through one catheter than the other. A pulsatile pump (70 pulses/min) may be necessary to disrupt laminar flow or streaming in order to accomplish a more optimal distribution of the chemotherapy (13, 47).

At times, especially in relatively hypovascular neoplasms, dynamic CT is performed while 30% contrast material is injected through catheters selectively placed in the vessels supplying the neoplasm (CT-angio). The injection rate is usually 1 to 2 ml/s for a total of 60 to 120 ml. Although the rate still does not duplicate the infusion rate for the chemotherapeutic agent, it more closely simulates the treatment conditions.

As soon as the catheter is placed into the aorta, aqueous heparin, 45 U/kg, is injected except in patients who are actively bleeding (4). During selective catheter placement, 2 to 3 ml aliquots of heparinized saline (1000 U/500 ml of normal saline) are injected every 2 to 3 minutes. Throughout each 24-hour period of the infusion, 15,000 to 25,000 U of aqueous heparin are given either intravenously or intra-arterially to maintain the clotting parameters at 1.5 to 2 times normal. The aqueous heparin is miscible with most chemotherapeutic agents except doxorubicin; with this agent the aqueous heparin is administered by an alternate route either intravenously or intra-arterially.

Carcinoma of the Uterine Cervix

Carcinoma of the cervix occurs in approximately 16,000 women each year in the United States, with an overall mortality of 40%. Squamous cell carcinoma accounts for about 95% and adenocarcinoma for 4 to 5% of the cases (36).

The conventional treatment of squamous cell carcinoma of the uterine cervix has been radiation therapy or surgery, or both. Carcinoma-in-situ, stage 0 (Table 1), is treated by conservative or radical surgery or by radiotherapy, or both, with cure rates approaching 90 to 95%. For a small carcinoma (stage 1 or 2) confined to the cervix, the results of either radiation therapy or surgery are comparable with the

Table 1 Clinical staging system for carcinoma of the uterine cervix

Stage 0	Carcinoma in situ, intra-epithelial carcinoma
Stage 1	Tumor confined to cervix
Stage 2	Tumor extends beyond the cervix but not the pelvic wall or lower third of the vagina
Stage 3	Tumor extends to pelvic wall or lower third of vagina. Those patients with hydronephrosis or a nonfunctioning kidney should be included
Stage 4	Tumor extends beyond the true pelvis or clinically involves the mucosa of the bladder or rectum

5-year-survival rates ranging from 80 to 85%. The selection of treatment has come to be determined by the patient's preference or the experience of the gynecologist and radiotherapist rather than the effectiveness of the modality. However, with patients with locally advanced cancers, such as bulky tumors (6 cm or larger in diameter) of stage 2 or 3, treatment yields a 5-year-survival rate of 20 to 40%. Radiation therapy has been preferred and 25 to 40% of patients so treated have had local recurrence within the radiated field. Those patients with stage 4 tumors treated almost exclusively by radiation therapy, have a 0 to 17% 5-year-survival rate (30, 36).

Persistence or local recurrence is often associated with intractable pain, bleeding, foul discharge, and fistulas between the rectum, bladder, vagina, and, also, small bowel. In these patients palliation has been difficult to accomplish by systemic chemotherapy. During the past three decades, arterial infusion of chemotherapeutic agents has been utilized to increase the local concentration of drugs, but responses have been poor and of short duration.

Intra-Arterial Therapy

In 1952 Cromer et al. (5) reported on the intra-aortic injection of nitrogen mustard in 16 patients with carcinoma of the cervix and vagina. They observed regression of local disease in eight patients and a reduction in size of the pelvic tumor in four patients. Krakoff and Sullivan (14), using the percutaneous approach, also found some objective benefit in three of six patients with carcinoma of the cervix after the intra-aortic injection of nitrogen mustard. Sullivan et al. (39) used catheters implanted surgically into the internal iliac arteries for the infusion of methotrexate and noted total or partial tumor regression in all four of their evaluated patients with carcinoma of the cervix. Trussel and Mitford-Barbeton (42) also delivered methotrexate into catheters placed surgically into the internal iliac arteries in patients with stage 2 or 3 carcinoma of the cervix who had not been previously treated by radiation therapy. A 50% reduction in tumor volume was achieved in half of their patients. Three of the 14 patients died of hemorrhage despite the use of citrovorum rescue factor (42). Hulka and Bissel (9) also infused 5-fluorouracil, floxuridine, or methotrexate selectively into the internal iliac arteries in a group of 13 patients with carcinoma of the cervix and vagina. These investigators observed a complete remission in four patients with stages 3 and 4 disease who also underwent irradiation after chemotherapy. Three patients were alive and free of cancer 13 to 40 months after infusion. Intra-arterial Fluorescite with Wood's light illumination was used to assess distribution. Morrow et al. (24) infused bleomycin through catheters placed in the aorta or common or internal iliac arteries. Two of 16 patients showed partial responses. Lifshitz et al. (17) using intra-aortic methotrexate alone or in combination with vincristine observed tumor regression in 3 of 14 patients, with a mean survival time of 13 months, compared with 7.9 months for the nonresponders. The three patients who experienced objective tumor response had all received a combination of methotrexate and vincristine. None of the patients treated with methotrexate alone had tumor regression. Swenerton et al. (40) used intra-aortic or common iliac artery infusion of a combination of vincristine, bleomycin, and mitomycin C over 66 hours at 6-week intervals. Of 20 patients treated, three had partial responses and five had less than 50% shrinkage of tumor. Of the two partial responders, one lived 93 months and the other more than 113 months. Ohta (27) and Oku et al. (28) suggested employing intra-arterial infusion before definitive radiation therapy.

Anatomic considerations. The uterus, corpus and cervix are supplied by the uterine arteries, which originate from the anterior division of each internal iliac artery. It usually has a "U" configuration (Fig. **1c**): the descending portion along the pelvic side walls, the transverse portion that becomes more tortuous with pregnancies and age, and the ascending portion, which travels along the body of the uterus to terminate in the fundal and adnexal branches. The mural branches alter their configuration and size with the cycle. The fundal branches communicate with the branches of the opposite uterine artery, while the adnexal branches join the ovarian branches, which arise from the anterior aspect of the aorta. Each cervicovaginal branch originates near the junction of the second and third portion of each uterine artery. The vaginal artery, usually coming directly from the internal iliac artery, nourishes the posterior vagina and communicates with the vaginal branch of the cervicovaginal artery. Numerous variations exist in the take-off of these vessels, but the terminal branches are most consistent.

Technical considerations. The placement of the catheters into both internal iliac arteries, selectively into the main trunks, the anterior divisions, the vaginal arteries from the internal pudendals, or the uterine arteries depends on the blood supply to the tumors and the flow distribution as evaluated by angiography, radionuclide flow study, and CT-angio.

In most patients with carcinoma of the cervix, the uterine arteries can be selectively catheterized after puncture of the contralateral femoral arteries (Fig. **3**). This is only of value if the neoplasm is confined to the cervix and the immediately adjacent area. More frequently, intra-arterial therapy is delivered to patients with stage 3 and stage 4 carcinomas of the cervix in whom the disease extends to the

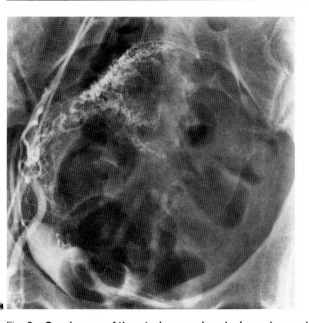
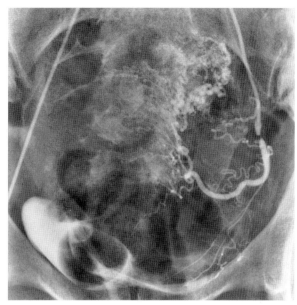

b

Fig. 3   Carcinoma of the uterine cervix: uterine artery catheterization
a Ipsilateral right uterine artery catheterization (arterial phase). **b** Contralateral left uterine artery catheterization (arterial phase)

pelvic side walls, the vagina, the bladder, and the iliac lymph nodes. This necessitates infusion of both anterior divisions and at times the initial branches of the posterior divisions. The distribution can be confirmed by CT-angio and radionuclide studies. Because the flow rate used in the radionuclide flow study is similar to the chemotherapy infusion rate, the radionuclide flow study is used to monitor the catheter position and the dose of the drugs to be delivered into each artery.

For example, in a patient with a hypervascular carcinoma of the uterine cervix as defined by angiography through catheters placed in the main trunk of the internal iliac arteries, the radionuclide flow study demonstrated the flow distribution to be almost exclusively to the true pelvis. Therefore, the position of the catheters was adequate and more selective placement was not necessary. On the other hand, in the patient with a hypovascular tumor (most squamous cell carcinomas of the cervix are relatively hypovascular), catheter placement in the internal iliac artery may not only infuse the true pelvis but also the buttocks. Embolization of the superior and inferior gluteal arteries with stainless steel coils or segments of Gelfoam will prevent the infusion of the buttocks and redistribute the chemotherapy to the true pelvis. However, pudendal flow may be increased, resulting in increased local toxicity (Fig. **2b**).

Criteria for Response

After three courses of intra-arterial infusion of chemotherapy, the patients were evaluated by the gynecologist and radiotherapist to assess the response for a trial of curative radiotherapy. The response criteria included agreement by the examiners that the neoplasm had decreased by at least 50%. When applicable, evaluation of response took into consideration pain relief, cessation of bleeding, significant improvement as measured by imaging studies, and conversion of the tumor histologic pattern to a benign appearance, as seen on biopsy specimens obtained after chemotherapy.

Clinical Experience

Group I. At our hospital, nine patients with squamous cell carcinoma of the uterine cervix were treated with cisplatin (120 mg/m^2 over 2 hours). The drug was delivered through percutaneously placed catheters into each internal iliac artery (3). Of these patients, six had unresectable pelvic recurrences after radiation therapy, and three patients had previously untreated large volume primary tumors. Three patients (33%) experienced partial responses, including two with pelvic recurrences and one with a previously untreated tumor. The durations of responses were 6, 6, and 3 months. The previously untreated patient demonstrated a marked reduction in tumor volume and after three infusions of cisplatin, at intervals of 1 month, began radiation therapy. She remains free of disease 7 months after the initia-

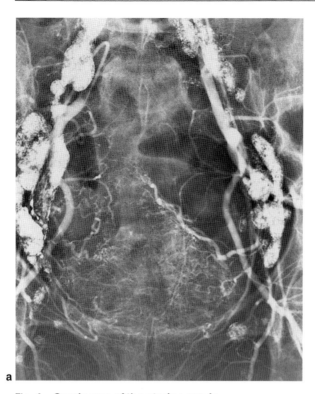 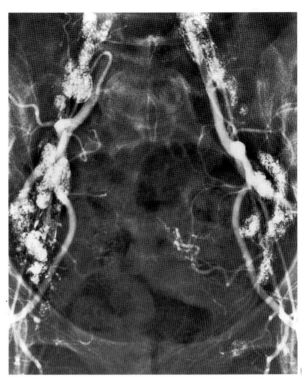

a

Fig. 4   **Carcinoma of the uterine cervix**
a Hypervascular carcinoma of the cervix before intra-arterial therapy. **b** Postinfusion chemotherapy; there is marked improvement

tion of therapy. Several patients also had significant pain relief (Fig. **4**).

Group II: intra-arterial induction chemotherapy. Forty-seven patients with stage 3 and stage 4 carcinoma of the uterine cervix were treated under a protocol that consisted of a combination of agents: Vincristine (2 mg) by intravenous administration with the intra-arterial infusion of mitomycin C ($10 \, mg/m^2$ over 24 hours every other course), bleomycin (20 to 40 mg/m^2 over 24 hours), and cisplatin ($120 \, mg/m^2$ over 2 hours). Vincristine was soon deleted from the protocol because of the myelosuppression that resulted. After three cycles spaced 3 weeks apart, the patients were re-evaluated.

Of the 47 patients treated, 42 were evaluable. Twenty-nine of the 42 patients (69%) had a partial response to the treatment with a reduction of the tumor by more than 50%. Nine additional patients had stable disease or less than 50% reduction in the size. Two patients had progressive disease, and two other patients experienced treatment-related deaths due to renal failure and bleomycin pulmonary toxicity.

Thirty-eight partial-response and stable-disease patients underwent radiation therapy and 21 of the 42 evaluable patients (50%) remained disease-free with the follow-up of 6 to 42 months and a median

survival of 18 months. Seventeen patients relapsed, with a time to relapse of 0 to 35 months, and a median survival after relapse of 3 months.

It should also be noted that of 29 patients who had responded to chemotherapy 20 (69%) remained disease-free and only one of the patients with stable disease or less than partial response remained disease free (12).

Group III: intra-arterial therapy in irradiated patients. Another group treated during the same period consisted of 50 patients who had recurrent carcinoma of the cervix after radiation therapy or surgery, or both. Most of them had severe pelvic pain, vaginal bleeding, or edema of the extremity. The median survival of these patients was reported to be 3 months. For palliation, these patients underwent intra-arterial chemotherapy or chemoembolization with Ivalon and cisplatin.

Complications. All patients experienced nausea, vomiting, and alopecia. No significant thrombocytopenia was experienced as long as mitomycin C was given every other course. Chemodermatitis was seen, which was characterized by hyperpigmentation without blistering or ulceration. Neuropathy was occasionally experienced with pain and paresthesia along the buttocks and posterior leg, which resolved over weeks to months. Catheter-related problems were few and did not require interruption of therapy (7, 12).

Comment

Percutaneously placed internal iliac artery catheterization is feasible and associated with few complications. Vincristine and mitomycin C has been discontinued because of hematopoietic suppression and replaced by cytosine arabinoside (Ara-C). This approach can adequately reduce tumor bulk, improve the disease virtually to a stage II, and enable the patient to undergo "curative" pelvic irradiation. The impact of this therapeutic modality on survival and local recurrence has yet to be determined.

Urinary Bladder

Carcinoma of the urinary bladder, 2% of patients with malignant disease, affects approximately 40,000 Americans (3:1 male to female ratio) and is responsible for 10,800 deaths each year. Ninety-seven percent of all bladder tumors are epithelial in origin: 90% of these are transitional cell type, 6 to 7% are squamous cell carcinoma, and 1 to 2% are adenocarcinoma. These neoplasms are prone to recur and recurrent tumors are likely to be more aggressive. Accurate staging of the bladder neoplasms is most important in the treatment planning, because recurrent tumors tend to occur when the tumors are understaged and undertreated. At the time of diagnosis, 15% of cases are found to be invasive cancers and 15% will eventually progress in grade and stage to invasive disease (32, 36).

Intra-arterial therapy is confined to patients with advanced carcinoma of the bladder (stage D) with local extension or regional metastases (stage D_1), who are usually treated by pelvic or extended field irradiation that yields a 16 to 17% 5-year-survival

Table **2** Clinical staging system for carcinoma of the bladder

Stage 0	Tumor confined to mucosa (carcinoma in situ)
Stage A	No tumor penetration beneath lamina propria
Stage B_1	Tumor invades muscularis but does not extend more than halfway through the muscle layer
Stage B_2	Tumor extends more than halfway through muscle layer but does not invade perivesical tissues
Stage C	Tumor has penetrated into perivesical connective tissue
Stage D_1	Tumor fixed, invading adjacent organs, or with lymph node invasion below origin of common iliac arteries
Stage D_2	Tumor with lymph node invasion beyond origin of common iliac arteries

rate when a few nodes are involved (Table **2**) (22, 45). In patients with extrapelvic metastases (stage D_2) the median survival rate is 13 weeks if left untreated. There are no long-term survivors for stage D_2 disease with any form of therapy.

Systemic Chemotherapy

Systemic chemotherapy has been given to patients with advanced bladder neoplasms (stage D), both after recurrences as well as after failure to respond to surgery and radiation therapy (4, 8, 15, 19, 20, 22, 33, 37, 38, 41, 48–51). Single agents such as cisplatin, methotrexate, bleomycin, doxorubicin, 5-fluorouracil, mitomycin C, and cyclophosphamide have yielded partial responses. The most effective agent is cisplatin with objective response rates ranging from 33 to 45% (48–50). The use of cisplatin is frequently restricted in a population, mostly elderly, with renal insufficiency and frequent complications of obstructive uropathy (7). Mitomycin C, a modestly nephrotoxic agent, has previously been reported to be effective in the treatment of bladder carcinoma. Early and associated (6) described a 21% response rate in 1973. Varying response rates ranging from 10 to 33% have been reported since then (6). Response rates with doxorubicin have varied greatly, with initial reports of 36% (51). The CISCA protocol consisting of cisplatin, cyclophosphamide, and doxorubicin (Adriamycin) has been successful for palliation and partial response (38). With pulmonary metastases, there is a 61% response rate, whereas for all other sites it is 30%. The median survival time is 40 weeks when CISCA is used (33).

Harker and colleagues (8) with a combination of cisplatin, methotrexate, and vinblastine showed a 56% response rate (28% complete response rate). Sternberg et al. (37) reported a 67% response rate with a 40% complete remission rate with a combination of methotrexate, vinblastine, doxorubicin, and cisplatin (37).

Intra-Arterial Therapy

In 1961, Byron et al. (2) reported on their experience with intra-arterial infusion of ten patients with bladder cancer who failed to respond. The use of intra-arterial chemotherapy was reported by Nevin et al. (25), who also surgically implanted catheters into each internal iliac artery. 5-fluorouracil was infused for 10 days and then every other week for 3 months, when it was given as an adjunct to radiation therapy. Regression of local disease was seen in six of ten patients. A mean survival time of 25 months was noted in the complete responders. The effect of intra-arterial mitomycin C was described by Ogata et al. (26). Fourteen of the 28 patients responded but, because of the dosage, myelosuppression and local irritation were significant (26).

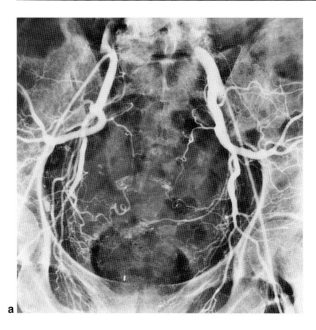
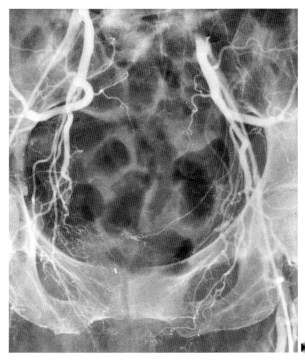

Fig. 5   Carcinoma of the urinary bladder
a A relatively hypervascular carcinoma of the bladder: before intra-arterial chemotherapy
b After three courses of infusion chemotherapy, there is a dramatic decrease in tumor vascularity and reduction of tumor

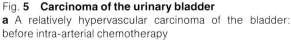

With the introduction of newer agents and the percutaneous approach, patients with stage D carcinomas of the bladder were treated at our hospital by a combination of intra-arterial and intravenous chemotherapy (4, 18–21, 43).

Anatomic Considerations. The bladder is supplied by the superior and inferior vesical arteries, derived from the anterior trunk of the internal iliac artery. With anatomic variation, the vesical arteries may originate from the obturator and inferior gluteal arteries, and in the female additional branches are derived from the uterine and vaginal arteries (46). When the neoplasm extends to adjacent soft tissues, viscera, and pelvic lymph nodes, the vascular supply to the whole pelvis is included in the territory to be infused (Fig. **5**).

Clinical Experience

Group I. In the initial group of 18 patients treated by intra-arterial cisplatin alone, nine (50%) experienced a symptom-free survival of more than 100 weeks (Fig. **3**).

Group II. The second group of 29 patients received intra-arterial 5-fluorouracil, and doxorubicin and mitomycin C were added intravenously. Seventeen (58.6%) achieved an objective response with a median survival time of 52 weeks compared with 28 weeks for the 12 nonresponders (18, 20, 21).

Group III. These encouraging results stimulated the most recent trial in 38 patients with locally advanced bladder carcinoma or with nodal metastases who were treated with combined intravenous and intra-arterial CISCA chemotherapy. Twelve patients were unresectable and 26 patients had lymph node metastases. Histologically, 29 patients had transitional cell carcinoma, seven patients with transformation to a histologic subtype of transitional cell carcinoma, and two patients had squamous cell carcinoma. Those patients with locally advanced disease received three cycles of intra-arterial infusion combined with intravenous CISCA therapy spaced 1 month apart. Patients with additional nodal metastases outside of the pelvis received intravenous chemotherapy initially, followed by intra-arterial infusion into each internal iliac artery (18, 20, 21).

Chemotherapy. Cyclophosphamide ($650 \, mg/m^2$) and doxorubicin ($50 \, mg/m^2$) were delivered intravenously on the day of catheter placement. The next day after adequate hydration, intra-arterial cisplatin (75 to $100 \, mg/m^2$) was infused along with intravenous mannitol ($40 \, g$) for diuresis. Each intra-arterial line was maintained with $7500 \, U$ of aqueous heparin for a total dose of $15,000 \, U$ over each 24-hour period.

Results. An overall complete remission rate of 50% was achieved with an 18% objective pelvic response rate; 32% failed to respond to chemotherapy

(Fig. 3). Responses by histologic subtypes revealed that patients with pure transitional cell carcinoma had a 62% complete remission rate. Those patients with transformation had 14% complete remission, and neither of the two patients with squamous cell carcinoma responded to this chemotherapy. A significant difference in the incidence of responses among patients with transitional cell carcinoma and those with transformation was seen (p <0.02). Complete remissions were independent of the site of disease. Nineteen patients achieved a complete remission with a mean duration of 86 weeks and a median of 81 weeks (range, 33 to 172) (18–21).

Complications. The toxicity with this regimen was moderate. Two patients had cardiac toxicity, defined as a greater than 10% decrease in ejection fraction, but no patient had symptomatic cardiac toxicity from doxorubicin. Renal toxicity, a greater than 0.4 mg/dl increase in the baseline serum creatinine level, occurred in four patients but did not require dialysis. Ten to 15% of the patients developed pain in the distribution of the sciatic nerve requiring continuous pain medication for a prolonged period up to 6 months. A clinical hearing loss occurred in four patients and peripheral neuropathy was experienced by three patients. Two patients had asymptomatic occlusion of the internal iliac arteries. Infectious complications, most frequently in the urinary tract, were found in 7.4% of patients whose courses were associated with a culture-negative leukopenic fever and 16% with culture-positive infections.

Comment

Intra-arterial chemotherapy is for those patients with advanced carcinoma of the bladder in whom the pelvic component of the disease represents the major tumor population or in whom there is residual disease after successful control of diffuse metastases.

For patients seen initially with hydronephrosis, percutaneous nephrostomies are performed by the radiologist to preserve renal function before chemotherapy, especially if cisplatin is to be given.

External Genitalia

Carcinoma of the penis, almost invariably squamous cell carcinoma, accounts for less than 1% of malignancies in men in the United States. Tumors of the male urethra are extremely rare, with only about 450 cases recorded. Transitional cell carcinoma, adenocarcinoma, and squamous cell carcinoma are dependent on the specific site of origin. Surgery and radiation therapy comprise the treatment of choice for the primary lesion and the regional ilio-inguinal lymph node metastases (10, 29, 31, 34, 36). In the event of local or regional recurrent squamous cell carcinoma of the penis and urethra, intra-arterial chemotherapy has been used by the percutaneous approach.

Carcinoma of the vulva comprises about 3 to 4% of all female primary genital malignancies. Ninety percent of vulvar cancers are squamous cell carcinomas. Other malignancies include basal cell carcinoma, adenocarcinoma of the Bartholin duct and gland, Paget's disease, melanoma and sarcoma (23, 36). Thus far, intra-arterial therapy has been reserved for recurrent or metastatic disease.

Anatomic Considerations. The internal pudendal artery, a terminal branch of the anterior division of the internal iliac artery supplies the external genitalia. With extension to inguinal and iliac nodes, additional supply originates from the obturator branch of the internal iliac artery, the inferior epigastric from the external iliac artery, and the superficial epigastric and the superficial and deep external pudendal branches from the common femoral artery.

Technical Considerations. Contralateral puncture of each femoral artery and catheterization of each branch of the vascular supply to the neoplasm can be accomplished with an exaggerated cobra catheter configuration. Ispilateral puncture and catheterization is possible by forming a long reverse curve configuration.

At times, redistribution of supply can be accomplished by selective occlusion of the smaller branches of the common femoral arteries so that the entire neoplasm can be infused from the bilateral anterior divisions of the internal iliac arteries. If this is not possible, only a portion of the tumor can be treated on each occasion. Another alternative is the injection of a bolus of the chemotherapeutic agent or combination of agents into each vessel dividing the total dose according to the estimated percentage of supply.

Chemotherapy. Cisplatin (100 to 120 mg/m^2) and bleomycin (30 mg/m^2) are delivered sequentially over a 24-hour period while cyclophosphamide (650 mg/m^2) is administered intravenously. This combination is repeated at monthly intervals. The effectiveness of these agents should be obvious after the first infusion. If uncertain, a second infusion should be done before changing therapy.

Clinical Experience

Our experience with percutaneous intra-arterial transcatheter chemotherapy in patients with recurrent carcinoma of the penis, urethra, and vulva is limited. It is as yet too soon to evaluate the response rate. The longest disease-free follow-up is 1.5 years (Figs. **6, 7**).

Melanoma of the external genitalia is a rare tumor with a poor prognosis. Malignant melanoma of the vulva is usually treated by radical vulvectomy, bilat-

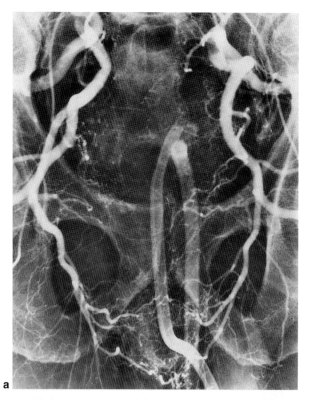

a

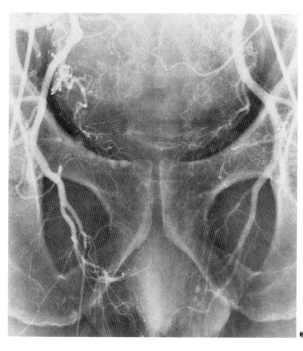

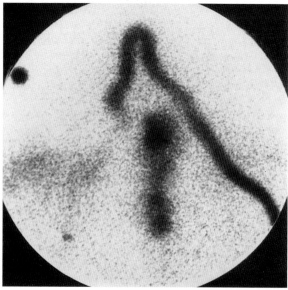

b

Fig. **6**   **Carcinoma of the penis**
a Hypervascular carcinoma of the penis supplied by the internal pudendal arteries
b Scintigraphy: injection of technetium-99m-macroaggregated albumin at a rate of 50 ml/h demonstrates the expected distribution of the infusion
c After intra-arterial chemotherapy, there is a marked improvement

eral inguinal node dissection, and at times a pelvic lymphadenopathy, yielding a 5-year survival of 50% (23). Two patients have received intra-arterial (internal iliac artery) cisplatin and dacarbazine (12). One had an excellent remission. She subsequently received external beam radiotherapy with a complete disappearance of the tumor. The other patient had an objective response and her residual disease is to be surgically excised.

Genitourinary Hemorrhage

Hemorrhage from neoplasms of the genitourinary tract has been successfully treated by the percutaneous transcatheter approach. Chronic bleeding is at times readily controlled by intra-arterial chemotherapy. Acute hemorrhage is more effectively managed by intra-arterial embolization or chemoembolization. Bleeding caused by radiation can be controlled by bilateral internal iliac artery embolization in 50% of patients (1, 16, 35).

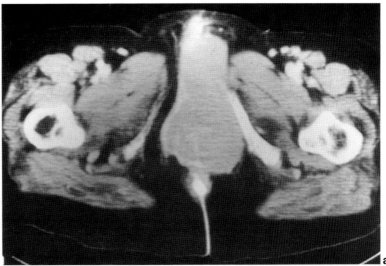

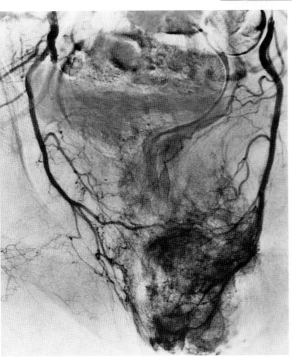

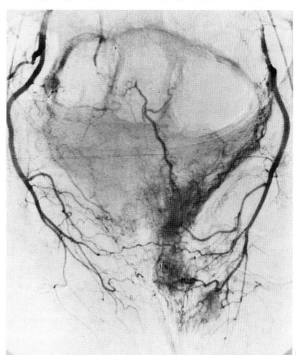

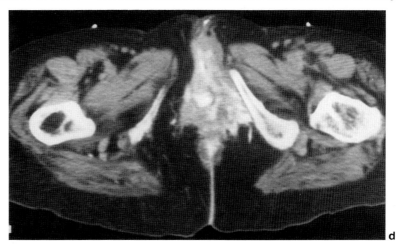

Fig. **7 Carcinoma of the vulva**
a Computed tomography demonstrates a mass in the vulva
b Bilateral internal pudendal arteriography opacifies the hypervascular carcinoma
c Bilateral internal pudendal arteriography after one course of intra-arterial chemotherapy reveals a dramatic decrease in vascularity and a response to treatment
d CT-angio at the same time as **c.** The accumulation of contrast material in the responding neoplasm confirms the distribution of the infusion

References

1. Bree RL, Goldstein HM, Wallace S. Transcatheter embolization of the internal iliac artery in the management of neoplasms of the pelvis. Surg Gynecol Obstet 1976;143:597–601.
2. Byron RL Jr, Perez FM, Yonemoto RH, Bierman HR, Gildenhorn HL, Kelly KH. Left brachial arterial catheterization for chemotherapy in advanced intra-abdominal malignant neoplasms. Surg Gynecol Obstet 1961;112:689–696.
3. Carlson JA, Freedman RS, Wallace S, Chuang VP, Wharton JT, Rutledge FN. Intra-arterial cisplatinum in the management of squamous cell carcinoma of the uterine cervix. Gynecol Oncol 1981;12:92–98.
4. Chong CDK. Bladder cancer: management of advanced disease. Tex Med 1987;83:51–54.
5. Cromer JK, Bateman JC, Berry GN, Kennelly JM, Klopp CT, Platt LI. Use of intra-arterial nitrogen mustard therapy in the treatment of cervical and vaginal cancer. Am J Obstet Gynecol 1952;63:538–548.
6. Early K, Elias EG, Mittleman A, Albert D, Murphy GP. Mitomycin C in the treatment of metastatic transitional cell carcinoma of the urinary bladder. Cancer 1973;31:1150–1153.
7. Hardaker WT, Stone RA, McCoy R. Platinum nephrotoxicity. Cancer 1974;34:1030–1032.
8. Harker WG, Meyers FJ, Freiha FS, Palmer J, Shortliffe LD, Hannigan JF, McWhirter KM, Frank MT. Cisplatin, methotrexate and vinblastine (CMV): an effective chemotherapy regimen for metastatic transitional cell carcinoma of the urinary tract: a Northern California Oncology Group study. J Clin Oncol 1985;3:1463–1470.
9. Hulka JF, Bissel NF. Combined intra-arterial chemotherapy and radiation treatment for advanced cervical carcinoma. Am J Obstet Gynecol 1965;91:486–490.
10. Jackson SM. The treatment of carcinoma of the penis. Br J Surg 1966;53:33–35.
11. Kaplan WD, D'Orsi CJ, Ensminger WD, Smith EH, Levin DC. Intra-arterial radionuclide infusion: a new technique to assess chemotherapy perfusion patterns. Cancer Treat Rep 1978;62:699–703.
12. Kavanaugh JJ. Regional chemotherapeutic approaches to the management of pelvic malignancies. Cancer Bull 1984;36:52–55.
13. Kim EE, Haynie TP, Wright KC, Lamki L, Wallace S, Gianturco C. Pulsatile versus steady infusion for hepatic chemotherapy. (Abstract). J Nucl Med 1984;25:41.
14. Krakoff IN, Sullivan RD. Intra-arterial nitrogen mustard in the treatment of pelvic cancer. Ann Intern Med 1956;48:839–850.
15. Kedia KR, Gibbons C, Persky L. The management of advanced bladder carcinoma. J Urol 1981;125:658–665.
16. Kobayashi I, Kusano S, Matsubayashi T, Uchida T. Selective embolization of the vesical artery in the management of massive bladder hemorrhage. Radiology 1980;136:345–348.
17. Lifshitz S, Railsback LD, Buchsbaum HJ. Intra-arterial pelvic infusion chemotherapy in advanced gynecologic cancer. Obstet Gynecol 1978;52:476–480.
18. Logothetis CJ, Samuels ML. Intra-arterial chemotherapy for malignant urothelial tumors. Cancer Bull 1984;36:47–52.
19. Logothetis C, Samuels M, Ogden S, Dexeus F, Johnson D, Swanson D, von Eschenbach A. Adjuvant chemotherapy for invasive bladder carcinoma: a preliminary report, meeting abstract. Proc Am Soc Clin Oncol 1985;4:108.
20. Logothetis CJ, Samuels ML, Odgen S, Dexeus F, Swanson D, Johnson DE, von Eschenbach A. Cyclophosphamide, doxorubicin and cisplatin chemotherapy for patients with locally advanced urothelial tumors with or without nodal metastases. J Urol 1985;134:460–464.
21. Logothetis CJ, Samuels ML, Wallace S, Chuang VP, Trindade A, Grant C, Haynie TP, Johnson DE. Management of pelvic complications of malignant urothelial tumors with combined intra-arterial and IV chemotherapy. Cancer Treat Rep 1982;66:1501–1507.
22. Miller LS. Preoperative irradiation for bladder cancer: the 2,000 versus 5,000 rad controversy. In: Johnson DE, Samuels ML, eds. Cancer of the urinary tract. New York: Raven 1979;81–88.
23. Morrow CP, Rutledge FN. Melanoma of the vulva. Obstet Gynecol 1972;39:745–752.
24. Morrow CP, DiSala PJ, Mangan CF, Lagasse LD. Continuous pelvic arterial infusion with bleomycin for squamous carcinoma of the cervix recurrent after irradiation therapy. Cancer Treat Rep 1977;61:1403–1405.
25. Nevin JE, Hoffman AA. Use of arterial infusion of 5-fluorouracil either alone or in combination with supervoltage radiation as a treatment for carcinoma of the prostate and bladder. Am J Surg 1975;130:544–549.
26. Ogata J, Migita N, Nakamura T. Treatment of carcinoma of the bladder by infusion of the anticancer agent (mitomycin C) via the internal iliac artery. J Urol 1973;110:667–670.
27. Ohta A. Basic and clinical studies on the simultaneous combination treatment of cervical cancer with a cytostatic agent and radiation. J Tokyo Med Coll 1978;36:529.
28. Oku T, Iwasaki M, Tojo S. Study on surgical chemotherapy for advanced cancer of the uterine cervix: particularly on the problem of clinical effect and drug concentration. Acta Obstet Gynaecol Jpn. 1979;31:1833.
29. Paulson DF, Perez CA, Anderson T. Cancer of the urethra and penis. In: DeVita VT Jr, Hellman S, Rosenberg SA, eds. Cancer: principles and practice of oncology. Philadelphia: Lippincott 1984:965–977.
30. Paunier JP, Delclos L, Fletcher GH. Causes, times of death and sites of failure in squamous cell carcinoma of the uterine cervix on intact uterus. Radiology 1967;85:555.
31. Ray B, Canto A, Whitmore WF Jr. Experience with primary carcinoma of the male urethra. J Urol 1977;117:591–594.
32. Richie JP, Shipley WV, Yagoda A. Bladder cancer. In: DeVita VT Jr, Hellman S, Rosenberg SA, eds. Cancer, principles and practice of oncology. Philadelphia: Lippincott 1984:915–928.
33. Samuels ML, Moran ME, Johnso DE, Bracken RB. CISCA combination chemotherapy for metastatic carcinoma of the bladder. In: Johnson DE, Samuels ML, eds. Cancer of the genitourinary tract. New York: Raven 1979:101–106.
34. Schelhammer PF, Spaulding JP. Carcinoma of the penis. In: Paulson DF, ed. Genitourinary surgery. Edinburgh: Churchill Livingstone 1983:629.
35. Schwartz PE, Goldstein HM, Wallace S, Rutledge F. Control of arterial hemorrhage using percutaneous arterial catheter technique in patients with gynecologic malignancy. Gynecol Oncol 1975;3:2760–2788.
36. Silverberg E. Cancer statistics. CA 1985;35:19–35.
37. Sternberg CN, Yagoda A, Scher HI, Watson RC, Hollander PS, Herr HW, Sogani PC, Morse MJ, Fair WR, Whitmore WF Jr. M-Vac: update of methotrexate (MTX), vinblastine (VLB), adriamycin (ADM), and cis-platinum (DDP) for urothelial tract cancer (Meeting Abstract). Proc Am Soc Clin Oncol 1985;4:105.
38. Sternberg JJ, Bracken RB. Combination chemotherapy (CISCA) for advanced urinary tract carcinoma: a preliminary report. JAMA 1977;238:2282–2287.
39. Sullivan RD, Wodd AM, Clifford P, Duff JK, Trussel R, Nary DK, Burchenal JH. Continuous intra-arterial methotrexate with simultaneous intermittent, intramuscular citrovorum factor therapy in carcinoma of the cervix. Cancer Chemother Rep 1960;8:1–6.
40. Swenerton KD, Evers JA, White GW, David A. Intermittent pelvic infusion with vincristine, bleomycin, and mitomycin C for advanced recurrent carcinoma of the cervix. Cancer Treat Rep 1979;63:1379–1381.
41. Torti FM, Harker WG. Chemotherapy of advanced transitional cell carcinoma of the uroepthelium. Cancer Chemother Pharmacol 1983;suppl2:51–54.
42. Trussel RR, de Mitford-Barberton GB. Carcinoma of the cervix treated with continuous intra-arterial methotrexate and intermittent intramuscular leucoxorin. Lancet 1981;1:971–972.
43. Wallace S, Chuang VP, Samuels ML, Johnson D. Transcatheter intra-arterial infusion of chemotherapy in advanced bladder cancer. Cancer 1982;49:640–645.
44. Wallace S, Medellin H, De Jongh DS, Gianturco C. Systemic heparinization for angiography. AJR 1972;116:204–209.
45. Whitmore WF, Batata MA. Preoperative irradiation with cystectomy for bladder cancer. In: Johnson DE, Samuels ML,

eds. Cancer of the genitourinary tract. New York: Raven 1977:89–100.

46. Woods D, Bechtel W, Charnsangavej C, Haynie TP, Kim EE, Carrasco CH, Wallace S. Gluteal artery occlusion: intra-arterial chemotherapy of pelvic neoplasms. Radiology 1985;155:341–343.

47. Wright KC, Wallace S, Kim EE, Haynie TP, Charnsangavej C, Chuang VP, Gianturco C. Pulsed arterial infusions: chemotherapeutic implications. Cancer 1986;57:1952–1956.

48. Yagoda A. Chemotherapy for advanced urothelial tract cancer: clinical cancer. Briefs 1984;6:13–24.

49. Yagoda A. Progress in chemotherapy for cancers of the urothelium. Urology 1984;23(suppl4):118–123.

50. Yagoda A, Watson RC, Gonzalez-Vitale JC, Grabstald H, Whitmore WF. Cisdiamminedichloroplatinum (II) in advanced bladder cancer. Cancer Treat Rep 1976;60:917–923.

51. Yagoda A, Watson RC, Whitmore WF, Grabstald H, Middleman MP, Krakoff IH. Adriamycin in advanced urinary tract cancer: experience in 42 patients and a review of the literature. Cancer 1977;39:279–285.

Bone Tumors

C. H. Carrasco, C. Charnsangavej, W. R. Richli and S. Wallace

Regional modes of treatment consisting of intra-arterial chemotherapy, arterial embolization, and intralesional injection of methylprednisolone are used with favorable results in the treatment of osteosarcoma, unresectable giant cell tumors, and eosinophilic granuloma, respectively.

Osteosarcoma

Osteosarcoma is an entity that comprises several subtypes of malignant bone-forming tumors that vary in their degree of aggressiveness. The high-grade intramedullary subtypes include the conventional (fibroblastic, chondroblastic, and osteoblastic), the small cell, and the telangiectatic osteosarcomas. These subtypes affect males slightly more frequently than females and have their peak incidence in the second decade of life. They occur most frequently in the metaphyses of the distal femur, the proximal tibia, and the proximal humerus. The etiology of osteosarcoma is unknown, but Paget's disease and radiation are known precursors in some instances.

Therapy

For many years, radical surgery was the principal mode of therapy for primary osteosarcoma and it generally yielded survival rates of approximately 20% (20). Radiation therapy, used for local control (6, 31, 33) and possibly for changed tumor cell viability to prevent implantation of cells dislodged during surgery, did not yield better results (20). The development of clinically apparent pulmonary metastases soon after potentially curative surgery (30, 38) suggests that in most patients osteosarcoma is microscopically disseminated at the time of diagnosis.

It has been demonstrated that various chemotherapeutic agents have activity against osteosarcoma (11, 18, 21, 24, 26, 44, 47, 55, 56). Their administration after resection of the primary tumor to treat the presumed microscopic metastases has been considered to be the prime reason for prolongation of disease-free survival in various series (12, 57). Moreover, advances achieved with chemotherapy have facilitated local resection with limb salvage rather than amputation (29, 37, 40, 51, 53). Preoperative chemotherapy and delayed surgery are used to treat the primary tumor and identify an effective chemotherapeutic agent for adjuvant therapy based on the degree of tumor necrosis (23, 49, 51). Rosen et al. (52) using a combination of various drugs, reported a 92% continuous disease-free survival rate for a median of 2 years in a group of 79 patients.

Intra-Arterial Chemotherapy

In an attempt to improve on the results of intravenously administered chemotherapeutic agents, some of these drugs were infused intra-arterially (1, 15, 25, 28, 29). In one study conducted at M. D. Anderson Hospital and Tumor Institute, cisplatin was demonstrated to be efficacious in osteosarcoma (2, 3, 4, 7, 16, 19, 27, 43, 44, 48, 50, 54) and was administered intra-arterially to 17 patients with osteosarcoma. The levels of the drug in the vein draining the region of the neoplasm, reflecting the local concentration, were higher than those of a peripheral vein, reflecting the systemic concentration (25).

Currently, preoperative intra-arterial cisplatin is administered to patients with localized osteosarcomas at M. D. Anderson Hospital and Tumor Institute to treat the primary tumor and determine the efficacy of this agent for adjuvant therapy. In this manner, the primary tumor is also downstaged so that a larger number of skeletally mature patients are able to undergo limb salvage surgery rather than amputation (5). Patients younger than 16 years of age receive seven courses of intra-arterial cisplatin alone spaced every 2 weeks. Older patients receive, in addition, intravenous doxorubicin before each of three to six courses of intra-arterial cisplatin.

Vigorous hydration with intravenous fluids is started on the night before the administration of cisplatin and continued for 24 hours afterward. Mannitol diuresis is obtained throughout the course of the infusion. Cisplatin at a dose of 120 to 200 mg/m^2 is diluted in 300 ml of 3% saline solution and administered intra-arterially over 2 to 24 hours.

Technical Considerations

Catheterization in the pediatric patients is done under general anesthesia, whereas in the older patients mild sedation and local anesthesia suffice. In patients with lower extremity tumors, the catheter is inserted via the contralateral femoral artery. The patients are anticoagulated immediately after insertion of the catheter with heparin 50 U/kg, and an equal dose is administered during the course of the infusion of cisplatin over 2 hours.

The catheters used should be of the smallest caliber that will allow a safe and atraumatic procedure to minimize the risk of thrombosis. We use 3.5 Fr catheters in the pediatric patients and 5 Fr catheters in older patients. In children, straight guide wires decrease the risk of vascular spasm.

Straight catheters are used to decrease the risk of chemotherapy-induced endothelial injury, which may occur when the tip of curved catheters rests on the vessel wall. A deflector wire is used to advance the catheter over the aortic bifurcation into the contralateral common iliac artery. For upper extremity neoplasms, the catheter's tip is preshaped in a gentle curve to engage the brachiocephalic vessels.

The tip of the arterial catheter should be placed proximal to the multiple branches, including hypertrophied periosteal-cortical arteries, that usually supply osteosarcomas. Laminar flow produces streaming and inadequate mixing of the infused solution with the flowing blood, which may result in inhomogeneous distribution leading to necrosis of normal tissue. Streaming can be altered with the use of a pulsatile pump (Gianturco) which creates turbulence and better mixing as the infusion exits the catheter's tip and thus a more homogeneous distribution of the infused drug. When a dominant vessel provides most of the blood flow to a tumor, it should be selectively infused at least once to achieve a greater cytotoxic effect (Fig. 1).

The main blood supply to osteosarcomas in the proximal femur is provided by the femoral circumflex arteries, branches of the deep femoral artery. Frequently, the segment of the deep femoral artery proximal to the origin of the circumflex arteries is so short that a catheter in this position is unstable and may dislodge into the superficial femoral artery resulting in an inadequate infusion. This is best avoided by placing the catheter's tip in the external iliac segment.

Osteosarcomas in the femoral diaphysis usually receive their blood supply from branches of both the superficial and deep femoral arteries, which requires alternating the infusions between these two vessels or infusing in the external iliac segment to cover the entire neoplasm. Proximal humeral osteosarcomas receive a predominant portion of their blood supply from the circumflex humeral arteries, which should be selectively infused at least once.

Evaluation of Response

Increasing reactive calcification and decrease in the soft tissue mass will be apparent by plain radiography and CT as the tumor regresses, but these features are not predictive of the degree of histologic tumor necrosis, which has significant prognostic implications for survival. On the other hand, total disappearance of the angiographic tumor vascularity (Fig. 2) usually translates into more than 90% histologic tumor necrosis, whereas residual tumor vascularity usually represents persistence of significant viable tumor (Fig. 3). Increase in the size of the tumor almost always indicates progression. After resection, the degree of tumor necrosis is assessed histologically with emphasis on the areas of residual angiographic vascularity. The most important predictor of prolonged continuous disease-free survival is the degree of response to preoperative chemotherapy. Patients with at least 90% tumor necrosis had a continuous disease-free survival at a minimum follow-up of 2 years of 91% compared with 14% for those with lesser degrees of necrosis.

Results

Pain relief occurs in most patients within days of the initial administration of cisplatin. Limb salvage surgery was possible in 24 of the initial 40 patients treated, whereas before preoperative chemotherapy, only six patients were considered candidates for the procedure. Currently, approximately 80% of our skeletally mature patients undergo limb salvage procedures. Sixty-five adult patients treated with preoperative intra-arterial cisplatin and systemic doxorubicin since 1980 were evaluated. Surgery was followed with adjuvant chemotherapy of doxorubicin and cisplatin until cisplatin toxicity and then changed to doxorubicin and dacarbazine. Since 1983, patients with less than 90% tumor necrosis in the resected specimen received high-dose methotrexate and bleomycin, cyclophosphamide, and dactinomycin. The overall disease-free survival is 65% and is superior to our historical controls (20%). The 28 patients treated since 1983 have a 75% disease-free

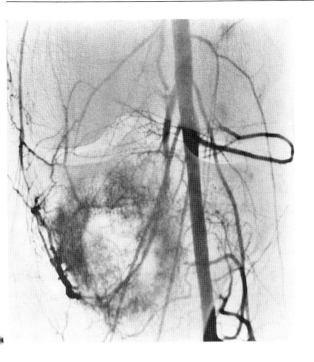

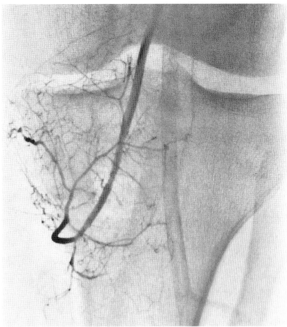

b

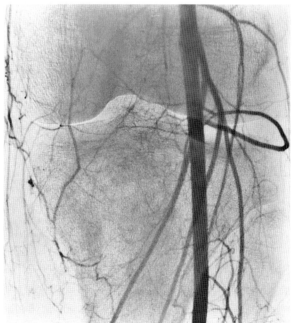

Fig. **1 Osteosarcoma of the proximal tibia. a** Popliteal arteriogram demonstrates a dominant inferior genicular artery supplying the tumor
b The dominant vessel was catheterized at the time of the second course of intra-arterial cisplatin
c Popliteal angiography before the third course of chemotherapy demonstrates occlusion of the genicular artery previously catheterized and total disappearence of the tumor vascularity. Greater than 90% tumor necrosis was observed in the resected specimen

c

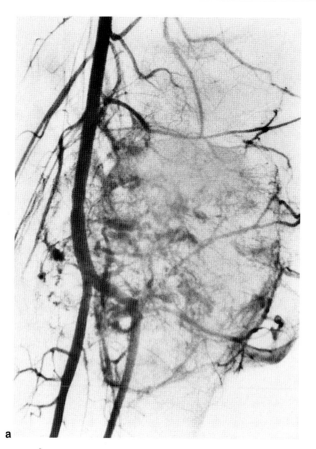
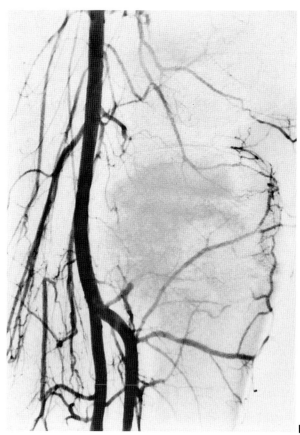

a   b

Fig. **2** **Osteosarcoma of the proximal tibia. a** Popliteal angiography demonstrates abundant tumor vascularity before treatment
b Complete disappearence of the tumor vascularity after two courses of chemotherapy. Histologic necrosis in the resected specimen was greater than 90%

survival at 2 years compared with 62% for those treated between 1979 and 1982.

Giant Cell Tumor of Bone

Giant cell tumor of bone is a locally aggressive neoplasm that affects women more frequently than men and has its peak incidence in the third decade of life, rarely occurring before the epiphyseal plate is united. The tumor is generally benign but has a high incidence (50%) of local recurrence after curettage and packing with bone. Rarely, giant cell tumors may give rise to distant metastases.

Embolization of Unresectable Giant Cell Tumors

Surgery is the treatment of choice for giant cell tumors. Radiation therapy is not frequently used because these tumors may undergo malignant transformation. Giant cell tumors involving the spine are relatively rare and occur more frequently in the sacrum, where surgical excision is often incomplete and associated with a high incidence of local recurrence. Alternative modes of therapy for unresectable giant cell tumors have included irradiation and embolization.

Embolization of skeletal neoplasms was initially performed as an adjunct to surgical resection for hypervascular tumors to decrease operative blood loss (8, 13, 22). Subsequently, this technique was used for palliation of pain caused by skeletal metastases (17) and later it was extended to management of patients with certain benign bone tumors, including giant cell tumors, who had failed other therapeutic modalities (9, 14, 32, 41, 58). Since giant cell tumors are very vascular, preoperative embolization has also been used to decrease intraoperative blood loss.

Technique

Angiography is performed to determine the tumor's vascular supply. For tumors located in the

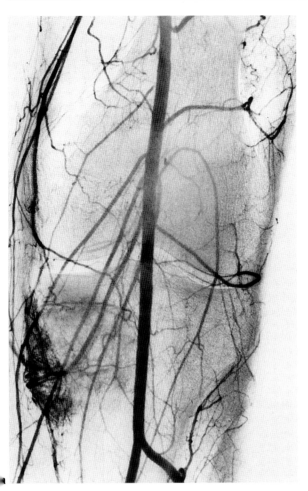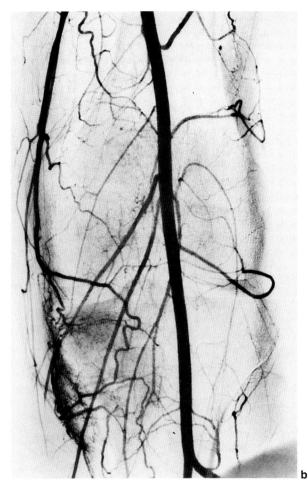

Fig. 3   **Proximal tibial osteosarcoma. a** Popliteal angiography before chemotherapy demonstrates tumor vascularity
b Popliteal angiography after three courses of chemotherapy, including one selective genicular infusion, demonstrates
persistent tumor vascularity. The resected specimen demonstrated almost no chemotherapy effect

thoracolumbar area, intercostal and lumbar angiography, including the level above and below the lesion, should be performed, particularly in patients previously operated on in whom vessels might have been ligated. An attempt to identify the anterior spinal artery, usually originating between the 10th thoracic and the 2nd lumbar levels on the left, should be made in each case. It should be stressed that failure to identify this vessel does not preclude the possibility of spinal cord injury. Sacral giant cell tumors receive their blood supply from branches of both internal iliac arteries, the middle sacral artery, and both 4th lumbar arteries.

Our preferred embolic materials are Ivalon 150 to 590 µm particles and Gelfoam pieces. On occasions, we have used dehydrated ethanol. Since partial reconstitution of the tumor's blood flow occurs invariably, the medium-sized arteries supplying the tumor should be maintained patent so that collateral flow will originate from these vessels rather than from adjacent vascular territories. Reembolization through the original feeding vessels is less difficult and probably more effective than embolization through far removed collaterals.

The procedure is performed at monthly intervals until symptomatic improvement occurs. The embolizations are then spaced at longer intervals, depending on the clinical course; repeat embolizations should be performed when recurrence of symptoms occurs. Embolization as a therapeutic alternative should be abandoned when there is no evidence of a clinical or radiologic response.

Results

Twenty-one patients with unresectable giant cell tumors were treated with arterial embolization during a period of 9 years. The tumors were located in the sacrum in 9, the thoraco-lumbar spine in 3, the ilium in 3, and involved both sacrum and ilium in 6 patients. Eighteen patients had received prior therapy, consisting of chemotherapy, irradiation, or surgery.

Ten patients (48%) had complete disappearance of their symptoms. Radiographic signs of healing consisting of reactive calcification at the periphery and in the center of the tumor (Fig. **4**) were noted in all of these patients. The median follow-up time was 2.5 months, ranging from 1 to 7 years. Recurrence of symptoms at an average of 45 months occurred in 4 patients. After reembolization, three of these patients were again rendered asymptomatic. One patient did not respond to reembolization and continued to progress after more than 3 years of an excellent response. Four patients (19%) had partial relief of their symptoms and two patients relapsed at 5 and 30 months, respectively. 5 of the 21 patients failed embolization, 4 of whom were dead at a median of 16 months after the initial embolization. 2 patients were lost to follow-up.

After embolization, seven patients received chemotherapy or irradiation. One patient underwent subsequent surgery for an iliac tumor that responded to embolization.

Complications

Apart from the side-effects of the embolization consisting of nausea, vomiting, low-grade fever, and pain, there were few complications. Ischemic neuropathy resulted in foot drop and foot numbness in three patients. One patient developed mild signs of rectal ischemia, which resolved without sequelae after embolization of the superior hemorrhoidal artery and both internal iliac arteries. One patient with a moderate but brief response died suddenly 10 days after reembolization for a relapse. An autopsy failed to reveal the cause of death.

Eosinophilic Granuloma of Bone

Eosinophilic granuloma (35, 46) is a distinct clinical and pathologic entity that represents the benign, localized form of histiocytosis X, which also includes the disseminated forms, Hand-Schüller-Christian disease and Letterer-Siwe disease (34). This unifying concept, however, has been questioned by some investigators who consider these entities separate despite certain histologic similarities (36, 39, 45).

Eosinophilic granuloma constitutes approximately 50 to 60% of all cases of histiocytosis X and is usually localized to one bone but occasionally affects several sites. It occurs during the first three decades of life and its highest incidence is in male children between the ages of 5 and 10 years. The lesions most frequently involve the skull and femur in patients younger than 20 years and the ribs and mandible in patients more than 20 years. Its etiology remains unknown.

The presenting symptom is usually pain in the area of the lesion that may be associated with a palpable or visible mass. The roentgenologic features usually consist of an osteolytic defect and periosteal reaction that may resemble a malignant bone tumor.

Intralesional Injection of Methylprednisolone

Although spontaneous healing of eosinophilic granulomas is known to occur, it usually requires some form of therapy. Isolated lesions have been treated succesfully with curettage or moderate doses of radiation therapy. Antineoplastic chemotherapy has also been used in some instances. Intralesional injection of methylprednisolone (10) constitutes an alternative mode of treatment.

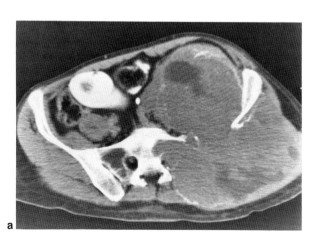 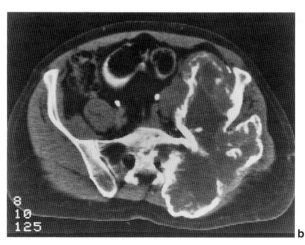

Fig. **4   Large iliac giant cell tumor. a** Computed tomography before the initial embolization

b Decrease in size and increased mineralized of the tumor noted after eight embolizations, 2 years later

Technique

After identification of a lesion suspected of representing an eosinophilic granuloma based on the clinical and roentgenographic findings, a percutaneous needle biopsy is performed under fluoroscopic guidance. General anesthesia is required in children, whereas local anesthesia suffices in the older patients. If the overlying cortex is intact, it is perforated with a small drill bit, and a spinal-type needle (18 to 20 G) is introduced through the orifice. Tissue is aspirated for cytologic analysis, and once the diagnosis is confirmed methylprednisolone sodium succinate, 125 mg, is infiltrated into the lesion.

Results

Twelve patients with 14 lesions in a series of 50 patients with eosinophilic granuloma were treated with intralesional injections of methylprednisolone sodium succinate at our hospital (42). Two patients required two injections. All patients treated experienced relief of pain within the first 1 to 2 weeks after the injection and did not require any additional therapy. Follow-up in 9 of the patients ranged from 25 to 48 months.

Radiographic features of healing occurred in all patients and were usually apparent 3 months after intralesional injection of methylprednisolone. These changes consisted of solidification of the periosteal reaction followed by a progressive decrease in the cortical thickening. The lytic area then gradually filled in with trabeculated bone attaining at times a completely normal architecture. Minimal cortical thickening may be the only residual evidence of the treated lesion (10, 42; Fig. 5).

The mechanism of action of intralesional injection of methylprednisolone in eosinophilic granuloma is not known, but the favorable results obtained have made it the therapeutic modality of choice in the management of isolated lesions at our hospital.

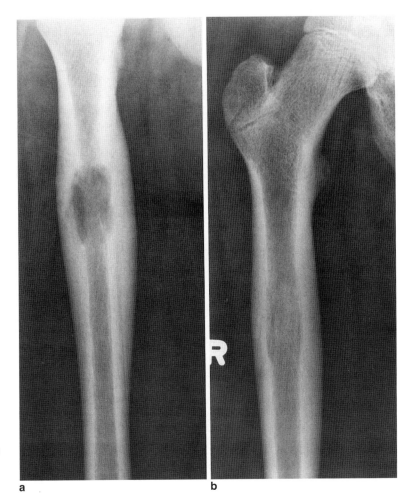

Fig. 5 **Eosinophilic granuloma in the femoral shaft. a** Before intralesional injection of methylprednisolone **b** Almost complete resolution of the lytic defect and the periosteal reaction are noted 1 year after treatment

a   b

References

1. Akahoshi Y, Takeuchi S, Chen S, Nishimoto T, Kikuike A, Yonezawa H, Yamamuro T. The results of surgical treatment combined with intra-arterial infusion of anti-cancer agents in osteosarcoma. Clin Ortho 1976;120:103–109.

2. Baum ES, Gynon P, Greenberg L, Krivit W, Hammond D. Phase II trial of cisplatin in refractory childhood cancer: children's cancer study group report. Cancer Treat Rep 1981;65:815–822.

3. Baum F, Greenberg L, Gaynon P. Use of cis-platinum diammine dichloride (CPDD) in osteogenic sarcoma (OS) in children. Proc Am Assoc Cancer Res and ASCO 1978;19:385.

4. Benjamin RS, Chuang VP, Wallace S. Preoperative chemotherapy for osteosarcoma (Abstract C-675). ASCO 1982;1:174.

5. Benjamin RS, Murray JA, Wallace S, Ayala A, Chawla SP, Raymond AK, Carrasco CH, Romsdahl MM, Papadopoulos NEJ, Plager C. Intra-arterial preoperative chemotherapy for osteosarcoma: a judicious approach to limb salvage. Cancer Bull 1984;36:32–36.

6. Cade S. Osteogenic sarcoma: a study based on 113 patients. J R Coll Surg Edinb 1955;1:79–111.

7. Calvo DB III, Patt YZ, Wallace S, Chuang VP, Benjamin RS, Pritchard JD, Hersh EM, Bodey GP, Mavligit GM. Phase I–II trial of percutaneous intra-arterial cis-diamminedichloroplatinum (II) for regionally confined malignancy. Cancer 1980;45:1278–1283.

8. Channon GM, William LA. Giant cell tumor of the ischium treated by embolization and resection: a case report. J Bone Joint Surg [B] 1982;64:164–165.

9. Chuang VP, Soo CS, Wallace S, Benjamin RS. Arterial occlusion: management of giant cell tumor and aneurysmal bone cyst. AJR 1981;136:1127–1130.

10. Cohen M, Zornoza J, Cangir A, Murray JA, Wallace S. Direct injection of methylprednisolone sodium succinate in the treatment of solitary eosinophilic granuloma of bone: a report of 9 cases. Radiology 1980;136:289–293.

11. Cortes EP, Holland JF, Wang JJ, Sinks LF, Blom J, Senn H, Bank A, Glidewell O. Amputation and adriamycin in primary osteosarcoma. N Engl J Med 1974;291:998–1000.

12. Cortes EP, Necheles TF, Holland JF, Glidewell O. Adriamycin (ADR) alone versus ADR and high dose methotrexate-citrovorum factor rescue (HDM-CFR) as adjuvant to operable primary osteosarcoma: a randomized study by cancer and leukemic group B (CALGB). Proc Am Assoc Cancer Res 1979;20:412.

13. Dick HM, Bigliani LU, Michelsen WJ, Johnston AD, Stinchfield FE. Adjuvant arterial embolization in the treatment of benign primary bone tumors in children. Clin Orthop 1979;139:133–141.

14. Eftekhari F, Wallace S, Chuang VP, Soo CS, Cangir A, Benjamin RS, Murray JA. Intra-arterial management of giant cell tumors of the spine in children. Pediat. Radiol 1982;12:289–293.

15. Eilber FR, Grant T, Morton DL. Adjuvant therapy for osteosarcoma: pre-operative treatment. Cancer Treat Rep 1978;62:213–216.

16. Ettinger LJ, Douglass HO Jr, Higby IJ, Mindell ER, Nime F, Ghoorah J, Freeman AI. Adjuvant adriamycin and cis-diammine-dichloroplatinum (cis-platinum) in primary osteosarcoma. Cancer 1981;47:248–254.

17. Feldman F, Casarella WJ, Dick HM, Hollander BA. Selective intra-arterial embolization of bone tumors. AJR 1975;123:130–139.

18. Finkelstein J, Hittle RE, Hammond UD. Evaluation of high dose cyclophosphamide regimen in childhood tumors. Cancer 1969;23:1239–1244.

19. Freeman AI, Ettinger LJ, Brecher ML. Cis-dichloro-diammineplatinum II in childhood cancer. Cancer Treat Rep 1979;63:1615–1620.

20. Friedman MA, Carter SK. The therapy of osteogenic sarcoma: current status and thoughts for the future. J Surg Oncol 1972;4:482–510.

21. Greesbeck HP, Cudmore JTP. Evaluation of 5-fluorouracil (5-FU) in surgical practice. Am Surg 1963;29:638–641.

22. Hilal SK, Michelsen JW. Therapeutic percutaneous embolization for extra-axial vascular lesions of the head, neck, and spine. J Neurosurg 1975;43:275–287.

23. Huvos AG, Rosen G, Marcove RC. Primary osteogenic sarcoma: pathologic aspects in 20 patients after treatment with chemotherapy, en bloc resection and prosthetic bone replacement. Arch Pathol Lab Med 1977;101:14–18.

24. Jaffe N. Osteogenic sarcoma: state of the art with high-dose methotrexate treatment. Clin Orthop 1976;120:95–102.

25. Jaffe N, Bowman R, Wang YM, Cangir A, Ayala A, Chuang V, Wallace S, Murray J. Chemotherapy for primary osteosarcoma by intra-arterial infusion: review of the literature and comparison with results achieved by the intravenous route. Cancer Bull 1984;36:37–42.

26. Jaffe N, Link M, Traggis D. The role of high-dose methotrexate in osteogenic sarcoma: sarcoma of soft tissue and bone in childhood. Nat Cancer Inst Monogr 1981;56:2101–2106.

27. Jaffe N, Knapp J, Chuang VP, Wallace S, Ayala A, Murray J, Cangir A, Wang A, Benjamin RS. Osteosarcoma: intra-arterial treatment of the primary tumor with cis-diamminedichloroplatinum II (CDP). Cancer 1983;51:402–407.

28. Jaffe N, Prudich J, Knapp J, Wang YM, Bowman R, Cangir A, Ayala A, Chuang V, Wallace S. Osteosarcoma: treatment of the primary tumor with intra-arterial high dose methotrexate (MTX-CF): pharmacokinetic, clinical, radiographic and pathologic studies (Abstract C-409). Proc Amer Assoc Cancer Res 1981;22:195.

29. Jaffe N, Watts H, Fellows KE, Vawter C. Local en bloc resection for limb preservation. Cancer Treat Rep 1978;62:217–223.

30. Jeffree CM, Price CHG, Sessons HA. The metastatic patterns of osteosarcoma. Br J Cancer 1975;32:87–107.

31. Jenkin RDT, Allt WEC, Fitzpatrick PJ. Osteosarcoma: an assessment of management with particular reference to primary irradiation and selective delayed amputation. Cancer 1972;30:393–400.

32. Keller FS, Rosch J, Bird CB. Percutaneous embolization of bony pelvic neoplasms with tissue adhesive. Radiology 1983;147:21–27.

33. Lee ES, Mackenzie DH. Osteosarcoma: a study of the value of preoperative megavoltage radiotherapy. Br J Surg 1964;51:252–274.

34. Lichtenstein L. Histiocytosis X: integration of eosinophilic granuloma of bone, "Letterer-Siwe disease", and "Schüller-Christian disease" as related manifestations of a single nosological entity. Arch Pathol Lab Med 1953;56:84–102.

35. Lichtenstein L, Jaffe JL. Eosinophilic granuloma of bone with report of a case. Am J Pathol 1940;16:595–604.

36. Lieberman PH, Jones CR, Dargeon HWK. A reappraisal of eosinophilic granuloma of bone, Hand-Schüller-Christian syndrome and Letterer-Siwe syndrome. Medicine (Baltimore) 1969;48:375–400.

37. Marcove RC. En bloc resection for osteogenic sarcoma. Can J Surg 1977;20:521–528.

38. Marcove RC, Mike V, Hajek JV, Levin AG, Hutter VP. Osteogenic sarcoma in childhood. NY STate J Med 1971;71:885–859.

39. McGavran MH, Spady HA. Eosinophilic granuloma of bone: a study of twenty-eight cases. J Bone Joint Surg [Am] 1960;42:979–992.

40. Morton DL, Eilber FR, Townsend CN, Grant TT, Mirra J, Weisenburger TH. Limb salvage from a multidisciplinary treatment approach for skeletal and soft tissue sarcomas of the extremity. Ann Surg 1976;184:268–278.

41. Murphy WA, Strecker WB, Schoenecker PL. Transcatheter embolization therapy of an ischial aneurysmal bone cyst. J Bone Joint Surg [Br] 1982;64:166–168.

42. Nauert C, Zornoza J, Ayala A, Harle TS. Eosinophilic granuloma of bone: diagnosis and management. Skeletal Radiol 1983;10:227–235.

43. Nitschke R, Starling KA, Vats T, Bryan H. Cis-diamminedichloroplatinum (NSC-119875) in childhood malignancies: a Southwest Oncology Group study. Med Pediatr Oncol 1978;4:127–132.

44. Ochs JJ, Freeman AI, Douglass HO, Higby DJ, Mindell R, Sinks T. Cis-dichloro-diammineplatinum (II) in advanced osteogenic sarcoma. Cancer Treat Rep 1978;62:239–245.

45. Otani S. A discussion on eosinophilic granuloma of bone, Letterer-Siwe disease and Schüller-Christian disease. J Mt Sinai Hosp 1957;24:1079–1092.
46. Otani S, Erlich JC. Solitary granuloma of bone simulating primary neoplasm Am J Pathol 1940;16:479–490.
47. Pinkel D. Cyclophosphamide in children with cancer. Cancer 1969;15:42–49.
48. Pratt CB, Hayes A, Green AA, Evans WE, Senzer N, Howarth CB, Ransom JL, Crom W. Pharmacokinetic evaluation of cisplatin in children with malignant solid tumors: a phase II study. Cancer Treat Rep 1981;65:1021–1026.
49. Rosen G, Caparros B, Huvos A, Kosloff MS, Nirenberg A, Cacavio A, Marcove RC, Lane JM, Mehta B, Urban C. Preoperative chemotherapy for osteogenic osteosarcoma: selection of postoperative adjuvant chemotherapy based on the response of the primary tumor to preoperative chemotherapy. Cancer 1982;49:1221–1230.
50. Rosen G, Caparros B, Nirenberg A, Cacavio A. Cisplatinum (DDP)-adriamycin (ADR) combination chemotherapy (CT) in evaluable osteogenic sarcoma (OS) [Abstract C-672]. ASCO 1982;1:173.
51. Rosen G, Marcove RC, Caparros B, Nirenberg A, Kosloff C, Huvos AG. Primary osteogenic sarcoma: the rationale for preoperative chemotherapy and delayed surgery. Cancer 1979;43:2163–2177.
52. Rosen G, Marcove RC, Huvos AG, Caparros BI, Lane JM, Nirenberg A, Cacavio A, Groshen S. Eight-year experience with adjuvant chemotherapy. J Cancer Res Clin Oncol 1983;106(suppl):55–67.
53. Rosen G, Murphy ML, Huvos AG, Guiterrez M, Marcove RC. Chemotherapy, en bloc resection and prosthetic bone replacement in the treatment of osteogenic sarcoma. Cancer 1976;37:1–11.
54. Rosen G, Nirenberg H, Caparros B, Juergens H, Tan C, Guiterrez M. Cisplatin in metastatic osteogenic sarcoma. In: Prestayko AW, Crooke ST, Carter SK, eds. Cisplatin: current status and new developments. New York: Academic Press 1980:465–475.
55. Sullivan MP, Sutow WW, Taylor G. L-phenylalanine mustard as treatment for osteogenic sarcoma in children. J Pediatr. 1963;63:227–237.
56. Sutow WW. Evaluation of dosage schedules of mitomycin C (NSC-26980) in children. Cancer Chemother Rep 1971;55:285–289.
57. Sutow WW, Sullivan MP, Wilbur JR, Cangir A. A study of adjuvant chemotherapy in osteogenic sarcoma. J Clin Pharmacol 1975;7:530–533.
58. Wallace S, Granmayeh M, de Santos LA, Murray JA, Romsdahl MM, Bracken RB, Jonsson K. Arterial occlusion of pelvic bone tumors. Cancer 1979;43:322–328.

Electrochemical Cancer Treatment

B. E. W. Nordenström

The mechanical transport of material in the blood and tissue fluid is known to be combined with transports via the capillary membranes produced by diffusion and by differences in hydrostatic and osmotic pressure. An endogenous system of electrical mass transport of material between organs and tissues has recently also been described (1, 2). This system can also be utilized for treatment of cancer. First, however, we must briefly describe how the electrical system of mass transport is powered and structured.

It was found that differences in electric charge occur between tissues as a result of differences in metabolic activity. They also occur between injured and non-injured tissue. Such differences develop in cancers as a result of internal necrosis or blood clots. The injury polarization of cancer is non-specific, and therefore useless in the differential diagnosis of the histological type of cancer. The degradation of a tissue injury will produce a levelling of the electric injury charge between the cancer and the surrounding tissue via the vascular-interstitial closed electric circuit (VICC), which is outlined in Fig. **1**. The VICC system is possible because the walls of arteries and veins are relatively insulating, surrounding the considerably more conductive blood plasma. At the level of the capillaries, ions can pass from the plasma to the interstitial tissue fluid, which closes the circuit. In this way blood vessels form a system for the structured transport of electric (ionic) current, while the interstitial fluid forms „unstructured" or variable

pathways for electric (ionic) current. Electric connections via the capillary membranes take place as electronic transport via segmentally contracted parts of arterial capillaries between the bloodstream and the interstitial tissue fluid, and as ionic transport through leaking pores between non-contracted endothelial cells of the capillaries. Electron transports by redox systems in the walls of the capillary endothelial cells is complex but well-established in the literature (1, 2).

Effects of Spontaneous Injury Polarization of Cancer

When a cancer produces electric polarization resulting from internal injury, the VICC system supplies pathways for the electric transport of ions and electrons in the walls of the contracted endothelial cells. The flow of electric current also leads to the development of structural modifications outside and inside cancers. Radiographically, we observe these as corona structures (1). These can be demonstrated in radiographs, theoretically explained and can be reproduced in experiments in vitro and in vivo. The corona structures may be seen as resulting from insufficient healing of cancerous lesions. It is understandable that a centrally developing necrosis of a cancer cannot lead to complete healing of the cancer, due to the persistence of viable cancer cells in the periphery which will continue to grow. This partly

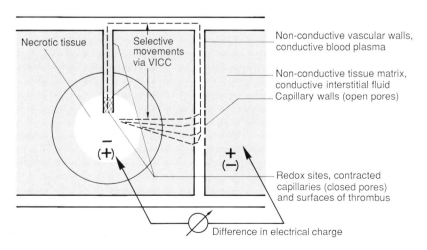

Fig. 1 Principles of the vascular-interstitial closed circuit
(simplified). Cancers often develop necrosis or bleeding which produces an electrical injury charge, a well-known concept, in relation to the surrounding tissue. The energy released is levelled over vessels and interstitial channels by ionic transport (the VICC system). In the circuit, "electrodes" are positioned as globular protein molecules in the cellular membranes of the endothelial cells. They are activated at segmental contractions of the arterial capillaries by the electric field which closes the ionic channels and interendothelial leaking effects of capillaries

Necrotic tissue

Selective movements via VICC

Non-conductive vascular walls, conductive blood plasma

Non-conductive tissue matrix, conductive interstitial fluid
Capillary walls (open pores)

Redox sites, contracted capillaries (closed pores) and surfaces of thrombus

Difference in electrical charge

depends on the development of new vessels. It has been shown in vitro in tissues that a flow of weak current ($\simeq 1$ µA) for several days can produce pathological "vessels" and "ducts" (1). Recently, it was possible for the first time to show accumulations of contrast medium around certain cancers of the lung, and sometimes around granulomas. In the opinion of the present author, this is due to the development of pathological vessels, which constitute important structures around polarizing lesions which develop by spontaneous necrosis, bleeding or infection, and supply blood to the growing periphery of the cancer.

Indications for Electrochemical Treatment of Cancer

This kind of cancer treatment is physicochemical in character, and might therefore be attempted in various organs. In order to accumulate a reasonable amount of information, only lung cancers and certain breast cancers have so far been treated. Many lung cancers are incurable by conventional techniques such as surgery, radiation treatment and chemotherapy. Therefore, mostly pulmonary metastases have been available for treatment. Occasionally, incurable primary lung cancers have been treated, as well as localized breast cancers, in cases where the patient has consistently refused conventional treatment techniques. Mostly only metastases in the periphery of the lung, up to a maximum of 4, and with a diameter of up to 5 cm, were accepted for treatment. Poor condition, high age and multiple peripheral metastases were considered as contraindications, in addition to other common contraindications.

Technique of Lung Cancer Treatment

To prevent pneumothorax, a F. 18–20 pleural draining tube is introduced under local anesthesia the day before the treatment. Continuous suction of about 20 cm H_2O is applied. Suitable electrodes for various purposes, as well as an electronic treatment device, have been developed. Local anesthesia is applied to the skin and underlying pleura where the tumor electrode is to be introduced. A 3 mm incision is made in the skin, and a thick needle is introduced to begin with through the chest wall to the lung. The same canal is used for the fluoroscopically-controlled introduction of the electrode into the center of the tumor. This usually requires two perpendicular planes. The reference electrode is introduced in the same way about three tumor diameters away from the surface of the tumor in the same lung lobe. The reference electrode may alternatively be introduced into a supplying vessel. A vascular Rotex electrode is then used, introduced through a femoral vessel, for example, using the Seldinger technique. Voltage is applied between the electrodes by means of an electronic instrument. Voltage must be applied and slowly reduced, to prevent electrical disturbance to the patient. Ordinary electrical precautions are carefully considered. The dose of current is measured in A × seconds = coulombs. Usually a maximum dose of 100–400 coulombs are used at 5–20 volts, although these figures may change in the future. When "pure" electrochemical treatment is combined with the use of chemotherapeutic agents, the latter may be infused into the tumor via particular electrodes, or accumulated in the tumor after intravascular infusion.

Healing of Cancers by Enhancement of Local Ionic Transports

The theory of cancer healing using direct current is based on several assumptions. When an electrode is introduced into a cancer, with another electrode outside the cancer in an afferent vessel or in the surrounding interstitial tissue, the paths taken by the flow of current from the external electrical source may partly be the same as those which occur in spontaneous injury polarization. By applying a positive electric potential to a tumor, for example, and a negative potential to a reference tissue electrode, electronegative ions will be attracted to the area of the tumor electrode, and electropositive ions will be repelled. The reverse will occur around the electronegative electrode. It is easy to see that a considerable distortion must be produced in the ionic microenvironment of the tissue fluid around an electrode in a cancer when a steady current is continuously applied. The currents applied are considerably higher than weak physiological currents, which slowly vary and fluctuate. Many different effects are produced by electric current in medical treatment. Some of them are summarized below.

Effects of Direct Current on Cancers

Distorted Ion Composition

This is introduced around a cancer electrode when there is a unidirectional flow of current at relatively high, unphysiological voltages. Cancer cells are more sensitive to changes in the microenvironment than normal cells. After a sufficient length of time, electrophoresis will seriously influence the growth of cancer cells so that they may die, deteriorate and become resorbed. This basic principle is fairly simple, and corresponds to the principles of all other conventional therapies except surgery. By using heat, cold, radiation, various chemicals, etc., we try to change the microenvironment to influence the cancer. Electrochemical treatment is in this respect only another variation of a well-established principle.

Development of Electrochemical Products

In addition to the transport of ions in the electric field, new electrochemical products develop at the electrode surfaces. Thus, at the anode (+), protons (H^+), O_2 and Cl_2 develop. The protons move electrophoretically out of the tumor and change the pH to approximately 2. This leads to an area of electrochemical destruction of tissue, which becomes black and dry. The center will be bleached by slowly diffusing Cl_2 gas. Correspondingly, OH^- ions will develop, also from water around the cathode. The pH will here be about 12, producing some basic, also dark-colored, reaction products in the tissue, and a pronounced production of H_2 gas. When a reference electrode is placed in the bloodstream, the bloodstream washes the reaction products away.

The development of gas at the anode ($Cl_2 + O_2$) and around the cathode (H_2) will produce an internal increase in pressure, with cavitation in the tissue. These effects may be of some importance in the reduction of cancer growth when the anode (+) or cathode (−) is placed in the tumor.

Electroosmotic Transport of Water

When current is passed between electrodes immersed in an electrolyte in the presence of narrow capillaries provided with a surplus of fixed electronegative charges, water will be transported by electroosmosis from the anode to the cathode (1). Electroosmosis occurs in this way in the VICC system spontaneously, and is partly responsible for producing the corona structures around cancers. It is easy to show that in the treatment of cancers by electrodes, direct current will transport water from the anode to the cathode. An anode (+) in a cancer will produce (together with the coagulation effects of protons) a black, dry gangrene in the cancer. The dehydration may also have affected the living conditions of the cells. When a cathode (−) is placed in a cancer, an accumulation of tissue fluid will take place in the tumor area and produce (together with some coagulation effects of OH^-) a dark-colored wet gangrene, which may also have an effect on the cancer cells.

Production of Microthromboses by Electric Current

An anode positioned in a cancer will produce an electropositive field around the electrode. The size and shape of the field may vary, depending on the shape of the electrodes, the conductive properties of the tissues, the distance between the anode and cathode, and the electrode voltage applied. Microthromboses tend to be produced in capillaries, even far out in the surrounding tissues, by accumulation of electronegative thrombocytes. They induce the blood coagulation process and produce cancer regression by blocking the surrounding local microcirculation. Long-standing anodic effects will therefore also produce emphysema-like deterioration of lung tissue around a tumor. The influence on the circulation may delay or prevent the resorption of destroyed tumor tissue.

The effect of the cathodic field on microcirculation is largely reversible, mainly produced on a temporary basis by an electroosmotic increase in the turgor pressure, with compression of the vessels. This tissue fluid effect is so marked that the interstitial edema fluid may even obstruct the circulation in vessels as wide as a pencil in experiments in dogs.

Electrophoretic Accumulation of Cells, "Leukotaxis"

Granulocytes have a strong electronegative charge on their surfaces. When relatively low voltages are applied (e.g. 100–2000 mV) these cells move, due to their charge, to the anodic (+) tissue by electrophoresis. The process of endogenous, spontaneous accumulation of granulocytes in injured tissue (the electropositive phase of polarization) was extensively studied in animal experiments. The accumulation of granulocytes was interpreted as an example of spontaneous electrophoresis in vivo. When granulocyte accumulation is induced by electrodes, the granulocytes collect until most capillaries, small vessels and interstitial tissues contain an abundance of these cells. The word „leukotaxis" does not explain the mechanism of granulocyte accumulation and should be abandoned (1).

Results of Electrochemical Treatment with the Anode in the Cancer

The evaluation of the effects of a cancer treatment usually requires several years. In the first series of treatments of incurable (negatively selected) cases, an evaluation was made of 26 cancers in 20 patients, of whom some were followed-up from 1978 to 1983. Some had only been followed-up over three years. The results of this preliminary study are presented in Fig. 2. According to this study, about 50 percent of the cases reacted favorably, i.e. either showed a definite regression of the tumor or a temporary decrease in size. Most patients died later on when the primary tumor recurred, or as a result of the growth of peripheral metastases. One patient with 4 fibrosarcoma metastases to the lungs which were treated, and one well-differentiated metastasis in the lung from a breast cancer, are still symptom-free 8 years after treatment. The details of these 26 cancers are described elsewhere (1).

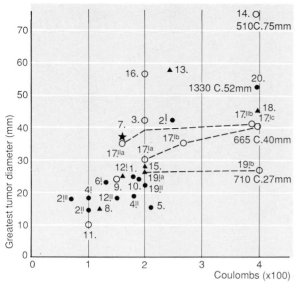

- ● Regression (12 metastatic tumors)
- ○ Progression (5 metastatic and 3 primary tumors)
- ▲ Indeterminate (3 metastatic and 2 primary tumors)
- ★● Thereafter ○(1 metastatic tumor)

Fig. 2 **Survey of the size, treatment dose and results** of the initial series of 26 lung cancers in 20 patients, with varying observation times (3–5 years) after treatment. Some tumors are sensitive, while others are relatively insensitive, to electrochemical treatment with the anode positioned in the tumor

Observations on Treatment Modifications

As the period of observation is still too short, only some preliminary results will be reported.

Effects of 20 Volts

When the electrode voltage was increased to 20 volts in 20 cases, no definitive improvements in the results could be observed compared with 10 volts. This is probably due to breakthrough effects in the tissues, as was found by using of as much as 40 volts.

Anodic and Cathodic Effects

Theoretically, it was assumed that the cancers should be made anodic (+) in the treatment. This is shown in a patient with a metastasis from a breast cancer before (Fig. **3a**) and 11 months after (Fig. **3b**) treatment. The tumor disappeared, and is still absent 5 years after treatment. Many cancers, however, did not decrease in size when the anodic field was applied. This was the case, for example, in half of the material from the first series of 26 cancers.

Due to unexpected circumstances, the effects of the cathodic field were tried in a patient with two large (5–6 cm diameter) leiomyoma metastases from a uterine tumor in the left lung (Fig. **4a, b**). As no

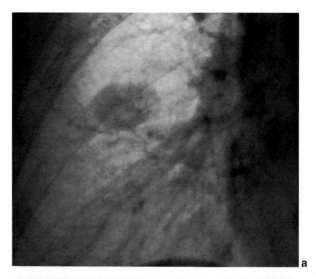

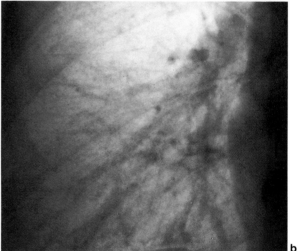

Fig. **3 The anode was always introduced into the cancer initially. a** In this case, the metastastic breast cancer in the lung disappeared 11 months after treatment **b** The patient is still healthy 3 years later

form of therapy had been able to arrest the tumor growth, and surgery was rejected, an attempt was made, at the patient's request, to stop the tumor growth. Similar electrodes were implanted into both tumors and 250 coulombs at 10 volts were applied (Figs. **4c, d**). This resulted in a progressive disappearance of the cathodic tumor (Figs. **4e, f**), while the anodic tumor continued to grow. During a second treatment session (Figs. **4g** and **h**) with the reversed polarity, the previously anodic, now cathodic tumor also started to regress (Fig. **4i**). After some time, however, it resumed its previous growth, leading to the patient's death (Fig. **4k**).

It is still not clear why in this case the cathodic (−) field was able to regress a tumor, while the anodic (+) tumor continued to grow. Temporary regres-

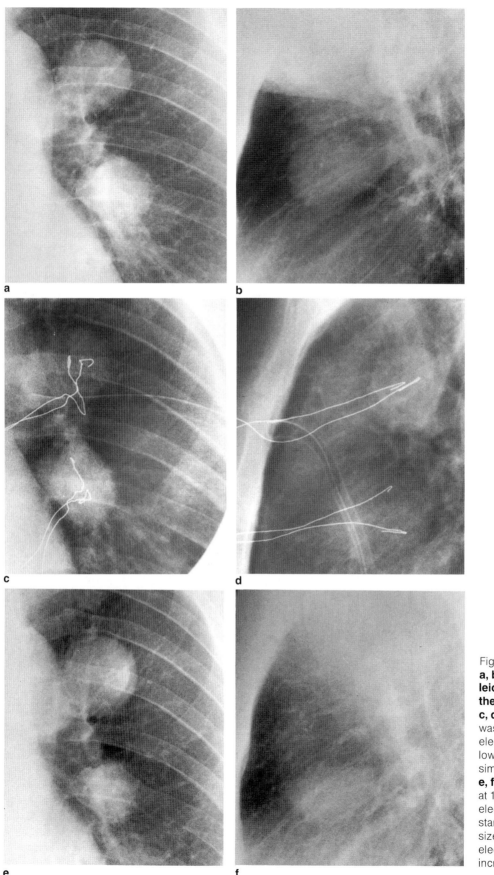

Fig. **4**
a, b Two metastatic leiomyosarcomas from the uterus
c, d The upper tumor was supplied with two electrodes (+) and the lower with two (−) of similar construction
e, f After 200 coulombs at 10 V, the electronegative tumor started to decrease in size, while the electropositive one increased

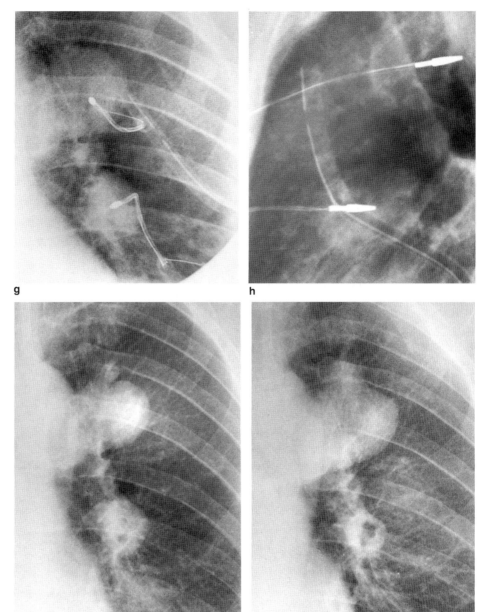

g, h New electrodes were introduced with the reverse polarity
i The new electronegative tumor initially started to decrease in size, and the new electropositive one continued to shrink
k Later on, the upper tumor started to increase while the lower one continued to decrease and subsequently disappeared. The patient died from other metastases

sion only occurred under reversed polarity in the previously anodic tumor. This resembles the selective sensitivity of tumors to radiation therapy, but it must be based on some other factor. An electrophoretic accumulation of charged immune bodies by the electronegative field may also be considered in the future.

Electrophoretic Accumulation of Charged Compounds

The terms chemotaxis and leukotaxis are today loose expressions without any real meaning (1). Considerable information already exists about the presence and function of the VICC system. Charged particles, cells and molecules move by electrophoresis in this system. Charged chemicals of various properties can therefore also be influenced when current is led over part of the VICC system between electrodes. Many of the induced field effects between electrodes can thereby be influenced in diseased tissue, such as chronic infections, cancer, and other diseases.

After preliminary electrophoretic studies in vitro and in animals, the chemotherapeutic anti-cancer agent doxorubicin was found to be electropositive. It was then possible to treat cancer locally in two ways, with doxorubicin in addition to the purely electrochemical treatments. The reasons for this additional procedure were that an increasing number of patients with large cancers were requesting any kind of help. It was therefore desirable to try to improve the possibilities of treating large tumors. In purely electrochemical treatments, only tumors of about 4–6 cm in diameter had been treated successfully.

The first combined electrochemical and chemotherapeutic approach was applied in 10 patients with incurable cancers. Electrodes had been constructed for the infusion of compounds into tissue (1). After percutaneous introduction of one electrode into the tumor and another into a supplying vessel, current was applied at 5–10 volts. An infusion of 50 mg of doxorubicin dissolved in 25–30 ml of sterile water was given for 10 minutes through the anodic (+) tumor electrode. The doxorubicin was thereby driven electrophoretically from the electrode through the cancer tissue at a high concentration and over a relatively long time. The toxic effects of the chemotherapeutic agent resulted in these cases in dense infiltrations into the tumor and its surrounding tissue. The infiltrations in the lung were largely resorbed. At a tentative early evaluation it seems possible to offer patients who are no longer suitable for other forms of treatment at least a reasonable palliation in this way.

The second combined electrochemical and chemotherapeutic treatment has only been performed in 5 patients with inoperable lung cancers. In these cases the cathode (−) was placed percutaneously into the tumor area. The anode was placed either in a supplying vessel or 10 cm outside the cancer in the lung parenchyma. During application of 5–10 volts between the electrodes, 50 mg of doxorubicin was slowly infused into a peripheral vein. During circulation of the drug, it was calculated that it should successively accumulate from the blood stream in the direction from outside of the cancer to the tissue around the eletronegative tumor electrode. In one case, a remarkable regression of the cancer occurred.

These two types of treatment must be tested separately before the third step is performed: a combination of the two previous methods of administration. A more detailed report on some of these attempts will follow (3, 4), including separate indications and tumor characteristics. In these studies, the concentration of doxorubicin was followed-up during and after treatment. Studies were made of the effects on blood electrolytes and blood morphology.

Conclusion

From theoretical, clinical and experimental studies, it has been found that purely electrochemical treatment of up to 4 cancers in the lungs, one with a maximum diameter of over 4 cm, had led to 10 years of cure at present. A temporary decrease or permanent arrest or disappearance was found in 50 percent of the initial series of 26 cancers in 20 patients when the anode was placed in the tumor. Certain cancers do not seem to react to these treatments, e. g. hypernephroma metastases, when the anode was placed in a large tumor. Metastases in the lung, even from well-differentiated breast cancers, have responded with complete regression. Lately it has been found that the cathodic field, in contrast to previous assumptions, was very effective in a 5 cm rhabdomyosarcoma, while a sarcoma of the same size with the same dose and in the same patient which was treated with the anode continued to grow. A series of tumor treatments with the cathodic field is therefore being performed. In the future, a preliminary testing of tumor sensitivity to the anodic or cathodic field will apparently become necessary. The electrical charge and content of immune bodies in the blood is therefore of particular interest. In addition to electrochemical cancer treatment, a combination with electrophoretic transport of a chemotherapeutic agent is likely to enhance the therapeutic possibilities. Depending on the polarity applied to the tumor in relation to the polarity of the chemotherapeutic agent, the drug can either be attracted in from the bloodstream or moved from a hollow electrode outward through the tumor. Both modes of electrophoretic movement of a compound may be used.

The introduction of new techniques for the treatment of cancer in patients is always difficult. A large and homogenous patient group, also including early clinical cases with good prognoses, and appropriate control cases, should be preferred for long-term series. It is not possible to obtain such optimum conditions for practical and ethical reasons. When both patients with good prognoses and those in whom the cancer is too far advanced have to be excluded, as well as control cases, any talk of "cure rates" is impossible. Nevertheless, sufficient descriptive case material may be obtained after an extended period by joint studies by different scientists and at various institutions. The present limitations of cancer treatment methods may thereby be widened. The multitude of variations of electrochemical treatment can in any case be used as a supplement to other cancer treatments.

References

1. Nordenström BEW. Biologically closed electric circuits: clinical, experimental and theoretical evidence for an additional circulatory system. Stockholm: Nordic Medical Publications, 1983: 1–358.
2. Nordenström BEW. An additional circulatory system: vascular-interstitial closed electric circuits (VICC). J. Biol Phys 1987; 15: 43.
3. Nordenström BEW. Electrochemical treatment of cancer: variable response to anodic and cathodic fields. Am J Clin Oncol (in press).
4. Nordenström BEW, Eksborg S, Beving H. Electrochemical treatment of cancer, I–III. Am J Clin Oncol (in press).

Embolization of the Spleen

R. F. Dondelinger and J. C. Kurdziel

Indications

Arterial embolization of the spleen may have two different objectives: either an interruption of arterial flow to the splenic artery or to one of its branches, or ablation of the splenic tissue by infarction. According to the aim of the procedure, splenic embolization may be considered as an alternative to splenectomy or ligation of the splenic artery (7, 31, 55, 57). Block of the flow in the splenic artery or of an intrasplenic branch is indicated as a preoperative modality or as treatment for arterial aneurysm, arteriovenous fistula, or in order to stop active arterial bleeding (30, 41, 50, 54). Most often, the procedure has to be carried out in emergency conditions. Usually, proximal obturation of the splenic artery is efficient in the control of hemorrhage, but does not induce significant infarction of the splenic tissue. After proximal occlusion of the splenic artery, vascular supply to the spleen is still maintained by the gastro-epiploic arteries, the left gastric artery, pancreatic and capsular splenic arteries, which perfuse the spleen at the level of the hilum. Embolization of the splenic artery has also been advocated for treatment of bleeding resulting from ruptured gastroesophageal varices (9, 20, 21, 23, 27, 54, 57), but portal hypertension has not been proved to be significantly influenced in all cases by arterial splenic embolization, when portal pressure was recorded (23, 37).

Embolization of the splenic tissue is mandatory in various hematologic conditions as an alternative to splenectomy in patients with poor general condition. The volume of the spleen may be subnormal, but in the vast majority of cases, splenomegaly is obvious. Since the intrasplenic arterial vascularization is represented by terminal vessels, an efficient infarction of the splenic tissue is obtained after embolization of the distal intrasplenic branches. Hypersplenism resulting from portal hypertension is certainly the main indication for arterial splenic embolization (1, 15, 21, 23, 24, 32, 34, 37, 38, 45–47, 54, 56).

The causes of hypersplenism are various. Most patients present with alcoholic or postnecrotic liver cirrhosis with a platelet count less than 60000 mm^3. These patients had also experienced at least one major episode of bleeding from ruptured gastro-esophageal varices. Embolization of the spleen has the advantage of retaining the organ in place, and a distal splenorenal shunt is still possible after correction of anemia and thrombocytopenia (21, 23).

Children with gastro-esophageal bleeding, signs of hypersplenism resulting from Gaucher's disease or atresia of the intrahepatic bile ducts, or portal vein thrombosis have also been submitted to splenic embolization (32, 40, 48, 51, 53). Embolization of the spleen has been advocated in patients who are on hemodialysis and show pancytopenia and splenomegaly, and in renal transplant patients in whom intolerance to immunosupressive medication after renal transplantation had to be corrected (22).

Thalassemia is also responsible for progressive hypersplenism, which requires an increase in the number of blood transfusions. Partial splenic embolization represents a valid alternative to splenectomy in this group of patients, in whom the risk of infections and lethal complications is particularly high after splenectomy (40). Idiopathic thrombocytopenic purpura may be corrected by embolization of the spleen (11, 19). The procedure is well tolerated in these patients, because the spleen is of normal volume or only moderately enlarged. The physiopathologic mechanism of thrombocytopenia correction is not completely elucidated. Infarction of the splenic tissue probably decreases sequestration of platelets in the spleen and reduces intrasplenic production of auto-antibodies directed against platelets. Splenic embolization has also been used in other pathologic conditions, such as in splenic lymphoma, chronic lymphatic leukemia, myeloid leukemia, myelofibrosis, hairy cell leukemia, polycythemia vera, hereditary spherocytosis, auto-immune hemolytic anemia, idiopathic hypersplenism, Felty's syndrome, and in patients who present with hypersplenism and cytopenia induced by anticancer chemotherapy. In the tumorous spleen, correction of hypersplenism and tumor mass reduction is expected (11, 18, 29, 33, 49).

Embolization Technique

Embolization of the spleen is performed after selective catheterization of the splenic artery by a femoral or an axillary approach. Standard preshaped cobra or sidewinder 5 Fr or 7 Fr catheters allow, in the vast majority of cases, an optimal catheterization of the splenic artery, the tip of the catheter being advanced at a sufficient distance from the ostium of the splenic artery. It is recommended that the splenic artery be catheterized as distally as possible in order to reduce possible reflux of embolic material into the gastric and pancreatic arteries originating from the splenic artery or into the other branches of the celiac artery or into the abdominal aorta. Balloon occlusion catheters or a coaxial technique may be used in a tortuous splenic artery in order to optimize distal catheterization (9, 23), but antegrade flow should be maintained in the splenic artery during embolization in order to prevent reflux of Gelfoam from the spleen into direct pancreatic arteries. The risk of inadvertent embolization of caudal pancreatic arteries by migrant embolic material is not clinically significant when larger particles are used as an embolization material. The branch of the splenic artery originating more proximally from the main trunk, and usually directed to the upper pole of the spleen, may be overlooked by a too distal catheterization.

Gelatin particles are the most commonly used material for embolization of the spleen (1, 22, 37, 45, 46, 47). The use of Gelfoam powder carries potential complications, such as pancreatitis and necrosis of the gastric wall (44, 52). Many other substances have been described, such as autologous clots (34), polyvinyl alcohol (11, 12), silicone microspheres (26), isobutyl-2-cyanoacrylate (23), and ethanol (36), but these materials do not offer significant advantages compared with gelatin. Particles of different size are injected, the smaller particles first in order to block the distal intrasplenic arteries, the larger particles to obturate the arteries more proximally at the splenic hilum. Formation of a plug of gelatin particles early in the procedure has to be avoided, since it may preclude a further correct embolization of the distal branches (32). Between 20 and 40 gelatin particles are necessary, according to the volume of the spleen.

The extent of infarction has to be assessed during the procedure. When a significant reduction in flow of contrast medium is observed in the splenic artery, embolization is stopped. At that moment, the extent of infarction generally corresponds to at least 80% of the splenic volume. Digital subtraction angiography can be performed during the procedure in order to assess progression and extent of embolization. Distribution of technetium(^{99m}Tc)-labeled Gelfoam particles within the spleen, detected with a gamma camera, makes control angiographies unnecessary. Assessment of the volume of embolized spleen seems to be as precise as with uniplanar angiography (6, 15).

Use of steel coils (2, 58) lodged in the splenic artery does not induce a satisfactory infarction of the splenic tissue. Coils are a safe embolization material, but the best long-term positive results are obtained when the coils are lodged in the branches at the splenic hilum (2, 58). Reduction of infectious complications resulting from splenic embolization is guaranteed by a strict aseptic angiographic technique.

Angiographic catheter exchange is avoided during the procedure. The patient is submitted to an antiseptic preparation before the procedure. A bath with providone-iodine is given the day before embolization and the puncture site is prepared. Antibiotics are administered systematically starting on the day of embolization, according to different protocols:

- Intramuscular injections of 1,000,000 U of penicillin G, associated with 3 mg/kg of gentamicin, for 5 days after embolization (46).
- A dosage of 0.5 g of cephalothin administered by four injections per day for 15 days after embolization (37).
- Tobramycin (1 mg/kg) and oxacillin (1 g) intravenously 30 minutes before the procedure (23).
- In children, gentamicin (10 mg/kg/day) and cefoxitin sodium (100 mg/kg/day) intravenously, continued for 5 days or longer (32).
- A 14-valency pneumococcal polysaccharide vaccine administered some days before embolization (32).

Fragments of gelatin are also soaked in an antibiotic solution before injection. Clinical tolerance of splenic embolization depends on the volume of the spleen, extent of embolization, embolization material, and of the underlying disease. Intra-arterial 2-chloroprocaine hydrochloride has been used during the procedure to control abdominal pain (39). Postembolization abdominal pain is usually tolerated by the patient and well-controlled by medication. Continuous epidural anesthesia has been used after embolization, but it rather complicates an otherwise easy procedure (46). A short hospital stay is necessary, ranging from 4 to 6 days, for patients who undergo embolization of a hematologic disorder, when the spleen is not enlarged. On the other hand, patients with an enlarged spleen or presenting with a complex underlying disease need longer hospitalization.

The local effect of arterial embolization on the spleen may be assessed by nuclear medicine studies, US or CT. ^{99m}Tc sulfur colloid scans and US are limited in their capability to demonstrate precisely the extent of embolization. CT allows the volume of infarcted zones in the spleen to be calculated and reflects transformation of infarcted tissue into fibrosis by measurement of growing density values on subsequent CT examinations (3, 8, 28) (Fig. **1**). CT shows zones of liquefaction observed at the early phase after embolization, detects such early complications as bleeding, intrasplenic or perisplenic abscesses, perisplenic effusions, and such late complications as thrombosis of the splenic vein or intrasplenic growth of the remaining splenic tissue. MRI is able to differentiate embolized areas in the spleen from persistent vascularized tissue and demonstrates transformation of infarcted zones into fibrous tissue.

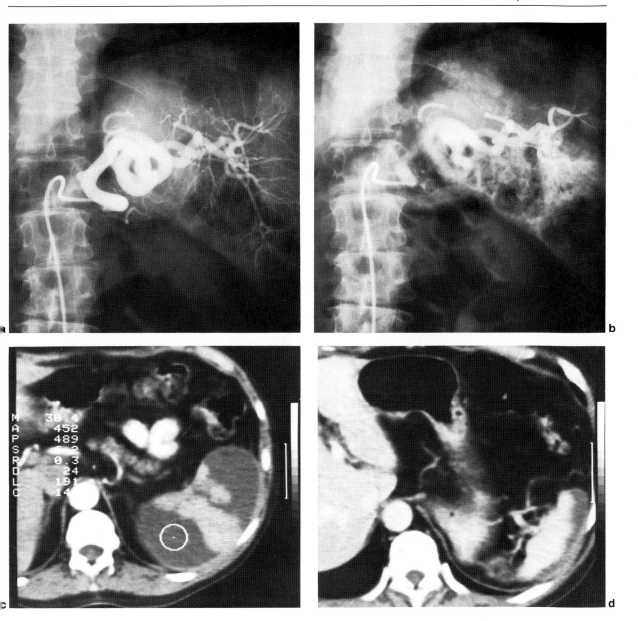

Fig. 1 **Hairy cell leukemia in a 65-year-old man.** Arterial embolization of the spleen for treatment of severe hypersplenism

a Splenic arteriography shows splenic enlargement
b After embolization with Gelfoam particles, angiography shows subtotal occlusion of intrasplenic arteries
c Control CT 2 months after embolization differentiates embolized areas (30 HU) from persistent splenic tissue
d Control 8 months after embolization shows shrinkage of the spleen and growth of remaining splenic tissue

Results

It is difficult to assess the clinical benefit from arterial embolization of the spleen, since the number of clinical trials is limited and most studies are based on a small number of patients. Individual reports and small series of cases are available in the literature, reporting patients who have been treated by embolization of the splenic artery for traumatic bleeding or aneurysm (30, 41, 50, 54) (Fig. **2**). However, integrated diagnostic and therapeutic management of trauma patients permits the treatment of splenic injuries with arterial embolization without subsequent surgery, even when the patient is in an unstable hemodynamic condition in selected cases. Five of seven patients have been treated in our experience. In two patients, the spleen ruptured 1 month after embolization.

Experimental studies in animals have shown that injection of gelatin particles in the splenic arteries

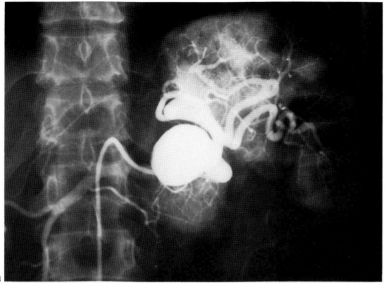

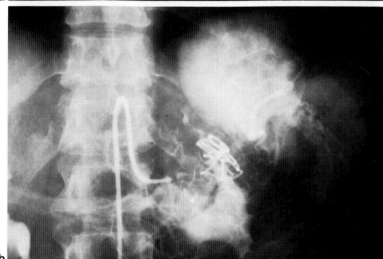

Fig. 2 **Radiologic treatment of an aneurysm of the splenic artery in a 48-year-old woman**

a Splenic arteriography confirms an aneurysm (3 by 3.5 cm) of the splenic artery

b Control arteriography after embolization of the aneurysmal sac with 3 Gianturco-Anderson-Wallace coils (5.7 cm). Notice persistent arterial perfusion of the spleen

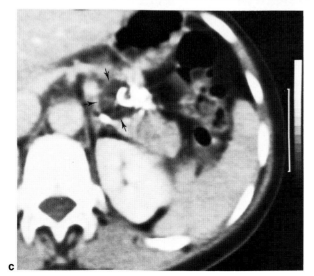

Fig. **2**
c CT 3 months after embolization confirms complete thrombosis of the aneurysm (arrow) and normal spleen

induces a persistent obliteration of the vessels 8 weeks after embolization (2, 11–14, 26, 27, 30, 38). At the early phase, 24 hours and 2 weeks after embolization, irregular zones of hemorrhagic infarction coexist with areas of normal splenic tissue. At the late phase, fibrosis replaces the areas of intrasplenic infarction. Leukocyte values were increased in all animals 24 hours after embolization, and hematocrit decreased by 20% during the first week after embolization (14). Experimental data in animals with a normal spleen show no influence on the lifetime of erythrocytes and no significant increase in circulating thrombocytes (11, 27).

The first embolization of the spleen in man was described by Maddison in 1973 (34). Among the studies collected from the literature, only a few reports contain a significant number of cases (22, 23,

32, 37, 40, 45, 46, 58). Generally, a partial emboliza-tion of the spleen varying from 30 to 80% is per-formed. Most of the patients reported earlier in the literature have been treated for hypersplenism (15, 24, 45, 46, 56, 58). Platelet count increases rapidly after splenic embolization in man and often a tem-porary hyperthrombocytosis is observed. In the study reported by Owman et al. (37) concerning 18 patients, 11 could be followed after the procedure, and six showed a platelet count greater than 100,000/mm^3 6 months after embolization; four had a normal platelet count 1 year after splenic embolization, as had two patients 2 years after treatment. Fourteen patients with cirrhosis and hypersplenism were alive 4 years after embolization. In a similar report, the frequency of bleeding episodes from gastro-esophageal varices was reduced to 0.4/year after splenic embolization, compared with 2.12 episodes before treatment (1). Also, in children, bleeding episodes decreased from 2.87 to 0.67 after splenic embolization (32). Yoshioka et al. (58) obtained an increase in platelets in 96%, even when coils had been used. In the study reported by Spigos et al. (46) analyzing the effect of splenic embolization in 13 patients, 7 being on immunosuppresive therapy, a significant increase in white cell count and platelets was noticed 2 weeks after embolization. Similar results are observed in the study by Gerlock et al. (22) composed of 6 patients under hemodialysis and one transplant patient. These early results have been confirmed by later experience (47). Pringle et al. (40) report on 6 patients with thalassemia and hyper-splenism who have been treated by splenic emboliza-tion. All patients showed correction of hypersplen-ism, reduction in the need of blood transfusions, and an obvious positive effect on growth in the children submitted to the procedure. Among 8 patients treat-ed for idiopathic thrombocytopenic purpura, long-term normalization of platelet count was observed in six in our experience (19) (Fig. **3**). In the other cases reported in the literature in which embolization was performed for idiopathic thrombocytopenic purpura before splenectomy or another surgical intervention, normalization of platelet count was achieved (11, 54).

A small number of splenic embolizations have been performed in patients with splenomegaly due to a malignant hemopathy. In this group of patients, splenectomy may be indicated in the late phase of the disease (35). Most patients present with a consider-ably enlarged spleen, causing abdominal compres-sion and organ displacement, signs of hypersplenism, and inadequate response to chemotherapy. Debulk-ing is probably the most beneficial effect gained from splenectomy or embolization. Hematologic response to surgery or embolization is unpredictable and life expectancy remains unchanged (16, 35). We have treated three patients with chronic lymphatic

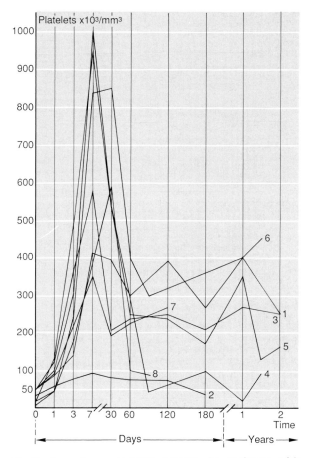

Fig. **3 Long-term platelet counts in patients with chronic auto-immune thrombocytopenia** after arterial splenic embolization

leukemia, two patients with myeloid splenomegaly, one patient with leukemic lymphosarcoma, one patient with hairy cell leukemia, one patient with polycythemia vera, and one patient with autoim-mune hemolytic anemia in whom an accessory spleen was left after splenectomy and was embolized. Posi-tive effects have been noticed to some degree in all patients with hypersplenism or with a need for blood transfusions, except the patient who had an acces-sory spleen embolized (Fig. **4**). Reduction in splenic volume is, however, limited in tumorous spleens after arterial embolization compared with the effect obtained in congestive or in normal spleens. Regen-eration of the splenic tissue growing from the hilum to the periphery occurs in almost all cases when viable splenic tissue is left in place.

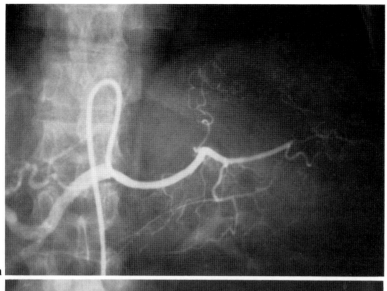

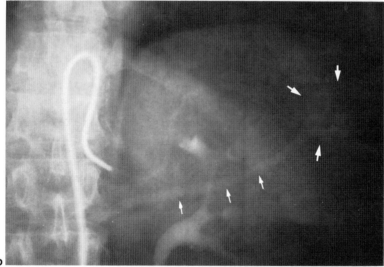

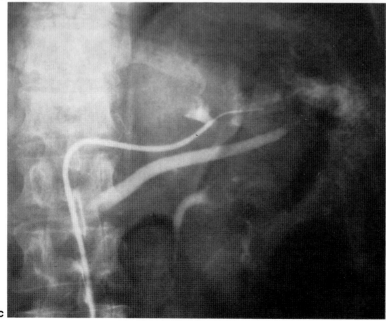

Fig. 4   **A 60-year-old woman with persistent auto-immune hemolytic anemia after splenectomy**
a, b Arteriography of the splenic artery shows a remaining accessory spleen (large arrows) drained by the small splenic vein (small snows)
c Control arteriography after embolization with 6 ml of absolute ethanol confirms embolization of the accessory spleen and stasis of contrast medium in the splenic vein

Complications

Arterial embolization of the spleen may be followed by serious infectious complications, compared with potential complications after embolization of other organs (11, 52, 54). Surgical splenectomy is not free from untoward side-effects and carries a definite number of complications and a mortality rate varying according to the underlying disease (43). Splenectomy done for a traumatic lesion of the spleen has a morbidity rate of 1.45% and a mortality rate from sepsis of 0.58%. Splenectomy done for treatment of spherocytosis carries a morbidity rate of 3.52% and a mortality rate from sepsis of 2.23% compared with a complication rate of 24.8% and 11%, respectively, when splenectomy is performed for cure of thalassemia. When the spleen is removed for trauma, the patient is at a 50 times higher risk of dying from fulminant sepsis than the population at large. This risk increases 200 to 800 times when splenectomy is performed in a patient with hemopathy (43, 58). Splenorrhaphy, partial splenectomy, and peritoneal implantation of fragments of splenic tissue after splenectomy lower significantly the risk of infectious postoperative complications (4, 5, 10, 17, 25). Splenectomized patients are at risk from overwhelming septicemia, bacterial meningitis, and pneumonia (4, 17, 42, 43). In half of the cases, *Streptococcus pneumoniae* is identified as the responsible germ; in 30% of the cases, *Hemophilus influenzae* or *Neisseria meningitidis* is present. In the majority of cases, fatal septicemia occurs during the 2 years after the spleen has been removed.

Arterial splenic embolization may also carry serious complications. The occurrence of a splenic abscess (2, 11, 27, 54, 56) is explained by the persistence of infarcted and necrotized splenic tissue, arrest of opsonizing function of the spleen after the circulation in the spleen has been stopped, and by backflow of digestive bacteria through the splenic vein to the spleen. Total embolization of the spleen induces a non-negligible postembolization mortality rate (11, 24), whereas partial splenic embolization carries a mortality rate of about 9% when reports concerning only a limited number of patients are considered (1, 9, 22, 23, 27, 32, 34, 38, 45, 46, 49, 56). Partial splenic embolization leaves functional splenic tissue in situ, which protects the patient from infections, but the minimal volume of splenic tissue necessary to maintain opsonic and immunologic functions of the spleen has not been determined. Experience certainly is an important factor in reducing complications, as shown by the low or absent mortality reported in the studies published containing a significant number of patients (22, 23, 32, 37, 46, 58). Among the other major postembolization complications, rupture of the spleen, necrosis of the gastric wall, renal insufficiency, acute pancreatitis,

pneumonia and thrombosis of the splenic vein have been described (27, 36, 37, 46, 52, 54). Minor complications are represented by abdominal pain in the left upper quadrant, slight fever, nausea and vomiting, paralytic ileus, pleural and peritoneal effusions, and platelike atelectasis in the left lower lobe. Children may present with an elevated temperature after splenic embolization for a longer time than adults (32). Strict aseptic angiographic technique, preventive systemic antibiotics and partial or repetitive splenic embolization, which has replaced total infarction of the spleen, have significantly diminished local complications after splenic embolization. In the group of renal transplant patients who are at particular risk from complications, Spigos (44) has observed one splenic abscess after partial embolization in 76 cases. Among 18 cirrhotic patients with portal hypertension studied by Owman et al. (37), 2 patients presented with a splenic abscess after subtotal embolization of the spleen; one death occurred, and 4 patients presented with thrombosis of the splenic vein. In the 6 immunosuppressed patients embolized by Gerlock et al. (22), no abscess occurred.

Conclusion

Splenic embolization is an alternative to surgical splenectomy in selected patients with various pathologic conditions. Results are comparable to surgery in hematologic disorders. The risk of complications should be prevented by strict observation of embolization technique and postprocedural antibiotic therapy.

References

1. Alwmark A, Bengmark S, Gullstrand P, Joelsson B, Lunderquist A, Owman T. Evaluation of splenic embolization in patients with portal hypertension and hypersplenism. Ann Surg 1982;196:518–524.
2. Anderson JH, Vuban A, Wallace S, Hester JP, Burke JS. Transcatheter splenic occlusion: an experimental study in dogs. Radiology 1987;125:95–102.
3. Balcar I, Seltzer SE, Davis D, Geller S. CT patterns of splenic infarction: a clinical and experimental study. Radiology 1984;151:723–729.
4. Belfanz JR, Nesbit ME Jr, Jarvis C. Overwhelming sepsis following splenectomy for trauma. J Pediatr 1976;88:458–463.
5. Benjamin JT, Komp DM, Shaw A. Alternatives to total splenectomy: two case reports. J Pediatr Surg 1978;13:137–140.
6. Berger JL, Gerlock AJ, Clanton JA, MacDonell RC Jr, Parris WCV, Kendall RI. Localization of gelfoam emboli after partial splenic embolization utilizing ^{99m}Tc-labeled emboli. Cardiovasc Intervent Radiol 1982;5:20–24.
7. Blain AW, Blain A. Ligation of the splenic artery, the operation of choice in selected cases of portal hypertension and Banti's syndrome. Ann Surg 1950;131:92–99.
8. Breiman RS, Beck JW, Korobkin M, Glenny R, Akwari OE, Heaston DK, Moore AV, Ram PC. Volume determinations using computed tomography. AJR 1982;138:329–333.
9. Bucheler E, Thelen M, Schirmer G. Katheterembolisation der Milzarterien zum Stopp der akuten Varizenblutung. RöFo 1975;122:224–229.

10. Burrington JD. Surgical repair of a ruptured spleen in children: report of eight cases. Arch Surg 1977;112:417–421.

11. Castaneda-Zuniga WR, Hammerschmidt DE, Sanchez R, Amplatz K. Nonsurgical splenectomy. AJR 1977;129:805–811.

12. Castaneda-Zuniga WR, Sanchez R, Amplatz K. Experimental observations on short and long-term effects of arterial occlusion with ivalon. Radiology 1978;126:783–787.

13. Chuang VP, Reuter SR. Selective arterial embolization for the control of traumatic splenic bleeding. Invest Radiol 1975;10:18–23.

14. Chuang VP, Reuter SR. Experimental diminution of splenic function by selective embolization of the splenic artery. Surg Gynecol Obstet 1975;140:715–720.

15. Conroy RM, Lyons KP, Kuperns JH, Juler GL, Joy I, Pribram HFW. New techniques for localization of therapeutic emboli using radionuclide labeling. AJR 1978;130:523–527.

16. Coon WN. The limited role of splenectomy in patients with leukemia. Surg Gynecol Obstet 1985;160:291–294.

17. Cooney DR, Dearth JC, Swanson SE, Dewanjee MK, Telander RL. Relative merits or partial splenectomy, splenic reimplantation and immunization in preventing postsplenectomy infection. Surgery 1979;86:561–569.

18. Dicato MA, Dondelinger RF. Embolisation partielle de la rate par hypersplenisme dans le syndrome myeloproliferatif avec insuffisance médullaire. Ann Med Nancy 1983;22:425–426.

19. Dondelinger RF, Kurdziel JC, Dicato MA, Driesschaert P. Partial splenic embolization in immune thrombocytopenia. Radiology 1985;157:337.

20. Dumont AE, Berman IR, Stahl WM. Significance of an enlarged splenic artery in patients with bleeding varices. Ann Surg 1972;175:466–471.

21. Esser G, Dux A. Embolisation der Milzarterie. RöFo 1982;137:324–329.

22. Gerlock AJ, MacDonell RC, Muhletaler CA, Parris WCV, Johnson HK, Tallent MB, Richie RE, Kendall RI. Partial splenic embolization for hypersplenism in renal transplantation. AJR 1982;138:451–456.

23. Goldman ML, Philip PK, Sarrafizadeh MS, Sarfeh IJ, Salam AA, Galambos JT, Powers SR, Balint JA. Intra-arterial tissue adhesive for medical splenectomy in humans. Radiology 1981;140:341–349.

24. Goldstein H, Wallace S, Anderson JH, Bree RL, Gianturco C. Transcatheter embolisation of abdominal tumors. Radiology 1976;120:539–542.

25. Grosfeld JL, Ranochak JE. Are hemisplenectomy and/or primary splenic repair feasible? J Pediatr Surg 1976;11:419–423.

26. Guilford WB, Scatliff JH. Transcatheter embolization of the spleen for control of splenic hemorrhage and in situ splenectomy: an experimental study using silicone spheres. Radiology 1976;119:549–554.

27. Günther R, Bohl J, Klose K, Anger J. Transkatheterembolisierung der Milz mit Butyl-2-Cyanoacrylat. RöFo 1980;133:158–163.

28. Heymsfield SB, Fulenwider T, Nordlinger B, Barlow R, Sones P, Kutner M. Accurate measurement of liver, kidney and spleen volume and mass by computerized axial tomography. Ann Intern Med 1979;90:185–187.

29. Hocking WG, Machleder HI, Golde DW. Splenic artery embolization prior to splenectomy in end-stage polycythemia vera. Am J Hematol 1980;8:123–127.

30. Katzen BT, Rossi R, Passariello R, Simonetti G, Transcatheter therapeutic arterial embolization. Radiology 1976;120:523–528.

31. Keramidas DC. The ligation of the splenic artery in the treatment of traumatic rupture of the spleen. Surgery 1979;85:530–533.

32. Kumpe DA, Rumack CM, Pretorius DH, Stoecker TJ, Stellin GP. Partial splenic embolization in children with hypersplenism. Radiology 1985;155:357–362.

33. Lokick J, Costello P. Splenic embolization to prevent dose limitation of cancer chemotherapy. AJR 1983;140:159–161.

34. Maddison FE. Embolic therapy of hypersplenism. Invest Radiol 1973;8:280–281.

35. Mentzer SJ, Osteen RT, Starnes HF, Moloney WC, Rosenthal D, Canellos G, Wilson RE. Splenic enlargement and hyperfunction as indications for splenectomy in chronic leukemia. Ann Surg 1987;205:13–17.

36. Mineau DE, Miller FJ, Lee RG, Nakashima EN, Nelson JA. Experimental transcatheter splenectomy using absolute ethanol. Radiology 1982;142:355–359.

37. Owman T, Lunderquist A, Alwmark A, Bjorjesson B. Embolization of the spleen for treatment of splenomegaly and hypersplenism in patients with portal hypertension. Invest Radiol 1979;14:457–464.

38. Papidimitriou J, Tritakis C, Karatzas G, Papaionnou A. Treatment of hypersplenism by embolus placement in the splenic artery. Lancet 1976;ii:1268.

39. Parris WCV, Gerlock AJ, MacDonnell RC. Intra-arterial chloroprocaine for the control of pain associated with partial splenic embolisation. Anesth Analg 1981;60:112–115.

40. Pringle KC, Spigos DG, Tan WS. Partial splenic embolization in the management of thalassemia major. J Pediatr Surg 1982;17:884–890.

41. Probst P, Castaneda-Zuniga WR, Gomes AS, Yonehiro EG, Delaney JP, Amplatz K. Nonsurgical treatment of splenic artery aneurysms. Radiology 1978;128:619–623.

42. Robinette CD, Fraumeni JF Jr. Splenectomy and subsequent mortality in veterans of the 1939–45 war. Lancet 1977;ii:127.

43. Singer DB. Postsplenectomy sepsis. Perspect Pediat Pathol 1973;1:285–311.

44. Spigos DG. Severe complications following partial splenic embolization. Br J Radiol 1982;55:320.

45. Spigos DG, Jonasson O, Felix E, Capek V. Transcatheter therapeutic embolization of hypersplenism. Invest Radiol 1977;2:418–423.

46. Spigos DG, Jonasson O, Mozes M, Capek V. Partial splenic embolization in the treatment of hypersplenism. AJR 1979;132:777–782.

47. Spigos DG, Tan WS, Mozes MF, Pringle K, Iossifides I. Splenic embolization. Cardiovasc Intervent Radiol 1980;3:382–388.

48. Stellin G, Kumpe DA, Lilly JR. Splenic embolization in a child with hypersplenism. J Pediatr Surg 1982;17:892–893.

49. Struyven J, Kuhn G, Jeanty P. Spleen embolization. Ann Radiol (Paris) 1981;24:404–405.

50. Tadavarthy SM, Knight L, Ovitt TW, Snyder C, Amplatz K. Therapeutic transcatheter arterial embolization. Radiology 1974;112:13–17.

51. Thanopoulos BD, Frimas CA. Partial splenic embolization in the management of hypersplenism secondary to Gaucher disease. J Pediatr 1982;101:740–743.

52. Vujic I, Lauver JW. Severe complications from partial splenic embolization in patients with liver failure. Br J Radiol 1981;54:492–495.

53. White JJ, Goldman ML, Lepow M. Correction of hypersplenism without splenectomy. J Pediatr Surg 1981;167:967–971.

54. Wholey MH, Chamorro HA, Rao G, Chapman W. Splenic infarction and spontaneous rupture of the spleen after therapeutic embolization. Cardiovasc Radiol 1978;1:249–253.

55. Witte CL, Corrigan JJ Jr, Witte MH, O'Mara RE. Splenic artery ligation in experimental hypersplenism. Surgery 1976;80:581–585.

56. Witte CL, Ovitt TW, van Wyck DB, Witte MH, O'Mara RE, Woolfenden JM. Ischemic therapy in thrombocytopenia from hypersplenism. Arch Surg 1976;11:1115–1121.

57. Witte CL, Witte MH, Renert W, O'Mara RE, Lilien DL. Splenic artery ligation in selected patients with hepatic cirrhosis and in Sprague-Dawley rats. Surg Gynecol Obstet 1976;142:1–12.

58. Yoshioka H, Kuroda C, Hori S, Tokunaga K, Tanaka T, Nakamura H, Shiozaki H, Ogawa Y, Mizunoya S, Okagawa K. Splenic embolization for hypersplenism using steel coils. AJR 1985;144:1269–1274.

Embolization of Arteriovenous Malformations

Pulmonary Arteriovenous Malformations

J. F. Reidy

Pulmonary arteriovenous malformations (PAVMs) are rare congenital vascular anomalies. Until recently, they were of diagnostic interest only and when seen the diagnosis could often be suggested from the chest radiographic appearances. If treatment was considered necessary then a thoracotomy and lung resection was offered. Altough there were good results with surgery, mortality rates of up to 5% were recorded. Recently, there has been a renewed interest by radiologists in PAVMs, since embolization has been offered as an alternative form of treatment. Embolization must now be considered to be safe and effective, often curative, and the procedure of choice for the treatment of PAVMs.

Clinical Features

PAVMs may occur as an isolated anomaly or in association with hereditary hemorrhagic telangectasia (HHT) or Rendu-Osler-Weber disease. In some reported series PAVMs are more commonly associated with HHT (10) but in others the majority are sporadic cases (4). When PAVMs are multiple, there is a stronger association with HHT. An incidence of 30 to 40% PAVMs has been described in HHT, and there is also an increased incidence in the unaffected relatives of these patients.

Although PAVMs can occur at any age, they are typically diagnosed in adult life with a mean age of about 40 years and they are more common in women than in men. They typically present with symptoms such as dyspnea and fatigue, but these may have been present for some years and even from childhood. Cyanosis, polycythemia, and digital clubbing may also have been present for some time.

Some form of cerebral vascular accident such as a stroke or transient ischemic attack may be an initial presenting feature. These cerebral ischemic episodes may be due to thrombosis associated with polycythemia or to a paradoxical embolus associated with the right to left shunting. About 10% of PAVMs present with some form of a stroke but recently an incidence of neurologic symptoms of up to 30% has been shown (3). When looked for there is often computed tomographic evidence of past ischemic cerebral episodes in patients who have had no clearcut episode of stroke. Bleeding and hemothorax are rare presentations of PAVMs. Sometimes isolated or multiple small PAVMs may be noted on chest radiographys taken for some other reason. Such patients may then have minimal or no symptoms related to the PAVM.

Indications

It is difficult to be rigid about the indications for embolization of PAVMs. When significant hypoxemia, decreased exercise tolerance, and significant right to left shunting occur, surgery has invariably been offered and embolization can now be offered as an alternative. If there was a conservative tendency to not operate on smaller PAVMs without significant right to left shunting, the increased awareness of cerebral complications and the relative safety and lesser morbidity of embolization techniques should encourage a more aggressive approach to their management. Unlike arteriovenous malformations elsewhere in the body, recurrence after embolization of simple PAVMs does not seem to occur and thus embolization of these lesions will usually be curative.

When there are multiple or diffuse PAVMs, surgery is more limited, since it would also mean resection of normal lung parenchyma for which surgery then carries an increased risk.

In both embolization and surgery all the PAVMs will not be occluded, but if a sufficient number of the larger lesions are embolized, there will be an improvement in the level of hypoxemia and the patient's associated symptoms. With careful embolization, this improvement should be achieved with less infarction of normal lung and less risk. Repeated embolizations can be performed when there are multiple lesions and when the first embolization has not effected sufficient improvement. Repeated embolizations carry no extra risk.

Investigations

In many instances a chest radiograph will either be diagnostic of or strongly suggest a PAVM. Tomography, CT, and intravenous digital angiography may have a role in confirming the diagnosis. If by whatever means the diagnosis of PAVM is clear, then the patient can be prepared for embolization on the same occasion as angiography. Nuclear medicine studies with injections of labeled microspheres into a peripheral vein can be useful as a baseline study to assess follow-up. The technique gives sensitive quantitative data regarding the right to left shunting.

If a patient has marked polycythemia, then a venesection before angiography would be advisable. Some degree of anticoagulation during the procedure and subsequent embolization is indicated, altough the amount of heparin given would depend on the type of embolization procedure, the length of the procedure, and the degree of polycythemia present. Good pulmonary angiography with or without digital angiography is necessary in order to define clearly all of the pulmonary vasculature. Demonstration of the precise arterial supply to all PAVMs is important, and multiple views may be helpful. These are important so that the position of the coil or balloon occlusion can be carefully planned.

In 1976 a radiologic classification of PAVMs was proposed (5). PAVMs were divided into solitary, multiple of varying sizes, multiple of uniform size, and diffuse types. More recently, a simple angiographic classification has been proposed (10) (Fig. 1). This is simpler and very appropriate to the

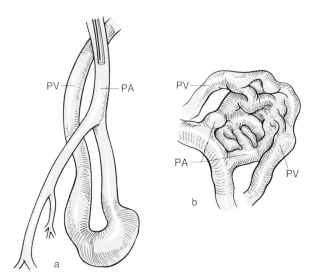

Fig. 1 **The two types of architecture seen in PAVMs** (10). **a** Simple type. **b** Complex type. Note the aneurysmal part consisting of a network of small branches or septations. Reproduced with permission from AJR 1983; 140: 683

assessment and evaluation before embolization. In White et al.'s 17 patients 79% of 91 PAVMs consisted of a single pulmonary artery to pulmonary vein communication that was usually aneurysmal and nonseptated. They described this as the simple type. This is the type that will usually be cured by appropriate embolization, but the large nonseptated malformation would allow any small embolus to pass freely through and into the systemic circulation. The remaining 21% of PAVMs were described as complex. They consisted of two or more connecting pulmonary artery branches feeding aneurysmal and septated communication, which was often cirsoid and with two or more draining veins. In some instances the malformation is diffuse, involving larger parts of the lung. This type is more difficult to embolize completely and effectively, but the risks of paradoxical emboli will be less than in the simple nonseptated type.

Embolization Techniques

The aim is to produce a permanent occlusion of the PAVM, so a nonabsorbable embolic agent must be used. In practice, steel coils or detachable balloons are used in most cases. Before embolization, it is important to demonstrate clearly the detailed anatomy of the PAVM and in particular its feeding artery or arteries.

In the most common form (the simple type) with a single feeding artery, the aim is to occlude the feeding artery just before it enters the aneurysmal part of the PAVM (Fig. 2). A more proximal occlusion could embolize branches to normal lung and possibly produce some pulmonary infarction. It is important to assess the diameter of the feeding artery because this must not be larger than the diameter of the coil or balloon to occlude it. If the diameter of the extruded coil or detachable balloon is less than that of the feeding artery, they could pass through the nonseptated aneurysmal part of the arteriovenous malformation and into the single draining vein, which is usually larger than the feeding artery. This would then produce systemic embolism with potentially catastrophic consequences. Whichever technique is used, it is important that the tip of the catheter is precisely placed and that, before detaching a balloon or pushing out a coil, this position and its relationship to the feeding artery is confirmed.

Whether detachable balloons or steel coils are used to occlude. PAVMs will largely depend on the personal preferences and experience of the interventional radiologist. Both techniques have advantages and disadvantages. Coils were first used to occlude PAVMs (8), and they are probably used more frequently because most interventional radiologists will be very familiar with them and they will be readily available in their departments (2, 6). Unlike detach-

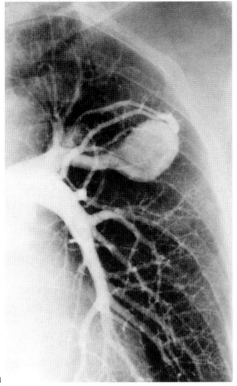

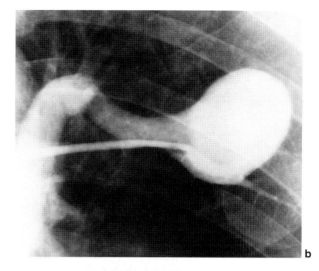

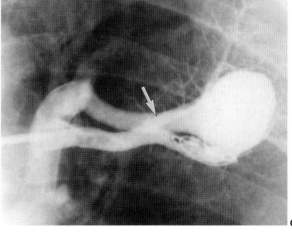

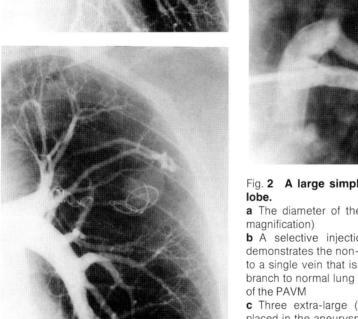

Fig. 2 A large simple PAVM involving the left upper lobe.

a The diameter of the feeding artery is 8 mm (including magnification)

b A selective injection into the single feeding artery demonstrates the non-septated aneurysmal sac that drains to a single vein that is larger than the artery. Note a small branch to normal lung that arises from the aneurysmal part of the PAVM

c Three extra-large (15 mm diameter) coils have been placed in the aneurysmal part as well as the distal feeding artery. They have reduced flow through the PAVM but have not occluded it. Observe the more proximal branch to normal lung (arrow) now more clearly demonstrated

d Following a second embolization procedure four more coils were placed in the more proximal feeding artery and there is now complete occlusion. It was not possible to place these coils between the original coils and the artery to normal univolved lung (black arrow, Fig. **2c**). This artery will have been occluded as well but this represents only a very small loss of normal lung. Perhaps in this case with a single lesion and a large feeding artery, balloon embolization would have allowed a more precise and certain occlusion

able balloons, no preparation is necessary and they are simple to use. Once the coil protrudes from the tip of the catheter, there is, however, no control of the precise positioning of the catheter and adjustments cannot be made. Large arteries may need multiple coils to effect complete occlusion, which should usually occur within about 15 to 20 minutes if it is going to occur.

A further advantage of using coils is that any conventional catheter can be used, provided it is tapered to 0.38. It is preferable that the catheter be made of polyethylene. Sometimes the diameter of the feeding vessel will be greater than that of the largest size standard coil (8 mm). In this situation special large coils are available and can be used to form a "bed" or "safety net" so that smaller coils will be trapped and not pass through the fistula. Large coils of up to 20 mm in diameter are now available and sometimes these can be placed into the aneurysmal portion of the PAVM before occlusion of the feeding artery with smaller coils. A theoretical disadvantage in the use of coils not shared by detachable balloons is that when the coil is partially occluding the feeding artery, any thrombus that forms may be detached and could embolize systemically. There is no clinical evidence to suggest that this does, in fact, occur.

Although detachable balloons are used less commonly, there are advocates for their use in PAVMs, particularly the group from the Johns Hopkins Hospital where there is a large experience (1). Detachable balloons have very definite advantages. When the balloon is inflated before detachment, its position and the occlusive effect can be checked by an injection of contrast medium through the introducing catheter. If the position is not satisfactory, the balloon can be deflated and the necessary adjustments made. This really is the only form of embolization device that is immediately reversible and thus allows very precise placement. Also when the balloon is inflated so that it occludes the artery, this occlusion will be immediately apparent.

A further advantage of detachable balloons is that it is not necessary to have the introducing catheter out as far as the proposed site of occlusion. These catheters with their balloons attached can be floated out or fluid-propelled so that the range extends well beyond the tip of the catheter. They do, however, require specialized large nontapered catheters that have to be introduced coaxially through introducing sheaths. There are two commercially available detachable balloon systems. One uses latex balloons on a very small (2 Fr) Teflon catheter, and with a range of sizes up to a maximum of 14 mm diameter (Ingenor, Paris). They used to need rather involved preparation, with hand tying of ligatures around the neck of the balloon, but more recently they come with a valved neck and need minimal preparation before use. The alternative system utilizes a silicone

balloon with a special valve mechanism that comes assembled for use (Becton Dickinson, Rutherford, N. J.). These balloons only come in two sizes (4 and 9 mm) and there is no variation on the shape of the round balloon.

A major disadvantage of detachable balloons is that they are expensive, making it difficult to keep a large stock on hand for just the occasional use. Although both systems have simplified and refined their techniques, much careful preparation is still necessary. Before embarking on any balloon embolization procedure, it is important to rehearse and practice techniques in order to minimize possible technical problems. The larger balloons need large nontapered catheters (9 Fr) that must be introduced via an introducer sheath. The large catheters, the coaxial catheter combinations plus the length of some of these procedures will increase the risk of embolic complications.

Premature detachment before inflation and occlusion is a risk, particularly with the silicone balloons. This is especially likely to occur when the balloon is just about to occlude the vessel in a high-flow fistula and extreme turbulence is produced. White and co-workers have suggested that a second distally placed nondetachable balloon catheter be placed to occlude the flow in the vessel before inflation of the detachable balloon (7). Alternatively, there may be problems detaching the latex balloons, and early deflation can occur with the contrast-filled silicone balloon.

In the less common complex PAVMs there are multiple feeding arteries and it may not be possible to occlude all of them. Even when this situation exists, occluding the major feeding arteries to the larger malformations will usually effect some improvement, as demonstrated by an increase in the oxygen saturation. If multiple PAVMs are present, it is best not to attempt too much at a single procedure and multiple embolization may be necessary. Although multiple detachable balloons can be used, coils in such situations are advantageous because they are much less expensive and the procedure will usually be shorter.

Complications

The complications of the embolization technique have already been discussed. The major complication that is unique to embolization of PAVMs is systemic or paradoxical embolism. This has only been occasionally described and is more likely to occur in the more common simple PAVM. Its clinical severity will depend on which artery the coil or balloon lodges in. It has been suggested that if a coil or balloon is too small and starts to pass through a PAVM, then asking an assistant to press on the carotids immediately would lessen the chance of the embolus passing into the carotid circulation. Especially with large catheters, prolonged procedures, and the presence of polycythemia, venous thrombus and paradoxical embolus are always likely. This risk can be minimized by preliminary venesection and the use of heparin during the embolization procedure.

The feeding artery to a PAVM will also supply some normal lung parenchyma. Even with a very careful and precise embolization, there is a likelihood of a small amount of normal lung parenchyma being infarcted. The more proximal the occlusion, the greater the amount of infarction that will occur. In a series of 40 patients who had a total of 145 PAVMs embolized, six were noted with mild to moderate pleuritic chest pain that began on the day after the procedure (7). The pain was described as lasting 2 to 5 days and all recovered with no ill effects.

Results

PAVMs are not common and there are few series of any size that detail results. The largest series consists of 40 patients who had 145 PAVMs successfully occluded (7). Silicone balloons were used in 142 PAVMs and the larger latex balloons in the remaining three. Details of the total number of PAVM's present in these patients were not given. No mention was made of PAVMs that were not occluded. In an earlier publication from the same group detailed physiologic observations were recorded in ten patients who had 58 of 71 visible PAVMs occluded (9). The arterial oxygen tension increased from an average of 43 to 64 mmHg. The average hemoglobin saturation increased from 79 to 92% after treatment. In a smaller group of four patients who had a total of 48 PAVMs, 30 were occluded with coils (6). A good catheter position was not obtained with one PAVM, whereas in two, each with two feeding arteries, only the larger ones were occluded. This suggests that embolization was not attempted in the other lesions. However, in these four cases with multiple PAVMs

the average oxygen tension on 100% oxygen was increased from 125 to 477 mm/Hg.

It would appear that in the simple type of PAVM by far the majority, embolization, whether by coils or detachable balloons, is a very effective, safe, and usually curative method of treatment. In the less common and more complex PAVMs it is more difficult to eradicate all of the malformation completely, but by embolizing the larger feeding vessels a significant clinical improvement can be effected. It is possible to repeat embolization procedures with no increased risk. Careful monitoring of the effect of embolization is essential.

References

1. Barth KH, White RI, Kaufman SL, Terry PB, Roland JM. Embolotherapy of pulmonary arteriovenous malformations with detachable balloons. Radiology 1982;142:599–606.
2. Castaneda-Zuniga W, Epstein M, Zollikofer C, Nath PH, Formanek A, Bem Shacher G, Amplatz K. Embolization of multiple pulmonary artery fistulas. Radiology 1980;134:309–310.
3. Deramond H, Remond A, Theibot J, Legars D, Trinez G.: Neurological manifestations revealing pulmonary arteriovenous fistulas. J Neuroradiol 1983;10:1–14.
4. Dines DE, Seward JB, Bernatex PE.: Pulmonary arteriovenous fistulas. Mayo Clin Proc 1983;58:176–181.
5. Higgins CB, Wexler L. Clinical and angiographic features of pulmonary arteriovenous fistulas in children. Radiology 1976;119:171–175.
6. Keller FS, Rösch J, Barker AF, Nath PH. Pulmonary arteriovenous fistulas occluded by percutaneous introduction of coil springs. Radiology 1984;152:373–375.
7. Mitchell SE, Kan JS, White RI. Interventional techniques in congenital heart disease. Semin Roentgenol 1985;20:290–311.
8. Portsmann W. Therapeutic embolisation of arteriovenous pulmonary fistula by catheter technique. In: Kelof O, ed. Current concepts in paediatric radiology. Berlin: Springer, 1977:23–31.
9. Terry PB, White RI, Barth KH, Kaufman SL, Mitchell SE. Pulmonary arteriovenous malformations: physiologic observations and results of therapeutic balloon embolisation. N Engl J Med 1983;308:1197–1200.
10. White RI, Mitchell SE, Kaufman SL, Kadir S, Chang R, Terry PB. Angioarchitecture of pulmonary arteriovenous malformations: an important consideration before embolotherapy. AJR 1983;140:681–686.

Peripheral Arteriovenous Malformations

A. Roche

Peripheral AVMs are either congenital vascular anomalies related to a developmental disorder of the circulatory system or acquired, mostly traumatic, lesions. Congenital AVMs frequently present as complex angiodysplasias diversely associating venous, arterial, and capillary anomalies. On the other hand, acquired AVMs are generally single arterial lesions or arteriovenous fistulas. Symptomatic congenital AVMs are more often difficult to treat than acquired ones, since they present frequently as diffuse and deep lesions requiring amputation, large mutilation, or are unresectable. Transcatheter embolization methods provide a new, safe, and efficacious therapeutic alternative when lesions are not resectable without serious damage or risk.

Clinical Presentation

The disorder includes diversely associated morphologic abnormalities, such as flat or slightly papular purplish-blue skin spots, (soft tissue masses, hypertrophy and lengthening (exceptionally shortening) of limb or of one of its segments, and unilateral varices whose constitutional nature is suggested by their presence since childhood.

Clinical examination has three main objectives:

– *Detection of arteriovenous communications* by observing pulsating varices, a continuous murmur with systolic reenforcement, or abnormal arterial pulsations, especially in the periarticular areas. These signs disappear after arterial compression at a more proximal level, whereas simple elevation of the limb does not lead to a significant depression of the varices.

– *Assessment of extension of the vascular malformation:* focal or superficial or, on the other hand, diffuse or deep. However, some malformations that clinically appear focal are found to be diffuse on arteriography. The clinical aspect of an associated cutaneous angioma allows one to suspect a deep involvement when it presents as a poorly limited or spottly lesion, however encouraging the superficial aspect might be. Conventional radiographs of the corresponding limb segments may also indicate a deep vascular malformation by discovering bone involvement.

– Regarding the fear of an *associated visceral localization* or of spontaneous complications, one must also distinguish the clinical type of the malformation: *immature angiomas,* growing and subsiding during childhood, which are capillary lesions with very few risks of complication and associated visceral angioma, and *mature angiomas,* presenting with a

lifelong development, either capillary, venous, or AVMs, which can present severe complications and deep visceral anomalies (6).

Classification

AVMs are classified as congenital and acquired.

– *Congenital* AVMs may be classified into systematized or disseminated angiodysplasia (angiomatous phakomatosis) sometimes with hereditary transmission, and sporadic localized and nonsystematized AVMs. Many eponyms and clinical classifications have been applied to systematized angiodysplasias. Klippel-Trenaunay syndrome, which is the most frequent peripheral systematized AVM, includes on the same side of the body: lengthening, hypertrophy, varices, and cutaneous angiomas; when clinical signs or arteriovenous fistula are added to these findings, the disease is commonly called Parkes-Weber syndrome (1). These anomalies are present from birth, but there is no family history of similar disorder (5, 10). They may involve the upper or the lower limb and sometimes both in a homolateral fashion. A crossed contralateral involvement has been exceptionally described.

– *Acquired* AVMs are due to a primitive degenerative or most often posttraumatic arterial wall lesion, responsible for rupture of the vessel, constitution of an aneurysm, and secondary arteriovenous fistula.

Embolization Procedure

Angiographic Evaluation

The approach of treatment of an AVM depends on its location, size, number of feeding vessels, and type of malformation. Such a rational approach necessitates an angiographic evaluation before therapy (4).

Key points are: determination of the angiographic type of the malformation: venous, capillar, arteriovenous; location, extension, and depth of the lesions; determination of the caliber of the feeding pedicles that determines the suitability of selective catheterization; and in case of arteriovenous fistula, presence or absence of an intervening nidus separating the arterial and venous components.

Angiographic type: Regarding the necessity for embolization techniques, patients can be subdivided into three groups, depending on the involvement of veins, the presence of telangiectasia, and the presence of arteriovenous fistula.

– Group I: the anomalies are purely venous, with dysplastic appearance of the veins and increased venous return probably related to abnormal microscopic arteriovenous communications. These venous anomalies can be associated with other specific signs of the other groups.

– Group II: telangiectasia is the basic lesions; its pattern is represented by vascular ectasias, 2 to 5 mm wide, opacified at the early arterial phase, with early drainage and persisting late opacification. The arterial feeders to these small anomalies are dilated and may be demonstrated only after selective injection in afferent branches.

– Group III: corresponds to the presence of macroscopic arteriovenous fistula: dilated and tortuous arteries with an early drainage into dilated veins.

Extension and depth of the lesions: The malformation is generally unilateral, even in cases in which it is diffuse. Truncular injection and anatomic identification of the feeders of the AVM allow assessment of the degree of extension: depth of the lesions (down to the bones or the deep muscular masses), and diffusion of the involvement to adjacent segments of the limb.

Bone involvement (15) can be generally attested by abnormal bone trabeculation pattern on plain films, but in some cases the identification of an osseous artery feeding the malformation is the only sign of this involvement. Selective opacification of articular arteries of the knee shows the involvement of the synovium in patients who present with hemarthrosis (Fig. **1**).

Phlebography or direct puncture of the AVM may be necessary to opacify the venous component of a low flow malformation.

Caliber of feeding pedicles. The caliber of the feeding arteries determines the conditions for selective catheterization necessary to avoid reflux of embolic material during embolization.

Nidus occlusion. When the nidus of the malformation is not definitively occluded, the ligation of the feeders is ineffective because of the development of new collateral vessels. Primary occlusion of this nidus is then the main objective, and particular care must be taken not to occlude the arterial pedicles before the true malformation is ablated.

Technique

Embolization should be adapted to different goals, depending on individual situations: occlusion of the nidus of the AVM without prior occlusion of the feeding pedicles that the embolus migrates along: occlusion of the arterial pedicles without risk of reflux; selective occlusion of the AVM by direct puncture in case of pure venous malformation; permanent occlusion to minimize the possibilities of

vascular repermeation; and choice of particles large enough to be trapped in the malformation.

Embolization has to be as complete as possible, which can be difficult, even impossible, to accomplish when the malformation is diffuse; multiple sessions of embolization are, therefore, necessary in treating the majority of patients. The principle of complete embolization results from the angiographic concept of vascular compartments. A vascular malformation is constituted by compartments that do or do not intercommunicate. Each compartment is fed by one or many vascular pedicles. Embolization is complete when all the compartments are occluded; each compartment can be thrombosed either by occlusion of all its afferent vessels or by embolization of only some well-chosen pedicles. This implies that a selective catheterization of vessels that feed the malformation is performed, in order to obtain an adequate morphologic and hemodynamic pretherapeutic assessment and to allow a distal occlusion (Fig. **2**).

Non-permanent agents such as gelatin sponge, are not suitable, since the vessels embolized with such material are systematically recanalized some weeks later. Calibrated Ivalon, a permanent embolus, can be adapted to embolization of the nidus of the malformation when it is not a too wide mesh structure. Silicone polymers and isobutyl-2-cyanoacrylate (IBC) are suitable materials; IBC seems to be mainly used since mixing it with Lipiodol slows down the polymerization and allows distal occlusion without prior proximal embolization. Gianturco-Wallace coils or detachable balloons may be very useful to occlude the large feeder of an arteriovenous fistula while minimizing the risks of inadvertent migration of the embolus. Absolute ethanol, sclerosing agents, or Ethibloc are suitable for treatment of venous malformations by direct puncture.

Radiopacity of the embolizing material is desirable; it can be easily achieved with IBC and Lipiodol, coils, large balloons, and barium and Ivalon.

The actual armamentarium, which includes usual catheters (single or coaxial systems), balloon catheters allowing blood flow changes in the explored vessels, solid and calibrated emboli, or liquid polymer agents, allows adequate management of almost all situations (2, 3).

Difficulties proceed from prior surgical ligations, which can preclude very selective arterial approach, high flow, and large arteriovenous communications without any intervening angiomatous tissue with risk of migration of the embolus to the pulmonary venous circulation. In the first case, an unusual arterial approach may be necessary after direct puncture of a deep artery distal to the ligation (Fig. **3**); in the second case, the flow can be slowed down either by inflating a balloon and working in the distal bed with

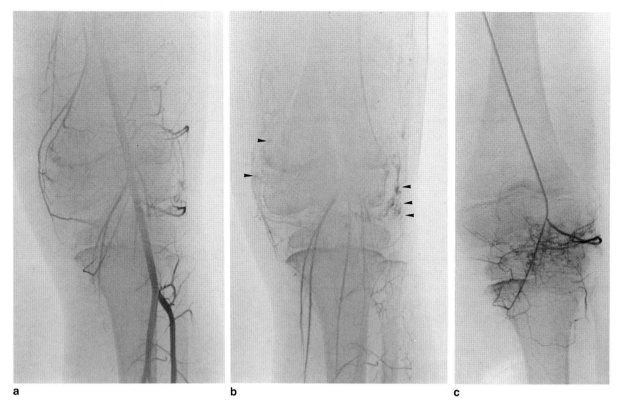

a   b   c

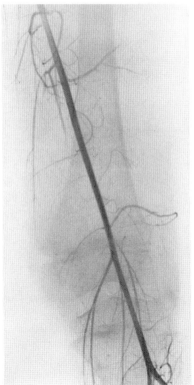

d

Fig. 1 **Young girl presenting with Klippel-Trenaunay syndrome complicated by recurrent hemarthrosis of the knee**
a, b Injection of the superficial femoral artery: synovial involvement is demonstrated on late film (arrowheads)
c Superselective injection of the periarticular arteries of the knee: small telan-
giectasic-like lesions are opacified in the periarticular area
d Control injection of the superficial femoral artery after embolization of the
articular pedicles. Permanent disappearance of the hemarthrosis

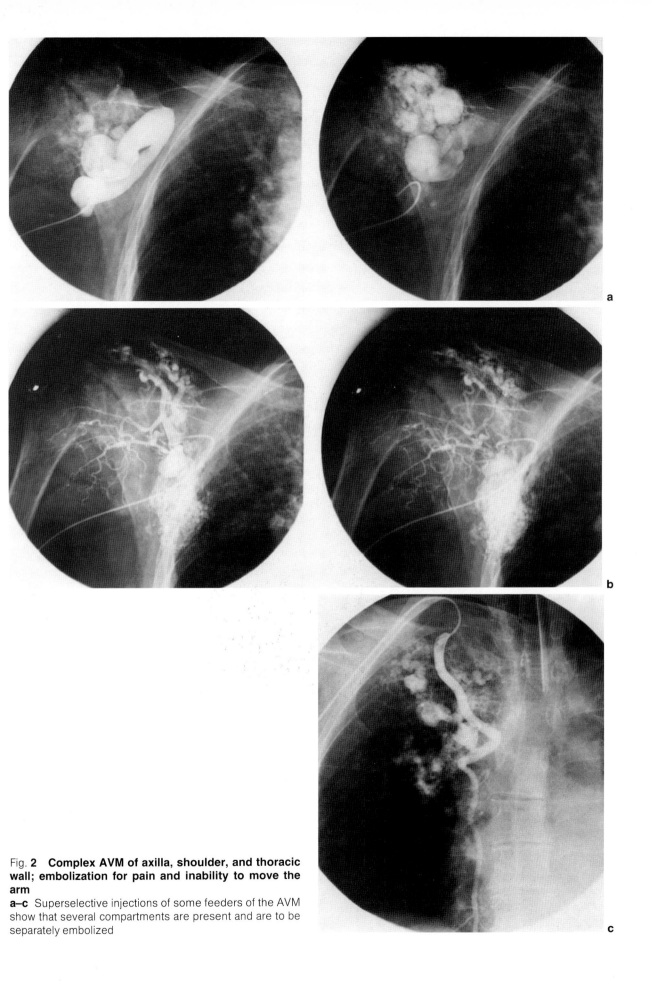

Fig. 2 Complex AVM of axilla, shoulder, and thoracic wall; embolization for pain and inability to move the arm
a–c Superselective injections of some feeders of the AVM show that several compartments are present and are to be separately embolized

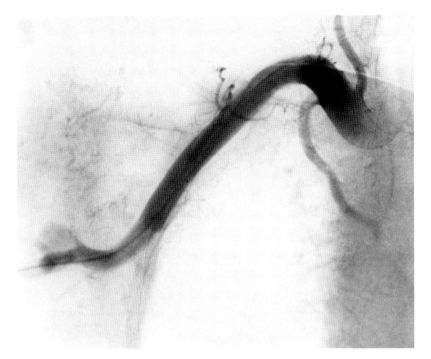

Fig. **2**
d Control after embolization with IBC and Lipiodol shows good devascularization of the AVM. Symptoms were improved by embolization

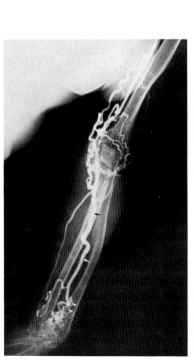

Fig. **3 AVM of the hand; previous partial amputation and surgical ligations that make catheterization of the malformation impossible by usual arterial approach**
a Descending opacification of the arterial system by femoral route. Multiple collateral arteries around the elbow; neither radial nor cubital arteries are usable; interosseous artery (arrow) is the main remaining artery feeding the AVM
b Direct puncture of the interosseous artery allowed catheterization and embolization of the malformation. Amputation could be avoided

a   b

Fig. **4 Young girl with Parkes-Weber syndrome,** presenting with pain and extensive bleeding ulcers. Diffuse lesions
a Injection of the superficial femoral artery
b, c Selective injections of pedicles of the deep femoral system. The extreme extensiveness of the AVM is evident; it precluded complete embolization despite five successive attempts. Amputation could not be avoided

a

b

c

a coaxial system, or when possible by direct manual compression of the venous component of the AVM.

The only real adverse factor is the extreme extensiveness of the lesions that makes it unlikely that all the feeding pedicles will be occluded (Fig. **4**); however, even if embolization techniques are clearly palliative in such situations, some apparently very complex malformations are found to have few compartments and are amenable to embolization through a few well-chosen pedicles.

Only a few series of peripheral AVM embolization have been reported since this technique has been available. Most of the reported cases are summarized in Table **1.** From 1975 to 1981, we explored by angiography 30 patients with AVM in order to plan treatment. Only 21 of them underwent embolization and are presently reported in the literature series.

Indications

Functional consequences of peripheral AVM include:

- *Postural disorders* related to leg length discrepancy or to functional impairment when a hand is involved.
- *Esthetic disorders* that are rarely bothersome; these are related to hypertrophy, varices, cutaneous angiomas, or to trophic disorders (edema, dermatitis, recurrent ulcers).
- *Pain* characterized by a feeling of heaviness that increases on walking, fatigue, or exposure to heat. Such pain often reduces strikingly the degree of activity of the patient. Pain manifestations are related to increased venous pressure; they are improved by elastic bandages, an activity that does not need standing in an upright position for a long

Table **1**

Authors (chronological order)	Patient sex/age	Location	Symptoms	A.V.F	Type	Number of embolizations	Previous treatments: Results, complications
Stanley (23)	F/29	Thigh	?	+	Deep, localized	1	Previous surgical ligation; good/disappearance of AVF
Olcott (21)	F/11	Thigh	Pain	+	?		Recurrence/hip disarticulation
	F/25	Arm	Pain, heart failure	+	?		Good
	F/24	Arm	Pain	+	?		Good
	F/21	Arm	Pain	+	?		Good
	F/22	Arm	Pain	+	?		Good
McErlean (17)	F/24	Lower limb	Pain	+	Deep diffuse fibrous dysplasia		Good (4 months)
Mitty (19)	F/23	Thigh	Pain	−	Deep, localized	1	Good (1 year)
Gedeon ((8)	F/23	Leg	Ulcerative lesions	+	Deep	4	Good/scarring/amputation avoided
Joyce (12)	F/9	Pelvis, lower limb	Heart failure	+	Deep, localized	3	Good/amputation avoided (18 mo)
	M/18	Pelvis and thigh	Heart failure	+	Deep, localized	3	Good/amputation avoided (18 mo)
Katzen (13)	F/28	Tibia	Pain	+	Osseous, localized	1	Good (1 year)/persistent AVM
Gomes (10)	F/20	Axilla	Pain, swelling in arm	+	Deep, localized	3	Good/reduction in symptoms
	F/13	Pelvis and leg	Enlargement, pathologic fracture	+	Deep, diffuse	3	Sepsis resolved/ peripheral nerve palsy/ hip disarticulation
	M/73	Foot	Pain, swelling, inability to walk	+	Deep, localized	2	Good/small skin slough
	M/43	Pelvis and leg	Enlargement, bleeding varix	+	Deep, diffuse	3	Good/varix resected
	M/33	Axilla and shoulder	Enlargement, cardiomegaly	+	Deep, diffuse	5	Good/reduction in shoulder and heart size
	M/17	Thigh and Knee	Pain, swelling	−	Diffuse, cavernous hemangioma	2	Improved/sciatic palsy resolved over 1 year
	F/13	Pelvis and thigh	Non-union	+	Deep, diffuse	2	Good/decreased pain/ internal fixation fracture
	F/17	Shoulder and arm	Pain, swelling	+	Deep, diffuse	1	Previous surgical ligation; decreased pain
	F/27	Foot	Pain, inability to walk	−	Cavernous hemangioma	1	Treated by direct puncture/Good/decreased swelling

Table **1**   (Continued)

Authors	Patient sex/age	Location	Symptoms	A.V.F	Type	Number of emboli-zations	Results complications
Personal series	M/57	Lower limb	Pain, inability to walk	+	Deep, diffuse	1	Improved/decreased pain
	F/15	Lower limb	Pain, bleeding ulcers	+	Deep, diffuse	5	Previous surgical liga-tions; scarring/recur-rence over 2 y, leg am-putation
	F/15	Lower limb	Bleeding ankle ulcers	+	Deep, osseous diffuse	2	Scarring (2 years)
	M/16	Lower limb	Pain	+	Deep, diffuse	2	Pain improved
	F/27	Lower limb, knee	Hemarthrosis	−	Deep, diffuse	2	Good: disappearance of bleeding
	M/19	Lower limb	Pain, ulceration of leg amputa-tion discussed	+	Deep, diffuse	4	Previous ligation; good: amputation avoided scarring of ulcerations
	M/31	Lower limb	Pain	+	Deep, diffuse	2	Previous surgical liga-tions; no improvement by embolization
	F/15	Lower limb	Pain, skin ulceration in-ability to walk	+	Deep, diffuse	1	Good; scarring of ulceration: ability to walk
	F/31	Lower limb, knee	Hemarthrosis	−	Deep, diffuse	1	Embolization localized to the knee: improved
	M/36	Lower limb	Pain, varix	−	Deep, diffuse	1	Previous surgical liga-tion; no improvement by embolization: localized muscular slough
	F/22	Lower limb, knee	Hemarthrosis	−	Deep, diffuse	1	Embolization localized to the knee: good
	F/14	Lower limb, knee	Hemarthrosis, pain	−	Deep, diffuse	1	Embolization localized to the knee: good
	F/6	Lower limb	Swelling, pain	−	Deep, diffuse	1	No improvement; stabil-ity of the symptoms
	F/42	Hand	Bleeding ulcer-ations, pain, varix amputa-tion considered	+	Deep, localized	1	Previous surgical liga-tions; good: amputation avoided; small skin slough
	M/44	Hand	Pain, bleeding ulcerations, amputation considered	+	Deep, localized	2	Previous partial amputa-tion; total amputation avoided
	M/32	Thoracic (ant. lat. post)	Swelling, car-diomegaly	+	Deep, localized	2	Preoperative emboliza-tion; partial surgical ex-cision
	F/70	Axilla and shoulder	Pain, inability to move the arm	+	Deep, osse-ous, localized	1	Improved: decreased pain and improvement in arm mobility

Table **1**   (Continued)

Authors	Patient sex/age	Location	Symptoms	A.V.F	Type	Number of emboli-zations	Previous treatments: Results, complications
Personal series (cont.)	M/36	Pelvis, lower limb	Pain, cardiomegaly	+	Deep, diffuse	3	Improved: decreased pain, reduction in heart size, temporary sexual impotence
	F/14	Thigh	Pain, enlargement	–	Deep, localized	1	Improved: persistence of enlargement
	F/30	Leg	Pain	–	Osseous, localized	1	Good, disappearance of pain
	M/50	Perineal	Pain	–	Venous angioma	1	Direct puncture; improved

time and that avoids any local trauma. In case of failure, venous surgery may be indicated.

In rare cases, the functional consequences are unbearable: incapacitating pain, which reduces the walking range in a young and active patient, extensive ulcers, which are sometimes hemorrhagic, recurrent hemarthroses involving mainly the knee and causing the same functional problems as hemophilia, heart failure due to a large arteriovenous fistula.

In our experience, it is worth noticing that half of the patients in group I were asymptomatic, that 75% of group II presented with knee hemarthrosis, and that only 7% in group III were asymptomatic. It seems, therefore, that symptoms are more severe in case of arteriovenous fistula and that patients with telangiectasias are specifically prone to hemarthrosis.

Such clinical settings used to be indications for aggressive surgical treatment: arterial ligation (its inefficacy is now recognized), excision (difficult or impossible to perform in case of diffuse or deep forms), even amputation in the most severe cases. Regarding the poor efficacy or the mutilating character of the surgical approaches (8), and the inefficiency of radiation therapy (14), embolization has been mainly advocated in such circumstances (9, 11–13, 16–22, 26, 27).

Results

Surgery

Szilagyi et al. (24) reported a series of 82 patients with limb angiodysplasia among whom 18 had undergone surgery. Results of surgical treatment depended on the superficial or deep location, and the focal or diffuse character of the lesion. Surgery included excision in the localized forms, and multiple arterial ligations, which may be associated with excision in the diffuse forms. The outcome was poor in 10% of the patients with localized forms, since the lesion increased in size after surgery. The results were good in the other nine patients, with no recurrence after total excision or no change in patient's status after partial excision. On the other hand, in the group of eight patients with diffuse and deep lesions, only once was the outcome good, two patients did not improve and in five the symptoms became severe and the malformation increased in size after surgery.

So, a good outcome is obtained after surgery, if excision is total and if a local lesion does not extend into deep tissues. On the other hand, total excision of an extensive lesion (in size and depth) is impossible, unless amputation is performed, and postoperative worsening is frequent.

Flanc (7) reported 50% good results in the focal form of limb angiodysplasia: however, the results are obtained in 75% of these only after amputation of a finger, a hand, or a foot. Szilagyi et al. (24, 25) proposed surgical abstention and elastic bandage in the diffuse forms and in the focal but deep malformations in which simple excision was not possible. In their series of 64 patients, who were treated according to these guidelines, they observed improvement, worsening, and no change in 12, 10 and 42 patients, respectively. Conservative treatment is, therefore, efficient in 20% of the patients but it does not preclude the development of the disorder in 15% of them. The value of such a protocol is not eliminating the other therapeutic modalities, in particular embolization, which was precluded by the previous multiple arterial ligations, which had no therapeutic effect (23).

Embolization

Which symptoms, are likely to be improved by embolization regarding their pathophysiology?

Extensive ulcers are certainly the consequence of increased venous pressure, but also result very likely from ischemia secondary to arteriovenous shunting. Topography of the ulcers, which is distal to the arteriovenous communication in our experience, is in favor of the latter hypothesis. Embolization may be efficient if it decreases the shunt.

On the other hand, pain does not have any clinical characteristic of ischemia because of decreased arterial flow. Its worsening with heat or the upright position makes it related to increased venous pressure. It increases in the presence of multiple arteriovenous communications. Lengthening is encountered in all arteriographic types. It is related to advanced bone growth depending on venous stasis. It is also seen in arteriovenous fistula and childhood phlebitis. It appears that embolization is unlikely to control pain and lengthening when the AVM is diffuse.

Soft tissue swelling depends on venous stasis, but the bulk of the malformation (either its arterial or venous components) per se sometimes accounts for an important part in the hypertrophy and can therefore be treated with embolization.

Clinical evolutive potential of limb angiodysplasias may be attested to by complications in the course of a previously well-tolerated Klippel-Trenaunay syndrome: appearance worsening of clinical signs of an arteriovenous fistula, recurrence of the malformation after incomplete excision or arterial ligation or a too proximal embolization. This evolutive potential seems to be difficult to predict; however, in our experience five of the eight patients with the most severe clinical manifestations were around their puberty phase and two young girls presented a worsening of the clinical condition at puberty. Therefore, when radical treatment of the malformation is not possible and if the clinical status allows it, it seems preferable not to start an agressive therapy until puberty. Besides morphologic changes, the outcome may be toward an extension in size and depth by recruitment of arterial feeders around the lesion. This occurs systematically in active AVMs (with high-flow arteriovenous fistulas) after an arterial ligation or an incorrect embolization.

Clinical results of embolization are shown in Table **1**.

Complications

Postembolization syndrome is common after AVM embolization; it is related to inadvertent muscular and cutaneous arterial occlusion; pain may be severe for 36 to 48 hours after embolization, requiring treatment with major analgesics.

More severe ischemic complications include extensive myonecrosis, skin slough, nerve palsy, and sexual impotence (in one case of large pelvic embolization). In the reported cases, only one patient with infected muscular necrosis necessitated local surgery; all other ischemic complications spontaneously resolved.

Major risks of embolization are inadvertent migration of embolus to the pulmonary circulation and reflux of particles toward the normal distal bed. Choice of particles large enough and superselective catheterization prevent these potential complications.

Conclusion

When conservative treatments become inefficacious, AVM embolization should now be performed before surgery if the malformation is diffuse, deep, unresectable, or requires amputation. Its palliative effects may be sufficient to avoid mutilating surgery and are better than those of arterial ligations, which have no therapeutic effect (23).

References

1. Andre JM. Les dysplasies vasculaires systématisées. Paris: Expansion Scientifique Française, 1973.
2. Berenstein A, Kricheff II. Catheter and material selection for transarterial embolization: technical considerations, I: catheters. Radiology 1979;132:619(630.
3. Berenstein A, Kricheff II. Catheter and material selection for transarterial embolization: technical considerations, II: materials. Radiology 1979;132:631–639.
4. Bliznak J, Staple TW. Radiology of angiodysplasias of the limb. Radiology 1974;110:35–44.
5. Coursley G, Ivins JC, Barker NW. Congenital arteriovenous fistulas in the extremities: an analysis of 69 cases. Angiology 1956;7:201–217.
6. Enjolras O, Reizine D, Riche MC, Merland JJ. Angiomes cervicocéphaliques superficiels: faut-il demander des examens complémentaires? Presse Méd 1985;14:1866–1870.
7. Flanc C. Congenital arteriovenous fistulas of the extremities. Aust NZ J Surg 1968;37:222–232.
8. Gedeon A, Manelfe C, Barret A, Pradere B. Angiodysplasie du membre inférieur avec mégadolichoartère et fistules artério-veineuses multiples: approche thérapeutique. Chirurgie 1980;106:409–414.
9. Gomes MMR, Bernatz PE. Arteriovenous fistulas: a review and ten-year experience at the Mayo Clinic. Mayo Clin Proc 1970;45:81–102.
10. Gomes AS, Busuttil RW, Baker JD, Oppenheim W, Machleder HI, Moore WS. Congenital arteriovenous malformations: the role of transcatheter embolization. Arch Surg 1983;118:817–825.
11. Gorlin RJ, Pindborg JJ, Cohen MM Jr, eds. Syndromes of the head and neck. New York: McGraw-Hill, 1976:412–417.
12. Joyce PF, Sundaram M, Riaz A, Wolverson MK, Barner HB, Hoffman RJ. Embolization of extensive peripheral angiodysplasias: the alternative to radical surgery. Arch Surg 1980;115:665–668.
13. Katzen BT, Said S. Arteriovenous malformation of bone: an experience with therapeutic embolization. AJR 1981;136:427–429.
14. Kaufman SL, Kumar AAJ, Roland JMA. Transcatheter embolization in the management of congenital arteriovenous malformations. Radiology 1980;137:21–29.

15. Letts RM. Orthopaedic treatment of hemangiomatous hypertrophy of the lower extremity. J Bone Joint Surg [Br] 1977;59:777–783.

16. Levin DC, Gordon DH, McSweeney J. Arteriography of peripheral hemangiomas. Radiology 1976;121:625–630.

17. McErlean DP, Shanik DG, Martin EA. Transcatheter embolisation of bone tumour arteriovenous malformations. Br Radiol 1978;51:414–419.

18. Malan E, Puglionisi A. Congenital angiodysplasias of the extremities. J Cardiovasc Surg (Torino) 1965;6:255–345.

19. Mitty HA, Kleiger B. Partial embolization of large peripheral hemangioma for pain control. Radiology 1978;127:671–672.

20. Natali J, Merland JJ. Superselective arteriography and therapeutic embolization for vascular malformations (angiodysplasias). J Cardiovasc Surg 1976;17:465–472.

21. Olcott C, Newton TH, Stoney RJ, Ehrenfeld WK. Intraarterial embolization in the management of arteriovenous malformations. Surgery 1976;79:3–12.

22. Ricketts RR, Finck E, Yellin AE. Management of major arteriovenous fistulas by arteriographic techniques. Arch Surg 1978;113:1153–1159.

23. Stanley RJ, Cubillo E. Nonsurgical treatment of arteriovenous malformations of the trunk and limb by transcatheter arterial embolization. Radiology 1975;115:609–612.

24. Szilagyi E, Elliot JP, DeRusso FJ, Smith RF. Peripheral congenital arteriovenous fistulas. Surgery 1965;57:61–81.

25. Szilagyi E, Smith RF, Elliot JP, Hageman JH. Congenital arteriovenous anomalies of the limbs. Arch Surg 1976;111:423–429.

26. Tice DA, Clauss RH, Keirle AM, Reed GE. Congenital arteriovenous fistulae of the extremities. Arch Surg 1963;80:130–135.

27. Weingarten A, Doyon D, Roche A, Curet P, Harry G. Place de l'arteriographie supersélective et de l'embolisation dans le traitement des angiodysplasies des membres avec shunt. J Radiol Electrol 1978;59:471–477.

Embolization of Varicoceles

E. Zeitler

Sclerotherapy of the internal spermatic vein using a catheter with entry in the groin is a procedure for percutaneous radiologic embolotherapy (4, 5, 10, 12, 20, 21). Possible forms of sclerosing and embolization for treatment of varicoceles are presented in Table **1**.

Prerequisites for percutaneous treatment are a secure diagnosis and the possibility of catheterization of the internal spermatic vein (testicular vein) through the inferior vena cava and renal vein. For the occlusion and the appropriate site of embolization, important suprainguinal anastomoses have to be phlebographically localized before the procedure (Fig. **1**).

Epidemiology

The frequency of varicoceles is related to age. They are only rarely diagnosed before the age of 10.

Table **1** Methods of percutaneous treatment of varicoceles

Sclerotherapy	Embolization
A. Hypertonic glucose 75% plus monoethanolamine	A. Gianturco coils
B. Varicocid	B. Detachable balloons
C. Aethoxysclerol	C. Bucrylate (isobutyl-2-cyanoacrylate)

Systematic screening investigations in recruits before their military service or in students showed asymptomatic varicoceles in 1 to 15% of young men (19). Apart from these varicoceles detected by screening methods, there are rare symptomatic forms that are

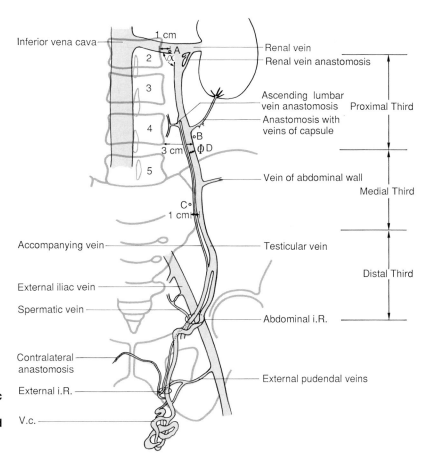

Fig. **1 Diagram showing anatomic situation, entry site, and the angle between the left testicular vein and the renal vein,** as well as the supra- and infra-inguinal anastomoses

detected when investigating conjugal infertility (3). Varicoceles are the most important cause of male infertility (10 to 60%) (4, 6).

Diagnosis

Clinical examination alone is not sufficient for a sure detection of varicoceles. Thus, before phlebography of the internal spermatic vein (Figs. **2, 3**), Doppler ultrasound investigation with a Valsalva maneuver or thermography of the upright patient should be done additionally (3, 6, 14, 15). The additional use of the Doppler ultrasound technique reduces the number of subclinical varicoceles considerably, so that phlebography can be used with much more accuracy.

Seminal Cytology

A reduction of sperm count and spermatozoic motility can be considered as an important indication for a varicocele. In addition to this non-specific effect on sperm count and motility, a distinct change in seminal cytology has been attributed to the influence of the varicoceles. An increased incidence of spermatozoa with elongated heads, "tapering forms", and of amorphous and immature sperm cells in semen have been described (11, 12). Although some investigators could confirm these findings and others could not, a prospective study has shown that the analysis of seminal cytology is of limited help in detecting subclinical varicoceles (7).

Diagnosis of a varicocele is made by means of:
– Inspection and palpation of the scrotum
– Ultrasound Doppler technique or thermography, or both
– Phlebography of the internal spermatic vein

Indications for the treatment of a varicocele are:
– Symptomatic varicocele
– Men wishing to procreate or with infertility known for 2 years. Often in these patients sperm count and spermatozoic motility are found to be reduced
– To maintain fertility of boys after the age of 12 years (15)

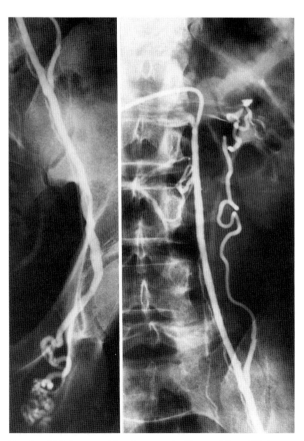

Fig. **2** **Phlebographic demonstration of insufficiency of the spermatic vein** with varicocele on the left side

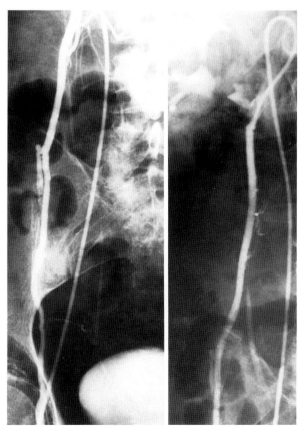

Fig. **3** **Phlebographic demonstration of insufficiency of the spermatic vein** with varicocele on the right side

Phlebography of the Internal Spermatic Vein

Phlebography is mainly performed by puncture and catheterization of the femoral vein (6). An approach by the right jugular vein can also be used (22). For phlebography of the internal spermatic vein, specially-developed catheters are used (2, 10, 13, 20). Selective catheterization of the left internal spermatic vein is possible in more than 95%. The rate is only reduced in patients with a periaortic venous ring and high tortuosity. From August 1977 to December 20, 1986, 2221 varicoceles were diagnosed in 2358 patients referred for phlebography of the internal spermatic vein; 1621 (73%) of these varicoceles were localized on the left side and 600 (27%) on the right.

We used sclerotherapy in 972 of the 1621 (60%) left isided varicoceles. In the other 40% we recommended surgery because of the presence of venous anomalies or because a safe positioning of the catheter was not feasible. In 68 patients (11%) with a right-sided phlebographically proved varicocele, a sclerotherapeutic occlusion was done some months later, because after the left-sided sclerotherapy no change in seminal cytology was seen. In these cases, no surgery was done primarily.

Complications

Before performing phlebography, the patient has to be informed about the possible side-effects and complications. Intolerance of contrast media and mechanical wall injuries of the spermatic vein are the most significant risks. In 1.5% of the patients, we encountered slight reactions to contrast medium and three severe reactions with cardiovascular symptoms (0.1%). Dissection of the venous wall or perforation of the internal spermatic vein were phlebographically seen in 1.5% of the patients.

Results

A phlebogram of the spermatic vein gives accurate information on the presence of incompetent ostial valves and reflux of contrast medium into the spermatic vein. Furthermore, it gives information about whether or not the reflux of contrast medium with a Valsalva test reaches the inguinal region. Reflux of contrast medium into the internal spermatic vein depends on:

- Site of the contrast medium injection into the renal vein or selectively into the internal spermatic vein.
- Position of the patient (a horizontal position of the patient or an upright oblique position with the table raised by 30°). When evaluating the grade of insufficiency of the spermatic vein, the way of applying contrast medium, too, has to be considered.

When the varicocele is evaluated by selective injection into the internal spermatic vein, venous insufficiency can be differentiated as follows:

Grade I: Contrast medium flows only in the proximal direction through the first valve and not further.

Grade II: Contrast medium flows only as far as the iliosacral joint. Reflux into this region may, e. g., signify a state following a surgical intervention together with ligature and can then not be defined as a varicocele. However, if there is a reflux through collateral veins to the testicular veins, recurrent varicocele must be assumed.

Grade III: Reflux of contrast medium reaches the testicle or the level of the pubis.

Further treatment depends greatly on the result of the phlebogram, since accompanying veins and venous plexuses are present in more than 50% of the patients with varicoceles. The venous variations can be divided into those in which sclerotherapy or local embolization is feasible and those in which embolization or sclerotherapy is either very difficult to perform or not possible at all. Thus, the variations of the internal spermatic vein in the presence of a left-sided varicocele may be classified as several types (Fig. **4**) (1). In types I and III, all percutaneous occlusion treatments are possible. In types II and IV, treatment is feasible if the catheter tip can be placed very close to the inguinal ligament. In type V with a periaortic ring, it is successful only in selected cases.

Percutaneous treatment by means of sclerotherapy or embolization is feasible in those cases in which there is only venous drainage into the renal vein or in the presence of several parallel veins proximal to the inguinal canal, which then reach a main stem. Embolization by detachable balloons or by bucrylate can also be performed in the presence of transverse connections to the paravertebral pelvic veins. In these cases sclerotherapy should, however, be avoided. If there are doubts about the presence of communicating veins to the kidneys or the pelvic organs, surgery has to be preferred. An alternative is the application of bucrylate or of a detachable balloon very proximally in the spermatic vein (9, 10, 14). A phlebogram of the internal spermatic vein is an absolute prerequisite for the choice of an optimal treatment modality, embolization, sclerotherapy, or surgery, and any percutaneous radiologic cure.

Radiologic Treatment

Percutaneous radiologic treatment can immediately follow phlebography, which is performed on an outpatient basis. This treatment can, as is shown in Table **1,** either be sclerotherapy or embolotherapy.

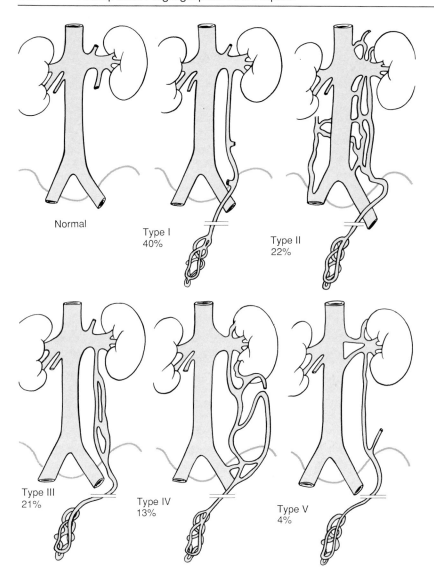

Normal

Type I
40%

Type II
22%

Type III
21%

Type IV
13%

Type V
4%

Fig. **4   Classification of the different types of spermatic variations** indicating the possibility of percutaneous treatment

Gianturco-Wallace-Coils

If Gianturco-Wallace coils are chosen (16, 17), the use of minicoils should be avoided, since these migrate more easily. When a safe position of the catheter in the internal spermatic vein is achieved, application of the coil does not pose any particular technical problem. Thrombotic occlusion of the vessel occurs within 20 minutes. Extraction of the coil because of complaints from patients was very seldom necessary.

Bucrylate (Isobutyl-2-Cyanoacrylate)

Embolization with bucrylate requires the application of a coaxial catheter system (10). The site of embolization must be situated inferior to the lowest anastomosis between the spermatic vein and the perirenal venous plexus or the paravertebral veins. According to Kunnen (10), the procedure should only be performed if the spermatic vein shows no parallel veins at the site of embolization. All catheters are continuously moistened through a T-adaptor with a solution of glucose 5%. After withdrawing the guide wire and proper positioning of the inner catheter for embolization, the patient is brought into a nearly horizontal position in order to stop blood flow in the spermatic vein. A first tuberculin syringe is filled with 1 ml glucose 10%. In a second syringe, the following substances are aspirated in sequence:

1. 0.1 ml 60% contrast medium
2. Between 0.3 and 0.6 ml of bucrylate
3. 0.1 ml 60% contrast medium.

Glucose 10%, 0.7 ml, is injected to push the entire embolus into the spermatic vein. As the coaxial embolization catheter is immediately pulled back,

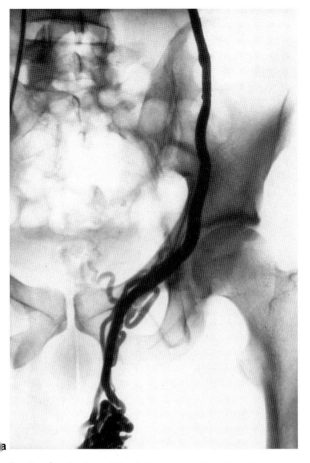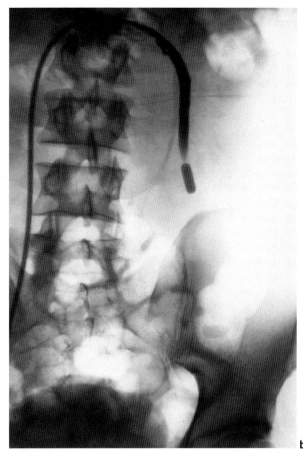

Fig. 5   **Occlusion of the left spermatic vein with a detachable balloon**
a Diagnostic phlebography
b Occlusion

the remaining 0.3 ml glucose 10% is injected in order to clean the catheter of bucrylate completely. The inner catheter is then withdrawn. The outer cobra catheter is pulled back into the caval vein and rinsed with glucose 5%. If any resistance is noticed while rinsing, adherence of residual bucrylate to the wall of the catheter is suspected. The outer catheter is also withdrawn. As soon as the tissue adhesive comes in contact with blood, it polymerizes to form a thrombus (2, 10).

Detachable Balloons

Application of detachable balloons (Fig. 5) with a special device introduced by White et al. (18) for embolotherapy of different indications is performed as follows: a special device for coaxial application of the balloon catheter is used via a diagnostic catheter placed in the internal spermatic vein. After accurate phlebographic control, the balloon catheter is filled with contrast medium to the diameter of the spermatic vein in order to avoid any slipping of the balloon. The balloon is placed inferior to the communication of the spermatic vein with collaterals. Only after safe fixation of the balloon, the catheter is removed and phlebographic control performed. Before definitive placement of the balloon, a change of site is possible by withdrawing the catheter into the guide catheter.

Sclerotherapy

After diagnostic phlebography, the sclerosing agent chosen for therapy (Varicocid, Aethoxysclerol) is applied if no outflow of contrast into the renal vein during phlebography is observed. In veins with a

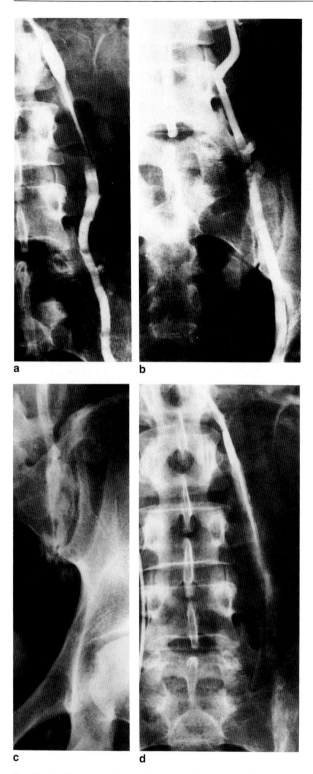

a   b

c   d

Fig. **6 Left spermatic vein sclerotherapy with occlusion balloon catheter**
a Demonstration of the occlusion balloon
b Spermatic vein insufficiency
c, d Control after effective sclerotherapy

narrow lumen the diagnostic catheter may be suitable for this procedure. When the diameter of the internal spermatic vein is larger, it is necessary to place an occlusion balloon catheter in the upper segment of the internal spermatic vein and to fill the balloon catheter with contrast medium in order to avoid outflow of the sclerosing agent into the renal vein or inferior vena cava. When several parallel veins that communicate are present, sclerotherapy may nevertheless be performed if the phlebogram taken in a semi-upright position of the patient on the tilting table rules out outflow into the renal vein. The catheter tip has to be located inferiorly to the last side communications. Before the application of the sclerosing agent, therefore, examination of whether the contrast medium reaches the testis and whether there is a reflux into the renal vein must be done.

Immediately after application of the contrast medium, 3 ml of sclerosing medium (Aethoxysclerol or Varicocid 1%) are injected and then 1 ml of contrast medium is injected again. Thus, the site of the drug is documented in between the contrast medium injections, and the position of the drug may, if necessary, be changed distally or proximally.

During sclerosis, the patient notices a dragging pain in the course of the spermatic vein, which decreases considerably within 15 minutes. Sclerosis is induced 30 minutes after injection. A control phlebogram has to be performed after the procedure. In case no complete occlusion has been obtained, a second dose of sclerosing medium can be injected. A second dose is required in 20% of patients. Figure **6** shows the site of the occlusion balloon catheter and the sclerosing agent. Although some regularly use a balloon catheter for sclerosis on the left side (14), it was required in only 15% of our patients.

Follow-Up After Treatment

After embolization or sclerotherapy, a compression bandage has to be applied to the groin. The patient can leave the radiologic department 2 hours after the procedure. We advise the patient not to have sexual intercourse for the next 2 days. If the patient complains of pain in the scrotum or if painful local thrombosis of the testicular vein is present, a suspensory should be used and cool water compresses are recommended.

Results

Results of percutaneous radiologic treatment do not really depend on the type of venous occlusion and are competitive with surgical results (Table **2**). Follow-up investigations after embolization using bucrylate (3, 10), detachable balloons (18), or sclerotherapy (1, 5, 8, 14) show comparable results.

Table **2** Persistence of varicoceles after therapy

	Persistent varicocele (%)
Surgical treatment	3–15
Sclerotherapy	2
Detachable balloon	2.7
Bucrylate	< 1

We studied the phlebographic outcome after sclerotherapy 3 to 12 months after spermatic vein occlusion in 277 of 1040 patients. A persistence of an incompetent spermatic vein, grade III, was found in 11 patients and led to a second-sclerotherapy. Phlebogram performed in these 11 patients showed an occlusion in six and venous patency in five (2%). These results have to be compared with the findings after surgical cure of varicoceles in which persistence is cited in 1 to 25% (6). We performed also a phlebogram of the internal spermatic vein in 105 patients in whom a surgical ligature was performed at least 1 year previously and who were referred for reevaluation of persistence of a varicocele. In 57% we found persistence or recurrence of the varicocele. In 23 cases a percutaneous sclerotherapy led to a permanent occlusion. In 37 cases a second surgical intervention was indicated.

Combination of Urologic and Radiologic Treatment

In case of a second surgical intervention it may be advisable to perform surgery in cooperation with the radiologist. The radiologist introduces a catheter into the internal spermatic vein and tries to mark the incompetent internal spermatic vein intraoperatively under fluoroscopic image intensifier control. A successful ligature may then also be proved during surgery by phlebography control.

Complications

Potential complications after occlusion treatment of the internal spermatic vein are:
- Local changes at the puncture site (groin, neck)
- Local changes in the scrotum, around testicular veins
- Local changes in the region of the internal spermatic vein in its retroperitoneal course
- Complications caused by embolization material

Local complications at the site of percutaneous puncture are extremely rare. We only encountered them twice in 1040 sclerotherapies.

After sclerotherapy, we detected local thrombophlebitis of the testicular vein in 20 patients (2%). In one patient a perforation of the spermatic vein led to a retroperitoneal hematoma causing a left-sided transient renal pyelectasis. Regression could be documented by a control urogram within 6 weeks. There were no other complications noted after sclerotherapy.

Displacement of a detachable balloon may represent a rare complication. White et al. (18) observed one case and we encountered also one case of embolization of the detachable balloon from the spermatic vein into the lower left pulmonary artery. No permanent damage resulted. A case of retroperitoneal fibrosis with urinary obstruction and pain over more than 9 months was reported (19). Surgical extraction of the Gianturco coil was necessary.

Applying bucrylate, entrapment of the catheter due to a rapid polymerization of the material in the spermatic vein is only encountered if the technique is not appropriate. This complication may require surgery. Altogether, there are no severe complications reported, independent of the choice of the sclerosing or embolization modality used.

Criteria for Evaluation of Results

Criteria for the evaluation of results are phlebography, the assessment of changes in the quality of semen, and finally the number of gravidities of the female partner. Results reported here would be incomplete if the situation of the women were not considered. Also, follow-up results reported by Comhaire et al. (3) show that radiologic treatment can have induced gravidity in 70% if medical evaluation of the female partner is normal.

A complete follow-up study of the patients we treated is difficult because of the fact that the patients are referred from different physicians and that they come from distant places to be diagnosed and cured. We received only 236 responses (39%) to a letter to 600 patients treated more than 2 years ago. In these 236 patients, 126 gravidities were confirmed (53%).

Choice of Occlusion Procedure

Primarly, perfect handling of the corresponding technique is a prerequisite for the choice of each occlusion procedure. This is especially important in embolization treatments using bucrylate, tissue adhesives, detachable balloon catheters, and Gianturco coils. In all techniques, significant complications are very rarely encountered. This is of particular significance because, in general, clinical findings are normal and there is just infertility to be cured, which only in rare cases causes subjective complaints. It is, therefore, important before treatment to examine whether there exists a definite wish for a child. Sometimes a combination of embolization and sclerotherapy might be advisable, since if several side veins are present and communicate, the application of a balloon or of bucrylate and distal proximal injection of a sclerosing agent may influence positively the results of treatment (8, 14).

An advantage of using a detachable balloon for occlusion of the internal spermatic vein is that this is a good training region for the technique. Independent of this, it is an expensive procedure.

So far, the significance of a right-sided varicocele is not known and needs further studies.

Conclusion

For the left spermatic vein the transfemoral approach and for the right the transjugular approach are safe and simple. All percutaneous techniques of spermatic vein occlusion are performed without general anesthesia and on an outpatient basis. They can be well-controlled and are as effective as surgical ligation. Sclerotherapy also is very convenient and economic.

References

1. Bahren W, Lenz M, Porst H, Wierschin W. Nebenwirkungen, Komplikationen und Kontraindikationen der perkutanen Sklerotherapie der V. spermatica interna zur Behandlung der idiopathischen Varikozele. RöFo 1983;138:172–179.
2. Bigot JM, Chatel A, Dectot H, Helenon C. Phelebographie spermatique rétrograde. Ann Radiol (Paris) 1978;21:515–523.
3. Comhaire F, Monteyne R, Kunnen M. The value of scrotal thermography as compared with selective retrograde venography of the internal spermatic vein for the diagnosis of "subclinical" varicocele. Fertil Steril 1976;27:694–698.
4. Glezerman M, Jecht EW, eds. Varicocele and male infertility II. Berlin: Springer, 1984.
5. Iaccarino V. Trattamento conservativo del varicocele: flebografia selettiva o scleroterapia delle vene gonadiche. Riv Radiol 1977;17:107–117.
6. Jecht EW, Zeitler E, eds. Varicocele and male infertility. Berlin: Springer, 1982.
7. Jecht EW, Muller R, Zieglwalner E. Varicocele and seminal cytology. In: Jecht EW, Zeitler E, eds. Varicocele and male infertility. Berlin, Springer 1982:35–40.
8. Jecht EW, Comhaire F. Andrology: Non-surgical treatment of varicocele. Proceedings of the 15th International Congress of Dermatology, Tokyo, Japan, May 23–28,1982.
9. Kaufman SL, Kader S, Barth KH, Smyth JW, Walsh PC, White RI. Mechanisms of recurrent varicocele after balloon occlusion or surgical ligation of the internal spermatic vein. Radiology 1983;147:435–440.
10. Kunnen M. Nonsurgical cure of varicocele by transcatheter embolization of the internal spermatic vein with bucrylate. In: Jecht EW, Zeitler E, eds. Varicocele and male infertility. Berlin: Springer,1982:154–161.
11. MacLeod J. Seminal cytology in the presence of varicocele. Fertil Steril 1965;16:735.
12. MacLeod J. Further observations on the role of varicocele in human male fertility. Fertil Steril 1969;20:545.
13. Riedl P. Selektive Phlebographie und Katheterthrombosierung der Vena testicularis bei primärer Varikozele. Wien Klin Wochenschr-Suppl 1979;91:3.
14. Riedl P, Kumpan W, Maier U, Stackl W, Lungmayr G. Long-term results after sclerotherapy of the spermatic vein in patients with varicocele. Cardiovasc Intervent Radiol 1985;8:46–49.
15. Sorensen R, Berger T, Kaufmann K, Hamm B. Venographie und Sklerotherapie von Varicocele bei Kindern und Jugendlichen. International Symposium on Therapeutic Interventional Radiology, Berlin, Nov 7–9, 1985.
16. Thelen M, Weissbach L, Schramm P. The treatment of idiopathic varicocele by transfemoral spiral occlusion of the left testicular vein. In: Jecht EW, Zeitler E, eds. Varicocele and male infertility. Berlin: Springer, 1982:147–152.
17. Weissbach L, Thelen M, Adolphs HD. Treatment of idiopathic varicoceles by transfemoral testicular vein occlusion. In: Jecht EW, Zeitler E, eds. Varicocele and male infertility. Berlin: Springer, 1982:192–197.
18. White RI, Kaufman SL, Barth KH, Kadir S, Smyth JW, Walsh PC. Occlusion of varicoceles with detachable balloons. Radiology 1981;139:327–334.
19. Wutz J. Epidemiology of idiopathic varicocele. In: Jecht EW, Zeitler E, eds. Varicocele and male infertility. Berlin: Springer, 1982:3–5.
20. Zeitler E, Jecht E, Richter EI, Seyferth W. Technik und Ergebnisse der Spermatika-Phlebographie bei 136 Männern mit primärer Sterilität. RöFo 1979;131:131–179.
21. Zeitler E, Jecht E, Richter EI, Seyferth W. Perkutane Behandlung männlicher Infertilität im Rahmen der selektiven Spermatika-Phlebographie mit Katheter. RöFo 1980;132:293–300.
22. Zollikofer CL, Formanek A, Castaneda-Zuniga W, Amplatz K. Modified technique for embolization of the internal spermatic vein. In: Jecht EW, Zeitler E, eds. Varicocele and male infertility. Berlin: Springer, 1982:162–172.

Embolization of Abdominal Aortic Aneurysms

P. Rossi and P. Pavone

Surgical treatment of abdominal aortic aneurysms is considered mandatory on the basis of the survival statistics of treated compared with untreated groups (9, 14). Higher 5-year survival rates (50 to 62%) are, in fact, obtained after elective aneurysmectomy with interposition of a graft, compared with the control group (10 to 19%) (9, 10, 16).

Surgical bypass procedures have a relatively low incidence of complications and a mortality rate ranging from 1,5 to 5% (9, 10). This is generally considered reasonable, since there is a high incidence of aneurysm rupture in the untreated group (35% of patients followed more than 2 years) (6, 11). Although it is impossible to predict early rupture, mortality following emergency surgery after rupture is very high (35 to 65%) (4, 6, 15).

Indications for prompt surgical treatment should include symptomatic patients, rapid expansion shown on follow-up diagnostic imaging, and size greater than 4 to 5 cm (10).

Aneurysmectomy and graft replacement are, however, major vascular surgical procedures and related mortality can dramatically increase when general risk factors are present. Extensive atherosclerotic disease can cause concomitant cardiac, renal, or cerebral vascular insufficiency, and in heavy smokers respiratory insufficiency can also be present. Arterial hypertension, either essential or due to a renovascular disorder, advanced age of the patient, and in rare cases (4%) the presence of a neoplastic disease can all be contra-indications to surgical intervention (17). Reported series show a surgical mortality rate as high as 60% in poor-risk patients (4, 16).

The clinical development of patients with asymptomatic abdominal aortic aneurysm treated conservatively as a result of operative contra-indications has been described (16). Death followed such treatment in 70.9% of patients. The cause of death was frequently related to general atherosclerotic (mostly coronary) involvement (55%), but rupture of the aneurysm continued to be a significant source of loss of life (27%) (8).

Alternative surgical procedures to aneurysmectomy should therefore be considered, especially in those cases in which aneurysms are symptomatic, of large size, or have a tendency to increase in diameter. The first surgical experiences, obtained before the development of a suitable vascular prosthesis, included attempts at external or internal reinforcement or constriction of the lumen of the aneurysm. Cellophane or muscle wrapping, fascia lata or metal banding, and intraluminal wiring have all been advocated for this purpose (2, 3, 12).

Of these techniques, the introduction of wires into the aneurysm through a needle that directly punctures the vascular wall after surgical exposure has recently been reproposed as a palliative measure in unresectable aneurysm (7). The thrombus produced by the wire contributes to the straightening and reinforcement of the aneurysmal sac, leaving the lumen of the aorta patent, with rapid axial flow to the iliac arteries. Using such a technique, a acceptable mortality rate is obtained in high-risk patients (12.5%) and a lower incidence of rupture is found at 2 years (14%) compared with a control group of patients (7). However, the risk of complete thrombosis of the aneurysm and the poor results at late follow-up (33% survival at 5 years) have limited the application of surgical aneurysmal wiring.

Bilateral axillofemoral bypass has been proposed as an alternative to surgical aneurysmectomy (8). In this procedure, ligation of the external iliac arteries is performed in order to stop the flow through the aneurysm and promote complete thrombosis of the aneurysmal sac. However, in the experience reported by Goldman et al. (5), in 3 out of 15 cases patency and continuous flow through the internal iliac artery prevented thrombosis of the aneurysm, with persistent risk of rupture.

Ligation of the iliac artery before its bifurcation is not feasible with the atraumatic surgical techniques used in extra-anatomic bypass. Percutaneous embolization techniques have therefore been used to obtain complete thrombosis of the aneurysmal sac, in association with axillobifemoral bypass to maintain peripheral flow.

Percutaneous Embolization Techniques

Percutaneous thrombosis of the aneurysm can be obtained either before or after surgical axillobifemoral bypass. There is no definitive agreement on this point, but a few considerations can be mentioned. By first performing the bypass procedure, one may avoid the need for percutaneously induced thrombosis in most cases. As reported by Goldman et al. (5), thrombosis was not achieved with this method in only 3 of 15 cases, in which simultaneous occlusion of both internal iliac arteries was required to obtain embolization of the aneurysm. This procedure also induced significant morphologic ischemic changes in the gluteal muscles. In one case the researchers were not able to control the flow through the internal iliac artery completely and the patient died subsequently from aneurysmal rupture.

We have found it more useful to perform embolization of the aneurysm immediately before surgical intervention (13). Using bilateral femoral percutaneous catheterization makes maneuvering easier and the introduction of various embolizing materials possible. The aim of obtaining bilateral occlusion of the common iliac arteries while keeping the internal iliac arteries patent further justifies this approach.

Berguer et al. (1) described a third technique with catheters passed bilaterally through surgically exposed common femoral arteries after axillobifemoral bypass. The use of Fogarty balloons without an inner lumen required catheterization through the axillary artery in order to inject the embolizing agents.

Percutaneous Approach and Materials

An approach through the axillary artery is mandatory when the procedure is performed after surgical bypass. The same route can be used when severe atherosclerotic involvement of the iliac arteries prevents catheterization through the femoral artery.

The ideal material for embolization of the common iliac artery by this route is represented by detachable balloons. However, balloons as large as 1 cm are needed. These are costly, and skill and experience are required in order to obtain precise detachment of the balloon in the iliac arteries by means of a coaxial catheter technique (18).

Coils can be used easily when the atherosclerotic involvement of the common iliac artery does not allow peripheral dislocation of the coil itself (Fig. 1).

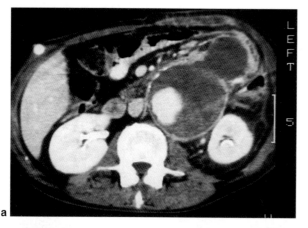

a

Fig. 1 Embolization of abdominal aortic aneurysm
a CT shows a huge bisaccular aneurysm of the abdominal aorta. Poor general condition of the patient prevented aneurysmectomy, and embolization was planned due to the high risk of rupture. The decision was made to perform axillobifemoral bypass immediately before CT and the angiographic procedure. The embolization was carried out through a left transaxillary approach due to bilateral external iliac artery occlusion

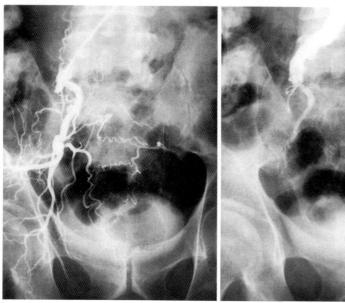

b   c

Fig. **1**
b The initial angiographic control shows the right hypogastric artery to be the only patent runoff vessel
c This branch was occluded with multiple Gianturco coils and Gelfoam pledgets

Large diameter coils (8 to 15 mm) have to be used in order to avoid dislocation in the external iliac artery. Multiple coils are advanced through the axillary route in the common iliac artery before embolization of the aneurysmal sac is started.

Bucrylate injection through the axillary artery can be used only postoperatively after surgical ligation of the external iliac artery (5). The glue is injected in the internal iliac arteries. However, occlusion of the peripheral branches of the hypogastric artery may cause ischemic changes of the gluteal muscles and in one of the cases reported a hematoma of the gluteal region developed after mild trauma (5).

A bilateral femoral approach is preferred when the procedure is performed preoperatively. Occlusion of both common iliac arteries can be obtained more easily with this approach, since more than one catheter can be advanced.

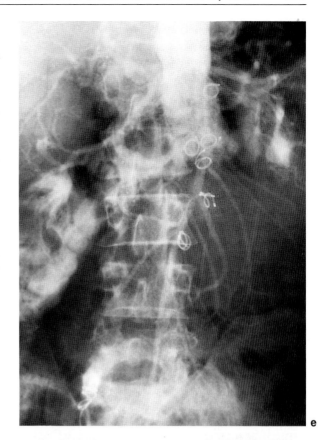

e

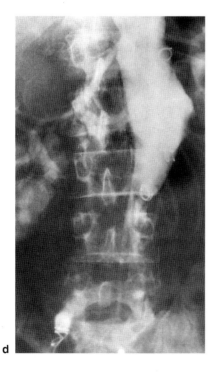

d

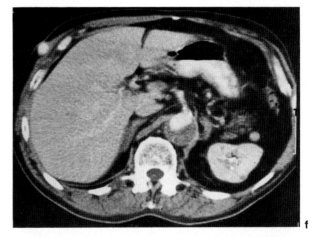

f

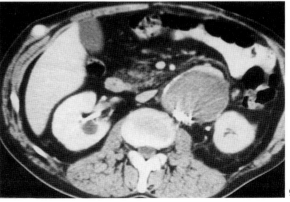

g

Fig. **1**
d After distal flow had completely discontinued, embolization of the aneurysm was carried out with further insertion of coils at the level of the distal abdominal aorta
e The final angiographic control shows extreme reduction of flow into the aneurysm. However, a coil is accidentally located at the origin of the superior mesenteric artery. Normal flow is present in this latter vessel
f, g The CT scans performed after embolization show complete thrombosis of the aneurysm. The coil into the mesenteric artery is also evident, although there is normal vascular enhancement of this vessel. The axillofemoral bypass is patent

On the basis of our experience, we suggest:

- Bilateral femoral catheterization
- Placement of an occlusion balloon catheter inflated in the left distal common iliac artery
- Coil embolization of the left common iliac artery through the right femoral catheter
- Placement of a second occlusion balloon catheter via the right femoral artery
- Embolization of the aneurysmal sac
- Occlusion of the right common iliac artery with coils
- Deflation and removal of both occlusion balloon catheters after complete thrombosis of the aneurysm and the iliac arteries is obtained

The bilateral occlusion balloons are inflated during the embolizing procedure in order to avoid distal embolization of thrombi or embolizing agents. In fact, in one of our patients emboli and a Gianturco coil were removed from the femoral artery during surgical intervention in axillofemoral bypass.

Bucrylate cannot be used through the transfemoral approach, since it might attach the catheter to the arterial wall when injected against antegrade flow.

Embolization of the Aneurysmal Sac

Aneurysmal thrombosis can be achieved only after distal runoff occlusion has been completed, as already described. Materials for aneurysmal embolization include mechanical or chemical agents.

Commercial coils even of large size are not particularly useful, since their dimensions are too small and too many would be needed for complete occlusion. Moreover, small coils can move freely in the flow inside the aneurysm and may dislodge cranially into a visceral branch of the aorta. In one of our cases, a coil dislodged at the origin of the mesenteric artery, although it did not result in thrombosis of the artery as shown at 2 years follow up.

A more suitable embolization technique with coils has been described (13). A homemade 70 cm coil can be formed using the outer spring coil of a commonly used stainless-steel movable-core guide wire. The coil can be advanced into the aorta mounted over the inner core of a movable core guide wire, using another 70 cm segment of the external coil of the guide wire as a pusher. Bending of the coil every 2 cm over a gas flame allows the coil itself to fold in the aneurysmal sac, resuming its position over the thrombosed walls. This technique also aims to reinforce the aneurysmal wall, preventing rupture even if minimal residual flow should remain.

Complete thrombosis of the aneurysm after stagnant flow has been obtained can be further speeded up by injection of hypertonic 50% glucose solution or thrombin. Also, temporary occlusion of the inlet flow with a large balloon catheter, advanced through the axillary artery and inflated below the renal arteries, may speed up thrombosis formation inside the aneurysm by completely excluding the flow through the aneurysmal sac for a few minutes.

Using the techniques described, thrombosis of the aneurysm rapidly extends cranially up to the level of the renal arteries. The presence of antegrade flow in these latter vessels avoids further cranial extension of the thrombus. The mechanism is the same as that involved in complete distal aortic occlusion observed in Leriche's syndrome.

The lumen of the aorta at the level of the renal arteries is usually reduced at follow-up examinations, but in no case in our experience or in those described in the literature was extension of the thrombus into the renal arteries observed.

Complications

A careful evaluation of the angiogram obtained before embolization is required for correct planning.

Patency of the inferior mesenteric artery could have dramatic consequences after occlusion, and also the presence of inferior polar renal arteries should be checked for the same reasons. The inferior mesenteric artery is usually occluded in abdominal aneurysms.

Complications might include dislocation of thrombi of embolizing material (coils) distal to the common iliac artery in cases performed preoperatively. Removal of such materials can be accomplished easily at surgery. Prevention includes the use of occlusion balloon catheters inflated in the distal common iliac arteries during the whole procedure.

Peripheral embolization of the internal iliac artery with bucrylate can induce ischemic alterations of the gluteal muscles with possibile chronic hematomas.

Finally, small coils delivered in the stagnant flow of the aneurysm can dislodge into visceral branches, although in one of our cases no occlusion of the mesenteric artery was observed at long-term follow-up despite coil embolization at its origin.

If the procedure is performed preoperatively, the patient experiences severe ischemic pain radiating to both hips and extremities.

Our suggestion in these cases is to perform an epidural anesthesia before the embolizing procedure to take advantage of spinal anesthesia also during embolization.

Conclusion

Percutaneous embolization of abdominal aortic aneurysms is a valid procedure to obtain interruption of flow through the vessel in inoperable cases. Extraanatomic axillobifemoral bypass performed before, or preferably after the procedure, guarantees peripheral flow.

The technique is satisfactory, and long-term follow-up of axillofemoral bypass shows results and patency rates that are similar to those obtained with aortobifemoral bypass.

New research in this field is oriented toward the percutaneous introduction of a graft or a stent through the aneurysm.

References

1. Berguer R, Schneider J, Wilner H. Induced thrombosis of inoperable abdominal aortic aneurysm. Surgery 1978;84:425–429.
2. Christian HA. Aneurysm of the thoracic aorta treated by wiring. Boston Med Surg J 1912;166:122–127.
3. Finney JMT. The wiring of otherwise inoperable aneurysms with report of cases. Ann Surg 1912;55:661–681.
4. Gardner RJ, Gardner NL, Tarnay TJ, Warden HE, James EC, Wafne AL. The surgical experience and a one to sixteen years follow up of 277 abdominal aortic aneurysm. Am J Surg 1978;135:26–230.
5. Goldman M, Sarrafizaden MS, Philip PX, Karmody AM, Leather RP, Parikh N, Powers SR. Bucrylate embolization of abdominal aortic aneurysms: an ajunct to non resective therapy. AJR 1980;135:1195–1200.
6. Hertzer NR, Beven EG. Abdominal aortic aneurysm: recognition and management. Postgrad Med 1977;61:72–80.
7. Hicks GL, Rob C. Abdominal aortic aneurysm wiring: an alternative method. J Surg 1976;131:664–667.
8. Leather RP, Dhiraj S, Goldman M, Rosenberg M, Karmody A. Non resective treatment of abdominal aortic aneurysms: use of acute thrombosis and axillo-femoral by-pass. Arch Surg 1979;114:1402–1408.
9. Magee HR, Cohen JR, Mellick SA. Ruptured abdominal aortic aneurysm: a review of 168 cases. Aust NZ J Surg 1977;47:48–54.
10. Moore HD. Abdominal aortic aneurysms. J Cardiovasc Surg 1976;17:47–53.
11. O'Donnel TF, Darling CR, Linton RR. Is 80 years too old for aneurysmectomy? Arch Surg 1976;111:1250–1257.
12. Power DA. The palliative treatment of aneurysms by wiring with Colt's apparatus. Br J Surg 1921;9:27–36.
13. Rossi P, Stipa S, Simonetti G, Cavallaro A, Passariello R. Transcatheter wiring of abdominal aortic aneurysm. Cardiovasc Intervent Radiol 1983;6:51–54.
14. Sink JD, Myers RT, James PM. Ruptured abdominal aortic aneurysms: review of 33 cases treated surgically and discussion of prognostic indicators. Am Surg 1976;42:303–307.
15. Stenstrom JD, Ford HS, MacKay MI, Hosie RT, Donald JC. Ruptured abdominal aortic aneurysm. Am Surg 1976;42:538–540.
16. Szilagyi DE, Smith RF, De Russo FJ, Elliot JP, Sherrin FW. Contribution of abdominal aortic aneurysmectomy to prolongation of life. Ann Surg 1966;164:678–699.
17. Szilagyi DE, Elliot JP, Berguer R. Coincidental malignancy and abdominal aortic aneurysm. Arch Surg 1967;95:402.
18. White RJ Jr, Kaufmann SL, Barth KH, De Caprio V, Stranbert JD. Embolotherapy with detachable silicone balloons: technique and clinical results. Radiology 1979;131:619–627.

Angiographic Management of Vascular Obstruction

The State of the Art

E. Zeitler

Percutaneous transluminal angioplasty (PTA), in both the original "Dotter method" (5) and the more recent differentiated form using variations of the Grüntzig balloon catheter (6, 7), has become an essential procedure for the therapy of peripheral arterial occlusive disease.

The advantages of PTA include:

- Nearly absent morbidity during the first 3 days after therapy (1 in 3000 treatments)
- The small complication rate, for which 1 to 2% require surgery
- The present favorable long-term results (50 to 70% patency rate after 5 years)
- The short hospitalization time and the availability of the procedure in all hospitals with experienced radiologists and angiographic equipment (2)

Despite these advantages, the procedure can still be improved with additional physical and medical treatment, optimization of instruments and techniques, and auxiliary methods of special indications (12).

Fundamentals of Percutaneous Transluminal Angioplasty

PTA is a modification of the diagnostic percutaneous catheter technique introduced by Seldinger (15) as a therapeutic method. It was one of the most important techniques at the beginning of interventional radiology (17).

Concerning this technique, the mechanistic principle consists of the fact that after the passage of the arterial obstruction under fluoroscopic control with a guide wire, the catheters, which are pressed through the obstructed area upon the guide wire, dilate the inner arterial lumen. For this purpose, Dotter and Judkins introduced a coaxial Teflon catheter system, which allowed the restoration of a free arterial lumen up to a diameter of 12 Fr (3.6 mm).

The disadvantage, obvious from the beginning, was that the entrance defect to the arterial wall had the same diameter as the restored free blood pathways. The patent lumen adequate to the diameter of the artery could be achieved after introduction of the balloon catheter, developed by Grüntzig (7). With this new catheter type, lesions at the puncture site and embolization risks were also reduced.

The pathomorphologic mechanism can be described as a "controlled traumatic injury," which

Table **1** Mechanisms of percutaneous transluminal angioplasty

- Rupture of the intima and media fibers
- Compression of the thrombus
- Compression of the media layers
- Distribution of the thrombus at the inner surface of the vessel
- Overstretching of the artery
- Mechanical destruction and embolization

leads to dilation with a free arterial lumen corresponding to that seen in histologic and angiographic examinations (3, 4, 10). The controlled traumatic injury can vary despite of the location and extention of the arteriosclerotic lesion and the balloon diameter used (Table **1**).

PTA can be divided into five steps:

- Pre-treatment angiography
- Dilation procedure
- Control angiography
- Patient care
- Follow-up control

The objectives of vascular dilation are:

- To enlarge the vessel lumen and increase blood flow
- To keep the vessel open
- To provide a smooth inner surface
- To prevent distal embolization

To reach this aim, a balloon dilation catheter should be able to reach the lesion, pass it, open it, and be removed, all with minimum trauma (1). This objective can be most easily realized in the dilation of isolated arteriosclerotic hemodynamically effective stenoses in the femoropopliteal arteries (Fig. **1**) as well as in the iliac arteries (Fig. **2**). In many cases the atherosclerotic changes are so severe that the dilation results only in rupture of the intima and media layers, and pressing the atheromatous material against media and adventitia results in overstretching the arterial outer diameter.

The improved blood flow with longitudinal shearing power forces the new patent lumen to remain open, and a neointima completes the healing process with smoothing of the inner arterial surface (10).

Fig. 1 **A 71-year-old man with gangrene of the right** ▶
foot. Angiographically, there is a high-grade femoral
stenosis
a before PTA
b after PTA

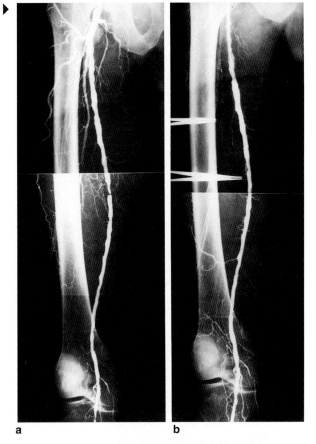

Fig. 2 **A 62-year-old woman with diabetes and gan-**
grene of the forefoot with claudication, moving dis-
tance 250 m
a Stenosis of the left external iliac artery
b Angiography after dilation from the contralateral side
▼

a   b

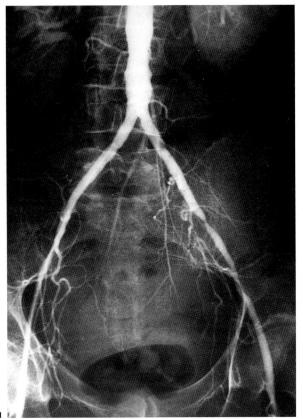

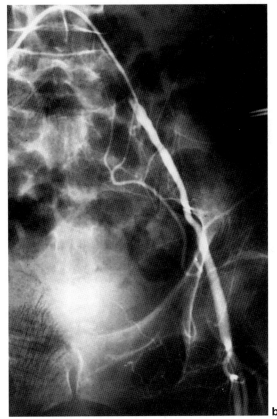

a

b

Technical Equipment

PTA must be performed in an angiographic laboratory with high resolution image-intensifier fluoroscopy and X-ray film documentation, including, if possible, digital subtraction angiography (DSA) (16). The mechanical technique of transluminal angioplasty, however, is also possible without DSA and in an operating room, if X-ray fluoroscopic control is available.

In addition to the typical angiographic instrumentation, individually adapted bypass catheters and balloon dilation catheters are necessary. The technical instrumentations and equipment are given in Table **2.**

There is no doubt that a safe percutaneous restoration of the free arterial bloodstream is only possible under x-ray control with image intensifier television technique. Nothing but this can guarantee an aseptic and safe procedure.

Catheter Introduction and Balloon Dilation

Without question, the retrograde puncture of the femoral artery in the groin can be more easily performed than the antegrade puncture. Therefore, dilation of an iliac artery stenosis can be performed from the ipsi- and contralateral sides. Only in a small number of cases can stenoses of the superficial femoral artery be treated from the contralateral side after retrograde puncture in the groin. Therefore, PTA of a femoropopliteal obstruction needs the antegrade puncture in the groin (Fig. **3**).

If available, DSA can prevent arterial wall perforation and helps in performing a safe passage of the obstructed area by using the mapping technique (16).

Balloon dilation needs adequate catheters in size and diameter. Clinical and experimental work has shown that polyethylene balloon catheters produce the best defined pressure against the arteriosclerotic wall (1). Several companies offer a wide range of balloon catheter material. The normal pressures varying between 4 and 12 atmospheres, applied three to four times and lasting 10 to 20 seconds, are in most cases sufficient for standard dilation.

Adjunct Drug Therapy

Accessory treatment before, during, and after PTA has the following goals:

- To avoid platelet aggregation leading to early rethrombosis
- To avoid acute thrombosis during the procedure when flow is reduced by the dilating catheter
- To avoid mechanically induced spasm
- To maintain peripheral perfusion during the catheter dilation and the subsequent manual compression of the arterial puncture site after catheter removal.

Various forms of adjunct drug therapy have been used so far, but without question the best additional drug therapy during and after PTA to prevent rethrombosis is not yet known. The recommendations that can be offered today (12) reflect the best early and long-term results, but prospective double-blind studies up to now are not available (Tab. **3**).

Table **2**   Equipment and instrumentation for percutaneous transluminal angioplasty

- Angiographic unit with high-resolution image intensifier fluoroscopy and X-ray film documentation

- For local anesthesia, contrast injection and saline application, disposable syringes and needles

- Scalpel, clamps, Seldinger needle, and catheter adapters

- Dilator with tapered tip and catheters, sheaths of different lengths for ipsi- and contralateral PTA

- Teflon-coated safety J guide wires 100, 200, and 260 cm

- Teflon or polyethylene catheters with straight and curved tips, with and without proximal side holes for angiography and bypassing the obstruction

- Dilating balloon catheters with polyvinyl chloride or polyethylene balloons with different lenghts (2 to 12 cm) and widths (3 to 12 mm)

- Coaxial balloon dilatation catheter systems with balloon diameter of 3 and 4 mm

- Manometer-controlled pressure injector

- Compresses, sponges, and electric pad or hot water bottle for keeping the foot warm before, during, and after PTA

Table **3**   Adjunct drug therapy

Premedication
  None or aggregation inhibitors: oral acetylsalicylic acid (ASA), 330 mg, two to three times daily, alone or combined with dipyridamole, 75 mg

After arterial catheterization
  To prevent early rethrombosis: Heparin intra-arterially, 5000 IU
  To prevent arterial spasm: oral calcium antagonists, nifedipine or nitroglycerin spray, 1% lidocaine (3 cc), or nitroglycerin intra-arterially

After successful PTA
  Anticoagulation: Heparin or warfarin or aggregation inhibitors: Twice daily, 230 mg, ASA, or two to three times daily ASA, 330 mg, plus dipyridamole, 75 mg

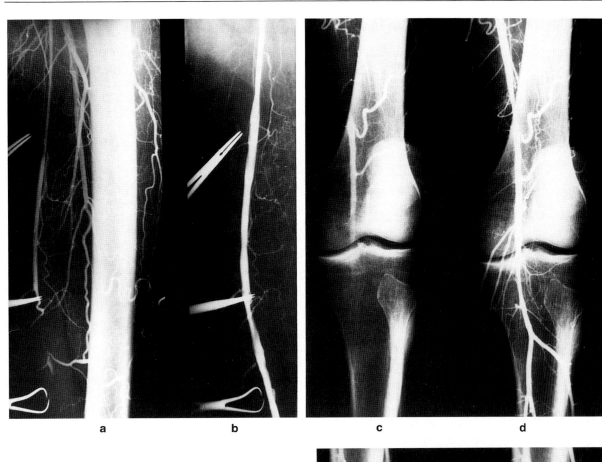

a   b   c   d

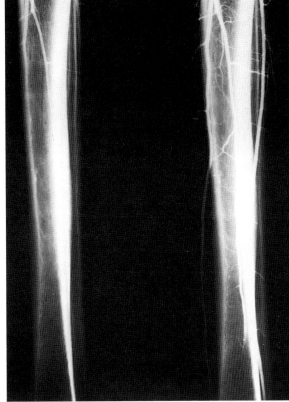

e   f

Fig. 3   **A 53-year-old man, with rest pain and gangrene of the left leg: angiography of the thigh**
a Before angioplasty occlusion of 4 cm length and bridge collaterals
b Control after balloon dilation
c Angiography of the popliteal artery with a distal occlusion of 5 cm length
d Control angiography after balloon dilation
e, f Arteries of the lower leg before and after angioplasty

Adjunct medical therapy before, during, and after PTA is of importance in ensuring the success of the mechanical treatment. The avoidance of early rethrombosis by platelets or fibrin thrombus is important for the clinical result after the mechanical dilation.

Indications for Percutaneous Transluminal Angioplasty

Twenty years after the first publication of this principle of treatment by Dotter and Judkins (5), PTA is accepted for use in several parts of the body. Table **4** shows in which obstructions of the arterial system of the upper and lower limbs the procedure has already been executed successfully. Contraindications include total occlusion of the aorta and the common and iliac arteries and also long segmental stenoses in the iliac and superficial femoral arteries (11, 14). These types of arteriosclerotic obstructions have a lower primary success rate and a reduced patency rate after 1 and 3 years (11, 18). Therefore, in patients with arteriosclerotic obstructions with rest pain and gangrene, vascular surgery is the primary method of choice. Alternatively, low-dose thrombolytic therapy intra-arterially in combination with balloon dilation in special cases can be used. In contrast to this, PTA is the method of primary choice in patients with rest pain and gangrene as well as with claudication with single or multiple arterial stenoses.

The possible complications of PTA can be bleeding at the point of puncture, pulsating hematoma, perforation of the artery at the point of obstruction, peripheral embolization, and early rethrombosis.

Table **4**   Suitable obstructions for percutaneous transluminal angioplasty of arteries of the extremities

Unilateral stenoses of common and external iliac arteries on both sides

Stenoses of common femoral artery

Stenoses of the deep femoral artery

Single or multiple short segmental stenoses of the superficial femoral artery

Occlusion of the superficial femoral artery with a length of less than 12 cm

Single or multiple segmental stenoses of the popliteal artery

Occlusion of the popliteal artery

Stenoses of the posterior tibial trunk

Stenoses of the proximal part of the lower leg arteries

Infrarenal aortic localized stenoses

Stenoses of the subclavian artery

Stenoses of the axillary artery

These complications occur between 5 and 12% and surgical operations are necessary in 1 to 3% of all angioplasty procedures. The complication rate also depends on the extension of the occlusion, the clinical stage, the sex of the patient, and the experience of the interventional radiologist.

After PTA, therefore, a 24-hour-hospitalization in most cases is recommended.

Clinical Treatment

Before PTA and to control the follow-up result by documentation of the clinical status, measurement of the ankle-arm pressure ratio (AAPR) by the Doppler method is essential. Additionally, measurement with the Doppler technique or oscillography after exercise can be done for detailed hemodynamic studies. Without question, pre- and post-angiograms can today be done with DSA. Intra-arterial as well as intravenous DSA gives similar results, but the peripheral outflow can be best demonstrated by intra-arterial DSA (16).

Angioplasty can be considered successful only after angiographic control, control of the ankle-arm pressure ratio, the pulse status, and clinical success. This can be best demonstrated with Doppler ultrasound measurement, in which ankle-arm pressure ratio is reduced more than 0.15, and with the improvement in the clinical situation, especially from gangrene to claudication.

In the future it will be increasingly tested whether the new developments, such as the application of laser technique and of mechanical instruments that effect an atherectomy or vaporization of the arteriosclerotic material, are able to extend the indications for PTA. This will depend extensively on the complication rate and on the long-term results. Hopes for an improvement in long-term results are pinned on the percutaneous application of expendable endoprostheses. There is no doubt that the method, inaugurated by Dotter and Judkins and modified by Grüntzig and others, is not only assured of its place in the therapy of peripheral vascular occlusive disease of the legs, but it also has to be regarded as an essential contribution to the treatment of a widespread disease, with low risk and with a reduction of costs.

References

1. Abele JE. Basic technology of balloon catheters. In: Dotter CT, Grüntzig AR, Schoop W, Zeitler E, eds. Percutaneous transluminal angioplasty: technique, early and late results. Berlin: Springer, 1983: 31–36.
2. Athanasoulis CA. Percutaneous transluminal angioplasty: general principles. AJR 1980;135:893–900.
3. Block PC, Baughman KL, Pasternak RC. Transluminal angioplasty: correlation of morphologic and angiographic findings in an experimental model. Circulation 1980;61:778–785.

4. Castaneda-Zuniga WR, Amplatz K, Laerum F. Mechanics of angioplasty: an experimental approach. Radiographics 1981;1:1–14.
5. Dotter CT, Judkins MP. Transluminal treatment of arteriosclerotic obstruction: description of a new technique and a preliminary report of its application. Circulation 1964;30:654–670.
6. Grüntzig A, Hopff H. Perkutane Rekanalisation chronischer arterieller Verschlüsse mit einem neuen Dilatationskatheter. Dtsch Med Wochenschr 1974;99:2502.
7. Grüntzig A. Die perkutane transluminale Rekanalisation chronischer Arterienverschlüsse mit einer neuen Dilatationstechnik. Baden-Baden: Witzstrock, 1977.
8. Hess, H. Clot lysis in peripheral arteries. In: Dotter CT, Grüntzig AR, Schoop W, Zeitler E, eds. Percutaneous transluminal angioplasty: technique, early and late results. Berlin: Springer, 1983:753–758.
9. Hess H, Mietaschk A, Bruckl R. Peripheral arterial occlusions: a 6 year experience with local low-dose thrombolytic therapy. Radiology 1987;163:753–758.
10. Leu HJ, Grüntzig A. Histopathologic aspects of transluminal recanalization. In: Zeitler E, Grüntzig A, Schoop W, eds. Percutaneous vascular recanalization: technique, application, clinical results. Berlin: Springer, 1978:39–50.
11. Murray RR, Hewes RC, White RI, Mitchell SE, Auster M, Chang R, Kadir S, Kinnison M, Kaufman SL. Long-segment femoropopliteal stenoses: is angiography a boom or bust? Radiology 1987;162:473–476.
12. Richter EI, Zeitler E. Percutaneous transluminal angioplasty: adjunct drug therapy. In: Dotter CT, Grüntzig AR, Schoopp W, Zeitler E, eds. Percutaneous transluminal angioplasty. Berlin: Springer, 1983:84–90.
13. Roth FJ, Cappius G, Fingerhut E. Radiological pattern at and after angioplasty. In: Dotter CT, Grüntzig AR, Schoop W, Zeitler E, eds. Percutaneous transluminal angioplasty: technique, early and late results. Berlin: Springer, 1983:73–83.
14. Schmidtke I, Roth FJ. Relapse treatment by percutaneous transluminal dilatation. In: Dotter CT, Grüntzig AR, Schoop W, Zeitler E, eds. Percutaneous transluminal angioplasty: technique, early and late results. Berlin: Springer, 1983:131–139.
15. Seldinger SJ. Catheter replacement of the needle in percutaneous arteriography: a new technique. Acta Radiol (Stockh) 1953;39:368–376.
16. Seyferth W, Dilbat G, Zeitler E, Bolle G. Digital subtraction angiography: a method of following percutaneous transluminal angioplasty. In: Dotter CT, Grüntzig AR, Schoop W, Zeitler E, eds. Percutaneous transluminal angioplasty: technique early and late results. Berlin: Springer, 1983:13–19.
17. Zeitler E, Grüntzig A, Schoop W, eds. Percutaneous vascular recanalization. Berlin: Springer, 1978.
18. Zeitler E, Richter EI, Seyferth W. Femoropopliteal arteries. In: Dotter CT, Grüntzig AR, Schoop W, Zeitler E, eds. Percutaneous transluminal angioplasty: technique, early and late results. Berlin: Springer 1983:105–114.

Techniques of Percutaneous Transluminal Angioplasty

F. Olbert and F. Karnel

For patients with incipient vascular conditions or chronic occlusions of arteries of the extremities, PTA is a widely used and well-established therapeutic procedure. It is a valid alternative to major surgical interventions in patients presenting with a suitable morphologic pattern of the occlusion and a sparing method of treatment, especially for high-risk patients (2, 5, 9, 10, 54, 56).

In addition, PTA has proved its value in the treatment of coronary heart disease (6, 7, 13, 17, 18, 25, 26, 39, 40, 53, 55). Indeed, indications for PTA have in recent times been considerably broadened. In the early years of vascular dilation only single stenoses of individual vessels were treated, but a number of centers have recently started using the technique to dilate stenoses involving as many as three different vessels. PTA is also used to dilate stenoses in extracranial cerebral vessels (4, 11, 20, 34, 37, 38). It has also been used to treat hypertension due to renal artery stenoses (16, 21, 24, 29, 31).

In many centers PTA is combined with local fibrinolysis using streptokinase or urokinase, a technique allowing the removal of thrombotic deposits in the stenosed vessel and even of total occlusions of thrombotic origin (13, 20, 22, 23, 45). Once patency has been achieved, the underlying stenosis may be dilated.

Recently, attempts to treat occlusions by combining percutaneous transluminal dilation with a laser technique have been reported (12).

Dotter in 1964 (9, 10) was the first researcher to develop a coaxial catheter system (Fig. **1a, b**), which

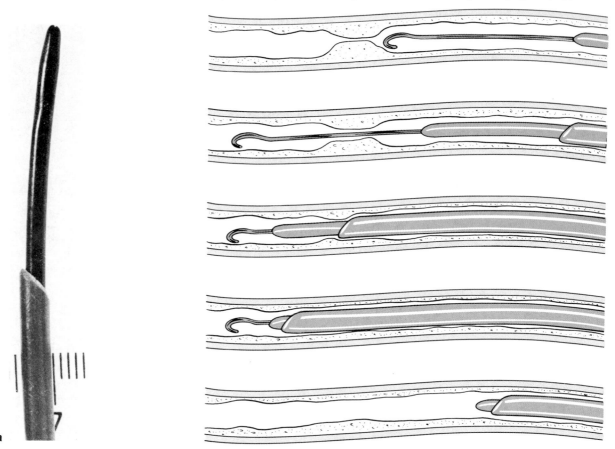

Fig. **1** **a The coaxial catheter system** developed by Dotter with the inner and outer catheters
b Dotter's recanalization technique. By gradually advancing the two catheters, the occluding material is forced apart
Reproduced with permission from A. Grüntzig (15)

he used successfully to treat stenosed and occluded femoral arteries. After antegrade puncture of the femoral artery in the inguinal region, an 8 Fr Teflon catheter was inserted according to the Seldinger technique and advanced up to the stenosis or occlusion. Subsequently, a 12 Fr catheter was advanced over it. Although this technique helped to remove occlusions and stenoses in many cases, it fairly frequently gave rise to peripheral embolism.

Van Andel (2) improved the Dotter technique in 1978 by developing a new catheter system (Fig. **2**) consisting of several catheters with lumens ranging from 8 to 12 Fr, permitting the gradual dilation of stenoses or occlusions.

In 1974, Grüntzig and Hopf (14, 15, 19, 27) revolutionized vascular dilation by developing the balloon catheter (Fig. **3**), which permitted the removal of stenoses or occlusions by inflating the balloon and thus applying pressure to the vascular wall. The introduction of such a balloon catheter into the artery, with the balloon folded around the catheter shaft in umbrella fashion, was much easier and greatly reduced the risk of damaging the vascular wall. Peripheral embolisms due to detached plaques became less frequent.

In 1977, Olbert developed, with the assistance of Hanecka, a catheter system (43, 44, 45) that is based on Olbert's concept of advancing the balloon and catheter to the stenosis or occlusion with minimal traumatization of the vascular wall. The principal feature of the system is that whenever the catheter is inserted into the vessel or moved in it, the balloon and the catheter have the same diameter, since the coaxial telescopic catheters are arranged in such a way that, as the inner catheter to which the distal end of the balloon is firmly connected moves forward, the balloon is stretched and its diameter is reduced to that of the outer catheter and arrested in that posi-

Fig. **2 The Van Andel catheter.** In order to avoid the abrupt change from one catheter lumen to the other, Van Andel uses a recanalization catheter with a continuously increasing outside diameter. The catheter is available in different sizes (8–12 Fr). Reproduced with permission from A. Grüntzig (15)

tion by means of a locking device at the proximal end of the catheter. Before the balloon is inflated, this locking device is released so that the distal tip of the catheter may move slightly toward the proximal end of the system. With the catheters currently in use, the total length of the balloon is only slightly reduced at its distal end, i. e., at the tip of the catheter (Fig. **4**).

Fig. **3 Longitudinal section of Grüntzig's double-lumen dilation catheter.** 1 Inner catheter with lateral channel; 2 enveloping catheter, folding around the inner catheter in umbrella fashion when deflated and unfolding during dilation. Reproduced with permission from A. Grüntzig (15)

Fig. **4 Longitudinal section of the Olbert catheter system.** 1 Outer catheter, to which the proximal end of the balloon is firmly fixed; 2 inner catheter, to which the distal end of the balloon is firmly fixed; 3 balloon, which can be stretched by shifting the inner catheter so that the balloon diameter becomes identical to that of the outer catheter; 4 space between inner and outer catheters, containing the pressure liquid (diluted contrast medium)

Since, during insertion into the vessel, the extended balloon has the same diameter as the catheter, additional traumatization of the vascular wall, plaque detachment, and the risk of consequent peripheral embolism are minimized. The balloon withstands pressures of up to 15 atm (Fig. **5**) without permanent deformation. Accordingly, the desired diameter of the inflated balloon can always be exactly controlled and no annular impressions will occur at the site of the stenosis during dilation (63, 64).

Since the outer diameter of the balloon is the same as that of the catheter, the catheter system can easily be inserted through the skin, the subcutaneous tissue, and the arterial wall once the guide wire is in place. Alternatively, the catheter may also be inserted with the help of a commercially available system of guide tubes permitting the painless exchange of catheters when different balloon or catheter diameters are required. The use of such a guide tube system is particularly advisable in the case of very obese patients.

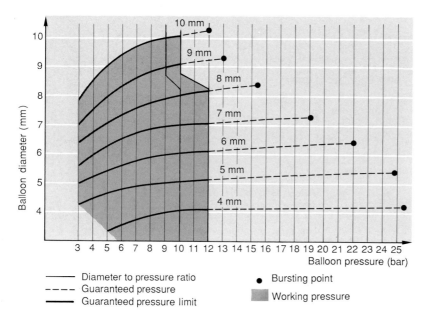

Fig. **5**   **Recording of balloon lumen to balloon pressure ratio** (Olbert catheter system). The desired lumen is reached below maximum pressure

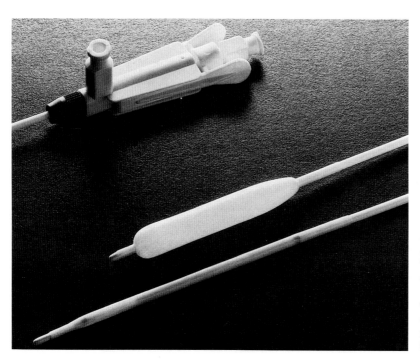

Fig. **6**   **The commercially available catheter.** In the uninflated state bottom the balloon at the distal end of the catheter has almost the same diameter as the rest of the catheter. When inflated (middle), it assumes the desired cylindrical shape. (Top): Locking device for the inner catheter, which is released on slight counterpressure, enabling the inner catheter to move backward and forward during dilation

The balloon currently available has a diameter of 4 to 10 mm and is guaranteed to withstand pressures of up to 12 atm (Fig. **6**). Rapid inflation and deflation of the balloon, such as is required for the rapid removal of multiple stenoses of the superficial femoral artery, is best achieved by means of the calibrated pressure regulator (45) coming with the catheter set (Fig. **7**).

Angiography before the intervention as well as for the purpose of documenting PTA is best performed by digital subtraction angiography, if available; alternatively, a 35 mm camera or a plate-film changer may be used (61, 62).

Digital subtraction angiography permits mapping, which greatly facilitates manipulations, since the guide wire and dilation catheter can be advanced and retracted, as it were, "on the stored image," and any changes in the direction of the guide wire of catheter can be effected under visual control (61). The amounts and concentrations of contrast medium required for digital subtraction angiography are much lower than in conventional angiography; documentation of the status during and after dilation is performed virtually painlessly. Accordingly, expensive nonionic contrast media can be dispensed with (45).

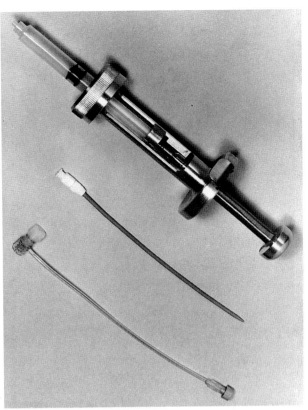

Fig. **7** **The catheter set** consists partly of a vascular dilation device and the manually operated calibrated pressure regulator to be used in particular for rapid dilation of vessels with multiple stenoses

Mechanism of Transluminal Dilation and Recanalization

Dotter was still of the opinion (9, 10) that during the dilation and recanalization process the arteriosclerotic material was pressed against the vascular wall. Now, after the introduction of the balloon catheter, the general view is that the success of PTA is due to deliberate and controlled rupturing of the intima. Indeed, these lesions are clearly visible immediately after the intervention and will heal within 6 months (5, 30).

Medication

In order to avoid complications in the course of the intervention, acetylsalicylic acid therapy should begin 3 days before the intervention at a dosage level of half a tablet (0.25 g) three times a day. Throughout the intervention, the catheter is rinsed with 1% heparin solution. In all, 5000 IU heparin are administered subcutaneously during the intervention. The patient stays in the hospital for 3 days and is administered 5000 IU heparin four times per day by subcutaneous injection. Follow-up treatment with 0.25 g acetylsalicylic acid three times a day is indicated for the next 6 months. Vascular spasms due to mechanical irritation of the intima by one or more dilation procedures performed on the same vascular portions, such as may occur particularly in the popliteal artery or near the trifurcation in the lower calf or in

the small peripheral branches distally to the site of renal artery dilation, can be successfully treated with 1% lidocaine solution or 10 mg nifedipine per os (45, 53, 57, 61).

Indications

The indications for PTA are the same as for surgery, with the exception of patients in stage II, who are never subjected to surgery. Their complaints, which occur only after prolonged walks or physical exercise, are considered primary indications for PTA. Such patients, in whom the intervention is performed for prophylactic reasons, have to be fully informed about possible complications (2, 10, 14, 15, 45, 56, 58, 60).

Whether angioplasty is indicated or not depends on the case history (walking distance, pain at rest) and clinical findings: we measure the blood pressure in the upper and lower extremities and check the pulse. The Doppler index is determined and plethysmography performed at rest and after exercise. The critical flow after exercise is 10 ml per 10 ml tissue.

The physical examination comprises a complete electrocardiographic study, evaluation of laboratory findings, especially coagulation time and renal function. Before the intervention, a chest radiograph and urinanalysis are made. In cases of impaired blood supply to the upper extremities neurologic findings are obtained, including electroencephalography, computed tomography, and cerebral scintigraphy. The intervention is performed in consultation with the angiologist and vascular surgeon.

Angioplasty Technique

The vessel is punctured by the Seldinger technique. Note should, however, be taken of the following aspects. Depending on whether a retrograde or antegrade puncture will be performed, the small incision into the skin preceding puncture should be made some 30 mm distally or proximally to the envisaged site of arterial puncture in order to achieve an oblique puncture channel and prevent any kinking of the guide wire or the catheter during insertion. When inserted through a steep puncture channel, the catheter is bound to kink and produce complications. The entire puncture channel down to the arterial wall is carefully infiltrated with 20 to 40 ml of a 1% lidocaine solution and slightly dilated with the blunt end of the incision instrument in order to facilitate advancement of the catheter through the connective tissue. For prolonged interventions, which may be painful because they take longer than the effects of local anesthesia, or for interventions that may necessitate the exchange of the catheter, when different catheter lengths or balloon diameters are required, a guide tube system should be used, not only to avoid unnecessary pain, but also to prevent any damage to the vascular wall that may arise when the catheter is exchanged for another one. The use of such a guide tube system greatly facilitates the intervention in patients with excessive fat deposits in the groin (2, 15, 41, 45, 58, 61).

Angioplasty in the Lower Extremities

Distal Abdominal Aorta and Pelvic Vessels

For unilateral or bilateral stenoses of the distal abdominal aorta (Fig. **8a, b**), the proximal portion of the common iliac artery or the external iliac artery can be examined and dilated at the same session. Larger stenoses in these regions result in an absence of femoral artery pulses in the groin, so the diagnostic intervention has to be made via the transaxillary route. Transluminal dilation can be performed immediately after angiography. The removal of such stenoses by means of PTA is far less strenuous for

the patient than surgery, involves relatively low risk, and considerably reduces the patient's stay in the hospital (45, 48).

Method

After ample local anesthesia of the axilla, puncturing of the axillary artery is performed with the patient's arm extended cranially at right angles and the shoulder region supported in such a way as to make the artery more easily palpable. After puncturing the vessel in this position, the guide wire is advanced as far as the aortic arch. In order to direct it into the thoracic or distal aorta, we use a catheter with a curved front end. Angiography is performed with a pigtail catheter. If angioplasty is required in the region of the distal abdominal aorta or in the central portion of the pelvic vessels, this catheter is exchanged for an 8 mm balloon catheter (Olbert catheter system), which is inserted via a system of guide tubes.

Once the balloon catheter has been pushed beyond the stenosis by means of a 0.035 guide wire, this guide wire is exchanged for a 0.025 guide wire, which permits the rinsing of the catheter with heparin solution during the entire intervention. The catheter should only be advanced or retracted with the guide wire in place.

Two, or sometimes even three, balloons are required to dilate the distal abdominal aorta. The balloon for primary dilation of the aortic stenosis is inserted via the transaxillary route, whereas the other two balloons are advanced from the groin via the retrograde route.

Pelvic vessels can be dilated by means of:
- The transaxillary technique (Fig. **9**)
- The ipsilateral retrograde technique (Fig. **10a, b**)
- The crossover technique (Fig. **11**).

Ipsilateral retrograde PTA means that the catheter is introduced via the inguinal region on the side of the lesion. The crossover technique permits dilation of a stenosed vessel after puncturing the contralateral femoral artery. In this case a sidewinder catheter is used, which is bent around in the aortic arch, retracted as far as the aortic bifurcation, and then advanced into the common iliac artery on the other side. Once the guide wire has been pushed beyond the stenosis, dilation with an 8 to 10 mm balloon can be performed.

Antegrade Puncture of the Femoral Artery

The vessel is punctured below the inguinal ligament. Since an oblique puncture channel is required, the skin is incised after local anesthesia some 40 mm

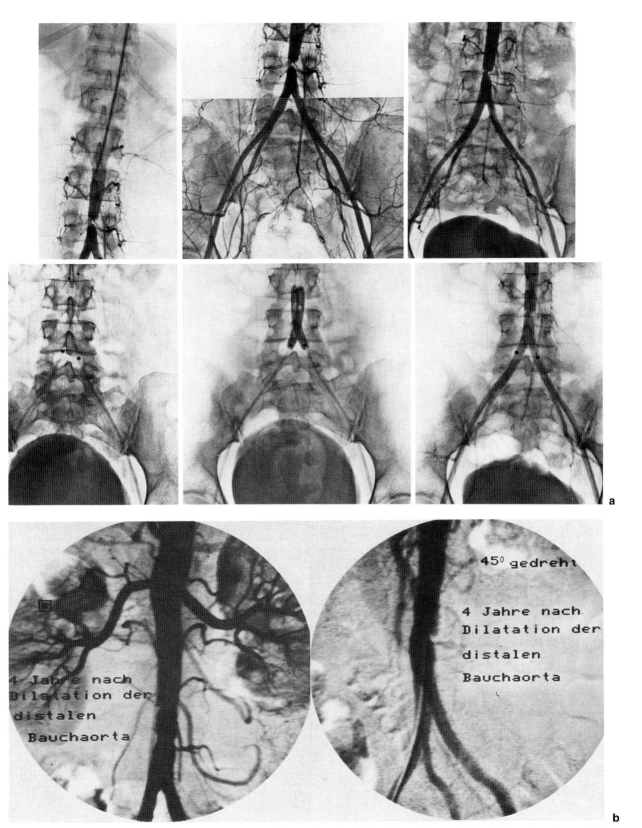

Fig. 8 **Distal stenosis of the aorta in a 45-year-old female patient.** Walking distance 100 to 200 m, dragging pain in both legs. **a** Transaxillary angiography revealed a sizable stenosis in the distal abdominal artery. Immediately after angiography, the distal aorta is initially dilated with an 8 mm balloon. In this way, the femoral pulse is restored bilaterally and the aortic stenosis can now be dilated by advancing an 8 mm balloon via the femoral artery

b Intravenous digital subtraction angiography performed 4 years after dilation shows only a minor deformation of the posterior aortic wall. The patient is free from pain and has an unlimited walking distance

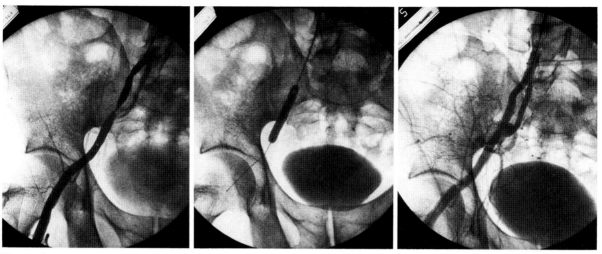

Fig. **9   Sizable stenosis of the right external iliac artery,** as visualized by transaxillary angiography during dilation by means of an 8 mm balloon in the course of the same session. Control angiography shows a normal vascular lumen

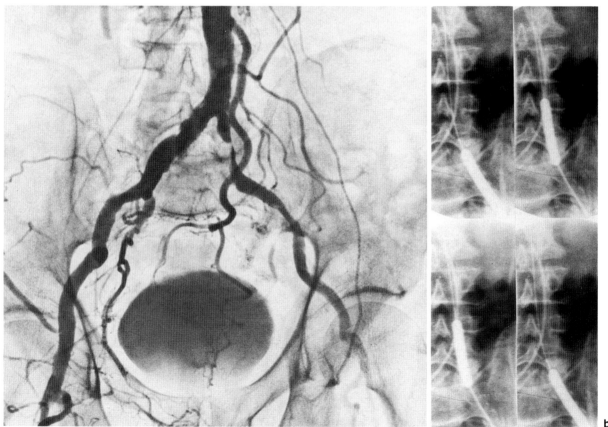

a

b

Fig. **10 a, b   Dilation of a severe stenosis in the left common iliac artery** by means of an 8 mm catheter introduced via the femoral route

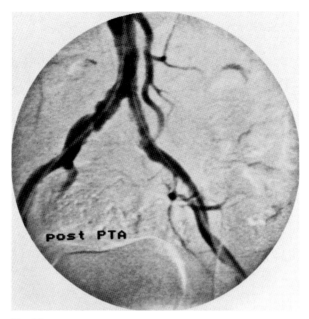

Fig. **10**
c Intra-arterial digital subtraction angiography performed immediately after the intervention reveals a normal vascular lumen

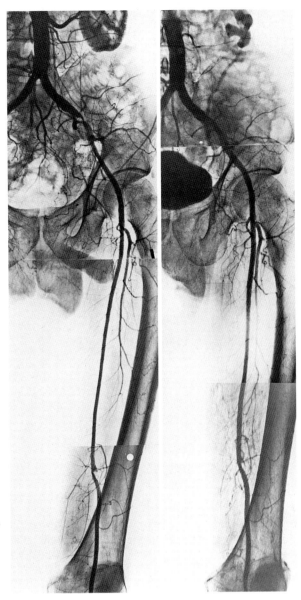

Fig. **11 Severe stenosis of the left external iliac artery** ▶
and moderately severe stenosis of the proximal
popliteal artery. The two stenosed vascular portions can
be successfully dilated in one session. Control angiography
shows a normal vascular lumen in both the external iliac
and popliteal arteries

above the envisaged puncture site. Note that after having punctured the vessel, the proximal end of the puncturing cannula is lowered as much as possible dorsally in order to allow the insertion of a guide wire into the superficial femoral artery. If this is not done, the guide wire will frequently tend to move into the deep femoral artery (2, 14, 15, 45, 60, 61).

Once the guide wire has been placed into the superficial femoral artery, we normally insert a system of guide tubes enabling us to exchange one catheter for another with a different length or a different balloon diameter without causing pain to the patient. The guide wire is pushed up to the

stenosis and the dilation catheter is then moved into the same position. Regardless of whether we treat a stenosed or an occluded vessel, several doses of 20 ml Macrodex are injected manually under relatively high pressure in order to achieve a so-called jet effect in the obliterated region and in this way prepare a preformed lumen for the guide wire. Experience has shown that after this procedure the guide wire and the catheter can be more readily passed through a stenosis or occlusion (Figs. **12, 13**).

Once the guide wire has been moved beyond the stenosis or occlusion, the dilation catheter is pushed beyond it as well while the guide wire is still in place.

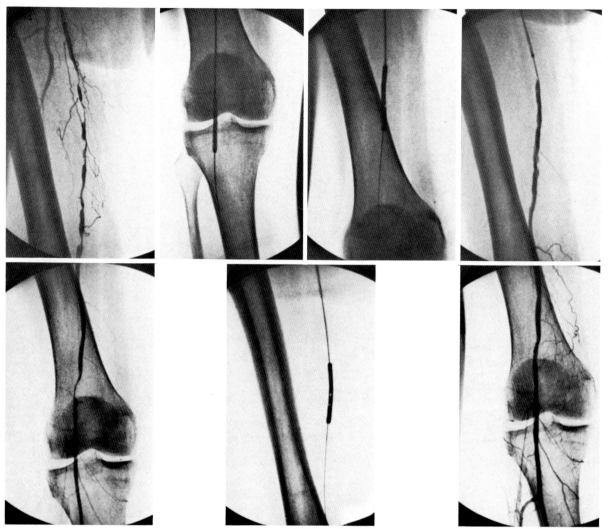

Fig. 12 **Multiple stenoses of the superficial femoral artery as well as severe stenosis in the right popliteal artery.**
Primary dilation of the distal stenosis in the popliteal artery. The catheter is then gradually retracted and alternatively inflated and deflated. In this way, the multiple stenoses of the superficial femoral artery are removed. For this type of intervention, the balloon pressure regulator shown in Figure **7** is indispensable

Then as for the pelvic arteries the 0.035 guide wire is replaced by a 0.025 guide wire. In this way the catheter and the vascular lumen distal to the stenosis or occlusion can be rinsed with heparin solution throughout the intervention.

In our experience dilation is best started at the distal end of the stenosis or occlusion and, in the case of longer occlusions, continued proximally. This procedure is repeated until the internal vascular wall in the obliterated region has become completely smooth. Throughout the intervention, the distal end of the guide wire will be distal to the vascular portion to be treated and, whenever the dilation catheter is moved along the guide wire, which serves as a splint, the balloon must be stretched. During these movements, the locking device at the proximal end of the catheter must be arrested. By applying a slight coun-

terpressure, the lock at the proximal end of the catheter is released and the balloon can be inflated for dilation. Dilation will always be followed by control angiography, which is now made in the form of digital subtraction angiography, a method requiring relatively small amounts of contrast medium. When this modern technique is used, mapping will greatly facilitate the dilation process itself, because in this case movements of the guide wire and catheter can be effected under visual control on what may be called a "preformed image" of the area to be dilated (62).

If necessary, stenoses or short occlusions of the superficial femoral artery can also be handled by the crossover technique.

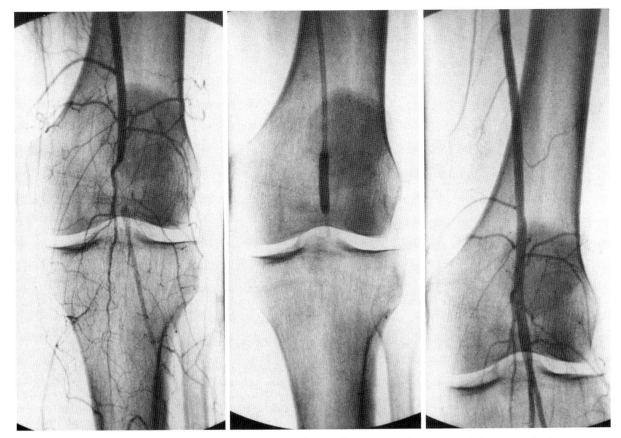

Fig. **13**   **A 40 mm occlusion of the proximal portion of the popliteal artery.** Patent vessel after recanalization

Angioplasty in the Upper Extremities

Today, transluminal dilation is also used to treat central stenoses of the subclavian artery, but also more peripheral stenoses of the subclavian and axillary arteries (3, 8, 28, 35, 36, 42). Compared with surgery, the intervention is relatively simple, involves a lower risk and reduces the patient's stay in hospital to 1 to 3 days. Such stenoses are dilated immediately after diagnosis by means of aortic arch angiography, which is now performed in the form of intra-arterial digital subtraction angiography. For this purpose the pigtail catheter introduced from the inguinal region according to the Seldinger technique is replaced by a dilation catheter of adequate diameter. Dilation as such is performed as described in the previous section (Figs. **14, 15**).

Angioplasty of the Renal Arteries in Hypertensive Patients

In the treatment of hypertension due to renal artery stenosis transluminal dilation has largely replaced surgery. Stenoses of a renal artery are now routinely visualized by means of intravenous digital subtraction angiography. During the same session, the blood samples required for the separate renin determinations can be taken from the left and right renal veins or the inferior vena cava both before and after stimulation with furosemide (32, 33, 46, 47, 49–52, 61).

Information on renal blood flow can be obtained from prior isotope examination and the kidney function can be assessed on the basis of renal clearance (1).

Dilation starts with angiography using a pigtail catheter (intra-arterial digital subtraction angiography), followed by probing of the renal artery with a sidewinder catheter. Once the inserted 0.035 guide wire has been moved beyond the stenosis, the dilation catheter is advanced and the guide wire exchanged for a 0.025 guide wire. After successful dilation, control angiography is performed using a pigtail catheter inserted into the aorta from the contralateral side.

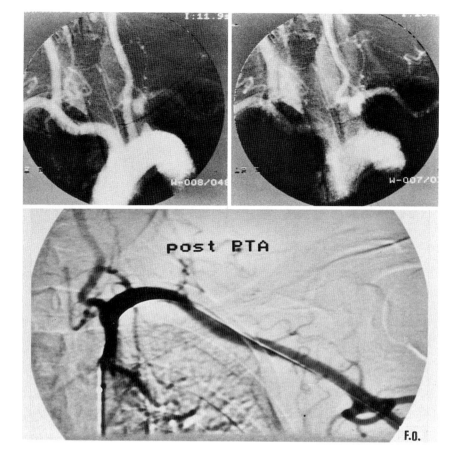

post PTA

F.O.

Fig. **14   Subclavian steal syndrome.** Blood pressure in the right arm: 160/90 mmHg; in the left arm: O. Subsequent to transluminal dilation, blood pressure readings are fairly comparable (right arm 160/90 mmHg, left arm 140/90 mmHg). The vertebral artery is clearly visible

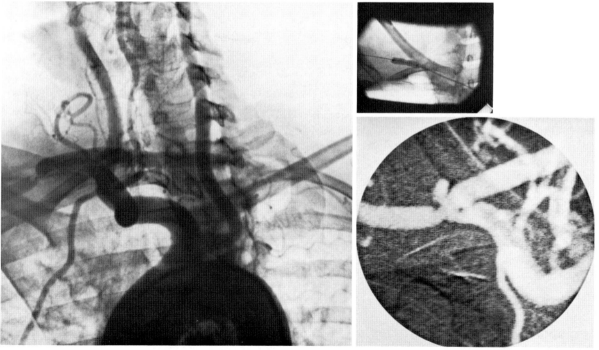

Fig. **15   Subclavio-Subclavian bypass for occlusion of the left subclavian artery.** After bypass surgery, impaired blood flow in the right upper extremity with spasms on exercise. Follow-up angiography revealed a stenosis in the anastomosed portion of the right axillary artery; after dilation the vessel is fully patent. Almost identical blood pressure readings for both arms: left arm 120/80 mmHg, right arm 110/80 mmHg

Complications

The complications are basically the same as may occur after arteriography, i. e., major hematomas, or, more rarely, dissections close to the puncture site or distal to it if caused by the guide wire or the catheter (Table **1**). Such complications will for the most part only arise because of insufficient experience of the radiologist and can generally be avoided. Embolism due to plaques has become rare (2 to 3%). Plaques may be trapped in the region of the popliteal artery or the trifurcation and have to be removed by percutaneous or surgical embolectomy within 6 hours. Thrombotic embolism, on the other hand, can be treated by lysis (streptokinase or urokinase) (Fig. **16**).

Table **1** Percutaneous transluminal angioplasty complications in 819 patients (1973–1985)

Overdilation	2
Arteriovenous fistula	2
Aneurysm	3
Hematoma	8
Embolic occlusion	13
Dissection plus occlusion	30
Total	58 (7.08%)

Immobilization of the patient after PTA should be reduced to a minimum and should be terminated after 24 hours at the latest. The compression bandage at the puncture site should fit tightly, but must

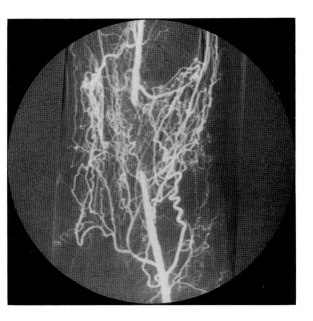

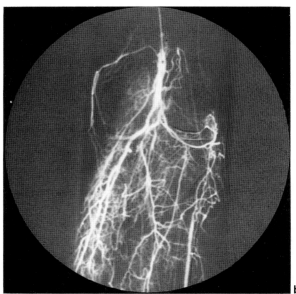

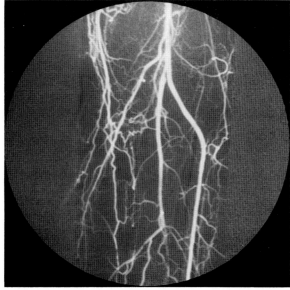

Fig. **16 a Occlusion (5 cm) of left superficial femoral artery**
b Peripheral embolic occlusion of popliteal artery after successful proximal recanalization
c Lysis therapy of the embolic occlusion with Urokinase (200000 IU urokinase intra-arterially). Successful recanalization of popliteal and anterior tibial arteries

on no account cause a reduction of blood supply to the limb by excessive compression. In order to avoid any additional strain on the diseased limb, the cross-over technique may be used to treat stenoses or short occlusions of the superficial femoral artery.

Immediate surgery is necessary if dilation of a renal artery results in a rupture, dissection, or acute thrombosis of the vessel.

If the intervention is carried out by an experienced physician, such complications are extremly rare. They may, however, occur in connection with central stenoses of the renal artery beginning immediately at the aortic wall. Elderly hypertensive patients may develop stenoses not only in the renal arteries, but also in the arteries of the extremities or in extracranial cerebral vessels. Before renal artery dilation, an examination of the extracranial cerebral vessels seems to be indicated, since the pressure decrease after dilation of the renal artery might in such cases lead to insufficient blood supply to the cerebral hemisphere.

References

1. Adam WE, Kaddatz R, Bitter F, Sigmund E. Untersuchungen über die Aussagekraft des Isotopennephrogramms bei einseitigen Nierenarterienstenosen. In: Pabst HW, ed. Nuklearmedizin, Radionuklide in der Haematologie: gegenwärtiger Stand der Therapie mit Radionukliden. Stuttgart: Schattauer, 1973:200–202.
2. van Andel GJ, ed. Percutaneous transluminal angioplasty. Amsterdam: Excerpta Medica, 1976.
3. Bachman DM, Kim RM. Transluminal dilatation for subclavian steal syndrome. AJR 1980;135:995–996.
4. Belán A, Veselá M, Vaněk I, Weiss K, Peregrin JH. Percutaneous transluminal angioplasty of fibromuscular dysplasia of the internal carotid artery. Cardiovasc. Intervent. Radiol 1982;5:79–81.
5. Castaneda-Zuniga WR, Formanek A, et al. The mechanism of balloon angioplasty. Radiology 1980;135:565–571.
6. Cowley MJ, Dorros G, Kelsey SF, et al. Acute coronary events associated with percutaneous transluminal coronary angioplasty. A J Cardiol 1984;53:12C–16C.
7. Dervan JP, Baim DS, Cherniles J, et al. Transluminal angioplasty of occluded coronary arteries: use of a movable guide wire system. Circulation 1983;68:776–784.
8. Van Dongen RJAM. Perkutane transluminale Katheterbehandlung supraaortaler Arterienobstruktionen. Angiology 1981;3:111–112.
9. Dotter CT, Judkins MP. Transluminal treatment of arteriosclerotic obstruction: description of a new technic and a preliminary report of its application. Circulation 1964;30:654–670.
10. Dotter CT, Grüntzig AR, Schoop W, Zeitler E, eds. Percutaneous transluminal angioplasty. Berlin: Springer, 1983.
11. Freitag G, Freitag J, Koch RD. Perkutane transluminale Angioplastik von Karotisstenosen. RöFo 1984;140:119–238.
12. Ginsburg R, Wexler L, Scott Mitchell R, Profitt D. Percutaneous transluminal laser angioplasty for treatment of peripheral vascular disease. Radiology 1985;156:619–624.
13. Gold HK, Cowley MJ, Palacious IF, et al. Combined intracoronary streptokinase infusion and coronary angioplasty during acute myocardial infarction. Am J Cardiol 1984;53:22C–125C.
14. Grüntzig A, Hopff H. Perkutane Rekanalisation chronischer arterieller Verschlüsse mit einem neuen Dilatationskatheter. Dtsch Med Wochenschr 1974;99:2502–2505.
15. Grüntzig A, ed. Die perkutane transluminale Rekanalisation chronischer Arterienverschlüsse mit einer neuen Dilatationstechnik. Baden-Baden; Witzstrock 1977.
16. Grüntzig A, Vetter W, Meier B, Kuhlmann U, Lütolf U, Siegenthaler W. Treatment of renovascular hypertension with percutaneous transluminal dilatation of a renal artery stenosis. Lancet 1978;i:801–802.
17. Grüntzig AR. Transluminal dilatation of coronary artery stenosis. Lancet 1978;i:263.
18. Grüntzig AR, Senning A, Siegenthaler WE. Nonoperative dilatation of coronary artery stenosis: percutaneous transluminal coronary angioplasty. N Engl J Med 1979;301:61–68.
19. Grüntzig AR, Meier B. Current status of dilatation catheters and guiding systems. Am J Cardiol 1984;53:92C–93C.
20. Hasso AN, Bird CR, Zinke DE, Thompson JR. Fibromuscular dysplasia of the internal carotid artery: percutaneous transluminal angioplasty. AJNR 1981;2:175–180.
21. Hedtler W, Sialer G, Pfeiffer A, Kuhlmann U, Lütolf U, Horst W. Isotopennephrographie als Erfolgs- und Verlaufskontrolle nach perkutaner transluminaler Dilatation von Nierenarterienstenosen. In: Schmidt HAE, Riccabona G, eds. 17. Internationale Jahrestagung der Gesellschaft für Nuklearmedizin, Innsbruck, 1975. Stuttgart: Schattauer, 1976:576.
22. Hess H. Clot lysis in peripheral arteries. In: Dotter CT, Grüntzig AR, Schoop W, Zeitler E, eds. Percutaneous transluminal angioplasty. Berlin: Springer, 1983:145–153.
23. Hollman J, Grüntzig AR, Douglas JS et al. Acute occlusion after percutaneous transluminal coronary angioplasty: a new approach. Circulation 1983;68:725–732.
24. Ingrisch H, Holzgreve H, Middeke N, Frey KW. Moderne röntgenologische Diagnostik und Therapie des Hochdruckes bei Nierenarterienstenosen. Klin Wochenschr 1980;58:1105–1113.
25. Ischinger T, Grüntzig AR, Hollman J, et al. Should coronary arteries with less than 60 per cent diameter stenosis be treated by angioplasty? Circulation 1983;68:148–154.
26. Kaltenbach M, Grüntzig A, Rentrop K, Bussmann W-D, eds. Transluminal coronary angioplasty and intracoronary thrombolysis. Berlin: Springer, 1982.
27. Katzen BT, Chang J. Percutaneous transluminal angioplasty with the Grüntzig balloon catheter. Radiology 1979;130:623–626.
28. Kobinia GS, Bergmann H Jr. Angioplasty in stenosis of the innominate artery. Cardiovasc Intervent Radiol 1983; 6:82–85.
29. Kuhlmann U, Grüntzig A, Vetter W, Furrer J, Lütolf U, Siegenthaler W. Renovaskuläre Hypertonie: Therapie durch perkutane transluminale Dilatation von Nierenarterienstenosen. Schweiz. Med Wochenschr 1978;108:1847–1859.
30. Leu HJ, Grüntzig A. Histopathologic aspects of transluminal recanalization. In: Zeitler E, Grüntzig A, Schoop W, eds. Percutaneous vascular recanalization. Berlin: Springer, 1978:19–50.
31. Mahler F, Krneta A, Haertel M. Treatment of renovascular hypertension by transluminal renal artery dilatation. Ann Intern Med 1979;90:56–57.
32. Mahler F. Transluminale Nierenarteriendilatation. Symposium, Lyon, 1982.
33. Mahler F, Probst B. Technique and complications of PTA in renal artery stenoses. VASA 1982;11:353–357.
34. Mathias K, Rohrbach R, Neff W, Ensinger H. Percutaneous transluminal dilatation (PTD) of carotid artery stenosis. In: Zeitler E, Grüntzig A, Schoop W, eds. Percutaneous vascular recanalization: technique, applications, clinical results. Berlin: Springer, 1978:66–72.
35. Mathias K, Staiger J, Thron A, Spillner G, Heiss HW, Konrad-Graf S. Perkutane Katheterangioplastik der Arteria subclavia. Dtsch Med Wochenschr 1980;105:16–18.
36. Mathias K. Perkutane transluminale Katheterbehandlung supraaortaler Arterienobstruktionen. Angiology 1981;3:47–50.
37. Mathias K, Bockenheimer S, von Reutern G, Heiss HW, Ostheim-Dzerowycz W. Katheterdilatation hirnversorgender Arterien. Radiologe 1983;23:208–214.
38. Mathias K. Dilatationsbehandlung hirnversorgender Arterien. Congres International d'Angeiologie. La Grande Motte, Frankfurt, April 7–13,1983.

39. Meier B, Grüntzig AR. Learning curve for percutaneous transluminal coronary angioplasty: skill technology or patient selection. Am J Cardiol 1984;53:65C–66C.

40. Meier B, Grüntzig AR, Hollman J, et al. Does length or eccentricity of coronary stenoses influence the outcome of transluminal dilatation? Circulation 1983;67:497–499.

41. Minar E, Ahmadi A, Ehringer H, Marosi L, Czembirek H, Konecny U. Perkutane transluminale Angioplastie (PTA) bei peripherer arterieller Verschlußkrankheit der unteren Extremitäten. Wien Klin Wochenschr 1986;98:33–40.

42. Motarjeme A, Keifer JW, Zuska AJ. Percutaneous transluminal angioplasty of the brachiocephalic arteries. AJR 1982;138:457–462.

43. Olbert F, Hanecka L. Transluminale Gefässdilatation mit einem modifizierten Dilatationskatheter. Fortschr Med 1977;95:867–869.

44. Olbert F, Muzika N, Mendel H, Schlegl A. Perkutane transluminale Gefäßdilatation: Langzeitergebnisse und Erfahrungsbericht mit einem neuen Kathetersystem: transaxilläre Technik. Wien Klin Wochenschr 1983;95:528–534.

45. Olbert F, Muzicka N, Schlegl A, eds. Transluminale Dilatation und Rekanalisation im Gefäßbereich. Nürnberg: Wachholz, 1985.

46. Olbert F, Ogris E, Muzika N, Schlegl A, Vacariu O, Diez W. Perkutane transluminale Angioplastie (PTA) im Bereich der Arteria renalis: Indikation, Technik und Ergebnisse. Wien Klin Wochenschr 1985;97:(Suppl 163):3.

47. Puijlaert CBAJ, Boomsma JUB, Ruijs JHJ, et. al. Transluminal renal artery dilatation in hypertension: technique results and complications in 60 cases. Urol Radiol 1981;2:201–210.

48. Roth FJ, Cappius G, Krings W. Seldom indications for angioplasty. Int Angiol. 1985;4:101–109.

49. Schwarten DE. Transluminal angioplasty of renal artery stenosis: 70 experiences. AJR 1980;135:969–974.

50. Sos TA, Sniderman KW. Percutaneous transluminal angioplasty. Semin Roentgenol 1981;16:26–41.

51. Sos TA, Pickering TG, Sniderman K, Saddekni S, Case DB, Silane MF, Vaughan ED, Laragh JH. Beneficial effects of percutaneous transluminal renal angioplasty on blood pressure in patients with renovascular hypertension due to atheroma and fibromuscular dysplasia. N Engl J Med 1983;309:274–279.

52. Tegtmeyer CJ, Teates CD, Crigler N, Gandee RW, Ayers CR, Stoddard M, Wellons HA Jr. Percutaneous transluminal angioplasty in patients with renal artery stenosis: follow-up studies. Radiology 1981;140:323–330.

53. Thornton MA, Grüntzig AR, Hollman J, et al. Coumadin and aspirin in prevention of recurrence after transluminal coronary angioplasty: a randomized study. Circulation 1984;69:721–727.

54. Wierny L, Plass R, Porstmann W. Long-term results in 100 consecutive patients treated by transluminal anigoplasty. Radiology 1974;112:543–548.

55. Williams DO, Grüntzig AR, Kent KM. et al. Efficacy of repeat percutaneous transluminal coronary angioplasty for coronary restenosis. Am J Cardiol 1984;53:32C–35C.

56. Zeitler E, Schoop W, Zahnow W. The treatment of occlusive arterial disease by transluminal catheter angioplasty. Radiology 1971;99:19–26.

57. Zeitler E, Reichold J, Schoop W, Loew W. Einfluß von Acetylsalicylsäure auf das Frühergebnis nach perkutaner Rekanalisation arterieller Obliterationen nach Dotter. Dtsch Med Wochenschr 1973;98:1285–1288.

58. Zeitler F, Grüntzig A, Schoop W, eds. Percutaneous vascular recanalization: technique, application, clinical results. Berlin: Springer, 1978.

59. Zeitler E. Complications in and after PTR. In: Zeitler E, Grüntzig A, Schoop W, eds. Percutaneous vascular recanalization. Berlin: Springer, 1978:120–125.

60. Zeitler E. Percutaneous dilatation and recanalization of iliac and femoral arteries. Cardiovasc Intervent Radiol 1980;3:207–212.

61. Zeitler E. Angioplasty. Plenary Session Proceedings of the 16th International Congress of Radiology, Hawaii, July 8–12,1985:45–50.

62. Zeitler E. Primary and late results of percutaneous transluminal angioplasty (PTA) in iliac and femoro-popliteal obliterations. Int Angiol 1985;4:81–85.

63. Zollikofer CL, Salomonowitz E, Brühlmann WF, Castaneda-Zuniga WR, Amplatz A. Dehnungs-, Verformungs- und Berstungscharakteristika häufig verwendeter Ballondilatationskatheter, Teil 1. RöFo 1986;144:40–46.

64. Zollikofer CL, Salomonowitz E, Brühlmann WF, Castaneda-Zuniga WR, Amplatz A. Dehnungs-, Verformungs- und Berstungscharakteristika häufig verwendeter Ballondilatationskatheter, Teil 2. RöFo 1986;144:189–195.

65. Starck EE, McDermott JC, Crummy AB, Turnipseed WD, Acher CW, Burgess JH. Percutaneous aspiration thromboembolectomy. Radiology 1985;156:61–66.

Percutaneous Transluminal Angioplasty of the Supra-Aortic Arteries

K. Mathias

It is estimated that annually 0.25% of the population of Western countries develop a stroke for the first time. The portion of the population with a definitive brain infarction amounts to 1.4%. Approximately 60% of the patients survive the cerebral infarction. Seventy-five percent of the strokes occur in persons over the age of 55 years. Minimal neurologic deficit is found in 40% of the patients, special care is required in another 40%, and total care in 10% (122).

A stroke may be caused by both extracranial and intracranial vascular disease. The emphasis in this chapter is on the treatment of the extracranial vessels responsible for a stroke syndrome, but attempts to treat intracranial vascular disease will be mentioned.

The treatment of atherothrombotic disease may be divided into four parts, for which the interventional radiologist is expected to help in the second and fourth parts insofar as the vascular lesions are amenable to catheter treatment:

– Management of the acute phase
– Measures to restore the circulation and arrest the pathologic process
– Physical therapy and rehabilitation
– Measures to prevent further strokes and progression of vascular disease

A comprehensive understanding of the pathophysiologic features of occlusive cerebrovascular disease has been gained by various methods. Doppler ultrasound and duplex scanning combining high resolution B-mode imaging and pulse Doppler analysis permit the determination of the location and extent of clinically significant stenotic arterial lesions with a high degree of accuracy. More recently, magnetic resonance imaging has the ability to visualize the arterial anatomy, and it can potentially be used to demonstrate arterial abnormalities and to measure blood flow.

Another non-invasive technique used to evaluate patients suspected of having a brain infarction is the determination of regional cerebral blood flow and cerebral blood volume using xenon inhalation procedures. Positron emission tomography and single-photon emission computed tomography are precise methods for measurement of regional blood flow and cerebral blood volume. Physiologic variables, such as oxygen consumption, glucose utilization, protein synthesis rate, and pH, can be mapped quantitively and will aid in the choice of different treatment modalities and the evaluation of treatment results.

Intravenous DSA permits a more definitive evaluation of the arterial system. However, impaired cardiac output and patient motion change the imaging quality for the worse, and an arterial study has to be performed to obtain adequate information. When the question of PTA of the supra-aortic arteries arises, an arterial study is necessary for demonstration of morphologic details of the lesion. In evaluating the risk of conventional or arterial DSA, it should be emphasized that an inaccurate diagnosis and consequently incorrect therapeutic decision has its own hazards.

Clinically, neurologic deficits are classified as transient or permanent.

– A transient ischemic attack (TIA) is a focal neurologic deficit, lasts less than 24 hours, and is confined to an area of the brain supplied by a specific artery.
– A prolonged reversible ischemic neurologic deficit (PRIND) is a transient neurologic impairment in which recovery occurs over 1 to 3 days.
– A crescendo transient ischemic attack is characterized by increasing frequency and severity of the events.
– A stroke in evolution is a neurologic deficit that worsens minute to minute or hour to hour.
– A completed stroke is a focal neurologic deficit confined to an area of the brain irrigated by a specific artery that has remained unchanged for more than 24 hours.

All these symptoms can be caused by a variety of occlusive vascular or embolic diseases. Arteriosclerosis is by far the leading cause of extra- and intracranial vascular disease. Degeneration of the subendothelial layer of the intima and the innermost fibers of the media together with focal deposits of lipids characterize the process leading to a fibrous plaque or complicated atheroma with subintimal hemorrhage, necrosis, and ulceration. Collagen exposed to the blood causes platelets to adhere to the eroded vessel wall. Thrombotic plugs form, break off, and embolize in distal arteries of brain and eye. Common sites of stenosis and ulceration are the regions of:

- The greater curvature of the aortic arch
- The proximal subclavian and innominate artery
- The ostium of the vertebral artery and
- The carotid bifurcation

Collateral pathways and their capacity influence the extent to which the cerebral blood flow is reduced by arteriosclerotic lesions. The main extracranial sources of collateral circulation when the internal carotid artery is occluded are anastomoses between the ophthalmic artery and branches of both external carotid arteries, the vertebral arteries, and cervical branches of the subclavian arteries. When the vertebral artery is occluded, anastomotic channels from the occipital, ascending cervical, and contralateral vertebral artery will open. Intracranial collaterals are supplied by the circle of Willis and leptomeningeal anastomoses. A common phenomenon is the steal of blood from the vertebrobasilar system to compensate for other ischemic vascular beds. The most frequent example is the subclavian steal syndrome.

A thorough angiographic workup is mandatory to show the morphologic characteristics and to evaluate the functional importance of occlusive vascular disease. Lesions can involve a single vessel, but more often multiple vessels are affected. Atherosclerotic plaques develop predominantly at the dorsal wall of the carotid artery. Therefore, lateral projections should not be omitted in the angiographic study. Additional findings related to arteriosclerosis are coiling, kinking, or angulation of supra-aortic arteries, which will produce problems not only for Dopplerultrasound examinations, but also for percutaneous dilation treatment.

Arteriosclerosis is by far the most frequent cause of an impaired cerebral circulation, but nonarteriosclerotic disorders must be taken into consideration (Table 1).

Technique

Dilation treatment of narrowed neck vessels has its historical root in a bougie technique using telescoping plastic or steel cannulas. After surgical exposure of the diseased vessel and arteriotomy, the instruments for graded dilation are introduced and are carefully moved forward through the narrow vessel segment. Vascular surgeons apply this technique in cases of arteriosclerotic lesions of the internal carotid artery near the skull base or in fibromuscular dysplasia. In our opinion, the development of balloon dilation catheters, which are available with numerous specifications, make these instruments superfluous.

Our experience with PTA of supra-aortic arteries is mainly based on the use of Grüntzig balloon dilation catheters. Other catheter types of similar construction are available from Olbert and Eschmann, but they are not produced in all the dimensions necessary for the treatment of the different neck vessels. The dilation catheter should have:

- Two channels for fast inflation and deflation of the balloon, flushing of the vessel, and manipulation of the guide wire
- A low profile balloon for easy passage of the stenosis and for catheter extraction without difficulties
- Safe balloons with working pressures of at least 6 to 8 atmospheres, according to the balloon diameter
- A constant "sausage" form of the balloon without balloon compliance at working pressure.

The catheter may be preshaped with a sidewinder configuration, but sometimes it is better to probe the vessel with a diagnostic catheter, to place the guide wire beyond the stenosis and to exchange the diagnostic catheter for a straight dilation catheter. The different dilation catheters used in the treatment of supra-aortic arteries are listed in Table 2.

The balloon of the dilation catheter must be completely emptied of air bubbles before being introduced into the vascular system to prevent gas embolization to the brain if the balloon should rupture during the treatment. Single use of the catheter is recommended to avoid catheter-related complications.

Table 1   Occlusive vascular diseases of the supra-aortic arteries

Arteriosclerosis
Fibromuscular dysplasia
Takayasu arteritis
Periarteritis nodosa
Giant cell arteritis
Thromboangiitis obliterans
Granulomatous arteritis
Allergic arteritis
Radiation-induced fibrosis

Table 2   Dimensions of dilation catheters

Artery	Catheter diameter (Fr)	Balloon diameter (mm)
Subclavian	7	8
Innominate	7	8 (10)
Common carotid	7	8
Internal carotid	7 (5)	6 (5)
External carotid	7 (5)	5
Vertebral	5	4 (3)

The patient is prepared in the same way as for other arterial procedures. No sedative premedication is given because this might obscure slight functional neurologic disturbances. Platelet aggregation inhibitors can be given to prevent formation and embolization of thrombi. We prefer an anticoagulation with 10000 IU of heparin immediately after introduction of the catheter.

The best percutaneous approach for PTA of the supra-aortic arteries is the femoral artery at the groin. In cases of severe iliac artery kinking, iliac artery occlusions or difficult right-sided subclavian artery obstructions, transaxillary catheterization provides an alternative approach. However, the procedure carries a greater risk than the femoral artery puncture because of the possibility of brachial plexus injury.

Following the arterial puncture, a sheath is inserted into the vessel allowing rapid catheter exchange and application of catheters with different diameters without hemorrhage at the puncture site.

The diagnostic catheter is advanced to the origin of the diseased supra-aortic artery and a control angiogram is performed to confirm location and degree of the narrowing. A control angiogram is mandatory when the stenosis is only documented by intravenous DSA. Under fluoroscopic observation, the catheter is carefully moved to the immediate vicinity of the stenosis, the stenosis is passed by a steerable guide wire in cases of a vertebral or carotid artery narrowing or a simple straight guide wire in subclavian or innominate artery stenosis (Fig. 1). The passage of the stenosis is visualized by intermittent injections of diluted contrast medium to avoid any vessel injury, especially a subintimal passage of plaque. The steerable guide wire offers the advantage of sufficient stiffening of the dilation catheter for the passage of the stenosis. When the guide wire tip is placed beyond the stenosis, the diagnostic catheter is exchanged for the dilation catheter. Before the dilation catheter is advanced into the stenosis, it must be prepared for the balloon inflation and deflation to

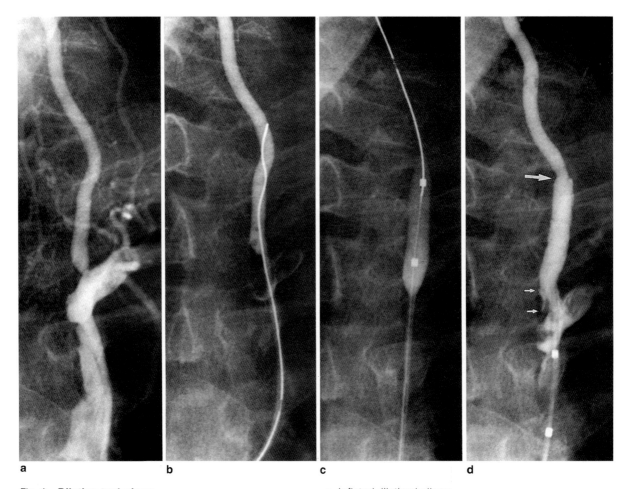

a   b   c   d

Fig. 1 **Dilation technique**
a Vertebral and subclavian artery stenosis
b Steerable guide wire advanced through stenosis

c Inflated dilation balloon
d Slight overdilation of vertebral artery and intimal cracking at the site of the plaque (arrow)

interrupt the blood flow as quickly as possible. It is useful to talk constantly with the patient in order to recognize early any ischemic brain reactions, because the cerebral ischemic tolerance of the patients varies greatly and a functional insufficiency vanishes within some seconds or a few minutes when the blood flow is restored and no embolism has occurred.

After sufficient dilation of the stenosis, the catheter ist pulled back, but the guide wire is left in place to allow easy repetition of dilation in case of significant residual stenosis. The control angiogram is best performed using DSA technique because it can be carried out with a small amount of contrast medium and with the guide wire still in position (72).

Continuous pressure monitoring permits the registration of the pressure gradient across the stenosis and the change of the pressure gradient after dilation. When the poststenotic pressure (back pressure) is reduced in carotid artery disease to less than 60 mmHg, the risk of a possible ischemic event is increased and special care is necessary. Additional monitoring techniques are transcranial Doppler ultrasound, conventional and on-line Fourier transformed electroencephalography and brainstem auditory-evoked potentials. In dilation treatment of cerebral arteries these methods prolong the treatment time, increasing the risk of the intervention. Therefore, we do without them. However, such neuromonitoring is valuable in local fibrinolysis of thrombotic cerebral artery disease requiring an infusion time of several hours (42).

Indications

The determinants for the indication to treat a supra-aortic artery lesion with radiologic interventional techniques are:

- General condition of the patient
- Type and duration of neurologic symptoms
- Localization of vascular obstructions
- Single or multiple vessel disease
- Angiographic morphology of obstructions

The general condition of the patient, his or her age, and additional diseases play a major role in the decision process for balloon dilation or local fibrinolysis. A history of myocardial infarction increases the operative mortality significantly. Patients with advanced coronary heart disease are better referred to the radiologist than to the vascular surgeon when the lesion is suited for a radiologic intervention, because far less stress will be induced in the patient in the angiographic laboratory in comparison to the operative theater. Life expectancy in patients with TIAs depends more on the state of the coronary than the cerebral arteries (1).

A thorough neurologic examination is mandatory before and after the treatment of the patient supplemented by a computed tomography scan of the head.

Vascular Territories for Percutaneous Transluminal Angioplasty

Subclavian Artery

Subclavian artery stenosis is most frequently encountered in the first segment of this artery, about 2 cm beyond its aortic origin. Hemodynamically significant stenosis leads to a reversed blood flow in the vertebral artery when the pressure gradient exceeds 15 mmHg. Some patients have a constantly reversed blood flow in the vertebral artery but are free of symptoms and do not need any treatment. This phenomenon can be explained by the favorable course of subclavian steal syndrome with a spontaneous improvement in 50% of the cases (14). Arm weakness and cerebral symptoms, such as vision disturbances, drop attacks, dizziness, syncope, and vertigo, are essential for the indication of PTA. In some of these patients a changing antegrade and retrograde blood flow can be observed and seems to be responsible for the complaints. Aortic arch angiography at rest may simulate a vertebral artery occlusion in some of these cases, but Doppler ultrasound and angiography immediately after an exercise test of the involved arm will prove its patency. The left subclavian artery is affected at least four times as often as the right one.

Obstructions of the subclavian artery beyond the origin of the vertebral artery will cause arm symptoms that are often more severe than in subclavian steal syndrome because a sufficient collateral circulation is missing.

Atherosclerosis is the underlying cause of the subclavian artery stenosis in most of the cases, but fibro-elastic bands in children, Takayasu disease, fibromuscular dyplasia, and fibrotic stenosis after radiation therapy have to be considered as further pathogenetic possibilities (41, 48). A rare indication for PTA is a stenotic Blalock-Taussig anastomosis (32).

Our experience is based on the treatment of 72 patients with subclavian artery obstructions (Table 3). In 63 cases the lesion was located on the left, in nine cases on the right side. Seven patients had subclavian artery occlusions (Fig. 2). Dilation was carried out in 59 patients by a transfemoral approach and in the remaining cases by a transaxillary approach. Galicha et al. (35) used a transbrachial route in five of six patients with a cut down of the brachial artery. In our opinion, surgical exposure of the artery is not necessary and even pulseless axillary arteries can be punctured with some experience. Sixty-seven patients complained of the typical symptoms of subclavian steal syndrome. The age of the

Table **3**   Results of proximal subclavian artery dilation in our patients

Type and location of obstruction	Treatment attempts	PTA successful	Good hemodynamic result
Left subclavian artery occlusion	6 (8%)	3 (50%)	2 (33%)
Left subclavian artery stenosis	57 (79%)	56 (98%)	52 (91%)
Right subclavian artery occlusion	1 (1%)	1 (100%)	1 (100%)
Right subclavian artery stenosis	8 (11%)	7 (88%)	6 (75%)
Total	72 (99%)	67 (93%)	61 (85%)

patients ranged from 14 to 79 years. One child had a fibro-elastic band at the origin of the left subclavian artery, and a 40-year-old man with Hodgkin disease had a radiation-induced peripheral subclavian artery stenosis. All other patients had atherosclerotic disease with manifestation of multiple stenotic lesions in nine of them (Fig. **3**).

Two of seven subclavian artery occlusions could not be recanalized, and in one patient an early reocclusion occurred. In one patient a right subclavian artery stenosis could not be passed. Another patient developed a TIA during probing of the left subclavian artery, and for that reason the treatment attempt was interrupted. In an additional five patients the dilation result was not satisfying leaving the stenosis unchanged, caused by an elastic band in one case and a residual stenosis in four cases. Rigid calcified stenoses or too small a balloon diameter are responsible for insufficient dilation results (77). Successful dilation is defined as:

– Improvement of the postangioplasty arteriogram: less than 30% residual stenosis
– Abatement of arterial lesion pressure gradient: pressure gradient less than 15 mmHg
– Improvement of clinical signs

The technical success rate of subclavian artery dilation is high with hemodynamic and angiographic improvement in 85% of subclavian artery obstructions in this series according to the criteria just

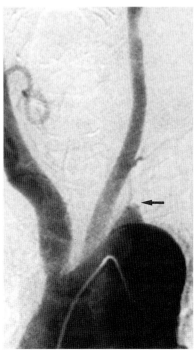 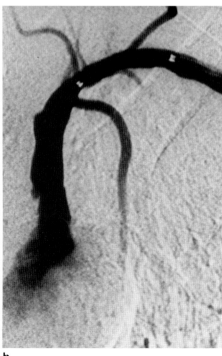

a   b

Fig. **2**   **a Subclavian artery occlusion** (arrow)
b Subclavian artery recanalized by a transaxillary approach

mentioned. Similar results with a primary patency rate of 80 to 95% have been obtained by other groups (4–6, 18, 20, 22, 39, 40, 68, 71, 74, 88, 97, 104, 105, 123) (Table **4**).

Recanalization of occluded subclavian arteries was attempted by some groups with a low success rate of 32% in 19 patients (35, 55, 67, 74, 81, 96, 124) (Table **5**). Our experiences are not quite so bad. We were able to restore a normal blood flow in the subclavian artery in four of seven patients (57%).

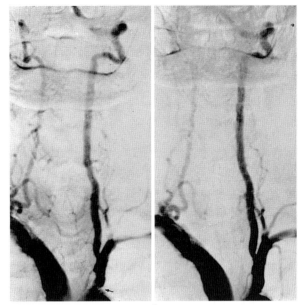

Fig. **3** **a Bilateral carotid artery occlusion and stenosis of the left subclavian artery** (arrow) **b** Improved blood flow to the cerebrum via a dominant left vertebral artery

a   b

Table **4**   Results of proximal sub-clavian artery dilation

References		Treatment attempts*	PTA successful	Compli-cations*
Damuth et al.	(22)	9	9	0
Galicha et al.	(35)	6	6	0
Gordon et al.	(39)	8	5	0
Grote et al.	(40)	12	12	0
Gunthaner and Schmitz	(41)	1 RI	1	0
Kachel et al.	(56)	21	21	0
Mathias	(74)	65 1RI	63	1 TIA
Motarjeme et al.	(81)	16	16	0
Olbert et al.	(88)	13	12	0
Pernes et al.	(90)	9	9	1 NL
Ringelstein et al.	(96)	27	26	1 DAE, 1 TO
Ritter et al.	(97)	3	3	0
Vitek et al.	(114)	13	13	0
Wilms et al.	(121)	23	21	1 DAE, 1 TO
Zeitler et al.	(124)	15	13	0
Total		241	230 (95%)	6 (2.5%)

* DAE: digital artery embolism; NL: nerve lesion; RI: radiation-induced stenosis; TIA: transient ischemic attack; TO: thrombotic occlusion

Table **5**   Results of proximal sub-clavian artery recanalization

References		Treatment attempts	PTA successful	Compli-cations
Galicha et al.	(35)	1	1	0
Kachel et al.	(56)	1	1	0
Mathias et al.	(74)	7	4	0
Motarjeme et al.	(81)	5	0	0
Ringelstein et al.	(96)	3	0	0
Zeitler et al.	(124)	2	0	0
Total		19	6 (32%)	0

Therefore, in our opinion an attempt of recanalization is worthwhile, because patients are not harmed so much by the procedure, and complications have not yet been encountered. On the other hand, one of two patients will lose his symptoms without the stress and risk of vascular surgery.

Follow-up data of blood pressure measurement, Doppler ultrasound, and mechanical oscillography are available for 61 of 67 of our dilated patients with a mean control period of 45 months. Two patients died during the follow-up period with a patent subclavian artery. Six patients had a residual or recurrent stenosis, but only two of these patients expressed any complaints and were referred for dilation again. A satisfying long-term result was found in 75% of all patients with attempted dilation.

Recurrent subclavian artery stenosis, which must be expected in 15% of the patients within 5 years, can be dilated again with good results, but a new PTA should be restricted to symptomatic patients. We have re-treated two patients with satisfying long-term results. Ringelstein et al. (96) and Wilms et al. (121) gained similar experiences with six patients.

Considering the low risk of the disease and the mediocre operative results, surgical intervention is only justified in well-selected patients who cannot be improved by PTA. Transthoracic reconstruction is obsolete today because of its high complicatation rate. Even extrathoracic reconstructions, such as axillo-axillary bypass, carotid-subclavian vein grafting, and subclavian-carotid transposition, are accompanied by a mortality of 4%, a 1-year reocclusion rate of 10%, and various other severe complications with an incidence of 2 to 13% (8, 25, 30, 31, 38, 51, 75, 98, 106, 119).

The embolic risk of subclavian artery dilation is low with an incidence of 3%. With the exception of one TIA, embolism involved only the digital arteries (96, 121). Ringelstein and Zeumer (95), using Doppler ultrasound flow measurements before, during, and after angioplasty of the subclavian arteries, have shown that, despite sufficient dilation, flow within the vertebral artery did not become orthograde immediately but did so gradually over a period of 20 seconds to several minutes. Delayed flow reversal may protect against cerebral embolism during and shortly after dilation. All reported complications of subclavian artery PTA produced only transient symptoms, and had a favorable outcome (74).

The number of patients in whom an occluded subclavian artery was recanalized is too small to permit an evaluation of the embolization risk. However, it can be concluded from the experiences with recanalization of femoral arteries that a comparable embolization rate of 3 to 5% must be expected.

Innominate Artery

Narrowing of the innominate artery exposes the patient to a higher degree of danger of cerebral infarction than subclavian artery obstructions. Occlusions of this vessel should be referred for surgical treatment because of the higher risk of dislocation of embolic material to the brain during recanalization. Transluminal dilation of innominate stenosis is accompanied by a lower complication risk than correction by vascular surgery, as far as reported experiences allow any judgment.

The technical approach is similar to the dilation of the proximal subclavian artery. As it feeds two cerebral arteries, the blocking of the artery should be kept as short as possible. The catheter can be introduced via the femoral or axillary artery. The balloon diameter will range from 8 to 10 mm.

We treated seven patients with an innominate artery stenosis, approaching the lesion in two cases by an axillary and in five cases by a femoral route. In all patients with atherosclerotic disease a good treatment result was achieved (Fig. 4). Additional 18 patients have been reported with similar favorable results (10, 18, 20, 24, 37, 56, 58, 64, 74, 81, 90, 113, 114, 124). We have some doubts regarding the usefulness of a "washout technique" as practiced by Derauf et al. (24). Additional blocking catheters may prevent cerebral embolism, but may become the source of platelet aggregation and intimal injury itself. Treatment time will increase with more complicated techniques accompanied by a higher risk of embolism and ischemic damage.

Inflammatory disease can be treated with good success in the same way as atherosclerotic lesions (58). It might be assumed that the risk of PTA in Takayasu disease is still less than in atherosclerosis, but the recurrence rate will be higher when the activity of the inflammatory process is not positively influenced. Table 6 gives an overview of the results of innominate angioplasty.

Vertebral Artery

The most common site of atherosclerotic vertebral artery stenosis is the origin of this vessel. At times plaques form as a ringlike extension from the subclavian artery to encircle the vertebral artery orifice. The left and right vertebral arteries are approximately equally affected by atherosclerosis, but there is some indication that when the two vessels are unequal in diameter, the smaller vessel is more frequently occluded. The intracranial vertebral artery, after it pierces the dura, is another frequent site of occlusive disease. Aside from these predilection sites, fibrous plaques and fatty streaks are distributed throughout the vertebral artery. However, ulceration in plaques is less frequent in the posterior circulation than in the carotid territory.

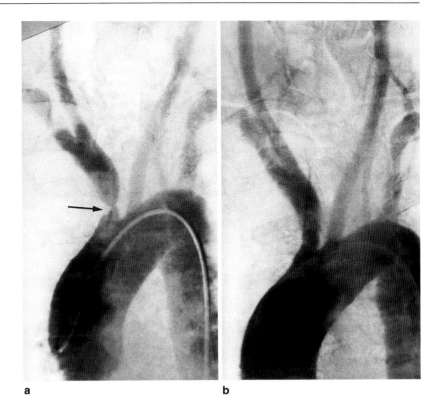

Fig. **4   a Innominate artery
stenosis** (arrow)
b Hemodynamically insignificant
residual stenosis after transfemoral
PTA

a   b

Another group of patients complaining of verte-bral-basilar insufficiency have intermittent vertebral artery compression by bony spurs of the cervical vertebral column. Naturally, these patients cannot be treated by PTA.

The ringlike, nonulcerated lesions at the ostium of the verberal artery are well suited for dilation. Bilateral vertebral artery disease is often encoun-tered (Fig. **5**). We have restricted our indication for dilation treatment to patients with characteristic clin-ical signs of vertebrobasilar involvement (Table **7**).

Transient vertigo, diplopia, or headache, occur-ring as solitary symptoms, should not be interpreted as a vertebrobasilar TIA. Also, some patients with dizziness will prove to have carotid TIA; hence, this symptom is not a reliable indicator of the vascular circuit that is involved. The clinical picture may vary in the vertebrobasilar system from episode to episode.

Unfortunately, not a single definitive study estab-

Table **6**   Results of innominate artery dilation

References		Dilation attempts*	PTA successful	Compli-cations*
Bergmann et al.	(10)	1	1	0
Derauf et al.	(24)	1 IO	1	0
Garrido and Garofolk	(37)	1	1	0
Kachel et al.	(56)	2	2	0
Kobinia and Bergmann	(58)	1 TA	1	0
Lowman et al.	(64)	1 IO	1	0
Mathias et al.	(74)	7	7	0
Motarjeme et al.	(81)	1	1	0
Pernes et al.	(90)	2	2	0
Roth et al.		2	2	0
Seurot et al.		2	2	0
Vitek et al.	(114)	2	2	0
Zeitler et al.	(124)	2	2	0
Total		25	25 (100%)	0

* IO: intraoperative; TA: Takayasu arteritis.

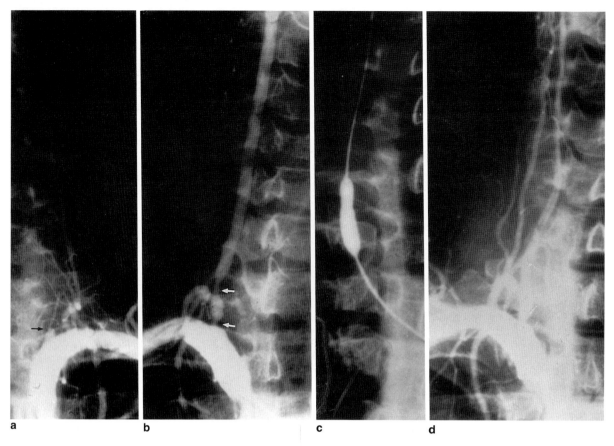

Fig. 5 **a Left vertebral artery occlusion, b right vertebral artery tandem stenosis** (arrow)
c A 5 Fr dilation catheter with inflated 4 mm balloon in the stenosis
d Slight residual stenosis at the origin of the vertebral artery. More distally located stenosis completely removed. Spastic reaction of vertebral artery

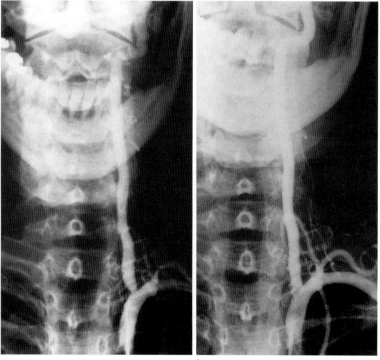

Fig. 6 **A 50-year-old woman with bilateral internal carotid artery occlusion, stenosis of left external carotid and vertebral artery**
a Stenosis of dominant left vertebral artery at the origin
b Normal vessel diameter after PTA

lishes the advantages or disadvantages of a given therapy for patients with well-defined vertebrobasilar disease. The Canadian Cooperative Study, including 86 patients with vertebrobasilar TIAs and 49 patients with slight nonprogressive vertebrobasilar strokes, demonstrated that aspirin reduced the risk of recurrent episodes, stroke, and death in men, but not in women (16). Reuther and Dorndorf (94) showed a slight, statistically insignificant trend favoring a beneficial effect of aspirin.

A wide range of surgical procedures is available, and can be effective. Reconstruction of the vertebral artery, bypass in the neck and extracranial-intracranial grafts have been used to back up the flagging posterior circulation, but today the indications are uncertain and the complications are considerable. The origin of the vertebral artery is not easily accessible by surgery, and the lumen is too small for endarterectomy. Therefore, the usual treatment is arteriotomy and a venous patch with a mortality and permanent morbidity of more than 5% (50).

Percutaneous angioplasty of vertebral artery stenosis was attempted by us in seven patients and succeeded in six of them (86%). In one case probing of the narrowed artery failed. With the availability of steerable guide wires, the chances of successful dilation certainly increased (Fig. 1). In one patient with two stenotic lesions of the right vertebral artery both

Table **7** Symptoms of vertebrobasilar insufficiency

Frequent	Rare
Ataxia	Noise or pounding in the ear or head
Dizziness	
Diplopia (vertical or horizontal)	Pain in the head or face
	Vomiting
Dysarthria	Hiccup
Transient vertigo	Memory lapse
Bifacial numbness	Confused behavior
Weakness or numbness of part or all of one or both sides of the body	Drop attacks
	Impaired hearing
Dysphagia	Deafness
Staggering	Hemiballismus
Veering to one side	Peduncular hallucinosis
Feeling of cross-eyedness	Forced deviation of the eyes
Park or blurred vision	
Tunnel vision	
Partial or complete blindness	
Pupillary change and ptosis	
Paralysis of gaze	

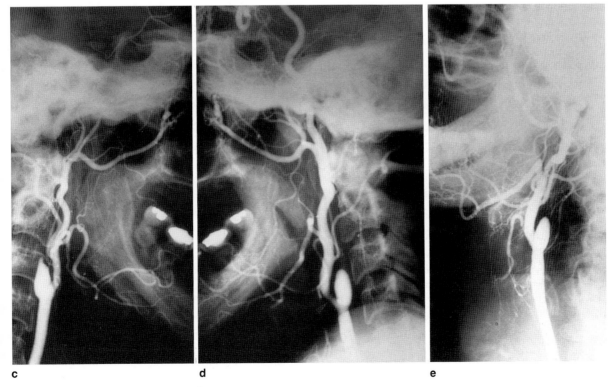

c   d   e

Fig. **6**   **c**   Right internal carotid occlusion
d   Left internal carotid occlusion and external stenosis (arrow)
e   Successful PTA of left external carotid stenosis

Table **8**   Results of vertebral
artery dilation

References		Treatment attempts*	PTA successful	Compli- cations*
Courtheoux et al.	(19)	24	21	1 TO
Kachel et al.	(56)	5	5	0
Mathias et al.	(74)	7	6	0
Motarjeme et al.	(80)	13	11	0
Smith et al.	(100)	1	1	0
Vitek et al.	(114)	4	4	1 TSO
Zeumer et al.	(125)	9	9 ?	0
Total		63	57 (90%)	2 (3%)

* TO: thrombotic occlusion; TSO: transient spastic occlusion

stenoses could be removed (Fig. **5**). In one female patient with bilateral internal carotid artery occlusion, dilation of a narrowed vertebral artery was performed uneventfully (Fig. **6**). Comparably favorable results are reported in the literature (19, 54, 56, 70, 73, 74, 79, 100, 103, 114, 125, 126) (Table **8**).

PTA can be performed on both vertebral arteries in one session (19). We have combined it with carotid and subclavian dilation in multiple vessel disease.

Complications of vertebral artery PTA are infrequently encountered (3%) and have not provoked brain infarctions even in post-PTA occlusions in two reported cases (19, 114). Sometimes spastic reaction can be observed (114), which we have seen in one patient in the poststenotic artery segment. Technical difficulties probing the vertebral artery may arise in patients with tortuosity of this vessel or an aberrant origin from the aortic arch.

Carotid Artery

The carotid artery may be divided into a cervical and an intracranial portion. The cervical segment extends from the innominate artery on the right and the aortic arch on the left to the skull base. However, the left common carotid arises from the innominate artery so often that this variant is scarcely recognized as such in diagnostic angiography, but plays an important role in PTA (62). The bifurcation of the common carotid artery usually is found at the level of the thyroid cartilage, but anatomic variations are great enough that it may be located anywhere within 5 cm of this site. The origin of the internal carotid is usually somewhat dilated, extending up to 2 cm from the origin before it assumes a uniform diameter: carotid bulb. Although the geometry of the bifurcation usually places the internal carotid posterior to the external, many variants exist, some in which the internal wraps around the external to a degree that the position appears almost reversed. Therefore, multiple projection angiography is mandatory before

PTA to evaluate the atherosclerotic lesion and the anatomic situation. Measurements made on the diameter of the bifurcation as most recently performed by Harrison and Marshall (43) in 102 normal persons gave the following results:

– Common carotid artery: 7.6 ± 1.6 mm
– Carotid bulb: 8.3 ± 1.9 mm
– Internal carotid beyond the bulb: 5.1 ± 1,1 mm
– Angle between external and internal: 36.4° ± 18.2°

The bifurcation area is also notable for the presence of the carotid body and sinus. The chemoreceptor function of the carotid body responds to a decrease in arterial oxygen tension, carotid blood flow, arterial pH, increase in arterial carbon dioxide tension, or blood temperature, in descending order of sensitivity. The carotid body has effects on respiration, blood pressure, and heart rate, being the only mediator of hypoxic ventilatory drive. Carotid endarterectomy produces an increase in the carbon dioxide tension and failure of response to hypoxia (115).

Stretching of the wall of the sinus produces activity of the carotid sinus nerve followed by sympathoinhibitory reflex hypotension and parasympathetic reduction in heart rate. Therefore, surveillance of blood pressure and heart rate during PTA of the carotid artery is recommended. Until now, we have not seen any significant changes of physiologic parameters during dilation treatment that can be related to mechanical irritation of the carotid bifurcation area.

The functional importance of the eye and brain and their sensitivity to ischemia have brought about many studies on development and stages of carotid atherosclerosis. Usually, the disease affects the carotid in a uni- or multifocal fashion, rather than diffusely. The intramural lesions occur most frequently at the bifurcation and curves. The majority are found in the first 2 cm from the origin of the internal carotid. The focus of atherosclerosis is determined to some degree by the local flow characteristics at the bifurcation. Most of the plaques develop at the rear wall of the internal carotid. Fewer lesions are seen in the intracranial portion in the siphon and at the stem of the anterior and middle cerebral arteries.

The hemodynamic significance of the stenosis is determined by:

- The cross-sectional area
- The length of the stenosis
- The velocity of blood flow
- The blood viscosity

Hemodynamically significant stenosis is defined as a stenosis reducing blood flow. In excised human internal carotid arteries the blood flow decreased when the lumen was constricted to a cross-sectional area of 4 to 5 mm^2. Clamping of the common carotid for treatment of intracranial aneurysms caused a sudden decrease in blood pressure when the lumen reached 2 mm in diameter (13). According to studies of Archie and Feldtman (3) normal blood flow is still present at up to 60% diameter and 90% area stenosis. A 40% flow reduction was documented at a 75% diameter and 94% area stenosis. Similar results were found in our animal experiments (66). Lesions in tandem produce cumulative effects only if separated by more than 3 cm.

These data are important for PTA in carotid artery disease and clearly indicate that a stenosis must be rather severe before significant reduction in blood flow occurs and dilation is justified. Asymptomatic carotid artery stenosis of less than 60% should not be treated by vascular surgery or PTA, but should be controlled in follow-up studies at 6-month intervals. Two-thirds of the patients will show no or insignificant progress of the stenosis within 1 year. On the other hand, 20% of carotid arteries with an 80 to 90% stenosis will develop an occlusion within 6 months.

The atherosclerotic plaque of the carotid artery may be complicated by layering platelet-fibrin complexes, ulceration, thrombus formation, hemorrhage into the wall of the atheroma, and arterial dissection. It is unclear if and what types of plaque complications play a role in PTA. Generally, stenoses with an angiographically smooth surface were preferentially selected for catheter dilation and rough plaques considered as "leave me alone lesions" because of an undue embolization risk. Reliable data supporting this working hypothesis are not available. In recent years, quite a number of reports on PTA of common, external, and internal carotid artery stenosis have been published (Table **9–11**).

In 12 patients with common carotid atherosclerosis PTA was performed successfully and without any complications (Fig. **7**) (11, 12, 33, 34, 48, 56, 61, 70, 73, 74, 80, 92, 107, 118, 124). Some investigators combined bifurcation endarterectomy with aortic arch vessel stenosis (57, 61). A definitive evaluation of the clinical importance of PTA of this vessel is not possible because of the small number of treated patients.

Patients with external carotid artery stenosis were more frequently treated by PTA because the embolization risk was generally considered to be much lower than in common or internal carotid obstruction (Table **10**). These therapeutic endeavors aim at an improved collateral circulation via the ophthalmic artery in cases of occluded internal carotids or create the precondition for extracranial-intracranial bypass grafting (Fig. **6**) (52, 74, 80, 84, 111, 112, 124). Although the EC/IC Bypass Study Group reported a failure of extracranial-intracranial bypass grafting to reduce the risk of ischemic stroke, in selected cases a combined radiologic and surgical treatment may be

Table **9**   Results of common carotid artery dilation

References		Treatment attempts*	PTA successful	Complications*
Freitag et al.	(34)	1	1	0
Hodgins and Dutton	(48)	1 TA	1	0
Kachel et al.	(56)	2	2	0
Kerber et al.	(57)	1 IO	1	0
Levien and Fritz	(61)	1 IO	1	0
Mathias et al.	(74)	1	1	0
Motarjeme et al.	(80)	1	1	0
Pritz and Smolin	(92)	1 IO	1	0
Tievsky et al.	(107)	1 PO	1	0
Wiggli and Gratzl	(118)	1	1	0
Zeitler et al.	(124)	1	1	0
Total		12	12 (100%)	0

* IO: intraoperative; PO: postoperative; TA: Takayasu arteritis.

Table **10**　Results of external carotid artery dilation

References		Treatment attempts*	PTA successful	Complications*
Jack et al.	(52)	6	5	1 TO
Mathias et al.	(74)	3	3	0
Motarjeme et al.	(80)	1 IO	1	0
Neuhaus et al.	(84)	2	2	0
Vitek et al.	(114)	19	18	0
Zeitler et al.	(124)	2	2	0
Total		33	31 (94%)	1 (3%)

* IO: intraoperative; TO: thrombotic occlusion.

Table **11**　Results of internal carotid artery dilation

References		Treatment attempts*			PTA successful	Complications*
Belan et al.	(7)	1 FMD			1	0
Dublin et al.	(27)	1 FMD			1	0
Freitag et al.	(34)		10 AS		7	2 TIA
Garrido and Montoya	(36)	1 FMD			1	0
Hasso et al.	(44)	3 FMD			3	0
Jooma et al.	(53)	1 FMD			1	1 ID
Kachel et al.	(56)		21 AS		19	2 TIA
Mathias et al.	(74)	1 FMD	11 AS	1 PO	12	1 TIA
Mullan et al.	(82)	1 FMD			1	0
Numaguchi et al.	(86)			1 PO	1	0
O'Leary and Clouse	(87)		1 AS		1	0
Ritter et al.	(97)		1 AS		1	0
Smith et al.	(99)	6 FMD	(5 IO)		6	0
Tsai et al.	(109)	1 FMD	25 AS	1 TA	27	0
Welch et al.	(117)	1 FMD			1	0
Wiggli and Gratzl	(118)		1 AS		1	0
Wilms et al.	(120)	1 FMD			1	0
Zeumer	(126)			3 PO	3	0
Total		18 FMD	70 AS	5 PO 1 TA		
			94		88 (94%)	6 (6%)

* AS: atherosclerotic; FMD: fibromuscular dysplasia; ID: intimal dissection; IO: intraoperative; PO: postoperative;
TA: Takayasu arteritis; TIA: transient ischemic attack.

worthwhile (29, 111, 112). The risk of PTA can be expected to be low considering only one thrombotic occlusion without brain infraction in 33 patients (52).

Fibromuscular dysplasia (FMD) is an uncommon, idiopathic vascular disease characterized by abnormalities of smooth muscle, fibrous and elastic tissue in small- and medium-sized arteries. In 1938, Leadbetter and Burkland (60) first described the condition in a 5-year-old hypertensive boy with renal artery stenosis. Similar angiographic and histologic changes were first reported in the extracranial internal carotid by Palubinskas and Ripley (89) in 1964 and subsequently were described in vertebral, external carotid, and intracranial arteries (2, 9, 41, 49, 69,

80). The true incidence of cephalic FMD is unkown, but FMD was observed in 0.67% of cases in 33,000 retrospectively reviewed cerebral angiograms with an 87% prevalence among women (45). Luescher et al. (65) observed cerebral manifestation of FMD in 26% of 92 patients.

In 1965, surgical resection was first performed in a patient with cerebral infarction and internal carotid FMD (17). Graduated arterial dilation was introduced 3 years later and became the most frequently used surgical procedure thereafter (78, 110).

In 1979, we treated our first female patient with internal carotid FMD by transluminal angioplasty (Fig. **8**) (69, 70). In the meantime, several reports

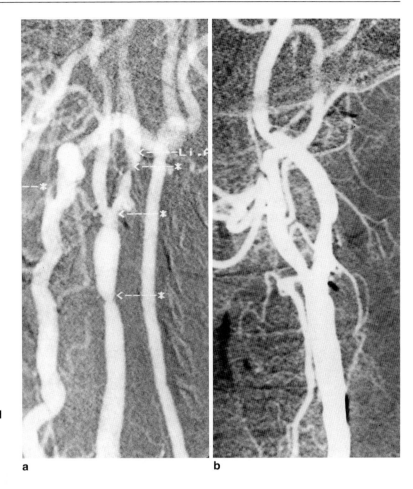

Fig. **7** **a** **Combined left common and
internal carotid artery stenosis**
(arrows)
b Normally patent vessel after PTA

a   b

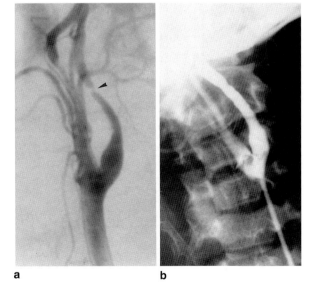

Fig. **8** **a** **Short stenosis of fibromuscular dysplasia of
the left internal carotid** (arrow)
b Stenosis removed. Slight spastic reaction

a   b

confirmed our opinion that PTA is an efficient procedure with low risk and offers a true choice in comparison to surgical repair in these patients (7, 27, 28,
36, 44, 53, 82, 99, 100, 109, 117, 120, 125, 126).
About 20% of all reported cases with internal carotid
stenosis treated by PTA concern FMD (Table **11**).

The treatment results of the patients were satisfying
and only one complication (intimal flap) was
reported by Jooma et al. (53). Surgical treatment of
FMD (99, 100) is no longer justified when PTA is
possible. The risk of damage to the arterial wall is
higher intra-operatively because visual control dur-

ing dilation does not meet radiologic standards (63).

The literature on the risk of stroke in asymptomatic atherosclerotic internal carotid stenosis seems in chaos. Some studies suggest an enormous risk, others very little, and few address the issue of whether the stroke occurs in the territory at risk and by what mechanism. In one study stroke without TIAs developed in 4.5% and TIAs occurred in 16.5% in patients with greater than 50% stenosis within 5 years (91). The cumulative stroke rate in another study was 7%, which the investigators estimated to be the same as the average risk of death in a normal population. Only the occurrence of a combined carotid and vertebral lesion increased the risk of cerebral ischemia significantly (47). From these data, it may be concluded that PTA of the internal carotid is not indicated in asymptomatic stenosis and single-vessel disease. Probably, the same is true for endarterectomy (46, 59).

Whether to operate on carotid lesions at all has recently been called into question, based on the prospect that the outlook for TIAs may be more benign than was once thought (46, 59). The risk factor of age, coexisting medical conditions, and others have been recognized to play a more major role in the outcome from surgery than was appreciated formerly. When the importance of stenotic severity is taken into account, the scanty data suggest that the real risk of stroke develops when the stenosis exceeds 80%. Moreover, it has become apparent that, in some hands, the risk of stroke from angiogram and surgery is greater than that of the lesion itself (93).

Therefore, we believe that PTA may be the minor risk for symptomatic patients with smooth, but high-degree stenosis, especially when the patient is in poor medical condition (Fig. 9). The number of patients belonging to the thus characterized group is not too large. Our own experience based on 11 patients has taught us that PTA of the internal carotid is technically feasible with a failure rate of about 10% and a good outcome of 90%. This opinion is supported by the good results of Freitag et al. (33, 34) and Kachel et al. (54, 56). In a series of 72 dilated patients with atherosclerotic disease five TIAs occurred, but no permanent impairment was observed (34, 56, 74, 97, 103). In comparison to these results even the best surgical reports describe a rate of minor and major stroke of 3% and a mortality of little less than 1% (46, 59, 93). A definitive

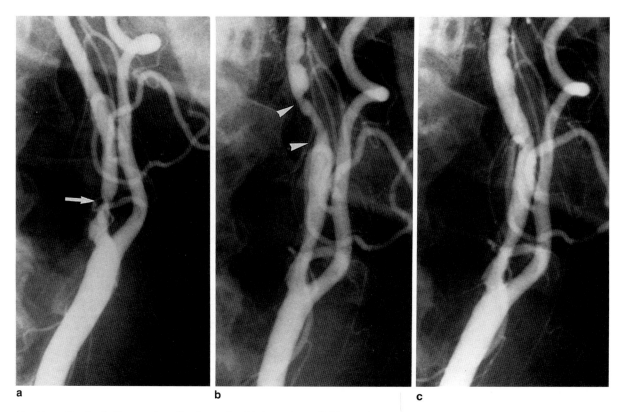

a   b   c

Fig. **9** **a Typical atherosclerotic stenosis of internal carotid** (arrow)
b Markedly improved vessel diameter, but considerable asymptomatic spasm immediately after PTA (arrows)
c Spasm resolved 10 minutes later without medication or clinical signs

evaluation of PTA in this territory is not possible at the present time because the number of cases is still too small and long-term results are scanty.

With the introduction of non-invasive scanning and DSA, the possibility of immediate postoperative stenosis or occlusion is now more extensively investigated than in the past and has shown a higher incidence of complications than usually appreciated on clinical grounds alone (93).

Early high-grade stenosis is not suited for PTA. However, catheter dilation can be performed in patients with residual and recurrent stenosis, which has to be expected in one-third of all operated patients (85, 93). When restenosis develops in a period from a few months up to 2 years, the finding is frequently a fibrous hyperplastic reaction. This type of stenosis is well suited for PTA (74, 86, 108, 126). Stenosis occurring beyond 2 years usually is caused by new atheroma (15). In these cases PTA will encounter the same risk as in the original atherosclerotic stenosis and, moreover, the disadvantage of a scarred, rigid arterial wall. No reports on PTA in this special situation exist.

Intracranial Artery Dilation

Stenotic lesions of the carotid siphon, the vertebral and the basilar arteries cannot be repaired by vascular surgery, but improvement of collateral blood flow may be attempted by extracranial-intracranial bypass. PTA was expected to become an alternative approach for such patients, but the preliminary results are not encouraging.

In the initial report of Sundt et al. (101) dilation of the vertebral and basilar arteries was carried out in four patients with severe recurrent or progressive vertebrobasilar insufficiency. The vertebral artery was exposed at the base of the skull by resecting the arch of the atlas. The balloon catheter was inserted, advanced through the stenosis of the vertebral or basilar artery, and PTA performed. In each case, there was relief of symptoms, despite a residual stenosis in one of the patients (101). The next four patients who underwent the treatment had a fatal outcome with vertebral occlusion, embolization, development of aneurysm, and arterial rupture (102). Smith et al. (100) reported another case of arterial rupture after dilation of a basilar stenosis.

The anatomic features of the intracranial arteries with their extremely thin walls make them more susceptible to rupture during PTA and are responsible for the poor results. The waning enthusiasm for the procedure is demonstrated by the fact that no further reports have been published since 1983 (103).

Another indication for intracranial dilation was reported by a Russian group (127). The investigators dilated 105 major cerebral vessels in 33 patients with subarachnoid hemorrhage due to ruptured aneurysm

and vasospasm. The effect of dilation was stable, and the functional state of the brain was ameliorated.

Local Fibrinolysis

Local application of fibrinolytic substances was introduced in the treatment of occlusive vessel disease by Dotter et al. in 1974 (26). Favorable results of this method in peripheral and coronary arteries have stimulated the attempt to apply the principles of intra-arterial fibrinolysis in cerebrovasular disease. At the present time, urokinase is preferentially used with a dosage of 40,000 IU/hr in vertebrobasilar and carotid siphon occlusions.

The indication for intra-arterial fibrinolysis in vertebrobasilar thrombosis is restricted to patients without signs of brain necrosis or hemorrhage in computed tomography and duration of coma less than 6 hours (83, 125). The excellent recovery of some patients indicates that brain tissue may survive even under prolonged ischemic conditions. Eight of 21 reported cases died despite local fibrinolysis, but nine patients recovered with only minor deficits (52, 83, 125).

Strokes in the carotid territory are frequent, but in contrast to vertebrobasilar occlusions life is rarely threatened. No improvement of clinical signs can be expected in cerebral areas, which are only supplied by end arteries, because reperfusion will always be too late to preserve brain tissue from irreversible ischemic damage. Treatment of 19 patients with occlusions of the distal carotid or the medial cerebral arteries has been reported (Table **12**). In seven cases no major neurologic deficit occurred, but one patient died from severe edema (23, 76, 126). At the present time, evidence is lacking that local fibrinolysis of the carotid territory will reduce the extent of cerebral damage or the mortality rate.

Combined Surgical and Radiologic Treatment

Dilation treatment can be combined with vascular surgery using both techniques, one after the other or simultaneously in one session. Possible indications are listed in Table **13**. Patients with multiple vessel disease are potential candidates for combined treatment, but some lesions are well suited for PTA, others for surgery.

The operative risk, which is increased in patients with multiple lesions at various supra-aortic arteries, can be reduced when a subclavian, vertebral, or carotid artery stenosis could be removed by PTA before surgery. In some cases of carotid fibromuscular dysplasia the artery was dilated after its surgical exposure (99, 100). One false aneurysm after intraoperative carotid dilation was reported by Lord et al. (63). In our opinion a percutaneous approach is just

Table **12**   Results of focal fibrinolysis

References		Treatment attempts*	Technical success	Clinical Outcome*	
Del Zoppo et al.	(23)	4 MCA	2	2 NMD, 2 MD	
Jack et al.	(52)	1 VBS	0		1 D
Miyakawa	(76)	2 MCA	2	2 NMD	
Nenci et al.	(83)	4 VBS	4	4 NMD	
Zeumer	(126)	16 VBS	9	5 NMD, 3 MD, 1 SD, 7 D	
		13 MCA + ICA	10	3 NMD, 6 MD, 3 SD, 1 D	
Total		21 VBS, 19 MCA + ICA		16 NMD, 11 MD, 4 SD, 9 D	
		40	27 (68%)	40% NMD	

* D: death; ICA: internal carotid artery; MCA: medial cerebral artery; MD: major deficit; NMD: no major deficit; SD: severe deficit; VBS: vertebrobasilar system.

Table **13**   Indications for combined treatment

PTA before vascular surgery

Dilation of external carotid stenosis before extracranial-intracranial bypass

Dilation of smooth internal carotid in bilateral stenoses with a rough contralateral internal carotid stenosis

Dilation of subclavian stenosis before subclavian-carotid bypass in common carotid occlusion

Dilation of subclavian stenosis before vertebral artery surgery

Simultaneous PTA and vascular surgery

Dilation of common carotid or innominate artery stenosis during deoppilation of carotid bifurcation

PTA after vascular surgery

Dilation of narrow bypass anastomosis

Recurrent carotid or subclavian stenosis after deoppilation

---

as effective as surgical exposure but is safer and more comfortable for the patient. Obliteration of the carotid bifurcation and dilation of the common carotid or distal internal carotid stenosis has been reported (116). As mentioned previously, PTA of postoperative stenosis of the internal carotid or subclavian artery may produce satisfying long-term results when restenosis occurs 6 to 24 months after surgery, because these lesions are not caused by atheroma, but consist of intimal hyperplasia and fibrosis. Embolization risk is minimal (107, 108). Even after bypass grafts, PTA my be helpful as described by Dacie and Lumley (21) in a 49-year-old man with amaurosis fugax and occlusion of the right internal carotid artery. The stricture of a Gore-Tex right external carotid anastomosis was successfully dilated.

References

1. Adams HP, Kassel NF, Mazuz H. The patient with transient ischemic attacks: is this the time for a new therapeutic approach? Stroke 1984;15:371–375.
2. Andersen PE. Fibromuscular hyperplasia of the carotid arteries. Acta Radiol [Diagn] (Stockh) 1970;10:90–101.
3. Archie JF, Feldman RW. Critical stenosis of the internal carotid artery. Surgery 1981;89:67–71.
4. Bachman DM, Kim RM. Transluminal dilatation for subclavian steal syndrome. AJR 1980;135:995–996.
5. Basche S, Ritter H, Gaerisch F, Grossmann K, Heerklotz I, Schumann E. Die perkutane transluminale Angioplastik der A. subclavia. Zentralbl Chir 1983;108:142–149.
6. Bean WJ, Rodan BA, Franqui DA. Subclavian steal: treatment with percutaneous transluminal angioplasty. South Med J 1984;77:1044–1046.
7. Belan A, Vesela M, Weiss K, Peregrin JH. Percutaneous transluminal angioplasty of fibromuscular dysplasia of the internal carotid artery. Cardiovasc Intervent Radiol 1982;5:79–81.
8. Bentley FR, Hollier LH, Batson RC. Axillo-axillary bypass for subclavian and innominate artery revascularization. Am Surg 1982;48:70–74.
9. Bergan JJ, MacDonald JR. Recognition of cerebrovascular fibromuscular hyperplasia. Arch Surg 1969;98:332–342.
10. Bergmann H, Kobinia G, Lederer B. Transluminale Dilatation einer Anonymastenose bei Aortenbogensyndrom. Wien Klin Wochenschr 1982;94:397–401.
11. Bockenheimer SA, Mathias K. Percutaneous transluminal angioplasty in arteriosclerotic internal carotid artery stenosis. AJNR 1983;4:791–792.
12. Bockenheimer SA, Mathias K. Percutaneous transluminal angioplasty in supra-aortic artery disease. Medica mundi 1983;28:87–89.
13. Brice JG, Dowsett DJ, Lowe RD. Haemodynamic effects of carotid artery stenosis. Br Med J 1964;2:1363–1368.
14. Buchwalsky R, Genswein R, Schlosser V, Blümchen G. Subclavian-Steal-Syndrom: postoperativer und spontaner Verlauf bei 27 Patienten über 3 Jahre. Thoraxchirurgie 1977;25:288–296.
15. Callow AD. Recurrent stenosis after carotid endarterectomy. Arch Surg 1982;117:1082–1095.
16. Canadian Cooperative Study Group: A randomized trial of aspirin and sulfinpyrazone in threatened stroke. N Engl J Med 1978;299:53–55.
17. Connet MC, Lansche JM. Fibromuscular hyperplasia of the internal carotid artery: report of a case. Ann Surg 1965;162:59–62.

18. Courtheoux P, Theron J, Maiza D, Derlon JM, Pelouze GA, Henriet JP, Evrard C, Commeau P. L'angioplastie endoluminale des sténosees atheromateuses des troncs supraaortiques: tronc artériel brachio-cephalique, artéres sousclaviéres. J Radiol 1984;65:845–851.

19. Courtheoux P, Tournade A, Theron J, Henriet JP, Maiza D, Derlon JM, Pelouze G, Evrard C. Transcutaneous angioplasty of vertebral artery atheromatous ostial stricture. Neuroradiology 1985;27:259–264.

20. Courtheoux P, Theron J, Maiza D, Henriet JP, Pelouze GA, Derlon JM, Commeau P, Evrard C. L'angioplastie endoluminale percutanée des sténoses atheromateuses des troncs supra-aortiques proximaux: tronc arteriel brachiocephalique, artéres sous-clavières. J Mal Vasc 1986;11:113–119.

21. Dacie JE, Lumley JS. Goretex graft-external carotid artery anastomotic stricture treated by percutaneous transluminal angioplasty. Cardiovasc Intervent Radiol 1985;8:191–194.

22. Damuth HD, Diamond AB, Rappoport AS, Renner JW. Angioplasty of subclavian artery stenosis proximal to the vertebral origin. AJNR 1983;4:1239–1242.

23. Del Zoppo GJ, Zeumer H, Herker LA. Thrombolytic therapy in stroke: possibilities and hazards. Stroke 1986;17:595–607.

24. Derauf BJ, Erickson DL, Castaneda-Zuniga WR, Cardella JF, Amplatz K. "Washout" technique for brachiocephalic angioplasty. AJR 1986;146:849–851.

25. Diethrich EB, Koopot R. Simplified operative procedure for proximal subclavian arterial lesions: direct subclavian-carotid anastomosis. Am J Surg 1981;142:416–421.

26. Dotter CT, Rösch J, Seaman AJ. Selective clot lysis with lowdose streptokinase. Radiology 1974;111:31–37.

27. Dublin AB, Baltaxe HA, Cobb CA. Percutaneous transluminal carotid angioplasty in fibromuscular dysplasia: case report. J Neurosurg 1983;59:162–165.

28. Dublin AB, Baltaxe HA, Cobb CA. Percutaneous transluminal carotid angioplasty and detachable balloon embolization in fibromuscular dysplasia. AJNR 1984;5:646–648.

29. EC/IC Bypass Study Group: Failure of extracranial-intracranial arterial bypass to reduce the risk of ischemic stroke. N Engl J Med 1985;313:1191–1197.

30. Edwards WH, Mulherin JL. The surgical approach to significant stenosis of the vertebral and subclavian arteries. Surgery 1980;87:20–28.

31. Eisenhardt HJ, Zehgke A, Pichlmaier H. Indikationstellung und operationstechnisches Vorgehen bei chronischen Verschlüssen des Truncus brachiocephalicus und der A. subclavian im Abschnitt I. Langenbecks Arch Chir 1980;351:161–169.

32. Fischer DR, Park SC, Neches WH, Beerman LB, Fricker FJ, Mathew RA, Zuberbuhler JR, Wedemeyer AL. Successful dilatation of a stenotic Blalock-Taussig anastomosis by percutaneous transluminal balloon angioplasty. Am J Cardiol 1985;55:861–862.

33. Freitag G, Freitag J, Koch RD. Perkutane transluminale Angioplastik von Karotisstenosen. RöFo 1984;140:209–212.

34. Freitag G, Freitag J, Koch RD, Wagemann W. Percutaneous angioplasty of carotid artery stenoses. Neuroradiology 1986;28:126–127.

35. Galicha JP, Bajaj AK, Vine DL, Roberts RW. Subclavian artery stenosis treated by transluminal angioplasty: six cases. Cardiovasc Intervent Radiol 1983;6:78–81.

36. Garrido E, Montoya J. Transluminal dilatation of internal carotid artery in fibromuscular dysplasia: a preliminary report. Surg Neurol 1981;16:469–471.

37. Garrido E, Garofola JH. Intraluminal dilatation of the innominate artery before extracranial-intracranial bypass: case report. Neurosurgery 1983;13:581–583.

38. Gerety RL, Andrus CH, May AG, Rob CG, Green R, DeWeese JA. Surgical treatment of occlusive subclavian artery disease. Circulation 1981;64 (Suppl 2):228–230.

39. Gordon RL, Haskell L, Hirsch M, Shifrin E, Weinman E, Romanoff H. Transluminal dilation of the subclavian artery. Cardiovasc Intervent Radiol 1985;8:14–19.

40. Grote R, Freyschmidt J, Walterbusch G. Die perkutane transluminale Angioplastik (PTA) von proximalen Subclaviastenosen. RöFo 1983;138:660–664.

41. Guthaner DF, Schmitz L. Percutaneous transluminal angioplasty of radiation-induced arterial stenoses. Radiology 1982;144:77–78.

42. Hacke W. Neuromonitoring during interventional neuroradiology. Cent Nerv Syst Trauma 1985;2:123–136.

43. Harrison MJG, Marshall J. Does the geometry of the carotid bifurcation affect its predisposition to atheroma? Stroke 1983;14:117–123.

44. Hasso AN, Bird CR, Zinke DE, Thompson JR. Fibromuscular dyplasia of the internal carotid artery: percutaneous transluminal angioplasty. AJR 1981;136:955–960.

45. Healton EB. Fibromuscular dysplasia. In: Barnett HJM, Mohr JP, Stein BM, Yatsu FM eds. Stroke. Edinburgh: Churchill Livingstone, 1986.

46. Heiss W-D. Carotis-Endarteriektomie: Schlaganfallprophylaxe bei symptomatischen und asymptomatischen Stenosen? Dtsch Med Wochenschr 1986;111:1867–1868.

47. Hennerici M, Rautenberg W. Stroke risk from symptomless extra cranial arterial disease. Lancet 1982;ii:1180–1183

48. Hodgins GW, Dutton JW. Transluminal dilatation for Takayasu's arteritis. Can J Surg 1984;27:355–357.

49. Huber P, Fuchs WA. Gibt es eine fibromuskuläre Hyperplasie zerebraler Arterien? RöFo 1967;107:119.

50. Imparato A, Riles T, Kim G. Vertebral artery reconstruction. Stroke 1981;12:125–129.

51. Iscovici X, Fabiani JN, Renaudin JM, Pernes JM, Gaux JC, Lemseffer M, Carpentier A. Lésions pré-vertebrales de l'artère sous-clavière: résultats à distance de la chirurgie réconstructice et de l'angioplastie percutanée. J Mal Vasc 1985;10:183–188.

52. Jack CR, Mehta BA, Boulos RS, Patel SC, Ausman JI, Malik GM. Interventional neuroradiology: Henry Ford Hospital experience with nonembolization procedures. Henry Ford Hosp Med J 1986;34:11

53. Jooma R, Bradshaw JR, Griffith HB. Intimal dissection following percutaneous transluminal carotid angioplasty for fibromuscular dysplasia. Neuroradiology 1985;27:181–182.

54. Kachel R, Ritter H, Großmann K, Glaser FH. Ergebnisse der perkutanen transluminalen Dilatation (PTD) von Hirngefässstenosen. RöFo 1986;144:338–342.

55. Kachel R, Ritter H: Perkutane Katheterrekanalisation (Angioplastie) eines Subklaviaverschlusses mit Subclavian-Steal-Syndrom. RöFo 1986;145:107–109.

56. Kachel R, Endert G, Basche S, Grossmann K, Glaser FH. Percutaneous transluminal angioplasty (dilatation) of carotid, vertebral, and innominate artery stenoses. Cardiovasc Intervent Radiol 1987;10:142–146.

57. Kerber CW, Cromwell LD, Loehden LO. Catheter dilatation of proximal carotid stenosis during distal bifurcation endarterectomy. AJNR 1980;1:348–349.

58. Kobinia GS, Bergmann H. Angioplasty in stenosis of the innominate artery. Cardiovasc Intervent Radiol 1983;6:82–85.

59. Krämer G, Grönniger J, Süß W, Hopf HC. Carotis-Thrombendarterektomie: Hoffnungen und nachweisbare Wirkungen. Dtsch Med Wochenschr 1986;111:1815–1817.

60. Leadbetter WF, Brukland CE. Hypertension in unilateral renal disease. J Urol 1938;39:611–628.

61. Levien LJ, Fritz VU. Intra-operative transluminal angioplasty in the management of symptomatic aortic arch vessel stenosis. S Afr J Surg 1985;23:49–52.

62. Lie TA, ed. Congenital anomalies of the carotid arteries. Amsterdam: Excerpta Medica 1968.

63. Lord RS, Graham AR, Benn IV. Radiologic control of operative carotid dilatation: aneurysm formation following balloon dilatation. J Cardiovasc Surg (Torino) 1986;27:158–162.

64. Lowman BG, Queral LA, Holbrook WA, Estes JT, Bayly B, Dagher FJ. The correction of cerebrovascular insufficiency by transluminal dilatation: a preliminary report. Am Surg 1983;49:621–624.

65. Luescher TF, Keller HM, Imhof HG, Greminger P, Kuhlmann U, Largiader F, Schneider E, Schneider J, Vetter W. Fibromuscular hyperplasia: extension of the disease and therapeutic outcome: results of the University Hospital Zürich Cooperative Study on Fibromuscular Hyperplasia. Nephron 1986;44 (Suppl. 1) 109–114.

66. Mathias K, Mittermayer C, Ensinger H, Neff W. Perkutane Katheterdilatation von Karotisstenosen: tierexperimentelle Untersuchungen. RöFo 1980;133:258–261.
67. Mathias K, Schlosser V, Reinke M. Katheterrekanalisation eines Subklaviaverschlusses. RöFo 1980;132:346–347.
68. Mathias K, Staiger J, Thron A, Spillner G, Heiss H-W, Konrad-Grad S. Perkutane Katheterangioplastik der Arteria subclavia. Dtsch Med Wochenschr. 1980;105:16–18.
69. Mathias K, Gospos C, Thron A, Ahmadi A, Mittermayer C. Percutaneous transluminal treatment of supraaortic artery obstruction. Ann Radiol (Paris) 1980;23:281–282.
70. Mathias K. Perkutane transluminale Katheterbehandlung supraaortaler Arterienobstruktionen. Int. Angiol 1981;3:47–50.
71. Mathias K, Heiss H-W, Gospos C. Subclavian-Steal-Syndrom: operieren oder dilatieren? Langenbecks Arch Chir 1982;356:279–283.
72. Mathias K, Haendle J. Katheterdilatation mit der digitalen Bildsubtraktion. Röntgenpraxis 1982;35:9–14.
73. Mathias K, Bockenheimer S, von Reutern G, Heiss H-W, Ostheim-Dzerowycz W. Katheterdilatation hirnversorgender Arterien. Radiologe 1983;23:208–214.
74. Mathias K. Katheterbehandlung der arteriellen Verschlusskrankheit supraaortaler Gefässe. Radiologe 1987; 27,547.
75. Metz L, Ulrich C. Zur Hämodynamik des karotido-subklavialen Bypass. Zentralbl Chir 1982;107:1041–1046.
76. Miyakawa T. The cerebral vessels and thrombosis. Rinsho Ketsueki 1984;25:1018–1021.
77. Moore TS, Russell WF, Parent AD, Parker JL, Smith RR. Percutaneous transluminal angioplasty in subclavian steal syndrome: recurrent stenosis and retreatment in two patients. Neurosurgery 1982;11:512–517.
78. Morris GC, Lechter A, Debakey ME. Surgical treatment of fibromuscular disease of the carotid arteries. Arch Surg 1968;96:636–647.
79. Motarjeme A, Keifer JW, Zuska AJ. Percutaneous transluminal angioplasty of the vertebral arteries. Radiology 1981;139:715–717.
80. Motarjeme A, Keifer JW, Zuska AJ. Percutaneous transluminal angioplasty of the brachiocephalic arteries. AJR 1982;138:457–462.
81. Motarjeme A, Keifer JW, Zuska AJ, Nabawi P. Percutaneous transluminal angioplasty for treatment of subclavian steal. Radiology 1985;155:611–613.
82. Mullan S, Duda EE, Patronas NJ. Some examples of balloon technology in neurosurgery. J Neurosurg 1980;52:321–329.
83. Nenci GG, Gresele P, Taramelli M, Agnelli G, Signorini E. Thrombolytic therapy for thromboembolism of vertebrobasilar artery. Angiology 1983;34:561–565.
84. Neuhaus KL, Rupprath G, Hellberg K, Kühn R, Tebbe U. Valvuloplastie und periphere Angioplastie mit Koronardilatationskathetern. Dtsch Med Wochenschr 1985;110:703–708.
85. Norwing B, Nilsson B, Olsson J-E. Progression of carotid disease after endarterectomy: a Doppler ultrasound study. Ann Neurol 1982;12:548–556.
86. Numaguchi Y, Puyau FA, Provenza LJ, Richardson DE. Percutaneous transluminal angioplasty of the carotid artery: its application in post surgical stenosis. Neuroradiology 1984;26:527–530.
87. O'Leary DH, Clouse ME. Percutaneous transluminal angioplasty of the cavernous carotid artery for recurrent ischemia. AJNR 1984;5:644–645.
88. Olbert F, Muzika N, Schlegl A, eds. Transluminale Dilatation und Rekanalisation im Gefässbereich. Nürnberg: Wachholz, 1985.
89. Palubinskas AJ, Ripley HR. Roentgen diagnosis of fibromuscular hyperplasia in extra-renal arteries. Radiology 1964;82:451.
90. Pernes JM, Bernot P, Seurot M, Angel C, Ferrer J, Renaudin JM, Fabiani JN, d'Allaines C, Gaux JC. Angioplastie endoluminale percutanée des troncs artériels supra-aortiques: résultats immediats et à distance. Presse Med 1984;13:1075–1078.
91. Podore PC, De Weese JA, May AG, Rob CG. Asymptomatic contralateral carotid artery stenosis: a five-year follow-up study following carotid endarterectomy. Surgery 1980;88:748–761.
92. Pritz MB, Smolin MF. Treatment of tandem lesions of the extracranial carotid artery. Neurosurgery 1984;15:233–236.
93. Raithel D, Schweiger H, Gentsch HH, Seyferth W, Zeitler E. Digital transvenous angiography in follow-up examinations after carotid reconstruction: early results. J Cardiovasc Surg (Torino) 1984;25:400–403.
94. Reuther R, Dorndorf W. Aspirin in patients with cerebral ischemia and normal angiograms or nonsurgical lesions: the results of a double-blind trial. In: Breddin K, Dorndorf W, Loew D, et al, eds. Acetylsalicylic acid in cerebral ischemia and coronary heart disease. Stuttgart: Schattauer, 1978:97.
95. Ringelstein EB, Zeumer H. Delayed reversal of vertebral artery blood flow following percutaneous transluminal angioplasty for subclavian steal syndrome. Neuroradiology 1984;26:189–198.
96. Ringelstein EB, Zeumer H, Brückmann H, Stübben G, Sturm KW. Atraumatische Diagnostik und semi-invasive Therapie des Subklaviaanzapfsyndroms mit Hilfe der perkutanen transluminalen Angioplastie (PTA): ein zeitgemäßes Konzept. Fortschr Neurol Psychiatr 1986;54:216–231.
97. Ritter H, Grossmann K, Basche S, Heerklotz I, Schiffmann R, Schumann E. Die perkutane transluminale Angioplastik (PTA) von Aortenbogenästen. RöFo 1982;136:365–370.
98. Sandmann W, Hennerici M, Kniemeyer H, Nüllen A, Aulich A, Kremer K. Early and late results after subclavian-carotid transposition. Thorac Cardiovasc Surg 1983;31:18–19.
99. Smith DC, Smith LL, Hasso AN. Fibromuscular dysplasia of the internal carotid artery treated by operative transluminal balloon angioplasty. Radiology 1985;155:645–648.
100. Smith RR, Moore TS, Russell WF. Transluminal angioplasty of the cerebral circulation. Clin Neurosurg 1983;31:117–134.
101. Sundt TM, Smith HC, Campbell JK, Vlietstra RE, Cuchiara RF, Stanson AW. Transluminal angioplasty for basilar artery stenosis. Mayo Clin Proc 1980;55:673–680.
102. Sundt TM, Smith HC, Piepgras DG, Campbell JK. Bypass and transluminal dilatation procedures for advanced occlusive disease of the posterior circulation. Neurosurg Rev 1982;5:65–72.
103. Takeuchi K. Application of percutaneous transluminal angioplasty (PTA) for stenotic lesions of the cephalic arteries. Jpn Ann Thorac Surg 1982;2:795–802.
104. Theron J, Courtheoux P, Henriet JP, Pelouze G, Derlon JM, Maiza D. Angioplasty of supraaortic arteries. J Neuroradiol 1984;11:187–200.
105. Theron J, Melancon D, Ethier R. "Pre"-subclavian steal syndromes and their treatment by angioplasty: hemodynamic classification of subclavian artery stenoses. Neuroradiology 1985;27:265–270.
106. Thompson BW, Smith HC, Campbell JK. Operative correction of proximal blocks of the subclavian or innominate arteries. J Cardiovasc Surg (Torino) 1980;21:125–130.
107. Tievsky AL, Druy EM, Mardiat JG. Transluminal angioplasty in postsurgical stenosis of the extracranial carotid artery. AJNR 1983;4:800–802.
108. Tisnado J, Vines FS, Barnes RW, Beachley MC, Cho SR. Percutaneous transluminal angioplasty following endarterectomy. Radiology 1984;152:361–364.
109. Tsai FY, Matovich V, Hieshman G, Shah DC, Mehringer CM, Tiu G, Higashida R, Pribram HF. Percutaneous transluminal angioplasty of the carotid artery. AJNR 1986;7:349–358.
110. Upson J, Raza ST. Fibromuscular dysplasia on internal carotid arteries: graduated internal dilation by arterial Fogarty catheter. NY State J Med 1976;76:972–974.
111. Vitek JJ, Morawetz RB. Percutaneous transluminal angioplasty of the external carotid artery: preliminary report. AJNR 1982;3:541–546.
112. Vitek JJ. Percutaneous transluminal angioplasty of the external carotid artery. AJNR 1983;4:796–799.
113. Vitek JJ, Raymon BC, Oh SJ. Innominate artery angioplasty. AJNR 1984;5:113–114.
114. Vitek JJ, Keller FS, Duvall ER, Gupta KL, Chandra-Sekar B. Brachiocephalic artery dilatation by percutaneous transluminal angioplasty. Radiology 1986;158:779–785.

115. Wade JG, Larson CP, Hickey RR. Effect of carotid endarterectomy on carotid chemoreceptor and baroreceptor functions in man. N Engl J Med 1970;282:823–825.

116. Wassmann H, Solymosi L. Revaskularisation langstreckig stenosierter oder nahezu verschlossener Karotiden. Neurochirurgia (Stuttg) 1985;28:131–133.

117. Welch EL, Lemkin JA, Geary JE. Grüntzig balloon dilatation for fibromuscular dysplasia of the internal carotid arteries. NY State J Med 1985;85:115–117.

118. Wiggli U, Gratzl O. Transluminal angioplasty of stenotic carotid arteries: case reports and protocol. AJNR 1983;4:793–795.

119. Williams SJ. Chronic upper extremity ischemia: current concepts in management. Surg Clin North Am 1986;66:355–375.

120. Wilms GE, Smits J, Baert AL, deWolf L. Percutaneous transluminal angioplasty in fibromuscular dysplasia of the internal carotid artery: one year clinical and morphological follow-up. Cardiovasc Intervent Radiol 1985;8:20–23.

121. Wilms G, Baert A, Dewaele D, Vermylen J, Nevelsteen A, Suy R. Percutaneous transluminal angioplasty of the subclavian artery: early and late results. Cardiovas Intervent Radiol 1987;10:123–128.

122. Wolf PA, Kannel WB, McGee DL. Epidemiology of strokes in Europe. In: Barnett HJM, Mohr JP, Stein BM, Yatsu FM, eds. Stroke. Edinburgh: Churchill Livingstone, 1986.

123. Zeitler E. Entwicklung und heutiger Stand der perkutanen transluminalen Angioplastie. Röntgenpraxis 1982;35:298–307.

124. Zeitler E, Berger G, Schmitt-Rüth R. Percutaneous transluminal angioplasty of the supra-aortic arteries. In: Dotter CT, Grüntzig AR, Schoop W, Zeitler E, eds. Percutaneous transluminal angioplasty. Berlin: Springer, 1983:245–261.

125. Zeumer H, Ringelstein EB, Hacke W. Gefäßrekanalisierende Verfahren der interventionellen Neuroradiologie. RöFo 1983;139:467–475.

126. Zeumer H. Vascular recanalizing techniques in interventional neuroradiology. J Neurol 1985;231:287–294.

127. Zubkov YN, Nikiforov BM, Shustin VA. Balloon catheter technique for dilatation of constricted cerebral arteries after aneurysmal SAH. Acta Neurochir. (Wien) 1984;70:65–79.

Percutaneous Transluminal Angioplasty of the Coronary Arteries

J. L. Struyven, C. Delcour, and E. Stoupel

Ten years had elapsed since Dotter described his coaxial technique for vessel dilation when Grüntzig in 1977 introduced the balloon angioplasty concept that has revolutionized the management of stenotic disease of blood vessels, especially those causing myocardial ischemia (14).

Equipment

Radiologic equipment

The basic requirements are the optimal visualization of coronary circulation from several different projections and the monitoring of the catheters and guide wire manipulations. Biplanar equipment can be helpful, but cranial and caudal angulations are mandatory. High-resolution image intensifiers are necessary for monitoring the dilation material. The possibility of momentarily increasing the X-ray dose allows improved spatial resolution, providing better visualization of the dilating material. This refinement uses pulse mode sequences of cineangiography in the fluoroscopy mode. Digital imaging of the coronary arteries includes direct digital vascular imaging and the mask-mode subtraction technique. A digital vascular imaging system can be considered as a recording device comparable to a 35 mm camera, but it

offers such advantages as immediate access to angiographic data and increased contrast discrimination. Both features are useful in percutaneous transluminal coronary angioplasty (PTCA). Digital subtraction coronary angiography can be performed in two ways, either by a high frame rate of up to 25 images per second or by electrocardiographic-triggered firing in late diastole. The 512 by 512 matrix currently used for digital coronography provides spatial resolution close to that of 35 mm cineangiography. However, contrast resolution is much better and permits the optimal localization of the dilating equipment and immediate evaluation of results after PTCA while using small quantities of contrast medium for the opacification of the coronary artery. The production of an angiographic map can be useful for coronary angioplasty to ensure proper direction and placement of the dilation catheters. In this special technique an unsubtracted angiogram is acquired in late diastole and processed through the computer by mask-mode subtraction, contrast reversal, and contrast enhancement algorithms. This image is stored in the computer memory and can be recalled and displayed on the videomonitor. Live fluoroscopic images can be superimposed on the map image to help direct the guide wire into the appropriate coronary branch and align the balloon over the

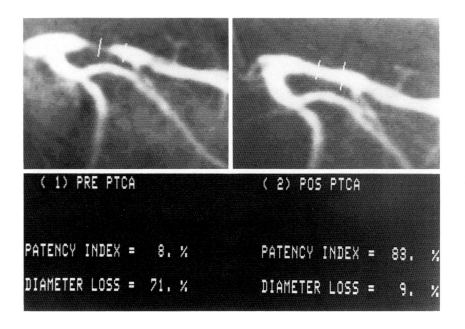

Fig. 1 **Pre- and post-PTCA quantitative study** using specially designed computer programs to calculate stenosis. Left anterior descending coronary artery in right anterior oblique projection

coronary stenosis. Digital data used for imaging can also be processed for quantification (29, 33, 34, 43) (Figs. **1, 2**).

Guide Catheters

Guide catheters are 9 Fr or 8 Fr preshaped catheters analogous to diagnostic catheters. The most important function of the guide catheter is to provide an optimal support for the advancement of the dilation catheter across the stenosis. Current catheters are composed of an outer layer of polyethylene or polyurethane for stiffness and memory. The middle layer is a wire matrix to transmit torque, and the inner layer of Teflon lubricates the passage of the dilation catheter.

Because the tip of a guide catheter is shorter and thinner, its potential for intimal disruption is higher than that of a diagnostic catheter. Some manufactureres provide "soft tip" catheters that may decrease this risk. The tip of such a catheter deforms when pressure is applied so that trauma and irritation to the vessel wall is decreased. Currently available left guide catheters include Judkins, Amplatz, and

Bourassa curves. In standard catheters the tip is in the same plane as the catheter. Some companies manufacture left coronary catheters that have the tip oriented 30 degrees anteriorly or posteriorly to facilitate catheterization of the left anterior descending artery or the left circumflex. Currently available right catheters include Judkins, Amplatz, David, and Al Gamal curves. Optimally, the catheter must be able to engage the ostium of the coronary artery selectively without occluding arterial inflow. Vessel occlusion seldom occurs in the left coronary artery, but ostial damping is a common problem in the right coronary artery. Catheters equipped with side holes allow wedging of the right coronary artery with ongoing arterial perfusion.

Brachial guide catheters are also avialable and can be especially useful in some difficult anatomic situations. Basically, a 9 Fr catheter is superior in terms of torque control, backup support, and contrast delivery, but its potential for intimal damage is higher than that of an 8 Fr catheter. Therefore, 8 Fr catheters with large lumina and increased stiffness in the shaft are tending to replace 9 Fr catheters (39, 44, 45).

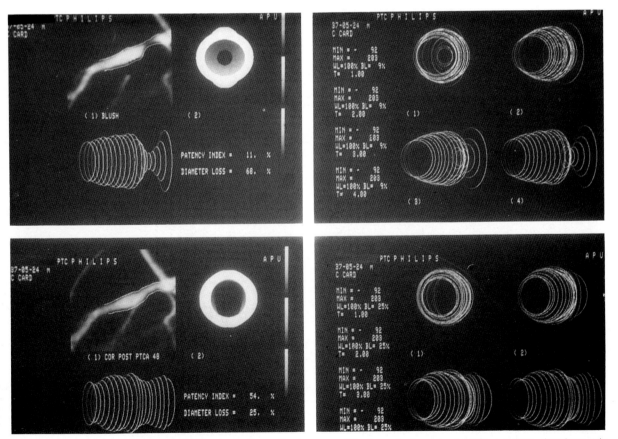

Fig. **2 Pre- and post-PTCA digitalized studies** allowing quantification of stenosis. In this program densitometric studies provide three-dimensional data

Dilation Catheters

The dilation catheters used in PTCA have undergone radical evolution since Grüntzig designed the G and DG catheters with a short guide wire affixed to the catheter tip. Since 1982, this design has been replaced by a movable or steerable guide wire that extends the dilating catheter, as described by Simpson and Robert. In this system a thin guide wire is inserted into the entire length of the lumen of the dilating catheter. The central lumen must have a sufficiently large diameter to allow movement of the guide wire and permit distal pressure measurement. Basically, the ballon size used is 3 mm in the outer diameter and 25 mm in length; radiopaque markers delineate the balloon. Likewise, balloon catheters are available in a number of sizes ranging from 2 mm for small vessels to 4.2 mm for bypasses. The most frequently used dilation catheters are manufactered by USCI (United States Catheter and Instrument Company), Schneider, and ACS (Advanced Cardiovascular System). Each has its merits and disandvantages. The ACS "concentric" system is designed

as a concentric balloon lumen and distal lumen, whereas the USCI "eccentric" system has an eccentric balloon lumen separated from the distal lumen. USCI currently uses polyvinyl chloride balloons, whereas ACS balloons are made of polyethylene. Experiments demonstrate that polyvinyl chloride balloons reach their specified diameter at approximately 5 atm and exceed it at higher inflation pressures. Polyethylene balloons exceed their stated diameter at 8 to 10 atm. A concentric lumen system allows rapid inflation and deflation of the balloon and a lower profile, whereas an eccentric lumen permits more accurate transstenotic pressure measurements. Polyethylene has a lower coefficient of friction compared with polyvinyl chloride. Another difference is the potential for overinflating polyvinyl chloride balloons, which may surpass the intended diameter by 0.2 to 0.5 mm. Over the past years, there has been an evolution in technology.

Hartzler designed an ultra-low profile catheter with a balloon directly bonded to a guide wire (ACS) (Fig. 3). The Monorail-Bonzel catheter can be

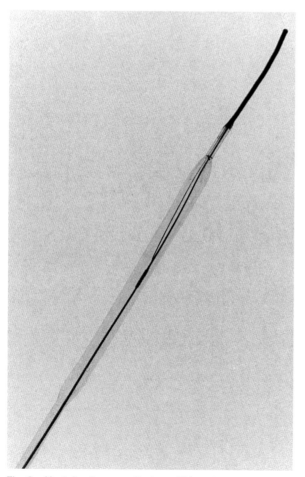

Fig. **3 Hartzler-type catheter.** This ultra low profile catheter is made of a balloon directly bonded to a guide wire

Fig. **4 Monorail-Bonzel catheter.** Arrow indicates the entrance of the guide wire into the shaft of the dilation catheter

removed and another inserted using the same guide wire because in this design the guide wire lumen is located only in the distal part of the catheter (USCI) (Fig. **4**). New balloon materials such as polyethylene terephthalate (USCI) offer a low friction coefficient and are able to withstand up to 20 atm of pressure even when regular pressure ranges from 6 to 10 atm. High pressure is sometimes mandatory to overcome extremely hard calcified lesions (5, 19, 20, 31, 39, 44).

Guide Wires

Steerable catheters using a thin guide wire improved the success rate of PTCA; before the advent of this technology, most of the failures resulted from inability to reach or to cross the stenosis. Manipulating the proximal end permits the guide wire to cross the stenosis and serve as a rail along which the balloon catheter can be moved without entering side branches or damaging the intima. Different types of guide wires are commercially available with diameters ranging from 0.010 to 0.018 and with various designs of the distal tip, including straight, high torque, J type, flexible, and floppy guide wires. Basic construction of a coronary guide wire includes a short distal segment without a core, to achieve maximum flexibility, and a malleable ribbon incorporated in the distal part of the wire to allow shaping of the tip. This design helps in negotiating acute angles.

Use of 300 cm guide wires allows dilation catheter exchange without moving either the leading catheter or the intracoronary guide wire and, most importantly, without recrossing the stenosis. In order to eliminate handling problems associated with a cumbersome 300 cm guide wire Stertzer and Myler designed a system with an extension wire added to the proximal end of the original intracoronary guide wire. Another inherent feature of a wire is the friction coefficient, which determines the maneuverability, especially in tortuous arteries. Now most guide wires are Teflon coated. The recording of pressure measurements is still possible even with the steerable catheter system, but pressure measurements are sometimes compromised when the guide wire diameter exceeds 0.016 (44).

Additional Equipment

Simpson designed a "reperfusion" catheter to be used in case of intimal dissection, restenosis, or vessel closure. This type is a 3 Fr coronary infusion catheter with multiple side holes at the tip. The catheter must be positioned over a guide wire in such a way that the side holes extend on either side of the stenosis or dissection, thereby allowing passive flow of blood across the lesion through the catheter (10).

Laser treatment of atherosclerotic plaque has been proposed to recanalize occluded or stenotic vessels. Argon or neodymium:yttrium-aluminum-garnet (Nd:YAG) laser assisted angioplasty uses the thermal properties of a metal-tipped laser fiber, sapphire tip, or lens tip to recanalize an obstructed artery or widen a high-degree stenosed artery that is subsequently treated by balloon angioplasty. Laboratory and clinical trials are underway, but at this early stage conclusive results have been obtained only in peripheral vessels. In coronary arteries, technical refinements and further experience are needed to establish both the role and the risks of laser angioplasty, but the laser certainly shows considerable potential in this field. Preliminary results have already been reported using tip-encapsulated fibers (6, 48). Concern over the problem of recurrence of stenosis is reflected by research on endoprostheses. Palmaz, Gianturco, Castanega-Zuniga, and others had developed different types of supportive endoprosthesis. The stent is made of continuous stainless steel tubular mesh. The graft is mounted on the balloon of the dilation catheter and expanded into the stenosis by inflating the balloon. The mesh retains its shape after balloon deflation and keeps the diameter of the vessel lumen as large as the diameter of the inflated balloon. The purpose of this device is to prevent immediate restenosis by intimal dissection, elastic restenosis, or late restenosis. More experience is necessary (13, 35, 49).

Technique

The procedure is performed with surgical backup available. The patient is asked to fast from midnight on the evening before the procedure. Several medications are given: verapamil, diltiazem, or nifedipine to prevent spasm, plus dipyridamole and aspirin to prevent platelet aggregation (11). After sedation (diazepam) and local anesthesia (lidocaine 2%), an 8 or 9 Fr introduction sheath is inserted into the femoral artery and intravenous heparin (10,000 U) is administered. If desired, a pacing electrode can be advanced through the femoral vein to the pulmonary artery to serve as a marker of the lesion and for use if bradycardia occurs.

An appropriate manifold system allows pressure recording through the distal end of both leading and dilation catheters. The manifold system allows intracoronary contrast, saline, and medication delivery. Hemostatic catheter and guide wire connectors prevent blood loss and ensure feasible blood pressure recording.

Subsequently, the appropriate leading catheter is carefully positioned in the ostium of the involved coronary artery, and the lesion is clearly demonstrated and located. Baseline angiography serves also to select the balloon size. Intracoronary nitrates prevent or minimize spasm at the site of intimal trauma.

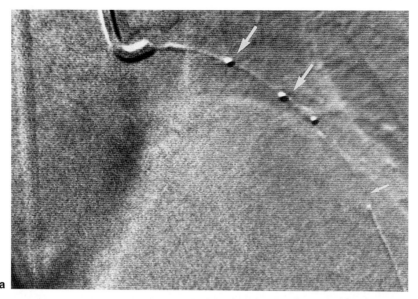

a

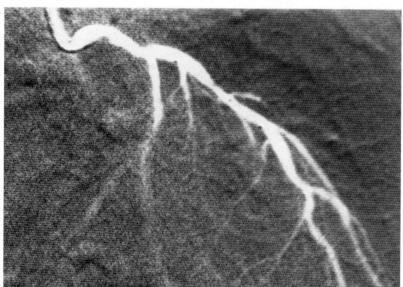

b

Fig. 5   a **Guide wire (small arrow) and dilation balloon (large arrows) are correctly located in the left arterior decending artery.** The large arrows indicate the radiopaque markers
b Digital subtraction coronary angiography (DSCA) with the dilation apparatus still in place. Right anterior oblique projection

The dilation catheter and guide wire are inserted into the leading catheter, and while the dilation catheter remains within the tip of the guiding catheter, the steerable guide wire is extended 7 to 10 cm beyond the distal end of the dilation catheter and carefully positioned beyond the stenosis in the appropriate artery (Figs. **5, 6**). Its position relative to vessel branches and stenosis is evaluated by a series of contrast injections. Use of digital subtraction angiography may be helpful in this situation, since contrast medium injections are difficult because of the dilation catheter located in the lumen of the guiding catheter. This guide serves as a rail permitting safe positioning of the balloon catheter in the lesion.

The fluoroscopic position of the radiopaque markers is used to confirm balloon positioning within the stenosis. When using the Monorail-Bonzel catheter, the guide wire is first inserted into the guiding catheter and advanced into the involved coronary artery, through the stenosis, and positioned in the distal part of the vessel. Contrast injections for localization are easily done in the absence of a dilation catheter. Then the dilation catheter is advanced over the guide wire and positioned within the target stenosis. Once optimal positioning is assured, transstenotic pressure is recorded and the balloon is inflated progressively until it assumes full cylindrical shape. In most cases transient constriction of the balloon by the coronary stenosis resolves once adequate distending pressure is developed. Optimal inflation pressure and inflation time are still controversial. Full cylindrical shape of the balloon is usually achieved using inflation

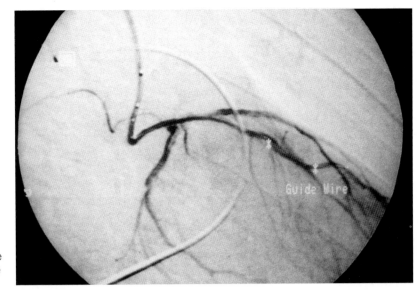

Fig. 6   Digital subtraction coronary angiography of a left anterior descending angioplasty. Injection of 1 ml. Asterisks indicate the location of the dilation apparatus in the right anterior oblique projection

pressures between 6 and 8 atm. As mentioned earlier, one must recall the indication that polyvinyl chloride balloons reach the stated diameter at a mean pressure of 5 atm and can be overinflated; those made from polyethylene exceed the stated diameter at a mean pressure of 8 to 10 atm. In the first case the angiographer may overdistend the artery, possibly leading to vessel dissection. In hard lesions or elastic stenoses it may be necessary to perform repeated, prolonged, or high-pressure inflations, which may necessitate changing balloons to avoid the risk of overdistension. Risk of side branch closure must be emphasized if there is a pre-existing ostial narrowing. In 1981, Grüntzig introduced the kissing balloon angioplasty technique, in which a guide wire is placed in both branches, allowing simultaneous positioning of dilation catheters in each. In our protocol, if potential side branch closure poses a risk, an additional wire is inserted into the side branch to provide easy access in case of closure. Immediate results of the procedure are assessed by angiographic evaluation or transstenotic gradient measurements (38).

Successful PTCA was defined by Grüntzig as at least a 20% reduction in the cross-sectional area of the stenosis and a residual gradient less than or equal to 15 mm Hg. We use slightly more stringent criteria than those defined by Grüntzig. In addition to requiring a 20% reduction in the stenosis, our designation of successful PTCA also requires that the residual stenosis be not more than 50% (Fig. **7**). Transstenotic gradient measurement is still controversial in estimating the degree of improvement, because its application has several serious sources of error, such as vessel tortuosity, collapse of the central lumen of the dilation catheter, presence of side holes in the guiding catheter, and presence of the balloon itself in the stenosis. In addition, dilation systems such as the Hartzler and the Monorail-Bonzel catheters do not allow transstenotic pressure evaluation. A residual postangioplasty gradient of less than 15 mmHg invariably indicates a good result, but the reverse is not true. Similarly, angiographic evaluation can be difficult due to eccentricity of the coronary lumen or presence of the dilation catheter in the guiding catheter. Angiographic evaluation is more convenient using digital angiography or Monorail-Bonzel-catheters. Once adequate dilation is achieved, the balloon catheter is withdrawn into the guiding catheter for further angiographic evaluation to assess adequate results. If the result is considered satisfactory, it is a common practice to leave the guide wire across the dilated segment for up to 5 minutes before the final angiographic evaluation. If hemodynamic deterioration occurs, the guide wire provides easy access to the lesion. If the lesion remains stable, the procedure is terminated or another significant lesion may be treated.

When angioplasty is completed, the patient is transferred to the recovery area with the femoral sheath still in place. When the heparin is considered to have been fully eliminated (4 to 5 hours), the sheath is removed and careful arterial compression is applied for 20 minutes. In addition to the benefit of anticoagulation, this method allows rapid reintroduction of diagnostic catheters or the dilation apparatus if the patient experiences reocclusion. Usually, the patient remains on bed rest for 18 to 24 hours. A stress test is performed 48 hours after PTCA, before discharge. Post-PTCA medications include aspirin, dipyridamole, and a calcium antagonist for at least 3 months (8, 12, 14, 20, 39, 42).

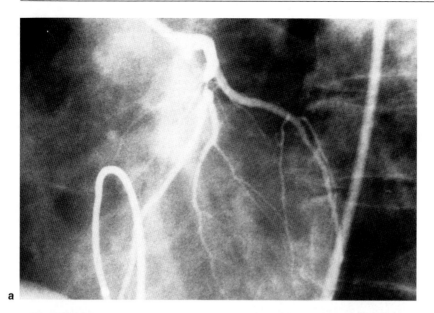

a

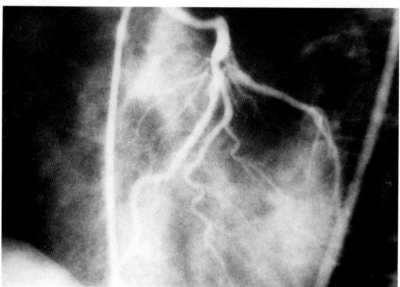

b

Fig. **7 a This angiogram demonstrates a 90% lesion of the left anterior descending artery** in left anterior oblique projection. **b Follow-up angiogram** after removal of the dilation apparatus: 10% residual stenosis

Complications

As a sophisticated form of cardiac catheterization, coronary angioplasty presents the usual risk related to vessel trauma at the insertion site. The larger caliber of angioplasty guiding catheters (diagnostic catheters are 5 or 7 Fr) and the frequent need to engage the catheter tip in the ostium is more likely to result in damage to the proximal coronary artery. Advancement of guide wires and dilation catheters may lead to intimal injury. The most common complications occur at the level of the dilation. Aggressive manipulation of the guide wire in a tortuous vessel and vigorous attempts to pass the dilation catheter through a tight stenosis can lead to plaque dissection or intimal disruption (Fig. **8**). The injury intentionally provoked by balloon inflation for PTCA results in variable degress of plaque rupture, intimal and medial disruption, and medial and adventitial stretching. These lesions are usually small, non-evolving, hemodynamically insignificant, and heal in a few weeks, as demonstrated by early follow-up studies.

Occasionally, large evolving dissections lead to total occlusion of the vessel. This is the result of compression of the lumen by the dissection flap, platelet aggregation, or thrombus formation. Vessel spasm can contribute to the complication. The process can be reversed by administration of intracoronary nitrates or by readvancement and reinflation of the dilation catheter (Fig. **9**). The complication rate

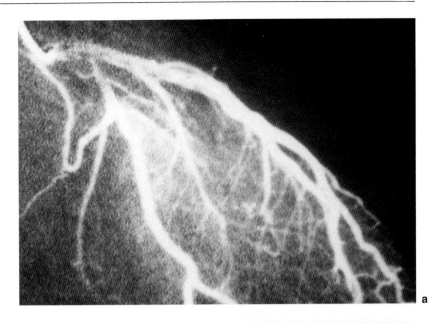

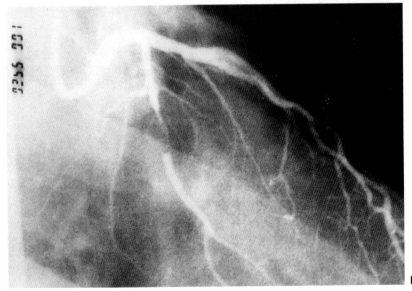

Fig. **8 a Angioplasty of a left circumflex coronary artery.**
Follow-up angiogram at the end of the procedure demonstrating arterial patency
b A 24-hour follwo-up angiogram. Electrocardiographic abnormalities and anginal symptoms were observed 12 hours after PTCA. Early dissection at the angioplasty site

increases when the lesions are eccentric, long, diffuse, or distal. Failure to reverse the obstruction mandates emergency coronary artery bypass surgery.

Myocardial damage can be obviated by using the previously described reperfusion catheter. If elapsed time between vessel occlusion and surgical reestablishment of coronary perfusion does not exceed 2 hours, transmural myocardial infarction is averted. However, the literature concerning emergency grafting after failed or complicated angioplasty reports higher mortality and morbidity than for elective surgery. In elective coronary bypass surgery operative mortality ranges from 1.2 to 2.4% in large series. When emergences surgery is performed after complicated PTCA, reported mortality is given as 3%.

Postoperative complication rates are also higher. However, one study does not report significant differences in mortality, although morbidity is significantly higher.

Embolization of atheromatous material has been reported but is fortunately seldom seen. Vessel wall perforation with a too stiff guide is a rare complication and can lead to pericardial blood loss. Rupture of the artery has been described. Side branches originating from within the stenosed segment of the coronary artery have a 14% risk of occlusion during angioplasty of the main branch. This complication can be obviated by the previously described kissing balloon technique (36). Ventricular fibrillation can also occur. Contrast medium is a potential source of

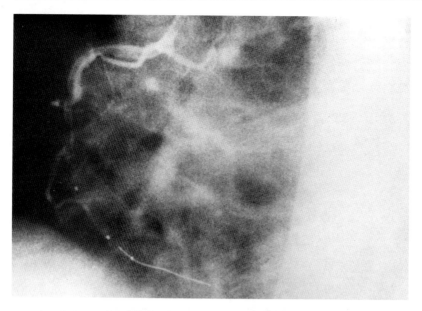

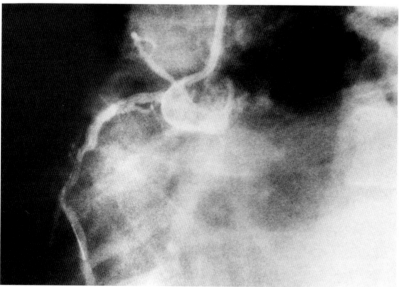

Fig. **9   a Post-angioplasty angiogram of a right coronary artery demonstrating an acute dissection.** The guide wire and balloon are still located beyond the stenosis
b Final result after redilation

complications, and the dose has to be limited. The use of a nonionic contrast medium decreases the risk (2, 3, 7, 25, 31, 37).

Indications

Anatomic Considerations

Morphologic aspects of a coronary lesion are important characteristics for predicting the hemodynamic success and complications risk of PTCA. Early typical indications for consideration of angioplasty include proximal, discrete, noncalcified, concentric, and subtotal lesions of a major coronary artery. These criteria identify lesions with a potentially high

success rate and low complication rate, and major improvements in equipment and technique in conjunction with increased operator experience have permitted the application of PTCA to less ideal lesions.

Long and eccentric lesions predispose to an increased risk of intimal dissection, and the tortuosity of the stenosed arterial segment also increases the risk. In these situations the failure and complication risk can be diminished by prolonged low-pressure inflations. The severity of the narrowing and the degree of calcification predict less successful dilation and the need for increased pressures compared with ideal lesions. Steerable guide wires, ultralow profile balloons, and soft and flexible catheters have allowed dilation of more distal and diffuse lesions. Multiple lesions in a single coronary artery carry a higher risk of intimal dissection.

The site of a lesion has to be taken into account, as for example a proximal left anterior descending or proximal left circumflex lesion close to the main stem. Angioplasty should be avoided if lesion characteristics predispose to intimal dissection that could involve the main stem (41).

Recanalization of a totally occluded artery can be achieved. The success rate is closely related to the elapsed time between the closure of the artery and the procedure. Unsuccessful attempts result from inability to advance the guide wire through the thrombus. Short occlusions and funnel-shaped entry ports are favorable for recanalization. Patients with a severe stenosis and a slow antegrade flow often experience total occlusion between diagnostic angiography and scheduled angioplasty. Recanalization in this group of patients is successful in up to 70%.

Clinical Considerations

Angina pectoris. Classically, PTCA is indicated in patients who have medically refractory angina, objective evidence of myocardial ischemia, normal left ventricular function, and who are surgical candidates. The ideal indication is the presence of a single, proximal, concentric non-calcified lesion. This attitude was based on the use of coronary artery surgery as the only available modality for myocardial revascularization but must now take into account the advent of an alternative effective and safe technique for reestablishing compromised myocardial blood flow. PTCA has become a primary therapeutic approach for many patients, and an increasing number of patients are now treated after routine coronary angiography when they meet the criterion of "medically uncontrolled angina".

Patients with severe stenosis of two or even three vessels and multiple lesions in a single artery are increasingly being considered as candidates for coronary angioplasty. In multiple vessel disease, therapeutic strategy has to take into account the severity and the location of the lesions. The most severe lesions must be dilated first, allowing less diseased vessels to protect the myocardium if dissection should occur. Patients with multivessel disease, including total occlusion, are probably best managed by surgery if the totally occluded artery supplies a large area of myocardium (4, 8, 14, 15, 17, 39).

Acute myocardial infarction. Thrombolytic therapy in acute myocardial infarction has been proved to be of little or no benefit for myocardial salvage, and furthermore the underlying stenosis is not treated.

The use of PTCA is advocated in the setting of acute myocardial infarction for two reasons: the reperfusion rate is higher than in thrombolytic therapy and an underlying lesion can be treated during the same procedure. Reperfusion is achieved by local thrombolytic therapy and possibly direct recanalization. A totally obstructed artery can be recanalized by traversing the thrombus with a guide wire. Since the risk is increased compared with elective PTCA, surgical backup is mandatory. The risks are related to possible intimal perforation and persistence or propagation of the thrombus despite numerous balloon inflations. Logistic problems must not be minimized, but potential benefits of the treatment are great: myocardial salvage and reduction of postinfarction complications, such as left ventricular failure, aneurysms, and life-threatening arrhythmias. However, controlled studies are required before emergency angioplasty can be endorsed as a routine procedure in myocardial infarction (16).

Angioplasty after coronary bypass surgery. Patients with prior bypass surgery may be candidates for angioplasty of the bypass itself or of the native coronary arteries. Progression of disease in native coronary arteries or graft stenosis is responsible for recurrence of symptoms yearly in 5% of patients. In native coronary arteries angioplasty can be used for stenosis distal to the graft or stenosis of a previously uninvolved artery. Narrowing in the vein grafts implanted for less than 3 years is usually related to fibrous dysplasia and represents a strong indication for angioplasty. Atheromatous changes and response to angioplasty are similar to that in native coronary atherosclerotic lesions. The presence of thrombus in the vein graft is a relative contra-indication, considering the risk of distal embolization. Internal mammary arteries are also suitable for angioplasty (46).

Results

Early Results

Primary success averages 90% in most series for single-vessel PTCA and has not changed despite the extension of indications to anatomically more difficult lesions. In our experience the success rate is 96% in a review of the last 200 patients. There is no significant difference in results with respect to the involved artery. Technically, the right coronary artery and the left circumflex artery are slightly more difficult to dilate than the left anterior descending artery. In our experience, total mortality was 0.5, and 3.2% of patients underwent emergency coronary artery bypass grafting. In the last 200 patients this figure decreased to 2%. PTCA in multivessel disease carries a lower success rate and a higher complication rate. In large series the overall success rate is less than 85% and the complication rate is twice the single-vessel complication rate (1, 4, 26, 30).

In coronary artery bypass graft angioplasty, the primary success rate is similar to that obtained in single-vessel disease.

Late Results and Recurrence

In patients undergoing angioplasty, morphologic and pressure gradient improvements correlate closely with clinical improvement and exercise testing. These improvements are maintained over several years but approximately 20% of patients again develop objective anginal symptoms as a result of restenosis of the dilated segment, which is manifested 1 to 6 months after PTCA. Restenosis is defined as a loss of greater than 50% of the gain in vessel diameter achieved at angioplasty. A clear distinction must be established between different types of artery restenosis. The first type, observed within 24 hours after angioplasty, is related to intimal dissection and is considered as a procedural complication. In the second type, restenosis is observed within the first month after PTCA and is related to the healing of the intimal dissection extending into the media and probably also to arterial spasm that increases the chance of restenosis. Recurrence of stenosis observed 3 to 6 months after PTCA is the third type. Experimental studies and pathologic findings suggest that local intimal proliferation and lipid uptake by smooth muscle result in restenosis. Numerous factors can be associated with restenosis: visible intimal tears, incomplete postangioplasty results, eccentric lesions. Statistical analyses demonstrate a higher incidence of restenosis in the left anterior descending artery. Further work is necessary to determine the pathogenesis and methods of prevention of recurrence of stenosis. The pharmacologic approach is probably the most promising in this field but requires further investigation. Theoretically, antiplatelet agents and anticoagulants are beneficial. Randomized studies have shown that calcium antagonists are of no benefit in preventing restenosis; however, in cases in which coronary spasm is well documented, these drugs can be effective. Recurrence rates in the literature vary from 17 to 31%, and is 21% in our own experience (4, 5, 9, 18, 21, 23, 24, 27, 28, 32, 47).

Conclusion

Coronary angioplasty is now widely considered as an acceptable therapeutic alternative for coronary artery disease. Further expansion of the technique is currently impeded by the recurrence of lesions, which will probably be resolved by pharmacologic interventions and technical improvements, such as intravascular stents. One other major challenge is the treatment of diffuse and multiple lesions. Randomized trials must define the respective roles of coronary artery bypass grafts and percutaneous transluminal coronary angioplasty. In this particular field, operator experience is undoubtedly the most important factor when comparing the respective merits of each modality. As indications for coronary angioplasty become more numerous and as the practice of angioplasty increases in complexity, training in angioplasty is required to provide optimal patient care. Current training should include a specific PTCA program that allows the physician to encounter a broad spectrum of cases and the difficulties that may arise.

Another consideration is the large radiation dose to which the operator is exposed during diagnostic procedures.

Angioplasty performed in an angiographic suite under local anesthesia generates substantially lower costs than coronary bypass surgery. In addition, avoidance of thoracotomy and more prompt recovery are significant advantages of PTCA. Comparative costs must take into account recurrence rates, repeated catheterizations, emergency surgery for complications, and elective surgery for angioplasty failure. When these factors are considered, PTCA costs are approximatively 55% of surgical management costs (22, 40).

References

1. Berger E, Williams DO, Reinert S, Most AS. Sustained efficacy of percutaneous transluminal coronary angioplasty. Am Heart J 1986;111:233–236.
2. Cowley MJ, Dorros G, Kelsey SK, Vanraden MJ, Detre KM. Acute coronary events associated with percutaneous transluminal coronary angioplasty: NHLBI PTCA registry experience. Am J Cardiol 1984;53:12–17.
3. Cowley MJ, Dorros G, Kelsey SF, Vanraden M, Detre KM. Emergency coronary bypass surgery after coronary angioplasty: the National Heart, Lung, and Blood Institute's percutaneous transluminal coronary angioplasty registry experience. Am J Cardiol 1984;53:22–26.
4. Cowley MJ, Vetrovec GW, Disciaascio G, Lewis SA, Hirsch PD, Wolgang TC. Coronary angiography of multiple vessels: short-term outcome and long-term results. Circulation 1985;72:1314–1320.
5. Cowley MJ, Vetrovec GW, Wolfgang TC. Efficacity of percutaneous transluminal coronary angioplasty: technique, patient selection, salutary results, limitations and complications. Am Heart J 1981;101:272–278.
6. Cumberland DC, Tayler DI, Procter AE. Use of lasers in percutaneous peripheral angioplasty. Semin Intervent Radiol 1986;3:65–68.
7. Dorros G, Cowley MJ, Simpson J, Bentivoglio LG, Block PC, Bourassa M, Detre K, Gosselin AJ, Grüntzig A, Kelsey SF, Kent KM, Mock MB, Mullin SM, Myler RK, Passamani ER, Stertzer SH, Williams DO. Percutaneous transluminal coronary angioplasty: report of complications from the NHLBI PTCA registry. Circulation 1983;67:723–732.
8. Dorros G, Stertzer SH, Cowley MJ, Myler RK. Complex coronary angioplasty: multiple coronary dilatations. Am J Cardiol 1984;53:126C–132C.
9. Essed CE, Van den Brand M, Becker AE. Transluminal coronary angioplasty and early restenosis: fibrocellular occlusion after wall laceration. Br Heart J 1983;49:393–396.

10. Ferguson T, Hinohara T, Simpson J, Stack R, Wechsler A. Catheter reperfusion to allow optimal coronary bypass grafting following failed transluminal coronary angioplasty. Ann Thorac Surg 1986;42:399–405.

11. Gelman JS, Felman RL, Scott E, Pepine CJ. Nicardipine for angina pectoris at rest and coronary arterial spasm. Am J Cardiol 1985;56:232–236.

12. George B, Myler R, Stertzer S, Clark D, Cote G, Shaw R, Fishman-Rosen J, Murphy M. Ballon angioplasty of coronary bifurcation lesions: the kissing balloon technique. Cathet Cardiovasc Diagn 1986;12:124–138.

13. Graag A, Lund G, Rysavy J, Castaneda F, Castaneda-Zuniga W, Amplatz K. Non-surgical placement of arterial endoprosthesis: a new technique using nitinol wire. Radiology 1983;147:261–263.

14. Grüntzig AR, Senning A, Siegenthaler WE. Nonoperative dilatation of coronary artery stenosis: percutaneous transluminal coronary angioplasty. N Engl J Med 1979;301:61–68.

15. Hartzler GO. Complex coronary angioplasty: an alternative therapy. Int J Cardiol 1985;9:133–137.

16. Hartzler GO, Rutheford BD, McConahay DR. Percutaneous transluminal coronary angioplasty: application for acute myocardial infarction. Am J Cardiol 1984;53:117C–121C.

17. Hartzler GO, Rutheford BD, McConahay DR, McCallister BD. Simultaneous multiple lesion coronary angioplasty: a preferred therapy for patients with multiple vessel disease [Abstract]. Circulation 1982;66:II–15.

18. Holmes DR Jr, Vlietstra RE, Smith HC, Vetrovec GW, Kent KM, Cowley MJ, Faxon DP, Grüntzig AR, Kelsey SF, Detre KM, Vanraden MJ, Mock MB. Restenosis after percutaneous transluminal coronary angioplasty (PTCA): a report from the PTCA registry of the National Heart, Lung, and Blood Institute. Am J Cardiol 1984;53:77C–81C.

19. Jain A, Demer LL, Raizner AE, Roberts R. Effect on inflation pressures on coronary angioplasty balloons. Am J Cardiol 1986;57:26–28.

20. Kaltenbach M, Beyer J, Walter S, Klepzig H, Schmidts L. Prolonged application of pressure in transluminal coronary angioplasty. Cathet Cardiovasc Diagn 1984;10:213–219.

21. Kaltenbach M, Kober G, Scherer D, Vallbracht C. Recurrence rate after successfull coronary angioplasty. Eur Heart J 1985;6:276–281.

22. Kelly M, Taylor G, Weston MH, Mikell F, Dove J, Batchelder J, Wellons H, Schneider J. Comparative cost of myocardial revascularization: percutaneous transluminal angioplasty and coronary artery bypass surgery. J Am Coll Cardiol 1985;5:16–20.

23. Kent KM, Bentivoglio LG, Block PC, Bourassa MG, Cowley MJ, Dorros G, Detre K, Gosselin AJ, Grüntzig A, Kelsey SF, Mock M, Mullin SMP, Passamani E, Myler RK, Simpson J, Stertzer SH, Vanraden M, Williams DO. Long-term efficacity of percutaneous transluminal coronary angioplasty (PTCA): report from NHLBI-PTCA registry. Am J Cardiol 1984;53:27C–32C.

24. Kent KM, Bentivoglio LG, Block PC, Cowley MJ, Dorros G, Gosselin AJ, Grüntzig A, Myler RK, Simpson J, Stertzer SH, Williams DO, Fisher L, Gillespie MJ, Mullin SM, Mock MB. Percutaneous transluminal coronary angioplasty: report from the NHLBI registry. Am J Cardiol 1983;49:2011.

25. Kern MJ, Eilen SD. Coronary vasospasm complicating PTCA. Am Heart J 1985;109:1098–1101.

26. Lamerton AJ, Nicolaides AN, Sutton D, Eascott HHG. The haemodynamic effects of percutaneous transluminal angioplasty Int Angiol 1985;4:93–97.

27. Leimgruber PP, Roubin GS, Anderson HV, Bredlau CE, Whitworth HB, Douglas JS, King SB III, Grüntzig AR. Influence of intimal dissection on restenosis after successful coronary angioplasty. Circulation 1985;72:530–535.

28. Leimgruber PP, Roubin GS, Hollman J, Cotsonis GA, Meier B, Douglas JS, King JB III, Grüntzig AR. Restenosis after successful coronary angioplasty in patients with single-vessel disease. Circulation 1986;73:710–717.

29. Mancini GB, Higgins C. Digital subtraction angiography: a review of cardiac applications. Digital subtraction angiography: a review of cardiac applications. Prog Cardiovasc Dis 1985;18:111–141.

30. Mata LA, Bosch X, David PR, Rapold H, Corcos T, Bourassa MG. Clinical and angiographic assessment 6 months after double vessel percutaneous coronary angioplasty. Am Coll Cardiol 1985;6:1239–1244.

31. Meier B, Grüntzig AR. Learning curve for percutaneous transluminal coronary angioplasty: skill technology or patient selection. Am J Cardiol 1984;53:65C–70C.

32. Meier B, King SP, Grüntzig AR. Repeat coronary angioplasty. J Am Coll Cardiol 1984;4:463–466.

33. Myerowitz P, Swanson D, Turnipseed W. Applications of digital subtraction angiography in cardiovascular diagnosis. Surg Clin North Am 1985;65:423–437.

34. Ovitt T, Newell J. Digital subtraction angiography: technology, equipment and techniques. Radiol Clin North Am 1985;23:177–184.

35. Palmaz J, Windeler SA, Garcia F, Tio FO, Sibbit RR, Reuter SR. Atherosclerotic rabbit aortas: expandable intraluminal grafting. Radiology 1986;160:723–726.

36. Pinkerton C, Slack J. Complex coronary angioplasty: a technique for dilatation of bifurcation stensoses. Angiology 1985;36:543–548.

37. Reul GJ, Cooley DA, Hallman GL. Coronary artery bypass for unsuccessful percutaneous transluminal coronary angioplasty. J Thorac Cardiovasc Surg 1984;88:685–694.

38. Robicsek F. Pitfalls in the application of residual coronary pressure gradient (RCPG) as an indicator of success or failure of transluminal coronary balloon angioplasty. Vasc Surg 1985;19:313–322.

39. Roubin GS, Grüntzig AR, Casarella WJ. Percutaneous coronary angioplasty: technique, indications and results. Cardiovasc Intervent Radiol 1986;9:261–272.

40. Serruys PM, De Feyter P, Soward A, Amidi A, Brower R. Does PTCA or CABG reduce the usage of anti-anginal medications? Eur Heart J 1985;6:87–90.

41. Slack JD, Pinkerton CA, Vantassel JW, Orr CM. Left main coronary artery dissection during percutaneous transluminal coronary angioplasty. Cathet Cardiovasc Diagn 1986;12:255–260.

42. Struyven J, Brion JP, Delcour C, Stoupel E, Vandermoten P, Degre S. Percutaneous transluminal coronary angioplasty: technical aspects, myocardial revascularization in acute conditions. Bibl Cardiol 1985;39:14–18.

43. Tobis J, Johnston W, Montelli S, Henderson E, Roeck W, Bauer B, Nalcioglu O, Henry W. Digital coronary roadmapping as an aid for performing coronary angioplasty. Am J Cardiol 1985;56:237–241.

44. Topol EJ, Myler RK, Stertzer SH. Selection of dilatation hardware for PTCA: 1985. Cathet Cardiovasc Diagn 1985;11:629–637.

45. Van Tassel R, Gobel F, Rydell M, Vlodaver Z, McCarter D. A less traumatic catheter for coronary arteriography. Cathet Cardiovasc Diagn 1985;11:187–199.

46. Waller BF, Rothbaum DA, Gorfinkel HJ, Ulbright TM, Linnemeier TJ, Berger SM. Morphologic observations after percutaneous transluminal balloon angioplasty of early and late aortocoronary saphenous vein bypass grafts. J Am Coll Cardiol 1984;4:784–792.

47. Williams DO, Grüntzig AR, Kent KM, Detre KM, Kelsey SF, To T. Efficacy of repeat percutaneous transluminal coronary angioplasty for coronary restenosis. Am J Cardiol 1984;53:32C–35C.

48. Wollenek G, Laufer G, Miholic J, Deutsch M, Wolner E. Experimental coronary angioplasty using a UV-excimer laser. Tex Heart Inst J 1985;12:339–343.

49. Wright KC, Wallace S, Charnsangavej C, Carrasco CH, Gianturco C. Percutaneous endovascular stents: an experimental evaluation. Radiology 1985;156:69–72.

Percutaneous Transluminal Angioplasty of the Renal Arteries

T. A. Sos, S. Crystal, and T. G. Pickering

The introduction and acceptance of percutaneous transluminal renal angioplasty (PTRA) over the past decade has had a tremendous impact on the current treatment of renovascular hypertension. The precise incidence of renovascular hypertension in the general population is not known; however, it has been estimated to occur in approximately 5% of hypertensive patients in the United States (6, 13).

It is a diagnosis of paramount clinical importance for two reasons. Firstly, it is the most common curable form of hypertension in any age group. Secondly, it is a potentially reversible cause of chronic renal failure.

The surgical alternative to PTRA in the treatment of renovascular hypertension encompasses several significant problems, i. e., it necessitates the use of general anesthesia, in high risk patients it poses a mortality rate as high as 5.9% (7), and morbidity, including nephrectomy, is not rare (7). Pharmacotherapy is not always successful in controlling blood pressure, and in cases of significant renal artery stenosis, lowering of blood pressure may result in diminished renal blood flow with concomitant ischemic atrophy or renal infarction (4).

For these reasons, since the introduction of the balloon angioplasty catheter by Grüntzig in 1974 (10) and the first PTRA, also by Grüntzig, in 1978 (11), PTRA is rapidly becoming accepted as an initial treatment of choice for correction of significant renal artery stenosis. Technologic advances in angiography, such as DSA, in combination with selective renal vein renin (RVR) sampling and assay (24), have made the diagnostic work-up less invasive, since arteriography is only performed in patients in whom the previous two studies have suggested the presence of a physiologically significant renal artery lesion.

Diagnosis of Renovascular Hypertension

Contemporary criteria for patient selection for PTRA (in addition to clinically demonstrated hypertension) range from angiographic documentation of a "significant," i. e., greater than 50% luminal diameter, renal artery stenosis to thorough documentation of renal pathophysiology by RVR sampling and assay and the evaluation of the effect of angiotensin-converting enzyme inhibitors, such as

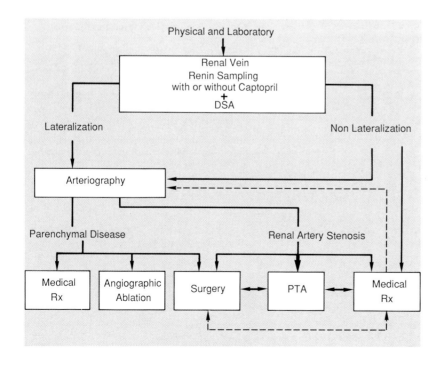

Fig. **1** **Evaluation of suspected renovascular hypertension.** DSA: intravenous digital subtraction angiography. PTA: percutaneous transluminal renal angioplasty

captopril (Fig. **1**). This is vital, since renal artery disease does not always produce hypertension and, even in a hypertensive patient, may not necessarily be the cause of the hypertension (5, 12). In fact, hypertension from any cause accelerates atheroma formation and may, in fact, be a consequence of essential hypertension. The correlation between arteriographic appearance and degree of ischemia is poor (5, 12).

The clinical findings of age, sex, smoking, the presence of a bruit, and difficulty in medical control of hypertension are nonspecific, suggestive findings that warrant further evaluation. Also judged as suitable candidates for PTRA are those patients with occlusive renal artery disease and dimished renal function.

Once selection criteria have been met, patients are not eliminated as candidates for renal angioplasty, even if they have severe medical or vascular diseases, including coexisting cerebral, coronary, or peripheral vascular disease. Other anatomic and pathologic contra-indications are only relative and include patients with stenotic renal arteries with coexistent significant renal artery aneurysms and patients with spontaneously dissected renal arteries. The only absolute contra-indication to renal angioplasty is a stenotic hypoplastic renal artery in a child with a hypoplastic aorta. These do not respond to angioplasty; repeated vigorous dilation can only rupture but never dilate these vessels.

Role of the Renin Angiotensin System

Plasma renin activity is usually normal or high in patients with renovascular hypertension, and it is almost never low (17). The pattern of renin secretion from the ischemic and contralateral kidney is one of unilateral hypersecretion coupled with contralateral suppression. In patients with unilateral renal artery stenosis, removal of the constriction (by PTRA or surgery) or treatment with angiotensin-converting enzyme inhibitors, such as captopril, often brings blood pressure back to normal. However, even in cases of renal artery stenosis with proved elevated renin levels, some degree of hypertension may remain, despite elimination of the stenosis, and with a return to normal renin values. This is often true in atheromatous patients in whom non-renin-mediated essential hypertension often coexists with renovascular hypertension, but cannot be predicted before PTRA.

Peripheral Plasma Renin Activity

Peripheral plasma renin activity (PRA) is an excellent screening test, especially enhanced by captopril stimulation. Eighty percent of patients with elevated PRA have renovascular hypertension (17).

Renal Vein Renin Determination

Selective RVR sampling and assay is undertaken in patients in whom the PRA is abnormally high (before or after Captopril) or in patients in whom the blood pressure has dramatically decreased after 25 mg of Captopril orally. The most commonly used approach in the analysis of RVR is to establish a ratio of the stenotic to the normal side and then to set the arbitrary "positive" ratios as 1.5 : 1. At the New York Hospital, we use a slightly more complicated but more reliable method of collecting and analyzing blood samples. Each renal vein sample is immediately followed by a control sample from the infrarenal inferior vena cava. Renin secretion can then be independently evaluated from each kidney according to the formula developed by Vaughan et al. (34). Here, renin secretion on each side is expressed as a ratio of secretion to systemic arterial level. In the normal state, $\frac{V-A}{A} \simeq 0.25$ on each side. In unilateral significant renovascular hypertension, ipsilateral $\frac{V-A}{A} \simeq 0.5$, and there is contralateral suppression, i.e., in the normal kidney, $\frac{V-A}{A} \simeq 0$. V is the RVR activity and A is the systemic arterial renin activity (which in practice is equal to that in the infrarenal inferior vena cava). In patients with bilateral renal artery stenosis the pattern of RVR often displays asymmetry, as in patients with unilateral renal artery stenosis, and usually lateralizes to the kidney with the greater degree of stenosis (18), although very rarely renin secretion is bilaterally suppressed if both kidneys are sufficiently diseased to have decreased sodium excretion. Thus, these patients become volume-dependent hypertensives.

Intravenous Digital Subtraction Angiography

Selective renal vein sampling before and after oral captopril is immediately followed by intravenous DSA for evaluation of the renal arteries. This involves a simple exchange of the renin sampling catheter for a multiple sidehole pigtail catheter inserted into the right atrium.

The value of intravenous DSA in the evaluation of renovascular hypertension has been thoroughly documented (3, 36). Studies have shown that intravenous DSA can be used to diagnose complete renal artery occlusion with a high degree of accuracy, although stenotic lesions are less well evaluated (3, 20, 36). Collateral flow is usually not accurately defined with intravenous digital subtraction angiography; however, visualization of collaterals is not essential in the diagnosis of renal artery occlusion on intravenous DSA. Visualization of a reconstituted distal renal artery is important only if surgical bypass or attempted recanalization by the angiographer is contemplated.

Since all arteries opacify with a digital intravenous study, many of which overlay each other, multiple contrast injections are usually necessary to delineate renal arterial disease adequately. Because of the large volume of contrast media needed, the technique is not suitable for those patients with abnormal renal function. Intra-arterial DSA is advantageous, since it requires only approximately one-sixth the total amount of contrast material used in conventional arteriographic technique.

Since the renal arteries originate slightly ventro-laterally from the aorta, the ipsilateral posterior oblique is the preferred position to visualize the renal artery ostium in question, i. e., left posterior oblique for the left renal artery origin. The ipsilateral anterior oblique is used to visualize the mid to distal renal artery. Standard injection rates for intravenous DSA are usually between 25 and 30 ml of contrast media injected at 35 ml/s. Bowel and patient motion often deteriorate the quality of the examination, especially the visualization of collateral pathways. To diminish artefacts, 1 mg of glucagon is given intravenously to reduce peristaltic activity, and an abdominal compression belt is applied.

Studies comparing the accuracy of intravenous DSA to conventional film screen arteriography have shown a concordance rate of approximately 80% with intravenous DSA giving a 5% false-positive rate, demonstrating lesions not shown on the arteriogram. Conversely, a 10% false-negative rate is seen. More difficult to viualize on intravenous DSA are lesions of the branch renal arteries (3, 36).

If these studies are positive, the patient is admitted to the hospital for abdominal aortography, with or without selective renal arteriography to identify main and branch renal artery stenosis.

Conventional film screen aortograms are the gold standard of renal artery imaging. Rapid filming sequence during the arteriogram is desired (four films per second), since the renal arteries fill slightly earlier than the superior mesenteric branches, due to their posterior placement on the abdominal aorta, as well as their relatively high flow (20% of cardiac output).

If the renal arterial lesions are well demonstrated by aortography, selective catheterization of the renal arteries should not be performed unless angioplasty is to be done at that time, since attempted selective catheterization may injure the artery.

However, in cases in which renal vascular hypertension is definitely suspected by RVR assay or other criteria, and in which aortography is negative, selective magnification arteriography must be carried out in several oblique or angulated views. This is especially true in children, in whom branch lesions of the renal arteries are frequent.

Before diagnostic arteriography, the necessary informed consent for it and PTRA are obtained, and a vascular surgeon is consulted or notified. At our institution, if, at arteriography, a renal artery stenosis is identified whose pathophysiologic significance and potential curability are supported by renin data, then PTRA is attempted immediately after the diagnostic arteriogram through the same puncture site.

A film of the abdomen should be obtained after angiography to evaluate renal size, hyperconcentration, and ureteral notching, signs of renal vascular hypertension, all of which are best shown on the "delayed film" of the hypertensive urogram.

Causes of Renal Artery Stenosis

Atheromatous Lesions

Atheromatous obstructions cause the majority of lesions affecting the renal artery, and represent 63% of all cases studied in the United States Cooperative Study on Renovascular Hypertension (35). They are classically seen in the proximal third of the renal artery (Fig. 2). Atheromatous disease of the abdominal aorta can also encroach on the renal artery ostium. Natural history studies have shown that stenoses secondary to atheroma, if medically treated, or left untreated, have a high probability of progression to complete occlusion. In one series, the average progression of disease, i. e., decrease in transluminal diameter, was estimated to be approximately 1.5% per month (21). Therefore, in patients with stenoses measuring 75 to 99% of the arterial diameter at angiography, approximately 40% would progress to complete occlusion after 1 year.

Response to dilation varies with the nature and location of the atherosclerotic lesion (25). Good results should be anticipated with short, isolated atherosclerotic lesions (Fig. 2) (8, 9, 15, 22, 25, 28). Ostial-type lesions, which in reality represent atherosclerotic disease of the aortic wall encroaching or engulfing the ostium, lessen the chance for successful PTRA (2). These stenoses often demonstrate transient response to dilation with return to the preangioplasty rate in a few days. This is most likely due to simple displacement of the plaques along the aortic wall away from the balloon catheter without actual compression of the plaques; therefore, they can recoil and resume their initial position. However, in a significant minority of ostial lesions, the stenosis is just within the origin of the renal artery, and is indistinguishable by angiography from the aortic plaque variety (Fig. 3). In these instances, successful long-term results are seen.

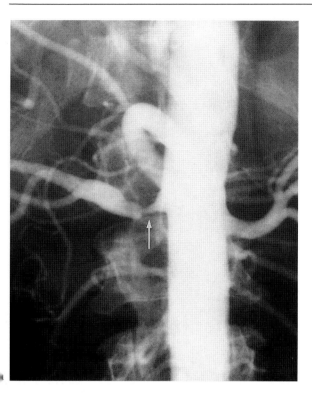

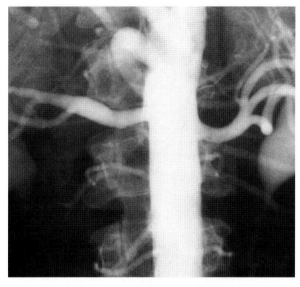

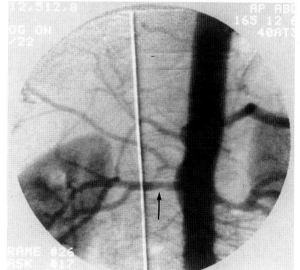

Fig. 2 **A 54-year-old hypertensive man with peripheral renin elevation, as well as renal vein renin levels lateralizing to the right kidney**
a Atherosclerotic stenosis of the proximal right renal artery is seen (arrow)
b Aortogram immediately after successful PTRA
c Intravenous DSA 5 years after PTRA demonstrates widely patent right renal artery (arrow). The patient was normotensive, off all medications

Fibromuscular Dysplasia

Fibromuscular dysplasia of the renal arteries is the most common cause of renovascular hypertension in the younger patient population, especially in females. They demonstrate the best response to angioplasty, approaching 100% (8, 9, 15, 25, 29). The most common variety is medial fibroplasia (65%), which exhibits the classic „string of beads" appearance. Aggressive overdilation of these lesions is not as necessary as with atherosclerotic lesions, because these lesions generally respond dramatically to PTRA and smooth out over time (Fig. 4). Balloon inflation pressures of 4 atmospheres are usually sufficient when dilating. The intimal variety of fibromuscular dysplasia, as well as Takayasu arteritis, are

exceptions to this rule and may require greater pressures to dilate (Fig. 5), show very poor initial response, but progressively improve to become fully dilated over the course of several months to years (27).

Fibromuscular lesions are often difficult to traverse and may require the use of Simmons or sidewinder-type catheters in combination with a floppy Bentson guide wire. In addition, the walls of the fibromuscular lesion are not as firm as with atherosclerotic lesions, and the guide wire must be withdrawn and redirected should resistance be encountered. An open-ended guide wire used in conjunction with a steerable-type wire in a coaxial fashion is often useful, as it is for branch lesions (26).

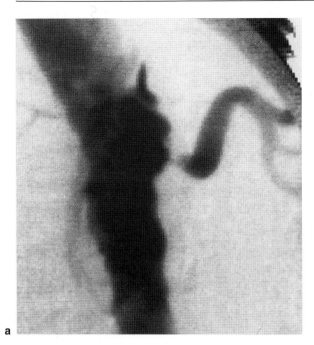
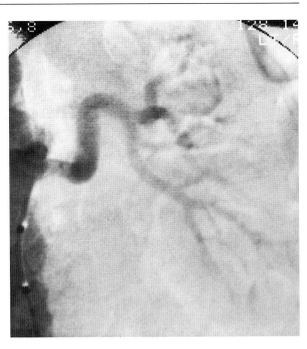

Fig. 3   A 75-year-old man with hypertension and renal failure on hemodialysis
a Intra-arterial DSA shows a solitary left kidney with severe atheromatous renal artery stenosis, which appears to be ostial
b After PTRA, a good result was obtained, renal function improved, and hemodialysis was not necessary at a 3-year follow-up. This stenosis must have been within the origin of the renal artery, and this differs from the "true ostial" lesion due to aortic wall atheroma, which responds poorly to angioplasty

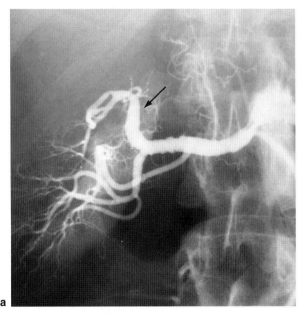
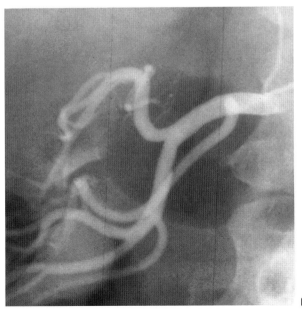

Fig. 4   A 42-year-old hypertensive woman and RVR lateralizing to the right
a Selective injection immediately after PTRA. Note improved filling of ventral branch of main renal artery (arrow), and slight overdilation of the previously diseased vessel
b Four years after PTRA. Right renal artery is morphologically normal. Blood pressure also returned to normal without medication

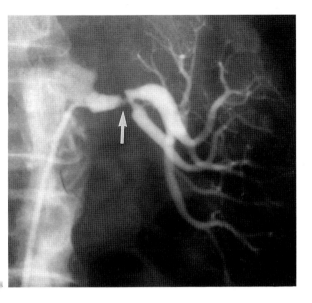

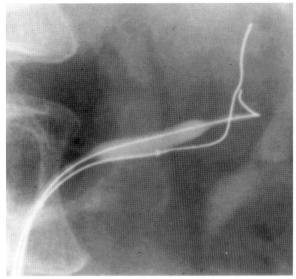

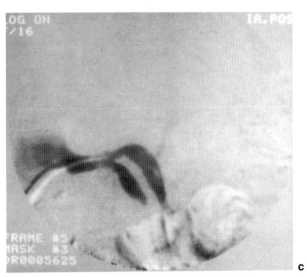

Fig. **5** **Uninephric 66-year-old man with hypertension and elevated serum creatinine**
a Selective left renal arteriogram: bifurcation lesion involving the proximal ventral and dorsal divisions (arrow). A 5 Fr visceral catheter inserted through a 7 Fr femoral arterial sheath

b Selective catheter withdrawn and a 4.5 Fr tibial type 3 mm balloon catheter positioned across upper lesion and inflated. Wire and identical uniflated balloon protect lower lesion; simultaneous kissing balloon inflations were not possible due to inability to pass both catheters completely across lesions

c After PTRA intra-arterial DSA shows successful dilation. Renal function improved. (Distal branches filled well on later frames, but dilation site was no longer opacified)

Techniques of Renal Angioplasty

As noted, once a lesion of the renal artery has been identified by preliminary studies and confirmed by arteriography, angioplasty is performed at the same time as the intra-arterial study (Fig. **6**). It is imperative that at any institution performing angioplasty, a team approach combining the knowledge and skills of internists, surgeons, and angiographers be utilized in selecting and caring for the patients undergoing angioplasty (30).

Choice of Puncture Site

Before PTRA is contemplated, it is routine to alert or consult a vascular surgeon. In a small percentage of cases, emergency surgery is required either to perform a renal bypass operation or to repair local puncture-site trauma. An intravenous DSA or a previous arteriogram before PTRA allows a logical approach to the procedure based on vascular anatomic and pathologic findings.

If a previous angiogram is not available, generally the right retrograde femoral arterial approach is preferable, since manipulation from the right femoral artery is more convenient and familiar to angiographers. If excessive tortuosity or obstructive or occlusive disease is encountered on the right, the left femoral route is usually the next choice. The axillary artery approach is not necessary, except in occlusion of the abdominal aorta or of both iliac arteries (31). However tempting it is to use the axillary artery in patients with caudally oriented renal arteries, it must be remembered that the subclavian arteries in these patients may also be tortuous

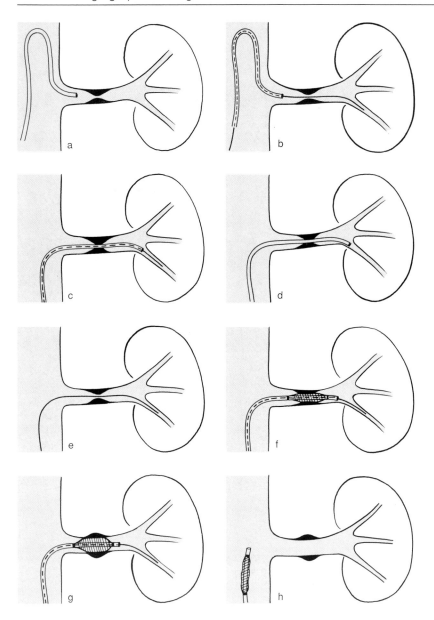

Fig. **6   Technique of renal angioplasty using shepherd's crook catheter**

and diseased. Also, local complications are far more frequent and severe when using the axillary route for routine angiography and are even higher when using 7 or 8 Fr catheters necessary for PTRA.

Crossing the Lesion – Catheter and Guide Wire Choices

The most difficult and dangerous part of the procedure is the atraumatic crossing of the renal arterial lesion. Before crossing a lesion, systemic heparinization is begun with 3000 to 4000 U of heparin intravenously. Approximately 100 to 300 µg of nitroglycerin is also infused into the renal artery directly. Additional adjunctive medications are shown in Table **1**. A variety of catheters and guide

wires have been used; however, the 5 Fr catheters have the advantage over larger selective catheters of retaining torque control for renal artery selection, while still being small enough to traverse tight lesions.

Once the renal artery orifice has been selected and appropriate medications administered, the lesion is then crossed (Fig. **6a**). Since subintimal dilations do not remain patent and can result in complete occlusion of the vessel, it is essential to keep the guide wire and catheter within the lumen when crossing the lesion. The initial attempt is usually made with a Bentson 0.035 inch guide wire, because of its softness and flexibility. The distal end can also be curved manually, giving it some degree of directionality as well. If attempts at using the Bent-

Table **1**   Adjunctive Medications in percutaneous transluminal renal angioplasty

Timing	Medication	Action	Route of administration*	Dose*	Onset of action	Peak action	Duration of action
Before PTRA	Aspirin (not used routinely)	Antiplatelet aggregation	PO	80–300 mg q.d.	~ 1 day		~ Few days (single dose)
During PTRA	Heparin sodium	Antithrombotic	IV or IA	2000–4000 U	Immediate	Immediate	~ 4 hours
	Nifedipine	Antispasmodic and spasmolytic	PO	10 mg	~ 10 min	~ ½ hour	~ 4 hours
	Nitroglycerin	Spasmolytic and antispasmodic	IA (local)	100–200 µg p.r.n.	~ Few seconds	~ Few seconds	~ Few minutes
After PTRA	Aspirin	Antiplatelet aggregation	PO	80–300 mg q.d.	~ 1 day		~ Few days (single dose)
Before, during, or after PTRA	Urokinase	Thrombolytic	IA (local)	150,000 U in ½ hour 80,000 U/hour × (up to) 24 hours	Immediate	Half life (20 min)	Half life (20 min)

* IA: intra-arterial; IV: intravenous, PO: orally; p.r.n.: as needed; q.d.: daily

son wire fail, a superb back-up is the combination of an 0.018 floppy, steerable platinum tibial-coronary-type guide wire alone, or in conjunction with the 0.035 inch open-ended guide wire.

The orientation of the renal artery arising from the aorta dictates catheter selection. Once an orifice has been selected and the lesion traversed with a guide wire, it is necessary to advance the catheter across the lesion. If the lesion is especially tight, or if the artery arises at a caudal angle from the aorta, advancing standard visceral type catheters (cobra) will succeed only in buckling it into the aorta, since the predominant vector force is cephalad. In most cases of PTRA, therefore, the Simmons of shepherd's crook-shaped catheter is preferred, because this catheter combines the advantages of the axillary approach with the relative simplicity, safety, and ease of the femoral technique. The shepherd's crook catheter can usually be safely reformed over the aortic bifurcation or, if that fails, in the superior mesenteric artery. Once formed, the catheter should be manipulated, especially in an atheromatous aorta, with a floppy guide wire extended through its tip. Approaching the renal lesion from below will result in a fluoroscopically visible "pop" into the renal artery origin. In fibromuscular dysplasia, and when the suprarenal aorta is relatively free of disease, the catheter may be pulled into the renal artery from above with or without the use of a guide wire. The floppy Bentson guide wire, which is very atraumatic, often springs across proximal stenoses spontaneously. Once the tip of the Simmons catheter is engaged in the renal ostium with the guide wire across the stenosis, withdrawal of the catheter from the femoral artery generates considerable force,

allowing the catheter to advance distally into the renal artery across the lesion, even over a very floppy guide wire (Fig. **6b, c**). If any resistance is encountered during manipulation, frequent test injections and appropriate spasmolytic therapy should be given. The shepherd's crook catheter selected should have a side arm long enough to cross the stenosis, but not long enough to enter the distal small branches (Fig. **6c**). After the stenosis is crossed, a test injection with dilute contrast is made to confirm the intraluminal position, and a pressure measurement is obtained (Fig. **6d**).

Having traversed the lesion, exchange must be made for a stiffer guide wire that will support the balloon catheter as it crosses the lesion (Fig. **6e**). In addition, vessel trauma must be carefully avoided; therefore, the guide wire most commonly used by us is a 0.035 inch heavy duty wire with a short straight floppy tip. This is the straight equivalent of the commonly used Rosen wire, which has a short floppy tip with a 1.5 mm tight J at its end. The diagnostic catheter is then exchanged for the balloon catheter, which has been preshaped over steam with a slightly curved tip to facilitate entrance of the catheter from the aorta into the renal artery (Fig. **6f**). Occasionally, resistance at the lesion is encountered, and further predilation with a 7 Fr van Andel-type catheter may be necessary. Continuous steady pressure should be applied to the catheter as it crosses the lesion. Sudden maneuvers may force the catheter up into the aorta and dislogde both the catheter and the guide wire from the renal artery.

The initial passage of the floppy guide wire can be facilitated by exaggerated respiratory motions of the patient, which alter the position and course of the renal arteries. These maneuvers are particularly useful with "beady" medial fibromuscular dysplastic lesions. Crossing these lesions requires a good deal of patience and time with sequential alternating advancement of the catheter and the guide wire, as well as frequent test injection and spasmolytic therapy.

Attempted recanalization and dilation of the completely occluded renal artery should be attempted only if the patient's clinical condition and kidney size warrant salvage (23). These are technically more difficult lesions to correct and should be attempted by a skilled and experienced angiographer. Visualization of the artery, both proximal and distal to the occlusion, is necessary before any attempt crossing. Abdominal aortography will almost always demonstrate the artery distal to the occlusion by collaterals. The proximal and distal artery should be in a relatively straight line. Recanalization is generally performed by using a more stiff and rigid 6 to 7 Fr shepherd's crook or Simmons catheter, which can select the renal artery orifice so that considerable forward pressure is applied as the catheter is withdrawn at the groin. A combination of catheter and guide wire maneuvers is used, starting with very gentle maneuvers, such as forced contrast injections, advancing relatively floppy guide wires, followed by more rigid ones, combined with initially gentle and later more forceful attempts to pull the catheter tip itself across the occlusion with or without the guide wire leading. Frequent test injections are needed to ensure the continued intraluminal presence of the catheter. Should perforation occur, frequent fluoroscopic examination is needed to preclude continued extravasation or retroperitoneal hemorrhage. If significant hemorrhage is seen, a balloon catheter is inflated proximal to the perforation while the patient is prepared for surgery and a bypass is attempted. If the kidney is not large enough to warrant surgical salvage, the perforated artery, if long enough, can be occluded by embolization. We have attempted 20 renal artery recanalizations and have succeeded in ten. In three of ten failures, the renal artery was perforated, but serious hemorrhage did not occur in any.

Branch and Bifurcation Lesions

The kissing balloon technique initially described for aortic bifurcation lesions (32) can be adapted for use in renal arterial lesions. If a stenosis arises at or in close proximity to a renal arterial bifurcation, this is a useful technique. The technique initially described utilizes a catheter entry site from each groin, with the balloon catheter traversing the lesion and a separate diagnostic catheter or wire protecting the orifice of the uninvolved branch during dilation. Should the uninvolved vessel become compromised after balloon inflation, the diagnostic catheter can be exchanged for a second balloon catheter and dilated.

An alternative approach described by us (30) utilizes a 6 or 7 Fr arterial sheath in the femoral artery, through which a 5 Fr selective catheter (cobra or similar shape) is advanced through the sheath into the proximal renal artery. Through this catheter, two 0.014 to 0.018 inch wires are sequentially placed in the involved branches. The kissing balloon technique can then be performed as described (Fig. 5). Lesions in small branches can be dilated with a similar technique (30), but using only a single 0.016 inch guide wire. This eliminates the need for the large, rigid, and traumatic 8 or 9 Fr guiding catheters.

Balloon Selection

Balloon size is selected by measuring the diameter of the renal artery on a standard arteriogram. Since the renal artery is magnified by 15 to 20% on standard angiograms, and at The New York Hospital we routinely use a balloon 1 mm greater than the angiographic diameter of the renal artery, in reality, the artery is overdilated by close to 2 mm (25). If there is doubt, it is best to start with a relatively small-sized balloon. This amount of overdilation must be proportionally reduced in vessels with an angiographic diameter less than 5 mm.

The quality and quantity of pain experienced during inflation of the balloon is a valuable indication of whether a proper-sized balloon has been used. Mild to moderate pain should diminish immediately on deflation and disappear within 1 or 2 minutes. Should the pain continue in intensity, one should suspect damage to the artery, i. e., rupture or occlusion. Very severe pain on inflation should be followed by immediate deflation to test dissipation of pain and ensure that a complication has not arisen. If the pain disappears rapidly on deflation, reinflation, even if painful, is usually safe. Persistent indentation (waist) of the balloon without pain and without elimination of indentation at either full inflation or during deflation also indicates the need for a 1 mm larger balloon. This is prudent, since a 30% or greater residual stenosis will likely lead to restenosis (25, 33).

Balloons are inflated with a 50% saline-contrast solution and are observed fluoroscopically both during inflation and deflation. We routinely inflate balloons for approximately 60 seconds, and in the renal arteries, reinflate one to two times. At low pressures and volumes, the balloon will form a cast of the artery, and this information allows proper positioning of the balloon, as well as indicating the success of the dilation. Various methods of balloon inflation and deflation have been tried, including automatic pumps. However, we think a simple syringe-stopcock combination with an interposed pressure gauge is the easiest and least expensive choice. A pressure of 4 to 10 atmospheres is usually adequate for most lesions. To prevent vessel wall injury, a floppy guide wire is left extending through the catheter tip during inflation. The deflated catheter is removed from the renal artery over a wire in order to protect the vessel and especially the dilated segment.

Spasm

Spasm of the main or branch renal arteries is a common occurrence during PTRA. Manipulation with the guide wire is the major cause of spasm, and, therefore, placement of the guide wire in small branches should, if possible, be avoided (1). The mechanical action of an angioplasty procedure is a controlled injury to the vessel wall and the plaque, which releases serotonin, thromboxane, and other vasoactive substances that can cause spasm or thrombosis, or both.

Calcium antagonists are very effective in preventing, diminishing, and reversing spasm. Nifedipine can be used prophylactically with dosages of 10 to 20 mg orally one half-hour before the procedure.

As was noted, nitroglycerin in dosages of 100 to 200 µg is used routinely before crossing the lesion and is also very effective to lyse spasm once it has occurred.

It should be remembered, however, that the most efficient treatment of spasm is avoiding it by very careful use of the guide wire. Spasm and thrombosis are often superimposed, with one causing the other, and a thorough understanding of, and experience with lytic agents is useful in performing PTRA.

Transplant Renal Arterial Stenosis

In a recent study the incidence of significant allograft renal artery stenosis was shown to be approximately 20% (14). These lesions occur in three locations: pre-anastomotic (atherosclerotic disease of the native vessels), anastomotic (granulation tissue with or without surgical technique), and postanastomotic (kinking, immune reactions) (16).

Renal transplant arteries are most frequently anastomosed to the recipient circulation in one of two ways: end-to-end to the hypogastric artery or end-to-side to the external iliac artery. Hypogastric anastomoses are usually approached via a retrograde contralateral femoral artery puncture, around the aortic bifurcation, or very rarely from the axilla. Conversely, end-to-side anastomoses are best approached retrogradely from the ipsilateral femoral artery (16).

Proximal (pre-anastomotic) lesions of the external iliac respond well to PTRA. Anastomotic lesions may require the use of high-pressure balloons to "crack" the tough fibrous elastic bands that are seen postsurgically (Fig. **7**). Multiple inflations may also be required to obtain a permanent result. Postanas-

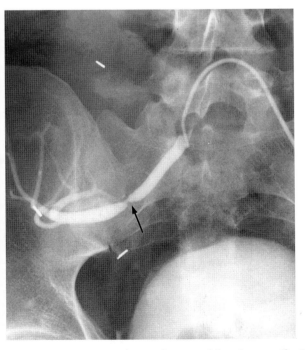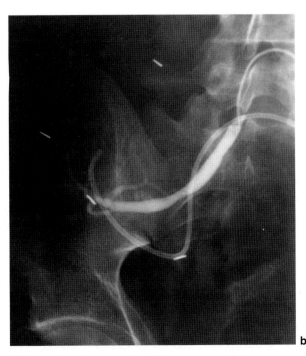

b

Fig. **7 Cadaver transplant to hypogastric artery: patient with hypertension and elevated serum creatinine**
a Stenosis at site of end-to-end anastomosis (arrow)
b Good anatomic PTRA result. Hypertension and renal function improved. (Note renin sampling catheter in renal vein)

tomotic lesions may be successfully dilated if the lesion is in an area of intimal hyperplasia often noted in this region.

Since transplanted kidneys receive no collateral supply, caution is needed when attempting to dilate these arteries. Occlusion of the vessel is a surgical emergency, and a vascular surgeon must be readily available.

Immediate Technical Success

Routinely, pressure measurements are used to monitor the procedure and evaluate outcome and results (Table 2, 3). A significant drawback to this method of evaluation of the technical success of angioplasty is the size of the balloon catheter straddling the lesion, which itself partially occludes the lumen (8, 9, 15, 22, 25, 28, 29).

Equally important, therefore, is the cosmetic result. PTRA is considered technically successful if the residual stenosis is less than 30%. According to Poiseuille's equation, doubling the radius will increase flow by 16 times. If a significant (greater than 30%) residual stenosis remains, the lesions are more likely to recur.

The technical success rate of PTRA in non-atheromatous lesions, typified by the medial form of fibromuscular dysplasia, approaches 100%. Such lesions are usually more difficult to traverse than dilate.

With atherosclerotic lesions, the success rate in crossing and adequately dilating non-ostial, non-occluded stenoses also approaches 100%. Ostial lesions have demonstrated initial success rates of approximately 75%. Recanalization and dilation of total renal artery occlusion is successful in 50% of cases.

Follow-Up

After PTRA, the blood pressure must be carefully monitored for approximately 24 to 48 hours, since marked hypo- and hypertensive episodes can occur. Despite pretreatment with angiotensin-converting enzyme inhibitors, the patient may become hypotensive. Conversely, diastolic pressures have been seen to increase dramatically but temporarily. The angiographer should be well schooled in treating these episodes.

Before renal angioplasty, the blood pressure should be controlled by angiotensin-converting enzyme inhibitors (captopril or enalopril, etc.), whenever possible. These medications interrupt the sequence by which renin mediates hypertension,

Table 2   Immediate and long-term clinical results of renal angioplasty in fibromuscular dysplasia

Reference		No. of Patients	Successfully dilated		Cured		Improved		Failed	
			No.	%	No.	%	No.	%	No.	%
Sos et al.	(25)	31	27	87	16	59	9	33	2	7
Tegtmeyer et al.	(29)	21	21	100	13	62	8	38	0	0
Geyskes et al.	(8)	21	21	100	10	48	10	48	1	5
Martin et al.	(15)	11	8	73	5	63	1	13	2	25
Grim et al.	(9)	10	9	90	5	56	4	44	0	0
Mean				90		58		35		7

Table 3   Immediate and long-term clinical results of renal angioplasty in unilateral – non-ostial atheroma

Reference		No. of Patients	Successfully dilated		Cured		Improved		Failed	
			No.	%	No.	%	No.	%	No.	%
Schwarten et al.	(22)	54	49	91	23	47	25	51	1	2
Geyskes et al.*	(8)	44	44	100	21	48	19	43	4	9
Sos et al.	(25)	20	15	75	4	27	9	60	2	13
Martin et al.	(15)	15	13	87	2	15	4	31	7	54
Grim et al.	(9)	15	15	100	1	7	7	47	7	47
Tegtmeyer et al.	(28)	13	11	84	3	27	8	73	0	0
Mean				89.5		28.5		41		21

* Includes some patients with bilateral disease

much the same way as successful dilation of the renal artery reduces renin output, and, therefore, its physiologic control of blood pressure. A successful PTRA might then precipitate a severe hypotensive episode if an angiotensin converting enzyme inhibitor was not used before the procedure.

Long-Term Results and Benefits

Blood Pressure

Nonatherosclerotic lesions. Patients with fibromuscular dysplasia demonstrate the best long-term response to angioplasty, since they rarely have coexistent essential hypertension; 90% are improved and of these, 60% are cured (Table **2**). Isolated focal nonatheromatous stenoses due to intimal fibroplasia or Takayasu arteritis show poor initial results; however, they often show good blood pressure and morphologic results at long-term follow-up (6 months to 2 years) (27). Young patients with hypoplastic aortas (Fig. **8**) and stenotic renal arteries, as well as patients with neurofibromatosis, show poor initial and long-term results (8, 9, 15, 25, 29).

Atherosclerotic Lesions. A review of 39 of our patients with focal nonoccluded, nonostial atheromatous vessels 3 years after PTRA showed clinical benefits in 87% (Table **3**). In 20 of these cases, angiographic follow-up demonstrated a restenosis or occlusion rate of 15%, with one of the restenosed arteries successfully redilated and normal after a 2-year follow-up (8, 9, 15, 22, 25, 28).

One quarter of ostial lesions show long-term blood pressure benefits (25, 33). Recanalized renal arteries have blood pressure benefits similar to nonoccluded, non-ostial lesions.

Renal Function

After successful renal artery angioplasty (or surgical revascularization), kidney size increases. Follow-up in 15 cases of successful PTRA showed an average increase in kidney area of 12 ± 7% after follow-up of 22 months (25).

Our experience with PTRA in 55 patients with serum creatinine greater than 2 mg/dl has shown that PTRA can be remarkably therapeutic (19); renal angioplasty was technically successful in 43 of the attempts, with a 1- to 2-year follow-up showing that 63% of the successful group had decreased serum

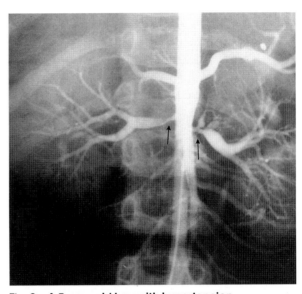

a

Fig. **8** **A 5-year-old boy with hypertension**
a The aorta is hypoplastic, with markedly stenotic renal artery origins (arrows)

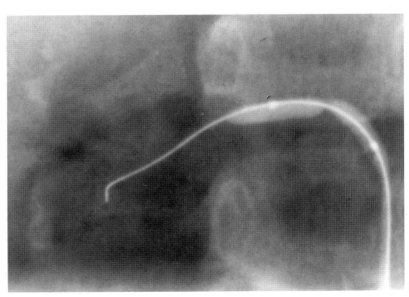

Fig. **8**
b Balloon profiles at inflation to 5 atmospheres: waists were not eliminated. Vigorous dilation with greater pressure was not and should not be attempted, because the artery could rupture and be damaged beyond surgical repair. Postdilation aortogram was unchanged

b

creatinine, whereas in the unsuccessful group, 79% had increased serum creatinine. Twelve percent of those in the successful group died, compared with 57% of patients in the unsuccessful group. Dialysis was eventually required in 14% of patients in the successful group and in approximately 50% in the other group.

Complications

After careful evaluation of almost 500 renal angioplasties attempted by us, it is clear that many of the risks of the renal angioplasty are also those of arteriography, which would have been performed even if an operation had been planned. The most common complication is puncture site injury, including hematomas in 4% of patients. Only four of these patients required an operation. Transient worsening of renal function was seen in 2%: however, permanent decrease was seen in another 2% of patients (many of whom had renal failure before angioplasty). Successful revascularization was possible in the 2% of patients in whom the renal artery was dissected. Nephrectomy was necessary in only two patients as a result of angioplasty. The 30-day mortality rate has been zero. As noted before, appropriate antispasmodic and antithrombotic treatment has diminished the incidence of complications, many of which are related to spasm and thrombosis. Distal embolization requiring surgery has occurred in less than 1% of patients.

Conclusion

When the diagnosis of renovascular hypertension has been made, renal angioplasty or revascularization should be attempted, because there is a high probability of cure or improvement. Short-term and long-term results of renal angioplasty with fibromuscular dysplasia are similar to those of the best surgical series, as are those of focal atheromatous lesions. Angioplasty should be the treatment of choice in such patients. On the other hand, patients with diffuse atheromatous disease show somewhat better results from surgical repair.

Since in the majority of patients angioplasty can be performed at the same time as diagnostic arteriography with relatively little trauma and low complication rates, it should be the initial treatment of choice. In addition, in the current setting of economic awareness, the low mortality and morbidity rates of renal angioplasty and the short hospitalization after the procedure are of great medical and economic benefit.

References

1. Beinart C, Sos TA, Saddekni S, Weiner MA, Sniderman KW. Arterial spasm during renal angioplasty. Radiology 1983;149:97–100.
2. Cicuto KP, McLean GK, Oleaja JA, Freiman DB, Grossman RA, Ring EJ. Renal artery stenosis: anatomic classification for percutaneous transluminal angioplasty. AJR 1981;137:599–601.
3. Clark RA, Alexander ES. Digital subtraction angiography of renal arteries: prospective comparison with conventional arteriography. Invest Radiol 1983;18:6.
4. Dollesy CT, Bulpitt CJ, eds. Management of hypertension: physiopathology and treatment. New York: McGraw-Hill, 1977:1038–1068.
5. Eyler WR, Clark MD, Garman JE, Rian RL, Meininger DE. Angiography of the renal arteries including a comparative study of renal arterial stenoses in patients with and without hypertension. Radiology 1962;78:879–891.
6. Foster JH, Dean RH, Pinkerton JA, Rhamky RK. Ten years experience with the surgical management of renovascular hypertension. Ann Surg 1973;177:755–766.
7. Foster JH, Maxwell MH, Franklin SS, Bleifer KH, Trippel OH, Julian OC, DeCamp PT, Varady PT. Renovascular occlusive disease: results of operative treatment. JAMA 1975;231:1043–1048.
8. Geyskes GG, Puylaert CBA, Dei HY, Dorhout Mees EJ. Follow-up study of 70 patients with renal artery stenosis treated by percutaneous transluminal dilatation. Br Med J 1983;287:333–336.
9. Grim CE, Luft FC, Yune HY, Klatte EC, Weinberger MH. Percutaneous transluminal dilatation in the treatment of renal vascular hypertension. Ann Intern Med 1981;95:439–442.
10. Grüntzig A, Hopff H. Perkutane Rekanalisation chronischer arterieller Verschlüsse mit einem neuen Dilatationskatheter: Modifikation der Dotter-Technik. Dtsch Med Wochenschr 1974;99:2502–2511.
11. Grüntzig A, Kuhlmann U, Vetter W, Meier B, Lutolf U, Siegenthaler W. Treatment of renovascular hypertension with percutaneous transluminal dilation of renal artery stenosis. Lancet 1978;i:801–802.
12. Holley KE, Hunt JC, Brown AL Jr, Kincaid OW, Sheps SG. Renal artery stenosis: a clinical pathological study in normotensive and hypertensive patients. Am J Med 1964;37:14–22.
13. Hunt JC, Strong CG. Renovascular hypertension mechanisms: natural history and treatment. Am J Cardiol 1973;32:562–574.
14. Lacombe M. Arterial stenosis complicating renal allotransplantation in man. Ann Surg 1975;181:283–288.
15. Martin ED, Mattern RF, Baer L. Renal angioplasty for hypertension: predictive factors for long-term success. AJR 1981;137:921–924.
16. Neithamer CD, Sniderman KW, Sprayregen S, Saddekni S, Srur MF, Rosenblit G, Sos TA. Transluminal angioplasty in allograft renal artery stenosis: methods and results. Semin Intervent Radiol 1986;3:2.
17. Pickering TG, Sos TA, Vaughan ED, Case DB, Sealey JE, Harshfield GA, Laragh JH. Predictive value and changes of renin secretion in hypertensive patients with unilateral renovascular disease undergoing successful renal angioplasty. Am J Med 1984;76:398–404.
18. Pickering TG, Sos TA, James GD, Vaughan ED, Sealey JE, Laragh JH. Comparison of renal vein renin activity in hypertensive patients with stenosis of one or both renal arteries. J Hypertens 1985;3(suppl 3):291–293.
19. Pickering TG, Sos TA, Saddekni S, Rozenblit G, James GD, Orenstein A, Helseth G, Laragh JH. Renal angioplasty in patients with azotaemia and renovascular hypertension. J Hypertens 1986;4:S667–S669.
20. Saddekni S, Sos TA, Srur M, Cohn DJ. Contrast administration and technique of digital subtraction angiography. Radiol Clin North Am 1985;23:275–291.
21. Schreiber MJ, Pohl MA, Novick AC. The natural history of atherosclerotic and fibrous renal artery disease. Urol Clin North Am 1984;11:383–392.

22. Schwarten DE, Yune HY, Klatte EC, Grim CE, Weinberger MH. Clinical experience with percutaneous transluminal angioplasty (PTA) of stenosed renal arteries. Radiology 1980;135:601–604.
23. Sniderman KW, Sos TA. Percutaneous transluminal recanalization and dilatation of totally occluded renal arteries. Radiology 1982;142:607–610.
24. Sos TA, Sniderman KW, Saddekni S, Weiner MA, Beinart C, Pickering TG, Case DB, Vaughan ED Jr, Laragh JH. Renal vein renin assay and digital intravenous angiography in patients with renovascular hypertension. Transluminal Angioplasties International Congress, January 27–29, 1983, Toulouse, France.
25. Sos TA, Pickering TG, Sniderman K, Saddekni S, Case DB, Silane MF, Vaughan ED, Larach JH. Percutaneous transluminal renal angioplasty in renovascular hypertension due to atheroma or fibromuscular dysplasia. N Engl J Med 1983;309:274–279.
26. Sos TA, Cohn DJ, Srur M, Wengrover SI, Saddekni S. A new open-ended guide wire catheter. Radiology 1985;154:817–818.
27. Srur MF, Sos TA, Saddekni S, Cohn DJ, Rozenblit G, Wetter EB. Intimal fibromuscular dysplasia and Takayasu arteritis: delayed response to percutaneous transluminal renal angioplasty. Radiology 1985;157:657–660.
28. Tegtmeyer CJ, Dyer R, Treates CD. Percutaneous transluminal dilatation of renal arteries. Radiology 1980;135:589–599.
29. Tegtmeyer CJ, Elson J, Glass TA. Percutaneous transluminal angioplasty: the treatment of choice for renovascular hypertension due to fibromuscular dysplasia. Radiology 1982;143:631–637.
30. Tegtmeyer CJ, Sos TA. Techniques of renal angioplasty. Radiology 1986;161:577–586.
31. Tegtmeyer CJ, Ayers CA, Wellons HA. The axillary approach to percutaneous renal artery dilatation. Radiology 1980;135:775–776.
32. Tegtmeyer CJ, Kellum CD, Kron IL, Mentzer RM. Percutaneous transluminal angioplasty in the region of the aortic bifurcation: the two-balloon technique with results and long-term follow-up study. Radiology 1985;157:661–665.
33. Tegtmeyer CJ, Kellum CD, Ayers C. Percutaneous transluminal angioplasty of the renal artery: results and long-term follow-up. Radiology 1984;153:77–84.
34. Vaughan ED, Buhler FR, Laragh JH, Sealey JE, Baer L, Bard RH. Renovascular hypertension: renin measurements to indicate hypersecretion and contralateral suppression, estimate renal plasma flow, and score for surgical curability. Am J Med 1973;55:402–414.
35. Veterans Administration Cooperative Study Group on Antihypertensive Agents. Effects of treatment on morbidity in hypertension. JAMA 1967;202:1028–1034.
36. Zabbo A, Novick AC. Digital subtraction angiography for noninvasive imaging of the renal arteries. Urol Clin North Am 1984;11:409.

Percutaneous Transluminal Angioplasty of the Iliac Arteries

G. Simonetti and F. Urigo

Dotter and Judkins (3) dilated iliac and femoro-popliteal arteries using Teflon coaxial catheters of gradually increasing diameters. Grüntzig and Hopff (4) successfully performed arterial dilation using a catheter having at the distal end a dilatable balloon of variable diameter and length according to the size of the vessel to be dilated and the extent of the lesion. With the introduction of balloon catheters, application of PTA was extended widely from the initial treatment of peripheral arterial stenoses to many other vascular districts (renal, celiomesenteric, supra-aortic, coronary arteries), so that now PTA is considered to be an effective alternative to surgical treatment (5, 6, 13–16). PTA was developed as a further step of angiographic technique. It should be performed only by expert angiographers, aiming to achieve a high percentage of success with a low incidence of complications, by sufficient knowledge of indications and limitations of the technique. Experimental and histologic studies (1, 2) of the mechanism of angioplasty have proved that dilation is related to laceration of the intima, overdistension of the media, and consequent increase in the arterial diameter and hence of its lumen. Atheromatous material can be fixed and distributed over a greater surface after PTA. Histologically, fixation of the intima has been shown to be stripped at several points in dilated arteries. The media is thinned and the muscular cells assume a corkscrew appearance. Two or 3 weeks after the dilation, cicatricial remodeling of the vascular wall occurs with new endothelium formation.

Indications

Stenotic or obstructive vascular disease of the iliac arteries, responsible for ischemic disease in the lower limbs and for impotentia coeundi, can be treated successfully by surgical revascularization or PTA. The indications for these different techniques depend on the nature and characteristics of the lesions. Surgical treatment of iliac arteries is indicated in the correction of particularly long obstructions and in aneurysms, where endarterectomy, bypass, and interposition of a prosthesis can be performed. PTA is indicated in isolated atherosclerotic lesions involving a short segment of the artery. How-

ever, multiple or extended lesions can also be successfully treated. Other important applications are stenoses due to fibromuscular dysplasia, arteritis, and in stenosis occurring in surgical vascular anastomoses. Recanalization of the iliac artery is indicated in the presence of a 1 to 4 cm occluded arterial segment. In the last 2 years, we had been using local infusion of urokinase before PTA when an occlusion was present. PTA was then performed only in cases that showed a partial recanalization after local thrombolysis, allowing the insertion of the angiographic guide wire and the balloon catheter through the residual arterial stenosis. Care must be taken not to create a false lumen or a vascular perforation, which may be followed by serious bleeding, controllable only by emergency surgery. The choice between surgery and PTA in iliac arteries as well as in other vascular territories should be based on clinical and functional evaluation, e.g., Doppler ultrasound and angiography, in order to define precisely the site, extent, and nature of the stenosis. Close collaboration between the vascular radiologist and the vascular surgeon is mandatory to establish an adequate therapeutic strategy.

Material and Methods

Aorto-iliac PTA requires Grüntzig catheters 7 or 8 Fr with a balloon of 8 to 12 mm in diameter and 3 to 8 cm in length. In 90% of the cases, we have used a homolateral femoral approach that is technically simple. When only a faint pulsation of the homolateral femoral artery is palpated, it can be punctured under Doppler guidance. In the other cases we have used a contralateral femoral or an axillary approach, depending on the distal or proximal location of the stenotic lesion in the iliac artery. Having chosen the adequate approach, a guide wire, straight or J-shaped with a movable core, is inserted. Once the guide wire has passed the stenosis, an angiographic catheter is introduced for angiography control to see if changes have taken place, if the lesion had been demonstrated angiographically weeks before. An arterial map of the vascular area to be treated is obtained. Leaving the guide wire in place, the catheter is exchanged for the balloon catheter, which is positioned at the level of the stenosis. The radiopaque markers on the extremities of the balloon are helpful for correct positioning. The balloon is inflated using a syringe filled with 50% diluted contrast medium under fluoroscopy control. The contrast medium is diluted to allow the balloon to deflate completely. Retention of nondiluted contrast medium in the balloon may hurt the angioplasty site at the end of PTA and make extraction of the catheter more difficult. During inflation of the balloon, a pressure of 4 to 5 atmospheres is reached, and monitored by a manometer in connection with the catheter. Balloon catheters allowing greater pressures (up to 16 atm) are now commercially available, making the compression of particularly hard atheromatous plaques easier. The balloon is either maintained inflated for 20 to 30 seconds and the procedure is repeated several times at short intervals, or for 60 to 90 seconds one or two times. Each time the dilation catheter is moved, the balloon must be completely deflated and the guide wire inserted to avoid iatrogenic lesions to the arterial wall by movements of the distal tip of the catheter. Finally, the Grüntzig catheter is changed for an angiographic catheter and control angiography is obtained to evaluate results of the treatment.

In iliac recanalization, PTA is preceded by local infusion of urokinase, using a catheter with lateral bores placed in the thrombosed artery. Infusion is administered over 24 to 48 hours in two cycles of 6 hours, with 3000 U/min in the first 24 hours, alternated with cycles of glucose; in the following 48 to 72 hours, dosage of urokinase is decreased to 2000 U/min. After PTA a therapy based on platelet anti-aggregation drugs is recommended for at least 6 months.

We usually do a follow-up examination every 6 months, consisting of a clinical and physiologic control and a Doppler examination. We have performed a further arteriography in 20% of the cases to evaluate doubtful findings, superimposed lesions, and eventually to perform an adjunctive PTA.

Results

Our personal experience dates from October 1973 (7, 8, 10, 11). Our series consists of 390 aortoiliac PTAs performed in 349 men and 41 women with an average age of 55 years. In 297 cases, we treated a unilateral stenosis and in 41 cases, a bilateral lesion (Fig. 1). In 44 cases, we recanalized an obstructed iliac artery (1 to 5 cm), and 22 recanalizations have been preceded by a local infusion of urokinase (Figs. 2, 3). In 8 patients we dilated a stenosis of the

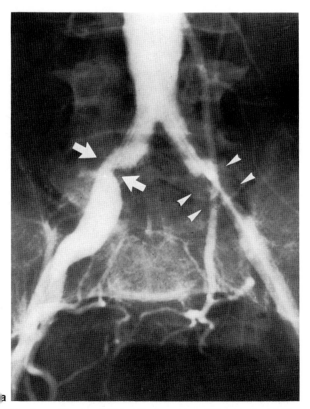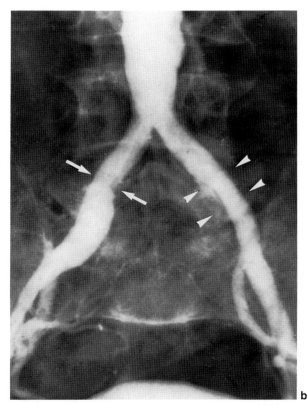

Fig. **1 a Severe bilateral stenoses of the common iliac arteries.** Functional occlusion of the left internal iliac artery
b After PTA resolution of the stenoses bilaterally, with a good patency of the left internal iliac artery

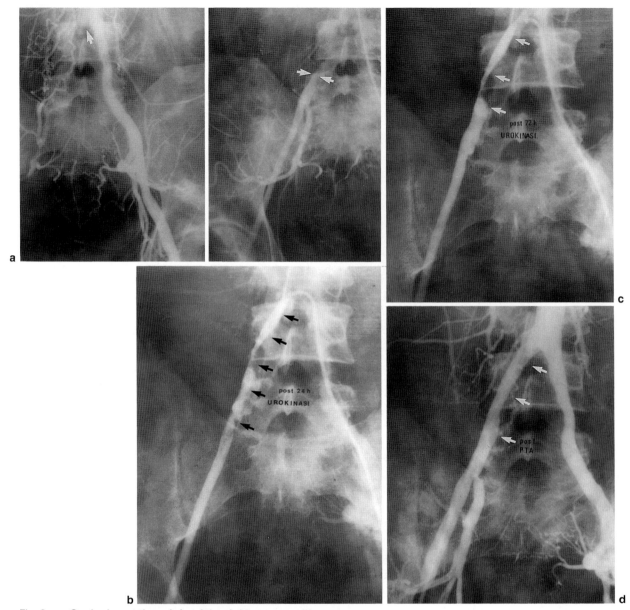

Fig. 2 a Occlusion at the origin of the right common iliac artery
b 24 hours after local infusion of urokinase, a recanalization of the vessel is achieved, with a residual thrombus
c 72 hours after administration of urokinase, the thrombus has resolved, a distal stenosis is shown
d Open lumen after PTA

abdominal aorta below the origin of the renal arteries (Fig. **4**) and in two patients an iliac PTA was also performed. In iliac stenoses we achieved an initial success rate in 96% of cases. Long-term follow-up from 1 to 10 years has shown good results. At 1 year of follow-up (264 patients), the patency rate was 94%; at 3 years of follow-up (193 patients), 90%, at 5 years of follow-up (82 patients), 80%, and at 10 years (31 patients), 78%. Ten of the 17 patients with iliac recanalization have had 3 to 6 years of follow-up, showing a lumen patency rate of 70%. Of

22 patients treated in the last 3 years, when recanalization was preceded by urokinase infusion, ten have been followed, with a satisfactory lumen patency rate observed in all controlled cases. Of the 8 aortic dilations, with 1 to 5 years of follow-up, 5 have shown a good lumen patency, and 3 patients were submitted some time later to surgery.

Stenoses and occlusions of the iliac arteries can be responsible for a reduced blood supply to the internal iliac artery, causing organic impotence. In our experience this occurred in 63% of the patients.

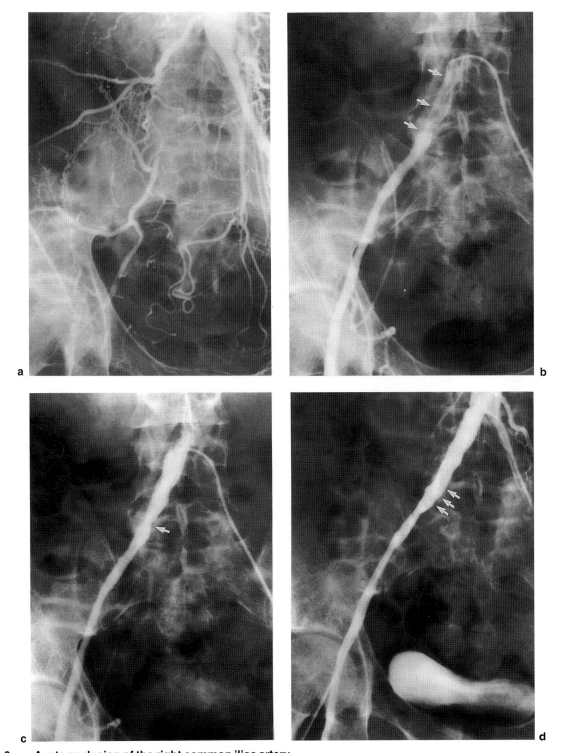

Fig. **3   a Acute occlusion of the right common iliac artery**
b 24 hours after local infusion of urokinase, the vessel is recanalized, with the presence of an intraluminal thrombus
c Dissolution of the thrombus after 72 hours of urokinase administration and residual distal stenosis is shown
d Result after PTA

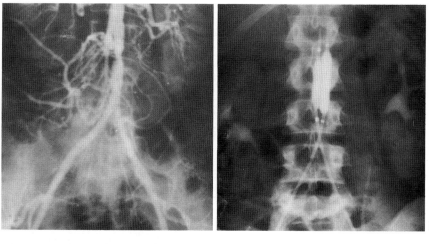

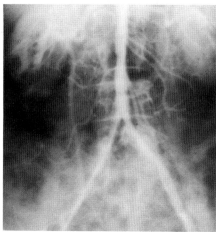

Fig. 4 **a Stenosis of the abdominal aorta** below the origin of the renal arteries
b A 10 and an 8 mm balloon catheter are placed at the level of the stenosis
c Result after PTA

Internal iliac revascularization following PTA has solved impotence that was due to inadequate blood supply in 32% of the cases. The internal iliac artery can be occluded due to a stenosis situated proximally to its ostium. This complication had occurred in 59 cases (15%). It can be significantly reduced by performing PTA inserting the balloon catheter by a transaxillary or a contralateral transfemoral approach. We have compared the results achieved by PTA and vascular surgery regarding aortoiliac recanalization in the last years (12). The surgical series was based on 102 patients (84 men, 18 women), with an average age of 58 years. These patients presented with stenoses and occlusions localized in the iliac artery. Those cases associated with hemodynamically significant lesions in the distal arteries were excluded from this study. Surgery of the iliac artery consisted of a thrombo-endoarterectomy in 88 cases, in associated angioplasty in 26 cases, bypass in 26 cases, and interposition of a vascular graft in 6 patients. Surgical results were excellent in 91%, early reoperation rate (1 to 6 months) due to recurrent thrombosis was 8% and the incidence of postoperative limb amputation was 8%. Patency of the treated vascular segments, after 1 to 5 years of follow-up, was satisfactory in 74% of the cases. No significant difference was recorded in the results in patients treated by various surgical techniques.

Complications

PTA is not entirely free from complications. Complications can occur at the puncture site of the artery (thrombosis, pseudoaneurysm, hematoma), at the level of the lesion (intimal dissection, thrombotic spasm, arterial wall perforation, vascular rupture), and distally from the lesion (embolization). According to the literature, the incidence of complications in relation to the entry point is about 3%, whereas at the level of the lesion and distally it is about 2%. In our series, three cases of thrombosis and eight hematomas were observed at the puncture site; 13 thromboses were seen at the level of the stenosis and one rupture of the artery (9). Concerning distal complications, 11 embolizations have been recorded.

Only four of these required a Fogarty procedure. In the other cases, intra-arterial urokinase was successfully infused. Knowing the mechanism of complications helps the operator to avoid them. Thrombosis at the puncture site is generally due to an intimal lesion or a thrombus that had formed in contact with the external surface of the catheter. This complication is best prevented by reducing the examination time, avoiding dissection at the entry point of the artery, and by applying a short manual compression distal to the emergence of the catheter and after removing it. The moderate bleeding brings out of the artery possible thrombi adherent to the catheter. Insertion and removal of the catheter are the most dangerous steps for the formation of a hematoma or a pseudoaneurysm. An arterial puncture leaving a tear that is larger than the catheter can cause formation of a hematoma. Careless removal of the catheter with the balloon not completely deflated can cause arterial stripping, making hemostasis problematic and a pseudoaneurysm more likely to occur. To prevent complications, it is fundamental to avoid exchange of the catheter for a smaller one. Catheters have to be changed in an increasing progression of their diameter. The Grüntzig balloon catheter must be removed with a spiral movement, to avoid stripping the artery, and the procedure has to be completed by an effective compression of the artery for at least 20 minutes. Thrombosis of the artery at the site of the lesion is usually secondary to a dissection, with an intimal flap protruding into the lumen. In this case, the thrombotic lesion is favored by the slowed blood circulation due to the inflated balloon that stayed too long in the artery.

Care must be taken when passing the stenosis with a guide wire and with the catheter. When a recanalization has been performed, we suggest repeated aspiration of blood and injection of heparin or urokinase to prevent significant distal embolization. Complications are best avoided by correct technique and an appropriate choice of dilation material. Regarding this choice, it is important not to be influenced by the high cost of the balloon. A low-cost balloon catheter often does not correspond to a satisfactory product and shows inadequate construction characteristics. For this reason in-depth knowledge of the material used for transluminal angioplasty is required. It is also important to consider that all balloon catheters are disposable. Re-usage can lead to complications and is restricted by law and by European community directives in some European countries. Through these directives, the re-use of diagnostic or therapeutic catheters by vascular radiologists or other operators is strictly prohibited.

Dilation has to be performed in the craniocaudal direction. Untoward movements of the guide wire or the catheter can perforate the arterial wall. The risk of complications increases with the presence of cal-cified lesions or working with a harder guide. It is important to avoid overinflation of the balloon and not to force the guide wire excessively in an attempt to pass a very narrow arterial tract. Repeated transstenotic manipulations aiming to achieve an optimal morphologic pattern of the dilated vessel might induce complications. It is wise to be satisfied with a fairly patent irregular lumen. In fact, a relative recanalization is enough, because increase of blood flow will provoke a remodeling of the vascular lumen. In future follow-up, the vessel shows a regular caliber.

Arterial rupture is one of the worst complications of PTA. It is due to disproportion between the inflated balloon and the arterial caliber, in relation to poor choice of balloon or overdistension ballooning. It is important to test the balloon before inserting the catheter and to follow all steps of the dilation under fluoroscopy. Distal embolization is a complication that occurs more frequently in recanalization. Frequent aspirations of blood in large quantity during the procedure are necessary. A local infusion of urokinase before PTA can be added.

Despite the complications just mentioned, their evolution is frequently benign. Simple therapeutic measures control most of the situations. However, help from a vascular surgeon is needed whenever the situation requires an immediate operation. A pseudoaneurysm must be treated surgically to prevent progressive dilation and further complications. A hematoma is easily controlled by local administration of hyaluronidase. Only a very large hematoma should be treated surgically. Thrombosis can be immediately treated by the radiologist using a local infusion of urokinase, through a contralateral catheter. In the rare unsuccessful case, a Fogarty procedure is needed. An intimal flap at the arterial puncture site, when complicated by thrombosis, must be treated surgically. Iliac artery perforation can produce a hematoma. A retroperitoneal hematoma must be monitored via ultrasound or computed tomography. In the presence of intraperitoneal blood, surgery must be performed rapidly. Arterial rupture is an absolute indication for surgery. The vascular radiologist can cooperate in the treatment by placing the inflated balloon proximal to the lesion, to reduce blood loss, while the patient is waiting for surgery.

Conclusion

PTA has been shown to be highly effective, playing a fundamental role in therapeutic strategy for aorto-iliac stenoses both for the medical and surgical approach. Some data will confirm the role of PTA: 5017 dilation catheters were sold in the United States in one month, 60,000 were sold in Europe in one year, and 30,000 PTAs are performed in one year worldwide. According to the literature, and comparing our results achieved by PTA and by surgical revascularization, PTA showed slightly better results than surgery. We also stress that the patients submitted to PTA had less advanced disease in comparison to the surgical patients. Indeed, the main indications for PTA are isolated lesions, consisting of stenoses and short obstructions. Surgery is indicated in atherosclerotic lesions of wide extent requiring more radical treatment. An unsuccessful PTA does not cause any damage in local vascular conditions and does not preclude subsequent surgical treatment. A bypass occlusion in most cases leads to a worse ischemic condition, and its surgical correction is not always satisfactory.

PTA is a slightly invasive procedure with a low incidence of easily managed complications. It can be performed under local anesthesia and needs a short hospitalization time; it can be repeated if necessary and does not preclude surgery whenever it is unsuccessful or impracticable.

References

1. Block PC, Fallon JT, Elmer D. Experimental angioplasty: lesson from the laboratory. AJR 1980;135:907.
2. Castaneda-Zuniga WR, Formanek A, Tadavarthy M, Vladaner Z, Edwards JE, Zollikofer C, Amplatz K. The mechanism of balloon angioplasty. Radiology 1980;135:565–571.
3. Dotter CT, Judkins MP. Transluminal treatment of arteriosclerotic obstruction: description of a new technic and a preliminary report of its application. Circulation 1984;30:653–670.
4. Grüntzig A, Hopff M. Perkutane Rekanalisation chronischer arterieller Verschlüsse mit einem neuen Dilatationskatheter: Modifikation der Dotter-Technik. Dtsch Med Wochenschr 1974;99:2052–2055.
5. Kadir SD, White R, Kaufman R, Bart KH, Williams GM, Burdick JF, O'Mara CF, Smith GW, Stonesifer GL, Ernst CB, Minken SL. Long-term results of aortoiliac angioplasty. Surgery 1983;94:10–14.
6. Montjarjeme A, Keifer JV, Zuska AJ. Angioplasty of the iliac arteries: new experiences. AJR 1980;135:937–944.
7. Simonetti G, Rossi P, Passariello R, Salvatori F. Indicazioni e risultati a distanza dell'angioplastica transluminale. Radiol Med (Torino) 1980;66:335–344.
8. Simonetti G, Rossi P, Passariello R, Caboni M, Castrucci M, Pesce B. Angioplastie transluminale percutanée des artères des membres inférieurs: étude suivie sur cinq années d'expérience. Radiol J CEPUR 1983;3:199–211.
9. Simonetti G, Rossi P, Passariello R, Faraglia V, Spartera C, Pistolesi R, Fiorani P. Iliac artery rupture: a complication of transluminal angioplasty. AJR 1983;140:989.
10. Simonetti G, Rossi P, Passariello R, Castrucci M, Pesce B. PTA in peripheral arteries. Ann Radiol (Paris) 1984;27:55–64.
11. Simonetti G, Bonomo L, Falappa PG, Feltrin GP, Fugazzola C, Lupatelli L, Montesi A, Petrillo G. Percutaneous transluminal angioplasty of iliac arteries. Ann Radiol (Paris) 1985;28:159–162.
12. Simonetti G, Urigo F, Guazzaroni M, Biglioli P, Dettori G, Bacciu PP. Iliac artery lesions : a comparison between percutaneous transluminal angioplasty and surgery. Ann Radiol (Paris) 1986;29:127–129.
13. Sos TA, Sniderman KW. Percutaneous transluminal angioplasty. Semin Roentgenol 1981;16:26–41.
14. Van Andel GJ. Transluminal iliac angioplasty: long term results. Radiology 1980;135:607–611.
15. Van Andel GJ. Long term results of iliac and femoral angioplasty. Ann Radiol (Paris) 1981;24:368.
16. Zeitler E. Percutaneous dilatation and recanalization of iliac and femoral arteries. Cardiovasc Intervent Radiol 1980;3:207–212.

Percutaneous Transluminal Angioplasty of the Femorotibial Arteries

E. Zeitler

The first atherosclerotic obstruction that Dotter and Judkins were able to recanalize in January 1964 (2, 3), was a superficial femoral artery lesion. It occurred in an 84-year-old woman with severe rest pain and a tight focal stenosis of the superficial femoral artery. She was considered to be an unacceptable candidate for femoropopliteal bypass surgery because of inadequate distal run-off. The procedure was successfully accomplished by passing a guide wire through the stenosis and then advancing a coaxial Teflon catheter system over the guide wire with a 12 Fr diameter. The leg was saved and the potential of percutaneous transluminal angioplasty (PTA) as a new technique was demonstrated.

Over the following years, the principle of this sort of examination with the coaxial Dotter catheter set, which can be executed in the angiography room without general anesthesia, has been tested in patients with intermittent claudication by teams in the Aggertalklinik, Engelskirchen (FRG) (5, 16–26) and in the Charité-Hospital, Berlin (GDR) (12, 13). These first systematic examinations in patients with occlusion of the superficial femoral artery in stage II according to Fontaine could be controlled by long-term follow-up observations of at most 10 years (5, 14, 15, 17).

In our first group with long-term follow-up study were 79 patients (72 men and 7 women, ages 41 to 71 years at the time of treatment, average age, 55.5 years), and 81 extremities were treated.

Twenty-one cases were recanalized with simple straight Teflon catheters of 7 or 8 Fr, and 59 occlusions were treated using the Dotter coaxial recanalization set. After 2 years, 44% of all living patients and 42 of all treated vessels were patent. After 8 years in 30% of the living patients, the artery treated was patent and was still patent 10 years later in 28% (14 of 50 surviving patients).

This study showed that very long occlusions (13 to 27 cm) show a tendency to an early reobliteration. After 5 years, all these were blocked again. The long-term result for short occlusions up to 3 cm was the most favorable. After 10 years, 9 of 22 patients treated still had patent arteries. This first study also showed that the group of non-smokers had the best long-term results; 31 were non-smokers, 42% with patent arteries, surviving more than 10 years. Cigarette smokers hat the worst results (11% with patent arteries).

PTA made essential progress with the inroduction of the balloon catheter by Grüntzig (4, 6–9). Its advantages consist in a reduction of the trauma of the artery at the point of puncture and in the specific dilation in the area of the localized arteriosclerotic lesion. In addition, in comparison to the coaxial Dotter set the number of complications at the point of puncture as well as the number of the peripheral embolies could be clearly reduced with the balloon catheter.

Obstructions of the femoral and popliteal arteries present the most frequent indications for PTA. Total occlusions of the superficial femoral artery beginning at its origins are no ideal indication for the mechanical balloon dilation technique. In these cases only the intra-arterial thrombolysis can be an alternative to bypass surgery.

Best indications for PTA in the femoropopliteal artery are:

– single or multiple isolated stenosis (Fig. **1**);
– short femoral or popliteal segmental occlusions up to 12 cm (Figs. **2, 3**) with best long-term results in femoropopliteal occlusions up to 5 cm in length (Fig. **4**);
– isolated stenosis in the popliteal artery and the posterotibial trunk.

The indication for PTA only exists in patients with clinical symptoms, such as claudication, rest pain, or gangrene and with a reduced ankle-arm pressure gradient (AAPG).

Technique

The examination takes place under local anesthesia on the angiographic examination table. Special problems can arise in antegrade puncture of the femoral artery in the groin. Such punctures can be quite difficult in obese patients, and it is therefore advantageous to hyperextend the hip by placing a cushion beneath the bed. In 1% the primary puncture occurs in the deep femoral artery instead of the common femoral or superficial femoral artery (5, 11, 26).

Under fluoroscopic control with injection of contrast medium, the position of the needle tip can be changed in several cases to the correct place. Sometimes a catheter (e.g., the right coronary Judkin's catheter) is very helpful or the use of steerable guide wires. Before definitive dilation can proceed, repeat

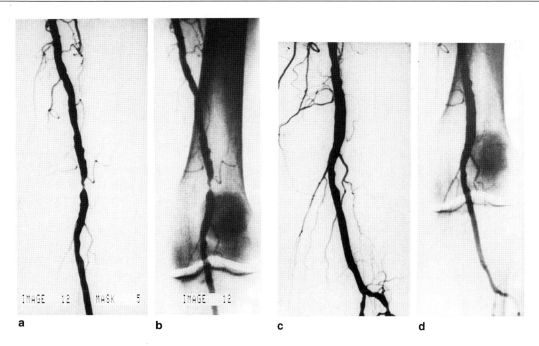

Fig. 1 A 52-year-old male patient with intermittent claudication, isolated stenosis at the transition from the superficial femoral artery to the popliteal artery
a DSA before PTA

b The comprehensive image for localization with the femur
c DSA after balloon dilation
d Comprehensive radiography

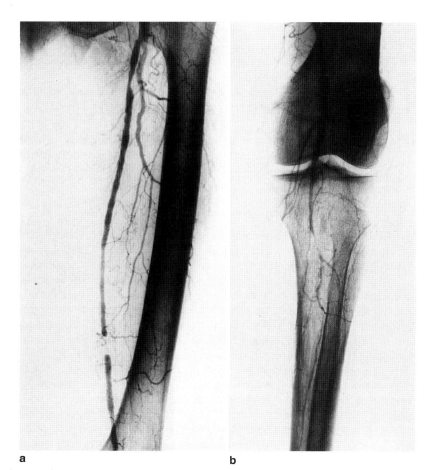

Fig. 2 A 77-year-old patient, whose right leg has already been amputated at the thigh. On the left side, gangrene of the big toe and rest pain
a, b Angiography before angioplasty with proof of a proximal femoral stenosis, of a femoral occlusion of 1 cm length at the adductor channel, of an extreme popliteal stenosis, and poor contrast of the arteries of the lower limb

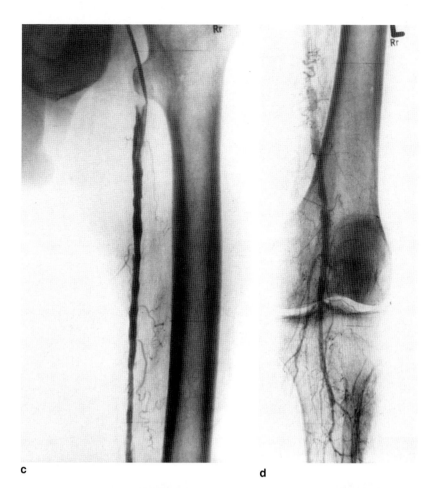

Fig. 2
c, d Angiography after successful
PTA by steps of the femoral
stenosis, of the femoral occlusion,
and of the popliteal stenosis. Cure of
the gangrene; 5 years later, no
gangrene and no rest pain

c

d

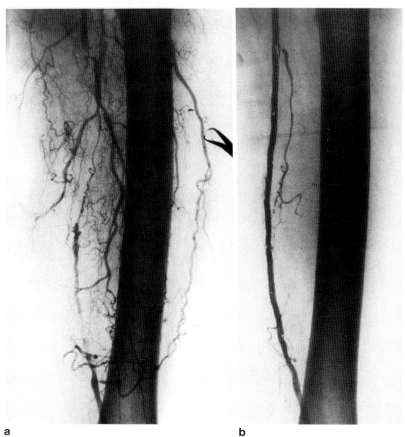

Fig. 3 **69-year-old male patient
with intermittent claudication**
a Angiography before PTA with
collateral circulation
b Successful removal of the
occlusion of 10 cm length by
balloon-dilation using the Grüntzig
technique

a

b

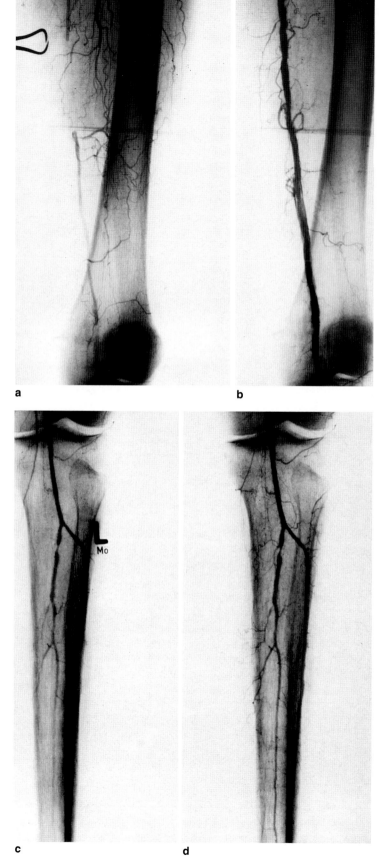

Fig. 4   **A 77-year-old female patient with diabetic gangrene and rest pain at the left leg**
a, b Arteries of the thigh before and after successful PTA of the femoral occlusion of 6 cm length; intimal cracking at the distal occlusion
c, d Angiography of the arteries of the lower limb with stenosis in the region of the tibiofibular trunk

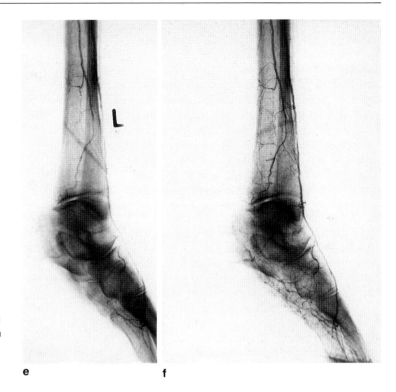

Fig. 4
e, f Distal angiography of the lower limb and the foot before and after successful PTA with remaining occlusion of the posterior tibial artery

e   f

angiography is necessary to delineate the individual obstructive lesions, which are then marked with towel clamps.

Independently of the use of polyethylene or Teflon catheters, one of the most important aspects of PTA lies in the safe intraluminal passage of the obstruction. Image intensifier fluoroscopy is essential for such a safe passage. DSA with its reduced requirements for contrast agents can help monitor the advancement of the guide wire and catheter as well as the extent of the dilation. In cases of occlusion the explosion method (10) can sometimes be helpful.

To ensure the intraluminal passage of the obstructive lesion, we use a Teflon catheter with proximal side holes by which we can follow the progress of the guide wire and catheter by intermittent contrast material injection. Such an arrangement using a Y-adapter also helps avoid entering collateral vessels.

When both the guide wire and initial catheter lie safely intraluminally beyond the obstruction, an appropriate balloon catheter is chosen for the dilation, depending on the size and the extent of the obstructing lesion.

The guide wire remains beyond the obstruction while the Teflon catheter is exchanged for the balloon catheter. Dilation is performed under manometric control. It is possible to distend the balloon by hand with a 2 to 5 ml syringe. A 20 ml syringe is recommended for the deflation of the balloon (1). Crossing the lesion is the most critical part of trans-

luminal angioplasty of the femoral or popliteal vessels. If the stenosis is concentric, the catheter is placed proximal to the lesion and a straight guide wire is gently and slowly advanced through the stenosis. Careful monitoring of this step under fluoroscopy is essential to ascertain that the guide wire advances smoothly and does not become hung up on the lesion.

If the stenosis is eccentric, the catheter is placed immediately proximal to the lesion and a guide wire will find the proper intraluminal pathway. Changing the direction of the catheter tip within the lesion, rotating the catheter and the curve of the wire tip helps to pass the distal part of the lesion.

To recanalize a femoral artery occlusion, the Teflon catheter with the tapered tip is placed directly at the beginning of the occlusion. With pressure, the mixture of saline and contrast material are injected to find the best way, which can be followed by the guide wire. It is possible to use a regular straight guide wire to go through the occlusion or a small-radius J wire to pass the occlusion at the time of contrast material injection under fluoroscopic control. In some cases, especially when the problem is to save the leg in diabetics with gangrene, it can be necessary to push guide wire and catheter with force through the lesion. In some cases it is necessary to use a stiff needle over the guide wire inside of the Teflon catheter.

After placing the guide wire tip and catheter tip distal to the obstruction, a spasmolytic agent can be injected and over the guide wire the Teflon catheter has to be exchanged for the balloon catheter.

It is important to have on hand many types of dilating catheters with balloons of different diameters and length. The choice of the proper dilating catheter depends on the diameter of the normal uninvolved artery proximal and distal to the arteriosclerotic obstruction. For the superficial or femoropopliteal arteries, we usually use dilating catheters with a 7 Fr shaft, a balloon diameter of 6 mm and a length varying between 4 and 10 cm. Before insertion of the dilating catheter, the balloon is tested, evacuated, and carefully wrapped around the catheter shaft.

In several cases an 8 Fr arterial sheath with a side arm for flushing is helpful in introducing the dilating catheter through the soft tissues of the groin. This is particularly necessary in patients with scarring or fibrosis from previous arteriography or surgery.

Balloon catheters that we have tested with good clinical results today are polyethylene catheters the expanding balloon catheter by Olbert, and the new small diameter catheter with 4 and 5 Fr.

After successful dilation, angiography is necessary to control the primary result (Tabl. 1) and look at the lower leg arteries for detection of peripheral embolization. If important residual stenoses exist, a second bypassing of the lesion and dilation is possible, and in cases with early rethrombosis an intra-arterial thrombolysis with urokinase or streptokinase can follow. Complications that need surgery were seen in 2.1% of patients with claudication and in 3.3% of patients with gangrene and rest pain (5).

Treatment

One diagnostic measure before every PTA is a clinical angiologic study to be used as documentation. The hemodynamic situation with determination of the arterial pressure at the ankle arteries as well as at the arm has to be determined whereby with the determination of the AAPG a good observation of the process is guaranteed. With an arterial pressure at the ankle of less than 50 mmHg, the extremity is in danger, with an AAPG of 0.8 or less and with the clinical symptoms of a localized obliteration or occlusion up to 12 cm, the indication for a PTA is always present.

Additional medical treatment is indicated in Table 2.

After treatment, the patient has to have a compression bandage, and he should stay in bed for 24 hours.

The results of femoropopliteal PTA depend on:
- The location of the obstruction
- The extent of the obstruction
- The clinical stage
- The peripheral outflow in the lower leg
- The concomitant medical therapy

Single femoropopliteal stenoses can be approached by ipsilateral antegrade arterial puncture in the groin. In cases with iliac artery and femoropopliteal stenoses it is possible to puncture the contralateral groin and dilate the stenosis in the iliac artery at the same time as the femoral artery stenosis. In cases with multiple stenoses or occlusions of the femoral artery, only the ipsilateral approach is effective.

For patients with ischemic rest pain and gangrene, revascularization therapy is urgently required to save the limb threatened with imminent amputation. Reconstructive surgery is best suited to limb salvage if a good peripheral outflow arterial system exists. Similar results can be obtained by PTA in selected cases, especially with stenosis and short occlusions in the distal femoral or popliteal artery. The advantage of the procedure are low costs and a low complica-

Table 1   Primary success rate. Control using digital subtraction angiography and arm-ankle pressure gradient (reduction of more than 0.2) between 3 and 10 days after percutaneous transluminal angioplasty

Obstruction	Location	%
Isolated stenoses	Superficial femoral artery	95
Multiple stenoses	Superficial femoral artery	85
Short occlusion (shorter than 3 cm)	Superficial femoral artery	91
Occlusion (up to 5 cm)	Superficial femoral artery	85
Occlusion (up to 10 cm)	Superficial femoral artery	80
Occlusion (larger than 12 cm)	Superficial femoral artery	59
Isolated stenoses	Popliteal artery	89
Multiple stenoses	Popliteal artery	78
Short occlusion	Popliteal artery	82
Total occlusion	Popliteal artery	54

Table 2   Medical drug therapy

Before and after PTA:	Acetylsalicylic acid (ASA) between 0.3 and 0.5 g, orally 2 to 3 times daily; calcium antagonists (nifedipine) orally
After catheterization:	Heparin 5000 IU intra-arterially Lidocaine 1%, 3 cc, ASA for at least 6 months or longer

tion rate, which allows the use of PTA also in high-risk patients who are not good candidates for vascular surgery.

The results of PTA for limb salvage are between 40 and 51% over a period of 6 months to 2 years. Major differences exist between patients with or without diabetes and between patients younger or older than 80 years.

Long-Term Results

Long-term results of PTA in the femoropopliteal area are available from several medical centers. It can definitely be demonstrated that early and later results with the balloon catheter technique according to Grüntzig are better than those of PTA when using single or coaxial Teflon catheters.

The first cooperative study (26) from 14 hospitals of 2337 patients has shown primary success after PTA with the balloon catheter in the femoropopliteal area in 87% and a rate of rethrombosis within the first 6 months of 15%. According to the life-table method, there was a patency rate of 64% after 5 years.

The differentiated analysis concerning stage and type of obliteration in our patients has revealed that the best results exist in isolated stenoses and short-distance occlusions, with a 5-year patency rate of more than 70% in patients with claudication and 66% in patients with rest pain or gangrene (Table 3).

Under these circumstances, and presuming that the treating physician has the necessary qualifications, the advantages of PTA can be summarized as follows:

– No anesthesia risk
– Practicable when there is a poor peripheral outflow
– Short stay at the hospital, which means lower costs
– Early mobilization and resumption of work
– With a primary success rate, there is a reduced risk of surgical treatment of the vessels
– Death rate of 0.1% and rate of complications needing surgery about 2%
– The long-term results can be compared with those after surgical reconstruction of the vessels
– In restenoses a second PTA is possible, thrombotic complications can be treated by an intra-arterial thrombolysis

Today PTA, therefore, is an accepted method in patients with localized obstructions of the femoral and popliteal arteries. If possible, it is indicated in patients with gangrene, rest pain and claudicatio intermittens. It is of high efficiency and needs, in addition, control of all risk factors. The interventional radiologist always needs to work in partnership with a vascular surgeon and if possible an internal medicine angiologist.

Table **3** Patency rate 5 years after successful percutaneous transluminal angioplasty

Obstruction	Claudication No.	Claudication %	Rest pain or gangrene No.	Rest pain or gangrene %
Isolated stenoses	140	75	73	68
Short occlusion (shorter than 3 cm)	58	70	59	66
Occlusion up to 10 cm	104	65	88	54

New developments, such as the application of laser or intravascular stents, must first prove their effectiveness in comparison to the balloon PTA of Grüntzig and the treatment with femoropopliteal stents.

References

1. Abele JT. Basic technology of balloon catheters. In: Dotter CT, Grüntzig AR, Schoop W, Zeitler E, eds. Percutaneous transluminal angioplasty: technique, early and late results. Berlin: Springer 1983:31–36.
2. Dotter CT, Judkins MP. Transluminal treatment of arteriosclerotic obstruction: description of a new technique and a preliminary report of its application. Circulation 1964;30:654–670.
3. Dotter CT, Judkins MP, Frische LH, Mueller R. The "nonsurgical" treatment of ilio-femoral arteriosclerotic obstruction. Radiology 1966;86:871–875.
4. Dotter CT, Judkins MP, Rösch J. Nichtoperative, transluminale Behandlung der arteriosklerotischen Verschlussaffektionen. RöFo 1968;109:125–133.
5. Dotter CT, Grüntzig AR, Schoop W, Zeitler E, eds. Percutaneous transluminal angioplasty: technique, early and late results. Berlin: Springer 1983.
6. Grüntzig A, Hopff H. Perkutane Rekanalisation chronischer arterieller Veschlüsse mit einem neuen Dilatationskatheter. Dtsch Med Wochenschr 1974;99:2502.
7. Grüntzig A, ed. Die perkutane transluminale Rekanalisation chronischer Arterienverschlüsse mit einer neuen Dilatationstechnik. Baden-Baden: Witzstrock 1977.
8. Grüntzig A. Die perkutane transluminale Rekanalisation: ein Vergleich der Dotter- und Dilatationstechnik. In: Alexander K, Cachovan M, eds. Diabetische Angiopathien. Baden-Baden: Witzstrock 1977.
9. Grüntzig A, Hirzel H, Goebel N, Gattiker R, Turina M, Myler R, Stertzer S, Kaltenbach M. Die perkutane transluminale Dilatation chronischer Koronarstenosen. Schweiz Med Wochenschr 1978;108:1721–1723.
10. Horvath L, Illés I, Varró J. Complications of the transluminal angioplasty excluding the puncture site complications. In: Zeitler E, Grüntzig A, Schoop W, eds. Percutaneous vascular recanalization. Berlin: Springer 1978:126–139.
11. Jang D, ed. Angioplasty. New York: McGraw-Hill 1986.
12. Portsmann W, Wierny L. Intravasale Rekanalisation inoperabler arterieller Obliterationen. Zentralbl Chir 1967;92:1586–1591.
13. Portsmann W. Ein neuer Korsett-Ballonkatheter zur transluminalen Rekanalisation nach Dotter unter besonderer Berücksichtigung von Obliterationen an den Beckenarterien. Radiol Diagn (Berl) 1973;2:239–244.
14. Richter E-I, Zeitler E. Percutaneous transluminal angioplasty: adjunct drug therapy. In: Dotter CT, Grüntzig AR, Schoop W, Zeitler E, eds. Percutaneous transluminal angioplasty. Berlin: Springer 1983:85–89.

15. Romaniuk P, Wierny L, Münster W. Langzeiteffektivität der angioplastischen Therapie iliakaler und femoro-poplitealer Obstruktionen im Vergleich zur Operation. In: Oeser H, ed. Angioplastisches Symposium, Berlin 4.–5. Juli 1985. Berlin: Schering 1986.

16. Schmidtke I, Zeitler E, Schoop W. Langzeitergebnisse der perkutanen Katheterbehandlung (Dotter-Technik) bei femoro-poplitealen Arterienverschlüssen im Stadium II. VASA 1975;4:210–226.

17. Schmidtke I, Zeitler E, Schoop W. Spätergebnisse (5–8 Jahre) der perkutanen Katheterbehandlung (Dotter-Technik) bei femoro-poplitealen Arterienverschlüssen im Stadium II. VASA 1978;7:4–15.

18. Zeitler E, Müller R. Erste Ergebnisse mit der Katheter-Rekanalisation nach Dotter bei arterieller Verschlußkrankheit. RöFo 1969;111:345–352.

19. Zeitler E, Schoop W, Zahnow W. The treatment of occlusive arterial disease by transluminal catheter angioplasty. Radiology 1971;99:19–26.

20. Zeitler E. Angiographische Probleme zur Diagnostik und Therapie der renovaskulären Hypertonie. In: Denck H, Flora G, Hilbe G, Piza F, eds. Renovasculäre Hypertonie. Wien: Wiener Medizinische Akademie 1971:113–117.

21. Zeitler E. Perkutane transluminale Verschlussrekanalisation und Stenosedilatation bei Angiopathia obliterans. Aktuel Chir 1971;6:143–154.

22. Zeitler E, Hüring HG, Schoop W, Schmidtke I. Mechanische Behandlung von Beckenarterienstenosen mit der perkutanen Kathetertechnik. Verh Dtsch Ges Herz Kreislaufforsch 1971;37:402–407.

23. Zeitler E. Transluminale Verschlussrekanalisation mit Angiographiekatheter. Herz Kreislaufforsch 1972;4:138–143.

24. Zeitler E, Reichold J, Schoop W, Loew D. Einfluss von Acetylsalicylsäure auf das Frühergebnis nach perkutaner Rekanalisation arterieller Obliterationen nach Dotter. Dtsch Med Wochenschr 1973;98:1285–1288.

25. Zeitler E, Schmidtke I, Schoop W, Giessler R, Dembski J, Mansjoer H. Ergebnisse nach perkutaner transluminaler Angioplastik bei über 700 Behandlungen. Röntgenpraxis 1976;29:78–81.

26. Zeitler E, Grüntzig A, Schoop W, eds. Percutaneous vascular recanalisation: technique, application, clinical results. Berlin: Springer 1978.

Percutaneous Transluminal Thrombus Aspiration

E. Starck, J. C. McDermott, and B. Crummy

In a broad sense, angioplasty is an interventional procedure, either surgical or radiologic, that results in improved blood flow in a previously diseased vessel. Dotter best defined transluminal angioplasty as "a method for fluoroscopically guided catheter treatment of vascular stenoses or obstructions" (3). From a radiologic approach, blood flow in a diseased vessel may be improved by one or more of the following methods:

- Coaxial catheter, "Dotter procedure," or balloon angioplasty
- Laser angioplasty
- Thrombolysis with streptokinase, urokinase, or tissue-specific plasminogen activator administration locally within the occlusion through a "drip" wire or catheter
- Percutaneous aspiration thromboembolectomy (PAT)

The common denominator in these methods is the use of a fluoroscopically directed catheter. Evolution of PAT and its subsequent development into a clinically useful procedure will be discussed.

History

Is it not more than possible that we can look ahead to percutaneous equivalents for embolectomy, thrombectomy, endarterectomy, and even graft placement? Dotter (4)

Surgery

The first successful surgical thromboembolectomy was performed by Lahey who removed an occluding embolus from a common femoral artery (16). Key (16) published the first sizable series of surgical embolectomies, and six of the ten were successful. The surgical treatment was refined by the introduction of vasodilators and anticoagulants. The development of the Fogarty balloon embolectomy catheter substantially improved the surgical treatment of arterial thrombo-embolic disease (8).

Radiology

Greenfield reported his experience with fluoroscopically guided transvenous aspiration of pulmonary emboli through a femoral venotomy (11). Buxton and Mueller reported successful removal of an iat-rogenic clot from the renal artery by transcatheter embolectomy (2). In this case report, an 8 Fr minimally tapered catheter with no sideholes was placed within the renal artery adjacent to the clot, and with aspiration the clot was successfully removed with restoration of patency. This was followed by a report of a more extensive experience by Milland et al. (17). Varying degrees of patency were restored in five occluded renal arteries in four patients by transcatheter thromboembolectomy using a Fogarty catheter. The investigators expressed concern about distal embolization of the clot on withdrawal of the Fogarty balloon catheter and angiographic catheter from the renal artery. Horvath et al. (14) suggested that percutaneous transluminal angioplasty (PTA)-related thromboemboli might be removed with catheter aspiration. However, no clinical experience was cited. Sniderman et al. (21) recorded experience in which post-PTA emboli were successfully aspirated with a catheter in five of six patients. We developed and refined catheters and sheaths for PAT and extended the procedure to treat thrombotic and embolic occlusions unrelated to angioplasty, including graft occlusions (22).

Materials

The following are the equipment and materials that are helpful in the performance of the PAT procedure. An angiography suite equipped with both DSA and mapping capabilities is helpful (6). An arteriogram performed by an intra-arterial DSA approach readily provides assessment of the pathologic changes within the vascular system and minimizes the contrast burden and discomfort to the patient. The mapping technique provides better control and facilitates selective catheterization and passage through stenotic or occlusive lesions. Furthermore, it reduces the risk of subintimal dissection as well as lessening the contrast burden to the patient.

The equipment required for the PAT procedure is a sheath, aspiration catheter, and guide wires. A floppy straight guide wire has often been the most helpful in traversing stenotic or occlusive lesions. A drip wire is helpful in the administration of thrombolytic agents.

The integral components to the sheath system are its size, length, hemostasis valve, sideport, and introducing Van Andel catheter. The sheath is thin-walled, 8 Fr in size, and approximately 45 cm in length. Since it is thin-walled, it will readily accept an 8 Fr aspiration catheter. The length of the sheath is altered depending on the site of the vascular occlusion (e.g., superficial femoral artery versus popliteal artery). The hemostasis valve is tightly fitting. This minimizes blood loss and can be readily exchanged if the sheath entraps thromboembolic material. The sideport provides ready access for medication administration (heparin, nitroglycerine, etc.) or contrast injection for follow-up arteriograms. Since there is a significant disparity between the size of the sheath and the guide wire, the sheath is introduced coaxially over a Van Andel catheter.

The advantages of the sheath system are several:

– It maintains arterial access so that multiple aspirations can be performed
– Its length can be tailored to protect uninvolved portions of the vessel as well as important collaterals that might have clot compressed into them during removal

Three different catheters are used for the aspiration procedure. In large vessel occlusion (e.g., superficial femoral artery, popliteal artery) a 7 Fr or 8 Fr catheter that is thin-walled and minimally tapered at its tip is used for aspiration. These two characteristics facilitate the removal of thromboembolic material of varying sizes on aspiration.

When an occlusion involves the trifurcation vessels, medications (nitroglycerin, nifedipine) are administered to reduce the incidence of spasm. After this, since these vessels are small in diameter and not only prone to go into spasm but also at risk for subintimal guide wire passage, a size 5 Fr straight catheter or 7 Fr Berenstein catheter tapered to 5 Fr are used in conjunction with a smaller guide wire to approach the clot. Once the clot is engaged, the guide wire is removed and the aspiration is performed.

Anticoagulants

Once the arterial access has been obtained and the site of occlusion has been traversed, a bolus of heparin is administered. The usual dose is approximately 5000 U intra-arterial or 100 U/kg body weight. The purpose of heparinization is to minimize continued thrombus formation during the interventional procedure.

Thrombolytic Agents

Currently, there are three commercially available thrombolytic agents. The first two commercially available agents are urokinase and streptokinase. The third agent is tissue-specific plasminogen activator. Before the administration of any thrombolytic agent, it is important to ascertain whether there are any contra-indications to such agents. The contra-indications to lytic therapy are: (10)

– Major surgery within the last 10 days
– Recent serious gastrointestinal or genitourinary bleeding
– Recent trauma, including cardiopulmonary resuscitation
– Severe uncontrolled hypertension
– Atrial fibrillation or known ventricular thrombi
– Subacute endocarditis
– Hemostatic defects secondary to either significant renal or hepatic disease
– Pregnancy
– Stroke within the previous weeks
– Diabetic hemorrhagic retinopathy
– Allergy to streptokinase
– Biopsy at an inaccessible site within the previous 10 days

Thrombolytic therapy (13, 15, 18, 20) is most often administered locally through either a catheter or drip wire embedded within the occluding material. Since there is a significant disparity in price between streptokinase and urokinase, we have been using the more economical streptokinase. However, recent experience suggests that urokinase may be safer and, with fewer complications, actually less expensive. Initially, a test dose of 10,000 U of streptokinase is administered over 10 to 15 minutes while the patient is monitored for any idiosyncratic reaction to the drug. Subsequently, 10,000 U of streptokinase are administered per hour for the next 6 hours. Then a follow-up arteriogram is performed.

If urokinase is the lytic agent, 100,000 U of urokinase are administered over 10 to 15 minutes and subsequently administered at the same dose per hour for the next 6 hours, at which time a follow-up arteriogram is performed.

Antispasmodics

In occlusions involving the renal artery, superior mesenteric artery, distal popliteal, or trifurcation vessels, where vascular spasm is common, before attempts at catheterization, a 10 mg capsule of nifedipine (in which holes have been punched in the capsule) is administered to the patient sublingually or nitroglycerin, is given. Nitroglycerin for intravenous or intra-arterial use is dispensed in 1 cc vials at a concentration of 5 mg/cc. This is diluted so that the final concentration is approximately 50 µg/cc. This is then administered intra-arterially in 2 to 3 cc aliquots before catheterization of vascular beds where spasm may be encountered.

Antiplatelet Therapy

Since the intima of the diseased portion of the vessel is oftentimes disrupted during balloon dilation or catheter aspiration, it provides an abraded surface on which platelets will readily aggregate. Because of this, aspirin, 325 mg by mouth per day, is administered daily following the angioplasty procedure indefinitely.

Performance of Percutaneous Aspiration Thromboembolectomy and its Algorithmic Approach

It is particularly important to remember that the procedure is flexible. The key consideration in the performance of PAT is the restoration of blood flow to an affected extremity by the catheter aspiration of thromboembolic debris (Fig. **1**). However, to achieve a successful outcome, local lysis or balloon angioplasty may be necessary.

Since the majority of our patients have presented with an acutely ischemic lower extremity, the preparation and performance of the PAT procedure in such cases will be considered here (Fig. **2**). However, the PAT procedure has been performed successfully in the renal and superior mesenteric arteries, as well as occluded grafts (e.g., femoropopliteal, femoral-femoral).

PAT has not been applied to the treatment of acutely threatened upper extremities. This is due to our concern for thromboembolic showering within the carotid or vertebral basilar system upon aspiration catheter movements.

When a patient with a cool and ischemic limb is seen, it is important that the radiologist examine the patient for the presence of femoral and distal pulses bilaterally. The skin of the affected extremity is examined for mottling and capillary fill. Finally, the affected lower extremity is assessed for propriocep-

tion and pain and temperature. Each groin in the patient is prepared. Arterial access for the diagnostic arteriogram is obtained by a retrograde common femoral artery puncture on the uninvolved extremity. Arteriograms of the abdominal aorta, pelvic vessels, and the affected lower extremity are then performed.

The importance of a diagnostic arteriogram before surgical or radiologic thromboembolectomy cannot be stressed enough. The arteriogram provides the radiologists and vascular surgeon with the pertinent arterial anatomic and pathologic conditions of the lower extremity. An intra-arterial DSA approach saves not only in the cost of film but more importantly reduces the time necessary to acquire information on the vascular anatomy. An attempt is made to differentiate whether the patient has an acute thrombotic occlusion superimposed on a critical stenosis, an embolic occlusion, or a chronic occlusion with an acute loss of an important collateral. Furthermore, the site of the occlusion is evaluated for its length and the flow distal to it.

If there is no evidence of aorto-iliac disease, and the occlusive segment is within either the superficial femoral artery, popliteal artery, or trifurcation vessels, an antegrade puncture of the common femoral artery in the involved site is performed. Once the needle is satisfactorily within the common femoral artery, a "map" (Fig. **2b**) can be generated by injecting a small amount of dilute contrast media. This will then facilitate the passage of a guide wire into the superficial femoral artery. A straight angiographic catheter or a Berenstein catheter may then be placed over the guide wire and advanced to the level of the occlusion.

Subsequently, a new "map" image is generated, detailing the site of occlusion and the run-off

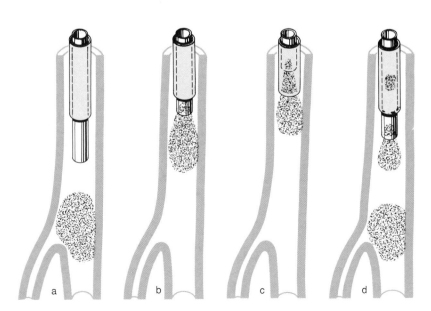

Fig. **1** **Diagram of PAT procedure**
a Coaxial sheath with aspiration catheter is positioned above the lodged embolus at the bifurcation of the vessel
b Embolus is withdrawn toward the sheath
c Embolus remodels to shape of sheath as it is withdrawn proximally
d Fragmentation of the embolus, a major part remains engaged within the tip of the aspiration catheter. Another part has become separated, which will be removed during the next aspiration procedure

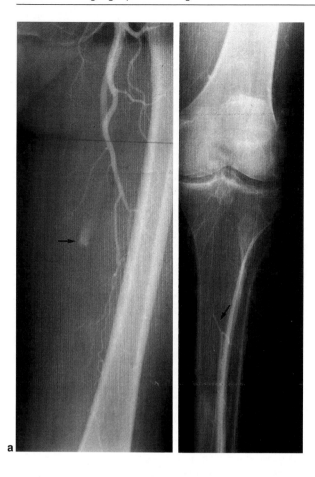

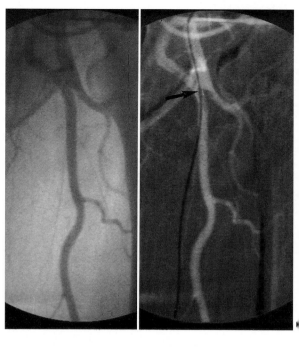

Fig. 2 PAT in embolic disease. A 78-year-old woman with bilateral cardiogenic embolization treated by balloon dilation and PAT without lysis
a Initial angiogram with embolic occlusion of the middle superficial femoropopliteal and proximal tibial arteries
b Pre PAT road map shows progression with complete occlusion of the superficial femoral artery

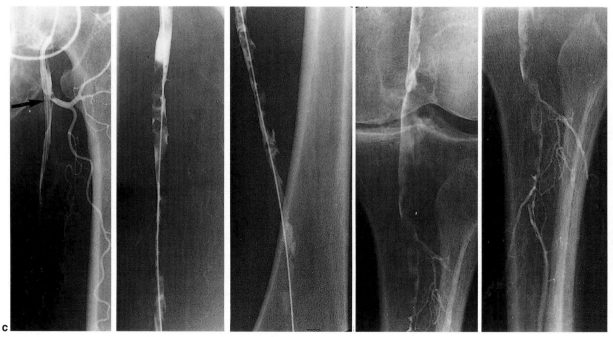

Fig. 2 c Thrombo-embolic material after balloon dilation

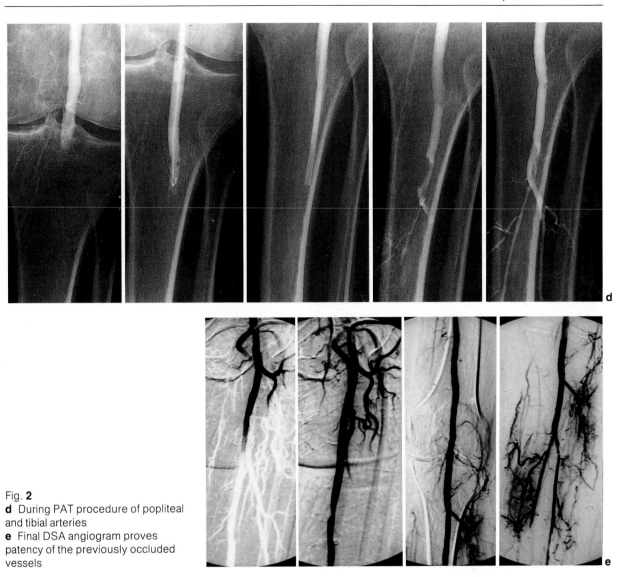

Fig. 2
d During PAT procedure of popliteal and tibial arteries
e Final DSA angiogram proves patency of the previously occluded vessels

immediately distal to it. The occlusion is then probed with a floppy tip straight guide wire. If the guide wire passes easily, there is a strong likelihood that a critical stenosis with subsequent thrombosis was the precipitating event. At this juncture the angiographic catheter is removed, leaving the guide wire in place. Over the guidewire, an 8 Fr sheath system loaded on a leading Van Andel catheter is placed. It is important that the tip of the sheath remain proximal to the occlusive site. The patient is then anticoagulated with 5000 U heparin. An appropriately sized balloon catheter is placed over the guide wire and advanced to the level of the occlusion. When the balloon dilation has been completed, thecatheter is removed, again leaving the guide wire in place. A follow-up arteriogram is performed, using the sideport of the vascular sheath. If the arteriogram demonstrates residual debris at the occlusive site, aspiration is performed.

When the major obstruction is located in the superficial femoral or popliteal artery, the aspiration catheter is moved back and forth while suction is applied. Then it is gradually withdrawn while suction is maintained until flowing blood enters the syringe. At this time, the catheter is removed and its contents are expelled into a gauze-draped basin. The thromboembolic material will be trapped on the gauze, but the blood will sift into the basin. The technique is similar for the tibial vessels except that the aspiration catheter is slowly withdrawn without being moved in a to-and-fro manner. Because these vessels are much smaller than the superficial femoral or popliteal artery, a to-and-fro movement might significantly abrade the vascular endothelium or precipitate spasm.

However, if the guide wire passes through the occlusive site with difficulty, the likelihood of a chronic occlusion is greater. Once the guide wire has been negotiated through the segment of occlusion and the distal run-off has been assessed, a balloon angioplasty is performed. The guide wire is left in place and contrast is injected through the side port of the sheath. If the follow-up arteriogram demonstrates reocclusion of the previously treated site, a small catheter or "drip" wire is lodged within the site of occlusion and thrombolytic therapy is initiated and continued for the next 6 hours. At this time, a follow-up arteriogram is performed. If the occlusive site is patent with satisfactory run-off, the procedure is then terminated. However, if there is residual debris present within the occlusive site, the aspiration catheter is placed through the sheath and advanced over the guide wire to the most inferior site of the occlusion. The guide wire is removed and an aspiration is then performed. In most instances, the thrombolytic therapy will have dissolved any fresh thrombus and the aspiration catheter is then able to remove undissolvable organized thrombus, or atherosclerotic debris, so that sufficient flow will be restored. In this manner, the initial balloon angioplasty fragments the occluding material and provides greater surface contact for thrombolytic therapy. The thrombolytic therapy serves to dissolve any fresh thrombus so that when the PAT is performed it is able to remove any residual fresh thrombus as well as undissolvable material. Thus, local thrombolytic therapy reduces the volume of material that needs to be removed by PAT, and PAT serves to reduce the time and the dose of local thrombolytic therapy.

The PAT procedure has also been applied to embolic occlusions unrelated to PTA (Table 1). In general, these embolic events are predominantly cardiac (1, 5, 7). When such patients were placed on lytic therapy (whether systemic or local), the systemic effects of such medication place a patient at increased risk of continued cardiac embolization. Since the majority of embolizations arise from the heart, lytic therapy increases the risk of lysis of the mural thrombus with subsequent intermittent and embolic showering. These patients may have no major underlying vascular disease and frequently do not present until several embolic events have occurred. Heparinization and several passes with an aspiration catheter will often suffice to restore vascular patency and sufficient flow. Thus, the PAT procedure in embolic phenomena to peripheral vascular sites has provided a less invasive alternative to the Fogarty procedure.

Results

Before a discussion of the PAT procedure, it is important to realize that the aspiration catheter is able to remove fresh, dissolvable thrombus, old non-dissolvable thrombus, and atherosclerotic debris. In contrast, lytic therapy can only dissolve fresh thrombus.

In the past 5 years, the PAT procedure has been found to be an efficacious tool in the restoration of blood flow in certain situations.

To date, 114 procedures in 111 extremities of 109 patients have been performed. PAT has been successful in the treatment of one of two renal artery occlusions, and three of three superior mesenteric artery occlusions. The angiographic length of occlusion has varied from 0.2 to 65 cm (mean, 13.8 cm). To date, PAT has not been performed in humans with upper extremity and cervical artery occlusions.

The clinical success is based on short-term follow-up ranging from approximately 1 week to 2½ years. The nature of the underlying disease usually is the deciding factor in determining the final outcome. No patient became worse by the PAT procedure itself. However, two below-the-knee amputations could not be avoided.

Percutaneous Aspiration Thromboembolectomy versus Fogarty Embolectomy

A comparison of PAT with Fogarty embolectomy is in order. First, the PAT procedure requires merely an antegrade common femoral artery puncture with subsequent sheath placement, rather than a groin incision and common femoral arteriotomy. Inherently then, vascular access for the PAT procedure is less traumatic.

The placement of a sheath is advantageous, since it protects the relatively normal portion of the vessel and perhaps a recent PTA site as well as important collaterals. Also, balloon abrasion of the endothelium is a well-known method of inducing atherosclerotic change in vessels. So the possibility

---

Table 1 Differential diagnosis of acutely threatened limbs

1. Embolic
   A. Cardiac: endocarditis, myocardial infarction, mitral stenosis, atrial fibrillation, left atrial myxoma
   B. Aneurysma: abdominal thoracic aortic aneurysms, popliteal aneurysm
   C. Ulcerated plaque in an atherosclerotic artery
2. Arterial thrombosis
   A. Subintimal hemorrhage within a critically stenotic lesion
   B. Trauma – subintimal flap – dissection
   C. Postsurgical, postcatheterization
3. Low-output congestive heart failure
4. Aortic dissection
5. Hematologic states, e.g. polycythemia
6. Graft thrombosis

exists that the Fogarty balloon may have adverse effects on the vessel wall (9). This may be obviated with the use of a sheath as recently described (19). Also, the sheath will prevent debris from occluding potentially important collaterals during extraction of clot. Experimental animal work has shown that the Fogarty balloon may force clot laterally into collateral vessels.

Fluoroscopic guidance, standard angiographic techniques, and the inherent characteristics of the aspiration catheter make PAT a more controlled procedure. Fluoroscopic monitoring of the guide wire, subsequent observation of catheter movement, and the ability to inject contrast media through the aspiration catheter provide greater control. Since the catheter is placed over a guide wire, it can be easily advanced to the site of the occlusion. Debris is then aspirated when suction is applied to the catheter, and the catheter is removed through the sheath so less of the arterial wall is exposed to abrasion than with the balloon-inflated Fogarty catheter. Finally, the presence of fluoroscopy and the ability to inject contrast serves to monitor the degree of success or failure in removing the thromboembolic material, and allows selective catheterization of branches such as the tibial arteries. The absence of fluoroscopy, the inability to inject contrast with the Fogarty procedure is a distinct disadvantage compared to the PAT procedure.

Recently, there have been reports of the use of portable fluoroscopy in the operating room to aid in the performance of Fogarty embolectomy (19). The placement of a Fogarty balloon catheter through a sheath placed after antegrade common femoral artery puncture has been reported (23). These represent distinct improvements in the standard method of the Fogarty balloon thrombo-embolectomy. However, the inherent limitations of the Fogarty catheter persist: it cannot be advanced over a guide wire, nor can contrast be injected to monitor the location of the catheter. Finally, the literature has isolated reports of advanced atherosclerosis occurring in patients after a Fogarty procedure (12). This may be related to catheter abrasion of the endothelium. To date, a similar experience has not been observed in the PAT patient population.

Complications

Ten hematomas were incurred; three of these required transfusion. One patient had cholesterol microembolizations to her lower extremity. One thrombotic occlusion occurred at the puncture site 48 hours after treatment, and this required surgical correction. Three antegrade dissections within the femoropopliteal region occurred during the antegrade movements with the aspiration catheter. However, luminal patency was restored after final balloon

dilation. The PAT procedure did not result in any deaths. However, one 88-year-old woman died approximately 11 days after the procedure from a myocardial infarction.

Conclusion

The PAT procedure represents another angioplastic tool for the restoration or improvement of blood flow in ischemic extremities. In this series the PAT procedure alone was insufficient in 20% of the cases. In 14% of the cases, PAT in combination with local lysis was sufficient to restore blood flow. In 29% of the patients balloon dilation, local thrombolytic therapy, and PAT were necessary to restore blood flow. Finally, in 37% balloon dilation and PAT were effective. As can be seen, PAT is now a third and major angioplastic tool in the restoration of blood flow. As emphasized previously, the PAT procedure is able to remove both dissolvable fresh thrombus and nondissolvable atherosclerotic debris. Thus, PAT can reduce the need for and duration of local thrombolytic therapy.

Finally, PAT represents an important alternative to the restoration of blood flow in the acutely threatened lower extremity when the aortoiliac system is patent. This technique is less invasive and more expeditious than the classic Fogarty procedure.

References

1. Abbott WM, Maloney RD, McCabe CC, Lee CE, Wirthlin LS. Arterial embolism: a 44 year perspective. Am J Surg 1982;143:460–474.
2. Buxton DR Jr, Mueller CF. Removal of iatrogenic clot by transcatheter embolectomy. Radiology 1974;111:39–41.
3. Castaneda-Zuniga W, ed. Transluminal angioplasty. New York: Thieme-Stratton 1983:1.
4. Dotter C. In: Castaneda-Zuniga W, ed. Transluminal angioplasty. New York: Thieme-Stratton 1983:2.
5. Connett MC, Murray DH Jr, Wenneker WW. Peripheral arterial emboli. Am J Surg 1984;148:14–19.
6. Crummy AB, Starck EE, McDermott JC, Turski PA, Peppler WW. Digital subtraction arteriography (DSA) "road map". Semin Intervent Radiol 1984;1:247–250.
7. Elliott JP, Hageman JH, Szilagyi E, Ramakrishnan V, Bravo JJ, Smith RF. Arterial embolization: problems of source, multiplicity, recurrence and delayed treatment. Surgery 1980;88:833.
8. Fogarty TJ, Cranley JJ, Krause RJ, Strasser ES, Hafner CD. A method for extraction of arterial emboli and thrombi. Surg Gynecol Obstet 1963;116:241–244.
9. Foster JH, Carter JW, Graham CP, Edwards WH. Arterial injury secondary to the use of the Fogarty catheter. Ann Surg 1970;171:971–978.
10. Gallant TE, Athanasoulis CA. Regional infusion of thrombolytic enzymes. In: Athanasoulis CA, Pfister RC, Greene RE, Roberson GH, eds. Interventional radiology. Philadelphia: Saunders 1982:376.
11. Greenfield LJ, Kimmell GO, McCurdy WC: Transvenous removal of pulmonary emboli by vacuum-cup catheter technic. J Surg Res 1960;9:347.
12. Greenwood LH, Hallett JW Jr, Yrizarry JM, Robison JG, Brown SB. Diffuse arterial narrowing after thromboembolectomy with the Fogarty balloon catheter. AJR 1984;142:141–142.

13. Hess H. Clot lysis in peripheral arteries. In: Dotter CT, Grüntzig AR, Schoop W, Zeitler E, eds. Percutaneous transluminal angioplasty. Berlin: Springer 1983:145–153.

14. Horvath L, Illes I, Varo J. Complications of the transluminal angioplasty excluding the puncture site complications. In: Zeitler E, Grüntzig A, Schoop W, eds. Percutaneous vascular recanalization. Berlin: Springer 1978:126–140.

15. Katzen BT. Low-dose streptokinase infusion for the treatment of arterial occlusions. In: Castaneda-Zuniga WR, ed. Transluminal angioplasty. New York: Thieme-Stratton 1983:31–40.

16. Key E. Embolectomy in treatment of circulatory disturbances in extremities. Surg Gynecol Obstet 1923;36:309–316.

17. Milland VG, Sher MH, Deterling RA Jr, Packard A, Morton JR, Harrington JT. Transcatheter thromboembolectomy of acute renal artery occlusion. Arch Surg 1978;113:1086–1092.

18. Risius B, Zelch MG, Graor RA, Geisinger MA, Smith JAM, Piraino DW. Catheter-directed low dose streptokinase infusion: a preliminary experience. Radiology 1984;150:349–355.

19. Robicsek F. Dye-enhanced fluoroscopy-directed catheter embolectomy. Surgery 1984;95:622–624.

20. Roth FJ, Cappius G, Schmitdke I. Early experience of catheter lysis. In: Dotter CT, Grüntzig AR, Schoop W, Zeitler E, eds. Percutaneous transluminal angioplasty. Berlin: Springer 1983:154–160.

21. Sniderman KW, Bodner L, Saddekni S, Srur M, Sos TA. Percutaneous embolectomy by transcatheter aspiration. Radiology 1984;150:357–361.

22. Starck E, McDermott JC, Crummy AB, Turnipseed WD, Acher CW, Burgess J. Percutaneous aspiration thromboembolectomy (PAT). Radiology 1985;156:61–66.

23. Zimmerman JJ, Cipriano PR, Haydon WG, Fogarty TJ. Balloon embolectomy catheter used percutaneously. Radiology 1986;158:260–262.

Local Arterial Thrombolysis

B. T. Katzen and A. van Breda

Since the discovery of thrombolytic agents, there has been interest in applying the benefits of lysis to peripheral vascular occlusive disease where thrombosis is an integral part of the pathophysiologic process. Enthusiasm has varied widely, and development has been limited by the relatively recent availability of thrombolytic agents for general use. The development of interventional vascular radiology in the past 10 to 15 years has been accompanied by increasing investigation of the applicability of these agents in peripheral vascular disease. Local thrombolysis is a technique that has evolved more recently and has continued to improve in safety and efficacy and should be familiar to all angiographers, particularly those performing transluminal angioplasty and other percutaneous interventions. Thrombolysis has become significant as an adjunct to angioplasty in two major areas: the treatment of thrombotic complications and the treatment of atherosclerotic occlusions associated with both thrombotic and atherosclerotic components. Additionally, catheter-directed lysis can be extremely valuable in the management of bypass graft occlusions. The following discussion reviews the current status of thrombolysis in the management of vascular disease.

History

Spontaneous thrombolysis of blood was first described by John Hunter in his *Treatise on the Blood* in 1794. Tillett and Garner discovered the exogenous thrombolytic activity of a streptococcal extract (28). Further investigation resulted in the isolation of the agent, streptokinase (SK), from β-hemolytic streptococci. Urokinase (UK) was isolated from human urine and evaluated for thrombolytic activity (21). The first clinical application of SK was reported in 1955, (29) and the first clinical evaluation of UK occurred shortly thereafter. Although other agents, such as acylated SK-plasminogen complex, which is a combination of SK and plasminogen, have been used intermittently in the intervening years, most clinical experience has involved SK and UK.

Initially, systemic thrombolytic administration was used to treat peripheral vascular disease. However, the increased effectiveness of a locally administered thrombolytic agent was recognized early in the clinical experience (6, 12, 14, 29). Difficulties with intra-arterial administration of high doses of SK and the resultant systemic thrombolytic effect limited the application of this technique. Nonetheless, local infusions of thrombolytic agents have been used since the early 1960s (5), and the angiographic application of this technique was emphasized by Dotter et al (10). This technique has the advantage of focusing the activity of SK at the site of the thrombosis, permitting lower doses and avoiding or minimizing the systemic fibrinolytic effect, but the method was not much used until 1981, when there was a revival of interest in regional thrombolysis (20). Over the past several years, a great deal more experience with this technique has resulted in a better, if still incomplete, understanding of its clinical utility and limitations.

Pharmacology of Fibrinolysis

The body's natural fibrinolytic and hemostatic systems are in equilibrium to preserve vascular integrity and patency. The fibrinolytic system can be activated by endogenous factors in the blood, vascular endothelium, and other tissues, or by thrombolytic agents (exogenous activators). Activation occurs by conversion of the inactive precursor plasminogen, present in circulating blood, or bound to fibrin in clot, to the active proteolytic enzyme plasmin, which hydrolyzes a solid clot into peptide fragments called fibrin degradation products. Plasminogen is synthesized rapidly, and if depleted during thrombolytic activity, returns to normal within 24 hours of cessation of therapy. Plasmin has a very short half-life due its nearly immediate inactivation in the blood by antiplasmin, a specific inhibitor. In a thrombus, the presence of fibrin prevents plasmin inactivation, allowing plasmin activity and fibrin breakdown. Activation of the fibrinolytic mechanism is normally controlled by specific inhibitors at various steps to maintain hemostasis and prevent fibrinolysis except in areas of high fibrin concentration, such as a thrombus (7).

To activate the fibrinolytic mechanism, endogenous activators must be released or exogenous activators administered. Agents such as nicotine are known to induce release of endogenous activators, but these are not clinically useful. Therefore exogenous activators are necessary to produce controlled therapeutic thrombolysis.

Streptokinase

The agent most frequently used for fibrinolytic therapy is streptokinase (SK), a non-enzymatic protein derived from β-hemolytic streptococci that activates fibrinolysis by combining in a 1:1 molar ratio with plasminogen to form an activator complex. The SK-plasminogen is effective in converting free plasminogen into plasmin. The effectiveness of SK is therefore dependent on a sufficient quantity of plasminogen to form the activator complex and act as a substrate for the conversion to plasmin.

SK is antigenic, and prior streptococcal infection induces a variety of antibodies, including a specific SK antibody that directly inactivates the agent by forming an irreversible complex in a 1:1 ratio. Therefore, all the antibody sites must be saturated by an initial loading dose of SK before subsequent doses can act systemically. Antibody titers can vary greatly from person to person. Calculation of the loading dose requirements was performed during initial clinical trials and was based on antibodies in a large patient sample population. Currently, a standardized loading dose of 250,000 U is used, since this dose will neutralize antibodies in 90% of the American population (27). Although the importance of antibodies in systemic fibrinolytic therapy is obvious, the role of antibodies during direct infusion of SK into clot is not known. The antigenicity of SK can cause occasional pyretic reactions (5 to 10% of patients) and cases of serum sickness (31, 37). Anaphylaxis has been reported, but is extremely rare (1) and may have been seen only in earlier preparations.

The half-life of SK is short; however, altered coagulation may persist for hours because of the depletion of fibrinogen and other clotting factors, as well as the presence of fibrin split products (3), which may produce an anticoagulant effect.

Urokinase

The other agent frequently used for fibrinolysis, urokinase (UK), differs from SK in several significant aspects. As opposed to SK, UK is non-antigenic, being derived from human fetal renal cell cultures. Since there are no antibodies to cause inactivation, no loading dose is necessary. Biochemically, UK is a direct plasminogen activator and does not form an intermediate activator complex. All molecules of plasminogen are converted to plasmin in a 1:1 ratio. Because of these characteristics, UK should have a more direct and predictable thrombolytic effect. To date, there has been much greater clinical experience with SK because of its greater availability and reduced cost, but further evaluation of these agents should clarify these differences.

The half-life of UK is short; however, as with SK, prolonged abnormalities after systemic use can result from depleted clotting factors.

Tissue Plasminogen Activator

Currently a new thrombolytic agent is being evaluated: tissue plasminogen activator (t-PA) (7). This agent is an endogenous activator of plasminogen that was originally prepared from human uterine tissue and is now being manufactured by biogenetic engineering techniques. It is normally present in a variety of tissues and is a more specific agent in that it will only activate plasminogen in the presence of fibrin, theoretically limiting its effect to areas of thrombus and avoiding depletion of fibrinogen systemically. Initial results have demonstrated that systemic fibrinogen levels can be significantly reduced, indicating further evaluation and understanding of mechanism of action is necessary. It is hoped that (t-PA) will provide more specific activity and a more predictable response; it may also obviate the need for local infusions (8, 9, 36, 38).

Angiographic Applications of Fibrinolytic Therapy

Postangioplasty or Angiographic Complications

Acute thrombosis may complicate angioplasty in 2 to 3% of patients (18). Because of the presence of fresh thrombus, these situations represent ideal applications of catheter-directed therapy and should be used before surgical intervention if the clinical setting permits. Factors that make these occlusions so amenable to thrombolysis include the acute nature of thrombus, the knowledge of vascular anatomy afforded by the preceding angiography, and the fact that an angiographic catheter is generally in place following the angioplasty. Thrombolysis is generally rapid in these patients, often within a few hours, and the success rates are high (30, 35).

These occlusions are often associated with significant spasm, most likely related to the trauma of angioplasty or the abnormal flap that may have occurred, and vigorous use of intra-arterial vasodilators should accompany therapy, particularly in the acute phase while waiting for initiation of the infusion. As in all patients with acute arterial occlusions, careful clinical assessment of the degree of ischemia should be made, and if neurologic deficit or motor abnormalities are present, immediate surgical intervention should be considered. However, these patients commonly have sufficient collateralization due to their underlying disease, so that tolerance of the occlusion may allow time for thrombolytic infusion.

Occlusions that occur after diagnostic angiographic procedures are generally the result of underlying disease such as diffuse atherosclerotic disease or arterial spasm. Low-dose infusions into areas including the puncture site have been performed with safety, although careful observation of the site being infused is made. The use of vasodilators may also be of value and is recommended.

Embolization after transluminal angioplasty should be approached with caution, since the nature of the embolic material is uncertain and may be atheromatous or thrombotic. Careful clinical assessment is made, and if thrombolytic therapy is used, rapid reperfusion should occur or surgical therapy should follow expeditiously. Because of the distal location of occlusion in these patients, clinical status may not allow time for infusion.

Occlusions of Native Vessels

The nature of an atherosclerotic occlusion is difficult to assess angiographically and may be purely atherosclerotic or be a combination of atheromatous plaque and superimposed thrombus. Most occlusions probably consist of both elements. Although recanalization of total occlusions is possible and can be associated with successful angioplasty, they may be associated with a higher risk of emboli, particularly in the iliac artery (18).

It has been our experience that the thrombotic component of many occlusions can be lysed with thrombolytic therapy (33). The likelihood of successful lysis is partially dependent on age of thrombus, but this may be difficult to evaluate angiographically and is difficult to assess clinically, since there may be little hemodynamic difference between a high-grade stenosis and total occlusion. Data show that success of thrombolysis in relatively acute occlusions of native vessels is high, with total success rates of 82 to 90% (33), but overall success rates of 75 to 80% were noted in occlusions greater than 3 weeks duration.

The angiographic appearance of occlusions can suggest a recent event even in the presence of chronic symptoms (Figs. 1, 2). An irregular proximal or distal end of an occlusion, the lack of well-developed collateral circulation, and an occlusion that does not begin or end at a collateral branch are all suggestive findings, especially in an appropriate clinical setting.

Because of the uncertainties just described, after review of the clinical and angiographic findings by all medical specialists involved, a trial of thrombolytic therapy is frequently used in native vessel occlusions. If lysis is successful, angioplasty or other intervention will follow, and if not, surgical therapy is used. Approximately 70% of native vessel occlusions treated electively have been demonstrated to undergo successful lysis (33).

Renal Artery Occlusions

Occlusions of the renal arteries can be associated with acute symptoms, severe hypertension, or in some cases be asymptomatic. Recent experience has shown that thrombolytic therapy can play a significant role in thrombus formation associated with renal artery disease.

An important group of patients, recently recognized, have presented with symptoms of pulmonary edema and deteriorating renal function, generally associated with anuria. They frequently have a past history of mild chronic renal failure, which has become worse during the acute episode and does not improve in conjunction with improvement in cardiac function. The presence of renal artery occlusion is confirmed by intra-arterial DSA, and the occluded renal artery orifice probed using selective angiography catheters (Fig. 3). UK was infused in all patients while keeping the catheter imbedded in the occluded segment, using techniques similar to those described in the treatment of native iliac artery occlusions. All patients were found to have one kidney that had been removed, or was extremely small due to atrophy or chronic renal artery occlusion. The other kidney had been stenotic and had superimposed thrombosis, leading to acute renal failure. Of 12 patients treated with catheter-directed fibrinolytic therapy, an average creatinine of 8.9 mg/dl was noted, with 9 of the 12 patients having been placed on dialysis acutely. The average duration of anuria was 3.7 days. Thrombolysis was successful in all patients with improved renal function in 10 of 12 patients. All nine patients in whom dialysis had been initiated were able to avoid subsequent dialysis because renal function studies returned to their previous levels.

Perhaps the largest problem is detecting the presence of renal artery occlusion and selecting patients for subsequent intervention. Most patients were presumed to have acute tubular necrosis and were screened using radionuclide flow studies. Unfortunately, these studies cannot differentiate acute tubular necrosis from bilateral renal artery thrombosis. In patients in whom acute tubular necrosis is suspected, renal ultrasound is performed, and if substantial renal parenchyma is found on one side, further evaluation by arterial DSA is performed to obtain more specific anatomic information.

In one patient being evaluated for renovascular hypertension, extensive fresh thrombosis was found in association with a renal artery stenosis and was successfully treated with low-dose thrombolysis. This was associated with an optimal blood pressure response, but little improvement in renal function. The clinical success in these patients confirms the importance of thrombolytic therapy in the management of renal artery occlusions and raises questions regarding the duration of ischemia the kidney can experience and still recover function. The potential benefits associated with successful therapy warrants the aggressive diagnosis in suspected patients, and attempts at thrombolytic therapy if possible.

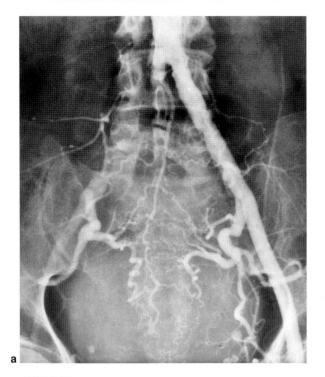

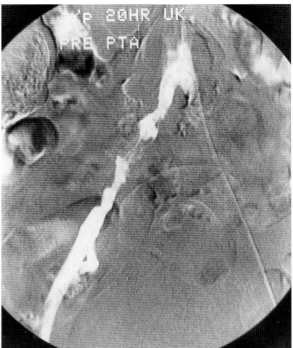

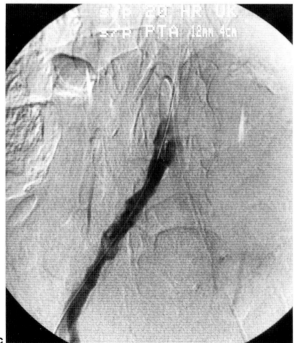

Fig. 1 **A 58-year-old man with an 8-year history of right hip claudication;** stable over the past 2 to 3 years
a Film screen angiography demonstrating a 5 to 6 cm occlusion of the right common iliac artery 2 cm from its origin with abundant collateralization from the contralateral hypogastric artery
b After 5 hours of 80,000 U/h of urokinase through a Simmons I catheter embedded in the common iliac occlusion, partial lysis of the occlusion is demonstrated. After 20 hours of urokinase at 80,000 U/h, restoration of antegrade flow was achieved, with a threadlike lumen in the mid-common iliac artery. Transluminal angioplasty was performed with a 12 mm outer diameter balloon
c Intra-arterial DSA after UK and angioplasty

Fig. 2 **A 76-year-old woman with left calf claudication for 6 months.** Peripheral arteriogram demonstrating a 12 cm left superficial femoral artery occlusion at the adductor canal

a Selective left superficial femoral arteriogram demonstrating an abrupt cut-off at the origin of the left superficial femoral artery and filling of a segment of superficial femoral artery proximal to the distal collateral. An open-ended guide wire was placed through a 5 Fr catheter, with the tip at the origin of the occlusion, demonstrating thrombus in the occluded segment. The open-ended guide wire was passed through the occluded segment

b The open-ended guide wire withdrawn to the proximal portion of the occlusion

c After 22 hours of UK at 50,000 U/hr, high-grade stenosis at the adductor canal was demonstrated

d Arterial DSA after angioplasty, demonstrating a widely patent segment

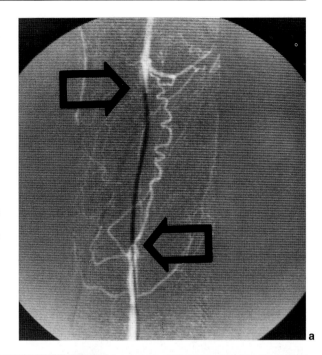

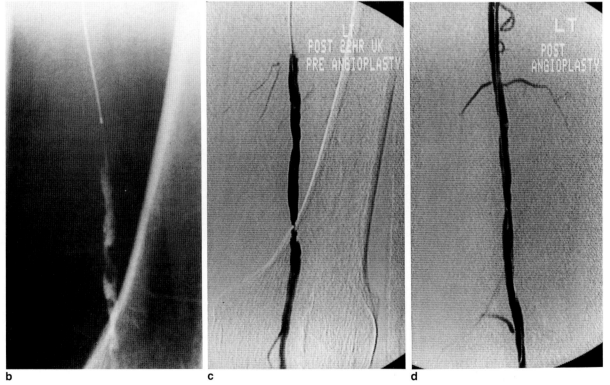

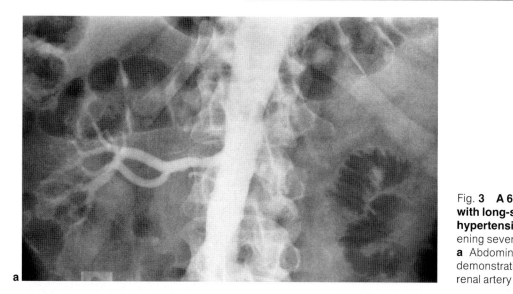

Fig. **3**   **A 60-year-old woman with long-standing history of hypertension,** recently worsening severely
a Abdominal aortogram demonstrating no filling of the left renal artery

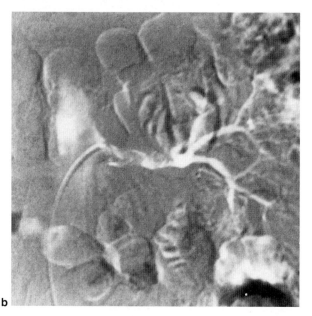

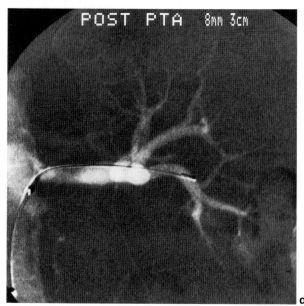

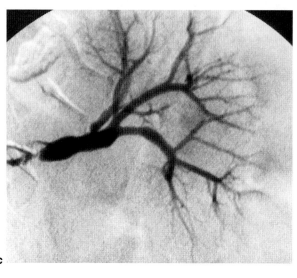

Fig. **3**
b After probing the left renal artery with a selective catheter, injection of contrast demonstrates patency, with abundant intraluminal thrombosis
c Following 12 h of UK at 80000 U/h, resolution of the thrombus is noted, with an underlying high-grade stenosis at the catheter tip
d DSA following balloon angioplasty demonstrates a widely patent lumen, with no evidence of distal occlusion

Thrombolysis of Occluded Bypass Grafts

Treatment of occluded arterial bypass grafts is another important application of catheter-directed thrombolysis (34). As with all forms of occlusions, thrombus is a manifestation of underlying disease and this method of therapy offers both diagnostic and therapeutic benefits (Fig. **4**). Stenoses at graft anastomoses can occur at both proximal and distal sites and can be difficult to document intra-operatively. In the case of saphenous vein bypass grafts, fibrinolytic therapy and transluminal angioplasty may save the saphenous vein and obviate the need for revision and replacement with synthetic material. There may be prognostic significance in the success of thrombolytic therapy; in two series, when poor run-off was the cause of graft occlusion, repeated occlusions occurred unless some other run-off was established surgically (25, 34). Patients with occluded bypass grafts present with other medical abnormalities, making them poor surgical candidates. Thrombolysis may also allow operation to be delayed in patients who are poor operative risks (34).

General principles of patient selection are similar to those described previously. Acute occlusions of grafts that are less than 6 weeks old are generally the

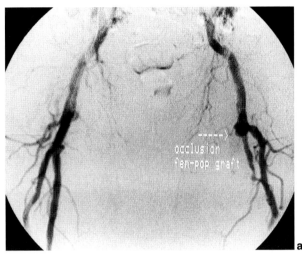

Fig. **4   A 70-year-old woman with 2-day-old occlusion of a femoropopliteal saphenous vein bypass graft** which had been placed 2 years earlier
a Arterial DSA from a contralateral approach, demonstrating the origin of the occluded bypass graft (arrow). Following anterograde puncture of the left common femoral artery, a 5 Fr catheter was placed in the vein graft, through which an open-ended guide wire was placed for infusion of urokinase

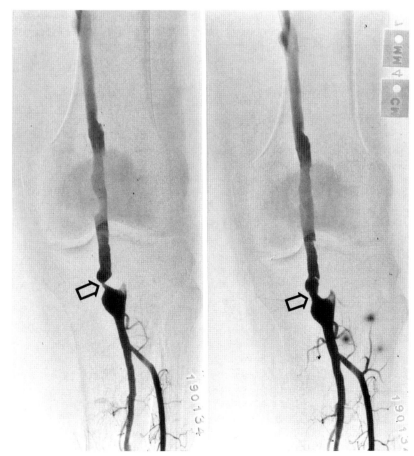

Fig. **4   b** After 14 h of lytic therapy, complete lysis is noted, with distal anastomotic stenosis (arrow)
c Angiogram after successful angioplasty of the distal stenosis

b   c

result of technical problems and are better treated surgically (39). This approach also avoids the potential problems of infusing a recent operative site. The clinical situation should be taken into account, and if operation is not feasible and there is a potential for limb loss, thrombolysis should be attempted.

There have been reports of extravasation of contrast during thrombolytic therapy performed in Dacron grafts, due to leakage through interstices of the graft (26). Most of these have been asymptomatic or insignificant, but significant bleeding can occur (34). In our experience this has not been noted with the use of UK. In the extremities, sites of infusion can be observed clinically, but intra-abdominal sites can bleed without being recognized early, and this potentially severe complication should be borne in mind.

Dosage and Selection of Fibrinolytic Agents

Since the initial description of catheter-directed fibrinolysis, several regimens for administration have been described using both SK and UK. Our therapeutic objective is to achieve successful clot lysis in the most expeditious fashion, with the least complications, and producing little or no systemic effect. Because of underlying arterial catheters and frequently present medical conditions that may be associated with higher risks of bleeding from systemic lysis, and the fact that catheter-directed therapy requires lower doses of the active agent, the technique of low-dose catheter-directed therapy has evolved. By delivering the fibrinolytic agent directly into the thrombus, it is possible to activate plasminogen bound to fibrin without activating circulating plasminogen. This important principle leads to greater efficacy when compared with the use of systemic doses to treat arterial occlusions and provides the basis for achieving no significant systemic effect. This concept was first demonstrated by Dotter who achieved successful lysis with doses as low as ¹⁄₂₀th of systemic doses (10).

Most subsequent series have reported use of SK in low doses (5000 to 10000 U/hr), because of its low cost and ready availability (2, 4, 10, 16, 20, 25, 30, 34).

Hess et al. (17) described a more rapid, higher dose SK infusion technique in which 1000 to 3000 U boluses were injected directly into the thrombus. After several minutes, and under fluoroscopic observation, thrombus and lytic products were vigorously aspirated, and the catheter advanced. This process was then repeated and the catheter advanced again. The duration of these infusions ranged from 1 to 5 hours, with the patient remaining on the angiographic table throughout the procedure. Overall, success rates were similar to those reported in low-dose, slower infusions, but this technique has not

been widely utilized in the United States, probably in part because of the time constraints in most angiography departments. Bleeding complications are reportedly lower, possibly because of the smaller total SK dose.

Higher rates of intra-arterial SK infusion have rarely been used for peripheral vascular occlusions, although they are common in the treatment of acute coronary occlusions. The necessity for rapid revascularization in coronary occlusions to prevent myocardial necrosis does not apply to most peripheral arterial occlusions. Limited experience with higher doses of SK fails to demonstrate any significant improvement in success rates or lysis time in the peripheral circulation.

More recently, investigators have been evaluating the use of UK for catheter-directed thrombolysis, and significant clinical differences appear to exist, leading to UK becoming the preferred agent. It is not neutralized by circulating antibodies, as is SK, and this may result in increased success rates (32). Additionally, there appears to be little or no systemic effect. We generally infuse 40,000 to 80,000 U/hr in a manner similar to that described for SK. Another protocol described by McNamara and Fisher (22) showed improved results using initial higher doses of UK followed by lower hourly dose rates. Infusions were started at 4000 U/min for 2 hours followed by 1000 U/min and included the use of concomitant heparinization. A recent series of 122 patients by Van Breda et al. (33) confirmed the higher success rates and reduced complication rates of infusions utilizing UK. Additionally, there seemed to be little significant difference between doses of 50,000 U/hr and doses exceeding 100,000 U/hr. MacNamara and Fischer (22) use an initial regimen of 4000 U/min for 2 hours, followed by longer infusion of 1000 U/min (60,000 U/hr). With this regimen, too, a higher success rate and lower incidence of bleeding were noted. Despite its increased cost, the increased safety and efficacy of UK make it the agent of choice for catheter-directed thrombolytic therapy.

Patient Care

Once fibrinolytic infusions are initiated, patients are placed in an intensive care unit for monitoring of the puncture site, bleeding parameters, and clinical status of the affected extremity. This includes frequent Doppler examinations and close observation for bleeding.

Periodic angiographic monitoring is performed by returning the patient to the angiographic suite, and the catheter is advanced, if necessary, as lysis progresses. Care is taken to minimize manipulation at the puncture site. The coaxial system allows advancement of the small infusion guide wire or catheter, without manipulation at the puncture site. Contamination of the puncture site during repeat manipulations probably occurs but has not been clinically significant. Nonetheless, because of the potentially devastating complications of vascular prostheses, these patients are given broad-spectrum antibiotics.

If no progress is noted during the first 6 to 12 hours, the infusion is terminated. Generally during this time, some evidence of lysis will be noted, possibly associated with clinical improvement. If no further progress is noted in the subsequent 12 to 24 hours, the infusion is stopped. All decisions are made in the context of the clinical status of the patient and therapeutic alternatives.

At the completion of thrombolytic therapy, angiography is again performed to outline any underlying stenosis or other cause of occlusion, which may then be treated immediately by angioplasty, if feasible, or surgery, if necessary. In patients in whom complete lysis is achieved and no underlying cause is found, consideration of long-term anticoagulation should be considered. Patients who are treated by angioplasty after lysis are not generally anticoagulated.

Hematologic Monitoring

Many attempts to avoid or minimize systemic effects during locally administered fibrinolysis have been made, a task made more difficult by the lack of a single laboratory parameter that predicts the likelihood of bleeding accurately. Thrombin time is the single most useful parameter (3), but significant bleeding can occur with a normal thrombin time. In addition, the thrombin time is altered in the presence of heparin, which some have used concomitantly during fibrinolytic infusions. Fibrinogen depletion occurs during systemic fibrinolysis but should be reduced during lower dose infusions, and depletion has been associated with an increased incidence of bleeding complications (30).

Recommendations for laboratory monitoring, based on our clinical experience, include a baseline coagulation profile of thrombin time, fibrinogen, partial thromboplastin time, and prothrombin time at the start of therapy, primarily to screen for unsuspected underlying abnormalities. Thrombin time and fibrinogen are repeated at 4 hours to identify patients with an abnormally rapid onset of systemic effect. This has been noted to occur clinically only in patients being infused with SK. If this occurs, the hourly dose is reduced or discontinued and lab work repeated in 4 hours. If no significant alteration is noted, the thrombin time and fibrinogen are repeated at 12 hours or immediately before the next angiographic check. If the fibrinogen declines to levels below 100 mg/dl the infusion is slowed or discontinued, and cryoprecipitate or fresh frozen plasm is given to restore fibrinogen levels. In clinical experience this has not been necessary during infusions of UK, since significant reduction in fibrinogen has only been rarely observed.

Some physicians recommend concomitant anticoagulation to reduce the risk of pericatheter thrombosis (22); however, this has been unnecessary in our experience when using a small coaxial infusion technique and avoiding the placement of catheters through areas of reduced flow.

The use of t-PA in peripheral arterial occlusions is currently under evaluation at lower doses than those used for myocardial infarction, and with techniques similar to those described earlier. At this time, there is insufficient data to make conclusions as to its efficacy or safety compared with UK.

Results

Results of catheter-directed fibrolytic infusions have varied as questions regarding agents of choice, technique, and dose have been evaluated in the literature (Table 1), ranging from 40 to 90%, with an

Table **1** Success rates of local thrombolysis of peripheral occlusions

References		No. cases	Drug	Dose (U/hr)	Success* (%)
Totty et al.	(30)	28	SK	5000	65
Risius et al.	(25)	56	SK	5000	92 (acute)
					38 (chronic)
Bernie et al.	(4)	16	SK	5000	75
Becker et al.	(2)	57	SK	5000	69
Wolfson et al.	(40)	50	SK	5000	80
Wook et al.	(41)	17	SK	5000	82
Eskridge et al.	(11)	27	SK	5000	52
Hess et al.	(17)	136	SK	1000–3000/5 min	69
Van Breda et al.	(32)	24	UK	40,000–60,000	79
McNamara and Fischer	(22)	93	UK	4000 U/min then 1000 U/min	81
Graor et al.	(13)	122	UK	40,000–80,000	83

* Success is defined as either complete lysis angiographically or lysis with significant clinical improvement

average of approximately 75%. Comparisons of success rates in various studies are difficult due to the many factors that may influence success. First, as is true in systemic thrombolysis, acute occlusions respond better than chronic ones. For example, angioplasty-induced thromboses respond quite well, with complete or significant lysis noted in most patients (33). In our experience with 18 postangioplasty thromboses, successful lysis was achieved in 17, the single failure due to extensive atheromatous disease with poor run-off.

A second general observation has been that short occlusions tend to be more successful than longer ones. Success rates in bypass grafts is similar to native vessel occlusions, with the same mechanical factors affecting success.

UK has been noted to produce higher success rates with reduced morbidity and is currently the agent of choice. Further studies by other investigators may confirm further improvement in results.

Complications: Recognition and Treatment

Although in our own experience the safety of fibrinolytic therapy has improved significantly, treatment is complex, technical, and complications can occur. These may result from the angiographic aspects of the procedure, such as puncture site thrombosis, or may be specific to the thrombolytic therapy, such as hemorrhage, distal embolization, or pericatheter thrombosis. Additionally, adverse reaction to some agents can occur.

Pericatheter Thrombosis

Development of thrombus along the angiographic catheter despite successful lysis being documented at the distal end has been reported in as many as 35% of infusions (2, 11, 22) and was noted by us occasionally in earlier experience. Several factors may contribute to this phenomenon, but poor flow in the presence of distal occlusion, coupled with the almost universal presence of diffuse vascular disease along the path of the catheter, is the primary reason for thrombosis, and the presence of an angiographic catheter further compromises flow and is probably the precipitating factor in thrombus formation. In addition, there may be an increased thrombogenic milieu in some patients with ongoing thrombosis. It has been our observation that this can occur in the presence of adequate systemic anticoagulation if flow is reduced severely (19).

For this reason, the smallest possible infusion device should be used, particularly in the more distal vessels, and the intravascular course of the infusion catheter should be kept to a minimum, i.e., antegrade puncture and access to the superficial femoral

artery, rather than approaching from the contralateral femoral artery. Use of coaxial systems using a 5 Fr catheter maintained in an approximal position and an open-ended guide wire positioned in the occlusion is the most ideal arrangement and is used most frequently. In cases of infusions of the superficial femoral artery or distally, the 5 Fr catheter may be used for distal manipulation, but once the open-ended guide wire is in place, the catheter is withdrawn to the approximate level of the lesser trochanter. Injection of contrast proximally in the artery, before initial distal manipulation, should be performed to assist in assessing the degree of flow around the catheter.

In cases of common iliac occlusion, open-ended guide wires and coaxial devices are not generally used except in occlusions of the more distal external iliac artery, or in cases of long segment graft occlusions.

Hemorrhage

The most significant potential problem with low-dose thrombolysis, as with systemic infusions, is hemorrhage, although the objective of low-dose infusions is to reduce this risk to negligible levels. The rate of bleeding in reported series varies from 4 to 25% (2, 4, 10, 13, 20, 22, 25, 34) and has been noted to be worse with SK than with UK in our most recent experience (32). Most bleeding occurs at the arterial puncture site, but bleeding at remote sites has been noted, including intracranial bleeding with SK. The use of concomitant heparinization adds to the risk of bleeding and may create confusion as to the cause of bleeding when it occurs. Local bleeding can generally be controlled by manual compression and terminating the infusion. Patients with known intracranial disease are at higher risk of bleeding if systemic effects occur, but can probably be treated more safely with low-dose UK. Similarly, patients with known gastrointestinal bleeding or other bleeding problems are not treated. Because of potentially life-threatening risks, thrombolytic therapy should not be undertaken without due considerations of the risk to benefit ratio and treatment alternatives. However, in our experience, low-dose UK has been used safely in patients with many underlying risk factors, including being used in intraoperative settings.

Laboratory monitoring of thrombolytic infusions does not accurately predict the likelihood of bleeding or of successful lysis. The risk of bleeding does seem to increase with length of infusion and we therefore attempt to limit the length of infusion to 24 hours (15, 23). Maintaining fibrinogen levels above 100 mg/dl may help prevent bleeding complications, and infusion of cryoprecipitate should be considered if fibrinogen declines below these levels. Additionally, thrombolysis of synthetic prosthetic grafts, especially those made of Dacron (24) carries the risk of extravasation through the graft interstices, which could possibly cause life-threatening hemorrhage, although this has not been noted in our clinical experience.

Embolization

Some patients experience dramatic worsening of ischemia during thrombolytic therapy; this is usually due to distal embolization of thrombotic material as lysis progresses. Careful angiographic evaluation after therapy may demonstrate some evidence of distal emboli (17, 20, 34, 40) but most often the clinical status improves within 1 hour as lysis progresses. Documented distal embolization, in most reports, has responded to continued thrombolytic therapy. If significant clinical deterioration persists longer than 1 hour, angiography should be repeated and surgical intervention performed if necessary, but, in general, continued thrombolytic therapy will result in clinical improvement.

Fatal bilateral renal embolization and mesenteric artery embolism have been reported during attempted lysis of aortic occlusions (41). In general, lysis of abdominal aortic occlusions is not recommended unless no therapeutic options are present, because of the amount of thrombus present reducing the likelihood of success and increasing the likelihood of complication.

Embolization of thrombus can occur due to contrast injection at the origin of an occlusion if injection is made too forcefully. These injections should be made carefully when occlusions are at the origin of a vessel, such as the superficial femoral artery, where thrombus could reflux into the profunda femoral artery. If reflux of thrombus should occur, initial thrombolytic therapy should be directed at this site, but surgery may be necessary if significant clinical deterioration occurs.

In general, all catheter manipulations during thrombolysis should be performed with caution, since the clot softens before total lysis.

Allergic Reactions

Early preparations of SK were associated with a high incidence of allergic reactions, including pyrexia, musculoskeletal pain, and even anaphylaxis. Allergic reactions to UK is extremely rare and is not generally clinically significant. Pretreatment with corticosteroids is not recommended, and antipyretic agents and symptomatic treatment is generally sufficient. If SK is being used, conversion to UK will avoid allergic manifestations.

Conclusion

Intra-arterial thrombolytic infusion has a definite role in today's management of peripheral vascular disease and is an important part of the interventional radiologist's armamentarium. In addition to its therapeutic benefits, it has contributed significantly to our understanding of the nature of atherosclerotic occlusion and has raised many questions, including those regarding the age of thrombus in the occluded vessel which may still be able to be lysed.

It is useful in occlusions related to vascular intervention, such as transluminal angioplasty or catheterization procedures, and also plays a significant role in the treatment of occlusions of native vessels and grafts. Careful clinical assessment of patients and consideration of therapeutic alternatives is necessary to minimize the risk and maximize benefits. The pharmacology and physiology of thrombolysis should be familiar to practicing angiographers and others interested in this field.

References

1. Baumgartner TG, Davis RG. Streptokinase induced anaphylactic reaction. Clin Pharmacol 1982;1:470–471.
2. Becker GJ, Rabe FE, Richmond BD, Yune HY, Dilley RS, Bang NU, Glover JL, Klatte EC. Low dose fibrinolytic therapy. Radiology 1983;148:668–670.
3. Bell WR, Meek AG. Guidelines for the use of thrombolytic agents. N Engl J Med 1979;301:1266–1270.
4. Bernie GA, Dandyk DF, Zierler RE, Thiele BL, Strandness DE. Streptokinase treatment of acute arterial occlusions. Ann Surg 1983;198:185–191.
5. Biggs JC. Thrombolytic therapy in arterial and venous thrombosis. Aust Ann Med 1970;19(suppl):19–24.
6. Boyles PW, Meyer WH, Graff J. Comparative effectiveness of intravenous and intra-arterial fibrinolysis therapy. Am J Cardiol 1960;6:439–445.
7. Collen D. On the regulation and control of fibrinolysis. Haemostasis 1980;43:77–89.
8. Collen D, Rijken DC, van Damme T, Billau A. Purification of human tissue-type plasminogen activator. Thromb Haemost 1982;48:294–296.
9. Collen D, Verstack M. Systemic thrombolytic therapy of acute myocardial infarction? Circulation 1983;68:462–465.
10. Dotter CT, Rösch J, Seaman AJ. Selective clot lysis with low-dose streptokinase. Radiology 1974;111:31–37.
11. Eskridge JM, Becker GJ, Rabe FE, Richmond BD, Holden RW, Yune HY, Klatte EC. Catheter related thrombosis and fibrinolytic therapy. Radiology 1983;149:429–432.
12. Freeman AH, Bang NV, Grossi LE. Factors affecting the formation and dissolution of experimental thrombi. Am J Cardiol 1960;6:426–429.
13. Graor RA, Risius B, Young J, Geisinger MA, Zelch MG, Smith JA, Ruschhaupt WF. Low-dose streptokinase for selective thrombolysis: systemic effects and complications. Radiology 1984;152:35–39.
14. Guril NJ, Callahan W, Hufnagel HV. High-dose short-term local urokinase for clearing femoral thrombi by vasodilatation and thrombolysis. J Surg Res 1976;20:381–386.
15. Hargrove WC, Barker CF, Berkowitz HD, Perloff LJ, McLean G, Freiman D, Ring EJ, Roberts B. Treatment of acute arterial and graft thromboses with low dose streptokinase. Surgery 1982;92:981–990.
16. Hargrove WC, Berkowitz HD, Freiman DB, McLean G, Ring EJ, Roberts B. Recanalization of totally occluded femoropopliteal vein grafts with low dose streptokinase infusion. Surgery 1982;92:890–895.
17. Hess H, Inguish H, Mietaschk A, Rath H. Local low dose fibrinolytic infusions of peripheral arterial occlusions. N Engl J Med 1982;307:1627–1630.
18. Katzen BT. Percutaneous transluminal angioplasty for arterial disease of the lower extremities. AJR 1984;142:23–25.

19. Katzen BT, Edwards KC, Albert AS, van Breda A. Low dose fibrinolysis in peripheral vascular disease. J Vasc Dis 1984;1:718–722.
20. Katzen BT, van Breda A. Low-dose streptokinase in the treatment of arterial occlusions. AJR 1981;136:1171–1178.
21. MacFarlane RG, Pilling J. Observations on fibrinolysis: plasminogen plasmin and antiplasmin content of human blood. Lancet 1946;ii:562–565.
22. McNamara TO, Fischer R. Thrombolysis of peripheral arterial and graft occlusions: improved results using high dose urokinase. AJR 1985;144:769–775.
23. Mori KW, Bookstein JJ, Heeney DJ, Bardin JA, Donnelly KJ, Rhodes GA, Dilley RB, Warmath MA, Bernstein EF. Selective streptokinase infusion: clinical and laboratory correlates. Radiology 1983;148:677–682.
24. Rabe FE, Becker GJ, Richmond BD, Yune HY, Holden RW, Dilley SR, Klatte EC. Contrast extravasation through dacron grafts: a sequela of low dose streptokinase therapy. AJR 1982;138:917–920.
25. Risius B, Zelch M, Graor R, Geisinger MA, Smith JAM, Piraino DW. Catheter-directed low dose streptokinase infusion: a preliminary experience. Radiology 1984;150:349–355.
26. Rosner NH, Doris PE. Contrast extravasation through a goretex graft: a sequela of low dose streptokinase therapy. AJR 1984;143:633–634.
27. Sharma GVRK, Cella G, Parisi AF, Sasahara AA. Thrombolytic therapy. N Engl J Med 1982;306:1268–1276.
28. Tillet WS, Garner RL. The fibrinolytic activity of hemolytic streptococci. J Exp Med 1933;58:485–502.
29. Tillet WS, Johnson AJ, McCarthy WF. The intravenous infusion of the streptococcal fibrinolytic principle (streptokinase) into patients. J Clin Invest 1955;34:169–175.
30. Totty WG, Gilula LA, McClennan BL, Ahmed P, Sherman L. Low dose intravascular thrombolytic therapy. Radiology 1982;143:59–69.
31. Totty WG, Romano T, Benian GM, Gilula LA, Sherman LA. Serum sickness following streptokinase therapy. AJR 1982;138:143–144.
32. Van Breda A, Katzen BT, Deutsch AS. Urokinase versus streptokinase in local thrombolysis. Radiology 1987;165:109–111.
33. Van Breda A, Katzen BT, Picus D, Steinberg DL. Intra-arterial urokinase infusion for treatment of acute and chronic arterial occlusions. Radiology 1986;161(P):104.
34. Van Breda A, Robinson JC, Feldman L. Local thrombolysis in the treatment of graft occlusions. J Vasc Surg 1984;1:103–112.
35. Van Breda A, Waltman AC. Low dose thrombolysis for arterial disease of the lower extremities. Int Angiol 1983;2:75–83.
36. Van de Werf F, Ludbrook PA, Bergmann SR. Coronary thrombolysis with tissue-type plasminogen activator in patients with evolving myocardial infarction. N Engl J Med 1984;310:609–613.
37. Weatherbee TC, Esterbrooks DJ, Katz DA. Serum sickness following selective intracoronary streptokinase. Curr Ther Res 1984;35:433–438.
38. Weimar W, Stibbe J, van Seyen AJ, Billiau A, de Somer P, Collen D. Specific lysis of an iliofemoral thrombus by administration of extrinsic (tissue-type) plasminogen activator. Lancet 1981;ii:1018–1020.
39. Whittemore AD, Clowes AW, Couch NP, Nannick JA. Secondary femoropopliteal reconstruction. Ann Surg 1981;193:35–42.
40. Wolfson RH, Kumpfe DA, Lutherford RB. Role of intra-arterial streptokinase in treatment of arterial thromboembolism. Arch Surg 1984;119:697–702.
41. Wook WA, Tisnado J, Cho SR. Visceral embolization during low dose fibrinolysis of aortic graft occlusion. AJR 1983;141:1055–1056.

Angiographic Management of Intestinal Ischemia

K. Mathias

Occlusive vessel disease of visceral arteries produces different clinical signs, depending on location and extension of the circulatory impairment as well as on the time involved in the development of the pathologic process. Acute and chronic mesenteric insufficiency must be differentiated according to complaints of the patient, acuteness of symptoms, and importance for the patient's life.

History

In the 15th century, Antonio Beneviene probably reported for the first time the occlusion of the superior mesenteric artery. In 1830, Cruveilhier described the pathologic findings of mesenteric artery occlusion. At that time, the collateral circulation between the celiac and superior mesenteric arteries via the superior pancreaticoduodenal artery, as mentioned, by Chaussier in 1818, was well known. Riolan (1580–1657), an anatomist in Paris, found the collateral pathway between the superior and inferior mesenteric artery (ramus anastomoticus magnus arteriae colicae sinistrae), but did not recognize its pathophysiologic importance. Chiene reported in 1868 the case of a 65-year-old woman with chronic occlusions of celiac and mesenteric arteries, but without pathologic signs of intestinal gangrene.

The details of acute embolic occlusion of the superior mesenteric artery were excellently described by Cohn (1860), Gerhardt (1863), and Kussmaul (1864). Litten examined in 1875 the pathophysiology of acute bowel ischemia by experimental ligation of the mesenteric artery. Elliot successfully resected a small bowel segment with ischemic gangrene for the first time in 1895. Obliteration of acute mesenteric occlusion was successfully performed by Klass in 1951.

The clinical picture of chronic mesenteric insufficiency was described by Howse (1878), Hasenfeld (1879), Schnitzler (1901), and Ortner (1902). Schnitzler proposed the term "dyspepsia intermittens arteriosclerotica," Ortner designated the disease as "dyspragia intermittens angiosclerotica intestinalis." The term "angine abdominale" is attributed to Bacelli (1904). The first operative correction of the disease followed more than 50 years later when Shaw and Maynard performed a superior mesenteric endarterectomy in 1958.

Table 1 Classification of mesenteric insufficiency

Acute	Chronic
Nonocclusive	Intestinal angina
Occlusive	Fibromuscular dysplasia
Arterial	Arteritis
Embolic	Tumor
Thrombotic	
Dissection	
Venous	
Portal Hypertension	
Tumor	

Today, the different types of mesenteric insufficiency are classified as listed in Table 1.

Pathophysiology

The abdominal viscera, including parenchymal organs, intestine, mesentery, and vessels, are supplied by 1000 ml/min of blood. The intestinal oxygen consumption is rather high with 80 ml/min. During digestion, the blood supply increases up to 4000 ml/min.

In acute mesenteric occlusions the short ischemic tolerance of the bowel is responsible for mucosal necrosis within a period of 3 hours and gangrene of the bowel wall in 6 to 12 hours after onset of symptoms.

Flow is diminished at rest when the cross-sectional area of the superior mesenteric artery is reduced more than 80%. In these cases the typical symptoms of abdominal angina will appear after every meal when a sufficient collateral network is missing.

Diagnosis

In all patients suspected of having acute or chronic mesenteric ischemia plain radiographs of the chest and abdomen are obtained followed by B-scan and Doppler ultrasound. The next step to the final diagnosis is angiography (1, 2, 4, 6, 20). Midstream abdominal aortography should be performed in anteroposterior and lateral projections. The lateral view is essential because occlusions or stenoses of the celiac, superior or inferior mesenteric arteries are usually obscured in the anteroposterior projection by the opacified abdominal aorta. If the aortogram does not reveal proximal vessel obstructions, selective visceral angiography, especially of the superior mesenteric artery, is performed to detect or rule out small arterial branch occlusions, mesentericoportal thrombosis or nonocclusive disease.

Acute Mesenteric Insufficiency

The acute impairment of the mesenteric circulation can be caused by arterial occlusions, mesenteric vein thrombosis, and nonocclusive vessel disease. The main stem of the celic, superior or inferior mesenteric artery can be occluded by:

- Arterial embolism
- Arterial thrombosis
- True or dissecting aortic aneurysm
- Aneurysm of mesenteric artery
- Compression of artery
- Traumatic artery occlusion.

Most of the patients (60 to 80%) have arterial embolism. Local thrombosis occurs in 20 to 30% of the cases. Nonocclusive vessel disease (synonyms: hemorrhagic necrotizing enteropathy, ischemic enteropathy, hemorrhagic necrosis of the intestine, non-occlusive mesenteric ischemia) is encountered in 20% of the patients and often begins with lingering symptoms.

The superior mesenteric artery is affected in 90% of visceral embolic artery occlusions because of the funnel form of the mesenteric origin and the straight course of the vessel in continuation of the aorta, which itself bends posteriorly and follows the lumbar lordosis. Embolism into the celic or inferior mesenteric artery is less frequently encountered.

Prerequisite for an acute thrombotic occlusion is a diseased vessel wall. Atherosclerosis, fibromuscular dysplasia, and the different types of angiitis, such as endangiitis obliterans, periarteritis nodosa. Takayasu's disease, are important pathogenetic factors. Preferentially, thrombotic occlusions occur in the main stem of the superior and inferior mesenteric arteries. A period of mesenteric artery stenosis, in 40% of the patients with the clinical signs of intermittent mesenteric insufficiency, precedes the thrombotic event.

The prognosis of acute visceral artery occlusions depends on the location and the functional state of the collaterals. The spontaneous course of acute occlusion of the superior mesenteric artery has a fatal outcome in all patients within a few days. A limited small bowel gangrene will follow an occlusion of one or several branches of the superior mesenteric artery. Occlusions of celiac and inferior mesenteric arteries produce no severe impairment of the afflicted organs and are generally survived with minor complications, such as transient upper abdominal pain or ischemic colitis.

The high risk of extended bowel infarction in superior mesenteric artery occlusion can be explained by the length of the supplied bowel, the 2-dimensional ramification of the mesenteric branches, and the isolation of mesenteric blood flow from surrounding tissues, the vascular tree being enveloped in the two mesenterial leaves. Main stem occlusions and peripheral occlusions of the vasa recta comprise the highest risk of bowel necrosis, whereas single branch occlusions are better tolerated because they permit blood flow via collaterals from the celic and inferior mesenteric arteries as well as the mesenteric arcades.

The acute mesenteric occlusion may cause a standstill of the blood flow in the whole mesenteric territory and will induce in this way a secondary mesenteric vein thrombosis. Then, the originally ischemic infarction changes into a hemorrhagic infarction with the characteristic blue-black appearance of the bowel wall. Mesenteric vein thrombosis may occur as a disease of its own in portal hypertension or tumor compression of portal veins. The mortality rate is high in these cases.

Diagnosis

When the diagnosis is suspected clinically, angiography is the method of choice for demonstrating mesenteric arterial or venous occlusion. Ultrasound examinations (simple Dopplerultrasound, duplexultrasound, angiodynamography) can be helpful but may fail in more peripheral arterial obstructions and acute low flow states.

Embolic and thrombotic mesenteric artery occlusion can be reliably diagnosed by angiography. In nonocclusive disease angiography helps to rule out embolic or atherosclerotic occlusions, but the radiologic signs are nonspecific and will only enhance the clinical suspicion of a low flow state. The most frequent sign of bowel ischemia is diffuse generalized vasoconstriction of the mesenteric artery and its branches. Strongly suggestive of nonocclusive disease are concentric narrowings interspersed among arterial segments of normal caliber.

My study, including 43 patients with acute mesenteric infarction, revealed a mortality of 81% (12). The patients had superior mesenteric embolism (53%), arterial mesenteric thrombosis (23%), venous mesenteric thrombosis (12%), and nonocclusive disease (12%). Comparable data are reported by other investigators (Table 2) (1, 3, 4, 9, 11, 14, 16).

The high mortality rate of acute mesenteric insufficiency has been nearly unchanged for the last decades. There is general consensus that immediate surgery consisting of embolectomy or resection of gangrenous bowel segments is the appropriate management of patients with occlusive forms of bowel ischemia. In patients with nonocclusive disease only resection of infarcted bowel loops is possible and the

Table **2** Mortality of acute mesenteric insufficiency

Reference	Year	No.	Mortality (%)
Ottinger and Austin (16)	1967	136	92
Huber (11)	1972	60	80
Mavor (14)	1972	71	83
Havia and Inberg (9)	1975	82	83
Boley (4)	1981	?	70
Beyer and Koster (1)	1985	101	75
Own study	1987	43	81
Total		493	84

clinical results are dismal. Alternative methods of treatment improving the prognosis are desirable.

Interventional Procedures

Immediate surgical exploration of patients with clinically suspected acute bowel ischemia (first look operation) should be consigned to the period before the introduction of aortography and mesenteric arteriography. Two arguments support this opinion. The margins of the ischemic zones of the bowel are not demarcated in the early stage of the disease, leaving the surgeon in doubt about the optimal resection borders. With immediate operation, the surgeon does not know what kind of circulatory disorder caused the bowel ischemia. Therefore, arteriography should be the first step in the management of these patients. With the catheter in place, it is reasonable and desirable to use this internal approach to the disease process therapeutically.

The following procedures are available:

– Fragmentation of main stem thrombus with catheter and guide wire to restore blood flow to the proximal jejunal and the right colonic arteries
– Extraction of thrombus from the mesenteric artery with the aid of balloon catheters and embolism into peripheral leg arteries where more time for local fibrinolysis exists
– Suction embolectomy
– Local fibrinolysis
– Infusion therapy with vasodilators

Fragmentation of the thrombus is an easy and quick procedure and will help in patients with main stem occlusion of the superior mesenteric artery, as we have seen in two cases (Fig. **1**). In a few minutes the blood flow is partially restored in proximal branches, diminishing the extent of bowel ischemia and improving the collateral circulation. This maneuver is combined with local fibrinolysis and vasodilator infusion. The perfusion treatment should go on in these

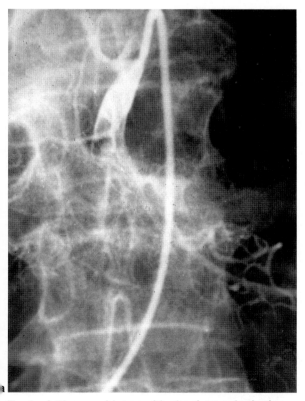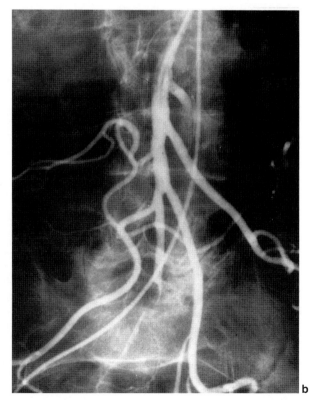

Fig. 1   **A 72-year-old man with absolute arrhythmia.**
a Thrombo-embolic occlusion of the superior mesenteric artery
b Fragmentation with guide wire and catheter followed by local urokinase infusion

patients during surgery. Surgery is postponed when symptoms of peritonitis are absent. Operation (so-called second look) is carried out 24 to 48 hours later to inspect the bowel and resect areas of compromised intestine.

Additional steps are taken in the meanwhile to reverse existing mesenteric vasoconstriction:

– Balancing of intravascular volume
– Intravenous low molecular weight dextran
– Improvement of low cardiac output
– Administration of intraluminal antibiotics
– Epidural and splanchnic nerve block
– Mesenteric arterial infusion of vasodilatory drugs

An alternative procedure to thrombus fragmentation is suction embolectomy. Suction embolectomy was carried out in one patient with an open-end 8 Fr catheter using a sheath in the femoral artery for easy catheter exchange. Complete removal of thrombus is not always possible in this way, but the thrombotic mass can be reduced. The residual thrombus will be rinsed with urokinase. Streptokinase is accompanied by a greater risk of bleeding, and early experiences with recombinant tissue plasminogen activator (rt-PA) are not as promising as thought in the beginning. A faster thrombus disintegration is paid for with a higher frequency of cerebral hemorrhage.

In balloon embolectomy a balloon catheter is passed beyond the thrombus, inflated, and cautiously extracted into the aorta. The thrombotic material will be carried away with the bloodstream to

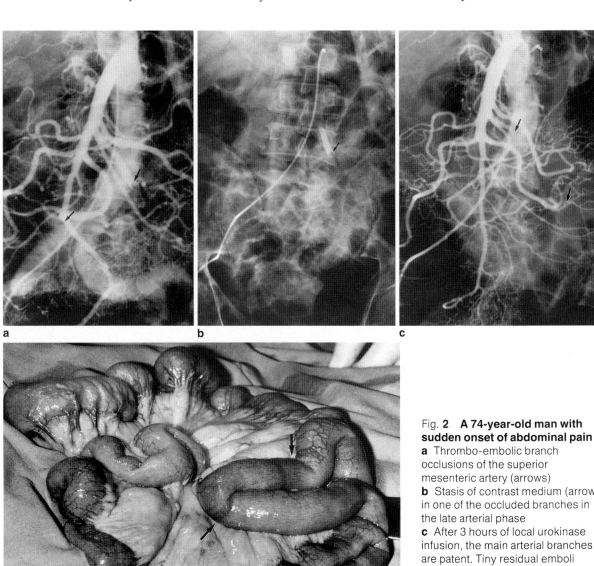

Fig. 2 **A 74-year-old man with sudden onset of abdominal pain**
a Thrombo-embolic branch occlusions of the superior mesenteric artery (arrows)
b Stasis of contrast medium (arrow) in one of the occluded branches in the late arterial phase
c After 3 hours of local urokinase infusion, the main arterial branches are patent. Tiny residual emboli (arrows)
d Intraoperatively, only a segmental discoloration of a small bowel segment was seen (arrows). No resection needed

peripheral vessels. This action necessitates treatment of the peripheral emboli with local fibrinolysis.

Local fibrinolysis is the preferred treatment modality in single or multiple thrombotic occlusions in peripheral mesenteric branches (Fig. **2**). In patients without signs of peritonitis we give 100,000 IU of urokinase per hour and continue the drug infusion as long as necessary for complete thrombus dissolution. We were able to reopen the superior mesenteric artery or branches of this vessel in three patients with this method without bowel infarction. Theiss et al. (23) report similarly favorable results in a patient treated with urokinase. When immediate operation is mandatory because of peritonitis we limit the urokinase dosage to 200,000 IU and have as yet not experienced prolonged bleeding during surgery. This experience is supported by Zschenker et al. (26) who treated mesenteric vein occlusion with thrombectomy, segmental small bowel resection, and local streptokinase infusion.

Patients with nonocclusive disease should be treated by intraarterial infusion of vasodilatory drugs. An additional application of vasodilators is also recommended in patients with occlusive forms of acute mesenteric insufficiency, because most of these patients have additional vasospasm, and infusion therapy will open collateral pathways. Several substances are investigated including phenoxybenzamine, tolazoline, diltiazem, prostaglandin E_1, Laevadosin, a mixture of adenosine di- and triphosphate, and papaverine (4, 21, 22). If the superior mesenteric arteriogram shows occlusion or vasoconstriction, 25 mg tolazoline or 2 ml of a mixture of adenosine di- and triphosphate are injected into the superior mesenteric artery. A positive response with reversal of vasoconstriction of the mesenteric vascular tree indicates that vasodilatory drug infusion will increase blood flow in mesenteric vessels. Even intensive opacification of the bowel wall in the capillary phase of a control arteriogram does not exclude deep mucosal necrosis of the small bowel.

We have gained more extensive experience with Laevadosin, but other drugs may achieve the same results, such as papaverine or prostaglandin E_1. We usually infuse a solution of 10 ml Laevadosin diluted in 40 ml physiologic sodium chloride with an arterial infusion pump at a rate of 12 ml/hr (13). To recognize systemic hemodynamic changes it is necessary to monitor continuously pulse rate, blood pressure, and central venous pressure. The infusion is continued while the patient is on the way to the operating room and for 1 or 2 days after operation. The duration of the infusion therapy depends on the angiographic presentation of the mesenteric vessels. If there is persistent segmental vasoconstriction, the infusion should be continued. When repeated mesenteric arteriography shows a normal vessel caliber, the infusion is discontinued and the catheter removed. If a second look operation is planned, mesenteric infusion is continued until the time of reexploration.

We suggest the algorithm for the management of patients with acute mesenteric insufficiency presented in Table **3**.

Table **3** Diagnosis and treatment of acute mesenteric insufficiency		Initial stage	Silent stage	Final stage
	Time	1–6 hours	7–12 (48) hours	More than 12 (48) hours
	Clinical signs	Abdominal pain shock signs diarrhea	Tolerable pain, no peristalsis, worsening general condition	Paralytic ileus, peritonitis
	Laboratory data	Normal	Increasing leukocytosis	
	Abdominal plain film	Normal	Gasless abdomen	Air-fluid levels, gas in bowel wall or portal veins
	Arteriography Mesenteric occlusion	Thrombus fragmentation Suction embolectomy Local fibrinolysis Infusion of vasodilators		Infusion of vasodilators
	Nonocclusive disease	Infusion of vasodilators (stages I and II)		
	Operative revascularisation	+++	+	0
	Bowel resection	0	+	++

A dramatic change in the poor prognosis of acute mesenteric insufficiency cannot be expected from interventional radiology, because a larger portion of the patients are referred to the hospital in an already poor general condition and with a far progressed stage of the disease. It can be estimated that the mortality rate can be reduced in the range of 10% by additional radiologic treatment. Boley (4) reported even better results with a survival rate of 46% in patients who were immediately managed by angiography and infusion therapy. Evaluating the main advantages of the radiologic treatment methods, it should be emphasized that the patients are only insignificantly stressed and are exposed to a minimal additional risk, but recover completely if the blood flow is restored in time. It is a pity that especially infusion therapy, which is easily performed and available nearly everywhere has not gained general acceptance as an additional valuable tool in the treatment of patients in whom surgery alone has not improved the prognosis in the last decades.

Chronic Mesenteric Insufficiency

Several terms are used to describe the state of chronic mesenteric insufficiency: angina abdominalis (Bacelli), Dyspragia intermittens angiosclerotica (Ortner), mesenteric arterial insufficiency (Derrick), angina intestinalis (Mikkelsen), and syndrome d'ischemie intestinale paroxystique (Leymarios).

Several diseases can chronically compromise the blood flow in the intestine (Table 4). Atherosclerosis is encountered as the most frequent organic cause of reduced bowel perfusion. The changes to the vessel wall are normally restricted to the origin of the three visceral arteries and to the first 2 to 3 cm of the main stems. Intimal thickening of the aorta leads to short ringlike stenoses, whereas atherosclerosis of a visceral artery extends over a longer artery segment of few centimeters. Peripheral stenotic lesions of arterial branches are less often seen.

Fibromuscular dysplasia, seen mostly in younger women and often combined with renal artery stenosis, and angiitis, are rare causes of visceral artery stenosis. In the past the compression syndrome of the celiac axis played a certain role in the scientific discussion as a possible disease entity, but nowadays the pathologic importance of compression of the celiac artery by the cruciate ligament is doubted. The intermittent complaints of patients are related to other diseases of upper abdominal organs, such as chronic pancreatitis or liver cirrhosis. A patient with celiac compression described by Saddekni et al. (19) was operated on with division of the cruciate ligament, but without clinical benefit. The patient developed periarterial fibrosis with celiac artery narrowing and was successfully dilated with relief of abdominal pains.

Occlusion of the infrarenal aorta and development of a collateral network from the mesenteric arteries to the iliac vessels also lead to mesenteric symptoms, because during walking blood is stolen from the mesenteric circulation.

Diagnosis

The triad of symptoms characterizing the state of chronic mesenteric insufficiency constists of:

- Intermittent, mostly severe abdominal pain attacks with variable location and related to the intake of food
- Malabsorption with fat and muscle fibers in the feces
- Auscultation: vascular bruits in the upper abdomen mostly to the left of the umbilicus

Nearly all patients complain of postprandial pain attacks. Symptoms of malabsorption are seen in 20% of the patients. The vascular bruits are produced by the turbulent flow in collateral vessels. The patients will characteristically lose weight. The pain is relieved by alcohol (vasodilation?), favoring alcohol abuse. Sometimes chronically reduced blood flow in the celiac and superior mesenteric arteries is responsible for the persistence of stomach and duodenal ulcers. The prognosis of chronic mesenteric ischemia is not well known, but in patients with higher degrees of stenosis there is always the risk of progression, acute artery occlusion, and bowel infarction.

The clinical diagnosis of chronic mesenteric insufficiency must be confirmed angiographically to rule out other diseases with similar symptoms, such as pancreatitis, cholecystitis, nephrolithiasis, or Crohn's disease. Direct and indirect angiographic signs of impaired mesenteric circulation, which are regularly observed, are:

- Narrowing or cutoff of opacified artery
- No or delayed opacification of one or more visceral arteries (comparison with appearance of contrast medium in renal arteries)
- Dilation of the left iliac, inferior mesenteric, and medial colonic arteries

Table **4** Causes of chronic mesenteric insufficiency

Atherosclerosis
Angiitis (endangiitis obliterans, Takayasu disease)
Fibromuscular dysplasia
External compression (tumor, aneurysm)
Congenital stenosis (coarctation of abdominal aorta, often combined with renal and mesenteric artery stenosis)
Steal syndromes (Leriche syndrome with iliofemoral steal, arteriovenous fistula)

– Opacification of collaterals between the different vascular areas (pancreatic arcades, Riolan's anastomosis)
– Thin vessels with insufficient filling

Stenosis or occlusion of only one of the three visceral arteries is normally hemodynamically compensated for by collateral blood flow. Symptoms in these patients should be judged sceptically and other possible diseases with similar signs should be excluded when discussing the therapeutic concept. Moreover, the functional quality of the collateral circulation should be evaluated, taking into account the number and diameter of collaterals and the flow velocity in comparison to other vascular beds.

Percutaneous Dilation Treatment

In the past, when the diagnosis of chronic mesenteric insufficiency was sufficiently documented, vascular surgery was the only treatment modality. Surgical reconstruction includes several procedures to restore mesenteric blood flow, including open thrombendarterectomy, bypass grafting, as well as transsection with reinsertion of visceral arteries. In patients with stenosis of the celiac axis and superior mesenteric

artery percutaneous angioplasty now offers an alternative method to increase the blood flow in the involved vascular territory.

The indication for catheter dilation depends on clinical and angiomorphologic criteria. All pathologic conditions responsible for the arterial narrowing, such as atherosclerosis, fibromuscular dysplasia, angiitis, postoperative scarring, or intimal proliferations after surgical correction, can be dilated successfully (5, 7, 8, 10, 13, 15, 17–19, 24, 25). An exception is external vessel compression by a space-occupying lesion or ligament. Both types of lesions are unsuited for angioplasty. Based on the fact that angioplasty has a much lower risk of complications for the patient than vascular surgery, it is much easier to confront the patient with the indication for an active treatment. In our opinion angioplasty should also be performed in patients with more or less asymptomatic stenoses, because it is impossible to predict the fate of the patient when thrombotic occlusion of the narrowed artery occurs. Such an occlusion may develop without clinically significant consequences, but, on the other hand, it may lead to bowel infarction in an unknown number of patients. Prophylactic dilation will prevent this event reliably.

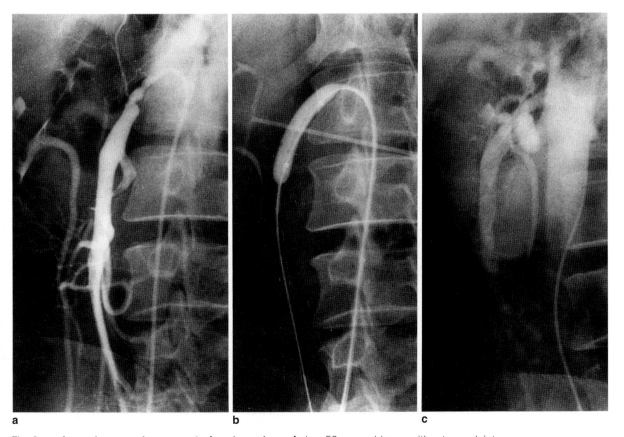

a   b   c

Fig. **3   a Irregular superior mesenteric artery stenosis** in a 58-year-old man without complaints
b Prophylactic dilation: balloon inflated, tip of guide wire in peripheral mesenteric artery branch
c Stenosis successfully dilated without residual narrowing

Celiac and mesenteric artery stenosis are approached by a transfemoral route. Castaneda-Zuniga et al. (5) recommend a transaxillary catheter insertion with the argumentation that probing the celiac axis and superior mesenteric and passage of the stenosis is easier by this approach. Our own experiences until now do not support this opinion. After angiographic documentation of location and degree of the stenosis, the narrowed arterial segment is passed by a type 1 or 2 sidewinder catheter under fluoroscopic control. During the passage of the stenosis, contrast medium is constantly injected to prevent subintimal placement of the catheter tip. In case the stenosis cannot be passed easily in this way a straight guide wire with movable core is used to palpate and pass the stenosis. With the tip of the catheter beyond the narrowed artery segment, a heavy-duty guide wire is placed with its tip more peripherally in the artery for safe catheter exchange and introduction of the dilation catheter. A catheter with a maximal balloon diameter of 5 or 6 mm and a balloon length of 2 to 4 cm is used. Alternatively, a preshaped dilation catheter can be inserted from the beginning of the intervention, but we prefer to probe the stenosis with a diagnostic catheter, the curvature of which can be more ideally adapted to the special anatomic situation.

Experience with this application of angioplasty has been limited with only casuistic reports (5, 7, 8, 10, 13, 15, 17–19, 24, 25). The relative rarity of abdominal angina is the reason, and larger treatment numbers cannot be expected in the near future. All investigators report uncomplicated dilations with convincing early results. We performed angioplasty in five patients with superior mesenteric artery stenosis and could improve the diameter of the narrowed artery segment considerably. Four patients had the typical signs of abdominal angina. In one patient the stenosis was detected incidentally and was treated prophylactically (Fig. 3). It may be speculated that the long-term results will be comparable to those of renal artery angioplasty with a recurrence rate of about 10% in atherosclerotic disease. The patients should be followed up by transvenous digital subtraction angiography.

References

1. Beyer D, Koster R. Bildgebende Diagnostik akuter intestinaler Durchblutungsstörungen. Berlin: Springer, 1985.
2. Boley SJ, Sprayregen S, Veith JF. An aggressive roentgenologic and surgical approach to acute mesenteric ischemia. In: Nyhus, LM, ed. Surgery Annual. New York: Appleton-Century-Crofts, 1973:355.
3. Boley SJ, Brandt LJ, Veith FJ. Ischemic disorders of the intestines. Curr Probl Surg 1978;15:1–14.
4. Boley SJ. Early diagnosis of acute mesenteric ischemia. Hosp Pract 1981;16:63–70.
5. Castaneda-Zuniga WR, Gomez A, Weens C, Ketchum D, Amplatz K. Transluminal angioplasty in the management of mesenteric angina. Röfo 1982;137:330–332.
6. Clar RA, Gallant TE. Acute mesenteric ischemia: angiographic spectrum. AJR 1984;142:555–562.
7. Furrer J, Grüntzig A, Kugelmeier J, Goebel N. Treatment of abdominal angina with percutaneous dilatation of an arteria mesenterica superior stenosis. Cardiovasc Intervent Radiol 1980;3:43–44.
8. Golden DA, Ring EJ, McLean GK, Friedman DB. Percutaneous transluminal angioplasty in the treatment of abdominal angina. AJR 1982;139:247–249.
9. Havia T, Inberg MV. Akuter Mesenterialgefässverschluss. Zentralbl Chir 1975;100:718–719.
10. Hodgins GW, Dutton JW. Transluminal dilatation for Takayasu's arteritis. Can J Surg 1984;27:355–357.
11. Huber FB. Darminfarkt nach stumpfem Bauchtrauma. Schweiz Med Wochenschr 1972;102:339–343.
12. Kern J. Die akute Mesenterialinsuffizienz – eine klinisch-radiologische Studie. Dissertation, Freiburg, 1982.
13. Mathias K. Kathetertherapie bei mesenterialen Durchblutungsstörungen. Med Chir Dig 1983;12:9–12.
14. Mavor GE. Acute occlusion of the superior mesenteric artery. Clin Gastroenterol 1972;1:639–646.
15. Noveline RA. Percutaneous transluminal angioplasty: newer applications. AJR 1980;135:983–988.
16. Ottinger L, Austen WG. A study of 136 patients with mesenteric infarction. Surg Gynecol Obstet 1967;124:251–257.
17. Roberts L, Wertman DA, Mills SR, Moore AV, Heaston DK. Transluminal angioplasty of superior mesenteric artery: an alternative to surgical revascualrization. AJR 1983;141:1039–1042.
18. Roth FJ. Seltene Indikationen zur Angioplastie. Röntgenpraxis 1982;35:308–311.
19. Saddekni S, Sniderman KW, Hilton S, Sos TA. Percutaneous transluminal angioplasty of nonatherosclerotic lesions. AJR 1980;135:975–982.
20. Schimanski K, Schmidt H. Chronische Verschlüsse der unpaaren Eingeweidearterien. In: Glauner R, Rüttimann A, Thurn P, Viamonte M, Vogler E, eds. Ergebnisse der medizinischen Radiologie. Stuttgart: Thieme, 1972:83–152.
21. Seemann WR, Kujat C, Urbanyi B, Kopp KH, Mathias K. Adenosin und Diltiazem: neue therapeutische Aspekte bei der Behandlung der mesenterialen Insuffizienz. Vasa 1984;13:65–71.
22. Seemann WR, Mathias K, Roren T, Urbanyi B, Kopp KH. Adenosine and Diltiazem: a new concept in the treatment of intestinal ischemia. Invest Radiol 1985;20:166–170.
23. Theiss W, Gullota U, Bonke S. Behandlung einer Mesenterialarterienembolie durch hochdosierte, lokale Urokinasegabe. Vasa 1982;11:213–217.
24. Uflacker R, Goldamy MA, Constant S. Resolution of mesenteric angina with percutaneous transluminal angioplasty of a superior mesenteric artery stenosis using a balloon catheter. Gastrointest Radiol 1980;5:367–369.
25. Werner W, Doker R, Timmermann J. Perkutane transluminale Angioplastie als Alternative zur chirurgischen Intervention bei Angina abdominalis. Vasa 1987;16:186–189.
26. Zschenker H. Über die Behandlung eines Mesenterialvenenverschlusses durch Thrombektomie, ausgedehnte Dünndarmresektion und nachfolgende Streptasebehandlung. Chirurg 1971;42:332–333.

Local Venous Thrombolysis

V. Iaccarino

Spontaneous recanalization of thrombophlebitis results in destruction of the venous valves, so that in about 75% of patients with iliofemoral thrombophlebitis a postphlebitic syndrome develops despite a 50% success rate in recanalization (7). Although thrombus organization occurs within 2 weeks, recanalization takes considerably longer. Heparin therapy decreases the incidence of significant pulmonary emboli associated with venous thrombosis, but it has not been effective in reducing the incidence of the postphlebitic syndrome (8). Surgical thrombectomy has been of little value clinically and is associated with significant morbidity and mortality (8). The goal of therapy in patients with deep vein thrombosis is to prevent pulmonary embolism and avoid the long-term disabling sequelae of the postphlebitic syndrome (5, 8).

Between 1973 and 1979 (2), systemic administration of urokinase was introduced in the treatment of venous thrombosis. The first articles (2) demonstrated that valuable clinical results were achieved with systemic administration of urokinase in 48% of patients with chronic venous obstruction. Chronic venous obstruction can be either completely eliminated (37%) or basically improved (12%) by late fibrinolysis, but sometimes it is necessary to prolong treatment up to 7 to 21 days. Volumetric studies demonstrated the absence of strong correlation between early phlebographic resolution of the thrombi and long-term valvular function, suggesting the possibility of subclinical rethrombosis (5).

Iliofemoral rethrombosis was demonstrated despite ongoing streptokinase therapy (3). The anatomic site of the venous thrombosis cannot be used to predict the success of fibrinolysis (1, 6), and completely obstructing thrombi are as easily lysed as partially obstructed veins (6). Urokinase represents the only fibrinolytic agent that can be used safely for long-term administration (11). Since good results are achieved with local fibrinolytic treatment in arterial occlusive disease (4), local administration of urokinase can also be used in deep vein thrombosis (8, 9). Urokinase improves the therapeutic effects and prevents or reduces complications.

Technique

Since 1980, we have performed local thrombolysis with urokinase in 32 patients affected by thrombosis of the iliofemoral veins and veins below the knee. Technique includes a preliminary phlebography for exact determination of morphology and extent of the thrombi. A 20-gauge needle catheter was positioned in a superficial vein of the foot below the venous plantar arch. An elastic bandage was applied to the lower limb, which was positioned with a 30 degree inclination. On three occasions a venous cutdown was required for cannulation, because of edema of the foot. Four patients needed catheterization of a dorsal foot vein, and in four patients an adjunctive transfemoral catheterization of the distal segment of the femoral thrombus was performed. In 20 patients, in whom venous thrombosis extended to both thighs and the iliac veins, a crossover transfemoral approach or a transbrachial catheterization was used for mechanical thrombolysis through the thrombus. Generally, a 7 Fr catheter was used. Commerically available catheters, 125 cm in length, are not long enough to reach the popliteal vein from the arm, so we used homemade catheters of adequate length. Multipurpose or Judkins right coronary catheters are also suitable. When the catheter is placed in the thrombus, small amounts of an anionic contrast medium diluted with saline and heparin are injected. The thrombography or opacification of the thrombi remains for a long time. J or straight guide wires are used. The popliteal vein has never been passed below the knee. In follow-up studies the catheter was withdrawn in the superficial femoral vein or in the iliac vein.

Thrombolytic infusion was performed by means of a peristaltic pump. For the first 24 hours, 100,000 to 200,000 U of urokinase were infused per hour with 300 U of heparin in 2 or 3 liters of saline. Coagulation time and fibrinogen were checked to adapt dose reduction when necessary (10). For long-term treatment, urokinase infusion was stopped for 2 hours every 12 hours. The elastic bandage of the limb was kept in place during treatment. Phlebographic control was performed about every 2 days, using a diluted anionic contrast medium. Follow-up at 24 months included clinical examinations and Doppler ultrasound. Oral anticoagulant therapy was given.

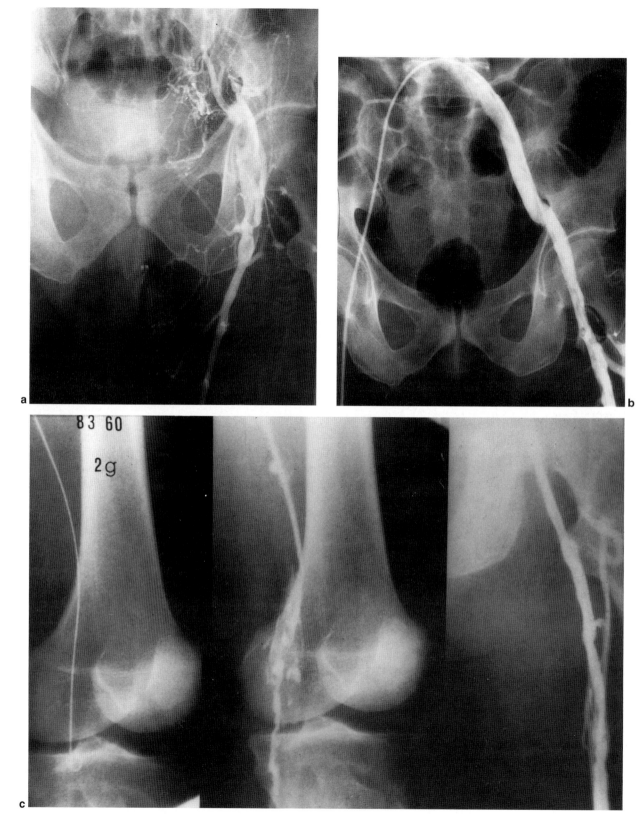

Fig. 1 **a Postsurgical deep vein thrombosis in a patient operated on 6 days before for inguinal hernia.** This patient developed phlegmatia alba dolens
b Contralateral transfemoral catheterization was performed
c This figure shows the result 6 days after therapy: complete patency of the iliac and femoral veins

Indications

Local thrombolysis is superior to systemic treatment. In the venous system, flow is slower than in the arteries. Urokinase binds directly to the thrombus, so significant systemic fibrinolysis is avoided. In systemic thrombolysis the contact of urokinase with the thrombus is reduced. Local venous thrombolysis is indicated in patients with phlegmatia alba dolens with rest pain, in phlegmatia coerulea dolens, and in postpartum or postoperative deep vein thrombosis. It is still indicated in extensive thrombosis (Fig. **1**), because of a direct and quick action on the clot and improved prevention of valvular destruction and subsequent postphlebitic syndrome. In our hypothesis the postphlebitic syndrome develops after spontaneous autothrombolysis. On the other hand, during pharmacologically induced thrombolysis, the clot is attacked immediately and valvular destruction is avoided.

Results

Complete destruction of thrombi was achieved in 85% of cases. In the other cases, there was at least a complete resolution of the clinical symptoms. In 20 cases, a complete resolution was observed after 72 hours of treatment, when therapy was started within 3 days of the onset of symptoms. The same results were obtained with a treatment of 92 hours in five patients. With an infusion of urokinase over 7 days, a complete lysis was obtained in three patients, in whom symptoms had appeared about 4 to 6 weeks before. In almost all patients, no postphlebitic syndrome was seen, even after 24 months of follow-up. Phlebography showed complete dissolution of thrombi.

We also achieved dissolution of thrombi in two women in whom therapy was started 45 days after the onset of symptoms. Another patient affected by deep vein thrombosis after a gunshot wound 60 days before and pulmonary embolism, was treated successfully with local therapy lasting 19 days. After 18 months, the patient had a mild postphlebitic syndrome only at the site of operation. Four patients required PTA of an iliofemoral stenosis at the end of drug therapy (Fig. **2**). Finally, we achieved patency of the right iliac vein and the inferior vena cava in one patient after thrombolysis and PTA. Although

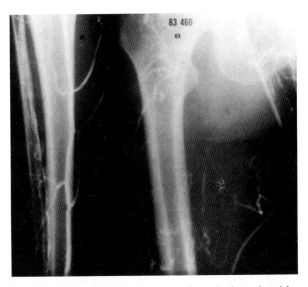

Fig. **2 a 50-year-old man developed thrombophlebitis of the right lower limb 25 days after femoral cardiac catheterization.** Thrombolytic therapy was performed for 11 days

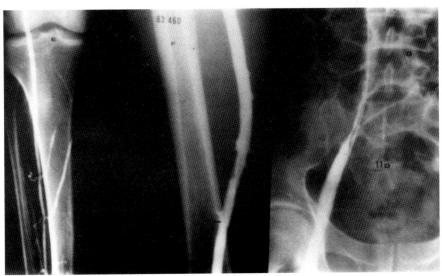

Fig. **2**
b At the end of therapy, a stenosis of the right common iliac vein was evident

b

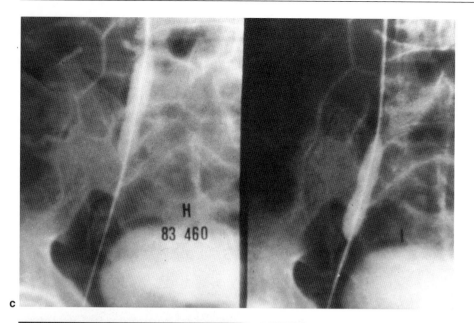

c

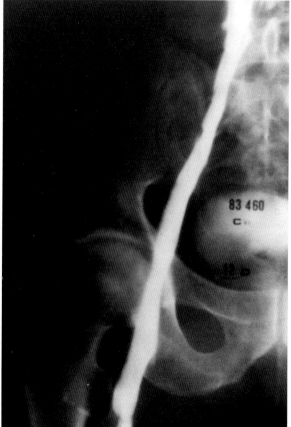

d

Fig. 2
c, d PTA was performed. This patient had a congenital deficiency of antithrombin 3 and was treated with oral anticoagulants

catheterization through the thrombus was performed for mechanical thrombolysis, no clinically significant pulmonary embolism was seen. Pulmonary embolism is, however, possible and we now insert a temporary Günther caval filter, that admits the catheter used for thrombolysis. Local thrombolysis was also performed within the first days after visceral surgery, using low doses of heparin and thrombolytic agents.

Conclusion

Local therapy permits restitutio ad integrum of the venous system of the lower limbs in patients not considered until now for treatment, even when the period since the onset of symptoms has been longer than 45 days.

Only Urokinase was used, because of the long duration of therapy. This drug is expensive, but the socio-economic costs of postphlebitic syndromes may be higher.

References

1. Arnesen H, Heilo A, Jakobsen E, et al. A prospective study of streptokinase and heparin in the treatment of deep venous thrombosis. Acta Med Scand 1978;203:457.
2. Bell WR. SK and UK in the treatment of pulmonary thromboembolism: from a national cooperative study. Thrombos Haemost 1976;35:57.
3. Dhall DP, Dawsona A, Mavorge G. Problems of resistant thrombolysis and early recurrent thrombosis in streptokinase therapy. Surg Gynecol Obstet 1978;146:15.
4. Dotter CT, Rösch J, Seaman AJ. Selective clot lysis with low-dose streptokinase. Radiology 1974;111:31.
5. Frantoni JC, Ness P, Simon TL. Thrombolytic therapy: current status. N Engl J Med 1975;293:1073.
6. Ghelin E, Thess W. Repeated phlebographic examination during and after fibrinolytic therapy with streptokinase and urokinase. Cardiovasc Radiol 1978;1:157.
7. Leveen HH, Diaz CA. Venous and arterial occlusive disease treated by enzymatic clot lysis. Arch Surg 1972;105:927.
8. Porter JM, Goodnight SH Jr. The clinical use of fibrinolytic agents. Am J Surg 1977;134:217.
9. Serradimigni A, Mathieu P, Leonetti J, et al. La place des thrombolytiques dans le traitement des thromboses veineuses profondes des membres inférieurs. Therapie 1978;33:75.
10. Tsapogas MJ, Peabody RA, Wu KT, et al. Controlled study of thrombolytic therapy in deep venous thrombosis. Surgery 1973;74:973–984.
11. Urokinase-Streptokinase Embolism Trial. A cooperative study: phase 2 results. JAMA 1970;214:2163.

Percutaneous Transluminal Angioplasty in the Venous System

V. Iaccarino

Percutaneous transluminal angioplasty (PTA) and local thrombolysis can be applied in the treatment of pre- and post-hepatic hypertension. In pre-hepatic portal hypertension, it is possible to perform PTA when one or several stenoses of the splenoportal tract caused by external compression, or secondary to pylephlebitis, are present. Treatment can also be applied before surgery, to occlude collateral vessels that may be a source of bleeding.

After transhepatic portography obtained by injecting contrast medium at a rate of 6–8 ml per second, it is important to measure portal pressures above and below the stenosis (11). We perform PTA of the portal vein up to a diameter of 12 mm. If no significant pressure gradient remains, we do not occlude portosystemic varices (Fig. 1). At the end of the procedure, the transhepatic tract is occluded with Spongostan, as a 9 Fr calloon catheter has been

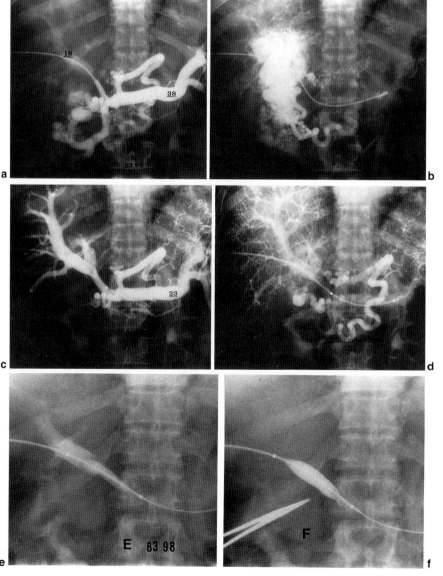

Fig. **1 a Patient with periduodenal varices** shown on endoscopy and radiology. Transhepatic catheterization through a stenosis of the portal vein shows periduodenal collateral vessels. Portal pressure was 18 cm H_2O, pressure in the splenic vein 38 cm H_2O
b Late-phase portography shows a huge portal cavernoma
c Dilation of the portal vein stenosis up to 12 mm. Pressure in the splenic vein decreased to 23 cm H_2O; the portal vein is well recanalized
d Immediate disappearance of the portal cavernoma and good opacification of the intrahepatic portal veins
e, f Spot films show the dilation procedure. The clip is placed over the stenosis. The stenosis of the splenic vein was related to a retropancreatic mass that was treated surgically

introduced through the liver parenchyma. It is also possible to perform thrombolysis in the portal vein with a percutaneous transhepatic approach. When reflux in the gastroesophageal veins is demonstrated by portography, these vessels must be occluded. The portographic control is repeated after embolization to ensure that complete occlusion is obtained. An occlusion balloon catheter is then introduced, and a slow infusion of urokinase is started, with the tip of the catheter placed as near as possible to the thrombi that have been fragmented by inflation of the balloon catheter. Results are usually satisfactory. This technique can be used whatever the underlying disease. In the cirrhotic patient with a high risk of bleeding, all varices present must be previously occluded.

PTA can also be used to create a portocaval intrahepatic shunt via the right internal transjugular approach. This non-surgical technique is indicated when a systemic portocaval or splenorenal shunt is not successful due to a marked persistent gradient between the inferior vena cava and the right atrium (inferior vena cava hypertension). Transhepatic portography is performed with a 16 G needle and highly opaque contrast medium. A catheter is placed in the portal system to record pressures. This is mandatory prior to any decision concerning an interventional approach in the treatment of portal hypertension (5, 11).

A modified Rosch cannula is introduced via the transjugular approach to the medial or left hepatic vein, which is reached under lateral fluoroscopy control. The needle is directed to the portal vein, which contains the transhepatic catheter (1, 2, 3, 5, 8, 9, 12, 18, 19). Good visualization of the catheter in the splenoportal trunk makes this difficult technique easier. This technique avoids multiple punctures of the hepatic parenchyma, and prevents perforation of the hepatic capsule, which is a major complication. When the portal vein has been catheterized, a high-pressure balloon dilation catheter of 7–8 mm in diameter is introduced over a long guide wire, and the liver parenchyma between the portal vein and the hepatic vein is dilated. Because of the pain caused by this technique, the patient is medicated with intravenous fentanyl.

Portal pressure does not generally change after an initial dilation. After a second dilation with a balloon catheter of 12 mm in diameter for 2–3 minutes, portal pressure is measured again. If necessary, dilations of up to 20–25 mm are performed. Two catheters of 12 mm in diameter can be placed side by side and inflated simultaneously (1, 2, 3, 8, 9). Portal pressure usually decreases significantly at the end of the procedure. A transbrachial control of the intrahepatic shunt is obtained after 2–3 weeks, showing a further decrease in the portal pressure (Fig. **2**). A cannula placed via the transjugular vein can also be left in

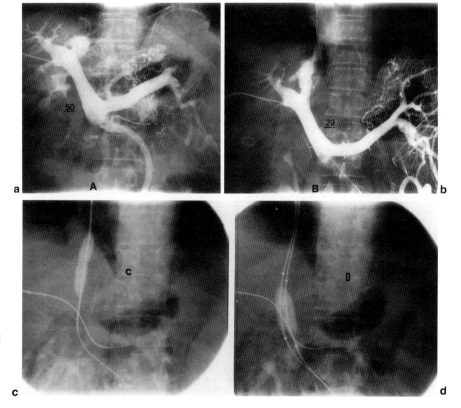

Fig. **2 a Transhepatic portography in a patient with portal hypertension, gastric varices and reflux into the inferior mesenteric vein.** Portal pressure was 50 cm H$_2$O
b Control after sclero-embolization of esophageal varices and porto-atrial intrahepatic shunt. Portal pressure decreased to 29 cm H$_2$O
c The spot films show the balloon catheter with a diameter of 8 mm during the dilation. Portal pressure was still elevated after the procedure
d Two balloon catheters with balloons of 20 mm in diameter were inflated for 5 min.

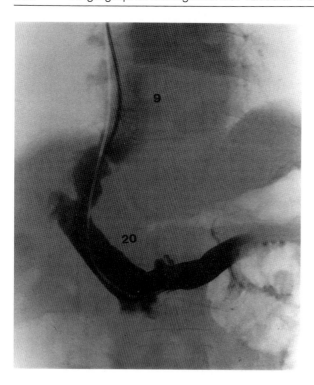

Fig. 2

e Control portography after 1 month via a transbrachial approach and catheterization of the shunt. The portal pressure was 20 cm H_2O, the pressure in the right atrium 9 cm H_2O

place after the second dilation of up to 12 mm to monitor pressure. If after 24 h, portal pressure has not decreased, dilation is repeated with a larger balloon. It is important to calibrate the portocaval shunt to avoid portosystemic encephalopathy (10). Venous PTA will be more frequently used when it becomes possible to place endovascular stents (4, 15, 16, 17) to obtain extended patency in intrahepatic shunts. The real patency of the shunt created by PTA is unknown, because until now this procedure has only been applied in patients with a short life-expectancy and follow-ups for more than a few months are not available (5). In the literature (2, 3, 6, 19), and in our experience (9), patency for 6 months has been reported. The hard consistency of the hepatic parenchyma in the cirrhotic patient determinates the patency of the shunt, especially if the diameter exceeds 12 mm. The risk of encephalopathy is, of course, also increased. Calibrated stents could be useful.

The risks associated with venous PTA in skilled hands are acceptable in very serious portal hypertension, especially if surgery is contra-indicated. In hepatic vein stenosis, this procedure is indicated, because there is no surgical alternative. In caval stenosis or partial caval obstruction, surgical venous by-pass fails all too frequently, and PTA is a valuable alternative therapy.

PTA is also effective in the dilation of a too narrow surgical portocaval shunt, especially in so-called calibrated shunts (7). The technique consists

of a phlebographic transanastomotic control of the shunt and pressure measurements in the portal vein, splenic vein and inferior vena cava. Portal pressure does not normally exceed 25 cm H_2O. If portal hypertension is present, and reflux in the gastroesophageal veins is demonstrated, two balloon catheters of 7–10 mm in diameter are introduced through the narrowed shunt. The metallic markers of the balloons are placed at the same level, and the balloons are inflated simultaneously through a Y connector. The dilation is generally difficult due to the anastomotic fibrosis, and has to be repeated until a marked reduction of the portal pressure is obtained. No bleeding has been seen, even after 4 years, in a few patients treated so far.

In post-hepatic hypertension, PTA is theoretically the first therapeutic approach for stenoses of the intrahepatic vena cava and the hepatic veins. For stenoses of the hepatic veins, it is possible to perform PTA not only via a transbrachial or a transjugular approach, but also via transhepatic puncture. This approach is more easily performed with ultrasound guidance, and is indicated in the case of atresia or marked stenosis with subsequent dilation of the hepatic veins (11, 21).

PTA of the inferior vena cava is useful above all in its pseudo-intrahepatic portion, when a significant atriocaval pressure gradient is recorded, and reflux of contrast medium in the hepatic veins is seen, as in pseudo- or hemodynamic Budd-Chiari syndrome (6, 14, 21).

PTA of the infrarenal vena cava and the iliac veins can be performed if extrinsic occlusion after surgery is present (4). Inferior cavography in anteroposterior and lateral projections is obtained, and caval pressures are recorded. PTA is performed via a transbrachial, transfemoral, or transjugular approach. The transbrachial puncture is preferred only if thrombosis of the iliac veins is present. It might be useful to perform local thrombolysis for 24 h prior to PTA, to avoid the high risk of pulmonary emboli in selected cases. Dilation of the iliac veins can also be performed to avoid an inferior vena cava syndrome.

Local thrombolysis of renal vein thrombosis is mainly indicated in nephrotic syndromes, such as those observed in collagen disease, but only in the early phase. As a result of their disease, these patients have a high level of fibrinogen, making thrombolysis very effective. In a patient affected for 30 days, thrombolysis has not been successful. Early treatment is mandatory in these cases to ensure successful thrombolysis.

PTA and thrombolysis can be successfully performed in the portal system and vena cava when significant pressure gradients have been demonstrated, and with careful management of the catheter systems.

References

1. Burgener FA, Gutierrez GH. Non surgical production of intrahepatic portosystemic shunts in portal hypertension with the double lumen balloon-catheter. RöFo 1979;130:686–688.
2. Burgener FA, Gutierrez GH. Produktion einer intrahepatischen porto-kavalen Fistel im Hund mit Leberzirrhose und Pfortaderhochdruck. RöFo 1984;141:327–332.
3. Burgener FA, Gutierrez GH, Logsdon GA. Angiographic, hemodynamic and histologic evaluation of portal hypertension poly-vinyl-alcohol injections. Radiology 1982;143:379–395.
4. Charnsangavej C, Carrasco CH, Wallace S, Wright KC, Osawa K, Richli W, Gianturco C. Stenosis of the vena cava: preliminary assessment of treatment with expandable metallic stents. Radiology 1986;161:295–298.
5. Colapinto RF, Stronel RD, Gildimer M. Formation of intrahepatic portosystemic shunts using a balloon-dilatation catheter: preliminary clinical experience. Can Med Assoc J 1982;126:267–268.
6. Duvauferrier R. Angioplasty in primary Budd-Chiari syndrome: report of 3 cases. J Radiol. 1985;66:725–729.
7. Henderson JM, El Khishen MA, Millikan WJ, et al. Management of stenosis of distal splenorenal shunt by balloon dilatation (ab). Radiology 1984;151:546.
8. Kerlan RK Jr, Sollenberger RD, Palubinskas AJ. Portalsystemic encephalopathy due to a congenital portocaval shunt. AJR 1982;139:1013.
9. Kimura K, Okuda K, Takara K, Schoichi M, Lesmana L. Membranous obstruction of the portal vein: a case report. Gastroenterology 1985;88:571.
10. Koch G, Rigler B, Tentzeris M, Schuy S, Sakulin M, Schmidt-Bloiber H. Der intrahepatische porto-cavale Shunt. Langenbecks Arch Chir 1973;333:237–244.

Percutaneous Transluminal Angioplasty of Arteriovenous Shunts

J. C. Gaux and P. Bourquelot

The treatment of chronic renal failure by maintenance hemodialysis requires arteriovenous fistulas (AVFs) that are subjected to repeated needle punctures. Late complications may include thrombosis and stenosis of AVFs. Surgical correction is the usual treatment, but it re-exposes the repaired shunt to the risk of infection and stenosis, or occlusion of the anastomosis. Non-operative therapy can avoid the hazards of surgery in many cases and prolong the survival rate.

Percutaneous transluminal methods are now proposed for the management of these patients: angioplasty for the relief of stenoses, and local thrombolytic therapy for acute thrombosis.

Anatomic Types of Vascular Access for Hemodialysis

It is widely accepted that the arteriovenous fistula (AVF) is the method of choice in achieving vascular access for maintenance hemodialysis. Since the first report by Brescia et al., different modifications have

been made with regard both to the site of the procedure and the type of anastomosis.

Three anatomic sites for the AVF can be distinguished: the distal forearm, the antecubital fossa at the elbow, and a proximal AVF using interposition materials, either homologous saphenous vein or heterologous shunts such as a bridge graft made of polytetrafluoroethylene (PTFE) or bovine carotid artery heterograft.

AVF in the Distal Forearm

AVF in the forearm has been the established technique for vascular access in hemodialysis treatment for the last 15 years. The fistula is usually constructed between the radial artery and the cephalic vein, if these vessels are available. The anastomosis may be performed side-to-side (Fig. **1**) or end-to-end, each technique having its advantages and disavantages (5). The region at the base of the thumb between the tendons of the extensor pollicis muscles can be a desirable site for vascular surgery for hemodialysis. The advantages of this surgical construction lie in the possibility of performing a new AVF at the distal forearm in case of failure, and having an extensive vascular segment for puncture (2).

AVF at the Elbow

This type of AVF location is chosen when a more distal fistula has failed, or when the forearm distal veins are unsuitable for the standard AVF. The following surgical constructions have been described, the choice of one of them depending on the anatomical status:

When either the cephalic or basilic vein in the forearm is still patent and of sufficient caliber, it is dissected free, placed in a U-shaped subcutaneous tunnel, and sutured end-to-side to the brachial artery in the antecubital fossae (Fig. **2a**). This construction results in the formation of a loop which is prominent under the skin.

If the veins in the forearm are inadequate or absent, a perforating vein at the elbow can be anastomosed end-to-side to the brachial artery (Fig. **2b**).

Another possibility is to dissect the basilic vein free up to the axillary vein, transpose it into a subcutaneous tunnel just at the anterior aspect of the upper arm, and then suture it end-to-side to the

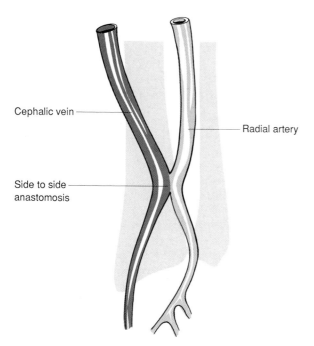

Fig. **1**   **An arteriovenous fistula (AVF)** between the side of the brachial artery and the side of the cephalic vein

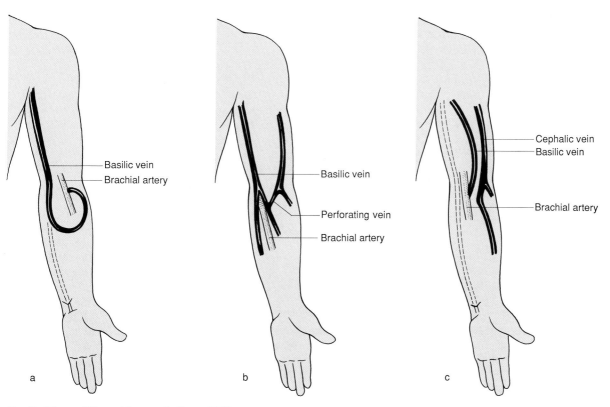

Fig. 2   Three different types of elbow AVF
a End-to-side anastomosis of the basilic vein to the brachial artery
b End-to-side anatomosis of the perforating vein to the brachial artery
c Subcutaneous positioning of the basilic vein, with end-to-side anastomosis to the brachial artery (19)

brachial artery in the antecubital fossa (Fig. **2c**). The superficial and anterior positioning of the vein thus makes it accessible for puncture.

Proximal Material Interpositions

The interposition either of homologous saphenous vein, or of prosthetic material (bovine carotid or PTFE grafts) for arteriovenous communications become an indication for access surgery if there is no possibility of constructing a direct AVF (3, 19).

The most frequent types of interposition are:

Bovine carotid or PTFE graft between the brachial artery at the elbow and the axillary vein. In this case, the prosthetic material is positioned in a subcutaneous tunnel at the volar aspect of the arm.

(b) Interposition of the prosthesis between the axillary artery and the axillary vein located on the contralateral side, when there is a blockage of the central veins.

Rarely, interposition of a graft may be carried out in the groin. The anastomosis can be made between the femoral artery and the saphenous vein, or the femoral artery and the femoral vein.

AVF Complications with Hemodynamic Consequences

Successful chronic hemodialysis requires vascular access with a flow rate well above 300 ml/min. The flow through the shunt can go as high as 3000 to 4000 ml/min (22). This relatively excessive flow can be altered by AVF complications with subsequent hemodynamic alterations, but in practice, when the flow is within 350–800 ml/min, most of the shunts remain patent for a long time. Complications occurring with AVFs are described below, and their consequences for the AVF blood flow are discussed.

Thrombosis

Complete loss of an AVF is often the result of thrombosis (10, 14). This is the most serious complication of internal AVFs, accounting for 87% of all fistula failures (16). Most of the synthetic (PTFE) or bovine grafts are subject to arterial or venous thrombosis. Poor venous run-off due to a narrow anastomosis, or an unsuspected proximal venous obstruction, are the most frequent cause of early fistula failure. Stenoses at the anastomotic site are most often a result of poor surgical management, and required revision or replacement of the AVF. Unsuspected proximal stenosis should not occur if a presurgical phlebogram is performed to assess the patency of the venous system up to the level of the axilla.

Late thrombosis usually occurs within 6–12 months, but is preceded by a period of weeks during which the fistula shows signs of failure, such as diminished thrill, difficulty in dialysis, or venous congestion in the hand. This type of thrombosis is most often caused by a stenosis of the proximal vein (within 1–5 cm of the anastomosis) related to intimal hyperplasia of the outflow vein or perivascular fibrosis secondary to repeated cannulations (15, 16), or both.

Thrombosis is also the most frequent cause of prosthetic shunt failure, and has been reported to occur early in 10–20% of patients supporting a bovine carotid heterograft (12). Causes include: surgical twisting or kinking of the graft during implantation; a stenosis on the venous side of the anastomosis; and an unsuspected central obstruction (10). Rarely, the narrowing can be located on the middle part of graft, due to: pseudointimal proliferation impinging on the lumen; dissection secondary to repeated puncture; pseudodiaphragmatic lesions that are thought to be fibrous; and aggressive arterial atherosclerosis.

Stenosis

Stenoses occur most often on the venous limb of the AVF, or within a graft, but exceptionally we can also observe a narrowing on the arterial side of the AVF (6).

Venous stenoses in both graft and internal fistulas generally occur at or within several centimeters of the anastomotic site. The cause of these venous stenoses is unclear. Stenoses located just at the venous anastomosis may result from surgical trauma or anastomosis of a large shunt vessel to a smaller vein. Proximal stenoses located at a distance from the anastomosis may be related to turbulent flow and shear stresses in a high pressure vein, resulting in accelerated atherosclerotic changes at the site of valves or venous bifurcations (7, 8). In addition, one may speculate that platelets damaged by the dialysis process may be adherent to the endothelium, thereby initiating the endovenous narrowing process by means of mural thrombus and eventual fibrosis (7).

Venous Aneurysms and Varicosities

Prolonged venous hypertension secondary to stenosis leads to incompetence of the valvular mechanism, with resultant retrograde flow and sital varicosities (7). This latter phenomenon may cause swelling of the entire hand and further ischemic changes. Varicosities may also be due to markedly increased flow through the fistula, with subsequent stasis on the distal capillary bed (22).

Venous aneurysms are caused by a number of factors, including: development of systemic pressure within the venous lumen; excessive flow; and poststenotic dilation. Usually these aneurysms appear very large and prominent clinically, but most often the angiographic aspect only shows a mild, tapered dilation because of the mural thrombosis and periadventitial fibrosis. Unless they are progressively enlarging, surgical management is unnecessary.

Venous or graft pseudoaneuysms are rare complications, usually secondary to: poor compression at the end of the dialysis, with hematoma formation at the needle puncture site, and postdilation technique, the false aneurysm occurring within 1–3 months following the procedure (6). In practice, such lesions are most often the consequence of balloon overinflation, with subsequent vascular wall rupture leading to the pseudoaneurysm formation (4, 6).

Arterial Steal

Although radial artery steal is not infrequently seen angiographically (7), clinical manifestations of arterial insufficiency are shomewhat rare, with a reported incidence of 0.4–2% (1, 20). Ischemia is due to a short-circuiting of blood flow when the ulnar or interosseous arteries are incapable of providing adequate flow to the hand.

Treatment of arterial steal, consists either in reducing excessive blood flow, if that is surgically possible, or in ligating the radial artery distally at the wrist.

Other Complications

Other complications (such as infection, pulmonary embolisms) do not always result in hemodynamic consequences for the graft. However, because of the high risk of graft infection, angioplasty is most often preferred to the surgical procedure when a stenosis is discovered. Some fibromuscular dysplastic lesions located on the arterial side of the AVF have been reported following malfunction of an AVF, but this is exceptional.

Excessive fistula flow can cause cardiac failure. Cardiac output increase is due to a combination of different factors, i.e. increased heart rate, decreased outflow, and increased inflow (22). Treatment consists of surgical banding to decrease flow through the AVF.

Technique of Percutaneous Transluminal Angioplasty

Thrombectomy and surgical revision expose the revised shunt to the risks of infection and stenosis of the anastomosis. PTA is an alternative to surgery, decreasing particularly the risk of postsurgical infection, which is a not infrequent complication, particularly with interposed grafts. Three technical problems will be discussed here: angiographic modalities, PTA procedures, and fibrinolytic therapy sometimes associated with PTA.

Angiographic Modalities

Angiography should be performed just before the dilation procedure, even if the lesions have already been documented previously (21). The procedure is performed as follows: cannulation of the arterialized venous limb of the AVF, or of the graft, by a retrograde approach with an 18 G Teflon sheath; compression by hand or by a tourniquet is done proximally in order to decrease the flow just before contrast injection. The association of the retrograde approach and compression permits the opacified blood to fill the fistula through the anastomotic site. In order to decrease patients' complaints during opacification, and the risk of post-angiographic thrombosis, one must utilize a low osmolality contrast medium such as ioxaglate or non-ionic compounds. Images are made by means of serial films with a rapid-sequences film changer. Most often we perform two views in order to suppress overlapping of venous branches which can hide a stenotic lesion. Today, it seems that the method of choice for angiographic imaging may be DSA, which allows diluted contrast medium (up to 50–60%) to be injected.

Dilation Procedure

After the predilation angiographic analysis, 5000 IU of heparin are injected into the venous limb of the fistula, to prevent thrombosis during the procedure. Usually, recording blood pressure across the lesion is not possible, or the curve is of poor quality except across the stenoses located at the proximal anastomotic site of the bovine heterograft. This is probably due to the low pressure level within the venous system in relation to stenoses near the anastomotic site, as well as to an occlusive catheter effect across the stenosis, associated with a loss of perfusion inflow into the collateral veins.

Catheterization of the venous limb fistula or graft is usually achieved with a balloon with a diameter of between 8 and 12 mm, depending on the angiographic estimate of the internal lumen (11). At present, all authors have abandoned the use of PVC balloons, because of their inability to support high pressure up to 12 atm. It is preferable to use polyethylene balloons, which can be inflated up to 12–17 atm, using either high-pressure Olbert balloon catheters or others which appear more suitable for dilating proximal anastomotic grafts. Balloon inflation is achieved under fluoroscopic control with a hand-held syringe connected to a pressure monitoring device, aiming not to exceed the maximal pressure limit. Most of the time, the balloon is kept inflated for up to 2–3 min, or until the balloon deformity disappears. If there is no change after three or four inflations, the procedure is terminated. Following angioplasty, a control angiogram must be obtained to monitor success and to rule out complications. In our experience (4, 6, 13) the angiographic quality of the dilation can be evaluated as follows: good results, if no residual stenosis or only mild narrowing (25%) is seen (Figs. 3–5); intermediate results, showing residual stenosis up to 50% and poor results, showing residual stenosis above 75%, associated with a lack of improvement in the dialysis flow.

Fibrinolytic Therapy

Many authors have developed a non-operative approach by using local fibrinolytic therapy, and if necessary a dilation of the obstructive lesions, to prevent reocclusion. The hematocrit, prothrombin time, and activated partial thromboplastin time are determined prior to the procedure; moreover, fibrinogen and fibrin split product levels are assayed after each course of declotting.

The fibrinolytic agents used depend on the authors' experience. Some use streptokinase, but others prefer to use urokinase (18, 24). The modalities of fibrinolytic agent injection differ: some prefer a continuous infusion of the product into the clot (2500 IU/h for streptokinase, or 10,000 IU/h for urokinase) while others inject a bolus of 2500–5000 IU at 5–15 min intervals (24). When declotting is achieved, a continuous intravenous perfusion of heparin is continued for 24–48 h, and angioplasty of the stenosis responsible is usually performed the day after declotting, to minimize the risk of bleeding.

Complications

Some complications were observed during the attempts at dilation, but most patients recover with appropriate therapy. Complications are unusual, occurring in 3–5% of dilations (8, 9). Thrombosis occurs if heparinization is not done or is insufficient. At the beginning of our experience (6), in a personal series of 35 patients, we observed 4 thromboses; one patient recovered with immediate perfusion of fibrinolytic agents, another through surgical throm-

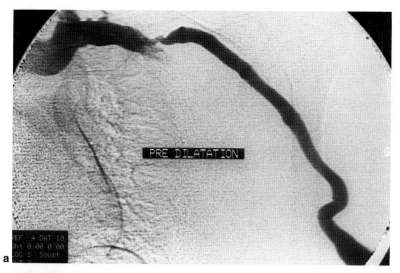

PRE DILATATION

a

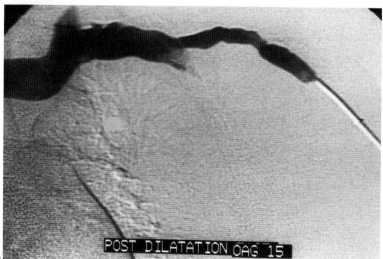

POST DILATATION OAG 15

b

Fig. 3   **PTA of the cephalic vein.** Digital subtraction angiography (DSA)
a Stenosis located at the end of the cephalic vein
b After PTA, no stenosis remains. Moderate spasm is identified upstream of the dilated zone

bectomy, and the remaining two failed to recover despite immediate surgical thrombectomy.

Balloon rupture is observed, resulting from overinflation during dilation of a hard stenosis. Usually balloon rupture results in tears in the vessel wall, with extravasation of contrast medium, leading several months later to a false aneurysm formation (6). Rarely, graft infection may follow angioplasty, but this complication usually resolves after antibiotic therapy without damage to the graft.

During fibrinolysis it is rare for patients to sustain a bleeding complication remote from the graft. Although clot migration is theoretically possible during fibrinolysis, it is in fact rare, and does not cause clinical problems (23, 24).

Indications and Results

Selection of patients for angioplasty is important, because results depend on two major parameters: the site of the stenosis, and the type of catheter used. Immediate results seem to be better with heterologous shunts. On the other hand, stenosis near the anastomosis is easier to dilate (6). Multiple stenoses along an autogenous vein are less suitable for angioplasty. When the stenosis is located near a proximal arteriovenous anastomosis, failure is not infrequent.

Using high-pressure balloons with long inflation times undoubtedly results in better initial results (8). Comparative results show a significantly higher initial patency rate with high-pressure balloons (91% versus 67%) (16). We obtained similar results: in 84 patients, 35 angioplasties were performed using normal polyethylene balloons, and 67 using high-

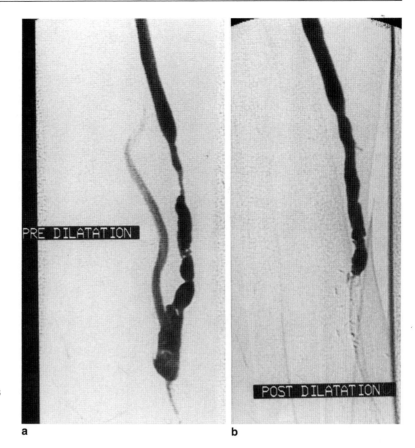

Fig. 4 **PTA of a fistula** (DSA)
a Stenosis at the mid part of the fistula.
Two lucent areas upstream of the
stenosis are due to surgical clip artefacts
b After PTA, mild irregularities of the
venous wall are noted

a   b

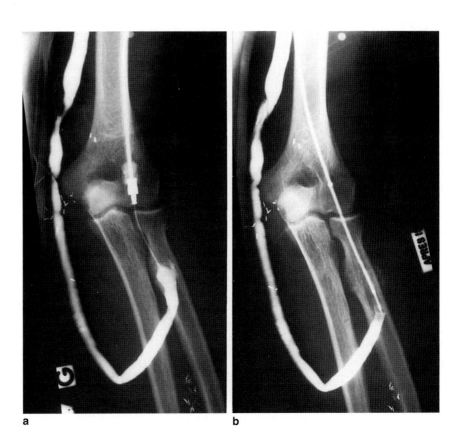

Fig. 5 **Loop PTFE graft
between the brachial artery
and vein**
a Stenosis distal to venous
anastomosis
b After PTA, no significant
stenosis remains

a   b

pressure balloons (13). The initial success was significantly greater with the high-pressure balloons (90% versus 66%).

Long-term patency rates are 70% at six months, 55% at one year, and 40–50% at two years. These results are the same with polyethylene balloons and high-pressure balloons (9) (Fig. **6**). The causative factors, high flow, turbulence and shear stresses, are still present, and lead to restenosis regardless of the method of dilation. In our experience, the anatomic type of the vascular access has no influence on late results and the patency rate is the same (Fig. **7**).

Restenosis may develop in a large proportion of patients. The interval between angioplasty and the development of restenosis, in most instances, is less than 6 months. The rate varies from 35% for autologous AVFs to 84% for heterologous shunts at the

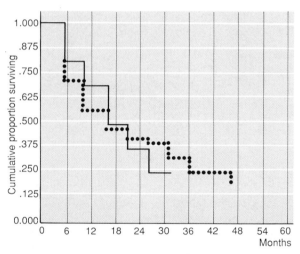

Fig. **6** **Comparison of the patency rates of AVF after PTA** using polyethylene balloon catheters (●) and high-pressure balloon catheters (—)

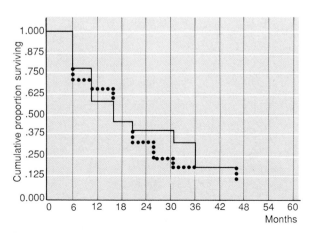

Fig. **7** **Comparison between the patency rates of grafts (●) and veins (—)** following PTA

site of the venous anastomosis. Repeated angioplasty can be performed, with a high success rate of 72%, which can prolong the life of a fistula for many years.

Some lesions are not suitable for angioplasty: lesions longer than 6 cm and segmental occlusions. In other cases, angioplasty can be performed, because it is a safe, usually simple procedure, with a low complication rate and high initially good results. Early detection of stenotic lesions by angiography at the first sign of dialysis inefficiency, or flow rates within the vessel below 200 ml/min, high venous pressure, and clots in the dialysis cannula, allow early reparative angioplasty prior to complete thrombosis of the fistula.

Local fibrinolytic therapy of thrombosed AVFs is an alternative to surgical thrombectomy and revision. Recent bruises or surgical incisions may constitute contra-indications. Thromboses in the early postoperative period (less than three weeks) are not suitable for local fibrinolysis, because the risk of hemorrhage at the site of anastomosis is high, the AVF is usually not developed, and rethrombosis is very frequent. In other cases, thrombolysis should be the first line of treatment for failed hemodialysis access shunts.

Immediate results depend on the anatomic type of the AVF, and on the cause of the thrombolysis, which is most often stenosis. In our experience with 42 clotted hemodialysis shunts, 21 (50%) were restored to function without surgical correction; 12 (29%) had restoration of flow, but required surgical correction of an underlying problem; and 9 (21%) showed no improvement. These results are similar to those of Zeit (24) with streptokinase. Mangiarotti reported a 65% success rate with urokinase (17). The anatomical type of AVF is an important factor affecting the results of fibrinolytic therapy. In 42 cases of AVF thrombosis, initial success, i.e. restoration to function without surgical therapy, is 75% in autologous AVFs, only 31% in bovine heterografts, and 40% in PTFE grafts. Young (23) reports six failures out of seven PTFE graft thromboses. Failure was due to bleeding from previous dialysis puncture sites such that fibrinolytic therapy had to be stopped. However, we do not believe that fibrinolytic therapy must be rejected in case of PTFE graft thromboses, because it is a safe procedure which can be successful in many cases (40%).

Long-term results show a 14% rate of rethrombosis at one month and 30% at six months. After this period, the patency is stable, about 60% at one and two years.

Conclusion

PTA of AVF stenoses has been widely accepted as an effective technique, because it is safe and prolongs the lifetime of dialysis access. Local thrombolytic therapy is efficient in many cases of thrombosis, especially with autologous AVFs; underlying stenoses may be treated by angioplasty or surgery.

Finally, close cooperation between the vascular surgeon and the radiologist is essential to the success rate.

References

1. Beven EG, Hertzer NR. Construction of arteriovenous fistulas for hemodialysis. Surg Clin North Am, 1975;55:1125–1136.
2. Bonallumi U, Civalleri D, Adami G, Gianetta E, Griffanti-Bartoli F. Utilization of the "anatomical snuffbox" for vascular access in haemodialysis. In: Kootstra G, Jörning PJG, eds. Access surgery: a review of current techniques for vascular access for haemodialysis, chemotherapy and total parenteral nutrition. Lancaster: MTP Press, 1983:15–20.
3. Butler HG, Baker LD, Johnson JM. Vascular access for chronic hemodialysis: polytetrafluoroethylene (PTFE) versus bovine heterograft. AM J Surg 1977;134:791–793.
4. Cattan S, Bourquelot P, Raynaud A, Seurot M, Gaux JC. Percutaneous transluminal angioplasty in stenosis of hemodialysis fistulas. In: Oliva L, Veiga-Pirez JA, eds. Interventional radiology 2. 1st ed. Amsterdam: Excerpta Medica 1981:336–340.
5. Forsberg B, Forsberg L, Lindstedt E, Westling H, White T. Side-to-side, side-to-end or end-to-end anastomosis for Cimino-Brescia fistula: preliminary report of a randomized study. In: Kootstra G, Jörning PJG, eds. Access surgery: a review of current techniques for vascular access for haemodialysis, chemotherapy and total parenteral nutrition. Lancaster: MTP Press, 1983:21–23.
6. Gaux JC, Bourquelot P, Raynaud A, Seurot M, Cattan S. Percutaneous transluminal angioplasty of stenotic lesions in dialysis vascular accesses. Eur J Radiol 1983;3:173–242.
7. Glanz S, Bashit B, Gordon DH, Butt K, Adamson R. Angiography of upper extremity: access fistulas for dialysis. Radiology 1982;143:45–52.
8. Glanz S, Gordon D, Butt K, Hong J, Adamson R, Sclafani S. Dialysis access fistulas: treatment of stenosis by transluminal angioplasty. Radiology 1984;152:637–642.
9. Glanz S, Gordon D, Butt K, Hong J, Adamson R, Sclafani S. Stenotic lesions in dialysis-access fistulas: treatment by transluminal angioplasty high-pressure balloons. Radiology 1985;156:236.
10. Gothlin J, Lindstedt E. Angiographic features of Cimino-Brescia fistulas. AJR 1975;125:582–590.
11. Gordon D, Glanz S, Butt K, Adamson R, Koenig M. Treatment of stenotic lesions in dialysis access fistulas and shunts by transluminal angioplasty. Radiology 1982;143:53–58.
12. Hertzer NR, Beven EG. Venous access using the bovine carotid heterograft. Arch Surg 1978;113:696–700.
13. Houle D. Prolongation de la durée de perméabilité des abords vasculaires d'hémodialyse chronique par angioplastie endoluminale percutanée: etude à propos de 102 examens [Dissertation]. Paris: 1985.
14. Hughes K, Adams FG, Hamilton DNH. The radiology of local complications of haemodialysis access devices. Clin Radiol 1980;31:489–496.
15. Hunter DW, So SKS, Castaneda-Zuniga WR, Coleman CE, Sutherland DE, Amplatz K. Failing thrombosed Brescia-Cimino arteriovenous dialysis fistulas. Radiology 1983;149:105–109.
16. Kinnaert P, Vereestraeten P, Toussaint C, van Geertruyden J. Nine years' experience with internal arteriovenous fistulas for heamodialysis: a study of some factors influencing the results. Br J Surg 1977;64:242–246.
17. Mangiarotti C, Canavese C, Thea A, Segoloni GP, Stratta P, Salodione M, Vercellone A. Urokinase treatment for arteriovenous fistulae declotting in dialyses patients. Nephron 1984;36:60–64.
18. Martin EC, Diamond NG, Casarella WJ. Percutaneous transluminal angioplasty in non-atherosclerotic disease. Radiology 1980;135:27–33.
19. Moris C, Kinnaert P. Arteriovenous fistulas at the elbow for maintenance haemodialysis. In: Kootstra G, Jörning PJG, eds. Access surgery: a review of current techniques for vascular access for haemodialysis, chemotherapy and total parenteral nutrition. Lancaster: MTP Press, 1983:25–30.
20. Russel JA, Abbot JA, Lim RC. Radial steal syndrome with arteriovenous fistulas for haemodialysis. Ann Intern Med 1971;75:387–394.
21. Staple TW. Retrograde venography of subcutaneous arteriovenous fistulas created surgically for hemodialysis. Radiology 1973;106:223–224.
22. Vanderwerf BA, Williams T, Koep LJ. Haemodynamics of arteriovenous fistulas. In: Kootstra G, Jörning PJG, eds. Access surgery. Lancaster, MTP Press Ltd. 1982:129–133.
23. Young AT, Hunter DW, Castaneda-Zuniga WR, So SKS, Mercado S, Cardella JF, Amplatz K. Thrombosed synthetetic hemodialysis access fistulas: failure of fibrinolytic therapy. Radiology 1985;154:639–642.
24. Zeit RM, Cope C. Failed hemodialysis shunts: one year of experience with aggressive treatment. Radiology 1985;154:353–356.

Percutaneous Laser-Assisted Angioplasty

T. C. McCowan and E. J. Ferris

Atherosclerotic cardiovascular disease is a major cause of morbidity and mortality in the world today. Pharmacologic agents have not been effective in severe disease, and surgical reconstruction, either endarterectomy or vascular bypass, has been the mainstay of therapy. In the last two decades percutaneous interventional radiologic techniques have proved valuable in treating many forms of vascular disease (7). Certain lesions, however, particularly those that are totally occlusive, diffuse, or highly calcified, are difficult or impossible to treat with current techniques (25, 26). Recently, optical fibers coupled to laser systems have been used in conjunction with percutaneous angiographic and balloon catheters to treat atherosclerotic lesions previously unmanageable without the application of laser energy (1–3). As with PTA, this offers the patient a therapeutic option that avoids the risks associated with major surgery and may reduce overall medical costs.

Materials and Methods

Laser

A laser is a device that converts electromagnetic radiation (light) of mixed frequencies into one or more discrete frequencies of highly amplified and coherent radiation. It is this high power and relatively monochromatic light output that is valuable in the laser's application to intravascular work. The basic design of a laser in shown in Figure 1. A variety of lasers are available for both clinical and experimental medical use. Some of the features of these lasers are listed in Table 1. Each laser offers unique

Table 1   Clinical and experimental medical lasers

Laser	Wavelength (nm)	Typical Maximum Power (W)
Argon ion	488, 514	< 20
CO_2	10,600	< 200
Excimer	193, 248, 308, 351	< 100
Helium-neon	632	< 0.05
Nd: YAG	1060	< 100

advantages and disadvantages in wavelength, energy levels, mode of operation (pulsed or continuous wave), tissue penetration and interaction, and delivery systems available (14, 15, 17, 20, 22).

The neodymium:yttrium-aluminum-garnet (Nd:YAG) laser has seen limited use in cardiovascular work. It has a principal wavelength of 1060 nm but can be altered to produce harmonic wavelengths of 355 and 532 nm. Average power outputs of greater that 100 W are obtainable. Both pulsed and continuous wave modes are available. The light output can be easily and efficiently transmitted through glass fibers and water. At its principal wavelength, it is poorly absorbed by blood, plaque, and normal vessel wall; thus, it is a very penetrating source of laser energy. This does, however, present problems in limiting the Nd:YAG laser's effects on adjacent normal tissue. The high-power output and relatively widespread availability of Nd:YAG systems has recently increased interest in their use in the vascular system.

The excimer (excited dimer) laser is currently the most intensely investigated of the new types of la-

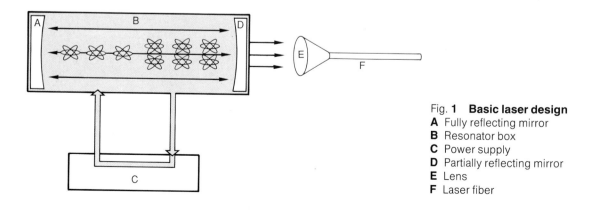

Fig. 1   Basic laser design
A Fully reflecting mirror
B Resonator box
C Power supply
D Partially reflecting mirror
E Lens
F Laser fiber

sers. There is some evidence that the excimer laser operates through a photoablation process to break chemical bonds. This occurs at a temperature well below that of other lasers and may cause less damage to normal surrounding tissue. A variety of wavelengths from 194 to 355 nm are available, depending on the chemical composition of the gases used. Currently, argon, krypton, and xenon coupled with fluoride or chloride are the active media being used. These highly toxic gases require special containment systems for safe clinical use. The excimer is operated exclusively in the pulsed mode and is able to attain very high-power densities per pulse. Difficulties remain in transmitting most excimer wavelengths through suitable fibers without significant loss of power or fiber damage. Water, blood, tissue, and plaque absorption varies with the particular wavelength generated.

The argon laser is still widely used for vascular work. Primary wavelengths are in the blue-green region at 488 and 514 nm. These wavelengths are easily transmitted through both glass fibers and water. Atherosclerotic plaque and normal vessel show relatively poor absorption of these wavelengths. Hemoglobin, however, exhibits very high absorption. This has particular significance when using the argon laser for direct energy application with an open-tipped fiber. Either a bloodless field or extremely close approximation to the lesion then becomes necessary. Maximum power levels for currently available argon lasers are in the range of 16 to 20 W. This laser can be operated in the continuous wave or pulsed mode. All patients at the University of Arkansas for Medical Sciences reported herein have been treated with an argon ion laser system.

Table **2** Laser ionics argon laser model 556A

Wavelength	514.5–454.5 nm
Emergent beam size	2 mm
Beam divergence	0.6 mrad
Maximum average output	14 W (continuous wave)

The specifics of this laser are given in Table **2**. Figure **2** is a picture of the argon ion laser with attached optical fiber.

Optical Fibers

Three factors are important in the selection of an optical fiber for use in the vascular system: toxicity, size and flexibility, and optical transmission (20, 22).

The fiber must obviously be nontoxic to human systems. Most vascular fiber optics are composed of a quartz-based compound with a plastic coating and are inert. These fibers are available in a variety of diameters and lengths. Other fibers are being developed for use with lasers that are unable to transmit their wavelengths through glass. Progress is being made, but the potential toxicity of these newer fibers, many of which are based on halide compounds, is still a concern.

Quartz-based fibers can be made in a variety of sizes easily adaptable to percutaneous intravascular work. Fibers 200 to 400 µm in diameter and in 2 to 4 m lengths are frequently used. They are relatively flexible but do not bend well around tight curves, such as those found in very tortuous vessels. Tactile feedback tends to be less than with commonly used catheters and guide wires. Additionally, current fi-

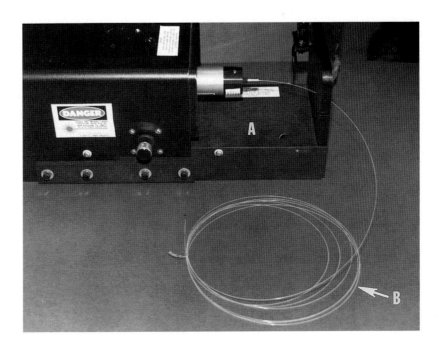

Fig. **2** **Argon laser with attached fiberoptic**
A Laser
B Optical fiber

bers are not easily steerable. This problem is being addressed by both attached wires and specially designed guiding catheters.

The fiber must allow safe and effective transmission of the desired laser wavelength. Argon and Nd:YAG laser wavelengths are easily transmitted through glass fibers with efficiencies greater than 90%. Excimer and carbon dioxide (CO_2) lasers will not transmit well through currently available fibers.

Tip

The fiber-tip configuration is extremely important in determining the mechanism of laser-tissue interaction. Three basic tip styles are currently used or being developed. Some of these tips are shown in Figure 3.

Metal-capped laser fibers have been extensively investigated for intravascular work (13, 23). This tip consists of a metal alloy bonded to the end of a quartz-based fiber. The size and shape can be tailored, although most clinical work has been done with 1.5 or 2.0 mm diameter tips. These tips heat very rapidly when the laser energy is applied and reach temperatures greater than 400°C in less than 3 seconds in saline. A small safety wire is attached to the tip in case it becomes detached from the fiber during use. The largest series of percutaneous laser angioplasty cases has been treated with this tip configuration, and this tip was used for all patients in the present report. The incidence of both thermal and mechanical perforation has been less with this type of tip than with the open-tipped fiber.

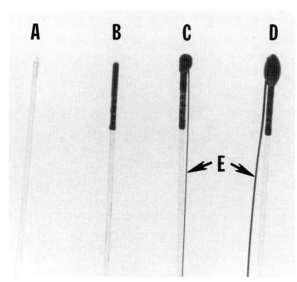

Fig. 3   **Optical fiber and tip configurations**
A A 300 µm open-tipped fiber
B A 300 µm cylindrical metal-capped (experimental) fiber
C A 1.5 mm metal-capped (clinical) fiber
D A 2.0 mm metal-capped (clinical) fiber
E Safety wire

An open-tipped fiber is demonstrated in Figure 3 (11, 20). In this configuration, the laser energy exits the fiber tip parallel to the fiber axis and is applied directly to the target tissue. This takes advantage of tissue absorption characteristics of the laser wavelength used but has been shown to have a higher complication rate, primarily related to thermal and mechanical perforation. The use of centering balloon delivery catheters may reduce the rates of these complications. This type of tip arrangement may also be usable in angioscopically guided laser angioplasty. The fiber might be used for both illumination (using low-power outputs) and application of laser energy (high power).

A lens-tipped fiber has been described that focuses the laser energy onto the target tissue for safer, more effective use of the energy and wavelength. This configuration has certain theoretical advantages, but it is still experimental.

Monitoring

The metal-capped fiber is easily seen at fluoroscopy, and the progress of the recanalization attempt can be monitored with frequent injections of contrast media. The result of the procedure can be documented with digital or plain film images.

Some investigators have advocated the use of angioscopy for monitoring the progress of laser angioplasty (8, 18, 21). Small fiber-optic catheters similar to those used in gastrointestinal and pulmonary endoscopy are now available for percutaneous use in the vascular system. Two angioscopic systems have been investigated and are depicted in Figure 4. One is a single catheter system with self-contained viewing and illuminating fibers, flush port, and occlusion balloon. Minimum diameter for this configuration is currently approximately 2.0 mm. The other system is a smaller fiber-optic catheter containing only viewing and illuminating fibers. It is available in a diameter of 1 mm. This system requires a coaxial guiding catheter to provide access to a flushing port and occlusion balloon. When used with the laser, they offer the theoretical advantage of direct three-dimensional visualization of the vessel interior, which would be of considerable value in improving the safety of laser angioplasty by allowing real-time monitoring of the procedure. The major problem with angioscopy is the need for vascular occlusion and a flush system to displace the blood from the lumen to allow visualization. This technique is under investigation.

Technique

Laser angioplasty is performed in the radiology department in a vascular interventional room especially equipped to handle the power and water

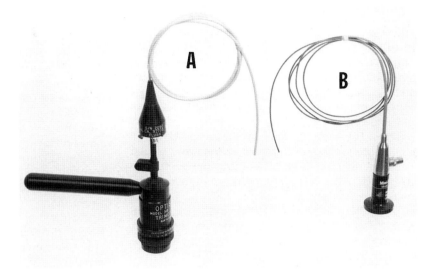

Fig. 4 **Angioscopes**
A Single balloon angioscope
B Coaxial angioscope

requirements of the laser. The patient is prepared and draped in the usual sterile manner. Nifedipine, 10 mg sublingual, is given before the procedure. The femoral artery is punctured at the groin, and the superficial femoral artery is cannulated in an antegrade fashion. A bloodless sheath is then placed in the artery. An angiogram is performed, and the level of the obstruction is localized with radiopaque markers. The laser fiber is advanced through the sheath to a position just proximal to the lesion. The metal tip is readily visible at fluoroscopy. The laser is turned on, and the fiber passed through the lesion with gentle axial pressure as a channel is created by the laser energy. Angiography is repeated to verify recanalization of the target segment. A guide wire is then advanced through this channel, and balloon angioplasty is performed to provide maximal lesion dilation. This is shown diagrammatically in Figure **5**. The patient is usually given 5000 U of heparin and 200 to 400 µg of nitroglycerin intra-arterially during the procedure. Heparin, 1000 U/h, is administered for 24 hours after the angioplasty. The patient is frequently discharged 2 days after the procedure and is placed on low-dose aspirin and followed at regular intervals with non-invasive ankle/brachial (A/B) Doppler pressure measurements (5, 10, 11, 19).

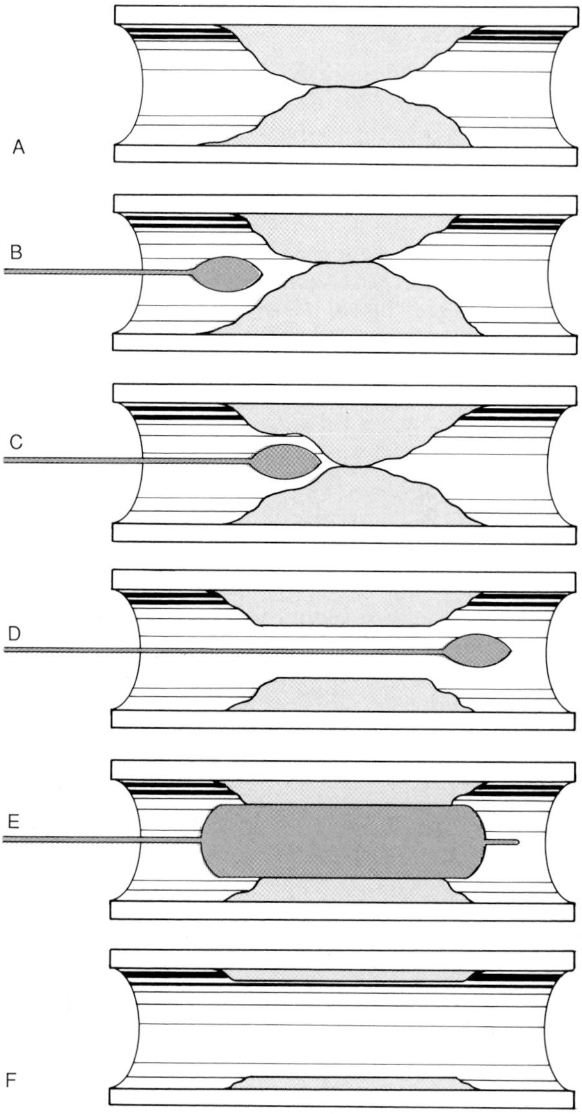

Fig. 5 **Technique of laser angioplasty** ▶
A Obstructed vessel
B Laser probe positioned at block
C Laser probe advancing into lesion
D Laser probe penetrates obstruction
E Dilation balloon catheter inserted and inflated
F Vessel opened, procedure complete

Tissue Effects

Atherosclerotic plaques are composed of a complex mixture of cells, lipids, and inorganic calcium salts. Although the physical effects of laser energy, such as depth and volume of tissue destruction per applied energy, can be easily documented, the biologic response of vascular lesions to laser irradiation is not fully understood (9, 12, 14, 15).

Three basic mechanisms have been proposed to explain the action of laser radiation on vascular tissue: thermal, mechanical/acoustic, and photoablative (20, 22). The relative importance of these interrelated mechanisms is frequently difficult to assess and quantify, since various factors influence the ultimate effects of the laser radiation on the tissue. Significant variables affecting the outcome of tissue irradiation include the laser wavelength, power, mode of operation (continuous wave versus pulsed), and type of delivery fiber. Also important is the thickness and calcium content of the lesion, and the status of the surrounding tissue milieu. The histologic effects of laser angioplasty with a metal-capped fiber in an experimental atherosclerotic model are shown in Figure 6.

The direct thermal effect is the most prominent and obvious action of laser radiation on vascular tissue. It is the primary mechanism for disolution of atherosclerotic plaque. A range of effects is produced, including inapparent disruption of intracellular processes, cellular death and breakdown, coagulation necrosis, tissue charring, and vaporization. Fatty, fibrous, and calcified atheromas show different responses to laser radiation.

Mechanical/acoustic tissue injury is primarily a by-product of the thermal effect of laser radiation and is caused by the kinetic interaction of expanding tissue, fluids, and gases with surrounding structures. When this interaction extends beyond the atheromatous plaque, the result is detrimental and accounts for much of the lateralization of injury into normal tissues. This effect is not a direct linear response but instead rapidly increases above a threshold of tissue energy absorption. Lateralization of injury can be reduced by allowing the tissue to cool between the applications of laser energy. Pulsed mode lasers may reduce tissue injury by this means.

Photoablation supposedly involves the direct interaction of high-energy photons with the intraolecular bonds of the tissue being irradiated to disrupt the lesion. This process occurs at a temperature below that of significant thermal and mechanical/acoustic effects, and lateralization of tissue injury is therefore markedly reduced. This is the proposed mechanism of action of the excimer laser. This theory is not totally accepted, however, and much of the decreased tissue damage may be due to the very short pulse duration of this laser with time for tissue cooling between pulses.

Indications

Currently, laser angioplasty is used as an adjunct to balloon PTA. Its major indication is in the treatment of peripheral vascular occlusive lesions that are too long or too heavily calcified to allow passage of conventional guide wires and catheters. The main locations of disease suitable to this therapy are the superficial femoral artery and the popliteal artery. Lesions in other areas, including the tibioperoneal trunk, iliac arteries, and the coronary arteries have been successfully treated with the laser, but the safety and effectiveness of laser angioplasty in these areas has not been fully established (4, 6).

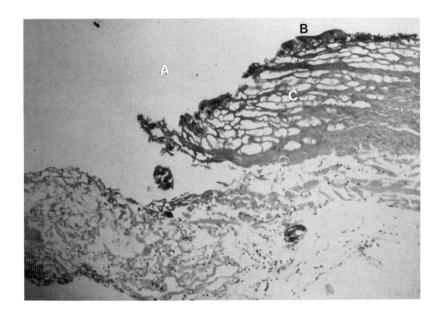

Fig. **6   Histologic effects of laser angioplasty with a 2.00 mm metal-capped fiber in experimental atherosclerotic model**
A Vaporized plaque
B Charred debris
C Coagulation necrosis in media

Complications

The majority of possible complications are similar to those of PTA (5, 11, 19). They are listed in Table **3**. Some of the immediate tissue effects of laser angioplasty may present as complications. The patient may experience pain in the area receiving the laser treatment. This most often is minor but may be severe. Acute thrombosis or arterial spasm may occur and lead to vascular compromise. These can usually be handled pharmacologically in a similar manner to the same complications seen in PTA as currently performed. The most feared complication, vascular perforation, is probably most related to technical and operator factors. Although the rate of vascular perforation is high in some series, it usually is minor and does not compromise the procedure. Metal-capped laser fibers have been shown to have a lower rate of mechanical and thermal perforation compared with open-tipped fibers. Distal embolization of the combustion products or fragments of an atherosclerotic lesion is a potential risk in any laser angioplasty procedure. It was originally hoped that the laser would be able to vaporize atherosclerotic lesions totally. Although some of the lesion is vaporized, a wide variety of breakdown products is produced. The potential toxic effects of these products has been a concern. However, most studies have shown these products to be primarily carbon dioxide, water, nitrogen, and short-chain organic molecules in various proportions. All appear readily absorbable in the blood and probably present no significant toxic problem for the body. Clinically significant embolization in reported series has been rare.

The long-term effects of laser angioplasty are largely unknown. Limited experimental animal studies and human clinical trials have shown no increase or acceleration in the formation of new atherosclerotic lesions. Aneurysm formation is apparently uncommon but has been documented in some experimental animals. The potential for causing mutagenic or neoplastic change is unknown. This potential has been largely a question focused on the ultraviolet lasers, such as the excimer. It is unlikely, however, that the effect could be more significant than the low risk associated with x-ray exposure during angiography.

In the series of patients at the University of Arkansas for Medical Sciences, five patients had complications related to the laser angioplasty procedure. These included distal embolization into the anterior tibial artery (treated with heparin), intravascular thrombosis related to slow blood flow in a patient with poor distal vessels (treated with heparin), and a small vascular perforation (no therapy required). One patient had transient renal failure secondary to contrast media administration. Another

Table **3** Possible complications of laser angioplasty

Early	Late
Hematoma	Reocclusion
Infection	Accelerated disease
Thrombosis	Aneurysm formation
Embolism	Mutagenesis
Vascular spasm	Neoplastic change
Pain	
Dissection	
Perforation	
Vessel rupture	
Contrast media reaction	

patient had bleeding from the groin puncture site that required surgical repair. None of these complications was believed to affect the patient's clinical outcome.

Clinical example. A 74-year-old man with a history of heart disease presented with left leg claudication at less than 1 block of walking (Fig. **7**). Additionally, he had ischemic changes in his fifth toe. A/B Doppler index was 0.42 in that leg. Angiogram revealed a 6 cm occlusion of the distal superficial femoral artery and proximal popliteal artery. The patient underwent laser angioplasty with a 2 mm metal-capped fiber. A total of 80 J (8 W for 10 seconds) of energy was delivered. A/B index was 0.73 24 hours after the procedure. He was discharged in 2 days. A/B index was 1.03 at 1 month, and he had no claudication or ischemic changes.

Results

The early results of laser angioplasty have ranged from mixed to encouraging (5, 10, 11). Most reports of laser angioplasty using the argon ion laser with an open-tipped fiber have had only moderate success at recanalization and have had a high incidence of complications, most notably vascular perforation and pain. A larger study using the argon ion laser and a metal-capped fiber has had much better results. Initial recanalization was achieved in 80 to 90% of the patients at the participating institutions. For the first 13 patients at the University of Arkansas for Medical Sciences, the target lesion was recanalized with laser angioplasty in 11 (85%). Ten of the 13 (77%) had improvement of the clinical symptoms. One-half of the lesions were considered impossible to treat with routine balloon angioplasty.

A/B Doppler pressures increased from 0.50 ± 0.13 preangioplasty to 0.73 ± 0.18 at 24 hours. The A/B index was 0.82 ± 0.17 at 1 month and 0.77 ± 0.19 at 6 months. Follow-up of a limited number of patients from the study institutions evaluating the argon ion laser with a metal-capped fiber shows a patency rate

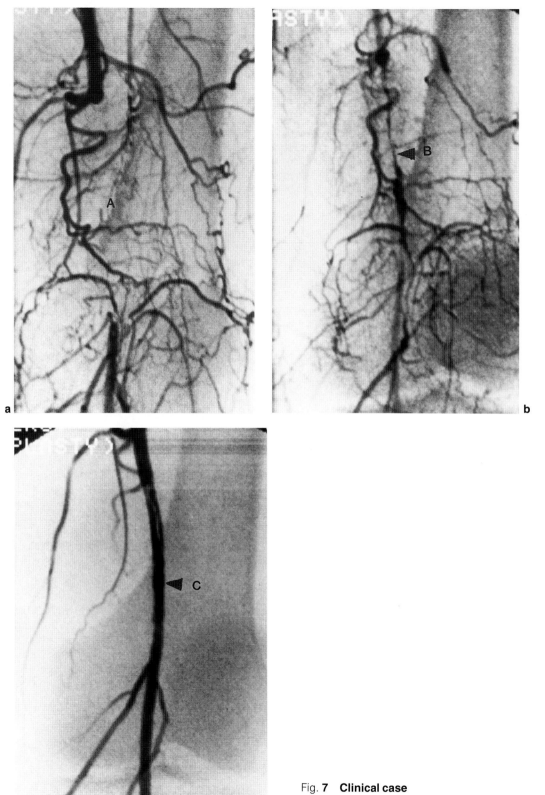

Fig. 7 Clinical case
a 6 cm occlusion of the distal SFA and proximal popliteal artery
b Laser channel created
c Patent vessel following balloon dilation

of approximately 80 to 85% at 1 year for the successfully recanalized lesions. This compares quite favorably with previously reported PTA and surgical bypass results (7, 25, 26).

Conclusion

Although laser angioplasty is a promising technique for the treatment of occlusive vascular disease, several problems remain to be addressed and solved. There is no consensus regarding the best type of laser and fiber system. Each laser has its own advantages and disadvantages, depending on the wavelengths produced and the absorption characteristics of the target tissue. The currently used fibers are very difficult to direct and maneuver. Probably the single largest obstacle is the development of techniques, either mechanical, physical, or pharmacologic, that allow maximal absorption of the laser energy in the diseased tissue while sparing the normal surrounding structures. Several options are being investigated. Differential absorption can be affected by selection of the laser wavelength and altering the power application sequence by pulsing the laser very rapidly (for example, 1000 pulses/second) with very high-power densities per pulse (megawatts/pulse) (16). Improved monitoring with steerable intravascular angioscopes may improve the ability to direct the laser energy at the target plaque.

One proposal that may increase the ratio of lesion to surrounding tissue-effects of laser angioplasty is the use of agents that selectively localize in atherosclerotic tissue and enhance the destructive effect of the laser energy. Tetracycline compounds have been found to localize in atherosclerotic lesions, probably based on an interaction with calcium. Hematoporphyrin derivative (currently most often used for its uptake in neoplastic lesions) is an injectable compound that is selectively concentrated in atherosclerotic plaques and alters the absorption of the tissue to laser light. Following radiation by light of the proper wavelength, both of these compounds produce a selective disruption of the atherosclerotic lesion (24).

Laser angioplasty has a proved value in the treatment of occlusive lesions in the larger vessels of the lower extremity that previously have or would have failed standard PTA techniques. Although laser angioplasty has been performed in the distal vessels of the lower extremity and even in the coronary arteries, its effectiveness and safety in these vascular systems is unproved. Laser angioplasty alone as currently practiced usually does not reestablish sufficient luminal diameter to provide adequate blood flow to maintain vessel patency without follow-up balloon angioplasty. Considerable effort is directly to developing laser angioplasty techniques that can be used as the primary and sole therapy for atherosclerotic occlusive disease. Randomized clinical trials comparing patency rates, complications, and costs with other modalities such as balloon-only PTA and surgical bypass, are needed to assess this promising technology fully.

References

1. Abela GS, Pepine CJ. Emerging applications of laser therapy for occlusive vascular disease. Cardiovasc Rev Rep 1985;6:269–278.
2. Choy DSJ, Stertzer SH, Myler RK, Marco J, Fournial G. Human coronary laser recanalization. Clin Cardiol 1984;7:377–381.
3. Choy DSJ, Stertzer SH, Rotterdam HZ, Sharrock N, Kaminov IP. Transluminal laser catheter angioplasty. Am J Cardiol 1982;50:1206–1208.
4. Crea F, Davies G, McKenna W, Pashazade M, Taylor K, Maseri A. Percutaneous laser recanalization of coronary arteries. Lancet 1986;ii:214–215.
5. Cumberland DC, Sanborn TA, Taylor DI, Moore DJ, Welsh CL, Greenfield AJ, Guben JK, Ryan TJ. Percutaneous laser thermal angioplasty: initial clinical result with a laser probe in total peripheral artery occlusions. Lancet 1986;i:1457–1459.
6. Cumberland DC, Starkey IR, Oakley GDG, Fleming JS, Smith GH, Goiti JJ, Taylor DI, Davis J. Percutaneous laser-assisted coronary angioplasty. Lancet 1986;ii:214.
7. Doubilet P, Abrams HL. The cost of underutilization: percutaneous transluminal angioplasty for peripheral vascular disease. N Engl J Med 1984;310:95–102.
8. Ferris EJ, Ledor K, Ben-Avi DD, Baker ML, Robbins KV, McCowan T, Sharma B. Percutaneous angioscopy. Radiology 1985;157:319–322.
9. Gerrity RG, Loop FD, Golding LAR, Ehrhart LA, Argenyi ZB. Arterial response to laser operation for removal of atherosclerotic plaques. J Thorac Cardiovasc Surg 1983;85:409–413.
10. Ginsburg R, Kim DS, Guthaner D, Toth J, Mitchell RS. Salvage of an ischemic limb by laser angioplasty: description of a new technique. Clin Cardiol 1984;7:54–58.
11. Ginsburg R, Wexler L, Mitchell RS, Profitt D. Percutaneous transluminal laser angioplasty for treatment of peripheral vascular disease. Radiology 1985;156:619–624.
12. Lee G, Ikeda RM, Herman I, Dwyer RM, Bass M, Hany H, Kozina J, Mason DT. The qualitative effects of laser irradiation on human arteriosclerotic disease. Am Heart J 1983;105:885–889.
13. Lee G, Ikeda RM, Chan MC, Dukich J, Lee MH, Theis JH, Bommer WJ, Reis RL, Hanna E, Mason DT: Dissolution of human atherosclerotic disease by fiber optic laser-heated metal cautery cap. Am Heart J 1984;107:777–784.
14. Isner JM, Clarke RH. The current status of lasers in the treatment of cardiovascular disease. IEEE J Quantum Elec 1984;QE-20:1406–1420.
15. Letokhov VS. Laser biology and medicine. Nature 1985;316:235–330.
16. Linsker R, Srinivasan R, Wynne JJ, Alonso DR. Far-ultraviolet laser ablation of atherosclerotic lesions. Lasers Surg Med 1984;4:201–204.
17. Litvack L, Grundfest WS, Beeder C, Forrester JS. Laser angioplasty: status and prospects. Semin Intervent Radiol 1986;3:75–81.
18. Litvack F, Grundfest WS, Lee ME, Carroll RM, Foran R, Chaux A, Berci G, Rose HB, Matloff JM, Forrester JS. Angioscopic visualization of blood vessel interior in animals and humans. Clin Cardiol 1985;8:65–70.
19. McCowan TC, Ferris EJ. Laser angioplasty: a new therapeutic option. Diagn Imag Clin Med 1986;8:86–91.
20. McCowan TC, Ferris EJ, Baker ML, Robbins KV. Laser angioplasty: some experimental observations. Semin Intervent Radiol 1986;3:168–173.

21. McCowan TC, Robbins KV, Uthman EO, Ferris EJ, Baker ML. Angioscopic monitoring of in vivo laser angioplasty. SPIE Opt Fibers Med Biol 1985;576:39–41.

22. Murphy-Chutorian D, Selzer P, Wexler L, Ginsburg R. Practical issues in laser angioplasty: a new technique. Contemp Surg 1985;27:13–20.

23. Sanborn TA, Faxon DP, Haudenschild CC, Ryan TJ. Experimental angioplasty: circumferential distribution of laser thermal energy with a laser probe. J Am Coll Cardiol 1984;5:934–938.

24. Spears JR, Serur JR, Shropshire D, Paulin S. Fluorescence of experimental atheromatous plaques with hematoporphyrin derivate. J Clin Invest 1983;71:395.

25. Van Andel GS, van Erp WFM, Krepel VM, Breslau PJ. Percutaneous transluminal dilatation of the iliac artery: long-term results. Radiology 1985;156:321–323.

26. Krepel VM, van Andel GS, van Erp WFM, Breslau PJ. Percutaneous transluminal angioplasty of the femoropopliteal artery: initial and long-term results. Radiology 1985;156:325–328.

Percutaneous Laser-Assisted Angioplasty: Clinical Results

I. Enge and A. Schilvold

Percutaneous transluminal angioplasty (PTA) has become widely accepted not only in the treatment of stenosis and obstructions of peripheral arteries of the extremities, but also in a variety of other vessels. Ten to 20% patients referred for lower leg ischemia are treated by PTA. In a number of cases, however, PTA may not be successful because this method depends on the ability to traverse the diseased area with the guide wire or the catheter. Thus, especially in patients with long standing, total occlusions, fibrous and calcified plaques, PTA will often fail.

Recanalization of hard plaques using laser energy is a new concept performed during the last years both experimentally (3, 5, 10, 16) and clinically (2, 11). The different approaches using laser energy for these purposes have not all been successful, mainly due to the small diameters of the channels created and the lack of steerability, which has led to an unacceptably high rate of perforation of the vessel wall. Recent reports on laser-assisted PTA in treatment of patients with intermittent claudication (2, 8, 9, 11) indicate growing interest for this as a potentially important tool for treatment of this commonly occurring disease.

Laser Technology

Laser (light amplification by stimulated emission of radiation) is based on the theories of Albert Einstein proposed in 1917. In 1960 the first working laser was produced, using a ruby as the lasing medium. In the following years, a number of new materials have resulted in new lasers with different properties. Several hundreds of lasing media are now known, although only a few are in practical use.

Laser light comes into existence when the atoms of a lasing material are hit by energy, bringing the atoms to an excited level. In order to produce laser light, the majority of atoms must be in an excited state (population inversion). The material may be a crystal, a liquid, or a gas. When the atoms return to a more stable condition containing less energy, the surplus energy of the atom is emitted in light quants called "photons". When the photon hits an excited atom, the atom will emit another photon in addition to the photon that hit the atom. Thus, two photons will be emitted, which in turn will hit another atom to produce four photons, and so on. In order to enhance the axial light, mirrors are positioned at each end of the tube containing the lasing medium. The light, consisting of photons, is thrown back and forth between the mirrors, contributing to the stimulated emission of (light) radiation. A small portion of the light slips through a window in one mirror, is focused in a lens, and passed on to a system of mirrors or an optic fiber for final use.

In order to pump energy into the system to bring the atoms to an excited level, an external power supply unit is necessary. Most commonly used are electrodes (anodes and cathodes) positioned on each side of the tube, "bombing" the atoms with electrons, which are temporarily absorbed in the atoms (excitation). A light source may also be used for energy delivery.

Laser light differs from ordinary light in several ways:
- The photons emitted from the purified medium all have the same wavelength (monochromatic).
- The light waves travel in the same phase (coherent).
- The light has only a slight divergence, the light waves traveling almost parallel (collimated).
- Light is able to carry considerable energy provided the light beam is sufficiently dense (Table 1). The light energy in a given laser beam is called power density (W/cm^2). The total energy delivered is expressed in W/s, called joules (J).

Medical Lasers

The most commonly used lasers in medicine are currently the argon, the neodymium:yttrium-aluminum-garnet (Nd:YAG) and the carbon dioxide (CO_2), based on the lasing medium. The light-tissue interaction depends on the wavelength of the laser beam, giving differences in absorption, transmission, scattering, and reflection.

The wavelengths of these lasers vary, being 488 and 514 nm (argon), 532, 1064, 1318 nm (Nd:YAG), and 10,600 nm (CO_2).

Although laser light from the CO_2 laser is totally absorbed in water (cytoplasma), light from the Nd:YAG laser will pass through water without being absorbed. A practical consequence from the field of ophthalmology is that light from the CO_2 laser will be absorbed in the cornea, whereas the Nd:YAG light will go all the way through the cornea, lens, and vitrous medium and be absorbed in the retina. The

Table **1**   Characteristics of laser light

Focal length of lens (mm)	50	125	250	340	430
Spot diameter (mm)	0.1	0.22	0.45	0.60	0.80
Power (W)	Power density (W/cm^2)				
80	1,020,000	210,000	50,000	16,000	3000
60	760,000	160,000	38,000	12,000	2000
40	510,000	105,000	25,000	8,000	1300
20	250,000	53,000	13,000	4,000	640
5	64,000	13,000	3,000	1,000	160

Absten, G. T., S. N. Joffe: Reprinted from Lasers in Medicine.

argon laser, having wavelengths near the absorption peak of hemoglobin (577 nm), will be absorbed by blood and blood-containing tissue.

Fiber Technology

The development of thin, flexible fibers to transport the laser light to the target tissue has been decisive for the development of percutaneous applications.

A normal, complete fiber may be well below 1 mm in diameter. The central light-transporting material is usually quartz, with a diameter of 0.2 to 0.3 mm. The quartz is surrounded by a cladding, having a lower refractive index than the core, thus reflecting the laser light back into the core. The outer layer consists of Teflon, which promotes the smooth passage down an instrument or a vessel and minimizes the clotting of blood to the fiber.

An important limitation of quartz fibers is their limited capability to transport different wavelengths. Light within the visible and near infrared range may be sent through these fibers. A quartz fiber may be connected to an argon and a Nd:YAG laser, but not to a CO_2 laser.

The technical solution to this problem is expected to be solved in the near future, as extensive research is being conducted.

Percutaneous Vascular Applications

Five years after the first tunneling of a thrombus using laser light by Choy et al. followed by in vitro and in vivo animal experiments, the initial report on percutaneous laser recanalization in vivo in a patient was published in 1984 (10) using a bare fiber to vaporize the plaque. Intra-operative laser recanalization was demonstrated the same year (4). However, several workers experienced considerable difficulties in achieving a patent lumen, the steerability was poor, and vessel wall perforation generally occurred in at least 10 to 25% of the cases (2, 11).

Consequently, development of modified fiber tips took place in the early 1980s in order to improve the short- and long-term results of laser treatment.

Light-tissue interaction. As already mentioned, using a bare fiber to irradiate the plaque has been disappointing when used percutaneously in vivo, even under direct visualization through an angioscope. These difficulties also included problems in creating a small channel for subsequent crossing with a guide wire to perform ordinary PTA. The noncontact technique necessary to prevent blowing the fiber tip was an additional problem during the procedure.

Based on the absorption characteristics of laser light, work has been carried out to enhance light absorption in the plaque (photodynamic therapy). The majority of experimental work carried out so far has dealt with phototherapy of neoplasms after absorption of photosensitizer in the neoplastic cells.

Hematoporphyrin derivatives and also tetracyclines are selectively bound to atheromatous plaques. The total amount of radiation energy should thus be reduced with less risk of vessel wall damage. The problem of intolerability of the substances, especially the hematoporphyrin derivatives when the skin of the patients is exposed to the sun, may be a limiting factor.

New substances, such as the carotenoids, which occur naturally in atheromatous plaques, are potentially interesting photosensitizers for future photodynamic therapy. Better understanding of the photochemical interaction, a better control of light dosimetry, and the development of new photosensitive substances will make this a potentially useful treatment modality in the future.

Laser balloon angioplasty is based on the combination of a laser fiber and a dilation balloon in one catheter. However, the radiation of light is from the interior of the balloon perpendicular to the vessel wall. The theoretical consideration behind the construction has been the possibility of welding the intima flap to the stretched vessel wall with the balloon inflated and thus reduce the risk of dissection and abrupt reclosure of the dilated vessel due to subintimal bleeding and elastic recoil. In addition, the experimental work done may indicate a smoother channel with the combined approach than with only PTA (18).

Another construction under investigation is a balloon catheter with a coaxial laser fiber firing forward to create an initial channel for subsequent dilation. Irregular and tortuous vessels may cause complications even if the fiber is likely to be fixed in the center of the vessel by the inflated balloon.

A variation in construction is an asymmetric balloon with a laser fiber, which is rotated during the procedure. The method is claimed to produce a larger and more regular channel in a controlled manner (12).

Selective ablation of the atheromatous plaque using spectroscopy to identify the target tissue is another investigational device. The catheter has a number of fibers that irradiate the plaque following automatic feedback from spectroscopic evaluation of the vessel in front of the catheter (6).

Better plaque recognition by direct vision through an angioscope (19) or by an ultrasound probe on the catheter tip are both methods undergoing clinical asessment. The former method, being dependent on a bloodless field in front of the lens, leaves the method more suitable for intra-operative use in the vessels, where the surgeon temporarily can shut off the blood flow during the procedure. Inflatable balloons designed to close the vessel have proved unsatisfactory, since the back flow from collaterals as well as the vasa vasorum contribute to inadequate hemostasis. Angioscopy, however, has an interesting future for diagnosis, control, and therapy with specially designed instruments that can be passed through the angioscope.

Contact laser ablation. The sapphire tip concentrates the laser energy in the immediate surroundings of the tip by deflecting the laser light within the tip. The tip itself may be heated to cause vaporization in addition to the laser light energy. The tip will act solely by application of laser light energy to the tissue when the tip is cooled during the procedure. Since it is a contact laser device, the operator will get a tactile feedback during the procedure. Clinical reports on successful laser recanalization of peripheral arterial occlusion have recently appeared (9).

The Laserprobe tip consists of a metal cap attached to an optic fiber. The laser energy delivered through the fiber is converted to heat within the cap. The heated laser probe will cause vaporization of occlusive organic material, producing a channel when brought into contact with the tissue. Based on the energy (joules) delivered through the fiber, a controlled thermal energy can be brought to the tissue.

The laser probe has an ovoid configuration, giving it good tracking abilities within the vessel lumen. Different sizes have been used, the 2 mm diameter probe being the size with which most of the clinical work has been done. An anchor wire is attached to the probe to secure its retrieval in case of detachment. A channel through the body of the instrument has been made to allow the laser probe to be passed over a guide wire.

A typical energy level to heat the laser probe to its working temperature of about 400°C will be 10 to 12 W to the probe tip within the vessel. The laser probe is a disposable device delivered with a SMA connector. Coupling to other generators is possible by using an adaptor. The laser probe can be used in connection with any laser generator, provided the laser light can be delivered through a fiber, the generator is giving a stable energy output at the energy level just mentioned, and coupling possibilities are present.

At 400°C, the organic material in the plaque will vaporize. Calcifications will not be affected, because the melting point is about 1800°C and the evaporation point is about 5000°C. Due to the vaporization of organic material, a channel with a diameter somewhat less than the diameter of the probe will be created after the first crossing. The channel can be widened a little more by passing the probe back and forth repeatedly. Experimental work was promising, showing significantly lower incidence of perforation of the vessel wall, a significant channel for crossing with a guide wire in less time than bare fiber technique (1, 7, 15, 17).

Cumberland et al. (8) have reported a total time varying from 5 to 120 seconds to cross an occlusion, which correspond to our experience with the laser probe.

Debris analysis. Analysis of the composition of vaporized organic material of atherosclerotic plaques in vitro using bare laser light has been done (13, 20). The particle size distribution was 10 to 50 μm, the vast majority (95%) being 10 to 20 μm, partly depending on whether Ringer's solution or CO_2 was used as irrigation.

The cytotoxicity of the particles tested was low or absent. The gases identified were air, traces of methane, acetylene, ethylene, ethane, propylene, and butane. Tetrafluorethylene was also identified. The latter was probably due to the Teflon jacket around the fiber. Whether the gas will be released using the laser probe is not known, since high temperatures are necessary to vaporize fluorocarbons. Clinical side effects of the debris have not been shown in vivo in patients treated with the laser probe. Further studies are necessary to obtain more detailed knowledge in this field.

Experimental work. The lasers described act through direct light-tissue interaction or through conversion to heat in a fiber tip.

The excimer laser (derived from excited dimer) uses a halide of a noble gas as the lasing medium. The wavelengths range from 193 to 351 nm in the commercially available models. The lasers are pulsed, having a short pulse width, but can reach a very high peak intensity. Especially as far as the 193 nm wavelength is concerned, the laser probably acts by breaking the molecular chemical bonds and not exerting thermal effects on the tissue. The possibility of nonthermal ablation of even calcified plaques without injuring the vessel wall has been postulated, and experimental work has been promising (14). However, there are problems that need further investigation.

In animal work, teratogenic effects have been shown, possibly due to splitting and recombination of genetic material, which is not denatured due to lack of thermal decomposition. There are also problems passing the light down a fiber; this is especially the case with the shorter wavelengths. The future role of the excimer laser in vessel recanalization has to be established through further experimental work in animals, as well as the solving of technical problems, as pointed out earlier.

Tunable dye lasers are capable of delivering various wavelengths according to the absorption peak of the target tissue. Different wavelengths can be obtained by irradiating an organic dye with a laser beam. The resulting beam that comes out of the liquid is composed of various wavelengths. The beam can be sent through a revolvable prism to select the wanted color.

Free electron lasers are also variable in the selection of wavelengths, giving new possibilities in diagnosis and treatment of diseases. The laser is still an experimental device.

Other lasers are under development. Some of them may have an extremely high peak power output, such as the X-ray laser, activated by an atom bomb for military purposes, capable of destroying missiles. The laser may have applications in the medical field in a more peaceful mode as well.

Lasers have an exciting future in medical diagnosis and treatment. In 1988 we are still at the beginning of the road. Lasers mentioned, as well as new developments, will be explored to become an increasingly important tool for physicians in several fields of medicine in the near future.

Clinical Application of Laser-Assisted Angioplasty Using a Metal-Capped Fiber Tip

Selection of Patients

A possible candidate for either operative treatment, PTA, or laser-assisted PTA is evaluated by clinical examination (vascular surgeon), vascular laboratory tests (ankle-arm pressure index, flow measurements), angiographic mapping, and usually also intra-arterial pressure gradient recordings.

The choice of treatment should be discussed and decided on in close cooperation between the vascular surgeon and the interventional radiologist. All this can be done on an out-patient basis. If percutaneous angioplasty is the method of choice, the reasons for this decision are explained to the patient, detailing the performance of the procedure, potential complications, and the anticipated beneficial effects.

At the present time, with limited experience in the use of laser-assisted PTA, we suggest that the laser should only be used when PTA has failed or operative intervention is considered to be contraindicated (8).

Preprocedural Patient Care

We recommend that the same precautions and instructions used for angiography and PTA be followed.

Technique

Local anesthesia is usually sufficient, but additional medication may be necessary. We recommend the percutaneous femoral route both for antegrade and retrograde catheterization. An 8 Fr sheath with valvular arrangement and flushing facilities is introduced into the artery to secure permanent access to the vessel during the procedure. Frequent flushing with heparin and saline solution (5000 IU/liter) is important to prevent clotting and embolization. We have encountered a problem of leakage of blood back through the valve irrespective of the different models used.

A ruler with radiopaque figures attached to the actual limb, and test injection of contrast medium, facilitate the exact localization of the diseased area (Fig. 1a, b). Under fluoroscopic guidance, attempts are then made with a soft-tipped guide wire to traverse the occlusion and perform a PTA. Only if the traditional PTA fails, is the laser technique applied. Following intra-arterial injection of 5000 IU of heparin, the probe is introduced and on reaching the obstructed site, the laser energy is switched on, heating the probe immediately. At the same time, by gentle pushing of the heated probe, it may penetrate the occluded area of the vessel and create a primary channel (Fig. 1c). The laser energy is usually only switched on for a period of 5 seconds using 10 to 12 W. It is important immediately after the activation of the laser, to withdraw the probe into the vessel lumen and move it back and forth for about 3 seconds to cool it down and prevent it from jamming in the channel. Repeated attempts to traverse the obstruction may be necessary. When this has been achieved, the procedure is continued as traditional

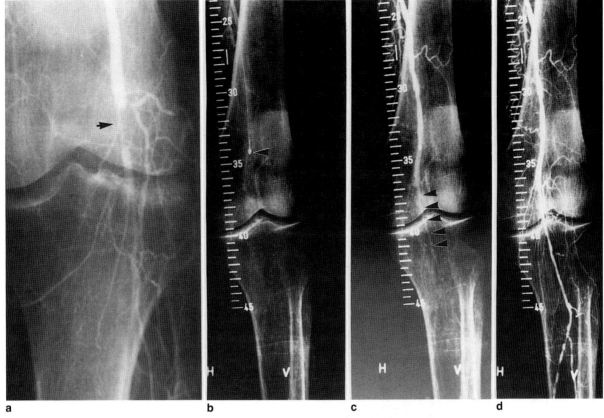

Fig. 1 **An 86-year-old woman with gradually increasing left lower leg ischemia to resting pain and gangrenous ulcerations on first toe and heel.** Admitted for an amputation performed on the first toe or even a lower leg amputation
a Before admittance, 95% stenosis was angiographically demonstrated of the lower part of the superficial femoral artery and almost total occlusion of the popliteal artery (arrow). When admitted, the popliteal artery was totally occluded and could not be traversed by conventional PTA technique
b Radiopaque device for markings. Laser probe (arrowhead) pushed at the site of the occlusion
c Laser probe passed through the occlusion (arrowhead). Contrast medium injected demonstrating the channel created
d After dilation using a balloon catheter 5 mm/4 cm, good pulsation was obtained in the popliteal artery.

PTA (Fig. **1d**). Finally, an angiographic check of the treated area and the peripheral arterial tree is performed.

Restenosis or occlusion may occur. Most of these cases can be successfully treated with repeated PTA.

As is experienced after PTA, longer occlusions have a lower patency rate. Laser-assisted PTA seems, however, justified in selected cases impossible to cross with the guide wire (Fig. **2**).

Postprocedural Patient Care and Follow-up

The patient remains in the hospital overnight. Search for possible complications will be done at the ward as well as a close clinical and vascular laboratory follow-up the next morning. The patient then will usually be discharged from the hospital on antiplatelet aggregation treatment (0.5 g aspirin daily). Further follow-up is done on an out-patient basis after 3, 6, and 12 months, including clinical and laboratory tests and,

in case of recurring ischemia, new angiographic mapping.

Complications

Known complications of PTA are hematoma and bleeding from the puncture site, spasm, formation of false aneurysm, thrombosis, dissection and perforation of the artery, arteriovenous fistulas, peripheral embolism, thrombotic occlusion, and occasionally recurrent obstruction. These complications may also occur after laser-assisted PTA. As already mentioned, the risk of perforation of the artery using the bare laser light energy (2, 11) is too high. Using the laser-heated probe, however, there is a lower frequency of such complications, although they may occur (8). This is also in accordance with our experience.

Complaints of pain during attempts to cross the occlusion with the laser probe may be an indication

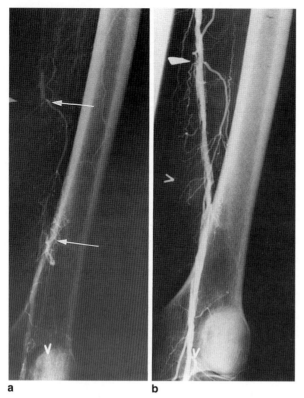

a   b

Fig. **2   A 72-year-old woman with increasing left lower leg ischemia for 6 months. Claudication distance, 20 meters.** Admitted for either surgery PTA
a Long segment occlusion of the left surperficial femoral artery (arrows)
b Angiographic results after laser-assisted PTA

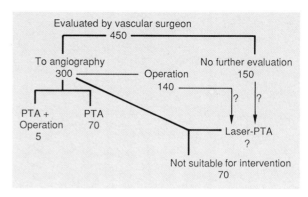

Fig. **3**   Patients treated for peripheral vascular disease

of subintimal dissection or perforation of the arterial wall. This should be confirmed or excluded by an angiogram before breaking off or continuing the procedure.

Potential Indications

Reflecting our strict indications for using laser, about 10 to 15% of patients referred would have laser-assisted PTA treatment. One argument against the philosophy of using laser only on strict indications would be that no one knows if the long-term results of PTA could lead to further improvement if laser light energy was used in all PTA procedures.

It should be stressed that, in some of the patients treated with laser-assisted PTA, the alternative would be an amputation. In others, for instance in diabetics, a lower level leg or only a toe amputation could be a beneficial result of recanalization of the main arteries to the leg, as we have seen in some patients.

What is then the number of patients to be treated by laser-assisted PTA? Following the introduction of

and fully acceptance of PTA as an alternative method to surgery for lower leg ischemia at our hospital, the number of patients operated on yearly for this disease decreased by about 25%. The number of patients referred for claudication in 1 year is about 450 (Fig. **3**).

By clinical evaluation one-third of these patients were not considered candidates for further examination or treatment because of either wrong diagnosis or too vague symptoms and complaints. Potential candidates for laser-assisted PTA may, however, be found among some of the 70 patients not considered fit for any intervention, some from the group operated on, and even some from the group who did not proceed to further evaluation by arteriography.

The consequences of this new therapeutic method are similiar to those resulting from a number of other interventional radiologic procedures: an increase in the number of patients who can be treated, in many cases avoiding surgery or being the only alternative treatment, avoiding general anesthesia and postoperative pain, and shortening the hospital stay. Some patients may be able to return to normal life and working acitivity. Socially, psychologically, and economically, this has a great impact on the patients as well as on our society.

From an investor's economic point of view, it is also important to assess the real benefit of investing in laser equipment. This again relates to the number of cases and type of lesions for which the combined laser-PTA method is considered decisive for the achievement of acceptable results. The laser technology, however, as well as other concepts and methods, are under rapid development. Some of these are already used in clinical trials for arterial recanalization. Even coronary artery occlusions have been treated in a limited number of cases with laser-assisted PTA. Further improvements of the laser probe and the technique seem to be needed before this indication is justified.

Conclusion

Laser-assisted PTA is a new adjunct in the treatment of patients with occlusive arterial disease. Short-term follow-up studies indicate this to be the method of choice – at least for the time being – in selected patients with lower leg ischemia having lesions suitable for PTA, but where this method of treatment has failed due to the nature of the atherosclerotic plaque. The long-term follow-up results are not yet available. Further development of equipment and introduction of other methods for treatment of such patients are under investigation.

References

1. Abela GS, Ferrech A, Crea F, Conti CR. "Hot tip", another method of laser vascular recanalization. LMS 1985;5:327–335.
2. Abela GS, Normann SJ, Cohen DM, Franzini D, Feldman RL, Crea F, Fenech A, Pepine CJ, Conti CR. Laser recanalization of occluded atherosclerotic arteries in vivo and in vitro. Circulation 1985;71:403.
3. Abela GS, Normann S, Cohen D, Feldman BL, Geiser EA, Conti CR. Effects of carbon dioxide Nd-YAG and argon laser radiation on coronary atheromatous plaques. Am J Cardiol 1982;50:1199–1205.
4. Choy DSJ, Stertzer SH, Myler RK, Marco J, Fournial G. Human coronary laser recanalization. Clin Cardiol 1984;7:377–381.
5. Choy DS, Stertzer SH, Rotterdam HZ, Sharrock N, Kaminov IP. Transluminal laser catheter angioplasty. Am J Cardiol 1982;50:1206–1208.
6. Cothren RM, Hayes GB, Kittrell C, Costello BJ, Sacks BA, Shearing A, Kramer JR, Feld MS. A novel laser catheter for removing atherosclerotic plaque. Circulation 1985;72(suppl3):402.
7. Crea F, Davies D, McKenna W, Pashazade M,Taylor K, Maseri A. Percutaneous laser recanalisation of coronary arteries. Lancet 1986;ii:214–215.
8. Cumberland DC, Tayler DI, Welsh CL, Guben JK, Sanborn TA, Moore DJ, Greenfield AJ, Ryan TJ. Percutaneous laser thermal angioplasty: initial clinical results with a laser probe in total peripheral occlusions. Lancet 1986;i:1457–1459.
9. Fourrier JL, Brunetaud JM, Prat A, Marache P, Lablanche JM, Bertrand ME. Percutaneous laser angioplasty with sapphire tip (letter). Lancet 1987;i:105.
10. Ginsburg R, Kim DS, Cuthener D, Toth J, Mitchell RS. Salvage of an ischemic limb by laser angioplasty: description of a new technique. Clin Cardiol 1984;7:54–58.
11. Ginsburg R, Wexler L, Mitchell RS, Pfofitt D. Percutaneous transluminal laser angioplasty for treatment of peripheral vascular disease: clinical experience with 16 patients. Radiology 1985;156:619–624.
12. Geschwind HJ, Boussignac G, Vielledent C, Teisseire B. Removal of atheromatous plaques with Nd-YAG laser. J Am Coll Cardiol 1985;5:545.
13. Grewe DD, Castaneda-Zuniga WR, Nordstrom LA, Gray RJ, Friedberg HD, Lillehei CW, Greatbatch W, Kosa NB. Debris analysis after laser photorecanalization of atherosclerotic plaque. Semin Intervent Radiol 1986;3:53–60.
14. Grundfest WS, Litvack IF, Goldenberg T, Sherman T, Morgenstern L, Carroll R, McDermid S. Pulsed ultraviolet lasers and the potential for safe laser angioplasty. Am J Surg 1985;150:220–226.
15. Lee G, Ikeda RM, Chan MC, Dukich J, Lee MH, Theis JH, Bommer WJ, Reis RL, Hanna E, Mason DT. Dissolution of human atherosclerotic disease by fiberoptic laser-heated metal cautery cap. Am Heart J 1984;107:777–778.
16. Lee G, Ikeda RM, Chan MC, Dukich J, Lee MH, Theis JH, Bommer WJ, Reis RL, Hanna E, Mason DT. Acute and chronic complications of laser angioplasty: vascular wall damage and formation of aneurysms in the atherosclerotic rabbit. Am J Cardiol 1984;53:290–293.
17. Sanborn TA, Faxon DP, Haudenschild CC, Ryan TJ. Experimental angioplasty: circumferential distribution of laser thermal energy with a laser probe. J Am Coll Cardiol 1985;5:934–938.
18. Serur JR, Sinclair IN, Spokojny AM, Paulin S, Spears JR. Laser balloon angioplasty (LBA): effect on the carotid lumen in the dog. Circulation 1985;72(suppl3):457.
19. Spears JR, Marais HJ, Serur J, Paulin S, Grossman W. In vivo coronary angioscopy. Circulation 1982;66(suppl2):366.
20. Vielledent CH, Geschwind HJ, Boussignac G, Gaujour B, Teisseire BP. Debris after laser arterial recanalization. LMS 1986;1:31–34.

Stents

Vascular Stents

A. H. Cragg, C. Zollikofer, and W. R. Castaneda-Zuniga

History

During the past few years, percutaneous transluminal angioplasty has been accepted as a primary treatment modality for numerous types of vascular occlusive disease, both arterial and venous. Restenosis of
previously dilated blood vessels, however, continues
to be a significant problem. In the iliac arteries, a
restenosis rate of only 5% is expected (9). Atherosclerotic ostial stenoses of the renal arteries,
however, have a very high restenosis rate. In the
coronary arteries, restenosis rates of 23 to 33% are
common (3). In the venous system stenoses of large
veins due to thrombosis or tumor compression are
very resistant to angioplasty. A mechanical means of
permanently propping a vessel open would have
broad clinical application and would improve the

usefulness of angioplasty. Likewise, an effective
means of delivering and fixing a vascular graft percutaneously would be useful. Atherosclerotic aortic
aneurysms are common in older patients who are
often not surgical candidates.

Percutaneous vascular grafting and stenting is an
idea that, like many old ideas, has enjoyed a renais-
sance in the last few years due to the availability of
new technology (Table 1). In 1969, 5 years after he
invented the technique of transluminal angioplasty,
Dotter (6) described a technique for transluminal
placement of coil spring endovascular stents (Fig. 1).
Although the idea was ingenious, research on the
method did not progress. With the explosion of
technology relating to transluminal angioplasty,
however, numerous investigators are now beginning
to expand on Dotter's idea by developing transluminally placed stents and grafts, which seek to complement the conventional techniques of surgical vascular reconstruction and percutaneous angioplasty.

The ideal percutaneous vascular stent or graft
must meet several criteria. The device must have a
good expansion ratio, i.e., one should be able to pass
a good-sized prosthesis through a relatively small
catheter. Expansion should be reliable and the stent
or graft must not migrate. Ideally, release of the
device should be controlled by an introducing instrument to allow precise placement. The prosthesis
must have a high patency rate without inducing
secondary stenosis from intimal hyperplasia or accelerated atherosclerosis. The ideal stent or graft has
not yet been developed, although a number of
ingenious designs now exist.

Although both techniques of percutaneous vascular stenting and percutaneous vascular grafting use
similar technology, their application is entirely
different. The purpose of stenting is to prop open a
conduit in the body which is obstructed. As might be
expected, the primary experimental and clinical
application of this technique is as an adjunct to
transluminal angioplasty. The primary aim of percutaneous vascular grafting is to create a smaller,
normal-sized lumen in areas of aneurysm or
arteriovenous fistula formation. In this way, per-

Table 1 Development of percutaneous vascular stenting
and grafting*

Dotter 1969	Stainless steel coils
Maass et al. 1982–1985	Expanding spring double-helix spirals Bovine spiral xenografts for hemodialysis Microporous PE/PU expand-able stent with integrated wire
Dotter et al. 1983	Thermal-shaped memory alloy
Cragg et al. 1983/1984	Thermal-shaped memory alloy
Wright et al. 1984	Expandable stainless steel grafts
Charnsangavej et al. 1985	Zig-Zag pattern
Palmaz et al. 1984/1985	Stainless steel wire mesh com-bined with PTA
Palmaz et al. 1985/1986	Modified tubular stent (combined with PTA balloon)
Medinvent 1985/1986	Stainless steel expandable wire mesh

* Numerous methods have been developed since the original description of the technique by Dotter in 1969.

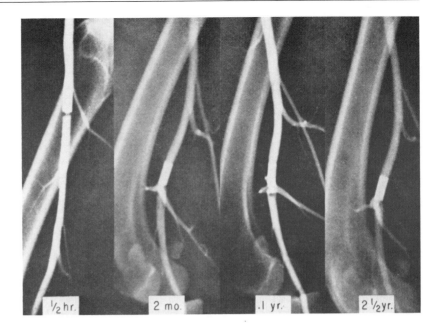

Fig. **1** **In Dotter's original technique, a stainless steel spring coil was advanced in coaxial fashion into an artery.** In several cases, including this one, Dotter demonstrated patency in canine arteries for longer than 2 years. Reprinted with permission from Dotter (6)

½ hr.   2 mo.   .I yr.   2 ½yr.

cutaneous vascular grafting may serve as an alternative to conventional surgical techniques for vascular grafting. Because of their different applications, it is useful to separate percutaneous vascular stenting and grafting and discuss them separately.

Vascular Stenting

After Dotter's original work on vascular stenting, it was not until 1983 that three independent investigators reported experimental results with different techniques for placement of vascular stents (4, 7, 11). Subsequent to these reports, a number of new techniques have arisen. The advantages and disadvantages of each technique are discussed.

Nitinol Stent

Both Dotter et al. (7) and Cragg et al. (4) have described the use of self-expanding nitinol spirals as vascular stents. Nitinol wire is a nickel-titanium alloy that has thermal memory characteristics for shape. When constrained to a certain shape, e.g., a spiral helix, and annealed at high temperature (500°C), the wire acquires a "memory" for that shape. If cooled below its transition temperature, which is variable depending on wire composition, the wire becomes soft and pliable. When the wire is then heated to its transition temperature, which is usually much lower than the annealing temperature, e.g., 35°C, the wire will rapidly resume its original helical shape.

In the technique described by Cragg et al. (4) nitinol coils were straightened in ice water and passed into canine aortas as straight wires (Fig. **2**). Since the transition temperature of the wire was

close to body temperature, when the coil contacted the blood it rapidly resumed its coil shape. The coil was then positioned in the aorta and released.

In Dotter's technique, nitinol spirals were twisted down on an inner catheter and passed into an artery coaxially through a guiding catheter. Since the transition temperature of the wire used by Dotter was higher than body temperature, the coil was transformed by injecting 20 to 30 ml of saline hated to 60°C into the blood vessel containing the coil.

The advantage of both of these techniques is the ability to place a large stent through a small hole. With Cragg's technique, nitinol spirals of any diameter could be passed through a 8 Fr catheter. This is not possible with stainless steel. The disadvantages of both techniques are the lack of precise control in their placement and the need for either cooling or heating during introduction.

Double-Helix Stent

The Maass stent (11, 12) is a double-helix constructed from flat surgical steel alloy (Fig. **3**). The bands that make up the stent are 5 to 8 mm wide. The stent is constrained on a flexible introducing instrument and has about a 4:1 expansion ratio. Thus, stents with diameters of 15 mm require a 4 mm (12 Fr) diameter catheter for introduction. The stent is fixed by expansion against the vessel wall. The prosthesis is incorporated by intimal proliferation and endothelialization.

The advantage of this technique is the external release mechanism that allows precise placement of the stent. A disadvantage is the large size of the introducing system that requires a surgical cutdown for placement of larger stents.

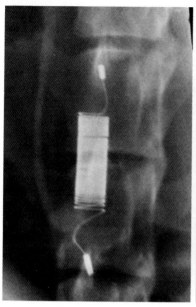

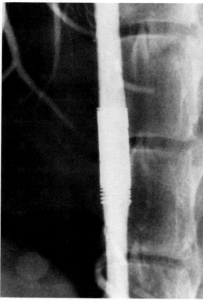

Fig. 2 **A tightly wound nitinol coil (0.8 by 3 cm) was placed percutaneously in a dog's abdominal aorta.** An aortogram obtained immediately after placement of the graft demonstrates some enlargement of the aortic lumen. Reprinted with permission from Cragg et al. (4)

Mesh Stent

Palmaz et al. (14, 16) have described a stent that is placed using an angioplasty catheter. The original stent consisted of a tubular mesh of stainless steel wires arranged in a crisscross pattern. The cross points of the stent were then soldered together. The present stent used by Palmaz et al. (17) is a continuous thin stainless steel tube in which longitudinal slots have been etched. The stent is mounted on a balloon catheter and expanded by inflation of the balloon (Fig. 4).

The advantage of the technique is the ability to combine the procedure with transluminal angioplasty and precisely place the stent. The expansion ratio of the stent is 3:1 or 4:1, which requires a catheter of about 12 Fr for placement of a 10 mm diameter stent.

Another stent similar to the original Palmaz stent is now being tested in Europe (8) (Fig. 5). This stent is constructed of stainless steel wire woven in a crisscross tubular pattern. Since the cross points of the stent are not soldered, as in the original Palmaz stent, the new stent is self-expanding. Stents up to

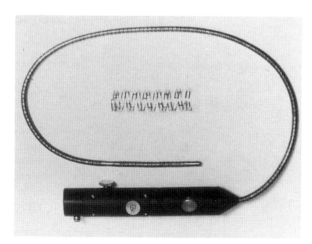

Fig. 3 **Maass helical stent and introducing apparatus.** The stent is torqued down on the introducer shaft and externally released

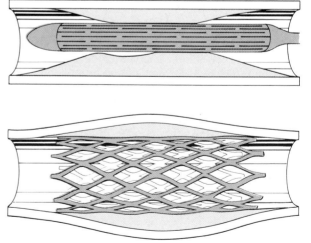

Fig. 4 **The Palmaz stent is a thin metallic tube in which slots have been etched.** The stent is mounted on an angioplasty catheter and expanded by inflation of the balloon. Reprinted with permission from Palmaz et al. (16)

15 mm in diameter can be introduced through a 9 Fr sheath.

Zig-Zag Stent

Wright et al. (18) and Charnsangavej et al. (1) have described a self-expanding stent constructed of stainless steel wire that is bent in a zig-zag configuration. The stents are compressed and pushed through a catheter. When released from the catheter, they expand against the wall of the blood vessel.

The advantages of this stent include its ease of introduction and its self-expanding properties. The expansile force and diameter of the stent can be easily adjusted by changing the wire size, number of bends in the wire, and length of the stent. Disadvantages of this technique include lack of an externally controlled release mechanism and lack of longitudinal flexibility.

Experimental and Clinical Applications of Percutaneous Vascular Stenting

To date, most reports on the experimental use of endovascular prostheses have stressed the feasibility of introduction and fixation. Early reports are now appearing concerning long-term patency of stents in both atherosclerotic and nonatherosclerotic stenoses.

Palmaz et al. (17) placed 2 to 4 mm stents in the aortas of 20 atherosclerotic rabbits. Follow-up to 24 weeks (five rabbits) demonstrated 100% patency

with no graft restenosis (17) short-term placement in the coronary arteries has also been successful (Fig. 6).

The Palmaz stent has also been placed across experimentally created portocaval shunts (15). The occlusion rate was high, however, reflecting the thrombogenic nature of endoprostheses in the venous system.

Clinical experience with endovascular stenting is still preliminary. The Maass helical stent and the zig-zag stent have been used in the treatment of venous stenoses. Charnsangavej et al. (2) treated two patients with compression of the superior and inferior vena cava by tumor (Fig. 7). Maass and Senning successfully used double helix spirals either alone or in combination with surgery to treat 12 patients with obstruction of the vena cava related to Budd-Chiari syndrome or thrombosis. Helical stents have also been placed in combination with surgical grafts in two patients with dissecting aortic aneurysms (Maass D: Personal communication).

The Medinvent wire mesh stent has been placed successfully across ten coronary and ten iliofemoral

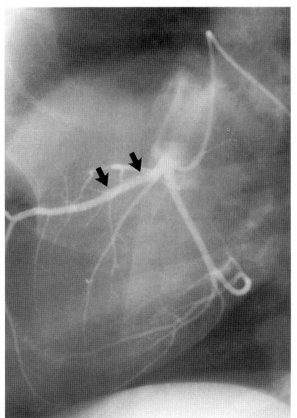

Fig. 6 **A Palmaz stent (arrows) has been placed in the proximal left anterior descending coronary artery of a dog** (arrows). There is wide patency of the lumen immediately after placement. (Case courtesy of J. Palmaz, M. D.)

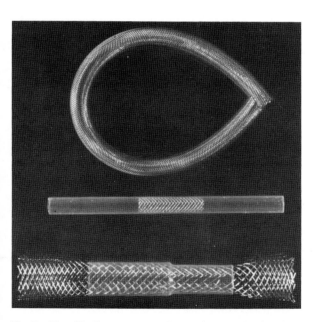

Fig. 5 **The Medinvent stent is a wire mesh that has longitudinal flexibility.** The stent is compressed by pulling on both ends. The stent is able to adapt to varying lumen sizes

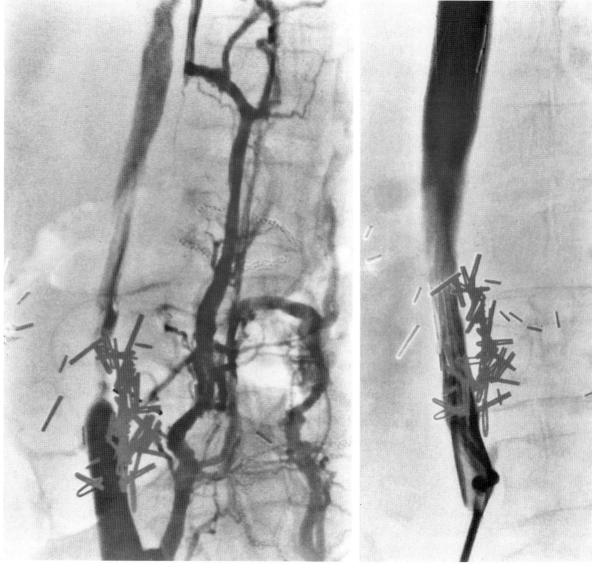

a   b

Fig. **7   a An 82-year-old woman with compression of the inferior vena cava by a retroperitoneal leiomyosarcoma.** Note large paravertebral collaterals
b Following placement of Gianturco stents, the caval lumen has increased and the collaterals have disappeared. One stent migrated to the hepatic segment of the vena cava and subsequently to the right ventricle. Reprinted with permission from Charnsangavej et al. (2)

stenoses (8). Zollikofer has successfully treated a stenosis of the common iliac vein with the Medinvent stent (Fig. **8**). To date there has been no controlled clinical trial of any endovascular stent; thus, the long-term efficacy of endovascular stenting is unknown.

Vascular Grafting

Percutaneous placement of an endovascular graft is an appealing idea that could find application in the treatment of unresectable aneurysms, anastomotic pseudoaneurysms, and arteriovenous fistula. The placement of an expansile, self-sealing, microporous prosthesis through a relatively small introducing catheter has been technically difficult. Cragg et al. (5) demonstrated the feasibility of the technique by placement of tight nitinol coils across experimentally created aortic and iliac aneurysms (Fig. **9**). Recently, attempts have been made to introduce fabric grafts that are expanded and supported by an expanding metal framework (10, 13). To date, there has been no clinical application of this technique.

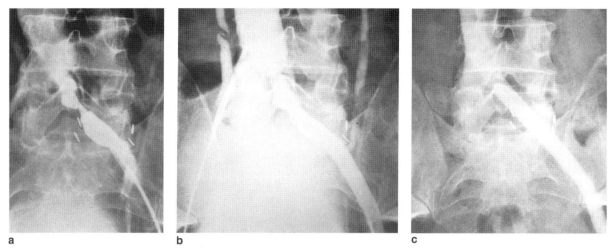

a   b   c

Fig. **8 a Stenosis of the left common iliac vein** is demonstrated in a patient with graft replacement of the external iliac vein
b After angioplasty of the common iliac vein, the lumen is increased in size. However, a persistent stenosis is noted
c After placement of a Medinvent mesh stent, the caliber of the vessel is increased and the stent is widely patent

Fig. **9 a Experimentally created fusiform abdominal aortic aneurysm** in a dog
b Four weeks after placement of nitinol graft, the aneurysm has been ablated and the graft lumen is widely patent. Reprinted with permission from Cragg et al. (5)

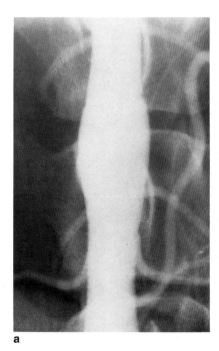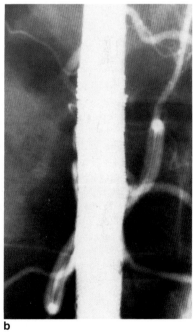

a   b

Conclusion

The techniques of vascular grafting and stenting are exciting offshoots of the original interventional vascular procedures described by Dotter and other pioneers in interventional radiology. Percutaneous vascular grafting and stenting are new procedures that must find their niche through experimentation and clinical trial just as angioplasty did 10 years ago. As refinement of these techniques occurs, broader clinical application will surely follow.

References

1. Charnsangavej C, Wallace S, Wright KC, Carrasco CH, Gianturco C. Endovascular stent for use in aortic dissection: an in vitro experiment. Radiology 1985;157:323–324.
2. Charnsangavej C, Carrasco CH, Wallace S, Wright KC, Ogawa K, Richli W, Gianturco C. Stenosis of the vena cava: preliminary assessment of treatment with expandable metallic stents. Radiology 1986;161:295–298.
3. Cowley MJ, Block PC. A review of the NHLBI PTCA registry data. In: Jang GD, ed. Angioplasty. New York: McGraw-Hill 1986:368–378.
4. Cragg AH, Lund G, Rysavy J, Castaneda F, Castaneda-Zuniga WR, Amplatz K. Nonsurgical placement of arterial

endoprostheses: a new technique using nitinol wire. Radiology 1983;147:261–263.

5. Cragg AH, Lund G, Rysavy JA, Salomonowitz E, Castaneda-Zuniga WR, Amplatz K. Percutaneous arterial grafting. Radiology 1984;150:45–49.

6. Dotter CT. Transluminally placed coil springs and arterial tube grafts: long-term patency in the canine popliteal artery. Invest Radiol 1969;4:329–332.

7. Dotter CT, Buschmann RW, McKinney MK, Rösch J. Transluminal expandable nitinol coil stent grafting: preliminary report. Radiology 1983;147:259–260.

8. Joffre F, Puel J, Knight CI, Kropf L, Wallensten H, Sigwart V, Courtault A. Use of a new type of self-expanding endovascular stent prosthesis: early clinical results (abstract). Radiology 1986;161(P):348.

9. Kadir S. Percutaneous transluminal angioplasty of the iliac and common femoral arteries and their branches. In: Jang GD, ed. Angioplasty. New York: McGraw-Hill 1986:36–60.

10. Lawrence DD, Charnsangavej C, Wright KC, Gianturco C, Wallace S. Percutaneous endovascular graft: an experimental evaluation [Abstract]. Radiology 1986;161(P):348.

11. Maass D, Demierre D, Deaton D, Largiader F, Senning A. Transluminal implantation of self-adjusting expandable prostheses: principles, techniques, and results. Prog Artif Organs 1983;24:979–987.

12. Maass D, Zollikofer CL, Largiader F, Senning A. Radiological follow-up of transluminally inserted vascular endoprosthesis: an experimental study using expanding spirals. Radiology 1984;152:659–663.

13. Maass D. Neue Methoden in der Gefässchirurgie. Neue Zürcher Zeitung 1986:Feb12:71.

14. Palmaz JC, Sibbitt RR, Reuter STR, Tio FO, Rice WJ. Expandable intraluminal graft: a preliminary study. Radiology 1985;156:73–77.

15. Palmaz JC, Sibbitt RR, Reuter STR, Garcia F, Tio FO. Expandable intrahepatic portacaval shunt stents: early experience in the dog. AJR 1985;145:821–825.

16. Palmaz JC, Sibbitt RR, Tio FO, Reuter STR, Peters JE, Garcia F. Expandable intraluminal vascular graft: a feasibility study. Surgery 1986;99:199–205.

17. Palmaz JC, Windeler SA, Garcia F, Tio FO, Sibbitt RR, Reuter STR. Atherosclerotic rabbit aortas: expandable intraluminal grafting. Radiology 1986;160:723–726.

18. Wright KC, Wallace S, Charnsangavej C, Carrasco CH, Gianturco C. Percutaneous endovascular stents: an experimental evaluation. Radiology 1985;156:69–72.

Expandable Stents

C. Charnsangavej, C. H. Carrasco, K. C. Wright, S. Wallace, and C. Gianturco

Despite developments in the management of stenosis of various tubular structures in various organs in the body, the results of those treatments are less than perfect and, at times, less than satisfactory. For example, angioplasty for stenotic atherosclerotic vessels, although effective, is associated with recurrent stenosis over a long period (9, 10, 14). Placement of biliary drainage catheter (internal or external) is often limited by infection due to the fact that the stent may be too small to provide adequate drainage (2, 12). Continuing research by interventional radiologists is based on the principle that a prosthesis should be small enough to allow placement by a percutaneous approach, strong enough to exert pressure against the extrinsic compression, and yet adequate enough to maintain patency of the tubular structures (5, 6, 13).

At the M. D. Anderson Hospital and Tumor Institute, a new prosthesis has been developed by Gianturco, called the Gianturco stent or expandable metallic stent (16). The stent is constructed of stainless steel wire bent in a zig-zag pattern, encircled to form a cylinder (Fig. 1). The stent can be compressed and introduced through a Teflon catheter of 8 to 12 Fr, depending on the caliber of the wire and the diameter of the stent. As the stent is released from the catheter, it expands to its original diameter. The expansile force varies with the caliber of the wire, the diameter and length of the stent, and the number and angle of the bends. It increases with an increase in the caliber of the wire, the diameter of the stent, and the number and angle of the bends, and decreases with the length.

The stent has been evaluated in various tubular structures in the body in experimental animals both in normal and simulated pathologic conditions. This

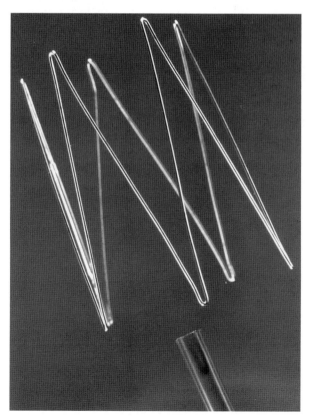

Fig. 1   **Expandable metallic stent**

report describes our experience with the Gianturco stent in experimental animals, and its clinical use in a selected group of patients with vena caval and tracheobronchial stenoses.

Experimental Studies

Normal Vena Cava and Jugular Veins

Seventeen stents were placed in the normal jugular vein, precava, and postcava of five normal mongrel dogs to evaluate patency of the veins and their branches at varying periods up to 6 months. The stents were observed for clot formation, migration, or perforation of the vessels.

The stents increased the diameter of the vessels to the original diameter of the stents in all dogs. There was no luminal narrowing, clot formation, or occlusion of the vessels. The orifice of the branches bridged by the stents remained patent in all vessels. There was no migration, except in one stent, where slight migration was observed during the first week after placement.

Within 4 weeks after placement, the stents were covered by a thin layer of white tissue, incorporated

into the wall of the vessel. Histologic examination revealed that this layer of tissue represented proliferation of the tunica intima and a covering of new endothelium. This endothelial proliferation was almost complete at 1 month and complete at 3 months.

Normal Aorta

Ten stents were placed in the abdominal and thoracic aorta of five normal mongrel dogs. Again, there was no migration, clot formation, or occlusion of the aorta and its branches.

The pathologic findings were the same as those observed in the vena cava. However, intimal proliferation covering the stent developed later than in the venous system. It took up to 12 weeks after placement for the entire stent to be fully covered.

Stenotic Inferior Vena Cava

To evaluate the ability of the Gianturco stent in a simulated pathologic condition, the stent was placed in the experimentally-induced stenotic vena cava in dogs. Stenosis of the inferior vena cava was created

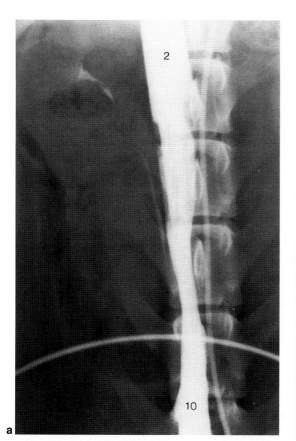 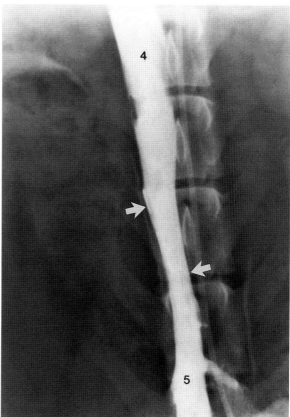

Fig. 2 **Expandable metallic stent in an experimentally induced stenotic vena cava**
a Inferior vena cavogram after creation of stenotic vena cava. The pressure gradient was 8 cm H_2O
b After placement of the stents (arrows), the pressure gradient was reduced to 1 cm H_2O

by the percutaneous injection of absolute ethanol into the paravascular retroperitoneal space. A significant stenosis was defined as a 50% decrease in the caval diameter or a pressure gradient across the stenosis of more than two times normal or 5 cm of saline, whichever was greater.

After a significant stenosis developed, stents were placed across the narrowed segment. Follow-up venography and pressure measurement were performed up to 4 months after placement.

Successful dilation and maintenance of patency of the inferior vena cava were observed in four of seven dogs (3) (Fig. 2). Early migration of the stents occurred in two dogs and resulted in occlusion of the inferior vena cava. At 4 months after stent placement, intimal proliferation covering the stents was demonstrated in all four dogs.

Experimental Aortic Dissection

Experimental aortic dissection was created by the injection of saline or contrast material through the intima in the wall of aortic specimens from human cadavers (4). The fluid in the wall of the aortic specimen separated the layers of the aortic wall, producing the intimal bulge and, compromising the lumen of the aorta. Placement of the stents resulted in compression of the intima toward the outer layer of the aorta. The fluid collection in the aortic wall diffusely dispersed in the wall or leaked into the lumen through the puncture site.

Tracheobronchial Tree

Eighteen stents were placed in the tracheobronchial tree of eight mongrel dogs. The stents expanded to their full diameter in all dogs, distending the trachea and bronchus and resulting in extrinsic compression of the esophagus in three of the eight dogs. Migration of the stents occurred in most stents placed in the trachea but only rarely when placed in the bronchus. Most dogs developed coughing as a result of tracheobronchial irritation, but there was no respiratory distress.

Pathologic examination revealed mucosal secretion covering the stent, with mucosal and submucosal inflammation in all dogs (15) (Fig. 3).

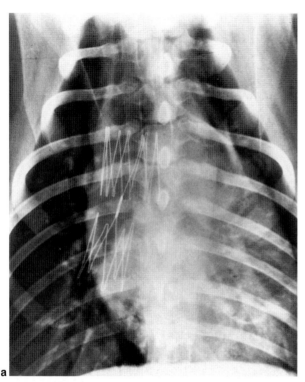

a

Fig. 3 Expandable metallic stent in the tracheobronchial tree

a Radiograph of the stents in the lower trachea and branches

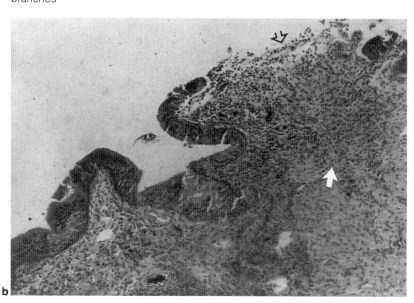

b

Fig. 3
b Photomicrograph of the trachea. Note the mucosal denudation (open arrow) and submucosal inflammation (arrow)

Biliary Duct

The stents were placed in the common bile duct of five normal mongrel dogs to determine the reaction of the ductal wall to the stent. The stents were left in place from 4 to 23 weeks. The common bile duct remained patent in all dogs. There was localized ductal dilation where the stent was placed. Mucosal denudation secondary to focal compression by the stent and chronic reactive inflammation were observed in the wall of the bile duct (1) (Fig. **4**).

Ureter

The stents were placed in the normal ureter and stenotic ureter created by the injection of absolute ethanol into the wall of the ureter in seven dogs. After placement of the stents, there was papillary mucosal proliferation between the wire struts. However, improvement in hydronephrosis of the obstructed kidney was observed in most dogs.

Small Vessels

Two types of metallic stents were designed for use in small vessels in experimental animals, the self-expanding metallic stent and the flexible balloon-expanded stent.

The self-expanding stent is constructed in a similar fashion of the original stent using the wire of 0.008 to 0.010 inch in diameter. The stents were successfully placed in peripheral and visceral arteries in dogs using a 5 to 9 Fr Teflon coaxial catheter system or an 8 Fr double-lumen polyethylene catheter. Good vascular patency was observed in all the 4 to 8 mm stents, whereas only 54% of the 3 mm stents remained patent (7). Local dilation of the arteries with stretching of the tunica media and internal elastic lamina was observed.

The flexible balloon-expanded stent was designed for introduction into small vessels subject to motion. The stent was made of surgical suture wire (0.006 inch) wrapped cylindrically, with bends adopting a sequential U and inverted U configuration every 360° (8) (Fig. **5**). The stent was wrapped tightly around a collapsed angioplasty balloon (25 mm long and 2.5 mm in diameter when fully inflated). The angioplasty balloon-stent unit was advanced to the area of interest. To release the stent, the balloon was inflated to maximal pressure, two or three times, until good stent expansion was observed. The

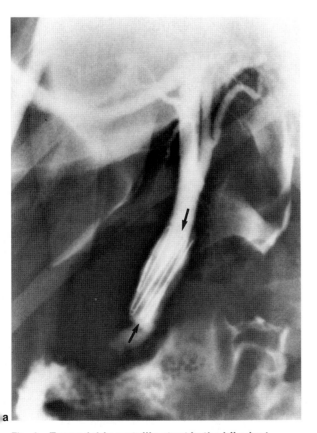
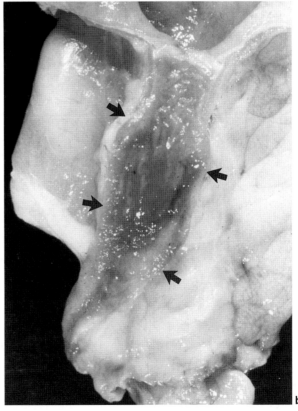

a   b

Fig. **4** **Expandable metallic stent in the bile duct**
a Cholangiogram after placement of the stent (arrows)
b Specimen of the bile duct 3 months after stent placement. Note local dilation of the bile duct (arrow)

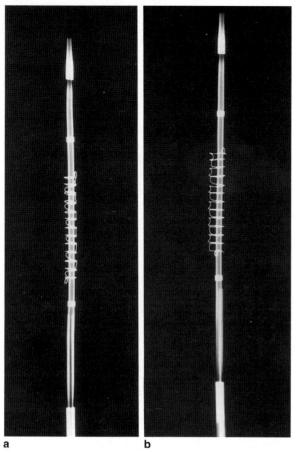

a   b

Fig. 5   **Flexible balloon-expanded stent for small vessels**

a Angioplasty balloon-stent unit in the collapsed state
b Angioplasty balloon-stent unit after balloon inflation showing complete expansion of the stent

Fig. 6   **Endovascular graft stent**
a The graft-stent unit

angioplasty catheter was then withdrawn while negative pressure was applied to the balloon. The stents were successfully tested in peripheral arteries in dogs (8) and in the coronary arteries.

Endovascular Graft-Stent

An arterial endovascular graft consisted of multiple stents in tandem connected to each other by metallic struts. The Dacron tubing was wrapped around the outside of the middle group of stents. The lead and trail stents acted as anchors for the graft, while the middle stents served to open the Dacron tubing when the device was released from the catheter (Fig. **6**). The graft-stent was introduced through an 11 Fr Teflon catheter.

The device was successfully placed in the normal abdominal and thoracic aorta of nine dogs. At follow-up of 7 to 35 weeks, all but one graft remained patent. At necropsy, there were fibroproliferative changes covering the graft and between the graft and

the vessel wall. The side branches bridged by the lead or trail stents remained patent, whereas the branches covered by the grafts were occluded (11).

Clinical Application

Expandable metallic stents were placed in stenotic vena cavae and tracheobronchial trees in eight patients who had malignant tumors involving these tubular structures, which had not responded to the conventional treatment or developed complications after the treatment. The procedures were performed with the approval of the Surveillance Committee of M.D. Anderson Hospital and Tumor Institute.

Stenotic Vena Cava

Five patients had vena caval stenosis (Table **1**). Three patients had superior vena caval syndrome from primary carcinoma of the lung with mediastinal involvement. The superior vena caval syndrome did

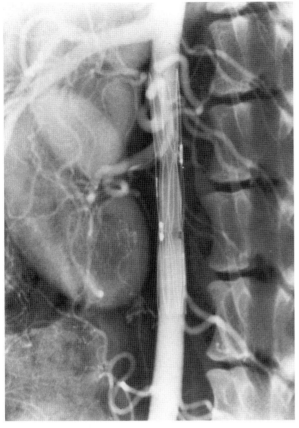

Fig. **6**
b Endovascular graft-stent in the abdominal aorta

c Gross specimen of the device in the abdominal aorta 35 weeks after placement

Table **1**   Clinical application of the expandable metallic stent in vena caval stenosis

Patient Age, Sex	Primary neoplasms	Prior treatment	Presenting symptoms	Stent placement	Results and complications
42F	Adenocarcinoma of the lung	Radiation therapy, chemotherapy	SVC syndrome	4 single stents	Relief of symptoms, died 3 weeks later from myelosuppression
82F	Leiomyosarcoma, retroperitoneal fibrosis	Surgery, radiation therapy	Edema of both lower legs	4 single stents	Relief of symptoms. Stent migration to the right ventricle, died 5 months later from progression of tumors
64M	Adeno carcinoma of the lung	Radiation therapy	SVC syndrome	1 double stent	Relief of symptoms, died 2 weeks later from pulmonary hemorrhage, complication of fibrinolytic therapy
56M	Metastatic melanoma to the liver	Chemotherapy, embolization	Edema of both lower legs	1 double stent	Symptomatic relief for 1 month. Tumor invasion of IVC
48F	Squamous cell carcinoma of the lung	Radiation therapy	SVC syndrome	1 double stent	Relief of symptoms, 3 months later follow-up responded to chemotherapy

* IVC: inferior vena cava, SVC: superior vena cava.

not improve after radiation therapy in all three patients, and in one of these three, surgical debulking was attempted but failed. The other two patients had inferior vena caval stenosis presenting with edema of both lower extremities. One patient had leiomyosarcoma in the retroperitoneum treated by surgical resection and radiation therapy, resulting in retroperitoneal fibrosis and inferior vena caval stenosis. The other patient had metastatic malignant melanoma to the liver and occlusion of the hepatic segment of the inferior vena cava.

After placement of the stents, immediate relief of the presenting symptoms was accomplished in all five patients (Fig. **7**). Two patients died whithin 1 month after placement of the stents from myelosuppression as a complication of chemotherapy and from pulmonary hemorrhage after fibrinolytic therapy to lyse the clot in the innominate and subclavian veins. In the patient with metastatic melanoma, edema of both legs recurred 1 months after stent placement due to tumor invasion into the stent and occlusion of the inferior vena cava. In the other two patients, the vena cava remained patent at 3 and 5 months of follow-up.

Complication of stent placement occurred in one patient because of underestimation of the size of the vena cava. The stent migrated from the stenotic segment and lodged in the right ventricle with no clinical consequence. The patient died 5 months later, at which time autopsy revealed that the stent in the right ventricle was covered by the endocardium and the one in the vena cava maintained the patency of the vena cava. Since then, modification of the stent was developed by attaching the barbs onto the stent and using double stents. This modification has allowed for better fixation of the stent to the wall of the vessel and better stabilization at the release of the stent.

Tracheobronchial Stenosis

The stents were placed in four patients with tracheobronchial stenosis (Table **2**). Two patients had malignant tumors, primary carcinoma of the lung in one and metastatic osteogenic sarcoma in the other, compressing the distal trachea and main stem bronchus. The other two patients had tracheobronchial stenosis after surgical resection of the primary tumors. One patient had recurrent pneumonia as a result of anastomotic stenosis and the other required positive pressure respirator to maintain the patency of a myocutaneous graft reconstruction.

The stents were placed into the tracheobronchial tree through a rigid bronchoscope or tracheostomy opening under fluoroscopic guidance. The stenoses were relieved in all patients except the one with

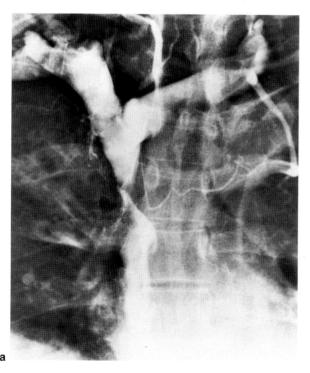
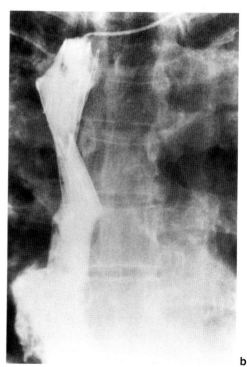

a

b

Fig. **7** **Expandable metallic stent in the superior vena cava in a 64-year-old man with a superior vena cava syndrome due to an adenocarcinoma of the lung**
a Before stent placement
b After stent placement

Table **2** Application of stents in tracheobronchial stenosis

Patient Age, Sex	Primary neoplasms	Prior treatments	Presenting symptoms	Stent placement	Results and complications
42F	Adenocarcinoma of the lung	Radiation therapy, chemotherapy, surgery	Collapse of myocutaneous graft, obstructing airway	1 single stent	Relief of symptoms, died 3 weeks later from myelosuppression
75M	Squamous cell carcinoma of the lung	Right upper lobectomy with sleeve resection	Stenosis of anastomotic site with recurrent pneumonia	3 single stents	Resolution of pneumonia, died 4 months later from brain metastases
67M	Squamous cell carcinoma of the left upper lobe	Radiation therapy, chemotherapy	Stenosis of the left main stem bronchus	2 single stents	No complications, died 2 weeks later from brain metastases
32F	Metastatic osteogenic sarcoma	Surgery	Pneumonia	2 single stents	Failed to relieve the stenosis. Died 1 week later

metastatic osteogenic sarcoma, in whom the expansile force of the stent was not sufficient to overcome the compression by the tumor. No patient developed respiratory irritation or distress after placement of the stents. Two patients died within 1 month of stent placement from complications of chemotherapy. The other two lived 2 to 4 months without any complications and later died from brain metastases.

Current Indications

Our experimental studies and early clinical applications indicate that placement of the stent in the vascular system, tracheobronchial tree, and biliary tract is possible with only minor complications. The stent can be placed in the vessels without clot formation or perforation. Local dilation with stretching of the tunica media and internal elastic membrane was observed in most vessels. The stent gradually becomes incorporated into the vascular wall by a proliferation of the tunica intima where the wires contact the wall. When placed in the normal bile duct and tracheobronchial tree, there is local dilation with foreign body inflammatory reaction developing around the stent.

The expandability of the stent also provides an advantage, since it not only neutralizes the extrinsic compression from fibrosis or tumor on the vessel wall but also prevents progression of the stenosis. However, the stents failed when they were placed in a thrombosed vessel or when the extrinsic force from ossified tumors was not overcome. The presence of tumors in the lumen of the vessel may also limit the use of the stent because the tumor may grow between the wire struts of the stent.

The results of our clinical trials are still early and limited, but with promising prospects. Indications and contraindications of stent placement are still to be defined. The current selection of patients is on the basis of little or no alternative therapy. It is hoped that the stent may provide palliation of immediate symptoms so that they can receive further definitive treatment. The stent also has considerable potential in the management of vascular dissection, aneurysm, and to prevent restenosis after balloon angioplasty for atherosclerotic disease.

References

1. Carrasco CH, Wallace S, Charnsangavej C, Richli W, Wright KC, Fanning T, Gianturco C. Expandable biliary endoprosthesis: an experimental study. AJR 1985;145:1279–1281.
2. Carrasco CH, Zornoza J, Bechtel WJ. Malignant biliary obstruction: complications of percutaneous biliary drainage. Radiology 1984;152:343–346.
3. Charnsangavej C, Carrasco CH, Wallace S, Wright KC, Ogawa K, Richli W, Gianturco C. Stenosis of the vena cava: preliminary assessment of treatment with expandable metallic stents. Radiology 1986;161:295–298.
4. Charnsangavej C, Wallace S, Wright KC, Carrasco CH, Gianturco C. Endovascular stent for use in aortic dissection: an in vitro experiment. Radiology 1985;157:323–324.
5. Cragg AH, Lund G, Rysavy JA, Salomonowitz E, Castaneda-Zuniga WR, Amplatz K. Percutaneous arterial grafting. Radiology 1984;150:45–49.
6. Dotter CT, Buschmann RW, McKinney MK, Rösch J. Transluminal expandable nitinol coil stent grafting: preliminary report. Radiology 1983;147:259–260.
7. Duprat G Jr, Wright KC, Charnsangavej C, Wallace S, Gianturco C. Self-expanding metallic stents for small vessels: an experimental evaluation. Radiology 1987;162:469–472.
8. Duprat G Jr, Wright KC, Charnsangavej C, Wallace S, Gianturco C. Flexible balloon-expanded stent for small vessels. Radiology 1987;162:276–278.
9. Hewes RC, White RJ Jr, Murray RR, Kaufman SL, Chang R, Kadir S, Kinnison ML, Mitchell SE, Auster M. Long-term results of superficial femoral artery angioplasty. AJR 1986;146:1025–1029.
10. Krepel VM, van Andel GJ, van Erp WFM, Breslan PJ. Percutaneous transluminal angioplasty of the femoropopliteal artery: initial and long-term results. Radiology 1985;156:325–328.
11. Lawrence DD Jr, Charnsangavej C, Wright KC, Gianturco C, Wallace S. Percutaneous endovascular graft: an experimental evaluation. Radiology 1987;163:357–360.

12. Mueller PR, van Sonnenberg E, Ferrucci JT. Percutaneous biliary drainage: technical and catheter-related problems in 200 procedures. AJR 1982;138:17–23.
13. Palmaz JC, Sibbitt RR, Reuter SR, Tio FO, Rice WJ. Expandable intraluminal graft: a preliminary study. Radiology 1985;156:73–77.
14. Van Andel GJ, van Erp WFM, Krepel VM, Breslan PJ. Percutaneous transluminal dilatation of the iliac artery: long-term results. Radiology 1985;156:321–323.
15. Wallace MJ, Charnsangavej C, Ogawa K, Carrasco CH, Wright KC, McKenna R, McMurthrey M, Gianturco C. Tracheobronchial tree: expandable metallic stents used in experimental and clinical applications. Radiology 1986;158:309–312.
16. Wright KC, Wallace S, Charnsangavej C, Carrasco CH, Gianturco C. Percutaneous endovascular stents: an experimental evaluation. Radiology 1985;156:69–72.

Clinical Results

F. Joffre and H. Rousseau

In the last ten years, PTA has assumed a predominant place in the treatment of atheromatous lesions as an alternative to surgical bypass. However, this technique is limited by the possibility of restenoses, which occur at a rate of approximately 30% after femoropopliteal and coronary artery angioplasty. In consequence, the use of metallic endovascular prosthesis, as a support of the vascular layers, can be an attractive approach for prevention of restenoses. Dotter (5) was the first to present an endovascular metallic stent placed in an artery of a dog, but the technique has been further developed only in the 1980s. Dotter (4) and Cragg (3) proposed circumferential prostheses (Nitinol), which return to the initial shape at body temperature, but this experimental study did not give satisfactory results.

Two other stents were experimented with: the auto-expansible prosthesis developed by Maass (13) is in simple or double helicoid shape; and the prosthesis designed by Gianturco (2), which is in a zig-zag shape. For percutaneous placement, portable catheters of a large diameter are used. Palmaz (18, 19) first experimented with this material, and recently Gianturco (25) proposed another type of prosthesis based on the same principle.

Although this principle is attractive, the inflexibility of the prosthesis makes selective catheterization difficult. All experimental studies done on animals have demonstrated the perfect tolerance of the body for this type of material, with the prosthesis being incorporated into the arterial layers in a few weeks. The stent that we have experimented with is totally different. The endovascular metallic "wall stent" is composed of wire netting stainless steel alloy multifilaments which are not attached together. Because the filaments are interlaced without fixation, they can be stretched longitudinally over the delivery system (6 Fr) during placement. The elasticity of the metal filaments allows controlled progressive deployment, spontaneous expansion of the prosthesis, and its fixation against the vascular wall, which generates permanent pre-established mural pressure (Fig. 1).

The delivery catheter is adapted to receive a 0.014 movable guide wire. Retention of the prosthesis on the delivery system is assured by means of an invaginated balloon-like structure (Fig. 2). Low hydraulic

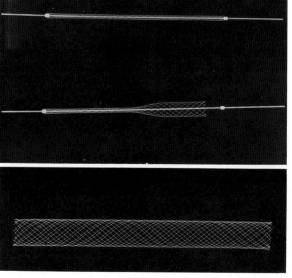

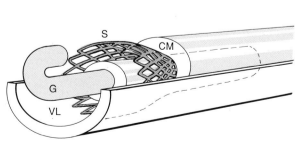

Fig. **1** **A partially enlarged prosthesis.** G: central guide wire inside the delivery catheter. CM: constraining membrane over the stretched stent (S) which can be progressively withdrawn. The stent pushes against the vascular layer (VL)

Fig. **2** **Delivery catheter.** The stent is stretched longitudinally, and covered by a constraining membrane. Low hydraulic pressure is used to permit frictionless eversion of the membrane and progressive release of the prosthesis

pressure permits almost frictionless eversion of the constraining membrane under control of a distal slide mechanism in such a way as to allow progressive release of the prosthesis. If the hydraulic pressure is removed from the annular channel of the coaxial system, the prosthesis is held tenaciously on the instrument tip. Even if only a small portion of the stent is still to be deployed, it can be retrieved, but not advanced.

We have done extensive experimentation on animals which showed good vascular patency and tolerance, and particularly a complete and homogenous intimalization covering the stent filaments.

Stents which traversed the ostia of collaterals were studied histologically. The collaterals remained patent. Filaments of the prosthesis were surrounded by new intima without significant reduction of the vascular lumen. The theoretical purpose of the endoprosthesis is to avoid recurrence of stenosis after PTA. For this reason, the first human implantations have been reserved for patients presenting with recurrence of arterial stenosis.

Three main indications have been proposed until now in the vascular system:

- arteriovenous fistulas for hemodialysis, which have restenosed: PTA is efficacious in only 50% of cases in the short and medium term (7, 8);
- peripheral arteries: the prosthesis is indicated in restenosis after PTA or iliac endarteriectomy and for complicated femoral artery stenoses which may easily recur after PTA (22, 23, 26);
- restenosis after coronary PTA.

Arteriovenous Fistulas

Hemodialysis for chronic renal insufficiency requires efficacious vascular access, achieved by the creation of an arteriovenous fistula (AVF) or graft interposition. The arteriovenous fistula is a non-physiologic vascular structure, wounded several times per week during many years; so it is not surprising to observe a significant incidence of stenosis, about 50% of AVFs. PTA is an attractive technique, but it does not always re-establish sufficient blood flow, and its effect is frequently transitory (3, 8, 10). The use of an endovascular prosthesis to support the vascular wall can improve or prolong the effect of PTA. We report here preliminary results on the use of a self-expanding metallic endoprosthesis in the treatment of 9 AVF stenoses.

Eight patients (3 females, 5 males) with 10 stenoses of short-circuit arteriovenous fistulas underwent percutaneous implantation of an endovascular prosthesis. Their ages ranged from 33 to 69 years. There were 8 lower arm AVFs and 1 Brescia-type femoral AVF. The stenoses were located as follows:

- 4 terminal stenoses, axillary/subclavian heterograft

- 1 proximal anastomotic stenosis, associated with an aneurysm and a graft thrombosis
- 1 long proximal, and 2 multiple diffuse irregular stenoses on the homograft vein.

Clinical symptoms were represented by venous hypertension, diminution of flow during dialysis, or in 2 cases, recurrent thrombosis. Fistulography was performed to evaluate the type of stenosis. Under local anesthesia, the puncture was directed to the graft, distal to the stenosis or collateral veins of the AVF. The delivery system is placed via a 6 Fr introducer catheter, and the stenosis passed with a guide wire. In 5 cases, PTA was performed with a balloon catheter of 8 mm in diameter at a pressure of above 10 bar for 1 min. In 2 cases, the prosthesis was placed directly. PTA was performed later on the stent. Follow-up angiography was performed after a few hours, and 1, 2, 3 and 6 months after the procedure. 2 patients had a 90% stenosis at the anastomotic site. The prosthesis was implanted without dilatation. Fistulography performed immediately after the procedure showed residual stenosis of 50%. Angiography performed 10 days after demonstrated only a 30% residual stenosis, i.e. progressive opening of the stenosis. Intravenous heparin (3000–5000 U) was administered intraoperatively, and antiplatelet aggregation medication (acetyl salicylic acid, dipyramidol) was given post-operatively for 6 months.

Results

In all cases, progressive opening of the prosthesis was noted after implantation. At the same time, the prestenotic dilated veins returned to normal. In one case, the prestenotic aneurysm disappeared by vascular remodeling. In two cases, follow-up angiography after 1, 2 and 3 months demonstrated radiolucent filling defects on the inner wall of the prosthesis, corresponding to intimal proliferation. This reaction progressed slowly, resulting in a concentric stenosis after 3 months. One of these patients can still undergo hemodialysis after one year in the same AVF, with progressive development of collateral circulation. In the remaining 6 cases, fistulography demonstrated intraluminal filling defects on the inner wall without significant reduction of the vascular diameter. In the last 2 patients, no PTA was performed. We have observed progressive widening of the prosthesis within 10 days, with almost complete disappearance of the stenosis. Fistulography after 1 month demonstrated a regular vascular wall.

No complications were observed intra- or postoperatively. Neither vascular wall trauma nor infection occurred. No hematoma occurred at the puncture site. The only immediate complication was thrombosis on a persistent stenosis. Thrombosis had already occurred several times before implantation of the prosthesis in an aneurysmal zone proximal to the stenosis. This post-implantation thrombosis was recanalized by local administration of streptokinase. This AVF remained patent after 9 months. No rethrombosis was seen. Histologic examination of one concentric stenosis demonstrated hyperplasia of a neo-intima rich in fibroelastic cells, and no evidence of "foreign body" cellular or inflammatory reaction. Subsequent fistulographies demonstrated that this phenomenon was progressive. This type of complication developed in multiple, long, irregular homograft stenoses. On the other hand, no intimal hyperplasia appeared in the short anastomotic stenoses, as the last 5 implantations, with a follow-up of 9 months, showed.

In all cases, this technique could repair initial surgical complications and preserve vascular function for at least 4 months, avoiding any other vascular approach.

Iliac and Femoropopliteal Arteries

Vascular prostheses were placed in the peripheral arteries in 21 patients (2 females, 19 males). Their mean age was 52 years, varying from 37 to 78. The implantations involved 7 iliac arteries which had been treated by PTA 6 months to 2 years previously (Fig. 3), one iliac restenosis following endarterectomy 5 years before, 11 superficial femoral, and 2 popliteal artery stenoses (Fig. 4). The stenoses were 2–6 cm in length, and the arterial diameter above the stenosis ranged from 4–6 mm. The stents used varied in size, ranging from 4.5–7 mm in diameter. The size of the stent matched the length of the stenosis and the vascular diameter. Implantation was carried out by a homolateral femoral retrograde catheterization for iliac stenoses, and by direct antegrade puncture for femoral stenoses. PTA was done with the balloon inflated for 1 min, the diameter of the balloon being equivalent to the diameter of the artery measured above the stenosis. A 0.014 guide wire was left in place after PTA, while the balloon catheter was withdrawn and replaced by the catheter carrying the stent. The catheter was introduced into the artery with a 6 Fr introducer. The stent was released progressively under fluoroscopy control. The prosthesis was placed so that it overlapped the stenosis.

Anticoagulant treatment was started at the moment of implantation: 3000–5000 U of intra-arterial

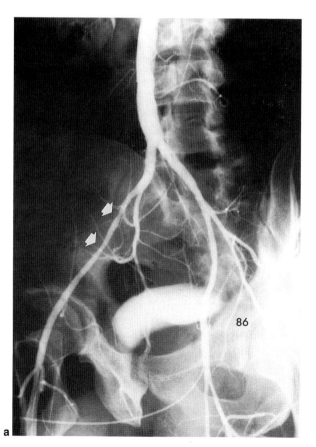
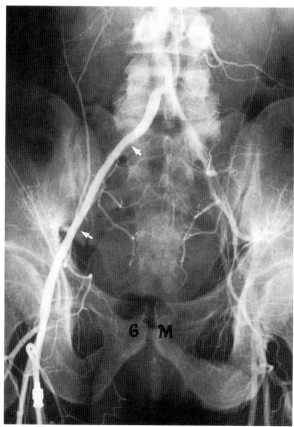

Fig. 3 **a PTA carried out 9 months** previously was considered satisfactory clinically and radiographically
b Restenosis, treated after PTA with a stent. Control 6 months later shows the regular appearance of the vessel wall

heparin, platelet anti-aggregating treatment for 6 months (300 mg of aspirin per day and 70 mg of dipyramidol per day).

Results

In 10 implantations, one partial obliteration of the superficial femoral artery was observed within 3 to 9 months. This partial obliteration was followed by the development of collateral arteries, but did not need surgery. An iliac artery thrombosis occurred 15 days after implantation of the prosthesis. The extremity of the stent was in contact with a false aneurysm at the origin of the iliac artery. This aneurysm was due to PTA carried out 2 years previously. The mechanism of secondary thrombosis can be explained by hemodynamic perturbations at the level of the false aneurysm. In the other cases, angiography controls showed arterial patency and also a thin, translucent border between the stent and the lumen. This border is negligible compared to the diameter of the vessel. It can be considered as a new intimalization of the stent, which is incorporated into the arterial wall. We also noted that the collateral branches covered by the stent remained patent. Neither recurrent stenosis nor migration of the stent were observed in any of these cases. In order to avoid immediate thrombosis, we administered 5000 U of streptokinase in situ. We have used this protocol in the last ten cases and noted the absence of general fibrinolysis, hemorrhagic complications, and lasting patency of the prosthesis.

Coronary Arteries

Despite the high rate of initial success and the low rate of complications with PTA of the coronary arteries, early restenosis is a major concern. The reported rates of restenosis following the procedure

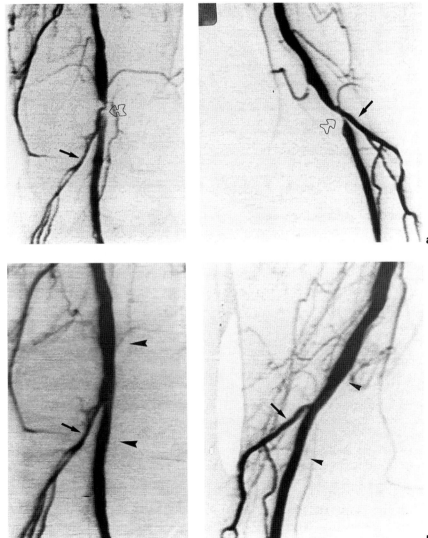

Fig. 4 **a Severe stenosis of the popliteal artery** in front and side views
b After stenting, the collateral covered by the stent is still patent

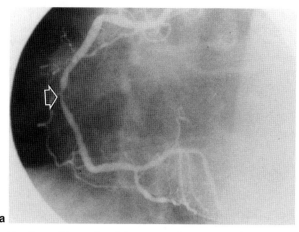
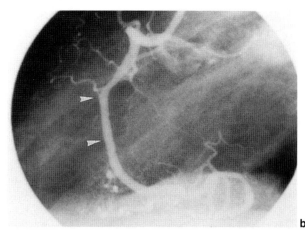

Fig. 5 a Stenosis of the second segment of the right coronary artery, which had been dilated 8 months previously. An endovascular stent was placed
b Satisfactory angiographic control

vary from 15–43% (11, 12, 14). This rate may reach 50% for patients with pluritruncal stenoses who have had multiple dilations. The highest incidence is found in the first 5 months after PTA. Our experience of endocoronary prostheses includes 22 patients (20 males and 2 females). Their mean age was 54 years, varying from 41 to 69. The stent was placed after selective catheterization of the coronary artery and after coronary angiography. The prosthesis was introduced by the coaxial technique with the help of a coronarography carrier.

Indications included:

- post-angioplasty restenosis in 21 patients. The mean delay in restenosis was 4–5 months (2–17 months). The prosthesis was placed at the level of the left anterior descending artery in 15 cases, in the right coronary artery in 4 cases, and in the circumflex artery in 2 cases (Fig. 5).
- focal stenosis at the level of a venous graft in the left anterior descending artery in one patient.

Results

No complications occurred in 15 cases. The mean follow-up was 4 months, varying from 1 to 12. All patients were non-symptomatic, with a negative effort test. Coronarography was done 15 days following implantation in 7 patients, and after 3 months in all cases, but did not reveal any restenosis.

Acute and subacute occlusions occurred in 7 cases. After implantation, coronary occlusion occurred either immediately, in 5 cases, or within 10 days in 3 cases. In situ streptokinase infusion was carried out 5 times with successful and stable results in 2 cases. Two patients with a high coronary risk, one of whom was refused by the surgeon, died. Failures can be explained by a previous myocardial

infarct in the territory of implantation in 3 cases, thrombosis in 1 case, inadequate heparinization in 1 case, and a mechanical complication following previous PTA or stent implantation in 1 case.

These results suggest that indications of stenting should be related to monotruncal stenoses which have good quality runoff. Patients presenting with myocardial necrosis in the territory of the implanted artery should be excluded from stenting. With regard to medical therapy, heparin was given preoperatively for 2 days and continued 9 days post-implantation of the stent. It was then administered subcutaneously for 6 weeks. In the last 9 patients, we administered 50,000 U of streptokinase in the coronary artery as a prophylactic measure. No thrombosis was observed.

Current Developments

According to recent pathological studies, restenosis originates within the arterial wall, and more precisely within the cracks and fissures generated by PTA (11, 21). The concept of sealing these fissures or cracks has led to the development of a new form of self-expanding scaffolding prosthesis, promising a new approach to the prevention of restenosis. Some conclusions can be drawn from the experimental results (27) and our preliminary clinical results. Stenting is feasible in all cases, regardless of the diameter of the artery or the site of implantation. The pressure applied to the wall of the artery is calculated in advance, and adjusted in order to avoid lesions or thromboses in the vessel wall. Migration of the stent and vascular lesions have not been observed. Tissue proliferation appears rapidly, leading to a perfectly regular and uniform vascular lumen. This tissue proliferation decreases thrombogenicity and atherogenicity of the stent. The collateral branches covered by the stent remain patent, as shown by histological and angiographic experimental results. It should be noted that the organism perfectly accepts the alloy of which the stent is made, since we noticed neither inflammatory tissue reactions nor rejection. The preliminary results from the first clinical application seem encouraging. Implantation of the stent does not present any major technical problems, and seems harmless. However, some questions still remain: The effect of the stent placed alone without PTA is unknown. Is it possible to use the stent alone without previous dilation of the stenosis with a balloon probe? Taking into consideration the good overall results of PTA, it is premature to generalize implantation of stents for all arterial stenoses after PTA. However, to avoid recurrence, the endoprosthesis could be placed prophylactically in the following circumstances:

– Complex arterial stenosis, considered until now as a bad indication for PTA.
– Stenoses or occlusion likely to recur, or lesions with a bad radiological result after PTA (extensive dissection) (1, 6, 15).
– Stenoses on hemodialysis fistulas which are known to have a high percentage of recurrence (50%), especially anastomotic stenoses.
– Another indication could include arterial stenoses which are classically not accessible to PTA due to the risk of embolus, such as carotid or vertebral artery stenoses (9, 16, 17, 24).

Theoretically, the stents allow dilation by immobilizing the atheromatous lesions. If the first dilation by the stent alone is not sufficient, we can try a second dilation with an angioplasty balloon inside the lumen of the stent. Gianturco (2) has also proposed treatment of aortic dissection by the same procedure. Indications for venous application could also been considered, as in the case of extrinsic compression by tumor or perivascular fibrosis. Finally, the creation of intrahepatic portocaval shunts has also been proposed.

References

1. Block PG, Fallon JT, Elmer D. Experimental angioplasty: lessons from the laboratory. AJR 1980;135:907–912.
2. Charnsangavej C, Wallace S, Wright KC, Carrasco CH, Gianturco C. Endovascular stent for use in aortic dissection: an in vitro experiment. Radiology 1985;157:323–325.
3. Cragg A, Lund G, Raysavy J, Castaneda F, Castaneda-Zuniga W, Amplatz K. Nonsurgical placement of arterial endoprosthesis: a new technique using nitinol wire. Radiology 1983;147:261–263.
4. Dotter C, Buschmann RW, McKinney MK, Rösch J. Transluminal expandable nitinol coil stent grafting: preliminary report. Radiology 1983;147:259–260.
5. Dotter C. Transluminal placed spring coils and arterial tube grafts: long term patency in the canine popliteal artery. Invest Radiol 1969;4:329–332.
6. Gardiner GA, Meyerovitz MF, Stokes KR, Clouse ME, Harrington DP, Bettmann MA. Complications of transluminal angioplasty. Radiology 1986;159:201–208.
7. Glanz S, Gordon D, Butt KMH, Adamson R, Sclafani SJA. Dialysis access fistulas: treatment of stenosis by transluminal angioplasty. Radiology 1984;152:637–642.
8. Hunter DW, Sos KS, Castaneda-Zuniga WR, Sutherland DER, Amplatz K. Failing or thrombosed Brescia-Cimino arteriovenous dialysis fistulas. Radiology 1983;149:105–109.
9. Iscovici X, Fabiani JN, Renaudin JM, Pernes JM, Gaux JC, Lemseffer M, Carpentier A. Lésions pré-vertébrales de l'artère sous-clavière: résultats à distance de la chirurgie reconstructrice et de l'angioplastie percutanée. J Mal Vasc 1985;10:183–188.
10. Lawrence PF, Miller FJ, Mineau DE. Balloon catheter dilatation in patients with failing arteriovenous fistulas. Surgery 1981;89:439–442.
11. Leimgruber PP, Roubin GS, Hollman J, Cotsonis GA, Meir B, Douglas JS, King SB III, Grüntzig AR. Restenosis after successful coronary angioplasty in patients with single-vessel disease. Circulation 1986;73:710–717.
12. Levine S, Ewels CJ, Rosing DR, Kent KM. Coronary angioplasty: clinical and angiographic follow-up. Am J Cardiol 1985;55:673–676.
13. Maass D, Demierre D, Deaton D, Largiader F. Transluminal implantation of self-adjusting expandable prosthesis: principles, techniques, and results. Prog Artif Organs 1983;24:979–987.
14. Mabin TA, Holmes DA, Smith HC, Vlietstra RE, Reeder GS, Bresnahan JF, Bove AA, Hammes LN, Elveback LR, Orszulak TA. Follow-up clinical results in patients undergoing percutaneous transluminal coronary angioplasty. Circulation 1985;71:754–760.
15. Martin EC, Diamond NG, Casarella WJ. Percutaneous transluminal angioplasty in non-atherosclerotic disease. Radiology 1980;135:27.
16. Montarjeme A, Keifer JW, Zuska AJ. Percutaneous transluminal angioplasty of the brachiocephalic arteries. AJR 1982;138:457–462.
17. Numaguchi Y, Puyau FA, Provenza LJ, Richardson DE. Percutaneous transluminal angioplasty of the carotid artery: its application to post-surgical stenosis. Neuroradiology 1984;26:527–530.
18. Palmaz JC, Sibbitt RR, Reuter SR, Tio FO, Rice WJ. Expandable intraluminal graft: a preliminary study. Radiology 1985;156:73–77.
19. Palmaz JC, Windeler SA, Garcia F, Tio FO, Sibbitt RR, Reuter SR. Atheroslerotic rabbit aortas: expandable intraluminal grafting. Radiology 1986;160:723–726.
20. Probst P, Cerny P, Owens A, Mahler F. Patency after femoral angioplasty: coprrelation of angiographic appearance with clinical findings. AJR 1983;140:1227–1232.
21. Samson RH, Sprayregen S, Veith FJ, Scher KA, Gupta SK, Ascer E. Management of angioplasty complications, unsuccessful prodecures and early and late failures. Ann Surg 1984;199:234–239.
22. Spence RK, Freiman DB, Gatenby R, Hobbs CL, Barker CF, Berkowitz HD, Roberts B, McClean G, Oleaga J, Ring EJ. Long-term results of transluminal angioplasty of the iliac and femoral arteries. Arch Surg 1981;116:1377–1386.
23. Tisdano J, Vines FS, Barnes RW. Percutaneous transluminal angioplasty following endarterectomy. Radiology 1984;152:361–364.
24. Wiggli U, Gratzi O. Transluminal angioplasty of stenotic carotid arteries: case reports and protocol. AJNR 1983;4:793–795.
25. Wright KC, Duprat G, Charnsangavej C, Wallace S, Gianturco C. Flexible balloon-expanded stent for small vessels. Radiology 1987;162:276–278.
26. Zeitler E, Richter EI, Roth FJ, Schoop W. Results of percutaneous transluminal angioplasty. Radiology 1983;146:57–60.
27. Rousseau H, Puel J, Joffre F, Sigwart U, Duboucher C, Imbert C, Knight C, Kropf L, Wallsten H. A new type of self-expanding endovascular stent prosthesis: experimental study. Radiology 1987;164:709–714.

Percutaneous Vena Cava Filtering

M. Darcy and W. R. Castaneda-Zuniga

Background

The development of vena caval filters was stimulated by the need to find a simple but effective method of preventing pulmonary embolism (PE), a disease seen with a frequency of 630,000 symptomatic cases per year in the United States (7). The high mortality of this disease (39% in some series) (7, 19) added further impetus to the search for effective therapy. Although anticoagulation is sufficient therapy in many cases, between 3 and 9% of patients with PE will have a second embolic event while on adequate anticoagulation (7, 42). In addition, a significant number of patients either have contra-indications to, or complications resulting from, anticoagulants (19, 32). This spurred the development of mechanical methods of embolism prevention.

The earliest attempts (around 1934) at mechanically preventing PE involved common femoral vein ligation. Unfortunately, patients frequently developed recurrent PE due to embolization from the "normal" leg or from the pelvic veins. Therefore, femoral vein ligation was abandoned in favor of inferior vena cava (IVC) ligation or plication. Although initially effective against PE, caval ligation carries a very high (up to 50%) operative mortality (42). The mortality is in part due to the magnitude of

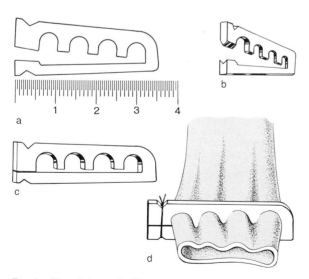

Fig. 1 **The Adams-DeWeese vena caval clip** which, when closed around the vena cava, partitions the lumen into four small channels

the operation but is also aggravated by the sudden decrease in cardiac output caused by the sudden restriction of venous return to the heart. In addition, caval occlusion leads to lower extremity edema and stimulates the opening of large collateral channels around the level of ligation. These collaterals can eventually enlarge enough to transmit emboli, thus contributing to the 7 to 50% recurrent embolization rate seen after caval ligation (3, 26). In the 1960s, IVC plication in various forms was developed to attempt to prevent PE while maintaining caval patency and thus avoiding the previously mentioned problems associated with caval occlusion. The most popular method of plication was the use of extrinsic clips (Fig. **1**), which were effective against PE while maintaining patency of the IVC in 70–80% of cases (23, 28). As expected, this lowered the rates of venous stasis problems and recurrent embolization. The operative mortality, however, was still prohibitively high (up to 40%) (26, 42).

The high operative mortality of IVC ligation or plication stimulated investigators to develop devices that could be placed within the caval lumen without having to resort to an abdominal operation. One of the early devices, the Eichelter sieve, had limited applicability, since it was mounted on a catheter that then protruded externally from the patient's femoral vein. This sieve was nondetachable and obviously long-term use was limited. Pate et al. (36) then developed in 1969 a springlike clip that would stretch the cava in one direction but thus narrowed the other dimension of the lumen to a slitlike opening, which was too narrow to allow passage of significant emboli. Neither of these devices received widespread acceptance.

Filters Currently Used

The first device to achieve more widespread acceptance was the Mobin-Uddin (MU) filter, which was introduced in 1967 (29). This filter consists of six metallic prongs anchored to a central hub and covered with a fenestrated Silastic membrane. The filter is introduced via a jugular or femoral approach using a carrying capsule loaded on a catheter (Fig. **2**). Once released from the capsule, the filter prongs spring out and anchor the filter within the cava. The apex of the filter points caudally (Fig. **3**). The Silastic fenestrations are each 3 mm in diameter. It was

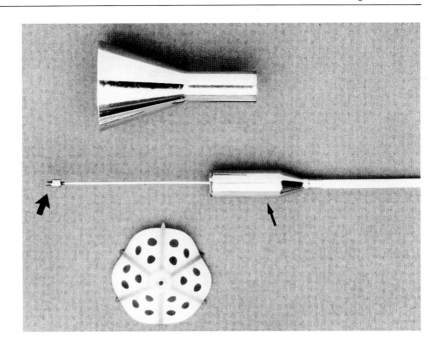

Fig. 2 **The Mobin-Uddin insertion set.** The filter screws onto the threaded end of the introducing wire (fat arrow). The loading cone (top) is then used to help load the filter into the carrier capsule (thin arrow)

hoped that the fenestrations would permit adequate blood flow to prevent IVC thrombosis, while still filtering clinically significant clots.

There has been extensive clinical experience with the MU filters. The MU effectively prevents all clots larger than 3 mm from embolizing. There are, however, several problems with this design. First, the carrier capsule is large (7 by 32 mm) and therefore requires a large hole in the vessel for insertion. In the past, a venous cut-down was required but, more recently, percutaneous methods of introduction have been described (20, 38). This involves dilating a tract into the vein with coaxial dilators and then inserting a 24 Fr sheath through which the filter capsule is passed into the venous system. Despite the large size of the sheath used, patients generally heal from this size of hole without difficulty.

An early problem with the MU filter was migration within the IVC from the site at which the filter was placed (31). This was primarily due to the original small size (23 mm maximal span across the prongs) of the filter, which did not allow all the prongs to engage adequately the caval wall when placed in a larger sized cava. Once the filter size was increased to 28 mm, migration became less frequent.

The major problem seen with the MU filter has been thrombosis of the IVC, which is seen in 50–70% of cases (26, 45). This appears to be due to the degree of caval blood flow restriction, since the addition of heparin bonded to the Silastic web failed to improve caval patency rates. Due to the high incidence of caval thrombosis, approximately 20% of patients developed significant venous stasis sequelae in the lower extremities (5). As with IVC ligation,

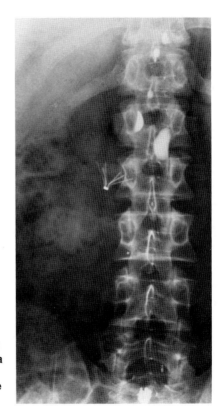

Fig. 3 **Typical orientation of a Mobin-Uddin filter within the vena cava**

patients can also develop large collateral channels around the filter and the thrombosed IVC (Fig. 4). Recurrent embolization is a potential risk and is seen in 3% of cases (31). Perforation of the IVC and adjacent structures (duodenum and ureter) is

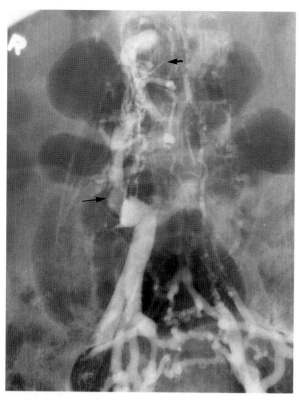

Fig. 4 **Complete occlusion of the inferior vena cava below a Mobin-Uddin filter** (short arrow). Note the enlarged collateral vessel (long arrow), which could allow transmission of emboli

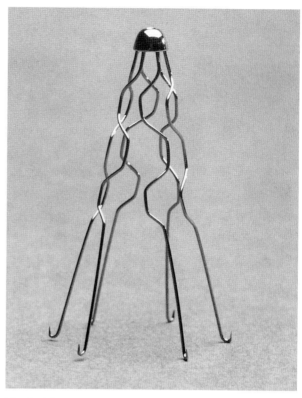

Fig. 5 **The Greenfield filter.** Note the hooks at the base of the filter which anchor the filter to the caval wall

another rare but described complication of MU filters (18, 30).

The next advance in filter technology came with the development of the Greenfield filter (GF) in 1973 (14). This filter consists of six stainless steel legs attached to a central hub and radiating out to form a cone (Fig. **5**). The opening between the legs varies from 2 mm at the hub to 6 mm near the base at the hooks. The tip of each leg has a hook to anchor it to the caval wall. Unlike the MU filter, there is no Silastic covering. The filter is also oriented differently with its apex pointing cephalad. The GF can be introduced via a femoral or jugular route using a carrier capsule mounted on a catheter (Fig. **6**). This capsule is also quite large (7.9 mm in diameter). In the past, insertion required a surgical venotomy; however, percutaneous introduction through a 24 Fr sheath has been described (10, 44).

The main advantage of the GF is that the rate of caval thrombosis is only 3 to 5% (27, 43, 45). The more open design of the GF causes less restriction to blood flow. The increased patency is also attributed to the inverted cone design. Emboli accumulate in the central cone tip with continued flow maintained at the periphery of the caval lumen. Also, the geometry of the cone shape dictates that a large part of the filter has to be filled with clot before there is a significant decrease in the cross-sectional area of the vena cava (14).

Clinical experience would suggest that the GF has good clot trapping characteristics. The rate of recurrent embolization is only 2% (15). Laboratory experience, however, indicates that the filter's efficiency is dependent on its position within the IVC. In vitro experiments passing various-sized particles or clots past the filter revealed a marked decrease in trapping efficiency when the filter was tilted within the IVC (Fig. **7**) (17, 24). Inserting the filter over a guide wire has been proposed as a way of keeping the GF better centered within the cava. Tilting of the filter can occur even with flawless insertion technique; however, one preventable cause of tilt is accidental discharge of the filter partially into a renal or iliac vein. This can usually be avoided by locating the renal and iliac veins with a preinsertion cavogram and then placing a metallic marker at the desired

Fig. 6 **The Greenfield filter introducing capsules.** The top capsule is for jugular access. The bottom capsule is for femoral insertion

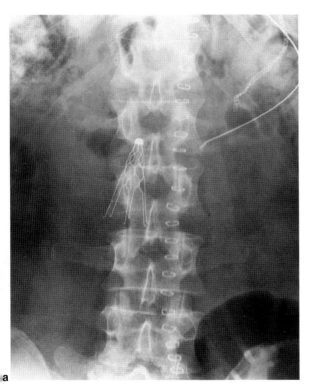

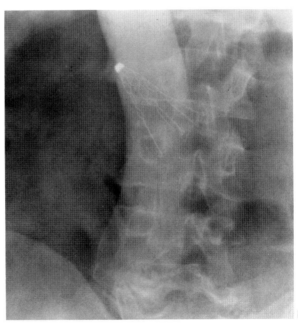

Fig. **7** **a A Greenfield filter showing good orientation,** with its long axis parallel to the direction of the inferior vena cava

b A Greenfield filter showing poor orientation, with a severe tilt within the inferior vena cava

level of placement to avoid confusion during manipulation of the filter.

Aside from the large insertion capsule, and the problem of filter tilt, the GF also suffers from problems with filter misplacement and migration. The renal and iliac veins are the most frequent sites of misplacement; however, GFs have been misplaced into hepatic veins, right spermatic vein, and the right atrium (1, 2, 15). In Greenfield's own series, 7% of filters inserted were misplaced. This may partially

relate to the fact that the carrier capsule is just barely longer than the filter itself. A slight slip of the hand could allow premature filter release from the capsule.

Postplacement migration of GFs is a complication seen in 28% of cases in Greenfield's own series (27). The degree of migration is usually small (<2 cm); however, the filter has been seen to migrate as far as the heart (4). Even small migrations, however, can have serious consequences. If the migration allows some of the filter legs to enter into a renal vein, then the filter will tilt with a resulting decrease in clot-trapping efficiency. Both cranial and caudal migrations have been seen. Caudal migration may actually represent perforation of the caval wall and should be closely watched for.

Migration of GFs has two preventable causes. If the legs of the filter are crossed within the carrier capsule, they may not spring open completely on release and thus may not adequately engage the caval wall. Once loaded in the capsule, the filter legs should be checked before insertion to ensure that they are not crossed. Similarly, the filter may not adequately engage the caval wall if the legs are tethered by blood clots that form within the capsule. This can be avoided by infusing heparinized saline through the capsule during insertion.

General Management of Filters

The indications for use of caval filters are listed in Table 1. In the past, the majority of filters were inserted because of problems with anticoagulation: treatment failure, complication of therapy, or contra-indications to anticoagulants. Only 18% of the filters placed by Greenfield were inserted prophylactically in patients without signs or symptoms of PE (13). There are two situations in which filters can be justified for prophylaxis. First is when a patient has a large free-floating, pedunculated thrombus in the pelvic veins or upper femoral vein. Norris et al. (33) showed that this type of thrombus is much more likely to embolize than a thrombus that is adherent to the vein walls. Perioperative prevention of PE is the other indication for a prophylactic filter. Certain operations carry a very high risk of PE, for example, total hip replacement carries a 25% risk (46). Considering the low morbidity associated with filter insertion, prophylactic use of a caval filter should be considered before high-risk operations, especially if it is known that the patient has venous thrombosis preoperatively. The development of newer filters that can be percutaneously retrieved may increase

Table 1   Indications for filter placement

Recurrent PE despite anticoagulation
Contra-indication to anticoagulation
Complication of anticoagulation
Prophylaxis (free-floating pelvic thrombi)
Prophylaxis (high-risk operation)
Massive life-threatening pulmonary embolism
Septic thrombophlebitis
PE in a cancer patient

the willingness of surgeons to utilize filters prophy-lactically during the perioperative period.

The other indications on the list are more controversial. In the past it was feared that in the patient with septic emboli, the filter could become contaminated and act as a focus of continuing bacteremia. Peyton et al. (37), however, demonstrated that filters and clots attached to them can be sterilized in vivo. Their experiment also suggested that dogs with septic embolization tolerated filter placement better than caval ligation, which has historically been the proposed method of treatment. Another controversial indication for insertion is the presence of deep vein thrombosis in a cancer patient. Primary use of filters (before anticoagulation) has been espoused in cancer patients due to the fact that these patients tolerate anticoagulants poorly and have a higher rate of recurrent PE (19%) while on anticoagulants (32).

Once the decision has been made to use a filter, the patient should first be evaluated with a cavogram. This demonstrates the size of the IVC, the location of the renal veins, and whether the thrombus extends into the IVC. Some investigators suggest doing this study by a left femoral vein approach, to avoid missing an anomaly, such as a double IVC, which can be seen in up to 3% of patients, according to Ferris (11).

The femoral and jugular insertion routes both have advantages and disadvantages. The jugular approach provides a straighter course into the IVC and thus helps keep the filter better centered during release. This approach also avoids the possibility of dislodging any thrombus that might be present within the pelvic veins. The disadvantages of the jugular approach are: most radiologists are less familiar with doing internal jugular punctures, the risk of air embolism through the sheath is slightly larger due to the negative intrathoracic pressure, and the large MU and GF capsules sometimes get caught on the eustachian valve. Aside from the problems already alluded to, the femoral route also can be difficult in older patients with tortuous vessels. In these patients it is sometimes difficult to advance the large MU and GF capsules up to the IVC. Overall, the jugular approach is preferable.

The preferred level of placement of the filter in most situations is immediately below the renal veins. This is to maintain patency of the renal veins should the IVC thrombose below the filter. The filter should be close to the renal veins so that if the cava should thrombose, there would not be a large stagnant dead space between the filter and renal veins in which to form suprafilter clots. The infrarenal location became less important after the GF was developed with its improved caval patency rate. Orisini and Tarrell (34) described the use of filters in the supra-renal cava with no ill effects. Indications for supra-renal placement are listed in Table 2 and primarily

Table **2** Indications for suprarenal filter placement

IVC thrombus above the renal veins
Renal vein thrombosis
Recurrent PE via a large left ovarian vein
Recurrent PE after previous IVC interruption

include any situation in which the clot extends to the level of the renal veins or when an infrarenal location would not provide adequate protection against embolization. Placement of GFs in the superior vena cava has been experimentally evaluated (21) and appears to be both safe and effective.

Postinsertion management of filters is relatively uncomplicated. The body's natural thrombolytic system tends to lyse the clots captured by the filter. Langham et al. (22) experimentally demonstrated that clots embolized to filters in dogs showed greater resolution within the first week in those dogs receiving anticoagulants compared with untreated dogs. After 2 weeks, however, the natural thrombolytic system of the dogs who had not received anticoagulants had caught up with the treated group and the overall percent of clot resolution was the same between the two groups (22). Thus, it appears that anticoagulation should not be necessary after filter insertion, unless to aid in symptomatic treatment of deep vein thrombosis.

Plain abdominal radiographs are one of the more useful and cost-effective methods of postinsertion follow-up. Filter integrity, angulation,and migration can all be evaluated by plain abdominal radiographs.

In addition, when using GFs, the span across the filter base should be checked. A decrease in the span suggests caval thrombosis with retraction of the IVC, whereas increased span suggests perforation of the filter legs out through the caval wall (27). Cavography and CT may be needed to evaluate further the filter or the IVC. CT is probably better for demonstration of caval perforation and pericaval hemorrhage. However, CT is probably not as good as cavography in evaluating intracaval thrombus (12). To date, ultrasound has not been demonstrated to be useful in evaluating filters.

Newer Filters

There are many newer filters being developed and tested in attempts to overcome the problems associated with both the MU and GF.

Bird's Nest Filter

This filter, developed by Roehm et al. (39, 41), is unlike the MU and GF in that it does not come preformed. It consists of four flexible 25 cm long 0.18 mm stainless steel wires that are formed into a tangle of wires during the insertion process (Figs. **8, 9**). There is a hook at the ends of each wire to anchor the filter. The main advantage of this filter is that it can be passed through an 8 Fr catheter (one-third the size of the 24 Fr sheath needed for introducing MU and GFs). Use of an 8 Fr introducing catheter should be less intimidating to the average radiologist. This smaller system should also eliminate the inability to pass the eustachian valve or a tortuous iliac vein, as is

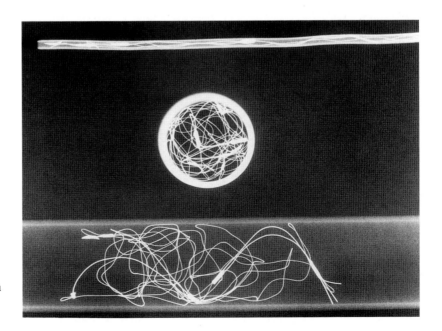

Fig. **8** **The bird's nest filter.**
The filter is shown loaded in an introducing catheter (top), and as it would appear within the inferior vena cava (bottom: side view; middle: end view)

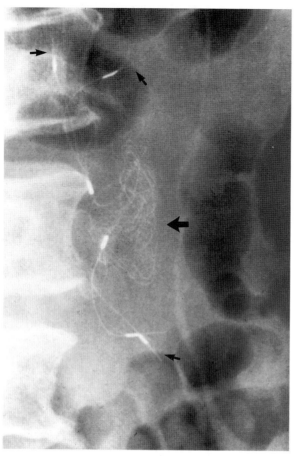

Fig. 9 The bird's nest filter within the inferior vena cava. Hooks (small arrows) are present at the top and bottom ends to anchor the filter within the inferior vena cava. The central tangle of wires (large arrow) provides the filtration

ing caval thrombosis. The only disadvantage to the Bird's nest filter is that the procedure for forming the filter within the IVC is somewhat complex.

Amplatz Filter

This filter was developed in 1984 at the University of Minnesota (24). The filter is constructed from an inert alloy (MP32N) and is formed into a spider configuration that sits with its apex directed caudally (Fig. **10**). There are 12 prongs attached to a central hub and wire loops are present on alternating prongs to limit penetration of the caval wall to 2 mm. The Amplatz filter is flexible and will collapse enough to allow percutaneous introduction through a 14 Fr catheter. This introducing catheter can be advanced past the desired area of placement before inserting the filter and thus there is no risk of premature filter release, as is seen with the GF.

The feature that was an innovation of the Amplatz filter is the caudal hook that can be snared and permits percutaneous retrieval (Fig. **11**). The filter is retrieved through a 14 Fr Teflon catheter. Thus, for the first time, it became possible to use a filter for short-term prophylaxis of PE. Animal experiments demonstrated that the retrieval process is technically easy. The prongs and hooks, however, get incorporated under an endothelial reaction so that percutaneous retrieval cannot be easily accomplished after 2 to 3 weeks (8). Although the filter can be placed from jugular or femoral venous access, the caudal hook dictates that a femoral approach be used for retrieval.

Another advantage to the Amplatz filter is that in vitro experiments indicate that the clot-trapping efficiency is not significantly affected by tilting of the filter within the vena cava and that when tilted, its effectiveness is superior to that of a tilted GF (24).

Clinical trials so far have included 25 patients. In all cases the insertion was quite easy. No patient has had symptoms of recurrent PE. To date, there have been three known complications: one caval throm-

sometimes a problem with GFs. Clinical experience with the Bird's nest filter in 200 patients suggests that it is a very effective filter, since the rate of recurrent embolization is only 1% (40). Also, the complication rate was low with only one patient (0.5%) develop-

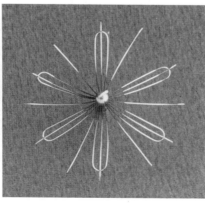

Fig. 10 The Amplatz vena cava filter, end and side views. The caudal hook (white arrow) allows percutaneous retrieval

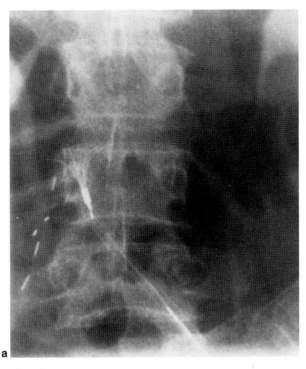
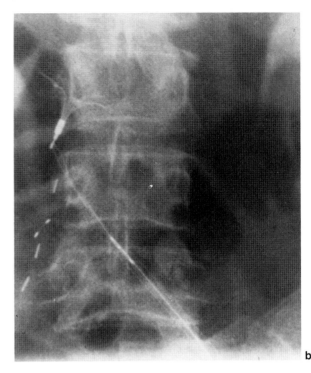

Fig. 11   Retrieval of the Amplatz filter
a A wire snare has been passed around the caudal hook of the filter
b The 14 Fr catheter is being passed over the filter

bosis, one filter misplaced into a right spermatic vein (9), and one patient who developed thrombus above the filter. The caval thrombosis occurred in a patient who had extensive caval thrombus before filter insertion. The misplaced filter was inserted using the original insertion set, which has since been modified to prevent a similar misplacement. Retrieval has been attempted in three patients in whom short-term prophylaxis against PE was desired. Retrieval was successful in all three and no complications occurred.

Basket Filter

The basket filter was designed in West Germany by Günther et al. (17). The filter consists of a basketlike network of 12 stainless steel wires with prongs extending from the cephalad end to anchor the filter (Fig. 12). A caudal hook was also incorporated in this design to allow percutaneous manipulation or retrieval.

There are several potential advantages to this filter. First, the filter can be introduced by either a

Fig. 12   The basket filter
a Side view. The prongs (straight arrow) anchor the filter in the inferior vena cava. The basket (long curved arrow) provides the filtration. The caudal hook (short curved arrow) allows percutaneous retrieval
b End view of the basket filter

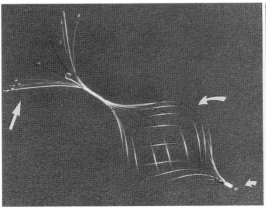
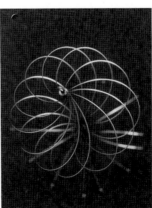

jugular or femoral route through a small 10 Fr sheath. The smaller size (relative to percutaneous GF insertion) of the introducing catheter makes insertion easier. Second, the filter has effectively three different planes of filtration (the caudal part of the basket, the cephalad part of the basket, and the prongs). Günther's data indicate that this provides superior filtration compared with other filters (17). Third, the basket helps keep the filter centered in the cava, which presumably helps improve filtration. Lastly, the caudal hook allows percutaneous manipulation or retrieval of the filter.

The basket portion, however, is quickly incorporated into the caval wall by an endothelial reaction. Thus, retrieval is limited to within 10 days after insertion, which in turn limits the practical application of this retrievability feature. A slight disadvantage to this filter is its 7.5 cm length, which could make it difficult to position the filter so as to avoid the renal veins and caval bifurcation (Fig. **13**). As of September 1986, their clinical experience included 10 human patients, one of whom developed caval thrombotic occlusion and died secondary to recurrent pulmonary embolism (16).

Nitinol Filters

Nitinol is an interesting alloy of nickel and titanium that has thermal memory properties. Nitinol wires can be formed into a desired shape on a jig and annealed at high temperature, which will give the wires a memory for that shape. When cooled down in an icebath, the wires become soft and pliable, but when rewarmed to body temperature, the wires will resume the shape in which they were annealed. Once they have resumed the memory shape, the wires become as rigid as stainless steel. The obvious advantage of this material is that, while in their cooled flexible state, the wires can be passed through a standard angiographic catheter that is much smaller than existing filter insertion systems.

There are two filters being developed using nitinol. Palestrant et al. (35) has devised a filter comprised of seven nitinol wires that form into anchoring hooks and a separate filtration plane (Fig. **14**). Cragg and Castaneda-Zuniga (6) devised a filter using a single nitinol wire that assumes a coil configuration in the IVC (Fig. **15**). Both filters have undergone laboratory evaluation but to date no clinical applications have been published. Palestrant's laboratory data suggest that his nitinol filter will trap emboli better than the GF or MU filters.

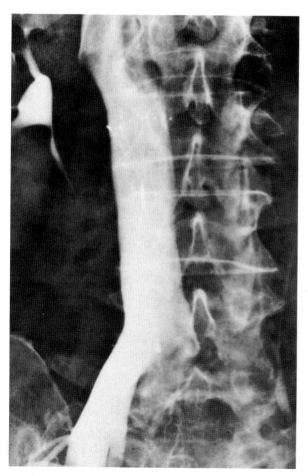

Fig. 13 The basket filter within an inferior vena cava.
Note that due to the basket filter's length, the filter extends from just below the renal veins to the caval bifurcation

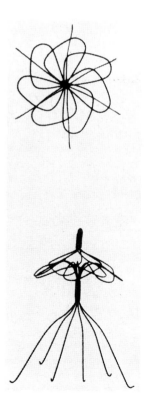

Fig. **14 Palestrant's nitinol caval filter.** The filter is viewed end-on (top) and from the side (bottom)

Helix Filter

Maass et al. (25) developed the helix filter, which consists of a spring steel band that assumes a spiral coil shape in the IVC (Fig. **16**). A horizontal watch-spring-type coil provides the filtration. The filter is held in place simply by elastic expansion against the walls of the cava. Their laboratory data indicate that this filter provides negligible resistance to blood flow and yet it consistently filters emboli 3.5 mm and larger. The design also makes transvenous removal feasible. One of the disadvantages is that the insertion applicator is 7 mm in diameter, which is considerably larger than insertion catheters for the Amplatz, basket, and bird's nest filters. Again, no clinical trials have yet been published.

Conclusion

The development of currently used filters, such as the GF, has provided a relatively safe and effective means of preventing pulmonary embolism. The morbidity and mortality associated with the surgical methods of caval interruption have been essentially eliminated. The ongoing development of the newer filters holds the promise of greater ease of insertion, a broader range of applications of filters, and possibly increased effectiveness.

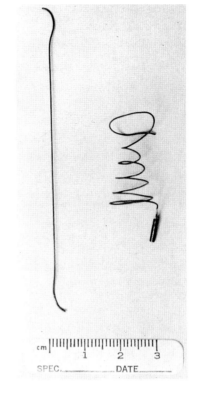

Fig. **15 Cragg's nitinol filter.** On the left the filter is in the cooled pliable state. On the right, the filter has regained its memory shape

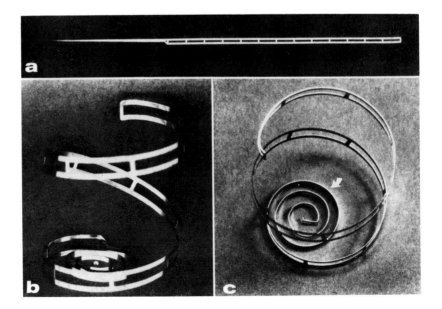

Fig. **16 The helix filter.** The watch-spring spiral (white arrow) provides the filtration. The remainder of the filter anchors the filter within the cava by elastic expansion

References

1. Aikens CW, Thurer RL, Waltman AC, Margolies MN, Schneider RC. A misplaced caval filter: its removal from the heart without cardiopulmonary bypass. Arch Surg 1980;115:1133.
2. Allen HA, Cisternino SJ, Otteson OE, Queral L, Dagher F. The Kimray-Greenfield vena caval filter: a case of unusual misplacement. Cardiovasc Intervent Radiol 1982;5:82–84.
3. Bernstein EF. The role of operative inferior vena caval interruption in the management of venous thromboembolism. World J Surg 1978;2:61–71.
4. Castaneda F, Herrera M, Cragg AH, Salomonowitz E, Lund G, Castaneda-Zuniga W, Amplatz K. Migration of a Kimray-Greenfield filter to the right ventricle. Radiology 1983;149:690.
5. Coleman C, Castaneda-Zuniga W, Amplatz K. Mobin-Uddin vena caval filters. Semin Intervent Radiol 1986;3:193–195.

6. Cragg A, Castaneda-Zuniga WR. Nitinol spiral vena caval filter. Semin Intervent Radiol 1986;3:227–230.
7. Dalen JE, Albert JS. Natural history of pulmonary embolism. Prog Cardiovasc Dis 1975;17:259–270.
8. Darcy MD, Hunter DW, Lund GB, Cardella JF, Amplatz K. Retrievable vena caval filter. Semin Intervent Radiol 1986;3:214–219.
9. Darcy MD, Smith TP, Hunter DW, Castaneda-Zuniga WR, Amplatz K. Misplacement of a vena caval filter in the retroperitoneum. J Cardiovasc Intervent Radiol 1987;10:37.
10. Denny DF, Cronan JJ, Dorfman GS, Esplin C. Percutaneous Kimray-Greenfield placement by femoral vein puncture. AJR 1985;145:827–829.
11. Ferris EJ. The inferior vena cava. In: Abrams HL, ed. Abrams angiography: vascular and interventional radiology; vol 1. Boston: Little, Brown 1983:949.
12. Gin-Chung L, Angtuaco TL, Ferris EJ, Hemendran RS, Reifsteck JE, Harshfield DL. Inferior vena caval filters: noninvasive evaluation. Radiology 1986;160:521–524.
13. Greenfield LJ. Current indications for and the results of Greenfield filter placement. J Vasc Surg 1984;1:502–504.
14. Greenfield LJ, McCurdy JR, Brown PP, Elkins RC. A new intracaval filter permitting continued flow and resolution of emboli. Surgery 1973;73:599–606.
15. Greenfield LJ, Peyton R, Crute S, Barnes R. Greenfield vena caval filter experience: late results in 156 patients. Arch Surg 1981;116:1451–1455.
16. Günther RW, Schild H. Basket filter for the prevention of pulmonary embolism. Semin Intervent Radiol 1986;3:220–226.
17. Günther RW, Schild H, Fries A, Storkel S. Vena caval filter to prevent pulmonary embolism: experimental study. Radiology 1985;156:315–320.
18. Irvin GL. Duodenal perforation with a vena caval umbrella. Am Surg 1972;38:635–637.
19. Kinasewitz GT, George RB. Management of thromboembolism: anticoagulants, thrombolytics, or surgical intervention? Chest 1984;86:106–111.
20. Knight L, Amplatz K, Nicoloff DM. Alternate method for introduction of inferior vena cava filter. Surg Gynecol Obstet 1974;138:762–864.
21. Langham MR, Etheridge JC, Crute SL, Greenfield LJ. Experimental superior vena caval placement of the Greenfield filter. J Vasc Surg 1985;2:794–798.
22. Langham MR, Hoffman MJ, Greenfield LJ. Effect of anticoagulation on the lysis of filter entrapped thromboembolism in dogs. J Surg Res 1985;38:391–399.
23. Leather RP, Clark WR, Powers SR, Parker FB, Bernard HR, Eckert C. Five year experience with the Morits vena cava clip in 62 patients. Arch Surg 1968;97:357–364.
24. Lund G, Rysavy JA, Salomonowitz E, Cragg AH, Kotula F, Castaneda-Zuniga W, Hunter DW, Coleman C, Amplatz K. A new vena caval filter for percutaneous placement and retrieval: experimental study. Radiology 1984;152:369–372.
25. Maass D, Demierre D, Wallsten H, Senning A. The helix filter: a new vena caval filter for the prevention of pulmonary embolism. J Cardiovasc Surg 1985;26:116–123.
26. Mansour M, Chang AE, Sindelar WF. Interruption of the inferior vena cava for the prevention of recurrent pulmonary embolism. Am Surg 1985;51:375–380.
27. Messmer JM, Greenfield LJ. Greenfield caval filters: long term radiographic follow-up study. Radiology 1985;156:613–618.
28. Miles RM, Richardson RR, Wayne L, Elsea PW, Stewart SB, Duncan D. Longterm results with the serrated teflon vena caval clip in the prevention of pulmonary embolism. Ann Surg 1969;169:881–891.
29. Mobin-Uddin K, Smith PE, Martines LD. A vena caval filter for the prevention of pulmonary embolus. Surg Forum 1967;18:209.
30. Mobin-Uddin K, Trinkle JK, Bryant LR. Present status of the inferior vena cava umbrella filter. Surgery 1971;70:914–919.
31. Mobin-Uddin K, Utley JR, Bryant LR. The inferior vena cava umbrella filter. Prog Cardiovasc Dis 1975;17:391–399.
32. Moore FD, Osteen RT, Karp DD, Steele G, Wilson RE. Anticoagulants, venous thromboembolism, and the cancer patient. Arch Surg 1981;116:405–407.
33. Norris CS, Greenfield LJ, Herrmann JB. Free-floating iliofemoral thrombus: a risk of pulmonary embolism. Arch Surg 1985;120:806–808.
34. Orsini RA, Jarrell BE. Suprarenal placement of vena caval filters: indications, techniques and results. J Vasc Surg 1984;1:124–135.
35. Palestrant AM, Prince M, Simon M. Comparative in vitro evaluation of the nitinol inferior vena cava filter. Radiology 1982;145:351–355.
36. Pate JW, Melvin D, Cheek RC. A new form of vena caval interruption. Ann Surg 1969;169:873–880.
37. Peyton JW, Hylemon MB, Greenfield LJ, Crute SL, Sugerman HG, Quershi GD. Comparison of Greenfield filter and vena caval ligation for experimental septic thromboembolism. Surgery 1983;93:533–537.
38. Rizk GK, Amplatz K. A percutaneous method of introducing the caval umbrella. AJR 1973;117:903–909.
39. Roehm JOF. The bird's nest filter: a new percutaneous transcatheter inferior vena cava filter. J Vasc Surg 1984;1:498–501.
40. Roehm JOF, Gianturco C, Barth MH. The bird's nest inferior vena cava filter. Semin Intervent Radiol 1986; 3:205–213.
41. Roehm JOF, Gianturco C, Barth MH, Wright KC. Percutaneous transcatheter filter for the inferior vena cava. Radiology 1984;150:225–257.
42. Silver D, Sabiston DC. The role of vena caval interruption in management of pulmonary embolism. Surgery 1975;77:1–10.
43. Simon M, Palestrant AM. Transvenous devices for the management of pulmonary embolism. Cardiovasc Intervent Radiol 1980;3:308–318.
44. Tadavarthy SM, Castaneda-Zuniga W, Salomonowitz E, Lund G, Cragg A, Hunter D, Coleman C, Amplatz K. Kimray-Greenfield vena caval filter: percutaneous introduction. Radiology 1984;151:525–526.
45. Wingerd M, Bernard VM, Maddison F, Towne JB. Comparison of caval filters in the management of venous thromboembolism. Arch Surg 1978;113:1264–1269.
46. Woolson ST, Harris WH. Greenfield vena caval filter for management of selected cases of venous thromboembolic disease following hip surgery. Clin Orthop 1986;204:201–206.

Foreign Body Retrieval

P. Rossi, P. Pavone

The widespread use of percutaneous techniques, both in the cardiovascular system and in the biliary and urinary systems, has led to an increase in the risks of dislocation of materials employed for catheterization. The removal of dislocated fragments, once performed surgically, has been achieved successfully over the last 20 years by means of the percutaneous technique, using angiographic materials.

An overview of this rare, but important problem will be given here, together with a discussion of the use of the angiographic techniques presently available for percutaneous removal and a presentation of our personal series.

The Nature of Intravascular Foreign Bodies and Causes of Dislodgment

Iatrogenic origins were involved in practically every case of an intravascular foreign body so far described (7), although vascular embolization associated with bullets has occasionally been reported, and becomes a relevant problem in war periods (12). Intravenous polyethylene catheters introduced for parenteral feeding of central venous pressure (CVP) monitoring account for the majority of intravascular foreign bodies (79,4% in the Bloomfield's review) (1).

The detachment of a distal segment of a catheter or CVP line can occur inadvertently during introduction. In most cases, the external needle produces damage during retrieval or repositioning of the catheter. Forceful introduction maneuvers are also to be avoided since kinking of the catheter can produce points of weakness, and detachment at this level can occur.

In other instances, no definitive cause of detachment is found, and it has been supposed that construction defects in the materials are present. For the same reason, the detachment of fragments of internal pacemakers, and of catheters used for ventriculoauriculostomy or decompression of hydrocephalus, may occur. Intravascular foreign bodies are rarely found after vascular or cardiac surgery, although recently a case of a fragment of a 36 Fr cardiopulmonary by-pass detached after coronary surgery with extracorporeal circulation has been published (21).

On the arterial side, fragments of angiographic catheters and guide wires are found more rarely.

Forceful maneuvers during selective catheterization, and faulty materials, may produce detachment of the distal part. Excessive aging or exposure to ionizing radiations are deleterious to polyurethane catheters, causing wall delamination and tip separation. Problems of this sort should become nonexistent with the increasing use of disposable and more reliable materials.

In addition, the unwanted dislodgment of Gianturco coils during percutaneous embolotherapy is considered a cause of iatrogenic foreign bodies (3). Inadvertent displacement of the tip of the catheter from the artery to be embolized, or partial protrusion of the proximal end of the coil from the origin of the embolized branch, are the most frequent causes for foreign bodies in the arterial tree. In other instances, the coil remains embedded in the tip of the catheter, and may be dislodged during removal of the catheter.

Materials employed for drainage, such as catheters, guide wires and endoprostheses, can be dislodged in the biliary and urinary systems during interventional maneuvers. Although stones might also be considered as foreign bodies, and their removal with percutaneous techniques has been widely used, this subject will not be discussed here.

A particular problem is posed by endoprostheses, which may be released initially in the wrong position, or dislodge proximally or, more frequently, distally to the biliary obstruction. Occluded endoprostheses need to be removed for replacement with new ones, and percutaneous retrieval is very effective.

The Site of Embolization

The site of embolization of the vascular foreign body depends on the site of introduction: arterial or venous (31).

Catheters dislodged through a venous access progress centrally and stop at different levels according to their size. Longer fragments remain with the proximal end in the superior vena cava, while the distal end stops against the wall of the right atrium or ventricle, or in the pulmonary artery. Smaller fragments migrate more distally, and usually reach the pulmonary arteries; only rarely do they stop in the right ventricle, trapped in the wall muscles. This is also the case with loose transvenous electrode pacemaker catheters, the distal end of which is usually firmly fixed into the wall of the right ventricle.

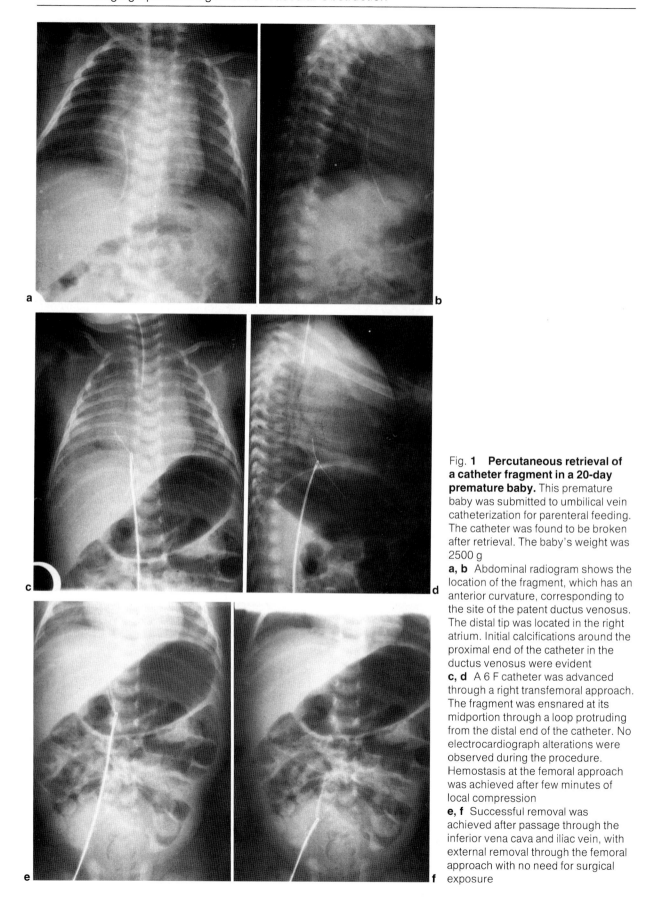

Fig. 1 Percutaneous retrieval of a catheter fragment in a 20-day premature baby. This premature baby was submitted to umbilical vein catheterization for parenteral feeding. The catheter was found to be broken after retrieval. The baby's weight was 2500 g

a, b Abdominal radiogram shows the location of the fragment, which has an anterior curvature, corresponding to the site of the patent ductus venosus. The distal tip was located in the right atrium. Initial calcifications around the proximal end of the catheter in the ductus venosus were evident

c, d A 6 F catheter was advanced through a right transfemoral approach. The fragment was ensnared at its midportion through a loop protruding from the distal end of the catheter. No electrocardiograph alterations were observed during the procedure. Hemostasis at the femoral approach was achieved after few minutes of local compression

e, f Successful removal was achieved after passage through the inferior vena cava and iliac vein, with external removal through the femoral approach with no need for surgical exposure

Catheter migration into the pulmonary vessels can also occur during percutaneous removal of fragments lodged in the cardiac chambers or in peripheral veins. This occurrence does not prevent successful removal. In some cases, the catheter is localized in a peripheral vein near the site of entry, with its tip in a side branch or outside the wall itself in the soft tissue.

In one of our cases, an umbilical vein catheter placed in a premature newborn baby broke at the level of the ductus venosus, and did not move from the site of dislodgment, remaining with the proximal end in the ductus itself and with the distal end free-floating into the right atrium. It was subsequently snared and removed through the inferior vena cava. Initial closure of the ductus and calcium deposits around the catheter fragment may have prevented further dislocation in this case (Fig. **1**).

On the arterial side, embolization is more directly related to the site of catheter dislodgment. More frequently, catheters are localized in peripheral vessels after dislodgment into the aorta. The rupture of the catheter during selective angiography causes dislocation into the branch being catheterized.

In the biliary system the site of dislodgment can either be the biliary system itself or the duodenum. Distal progression in the gastrointestinal tract may occur. Occluded endoprostheses pushed distally to perform a second internal drainage may dislocate into the distal gastrointestinal tract. In one of our cases, an endoprosthesis migrated to the level of the right colon, and stayed there without producing any symptoms for 5 months until the patient's death.

Complications when the Foreign Body Persists in the Vascular Bed

The presence of an intravascular foreign body can result in significant complications in a high percentage of cases (5). In the review of the literature reported by Fisher (7), only 12 out of 42 patients (29%) in whom the foreign body was not removed survived without significant complications in a long-term follow-up. Fourteen (33%) had non-fatal complications, and 16 (38%) died of causes related to the presence of the intravascular foreign body. The overall risk of complications was therefore 71% when the catheter was not removed.

Complications can arise immediately after catheter dislogment, as well as after an interval of months to years. Complications include perforation of the myocardium with a hemopericardium and cardiac tamponade, sepsis, pulmonary embolism, severe arrhythmias and cardiac arrest. Non-fatal complications vary from transitory arrhythmias to mild forms of sepsis, pulmonary embolism or endocarditis. All of these complications can also appear at a later stage if the catheter is not removed. Among later complications, endocarditis, perforations of cardiac valves, and mycotic aneurysm of the pulmonary artery have also been described (5).

Although endocarditis has been mentioned as a non-fatal complication, its final outcome cannot be foreseen. The intravascular foreign body can act as a route of entry for fungi to the body, and monilial endocarditis has also been described after a polyethylene catheter embolism (5). Contact between the dislodged catheter and the tricuspid valve may produce mechanical damage to the valve, initiating the process of endocarditis. Also, arrhythmias can evolve unpredictably from mild to severe forms, leading to cardiac arrest and death. Chronic mechanical damage to the myocardium can result in cardiac perforation due to the force of contraction on the retained catheter tip (22).

Catheters dislodged more peripherally into the vascular bed can induce the development of thrombi, which may become a source of repeated or even massive pulmonary embolism (14).

The high incidence of complications makes the removal of the foreign body mandatory in every case, although a few exceptional cases of unremoved foreign bodies which did not produce any kind of complication have occurred. Lamprecht (15) found, incidentally during autopsy, a 40 cm long fragment of a catheter located in the wall of the vena cava and the right atrium, dislodged 6 years previously. The catheter retained for the longest time in our series had been lodged in the superior vena cava and right ventricle for 5 years. The patient came to our attention after developing extrasystole and repeated pulmonary microembolisms.

The appearance of fatal late complications cannot be predicted, and there should therefore be no time delay between the dislodgment of the catheter and its removal. There are also medico-legal implications which stress the responsibility of the physician who performed the procedure, or that of the company producing the catheter itself.

The presence of a foreign body in the biliary system usually has no clinical significance. In one case, we left an endoprosthesis in a segmental biliary branch after proximal dislocation occurred during positioning. No complications were observed during follow up. In the case of an endoprosthesis dislodged into the right colon, relevant symptoms also did not appear.

Prompt removal should be ensured when the dislodged fragment is firmly embedded in the visceral wall. In two cases of internal drainage, we observed perforation of the duodenum due to prolonged decubitus of the internal catheter to the opposite duodenal wall. It is possible that dislodged materials might also produce internal perforation by the same mechanism. The use of endoscopic removal techniques should, however, be considered when the fragment is in the duodenum.

Percutaneous Removal

The non-surgical removal of intravascular foreign bodies was first proposed in 1964 by Thomas (29), who was able to grasp a fragment of a guide wire dislodged into the inferior vena cava by means of a bronchoscope forceps introduced through a saphenous cut-down. The rigidity of the instrument, however, restricted its use for catheters dislodged into main veins and the right atrium, and the assistance of a surgeon was still required.

Catheter removal using the percutaneous technique alone was described by Henley in 1969 (11). He employed the snare-loop technique developed on the principles described by Porstmann for percutaneous ductal closure (23). The snare-loop technique, also correctly proposed and described by Curry in the same year (4), has proved to be very reliable and easy to prepare in conventional angiography suites.

Retrieval Systems

Various techniques for percutaneous removal of intravascular foreign bodies have been described, and in many cases a combination of more than one technique has been employed for successful removal.

Snare-Loop

This is one of the earliest techniques employed (4, 17) and is certainly the most commonly used and the most useful in current practice. The system is composed of a very thin guide wire (0.0025 or less) folded in half at its midsection and inserted through a 7–8 Fr catheter. One of the distal ends of the guide wire is maneuvered by the radiologist, who modifies the loop which is formed by the folded guide wire and protrudes through the distal end of the catheter. Commercially available sets with more recently developed loops offer better technical results.

After percutaneous positioning of the catheter tip near the "lost" catheter fragment, various trials are performed to ensnare it by maneuvering the distal tip of the guide wire. For successful snaring, at least one end of the embolized fragment should be free-floating in the vessel lumen or in the cardiac chamber. After snaring the fragment, both ends of the guide wire are forcefully pulled out so that the fragment becomes fixed by the loop at the tip of the catheter.

Slow retrieval of the catheter is recommended, with particular care at the entry site. The use of a vascular Teflon sheath is suggested to facilitate passage through the soft tissues.

Hooked Catheters and Guide Wires

This technique employs a standard 7 Fr catheter with its distal end curved 180 degrees, or a pre-curved catheter, such as a sidewinder. This system is particularly useful when both distal ends of the embolized fragment are strongly adherent or embedded in the vessel or cadiac wall (25), preventing snaring.

With a rotatory motion of the catheter, the hooked fragment is gently pulled into a more peripheral vessel. Complete recovery of the system can be accomplished after the distal end of the catheter has been set free by snaring the tip with a second catheter introduced from the other side. Venotomy used in the first case has been discarded.

As an alternative to hooked catheters, guide wires with a deflecting tip have also been used (19). This system is rather rigid, however, and may cause damage to the vessel or endocardial wall. Its use should be limited to large vessels or the heart.

Helical Baskets (Dormia Ureteral Stone Baskets)

The Dormia basket can also be used to retrieve foreign bodies (9, 16). Its opening at the distal tip of a straight catheter allows maneuvering and snaring of the embolized fragment into the spirals. Of course, the presence of a free-floating end of the catheter is required, as in the snare loop technique.

This system may have some advantages in smaller vessels, since a small diameter is required for the complete opening of the basket. On the other hand, its maximum diameter opening is predetermined, and may not be of particular value in the heart. The helical basket has also been used to remove foreign bodies of larger caliber, such as intravascular bullets (27).

Grasping Devices

A number of grasping devices have been used to remove intravascular foreign bodies (20, 28). The first described case of percutaneous removal was actually performed with a myocardial biopsy catheter. Bronchoscopic forceps may also be used. Both of these systems require venous cut-down, and present limited manipulation ability and a certain risk of perforation.

Better results can be obtained with other grasping systems which are completely flexible (24) and where removal does not require venotomy when a Teflon sheath is used at the entry site. However, these systems may be extremely dangerous.

Balloon Catheters

Removal of peripheral foreign bodies using a Fogarty catheter has been described (18). The technique has the advantage of permitting the removal of fragments from small caliber vessels, conveying them into a larger vein in which manipulations or snaring with other devices can be performed.

As an alternative to the Fogarty balloon, occlusion balloon or angioplasty catheters can also be used. These catheters present an internal lumen and can be advanced using percutaneous techniques. Removal of vascular sheaths with the Grüntzig balloon advanced into the fragment has been recently described (8).

Personal Experience

Our series consists of 19 patients in whom the attempt to retrieve intravascular foreign bodies was made. In 15 cases, the foreign body was a broken intravenous catheter introduced through a subclavian approach for parenteral feeding or CVP monitoring. Three of the remaining 4 cases were broken tips of angiographic catheters, one in the iliac vein, one in the superior mesenteric artery, and the other a new 5 Fr catheter which broke in the right iliac artery after a perforation by a guide wire in the attempt at selective catheterization of the left hypogastric artery for embolization. In 2 of these cases, the retrieved catheter fragments showed friable polyurethane material, while the 5 Fr polyethylene catheter was lacerated by the guide wire. In the final case, the lost fragment represented the distal tip of an umbilical vein catheter introduced at birth in a 23-day old premature boy. All foreign bodies were radiopaque and could be identified in the radiographs of the region obtained in anteroposterior and lateral projections.

Before the retrieval attempt was carried out, contrast medium was injected at the level of dislodgment to visualize the presence of blood clots around the foreign body.

Techniques of removal included the use of hook catheters and the snare-loop technique (Figs. **1, 2**). Successful removal was obtained in 16 cases, while in 3 cases it was not possible to ensnare the loose fragment with the loop because the catheter had crossed the vessel wall and was lodged almost entirely in the soft tissue. In the first 2 successful cases the hook catheter technique alone was employed. In both cases, the catheter fragments were long and coiled up in the right atrium, with one tip embedded in the right ventricle or pulmonary artery. Retrieval with this technique was not difficult after hooking the fragment and applying repeated rotatory motions to the catheter so that the fragment was firmly caught. Saphenous cut-down was neces-

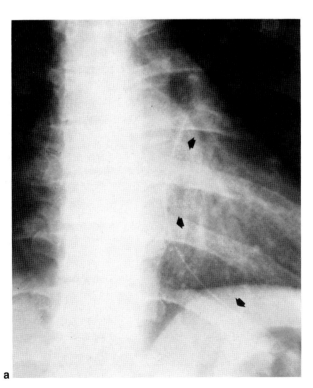

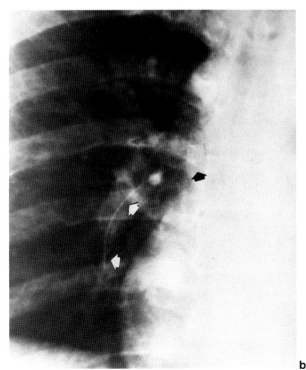

a   **b**

Fig. **2 a–e   Retrieval of a catheter fragment from the right ventricle.** The patient (a 29-year-old female) had undergone surgical intestinal by-pass in 1979 due to obesity. An intravenous feeding tube has been positioned, and had broken off during removal. After 3 years, the appearance of episodes of arrythmia recommended its removal
a The chest film showed the fragment to be located in the right ventricle (arrows)
b After initial maneuvers with a catheter for percutaneous removal, the catheter dislocated further into the right pulmonary artery (arrows)

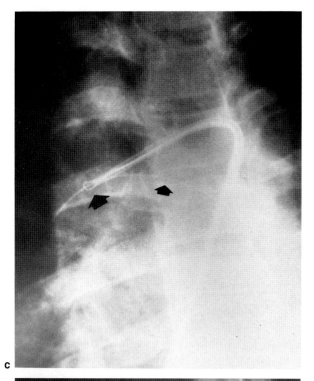

c

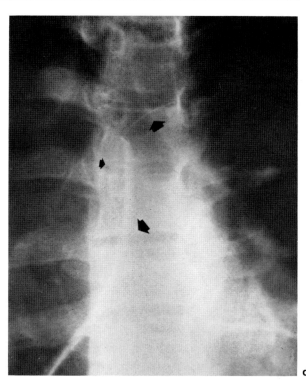

d

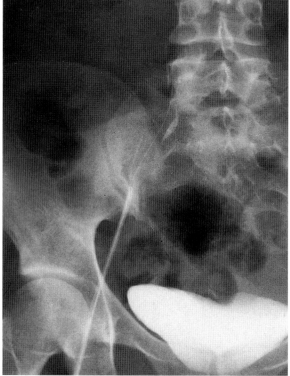

e

Fig. 2
c By advancing the catheter into this vessel, it was possible to ensnare the fragment with the loop
d, e The ensnared fragment during retrieval at the level of the pulmonary trunk and right atrium and, finally, at the level of the right iliac vein. The whole system was removed through the femoral vein approach with no need for surgical exposure. The patient had no complications, either during the procedure or in the follow-up

sary for the removal of the hooked fragment. In another case, it was possible to remove the catheter with a simple cutaneous incision after unsuccessful attempts with the snare-loop technique. The fragment was located with the proximal end in the superficial venous branch at the axilla and the distal end in the vertebral vein.

In the only arterial case, successful snaring of a catheter located in the superior mesenteric artery could have been accomplished, but during removal the curved tip of a cobra catheter entered the epigastric artery and disappeared from the main lumen of the femoral artery (Fig. **3**). No further attempt at catheter removal was needed.

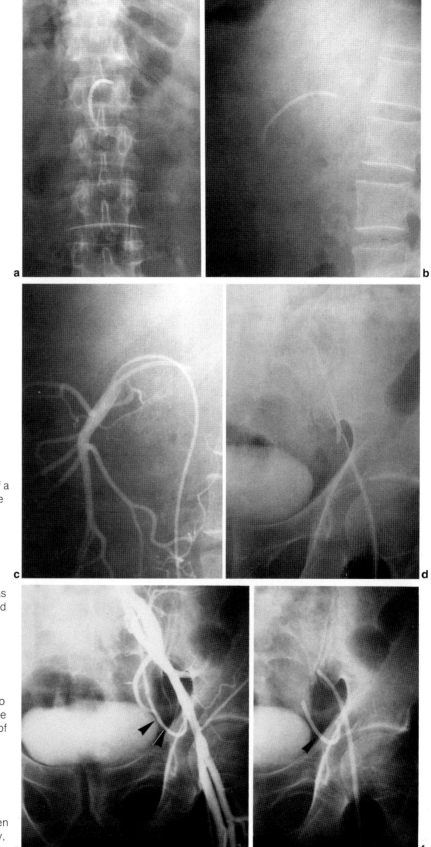

Fig. 3 **Retrieval of a broken catheter from the superior mesenteric artery.** The distal end of a cobra catheter had broken off into the superior mesenteric artery during diagnostic arteriography

a, b Anteroposterior and lateral projections show the site of dislodgment of the radiopaque catheter

c The superior mesenteric artery was selectively catheterized with a second cobra catheter, and injection demonstrated the relationship of the fragment to the vessel

d Using the snare-loop method, the fragment was retrieved down to the left femoral artery

e However, when it was attempted to pull the catheter out further, it became engaged in a small collateral branch of the left femoral artery, as shown on the angiogram (arrows: epigastric artery)

f The anteroposterior projection shows the position of the fragment, which is medial and anterior to the femoral artery. The decision was taken not to remove the fragment surgically, due to its stable position.

In the remaining 11 cases, complete percutaneous removal of the fragment was obtained. The technique employed in these cases included the use of the snare-loop technique alone in 3 cases, while in the remaining cases the fragment had to be dislocated using a hooked catheter or wire initially before successful removal with the snare-loop technique could be obtained.

No complications were encountered in our series.

Biliary System

Percutaneous removal techniques were employed in 9 cases in the biliary system following transhepatic drainage. In 7 cases, the foreign body was an endoprosthesis, while in 2 cases the distal flexible part of an exchange guide wire had broken off in the duodenum. The endoprostheses had to be repositioned due to insufficient drainage in 2 cases, and removed after occlusion in 5 cases. Repositioning was accomplished in our 2 cases by pulling the endoprostheses with an angioplasty balloon inflated inside its lumen.

Removal of occluded or non-functioning endoprostheses was obtained in 2 cases through the same transhepatic approach, since the guide wire was still inserted through the internal lumen of the endoprostheses. In both cases, balloon angioplasty catheters were employed. In 2 cases, the endoprostheses were pushed further distally, into the duodenum. In one of these 2 patients, the stent was reached through a nasogastric tube advanced under fluoroscopic guidance, snared, and removed through the nose (Fig. **4**). In the second patient, the endoprosthesis was left in place and migrated further distally with peristaltic bowel movement, reaching the right colon. No complications developed during the 5 months' follow-up before death. In the last case, removal of the endoprosthesis was carried out 2 years after its placement by puncturing the biliary tree at the level of the proximal end of the radiopaque stent, crossing its lumen with a guide wire, and subsequently using an angioplasty balloon for removal.

In the case of Carey – Coon's occluded stent, the silk suture in the subcutaneous layer can be used as guidance to advance a thin catheter to gain access to

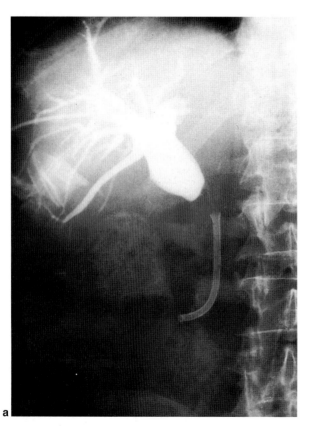
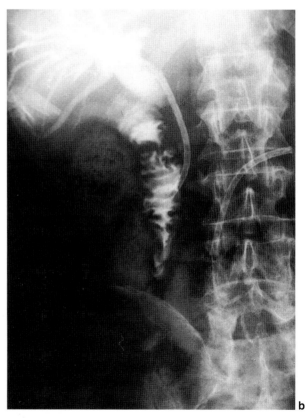

a

b

Fig. 4   Retrieval of a dislocated biliary endoprosthesis. The patient had been submitted to a percutaneous biliary procedure for a pancreatic carcinoma. Two months after insertion, the biliary endoprosthesis dislocated from its original site. A new biliary drainage was positioned in the dilated biliary tree
a After injection of contrast medium, the endoprosthesis is shown to be located 2 cm distal from the dilated biliary tree
b Internal drainage was carried out, pushing the dislocated stent into the duodenum

the biliary system at the level of the proximal end of the stent for removal (2).

Finally, percutaneous retrieval of distal fragments of exchange guide wires detached in the duodenum and the main bile duct was successfully obtained in 2 cases with the snare-loop technique using the same transhepatic approach.

Choice of the Retrieval System

Because of its reliability, the snare-loop technique should be considered first when attempting percutaneous removal of intravascular foreign bodies. This is particularly true when the catheter fragment is small and when it has been shown that at least one of its ends is free-floating in the vascular bed or in a cardiac chamber. Snare-loop catheter assembly can also be successful in retrieving embolized fragments from small segmental pulmonary branches.

As an alternative, if various attempts with the snare-loop system have failed, the redundant loop technique described by Dotter can be employed (6). This is possible only in the right atrium, where advancing the guide wire further causes it to form multiple convoluted loops, increasing the probability that the fragment will be ensnared.

In cases when the snare technique is not feasible because the fragment has both ends attached to the vascular wall, or the catheter fragments is very long, the "hook system" is a valid adjunct to the snare-loop technique. In fact, the main aim of the "hook system" is not to remove the lost catheter, but to dislocate it from the site of embolization, or to detach one end from the vessel wall, allowing

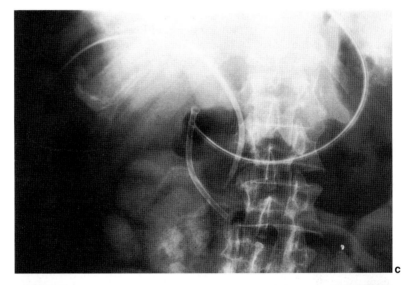

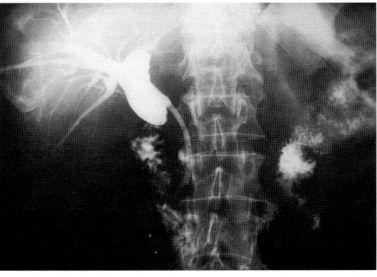

Fig. 4
c The snare-loop technique through a nasogastric tube was employed. The loop was advanced into the duodenum and maneuvered fluoroscopically. The stent was pulled back through the stomach and esophagus, and removed through the nose. No particular discomfort was felt by the patient during the whole procedure
d A second endoprosthesis was finally positioned for palliative treatment of the jaundice

retrieval with the snare-loop since at least one end of the catheter is free.

Particular care should be taken to hook the fragment firmly to the catheter in order to avoid further distal dislocation. The snare-loop catheter should be advanced at the same time from the contralateral femoral approach, to allow the fragment to be ensnared while the catheter is still hooked. The combined technique (hook system + snare loop) was employed sucessfully in 6 of our cases.

If the fragment is dislocated into a very peripheral, small-size vessel and maneuvering with the snare-loop is not possible, proximal dislocation for further ensnaring can be provided by using a balloon catheter. Angiographic occlusion balloons can be easily advanced distally to the fragment and, when inflated, can retrieve it proximally on the same principles as the Fogarty balloon embolectomy. Complete removal will still require use of the snare-loop technique, unless surgical exposure of the vein is performed.

Bullets dislodged into the cardiovascular system have been successfully removed using either the snare-loop technique or a Dormia basket (26).

Finally, no case is identical to another, and it may often be necessary to use more than one retrieval system at different stages of the procedure. The choice of system should therefore be tailored to each individual case, according to the nature of the foreign body, its location in the cardiovascular system, and the position of the terminal ends. Careful evaluation of the initial diagnostic work-up, plain radiographs, and angiographic studies, will indicate which approach is more appropriate and which technique should be employed.

Success of Percutaneous Removal

The success rate for percutaneous removal of cardiovascular foreign bodies is high, although no definitive statistical conclusions can be drawn. In fact, despite extensive experience, few large series have been reported in the literature, while most descriptions refer to individual cases. In the review of literature by Fischer in 1979 (7), out of 69 articles, only one documented a series of 6 cases, while the other papers did not publish more than 3 cases. Recently Uflaker (28) has reported his experience in 20 cases of cardiovascular foreign bodies, with successful retrieval accomplished in 95%. In our experience in intravascular foreign body retrieval, the success rate has been 84% (16 out of 19). In the 3 cases, the reason for failure was the positioning of the fragments outside the vessel walls.

Percutaneous removal should be attempted in every case. Surgical removal should be limited to the cases in which percutaneous removal has been unsuccessful.

Isolated reports of unsuccessful retrieval, in addition to our experience, indicate that in most of the cases the failures are due to the absence of a free end available for snaring or to further peripheral dislocation of the fragment before or during maneuvering.

The catheter can, in fact, dislodge in the pulmonary branches, making retrieval with the snare-loop technique difficult or impossible. This occurred in one of our cases, but successful retrieval with the snare-loop was accomplished after several attempts in the pulmonary artery (Fig. **2**).

Non-opaque catheters can also create particular problems during percutaneous retrieval attempts, although these are now rarer, since practically every catheter is either completely or partially radiopaque. Morse (21) was able to snare a large (36 Fr) non-opaque cannula after a contrast material injection had correctly shown the site of dislodgment.

Success of the therapy can also be claimed when only partial removal has been obtained and the catheter is further embolized into a safer location. In one of our cases, the catheter was left in the epigastric artery. Uflaker (30) also obtained the embolization of a fragment of a catheter into the deep femoral artery, after successful removal from the thoracic aorta. In both cases, no complications have been encountered with the retained fragments in long-term follow-up.

Complications

Complications in percutaneous removal of cardiovascular foreign bodies are rare, and no deaths have been attributed to this technique. Only Wendth (32) experienced a death, in one of his patients; this was due, however, to a ruptured abdominal aortic aneurysm after attempted removal with the local surgical approach and further major surgery.

During intracardiac retrieval, transient arrhythmias are common. Continuous electrocardiograph monitoring and availability of a defibrillator are mandatory in these cases. The occurrence of arrhythmias should not force one to discontinue the attempts at retrieval, unless ventricular tachycardia appears, although in the latter case a further attempt can be made before surgery is considered.

During retrieval from the cardiac chambers or the pulmonary arteries, patients may experience chest pain due to pulmonary microembolism. This happens more frequently if the catheter has been in place for a long period of time.

Contra-Indications to Percutaneous Removal

There is no absolute contra-indication to the percutaneous removal of intravascular foreign bodies. An attempt should be made in every case. Only in the case of embolization of a foreign body into the distal pulmonary vessels can failure be predicted, due to difficulties in manipulating the snare-loop assembly at these levels. However, an attempt can be made using all the techniques available.

One relative contra-indication may be excessive myocardial excitability due to mechanical stimulation. This can, however, be controlled pharmacologically. Another relative contra-indication is firm adherence of the fragment to the vessel or cardiac wall, as is the case in pacemaker catheters dislodged into the heart. A strong pull on the catheter fragment after ensnaring may cause a dangerous tear requiring immediate surgery. More gentle maneuvering is recommended in these cases, or a continuous traction on the fragment by means of external weights.

Finally, patient age is not a problem in any case. We have successfully retrieved a catheter fragment in a 23-day-old premature newborn baby weighing 2500 g. After removal of the fragment with a snare-loop assembly advanced through a 6 Fr catheter, only a few minutes of local compression to control hemorrhaging at the femoral vein puncture site were needed, and hematoma did not develop. During snaring maneuvers in the right atrium, no significant arrhythmias were observed, although the cardiac frequency was 110–120 beats per minute.

Removal of Foreign Bodies in the Biliary and Urinary Systems

The same retrieval techniques desribed for intravascular foreign body removal may be applied to the removal of materials dislodged into the biliary and urinary system (13, 10). The balloon angioplasty catheter advanced into the lumen of the endoprosthesis was particularly well suited both to the repositioning and removal of 5 biliary stents. The large caliber of the stents (12–16 Fr) allows easy passage of the 7 Fr catheter with a balloon diameter of 6 mm. Lubricating the catheter helps to reduce the probability of distal dislodgment while the catheter is being advanced.

Endoscopic techniques should be preferred in cases of distal dislocation in the duodenum. In the urinary system softer and smaller stents are usually employed. This allows removal with the snare-loop technique through the percutaneous approach, and only minimal dilation of the tract is needed to permit the passage of the bent stent.

References

1. Bloomfield DA. The non surgical retrieval of intracardiac foreign bodies: an international survey. Cathet Cardiovasc Diagn 1978;4:1.
2. Brown AS, Mueller PR, Ferrucci JT. Transhepatic removal of obstructed Carey-Coons biliary endoprostheses. Radiology 1986;159:555.
3. Chuang VP. Non-operative retrieval of Gianturco coils from abdominal aorta. AJR 1979;132:996.
4. Curry JL. Recovery of detached intravascular catheter or guide wire fragments: a proposed method. Radiology 1969;105:894.
5. Doering RB, Stenmer EH, Connolly JE. Complications of indwelling venous catheter with particular reference to catheter emboli. AJR 1967;114:259.
6. Dotter CT, Rösch J, Bilbao M. Transluminal extraction of catheter and guide fragments for the heart and great vessels: 29 collected cases. AJR 1971;111:467.
7. Fisher RG, Ferreyro R. Evaluation of current techniques for nonsurgical removal of intravascular iatrogenic foreign bodies. AJR 1979;130:541.
8. Greenwood LH, Sravaa EB, Morse SS, Denny DF. Intravascular foreign body retrieval with balloon angioplasty catheter. J Intervent Radiol 1986;1:33.
9. Harnick E, Rohmer J. Atraumatic retrieval of catheter fragments from the central circulation of children. Eur J Cardiol 1974;1:421.
10. Harris Yones EP, Fataar S, Tuft RJ. Repositioning of biliary endoprosthesis with Grüntzig balloon catheters. AJR 1982;138:771.
11. Henley FT, Ballard JW. Percutaneous removal of flexible foreign body from the heart. Radiology 1969;92:176.
12. Hiebert CA, Gregory FJ. Bullet embolism from the head to the heart. JAMA 1974;229:442.
13. Honikman SP, Mueller PR, Ferrucci JT, van Sonnenberg E, Kopans DB. Malpositioned biliary endoprosthesis retrieval using a vascular balloon catheter. Radiology 1982;144:423.
14. Knutson H, Steinberg K. Pulmonary embolus with foreign body. Nord Med 1959;62:1491.
15. Lamprecht W. Zur Kasuistik iatrogener intrakardialer Fremdkörper. Chirurg 1965;36:182.
16. Lassers BW, Pickering D. Removal of a iatrogenic foreign body from the aorta by means of ureteric stone catcher. Am Heart J 1967;73:375.
17. Masumi RA, Ross AM. Atraumatic nonsurgical technique for removal of broken catheters from cardiac cavities. N Engl J Med 1967;277:195.
18. Mathur AP, Pochaczensky R. Fogarty balloon catheter removal of catheter fragment in subclavian vein. JAMA 1971;217:481.
19. McSweeney WY, Schwartz DC. Retrieval of a catheter foreign body from the right heart using a guidewire deflector system. Radiology 1971;100:61.
20. Millan VG. Retrieval of intravascular foreign bodies using a modified bronchoscopic forceps. Radiology 1978;129:587.
21. Morse SS, Strauss EB, Hashim SW, Greenwood LH, Denny DF, Sniderman KN. Percutaneous retrieval of an unusually large, nonopaque intravascular foreign body. AJR 1986;146:863.
22. Nathan DA, Center S. Perforation during indwelling catheter pacing. Circulation 1966;33:128.
23. Porstmann W, Wierny L, Warnke H. Closure of persistent ductus arteriosus without thoracotomy. German Med Monthly 1967;12:1.
24. Rabinov K, Simon M. A new selective catheter with multidirectional controlled tip. Radiology 1969;92:172.
25. Rossi P. Hook catheter technique for transfemoral removal of foreign body from right side of the heart. AJR 1970;109:101.
26. Rossi P. Percutaneous removal of intravascular foreign bodies. In: Wilkins RA, Viamonte M, eds. Interventional radiology. Oxford: Blackwell 1982:359–369.
27. Ruff RJ, Alspaugh JP, Peterman S, Ludi G, Hamner L, Martin LG, Chuang VP, Casarella WJ. Percutaneous basket retrieval of an intravascular bullet. J Intervent Radiol 1986;1:29.
28. Smith NP, Bolvin MR, Bolos JM. Transjugular removal of foreign body from the right atrium by endoscopic forceps. J Thorac Cardiovasc Surg 1968;55:594.
29. Thomas J, Sinclair Smith B, Bloomfield D, Davachi A. Non surgical retrieval of broken segment of steel spring guide from right atrium and inferior vena cava. Circulation 1964;30:106.
30. Uflaker R, Lima S, Melichar AC. Intravascular foreign bodies: percutaneous removal. Radiology 1986;160:731.
31. Wellman KF, Reinhard A, Salazar EP. Polyethylene catheter embolism. Circulation 1968;37:380.
32. Wendth AJ, Cross VF, Moriarty DJ, Vitale P, Lopez F. Retrieval of an intracardiac foreign body. Angiology 1972;23:329.

Interventional Procedures in the Digestive Tract

Dilation of Esophageal Strictures

G. Simonetti and G. B. Meloni

Several types of esophageal stenoses have been reported in the literature, including peptic stenoses, ectopic gastric mucosal stenoses (Barrett's esophagus), caustic stenoses, iatrogenic stenoses, achalasia, and neoplastic strictures.

The therapeutic possibilities for stenoses are numerous, and vary according to the etiology. In recent years, nonsurgical techniques have been preferred to surgical ones in the therapy of esophageal stenoses.

The first attempt to treat impaired swallowing dates back to the 16th century, when Fabricius ab Aquapendente (1537–1619), using a wax taper, pushed an esophageal foreign body into the stomach, thus becoming the first to perform a blind bougienage (6). Wax was the material chosen for many years for constructing dilators. The word "bougie" is derived from the Algerian town "Boujiyah", a medieval center for wax candle trade.

Among the bougies that have been widely used recently are those designed by Chevalier Jackson (8): one is made of a strong wire shaft connected to the dilating part, which has an olive-shaped end (Fig. 1a); the other is a graduated rod with a rounded end (Fig. 1b). The olive-shaped part offers the advantage

of reducing to a minimum the risk of creating a false passage. A notable improvement in results has been achieved by the use of a metallic guide wire. The bougie can be pushed over the previously positioned guide through the stenosis without any danger of perforation.

The Eder-Puestow model (11) (Fig. 1e) and Celestine's device (4) (Fig. 1f), both equipped with a metallic guide wire, have been adopted in recent years in most centers.

Another technique is represented by self-bougienage using mercury-filled bougies. The most commonly used are those described by Hurst and Maloney (Fig. 1c–d), especially in repeated treatment of achalasia and postsurgical stenoses. The patient pushes the bougie several times through the stenosis. These dilations are repeated several times every 3 to 10 days and over long periods (10 to 30 years). Weight, length, and size of the bougie can be adapted to each individual patient.

Dilation in achalasia requires the use of a dilating part, which must be larger than the cricopharyngeal sphincter. The difficulty of introducing such a device can be overcome by using a dilator that can be expanded after it is placed in the esophagus. Russel

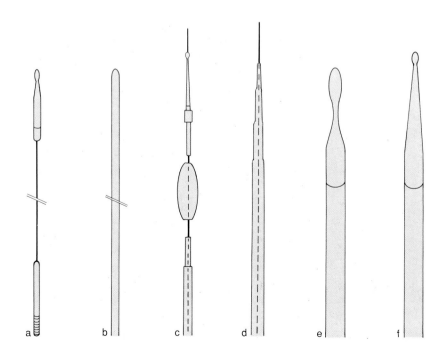

Fig. **1 Devices for esophageal bougienage**
a Jackson's olive-shaped end bougie
b Jackson's rounded end bougie
c Hurst's mercury-filled bougie
d Maloney's mercury-filled bougie
e Eder-Puestow's bougie
f Celestine's bougie

(12) and Plummer (10) were the first to adopt a pneumatic balloon for dilating achalasic strictures.

A radical improvement in esophageal dilation has been achieved by the use of the Grüntzig-type balloon catheter. The first type of coaxial balloon catheter, made of polyvinyl, was designed by Grüntzig and Hopff (7). It was initially used for percutaneous dilation of femoral and iliac arterial stenoses, subsequently in the coronary arteries, and generally in the entire vascular system.

The great therapeutic success achieved by this new procedure has encouraged its use in the treatment of many different pathologic strictures outside the vessels, such as in the urinary, biliary, and gastrointestinal tracts (2, 3, 9).

The Grüntzig balloon catheter, which was initially available with a balloon diameter of a maximum size of 8 mm, was first used in severe esophageal strictures associated with bougie dilation (9). Further improvements and new balloon catheter models have led to disuse of traditional bougienage. In fact, several types of balloon catheters, with shapes and dimensions especially designed for the esophagus, are now available.

When the balloon is inflated, it applies radial and stationary forces on the stenotic wall (Fig. **2a**) (5). This is a great advantage in comparison to bougies, which have to be larger than the stenotic lumen to obtain satisfactory dilation. Bougies apply an axial force on the wall at the level of the stenosis (Fig. **2b**), but also above the stricture. The axial force, which is the predominant component when the bougie is pushed through the stenosis, induces lesions if it is applied in a pathologic esophagus.

Transluminal dilation of esophageal stenoses with Grüntzig-type balloon catheters, performed under fluoroscopic control, is called transluminal esophagoplasty (TEP).

Material

Equipment necessary for TEP includes a balloon catheter, an angiography guidewire, a manometer, a syringe, a stopcock, and diluted contrast medium. For esophageal dilation, we use a modified Grüntzig-type polyethylene balloon catheter, with a double coaxial lumen of 90 cm in length. The diameter of the balloon varies between 8 and 40 mm, according to the diameter of the stricture. Length of the balloon ranges from 8 to 20 cm. Two radiopaque markers are placed at the ends of the balloon (Fig. **3b**). Standard balloon catheters available have basically the same structure.

Balloon size is limited and excess inflation pressure does not increase expansion of the balloon. Overinflation is the most common cause of balloon rupture. We prefer the rigiflex soft tip dilation balloon catheter. The guide wire used is a "J" 0.038

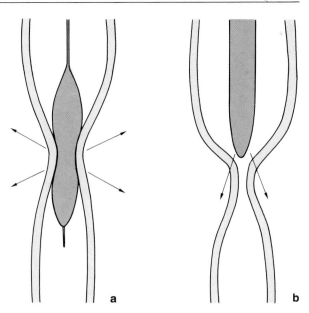

Fig. **2 a Balloon inflated: radial forces**
b Bougienage: axial forces

angiographic guide wire, 180 cm in length. The pressure is monitored by a manometer calibrated in atmospheres. A disposable 20 ml syringe is used for inflation of a 20 mm balloon. With a larger balloon, a 60 ml syringe is necessary. The stopcock, preferably metallic, is inserted between the catheter and the syringe and allows constant pressure to be maintained during inflation. Contrast medium diluted to 50% with saline is used for inflation of the balloon. The low concentration of iodine avoids crystallization of contrast and possible damage to the balloon.

Method and Technique

Before dilation, the esophageal stenosis has to be fully documented radiographically. The radiologic examination of the upper gastrointestinal tract is preferably performed using the double-contrast technique, which enables accurate demonstration of the site, morphologic characteristics, and extension of the lesion.

Endoscopic examination is always performed in addition to the radiologic diagnostic workup. Histologic diagnosis can thus be established in doubtful cases by multiple biopsies. In peptic stenoses measurement of the pH and endoluminal esophageal manometry should be performed.

Careful anatomic and clinical study is mandatory for planning an effective therapeutic strategy. TEP is carried out in the radiologic suite, under fluoroscopy guidance. With the patient in the upright position, the guide wire is introduced transorally through the stenosis into the stomach. In the presence of a particularly narrow or tortuous esophageal stricture,

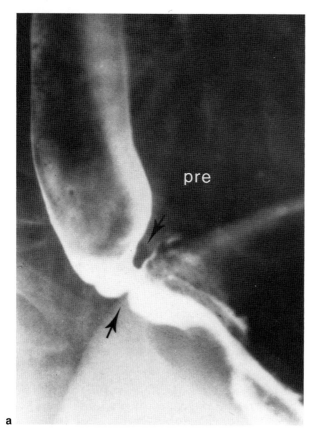

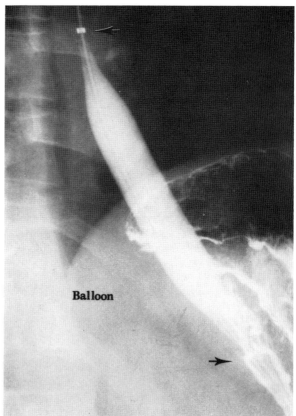

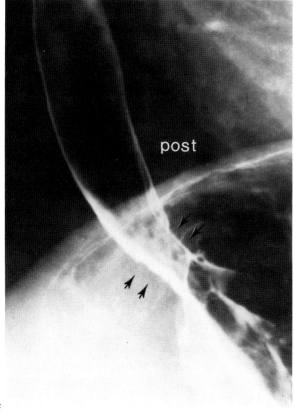

Fig. **3   Male, age 58 years. Peptic stenosis.** An anti-reflux surgical plastic operation (Nissen-Rossetti) was associated with TEP
a Pre-TEP
b Balloon inflated. Radiopaque markers (arrows)
c Post-TEP

catheterization even with the guide wire can be difficult. Insertion of the guide wire is facilitated by previous placement of a nasogastric tube provided with a bore at the distal end. When the guide wire has been correctly placed, the dilation catheter is inserted over the guide wire, which has been previously covered with an anesthetic gel. The balloon is positioned at the level of the stenosis. The balloon is inflated under fluoroscopic control, and the diluted contrast material injected by hand. The balloon should be inflated gradually until it reaches its maximum diameter at a pressure of 2 to 4 atm. Dilation is repeated three to five times in each session, the balloon is kept inflated for no more than 3 to 4 minutes at a time to prevent ischemia of the esophageal wall, which could cause necrosis.

At the end of the procedure, radiologic control is performed using hydrosoluble contrast media, to rule out complications and to evaluate the result. It is possible to observe misleading radiologic results immediately after TEP due to spasms of the esophagus. In our experience we have obtained good results repeating the dilation every 3 to 4 days, for a period of at least 2 to 3 weeks. The average number of sessions are five to seven for each patient.

We use balloons of increasing diameter in order to achieve a progressive, gradual dilation. In severe strictures progressive dilation can be achieved using balloons with a diameter starting from 8 to 20 mm, but generally a balloon with a diameter of 15 to 20 mm is used for the treatment of achalasia. The diameter of the balloon is then increased to 35 to 40 mm in the final session. TEP does not require additional medical treatment. Cooperation of the patient is essential in order to modulate dilation according to the symptoms provoked. Sedation is only necessary with children, using 5 to 20 mg of intravenous diazepam, or in patients unable to cooperate, using general anesthesia.

TEP may also be performed under endoscopic control. However, endoscopy has disadvantages, such as direct vision of the proximal part of the stricture only and greater discomfort for the patient.

Indications

TEP is indicated in the treatment of peptic, postsurgical, caustic, and neoplastic stenoses, including achalasia and Barrett's esophagus.

Peptic Stenoses

Peptic stenoses involve the distal end of the esophagus (Fig. **3**). They are caused by incontinence of the lower esophageal and cardial sphincters. In most cases a hiatal hernia is present. In Barrett's esophagus, the heterotopic gastric mucosa can cause an esophageal stenosis, which is located more proximally with a variable narrowing of the esophageal lumen. TEP can be the first step in the therapeutic approach, but should be followed by antireflux surgery. Patients who are not suitable for digestive surgery due to age or poor general condition, should undergo medical treatment to achieve a decrease in symptoms caused by gastroesophageal reflux.

Postoperative Stenoses

Intrathoracic and cervical surgical esophagogastric anastomoses are followed by stenoses in 5 to 25% of the cases (Fig. **4**). In esophagointestinal anastomoses following total gastrectomy and in transsection anastomoses performed for treatment of esophageal varices, the incidence of postsurgical stenoses varies from 3 to 7%. The stricture can occur in the early postoperative period, caused by improper surgical technique, or more frequently in the follow-up period due to hyperplastic healing of inflammatory complications. Even when an esophageal fistula is present, most often situated proximally to the stenotic tract, TEP can be successfully performed. Dilation of the stricture decreases intraluminal esophageal pressure, resulting in resolution of the fistula (Fig. **5**).

Caustic Stenoses

Ingestion of acid or alkali creates lesions of the esophageal wall of variable severity, depending on amount and concentration of the substance swallowed (Fig. **5**). Contact between the caustic agent and the esophageal wall causes immediate necrosis, which can extend to the muscular layers in severe cases. Lesions may include the whole esophagus, but are most important at the level of physiologic sphincters. The reparative process is almost always the cause of a stenosing scar. The deeper the initial lesion, the more marked and severe is the stenosis. The stenosis is narrow, has an irregular shape, and is diffuse, in many cases including the entire esophagus. TEP is performed after a minimum of 15 to 20 days, to allow stabilization of the inflammatory lesions. TEP of caustic stenoses located in a recently scarred, fragile esophageal wall requires particular care during dilation. TEP does not show excellent results regularly, but is however, the treatment of choice.

Achalasia

The aim of TEP is to perform a nonsurgical disruption of the lower esophageal and cardial sphincter, distending the circular muscular fibers beyond the limits of elasticity (Fig. **6**). Function of the sphincter is not compromised due to the residual contractibility of the muscular ring, the unaltered activity of the longitudinal muscular fibers, and the preservation of

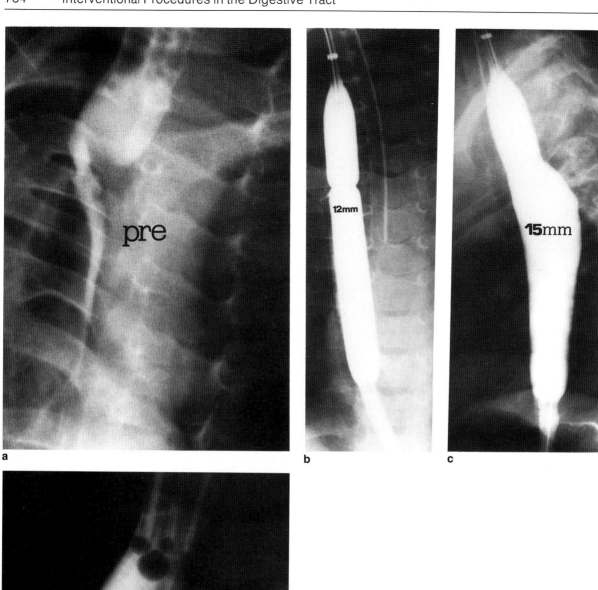

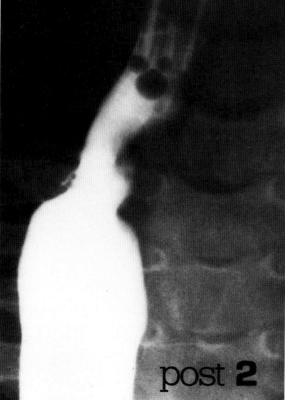

Fig. **4   Male, age 3 years. Postoperative stenosis** in patient submitted to an esophagoesophageal anastomosis for esophageal atresia. General anesthesia was given during TEP

a Before TEP

b 12 mm, and **c** 15 mm balloons used in the first two sessions

d After two dilations

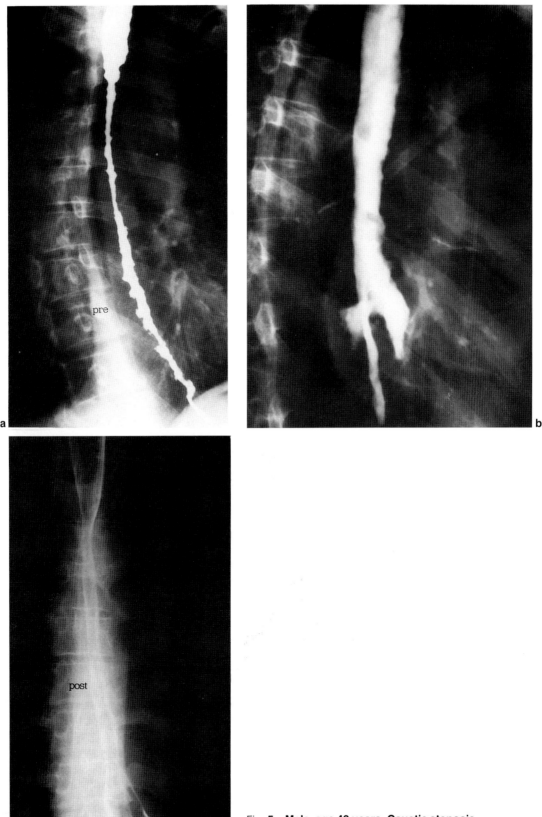

Fig. **5 Male, age 43 years. Caustic stenosis**
a Long and irregular stricture
b Esophageal perforation resolving
c After TEP, disappearance of the lesion

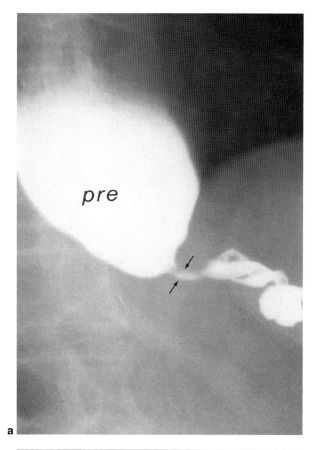

a

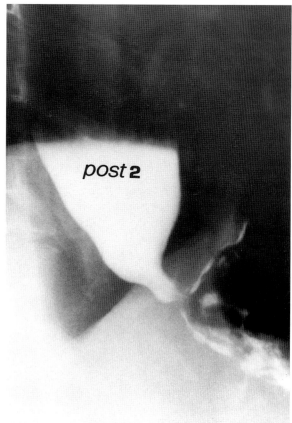

b

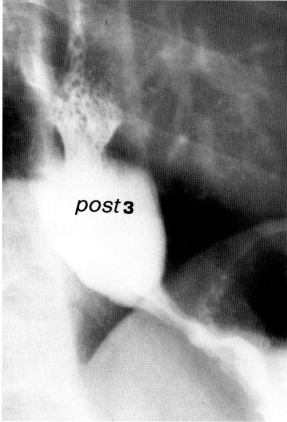

c

Fig. 6   Male, age 36 years. Achalasic stenosis
a Megaesophagus
b After two sessions with 15 mm balloon
c After the third session with 30 mm balloon
d A 35 mm balloon used in the fourth and fifth sessions
e After TEP, a satisfactory dilation of the stricture was achieved associated with a reduction of megaesophagus

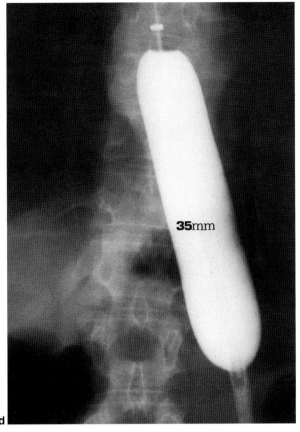

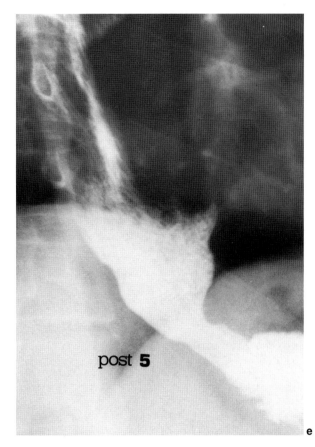

d   e

Fig. **6 d, e**

the angle of His. When, after TEP incontinence of the lower esophageal sphincter with gastro-esophageal reflux is present, antireflux plastic surgery can be performed. TEP has positive results competitive with surgery (1). TEP should, therefore, be considered the treatment of choice, and only in case of failure should surgery be attempted.

Neoplastic Stenoses

Carcinoma of the esophagus is localized preferentially in the middle and lower third (Fig. **7**). Furthermore, mediastinal lymph node metastases and central bronchogenic carcinoma associated with direct infiltration of the esophageal wall can cause malignant esophageal strictures. Neoplastic stenoses can be severe, angulated, and contain fistulas. The neoplastic esophageal wall is particularly fragile and may be easily lacerated during TEP. TEP with or without associated radiotherapy, can be advocated as a palliative treatment in patients who are not fit to undergo surgery, since the disappearance or reduction of symptoms improves the quality of life in patients with cancer. TEP makes the placement of an endoprosthesis, such as a Celestine tube, easier (Fig. **7e**), which avoids recurrence of symptoms and makes future dilation unnecessary.

Results

TEP was performed in 63 patients, 47 males and 16 females, aged from 3 to 74 years. In 11 cases a peptic stenosis was present, in three patients, Barrett's esophagus, in 35 patients, a postoperative stenosis, in six patients, a caustic stenosis, and in four patients, a neoplastic stricture. Achalasia was the cause of narrowing in four patients. In eight patients the stricture was located in the cervical esophagus, in 25 patients, in the thoracic esophagus, and in 30 patients, in the abdominal segment of the esophagus. Length of the stenosis varied between 2 cm (peptic and postoperative stenoses) and 20 cm (caustic stenoses).

The esophageal stricture evaluated by radiology and endoscopy varied from 50% in moderate stenoses to more than 90% in severe stenoses. Symptoms were thoracic pain, gastroesophageal reflux, and dysphagia. Dysphagia is a constant symptom, which is the best clinical parameter to evaluate efficacy of the treatment besides stricture reduction shown by radiologic and endoscopic examinations. Severity of dysphagia and degree of stenosis are not strictly correlated. Complete disappearance of dysphagia and only partial reduction of the stricture are common. Patients treated by TEP and with a follow-

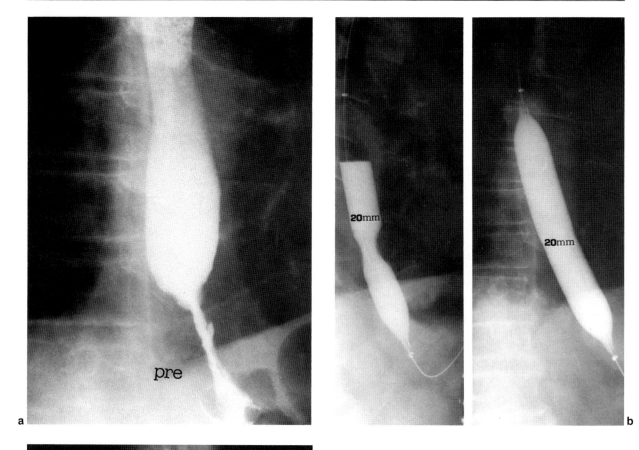

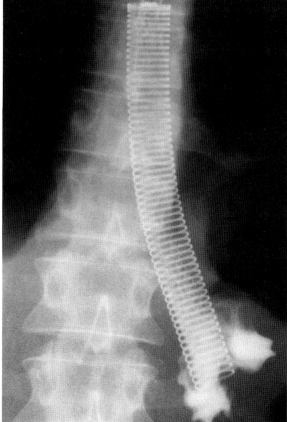

Fig. 7   **Male, age 69 years. Neoplastic stenosis**
a Irregular stricture in the lower esophagus
b A 20 mm balloon partially and completely inflated
c After the third dilation, the diameter of the lumen allows positioning of an endoprosthesis

Table **1** Transluminal esophagoplasty: 12 to 24 months follow up

	Cases	Dysphagia	
		Reduction	Disappearance
Peptic stenoses	11	2	9
Barrett's esophagus	3	1	2
Postoperative stenoses			
Cervical esophagogastric anastomoses	7	2	5
Intrathoracic esophagogastric anastomoses	5	1	4
Esophagointestinal anastomoses	15	1	14
Transection anastomoses	6	2	4
Esophago-esophageal anastomoses	2	–	2
Caustic stenoses	6	2	4
Achalasia	4	2	2
Neoplastic stenoses	4	2	2
	63		

up of 12 to 24 months have been divided into two groups according to clinical symptoms (Table **1**):

– Patients with complete disappearance of dysphagia
– Patients with reduction of dysphagia

In most of the patients, complete disappearance of symptoms has been obtained. In the remaining group, a notable reduction has been achieved. Treatment was efficient to some degree in all patients. General anesthesia was necessary in a 3-year-old boy with a postoperative stenosis of the thoracic esophagus (Fig. **7**).

Complications

Perforation is the most dangerous complication that can occur during TEP. The risk of perforation during placement of the guide wire and the catheter with fluoroscopic guidance is almost nonexistent, but perforation can occur during the dilation of neoplastic or caustic stenoses due to the fragility of the esophageal wall. Two cases of perforation resulting in mediastinitis have been observed, one patient had a caustic stenosis (Fig. **5**), one a neoplastic stricture. A mucosal tear in the esophagus is more frequent and without significant consequences. Two patients who had undergone subtotal esophageal resection and cervical Akiyama-type esogastric anastomosis developed inhalation pneumonia. Rupture of the balloon has occurred seven times without clinically significant complications.

Conclusion

The advantages of TEP using Grüntzig-type balloon catheters are: diminished risk, good tolerance, repeatability, easy performance, immediate disappearance of reduction of dysphagia, and the possibility of treatment on an out-patient basis. Dilation with bougies carries a higher perforation risk. significant discomfort for the patients, requires topical or general anesthesia (10% of cases).

Radiologic control allows direct vision of the guide wire and the catheter, avoiding the creation of a false lumen and allowing easy correct positioning of the balloon within the stricture and immediate control of the results. Endoscopic control provides direct vision of the proximal part of the stricture only, without control of the passage of the stricture and placement of the catheter.

TEP resolves or reduces dysphagia, avoiding feeding problems. Caustic stenoses are the most difficult to treat and generally require prolonged treatment. Best results are obtained in short esophageal strictures. In patients who present with a long stenotic tract, partial resolution of dysphagia is observed. In achalasia, results are the same as those after surgery.

References

1. Bucharach W, Word Boyce HD, Jackson D. Problems in swallowing and esophageal carcinoma. Heart Lung 1981;3:525–531.
2. Ball SW, Siegel RS, Goldthorn JC, Kosloske AM. Colonic strictures in infants following intestinal ischemia: treatment by balloon catheter dilatation. Radiology 1983;149:469–472.
3. Banner MP, Pollack HM, Ring EJ, Wein AJ. Catheter dilatation of benign urethral strictures. Radiology 1983;147:427–433.
4. Celestine JR, Campbell WB. A new and safe system for esophageal dilatation. Lancet 1981;i:74–75.
5. Dawson SL, Mueller PR, Ferrucci JT Jr, Richter JM, Shapiro RH, Butch SJ, Simeone JF. Severe esophageal strictures: indications for balloon catheter dilatation. Radiology 1984;153:631–635.
6. Earlam R, Cunha-Melo JR. Benign oesophageal strictures: historical and technical aspects of dilatation. Br J Surg 1981;68:829–836.
7. Grüntzig A, Hopff H. Perkutane Rekanalisation chronischer Arterienverschlüsse mit einem neuen Dilatationskatheter. Dtsch Med Wochenschr 1974;99:2502.
8. Jackson C, ed. Bronchoscopy and esophagoscopy. Philadelphia: Saunders 1922.
9. London RL, Trotman BW, Di Marino AJ Jr, Oleaga JA, Freiman DB, Rosato EF. Dilatation of severe esophageal strictures by an inflatable balloon catheter. Gastroenterology 1981;80:173–175.
10. Plummer HS. Cardiospasm: with a report of cases. Northwest Lancet 1906;26:419–424.
11. Puestow KL. Conservative management of occlusive diseases of the esophagus. Am J Gastroenterol 1955;24:224–232.
12. Russel JC. Diagnosis and treatment of spasmodic stricture of the esophagus. Br Med J 1898;1:1450–1451.

Percutaneous Gastrostomy

J. H. Boverie and F. Longtain

Gastrostomy or jejunostomy is an established surgical procedure used either for nutritional support when oral intake is inadequate or for organic obstruction decompression. Surgical techniques for gastrostomy insertion are generally described as temporary (serosa-lined, Stamm type) or permanent (mucosa-lined, Glassman type) (8). In children it is commonly used in the management of esophageal strictures. In elderly patients, indications for this important treatment adjunct are dysphagia from upper alimentary tract cancer (head and neck, pharyngeal or esophageal, esophageal repercussion from lung or mediastinal carcinoma) or neurologic swallowing dysfunction from stroke, organic brain diseases, or psychiatric disorders. Gastrostomy, although relatively simple and effective and sometimes performed under local anesthesia, requires general anesthesia for patients who are in poor condition in up to 25% of cases. There is a substantial operative risk. In recent studies 3 to 35% of adult patients had complications, with 7% being major, such as wound dehiscence, gastric perforation, hemorrhage, lung aspiration, peritonitis or postoperative respiratory distress (8, 14, 15). For this reason there is increasing emphasis on radiologic diagnosis of complications of gastrostomy feeding tubes (9, 18) and more importantly, on interventional radiology as a nonsurgical alternative.

Technique

Until now, two major techniques have been described. The first is a combined endoscopic percutaneous method, (5, 6) and the second has been taken directly from other interventional radiologic procedures, such as intra-abdominal collection management, including Seldinger or trocar methods. The latter has several advantages: expertise in endoscopy is not required; the alimentary tract need not be patent proximal to the stomach (pharyngeal or esophageal stricture obstruction precludes endoscopy); and only one operator is necessary.

Only the radiologic methods will be discussed here. The basic procedure consists of introducing a large feeding catheter through the anterolateral wall of the abdomen and the near anterior gastric wall into the gastric lumen or after passing the pylorus into the proximal jejunum. Percutaneous methods are still in their early stages and during the last 6

years several small series were reported in radiologic literature (3, 4, 7, 16, 17). In 1986, Van Sonnenberg et al. (12, 13) summarized, by laboratory evaluation of all procedures and clinical applications (40 cases), the importance of the choice between Seldinger and trocar techniques, the effect of fluoroscopic-sonographic combined guidance, as well as the knowledge of the exact puncture site. They pointed out the role catheter design plays in safety, and questioned whether or not it is imperative to appose the anterior gastric wall to the abdominal wall. Van Sonnenberg et al.'s conclusions are: a variety of methods are feasible for percutaneous gastrostomy; and major complications may be avoided with proper care and with appropriately designed tools. Therefore, it seems preferable first to schematically describe the principles of a standard technique using the Seldinger method as recommended by Wills and Oglesby (16, 17) and then to discuss other available modalities in relation to specific situations.

Preprocedure Steps and Imaging Modalities

All manipulations are performed in a radiologic suite under fluoroscopic control. A nasogastric tube is positioned and gastric distension achieved through it. It brings the anterior wall of the stomach in contact with the anterior abdominal wall, making the puncture easier and safer. The effect of infusion, usually more than 500 ml, is observed fluoroscopically. If the nasogastric tube is too distal, air escapes into the duodenum and gastric distension is difficult to maintain. Glucagon, 1 or 2 ml intravenously, is also used routinely to help augment gastric distension. It is then necessary to localize the adjacent organs that must be avoided during the puncture procedure.

If available, computed tomography provides an evaluation of the relationship of the left liver lobe and the transverse colon to the stomach, but during preprocedure steps, the best methods are real-time US, abdominal plain film, and C-arm fluoroscopy to obtain a cross-table lateral view of the patient in a supine position. Gas or rarely contrast medium instilled in the rectum allows the identification of the colon on plain film. Part of left liver lobe covering the anterior gastric wall is well visualized by ultrasound. Cross-table lateral view and US may also

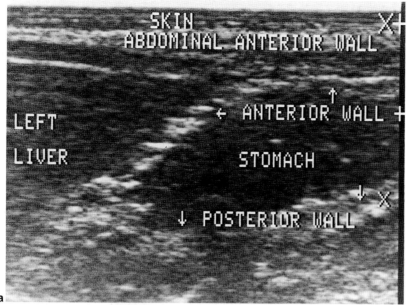

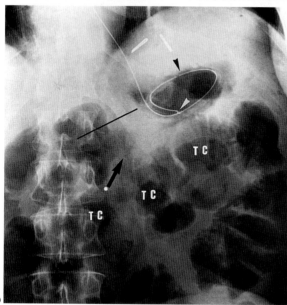

Fig. 1   **Preprocedure steps**

a A longitudinal sonogram shows the relationship between the stomach, the abdominal wall and the partially overhanging left lobe. Injecting water-soluble contrast medium into the stomach improves viewing of the anterior and posterior walls. Depth measurement from the skin is possible, and the feasibility of vertical and oblique puncture directions can be assessed

b The straight line is the projection of the liver area on the plain film. White mark indicates the puncture site selected. The transverse colon (TC) is well documented by spontaneous air contrast. In this difficult case, the arrow indicates the upper left oblique axis required to reach the gastric lumen. The nasogastric tube (arrowheads) is coiled into the fundus

be helpful for depth measurement to the stomach wall, which is usually between 3 and 5 cm.

These landmarks are easily drawn on the patient's skin, defining a window for the puncture site. The inferior epigastric artery and the most ventral portion of the stomach where the major arteries and veins are positioned must also be avoided. Elective puncture site is then over the distal gastric body in front of the mid to outer third of the rectus abdominis muscle with a generally left subcostal approach (Fig. 1).

Puncture

Puncture involves sterilization of the skin and local anesthesia infiltrating to the depth of the peritoneal surface. A small skin nick is made with a scalpel blade and soft tissues are dissected. Under fluoroscopic guidance, an 18 to 21 gauge needle with a Teflon sheath (e.g., Lunderquist needle) is advanced into the cutaneous orifice toward the anterior gastric wall. The gastric lumen is gained directly or sometimes by initial insertion into the peritoneal cavity. As vertical as possible an approach is desirable. When the gastric lumen is entered, a sensation of decreased resistance is often felt. After removal of the needle, injection of a contrast agent into the sheath confirms its good location. A 0.97 mm guide wire is passed into the stomach through the sheath and is coiled within the fundus. Progressively larger dilators beginning at 6 Fr and going to as high as

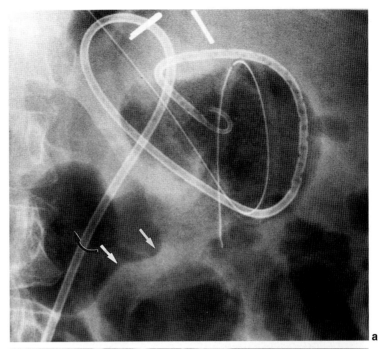

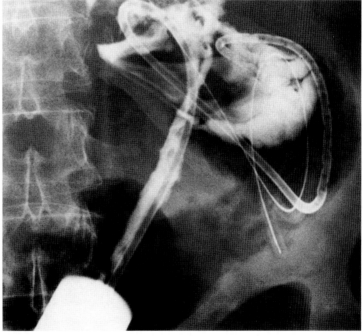

Fig. **2 Initial feeding tube placement**
a Initial anchored 9 Fr pigtail catheter
with multiple side holes coiled in the
proximal stomach. The puncture site is
indicated by a curved arrow. Note the
prominent fold on the greater curve
caused by a small intramural bleeding
point without morbidity (arrow)
b On day 7, a mature tract is confirmed
by sinogram along the initial feeding tube.
Safe tube exchange is then possible

18 Fr are successively passed over an exchange heavy
duty guide wire.

Feeding Tube Placement

Catheters used as gastrostomy tubes must have distal
assembly to prevent dislodgment. The simplest temporary device is an 8 Fr pigtail catheter. In nearly all
cases a 10 Fr Cope nephrostomy catheter is directly
placed in the gastric fundus or farther distally as
necessary. It should tolerate most enteric feeding but
no puréed food. For puréed food, a softer 12 Fr Cope

loop catheter is the ideal initial feeding catheter tube
(4, 10, 11, 13, 18). After placement, it is recommended to clamp or place the tube under suction for
12 to 24 hours before attempting feeding. Contrast is
also injected to check for gastric leakage. As the
tract matures, usually in 1 week (12), the initial
catheter can, if necessary, be exchanged for a definitive 12 to 16 Fr Foley catheter or a self-forming cross-
limb pediatric feeding tube. Catheters are affixed to
the skin by a molnar disk secured to the skin by
adhesives (Fig. **2**).

Other Modalities and Specific Situations

Gastric distending agents can be either air or water-soluble contrast medium. Air is to be preferred, to reduce the chances of aspiration or fluid spillage in the peritoneal cavity (4, 13, 17). Fluoroscopic visualization is not affected. Disadvantages are: Maximum gastric distension (if possible approximately 1000 ml) is preferable because it provides added firmness to the gastric wall (17); otherwise the stomach wall may be pushed rather than punctured, particularly by trocar technique (7); and depth measurement cannot be assessed accurately by ultrasound (13). On the other hand, patients in whom nasogastric tube passage is impeded present a special problem. Effervescent granules can be tried (4, 12, 17), but stasis with respiratory distress is to be feared.

According to Wills and Oglesby (17), a 5 Fr angiographic catheter with a guide wire is correctly placed through the stenosis under fluoroscopic control in nearly all cases. A 22 gauge Chiba needle direct puncture aimed toward intragastric air is also feasible (13, 17). Ho et al. (3, 4) recommend use of a 22 gauge skinny needle with a 20 gauge Teflon sheath before feeding tube insertion. With his technique one is obliged to perform numerous exchanges of guide wires (0.35 to 0.98 mm) as well as dilators, without any real benefit.

As pointed out by many investigators (12, 16, 17), inherent to fine-needle puncture of the gastric wall is guide wire buckling into the peritoneal cavity and forcing dilators or catheters to make an abrupt turn as they enter the gastric lumen. When fine-needle puncture is necessary, Van Sonnenberg et al. (11) recommend new coaxial device with a 22 gauge removable hub needle, which acts as a guide wire and is replaced by an 18 gauge cannula. Only one 0.96 mm guide wire is used.

Until now, a simple trocar method has been less used (7, 16, 17). A well-tapered trocar, 9 to 12 Fr, with a catheter over it (e.g., Stamey trocar catheter) is passed directly into the stomach. The trocar is then withdrawn and a mushroom or balloon tip catheter is left in place. Trocar technique offers the simplicity to fewer device exchanges (J guide wire or dilator), and larger soft tubes may be inserted initially. On the other hand, puncture is more hazardous, with a potential risk of hemorrhage or gastric leakage.

An intragastric balloon sutured to the nasogastric tube has also been developed (10). When inflated by contrast medium, it provides support and firmness for the compliant stomach and offers a good target fluoroscopically or sonographically. Trocar technique is becoming easier; nevertheless, this technique is limited by its lack of utility in patients with upper alimentary tract obstruction and by the risk of aspiration occurring with puncture of the large-volume, fluid-containing balloon. It seems preferable to convert a gastrostomy feeding tube to a gastroenterostomy tube. Reasons are: poor gastric emptying; gastroesophageal reflux and concomitant aspiration is minimized; feeding can be initiated sooner; anchoring with a more distally seated catheter is safer; enteric decompression in patients with chronic partial obstruction is also possible (2). Ho et al. (4) used a 9 Fr curved tipped Kifa catheter over a 0.96 mm J guide wire, which can be manipulated through the pylorus and advanced to the ligament of Treitz. Finally, a 10 Fr pediatric feeding tube is left in place (Fig. 3). Other devices such as the Dobhoff surgical tube and even the simple Bilbao-Dotter type of radiologic tubes can be easily manipulated.

A more sophisticated recent method for gastrostomy and gastroenterostomy has been experienced by Van Sonnenberg et al. (12) and developed by Alzate et al. (1). A specially designed jejunostomy set comprises catheters to insert by the Seldinger or the trocar technique. It uses dilators with a coaxial peel-away sheath enabling 9 to 12 Fr, soft, multihole feeding tubes to be placed into the stomach or bowel at the initial procedure. This tube has a very helpful retention device (friction lock), which, when unexpanded, easily slides through the peel-away sheath and when expanded is larger than 20 Fr.

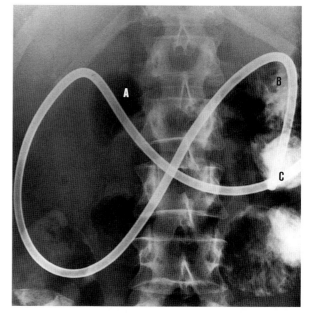

Fig. **3 Optimal final gastrostomy converted to gastroenterostomy.** Over a 0.96 mm guide wire, a 9-12 Fr soft feeding tube is manipulated through the pylorus beyond the duodenojejunal flexure and anchored safely. A: bulbar cap; B: Duodenojejunal flexure; C: stetting control by contrast injection

Complications

To date, there are 185 cases of percutaneous gastrostomy or enterostomy reported in eight recent series, and nine cases have been attempted with success in our institution. Only one death is described from respiratory distress during sedative preparation and before any procedure was performed (13). The major theoretical risks are leakage of gastric contents and peritoneal catheter dislodgement. The symptoms will be severe acute abdominal pain and peritonitis. Only five cases (2.5%) have been reported. Wills and Olgesby (17) suggest that manipulations induce a fibrotic reaction between abdominal and gastric anterior walls. An animal experimental study (18) supports this fact. Autopsy examinations demonstrated mature gastrocutaneous tracts after 7 days. Clinically, it is emphasized that in ten cases of catheter withdrawal, replacement through the tract shows no difficulty either. Bleeding is also a potential problem, but no significant bleeding has been reported yet. Radiologists should be further encouraged by the lack of significant complications at discharge and in patients with longer survival.

Conclusion

Current reports suggest that this interventional radiologic technique is an effective alternative to surgical gastrostomy. It is our opinion that major complications must be avoided by the greatest care being given to the preprocedure steps. The Seldinger guide wire exchange method remains the safest technique in most cases.

References

1. Alzate GD, Coons HG, Elliot J, Patrick PH. Percutaneous gastrostomy for jejunal feeding: a new technique. AJR 1986;147:822–825.
2. Bazre HJS. Percutaneous catheter drainage of closed-loop small bowel obstruction. AJR 1983;141:797–798.
3. Ho CS. Percutaneous gastrostomy for jejunal feeding. Radiology 1983;149:595–596.
4. Ho CS, Gray RR, Goldfinger M, Rosen IE, McPherson RR. Percutaneous gastrostomy for enteral feeding. Radiology 1985;156:349–391.
5. Larson DE, Fleming CR, Ott BJ, Schroeder KW. Percutaneous endoscopic gastrostomy: simplified access for enteral nutrition. Mayo Clin Proc 1983;58:103–107.
6. Ponsky JL, Gauderer MWL, Stellato TA. Percutaneous endoscopic gastrostomy: review of 150 cases. Arch Surg 1983;118:913–914.
7. Prenshaw RM. A percutaneous method for inserting a feeding gastrostomy tube. Surg Gynecol Obstet 1981;152:659–660.
8. Shellito PC, Malt RA. Tubes gastrostomy, techniques and complications. Ann Surg 1985;201:180–185.
9. Vade A, Jafris ZH, Agha FP, Vidyasagar MS, Coran AG. Radiologic evaluation of gastrostomy complications. AJR 1983;141:325–330.
10. Van Sonnenberg E, Cubberley DA, Brown LK, Wittich GR, Lyons JW, Stauffer AE. Percutaneous gastrostomy: use of intragastric balloon support. Radiology 1984;152:531–532.
11. Van Sonnenberg E, Wittich GR, Schiffman HR, Cabrera OA, Willson SA, Quinn SF, Casola G, Hayne LA, Polansky AD. Percutaneous drainage access: a simplified coaxial technique. Radiology 1986;159:266–268.
12. Van Sonnenberg E, Wittich GR, Brown LK, Fanenbaum LB, Campbell JZ, Cubberley DA, Gibbs JF. Percutaneous gastrostomy and gastroenterostomy, 1: techniques derived from laboratory evaluation. AJR 1986;146:577–580.
13. Van Sonnenberg E, Wittich GR, Cabrera OA, Quinn SF, Casola G, Lee AA, Princenthal RA, Lyons JW. Percutaneous gastrostomy and gastroenterostomy, 2: clinical experience. AJR 1986;146:581–586.
14. Wasiljew BK, Ujiki GT, Beal JM. Feeding gastrostomy: complications and mortality. Am J Surg 1982;143:194–195.
15. Wilkinson WA, Pickleman J. Feeding gastrostomy: a reappraisal. Ann Surg 1982;195:273–275.
16. Wills JS, Oglesby JT. Percutaneous gastrostomy. Radiology 1983;149:449–453.
17. Wills JS, Oglesby JT. Percutaneous gastrostomy: further experience. Radiology 1985;154:71–74.
18. Wolf EL, Frager D, Beneventano TC. Radiologic demonstration of important gastrostomy tube complications. Gastrointest Radiol 1986;11:20–26.

Percutaneous Management of Fistulas in the Digestive Tract

J. H. Boverie and A. Remont

Abdominal surgery is the main cause for enterocutaneous fistulas, but these can also arise as complications of inflammatory or neoplastic disease as well as trauma or radiation therapy (3, 4, 15, 16). These fistulas originate from an internal orifice in the intestinal wall and also in the biliary or pancreatic ducts and lead to the skin by abnormal abdominal tracts. They drain a mixture of gastrointestinal juices and pus or necrotic matter. Until recently, the radiologic study was limited to the identification of the morbid anatomy. Now, technical advances in interventional radiology have made possible selective catheterization of the most tortuous tracts and drainage of effluents (1, 6, 7, 12, 13, 17). In 1982, McLean et al. (9) reported their first experiences in radiologic percutaneous management of high-output postoperative enterocutaneous fistulas.

Clinical and Therapeutic Features

Gastrointestinal secretions (salivary, gastroduodenal, biliary, pancreatic) that may amount to as much as 8000 ml/day are mostly absorbed in the ileocolon. Quantity and quality of the bowel effluent lost per day – percentage of electrolytes and activated proteolytic enzymes – determine the seriousness of an enterocutaneous fistula. Therefore, high-output fistulas draining at least 300 ml to as much as 4000 ml a day usually arise from a lesion located between the inferior third of the esophagus and the ligament of Treitz (Table 1). Low-output fistulas

draining less than 100 ml arise from the ileum or colon, except in case of malfunction of intestinal absorption (4, 14).

When medically controlled, they become mature with a fibrous tract. Patient morbidity results only from long-term discomfort (3). High-output fistulas are dramatically morbid with: necrosis perforating the intestinal wall; sentinel abscess at the internal opening; intra-abdominal propagation of sepsis and collections of associated abscesses; multiple tracts interlaced beneath the skin leading to an external opening and skin maceration (Figs. **1, 2, 3**).

At the present time, medical treatment is given first except for the most serious peritonitis, which requires surgical management by enterostomy and abdominal cavity irrigation. Fluid losses, electrolyte and acid-base imbalance, and induced cardiorespiratory or renal dysfunctions are corrected. Digestive secretions are reduced by nasogastric suction and antisecretory drugs (anticholinergic-cimetidin-somatostatin). Enteral or parenteral hyperalimentation improves patient resistance and allows nonseptic fistulas to heal. Surgery is indicated when fistulas do not show a significant output decrease after 6 weeks or if the output decreases without spontaneous closure. It is now clear that resection and end-to-end anastomosis is preferred in surgical patients. In the last 10 years this management allowed a reduction of mortality due to sepsis from 45 to 67% to 6 to 20% (2, 3, 4, 5, 14, 15, 16).

Principles of Radiologic Drainage

The main cause for a medical treatment failure or for the still high surgical mortality is also emphasized in the surgical literature: "as long as a tract is bathed in gastric secretions, abscesses cannot easily heal and fistula output cannot decrease much. Skin maceration remains important." It would be useful to combine a controlled drainage of effluents with conservative management (4, 5, 17). This problem is ill-solved by blindly-placed surgical sump drains, since the perforation and its localization are not detectable until about 1 to 2 weeks postoperatively and endoluminal drainage is seldom used (8, 17). On the other hand, it seems possible to allow true controlled external drainage by interventional radiologic percutaneous management with diversion of the intestinal effluent. Basic manipulations are: probe the fis-

Table 1   Origin of the alimentary tract perforation relating to high-output and low-output fistulas

Location	No. cases	High-output (%)	Low-output (%)
Duodenum	13	100	–
Jejunum	11	100	–
Ileum	10	30	70
Colon	8	12	88
Bile duct	3	100	–
Pancreatic duct	2	100	–
Stomach	1	100	–
Esophagus	1	100	–
Total	49	71	29

tulous tracts; find the internal orifice and catheterize it; secure an internal-external drainage device in the lumen of the bowel, of the biliary or the pancreatic tracts, and control leaks around the internal orifice with contact drains; separately drain an abscessed cavity.

Before starting the radiologic treatment, consultation with the referring physician and careful review of previous radiologic examinations (e.g., computed tomography) provide the radiologist with a satisfactory understanding of the clinical problem. Crucial questions are: what is the underlying disease and of what type is the surgical anastomosis? what is the supposed origin of the fistula? is it a high-output or a low-output fistula and what does the lost fluid consist of? what surgical sump drains are left and where do they lead to? Multiduct and Penrose tubing drains must be withdrawn before any manipulation.

Methods and Equipment

Imaging Modalities

US and CT are seldom useful except for checking drain positions or for draining an abscess that does not communicate directly with the external fistula (6, 13). Since the three-dimensional tortuous orientation of tracts is unpredictable, insertion of radiopaque catheters and injection of contrast medium are always done under fluoroscopic control. The most appropriate positioning of the patient is determined for the remainder of the examination. A C-arm angiographic table limits the difficult mobilization of monitored patients because of a tube-image intensifier couple that is mobile in three directions.

Fistulogram and Cannulation

Before opacification, a plain film of the abdomen helps to locate surgical anastomosis clips, drains left in place, and opacities or lucencies outside the alimentary tract that may indicate propagation of an abscess (10). The fistulogram is best performed by injecting the contrast agent directly from the cutaneous opening in order to demonstrate the main axis and to avoid false passages in the secondary subcutaneous tracts at the time of cannulation. Very large openings are obturated by a sterile rubber plug with a central hole for introduction of a catheter-tipped syringe.

Skin is protected by sterile dressing and a slight pressure produces a cupping effect without excessive pain for the patient. A colostomy enema adaptor may also be used. Small or medium openings are opacified by an end-hole straight catheter of 5 to 14 Fr introduced superficially. Obturation is achieved by pressing gauze around the opening.

A water-soluble contrast agent is slowly injected and spot films of several projections are taken to delineate the anatomy of the tracts. We prefer a povidone-containing solution. The enhanced viscosity slows down the absorption, leading to a better opacification of deep tracts and communicating abscesses often collected in the nearest dependent spaces: perihepatic, perisplenic, paracolic gutters and pelvis (Fig. 1). The Seldinger method facilitates the cannulation of opacified tracts. A straight end-hole angiographic catheter of 5 to 7 Fr, narrower than the diameter of the fistula to allow torquing movements, is mounted over a 0.89 to 0.97 mm J-shaped guide wire. Guide wire and catheter are gently advanced as far as possible in the tracts. Their irregularities are negotiated with the 3 mm J wire protruding from the catheter tip. This is the safest way to avoid false passages in the surrounding necrotic tissues and risk of sepsis propagation. The guide wire may be anchored to the internal opening and the catheter advanced into the bowel's lumen over it. The guide wire often coils into large abscess ramifications. They must be explored by exchanging catheter and choosing a curvature fitting the anatomy to find a tract that may branch and go into a collected abscess cavity. This cavity is often the

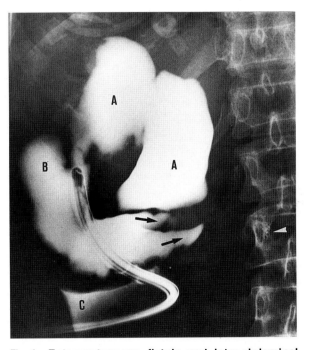

Fig. **1 Enterocutaneous fistula and intra-abdominal spread of infection.** Post-Roux-en-Y duodenojejunal anastomotic complication. During fistulogram, more or less collected abscesses are identified. A: Anteroposterior sub-hepatic spaces; B: Lateral extension toward subphrenic recess; C: Downward spread into the paracolic gutter. Inner branchings seem to point to duodenal stump (arrows) in front of surgical clips (arrowheads). No connection with bowel lumen is apparent. Sump drain is placed through the tract and abscesses are drained (see also Fig. **2**)

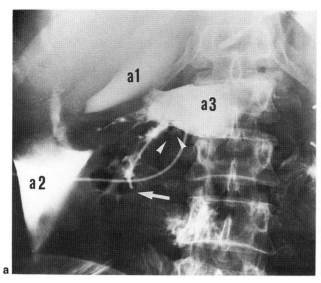
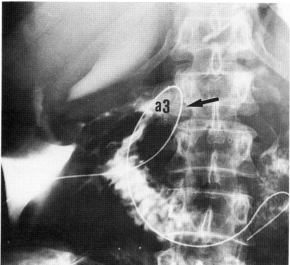

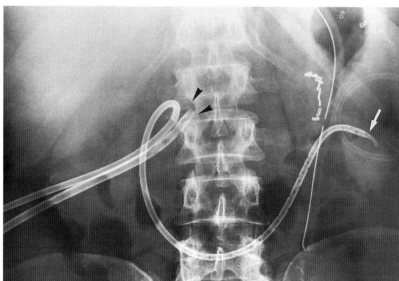

Fig. 2 **High-output fistula management sequence.**
(Same case as Fig. 1)
a After drainage of large abscesses, residual cavities can be seen (a1, a2). New communicating abscess (a3) is discovered beside duodenal stump (arrowheads). Angiographic tube is passed through it and bowel perforation is gained (left arrow). Guide wire is deeply introduced into lumen loop (right arrow)
b Pigtail Ring multiple side-hole catheter is anchored within the lumen and its extremity pushed as far as possible into the afferent loop (arrow). Sump drain is placed. After high suction, the sentinel abscess resolves quickly (a3, arrowheads)

"sentinel abscess" near the site of bowel perforation. The catheter tip is directed to the entrance of the abscess and the guide wire is advanced. Access to the bowel's lumen is gained by crossing the abscess cavity with the catheter (Fig. **2a**). If the intestinal orifice is not apparent, all the encountered abscesses and fistula secretions must be drained. Over the next few days, removal of purulent material will make manipulations easier, and the internal opening will be more readily apparent (6, 13) (Figs. **1, 2a**).

Draining Modalities

A stiff Lunderquist guide wire replaces the J-shaped one. It will serve as a support for inserting the internal-external drainage device in the bowel's lumen. Width of the internal opening is estimated

from the fistulogram and the known caliber of the withdrawn angiographic catheter. The draining device will be slightly narrower and its passage through the tract will be facilitated by use of a water-soluble surgical lubricant in order to avoid enlarging the hole in the bowel's wall.

Three situations bear discussion: High-output fistulas on a blind loop occur after gastrojejunostomy, hepatogastrointestinal or pancreatic surgery. Perforation results from a stasis in an afferent loop, the orifice is terminal due to suture breakdown of the stump. Ring-Lunderquist pigtail multiple side-hole biliary catheters of 8.3 to 12 Fr give ideal drainage, since the tapered tip facilitates insertion in the axis of the terminal orifice and the 40 lateral holes allow the pigtail to be pushed far into the loop below the perforation and the static fluid to be sucked up

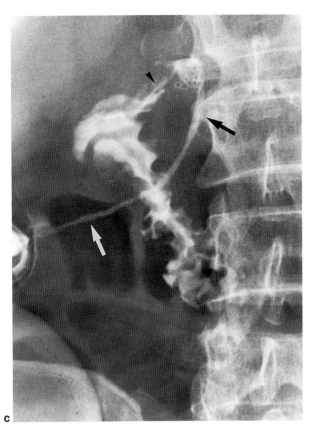

Fig. 2

c From the third week on, mature regular tract appears (arrows). Figure **2c** is the last control fistulogram before definitive closure

(Fig. **2b**). (2) For high-output fistulas with lateral perforation, T-tubes are better used because their horizontal limbs, fashioned with side holes; they control the flow of intestinal contents from above and below the site of perforation. Placement technique of a T-tube is identical to that described by Millan et al. (11) for drainage of the bile duct. An angiographic catheter of 4 to 5 Fr is passed, and the T-tube is introduced over the guide wire, the distal limb coiled and compressed over the long limb. Both are advanced in the bowel's lumen. Gentle traction is applied to the external limb of the T tube and the horizontal limbs are brought into alignment with the axis of the bowel's lumen (Fig. **3**). For low-output fistulas, endhole straight drainage catheters of 8 to 14 Fr customized to individual cases by cutting side holes, or multiple side-hole Ring-Lunderquist catheters, 6.6 Fr suffice to control intestinal contents. Small 4 to 9 Fr angiographic pigtail catheters may also be useful. After removal of the guide wires, contrast material is injected to confirm proper functioning of the internal-external drainage. Leaks are always present around the internal opening.

Evacuation of Cavity Contents

Dual lumina 8 to 30 Fr surgical sump drains, with an end hole cut in their tips to allow passage of a guide wire, permit continuous suction and irrigation. They are placed next to the internal orifice to control leakage of bowel contents and in communicating abscesses. If the tract is too narrow, straight drainage catheters may serve as contact drains. A 15 Fr tapered-tip catheter with 1 drain end-hole and 5 drain side-holes is well anchored within the sentinel abscess and its flexibility permits it to negotiate the most sinuous tracts. Irrigation is achieved by a Ring-Lunderquist catheter placed next to it. Endoluminal drain is set to low suction, sump drains are set to continuous high suction (Figs. **2b, 3b**).

Controls

A four-parameter chart allows one to follow the efficacy of the drainage procedure (Fig. **4**). Temperature increases on the day after manipulations, then drops quickly. It is back to normal in one week. Sump drain output decreases with the thermic curve to less than 50 ml after 8 days. Endoluminal tube output reaches 3000 ml at the beginning by evacuation of the static, then becomes equivalent to the normal gastrointestinal tract contents. Skin maceration resolves in 30 days, and the orifice closes around the drains. An anomaly in these curves indicates bad positioning, which may be corrected, or a failure due to spread of the infection. If only fever persists, another cause must be looked for (e.g., infection around the parenteral hyperalimentation catheter).

As early as the third week after sump drain removal, the fistulogram may show a mature fibrous tract. When the whole length of the fistula appears straight without branches or communications with residual cavities, the endoluminal drain is removed and a straight multiple side-hole catheter is placed in contact with the internal opening. It will soon be possible to clamp it without leaks. The fistula closes spontaneously in about 4 to 6 weeks (Fig. **2c**). For high-output fistulas results seem excellent, and it is advantageous to start the radiologic management as soon as a postoperative complication is recognized, usually 2 weeks postoperatively.

Results

All 12 patients treated by McLean et al. (9) were cured in 4 to 6 weeks without the need for surgery. Of 35 patients treated for surgical fistula in our institution, 32 were cured (91.4%) in 2 to 8 weeks. Five patients had a nonsurgical spontaneous fistula. Whether they be high or low output, these are the most difficult fistulas to treat by interventional radiology, especially if their cause is an inflammatory disease such as Crohn's disease, diverticulitis, or

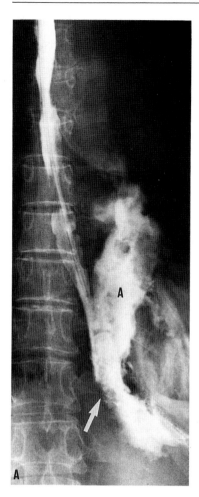

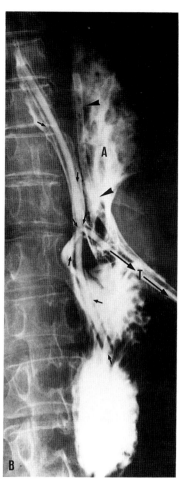

Fig. **3** **Lateral site perforation treatment using T-tube.** Emetic esophagogastric rupture
a Initial status. Total esophagogastric discontinuity (arrow) and large communicating mediastinal abscess (A)
b T-tube placement. Proximal limb into esophageal lumen (upper arrows) and distal limb into stomach (lower arrows) are in alignment with the esophagogastric axis and effluents drained by the main limb (T). Sump drain is in abscess (arrowheads)

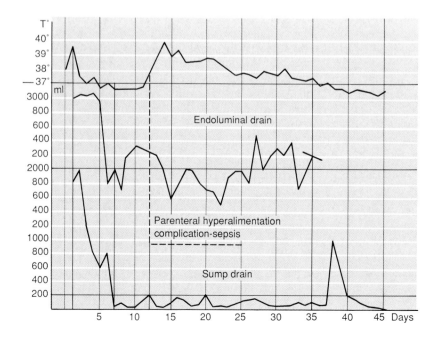

Fig. **4** **Typical chart during enterocutaneous drainage**
Fever peak always follows drain placement. Temperature drops quickly thereafter and sump drain output too. During first few days, endoluminal drain output is very high (static evacuation). Next, it decreases to normal value of digestive secretions. On day 12, output curves remain good while temperature increases because of parenteral, not radiologic, complication. On day 35, endoluminal drain is removed. Note the concomittant small peak of sump output. Fistula becomes mature and closes spontaneously on day 45

radiation therapy complication (Table **2**). Patients with low-output fistulas are not referred to the radiology department unless they have undergone medical management for at least 4 weeks. Results are not as good: 58% of 14 patients. Postoperative complications have, nevertheless, favorably evolved in 75% of cases, whereas only 50% evolved well when a medical disease was at the origin of the fistula. Colon fistulas are particularly difficult to manage. Fecal matter prevents effective internal-external endoluminal drainage. Drainage duration will always be longer, 4 to 12 weeks, than for high-output fistulas (Table **3**).

Table **2**   Outcome of percutaneous management of high-output fistulas

Etiology	No. case	Successful* (%)	Drainage duration (weeks)
Subtotal surgical complications			
Gastroduodenal	11	100	2 to 6
Biliary tract	7	100	3 to 6
Pancreatic	6	83+	4 to 7
Intestinal	5	100	2 to 4
Emetic esophagogastric rupture	1	100	7
	30	29–97	mean: 4
Subtotal primary diseases			
Traumatic	2	100	3 to 4
Radiation injury	3	33+	4 to 8
	5	3–60	mean: 6
Total	35	32–91.5	mean: 5

* Healing without need for surgical treatment.
+ Failure of catheterization.
+ Failure of draining methods.

Table **3**   Outcome of percutaneous management of low-output fistulas

Etiology	No. case	Successful (%)	Drainage duration (weeks)
Subtotal surgical complications			
Intestinal	2	50*	4 to 7
Appendectomy	1	100	7
Hysterectomy	1	100	12
	4	3–75	mean: 8
Subtotal primary disease			
Diverticulitis	5	60	7 to 16
Crohn's disease	3	33	9
Radiation injury	2	50	9
	10	5–50*	mean: 10
Total	14	5–58	mean: 9

* Failure of draining methods.

Patient Preparation and Nursing Care

No specific premedication is required to perform endoluminal or communicating abscess drainage. Local anesthesia in the form of lidocaine 1% injectable helps for painful cutaneous lesions. However, it is better to avoid it so as not to aggravate the local situation. Anxiety may often be the principal cause for patient discomfort during the procedure. Tranquilizers, such as diazepam, may then be given intravenously as needed.

Although the environment is septic, manipulations should be done under sterile field and operator conditions. Prophylactic antibiotic coverage is instituted routinely before the procedure and continued until a mature tract appears.

Nursing care is very important. To protect the skin around the cutaneous opening from local infection, it is better whenever possible to fix drains with a circular plastic ostomy ring-disk. This device is secured to the skin by a precoated adhesive surface. Drains are then sewn to the plastic ring. Skin sutures are thus avoided and the cutaneous opening remains open to air, minimizing maceration. If the loss of cutaneous tissues is too large, sterile exchange dressings are placed over the drains for protection and appropriate local care is given according to dermatologic treatment. Drains are connected to a drainage bag or put on suction. Output of the endoluminal drainage is regularly quantified, as is sump drain effluent. The ability of patients to tolerate endoluminal drainage clamping for 2- to 4-hour periods without excessive leakage of effluent contents by sump drains is also a good method of checking the healing effect. The nurse also has to check for the proper alignment of drains to prevent inadvertent dislodgment. Postprocedure irrigations are routinely performed in the ward with normal saline in appropriate volume in order to maintain their patency. Antiseptics, such as povidone-iodine, may also be instilled in the cavities. Patients are frequently discharged with a straight catheter in the tract when the endoluminal drain is removed. Nursing care is continued at home.

Complications

Complications are minor for the most part and can be avoided by careful manipulations. Bleeding of a necrotic enterocutaneous fistula is frequent but transient. Any tentative drainage must be stopped when severe bleeding occurs. Bacteriologic or mycotic infection is avoided by sterile work conditions. False passages with punctures by a guide wire or a catheter are the major risk: in the fistula or in its abscess branches, the risk is of infection spread; during catheterization of the intestinal perforation, the risk is of enlargement of the internal opening or

of perforating a neighboring loop; for deep abdominal lesions, the risk is of puncturing a vessel. Pyogenic septa of a collected abscess can also be ruptured if the injection of contrast agent is too vigorous. Fluoroscopic guidance in the course of the manipulation is the best protection.

Conclusion

Percutaneous management of high-output enterocutaneous fistulas is a valuable nonsurgical therapy for heavy care patients. Nevertheless, it should be emphasized that it is not an easy technique. Numerous manipulations and controls under fluoroscopy are required over many days. The difficulty does not lie in the cannulation or even in the setting of the endoluminal drainage, but rather in the identification and drainage of all fistula-associated abscessed cavities. Not all patients will respond to conservative treatment alone. Surgery is indicated after a tentative drainage of at least 8 weeks, or for uncontrolled peritonitis. However, in all cases, controlling intestinal output and decreasing the amount of infection will increase the chances of a successful outcome and will minimize skin maceration and local infection. Low-output, long-duration fistulas are also a relative indication.

References

1. Alexander ES, Weinberg S, Clark RA, Belkin RD. Fistulas and sinus tracts: radiographic evaluation, management and outcome. Gastrointest Radiol 1982;7:135–140.
2. Coutsoftides T, Fazio VW. Small intestine cutaneous fistulas. Surg Gynecol Obstet 1979;149:333–336.
3. Fazio VW, Coutsoftides T, Steiger E. Factors influencing the outcome of treatment of small bowel cutaneous fistula. World J Surg 1983;7:481–488.
4. Fischer JE. The pathophysiology of enterocutaneous fistulas. World J Surg 1983;7:446–450.
5. Harju E, Pessi T, Koikkalainen T, Kuskinen A. The treatment of high enterocutaneous fistula with surgical drainage and total parenteral nutrition. Int Surg 1985;70:33–38.
6. Kerlan RK Jr, Jeffrey RB Jr, Pogany AC, Ring EJ. Abdominal abscess with low-output fistula: successful percutaneous drainage. Radiology 1985;155:73–75.
7. Kerlan RK, Pogany AC, Ring EJ. A simple method for insertion of large untapered catheter. AJR 1983;141:792.
8. Levy E, Parc R, Bloch P, Legros A, Hannoun L, Nordlinger B, Huguet C, Loygue J. Transorificial intubation with direct neutralisation of the digestive juices in cases of gastric or duodenal lesions: principle and application of a new treatment for severe postoperative peritonitis of a gastric or duodenal origin. Ann Chir 1982;36:419–423.
9. McLean GK, Mackie JA, Feiman DB, Ring EJ. Enterocutaneous fistulae: interventional radiologic management. AJR 1982;138:615–619.
10. Meyers MA. Intraperitoneal spread of infections. In: Meyers MA, ed. Dynamic radiology of the abdomen: normal and pathologic anatomy. Berlin: Springer 1982:27–54.
11. Millan VG, Bramhavar DM, Kwon OJ, Paul RE Jr. Percutaneous replacement of biliary T tubes. AJR 1979;132:140–141.
12. Palestran AM, Rad FF. Cannulation of catheter tracts and narrowed channels. Radiology 1982;143:561–562.

13. Papanicolaou N, Mueller PR, Ferruci JT Jr, Dawson SL, Johnson RD, Simeone JF, Butch RJ, Wittenberg J. Abscess fistula association: radiologic recognition and percutaneous management. AJR 1984;143:811–815.
14. Reber HA. Abdominal abscesses and gastrointestinal fistulas. In: Sleisenger MH, Fordtran JS, eds. Gastrointestinal disease. Philadelphia: Saunders 1983:319–335.
15. Soeters PB, Ebeid AM, Fischer JE. Review of 404 patients with gastrointestinal fistulas: impact of parenteral nutrition. Ann Surg 1979;190:189–202.
16. Sternquist JC, Bubrick MP, Hitchock CR. Enterocutaneous fistula. Dis Colon Rectum 1978;21:578–581.
17. Tarazi R, Coutsoftides T, Steiger E, Fazio VW. Gastric and duodenal cutaneous fistulas. World J Surg 1983;7:463–473.

Percutaneous Lysis of the Vertebral Disk

J. Théron

Chymopapain (Chymodiactin, Discase, Lekopain) is a proteolytic enzyme extracted from the latex of a tropical tree *(Carica Papaya)*. It was discovered in 1934 by Jansen and Balls (29). Experimental studies on various animal species have demonstrated that chymopapain injected into the intervertebral disk has no action on collagen but produces a depolymerization of the mucopolysaccharides, reducing the ability of the disk gel to retain water (53, 61, 66).

In 1964 Smith (58) proposed using chymopapain to treat disk herniations percutaneously in order to reduce the pressure they exert on the nerve roots (21, 57, 61).

The results of recent double-blind studies (19, 31), of seven open studies (1, 4, 9, 22, 30, 36, 38, 40, 41, 50, 51, 52, 63, 73, 75), of a long-term study on 105 patients (32), and of a recent veterinary study on the treatment of disk herniations in dogs (showing similar results to those obtained in man) (67) have left little doubt as to the true efficacy of chymopapain in the treatment of disk herniations. They have finally supplanted the controversial studies (10, 55) that caused chymopapain to be withdrawn from the American market for several years.

Comparison Between Surgery and Chemonucleolysis

The advantages and disadvantages of the techniques of surgery and chemonucleolysis should be explained to the patient when inefficacy of the medical treatment forces the change to a more active treatment.

Chemonucleolysis has results at least comparable to those of surgery, does not change the spinal balance as much as surgery does, with consequently less post-treatment low back pain and recurrent disk herniations at another intervertebral levels, does not carry the risk of arachnoiditis and epidural fibrosis, and does not rule out, in case of poor results, the possibility of later surgery (15, 28).

Conversally, there is a risk of allergic complication, although minor, which should be explained to the patient, and the final result sometimes takes longer than with surgery. The patient should be well informed of the frequent irregularity in improvement of symptoms for several weeks. This irregularity appears to be, in my opinion, a major negative point to be considered by the patient in his choice of chymopapain. Many patients are often psychologically exhausted by prolonged bed rest and the use of various treatments and they do not readily accept a new therapeutic attempt, which promises them variable progressive improvement compared with surgery, which, whatever its possible secondary disadvantages, often has immediate good results, at least on the radiculalgia. Also, surgery will finally be proposed to them in the event of failure of the chymopapain treatment.

Indications for Chemonucleolysis

Our indications for chemonucleosis are broader than those of most clinicians. We do not use this technique on pregnant women or on disk herniations complicated by major neurologic signs, such as cauda equina syndrome. Otherwise, we believe that other absolute and relative contra-indications have to be discussed for each case.

Narrow lumbar canal. Before ruling out chemonucleolysis for patients presenting a narrow spinal canal recognized on measurements performed on CT (48), we believe that careful radiologic investigations are necessary to determine the degree, the extent, and the mechanism of the narrowness of the canal. We perform chemonucleolysis when the intervertebral disk is the main cause of compression of the inside of a congenitally narrow canal: chemonucleolysis may be efficient in a disk herniation which has decompensated for a narrow lumbar canal (Figs. **1, 2**). Conversely, we do not perform chemonucleolysis when the narrowness of the canal is extensive, compressive, as visualized on a venogram of the epidural veins on a long spinal segment, or when the narrow lumbar canal has been decompensated by an osseous lesion (degenerative changes of the vertebral body or of the facet joints). Chemonucleolysis would have no effect on these two types of lesions (Fig. **3**).

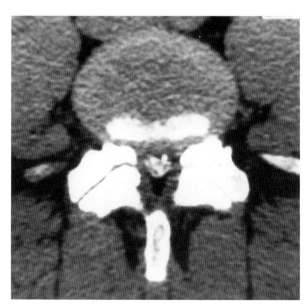

Fig. **1 Narrow lumbar canal decompensated by an L4–L5 disk herniation.** The compression of the inside of the canal is mainly due to the disk, which was successfully treated by chemonucleolysis. CT performed after myelography. Narrow concentric canal with thick articular processes and narrow transversal interspace between them. The ligamentum flavum is thick and elongated. Compression of the dural sac by the disk bulging is demonstrated

Low back pain. We perform chemonucleolysis to treat disabling lumbar pain without radiculalgia on condition that the preliminary radiologic investigations have provided evidence that a disk is responsible for the symptoms (Fig. **4**).

Large disk herniation. This may be treated successfully using chemonucleolysis, although some investigators report that only small disk herniations can be treated with this technique (Fig. **5**).

Disk herniation with paresis. This may be successfully treated using chemonucleolysis. However, we believe that it is justified to recommend surgery when the paresis does not regress rapidly (it usually regresses in the hours after the injection), knowing however, that surgery will not necessarily have a better result.

Epidural leakage on the discogram. Evidence of epidural leakage does contra-indicate the injection of chymopapain. Dura mater is impervious to it. However, it seems important in this case, to inject chymopapain very slowly to allow enough time for the fixation of the enzyme on the disk material (Fig. **6**).

Extruded disk herniation. In our opinion, there is no radiologic sure sign of extruded disk herniation. On the CT, a disk fragment at a level above or below the vertebral interspace is a suspicious but not certain sign. Moreover a disk herniation that has migrated behind the vertebral body may be successfully treated by chemonucleolysis on the condition that it is connected to the intervertebral disk where the enzyme is injected. Only detached fragments will not be treated and are a definite contra-indication if it is possible to recognize them with certainty on preliminary investigations.

Elderly patients. We regularly treat elderly patients (a few of whom are over 80) who have been refused surgery. The efficacy of chemonucleolysis is certainly not as good as for younger patients, but we believe that it is worth trying to give the patient the chance of a more active life.

Patients previously treated with chymopapain. A second injection of chymopapain for recurrent symptoms at a level already treated by chemonucleolysis or for a disk herniation at another disk level has long been a contra-indication, to avoid the potential allergic risk. Nevertheless, Sutton (62) has recently

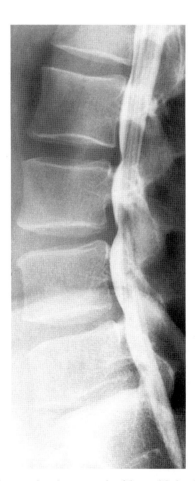

Fig. **2 Narrow lumbar canal with multiple disk bulgings.** Left radiculalgia. Successful treatment at the L5–S1 disk level by chemonucleolysis. The other disk levels were not treated. The narrow canal and multiple disk bulgings are seen on the myelogram (lateral projection)

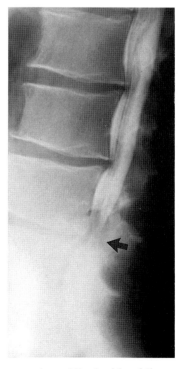

Fig. **3 Compression of the inside of the canal mainly due to an osseous compression.** Lateral myelogram clearly demonstrates the narrowing of the canal (arrow). This kind of narrow canal should not be treated by chemonucleolysis

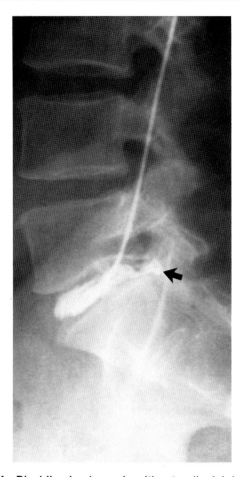

Fig. 4 **Disabling lumbar pain without radiculalgia.** The preliminary radiologic investigations were insignificant but put suspicion on the L5–S1 disk level. A diskogram was performed which demonstrated an abnormal disk with a thin disk herniation (arrow). The lumbar pain was exacerbated by the injection of contrast media into the disk. Chemonucleolysis of the disk had a very good result. Note the approach to the L5–S1 intervertebral disk by the curved needle

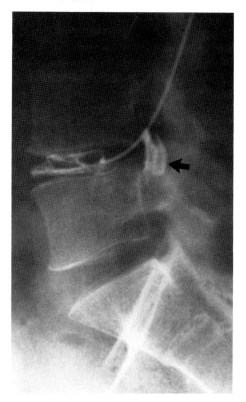

Fig. **5** **A large disk herniation successfully treated by chemonucleolysis.** L4–L5 diskogram. Unusual opacification of a large disk herniation (arrow). Note the approach to the curved needle to the L4–L5 intervertebral disk

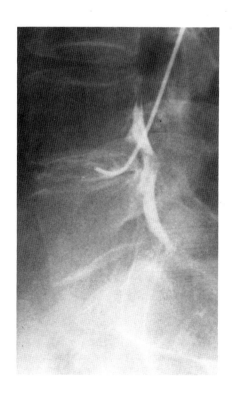

Fig. **6** **L4–L5 disk herniation.** Epidural leakage of contrast material on the diskogram. Very good result after nucleolysis. Note the approach to the L4–L5 intervertebral disk by the curved needle

reported a series of successful second injections on 35 patients without complication.

Development of new sensibilization tests will perhaps allow a better selection of patients in future (46). Presently, in case of recurrent symptoms on a previously treated disk, we first try an injection of triamcinolone hexacetonide in the disk. This has been effective in several cases of our early experience with this drug.

Disk calcifications. Calcifications do not represent a contraindication to chemonucleolysis in our experience.

Disk herniations on spondylolisthesis. A disk herniation arising at the level of or above a spondylolisthesis is not a contra-indication to chemonucleolysis in our experience.

Patients with previous disk surgery. When disk herniation arises at another disk level than that of the diskectomy, chemonucleolysis is routinely used.

When the problem seems to arise from the operated level, the point is usually to provide evidence that the abnormal densities visualized on CT are a recurrent disk herniation and not an epidural fibrosis. The use of diskography followed by a CT appears to us a major advance in the management of these numerous patients (27) (Fig. **7**).

When there is evidence of a recurrent disk herniation, we presently attempt an injection of triamcinolone hexacetonide, with encouraging results. At the beginning of our experience with chemonucleolysis (65), we reported a few cases of chymopapain injections with rather poor results. We now assume that these injections, done before the use of regular CT and even more before the use of the CT-diskogram, were probably performed on epidural fibrosis cases. Whatever the progress in the investigations, chemonucleolysis on an operated disk remains a difficult and still controversial problem.

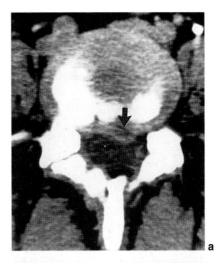

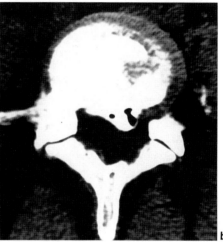

Fig. **7   Recurrent L4–L5 disk herniation after surgery.** Successful treatment by triamcinolone hexacetonide
a CT showing an opacity (arrow) that could correspond to either a recurrent disk herniation or to epidural fibrosis
b CT after the L4–L5 diskogram clearly demonstrates that the opacity is in connection with the remaining disk and corresponds to a recurrent disk herniation

Radiologic Investigations

Before Chemonucleolysis

Chemonucleolysis is a major therapeutic tool that should only be used, like surgery, with the maximum of information at hand.

With the quality of new equipment, CT alone may provide sufficient information to perform chemonucleolysis on uncomplicated cases with straightforward clinical signs correlating well with the level of obvious CT findings (11). These, in our opinion, are not the most frequent cases.

Many patients are referred having already undergone a myelogram. This technique is easy to perform and usually well tolerated, visualizes the relationship between intervertebral disk and nerve root, provides, on the lateral projection, good information on

the relationship between intervertebral disk and canal margins (Fig. **1, 3**), and allows us to rule out a tumor at the level of the conus medullaris.

Conversely, many L5-S1 disk herniations cannot be demonstrated because of the width of the epidural space at this level (Fig. **2**). Lateral disk herniations cannot be demonstrated. Many cases of disk bulging (protrusions) are often demonstrated on the lateral projection: these bulgings have been frequently found on asymptomatic patients (26, 42) and may also correspond to a normal disk (65). Some investigators have described various signs to differentiate normal from bulgings (33). We personally believe that the question often remains open after the myelogram and that it is better not to use the word "protrusion" but to use the word "bulging" when it is the only abnormal sign visualized on the procedure.

CT is atraumatic, shows disk herniations well, visualizes the facet joints, and permits measurements of the spinal canal and of the lateral recesses. Conversely, CT frequently shows multiple or questionable bulgings which are difficult to correlate with the clinical symptoms. It has been shown on totally asymptomatic patients that 20% of the CTs of patients younger than 40 years and 50% of patients older than 40 years could be read by several radiologists as abnormal (74).

This is one of the reasons why we use lumbar phlebography frequently (63), which seems to us to provide interesting complementary information to CT in giving a precise "mapping" of the limitations of the compression of the epidural space (64).

This procedure shows few false-negative results in radiculalgias, even on lateral herniations or at the L5-S1 level. The only possible false-negative results are at L4-L5 when the herniation is strictly on the midline and when the opacification of the veins is poor, usually because of a suboptimal technique. Also, the procedure frequently provides a decising argument on the abnormality of a disk bulging, showing that it compresses the epidural space. A disk bulging on a wide spinal canal may not be compressive for the epidural veins on the venogram and consequently will not compress the nerve root which is in contact with them (63). Sometimes the procedure shows that a narrow canal demonstrated on CT or on the myelogram does not compress the epidural veins or else compresses only for a short segment (Fig. 2). The venogram demonstrates the short distance between the longitudinal epidural veins characteristic of the congenital narrow canal (64) and shows the interruption of the veins in front of the herniation which is responsible for the symptoms and may be treated by chemonucleolysis on condition that CT or myelogram confirms that the venous interruption corresponds to a disk herniation and not to degenerative changes on the vertebral body or the facet joints.

Conversely, phlebography is technically more difficult to perform than CT or a myelogram and requires angiography training, provides poor information in lumbar pain without radiculalgia, is not specific, as already mentioned, and cannot differentiate between a venous compression due to an anterior (disk herniation) or posterior (facet joints) lesion.

The last step in the radiologic investigation is provided immediately before chemonucleolysis by the diskogram (18, 45), which is performed via an extradural approach (68–71) because of the toxicity of the enzyme for the nervous structures.

We perform diskography in every case to get final confirmation on the abnormality of the disk to be treated, to exacerbate, in the best cases, the painful

symptoms, which gives one more confirmation of the responsibility of the disk and seems to be a good prognostic sign for the outcome of chemonucleolysis (65), and to visualize an epidural leakage of the contrast medium or, rarely, a venous opacification. Diskography frequently, remains the final and only procedure helpful in demonstrating the disk origin of lumbar pain without radiculalgia (Fig. 4).

After Chemonucleolysis

Radiologic investigations are, in our opinion, rather disappointing.

An empty disk phenomenon may be demonstrated (Fig. 8) or a decrease in the size of the disk herniation; but frequently the herniation shows no marked decrease (Fig. 8), even when the patient is free of symptoms (2, 16, 23, 34, 39, 54, 60). We do not perform a CT anymore after chemonucleolysis: one of the reasons is that the patient usually finds it hard to accept that the herniation he has been treated for may still be present. The few cases of postchemonucleolysis myelograms performed on patients successfully treated have shown findings (22, 40, 60) comparable to the CT.

Plain films usually show a narrowing of the intervertebral space (Fig. 9) after chemonucleolysis (3), which, for some investigators, could in part explain the improvement in the symptoms by the modification produced in the relationships between disk herniation and nerve root (23, 60). However this narrowing is not a significant sign of good prognosis, and we do not usually perform plain films in the followup of the patient.

Some investigators have demonstrated the possibility of regeneration of a normal intervertebral space after chemonucleolysis (8); this would be an argument for performing a second chemonucleolysis on the same disk in case of recurrent pain (62).

The first reports of magnetic resonance imaging obtained after chemonucleolysis do not seem, in our opinion, to provide new information in the follow-up of the patients (44).

It is of the utmost importance to inform the sugeons that the demonstration of herniation still present on the CT is not an argument for performing surgery rapidly on a patient whose symptoms improve by gradual steps.

Patients with Previous Surgery

Radiologic investigations are identical when the herniation is located at another level. Conversely, at the operated level, as already mentioned, the diagnosis of recurrent herniation versus epidural fibrosis has been markedly improved by the use of the CT diskogram (27): the disk is injected but not the epidural fibrosis (Fig. 7).

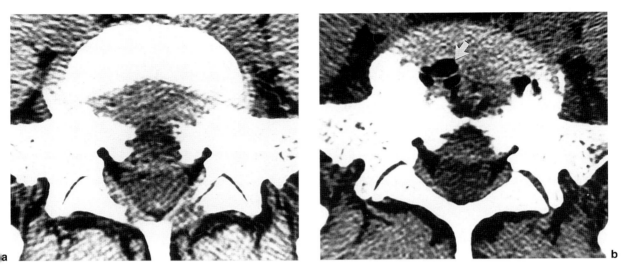

Fig. 8 **Successful treatment by chemonucleolysis.** CT does not show modifications of the disk herniation
a L5–S1 disk herniation before chemonucleolysis
b After chemonucleolysis, disk bulging is the same, although the symptoms have cleared. Note the commom empty disk phenomenon (arrow) demonstrated after chemonucleolysis

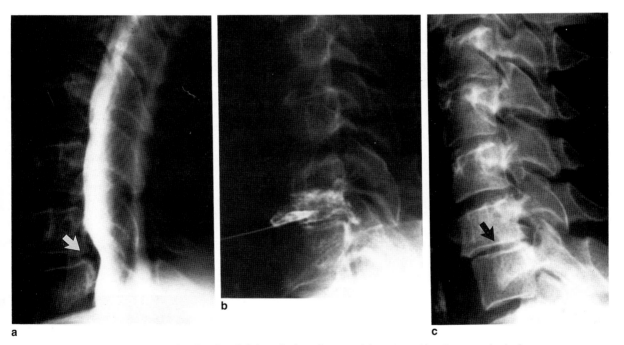

Fig. 9 **Cervicobrachial neuralgia, C6–C7 disk herniation.** Successful treatment by chemonucleolysis
a Cervical myelography, C6–C7 disk bulging (arrow)
b Cervical diskogram anterolateral approach. Degenerated disk. The radiculalgia was exacerbated by the injection of contrast media
c Plain film performed 2 months after chemonucleolysis. Note the marked narrowing of the C6–C7 vertebral interspace (arrow), to be compared with a

Technique of Lumbar Chemonucleolysis

Chemonucleolysis is performed in the radiology department under strict sterile conditions. The patient is positioned on the right side; this side was selected to rule out the risk of puncture of the caecum, which may happen when the approach to the disk is too anterior and the patient is positioned on the left side. The approach should be posterolateral, and it is mandatory not to puncture the dural sac.

The patient is put on a neuroleptanalgesic by an anesthesiologist who remains present during the entire procedure. However, some investigators have reported chemonucleolysis on out-patients (39). It is more comfortable to have an anteroposterior and lateral fluoroscopic unit.

The needle is an 18 G, which is curved with a clamp before the procedure to facilitate the puncture of the L5-S1 intervertebral disk (Fig. **4**). We believe that the rather large diameter of the needle facilitates its handling and also lowers the risk of puncturing a nerve root.

The correct lateral position should be checked by fluoroscopy before starting. We do not use precise measurements to localize the point of entry of the needle on the skin. The target to be reached is for us the posterior margin of the disk on the lateral projection which corresponds to its left posterolateral angle on a frontal overview. A too posterior approach of the needle will cause it to be stopped by the facet joints (Fig. **4**) and increases the risk of puncturing the dural sac; a too anterior approach will make the necessary rotation of the curved needle to reach the center of the disk after its puncture more difficult (Figs. **5, 6**).

Because of the iliac crest, the puncture of the L5-S1 intervertebral disk is more difficult than the L3-L4 and L4-L5 levels, but with some experience the puncture is almost always successful. The correct position of the extremity of the needle at the center of the disk should be checked on lateral fluoroscopy before performing the diskography. Diskography is systematically used for the reasons previously mentioned. Injection of chymopapain may immediately follow diskography and should be performed slowly to rule out reflux out of the disk at the site of puncture; when there is evidence of an epidural leakage on the diskogram, the injection is performed even more slowly.

The anesthesiologist is told when the injection is begun so that anaphylactic shock can be detected immediately. Before removing the needle, we inject 0,25 ml of ethanol, mainly to prevent an infectious complication.

Injection of chymopapain has, in our experience, been canceled when a venous injection was observed on the diskogram to prevent the risk of systemic injection of chymopapain. The risk is actually minimal at this dilution. We never had an injection of the subarachnoid spaces in our experience. It would have been, of course, an absolute contra-indication to the injection of chymopapain.

We have also canceled the injection when the diskogram did not confirm the findings of the preliminary investigations; this may happen when the diskogram was used in case of radiculalgia on insufficient investigation, or when the diskogram was the last and possibly only significant procedure to study a problem of disabling lumbar pain without radiculalgia.

Follow-up

The radiculalgia frequently clears up immediately after the chemonucleolysis procedure, but the patient experiences lumbar pain that is better relieved by anti-inflammatory drugs than by analgesics. A 1-week prescription of these is usually given and the patient is discharged in most cases 2 days after the procedure.

It is very important to explain to the patient that the chymopapain is going to keep treating the intervertebral disk for the following 6 weeks and consequently that he has to rest as much as possible. He should be informed of the frequent fluctuation in the symptoms with possible recurrence of the radiculalgia even when it had cleared rapidly after the procedure. This recurrence of the radiculalgia may be stronger than the original one. It appears, in our experience, around the 10th day after the procedure, clears up in 2 or 3 days on anti-inflammatory drugs; and does not imply a bad outcome of the treatment.

This fluctuation in the symptoms explains the frequent psychologic difficulties of the patient isolated at home with no contact with a medical environment.

For this reason, patients are now seen every week at a post-treatment consultation. A new clinical evaluation permits appreciation of the evolution of the symptoms. A very helpful complementary therapeutic tool has been provided, in our experience, by mesotherapy, according to Mrejen's technique (12, 49) and its use depends on the remaining symptoms. Complementary infiltration of the facet joints (24, 47, 56) that we used at the beginning of our experience has been markedly reduced in number since we started using mesotherapy.

Physiotherapy is started around the third week after the procedure (59).

Follow-up of the patients during the first weeks after the procedure is very important to improve the final results and markedly reduce the number of operated patients who, retrospectively, were often operated on much too early at the beginning of our experience (28).

A result should only be considered as a failure when no improvement has been observed after the 6th week (13). The date when the patient can start working full time again depends on the type of work and on the mental state of the patient, but it is rarely before the 8th week (13). Clinical evaluations performed 1 year after treatment are comparable to those during the third month. Results are stable.

Results

Our personal experience now includes 700 cases. Of the first 100 patients, the results have been as follows for predominant radiculalgia: very good or good: 67% and fair: 12.2%, for a success rate of 79.2% and a failure rate of 20.8%. For predominantly lumbar pain, the results were very good or good: 44%, and fair: 28%, for a success rate of 72% and a failure rate of 28%.

These results have been obtained with only the phlebography and the myelography as preliminary investigative procedures without respecting the usual contra-indications. A long-term study performed on these first or patients (14) has showed 72% of good results, confirming the long-term study performed on patients followed for 10 years (32).

Our personal results improved in two stages. First, the second 100 patients had physiotherapy (59), which was not used after chemonucleolysis for the first 100 patients. The results for predominant radiculalgia are: very good or good: 79.4%, and fair: 3.6%, for a success rate of 83% and a failure rate of 17%. For predominantly lumbar pain, the results are: very good or good: 70.5%, for a success rate of 70.5% and a failure rate of 29.5%.

The second stage was the recent addition of better information provided by high-definition CT, better follow-up of the patients and particularly the use of mesotherapy as a complementary therapeutic tool. These have provided much better results on the last 50 patients (minimum follow-up, 3 months) and a marked decrease in the number of patients operated on (only two patients). Selection of patients has been the same as before and has not followed the usual strict contra-indications. The results for predominant radiculalgia are: very good or good: 76%, and fair: 16%, for a success rate of 92% and a failure rate of 8%. For predominantly lumbar pain, the results are: very good or good: 75%, and fair: 5%, for a success rate of 80% and a failure rate of 20%.

It will be noted, comparing the data, that in the first stage of improvement (physiotherapy) the poor results have remained the same as for the first 100 cases, but the number of fair results have become very good or good. In the second stage of improvement, the number of poor results has significantly decreased.

Complications

After Watts (73), Bouillet (5, 6) reported two studies on complications of chemonucleolysis, the first one on 4880 cases and the most recent one on 18,925 cases. Benign allergic complications (cutaneous rash, Quincke's edema) have a 2% frequency; anaphylactic shock is extremely rare (0,2%). Septic diskitis has a 0.27% frequency and has been cured by antibiotics.

Some neurologic complications are benign (sphincter disorders, 0.8%, transitory radicular deficit, 0.6%). There were, in this study, 0.06% cauda equina snydromes due to the collapse of the disk with increased bulging of the herniation. They were all cured by medical treatment or by surgery. The other neurologic complications are serious (one paraplegia, one comitial "etat de mal", one subarachnoid hemorrhage); their mechanisms remain unclear.

MacCulloch (38) has compared the mortality (0.3%) and morbidity (0.2%) of disk surgery to those of chemonucleolysis (0.02% and 0.05%, respectively, in United States). The conclusions of these studies are that the use of chymopapain as a method of treatment exposes the patient to risks that are extremely rare, and inherent in any kind of therapeutic procedure.

Alternatives to Chymopapain: Aprotinin, Triamcinolone Hexacetonide

Aprotinin has been proposed for the same indications as chymopapain (35). Its immediate tolerance is good and its efficacy on the painful symptoms is fairly good (57% good results and 11% fair results in the series of Kraemer and Laturnus).

In our personal experience, aprotinin did not appear as efficient as chymopapain, and we had patients who had bad results with aprotinin who have been cured with chymopapain.

After attempts of intradiskal injections of steroids (17, 25), it has recently been proposed to inject triamcinolone hexacetonide (7) instead of chymopapain. The word "nucleoorthesis" has been proposed for this procedure, whose early results seem to be promising. In our personal experience we have successfully treated with this drug one patient who had been treated 5 years before with chymopapain and presented with a recurrence at the same level.

At the present time, we use it routinely for cervical disk herniations and reserve chymopapain as the basic drug for lumbar injections until more cases have been reported.

Cervical Chemonucleolysis

We have treated a short series of patients by cervical chemonucleolysis, whose results, comparable to the lumbar ones, have been reported (37) (Fig. **9**).

Because of the frequent uncomfortable intensity of the postnucleolysis cervic algias and of the potentially higher risk of injecting chymopapain in front of the spinal cord, we have preferred for the time being to use less aggressive drugs, such as aprotinin.

We presently use triamcinolone hexacetonide. All the patients present with cervicobrachial neuralgias resisting medical treatment. The preliminary investigations include a myelogram and a CT following the myelogram. We do not use cervical phlebography as much as before because of the very good information obtained with these two procedures. Their findings and the clinical signs usually permit one to focus on one or two disks.

Diskography is then performed to confirm degeneration of the disk. In the best cases, it exacerbates the cervicobrachial neuralgia with the injection of the contrast. This provides evidence of the involvement of the disk in the present symptoms. Triamcinolone hexacetonide is then slowly injected into the disk.

In the best cases, the cervicobrachial neuralgia clears rapidly. We advise wearing a Schantz-like collar for 3 weeks. The early results are presently very encouraging. In cases with poor results, pressently rare, the patient is operated on without repeating the radiologic investigations already performed.

This type of treatment has, in our opinion, a very interesting position following medical treatment and preceding surgery.

Conclusion

Chemonucleolysis is an efficient technique for treatment of disk herniation. Its complications are extremely rare and its results are at least as good as surgery.

Arguments too often based on business and economic reasons have slowed down the spread of its use for too many years. Unfortunately, the same erroneous arguments still keep being advanced against this technique, denying the evidence. Fortunately, the technique is now used in many countries and is being increasingly used.

Its indications are, in our opinion, much wider than the classic ones as long as the preliminary investigations provide enough information to make a precise therapeutic decision.

When chemonucleolysis may be used, it should be systematically proposed to the patient before surgery. Follow-up of the patient is essential and markedly affects the final outcome. It is of great importance not to operate too early on a patient whose improvement is slow to appear or who presents with a hyperalgic transitory recurrence of the radiculalgia. There is no reliable relationship between the improvement of the clinical signs and the decrease of the herniation on CT.

New areas of research are the use of new drugs for intradiskal injections and the development of percutaneous diskectomy techniques (20, 43).

References

1. Benoist M, Bouillet R, Mulhollan D. Chemonucleolysis: results of a european survey. Acta Orthop Belg 1983;49:32–46.
2. Benoist M, Deburge A, Heripret G, Busson J, Rigot J, Cauchoix J. Treatment of lumbar disk herniation by chymopapain chemonucleolysis: a report on 120 patients. Spine 1982;7:613–617.
3. Bonneville JF, Runge M, Clere P, Bonnet D, Mawazini H. Radiological evaluation of the disc space after chemonucleolysis. AJNR 1985;6:476–479.
4. Bouillet R, van de Putte L. Le traitement de la lombosciatique par injection de chymopapaine dans le disque intervertébral: une expérimentation de sept années. Acta Orthop Belg 1979;45:15–32.
5. Bouillet R. Complications de la nucléolyse. Acta Orthop Belg 1983;49:49–77.
6. Bouillet R. Complications de la nucléolyse discale par la chymopapaine. Acta Orthop Belg 1987;53:250.
7. Bourgeois P, Frot B, Folinais D, David M, Benacerraf R, Palazzo E, Vigneron AM, Kahn MF. Traitement de la lombosciatique par hernie discale par nucléoorthèse à l'hexacetonide de triamcinolone. Presse Méd 1986;15:2073.
8. Bradford DS, Cooper KM, Oegema TR. Chymopapain chemonucleolysis and nucleus pulposus regeneration. J Bone Joint Surg [Am] 1983;65:1220–1231.
9. Brown JE. Clinical studies on chemonucleolysis. Clin Orthop 1969;67:94–99.
10. Brown MD, Daroff RB. The double blind study on comparing disease and placebo: an editorial comment. Spine 1977;2:233–236.
11. Carrera GE, Williams AL, Haughton VM. Computed tomography in sciatica. Radiology 1980;137:433–437.
12. Chos D. La mésothérapie a trouvé un support semeiologique. Généraliste 1986;818:28.
13. Clere P, Runge M, Bouchareb M, Bonneville JF. Chimionucléolyse. In: Duvauferrier R, Ramée A, Guibert JL, eds. Radiologie et echographie interventionnelles. Montpellier: Axone 1986:187–197.
14. Debas J. Chimionucléolyse dans le traitement des sciatiques discales: devenir des patients après un an d'évolution [Dissertation]. University of Caen 1987.
15. Deburge A, Benoist M, Rocolle J. La chirurgie dans les échecs de la nucléolyse. Rev Chir Orthop 1984;70:637–641.
16. Drouillard J, Lavignolle B, Philippe JC, et al. Scanographie et chimionucléolyse des hernies discales. J Radiol 1982;63:267–272.
17. Feffer HL. Treatment of low back and sciatic pain by the injection of hydrocortisone into degenerated intervertebral discs. J Bone Joint Surg [Am] 1956;38:585.
18. Feinberg SB. The place of diskography in radiology as based on 2320 cases. AJR 1964;92:1275–1281.
19. Fraser RD. Chymopapain for the treatment of intervertebral disc herniation: a preliminary of double blind study. Spine 1982;7:608–712.
20. Friedman WA. Percutaneous discectomy: an alternative to chemonucleolysis. Neurosurgery 1983;13:542–547.
21. Garvin PJ, Jennings RB, Stern IJ. Enzymatic digestion of the nucleus pulposus: a review of experimental studies with chymopapain. Orthop Clin North Am 1977;8:27–35.

22. Gentry R, Strother CM, Turski PA, Javid MJ, Sackett JF. Chymopapain chemonucleolysis: correlation of diagnostic radiographic factors and clinical outcome. AJNR 1985;6:311–320.

23. Gentry LR, Turski PA, Strother CM, Javid MJ, Sackett JF. Chymopapain chemonucleolysis, CT changes after treatment. AJR 1985;145:361–369.

24. Ghormley RK. Low back pain. JAMA 1933;10:1773–1777.

25. Graham CE. Chemonucleolysis: a double blind study comparing chemonucleolysis with intradiscal hydrocortisone. Clin Orthop 1976;117:171–192.

26. Hitselberger WF, Witten RM. Abnormal myelograms in asymptomatic patients. J Neurosurg 1968;28:204–206.

27. Houang B, Vital JM, Pinol H, Daljiat R, Senegas J, Caillet JM. Discographie computerisée et rachis opéré: intérêt dans les récidives de hernies discales: etude de 15 cas. Société Française de Neuroradiologie 1986.

28. Houtteville JP, Toumi K. Surgical findings and results after chemonucleolysis failure in sciatica. In: Bonneville JF, ed. Focus on chemonucleolysis. Berlin: Springer 1986:116–121.

29. Jansen EF, Balls AK. Chymopapain: a new crystalline proteinase from papaya latex. J Biol Chem 1941;137:459–469.

30. Javid MJ. Treatment of herniated lumbar disk syndrome with chymopapain. JAMA 1980;243:2043–2048.

31. Javid MJ. Safety and efficacy of chymopapain (chymodiactin) in herniated nucleus pulposus with sciatica: result of a randomized double blind study. JAMA 1983;249:2489–2494.

32. Javid MJ. Efficacy of chymopapain chemonucleolysis: a long term review of 105 patients. J Neurosurg 1985;62:662–666.

33. Kieffer SA, Sherry RG, Wellenstein DE, King RG. Bulging lumbar intervertebral disk: myelographic differentiation from herniated disk with nerve root compression. AJR 1982;138:709–716.

34. Konings JG, Williams FJ, Deutman R. The effects of chemonucleolysis as demonstrated by computerized tomography. J Bone Joint Surg [Br] 1984;66:417–421.

35. Kraemer J, Laturnus H. Lumbar intradiscal instillation with aprotinin. Spine 1982;7:73–74.

36. Lavignolle B, Senegas J, Vital JM, Allard M, Baulny D, Rivel J. La chimionucléolyse. In Senegas J, ed. Journée de pathologie rachidienne. Bordeaux: Bergeret 1984:141–170.

37. Lazorthes Y, Theron J. Chemonucleolysis of cervical discs: preliminary results in 15 cases of root compression. In: Sutton J, ed. Current concepts in chemonucleolysis. London: Royal Society of Medicine 1985:217–223. (International congres symposium series, no 72.)

38. MacCulloch JA. Chemonucleolysis: experience with 2000 cases. Clin Orthop 1980;146:128–135.

39. MacCulloch JA. Out patient discolysis with chymopapain. Orthopedics 1983;6:1624–1627.

40. MacNab I, MacCulloch JA, Weiner DS, Hugo EP, Galway RD, Dall D. Chemonucleolysis. Can J Surg 1971;14:280–289.

41. MacNab I. Chemonucleolysis. Clin Neurosurg 1973;20:183–192.

42. MacRae DL. Asymptomatic intervertebral disc protrusions. Acta Radiol (Stockh) 1956;46:9–27.

43. Maroon JC, Onik G. Percutaneous automated discectomy: a new method for lumbar discremoval. J Neurosurg 1987;66:143–146.

44. Masaryk TJ, Boumphrey F, Modic MT, Tamborello C, Ross JS, Brown MD. Effects of chemonucleolysis demonstrated by MR imaging. J Comput Assist Tomogr 1986;10:917–923.

45. Massare C. Discographie. In: Fischgold H, ed. Traité de radiodiagnostic; vol 15. Paris: Masson 1971:39–49.

46. Monneret-Vautrain DA, Mouton C, Laxenaire MC, Roland J, Aussedat P, Occelli G, Gerard H. Détection d'une sensibilisation à la chymopapaine: bilan chez 111 candidats à la chimionucléolyse. Sem Hop Paris 1986;62:3499–3504.

47. Mooney V, Robertson J. The facet syndrome. Clin Orthop 1975;115:149–156.

48. Morvan G, Massare C. Tomodensitometric measurements of the lumbar spinal canal. J Belge Radiol 1982;65:397–402.

49. Mrejen D. Mésothérapie ponctuelle systématisée: bases neuroendocriniennes, applications thérapeutiques. 1987.

50. Norby EJ, Lucas GLA. A comparative analysis of lumbar disk disease treated by laminectomy or chemonucleolysis. Clin Orthop 1973;39:119–129.

51. Onofrio BM. Injection of chymopapain into intervertebral disc: preliminary report on 72 patients with symptoms of disc disease. J Neurosurg 1975;42:384–388.

52. Parkinson D, Shields C. Treatment of protruded lumbar intervertebral discs with chymopapain. J Neurosurg 1973;39:203–208.

53. Rolland G. Biochimie, pharmacologie et toxicologie de la chymopapaine. Vie Méd 1981;2–3(Jan):109–114.

54. Runge M, Clere P, Bonneville JF. Scanner et nucléolyse. In: Bonneville JF, ed. Focus on chemonucleolysis. Berlin: Springer 1986:79–85.

55. Schwetschenau PR, Ramirez A, Johnston J, Barnes E, Wiggs C, Martins AN. Double blind evaluation on intradiscal chymopapain for herniated lumbar discs: early results. J Neurosurg 1976;45:622–627.

56. Shealy CN. Percutaneous radiofrequency denervation of spinal facets. J Neurosurg 1975;44:448–451.

57. Smith L, Garvin PJ, Gesler RM. Enzyme dissolution of the nucleus pulposus. Nature 1963;168:1311–1312.

58. Smith L. Enzyme dissolution of the nucleus pulposus in humans. JAMA 1964;187:137–140.

59. Solassol A, Allas T, Theron J. Intérêt de la rééducation dans les suites de la chimionucléolyse discale lombaire. Ann Réadapt Med Phys 1984;26:379–390.

60. Spencer DL, Miller JAA. The mechanism of sciatic pain relief by chemonucleolysis. Orthopedics 1983;6:1600–1603.

61. Stern IJ, Smith L. Dissolution by chymopapain "in vitro" of tissues from normal and prolapsed intervertebral discs. Clin Orthop 1967;50:269–277.

62. Sutton JC. Repeat chemonucleolysis. In: Sutton JC, ed. Current concept in chemonucleolysis. London: Royal Society of Medicine. 1985:225–235. (International congress and symposium series; no 72.

63. Theron J, Moret J. Spinal phlebography. Berlin: Springer 1978.

64. Theron J. Spinal phlebography in the stenosis of the lumbar canal. In: Wackenheim, A, Babin E, eds. The narrow lumbar canal. Berlin: Springer 1980:75–82.

65. Theron J, Blais M, Casasco A, Courtheoux P, Adam Y, Derlon JM, Houtteville JP. Therapeutic radiology of the lumbar spine: chemonucleolysis, infiltration and coagulation of posterior spinal articulations. J Neuroradiol 1983;10:209–230.

66. Thomas L. Reversible collapse of rabbit ears after intravenous papain and prevention of recovery by cortisone. J Exp Med 1956;104:245–352.

67. Tan P. La chimionucléolyse en pratique vétérinaire: intérêts et limites [Dissertation]. University of Nantes 1986.

68. Troisier O. Nucléolyse chimique: discographie par voie latérale: intérêt de l'image de 3/4. Presse Med 1971;79:238.

69. Troisier O, Gozlan E, Durey A, Rodineau J, Gounot-Halbout MC, Pelveray B. Traitement des lombosciatiques par injection intradiscale d'enzymes protéolytiques (nucléolyse): 80 observations. Nouv Presse Med 1980;9:227–230.

70. Troisier O. Technique de la discographie extradurale. J Radiol 1982;63:571–578.

71. Wadell G, MacCulloch JA. Lateral lumbar discography. Br J Radiol 1978;51:498–502.

72. Watts C, Knighton R, Roulhac G. Chymopapain treatment of intermittent disc disease. J Neurosurg 1975;42:374–383.

73. Watts C. Complications of chemonucleolysis for lumbar disc disease. Neurosurgery 1977;1:2–5.

74. Wiesel SW, Tsourmas N, Feffer HL, Citrin CH, Patronas N. A study of computer-assisted tomography. Spine 1984;9:549–551.

75. Wiltsee LL, Midelle H, Yvan HA. Chymopapain nucleolysis in lumbar disk disease. JAMA 1975;231:474–479.

Percutaneous Lysis of Neural Structures

Celiac Plexus

J. C. Kurdziel and R. F. Dondelinger

Indications

The pathways of upper abdominal visceral pain are nerves converging in the celiac plexus, which conveys afferent and efferent sympathetic and parasympathetic preganglionic fibers and also sensitive nerves in the upper abdomen. There are usually 3 celiac ganglia, approximately 2 cm in diameter. However, they may vary both in number (from 1 to 6), and in size. They are located in the retroperitoneal space around and in front of the abdominal aorta in a constant relationship with the origin of the celiac and the superior mesenteric arteries. The right ganglia are located slightly more cephalad and close to the inferior vena cava (22). In addition, the afferent sensitive fibers originating from the intraperitoneal organs, from the kidneys, and from the adrenals end in the splanchnic nerves, which are involved in transmitting abdominal pain. Pain may be caused by irritation, tumor invasion, and compression or by entrapment due to fibrosis. Since the first description of splanchnic nerve neurolysis (16), only a few reports in the literature support percutaneous nerve block as a palliative method for treating severe abdominal pain (1, 3, 5, 7, 9–15, 18, 20, 21).

Malignant tumors situated in the upper abdomen and originating from the pancreas, stomach and duodenum, proximal small intestine, liver, and biliary system and from compressing lymph nodes or the dilated urinary system may generate intolerable upper abdominal pain, which does not respond satisfactorily to opiate medication or radiation therapy and significantly reduces the quality of life for preterminal oncologic patients. Percutaneous neurolysis of the celiac plexus and the splanchnic nerves represents an interesting alternative for patients receiving large doses of analgesic drugs and who are unable to undergo surgery, because of their poor general condition and usually advanced disease.

Celiac plexus block has also been advocated for treatment of abdominal pain in Crohn's disease, visceral neuropathy, and diabetic radiculopathy (4). Pain related to chronic pancreatitis may represent an indication per se for surgery. The mechanism of pain in chronic pancreatitis is not clear. Surgical treatment can be delayed if pain is relieved by percutaneous nerve block (1). Most of these patients are not severely disabled, and they are only seldom opiate addicts. Pain may also subside spontaneously after calcifications and pancreatic insufficency have appeared (23). In acute pancreatitis, block of the celiac plexus achieves apart from the analgesic effect, inhibition of the adrenoceliac circuit, which is responsible for secretion of vasoconstrictive substances, causing pancreatic ischemia and increase in edema of the pancreatic gland (7).

Technique

Radiographic guidance for correct deposit of the neurolysing substance has been suggested and been shown to be superior to a blind approach (2). Classically, vertebral landmarks have been used (3). The percutaneous puncture of the celiac plexus is performed with a 22 G needle, which is advanced alongside the lateral aspect of the vertebral body at the level of T12, or L1, until contact with the spine is lost.

A more precise localization of the celiac plexus may be obtained during angiographic control because its relationship to the celiac and the superior mesenteric arteries is constant (13, 15). A catheter is placed in the abdominal aorta and a profile aortogram is obtained. The tip of the aortic catheter is positioned at the level of the origin of the celiac artery, determined on a profile arteriogram of the abdominal aorta. A posterolateral puncture is used, with sagittal fluoroscopy control and guided by the aortic catheter. The approximate paravertebral puncture site is determined on the skin in a similar way as for high translumbar aortography. US has also been used to guide the percutaneous approach to the celiac plexus, since the abdominal aorta and the origin of the visceral arteries are often recognizable. Under sonographic control, precise placement of the needle tip may, however, become difficult when massive tumor invasion is present in the preaortic space or when vascular landmarks are not well demonstrated. CT has been advocated for many years (4, 8, 10, 11, 14, 17, 18, 20, 21) for guiding percutaneous needle positioning before neurolysis. CT allows exquisite precision in the placement of the needle tip, even when major anatomic changes have occurred as a result of tumor invasion or when only poor retroperitoneal fat layers are present. Furthermore, CT eliminates almost completely the risk of inadvertent injection of the neurolytic agent into vascular structures, abdominal viscera, such as the pancreas, or within the tumor. Direct injection of phenol or ethanol in the tumor mass may also have an analgesic effect. CT accurately demonstrates pathways of diffusion of the injected substance after percutaneous injection. If alcohol spreads too far laterally in the anterior pararenal space, the position of the needle tip has to be corrected. The procedure can be performed on an out-patient basis and even in very debilitated patients. Several techniques of percutaneous neurolysis of the celiac plexus are described under CT guidance. No premedication is given. Factors of blood clotting are checked before the procedure.

Anterior Approach

For the anterior percutaneous approach, the patient assumes a supine position on the CT table. The level of T12 is determined on a digital radiograph of the abdomen. Cross-sections are performed at this level after intravenous bolus injection of contrast medium in order to identify the origin of the celiac and the superior mesenteric arteries. In this way, precise localization of the celiac ganglia is determined, since vascular structures represent the most constant landmarks. CT is also able to show these nerve structures themselves, if regional anatomy is not disturbed by tumor growth and if surrounding fat planes are not obliterated (6).

The puncture site is drawn on the skin of the patient in such a way that the needle will be inserted by an anterior approach, perpendicular to the midline, and reach the pre-aortic retroperitoneal fat via an axial plane. A small cutaneous incision is made with a blade. A 22 G Chiba needle is placed after local anesthesia, and CT cross-sections are obtained to determine the precise needle tip localization immediately below the celiac artery in contact with the anterior aspect of the aorta (Fig. **1a**). Diluted contrast medium, 1 ml, is injected through the needle, and confirms extravascular position of the needle tip if permanent staining of contrast is observed in the retroperitoneal fat (Fig. **2b**). Contrast medium may also be mixed with alcohol before administration. Injection of air as a marker of diffusion has been suggested. A 19 G needle with a plastic sheath may also be used. (10). Only the sheath is left in place during injection of alcohol. When the procedure is performed during a period of pain, a preliminary test injection of 10 ml of lidocaine (1%) relieves pain immediately and also confirms thereby the correct needle tip position. A splanchnic or a celiac test block with local anesthetic several days before the procedure has been recommended. Aspiration with a syringe for 20 seconds confirms that the needle tip is not located in the lumen of a small vein.

Neurolysis is accomplished by slow injection of 25 to 40 ml of a sterile solution of ethanol of variable

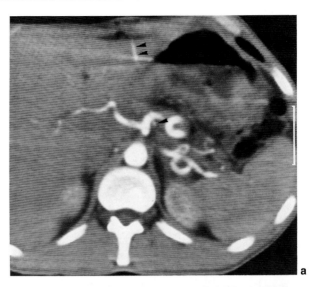

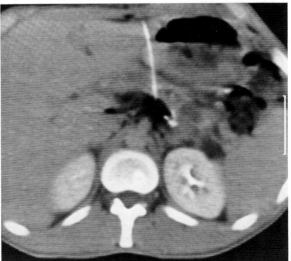

Fig. **1 A 34-year-old man with chronic pancreatitis, severe abdominal pain.** Percutaneous block of the celiac plexus was performed
a Determination of the celiac plexus around the origin of the celiac artery. Intravenous injection of contrast during CT shows the celiac artery. Percutaneous needle placement (arrows) by an anterior approach
b Control scan after injection of 80 ml of absolute ethanol demonstrates adequate local diffusion around the origin of the celiac artery

concentrations (30 to 95%) at each side of the celiac artery. Even an amount as high as 80 ml of alcohol injected does not induce complications (17). On some occasions, ethanol may diffuse on both sides of the celiac artery without changing the position of the needle. Ethanol is always recognized on CT sections by negative fat-like densities (Figs. **1b, 2c**). If no local anesthetic has been injected, the patient may experience at the beginning of the injection of ethanol or phenol a transient localized back pain, which con-

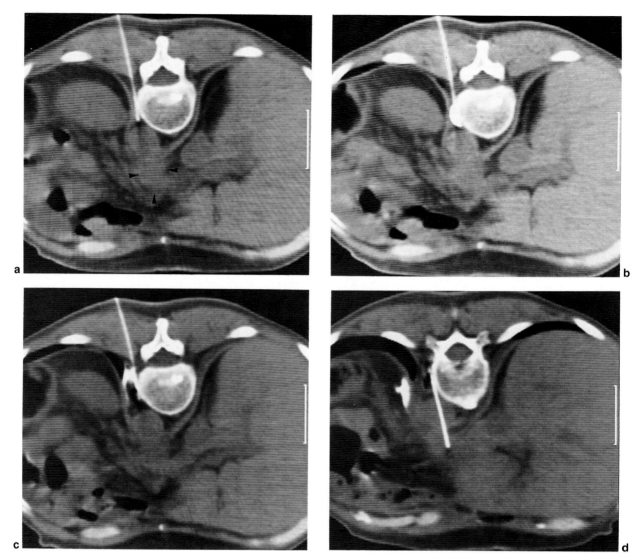

Fig. 2   A 61-year-old man with tumor recurrence (arrows) after gastrectomy for carcinoma. Severe abdominal pain is present
a Splanchnic nerve block by a posterior approach. Retrocrural needle placement is at the level of T12
b Test injection of 1 ml of contrast
c Adequate retrocrural diffusion after injection of 25 ml of ethanol
d Blockage of the celiac plexus by a percutaneous posterior and transaortic approach. Tip of the needle is in a correct pre-aortic position

firms optimal needle placement. Control CT sections in a rostral and in a caudal direction show diffusion of ethanol, which mixes with the previously injected contrast material. Contralateral infiltration of the pre-aortic retroperitoneal fat is mandatory when diffusion of ethanol to the opposite side is insufficient. Although easy to perform, this technique may imply a transhepatic, transgastric, transpancreatic, and sometimes a transcolic needle passage that theoretically increases the risk of complications.

Posterior Approach

During the posterolateral approach, the patient lies in a prone position. After localizing the origin of the celiac and the superior mesenteric arteries by the intravenous bolus injection technique, the needle tip is brought into an anterolateral location, adjacent to the aorta via a paraspinal puncture. Needle passage through the kidneys can always be avoided. Sometimes a caudocranial angled needle pathway is necessary to avoid the posterior costophrenic sulcus of the pleura. In this way, the risk of pneumothorax is eliminated. During oblique puncture, the entry point at the skin may be located 10 mm below the left renal vein. Since the right posterolateral approach may be hampered by the presence of the inferior vena cava, a transaortic puncture from the left side may be helpful in order to reach the ganglia located at the right side of the celiac artery (14) (Fig. **2d**). The transcrural passage of the Chiba needle can be particularly painful.

Splanchnic nerve neurolysis is best performed by a posterior percutaneous approach. The needle is inserted into the retrocrural space at the level of T12 (Fig. **2a**). Ethanol, 25 ml, is injected on both sides. This posterior approach requires a separate plan for both sides, which implies a larger number of supervisory CT sections. A single needle technique has also been proposed (7). The needle is emptied of alcohol using 1 to 2 ml of saline before withdrawal. Percutaneous neurolysis of the celiac plexus should be performed first. Neurolysis of the splanchnic nerves is added if the analgesic effect seems insufficient.

Results

Since pain is a subjective sensation, quantifying abdominal pain decrease is difficult. Nevertheless, interrogation of the patient after the procedure and reduction or cessation of analgesic drug use provide a more or less objective approximation of the success rate. The results of neurolysis can be assessed clinically immediately after the procedure and again after variable time intervals until the patient's death. Long-term pain ablation or reduction is difficult to follow, because of the progression of the underlying malignant disease. There are only a limited number of reports in the literature available, with a small number of patients studied. In addition to variations in the techniques reported, there are also differences in duration of clinical follow-up and quantification of pain relief. Subjective evaluation of pain and interference with analgesic requirements give different results for each patient, but the use of both criteria for effectiveness of neurolysis should provide more objective information. Moreover, the timing of the treatment during the course of the disease is important. It has been suggested that nerve blockage should be performed as soon as possible, before addiction to opiate analgesics. Overall results obtained with percutaneous nerve block are comparable to those of surgical splanchnicectomy (19).

Early experience with percutaneous sympathetic nerve blockage has shown inconstant results, varying from 33 to 75% (21). Although guidance methods, percutaneous approach, and the substance injected varied considerably in the techniques reported so far in the literature, recent positive clinical results obtained do not differ significantly in cancer patients, varying from 73 to 87% (4, 10, 13, 18, 20). Our experience is based on treatment of 30 patients with intractable abdominal pain originating from a malignant tumor in 25 cases, from chronic pancreatitis in three cases, and other causes in two cases. In patients with upper abdominal cancer overall positive results were obtained in 87%. Of three patients with chronic pancreatitis, one remained completely pain-free.

Pain resulting from pancreatitis does not respond as well to percutaneous neurolysis as pain associated with cancer. Lateral pancreaticojejunostomy (Puestow procedure) produces satisfactory long-term pain relief in more than 70% of selected patients (23). Injection of steroids instead of neurolytic agent has also been suggested (12).

Potential failure of percutaneous neurolysis is due to anatomic variations of the celiac plexus, e.g., unilateral predominance of celiac ganglia, inadequate needle tip position, or an inadequate diffusion of ethanol. Some patients are difficult to free from opiate medication. Pain recurrence can be related to advanced tumor growth with involvement of other pain pathways such as parietal nerves or regeneration of incomplete neurolized nerve fibers. Pain in pancreatic cancer or chronic pancreatitis may also result from ductal dilation. The procedure can be easily repeated, when necessary. It is important to note that neither the beneficial effect of percutaneous celiac and splanchnic neurolysis nor its duration can be predicted by morphologic criteria. Life expectancy in these patients is not altered, since the procedure does not arrest progression of the underlying disease, but quality of life is dramatically improved in many patients.

Complications

Serious complications related to the procedure are almost nonexistent. Systematic use of CT for guidance prevents puncture of the spinal canal, the intervertebral disks, and vascular structures. Transient orthostatic hypotension due to intestinal pooling of blood from intestinal vasoplegia, and temporary back pain are common after celiac plexus neurolysis. A persistent motor diarrhea may be found on rare occasions. Constipation may be improved due to the sympatholytic effect. Chemical peritonitis as a result of inadvertent alcohol injection into the peritoneal cavity has been reported (4).

Pleuritic pain, pneumothorax, haematuria, bleeding, acute pancreatitis, septicemia, sexual dysfunction, and malignant seeding are potential untoward effects that may follow puncture of the pancreas by the anterior approach due to inadequate needle placement. Paraplegia has been described as a potential complication of percutaneous neurolysis by the posterolateral approach, possibly related to intrathecal diffusion of ethanol along nerve fibers of the lumbar plexus or the puncture of a lumbar artery resulting in medullary ischemia (5, 9, 21). These complications were mainly due to the more imprecise fluoroscopy control used (as opposed to CT).

References

1. Bell SN, Cole R, Roberts-Thomson IC. Coeliac plexus block for control of pain in chronic pancreatitis. Br Med J 1980;281:1604.
2. Bonica JJ, ed. The management of pain. Philadelphia: Lea and Febiger 1954:229–230,1380–1389.
3. Bridenbaugh LD, Moore DC, Campbell DD. Management of upper abdominal cancer pain: treatment with celiac plexus block with alcohol. JAMA 1964;190:877–880.
4. Buy JN, Moss AA, Singler RC. CT guided coeliac plexus and splanchnic nerve neurolysis. J Comput Assit Tomogr 1982;6:315–319.
5. Cherry D, Lamberty J. Paraplegia following celiac plexus block. Anaesth Intens Care 1984;12:59–72.
6. Dal Pozzo G, Bozza A, Fargnoli R, Brizzi E. CT identification of coeliac ganglia. Eur J Radiol 1985;111:24–26.
7. Filshie J, Golding S, Robbie DS, Husband J. Unilateral computerised tomography guided coeliac plexus block: a technique for pain relief. Anaesthesia 1983;38:498–503.
8. Floyd JB. Pancreatitis and adrenocoeliac blockade: the possible role of the adrenals. (Unpublished data.)
9. Galizia EJ, Lahiri SK. Paraplegia following coeliac plexus block with phenol. Br J Anaesth 1974;46:539–540.
10. Haaga JR, Kori SH, Eastwood DW, Borkowski GP. Improved technique for CT-guided celiac ganglia block. AJR 1984;142:1201–1204.
11. Haaga J, Reich N, Havrilla T, Alfidi R. Interventional CT scanning. Radiol Clin North Am 1977;15:449–456.
12. Hanowell S, Kennedy S, MacNamara T, Lees D. Celiac plexus block: diagnosis and therapeutic applications in abdominal pain. South Med J 1980;33:1330–1332.
13. Hegedus V. Relief of pancreatic pain by radiography-guided block. AJR 1979;133:1101–1103.
14. Ischia S, Luzzani A, Ischia A, Faggion S. A new approach to the neurolytic block of the coeliac plexus: the transaortic technique. Pain 1983;16:33–341.
15. Jackson S, Jacobs J, Epstein R. A radiographic approach to coeliac plexus block. Anesthesiology 1969;31:373–375.
16. Kappis M. Sensibilität und lokale Anästhesie im chirurgischen Gebiet der Bauchhöhle mit besonderer Berücksichtigung der Splanchnicus-Anästhesie. Beitr Klin Chir 1919;115:161–175.
17. Moore D, Bush W, Burnett L. Celiac plexus block: a roentgenographic, anatomic study of technique and spread of solution in patients and corpses. Anesth Analg 1981;60:369–379.
18. Muehle C, van Sonnenberg E, Casola G, Wittich G, Polansky A. Radiographically guided alcohol block of the celiac ganglia. Semin Intervent Radiol 1987;4:195–199.
19. Sadar SE, Copperman AM. Bilateral thoracic sympathectomy-splanchnicectomy in the treatment of intractable pain due to pancreatic carcinoma. Cleve Clin Q 1974;41:185–188.
20. Schild H, Günther R, Hoffman J, Goedecke R. CT gesteuerte Blockade des Plexus coeliacus mit ventralem Zugang. RöFo 1983;139:202–205.
21. Thompson GE, Moore DC, Bridenbaugh LD, Artin RY. Abdominal pain and alcohol celiac plexus nerve block. Anesth Analg 1977;56:1–5.
22. Ward E, Rorie D, Nauss L, Bahn R. The celiac ganglia in man: normal anatomic variations. Anesth Analg 1979;58:461–465.
23. Warshaw AL. Pain in chronic pancreatitis: patients, patience and the impatient surgeon. Gastroenterology 1984;86:987–999.

Sympathetic Chain

J. C. Kurdziel and R. F. Dondelinger

Thoracic Sympathetic Chain

Surgical Sympathectomy

Temporary blockage and surgical stellate ganglionectomy have been advocated in the past as a treatment for vasospastic disorders of the upper limbs (6). Approach, type, and extent of surgical upper thoracic sympathectomy have long been controversial. Although resection of the stellate ganglion or T1, together with the upper thoracic sympathetic chain, was thought to be indispensable in order to achieve sympathetic denervation of the upper limb, preservation of T1 or of its upper part has become standard (4, 37). Anatomic variations may render partial excision of T1 hazardous, and removal of the inferior third of the stellate ganglion may expose the patient to a Horner syndrome (47). Surgical experience has shown that the major sympathetic innervation of the upper limbs is connected with the ganglia below T1 (41). Usually, the sympathetic chain is resected at T2 and T3, and possibly T4 (5, 41, 44, 47). A more extensive ablation of thoracic ganglia downward is also recommended by some (28, 30, 43).

Although it seems difficult to isolate the upper limbs entirely from the sympathetic nervous system, limited surgical resections of upper thoracic ganglia give acceptable clinical results. Upper thoracic sympathectomy by y posterior, anterior, or supraclavicular approach has been described (2, 3, 16, 41, 44). The transaxillary route is the favored technique, using a transpleural approach (3).

Alternative Techniques

Several attempts have been made to replace surgical thoracic sympathectomy by closed percutaneous and less invasive alternatives. Endoscopic transpleural electroresection of the upper thoracic sympathetic chain through a fiber-optic scope was popularized by Kux et al. (26). Weale (46) and Malone et al. (31) performed percutaneous transpleural electrocoagulation of the upper thoracic sympathetic chain. Dissection or destruction of the sympathetic chain by these techniques is performed under direct vision. The fiber-optic device is inserted into the pleural cavity under general anesthesia after a pneumothorax has been created. These endoscopic techniques are limited by pleural adhesions. A

Horner syndrome is unlikely, since the upper part of T1 is inaccessible by transpleural endoscopy.

Fluoroscopy-guided percutaneous phenol lysis of the thoracic sympathetic chain was mentioned by Reid et al. (36) but should be abandoned, since the risk of a pneumothorax is considerable.

Wilkinson (48) suggested percutaneous radiofrequency destruction of the thoracic sympathetic chain under fluoroscopic supervision. Six radiofrequency lesions are needed at three different sites adjacent to T2 and T3. In order to be certain that complete interruption of the sympathetic chain has been achieved, the current is applied at two different positions of the electrode for each level. Electrical stimulation is necessary before each lesion so that no intercostal nerve is hurt. We have recently described percutaneous phenol neurolysis of the upper thoracic sympathetic chain under CT supervision (12). These techniques using 18 to 22 G needles obviate the need for a pneumothorax. Cosmetic effects are of no concern, since only a small puncture of the skin is necessary. Percutaneous needle techniques are not limited by pleural adhesions. Due to the small gauge of needle used, vascular damage is unlikely to occur.

Indications

Indications for surgical upper thoracic sympathectomy or other alternative techniques are very diverse, and some of them are based on empirical observations only. They include: primary Raynaud's disease, palmar and axillary hyperhidrosis, thoracic outlet syndrome, secondary Raynaud's syndrome, occlusive arteriopathy, occupational digital arteriolar occlusion, causalgia, post-traumatic dystrophy, distal arterial emboli (47), distal arteritis (45), syringomyelia (42), frostbite ulceration (5), intractable ventricular tachycardia (13), and Prinzmetal's angina (17).

Technique

The procedure is carried out on an out-patient basis without premedication. The patient is placed in a prone position on the CT table. A frontal digitalized radiograph of the thorax is obtained. The level of T3 is selected, and an axial cut, 8 mm thick, is made. The appropriate level for the percutaneous approach is determined from supplementary adjacent slices if the posterior arch of the third rib overlies on the first slice. The puncture site is chosen and marked on the patient's skin. After disinfection, local anesthesia is induced. A small cutaneous incision is made with a blade. A 22 gauge Chiba needle is inserted percutaneously along the lateral aspect of the vertebral body of T3. The tip of the needle is located in front of the head of the third rib. The needle path must be extrapleural. Correct angulation of the needle and location of its tip are checked by control CT slices during progression of the Chiba needle (Fig. **1a**). Puncture of vertebral periosteum, a vertebral disk, or the lung and pleura can be avoided by use of control scans. The procedure should be entirely free from pain. Inadvertent puncture of the vertebral periosteum or disk causes local back pain, puncture of an intercostal nerve produces sudden pain along the intercostal space, and violation of the pleura provokes coughing. When the correct position of the

needle tip has been ascertained by control CT scans, 0.5 ml of diluted iodine contrast medium is injected through the Chiba needle. The contrast medium accumulates around the needle tip, indicating the future site and diffusion of the phenol (Fig. **1b**). If the contrast medium spreads anteriorly into the posterior mediastinum, the needle must be withdrawn a few millimeters and diffusion of contrast medium checked again. If the contrast medium extends into the vertebral canal or posteriorly along the extrapleural space, the needle must be advanced and its new position checked. By varying the window settings, it can be determined that no air has entered the pleural space and no alveolar hemorrhage has occurred. Neurolysis of the upper thoracic sympathetic chain is obtained by injecting 5 to 15 ml of a solution of phenol 400 mg, glycerin 2.5 g, and water to 5 ml for 1 to 3 minutes. During the administration of

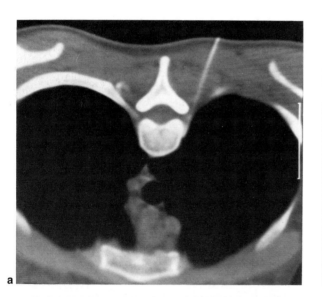

a

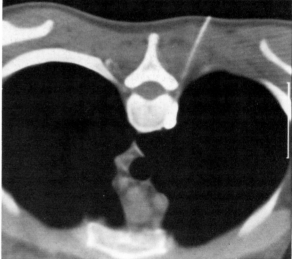

b

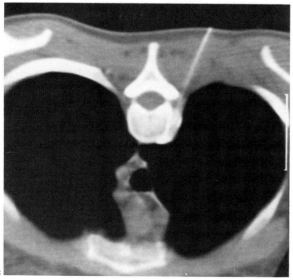

c

Fig. **1 Percutaneous phenol neurolysis of the left upper thoracic sympathetic chain with CT control.**
a The tip of the 22 gauge needle is located between the vertebral periosteum and the pleura at the level of T3
b Local staining of 1 ml of contrast medium injected through the 22 gauge needle
c The phenol has mixed with the contrast media at the end of injection. The pleura is slightly displaced. No phenol has spread in the mediastinum or in the vertebral canal

phenol, the patient is asked to report any changes in his upper limb. Usually, a sensation of heat is felt progressing from the arm down to the hand. The patient is able to locate and to grade the sensation of warmth and dryness in his hand and fingers. Physical examination of the hand during the procedure confirms an increase in skin temperature, cessation of sweating, coloration of the skin, and dilation of peripheral veins. At the same time, of a homolateral Horner syndrome is carefully watched for. Should a slight droop of the eyelid or an anisocoria be observed, injection of phenol is stopped. Otherwise, the injection is completed up to a volume of 5 to 15 ml until a maximum subjective effect is felt by the patient. The Chiba needle is withdrawn and adjacent rostral and caudal CT slices confirm diffusion of the injected phenol, which has mixed poorly with the contrast medium (Fig. **1c**). Usually, diffusion extends from T2 to T3 or from T1 to T4. A very slight rostral angulation of the needle favors diffusion of phenol in the upper thoracic direction. The patient is kept under observation in the Radiology Department for 1 hour before discharge. A chest radiograph confirms absence of local complications and demonstrates the spread of phenol.

Results

Results obtained by surgical upper sympathectomy vary largely according to indications. Obviously, best results are achieved in patients with hyperhidrosis. A complete cessation of excessive palmar sweating is noted in 94 to 99% (14, 39), and the results remain constant at long-term follow-up (1, 15, 18). Compensatory sweating may appear in 29 to 59% (15, 43). Patients with the so-called primary Raynaud's disease, by contrast, show good results only in 22 to 56% (4, 24, 47). Vasomotor syndromes recur in 48 to 78% (33, 47) during the first years after the procedure. Patients with Raynaud's disease form a heterogeneous group; 11% develop evidence of connective tissue disease during follow-up (4). The underlying progressive disease may account for the vanishing sympatholytic effect. Arteriosclerotic disease of the upper limbs responds well to thoracic sympathectomy. Regression of trophic ischemic changes of the fingers may be seen in up to 89% of patients (29). The closed percutaneous procedures offer competitive results to surgery (28, 46, 48).

Kux (28) reports 93% satisfactory results in palmar hyperhidrosis treated with endoscopic sympathectomy. Weale (46) reports good results in nine of ten patients treated with endoscopic electrocoagulation. Wilkinson (48) has obtained positive results in five of six procedures performed in hyperhidrosis and in nine of ten procedures done for Raynaud's disease or arteriosclerosis with application of radiofrequency (48). We have noticed positive long-term results in 13/18 procedures done for hyperhidrosis. Positive long-term results were obtained in 7 of 14 (50%) procedures done for Raynaud's disease. Among 14 limbs treated for Raynaud's disease, complete disappearance of symptoms was observed in four cases after follow-up period of 11, 11, 19, and 21 months, respectively. In 4 cases symptoms returned, in three cases after 12 months and in one case after 16 months. Three procedures produced an acceptable result with significant reduction of symptoms after a follow-up period of 10, 10, and 11 months, respectively. Three procedures were not followed by any change.

CT prevents incorrect diffusion of phenol by correct needle tip positioning. It may be objected that phenol induces only an incomplete neurolysis, as shown by experimental data. Even after careful surgical resection of the thoracic sympathetic chain, recurrence of vasomotor signs in the upper limbs are observed (41, 44). Reappearance of symptoms is thought to be related to nervous regeneration (22) or development of new sympathetic pathways through remaining structures despite excision, or both (7). The ease of performance of CT-guided phenol thoracic sympatholysis may change the actual reluctance to propose an interventional procedure in vasomotor syndromes of the upper limbs as long as the patient is not socially and professionaly disabled. This procedure, performed on an out-patient basis, could be recommended in these patients as an alternative to medical treatment even if clinical signs are moderate. The procedure may be repeated if the effect vanishes.

Complications

Surgical upper thoracic sympathectomy has almost no operative mortality (18, 39) but carries a significant number of complications (47). A Horner syndrome may be induced in up to 22% (1) if resection is performed below T1, and it has been reported to occur in 56% if the lower half or third of the stellate ganglion is included in the resection (47). Acute postoperative complications are seen in 0.1 to 33% (29, 39). Pneumothorax or hemothorax can be observed. Vascular damage to the subclavian vessels and injury to the phrenic nerve or brachial plexus occasionally occur during the supraclavicular approach (14). Chest wall pain, intercostal neuralgia, and dysesthesia at the incision site are other reported complications (5). Hospital stay is 6 to 12 days (18, 43). The high potential for side effects in surgical sympathectomy ill suits the rather benign diseases for which these patients are generally operated on. Progress in medical therapy, together with increased understanding of capillary vasomotion, and the overall good prognosis of primary vasomotor syndromes account for the loss of popularity of surgical treatment.

Closed percutaneous procedures have less potential for complications than surgery, but are not entirely free from untoward side effects. One in ten procedures had to be abandoned by Weale (46). Intercostal artery bleeding has been observed by Kux (28) in 1 of 124 cases and could be managed endoscopically. No Horner syndrome occurred in 166 patients treated by Kux (27), and Weale (46) reports one temporary Horner syndrome in a study of ten procedures. Wilkinson (48) reported 1 in 27 permanent partial Horner syndrome and 3 in 27 pneumothorax. We experienced 1 in 21 patients with pneumothorax that had to be drained, and 3 in 21 temporary incomplete Horner syndromes. CT guidance should, at least theoretically, eliminate the risk of pneumothorax. It is probably more difficult to avoid the danger of a Horner syndrome with percutaneous needle techniques. During phenol neurolysis, precise needle placement, reduced volume of phenol, control of pathways of diffusion with CT, and clinical observation of the patient during the procedure are mandatory, but the risk of a Horner syndrome is the price to pay for the advantages offered by a single percutaneous puncture technique.

Other possible disagreeable side effects (myalgia, neuralgia, compensatory sweating in other parts of the body, hands too dry, stuffy nose, hypersensitivity to cold) are inherent in the destruction of the sympathetic chain and may be encountered during any technique of sympathectomy. We have observed intractable neuralgia lasting for 4 months in one patient with Raynaud's disease.

Lumbar Sympathetic Chain

Indications

Percutaneous blockage of the lumbar sympathetic chain is mainly indicated in advanced atherosclerotic disease of the lower limbs. Other indications listed for percutaneous blockage of the thoracic sympathetic chain may also apply for the lumbar level.

Treatment of occlusive arterial disease of the lower limbs includes exercise, medical treatment, vascular reconstruction, percutaneous transluminal angioplasty, and interruption of the lumbar sympathetic chain. Surgical sympathectomy represents a last resource in many elderly end-stage disease patients. They show a poor run-off and are not eligible for vascular reconstruction. Lumbar sympathectomy is supposed to improve vasomotion of the capillaries, influence trophic lesions of the extremities, reduce rest pain and delay amputation. In these patients percutaneous blockage of the lumbar sympathetic chain represents a simple therapeutic alternative to surgery. Percutaneous neurolysis of the lumbar sympathetic chain with injection of phenol was first described by Haxton (21) and

popularized by Reid et al. (36) on the basis of more than 5000 injections.

Radiologic control of percutaneous needle placement was achieved in the past either by uniplanar or by biplanar fluoroscopy (36, 38). More recently, CT has been advocated as a useful imaging modality in the guidance of percutaneous lumbar sympatholysis (10, 19, 31). The advantages of CT in the control of needle placement during percutaneous lumbar sympatholysis are unequivocal. The excellent anatomic display that distinguishes CT makes the occurrence of technical failure unlikely.

Technique

The procedure is carried out on an out-patient basis. No sedation or other preparation of the patient is mandatory. In thin patients a small amount (50 ml) of contrast medium is given intravenously in order to localize the opacified ureters in a fatless retroperitoneal space on CT cross-sections. The patient is placed in a prone position on the CT table. A digital radiograph of the abdomen is made, on which the levels of L2 and L4 are determined (Fig. **2a**).

The lumbar sympathetic chain is composed of four or five ganglia, which are located close to the anterolateral aspect of the spine, in front of the psoas muscle, behind the aorta and the inferior vena cava, and medial to the ureters. Cross-sections at these two levels allow the appropriate percutaneous approach of the needle to the sympathetic chain to be planned (entry point of the skin, angulation of the needle to the midline, depth of the needle tip) similar to percutaneously CT guided biopsy techniques (11). The puncture site on the skin is determined in such a way that the needle can be inserted in an oblique medial direction, avoiding on its course the transverse spinal process, the kidneys, or intestinal loops that might be in an unusual location (postnephrectomy, for example). After the puncture site has been drawn on the skin, the back of the patient is draped and prepared. Local anesthesia is used. A 22 gauge Chiba needle is inserted at the level of L2 (Fig. **2b**) and subsequently of L4 (Fig. **2d**) in a strict axial plane. Increasing experience with CT control makes fewer control scans necessary to assess proper placement of the needle tip, which should always be surrounded by fat on the control scan before injection. Diluted contrast medium, 1 cc, is then injected through the Chiba needle. Permanent staining of contrast in the retroperitoneal fat, which is observed on control scans, confirms the extravascular location of the needle tip and allows safe injection of the neurolytic substance (Figs. **2c, 2e**).

Neurolysis is induced by slow injection of a sterile solution of phenol. A slight resistance is felt at the glass syringe during injection of phenol. The patient may experience a transient sensation of slight lumbar

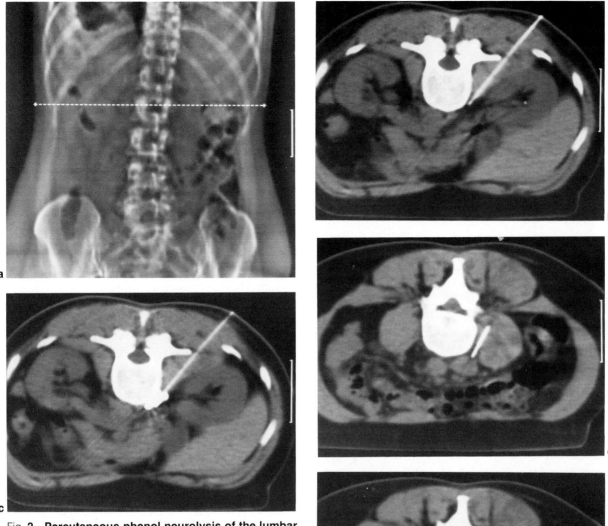

Fig. 2 Percutaneous phenol neurolysis of the lumbar sympathetic chain. a The level of L2 and subsequently of L4 are determined on a digital radiograph of the abdomen. The patient is in a prone position
b The tip of the 22 gauge needle is located in an adequate position, close to the spine and behind the inferior vena cava at the level of L2
c Accumulation of 1 ml of contrast medium around the needle tip at L2
d The needle tip is in contact with the inferior vena cava at the level of L4
e Local spread of contrast media around the needle tip at the level of L4. The inferior vena cava is slightly displaced medially

pain at the beginning of injection of phenol but injection of a local anesthetic through the Chiba needle is not required. Control CT sections show the diffusion of phenol that mixes with the previously injected contrast medium and spreads also in a cranial and a caudal direction. At L2, 5 to 10 ml of the solution of phenol are injected; at L4, a maximum of 10 to 15 ml are used. The entire length of the lumbar sympathetic chain has to be infiltrated from L1 to L5 in order to achieve satisfactory clinical results. The needle is rinsed with 1 ml of saline before withdrawal. If bilateral lumbar sympatholysis is indicated, one side only should be treated per session and a time interval of several weeks should be observed before the opposite side is treated. Length of the procedure with CT control is about 30 minutes.

Results

In severe arteriosclerosis, surgical lumbar sympathectomy has a positive effect in 30% (23) of end-stage disease patients and in 55% (35) of subjects who are in stage III or IV, after follow-up of 1 year. A 2-year limb salvage may be obtained in 63.5% of patients in this group (40). The majority of patients referred for percutaneous lumbar sympatholysis are elderly (63% over 70 years old) and not eligible for surgical sympathectomy because of poor general condition, diffuse vascular disease, or extensive surgical history (25). Precision in the placement of the needle tip during percutaneous neurolysis with CT control guarantees technical success. Healing, regression, and limitation of trophic changes at the periphery of the lower limbs, disappearance of rest pain, improvement in pain-free walking distance, subjective sensation of heat in the foot, and objective increase in local skin temperature are the main criteria by which the clinical benefit gained from the procedure is judged.

The effect of percutaneous lumbar sympatholysis on clinical staging of occlusive arterial disease after 141 procedures that were performed in 112 patients is detailed in Table 1.

Table 1   Effect of percutaneous lumbar sympatholysis on clinical staging

	No.	%
Stage IV before treatment		
Stage II after treatment	18	25
Stage III after treatment	18	25
Comfort	13	18
Unchanged	23	32
Total	72	51
Stage III before treatment		
Stage II after treatment	24	63
Comfort	4	11
Unchanged	10	26
Total	38	27
Stage II before treatment		
Stage I after treatment	8	26
Comfort	13	42
Unchanged	9	29
Impaired	1	3
Total	31	22

Percutaneous lumbar phenol sympatholysis has similar results to surgery. Considering all patients, a positive effect was obtained in 70% from percutaneous lumbar sympatholysis. In 25% of stage IV disease, clinical improvement of two stages was noticed, in 25%, an improvement of one stage; 50% of the patients remained in the same clinical stage after the procedure but showed some signs of improvement. Prognosis of trophic lesions located on the anterior foot is better than that of ulcers of the heel (34). Patients in stage III showed a beneficial effect in 74% with rest pain vanishing at night in 63%. These findings correlate with other statements that claim an overall clinical success rate of about 50% (20, 32, 34). The positive effect of 67% noticed in patients who are in stage IV is comparable to other positive results from the published material, varying from 66 (34) to 76% (36). It is more difficult to appreciate results of percutaneous lumbar sympatholysis in stage II patients. The 68% positive results noticed in this study are inferior to other published data (77 to 94%) (8, 9, 25, 34, 36).

There is no doubt that percutaneous lumbar sympatholysis has undeniable advantages over surgical sympathectomy. Initial results are superimposable with surgery and long-term results do not seem to differ from those following sympathectomy either. If the sympatholytic effect vanishes, repetition of the percutaneous procedure is readily accepted by the patient (9). CT control guarantees constant technical success of the percutaneous procedure, but does not influence definite results significantly. Lastly, reduction of hospital stay and medical costs by percutaneous lumbar sympatholysis associated with percutaneous transluminal angioplasty has a positive effect on public health policy, which is not negligible in the treatment of such widespread disease as arterial occlusion of the lower limbs.

Complications

Surgical lumbar sympathectomy carries a significant mortality rate (1 to 6%) (23), which may even be higher in diabetic and polyvascular patients. This surgical risk is out of proportion with the life expectancy in elderly patients, all the more so becauce the procedure is only a last resource and does not arrest progression of the underlying disease. Percutaneous lumbar sympathectomy is a procedure more easily tolerated by the patient. It can be performed on an out-patient base, even if surgery is not feasible. It has a low morbidity rate and can be repeated. The inadequate placement of the needle tip possible with conventional radiologic control (36) may result in inadvertent injection of phenol into the intervertebral disk, vertebral canal, pleura, aorta, inferior vena cava, kidneys, renal vessels, ureters, duodenum, psoas muscle, and intestines. These complications have been observed in 5% of the cases (34) during conventional radiologic control but can be avoided with the systematic use of CT. Urinary obstruction caused by periureteral fibrosis due to injection of phenol has been known to occur. Correct percutaneous needle placement in the retroperitoneal space without damage to abdominal organs is still possible with CT control even if protruding osteophytes or severe scoliosis of the lumbar spine are present or if major anatomic changes (large renal cyst, nephrectomy) or the absence of retroperitoneal fat layers make needle guidance with fluoroscopic control problematical. Thus, the risk of retroperitoneal irritation provoked by a too massive retroperitoneal injection of phenol is minimized.

The frequency of other complications related to the procedure, such as neuralgia (14 to 25%) (34, 36) or impotence is independent of the radiologic control modality but is related to the volume and to the pathways of diffusion of phenol. Precise documentation by CT adds to medical confidence in percutaneous neurolysis. Use of CT does not lengthen the procedure. The absence of significant complications suits the ease and rapidity with which the procedure is performed. Many patients complain, however, of neuritic pain in the lumbar region or irradiating to the thigh, which may persist for several weeks. One patient experienced a left pleural chylous effusion and ascites as a result of puncture of the thoracic duct, which regressed spontaneously. Another patient showed signs of mild transient peritonitis by irritation of a too anterior injection of phenol. Of 112 patients, five died within 1 week after percutaneous lumbar sympatholysis from cardiac and respiratory failure, which illustrates the fragility of these elderly polyvascular patients. In four of five patients, no direct relationship between the procedure and cause of death could be established.

References

1. Adar R, Kruchin A, Zeweig A, Mozes M. Palmar hyperhidrosis and its surgical treatment: a report of 100 cases. Ann Surg 1977;186:34–41.
2. Adson AW, Brown GE. The treatment of Raynaud's disease by resection of the upper thoracic and lumbar sympathetic ganglia and trunks. Surg Gynecol Obstet 1929;48:457–603.
3. Atkins HJB. Peraxillary approach to the stellate and upper thoracic sympathetic ganglia. Lancet 1949;ii:1152.
4. Baddeley RM. The place of upper dorsal sympathectomy in the treatment of primary Raynaud's disease. Br J Surg 1965;52:426–430.
5. Berguer R, Smit R. Transaxillary sympathectomy (T2 to T4) for relief of vasospastic sympathectic pain of upper extremities. Surgery 1981;89:764–769.
6. Brunning F. Zur Technik der kombinierten Resektions-Methode sämtlicher sympathischen Nervenbahnen am Halse. Zentralbl Chir 1923;50:1056–1059.
7. Cloward RB. Upper thoracic sympathectomy: surgical technique. Surgery 1969;66:1120–1124.
8. Courtheoux P, Theron J, Evrard C, Maiza D, Oriot G. La sympathectomie chimique lombaire: un nouvel acte de radiologie thérapeutique. Ann Radiol (Paris) 1982;25:429–431.
9. Cousins MJ, Reeve TS, Glynn CJ, Walsh JA, Cherry DA. Neurolytic lumbar sympathetic blockade: duration of denervation and relief of rest pains. Anaesth Intens Care 1979;7:121–135.
10. Dondelinger R. CT guided percutaneous biopsy. J Belge Radiol 1982;65:227–243.
11. Dondelinger R, Kurdziel JC. Percutaneous phenol neurolysis of the lumbar sympathetic chain with computed tomography control. Ann Radiol (Paris) 1984;27:376–379.
12. Dondelinger RF, Kurdziel JC. Tomodensitométrie d'intervention. In: Vasile N ed. Tomodensitiométrie corps entier. Paris: Vigot 1986:603–604.
13. Estes EH Jr, Izlar HL Jr. Recurrent ventricular tachycardia: a case successfully treated by bilateral cardiac sympathectomy. Am J Med 1961;31:493–495.
14. Gastonguay YR, Youhe P, Meere CP, Grondin CM. Traitement chirurgical des syndromes du défilé thoracique avec phénomènes de Raynaud. Ann Chir [Chir Thorac Cardiovasc] 1979;33:234–237.
15. Gjerris F, Olesen HP. Palmar hyperhidrosis: long-term results following high thoracic sympathectomy. Acta Neurol Scand 1975;51:167–172.
16. Goetz RH, Marr JAS. The importance of the second thoracic ganglion for the sympathetic supply of the upper extremities, with a description of two new approaches for its removal in cases of vascular disease: a preliminary report. Clin Proc 1944;3:102–114.
17. Grondin CM, Limet R. Sympathetic denervation in association with coronary artery graft in patients with Prinzmetal's angina. Ann Thorac Surg 1977;23:111–115.
18. Gruss JD, Bartels D, Stojanovic R. Indications opératoires et résultats de la sympathectomie thoracique. J Chir (Paris) 1976;112:307–314.
19. Haaga JR, Reich NE, Havrilla TR, Alfidi RJ. Interventional CT scanning. Radiol Clin North Am 1977;15:449–456.
20. Haimovici H, Steinman C, Karson IH. Evaluation of lumbar sympathectomy: advanced occlusive arterial disease. Arch Surg 1964;89:1089–1091.
21. Haxton HA. Chemical sympathectomy. Brit Med J 1949;1:1026–1028.
22. Haxton HA. The technique and results of upper limb sympathectomy. J Cardiovasc Surg (Torino) 1970;11:27–34.
23. Imparato AM. Lumbar sympathectomy: role in treatment of occlusive arterial disease in the lower extremities. Surg Clin North Am 1979;59:719–735.
24. Johnston ENM, Summerly R, Birnstingle M. Prognosis in Raynaud's phenomenon after sympathectomy. Br Med J 1965;1:962–964.
25. Keane FBV. Phenol lumbar sympathectomy for severe arterial occlusive disease in the elderly. Br J Surg 1977;64:519–521.
26. Kux M, Fritsch A, Kokoschka R. Endoscopic thoracic sympathectomy for the treatment of Raynaud's phenomenon and disease. Eur Surg Res 1976;8:32–33.
27. Kux M. Thoracic endoscopic sympathectomy for treatment of upper limb hyperhidrosis. Lancet 1977;i:1320.
28. Kux M. Thoracic endoscopic sympathectomy for palmar and axillary hyperhidrosis. Arch Surg 1978;113:264–266.
29. Laubach K, Linder F, Piotrowski W. Thorakale transaxillare Sympathektomie: Indikation, Technik und Frühergebnisse. Dtsch Med Wochenschr 1972;97:745–749.
30. Linton R ed. In: Atlas of vascular surgery. Philadelphia: Saunders 1973:486–487.
31. Malone PS, Duignan JP, Hederman WP. Transthoracic electrocoagulation TTEC: a new and simple approach to upper limb sympathectomy. Ir Med J 1982;75:20–21.
32. Mashian A, Soroker D, Pasik S, Mashiah T. Salvage of ischaemic limb by phenol sympathectomy. Age Ageing 1982;11:127–129.
33. Mattassi R, Meile F, D'Angelo F. Thoracic sympathectomy: review of indications, results and surgical techniques. J Cardiovasc Surg 1981;22:336–339.
34. Milleret R, Lavaud S, Gravier R. La sympathectomie au phénol dans le traitement des artériopathies chroniques oblitérantes des membres inférieurs. J Chir (Paris) 1980;117:317–320.

35. Postlewaithe JC. Lumbar sympathectomy: a retrospective study of 142 operations on 100 patients. Br J Surg 1973;60:789–791.

36. Reid W, Watt JK, Gray TG. Phenol injection of the sympathetic chain. Br J Surg 1970;57:45–50.

37. Rob C, Smith R eds. Vascular surgery; vol 3. Philadelphia: Lippincott 1968:215–218.

38. Rosen RJ, Miller DL, Imparato AM, Riles TS. Percutaneous phenol sympathectomy in advanced vascular disease. AJR 1983;141:597–600.

39. Shih CJ, Wang YC. Thoracic sympathectomy for palmar hyperhidrosis: report of 457 cases. Surg Neurol 1978;10:291–296.

40. Skilton JS, Ashton F. Lumbar sympathectomy in the salvage of ischaemic limbs. Br J Clin Pract 1974;28:339–342.

41. Smithwick HR. Modified dorsal sympathectomy for vascular spasm (Raynaud's disease) of the upper extremity: a preliminary report. Ann Surg 1936;104:339–351.

42. Soltesz L, Sandor GY. Sympathicus-Operationsversuch zur Beeinflussung der Syringomyelie. Orv Hetil 1957;98:740–744.

43. Sternberg A, Brickman S, Kott I, Reiss R. Transaxillarly thoracic sympathectomy for primary hyperhidrosis of the upper limbs. World J Surg 1982;6:458–463.

44. Telford ED. The technique of sympathectomy. Br Med Surg 1935;23:448–450.

45. Touati Y, Mathieu JP, Houel F, Impert P. Indications actuelles de la sympathectomie dorsale supérieure. J Mal Vasc 1982;7:187–192.

46. Weale FE. Upper thoracic sympathectomy by transthoracic electrocoagulation. Br J Surg 1980;67:71–72.

47. Welch E, Geary J. Current status of thoracic dorsal sympathectomy. J Vasc Surg 1984;1:202–214.

48. Wilkinson HA. Percutaneous radiofrequency upper thoracic sympathectomy: a new technique. Neurosurgery 1984;15:811–814.

Index